Fundamentals of Investments
VALUATION AND MANAGEMENT

The McGraw Hill Series in Finance, Insurance, and Real Estate

Financial Management

Block, Hirt, and Danielsen
Foundations of Financial Management
Eighteenth Edition

Brealey, Myers, and Marcus
Fundamentals of Corporate Finance
Eleventh Edition

Brealey, Myers, and Allen
Principles of Corporate Finance
Fourteenth Edition

Brooks
FinGame Online 5.0

Bruner, Eades, and Schill
Case Studies in Finance: Managing for Corporate Value Creation
Eighth Edition

Cornett, Adair, and Nofsinger
Finance: Applications and Theory
Sixth Edition

Cornett, Adair, and Nofsinger
M: Finance
Sixth Edition

DeMello
Cases in Finance
Third Edition

Higgins
Analysis for Financial Management
Thirteenth Edition

Ross, Westerfield, Jaffe, and Jordan
Corporate Finance
Thirteenth Edition

Ross, Westerfield, Jaffe, and Jordan
Corporate Finance: Core Principles and Applications
Seventh Edition

Ross, Westerfield, and Jordan
Essentials of Corporate Finance
Eleventh Edition

Ross, Westerfield, and Jordan
Fundamentals of Corporate Finance
Thirteenth Edition

Shefrin
Behavioral Corporate Finance: Decisions That Create Value
Second Edition

Investments

Bodie, Kane, and Marcus
Essentials of Investments
Twelfth Edition

Bodie, Kane, and Marcus
Investments
Thirteenth Edition

Jordan, Miller, and Dolvin
Fundamentals of Investments: Valuation and Management
Tenth Edition

Sundaram and Das
Derivatives: Principles and Practice
Second Edition

Financial Institutions and Markets

Rose and Hudgins
Bank Management and Financial Services
Ninth Edition

Rose and Marquis
Financial Institutions and Markets
Eleventh Edition

Saunders and Cornett
Financial Institutions Management: A Risk Management Approach
Tenth Edition

Saunders and Cornett
Financial Markets and Institutions
Eighth Edition

International Finance

Eun and Resnick
International Financial Management
Tenth Edition

Real Estate

Brueggeman and Fisher
Real Estate Finance and Investments
Seventeenth Edition

Ling and Archer
Real Estate Principles: A Value Approach
Seventh Edition

Financial Planning and Insurance

Allen, Melone, Rosenbloom, and Mahoney
Retirement Plans: 401(k)s, IRAs, and Other Deferred Compensation Approaches
Twelfth Edition

Altfest
Personal Financial Planning
Second Edition

Kapoor, Dlabay, Hughes, and Hart
Focus on Personal Finance: An Active Approach to Help You Achieve Financial Literacy
Seventh Edition

Kapoor, Dlabay, Hughes, and Hart
Personal Finance
Fourteenth Edition

Walker and Walker
Personal Finance: Building Your Future
Second Edition

Tenth Edition

Fundamentals of Investments
VALUATION AND MANAGEMENT

Bradford D. Jordan
University of Florida

Thomas W. Miller Jr.
Mississippi State University

Steven D. Dolvin, CFA
Butler University

FUNDAMENTALS OF INVESTMENTS: VALUATION AND MANAGEMENT, TENTH EDITION

Published by McGraw Hill LLC, 1325 Avenue of the Americas, New York, NY 10019. Copyright ©2024 by McGraw Hill LLC. All rights reserved. Printed in the United States of America. Previous editions ©2021. No part of this publication may be reproduced or distributed in any form or by any means, or stored in a database or retrieval system, without the prior written consent of McGraw Hill LLC, including, but not limited to, in any network or other electronic storage or transmission, or broadcast for distance learning.

Some ancillaries, including electronic and print components, may not be available to customers outside the United States.

This book is printed on acid-free paper.

1 2 3 4 5 6 7 8 9 LWI 28 27 26 25 24 23

ISBN 978-1-264-41281-5 (bound edition)
MHID 1-264-41281-9 (bound edition)
ISBN 978-1-266-82401-2 (loose-leaf edition)
MHID 1-266-82401-4 (loose-leaf edition)

Portfolio Manager: *Sarah Hutchings*
Senior Product Developer: *Christina Kouvelis*
Marketing Manager: *Sarah Hurley*
Content Project Managers: *Pat Frederickson; Tammy Juran*
Manufacturing Project Manager: *Rachel Hirschfield*
Senior Designer: *Matt Diamond*
Senior Content Licensing Specialist: *Beth Cray*
Cover Image: *Glow Images*
Compositor: *Straive*

All credits appearing on page or at the end of the book are considered to be an extension of the copyright page.

Library of Congress Cataloging-in-Publication Data

Names: Jordan, Bradford D., author. | Miller, Thomas W., author. | Dolvin, Steven D., author.
Title: Fundamentals of investments : valuation and management / Bradford D. Jordan, University of Kentucky,
   Thomas W. Miller Jr., Mississippi State University, Steven D. Dolvin, Butler University.
Description: Tenth Edition. | Dubuque, IA : McGraw Hill Education, [2023] | Revised edition of the authors'
   Fundamentals of investments, [2021] | Audience: Ages 18+ | Summary: "Traditionally, investments textbooks
   tend to fall into one of two camps. The first type has a greater focus on portfolio management and covers a
   significant amount of portfolio theory. The second type is more concerned with security analysis and generally
   contains fairly detailed coverage of fundamental analysis as a tool for equity valuation. Today, most texts try to
   cover all the bases by including some chapters drawn from one camp and some from another"—
Provided by publisher.
Identifiers: LCCN 2022046367 | ISBN 9781264412815 (hardcover ; alk. paper)
Subjects: LCSH: Investments.
Classification: LCC HG4521 .C66 2023 | DDC 332.6–dc23/eng/20221028
LC record available at https://lccn.loc.gov/2022046367

The Internet addresses listed in the text were accurate at the time of publication. The inclusion of a website does not indicate an endorsement by the authors or McGraw Hill LLC, and McGraw Hill LLC does not guarantee the accuracy of the information presented at these sites.

To my late father, S. Kelly Jordan Sr., a great stock picker.

BDJ

To my late mother and sister—let perpetual light shine upon them; my wife, Carolyn; and Thomas III, Emily, and Bennett.

TWM JR.

To my wife, Kourtney, and the "three L's"—my greatest investment in this life.

SDD

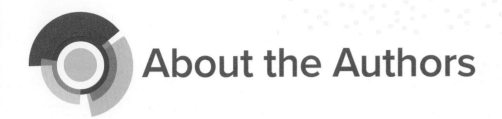

About the Authors

Bradford D. Jordan
Warrington College of Business, University of Florida

Bradford D. Jordan is Visiting Scholar at the University of Florida. He previously held the duPont Endowed Chair in Banking and Financial Services at the University of Kentucky, where he was department head for many years. He specializes in corporate finance and securities valuation. He has published numerous articles in leading finance journals, and he has received a variety of research awards, including the Fama/DFA Award.

Dr. Jordan is coauthor of *Corporate Finance* 13e, *Corporate Finance: Core Principles and Applications* 7e, *Fundamentals of Corporate Finance* 13e, and *Essentials of Corporate Finance* 11e, which collectively are the most widely used business finance textbooks in the world.

Thomas W. Miller Jr.
College of Business, Mississippi State University

Tom Miller is Professor of Finance and holder of the Jack R. Lee Chair in Financial Institutions and Consumer Finance at Mississippi State University. He has a long-standing interest in derivative securities and investments and has published numerous articles on various topics in these areas. His latest research interest is in the areas of option time decay and the workings and regulation of small-dollar loan markets. Professor Miller has been honored with many research and teaching awards. He is a co-author (with David Dubofsky) of *Derivatives: Valuation and Risk Management* (Oxford University Press). Professor Miller's interests include playing blues and jazz on tenor saxophone.

Steven D. Dolvin, CFA
Lacy School of Business, Butler University

Dr. Steven D. Dolvin, CFA, is Professor of Finance and holder of the Eugene Ratliff Endowed Chair in Finance at Butler University. He teaches primarily in the area of investments, but he also oversees student-run portfolios in both public and private equity. He has received multiple teaching awards and has also published numerous articles in both academic and practitioner outlets. His principal areas of interest are venture capital, financial education, retirement investing, ESG factors, and behavioral finance. His prior experience includes work in both corporate finance and investments, and he currently provides investment consulting for both individuals and businesses. Professor Dolvin is also a CFA Charterholder and is involved in his local CFA society.

Preface

So why *did* we write this book?

As we toiled away, we asked ourselves this question many times, and the answer was always the same: *Our students made us.*

Traditionally, investments textbooks tend to fall into one of two camps. The first type has a greater focus on portfolio management and covers a significant amount of portfolio theory. The second type is more concerned with security analysis and generally contains fairly detailed coverage of fundamental analysis as a tool for equity valuation. Today, most texts try to cover all the bases by including some chapters drawn from one camp and some from another.

The result of trying to cover everything is either a very long book or one that forces the instructor to bounce back and forth between chapters. This frequently leads to a noticeable lack of consistency in treatment. Different chapters have completely different approaches: Some are computational, some are theoretical, and some are descriptive. Some do macroeconomic forecasting, some do mean-variance portfolio theory and beta estimation, and some do financial statements analysis. Options and futures are often essentially tacked on the back to round out this disconnected assortment.

The goal of these books is different from the goal of our students. Our students told us they come into an investments course wanting to learn how to make investment decisions. As time went by, we found ourselves supplying more and more supplemental materials to the texts we were using and constantly varying chapter sequences while chasing this elusive goal. We finally came to realize that the financial world had changed tremendously, and investments textbooks had fallen far behind in content and relevance.

What we really wanted, and what our students really needed, was a book that would do several key things:

- Focus on students as investment managers by giving them information they can act on instead of concentrating on theories and research without the proper context.
- Offer strong, consistent pedagogy, including a balanced, unified treatment of the main types of financial investments as mirrored in the investment world.
- Organize topics in a way that would make them easy to apply—whether to a portfolio simulation or to real life—and support these topics with hands-on activities.

We made these three goals the guiding principles in writing this book. The next several sections explain our approach to each and why we think they are so important.

Who Is This Book For?

This book is aimed at introductory investments classes with students who have relatively little familiarity with investments. A typical student may have taken a principles of finance class and had some exposure to stocks and bonds, but not much beyond the basics. The introductory investments class is often a required course for finance majors, but students from other areas often take it as an elective. One fact of which we are acutely aware is that this may be the only investments class many students will ever take.

We intentionally wrote this book in a relaxed, informal style that engages the student and treats him or her as an active participant rather than a passive information absorber. We think the world of investments is exciting and fascinating, and we hope to share our considerable enthusiasm for investing with the student. We appeal to intuition and basic principles whenever possible because we have found that this approach effectively promotes understanding. We also make extensive use of examples throughout, drawing on material from the world around us and using familiar companies wherever appropriate.

By design, the text is not encyclopedic. As the table of contents indicates, we have a total of 21 chapters. Chapter length is about 30 to 40 pages, so the text is aimed at a single-term course; most of the book can be covered in a typical quarter or semester.

Aiming the book at a one-semester course necessarily means some picking and choosing with regard to both topics and depth of coverage. Throughout, we strike a balance by introducing and covering the essentials while leaving some of the details to follow-up courses in security analysis, portfolio management, and options and futures.

How Does the Tenth Edition of This Book Expand Upon the Goals Described Above?

Based on user feedback, we have made numerous improvements and refinements in the tenth edition of *Fundamentals of Investments: Valuation and Management.* We updated an appendix containing useful formulas. We updated every chapter to reflect current market practices and conditions, and we significantly expanded and improved the end-of-chapter material, particularly online.

To give some examples of our additional new content within individual chapters:

- **Chapter 1** contains updates on historical returns for small-company stocks, large-company stocks, long-term government bonds, and Treasury bills, as well as U.S. inflation rates.

- **Chapter 2** provides an updated calculation of margin interest to reflect the industry standard methodology, as well as a discussion of "meme risk" with regard to short selling.

- **Chapter 4** contains an expanded treatment of exchange traded funds (ETFs), including discussion of the latest types.

- **Chapter 5** expands the section on alternative sources of public funding (crowdfunding, ICOs) to include SPACs (special purpose acquisition companies). There is also updated material on the organization of the NYSE.

- **Chapter 6** contains an updated example featuring CVS Health Corporation.

- **Chapter 7** contains a screen showing a history of earnings surprises for Under Armour, Inc. Also included is a graph of the dramatic COVID-19 Crash of 2020.

- **Chapter 9** contains a discussion of the new Secured Overnight Financing Rate (SOFR), which is replacing the familiar London Interbank Offered Rate (LIBOR). It also has a brief discussion on negative government bond yields and an updated discussion of inflation indexed TIPS bonds.

- **Chapter 12** contains new discussion about tracking earnings surprises.

- **Chapter 13** provides an updated calculation of the Information Ratio to match the industry standard, as well as a new section on finding performance measures using industry sources.

- **Chapter 14** contains an explanation of futures quotes for Ultra T-Bonds. Also, the initial spot-futures parity example is now about gold, and it expands to include storage costs. The final spot-futures parity example is about stock indexes and the treatment of dividends.

- **Chapter 17** contains a new section on cryptocurrency and its role as an alternative asset.

- **Chapter 18** contains a new Investment Updates concerning high-yield bonds.

We continue to emphasize the use of the web in investments analysis, and we integrate web-based content in several ways. First, wherever appropriate, we provide a commented link in the margin. These links send readers to selected, particularly relevant websites. Second, our *Work the Web* feature, expanded and completely updated for this edition, appears in most chapters. These boxed readings use screenshots to show students how to access, use, and interpret various types of key financial and market data. Finally, new end-of-chapter problems rely on data retrieved from the web.

We continue to provide *Spreadsheet Analysis* exhibits, which we have enhanced for this edition. These exhibits illustrate directly how to use spreadsheets to do certain types of important problems, including such computationally intensive tasks as calculating Macaulay duration, finding Black-Scholes option prices, and determining optimal portfolios based on Sharpe ratios. We also continue to provide, where relevant, readings from a variety of real-life financial sources, which have been thoroughly updated for this edition.

Bloomberg Integration

The most impactful change in the tenth edition is the integration of Bloomberg throughout the textbook. Bloomberg is widely considered the most important investment data and analysis platform in the world, so we are excited to have it a part of this edition.

Throughout the text, we incorporate Bloomberg content for figures and tables, giving students insight into the power of the platform, as well as familiarity with the layout and structure. At the beginning of each section, we also identify a list of Bloomberg functions that are specific to the section's content. This will enable students to better explore Bloomberg on their own.

At the end of each chapter, we provide a set of newly created Bloomberg questions, which instructors can assign to students. With the growing number of Bloomberg labs within business schools, these questions will allow instructors to better integrate the platform into their classes and show students the power of the tool, as well as how the investments content is used in the "real world."

CFA™ Mapping

Consider this description provided by the CFA Institute: "First awarded in 1963, the Chartered Financial Analyst (CFA) charter has become known as the gold standard of professional credentials within the global investment community. Investors recognize the CFA designation as the definitive standard for measuring competence and integrity in the fields of portfolio management and investment analysis." The importance and growing significance of the CFA charter are compelling reasons to integrate CFA curriculum material into our tenth edition.

Among the requirements to earn the CFA charter, candidates must pass three sequential levels of comprehensive exams. Each exam asks questions on a wide array of subject areas concerning the investment process. To help candidates study for the exams, the exams at each level are divided into so-called study sessions. Each of these study sessions has a core set of readings designed to help prepare the candidate for the exams. We carefully examined the content of each reading (updated for the 2016 exams), as well as the stated learning outcomes, to determine which areas we covered in the eighth edition. Importantly, we also considered which areas might be added to the tenth edition.

In total, our textbook contains material that touches over 75 percent of the readings from Level I of the CFA exam. Topics that we do not address from Level I, such as basic statistics, accounting, and economics, are likely addressed in prerequisite courses taken before the investments course. In addition, we present some higher-level material: We touch on about 35 percent and 50 percent of the readings from the Level II and III exams, respectively.

Of course, we make no claim that our textbook is a substitute for the CFA exam readings. Nonetheless, we believe that this tenth edition provides a terrific framework and introduction for students looking to pursue a career in investments—particularly for those interested in eventually holding the CFA charter. To provide a sense of studying for the CFA, the tenth edition continues to include an end-of-chapter case review. Kaplan Schweser, a leading purveyor of CFA exam preparation packages, graciously provided extensive material from which we chose these case reviews. In addition, we have added additional Kaplan Schweser practice exams and questions to our online learning system, Connect.

We provide mapping between the textbook and the CFA curriculum as follows: Each chapter opens with a CFA Exam box citing references to specific readings from the CFA curriculum that are covered within the chapter. The topic is identified, and we indicate which level and study session the reading comes from. We label these topics CFA1, CFA2, CFA3, and so on, for easy reference. End-of-chapter problems in the book and in Connect are also labeled with these tags. Over 95 percent of our end-of-chapter material is related to the CFA exam. We believe that this integration adds tremendous value to the tenth edition.

How Is This Book Relevant to the Student?

Fundamental changes in the investments universe drive our attention to relevance. The first major change is that individuals are being asked to make investment decisions for their own portfolios more often than ever before. There is, thankfully, a growing recognition that traditional "savings account" approaches to investing are decidedly inferior. At the same time, the use of employer-sponsored "investment accounts" has expanded enormously. The second major change is that the investments universe has exploded with an ever-increasing number of investment vehicles available to individual investors. As a result, investors must choose from an array of products, many of which are very complex, and they must strive to choose wisely.

Beyond this, students are more interested in subjects that affect them directly (as are we all). By taking the point of view of the student as an investor, we are better able to illustrate and emphasize the relevance and importance of the material.

Our approach is evident in the table of contents. Our first chapter is motivational; we have found that this material effectively "hooks" students and even motivates a semester-long discourse on risk and return. Our second chapter answers the student's next natural question: "How do I get started investing and how do I buy and sell securities?" The third chapter surveys the different types of investments available. After only three chapters, very early in the term, students have learned something about the risks and rewards from investing, how to get started investing, and what investment choices are available.

We close the first part of the text with a detailed examination of mutual funds. Without a doubt, mutual funds have become the most popular investment vehicles for individual investors. There are now more mutual funds than there are stocks on the NYSE! Given the size and enormous growth in the mutual fund industry, this material is important for investors. Even so, investments texts typically cover mutual funds in a cursory way, often banishing the material to a back chapter under the obscure (and obsolete) heading of "investment companies." Our early placement lets students quickly explore a topic they have heard a lot about and are typically interested in learning more about.

How Does This Book Allow Students to Apply Their Investments Knowledge?

After studying this text, students will have the basic knowledge needed to move forward and actually act on what they have learned. We have developed two features to encourage students in making decisions as an investment manager. Learning to make good investment decisions comes with experience, while experience (regrettably) comes from making bad investment decisions. As much as possible, we press our students to get those bad decisions out of their systems before they start managing real money!

Not surprisingly, most students don't know how to get started in buying and selling securities. We have learned that providing some structure, especially with a portfolio simulation, greatly enhances the experience. Therefore, we have a series of *Getting Down to Business* boxes. These boxes (at the end of each chapter) usually describe actual trades for students to explore. The intention is to show students how to gain real experience with the principles and instruments covered in the chapter.

How Does This Book Maintain a Consistent, Unified Treatment?

In most investments texts, depth of treatment and presentation vary dramatically from instrument to instrument, which leaves the student without an overall framework for understanding the many types of investments. We stress early on that there are essentially only four basic types of financial investments—stocks, bonds, options, and futures. In Parts 2 through 6, our simple goal is to take a closer look at each of these instruments. We take a unified approach to each by answering these basic questions:

1. What are the essential features of the instrument?
2. What are the possible rewards?
3. What are the risks?
4. What are the basic determinants of investment value?
5. For whom is the investment appropriate and under what circumstances?
6. How is the instrument bought and sold, and how does the market for the instrument operate?

By covering investment instruments in this way, we teach students what questions to ask when looking at any potential investment.

Unlike other introductory investments texts, we devote several chapters beyond the basics to the different types of fixed-income investments. Students are often surprised to learn that the fixed-income markets are so much bigger than the equity markets and that money management opportunities are much more common in the fixed-income arena. Possibly the best way to see this is to look at recent CFA exams and materials and note the extensive coverage of fixed-income topics. We have placed these chapters toward the back of the text because we recognize not everyone will want to cover all this material. We have also separated the subject into several shorter chapters to make it more digestible for students and to allow instructors more control over what is covered.

Assurance-of-Learning Ready

Many educational institutions today are focused on the notion of assurance of learning, an important element of some accreditation standards. This edition is designed specifically to support your assurance-of-learning initiatives with a simple, yet powerful, solution.

Each Test Bank question for this book maps to a specific chapter learning objective listed in the text. You can use the Test Bank software to easily query for learning outcomes and objectives that directly relate to the learning objectives for your course. You can then use the reporting features of the software to aggregate student results in similar fashion, making the collection and presentation of assurance-of-learning data simple and easy.

Acknowledgments

We have received extensive feedback from reviewers at each step along the way, and we are very grateful to the following dedicated scholars and teachers for their time and expertise:

Aaron Brown, University of California–San Diego

Aaron Phillips, California State University–Bakersfield

Adam Schwartz, Washington and Lee University

Aidong Hu, Sonoma State University

Alan Wong, Indiana University Southeast

Allan O'Bryan, Rochester Community & Technical College

Allan Zebedee, San Diego State University

Anandi Banerjee, Queens University of Charlotte

Ann Hackert, Idaho State University

Armand Picou, Texas A&M University

Ashley G. Geisewite, Southwest Tennessee Community College

Ashraf Almordaah, Los Angeles City College

Benito Sanchez, Kean University

Bruce Grace, Morehead State University

Carl R. Chen, University of Dayton

Carla Rich, Pensacola Junior College

Caroline Fulmer, University of Alabama

Charles Appeadu, University of Wisconsin-Madison

Cheryl Frohlich, University of North Florida

Christos Giannikos, Bernard M. Baruch College

Crystal Ayers, College of Southern Idaho

Dale Prodzinski, Davenport University

David Dubofsky, TCU

David Hunter, University of Hawaii-Manoa

David Louton, Bryant College

David Loy, Illinois State University

David Peterson, Florida State University

David Stewart, Winston-Salem State University

Deborah Murphy, University of Tennessee-Knoxville

Dina Layish, Binghamton University

Donald Lennard, Park University

Donald Wort, California State University-East Bay

Dwight Giles, Jefferson State Community College

Edward Miller, University of New Orleans

Eric Robbins, Pennsylvania State University

Felix Ayadi, Fayetteville State University

Frederick Lambert, Liberty University

Gary Engle, University of Wisconsin-Milwaukee

Gay B. Hatfield, University of Mississippi

Georg Grassmueck, Lycoming College

George Jouganatos, California State University-Sacramento

Gioia Bales, Hofstra University

Gregory Charles, Portland Community College

Haigang Zhou, Cleveland State University

Herb Meiberger, San Francisco State University

Howard Van Auken, Iowa State University

Howard W. Bohnen, St. Cloud State University

Imad Elhaj, University of Louisville

It-Keong Chew, University of Kentucky

James Forjan, York College of Pennsylvania

Jeff Brookman, Idaho State University

Jeff Edwards, Portland Community College

Jeff Manzi, Ohio University

Jennifer Morton, Ivy Technical Community College of Indiana

Ji Chen, University of Colorado

Jim P. DeMello, Western Michigan University

Jim Tipton, Baylor University

Joan Anderssen, Arapahoe Community College

Joe Brocato, Tarleton State University

Joe Walker, University of Alabama-Birmingham

John Bockino, Suffolk County Community College

John Clinebell, University of Northern Colorado

John Daley, University of Colorado at Denver

John Finnigan, Marist College

John Guest, Delgado Community College

John Ledgerwood, Bethune-Cookman College

John Paul Broussard, Rutgers, The State University of New Jersey

John Romps, St. Anselm College

John Stocker, University of Delaware

John Wingender, Creighton University

Johnny Chan, University of Dayton

Jonathan Kalodimos, Oregon State University

Jorge Omar R. Brusa, University of Arkansas

Karen Bonding, University of Virginia

Keith Fevurly, Metropolitan State College of Denver

Kenneth Kang, Idaho State University

Kerri McMillan, Clemson University

Ladd Kochman, Kennesaw State University

Lalatendu Misra, University of Texas at San Antonio

Lawrence Blose, Grand Valley State University

Linda Martin, Arizona State University

Lisa Schwartz, Wingate University

Lyle Bowlin, Southeastern University

M. J. Murray, Winona State University

Majid R. Muhtaseb, California State Polytechnic University

Marc LeFebvre, Creighton University

Marek Kolar, Trine University

Margo Kraft, Heidelberg College

Marie Kratochvil, Nassau Community College

Matthew Fung, Saint Peter's College

Michael C. Ehrhardt, University of Tennessee-Knoxville

Michael Gordinier, Washington University

Michael Milligan, California State University-Northridge

Michael Nugent, SUNY-Stony Brook

Michael Radin, Montclair State University

Micki Pitcher, Davenport University

Mukesh Chaudhry, Indiana University of Pennsylvania

Naresh Bansal, Saint Louis University

Nolan Lickey, Utah Valley State College

Nozar Hashemzadeh, Radford University

Patricia Clarke, Simmons College

Paul Bolster, Northeastern University

Paul Fosbre, Kean University

Percy S. Poon, University of Nevada, Las Vegas

Ping Hsao, San Francisco State University

Praveen K. Das, University of Louisiana-Lafayette

Rahul Verma, University of Houston

Randall Wade, Rogue Community College

Richard Curry, University of Cincinnati

Richard Followill, University of Northern Iowa

Richard Hamlet, Tidewater Community College

Richard Lee Kitchen, Tallahassee Community College

Richard Proctor, Siena College

Richard W. Taylor, Arkansas State University

Robert A. Uptegraff Jr., Oakland University

Robert Friederichs, Alexandria Technical College

Robert Kao, Park University

Robert Kozub, University of Wisconsin-Milwaukee

Robert L. Losey, University of Louisville

Roger Kerkenbush, University of Wisconsin-Platteville

Ronald Christner, Loyola University-New Orleans

Samira Hussein, Johnson County Community College

Sammie Root, Texas State University-San Marcos

Samuel H. Penkar, University of Houston

Scott Barnhart, Clemson University

Scott Beyer, University of Wisconsin-Oshkosh

Scott Gruner, Trine University

Sergiy Saydometov, Dallas Baptist University

Stephen Chambers, Johnson County Community College

Stephen Huffman, University of Wisconsin, Oshkosh

Steven Lifland, High Point University

Stuart Michelson, University of Central Florida

Thomas Johansen, Fort Hays State University

Thomas M. Krueger, University of Wisconsin-La Crosse

Thomas Willey, Grand Valley State University

Tim Samolis, Pittsburgh Technical Institute

Vernon Stauble, San Bernardino Valley College

Violeta Diaz, St. Mary's University

Vivian Nazar, Ferris State University

Ward Hooker, Orangeburg-Calhoun Technical College

William Compton, University of North Carolina-Wilmington

William Elliott, Oklahoma State University

William Lepley, University of Wisconsin–Green Bay

Xu Sun, Utah Valley University

Yvette Harman, Miami University of Ohio

Zekeriya Eser, Eastern Kentucky University

We thank Scott Ehrhorn of Liberty University for developing the Test Bank. We thank R. Douglas Van Eaton, CFA, for providing access to *Schweser*'s preparation material for the CFA exam. We would especially like to acknowledge the careful reading and helpful suggestions made by professor David A. Dubofsky at TCU.

Special thanks to professor Bidisha Chakrabarty at Saint Louis University, Carolyn Moore Miller and Kameron Killian for their efforts. Steve Hailey and Emily Bello did outstanding work on this text. To them fell the unenviable task of technical proofreading and, in particular, carefully checking each calculation throughout the supplements.

We are deeply grateful to the select group of professionals who served as our development team on this edition: Sarah Hutchings, Portfolio Manager; Christina Kouvelis, Senior Product Developer; Sarah Hurley, Marketing Manager; Matt Diamond, Senior Designer; Marianne Musni, Program Manager; Pat Frederickson, Lead Core Content Project Manager; and Tammy Juran, Lead Assessment Content Project Manager.

Bradford D. Jordan

Thomas W. Miller Jr.

Steven D. Dolvin, CFA

Coverage

This book was designed and developed explicitly for a first course in investments taken either by finance majors or nonfinance majors. In terms of background or prerequisites, the book is nearly self-contained, but some familiarity with basic algebra and accounting is assumed. The organization of the text has been designed to give instructors the flexibility they need to teach a quarter-long or semester-long course.

To present an idea of the breadth of coverage in the tenth edition of *Fundamentals of Investments*, the following grid is presented chapter by chapter. This grid contains some of the most significant new features and a few selected chapter highlights. Of course, for each chapter, features like opening vignettes, *Work the Web, Spreadsheet Analysis, Getting Down to Business, Investment Updates*, tables, figures, examples, and end-of-chapter material have been thoroughly reviewed and updated.

Chapters	Selected Topics of Interest	Learning Outcome/Comment
PART ONE Introduction		
Chapter 1 A Brief History of Risk and Return	Dollar returns and percentage returns. Return variability and calculating variance and standard deviation.	Average returns differ by asset class. Return variability also differs by asset class.
	Arithmetic versus geometric returns.	Geometric average tells you what you actually earned per year, compounded annually. Arithmetic returns tell you what you earned in a typical year. Dollar-weighted average returns adjust for investment inflows and outflows.
	The risk-return trade-off. *Updated material: World stock market capitalization.*	Historically, higher returns are associated with higher risk. Estimates of future equity risk premiums involve assumptions about the risk environment and investor risk aversion.
Chapter 2 The Investment Process	The investment policy statement (IPS).	By knowing their objectives and constraints, investors can capture risk and safety trade-offs in an investment policy statement (IPS).
	Investor objectives, constraints, and strategies. *New material: Updated risk tolerance questionnaire.* Investment professionals and types of brokerage accounts. *New material: Coverage of portfolio margin.* Retirement accounts.	Presentation of issues like risk and return, resource constraints, market timing, and asset allocation. Discussion of the different types of financial advisors and brokerage accounts available to an individual investor. Readers will know the workings of company-sponsored plans, such as a 401(k), traditional individual retirement accounts (IRAs), and Roth IRAs.
	Short sales.	Description of the process of short-selling stock and short-selling constraints imposed by regulations and market conditions.

Chapters	Selected Topics of Interest	Learning Outcome/Comment
	Forming an investment portfolio.	An investment portfolio must account for an investor's risk tolerance, objectives, constraints, and strategies.
Chapter 3 Overview of Security Types	Classifying securities.	Interest-bearing, equity, and derivative securities.
	NASD's new TRACE system and transparency in the corporate bond market.	Up-to-date discussion of new developments in fixed income with respect to price, volume, and transactions reporting.
	Equity securities.	Obtaining price quotes for equity securities.
	Derivative securities: Obtaining futures contract and option contract price quotes using the internet.	Defining the types of derivative securities, interpreting their price quotes, and calculating gains and losses from these securities.
Chapter 4 Mutual Funds, ETFs, and Other Investment Companies	Advantages and drawbacks of investing in mutual funds.	Advantages include diversification, professional management, and minimum initial investment. Drawbacks include risk, costs, and taxes.
	Investment companies and types of funds.	Covers concepts like open-end versus closed-end funds and net asset value.
	Mutual fund organization, creation, costs, and fees.	Presents types of expenses and fees like front-end loads, 12b-1 fees, management fees, and turnover.
	Short-term funds, long-term funds, and fund performance. *New section: Socially responsible investing.*	Discussion of money market mutual funds versus the variety of available stock and bond funds and how to find their performance.
	Special funds like closed-end funds, exchange-traded funds, and hedge funds.	The closed-end fund discount mystery and discussion of exchange-traded funds (ETFs), exchange-traded notes (ETNs), hedge fund investment styles, and the perils of leveraged ETFs.
PART TWO Stock Markets		
Chapter 5 The Stock Market	Private vs. public equity and primary vs. secondary markets.	The workings of an initial public offering (IPO), a seasoned equity offering (SEO), the role of investment bankers, and the role of the Securities and Exchange Commission (SEC).
	NYSE and Nasdaq.	The role of dealers and brokers, the workings of the New York Stock Exchange (NYSE), and Nasdaq market operations.
	Stock indexes, including the Dow Jones Industrial Average (DJIA) and the Standard and Poor's 500 index (S&P 500).	The components of the DJIA and their dividend yields. The difference between price-weighted indexes and value-weighted indexes.
Chapter 6 Common Stock Valuation	The basic dividend discount model (DDM) and several of its variants, like the two-stage dividend growth model.	Valuation using constant growth rates and nonconstant growth rates.
	The residual income model and the free cash flow model.	Valuation of non-dividend-paying stocks. Valuation of stocks with negative earnings.

Chapters	Selected Topics of Interest	Learning Outcome/Comment
	New Material: Secured Overnight Financing Rate (SOFR), which is replacing LIBOR.	
Chapter 10 Bond Prices and Yields	Straight bond prices and yield to maturity (YTM).	Calculate straight bond prices; calculate yield to maturity.
	The concept of duration and bond risk measures based on duration.	Calculate and interpret a bond's duration. The dollar value of an 01 and the yield value of a 32nd.
	Dedicated portfolios and reinvestment risk. Immunization.	Learn how to create a dedicated portfolio and show its exposure to reinvestment risk. Minimize the uncertainty concerning the value of a bond portfolio at its target date.
PART FOUR Portfolio Management		
Chapter 11 Diversification and Risky Asset Allocation	Expected returns and variances.	Calculating expected returns and variances using equal and unequal probabilities.
	Portfolios and the effect of diversification on portfolio risk. The importance of asset allocation.	Compute portfolio weights, expected returns, variances, and why diversification works. The effect of correlation on the risk-return trade-off.
	The Markowitz efficient frontier and illustrating the importance of asset allocation using three securities.	Compute risk-return combinations using various portfolio weights for three assets.
Chapter 12 Return, Risk, and the Security Market Line	Diversification, systematic and unsystematic risk.	Total risk comprises unsystematic and systematic risk; only unsystematic risk can be reduced through diversification.
	The security market line and the reward-to-risk ratio.	The security market line describes how the market rewards risk. All assets will have the same reward-to-risk ratio in a competitive financial market.
	Measuring systematic risk with beta. Calculating beta using regression.	The average beta is 1.00. Assets with a beta greater than 1.00 have more than average systematic risk.
	The capital asset pricing model (CAPM).	Expected return depends on the amount and reward for bearing systematic risk as well as the pure time value of money.
	Extending CAPM.	One of the most important extensions of the CAPM is the Fama-French three-factor model.
Chapter 13 Performance Evaluation and Risk Management	Performance evaluation measures.	Calculate and interpret the Sharpe ratio, the Sortino ratio, the Treynor ratio, and Jensen's alpha. Also, calculate alpha using regression, calculate an information ratio, and calculate a portfolio's R-squared.
	Sharpe-optimal portfolios.	The portfolio with the highest possible Sharpe ratio given the assets comprising the portfolio is Sharpe optimal.

Chapters	Selected Topics of Interest	Learning Outcome/Comment
	Value-at-Risk (VaR).	VaR is the evaluation of the probability of a significant loss.
	Example showing how to calculate a Sharpe-optimal portfolio.	Combines the concepts of a Sharpe ratio, a Sharpe-optimal portfolio, and VaR.
PART FIVE Futures and Options		
Chapter 14 Mutual Funds, ETS, and Other Fund Types	The basics of futures contracts and using them to hedge price risk. Detailed example: hedging an inventory using futures markets.	Futures quotes from the internet and financial press, short and long hedging, futures accounts.
	Updated material: Spot-futures parity.	Basis, cash markets, and cash-futures arbitrage.
	Stock index futures.	Index arbitrage, speculating with stock index futures, and hedging stock market risk with stock index futures.
	Hedging interest rate risk with futures.	We show how to use portfolio duration when deciding how many futures contracts to use to hedge a bond portfolio.
Chapter 15 Stock Options	Option basics and option price quotes.	The difference between call and put options, European and American options, online option price quotes, and option chains.
	Option intrinsic value.	Know how to calculate this important aspect of option prices.
	Option payoffs and profits.	Diagram long and short option payoffs and profits for calls and puts.
	Using options to manage risk and option trading strategies.	Protective puts, covered calls, and straddles.
	Option pricing bounds and put-call parity.	Upper and lower pricing bounds for call and put options. Showing how a call option price equals a put option price, the price of an underlying share of stock, and appropriate borrowing.
Chapter 16 Option Valuation	The one-period and two-period binomial option pricing models.	How to compute option prices using these option pricing models—by hand and by using an online option calculator.
	The Black-Scholes option pricing model.	How to compute option prices using this famous option pricing model—by hand and by using an online option calculator.
	Measuring the impact of changes in option inputs.	Computing call and put option deltas.
	Hedging stock with stock options.	Using option deltas to decide how many option contracts are needed to protect a stock's price from feared declines in value.
	Employee stock options (ESOs) and their valuation.	Features of ESOs, repricing ESOs, and ESO valuation.
PART SIX Topics in Investments **Chapter 17** Alternative Investments	Benefits and risks of alternative investments.	Understanding how alternative investments affect the stability and diversity of a portfolio.

Instructors
The Power of Connections

A complete course platform

Connect enables you to build deeper connections with your students through cohesive digital content and tools, creating engaging learning experiences. We are committed to providing you with the right resources and tools to support all your students along their personal learning journeys.

65%
Less Time Grading

Laptop: Getty Images; Woman/dog: George Doyle/Getty Images

Every learner is unique

In Connect, instructors can assign an adaptive reading experience with SmartBook® 2.0. Rooted in advanced learning science principles, SmartBook 2.0 delivers each student a personalized experience, focusing students on their learning gaps, ensuring that the time they spend studying is time well-spent.
mheducation.com/highered/connect/smartbook

Affordable solutions, added value

Make technology work for you with LMS integration for single sign-on access, mobile access to the digital textbook, and reports to quickly show you how each of your students is doing. And with our Inclusive Access program, you can provide all these tools at the lowest available market price to your students. Ask your McGraw Hill representative for more information.

Solutions for your challenges

A product isn't a solution. Real solutions are affordable, reliable, and come with training and ongoing support when you need it and how you want it. Visit **supportateverystep.com** for videos and resources both you and your students can use throughout the term.

Students
Get Learning that Fits You

Effective tools for efficient studying

Connect is designed to help you be more productive with simple, flexible, intuitive tools that maximize your study time and meet your individual learning needs. Get learning that works for you with Connect.

Study anytime, anywhere

Download the free ReadAnywhere® app and access your online eBook, SmartBook® 2.0, or Adaptive Learning Assignments when it's convenient, even if you're offline. And since the app automatically syncs with your Connect account, all of your work is available every time you open it. Find out more at **mheducation.com/readanywhere**

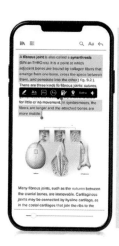

"I really liked this app—it made it easy to study when you don't have your textbook in front of you."

- Jordan Cunningham, Eastern Washington University

iPhone: Getty Images

Everything you need in one place

Your Connect course has everything you need—whether reading your digital eBook or completing assignments for class—Connect makes it easy to get your work done.

Learning for everyone

McGraw Hill works directly with Accessibility Services Departments and faculty to meet the learning needs of all students. Please contact your Accessibility Services Office and ask them to email accessibility@mheducation.com, or visit **mheducation.com/about/accessibility** for more information.

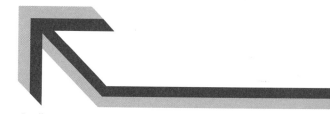

Features

Pedagogical Features

From your feedback, we have included many pedagogical features in this text that will be valuable learning tools for your students. This walkthrough highlights some of the most important elements.

Chapter Openers

These short introductions for each chapter present scenarios and common misconceptions that may surprise you. An explanation is more fully developed in the chapter.

CFA™ Exam Map

This feature maps topics within each chapter to readings from the CFA™ curriculum.

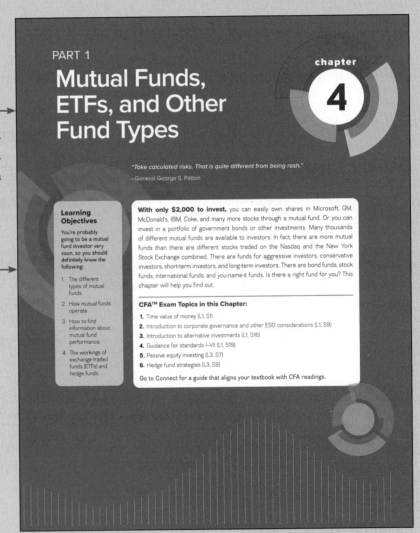

PART 1

Mutual Funds, ETFs, and Other Fund Types

chapter

4

"Take calculated risks. That is quite different from being rash."
–General George S. Patton

Learning Objectives

You're probably going to be a mutual fund investor very soon, so you should definitely know the following:

1. The different types of mutual funds.
2. How mutual funds operate.
3. How to find information about mutual fund performance.
4. The workings of exchange-traded funds (ETFs) and hedge funds.

With only $2,000 to invest, you can easily own shares in Microsoft, GM, McDonald's, IBM, Coke, and many more stocks through a mutual fund. Or you can invest in a portfolio of government bonds or other investments. Many thousands of different mutual funds are available to investors. In fact, there are more mutual funds than there are different stocks traded on the Nasdaq and the New York Stock Exchange combined. There are funds for aggressive investors, conservative investors, short-term investors, and long-term investors. There are bond funds, stock funds, international funds, and you-name-it funds. Is there a right fund for you? This chapter will help you find out.

CFA™ Exam Topics in this Chapter:

1. Time value of money (L1, S1)
2. Introduction to corporate governance and other ESG considerations (L1, S9)
3. Introduction to alternative investments (L1, S16)
4. Guidance for standards I–VII (L1, S19)
5. Passive equity investing (L3, S7)
6. Hedge fund strategies (L3, S9)

Go to Connect for a guide that aligns your textbook with CFA readings.

Check This

Every major section in each chapter ends with questions for review. This feature helps students test their understanding of the material before moving on to the next section.

CHECK THIS

4.1a	What are some advantages of investing in mutual funds?
4.1b	What are some drawbacks of investing in mutual funds?

Key Terms

Key terms are indicated in bold and defined in the margin. The running glossary in the margin helps students quickly review the basic terminology for the chapter.

risk-free rate
The rate of return on a riskless investment.

print money to pay its expenses, Treasury bills are virtually free of any default risk. Thus, we will call the rate of return on such debt the **risk-free rate**, and we will use it as a kind of investing benchmark.

A particularly interesting comparison involves the virtually risk-free return on T-bills and the risky return on common stocks. The difference between these two returns can be interpreted as a measure of the *excess return* on the average risky asset (assuming that the stock of

---

Key Websites

Websites are called out in the margin, along with a notation of how they relate to the chapter material.

There are many sites devoted to the fine art of short selling. Try www.bearmarketcentral.com.

SHORT SALES: SOME DETAILS

When you short a stock, you must borrow it from your broker, so you must fulfill various requirements. First, there is an initial margin and a maintenance margin. Second, after you sell the borrowed stock, the proceeds from the sale are credited to your account, but you cannot use them. They are, in effect, frozen until you return the stock. Finally, if any dividends are paid on the stock while you have a short position, you must pay them.

To illustrate, we will again create an account balance sheet. Suppose you want to short 100 shares of AT&T (T) when the price is $30 per share. This short sale means you will borrow shares of stock worth a total of $30 × 100 = $3,000. Your broker has a 50 percent initial

---

Investment Updates

These boxed readings, reprinted from various business press sources, provide additional real-world events and examples to illustrate the material in the chapter. Some articles from the past two years highlight very recent events, and others present events of more historical significance.

INVESTMENT UPDATES

SOME EXAMPLE DISCLOSURES

1. Regarding Communicating and Sending Trades to Your Broker via E-mail

"Raymond James does not accept private client orders or account instructions by e-mail. This e-mail (a) is not an official transaction confirmation or account statement; (b) is not an offer, solicitation, or recommendation to transact in any security; (c) is intended only for the addressee; and (d) may not be retransmitted to, or used by, any other party. This e-mail may contain confidential or privileged information; please delete immediately if you are not the intended recipient. Raymond James monitors e-mails and may be required by law or regulation to disclose e-mails to third parties."

2. Regarding Stock Analyst Reports

"This material provides general information only. Neither the information nor any views expressed constitute an offer, or an invitation to make an offer, to buy or sell any securities or other investment or any options, futures, or derivatives related to such securities or investments. It is not intended to provide personal investment advice and it does not take into account the specific investment objectives, the financial situation, and the particular needs of any specific person who may receive this material. Investors should seek financial advice regarding the appropriateness of investing in any securities, other investment, or investment strategies discussed in this report and should understand that statements regarding future prospects may not be realized. Investors should note that income from securities or other investments, if any, may fluctuate and that price or value of such securities and investments may rise or fall. Accordingly, investors may receive back less than originally invested. Past performance is not necessarily a guide to future performance. Any information relating to the tax status of financial instruments discussed herein is not intended to provide tax advice or to be used by anyone to provide tax advice. Investors are urged to seek tax advice based on their particular circumstances from an independent tax professional."

Work the Web

Various screenshots appear throughout the text. These exercises illustrate how to access specific features of selected websites in order to expand students' knowledge of current investment topics.

WORK THE WEB

You can find the short interest for the current month in many financial publications. But what if you want a longer history of the shares sold short for a particular company? At nasdaq.com, you can find the short interest for companies listed on the Nasdaq for the previous year. We went to the site in early 2022 and looked up Tesla (TSLA), and here is what we found:

As you can see, the short interest in Tesla fell from about 39 million shares in June 2021 to about 22 million shares in December. Why would you want a history of short sales? Some investors use short sales as a technical indicator, which we discuss in a later chapter. Here's a question for you: What do you think "Days to Cover" means? It is the ratio of short interest to average daily share volume. Thus, "Days to Cover" measures how many days of

normal trading would be necessary to completely cover all outstanding short interest. Days to Cover is also sometimes referred to as the Short Interest Ratio, and many investors actually track this ratio over time to determine changing market sentiment. As an example, check out the following graph from Bloomberg.

Another commonly used measure of short interest is the *percentage of float*. This metric measures the percentage of a firm's outstanding shares that are currently being shorted. Some stocks have large short interest positions because they have a large number of shares outstanding (think about Apple). Days to Cover and percentage of float help to standardize the way short interest is presented, which makes the information more meaningful.

TSLA > TSLA SHORT INTEREST

TSLA Short Interest

SETTLEMENT DATE	SHORT INTEREST	AVG. DAILY SHARE VOLUME	DAYS TO COVER
12/31/2021	22,471,754	23,331,804	1
12/15/2021	25,817,321	22,805,635	1.132059
11/30/2021	26,570,674	24,911,984	1.066582
11/15/2021	25,702,669	36,054,532	1
10/29/2021	28,075,921	32,901,460	1
10/15/2021	30,337,020	17,943,717	1.690676
09/30/2021	29,205,723	20,300,731	1.438654
09/15/2021	26,999,741	16,561,475	1.630274
08/31/2021	27,432,219	17,361,855	1.580028
08/13/2021	26,828,057	17,287,331	1.551891
07/30/2021	29,914,139	20,929,992	1.429248
07/15/2021	32,355,387	21,704,535	1.49072
06/30/2021	34,093,281	25,464,832	1.338838
06/15/2021	39,363,717	21,688,018	1.814998

Source: www.nasdaq.com, accessed January 2022.

Spreadsheet Analysis

Self-contained spreadsheet examples show students how to set up spreadsheets to solve problems—a vital part of every business student's education.

SPREADSHEET ANALYSIS

Using a Spreadsheet to Calculate Average Returns and Volatilities

Here is an Excel spreadsheet summarizing the formulas and analysis needed to calculate average returns and standard deviations using the 1990s as an example:

	A	B	C	D	E	F	G	H
1								
2		Using a spreadsheet to calculate average returns and standard deviations						
3								
4		Looking back in the chapter, the data suggest that the 1990s were one						
5		of the best decades for stock market investors. We will find out just how good by						
6		calculating the average returns and standard deviations for this period. Here are the						
7		year-by-year returns on the large-company stocks:						
8								
9		Year	Return (%)	Year	Return (%)			
10		1990	−3.10	1995	37.58			
11		1991	30.46	1996	22.96			
12		1992	7.62	1997	33.36			
13		1993	10.08	1998	28.58			
14		1994	1.32	1999	21.04			
15								
16		Average return (%):		18.99				

Summary and Conclusions

Each chapter ends with a summary that highlights the important points of the chapter. This material provides a handy checklist for students when they review the chapter.

2.5 Summary and Conclusions

In this chapter, we cover many aspects of the investing process—which we summarize by the chapter's important concepts.

1. **The importance of an investment policy statement.**
   A. The investment policy statement (IPS) identifies the objectives (risk and return) of an investor, as well as the constraints the investor faces in achieving these objectives.
   B. The IPS provides an investing "road map" and will influence the strategies, type of account, and holdings an investor chooses.

2. **The various types of securities brokers and brokerage accounts.**
   A. Opening a brokerage account is straightforward and really much like opening a bank account. You supply information and sign agreements with your broker. Then you write a check and provide instructions on how you want your money invested.
   B. Brokers are traditionally divided into three groups: full-service brokers, discount brokers, and deep-discount brokers. What distinguishes the three groups is the level of service they provide and the resulting commissions they charge. In recent years, the boundaries among the groups have blurred.
   C. Your broker does not have a duty to provide you with guaranteed purchase and sale recommendations. However, your broker does have a duty to exercise reasonable care in formulating recommendations. Your broker has a legal duty to act in your best interest. However, your broker relies on commissions generated from your account.

Getting Down to Business

For instructors looking to give their students a taste of what it means to be an investment manager, this feature (at the end of each chapter) acts as a first step by explaining to students how to apply the material they just learned. The *Getting Down to Business* boxes encourage students—whether for practice in a trading simulation or with real money—to make investment decisions, and they also give some helpful tips to keep in mind. These boxes include a link to a handy blog written by the authors.

GETTING DOWN TO BUSINESS

This chapter covered the basics of policy statements, brokerage accounts, some important trade types, and, finally, some big-picture issues regarding investment strategies. How should you, as an investor or investment manager, put this information to work?

The answer is that you need to open a brokerage account! Investing is like many activities: The best way to learn is by making mistakes. Unfortunately, making mistakes with real money is an expensive way to learn, so we don't recommend trying things like short sales with real money, at least not at first.

Instead, to learn how to trade and gain some experience with making (and losing) money, you should open a Stock-Trak account (or a similar simulated brokerage account). Take it seriously. Try various trade types and strategies and see how they turn out. The important thing to do is to follow your trades and try to understand why you made or lost money and also why you made or lost the amount you did.

In a similar vein, you should carefully review your account statements to make sure you understand exactly what each item means and how your account equity is calculated.

After you have gained some experience trading "on paper," you should open a real account as soon as you can pull together enough money. Try visiting some online brokers to find out the minimum amount you need to open an account. The amount has been declining. In fact, in 2019, you could open a TD Ameritrade account with no minimum, although you would need $2,000 to open a margin account.

Looking back at Chapter 1, you know that it's important to get started early. Once you have a real account, however, it's still a good idea to keep a separate "play money" account to test trading ideas to make sure you really understand them before committing your precious real money.

For the latest information on the real world of investments, visit us at jmdinvestments.blogspot.com.

Chapter Review Problems and Self-Test

1. **The Account Balance Sheet (LO2, CFA2)** Suppose you want to buy 10,000 shares of American Airlines (AAL) at a price of $30 per share. You put up $200,000 and borrow the rest. What does your account balance sheet look like? What is your margin?

2. **Short Sales (LO4, CFA3)** Suppose that in the previous problem you shorted 10,000 shares instead of buying. The initial margin is 60 percent. What does the account balance sheet look like following the short?

3. **Margin Calls (LO3, CFA2)** You purchased 500 shares of stock at a price of $56 per share on 50 percent margin. If the maintenance margin is 30 percent, what is the critical stock price?

Answers to Self-Test Problems

1. The 10,000 shares of American Airlines cost $300,000. You supply $200,000, so you must borrow $100,000. The account balance sheet looks like this:

Assets		Liabilities and Account Equity	
10,000 shares of AAL	$300,000	Margin loan	$100,000
		Account equity	200,000
Total	$300,000	Total	$300,000

Chapter Review Problems and Self-Test

Students are provided with one to three practice problems per chapter with worked-out solutions to test their abilities in solving key problems related to the content of the chapter.

Bloomberg Content

Through an exclusive agreement, the book contains three Bloomberg elements in each chapter. First, at the beginning of each section provides a list of related functions. Second, the end of chapter material contains a set of Bloomberg focused exercises. Third, Bloomberg screenshots are used throughout each chapter to illustrate key concepts. This set of material enables students to gain exposure to Bloomberg.

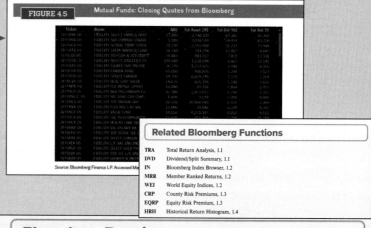

FIGURE 4.5 Mutual Funds: Closing Quotes from Bloomberg

Source: Bloomberg Finance L.P. Accessed Ma

Related Bloomberg Functions

TRA	Total Return Analysis, 1.1
DVD	Dividend/Split Summary, 1.1
IN	Bloomberg Index Browser, 1.2
MRR	Member Ranked Returns, 1.2
WEI	World Equity Indices, 1.2
CRP	County Risk Premiums, 1.3
EQRP	Equity Risk Premium, 1.3
HRH	Historical Return Histogram, 1.4

Bloomberg Exercises

1. Analyze the price and NAV of the ETF with the ticker symbol SPY. Why is the difference so small? **(NAV)**

2. Look up the management team for the Fidelity Magellan (FMAGX) mutual fund. **(MGMT)**

3. Conduct a fund screening to identify the "best" U.S. large-cap value funds. **(FSRC)**

4. Examine the largest positions held by the ETF with the ticker symbol XLY. Is this a diversified set? **(MEMB)**

Test Your Investment Quotient

An average of 15 multiple-choice questions are included for each chapter, many of which are taken from past CFA exams. This text is unique in that it presents CFA questions in multiple-choice format—which is how they appear on the actual exam. Answers to these questions appear in Appendix A.

Test Your Investment Quotient

1. **Investment Objectives (LO1, CFA9)** An individual investor's investment objectives should be expressed in terms of:
   a. Risk and return.
   b. Capital market expectations.
   c. Liquidity needs and time horizon.
   d. Tax factors and legal and regulatory constraints.

2. **Asset Allocation (LO1, CFA5)** Which of the following best reflects the importance of the asset allocation decision to the investment process? The asset allocation decision:
   a. Helps the investor decide on realistic investment goals.
   b. Identifies the specific securities to include in a portfolio.
   c. Determines most of the portfolio's returns and volatility over time.
   d. Creates a standard by which to establish an appropriate investment horizon.

3. **Leverage (LO3, CFA2)** You deposit $100,000 cash in a brokerage account and purchase $200,000 of stocks on margin by borrowing $100,000 from your broker. Later, the value of your stock holdings falls to $150,000, whereupon you get nervous and close your account. What is the percentage return on your investment (ignore interest paid)?
   a. 0 percent
   b. −25 percent
   c. −50 percent
   d. −75 percent

4. **Leverage (LO4, CFA3)** You deposit $100,000 cash in a brokerage account and short sell $200,000 of stocks. Later, the value of the stocks held short rises to $250,000, whereupon you get nervous and close your account. What is the percentage return on your investment (ignore interest paid)?

CFA Exam Review by Schweser

Unique to this text! These reviews are excerpted from Schweser, a leader in CFA exam preparation. Each review addresses chapter content but in a way that is consistent with the format of the actual CFA exam.

CFA Exam Review by Kaplan Schweser

[CFA1, CFA7, CFA8, CFA9]
Barbara Analee, a registered nurse and businesswoman, recently retired at age 50 to pursue a life as a blues singer. She had been running a successful cosmetics and aesthetics business. She is married to Tom, a retired scientist (age 55). They have saved $3 million in their portfolio and now they want to travel the world. Their three children are all grown and out of college and have begun their own families. Barbara now has two grandchildren. Barbara and Tom feel that they have achieved a comfortable portfolio level to support their family's needs for the foreseeable future.

To meet their basic living expenses, Tom and Barbara feel they need $75,000 per year in today's dollars (before taxes) to live comfortably. As a trained professional, Barbara likes to be actively involved in intensively researching investment opportunities. Barbara and Tom want to be able to provide $10,000 per year (pretax) indexed for inflation to each of their grandchildren over the next 10 years for their college education. They also want to set aside $15,000 each year (pretax) indexed for inflation for traveling for Barbara's musical performances around the United States. They have no debt. Most of their portfolio is currently in large-cap U.S. stocks and Treasury notes.

They have approached Pamela Jaycoo, CFA, for guidance on how to best achieve their financial goals. Inflation is expected to increase at an annual rate of 3 percent into the foreseeable future.

1. What is the Analees' return objective?
   a. 6.67 percent
   b. 6.17 percent
   c. 3.83 percent

2. What is their tolerance for risk?
   a. Average
   b. Below average
   c. Above average

What's on the Web?

These end-of-chapter activities show students how to use and learn from the vast amount of financial resources available on the internet.

What's on the Web?

1. **Risk Tolerance** As we discussed in the chapter, risk tolerance is based on an individual's personality and investment goals. There are numerous risk tolerance questionnaires on the web. One, provided by Merrill Lynch, is located at www.ml.com. Go to the website, search for Identifying Your Investor Profile, and take the quiz. How conservative or aggressive are you?

2. **Short Interest** You can find the number of short sales on a particular stock at finance.yahoo.com. Go to the site and find the number of shares short sold for ExxonMobil (XOM) under the "Statistics" link. How many shares are sold short in the current month? What about the previous month? What do "Percent of Float" and "Short Ratio" mean?

3. **Broker Call Money Rate** What is the current broker call money rate? To find out, go to www.bankrate.com and look up the call money rate.

Resources

Teaching and Learning Supplements

We have developed a number of supplements for both teaching and learning to accompany this text. Each product has been significantly revised for the tenth edition.

Digital Solutions

Student Support within Connect

Student-Narrated PowerPoints
Students all learn differently, and these chapter PowerPoints were created with that rationale in mind. The interactive presentations provide detailed examples demonstrating how to solve key problems from the text. The slides are accompanied by an audio narration.

Excel Templates
Corresponding to most end-of-chapter problems, each template allows the student to work through the problem using Excel, reinforcing each concept. Each end-of-chapter problem with a template is indicated by an Excel icon in the margin beside it.

Instructor Support within Connect

PowerPoint Presentation, *prepared by Thomas W. Miller Jr.,* Mississippi State University
This product, created by one of the authors, contains over 300 slides with lecture outlines, examples, and images and tables from the text.

Instructor's Manual, *prepared by Steven D. Dolvin, CFA,* Butler University
Developed by one of the authors, the goals of this product are to outline chapter material clearly and provide extra teaching support. The first section of the Instructor's Manual includes an annotated outline of each chapter with suggested websites, references to PowerPoint slides, teaching tips, additional examples, and current events references.

Solutions Manual, *prepared by Steven D. Dolvin, CFA,* Butler University
The Solutions Manual contains the complete worked-out solutions for the end-of-chapter questions and problems.

Test Bank, *prepared by Scott Ehrhorn,* Liberty University
With almost 1,500 questions, this Test Bank, in Microsoft Word, provides a variety of question formats (true-false, multiple-choice, fill-in-the-blank, and problems) and levels of difficulty to meet any instructor's testing needs.

Test Builder in Connect
Available within Connect, Test Builder is a cloud-based tool that enables instructors to format tests that can be printed or administered within an LMS. Test Builder offers a modern, streamlined interface for easy content configuration that matches course needs, without requiring a download.

Test Builder allows you to:
- access all test bank content from a particular title.
- easily pinpoint the most relevant content through robust filtering options.

- manipulate the order of questions or scramble questions and/or answers.
- pin questions to a specific location within a test.
- determine your preferred treatment of algorithmic questions.
- choose the layout and spacing.
- add instructions and configure default settings.

Test Builder provides a secure interface for better protection of content and allows for just-in-time updates to flow directly into assessments.

McGraw Hill Customer Care Contact Information

At McGraw Hill, we understand that getting the most from new technology can be challenging. That's why our services don't stop after you purchase our products. You can e-mail our Product Specialists 24 hours a day to get product training online. Or you can search our knowledge bank of Frequently Asked Questions on our support website. For Customer Support, call **800-331-5094,** or visit **www.mhhe.com/support.** One of our Technical Support Analysts will be able to assist you in a timely fashion.

 ReadAnywhere®

Read or study when it's convenient for you with McGraw Hill's free ReadAnywhere® app. Available for iOS or Android smartphones or tablets, ReadAnywhere gives users access to McGraw Hill tools including the eBook and SmartBook® 2.0 or Adaptive Learning Assignments in Connect. Take notes, highlight, and complete assignments offline – all of your work will sync when you open the app with Wi-Fi access. Log in with your McGraw Hill Connect username and password to start learning – anytime, anywhere!

Proctorio: Remote Proctoring & Browser-Locking Capabilities

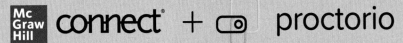

Remote proctoring and browser-locking capabilities, hosted by Proctorio within Connect, provide control of the assessment environment by enabling security options and verifying the identity of the student.

Seamlessly integrated within Connect, these services allow instructors to control the assessment experience by verifying identification, restricting browser activity, and monitoring student actions.

Instant and detailed reporting gives instructors an at-a-glance view of potential academic integrity concerns, thereby avoiding personal bias and supporting evidence-based claims.

Brief Contents

Contents

A Brief History of Risk and Return

"All I ask is for the chance to prove that money can't make me happy."

–Spike Milligan

Who wants to be a millionaire? Actually, anyone can retire as a millionaire. How? Consider this: Suppose you invest $3,000 on your 25th birthday. You have the discipline to invest $3,000 on each of your next 39 birthdays until you retire on your 65th birthday. How much will you have? The answer might surprise you. If you earn 10 percent per year, you will have about $1.46 million. Are these numbers realistic? Based on the history of financial markets, the answer appears to be yes. For example, over the last 100 or so years, the widely followed Standard & Poor's index of large-company common stocks has actually yielded about 12 percent per year.

CFA™ Exam Topics in This Chapter:

 1. Time value of money (L1, S1)

 2. Common probability distributions (L1, S2)

 3. Sampling and estimation (L1, S2)

 4. Portfolio risk and return: Part I (L1, S17)

 5. Analysis of dividend and share repurchases (L2, S6)

 6. Portfolio performance evaluation (L3, S13)

Go to Connect for a guide that aligns your textbook with CFA readings.

The study of investments could begin in many places. After thinking it over, we decided that a brief history lesson is in order, so we start our discussion of risk and return by looking back at what has happened to investors in U.S. financial markets since 1925. In 1931, for example, the stock market lost 43 percent of its value. Just two years later, the market reversed itself and gained 54 percent. In more recent times, the stock market lost about 25 percent of its value on October 19, 1987, alone, and it gained almost 40 percent in 1995. From 2003 through 2007, the market gained about 80 percent. In 2008, the market fell almost 40 percent. In 2009, the market reversed course again, and through 2018 the market recovered from its large losses (and more), as the return over this nine-year period was over 200 percent.

So what should you, as a stock market investor, expect when you invest your own money? In this chapter, we study close to a century of market history to find out. We pay particular attention to the historical relation between risk and return. As you will see, this chapter has a lot of very practical information for anyone thinking of investing in financial assets such as stocks and bonds. For example, suppose you were to start investing in stocks today. Do you think your money would grow at an average rate of 5 percent per year? Or 10 percent? Or 20 percent? This chapter gives you an idea of what to expect (the answer may surprise you). The chapter also shows how risky certain investments can be, and it gives you the tools to think about risk in an objective way.

Our primary goal in this chapter is to see what financial market history can tell us about risk and return. Specifically, we want to give you a perspective on the numbers. What is a high return? What is a low return? More generally, what returns should we expect from financial assets such as stocks and bonds, and what are the risks from such investments? Beyond this, we hope that by studying what *did* happen in the past, we will at least gain some insight into what *can* happen in the future.

Not everyone agrees on the value of studying history. On the one hand, there is philosopher George Santayana's famous comment, "Those who do not remember the past are condemned to repeat it." On the other hand, there is industrialist Henry Ford's equally famous comment, "History is more or less bunk." These extremes aside, perhaps everyone would agree with Mark Twain, who observed, with remarkable foresight (and poor grammar), that "October. This is one of the peculiarly dangerous months to speculate in stocks in. The others are July, January, September, April, November, May, March, June, December, August, and February."

Two key observations emerge from a study of financial market history. First, there is a reward for bearing risk, and, at least on average, that reward has been substantial. That's the good news. The bad news is that greater rewards are accompanied by greater risks. The fact that risk and return go together is probably the single most important fact to understand about investments, and it is a point to which we will return many times.

1.1 Returns

We wish to discuss historical returns on different types of financial assets. First, we need to know how to compute the return from an investment. We will consider buying shares of stock in this section, but the basic calculations are the same for any investment.

DOLLAR RETURNS

If you buy an asset of any type, your gain (or loss) from that investment is called the *return* on your investment. This return will usually have two components. First, you may receive some cash directly while you own the investment. Second, the value of the asset you purchase may change. In this case, you have a capital gain or capital loss on your investment.[1]

Related Bloomberg Functions
TRA   Total Return Analysis
DVD   Dividend/Split Summary

---

[1] As a practical matter, what is and what is not a capital gain (or loss) is determined by the Internal Revenue Service. Even so, as is commonly done, we use these terms to refer to a change in value.

To illustrate, suppose you purchased 200 shares of stock in Harley-Davidson (ticker symbol: HOG) on January 1. At that time, Harley was selling for $50 per share, so your 200 shares cost you $10,000. At the end of the year, you want to see how you did with your investment.

The first thing to consider is that over the year, a company may pay cash dividends to its shareholders. As a stockholder in Harley, you are a part owner of the company, and you are entitled to a portion of any money distributed. If Harley chooses to pay a dividend, you will receive some cash for every share you own.

In addition to the dividend, the other part of your return is the capital gain or loss on the stock. This part arises from changes in the value of your investment. For example, consider these two cases:

	Case 1	Case 2
Ending Stock Price	$ 55.60	$ 39.80
January 1 value	10,000	10,000
December 31 value	11,120	7,960
Dividend income	80	80
Capital gain or loss	1,120	−2,040

At the beginning of the year, on January 1, the stock was selling for $50 per share. As we calculated above, your total outlay for 200 shares is $10,000. Over the year, Harley paid dividends of $.40 per share, which means that by the end of the year, you received dividend income of:

$$\text{Dividend income} = \$.40 \times 200 = \$80$$

In Case 1, suppose that as of December 31, a HOG share was selling for $55.60, meaning that the value of your stock increased by $5.60 per share. Your 200 shares would be worth $11,120, so you have a capital gain of:

$$\text{Capital gain} = (\$55.60 - \$50) \times 200 = \$1,120$$

On the other hand, if the price had dropped to, say, $39.80 (Case 2), you would have a capital loss of:

$$\text{Capital loss} = (\$39.80 - \$50) \times 200 = -\$2,040$$

Notice that a capital loss is the same thing as a negative capital gain.

total dollar return
The return on an investment measured in dollars that accounts for all cash flows and capital gains or losses.

The **total dollar return** on your investment is the sum of the dividend income and the capital gain (or loss):

$$\text{Total dollar return} = \text{Dividend income} + \text{Capital gain (or loss)}$$

In Case 1, the total dollar return is thus given by:

$$\text{Total dollar return} = \$80 + \$1,120 = \$1,200$$

Overall, between the dividends you received and the increase in the price of the stock, the value of your investment increased from $10,000 to $10,000 + $1,200 = $11,200.

A common misconception often arises in this context. Suppose you hold on to your Harley-Davidson stock and don't sell it at the end of the year. Should you still consider the capital gain as part of your return? Isn't this only a "paper" gain and not really a cash gain if you don't sell it?

The answer to the first question is a strong yes, and the answer to the second is an equally strong no. The capital gain is every bit as much a part of your return as the dividend, and you should certainly count it as part of your return. The fact that you decide to keep the stock and don't sell (you don't "realize" the gain) is irrelevant because you could have converted it to cash if you had wanted to. Whether you choose to do so is up to you.

After all, if you insist on converting your gain to cash, you could always sell the stock and immediately reinvest by buying the stock back. There is no difference between doing this and just not selling (assuming, of course, that there are no transaction costs or tax consequences from selling the stock). Again, the point is that whether you actually cash out and buy pizzas (or whatever) or continue to hold the investment doesn't affect the return you actually earn.

PERCENTAGE RETURNS

It is usually more convenient to summarize information about returns in percentage terms than in dollar terms because that way your return doesn't depend on how much you actually invested. With percentage returns, the question we want to answer is: How much do we get for each dollar we invest?

To answer this question, let P_t be the price of the stock at the beginning of the year. Let D_{t+1} be the dividend paid on the stock during the year. The following cash flows are the same as those shown earlier, except that we have now expressed everything on a per-share basis:

	Case 1	Case 2
January 1 stock price, P_t	$50.00	$50.00
December 31 stock price, P_{t+1}	55.60	39.80
Dividend income, D_{t+1}	.40	.40
Capital gain or loss	5.60	−10.20

In our example, the price at the beginning of the year was $50 per share and the dividend paid during the year on each share was $.40. If we divide the dividend by the beginning stock price, the result is the **dividend yield**:

$$\text{Dividend yield} = D_{t+1}/P_t \tag{1.1}$$
$$= \$.40/\$50 = .0080, \text{ or } .80\%$$

This calculation says that for each dollar we invested, we received .80 cents in dividends.

The second component of our percentage return is the **capital gains yield.** This yield is calculated as the change in the price during the year (the capital gain) divided by the beginning price. With the Case 1 ending price, we get:

$$\text{Capital gains yield} = (P_{t+1} - P_t)/P_t \tag{1.2}$$
$$= (\$55.60 - \$50.00)/\$50.00$$
$$= \$5.60/\$50 = .1120, \text{ or } 11.20\%$$

This 11.20 percent yield means that for each dollar invested, we got about 11 cents in capital gains (HOG heaven).

Putting it all together, per dollar invested, we get .80 cent in dividends and 11.20 cents in capital gains for a total of 12.00 cents. Our **total percent return** is 12 cents on the dollar, or 12.00 percent. When a return is expressed on a percentage basis, we often refer to it as the *rate of return,* or just "return," on the investment. Notice that if we combine the formulas for the dividend yield and capital gains yield, we get a single formula for the total percentage return:

$$\text{Percentage return} = \text{Dividend yield} + \text{Capital gains yield}$$
$$= D_{t+1}/P_t + (P_{t+1} - P_t)/P_t \tag{1.3}$$
$$= (D_{t+1} + P_{t+1} - P_t)/P_t$$

To check our calculations, notice that we invested $10,000 and ended up with $11,200. By what percentage did our $10,000 increase? As we saw, our gain was $11,200 − $10,000 = $1,200. This is an increase of $1,200/$10,000, or 12.00 percent.

dividend yield
The annual stock dividend as a percentage of the initial stock price.

capital gains yield
The change in stock price as a percentage of the initial stock price.

total percent return
The return on an investment measured as a percentage that accounts for all cash flows and capital gains or losses.

WORK THE WEB

To look up information on common stocks using the web, you need to know the "ticker" symbol for the stocks in which you are interested. Look up ticker symbols in many places, including one of our favorite sites, finance.yahoo.com. Here we have looked up (using the "Quote Lookup" link) and entered ticker symbols for Tesla and some well-known "tech" stocks: Apple,

Microsoft, Amazon, and Meta (better known as Facebook). Our results are shown below.

As you can see, we get the price for each stock, along with information about the change in price and volume (number of shares traded). You will find a lot of links to hit and learn more, so have at it!

Symbol	Last Price	Change	Chg %	Currency	Market Time	Volume	Shares	Avg Vol (3m)	Day Range		52-Wk Range		Day Chart	Market Cap
AAPL	137.59	+0.24	+0.17%	USD	4:00PM EDT	137.426M	-	98.074M	132.61	140.43	123.13	182.94		2.227T
MSFT	252.56	-0.58	-0.23%	USD	4:00PM EDT	39.018M	-	33.772M	248.46	258.54	243.00	349.67		1.889T
AMZN	2,151.82	+5.44	+0.25%	USD	4:00PM EDT	4.975M	-	4.022M	2,100.20	2,197.41	2,048.11	3,773.08		1.095T
FB	193.54	+2.25	+1.18%	USD	4:00PM EDT	31.305M	-	33.601M	187.87	197.91	169.00	384.33		523.781B
TSLA	663.90	-45.52	-6.42%	USD	4:00PM EDT	47.859M	-	27.085M	633.00	721.58	571.22	1,243.49		687.807B

Source: finance.yahoo.com.

EXAMPLE 1.1 | Calculating Percentage Returns

Suppose you buy some stock in Concannon Plastics for $35 per share. After one year, the price is $49 per share. During the year, you received a $1.40 dividend per share. What is the dividend yield? The capital gains yield? The percentage return? If your total investment was $1,400, how much do you have at the end of the year?

Your $1.40 dividend per share works out to a dividend yield of:

$$\text{Dividend yield} = D_{t+1}/P_t$$
$$= \$1.40/\$35$$
$$= .04, \text{ or } 4\%$$

The per-share capital gain is $14, so the capital gains yield is:

$$\text{Capital gains yield} = (P_{t+1} - P_t)/P_t$$
$$= (\$49 - \$35)/\$35$$
$$= \$14/\$35$$
$$= .4, \text{ or } 40\%$$

The total percentage return is thus 4% + 40% = 44%.

If you had invested $1,400, you would have $2,016 at the end of the year. To check this, note that your $1,400 would have bought you $1,400/$35 = 40 shares. Your 40 shares would then have paid you a total of 40 × $1.40 = $56 in cash dividends. Your $14 per share gain would give you a total capital gain of $14 × 40 = $560. Add these together and you get $616, which is a 44 percent total return on your $1,400 investment.

A NOTE ON ANNUALIZING RETURNS

So far, we have only considered annual returns. Of course, the actual length of time you own an investment will almost never be exactly a year. To compare investments, however, we will usually need to express returns on a per-year or "annualized" basis, so we need to do a little bit more work.

For example, suppose you bought 200 shares of Cisco Systems (CSCO) at a price of $30 per share. In three months, you sell your stock for $31.50. You didn't receive any dividends. What is your return for the three months? What is your annualized return?

In this case, we say that your *holding period,* which is the length of time you own the stock, is three months. With a zero dividend, you know that the percentage return can be calculated as:

$$\text{Percentage return} = (P_{t+1} - P_t)/P_t = (\$31.50 - \$30)/\$30 = .0500, \text{ or } 5.00\%$$

This 5.00 percent is your return for the three-month holding period, but what does this return amount to on a per-year basis? To find out, we need to convert this to an annualized return, meaning a return expressed on a per-year basis. Such a return is often called an **effective annual return,** or **EAR** for short. The general formula is:

$$1 + EAR = (1 + \text{Holding period percentage return})^m \qquad (1.4)$$

where *m* is the number of holding periods in a year.

In our example, the holding period percentage return is 5.00 percent, or .0500. The holding period is three months, so there are four (12 months/3 months) periods in a year. We calculate the annualized return, or *EAR,* as follows:

$$
\begin{aligned}
1 + EAR &= (1 + \text{Holding period percentage return})^m \\
&= (1 + .0500)^4 \\
&= 1.2155
\end{aligned}
$$

Thus, your annualized return is 21.55 percent.

effective annual return (EAR)
The return on an investment expressed on a per-year, or "annualized," basis.

EXAMPLE 1.2 | **Annualized Returns**

Suppose you buy stock in Moderna (MRNA) at a price of $28 per share. Four months later, you sell for $29.40 per share. No dividend is paid. What is your annualized return on this investment?

For the four-month holding period, your return is:

$$\text{Percentage return} = (P_{t+1} - P_t)/P_t = (\$29.40 - \$28)/\$28 = .05, \text{ or } 5\%$$

There are three four-month periods in a year, so the annualized return is:

$$1 + EAR = (1 + \text{Holding period percentage return})^m = (1 + .05)^3 = 1.1576$$

Subtracting the one, we get an annualized return of .1576, or 15.76 percent.

EXAMPLE 1.3 | **More Annualized Returns**

Suppose you buy stock in Johnson & Johnson (JNJ) at a price of $60 per share. Three years later, you sell it for $64.50. No dividends were paid. What is your annualized return on this investment?

The situation here is a bit different because your holding period is now longer than a year, but the calculation is basically the same. For the three-year holding period, your return is:

$$\text{Percentage return} = (P_{t+1} - P_t)/P_t = (\$64.50 - \$60)/\$60 = .075, \text{ or } 7.5\%$$

How many three-year holding periods are there in a single year? The answer is one-third, so *m* in this case is 1/3. The annualized return is:

$$
\begin{aligned}
1 + EAR &= (1 + \text{Holding period percentage return})^m \\
&= (1 + .075)^{1/3} \\
&= 1.0244
\end{aligned}
$$

Subtracting the one, we get an annualized return of .0244, or 2.44 percent.

Now that you know how to calculate returns on a hypothetical stock, you should calculate returns for real stocks. The nearby *Work the Web* box using finance.yahoo.com describes how to begin. Meanwhile, in the next several sections, we will take a look at the returns that some common types of investments have earned over the last 96 years.

CHECK THIS

1.1a   What are the two parts of total return?

1.1b   What is the difference between a dollar return and a percentage return? Why are percentage returns usually more convenient?

1.1c   What is an effective annual return (EAR)?

1.2 The Historical Record

We now examine year-to-year historical rates of return on five important categories of financial investments. These returns represent what you would have earned if you had invested in portfolios of the following asset categories:

1. Large-company stocks. The large-company stock portfolio is based on the Standard & Poor's (S&P's) 500 index, which contains 500 of the largest companies (in terms of total market value of outstanding stock) in the United States.

2. Small-company stocks. This is a portfolio composed of stock of smaller companies, where "small" corresponds to the smallest 20 percent of the companies listed on the New York Stock Exchange, again as measured by market value of outstanding stock.

3. Long-term corporate bonds. This is a portfolio of high-quality bonds with 20 years to maturity.

4. Long-term U.S. government bonds. This is a portfolio of U.S. government bonds with 20 years to maturity.

5. U.S. Treasury bills. This is a portfolio of Treasury bills (T-bills for short) with a three-month maturity.

If you are not entirely certain what these investments are, don't be overly concerned. We will have much more to say about each in later chapters. For now, just accept that these are some important investment categories. In addition to the year-to-year returns on these financial instruments, the year-to-year percentage changes in the Consumer Price Index (CPI) are also computed. The CPI is a standard measure of consumer goods price inflation. We discuss the CPI in more detail in a later chapter.

Here is a bit of market jargon for you. A company's *total market capitalization* (or market "cap" for short) is equal to its stock price multiplied by the number of shares of stock. In other words, it's the total value of the company's stock. Large companies are often called "large-cap" stocks, and small companies are called "small-cap" stocks. We'll use these terms frequently.

A FIRST LOOK

Before examining the different portfolio returns, we first take a look at the "big picture." Figure 1.1 shows what happened to $1 invested in these different portfolios at the beginning of 1926 and held over the 96-year period ending in 2021 (for clarity, the long-term corporate bonds are omitted). To fit all the information on a single graph, some modification in scaling is used. As is commonly done with financial time series, the vertical axis is scaled so that equal distances measure equal percentage (as opposed to dollar) changes in value. Thus, the distance between $10 and $100 is the same as that between $100 and $1,000 because both distances represent the same 900 percent increases.

Looking at Figure 1.1, we see that the small-company investment did the best overall. Every dollar invested grew to a remarkable $56,033.70 over the 96 years. The larger common stock portfolio did less well; a dollar invested in it grew to $14,086.37.

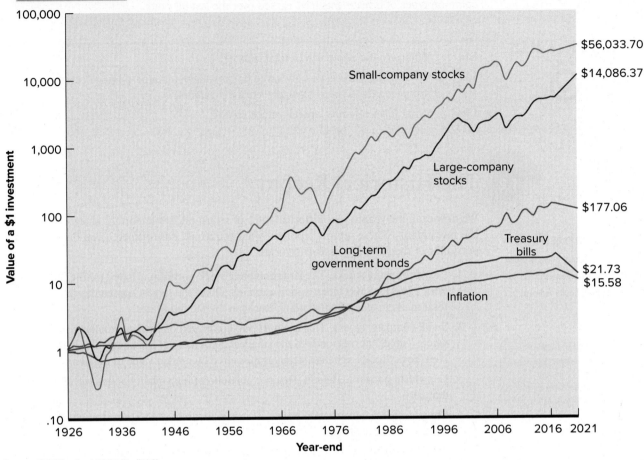

Source: *SBBI Yearbook* 2022 (Kroll LLC).

At the other end, the T-bill portfolio grew to only $21.73. This is even less impressive when we consider the inflation over this period. As illustrated, the increase in the price level was such that $15.58 is needed just to replace the original $1.

Given the historical record, why would anybody buy anything other than small-company stocks? If you look closely at Figure 1.1, you will probably see the answer—risk. The T-bill portfolio and the long-term government bond portfolio grew more slowly than did the stock portfolios, but they also grew much more steadily. The small stocks ended up on top, but, as you can see, they grew quite erratically at times. For example, the small stocks were the worst performers for about the first 10 years and had a smaller return than long-term government bonds for almost 15 years.

A LONGER-RANGE LOOK

The data available on the stock returns before 1925 are not comprehensive, but it is nonetheless possible to trace reasonably accurate returns in U.S. financial markets as far back as 1801. Figure 1.2 shows the values, at the end of 2021, of $1 invested since 1801 in stocks, long-term bonds, short-term bills, and gold. The CPI is also included for reference.

FIGURE 1.2 Financial Market History

Total return indexes (1801–2021)

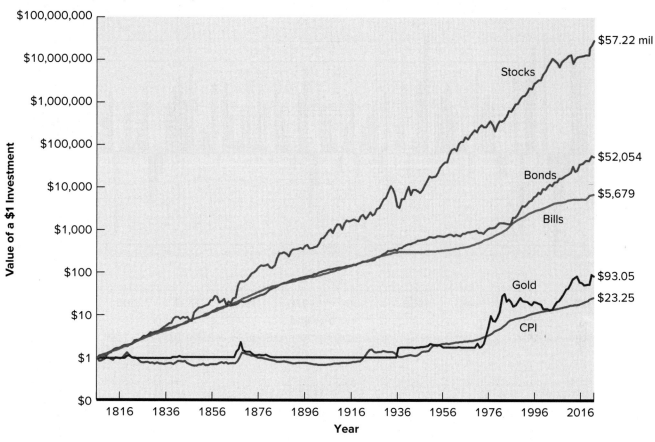

Sources: Jeremy J. Siegel, *Stocks for the Long Run*, 3rd ed. (New York: McGraw-Hill, 2003); update through 2009 provided by Jeremy J. Siegel; update through 2015 from Global Financial Data (www.globalfinancialdata.com) and Professor Kenneth R. French, Dartmouth College. Update through 2021 from *SBBI Yearbook 2022* (Kroll LLC), other sources.

Inspecting Figure 1.2, we see that $1 invested in stocks grew to an astounding $57.22 million over this 221-year period. During this time, the returns from investing in stocks dwarf those earned on other investments. Notice also in Figure 1.2 that, after 170 years, gold managed to outpace inflation beginning in the 1970s.

What we see thus far is that there has been a powerful financial incentive for long-term investing. The real moral of the story is this: Get an early start!

A CLOSER LOOK

To illustrate the variability of the different investments and inflation, Figures 1.3 through 1.6 plot the year-to-year percentage returns in the form of vertical bars drawn from the horizontal axis. The height of a bar tells us the return for the particular year. For example, looking at the long-term government bonds (Figure 1.5), we see that the largest historical return (47.14 percent) occurred in 1982. This year was a good year for bonds. In comparing these charts, notice the differences in the vertical axis scales. With these differences in mind, you can see how predictably the Treasury bills (bottom of Figure 1.5) behaved compared to the small-company stocks (Figure 1.4).

The returns shown in these bar graphs are sometimes very large. Looking at the graphs, we see, for example, that the largest single-year return was a remarkable 153 percent for

FIGURE 1.3

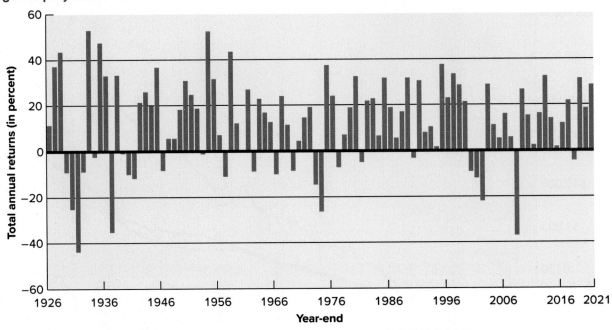

Year-to-Year Total Returns on Large-Company Stocks: 1926–2021

Large-company stocks

Source: Professor Kenneth R. French, Dartmouth College through 2015. Update through 2021, *SBBI Yearbook 2022* (Kroll LLC).

FIGURE 1.4

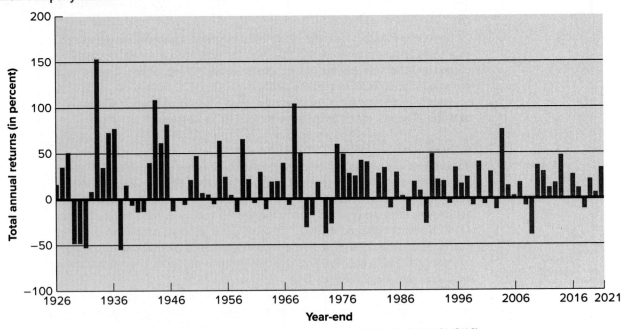

Year-to-Year Total Returns on Small-Company Stocks: 1926–2021

Small-company stocks

Source: Professor Kenneth R. French, Dartmouth College through 2015. Update through 2021, *SBBI Yearbook 2022* (Kroll LLC).

Long-term U.S. government bonds

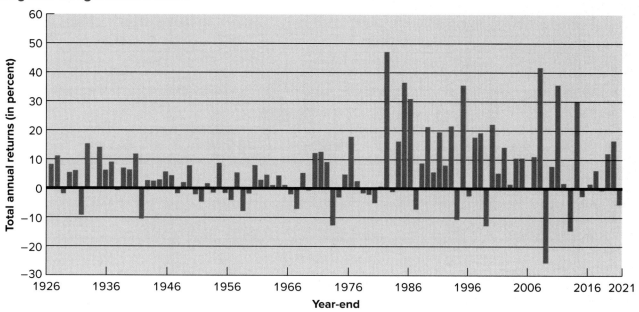

U.S. Treasury bills

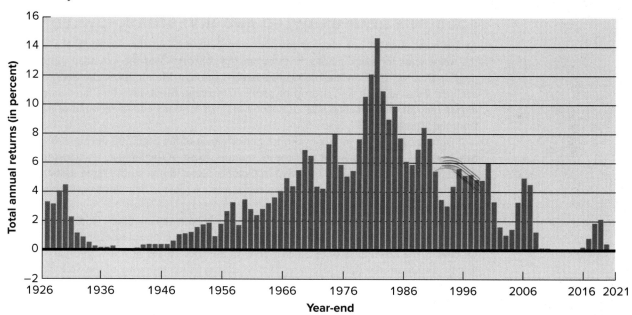

Source: Global Financial Data (www.globalfinancialdata.com) through 2015. Update through 2021, *SBBI Yearbook 2022* (Kroll LLC).

small-company stocks in 1933. In the same year, the large-company stocks returned "only" 53 percent. In contrast, the largest Treasury bill return was 14.6 percent in 1981. The Treasury bill return was near zero in a number of recent years. For future reference, the actual year-to-year returns for the S&P 500, long-term U.S. government bonds, U.S. Treasury bills, and the CPI are shown in Table 1.1.

FIGURE 1.6 | Year-to-Year Inflation: 1926–2021

Inflation cumulative index and rates of change

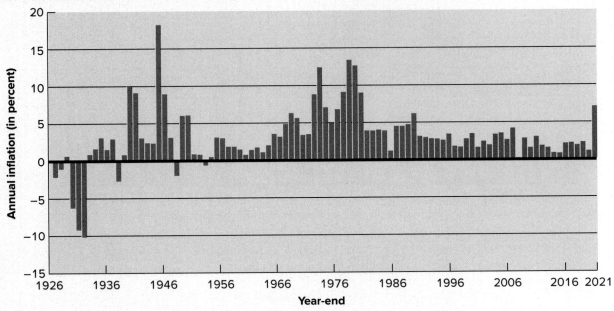

Source: Global Financial Data (www.globalfinancialdata.com) through 2015. Update through 2021, *SBBI Yearbook 2022* (Kroll LLC).

2008: THE BEAR GROWLED AND INVESTORS HOWLED

As we mentioned in our chapter introduction, 2008 entered the record books as one of the worst years for stock market investors in U.S. history. Over the extended period beginning in October 2007 (when the decline began) through March 2009, the S&P 500 index declined from 1,576 to 677, a drop of about 57 percent. Stock investors fared much better during the rest of 2009. The S&P 500 stood at 1,115 at year's end—a rebound of 65 percent from the March low.

Figure 1.7 shows the month-by-month performance of the S&P 500 during 2008. As indicated, returns were negative in 8 of the 12 months. Most of the damage occurred in the fall, with investors losing almost 17 percent in October alone. Small stocks fared no better. They fell 37 percent for the year (with a 21 percent drop in October), their worst performance since losing 58 percent in 1937.

As Figure 1.7 suggests, stock prices were highly volatile during 2008. Oddly, the S&P had 126 up days and 126 down days (remember the markets are closed weekends and holidays). Of course, the down days were much worse on average. To see how extraordinary volatility was in 2008, consider that there were 18 days during which the value of the S&P changed by more than 5 percent. There were only 17 such moves between 1956 and 2007!

The drop in stock prices in 2008 was a global phenomenon, and many of the world's major markets were off by much more than the S&P. China, India, and Russia, for example, all experienced declines of more than 50 percent. Tiny Iceland saw share prices drop by more than 90 percent for the year. Trading on the Icelandic exchange was temporarily suspended on October 9. In what has to be a modern record for a single day, stocks fell by 76 percent when trading resumed on October 14.

Did U.S. investors encounter any bright spots? The answer is yes: As stocks plummeted, bonds soared, particularly U.S. Treasury bonds. In fact, long-term Treasuries gained over 40 percent in 2008, while shorter-term Treasury bonds were up 13 percent. Long-term corporate bonds did not fare as well but still managed to finish in positive territory, up 9 percent. These returns were especially impressive considering that the rate of inflation, as measured by the CPI, was essentially zero.

TABLE 1.1 Year-to-Year Total Returns: 1926–2021

Year	Large-Company Stocks	Long-Term U.S. Government Bonds	U.S. Treasury Bills	Consumer Price Index	Year	Large-Company Stocks	Long-Term U.S. Government Bonds	U.S. Treasury Bills	Consumer Price Index
1926	11.14%	8.26%	3.30%	−1.12%	1975	37.23%	4.86%	5.87%	6.94%
1927	37.13%	11.15%	3.15%	−2.26%	1976	23.93%	17.86%	5.07%	4.86%
1928	43.31%	−1.90%	4.05%	−1.16%	1977	−7.16%	2.57%	5.45%	6.70%
1929	−8.91%	5.41%	4.47%	.58%	1978	6.57%	−1.61%	7.64%	9.02%
1930	−25.26%	6.08%	2.27%	−6.40%	1979	18.61%	−2.08%	10.56%	13.29%
1931	−43.86%	−9.26%	1.15%	−9.32%	1980	32.50%	−4.96%	12.10%	12.52%
1932	−8.85%	15.37%	.88%	−10.27%	1981	−4.92%	.69%	14.60%	8.92%
1933	52.88%	−.04%	.52%	.76%	1982	21.55%	47.14%	10.94%	3.83%
1934	−2.34%	14.16%	.27%	1.52%	1983	22.56%	−1.14%	8.99%	3.79%
1935	47.22%	6.24%	.17%	2.99%	1984	6.27%	16.29%	9.90%	3.95%
1936	32.80%	9.05%	.17%	1.45%	1985	31.73%	36.59%	7.71%	3.80%
1937	−35.26%	−.69%	.27%	2.86%	1986	18.67%	30.93%	6.09%	1.10%
1938	33.20%	6.96%	.06%	−2.78%	1987	5.25%	−7.14%	5.88%	4.43%
1939	−.91%	6.34%	.04%	.00%	1988	16.61%	8.75%	6.94%	4.42%
1940	−10.08%	11.88%	.04%	.71%	1989	31.69%	21.30%	8.44%	4.65%
1941	−11.77%	−10.51%	.14%	9.93%	1990	−3.10%	5.66%	7.69%	6.11%
1942	21.07%	2.70%	.34%	9.03%	1991	30.47%	19.47%	5.43%	3.06%
1943	25.76%	2.50%	.38%	2.96%	1992	7.62%	8.08%	3.48%	2.90%
1944	19.69%	2.94%	.38%	2.30%	1993	10.08%	21.53%	3.03%	2.75%
1945	36.46%	5.69%	.38%	2.25%	1994	1.32%	−10.64%	4.39%	2.67%
1946	−8.18%	4.41%	.38%	18.13%	1995	37.58%	35.66%	5.61%	2.54%
1947	5.24%	−1.77%	.62%	8.84%	1996	22.96%	−2.54%	5.14%	3.32%
1948	5.10%	2.03%	1.06%	2.99%	1997	33.36%	17.70%	5.19%	1.70%
1949	18.06%	7.91%	1.12%	−2.07%	1998	28.58%	19.22%	4.86%	1.61%
1950	30.58%	−2.12%	1.22%	5.93%	1999	21.04%	−12.76%	4.80%	2.68%
1951	24.55%	−4.64%	1.56%	6.00%	2000	−9.10%	22.16%	5.98%	3.39%
1952	18.50%	1.69%	1.75%	.75%	2001	−11.89%	5.32%	3.33%	1.55%
1953	−1.10%	−1.54%	1.87%	.75%	2002	−22.10%	14.23%	1.61%	2.38%
1954	52.40%	8.77%	.93%	−.74%	2003	28.68%	1.51%	1.03%	1.88%
1955	31.43%	−1.63%	1.80%	.37%	2004	10.88%	10.53%	1.43%	3.26%
1956	6.63%	−4.04%	2.66%	2.99%	2005	4.91%	−2.54%	3.30%	3.42%
1957	−10.85%	5.44%	3.28%	2.90%	2006	15.80%	.11%	4.97%	2.54%
1958	43.34%	−7.80%	1.71%	1.76%	2007	5.49%	11.07%	4.52%	4.08%
1959	11.90%	−1.81%	3.48%	1.73%	2008	−37.00%	41.78%	1.24%	.09%
1960	.48%	8.04%	2.81%	1.36%	2009	26.46%	−25.61%	.15%	2.72%
1961	26.81%	2.94%	2.40%	.67%	2010	15.06%	7.73%	.14%	1.50%
1962	−8.78%	4.67%	2.82%	1.33%	2011	2.11%	35.75%	.06%	2.96%
1963	22.69%	1.14%	3.23%	1.64%	2012	16.00%	1.80%	.08%	1.74%
1964	16.36%	4.45%	3.62%	.97%	2013	32.39%	−14.69%	.05%	1.50%
1965	12.36%	1.15%	4.06%	1.92%	2014	13.69%	29.76%	.03%	.76%
1966	−10.10%	−2.01%	4.94%	3.46%	2015	1.38%	−2.61%	.06%	.73%
1967	23.94%	−7.02%	4.39%	3.04%	2016	11.96%	1.75%	.20%	2.07%
1968	11.00%	5.36%	5.49%	4.72%	2017	21.83%	6.24%	.80%	2.11%
1969	−8.47%	−.67%	6.90%	6.20%	2018	−4.38%	−.57%	1.81%	1.91%
1970	3.94%	12.24%	6.50%	5.57%	2019	31.49%	12.16%	2.15%	2.29%
1971	14.30%	12.67%	4.36%	3.27%	2020	18.40%	16.65%	.45%	1.36%
1972	18.99%	9.15%	4.23%	3.41%	2021	28.71%	−5.41%	.04%	7.04%
1973	−14.69%	−12.66%	7.29%	8.71%					
1974	−26.47%	−3.05%	7.99%	12.34%					

Source: Author calculations based on data obtained from Global Financial Data (www.globalfinancialdata.com) and Professor Kenneth R. French, Dartmouth College through 2015. Update through 2021, *SBBI Yearbook 2022* (Kroll LLC).

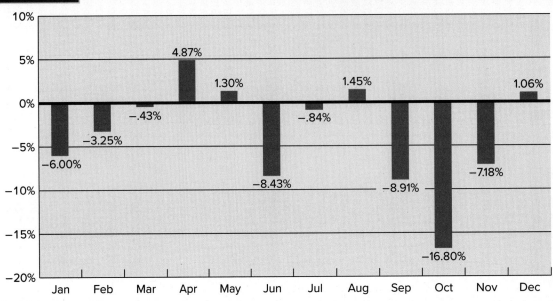

FIGURE 1.7   S&P 500 Monthly Returns: 2008

Source: Author calculations.

What lessons should investors take away from this very recent bit of capital market history? First, and most obviously, stocks have significant risk! But note a second, equally important lesson: Depending on the mix, a diversified portfolio of stocks and bonds probably would have suffered in 2008, but the losses would have been much smaller than those experienced by an all-stock portfolio. In other words, diversification matters, a point we will examine in detail in our next chapter.

CHECK THIS

1.2a   With 20/20 hindsight, which investment category performed best for the period 1926–1935?

1.2b   Why doesn't everyone just buy small-company stocks as investments?

1.2c   What was the smallest return observed over the 93 years for each category of investments? Approximately when did it occur?

1.2d   About how many times did large-company stocks (common stocks) return more than 30 percent? How many times did they return less than −20 percent?

1.2e   What was the longest "winning streak" (years without a negative return) for large-company stocks? For long-term government bonds?

1.2f   How often did the T-bill portfolio have a negative return?

 1.3 Average Returns: The First Lesson

Related Bloomberg Functions

CRP   Country Risk Premium

EQRP   Equity Risk Premium

As you've probably begun to notice, the history of financial market returns in an undigested form is complicated. What we need are simple measures to accurately summarize and describe all these numbers. Accordingly, we discuss how to go about condensing detailed numerical data. We start by calculating average returns.

TABLE 1.2	Average Annual Returns: 1926–2021	
Investment		**Average Return**
Large-company stocks		12.3%
Small-company stocks		16.3
Long-term corporate bonds		6.4
Long-term government bonds		6.0
U.S. Treasury bills		3.3
Inflation		3.0

Source: *SBBI Yearbook 2022* (Kroll LLC).

CALCULATING AVERAGE RETURNS

The obvious way to calculate average returns on the different investments in Figures 1.3 to 1.5 is to add up the yearly returns and divide by 96. The result is the historical average of the individual values. For example, if you add the returns for large-company common stocks for the 96 years, you will get about 1,181 percent. The average annual return is thus 1,181/96 = 12.3. You can interpret this 12.3 percent just like any other average. If you picked a year at random from the 96-year history and you had to guess the return in that year, the best guess would be 12.3 percent.

AVERAGE RETURNS: THE HISTORICAL RECORD

Table 1.2 shows the average returns for the investments we have discussed. Because these averages do not reflect the impact of inflation, we include an average inflation rate. Notice that over this 96-year period, the average inflation rate was 3 percent per year while the average return on U.S. Treasury bills was 3.3 percent per year. Thus, the average return on Treasury bills exceeded the average rate of inflation by only .3 percent per year. At the other extreme, the return on small-company common stocks exceeded the rate of inflation by about 16.3% − 3% = 13.3%. For large-company stocks, we get 12.3% − 3% = 9.3% per year.

RISK PREMIUMS

Now that we have computed some average returns, it seems logical to see how they compare with each other. Based on our discussion above, one such comparison involves government-issued securities. These are free of much of the variability we see in, for example, the stock market.

The government borrows money by issuing debt, that is, bonds. Bonds come in different forms, but we will focus on Treasury bills. Treasury bills have the shortest time to maturity of the different types of government debt. Because the government can always raise taxes or print money to pay its expenses, Treasury bills are virtually free of any default risk. Thus, we will call the rate of return on such debt the **risk-free rate,** and we will use it as a kind of investing benchmark.

risk-free rate
The rate of return on a riskless investment.

A particularly interesting comparison involves the virtually risk-free return on T-bills and the risky return on common stocks. The difference between these two returns can be interpreted as a measure of the *excess return* on the average risky asset (assuming that the stock of a large U.S. corporation has about average risk compared to all risky assets). Using the values in Table 1.2, we see that this excess return is 12.3% − 3.3% = 9%.

We call this the "excess" return because it is the additional return we earn by moving from a virtually risk-free investment to a risky one. Because this excess return can be interpreted as a reward for bearing risk, we will call it a **risk premium.**

risk premium
The extra return on a risky asset over the risk-free rate; the reward for bearing risk.

THE U.S. EQUITY RISK PREMIUM: HISTORICAL AND INTERNATIONAL PERSPECTIVES So far in this chapter, we have studied returns in U.S. stock and bond markets in the period 1926–2021. As we have discussed, the historical U.S. stock market risk premium has been substantial. Of course, whenever we use the past to predict the future, there is a danger that the past period isn't representative of what the future will hold. Perhaps U.S. investors got lucky over this period and earned particularly large returns. As we have noted, data from earlier years are available, although not of the same quality. The U.S. equity risk premium in the pre-1926 era was smaller than it was in the post-1926 era. Using U.S. return data from 1801 to 2006, the historical equity risk premium was 5.4 percent.

Thanks to Professors Elroy Dimson, Paul Marsh, and Michael Staunton, data from earlier periods and other countries are now available to help us take a closer look at equity risk premiums. Over the period 1900–2005, the U.S. historical equity risk premium is the eighth highest at 7.4 percent (which differs from our estimate below because of the different time periods examined). The overall world average risk premium is 7.1 percent. It seems clear that U.S. investors did well, but not exceptionally so relative to many other countries. The top-performing countries were the United States, Australia, and France; the worst performers were Denmark and Norway. Germany, Japan, and Italy might make an interesting case study because they had the highest stock returns over this period (despite World Wars I and II), but they also had the highest risk.

What is a good estimate of the U.S. equity risk premium going forward? Unfortunately, nobody can know for sure what investors expect in the future. If history is a guide, the expected U.S. equity risk premium could be 7.4 percent based on estimates from 1900–2005. We should also be mindful that the average world equity risk premium was 7.1 percent over this same period. On the other hand, the earlier period (1801–1925) suggests lower estimates. Taking a slightly different approach, Professor Ivo Welch asked the opinions of 226 financial economists regarding the future U.S. equity risk premium. The median response was 7 percent.

Estimates of the future U.S. equity risk premium that are somewhat higher or lower could be reasonable, especially if we have good reason to believe the past is not representative of the future. The bottom line is that any estimate of the future equity risk premium will involve assumptions about the future risk environment as well as the amount of risk aversion of future investors.

THE FIRST LESSON

From the data in Table 1.2, we can calculate risk premiums for the five different categories of investments. The results are shown in Table 1.3. Notice that the risk premium on T-bills is shown as zero in the table because they are our riskless benchmark. As we previously noted, looking at Table 1.3, we see that the average risk premium earned by the large-company common stock portfolio is 12.3% − 3.3% = 9%. This difference is a significant reward. The fact that it exists historically is an important observation, and it is the basis for our first lesson: Risky assets, on average, earn a risk premium. Put another way, there is a reward, on average, for bearing risk.

Why is this so? Why, for example, is the risk premium for small stocks so much larger than the risk premium for large stocks? More generally, what determines the relative sizes of the risk premiums for the different assets? These questions are at the heart of the modern theory of investments. We will discuss the issues involved many times in the chapters ahead. For now, part of the answer can be found by looking at the historical variability of the returns of these different investments. To get started, we now turn our attention to measuring variability in returns.

TABLE 1.3	Average Annual Returns and Risk Premiums: 1926–2021		
Investment		Average Return	Risk Premium
Large-company stocks		12.3%	9.0%
Small-company stocks		16.3	13.0
Long-term corporate bonds		6.4	3.1
Long-term government bonds		6.0	2.7
U.S. Treasury bills		3.3	—

Source: SBBI Yearbook 2022 (Kroll LLC). Author calculations.

1.4 Return Variability: The Second Lesson

We have already seen that the year-to-year returns on common stocks tend to be more volatile than returns on, say, long-term government bonds. We now discuss measuring this variability so we can begin examining the subject of risk.

Related Bloomberg Functions

HRH   Historical Return Histogram

FREQUENCY DISTRIBUTIONS AND VARIABILITY

To get started, we can draw a *frequency distribution* for large-company stock returns like the one in Figure 1.8. What we have done here is to count the number of times that an annual return on the large-company stock portfolio falls within each 10 percent range. For example, in Figure 1.8, the height of 20 for the bar within the interval 10 percent to 20 percent means that 20 of the 96 annual returns are in that range. Notice also that most of the returns are in the −10 to 40 percent range.

Now we need to measure the spread in these returns. We know, for example, that the return on large-company stocks in a typical year was 12.3 percent. We now want to know by how much the actual return differs from this average in a typical year. In other words, we need

FIGURE 1.8	Frequency Distribution of Returns on Large-Company Common Stocks: 1926–2021

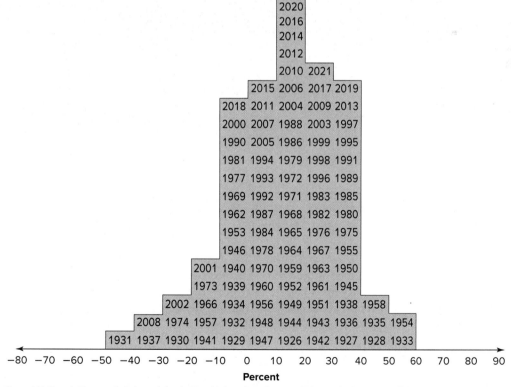

Source: Professor Kenneth R. French, Dartmouth College, through 2015. Update through 2021, *SBBI Yearbook 2022* (Kroll LLC).

a measure of the volatility of returns. The **variance** and its square root, the **standard deviation,** are the most commonly used measures of volatility. We describe how to calculate them next. If you've already studied basic statistics, you should notice that we are calculating an ordinary sample variance and standard deviation, just as you may have done many times before.

THE HISTORICAL VARIANCE AND STANDARD DEVIATION

The variance essentially measures the average squared difference between the actual returns and the average return. The bigger this number is, the more the actual returns tend to differ from the average return. Also, the larger the variance or standard deviation is, the more spread out the returns will be.

The way we calculate the variance and standard deviation depends on the specific situation. In this chapter, we are looking at historical returns. Therefore, the procedure we describe here is the correct one for calculating the *historical* variance and standard deviation. If we were examining projected future returns, then the procedure would be different. We describe this procedure in a later chapter.

To illustrate how we calculate the historical variance, suppose a particular investment had returns of 10 percent, 12 percent, 3 percent, and −9 percent over the last four years. The average return is $(.10 + .12 + .03 - .09)/4 = .04$, or 4 percent.

Notice that the return is never actually equal to .04, or 4 percent. Instead, the first return deviates from the average by $.10 - .04 = .06$, the second return deviates from the average by $.12 - .04 = .08$, and so on. To compute the variance, we square each of these deviations, add them up, and divide the result by the number of returns less 1, or 3 in this case. These calculations are summarized in the following table:

Year	(1) Actual Return	(2) Average Return	(3) Deviation (1) − (2)	(4) Squared Deviation
1	.10	.04	.06	.0036
2	.12	.04	.08	.0064
3	.03	.04	−.01	.0001
4	−.09	.04	−.13	.0169
Totals	.16		.00	.0270

In the first column, we write down the four actual returns. In the third column, we calculate the difference between the actual returns and the average by subtracting out 4 percent. Finally, in the fourth column, we square the numbers in Column 3 to get the squared deviations from the average.

The variance can now be calculated by dividing .0270, the sum of the squared deviations, by the number of returns less 1. Let Var(R) or σ^2 (read this as "sigma squared") stand for the variance of the return:

$$\text{Var}(R) = \sigma^2 = .027/(4 - 1) = .009$$

The standard deviation is the square root of the variance. So, if SD(R) or σ stands for the standard deviation of the return:

$$\text{SD}(R) = \sigma = \sqrt{.009} = .09487$$

The square root of the variance is used because the variance is measured in "squared" percentages and thus is hard to interpret. The standard deviation is an ordinary percentage, so the answer here could be written as 9.487 percent.

In the table above, notice that the sum of the deviations is equal to zero. This will always be the case, and it provides a good way to check your work. In general, if we have N historical returns, where N is some number, we can write the historical variance as:

$$\text{Var}(R) = \frac{1}{N - 1} [(R_1 - \overline{R})^2 + \cdots + (R_N - \overline{R})^2]$$

This formula tells us to do what we did above: Take each of the N individual returns (R_1, R_2, . . . , R_N) and subtract the average return, $\overline{R}$; square the results and add up all these squares; and, finally, divide this total by the number of returns minus 1 (i.e., $N - 1$).[2] The standard deviation is the square root of Var(R). In many areas, including finance, standard deviations are used to measure variability.

EXAMPLE 1.4   **Calculating the Variance and Standard Deviation**

From Table 1.1, we see that the large-company stocks and long-term government bonds had these returns for the years 2012–2015:

Year	Large-Company Stocks	Long-Term Government Bonds
2012	.1600	.0180
2013	.3239	−.1469
2014	.1369	.2976
2015	.0138	−.0261

What are the average returns? The variances? The standard deviations?

To calculate the average returns, we add up the returns and divide by four. The results are:

Large-company stocks, average return $= \overline{R} = .6346/4 = .1587$

Long-term government bonds, average return $= \overline{R} = .1426/4 = .0357$

To calculate the variance for large-company stocks, we can summarize the relevant calculations (with rounding) as follows:

Year	(1) Actual Return	(2) Average Return	(3) Deviation (1) – (2)	(4) Squared Deviation
2012	.1600	.1587	.0013	.000002
2013	.3239	.1587	.1653	.027308
2014	.1369	.1587	−.0218	.000473
2015	.0138	.1587	−.1449	.020982
Totals	.6346		.0000	.048765

Because there are four years of returns, we calculate the variance by dividing .0488 (rounded from .048765 above, to keep everything at 4 decimal places) by (4 − 1) = 3:

	Large-Company Stocks	Long-Term Government Bonds
Variance (σ^2)	.0488/3 = .0163	.1061/3 = .0354
Standard deviation (σ)	$\sqrt{.0163} = .1277$	$\sqrt{.0354} = .1881$

For practice, verify that you get the same answers that we do for long-term government bonds. Notice that the standard deviation for long-term government bonds, 18.81 percent, is actually higher than the standard deviation for large-company stocks, 12.77 percent, over this short period. Why is this relationship unusual?

THE HISTORICAL RECORD

Figure 1.9 summarizes much of our discussion of capital market history so far. It displays average returns, standard deviations, and frequency distributions of annual returns on a

---

[2] The reason for dividing by $N - 1$ rather than N is based on statistical sampling theory, which is beyond the scope of this book. Remember that to calculate a variance about a sample average, you need to divide the sum of squared deviations from the average by $N - 1$.

FIGURE 1.9

Historical Returns, Standard Deviations, and Frequency Distributions: 1926–2021

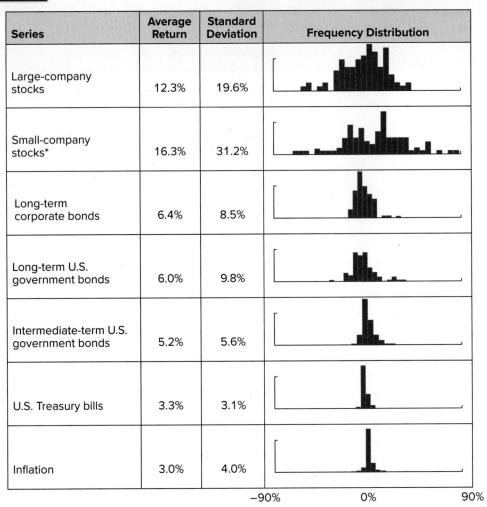

Series	Average Return	Standard Deviation	Frequency Distribution
Large-company stocks	12.3%	19.6%	
Small-company stocks*	16.3%	31.2%	
Long-term corporate bonds	6.4%	8.5%	
Long-term U.S. government bonds	6.0%	9.8%	
Intermediate-term U.S. government bonds	5.2%	5.6%	
U.S. Treasury bills	3.3%	3.1%	
Inflation	3.0%	4.0%	

−90%   0%   90%

* The 1933 small-company stocks total return was 152.9 percent and is not shown here.

Source: *SBBI Yearbook 2022* (Kroll LLC).

common scale. For example, in Figure 1.9, notice that the standard deviation for the small-stock portfolio (31.2 percent per year) is more than 10 times larger than the T-bill portfolio's standard deviation (3.1 percent per year). We will return to discuss these facts momentarily.

NORMAL DISTRIBUTION

normal distribution
A symmetric, bell-shaped frequency distribution that is completely defined by its average and standard deviation.

For many different random events in nature, a particular frequency distribution, the **normal distribution** (or *bell curve*) is useful for describing the probability of ending up in a given range. For example, the idea behind "grading on a curve" is based on the fact that exam scores often resemble a bell curve.

Figure 1.10 illustrates a normal distribution and its distinctive bell shape. As you can see, this distribution has a much cleaner appearance than the actual return distributions illustrated in Figure 1.8. Even so, like the normal distribution, the actual distributions do appear to be at least roughly mound shaped and symmetric. When this shape is observed, the normal distribution is often a very good approximation.

Also, keep in mind that the distributions in Figure 1.9 are based on only 96 yearly observations, while Figure 1.10 is, in principle, based on an infinite number. So, if we had been able to observe returns for, say, 1,000 years, we might have filled in a lot of the irregularities and

FIGURE 1.10

The Normal Distribution: Illustrated Returns Based on the Historical Return and Standard Deviation for a Portfolio of Large-Company Common Stocks

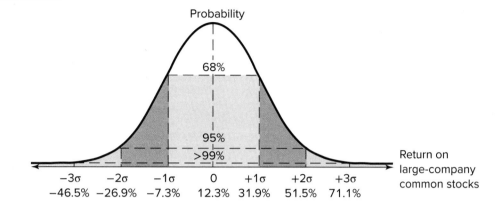

ended up with a much smoother picture. For our purposes, it is enough to observe that the returns are at least roughly normally distributed.

The usefulness of the normal distribution stems from the fact that it is completely described by the average and the standard deviation. If you have these two numbers, then there is nothing else you need to know. For example, with a normal distribution, the probability that we end up within one standard deviation of the average is 68 percent, or about 2/3. The probability that we end up within two standard deviations is about 95 percent. Finally, the probability of being more than three standard deviations away from the average is less than 1 percent. These ranges and the probabilities are illustrated in Figure 1.10.

To see why this range is useful, recall from Figure 1.9 that the standard deviation of returns on the large-company common stocks is 19.6 percent. The average return is 12.3 percent. So, assuming that the frequency distribution is at least approximately normal, the probability that the return in a given year is in the range of −7.3 percent to 31.9 percent (12.3 percent plus or minus one standard deviation, 19.6 percent) is about 2/3. This range is illustrated in Figure 1.10. In other words, there is about one chance in three that the return will be *outside* this range. Therefore, if you buy stocks in large companies, you should expect to be outside this range in one year out of every three. This reinforces our earlier observations about stock market volatility. However, there is only a 5 percent chance (approximately) that we would end up outside the range of −26.9 percent to 51.5 percent (11.9 percent plus or minus 2 × 19.8 percent). These points are also shown in Figure 1.10.

THE SECOND LESSON

Our observations concerning the year-to-year variability in returns are the basis for our second lesson from capital market history. On average, bearing risk is handsomely rewarded, but, in a given year, there is a significant chance of a dramatic change in value. Thus, our second lesson is this: The greater the potential reward, the greater the risk.

Thus far in this chapter, we have emphasized the year-to-year variability in returns. We should note that even day-to-day movements can exhibit considerable volatility. For example, on March 16, 2020, the Dow Jones Industrial Average (DJIA) plummeted almost 3,000 points, or about 13 percent, the worst day ever in terms of points. But the biggest percentage decline was on October 19, 1987, a day known as "Black Monday." On that day alone, the DJIA lost an astonishing 23 percent. The biggest single day gains and losses for the Dow going back to 1896 are summarized in Table 1.4. Many of the biggest gains and losses occurred in the spring of 2020, thanks to the onset of the COVID-19 pandemic and the uncertainty that was created.

TABLE 1.4

Good Times, Bad Times (You Know I've Had My Share): The Best and Worst Days for the DJIA: May 1896 to May 2022

Panel A. The Best Days

Date	Index Level	Point Increase	Rank	Date	Index Level	Percentage Increase
2020-03-24	20,704.61	2,112.98	1	1933-03-15	62.10	15.34%
2020-03-13	23,185.62	1,985.00	2	1931-10-06	99.34	14.87%
2020-04-06	22,679.99	1,627.46	3	1929-10-30	258.47	12.34%
2020-03-26	22,552.17	1,351.62	4	1920-03-24	20,704.91	11.37%
2020-03-02	26,703.32	1,293.96	5	1932-09-21	75.16	11.36%
2020-03-04	27,090.86	1,173.45	6	2008-10-13	9,387.61	11.08%
2020-03-10	25,018.16	1,167.14	7	2008-10-28	9,065.12	10.88%
2018-12-26	22,878.45	1,086.25	8	1987-10-21	2,027.85	10.15%
2020-03-17	21,237.38	1,048.86	9	1932-08-03	58.22	9.52%
2008-10-13	9,387.61	936.42	10	1932-02-11	78.60	9.47%

Panel B. The Worst Days

Date	Index Level	Point Decrease	Rank	Date	Index Level	Percentage Decrease
2020-03-16	20,188.52	−2,997.10	1	1987-10-19	1,738.74	−22.61%
2020-03-12	21,200.62	−2,352.60	2	2020-03-16	20,188.52	−12.93%
2020-03-09	23,851.02	−2,013.76	3	1929-10-28	260.64	−12.82%
2020-06-11	25,128.17	−1,861.82	4	1929-10-29	230.07	−11.73%
2020-03-11	23,553.22	−1,464.94	5	2020-03-12	21,200.62	−9.99%
2020-03-18	19,898.92	−1,338.46	6	1929-11-06	232.13	−9.92%
2020-02-27	25,766.64	−1,190.95	7	1899-12-18	58.27	−8.72%
2018-02-05	24,345.75	−1,175.21	8	1932-08-12	63.11	−8.40%
2022-05-18	31,490.07	−1,164.52	9	1907-03-14	76.23	−8.29%
2022-05-05	32,997.97	−1,063.09	10	1987-10-26	1,793.93	−8.04%

Source: S&P Global

This discussion highlights the importance of looking at returns in terms of percentages rather than dollar amounts or index points. For example, the 5.79-point drop in the DJIA on August 12, 1932, marked the eighth worst percentage drop in the history of the index. A 5.79-point loss in the DJIA in today's market, however, would hardly be noticed. This is precisely why we relied on percentage returns when we examined market history in this chapter.[3]

Now that you know how to calculate and, more important, interpret average returns and standard deviations, the nearby *Spreadsheet Analysis* box shows how to do the calculations using Excel, which can really speed up things when we have a lot of data.

---

[3] By the way, as you may have noticed, what's kind of weird is that many of the worst days in the history of the DJIA occurred in October. We have no clue as to why. Furthermore, looking back at the Mark Twain quote near the beginning of the chapter, how do you suppose he knew? Sounds like a case for *CSI: Wall Street.*

SPREADSHEET ANALYSIS

Using a Spreadsheet to Calculate Average Returns and Volatilities

Here is an Excel spreadsheet summarizing the formulas and analysis needed to calculate average returns and standard deviations using the 1990s as an example:

	A	B	C	D	E	F	G	H
1								
2	**Using a spreadsheet to calculate average returns and standard deviations**							
3								
4	Looking back in the chapter, the data suggest that the 1990s were one							
5	of the best decades for stock market investors. We will find out just how good by							
6	calculating the average returns and standard deviations for this period. Here are the							
7	year-by-year returns on the large-company stocks:							
8								
9		*Year*	*Return (%)*	*Year*	*Return (%)*			
10		1990	−3.10	1995	37.58			
11		1991	30.46	1996	22.96			
12		1992	7.62	1997	33.36			
13		1993	10.08	1998	28.58			
14		1994	1.32	1999	21.04			
15								
16		Average return (%):		18.99				
17		Standard deviation (%):		14.16				
18								
19	The formulas we used to do the calculations are just =AVERAGE(C10:C14;E10:E14)							
20	and =STDEV(C10:C14;E10:E14). Notice that the average return in the 1990s was 18.99							
21	percent per year, which is larger than the long-run average of 11.9 percent. At the same							
22	time, the standard deviation, 14.16 percent, was smaller than the 20.0 percent long-run value.							

EXAMPLE 1.5 | **Investing in Growth Stocks**

The term *growth stock* is frequently a euphemism for small-company stock. Are such investments suitable for "widows and orphans"? Before answering, you should consider the historical volatility. For example, from the historical record, what is the approximate probability that you will actually lose 16 percent or more of your money in a single year if you buy a portfolio of such companies?

Looking back at Figure 1.9, we see that the average return on small stocks is 16.3 percent and the standard deviation is 31.2 percent. Assuming that the returns are approximately normal, there is about a 1/3 probability that you will experience a return outside the range of −14.9 percent to 47.5 percent (16.3% = 31.2%).

Because the normal distribution is symmetric, the odds of being above or below this range are equal. There is thus a 1/6 chance (half of 1/3) that you will lose more than 14.9 percent, so you should expect this to happen once in every six years, on average. Such investments can thus be *very* volatile, and they are not well suited for those who cannot afford the risk.

CHECK THIS

1.4a   In words, how do we calculate a variance? A standard deviation?

1.4b   What is the second lesson from financial market history?

1.5 More on Average Returns

Thus far in this chapter, we have looked closely at simple average returns. But there is another way of computing an average return. The fact that average returns are calculated two different ways leads to some confusion, so our goal in this section is to explain the two approaches and also explain the circumstances under which each is appropriate. In addition, we include a measure of return that accounts for investor decisions to add funds to or remove funds from an investment.

ARITHMETIC VERSUS GEOMETRIC AVERAGES

Let's start with a simple example. Suppose you buy a particular stock for $100. Unfortunately, the first year you own it, it falls to $50. The second year you own the stock, its price increases to $100, leaving you where you started (no dividends were paid).

What was your average return on this investment? Common sense seems to say that your average return must be exactly zero since you started with $100 and ended with $100. But if we calculate the year-by-year returns, we see that you lost 50 percent the first year (you lost half of your money). The second year, you made 100 percent (you doubled your money). Your average return over the two years was thus $(-50\% + 100\%)/2 = 25\%$! So which is correct, 0 percent or 25 percent?

The answer is that both are correct; they just answer different questions. The 0 percent is called the **geometric average return.** The geometric average return answers the question *"What was your average compound return per year over a particular period?"*

The 25 percent is called the **arithmetic average return.** The arithmetic average return answers the question *"What was your return in an average year over a particular period?"*

Notice that, in previous sections, the average returns we calculated were all arithmetic averages, so you already know how to calculate them. What we need to do now is (1) learn how to calculate geometric averages and (2) learn the circumstances under which one average is more meaningful than the other.

Finally, the order and size of losses and gains matter to your portfolio. The nearby *Investment Updates* box provides an important example.

geometric average return
The average compound return earned per year over a multiyear period.

arithmetic average return
The return earned in an average year over a multiyear period.

CALCULATING GEOMETRIC AVERAGE RETURNS

If we have N years of returns, the geometric average return over these N years is calculated using this formula:

$$\text{Geometric average return} = [(1 + R_1) \times (1 + R_2) \times \cdots \times (1 + R_N)]^{1/N} - 1 \qquad (1.5)$$

This formula tells us that four steps are required:

1. Take each of the N annual returns $R_1, R_2, \ldots, R_N$ and add a 1 to each (after converting them to decimals!).
2. Multiply all the numbers from Step 1 together.
3. Take the result from Step 2 and raise it to the power of $1/N$.
4. Finally, subtract 1 from the result of Step 3. The result is the geometric average return.

To illustrate how we calculate a geometric average return, suppose a particular investment had annual returns of 10 percent, 12 percent, 3 percent, and −9 percent over the last four years. The geometric average return over this four-year period is calculated as

INVESTMENT UPDATES

INVESTMENT RETURNS: CRUEL MATH?

If your portfolio experiences a 20 percent loss, what return is necessary to bring your portfolio back to "even"? Many investors might simply say 20 percent, but they would be very much incorrect. In fact, you would need to earn 25 percent just to overcome the 20 percent loss and break even. This is the reality (or cruelty) of math, and it is a function of the key principle of finance: compounding.

This issue became particularly relevant in the wake of the 2008 financial crisis. For example, as Table 1.1 reports, large-cap U.S. stocks lost 37 percent in 2008. In 2009 and 2010, the market recovered, earning 26.46 percent and 15.06 percent, respectively. While these two returns add up to 41.52 percent, thereby "exceeding" the loss of 2008, investor portfolios were still underwater. In fact, $1 held at the beginning of 2008 would only be worth $.92 at the end of 2010.

This example illustrates that to offset losses, you need even bigger gains to get back to where you started. And, as the table below illustrates, this effect is more pronounced for higher levels of loss.

Loss	Gain Needed to Break Even
−5%	5.26%
−10%	11.11%
−15%	17.65%
−20%	25.00%
−25%	33.33%
−30%	42.86%
−35%	53.85%
−40%	66.67%
−45%	81.82%
−50%	100.00%

$(1.10 \times 1.12 \times 1.03 \times .91)^{1/4} - 1 = .0366$, or 3.66%. In contrast, the average arithmetic return is $(.10 + .12 + .03 - .09)/4 = .04$, or 4 percent.

One thing you may have noticed in our examples thus far is that the geometric average returns seem to be smaller. It turns out that this will always be true (as long as the returns are not all identical, in which case the two "averages" would be the same). To illustrate, Table 1.5 shows the arithmetic averages and standard deviations from Figure 1.9, along with the geometric average returns.

As shown in Table 1.5, the geometric averages are all smaller, but the magnitude of the difference varies quite a bit. The reason is that the difference is greater for more volatile investments. In fact, there is a useful approximation. Assuming all the numbers are expressed in decimals (as opposed to percentages), the geometric average return is approximately equal to the arithmetic average return minus half the variance. For example, looking at the large-company stocks, the arithmetic average is .123 and the standard deviation is .196, implying that the variance is .0384. The approximate geometric average is thus $.123 - .0384/2 = .104$, which is very close to the actual value of .105.

TABLE 1.5 — **Geometric versus Arithmetic Average Returns: 1926–2021**

Series	Geometric Mean	Arithmetic Mean	Standard Deviation
Large-company stocks	10.5%	12.3%	19.6%
Small-company stocks	12.1	16.3	31.2
Long-term corporate bonds	6.1	6.4	8.5
Long-term government bonds	5.5	6.0	9.8
Intermediate-term government bonds	5.0	5.2	5.6
U.S. Treasury bills	3.3	3.3	3.1
Inflation	2.9	3.0	4.0

Source: *SBBI Yearbook 2022* (Kroll LLC).

EXAMPLE 1.6

Calculating the Geometric Average Return

Calculate the geometric average return for the large-company stocks for the years 2012–2015 in Table 1.1.

First, convert percentages to decimal returns, add one, and then calculate their product.

Year	Large-Company Stocks	Product
2012	16.00	1.1600
2013	32.39	× 1.3239
2014	13.69	× 1.1369
2015	1.38	× 1.0138
		1.7701

Notice that the number 1.7701 is what our investment is worth after five years if we started with a $1 investment. The geometric average return is then calculated as:

$$\text{Geometric average return} = 1.7701^{1/4} - 1 = .1534, \text{ or } 15.34\%$$

Thus, the geometric average return is about 15.34 percent in this example. In contrast, in Example 1.4, the average arithmetic return was calculated as 15.87 percent. Here is a tip: If you are using a financial calculator, you can put $1 in as the present value, $1.7701 as the future value, and 4 as the number of periods. Then, solve for the unknown rate. You should get the same answer for the geometric average as we did here.

EXAMPLE 1.7

More Geometric Averages

Take a look back at Figure 1.1, which showed the value of a $1 investment after 96 years. Use the value for the small-company stock investment to check the geometric average in Table 1.5.

In Figure 1.1, the small-company investment grew to $56,033.70 over 96 years. The geometric average return is thus:

$$\text{Geometric average return} = 56,033.70^{1/96} - 1 = .1206, \text{ or about } 12.1\%$$

This 12.1% matches the value shown in Table 1.5.

ARITHMETIC AVERAGE RETURN OR GEOMETRIC AVERAGE RETURN?

When we look at historical returns, the difference between the geometric and arithmetic average returns isn't too hard to understand. To put it slightly differently, the geometric average tells you what you actually earned per year on average, compounded annually. The arithmetic average tells you what you earned in a typical year. You should use whichever one answers the question you want answered.

A somewhat trickier question concerns forecasting the future, and there is a lot of confusion about this point among analysts and financial planners. The problem is as follows: If we have *estimates* of both the arithmetic and geometric average returns, then the arithmetic average is probably too high for longer periods and the geometric average is probably too low for shorter periods.

The good news is that there is a simple way of combining the two averages, which we will call *Blume's formula*.[4] Suppose we calculated geometric and arithmetic return averages from

---

[4] Credit for this elegant result is due to Marshall Blume ("Unbiased Estimates of Long-Run Expected Rates of Return,"*Journal of the American Statistical Association*, September 1974, pp. 634–638).

N years of data and we wish to use these averages to form a T-year average return forecast, $R(T)$, where T is less than N. Here's how we do it:

$$R\left(T\right) = \left(\frac{T-1}{N-1} \times \text{Geometric average}\right) + \left(\frac{N-T}{N-1} \times \text{Arithmetic average}\right)$$

For example, suppose that, from 25 years of annual returns data, we calculate an arithmetic average return of 12 percent and a geometric average return of 9 percent. From these averages, we wish to make 1-year, 5-year, and 10-year average return forecasts. These three average return forecasts are calculated as follows:

$$R(1) = \left(\frac{1-1}{24} \times 9\%\right) + \left(\frac{25-1}{24} \times 12\%\right) = 12\%$$

$$R(5) = \left(\frac{5-1}{24} \times 9\%\right) + \left(\frac{25-5}{24} \times 12\%\right) = 11.5\%$$

$$R(10) = \left(\frac{10-1}{24} \times 9\%\right) + \left(\frac{25-10}{24} \times 12\%\right) = 10.875\%$$

Thus, we see that 1-year, 5-year, and 10-year forecasts are 12 percent, 11.5 percent, and 10.875 percent, respectively.

This concludes our discussion of geometric versus arithmetic averages. One last note: In the future, when we say "average return," we mean arithmetic average unless we explicitly say otherwise.

EXAMPLE 1.8

Forecasting Average Returns

Over the 96-year period 1926–2021, the geometric average return for large-company stocks was 10.5 percent and the arithmetic average return was 12.3 percent. Calculate average return forecasts for 1, 5, 10, and 25 years into the future.

In this case, we would use Blume's formula with values of $T = 1$, 5, 10, and 25 and $N = 96$:

$$R(T) = \frac{T-1}{95}\left(\times 10.5\%\right) + \frac{96-T}{95}\left(\times 12.3\%\right)$$

T	$R(T)$
1	12.3%
5	12.2
10	12.1
25	11.8

Notice that the short-term forecasts are closer to the arithmetic average return and the longer-term forecasts are moving closer to the geometric average return.

DOLLAR-WEIGHTED AVERAGE RETURNS

Suppose an investment had returns of 10 percent and −5 percent over the last two years. You know how to compute the arithmetic average (2.50 percent) and the geometric average (2.23 percent). You might not know that these average returns are accurate only if the investor made a single deposit at the start of the two-year period.

Many investors, however, make deposits or withdrawals through time. For example, some people add money to their investments over time as they save for retirement. Some people might be forced to withdraw funds to meet unexpected needs. Other investors attempt to "time the market" by adding funds because they believe their investments will soon increase in value. These "market timers" also sell part (or all) of their investments before an anticipated decline.

Whether investors can be successful at market timing is a topic of much debate, and one that we address in later chapters. Still, it is important to know how to calculate the return of

	A	B	C	D	E	F	G	H
1								
2		Calculating dollar-weighted average returns						
3								
4	To find a rate of return that equates a series of uneven cash flows, we must identify							
5	when the cash flows were made and we must know their size. Then, we can use							
6	the built-in IRR function in Excel to calculate the dollar-weighted average return.							
7								
8		*Time*	*Cash Flow*					
9		0	−$1,000					
10		1	−$4,000					
11		2	$4,845					
12								
13			−2.6%	=IRR(C9:C11)				
14								
15	Note, Time 0 is the beginning of Year 1, while Time 1 is the end of Year 1.							
16								
17	Using the IRR function, we calculate a dollar-weighted average return of −2.6%.							
18								
19								

dollar-weighted average return
Average compound rate of return earned per year over a multiyear period accounting for investment inflows and outflows.

an investment when an investor makes deposits and withdrawals. The relevant return measure in this case is called the **dollar-weighted average return.**

As an example, assume that you invest $1,000. After earning 10 percent the first year, you decide to invest another $4,000 (perhaps hoping the investment repeats its performance). Unfortunately for you, the return in Year 2 was −5 percent. What was your net return?

To begin to answer this question, you need to know the ending value of your investment. At the end of the first year, your account had a value of $1,100, which is the initial investment plus the 10 percent return. You then deposited another $4,000, bringing the account value to $5,100 at the beginning of Year 2. After losing 5 percent in Year 2, your final value is $4,845.

Before we set out to calculate your exact return, you know that your return is negative. After all, you deposited $5,000 out of your own pocket, but at the end of two years the investment is worth only $4,845. So, the arithmetic and geometric averages, which were both positive, do not account for this case.

To calculate the dollar-weighted average return, we need to find the average rate of return that equates our cash outflows to our cash inflows. In other words, what is the rate that makes the net present value of the investment equal zero? Here is a summary of your cash flows for this investment:

Time:	0	1	2
Cash flow:	−$1,000	−$4,000	+$4,845

In this summary, the negative cash flows are the deposits you made. The positive cash flow is the amount you have in the investment at the end of Year 2.

In a corporate finance class, this calculation is known as the *internal rate of return,* or *IRR.* Finding the IRR requires trial and error unless you use a financial calculator or spreadsheet. To see how to do this in Excel, you can look at the nearby *Spreadsheet Analysis* box.

The dollar-weighted rate of return for this investment is −2.6 percent. This makes sense because you had the greatest amount invested during the period when the return was the lowest, and you had the least amount invested when the return was the highest.

You know that the geometric average is always less than or equal to the arithmetic average. How about the relationship between the geometric average and the dollar-weighted average return? As you might guess, the relationship depends on when deposits and withdrawals were made. The geometric average return could be greater than, less than, or equal to the dollar-weighted average return. In fact, the geometric average is a special case of the dollar-weighted return, where the additional inflows and outflows happen to be zero.

CHECK THIS

1.5a Over a 5-year period, an investment in a broad market index yielded annual returns of 10, 16, −5, −8, and 7 percent. What were the arithmetic and geometric average annual returns for this index?

1.5b Over a 25-year period, an investment in a broad market index yielded an arithmetic average return of 4 percent and a geometric average return of 3.6 percent. Using Blume's formula, what would be the 5-year and 10-year average return forecasts?

1.5c Why is it important to control for the flow of funds into and out of an investment when calculating returns?

Risk and Return

In previous sections, we explored financial market history to see what we could learn about risk and return. In this section, we summarize our findings and then conclude our discussion by looking ahead at the subjects we will be examining in later chapters.

THE RISK-RETURN TRADE-OFF

Figure 1.11 shows our findings on risk and return from Figure 1.9. What Figure 1.11 shows is that there is a risk-return trade-off. At one extreme, if we are unwilling to bear any risk at all,

FIGURE 1.11 Risk-Return Trade-Off

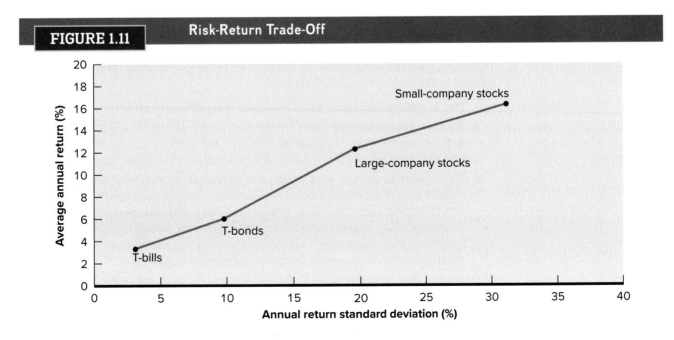

but we are willing to forgo the use of our money for a while, then we can earn the risk-free rate. Because the risk-free rate represents compensation for waiting, it is often called the *time value of money.*

If we are willing to bear risk, then we can expect to earn a risk premium, at least on average. Further, the more risk we are willing to bear, the greater is the risk premium. Investment advisors like to say that an investment has a "wait" component and a "worry" component. In our figure, the time value of money is the compensation for waiting and the risk premium is the compensation for worrying.

There are two important caveats to this discussion. First, risky investments do not *always* pay more than risk-free investments. Indeed, that is precisely what makes them risky. In other words, there is a risk premium *on average,* but over any particular time interval, there is no guarantee. Second, we have intentionally been a little imprecise about what we mean exactly by risk. As we will discuss in the chapters ahead, investors are not compensated for all risks. Some risks are cheaply and easily avoidable, and no reward is expected for bearing them. It is only those risks that cannot be easily avoided that are compensated (on average).

A LOOK AHEAD

In the remainder of this text, we focus almost exclusively on financial assets. An advantage of this approach is that it is limited to four major types: stocks, bonds, futures, and options, in the order that we cover them. This means that we will not be discussing collectibles such as classic automobiles, baseball cards, coins, fine art, or stamps. It's not that these are unimportant; rather, they are very specialized. Instead of treating them superficially, we leave a discussion of them for another day (and another book).

As we've indicated, to understand the potential reward from an investment, it is critical to first understand the risk involved. There is an old saying that goes like this: It's easy to make a small fortune investing in _____ (put your favorite investment here)—just start with a large fortune! The moral is that the key to successful investing is to make informed, intelligent decisions about risk. For this reason, we are going to pay particular attention to the factors that determine the value of the different assets we discuss and the nature of the associated risks.

One common characteristic that these assets have is that they are bought and sold around the clock and around the world in vast quantities. The way they are traded can be very different, however. We think it is important and interesting to understand exactly what happens when you buy or sell one of these assets, so we will be discussing the different trading mechanisms and the way the different markets function.

1.7 Summary and Conclusions

This chapter presents some important concepts for investors, including the following items—grouped by the chapter's important concepts.

1. **How to calculate the return on an investment using different methods.**

   A. We show how to calculate dollar returns and percentage returns over a time period. Returns have two parts: a capital gain (or loss) and dividend income. We also show how to convert returns over a period different from a year into annualized returns.

   B. We demonstrate the two ways to calculate average returns over time: the arithmetic method and the geometric method. The arithmetic average return answers the question "What was your return in an average year over a particular period?" The geometric average return answers the question "What was your average compound return per year over a particular period?" Generally, when investors say "average return," they are referring to arithmetic average unless they explicitly say otherwise.

   C. We also examine the effect of fund flows into and out of an investment. This case calls for calculating the dollar-weighted average return.

2. **The historical returns on various important types of investments.**

GETTING DOWN TO BUSINESS

This chapter took you through some basic, but important, investment-related calculations. We then walked through the modern history of risk and return. How should you, as an investor or investment manager, put this information to work?

The answer is that you now have a rational, objective basis for thinking about what you stand to make from investing in some important broad asset classes. For the stock market as a whole, as measured by the performance of large-company stocks, you know that, on average, you might realistically expect to make about 12 percent or so per year.

Equally important, you know that you won't make 12 percent in any one year; instead, you'll make more or less. You know that the standard deviation is about 20 percent per year, and you should know what that means in terms of risk. In particular, you need to understand that in one year out of every six, you should expect to lose more than 8 percent (12 percent minus one standard deviation), so this will be a relatively common event. The good news is that in one year out of six, you can realistically expect to earn more than 32 percent (12 percent plus one standard deviation).

The other important, practical thing to understand from this chapter is that a strategy of investing in very-low-risk assets (such as T-bills) has historically barely kept up with inflation. This might be sufficient for some investors, but if your goal is to do better than that, then you will have to bear some amount of risk to achieve it.

For the latest information on the real world of investments, visit us at jmdinvestments.blogspot.com.

A. In order of their historical return from highest to lowest, we discuss returns on some important portfolios, including:

- *Small-company stocks.* This is a portfolio composed of the smallest (in terms of total market value of outstanding stock) of the companies listed on major U.S. exchanges.
- *Large-company stocks.* This portfolio is based on the Standard & Poor's 500 index. This index contains 500 of the largest companies (in terms of total market value of outstanding stock) in the United States.
- *Long-term U.S. government bonds.* This is a portfolio of U.S. government bonds with 20 years to maturity.
- *U.S. Treasury bills.* This is a portfolio of Treasury bills (T-bills for short) with a three-month maturity.

B. One important historical return fact is that U.S. T-bill returns have barely outpaced inflation. Therefore, an investor must invest in stocks or bonds to earn a return higher than the inflation rate.

3. **The historical risks on various important types of investments.**

A. Historically, the risk (as measured by standard deviation of returns) of the portfolios described above is highest for small-company stocks. The next highest risk is for large-company stocks, followed by long-term government bonds and Treasury bills.

B. We draw two key lessons from historical risk:

- Risky assets, on average, earn a risk premium. That is, there is a reward for bearing risk. However, this expected reward is not realized each year.
- The greater the potential reward from a risky investment is, the greater the risk is.

4. **The relationship between risk and return.**

A. When we put these two key lessons together, we concluded that there is a risk-return trade-off.

B. The only way to earn a higher return is to take on greater risk.

Key Terms

arithmetic average return 24
capital gains yield 4
dividend yield 4
dollar-weighted average return 28
effective annual return (EAR) 6
geometric average return 24
normal distribution 20

risk premium 15
risk-free rate 15
standard deviation 18
total dollar return 3
total percent return 4
variance 18

Related Bloomberg Functions

TRA	Total Return Analysis, 1.1
DVD	Dividend/Split Summary, 1.1
IN	Bloomberg Index Browser, 1.2
MRR	Member Ranked Returns, 1.2
WEI	World Equity Indices, 1.2
CRP	County Risk Premiums, 1.3
EQRP	Equity Risk Premium, 1.3
HRH	Historical Return Histogram, 1.4

Chapter Review Problems and Self-Test

1. **Calculating Returns (LO1, CFA1)**   You bought 400 shares of Metallica Heavy Metal, Inc., at $30 per share. Over the year, you received $.75 per share in dividends. If the stock sold for $33 at the end of the year, what was your dollar return? Your percentage return?

2. **Calculating Returns and Variability (LO3, CFA4)**   Using the following returns, calculate the arithmetic average returns, the variances, the standard deviations, and the geometric returns for the following stocks:

Year	Michele, Inc.	Janicek Co.
1	12%	5%
2	−4	−15
3	0	10
4	20	38
5	2	17

3. **Forecasting Returns (LO4)**   Over a 30-year period, an asset had an arithmetic return of 12.8 percent and a geometric return of 10.7 percent. Using Blume's formula, what is your best estimate of the future annual returns over the next 5 years? 10 years? 20 years?

Answers to Self-Test Problems

1. **Your dollar return is your gain or loss in dollars. Here, we receive $.75 in dividends on each of our 400 shares, for a total of $300. In addition, each share rose from $30 to $33, so we make $3 × 400 shares = $1,200. Our total dollar return is thus $300 + $1,200 = $1,500.**

   Our percentage return (or just "return" for short) is equal to the $1,500 we made divided by our initial outlay of $30 × 400 shares = $12,000; so $1,500/$12,000 = .125, or 12.5%. Equivalently, we could have just noted that each share paid a $.75 dividend and each share gained $3, so the total dollar gain per share was $3.75. As a percentage of the cost of one share ($30), we get $3.75/$30 = .125, or 12.5%.

2. First, calculate arithmetic averages as follows:

Michele, Inc.	Janicek Co.
12%	5%
−4	−15
0	10
20	38
2	17
30%	55%
Average return: 30%/5 = 6%	55%/5 = 11%

Using the arithmetic averages above, calculate the squared deviations from the arithmetic average returns and sum the squared deviations as follows:

Michele, Inc.	Janicek Co.
$(12 - 6)^2 = 36$	$(5 - 11)^2 = 36$
$(-4 - 6)^2 = 100$	$(-15 - 11)^2 = 676$
$(0 - 6)^2 = 36$	$(10 - 11)^2 = 1$
$(20 - 6)^2 = 196$	$(38 - 11)^2 = 729$
$(2 - 6)^2 = 16$	$(17 - 11)^2 = 36$
384	1,478

Calculate return variances by dividing the sums of squared deviations by four, which is the number of returns less one.

Michele: $384/4 = 96$ Janicek: $1,478/4 = 369.5$

Standard deviations are then calculated as the square root of the variance.

Michele: $\sqrt{96} = .098$, or 9.8%   Janicek: $\sqrt{369.5} = .1922$, or 19.22%

Geometric returns are then calculated as:

Michele: $[(1 + .12)(1 - .04)(1 + .00)(1 + .20)(1 + .02)]^{1/5} - 1 = .0565$, or 5.65%
Janicek: $[(1 + .05)(1 - .15)(1 + .10)(1 + .38)(1 + .17)]^{1/5} - 1 = .0965$, or 9.65%

3. To find the best forecast, we apply Blume's formula as follows:

$$R(5) = \left(\frac{5-1}{29} \times 10.7\%\right) + \left(\frac{30-5}{29} \times 12.8\%\right) = 12.51\%$$

$$R(10) = \left(\frac{10-1}{29} \times 10.7\%\right) + \left(\frac{30-10}{29} \times 12.8\%\right) = 12.15\%$$

$$R(20) = \left(\frac{20-1}{29} \times 10.7\%\right) + \left(\frac{30-20}{29} \times 12.8\%\right) = 11.42\%$$

Test Your Investment Quotient

IQ

1. **Prices and Returns (LO1, CFA1)**   You plan to buy a common stock and hold it for one year. You expect to receive both $1.50 from dividends and $26 from the sale of the stock at the end of the year. If you wanted to earn a 15 percent rate of return, what is the maximum price you would pay for the stock today?
   a. $22.61
   b. $23.91
   c. $24.50
   d. $27.50

2. **Returns (LO1, CFA1)** A portfolio of non-dividend-paying stocks earned a geometric mean return of 5 percent between January 1, 2010, and December 31, 2016. The arithmetic mean return for the same period was 6 percent. If the market value of the portfolio at the beginning of 2010 was $100,000, the market value of the portfolio at the end of 2016 was *closest* to:

   a. $135,000
   b. $140,710
   c. $142,000
   d. $150,363

3. **Standard Deviation (LO4, CFA4)** Which of the following statements about standard deviation is true? Standard deviation:

   a. Is the square of the variance.
   b. Can be a positive or negative number.
   c. Is denominated in the same units as the original data.
   d. Is the arithmetic mean of the squared deviations from the mean.

4. **Normal Distribution (LO4, CFA2)** An investment strategy has an expected return of 12 percent and a standard deviation of 10 percent. If the investment returns are normally distributed, the probability of earning a return less than 2 percent is closest to:

   a. 10 percent
   b. 16 percent
   c. 32 percent
   d. 34 percent

5. **Normal Distribution (LO4, CFA2)** What are the mean and standard deviation of a standard normal distribution?

	Mean	Standard Deviation
a.	0	0
b.	0	1
c.	1	0
d.	1	1

6. **Normal Distribution (LO4, CFA2)** Given a data series that is normally distributed with a mean of 100 and a standard deviation of 10, about 95 percent of the numbers in the series will fall within which of the following ranges?

   a. 60 to 140
   b. 70 to 130
   c. 80 to 120
   d. 90 to 110

7. **Asset Types (LO3)** Stocks, bonds, options, and futures are the four major types of:

   a. Debt.
   b. Real assets.
   c. Equity.
   d. Financial assets.

8. **Investment Returns (LO1, CFA1)** Suppose the value of an investment doubles in a one-year period. In this case, the rate of return on this investment over that one-year period is what amount?

   a. 100 percent even if the gain is not actually realized.
   b. 200 percent even if the gain is not actually realized.
   c. 100 percent only if the gain is actually realized.
   d. 200 percent only if the gain is actually realized.

9. **Historical Returns (LO2)** Which of the following asset categories has an annual returns history most closely linked to historical annual rates of inflation?

   a. U.S. Treasury bills
   b. Corporate bonds
   c. Large-company stocks
   d. Small-company stocks

10. **Historical Returns (LO2)** Based on the annual returns history since 1926, which asset category, on average, has yielded the highest risk premium?
    a. U.S. government bonds
    b. Corporate bonds
    c. Large-company stocks
    d. Small-company stocks

11. **Stat 101 (LO1, CFA1)** Over a four-year period, an investment in Outa'synch common stock yields returns of -10, 40, 0, and 20. What is the arithmetic return over this period?
    a. 5 percent
    b. 7.5 percent
    c. 10 percent
    d. 12.5 percent

12. **Stat 101 (LO4, CFA2)** You calculate an average historical return of 20 percent and a standard deviation of return of 10 percent for an investment in Stonehenge Construction Co. You believe these values well represent the future distribution of returns. Assuming that returns are normally distributed, what is the probability that Stonehenge Construction will yield a negative return?
    a. 17 percent
    b. 33 percent
    c. 5 percent
    d. 2.5 percent

13. **Stat 101 (LO4, CFA2)** Which of the following statements about a normal distribution is incorrect?
    a. A normal distribution is symmetrically centered on its mean.
    b. The probability of being within one standard deviation from the mean is about 68 percent.
    c. The probability of being within two standard deviations from the mean is about 95 percent.
    d. The probability of a negative value is always one-half.

14. **Normal Distribution (LO4, CFA2)** Based on a normal distribution with a mean of 500 and a standard deviation of 150, the z-value for an observation of 200 is closest to:
    a. -2.00
    b. -1.75
    c. 1.75
    d. 2.00

15. **Normal Distribution (LO4, CFA4)** A normal distribution would least likely be described as:
    a. Asymptotic.
    b. A discrete probability distribution.
    c. A symmetrical or bell-shaped distribution.
    d. A curve that theoretically extends from negative infinity to positive infinity.

Concept Questions

1. **Risk versus Return (LO3, CFA4)** Based on the historical record, rank the following investments in increasing order of risk. Rank the investments in increasing order of average returns. What do you conclude about the relationship between the risk of an investment and the return you expect to earn on it?
   a. Large stocks
   b. Treasury bills
   c. Long-term government bonds
   d. Small stocks

2. **Return Calculations (LO1, CFA1)** A particular stock had a return last year of 4 percent. However, you look at the stock price and notice that it actually didn't change at all last year. How is this possible?

3. **Returns Distributions (LO4, CFA4)** What is the probability that the return on small stocks will be less than -100 percent in a single year (think about it)? What are the implications for the distribution of returns?

4. **Arithmetic versus Geometric Returns (LO1, CFA1)** What is the difference between arithmetic and geometric returns? Suppose you have invested in a stock for the last 10 years. Which number is more important to you, the arithmetic or geometric return?

5. **Blume's Formula (LO1)** What is Blume's formula? When would you want to use it in practice?

6. **Inflation and Returns (LO1, CFA4)** Look at Table 1.1 and Figures 1.5 and 1.6. When were T-bill rates at their highest? Why do you think they were so high during this period?

7. **Inflation and Returns (LO1, CFA4)** The returns we have examined are not adjusted for inflation. What do you suppose would happen to our estimated risk premiums if we did account for inflation?

8. **Taxes and Returns (LO1)** The returns we have examined are not adjusted for taxes. What do you suppose would happen to our estimated returns and risk premiums if we did account for taxes? What would happen to our volatility measures?

9. **Taxes and Treasury Bills (LO1)** As a practical matter, most of the return you earn from investing in Treasury bills is taxed right away as ordinary income. Thus, if you are in a 40 percent tax bracket and you earn 5 percent on a Treasury bill, your aftertax return is only $.05 \times (1 - .40) = .03$, or 3 percent. In other words, 40 percent of your return goes to pay taxes, leaving you with just 3 percent. Once you consider inflation and taxes, how does the long-term return from Treasury bills look?

10. **The Long Run (LO4, CFA4)** Given your answer to the last question and the discussion in the chapter, why would any rational person do anything other than load up on 100 percent small stocks?

Questions and Problems

Core Questions

1. **Calculating Returns (LO1, CFA1)** Suppose you bought 100 shares of stock at an initial price of $37 per share. The stock paid a dividend of $.28 per share during the following year, and the share price at the end of the year was $41. Compute your total dollar return on this investment. Does your answer change if you keep the stock instead of selling it? Why or why not?

2. **Calculating Yields (LO1, CFA1)** In Problem 1, what is the capital gains yield? The dividend yield? What is the total rate of return on the investment?

3. **Calculating Returns (LO1, CFA1)** Rework Problems 1 and 2 assuming that you buy 500 shares of the stock and the ending share price is $34.

4. **Historical Returns (LO3)** What is the historical rate of return on each of the following investments? What is the historical risk premium on these investments?

   a. Long-term government bonds
   b. Treasury bills
   c. Large stocks
   d. Small stocks

5. **Calculating Average Returns (LO1, CFA1)** The rates of return on Cherry Jalopies, Inc., stock over the last five years were 17 percent, 11 percent, −2 percent, 3 percent, and 14 percent. Over the same period, the returns on Straw Construction Company's stock were 16 percent, 18 percent, −6 percent, 1 percent, and 22 percent. What was the arithmetic average return on each stock over this period?

6. **Calculating Variability (LO4, CFA4)** Using the information from Problem 5, calculate the variances and the standard deviations for Cherry and Straw.

7. **Return Calculations (LO1, CFA1)** A particular stock has a dividend yield of 1.2 percent. Last year, the stock price fell from $65 to $59. What was the return for the year?

8. **Geometric Returns (LO1, CFA1)** Using the information from Problem 5, what is the geometric return for Cherry Jalopies, Inc.?

9. **Arithmetic and Geometric Returns (LO1, CFA1)** A stock has had returns of 21 percent, 12 percent, 7 percent, −13 percent, −4 percent, and 26 percent over the last six years. What are the arithmetic and geometric returns for the stock?

Intermediate Questions

10. **Returns and the Bell Curve (LO4, CFA2)** An investment has an expected return of 11 percent per year with a standard deviation of 24 percent. Assuming that the returns on this investment are at least roughly normally distributed, how frequently do you expect to earn between −13 percent and 35 percent? How often do you expect to earn less than −13 percent?

11. **Returns and the Bell Curve (LO4, CFA2)**   An investment has an expected return of 12 percent per year with a standard deviation of 6 percent. Assuming that the returns on this investment are at least roughly normally distributed, how frequently do you expect to lose money?

12. **Using Returns Distributions (LO4, CFA4)**   Based on the historical record, if you invest in long-term U.S. Treasury bonds, what is the approximate probability that your return will be below −3.8 percent in a given year? What range of returns would you expect to see 95 percent of the time? 99 percent of the time?

13. **Using Returns Distributions (LO2, CFA4)**   Based on the historical record, what is the approximate probability that an investment in small stocks will double in value in a single year? How about triple in a single year?

14. **Risk Premiums (LO2)**   Refer to Table 1.1 for large-company stock and T-bill returns for the period 1973–1977:

    a. Calculate the observed risk premium in each year for the common stocks.
    b. Calculate the average returns and the average risk premium over this period.
    c. Calculate the standard deviation of returns and the standard deviation of the risk premium.
    d. Is it possible that the observed risk premium can be negative? Explain how this can happen and what it means.

15. **Geometric Return (LO1, CFA1)**   Your grandfather invested $1,000 in a stock 50 years ago. Currently the value of his account is $324,000. What is his geometric return over this period?

16. **Forecasting Returns (LO1)**   You have found an asset with a 12.60 percent arithmetic average return and a 10.24 percent geometric return. Your observation period is 40 years. What is your best estimate of the return of the asset over the next 5 years? 10 years? 20 years?

17. **Geometric Averages (LO2)**   Look back to Figure 1.1 and find the value of $1 invested in each asset class over this 96-year period. Calculate the geometric return for small-company stocks, large-company stocks, long-term government bonds, Treasury bills, and inflation.

18. **Arithmetic and Geometric Returns (LO1, CFA1)**   A stock has returns of −9 percent, 17 percent, 9 percent, 14 percent, and −4 percent. What are the arithmetic and geometric returns?

19. **Arithmetic and Geometric Returns (LO1, CFA1)**   A stock has had the following year-end prices and dividends:

Year	Price	Dividend
0	$13.25	—
1	15.61	$.15
2	16.72	.18
3	15.18	.20
4	17.12	.24
5	20.43	.28

What are the arithmetic and geometric returns for the stock?

20. **Arithmetic versus Geometric Returns (LO1, CFA1)**   You are given the returns for the following three stocks:

Year	Stock A	Stock B	Stock C
1	8%	3%	−24%
2	8	13	37
3	8	7	14
4	8	5	9
5	8	12	4

Calculate the arithmetic return, geometric return, and standard deviation for each stock. Do you notice anything about the relationship between an asset's arithmetic return, standard deviation, and geometric return? Do you think this relationship will always hold?

Spreadsheet Problems

21. **Return and Standard Deviation (LO4, CFA4)**   The 1980s were a good decade for investors in S&P 500 stocks. To find out how good, construct a spreadsheet that calculates the arithmetic

average return, variance, and standard deviation for the S&P 500 returns during the 1980s using spreadsheet functions.

22. **Dollar-Weighted Average Return (LO3, CFA6)** Suppose that an investor opens an account by investing $1,000. At the beginning of each of the next four years, he deposits an additional $1,000 each year, and he then liquidates the account at the end of the total five-year period. Suppose that the yearly returns in this account, beginning in Year 1, are as follows: −9 percent, 17 percent, 9 percent, 14 percent, and −4 percent. Calculate the arithmetic and geometric average returns for this investment, and determine what the investor's actual dollar-weighted average return was for this five-year period. Why is the dollar-weighted average return higher or lower than the geometric average return?

CFA Exam Review by Kaplan Schweser

[CFA1, CFA6]

Mega Marketing, an advertising firm specializing in the financial services industry, has just hired Kinara Yamisaka. Ms. Yamisaka was a finance major in college and is a candidate for the CFA program. She was hired to provide the firm with more depth in the area of investment performance analysis.

Mega is preparing advertising information for Vega Funds Limited. Vega has provided the following five-year annual return data, where Year 5 is the most recent period:

Vega Funds Limited	
Year	Return
1	−10%
2	25
3	−5
4	30
5	5

To assess her understanding of returns, Ms. Yamisaka's supervisor asks her to calculate a number of different returns, including arithmetic, geometric, annualized, and money- (or dollar-)weighted returns. He also asks her to determine the impact of the following cash flow scenarios on Vega's returns:

Cash Flows	Scenario 1	Scenario 2	Scenario 3
Beginning market value	$100	$100	$100
End of Year 2 deposit (withdrawal)	$0	$20	($10)

1. What is Vega's geometric average return over the five-year period?
   a. 7.85 percent
   b. 9.00 percent
   c. 15.14 percent

2. What are Vega's money- (or dollar-)weighted average returns over the five-year period for Scenarios 2 and 3?

	Scenario 2	Scenario 3
a.	7.78%	7.96%
b.	7.96%	7.78%
c.	9.00%	7.85%

3. Ms. Yamisaka has determined that the average monthly return of another Mega client was 1.63 percent during the past year. What is the annualized rate of return?
   a. 5.13 percent
   b. 19.56 percent
   c. 21.41 percent

4. The return calculation method most appropriate for evaluating the performance of a portfolio manager is:
   a. Holding period.
   b. Geometric.
   c. Money-weighted (or dollar-weighted).

Bloomberg Exercises

1. Generate a histogram of the historical returns for the S&P 500 Index (SPX) over the last 10 years. (HRH)
2. Calculate the total return for someone who held Intel (INTC) stock from January 2, 2019, to January 2, 2022. (TRA)
3. Collect the current equity risk premiums for the United States and China. (CRP)
4. Identify which world stock market has had the best year-to-date return. (WEI)

What's on the Web?

1. **Ticker Symbols**   Go to finance.yahoo.com and look up the ticker symbols for the following companies: 3M Company, International Business Machines, Dell, Advanced Micro Devices, Amazon, and Bed Bath & Beyond.
2. **Average Return and Standard Deviation**   Go to finance.yahoo.com and enter the ticker symbol for your favorite stock. Now look for the historical prices and find the monthly closing stock price for the last six years. Calculate the annual arithmetic average return, the standard deviation, and the geometric return for this period.

The Investment Process

"Don't gamble! Take all your savings and buy some good stock and hold it till it goes up. If it don't go up, don't buy it."

–Will Rogers

Learning Objectives

Don't sell yourself short. Instead, learn about these key investment subjects:

1. The importance of an investment policy statement.

2. The various types of securities brokers and brokerage accounts.

3. How to trade on margin, including calculating the initial and maintenance margins.

4. The workings of short sales.

Are you planning to take a road trip on your upcoming fall or spring break? If so, you might do quite a few things to prepare for this adventure. Among them, you will probably consult an online road map to determine the best route to get you to your destination. You might also check for any expected construction delays. If you find any, you might look for ways to change your route. While road-trip planning might seem unrelated to investing, this process is similar to the approach that you should take with your investment portfolio. For example, investors need to understand their current financial position, as well as where they want to be in the future—like at retirement. Investors also need to identify any constraints that might keep them from reaching their goals.

To help you along your way, we discuss the general investment process in this chapter. We begin with the investment policy statement, which serves as the investor's "road map." We then discuss how you go about buying and selling stocks and bonds.

CFA™ Exam Topics in this Chapter:

1. Time value of money (L1, S1)
2. Market organization and structure (L1, S11)
3. Security market indexes (L1, S11)
4. Market efficiency (L1, S11)
5. Portfolio management: An overview (L1, S17)
6. Basics of portfolio planning and construction (L1, S18)
7. Overview of asset allocation (L3, S3)
8. Overview of private wealth management (L3, S10)
9. Topics in private wealth management (L3, S10)

Go to Connect for a guide that aligns your textbook with CFA readings.

The Investment Policy Statement

Different investors will have very different investment objectives and strategies. For example, some will be active, buying and selling frequently; others will be relatively inactive, buying and holding for long periods of time. Some will be willing to bear substantial risk in seeking out returns; for others, safety is a primary concern. In this section, we describe the investment policy statement, which is designed to reflect these choices.

The investment policy statement, or IPS, is typically divided into two sections: objectives and constraints. In thinking about investor objectives, the most fundamental question is: Why invest at all? For the most part, the only sensible answer is that we invest today to have more tomorrow. In other words, investment is simply deferred consumption; instead of spending today, we choose to wait because we wish to have (or need to have) more to spend later.

Given that we invest now to have more later, the particular objectives identified will depend on, among other things, the time horizon, liquidity needs, and taxes. We discuss these and other issues next.

OBJECTIVES: RISK AND RETURN

Probably the most fundamental decision that an investor must make concerns the amount of risk to take. Most investors are *risk-averse,* meaning that, all else equal, they dislike risk and want to expose themselves to the minimum risk level possible. However, as our previous chapter indicated, larger returns are generally associated with larger risks, so there is a trade-off. In formulating investment objectives, the individual must therefore balance return objectives with risk tolerance.

An individual's tolerance to risk is affected by not only the person's ability to take on risk, but also the individual's willingness to take risk. First, some investors are able to take on more risk, possibly due to a larger beginning portfolio or a longer time horizon. Second, although some investors are well suited to take on risk, they are not willing to do so. Thus, risk tolerance is impacted by both an investor's ability and willingness to take on risk.

Attitudes toward risk are strictly personal preferences, and individuals with very similar economic circumstances can have very different degrees of risk aversion. For this reason, the first thing that must be assessed in evaluating the suitability of an investment strategy is risk tolerance. Unfortunately, this is not an easy thing to do. Most individuals have a difficult time articulating in any precise way their attitude toward risk (what's yours?). One reason is that risk is not a simple concept; it is not easily defined or measured. Nevertheless, the *Investment Updates* box contains information on a short quiz that might help you assess your attitude toward risk. When you take the quiz, remember there are no right or wrong answers.

INVESTOR CONSTRAINTS

In addition to attitude toward risk, an investor's investment strategy will be affected by various constraints. We discuss five of the most common and important constraints next.

RESOURCES Probably the most obvious constraint, and the one to which many students can most easily relate, is *resources.* Obviously, if you have no money, you cannot invest at all. Beyond that, certain types of investments and investment strategies generally have minimum requirements.

What is the minimum resource level needed? The answer to this question depends on the investment strategy, so there is no precise answer. Through mutual funds, initial investments in the stock market can be made for amounts as small as $250—sometimes even less. Investors interested in actively making trading decisions need their own account. This account should contain at least a few thousand dollars, but more is better. Why? When buying and selling securities, the investor's account must cover brokerage commissions, account fees, and other costs.

HORIZON The investment *horizon* refers to the planned life of the investment. For example, individuals frequently save for retirement, where the investment horizon, depending on your age, can be very long. On the other hand, you might be saving to buy a house in the near future, implying a relatively short horizon.

INVESTMENT UPDATES

INVESTOR PROFILE QUESTIONNAIRE

On its website, Charles Schwab provides a publicly available risk tolerance survey, or questionnaire. The survey helps investors determine two important investment-related items: time horizon and risk tolerance. While time horizon is likely related to a person's age, it is more a factor of when money will be needed and at what rate. The longer the time horizon, the more risk an investor is able to take. Risk tolerance, on the other hand, addresses the level of risk an investor is willing to take. Understanding these two elements allows an investor to craft an appropriate asset allocation plan.

Taking the Test

To get a better perspective of your ability and willingness to take on risk, you should take the survey that Charles Schwab provides (see source below). Using calculated time horizon and risk tolerance scores, investors can use the chart below to determine their overall "Investor Profile," which ranges from conservative to aggressive. With this result, investors can then select assets (and portfolios) that match the appropriate investment strategy.

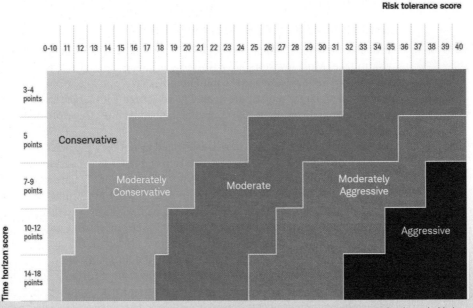

Source: Charles Schwab & Co., Inc., "Investor Profile Questionnaire." Accessed January 2022. www.schwab.com/public/file/P-778947/InvestorProfileQuestionnaire.pdf.

The reason that horizon is important is evident in our previous chapter. It is true that stocks outperformed other investments in the long run, but there were short periods over which they did much worse. This means that, if you have to pay tuition in 30 days, stocks are probably not the best investment for that money. Thus, in thinking about the riskiness of an investment, one important factor is when the money will be needed. This is why most risk tolerance surveys include questions about the investor's time horizon.

LIQUIDITY Some investors might have to sell an asset quickly. In such cases, the asset's *liquidity* is particularly important. An asset with a high degree of liquidity is one that can be sold quickly without a significant price concession. Such an asset is said to be liquid.

Liquidity has two related parts. One part of liquidity is the ease with which an asset can be sold. The other part is how much you have to lower the price to sell the asset quickly. Liquidity is difficult to measure precisely, but some assets are clearly much more liquid than others. A good way to think about liquidity is to imagine buying an asset and then immediately reselling it. The less you would lose on this "round-trip" transaction, the more liquid is the asset.

TAXES Different types of investments are taxed very differently. When we talk about the return on an investment, what is really relevant is the *aftertax* return. As a result, taxes are a vital consideration. Higher tax bracket investors will naturally seek investment strategies with favorable tax treatments, while lower tax bracket (or tax-exempt) investors will focus more on pretax returns.

In addition, the way in which an investment is held can dramatically affect its tax status. The tax laws and other rules are in a constant state of flux. For example, the Tax Cuts and Jobs Act of 2017 changed the tax rates faced by both individuals and corporations. It also changed the list of items that qualify as a valid tax deduction. So, we will stick to broad principles.

The general idea is that certain types of accounts, particularly retirement savings accounts, receive preferential tax treatment. The tax break can be enormous, and, as a result, the amount you can invest each year in these accounts is strictly limited. There are also rules regarding when you can withdraw the money, and it is important to pay careful attention to them.

Taxes impact almost every step of the investment process, from the type of account you choose to the nature and length of the investments themselves. Thus, we will discuss taxes throughout the remainder of the book, and throughout the rest of this chapter in particular. For now, though, consider a simple example on the impact of taxes.

If you started with $1 and were fortunate enough to make an investment that earned 100 percent (i.e., "a double"), then you would end up with $2. What if you were fortunate enough to do this 20 times? So, your $1 became $2, which became $4, and so on. After 20 investments, you would have just over $1 million in pre-tax income ($1,048,576 to be precise).

What about the tax implications? If this is a tax-deferred account, then you pay tax all at the end. If you are in the 35 percent tax bracket, then you would end up with about $650,000— much less than the original amount. However, what if you have to pay tax each time you liquidate one of the investments? So, your $1 becomes $1.65 instead of $2, which becomes $2.72 instead of $4, and so on. Well, in this case, you only end up with $22,370! How can it be so much lower? This is the power of compounding, and this simple example illustrates that deferring taxes can be a powerful tool for accumulating wealth.

UNIQUE CIRCUMSTANCES Almost everyone will have some special or unique requirements or opportunities. For example, many companies will match certain types of investments made by employees on a dollar-for-dollar basis (typically up to some maximum per year). In other words, you double your money immediately with complete certainty. It is difficult to envision any other investment with such a favorable payoff. Therefore, investors should probably seize this opportunity even though there could be some undesirable liquidity, tax, or horizon considerations.

The list of possible special circumstances is essentially endless; here we consider a few examples. The number of dependents and their needs will vary from investor to investor. Therefore, the need to provide for dependents will be an important constraint for some investors. Some investors want to invest only in companies whose products and activities they consider to be socially or politically suitable. Some investors want to invest primarily in their own community or state. Other investors, such as corporate insiders, face regulatory and legal restrictions on their investing. Elected officials may have to avoid (or at least ethically should avoid) some types of investments out of conflict of interest concerns.

STRATEGIES AND POLICIES

Once the IPS is in place, the investor must determine the appropriate strategies to achieve the stated objectives. Investors need to address four key areas when they devise their investment strategy. These key areas are investment management, market timing, asset allocation, and security selection. We discuss each of these next.

INVESTMENT MANAGEMENT A basic decision that all investors make is who manages their investments. At one extreme, investors make all of the buy and sell decisions themselves. At the other extreme, investors make no buy and sell decisions. Instead, the investor hires someone to manage their investments.

Often investors make some investment decisions and hire professional managers to make others. For example, suppose you divide your money among four different mutual funds.

For more risk tolerance quizzes, visit www.fool.com and www.soundmindinvesting.com.

Want to have a career in financial advice? See www.cfainstitute.org and www.cfp.net.

In this case, you have hired four different money managers. However, you decided what types of mutual funds to buy. Also, you chose the particular funds within each type. Finally, you decided how to divide your money among the funds.

At first blush, managing your money yourself might seem to be the cheapest way to go because you do not pay management fees. Upon reflection, this is not a cheap decision. First, you must consider the value of your time. For some investors, researching investments and making investment decisions is something of a hobby. For most investors, however, it is too time-consuming. The value of your time is a powerful incentive to hire professional money managers. Also, for some strategies, the costs of doing it yourself can exceed those of hiring someone even after considering fees. This higher cost is due to the higher level of commissions and other fees that individual investors might have to pay. For example, it might not be a bad idea for some of your investment to be in real estate, but a small investor will find it difficult to directly acquire a sound real estate investment at reasonable cost.

An interesting question regarding professional money managers concerns their performance. It certainly seems logical to argue that by hiring a professional investor to manage your money, you would earn more, at least on average. Surely the pros make better investment decisions than the amateurs! Surprisingly, this outcome is not necessarily true. We will return to this subject in a later chapter. For now, we simply note that the possibility of a superior return might not be a compelling reason to prefer professional management.

MARKET TIMING A second basic investment decision you must make is whether you will try to buy and sell in anticipation of the future direction of the overall market. For example, you might move money into the stock market when you think stock prices will rise. Or you might move money out of the stock market when you think stock prices will fall. This trading activity is called **market timing**. Some investors actively move money around to try to time short-term market movements. Other investors are much less active, but they still try to time long-term market movements. At the extreme, a fully passive strategy is one in which you make no attempt to time the market.

Market timing certainly seems like a reasonable thing to do. After all, why leave money in an investment if you expect it to decrease in value? You might be surprised that a common recommendation is that investors avoid trying to time the market. Why? As we discuss in more detail in a later chapter, the simple reason is that successful market timing is, to put it mildly, extremely difficult. To outperform a completely passive strategy, you must be able to accurately predict the future. If you make even a small number of bad calls, you will likely never catch up.

ASSET ALLOCATION Another fundamental decision that you must make concerns the distribution of your investment across different types of assets. We saw in Chapter 1 that different asset types—small stocks, large stocks, bonds—have distinct risk and return characteristics. In formulating your investment strategy, you must decide what percentage of your money will be placed in each of these broad categories. This decision is called **asset allocation**.

An important asset allocation decision for many investors is how much to invest in common stocks and how much to invest in bonds. There are some basic rules of thumb for this decision, one of the simplest being to split the portfolio into 60 percent stocks and 40 percent bonds. A slightly more sophisticated rule of thumb is that your equity percentage should be equal to your age subtracted from 100 (or, sometimes, 120). Under this rule, a 22-year-old college student should have $100 - 22 = 78$ percent (or $120 - 22 = 98$ percent) of their portfolio in stocks. This approach gradually reduces your exposure to stocks as you get older. Most of the major investment firms, as well as many websites, maintain recommended asset allocation schemes, which can be custom-tailored for individuals depending on their risk tolerance, wealth, and retirement goals.

SECURITY SELECTION Finally, after deciding who will manage your investments, whether you will try to time the market, and the various asset classes you wish to hold, you must decide which specific securities to buy within each class. This is termed **security selection**.

For example, you might decide that you want 30 percent of your money in small stocks. This is an asset allocation decision. Next, however, you must decide which small stocks

market timing
Buying and selling in anticipation of the overall direction of a market.

asset allocation
How an investor spreads portfolio dollars among broad asset classes.

security selection
Selection of specific securities within a particular class.

to buy. Here again you must choose an active strategy or a passive strategy. With an active strategy, you would try to identify those small stocks that you think will perform best in the future. In other words, you are trying to pick "winners." Investigating particular securities within a broad class in an attempt to identify superior performers is often called *security analysis.*

With a passive security selection strategy, you might acquire a diverse group of small stocks, perhaps by buying a mutual fund that holds shares in hundreds of small companies (such funds are discussed in detail in a later chapter).

A useful way to distinguish asset allocation from security selection is to note that asset allocation is a macro-level activity. That is, the focus is on whole markets or classes of assets. Security selection is a much more micro-level activity. The focus of security selection is on individual securities.

If we consider the active versus passive aspects of asset allocation and security selection simultaneously, four distinct investment strategies emerge. These strategies appear in the following two-by-two table:

	Security Selection	
Asset Allocation	**Active**	**Passive**
Active	I	II
Passive	III	IV

With Strategy I, we actively move money between asset classes based on our beliefs and expectations about future performance. In addition, we try to pick the best performers in each class. This is a fully active strategy. At the other extreme, Strategy IV is a fully passive strategy. In this strategy, we seldom change asset allocations or attempt to choose the likely best performers from a set of individual securities.

With Strategy II, we actively vary our holdings by class, but we do not try to choose particular securities within each class. With this strategy, we might move back and forth between short-term government bonds and small stocks in an attempt to time the market. Finally, with Strategy III, we do not vary our asset allocations, but we do select individual securities. A die-hard stock picker would fall into this category. Such an investor holds 100 percent stocks and concentrates solely on buying and selling individual companies.

Between asset allocation and security selection, which one do you think is most important to the success of a portfolio? Because the news media tend to concentrate on the success and failure of individual stocks, you might be inclined to think security selection is the most important element of a successful investing strategy. Research shows, however, that asset allocation is the most important determinant of portfolio returns. In fact, many experts suggest that about 90 percent of the performance of a portfolio is determined by asset allocation, while only 10 percent is from security selection.

How is this result possible? Well, consider the Crash of 2008. If at the beginning of 2008 you had allocated all your money to bonds (as opposed to stocks), you would have done much better than an investor who had heavily allocated to stocks. This outcome could happen even if the stock investor was excellent at selecting stocks. The idea is that equities tend to move together, so even good stocks can do poorly if all equities are doing poorly.

CHECK THIS

2.1a   What does the term "risk-averse" mean?

2.1b   What are some of the constraints investors face in making investment decisions?

2.1c   What is asset allocation?

2.2 Investment Professionals

Related Bloomberg Functions

BAS   Broker Activity Summary

RANK   Broker Ratings

Suppose you have created your IPS, detailing your objectives and constraints. So, what comes next? One way to get started is to open an account with a securities broker, such as Charles Schwab, E*TRADE, or Merrill Lynch. Such accounts are often called *brokerage* or *trading accounts*. Opening a trading account is straightforward and really much like opening a bank account. You will be asked to supply some basic information about yourself and to sign an agreement (often called a *customer's agreement*) that spells out your rights and obligations, as well as those of your broker. You then give your broker a check and instructions on how you want the money invested.

To illustrate, suppose that instead of going to Disneyland, you would rather own part of it. So, you open an account with $25,000. You instruct your broker to purchase 100 shares of Walt Disney stock and to retain any remaining funds in your account. Your broker will locate a seller and purchase the stock on your behalf. Say shares of stock in The Walt Disney Company are selling for about $150 per share, so your 100 shares will cost $15,000. In addition, for providing this service, your broker will generally charge you a commission. How much depends on a number of things, including the type of broker and the size of your order, but on this order, $20 wouldn't be an unusual commission charge. After paying for the stock and paying the commission, you would have $9,980 left in your account. Your broker will hold your stock for you. At a later date, you can sell your stock by instructing your broker to do so. You would receive the proceeds from the sale, less another commission charge. You can always add money to your account and purchase additional securities, and you can withdraw money from your account or even close it altogether.

In broad terms, this basic explanation is really all there is to it. As we begin to discuss in the next section, however, a range of services are available to you, and there are important considerations that you need to take into account before you actually begin investing.

CHOOSING A BROKER/ADVISOR

The first step in opening an account is choosing a broker. Brokers are traditionally divided into three groups: full-service brokers, discount brokers, and deep-discount brokers. What distinguishes the three groups is the level of service they provide and the resulting commissions they charge.

With a deep-discount broker, essentially the only services provided are account maintenance and order execution—that is, buying and selling. You generally deal with a deep-discount broker using the internet (see the next section, "Online Brokers and Robo-Advisors").

At the other extreme, a full-service broker will provide investment advice regarding the types of securities and investment strategies that might be appropriate for you to consider (or avoid). The larger brokerage firms do extensive research on individual companies and securities, as well as maintain lists of recommended (and not recommended) securities. They maintain offices throughout the country, so, depending on where you live, you can actually stop in and speak to the person assigned to your account. A full-service broker will even manage your account for you if you wish. In this case, the broker is said to have *discretion* over the account.

Today, many full-service brokers are trying to specialize in wealth management. That is, these brokers manage many aspects of financial planning for high-net-worth investors. These high-net-worth accounts are exactly what you think they are—accounts with a lot of money in them. Particularly on the full-service side, many brokers have moved toward an advisory-based relationship with their clients. So, rather than charging commissions on every transaction, the investment advisor charges an annual fee, say 1 percent, based on the balance in the account. This fee covers all services associated with advice and trading. An advisory-based relationship brings potential benefits to the client *and* advisor. For example, without commissions, the advisor has little incentive to trade an account actively. As a result, the interests of the client and the advisor may be more closely aligned.

Discount brokers fall somewhere between the two cases we have discussed so far, offering more investment counseling than the deep-discounters and lower commissions or fees than the full-service brokers. Which type of broker should you choose? It depends on how much advice and service you need or want. If you are the do-it-yourself type, then you may seek out the lower commissions. If you are not, then a full-service advisor might be more suitable. Investors might begin with a full-service broker, and then, as they gain experience and confidence, move on to a discount broker or a deep-discount broker. In contrast, some investors might begin with a discount broker when they have less money and move to a full-service broker as the advice becomes more meaningful.

We should note that the brokerage industry is quite competitive, and differences between broker types seem to be blurring. Full-service brokers frequently discount commissions or fees to attract new customers (particularly those with large accounts), and you should not hesitate to ask about commission rates. Similarly, discount brokers have begun to offer securities research and extensive account management services. Basic brokerage services have become like commodities, and, more and more, brokerage firms are competing by offering financial services such as retirement planning, credit cards, and check-writing privileges, to name a few.

ONLINE BROKERS AND ROBO-ADVISORS

The most important recent change in the brokerage industry is the rapid growth of online brokers, also known as *e-brokers* or *cyberbrokers*. With an online broker, you place buy and sell orders over the internet or through an app on your smartphone.

Before 1995, online accounts essentially did not exist. By 2019, many millions of investors were buying and selling securities online. Online investing has fundamentally changed the discount and deep-discount brokerage industry by slashing costs dramatically. In a typical online trade, no human intervention is needed by the broker as the entire process is handled electronically, so operating costs are held to a minimum. As costs have fallen, so have commissions. Even for relatively large trades, online brokers typically charge less than $20 per trade. Many online brokers have even started offering free trades, relying on their other services to generate revenue. Budget-minded investors and active stock traders especially welcome free trades.

Competition among online brokers is fierce. Some take a no-frills approach, offering only basic services and very low commission rates. Others, particularly the larger ones, charge a little more but offer a variety of services, including research and various banking services such as check-writing privileges, credit cards, debit cards, and even mortgages. As technology continues to improve and investors become more comfortable using it, online brokerages will almost surely become the dominant form because of their enormous convenience—and low commission rates.

More recently, firms like Robinhood have attracted many investors. These investors tend to be younger and new to the markets. Users can open accounts via a smartphone app, and they can do so with no minimum deposit. Once the account is up and running, most trades can be made with no commissions. While the service is cheap, there are some trade-offs. Robinhood has more limited access to things like mutual funds and retirement accounts. You may also be wondering how they stay in business. Much of their income comes from getting paid to send orders to particular market makers, which we discuss in a later chapter.

An example of this industry transformation is the recent advent of so-called *robo-advisors*. Under this approach, most advice given to the investor is made without consulting a human. In this process, an investor answers a series of questions designed to evaluate risk tolerance, time horizon, and investment capacity, among other things. Based on these answers, the robo-advisor recommends an asset allocation and associated investments, which are typically funds rather than individual securities. The goal of this process is to provide objective advice while lowering costs. As time progresses, it will be interesting to see if the machines are able to give better advice than humans.

INVESTOR PROTECTION

THE FEDERAL DEPOSIT INSURANCE CORPORATION You probably know that a U.S. government agency called the Federal Deposit Insurance Corporation, or FDIC, protects money deposited into bank accounts. In fact, the FDIC currently insures deposits up to $250,000 per account in nearly every bank and thrift in the United States. However, savers have not always had deposit insurance.

In the 1920s and early 1930s, many banks failed. When these banks failed, the money held in bank accounts vanished. To help restore faith in the banking system, the U.S. Congress created the FDIC in 1933. So far, so good. Since the start of FDIC insurance on January 1, 1934, no depositor has lost a single cent of insured funds as a result of a bank failure.

However, the FDIC insures only bank deposits. That is, the FDIC does not insure stocks, bonds, mutual funds, or other investments offered by banks, thrift institutions, and brokerage firms—even those calling themselves investment banks.

INVESTMENT FRAUD Suppose someone swindles you by selling you shares in a fictitious company. Or suppose someone sells you shares in a real company but does not transfer ownership to you. These two situations are examples of investment fraud.

The U.S. Sentencing Commission reports that the median loss reported in a typical securities fraud case is over $2 million. Further, experts estimate that losses from investment fraud in the United States range from $10 billion to $40 billion a year. You should know that "insurance" for investment fraud does not exist in the United States, but state and federal securities agencies were established to help investors deal with cases of investment fraud. Of course, investors can help protect themselves against fraud by dealing with reputable firms.

THE SECURITIES INVESTOR PROTECTION CORPORATION Even reputable investment firms can go bankrupt or suffer financial difficulties. Fortunately for investors, all reputable brokerage firms belong to the **Securities Investor Protection Corporation (SIPC)**. In fact, almost all brokerage firms operating in the United States are required to be members of the SIPC. The SIPC insures your brokerage account for up to $500,000 in cash and securities, with a $250,000 cash maximum.

Securities Investor Protection Corporation (SIPC)
Insurance fund covering investors' brokerage accounts with member firms.

If you want to learn more about the SIPC, go to www.sipc.org.

Congress chartered the SIPC in 1970, but the SIPC is not a government agency; it is a private insurance fund supported by the securities industry. The SIPC has a narrow, but important, focus: restore funds to investors who have securities in the hands of bankrupt or financially troubled brokerage firms. When a brokerage firm is closed as a result of financial difficulties, sometimes customer assets are missing. In this case, the SIPC works to return customers' cash, bonds, stock, and other eligible securities. Without the SIPC, investors at financially troubled brokerage firms might lose their securities or money forever.

Not every loss is protected by the SIPC. For example, the SIPC does not guarantee the value of securities held in an SIPC-covered brokerage account. In other words, you can still lose everything in an SIPC-covered account if the value of your securities falls to zero.

The SIPC gained the national spotlight with the Bernard "Bernie" Madoff scandal in 2009. Mr. Madoff ran a hedge fund that was really just a Ponzi scheme. In this system, Mr. Madoff took deposits from investors. Rather than investing the money, however, he created fictitious reports to detail investors' alleged holdings. If an investor wanted to withdraw funds, Mr. Madoff used deposits by subsequent investors to fund the payout. The Madoff case is one of the largest investment fraud cases in Wall Street history, topping $65 billion.

BROKER-CUSTOMER RELATIONS

There are several other important things to keep in mind when dealing with a broker or advisor. First, any advice you receive is not guaranteed. Far from it—buy and sell recommendations carry the explicit warning that you rely on them at your own risk. As an example of some common disclosures, check out the *Investment Updates* box. Your broker does have a duty to exercise reasonable care in formulating recommendations and to not recommend anything grossly unsuitable, but that is essentially the extent of it.

To learn more about dispute resolution, visit www.finra.org.

Second, your broker or advisor works as your agent and has a legal duty to act in your best interest. In this case, your investment representative is referred to as being a *fiduciary*. Brokerage firms, however, are in the business of generating brokerage commissions. This fact will probably be spelled out in the account agreement that you sign. There is, therefore, the potential for a conflict of interest. On rare occasions, a broker is accused of "churning" an account, which refers to excessive trading for the sole purpose of generating commissions. In general, you are responsible for checking your account statements and notifying your broker in the event of any problems, and you should certainly do so. With an advisory relationship, churning is less likely.

Finally, in the unlikely event of a significant problem, your account agreement will probably specify very clearly that you must waive your right to sue and/or seek a jury trial.

SOME EXAMPLE DISCLOSURES

1. Regarding Communicating and Sending Trades to Your Broker via E-mail

"Raymond James does not accept private client orders or account instructions by e-mail. This e-mail (a) is not an official transaction confirmation or account statement; (b) is not an offer, solicitation, or recommendation to transact in any security; (c) is intended only for the addressee; and (d) may not be retransmitted to, or used by, any other party. This e-mail may contain confidential or privileged information; please delete immediately if you are not the intended recipient. Raymond James monitors e-mails and may be required by law or regulation to disclose e-mails to third parties."

2. Regarding Stock Analyst Reports

"This material provides general information only. Neither the information nor any views expressed constitute an offer, or an invitation to make an offer, to buy or sell any securities or other investment or any options, futures, or derivatives related to such securities or investments. It is not intended to provide personal investment advice and it does not take into account the specific investment objectives, the financial situation, and the particular needs of any specific person who may receive this material. Investors should seek financial advice regarding the appropriateness of investing in any securities, other investment, or investment strategies discussed in this report and should understand that statements regarding future prospects may not be realized. Investors should note that income from securities or other investments, if any, may fluctuate and that price or value of such securities and investments may rise or fall. Accordingly, investors may receive back less than originally invested. Past performance is not necessarily a guide to future performance. Any information relating to the tax status of financial instruments discussed herein is not intended to provide tax advice or to be used by anyone to provide tax advice. Investors are urged to seek tax advice based on their particular circumstances from an independent tax professional."

Instead, you agree that any disputes will be settled by arbitration and that arbitration is final and binding. Arbitration is not a legal proceeding, and the rules are much less formal. In essence, a panel is appointed by a self-regulatory body of the securities industry to review the case. The panel will be composed of a small number of individuals who are knowledgeable about the securities industry, but a majority of them will not be associated with the industry. The panel makes a finding, and absent extraordinary circumstances, its findings cannot be appealed. The panel does not have to disclose factual findings or legal reasoning.

CHECK THIS

2.2a   What are the differences between full-service and deep-discount brokers?

2.2b   What is the SIPC? How does SIPC coverage differ from FDIC coverage?

2.3 Types of Accounts

The account agreement that you sign has a number of important provisions and details specifying the types of trades that can be made and who can make them. Another important concern is whether the broker will extend credit and, if so, the terms under which credit will be extended. We discuss these and other issues next.

cash account
A brokerage account in which all transactions are made on a strictly cash basis.

CASH ACCOUNTS

A **cash account** is the simplest arrangement. Securities can be purchased to the extent that sufficient cash is available in the account. If additional purchases are desired, then the needed funds must be promptly supplied.

margin account
A brokerage account in which, subject to limits, securities can be bought and sold on credit.

MARGIN ACCOUNTS

With a **margin account**, you can, subject to limits, purchase securities on credit using money loaned to you by your broker. Such a purchase is called a *margin purchase.* The interest rate you pay on the money you borrow is based on the broker's **call money rate**, which is, loosely, the rate the broker pays to borrow the money. You pay some amount over the call money rate, called the *spread;* the exact spread depends on your broker and the size of the loan, as well as your own history with the broker.

Suppose the call money rate has been hovering around 4 percent. If a brokerage firm charges a 2.5 percent spread above this rate on loan amounts under $10,000, then you would pay a total of about 6.5 percent. However, this is usually reduced for larger loan amounts. For example, the spread may decline to .75 percent for amounts over $100,000.

Several important concepts and rules are involved in a margin purchase. For concreteness, we focus on stocks in our discussion. The specific margin rules for other investments can be quite different, but the principles and terminology are usually similar.

In general, when you purchase securities on credit, some of the money is yours and the rest is borrowed. The amount that is yours is called the **margin**. Margin is usually expressed as a percentage. For example, if you take $7,000 of your own money and borrow an additional $3,000 from your broker, your total investment will be $10,000. Of this $10,000, $7,000 is yours, so the margin is $7,000/$10,000 = .70, or 70 percent.

It is useful to create an account balance sheet when thinking about margin purchases (and some other issues we'll get to in just a moment). To illustrate, suppose you open a margin account with $5,000. You tell your broker to buy 100 shares of Merck & Co. (MRK). Shares in Merck are selling for $80 per share, so the total cost will be $8,000. Because you have only $5,000 in the account, you borrow the remaining $3,000. Immediately following the purchase, your account balance sheet would look like this:

Assets		Liabilities and Account Equity	
100 shares of MRK	$8,000	Margin loan	$3,000
		Account equity	5,000
Total	$8,000	Total	$8,000

On the left-hand side of this balance sheet, we list the account assets, which in this case consist of the $8,000 in MRK stock you purchased. On the right-hand side, we first list the $3,000 loan you took out to help you pay for the stock. This amount is a liability because, at some point, the loan must be repaid. The difference between the value of the assets held in the account and the loan amount is $5,000. This amount is your *account equity,* that is, the net value of your investment. Notice that your margin is equal to the account equity divided by the value of the stock owned and held in the account: $5,000/$8,000 = .625, or 62.5 percent.

EXAMPLE 2.1 | **The Account Balance Sheet**

You want to buy 1,000 shares of Devon Energy (DVN) at a price of $48 per share. You put up $36,000 and borrow the rest. What does your account balance sheet look like? What is your margin?

The 1,000 shares of DVN cost $48,000. You supply $36,000, so you must borrow $12,000. The account balance sheet looks like this:

Assets		Liabilities and Account Equity	
1,000 shares of DVN	$48,000	Margin loan	$12,000
		Account equity	36,000
Total	$48,000	Total	$48,000

Your margin is the account equity divided by the value of the stock owned:

$$\text{Margin} = \$36,000/\$48,000$$
$$= .75, \text{ or } 75 \text{ percent}$$

initial margin
The minimum margin that must be supplied on a securities purchase.

INITIAL MARGIN When you first purchase securities on credit, there is a minimum margin that you must supply. This percentage is called the **initial margin**. The minimum percentage (for stock purchases) is set by the Federal Reserve (the "Fed"). However, the exchanges and individual brokerage firms may require higher initial margin amounts.

The Fed's power to set initial margin requirements was established in the Securities Exchange Act of 1934. In subsequent years, initial margin requirements ranged from a low of 45 percent to a high of 100 percent. Since 1974, the minimum has been 50 percent (for stock purchases), and the rate is currently specified in Federal Reserve Board Regulation T. In other words, if you have $10,000 of your own cash, you can borrow up to an additional $10,000, but no more.

We emphasize that these initial margin requirements apply to stocks. In contrast, for the most part, there is little initial margin requirement for government bonds. On the other hand, margin is not allowed at all on certain other types of securities.

EXAMPLE 2.2 **Calculating Initial Margin**

Suppose you have $3,000 in cash in a trading account with a 50 percent initial margin requirement. What is the largest order you can place (ignoring commissions)? If the initial margin were 60 percent, how would your answer change?

When the initial margin is 50 percent, you must supply half of the total (and you borrow the other half). So, $6,000 is the largest order you could place. When the initial margin is 60 percent, your $3,000 must equal 60 percent of the total. In other words, it must be the case that

$$\$3,000 = .60 \times \text{Total order}$$
$$\text{Total order} = \$3,000/.60$$
$$= \$5,000$$

As this example illustrates, the higher the initial margin required, the less you can borrow. When the margin is 50 percent, you can borrow $3,000. When the margin is 60 percent, you can borrow only $2,000.

---

maintenance margin
The minimum margin that must be present at all times in a margin account.

MAINTENANCE MARGIN In addition to the initial margin requirement set by the Fed, brokerage firms and exchanges generally have a **maintenance margin** requirement. For example, the New York Stock Exchange (NYSE) requires a minimum of 25 percent maintenance margin. This amount is the minimum margin required at all times after the purchase.

The maintenance margin set by your broker is sometimes called the "house" margin requirement. The level is established by your broker, who may vary it depending on what you are buying. For low-priced and very volatile stocks, the house margin can be as high as 100 percent, meaning no margin at all.

margin call
A demand for more funds that occurs when the margin in an account drops below the maintenance margin.

A typical maintenance margin might be around 30 percent. If your margin falls below 30 percent, then you may be subject to a **margin call**, which is a demand by your broker to add funds to your account, pay off part of the loan, or sell enough securities to bring your margin back up to an acceptable level. In some cases, you will be asked to restore your account to the initial margin level. In other cases, you will be asked to restore your account to the maintenance margin level. If you do not, or cannot, comply, your securities will likely be sold. The loan will be repaid out of the proceeds, and any remaining amounts will be credited to your account.

To illustrate, suppose your account has a 50 percent initial margin requirement and a 30 percent maintenance margin. Suppose stock in Vandelay Industries is selling for $50 per share. You have $20,000, and you want to buy as much of this stock as you possibly can. With a 50 percent initial margin, you can buy up to $40,000 worth, or 800 shares. The account balance sheet looks like this:

Assets		Liabilities and Account Equity	
800 shares @ $50/share	$40,000	Margin loan	$20,000
		Account equity	20,000
Total	$40,000	Total	$40,000

Unfortunately, right after your purchase, Vandelay Industries reveals that it has been artificially inflating earnings for the last three years (this action is not good). Share prices plummet to $35 per share. What does the account balance sheet look like when this happens? Are you subject to a margin call?

To create the new account balance sheet, we recalculate the total value of the stock. The margin loan stays the same, so the account equity is adjusted as needed:

Assets		Liabilities and Account Equity	
800 shares @ $35/share	$28,000	Margin loan	$20,000
		Account equity	8,000
Total	$28,000	Total	$28,000

As shown, the total value of your "position" (i.e., the stock you hold) falls to $28,000, a $12,000 loss. You still owe $20,000 to your broker, so your account equity is $28,000 − $20,000 = $8,000. Your margin is therefore $8,000/$28,000 = .286, or 28.6 percent. You are below the 30 percent minimum, so you are subject to a margin call.

THE EFFECTS OF MARGIN Margin is a form of *financial leverage*. Any time you borrow money to make an investment, the impact is to magnify both your gains and losses, hence the use of the term "leverage." The easiest way to see this is through an example. Imagine that you have $30,000 in an account with a 60 percent initial margin. You now know that you can borrow up to an additional $20,000 and buy $50,000 worth of stock (why?). The call money rate is 5.50 percent; you must pay this rate plus a .50 percent spread. Suppose you buy 1,000 shares of Verizon (VZ) at $50 per share. One year later, shares in Verizon are selling for $60 per share. Assuming the call money rate does not change and ignoring dividends, what is your return on this investment?

At the end of the year, your 1,000 shares are worth $60,000. You owe 6 percent interest on the $20,000 you borrowed, or $1,200. If you pay off the loan with interest, you will have $60,000 − $21,200 = $38,800. You started with $30,000 and ended with $38,800, so your net gain is $8,800. In percentage terms, your return was $8,800/$30,000 = .2933, or 29.33 percent.

How would you have done without the financial leverage created from the margin purchase? In this case, you would have invested just $30,000. At $50 per share, you would have purchased 600 shares. At the end of the year, your 600 shares would be worth $60 apiece, or $36,000 total. Your dollar profit is $6,000, so your percentage return would be $6,000/$30,000 = .20, or 20 percent. If we compare this to the 29.33 percent that you made above, it's clear that you did substantially better by leveraging.

The downside is that you would do much worse if Verizon's stock price fell (or didn't rise very much). For example, if Verizon shares had fallen to $40 a share, you would have lost (check these calculations for practice) $11,200, or 37.33 percent, on your margin investment, compared to $6,000, or 20 percent, on the unmargined investment. This example illustrates how leveraging an investment through a margin account can cut both ways.

EXAMPLE 2.3 | **A Marginal Investment?**

A year ago, you bought 300 shares of Coca-Cola Co. (KO) at $55 per share. You put up the 60 percent initial margin. The call money rate plus the spread you paid was 8 percent. What is your return if the price today is $50? Compare this to the return you would have earned if you had not invested on margin.

Your total investment was 300 shares at $55 per share, or $16,500. You supplied 60 percent, or $9,900, and you borrowed the remaining $6,600. At the end of the year, you owe $6,600 plus 8 percent interest, or $7,128. If the stock sells for $50, then your position is worth 300 × $50 = $15,000. Deducting the $7,128 leaves $7,872 for you. Because you originally invested $9,900, your dollar loss is $9,900 − $7,872 = $2,028. Your percentage return is −$2,028/$9,900 = −.2048, or −20.48 percent.

If you had not leveraged your investment, you would have purchased $9,900/$55 = 180 shares. These would have been worth 180 × $50 = $9,000. You therefore would have lost $900; your percentage return would have been −$900/$9,900 = −.0909, or −9.09 percent, compared to the −20.48 percent that you lost on your leveraged position.

EXAMPLE 2.4

How Low Can It Go?

In our previous example (Example 2.3), suppose the maintenance margin was 40 percent. At what price per share would you have been subject to a margin call?

To answer, let P^* be the critical price. You own 300 shares, so, at that price, your stock is worth $300 \times P^*$. You borrowed \$6,600, so your account equity is equal to the value of your stock less the \$6,600 you owe, or $(300 \times P^*) - \$6,600$. We can summarize this information as follows:

$$\text{Amount borrowed} = \$6,600$$
$$\text{Value of stock} = 300 \times P^*$$
$$\text{Account equity} = (300 \times P^*) - \$6,600$$

From our preceding discussion, your percentage margin is your dollar margin (or account equity) divided by the value of the stock:

$$\text{Margin} = \frac{\text{Account equity}}{\text{Value of stock}}$$
$$= \frac{(300 \times P^*) - \$6,600}{300 \times P^*}$$

To find the critical price, we will set this margin equal to the maintenance margin and solve for P^*:

$$\text{Maintenance margin} = \frac{(\text{Number of shares} \times P^*) - \text{Amount borrowed}}{\text{Number of shares} \times P^*}$$

Solving for P^* yields:

$$P^* = \frac{\text{Amount borrowed/Number of shares}}{1 - \text{Maintenance margin}}$$

Finally, setting the maintenance margin equal to 40 percent, we obtain this critical price, P^*:

$$P^* = \frac{\$6,600/300}{1 - .40}$$
$$= \frac{\$22}{.60} = \$36.67$$

At any price below \$36.67, your margin will be less than 40 percent and you will be subject to a margin call. So, \$36.67 is the lowest possible price that could be reached before you are subject to a margin call.

As Example 2.4 shows, you can calculate the critical price (the lowest price before you get a margin call) as follows:

$$P^* = \frac{\text{Amount borrowed/Number of shares}}{1 - \text{Maintenance margin}} \tag{2.1}$$

For example, suppose you had a margin loan of \$40,000, which you used to purchase, in part, 1,000 shares. The maintenance margin is 37.5 percent. What's the critical stock price, and how do you interpret it?

See if you don't agree that the critical stock price, P^*, is \$40/.625 = \$64. The interpretation is straightforward: If the stock price falls below \$64, you are subject to a margin call.

To help make the concept of margin clear, we focused on a portfolio with only one stock in it. In most cases, however, an investor has a portfolio containing many different securities. So, how does margin work in this case? Well, any time you borrow money, you begin trading on margin. The margin process from that point is similar, except that we focus on the overall value of our portfolio. So, while investors do not get a margin call if the price of one particular stock falls, they do get one if their overall portfolio value falls too much.

ANNUALIZING RETURNS ON A MARGIN PURCHASE

Things get a little more complicated when we consider holding periods different from a year on a margin purchase. For example, suppose the call money rate is 9 percent and you pay a spread of 2 percent over that. You buy 1,000 shares of Verizon (VZ) at \$60 per share, but you put up only half the money. In three months, Verizon is selling for $63 per share and you sell your shares. What is your annualized return assuming no dividends are paid?

In this case, you invested $60,000, half of which ($30,000) is borrowed. How much do you have to repay in three months? Here we have to adjust for the fact that the interest rate is 11 percent per year, but you only borrowed the money for three months. In this case, the amount you repay is equal to the amount you borrowed plus the interest. For margin loans, the interest is typically calculated using an Annual Percentage Rate, or APR. For simplicity, the industry also typically assumes a 360-day fiscal year. So, interest is calculated as:

$$\text{Interest Cost} = \text{Amount borrowed} \times \text{Interest rate per year} \times \frac{\text{Days held}}{360}$$

In our case, 3 months is one-fourth of the 360-day year, or 90 days. So, plugging in our numbers, we get:

$$\text{Interest Cost} = \$30,000 \times .11 \times \frac{90}{360}$$
$$= \$825$$

So, the amount we repay is the $30,000 borrowed plus $825 of interest, for a total of $30,825. When you sell your stock, you get $63,000, of which $30,825 is used to pay off the loan, leaving you with $32,175. You invested $30,000, so your dollar gain is $2,175, and your percentage return for your three-month holding period is $2,175/$30,000 = .0725, or 7.25 percent.

Finally, we could convert this 7.25 percent to an annualized return. There are four three-month periods in a year, so:

$$1 + EAR = (1 + \text{Holding period percentage return})^m$$
$$= (1 + .0725)^4$$
$$= 1.3231$$

Thus, your annualized return is 32.31 percent.

HYPOTHECATION AND STREET NAME REGISTRATION

As part of your margin account agreement, you must agree to various conditions. We discuss two of the most important next.

HYPOTHECATION Any securities you purchase in your margin account will be held by your broker as collateral against the loan made to you. This practice protects the broker because the securities can be sold by the broker if the customer is unwilling or unable to meet a margin call. Putting securities up as collateral against a loan is called **hypothecation**. In fact, a margin agreement is sometimes called a *hypothecation agreement*. In addition, to borrow the money that it loans to you, your broker will often rehypothecate your securities, meaning that your broker will pledge them as collateral with its lender, normally a bank.

hypothecation
Pledging securities as collateral against a loan.

STREET NAME REGISTRATION Securities in a margin account are normally held in **street name**. This means that the brokerage firm is actually the registered owner. If this were not the case, the brokerage firm could not legally sell the securities should a customer refuse to meet a margin call or otherwise fail to live up to the terms of the margin agreement. With this arrangement, the brokerage firm is the "owner of record," but the account holder is the "beneficial owner."

street name
An arrangement under which a broker is the registered owner of a security.

When a security is held in street name, anything mailed to the security owner, such as an annual report or a dividend check, goes to the brokerage firm. The brokerage firm then passes these on to the account holder. Street-name ownership is actually a great convenience to the owner. In fact, because it is usually a free service, even customers with cash accounts generally choose street-name ownership. Some of the benefits are:

1. Because the broker holds the security, there is no danger of theft or other loss of the security. This is important because a stolen or lost security cannot be easily or cheaply replaced.

2. Any dividends or interest payments are automatically credited, and they are often credited more quickly (and conveniently) than they would be if the owner received the check in the mail.

3. The broker provides regular account statements showing the value of securities held in the account and any payments received. Also, for tax purposes, the broker will provide all the needed information on a single form at the end of the year, greatly reducing the owner's record-keeping requirements.

RETIREMENT ACCOUNTS

COMPANY-SPONSORED PLANS If you are employed by a company, particularly a medium- or large-sized company, you will probably have access to a company-sponsored retirement plan such as a 401(k). In a typical plan, you (as the employee) can decide how much money you contribute to the plan by making deductions from your paychecks. In many cases, your employer also makes contributions to the plan. For example, your company could make dollar-for-dollar matching contributions up to a certain percentage of your salary. Even after your contributions hit the maximum amount your employer will match, you can still contribute additional funds. The amount of your total contribution is limited by the Internal Revenue Service (IRS). As of 2022, the contribution limit is $20,500 for workers under the age of 50 and $27,000 for those 50 and above. These limits are evaluated annually and adjusted for inflation when deemed appropriate.

To see how good your potential employer's 401(k) is, visit www.brightscope.com.

You decide how your 401(k) contributions are invested. Although some companies have retirement plans that allow employees to choose almost any security, most plans use a "menu" format. That is, the company provides a set, or a menu, of investment choices for its employees. Most likely, these choices are mutual funds. Mutual funds have become so important that we devote an entire chapter to them (see Chapter 4).

The general investing approach described earlier in this chapter applies to your retirement plan. You decide your percentage allocations to asset classes (like stocks, bonds, and T-bills) and then choose particular assets (e.g., mutual funds) in each asset class. For example, you might decide that you want 75 percent of your retirement funds invested in stocks. Then, you have to decide whether you want to invest in U.S. stocks, stocks in other regions of the world, stocks in specific countries, large-company stocks, small-company stocks, or a combination of these categories.

What happens if an employee doesn't select from the menu? In this case, employers identify a default investment option. Most employers generally select a *target date fund,* also called a *life-cycle fund.* This type of investment is designed to fit investors with a particular retirement date. For younger investors, the fund would use more equity, and for those nearer to retirement, more fixed income would be used. We discuss this type of fund, and many others, in another chapter.

The primary benefit of company-sponsored plans is that they are considered "qualified" accounts for tax purposes. In a qualified account, any money that you deposit into the account is deducted from your taxable income. As a result, your yearly tax bill will be lower, and the net out-of-pocket cost of your deposit is lower. For example, if you are in the 15 percent tax bracket and decide to deposit $12,000 next year, your net out-of-pocket cost is only $10,200. Why? You will pay $1,800 (= .15 × $12,000) less in taxes than you would if you had not made this deposit. Of course, nothing is free. You must pay taxes on the withdrawals you make during retirement.

INDIVIDUAL RETIREMENT ACCOUNTS (IRAs) People who do not have access to a company-sponsored plan, or those who want another retirement account, can use individual retirement accounts (IRAs). Because an IRA is set up directly with a broker or a bank, these accounts can contain a wide range of assets. In 2022, the maximum contribution to an IRA was $6,000 for those under the age of 50 and $7,000 for those 50 and above. Annoyingly, the amount you can contribute falls as your income rises above certain levels. As a result, IRA accounts are not available for every investor.

In terms of tax treatment, there are basically two types of IRAs. With the first type, you pay taxes today on money you earn. If you then invest these aftertax dollars in a retirement savings account, you pay no taxes at all when you take the money out later. This means that dividends, interest, and capital gains are not taxed, which is a big break. This type of account is called a Roth individual retirement account (Roth IRA).

With the second type of account, you do not pay taxes on the money you earn today if you invest it. Such accounts are "tax-deferred" and are similar to the way most employer-sponsored retirement accounts (such as 401(k) plans) are set up. Later, when you retire, you owe income taxes on whatever you take out of the account.

The two types of accounts really come down to this: You either pay taxes today and do not pay taxes later, or vice versa. It would be great if you could invest pretax dollars and never pay taxes. Alas, this is tax avoidance—which is illegal. Therefore, investors must decide whether to pay taxes now or pay taxes later.

Some circumstances make a Roth IRA preferable to a more traditional tax-deferred IRA. For example, younger investors who are currently in a low tax bracket might be well suited for a Roth IRA. The reason is that the benefit of tax-free investment growth outweighs the cost of making contributions with income left after taxes. From a behavioral standpoint, a Roth might also be preferred. When determining the amount to contribute, an investor is prone to pick a dollar amount, say, the maximum $6,000. With the Roth IRA, however, investors are actually "investing" more because they are also paying the tax on that portion up front. In any case, whether you choose a Roth or a traditional IRA will depend on personal characteristics like your age and your tax bracket.

CHECK THIS

2.3a	What is the difference between a cash and a margin account?
2.3b	What is the effect of a margin purchase on gains and losses?
2.3c	What is a margin call?

2.4 Types of Positions

Related Bloomberg Functions

SI   Short Interest

SPOS Short Positions

SIA   Short Interest Analysis

Once you have created your investment policy statement and decided which type of investment professional you will employ, your next step is to determine the types of positions you will hold in your account. The two basic positions are long and short.

An investor who buys and owns shares of stock is said to be *long* in the stock or to have a *long position*. An investor with a long position will make money if the price of the stock increases and, conversely, lose money if it goes down. In other words, a long investor hopes that the price will increase.

Now consider a different situation. Suppose you thought, for some reason, that the stock in a particular company was likely to decrease in value. You obviously wouldn't want to buy any of it. If you already owned some, you might choose to sell it.

short sale
A sale in which the seller does not actually own the security that is sold.

Beyond this, you might decide to engage in a **short sale**. In a short sale, you actually sell a security that you do not own. This is referred to as *shorting* the stock. After the short sale, the investor is said to have a *short position* in the security.

Financial assets of all kinds are sold short, not just shares of stock, and the terms "long" and "short" are universal. However, the mechanics of a short sale differ quite a bit across security types. Even so, regardless of how the short sale is executed, the essence is the same. An investor with a long position benefits from price increases, and as we will see, an investor with a short position benefits from price decreases. For the sake of illustration, we focus here on shorting shares of stock. Procedures for shorting other types of securities are discussed in later chapters.

BASICS OF A SHORT SALE

How can you sell stock you don't own? It is easier than you might think: You borrow the shares of stock from your broker and then you sell them. At some future date, you will buy the same number of shares that you originally borrowed and return them, thereby eliminating the short position. Eliminating the short position is often called *covering the position* or, less commonly, *curing the short*.

You might wonder where your broker will get the stock to loan you. Normally, it will come from other margin accounts. Often, when you open a margin account, you are asked to sign a loan-consent agreement, which gives your broker the right to loan shares held in the account. If shares you own are loaned out, you still receive any dividends or other distributions, and you can sell the stock anytime you wish. In other words, the fact that some of your stock may have been loaned out is of little or no consequence as far as you are concerned.

An investor with a short position will profit if the security declines in value. For example, assume that you short 200 shares of General Electric (GE) at a price of $100 per share. You receive $20,000 from the sale (more on this in a moment). A month later, the stock is selling for $80 per share. You buy 200 shares for $16,000, and this "round-trip" closes (or covers) your short position. Because you received $20,000 from the sale and it cost you only $16,000 to cover, you made $4,000.

Conventional Wall Street wisdom states that the way to make money is to "buy low, sell high." With a short sale, we hope to do exactly that, just in the opposite order—"sell high, buy low." If a short sale strikes you as a little confusing, it might help to think about the everyday use of the terms. Whenever we say that we are "running short" on something, we mean we don't have enough of it. Similarly, when someone says, "don't sell me short," they mean don't bet on them not to succeed.

EXAMPLE 2.5   **The Long and Short of It**

Suppose you short 2,000 shares of Under Armour (UA) at $15 per share. Six months later, you cover your short. If Under Armour is selling for $10 per share at that time, did you make money or lose money? How much? What if you covered at $20?

If you shorted at $15 per share and covered at $10, you originally sold 2,000 shares at $15 and later bought them back at $10, so you made $5 per share, or $10,000. If you covered at $20, you lost $10,000.

SHORT SALES: SOME DETAILS

There are many sites devoted to the fine art of short selling. Try www.bearmarketcentral.com.

When you short a stock, you must borrow it from your broker, so you must fulfill various requirements. First, there is an initial margin and a maintenance margin. Second, after you sell the borrowed stock, the proceeds from the sale are credited to your account, but you cannot use them. They are, in effect, frozen until you return the stock. Finally, if any dividends are paid on the stock while you have a short position, you must pay them.

To illustrate, we will again create an account balance sheet. Suppose you want to short 100 shares of AT&T (T) when the price is $30 per share. This short sale means you will borrow shares of stock worth a total of $30 × 100 = $3,000. Your broker has a 50 percent initial margin and a 40 percent maintenance margin on short sales.

An important thing to keep in mind with a margin purchase of securities is that margin is calculated as the value of your account equity relative to the value of the securities purchased. With a short sale, margin is calculated as the value of your account equity relative to the value of the securities sold short. Thus, in both cases, margin is equal to equity value divided by security value.

In our AT&T example, the initial value of the securities sold short is $3,000 and the initial margin is 50 percent, so you must deposit at least half of $3,000, or $1,500, in your account. With this in mind, after the short sale, your account balance sheet is as follows:

Assets		Liabilities and Account Equity	
Proceeds from sale	$3,000	Short position	$3,000
Initial margin deposit	1,500	Account equity	1,500
Total	$4,500	Total	$4,500

As shown, four items appear on the account balance sheet:

1. *Proceeds from sale.* This is the $3,000 you received when you sold the stock. This amount will remain in your account until you cover your position. Note that you will not earn interest on this amount—it will just sit there as far as you are concerned.

2. *Margin deposit.* This is the 50 percent margin that you had to post. This amount will not change unless there is a margin call. Depending on the circumstances and your particular account agreement, you may earn interest on the initial margin deposit.

3. *Short position.* Because you must eventually buy back the stock and return it, you have a liability. The current cost of eliminating that liability is $3,000.

4. *Account equity.* As always, the account equity is the difference between the total account value ($4,500) and the total liabilities ($3,000).

We now examine two scenarios: (1) the stock price falls to $20 per share and (2) the stock price rises to $40 per share.

If the stock price falls to $20 per share, then you are still liable for 100 shares, but the cost of those shares is now just $2,000. Your account balance sheet becomes:

Assets		Liabilities and Account Equity	
Proceeds from sale	$3,000	Short position	$2,000
Initial margin deposit	1,500	Account equity	2,500
Total	$4,500	Total	$4,500

Notice that the left-hand side doesn't change. The same $3,000 you originally received is still held, and the $1,500 margin you deposited is still there also. On the right-hand side, the short position is now a $2,000 liability, down from $3,000. Finally, the good news is that the account equity rises by $1,000, so this is your gain. Your margin is equal to account equity divided by the security value (the value of the short position), $2,500/$2,000 = 1.25, or 125 percent.

However, if the stock price rises to $40, things are not so rosy. Now, the 100 shares for which you are liable are worth $4,000:

Assets		Liabilities and Account Equity	
Proceeds from sale	$3,000	Short position	$4,000
Initial margin deposit	1,500	Account equity	500
Total	$4,500	Total	$4,500

Again, the left-hand side doesn't change. The short liability rises by $1,000, and, unfortunately for you, the account equity declines by $1,000, the amount of your loss.

To make matters worse, when the stock price rises to $40, you are severely undermargined. The account equity is $500, but the value of the stock sold short is $4,000. Your margin is $500/$4,000 = .125, or 12.5 percent. Since this is well below the 40 percent maintenance margin, you are subject to a margin call. You have two options: (1) buy back some or all of the stock and return it or (2) add funds to your account.

EXAMPLE 2.6	A Case of the Shorts

You shorted 5,000 shares of Layton Industries at a price of $30 per share. The initial margin is 50 percent, and the maintenance margin is 40 percent. What does your account balance sheet look like following the short?

Following the short, your account becomes:

Assets		Liabilities and Account Equity	
Proceeds from sale	$150,000	Short position	$150,000
Initial margin deposit	75,000	Account equity	75,000
Total	$225,000	Total	$225,000

Notice that you shorted $150,000 worth of stock, so, with a 50 percent margin requirement, you deposited $75,000.

EXAMPLE 2.7

Margin Calls

In our previous example (Example 2.6), at what price per share would you be subject to a margin call?

To answer this one, let P^* be the critical price. The short liability then is 5,000 shares at a price of P^*, or $5,000 \times P^*$. The total account value is $225,000, so the account equity is $225,000 - 5,000P^*$. We can summarize this information as follows:

$$\text{Short position} = 5,000 \times P^*$$

$$\text{Account equity} = \$225,000 - 5,000 \times P^*$$

Notice that the total account value, $225,000, is the sum of your initial margin deposit plus the proceeds from the sale, and this amount does not change. Your margin is the account equity relative to the short liability:

$$\begin{aligned}
\text{Margin} &= \frac{\text{Account equity}}{\text{Value of stock}} \\
&= \frac{(\text{Initial margin deposit} + \text{Short proceeds}) - \text{Number of shares} \times P^*}{\text{Number of shares} \times P^*} \\
&= \frac{(\$150,000 + \$75,000) - 5,000 \times P^*}{5,000 \times P^*}
\end{aligned}$$

To find the critical price, we will set this margin equal to the maintenance margin and solve for P^*:

$$\text{Maintenance margin} = \frac{(\text{Initial margin deposit} + \text{Short proceeds}) - \text{Number of shares} \times P^*}{\text{Number of shares} \times P^*}$$

Solving for P^* yields:

$$P^* = \frac{(\text{Initial margin deposit} + \text{Short proceeds})/\text{Number of shares}}{1 + \text{Maintenance margin}}$$

Finally, setting the maintenance margin equal to 40 percent, we obtain this critical price, P^*:

$$P^* = \frac{\$225,000/5,000}{1.40} = \$32.14$$

At any price above $32.14, your margin will be less than 40 percent, so you will be subject to a margin call. Thus, $32.14 is the highest possible price that could be reached before you are subject to a margin call.

As Example 2.7 shows, you can calculate the critical price on a short sale (the highest price before you get a margin call) as follows:

$$P^* = \frac{(\text{Initial margin deposit} + \text{Short proceeds})/\text{Number of shares}}{1 + \text{Maintenance margin}}$$

For example, suppose you shorted 1,000 shares at $50. The initial margin is 50 percent and the maintenance margin is 40 percent. What's the critical stock price, and how do you interpret it?

Noting that the initial margin deposit is $25,000 (50 percent of the short proceeds), see if you don't agree that the critical stock price, P^*, is $75/1.40 = \$53.57$. So, if the stock price rises above $53.57, you're subject to a margin call.

We should remind you, however, that while we have focused on individual stock positions, margin works at the portfolio level. So, it is possible for an investor to use margin to go long some stocks and go short others at the same time. Margin calls are triggered by a decline in the overall portfolio equity value and not necessarily by the change in price of any single security.

At this point, you might wonder whether short selling is a common practice among investors. Actually, it is quite common, and a substantial volume of stock sales are initiated by short-sellers. In fact, the amount of stock held short for some companies can be several tens of millions of shares, and the total number of shares held short across all companies can be several billion shares. To measure the extent of short selling in a particular stock, many

You can find the short interest for the current month in many financial publications. But what if you want a longer history of the shares sold short for a particular company? At nasdaq.com, you can find the short interest for companies listed on the Nasdaq for the previous year. We went to the site in early 2022 and looked up Tesla (TSLA), and here is what we found:

As you can see, the short interest in Tesla fell from about 39 million shares in June 2021 to about 22 million shares in December. Why would you want a history of short sales? Some investors use short sales as a technical indicator, which we discuss in a later chapter. Here's a question for you: What do you think "Days to Cover" means? It is the ratio of short interest to average daily share volume. Thus, "Days to Cover" measures how many days of

normal trading would be necessary to completely cover all outstanding short interest. Days to Cover is also sometimes referred to as the Short Interest Ratio, and many investors actually track this ratio over time to determine changing market sentiment. As an example, check out the following graph from Bloomberg.

Another commonly used measure of short interest is the *percentage of float*. This metric measures the percentage of a firm's outstanding shares that are currently being shorted. Some stocks have large short interest positions because they have a large number of shares outstanding (think about Apple). Days to Cover and percentage of float help to standardize the way short interest is presented, which makes the information more meaningful.

TSLA > TSLA SHORT INTEREST

TSLA Short Interest

SETTLEMENT DATE	SHORT INTEREST	AVG. DAILY SHARE VOLUME	DAYS TO COVER
12/31/2021	22,471,754	23,331,804	1
12/15/2021	25,817,321	22,805,635	1.132059
11/30/2021	26,570,674	24,911,984	1.066582
11/15/2021	25,702,669	36,054,532	1
10/29/2021	28,075,921	32,901,460	1
10/15/2021	30,337,020	17,943,717	1.690676
09/30/2021	29,205,723	20,300,731	1.438654
09/15/2021	26,999,741	16,561,475	1.630274
08/31/2021	27,432,219	17,361,855	1.580028
08/13/2021	26,828,057	17,287,331	1.551891
07/30/2021	29,914,139	20,929,992	1.429248
07/15/2021	32,355,387	21,704,535	1.49072
06/30/2021	34,093,281	25,464,832	1.338838
06/15/2021	39,363,717	21,688,018	1.814998

Source: www.nasdaq.com, accessed January 2022.

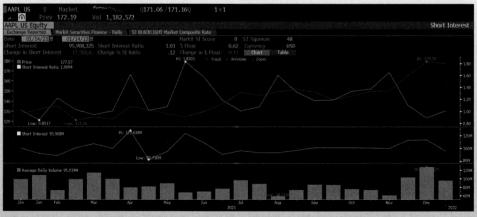

Source: Bloomberg Finance L.P.

SHACKLING SHORT SELLERS: THE 2008 SHORTING BAN

A paper by Ekkehart Boehmer, Charles Jones, and Xiaoyan Zhang examines the short selling ban imposed by the Securities and Exchange Commission in 2008. Here is the major conclusion the authors draw:

> Stocks subject to the ban suffered a severe degradation in market quality, as measured by spreads, price impacts, and intraday volatility. Price effects are a bit harder to assign to the ban, as there is substantial confounding news about TARP and other government programs to assist the financial sector on the day that the ban is announced and implemented. When we look at firms that are added later to the ban list (and which are generally much less affected by the news about TARP, for example),

we do not find a price bump at all. In fact, these stocks consistently underperform during the whole period the ban is in effect. This suggests that the shorting ban did not provide much of an artificial boost in prices.

Essentially, market liquidity suffered, which increased both trading costs and volatility. In fact, after controlling for other market forces, the researchers found that the ban had no positive impact on prices, which was a primary goal of the imposed ban. So, it doesn't appear that the ban really worked.

Source: Ekkehart Boehmer, Charles M. Jones, and Xiaoyan Zhang, "Shackling Short Sellers: The 2008 Shorting Ban," *Review of Financial Studies* 26, no. 6 (2013), pp. 1363–1400.

---

short interest
The amount of common stock held in short positions.

investors refer to **short interest**, which is the amount of common stock held in short positions. The *Work the Web* box shows how to find short interest for a particular company.

SHORT-SALE CONSTRAINTS

uptick rule
Rule for short sales requiring that before a short sale can be executed, the last price change must be an uptick.

Although short selling stock is relatively easy, you do need to be aware of some constraints related to this type of position. For example, all sell orders marked as short sales were previously subject to the **uptick rule**. According to the uptick rule, a short sale can be executed only if the last price change was an uptick. For example, suppose the last two trades were executed at 55.50 and then 55.63. The last price change was an uptick of .13, so a short sale can be executed at a price of 55.63 or higher. Alternatively, suppose the last two trades were executed at 55.50 and 55.25, where the last price change was a downtick of .25. In this case, a short sale can be executed only at a price higher than 55.25.

Regulators originally enacted the uptick rule to make it more difficult for speculators to drive down a stock's price by repeated short sales, often called a "bear raid." While the uptick rule originated on the NYSE, the Nasdaq adopted a similar rule in 1994. In 2004, the Securities and Exchange Commission (SEC) decided to test whether the uptick rule was still necessary. In particular, the SEC believed that increased market liquidity made this type of speculative trading less feasible. So, the SEC repealed the uptick rule in June 2007—ironically, just in time for one of the worst market crashes in history.

Without an uptick rule in place, in 2008 the SEC resorted to a complete ban on short selling in an original set of 799 financial companies. The SEC's goal was to limit the downward slide in the market, which the SEC perceived to be strongly related to excessive short selling. Even after the ban, however, financial stocks continued to slide. Combined with other negative effects, many insiders question how effective this ban actually was. Check out our *Investment Updates* box for some additional insight on the short selling ban.

After the markets began to recover in 2009, the SEC reconsidered its decision to eliminate the uptick rule. After much public discussion and comment, the SEC decided to adopt a modified, or alternative, uptick rule. The new rule, which was approved in 2010, does not apply any short-sale constraints until a stock declines by 10 percent in a single day. If this decline occurs, then any subsequent short sale is subject to the uptick rule.

Besides government intervention, short-sellers face other constraints. For example, there might not be enough shares available to short, whether from your particular broker or across the entire market. Without shares available to borrow, the short sale cannot take place. This constraint can create effects similar to those of the outright ban instituted by the SEC: reduced liquidity, increased volatility, and inefficient pricing.

We conclude our discussion of short sales with a very important observation. With a long position, the most you can ever lose is your total investment. In other words, if you buy $10,000 worth of stock, $10,000 is the most you can lose because the worst that can happen is the stock price drops to zero. However, if you short $10,000 in stock, you can lose much more than $10,000 because the stock price can keep rising without any particular limit. The possibility for large losses becomes even greater when trading in so-called *meme stocks*.

Meme stocks are those that are being widely followed on social media and have gained a cult-like following. One recent example is a trading frenzy that occurred in GameStop (GME). After a number of positive blog posts, shares in GME rose from around $18 on January 8, 2021, to a high of $325 on January 29, 2021. Investors with short positions suffered. As of early 2022, shares were still trading around $120 per share.

As our previous chapter showed, on average, stock prices tend to rise. Of course, not all share prices rise over time. Still, potential short-sellers should remember the following classic bit of Wall Street wisdom: "He that sells what isn't his'n, must buy it back or go to prison!"[1]

CHECK THIS

2.4a What is a short sale?

2.4b Why might an investor choose to short a stock?

2.4c What is the maximum possible loss on a short sale? Explain.

2.5 Forming an Investment Portfolio

Related Bloomberg Functions

REIT   Real Estate Investment Trusts

Let's review the investment process so far. We began by crafting our investment policy statement, detailing our objectives and constraints. Next, we discussed the type of investment professional that might best fit our situation. Then, once the account was opened, we considered whether we wanted a traditional cash account or if we were interested in increasing financial leverage (i.e., risk) using margin. Last, we had to decide whether we wanted to include long or short positions (or both) in our portfolio. With this basic structure in place, we can now consider actual examples of how we would put this process into practice.

In this section, we give you an example of how to use risk tolerance scores and other investor characteristics to create an asset allocation for an actual portfolio. Of course, many approaches are possible, and we can touch on only a few.

SOME RISK TOLERANCE SCORES

To start, we gave a risk tolerance quiz to 10 students, staff, and faculty at a well-known university. Their ages and risk tolerance scores, as well as some other information, appear in Table 2.1 (their names are changed, but no one is innocent).

TABLE 2.1	Risk Tolerance Test Results				
Name	**Age**	**Sex**	**Investment Experience**	**Score**	
Lynn	23	F	Little or none	13	
Lucy	50	F	Little or none	19	
Isabel	28	F	Little or none	37	
Brigit	38	F	Little or none	35	
Lauren	22	F	Little or none	19	
Patrick	29	M	Little or none	20	
Imelda	59	F	Less than average	18	
Homer	54	M	Average	27	
Bart	25	M	Average	38	
Marie	21	F	More than average	40	

---

[1] Of course, the same is true for "she that sells what isn't hers'n"; it just doesn't rhyme as well.

As you can see, the risk tolerance scores have a wide range: from 13 to 40. The higher the score, the higher the risk tolerance. If you look closely, you will see that the average score for the males and females in this tiny set of quiz takers is about the same. The average score for those investors with little or no investment experience, however, is 24. Those with at least some investment experience have an average score of 31. What do you think these scores mean?

RISK AND RETURN

In addition to time horizon, risk tolerance is the first thing to assess in evaluating the suitability of an investment strategy. Let's look at the test results for Marie and Imelda.

Marie and Imelda each have sufficient cash reserves. That is, both Marie and Imelda have at least six months' living expenses readily available in a money market account. Of course, these amounts are not the same, largely because of housing and transportation cost differences. Having a sufficient cash reserve means that Marie and Imelda can safely proceed with building an investment portfolio.

MARIE Marie is a 21-year-old accounting student with more than average investment experience. According to the *Investment Updates* quiz, her long time horizon and score of 40 mean Marie should take an aggressive investment approach, which means a heavy allocation to stocks. Okay, but how much of her portfolio should she devote to stocks?

To help determine Marie's percentage stock allocation, we will use the general rule of thumb we mentioned earlier in the chapter: the "100 minus age rule." That is, an investor's percentage allocation to stock should be equal to the investor's age subtracted from 100. For Marie, this is $100 - 21 = 79$ percent (let's call it 80 percent). Given Marie's aggressive nature, she might even want to consider subtracting her age from 110, or even 120, which would result in a higher allocation to equity.

Marie has 30+ years to retirement, so she does not have to worry about short-term market volatility. In addition, she is studying diligently so that she can begin her auditing career and earn a steady and relatively high income. Therefore, for now, having at least 80 percent of her investments devoted to stock seems appropriate.

IMELDA Imelda is a 59-year-old college professor with many advanced degrees. Combined with her short time horizon until retirement, Imelda's score of 18 means that she should take a conservative or, at the most, moderately conservative approach.

For Imelda, the rule of thumb shows that she should consider having a portfolio with $100 - 59 = 41$ percent in stocks (let's call it 40 percent). Imelda has 5+ years to retirement, but many years left to enjoy life. Therefore, Imelda has to worry about market volatility in the short term. Her worry stems from the fact that her lofty income will not be available to her when she retires. As a result, Imelda will really have to think long and hard about whether 40 is the appropriate percentage to have invested in stock. Further, using margin would be inappropriate because the added risk would not be consistent with her risk tolerance.

INVESTOR CONSTRAINTS

In our example, both Marie and Imelda have sufficient *resources*[2] to set up the brokerage accounts that they will use for their investment portfolio, but they have different investment *horizons.* For simplicity, we will assume that both investors prefer highly *liquid* investments. With respect to *taxes,* Marie is currently in a low tax bracket. Therefore, she is likely to elect to pay taxes now and invest in a Roth IRA if given the choice. Imelda will most likely defer taxes because she is currently in a high tax bracket. So Imelda will most likely try to invest as many pretax dollars as she can. Marie and Imelda will both have to factor in *special circumstances.* For example, Marie might very well have some dependents to support beginning in the next five years or so. Imelda has adult children, but her grandchildren will certainly appreciate her financial support in the years ahead.

---

[2] All investor constraints, strategies, and policies appear in *italics.*

STRATEGIES AND POLICIES

Learn more about investing as an individual at www.aaii.com.

With respect to *investment management,* both Marie and Imelda want to avoid the time-consuming activities associated with managing their own investment portfolios. However, each will monitor her portfolio on a monthly basis. Marie and Imelda are convinced that attempts at *market timing* will result in investment underperformance. In addition, both think that *security selection* is a dangerous trap for the unwary. As a result, they both decide to invest in some passively managed mutual funds (but they have not told us which ones).

Both investors have yet to decide on their *asset allocation.* The asset allocation strategy should provide the highest rate of return given the acceptable level of risk and after accounting for portfolio constraints. Based on their financial resources, financial goals, time horizon, tax status, and risk tolerance, our investors could select their initial asset allocations from those provided in Figure 2.1.

In addition, you can see that our investors have set holding limits on each asset class. That is, they want to make sure that they do not overinvest in any particular asset class. You should know that overinvesting can happen if one asset class performs well in relation to the others.

FIGURE 2.1   AAII Asset Allocation Models

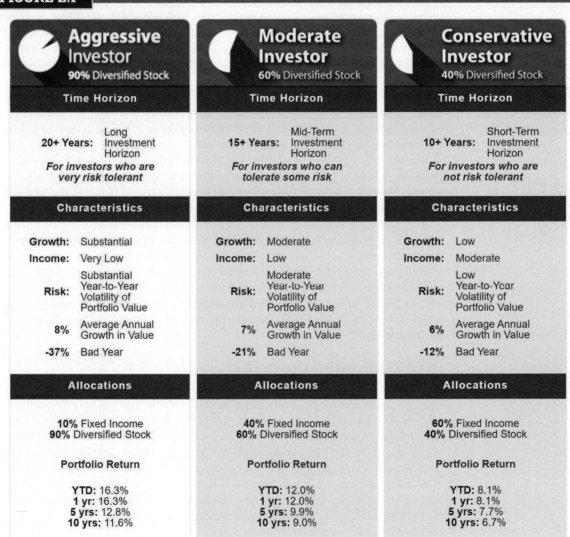

Source: www.aaii.com/asset-allocation, accessed January 2022.

MORE ON ASSET ALLOCATION

ALLOCATION BY INVESTOR PROFILE Earlier in this chapter, you learned that asset allocation is more important than security selection. Many factors affect asset allocation decisions. Not all investors will choose the same asset allocation. Consider the asset allocation guidelines given for three types of investors in Figure 2.1. How would you classify Marie and Imelda? Which investor profile fits you?

STRATEGIC VERSUS TACTICAL ALLOCATION As objectives or constraints change, investors will modify their asset allocation. Generally, these changes are infrequent. In other words, a properly selected asset allocation will be relatively stable. This targeted allocation is referred to as *strategic allocation*. Over time, because asset classes have relatively higher or lower returns, the portfolio will be rebalanced to the targeted strategic allocation.

What if you were actively following the financial markets and you thought that stocks were overvalued relative to bonds? Or suppose you thought that international stocks would perform better than U.S. stocks? In cases like these, you might use a *tactical asset allocation*. With a tactical asset allocation, you attempt to make smaller, short-term changes to your strategic allocation. The purpose? You are trying to capture added return.

After a period of time, you would shift your allocation back to the longer-term strategic allocation. Note well, however, that this tactical asset allocation approach is similar to market timing. You should be aware that considerable debate exists on whether tactical allocation is truly beneficial.

CHECK THIS

2.5a Besides risk tolerance, what are some other constraints, strategies, and policies that investors use in forming an investment portfolio?

2.5b Why could two investors of the same age wind up with different investment portfolios?

2.5c What is the difference between strategic and tactical asset allocation?

 2.5 Summary and Conclusions

In this chapter, we cover many aspects of the investing process—which we summarize by the chapter's important concepts.

1. **The importance of an investment policy statement.**

   A. The investment policy statement (IPS) identifies the objectives (risk and return) of an investor, as well as the constraints the investor faces in achieving these objectives.

   B. The IPS provides an investing "road map" and will influence the strategies, type of account, and holdings an investor chooses.

2. **The various types of securities brokers and brokerage accounts.**

   A. Opening a brokerage account is straightforward and really much like opening a bank account. You supply information and sign agreements with your broker. Then you write a check and provide instructions on how you want your money invested.

   B. Brokers are traditionally divided into three groups: full-service brokers, discount brokers, and deep-discount brokers. What distinguishes the three groups is the level of service they provide and the resulting commissions they charge. In recent years, the boundaries among the groups have blurred.

   C. Your broker does not have a duty to provide you with guaranteed purchase and sale recommendations. However, your broker does have a duty to exercise reasonable care in formulating recommendations. Your broker has a legal duty to act in your best interest. However, your broker relies on commissions generated from your account.

Therefore, on rare occasions, a broker is accused of "churning" an account (i.e., promoting excessive trading). When you open your brokerage account, you generally agree that disputes will be resolved by binding arbitration.

3. **How to trade on margin, including calculating the initial and maintenance margins.**

A. If you have a "cash account," you can purchase securities only to the extent that you can pay for them in full. If you want to buy more stock, you must deposit more cash into your account.

B. If you have a "margin account," you can purchase securities on credit using money loaned to you by your broker. Generally, you can borrow only half the amount needed to buy the securities.

C. When you first purchase securities on credit, you must supply a specified minimum amount of money. This minimum amount of money is called the initial margin.

D. After you have purchased securities on margin, the securities can decline in value. If they do, you must follow established rules concerning the amount of money you must keep in your account. This minimum is called the maintenance margin. If your account balance falls below the maintenance margin level, you will receive a margin call. In this chapter, we show you how to calculate initial and maintenance margin levels and their effects on your returns.

4. **The workings of short sales.**

A. An investor who buys and owns shares of stock is said to be long in the stock, or to have a long position. An investor with a long position makes money only if the price of the stock increases.

B. If you think, for whatever reason, that shares of stock in a particular company are likely to decline in value, you can engage in a short sale. In a short sale, you actually sell a security that you do not own. This is referred to as shorting the stock. After the short sale, the investor is said to have a short position in the security. An investor with a short position makes money only if the shares decrease in value.

C. In this chapter we describe in detail the short-sale process for shares of stock. We also stress the potentially unlimited losses that can arise from a short position.

GETTING DOWN TO BUSINESS

This chapter covered the basics of policy statements, brokerage accounts, some important trade types, and, finally, some big-picture issues regarding investment strategies. How should you, as an investor or investment manager, put this information to work?

The answer is that you need to open a brokerage account! Investing is like many activities: The best way to learn is by making mistakes. Unfortunately, making mistakes with real money is an expensive way to learn, so we don't recommend trying things like short sales with real money, at least not at first.

Instead, to learn how to trade and gain some experience with making (and losing) money, you should open a Stock-Trak account (or a similar simulated brokerage account). Take it seriously. Try various trade types and strategies and see how they turn out. The important thing to do is to follow your trades and try to understand why you made or lost money and also why you made or lost the amount you did.

In a similar vein, you should carefully review your account statements to make sure you understand exactly what each item means and how your account equity is calculated.

After you have gained some experience trading "on paper," you should open a real account as soon as you can pull together enough money. Try visiting some online brokers to find out the minimum amount you need to open an account. The amount has been declining. In fact, in 2019, you could open a TD Ameritrade account with no minimum, although you would need $2,000 to open a margin account.

Looking back at Chapter 1, you know that it's important to get started early. Once you have a real account, however, it's still a good idea to keep a separate "play money" account to test trading ideas to make sure you really understand them before committing your precious real money.

For the latest information on the real world of investments, visit us at jmdinvestments.blogspot.com.

Key Terms

Related Bloomberg Functions

Chapter Review Problems and Self-Test

1. **The Account Balance Sheet (LO2, CFA2)**   Suppose you want to buy 10,000 shares of American Airlines (AAL) at a price of $30 per share. You put up $200,000 and borrow the rest. What does your account balance sheet look like? What is your margin?

2. **Short Sales (LO4, CFA3)**   Suppose that in the previous problem you shorted 10,000 shares instead of buying. The initial margin is 60 percent. What does the account balance sheet look like following the short?

3. **Margin Calls (LO3, CFA2)**   You purchased 500 shares of stock at a price of $56 per share on 50 percent margin. If the maintenance margin is 30 percent, what is the critical stock price?

Answers to Self-Test Problems

1. **The 10,000 shares of American Airlines cost $300,000. You supply $200,000, so you must borrow $100,000. The account balance sheet looks like this:**

Assets		Liabilities and Account Equity	
10,000 shares of AAL	$300,000	Margin loan	$100,000
		Account equity	200,000
Total	$300,000	Total	$300,000

Your margin is the account equity divided by the value of the stock owned:

$$\text{Margin} = \$200,000/\$300,000$$
$$= .6667, \text{ or } 66.67\%$$

2. **Following the short, your account is as follows:**

Assets		Liabilities and Account Equity	
Proceeds from sale	$300,000	Margin loan	$300,000
Initial margin deposit	180,000	Account equity	180,000
Total	$480,000	Total	$480,000

Notice that you shorted $300,000 worth of stock, so, with a 60 percent margin requirement, you deposited $180,000.

3. **The lowest price to which the stock can drop before you receive a margin call is:**

$$P^* = \frac{\text{Amount borrowed/Number of shares}}{1 - \text{Maintenance margin}}$$

You borrowed $500 \times \$56 \times .50 = \$14,000$. Therefore:

$$P^* = \frac{\$14,000/500}{1 - .30} = \$40.00$$

You will receive a margin call if the stock drops below $40.00.

Test Your Investment Quotient

1. **Investment Objectives (LO1, CFA9)**   An individual investor's investment objectives should be expressed in terms of:

   a. Risk and return.
   b. Capital market expectations.
   c. Liquidity needs and time horizon.
   d. Tax factors and legal and regulatory constraints.

2. **Asset Allocation (LO1, CFA5)**   Which of the following best reflects the importance of the asset allocation decision to the investment process? The asset allocation decision:

   a. Helps the investor decide on realistic investment goals.
   b. Identifies the specific securities to include in a portfolio.
   c. Determines most of the portfolio's returns and volatility over time.
   d. Creates a standard by which to establish an appropriate investment horizon.

3. **Leverage (LO3, CFA2)**   You deposit $100,000 cash in a brokerage account and purchase $200,000 of stocks on margin by borrowing $100,000 from your broker. Later, the value of your stock holdings falls to $150,000, whereupon you get nervous and close your account. What is the percentage return on your investment (ignore interest paid)?

   a. 0 percent
   b. −25 percent
   c. −50 percent
   d. −75 percent

4. **Leverage (LO4, CFA3)**   You deposit $100,000 cash in a brokerage account and short sell $200,000 of stocks. Later, the value of the stocks held short rises to $250,000, whereupon you get nervous and close your account. What is the percentage return on your investment (ignore interest paid)?

   a. 0 percent
   b. −25 percent
   c. −50 percent
   d. −75 percent

5. **Account Margin (LO3, CFA2)**   You deposit $100,000 cash in a brokerage account and purchase $200,000 of stocks on margin by borrowing $100,000 from your broker. Later, the value of your stock holdings falls to $175,000. What is your account margin in dollars?

   a. $50,000
   b. $75,000
   c. $100,000
   d. $150,000

6. **Account Margin (LO3, CFA2)**   You deposit $100,000 cash in a brokerage account and purchase $200,000 of stocks on margin by borrowing $100,000 from your broker. Later, the value of your stock holdings falls to $150,000. What is your account margin in percent?

   a. 25 percent
   b. 33 percent
   c. 50 percent
   d. 75 percent

7. **Account Margin (LO4, CFA3)** You deposit $100,000 cash in a brokerage account and short sell $200,000 of stocks on margin. Later, the value of the stocks held short rises to $225,000. What is your account margin in dollars?

   a. $50,000
   b. $75,000
   c. $100,000
   d. $150,000

8. **Account Margin (LO4, CFA3)** You deposit $100,000 cash in a brokerage account and short sell $200,000 of stocks on margin. Later, the value of the stocks held short rises to $250,000. What is your account margin in percent?

   a. 20 percent
   b. 25 percent
   c. 33 percent
   d. 50 percent

9. **Margin Calls (LO3, CFA2)** You deposit $100,000 cash in a brokerage account and purchase $200,000 of stocks on margin by borrowing $100,000 from your broker, who requires a maintenance margin of 30 percent. Which of the following is the largest value for your stock holdings for which you will still receive a margin call?

   a. $200,000
   b. $160,000
   c. $140,000
   d. $120,000

10. **Margin Calls (LO4, CFA3)** You deposit $100,000 cash in a brokerage account and short sell $200,000 of stocks. Your broker requires a maintenance margin of 30 percent. Which of the following is the lowest value for the stocks you are holding short for which you will still receive a margin call?

    a. $260,000
    b. $240,000
    c. $220,000
    d. $200,000

11. **Investment Decisions (LO1, CFA8)** Which of the following investment factors, strategies, or tactics is the least relevant to a passive investment policy?

    a. Market timing
    b. Asset allocation
    c. Political environment
    d. Tax status

12. **Investment Decisions (LO1, CFA5)** Which of the following investment factors, strategies, or tactics is most associated with an active investment policy?

    a. Market timing
    b. Asset allocation
    c. Security selection
    d. Tax status

13. **Investment Decisions (LO1, CFA9)** Which of the following investment strategies or tactics will likely consume the greatest amount of resources, time, effort, and so on, when implementing an active investment policy?

    a. Market timing
    b. Asset allocation
    c. Security selection
    d. Tax strategy

14. **Investment Decisions (LO1, CFA5)** Which of the following investment strategies or tactics is likely the most relevant in the decision to short sell a particular stock?

    a. Market timing
    b. Asset allocation
    c. Security selection
    d. Tax strategy

15. **Investment Constraints (LO1, CFA3)** Which of the following investment constraints is expected to have the most fundamental impact on the investment decision process for a typical investor?

   a. Investor's tax status
   b. Investor's term structure
   c. Investor's need for liquidity
   d. Investor's time horizon

Concept Questions

1. **Margin (LO3, CFA2)** What does it mean to purchase a security on margin? Why might you do it?

2. **Short Sales (LO4, CFA3)** What does it mean to sell a security short? Why might you do it?

3. **Margin Requirements (LO3, CFA2)** What is the reason margin requirements exist?

4. **Allocation versus Selection (LO1, CFA5)** What is the difference between asset allocation and security selection?

5. **Allocation versus Timing (LO1, CFA7)** Are market timing and tactical asset allocation similar? Why or why not?

6. **Brokers versus Advisors (LO2, CFA9)** To an investor, what is the difference between using an advisor and using a broker?

7. **Broker-Customer Relations (LO2, CFA9)** Suppose your broker tips you on a hot stock. You invest heavily, but, to your considerable dismay, the stock plummets in value. What recourse do you have against your broker?

8. **Long vs. Short Profits (LO4, CFA3)** An important difference between a long position in stock and a short position concerns the potential gains and losses. Suppose a stock sells for $18 per share and you trade 500 shares. What are your potential gains and losses for each type of position?

9. **Liquidity (LO4, CFA3)** The liquidity of an asset directly affects the risk of buying or selling that asset during adverse market conditions. Describe the liquidity risk you face with a short stock position during a market rally and a long stock position during a market decline.

10. **Taxes (LO4, CFA8)** How will personal tax rates impact the choice of a traditional IRA versus a Roth IRA?

Questions and Problems

Core Questions

1. **Calculating Margin (LO3, CFA2)** Carson Corporation stock sells for $17 per share, and you've decided to purchase as many shares as you possibly can. You have $31,000 available to invest. What is the maximum number of shares you can buy if the initial margin is 60 percent?

2. **Margin (LO3, CFA2)** You purchase 275 shares of 2nd Chance Co. stock on margin at a price of $53. Your broker requires you to deposit $8,000. What is your margin loan amount? What is the initial margin requirement?

3. **Margin Return (LO3, CFA2)** In Problem 2, suppose you sell the stock at a price of $62. What is your return? What would your return have been had you purchased the stock without margin? What if the stock price is $46 when you sell the stock?

4. **Margin (LO3, CFA2)** Repeat Problems 2 and 3 assuming the initial margin requirement is 70 percent. Does this suggest a relationship between the initial margin and returns?

5. **Margin Purchases (LO3, CFA2)** You have $26,000 and decide to invest on margin. If the initial margin requirement is 50 percent, what is the maximum dollar purchase you can make?

6. **Margin Calls (LO3, CFA2)** You buy 500 shares of stock at a price of $38 and an initial margin of 50 percent. If the maintenance margin is 35 percent, at what price will you receive a margin call?

7. **Margin Calls (LO3, CFA3)** You decide to buy 1,600 shares of stock at a price of $64 and an initial margin of 65 percent. What is the maximum percentage decline in the stock before you will receive a margin call if the maintenance margin is 40 percent?

8. **Margin Calls on Short Sales (LO4, CFA3)**   The stock of Flop Industries is trading at $48. You feel the stock price will decline, so you short 1,000 shares at an initial margin of 60 percent. If the maintenance margin is 30 percent, at what share price will you receive a margin call?

9. **Margin Calls on Short Sales (LO4, CFA3)**   You sold short 1,000 shares of stock at a price of $36 and an initial margin of 55 percent. If the maintenance margin is 35 percent, at what share price will you receive a margin call? What is your account equity at this stock price?

10. **Taxes and Returns (LO1, CFA8)**   You purchased a stock at the end of last year at a price of $84. At the end of this year, the stock pays a dividend of $2.10 and you sell the stock for $101. What is your return for the year? Now suppose that dividends are taxed at 15 percent and long-term capital gains (over 11 months) are taxed at 30 percent. What is your aftertax return for the year?

Intermediate Questions

11. **Calculating Margin (LO3, CFA2)**   Using the information in Problem 1, construct your equity account balance sheet at the time of your purchase. What does your balance sheet look like if the share price rises to $24? What if it falls to $14 per share? What is your margin in both cases? Round the number of shares down to the nearest number of whole shares.

12. **Calculating Margin (LO3, CFA2)**   You've just opened a margin account with $20,000 at your local brokerage firm. You instruct your broker to purchase 500 shares of Landon Golf stock, which currently sells for $60 per share. What is your initial margin? Construct the equity account balance sheet for this position.

13. **Margin Call (LO3, CFA2)**   Suppose you purchase 500 shares of stock at $48 per share with an initial cash investment of $8,000. If your broker requires a 30 percent maintenance margin, at what share price will you be subject to a margin call? If you want to keep your position open despite the stock price plunge, what alternatives do you have?

14. **Margin and Leverage (LO3, CFA2)**   In Problem 13, suppose the call money rate is 5 percent and you are charged a 1.5 percent premium over this rate. Calculate your return on investment for each of the following share prices one year later. Ignore dividends.

    a. $56
    b. $48
    c. $32

    Suppose instead you had purchased $8,000 of stock with no margin. What would your rate of return have been now?

15. **Margin and Leverage (LO3, CFA2)**   Suppose the call money rate is 5.6 percent, and you pay a spread of 1.2 percent over that. You buy 1,000 shares at $40 per share with an initial margin of 50 percent. One year later, the stock is selling for $45 per share and you close out your position. What is your return assuming no dividends are paid?

16. **Margin and Leverage (LO3, CFA2)**   Suppose the call money rate is 4.5 percent, and you pay a spread of 2.5 percent over that. You buy 800 shares of stock at $34 per share. You put up $15,000. One year later, the stock is selling for $48 per share and you close out your position. What is your return assuming a dividend of $.64 per share is paid?

17. **Margin Interest (LO3, CFA2)**   Suppose you take out a margin loan for $65,000. The rate you pay is an 8.7 percent effective rate. If you repay the loan in six months (or 180 days), how much interest will you pay?

18. **Margin Interest (LO3, CFA2)**   Suppose you take out a margin loan for $75,000. You pay a 6.4 percent effective rate. If you repay the loan in 60 days, how much interest will you pay?

19. **Annualized Returns (CFA1)** Suppose you hold a particular investment for seven months. You calculate that your holding period return is 14 percent. What is your annualized return?

20. **Annualized Returns (CFA1)** In Problem 19, suppose your holding period was five months instead of seven. What is your annualized return? What do you conclude in general about the length of your holding period and your annualized return?

21. **Annualized Returns (CFA1)** Suppose you buy stock at a price of $57 per share. Five months later, you sell it for $61. You also received a dividend of $.60 per share. What is your annualized return on this investment?

22. **Calculating Returns (CFA1)** Looking back at Problem 12, suppose the call money rate is 5 percent and your broker charges you a spread of 1.25 percent over this rate. You hold the stock for 6 months (or 180 days) and sell at a price of $65 per share. The company paid a dividend of $.25 per share the day before you sold your stock. What is your total dollar return from this investment? What is your effective annual rate of return?

23. **Short Sales (LO4, CFA3)** You believe that Rose, Inc., stock is going to fall and you've decided to sell 800 shares short. If the current share price is $47, construct the equity account balance sheet for this trade. Assume the initial margin is 100 percent.

24. **Short Sales (LO4, CFA3)** Repeat Problem 23 assuming you short the 800 shares on 60 percent margin.

25. **Calculating Short Sale Returns (LO4, CFA3)** You just sold short 750 shares of Wetscope, Inc., a fledgling software firm, at $96 per share. You cover your short when the price hits $86.50 per share one year later. If the company paid $.75 per share in dividends over this period, what is your rate of return on the investment? Assume an initial margin of 60 percent.

26. **Short Sales (LO4, CFA3)** You believe the stock in Freeze Frame Co. is going to fall, so you short 600 shares at a price of $72. The initial margin is 50 percent. Construct the equity balance sheet for the original trade. Now construct equity balance sheets for a stock price of $63 and a stock price of $77. What is your margin at each of these stock prices? What is your effective annual return if you cover your short position at each of these prices in five months?

Spreadsheet Problems

27. **Short Sales (LO4, CFA3)** You believe that Thorn Enterprises stock is going to fall, so you have decided to short sell 1,000 shares at a price of $32. Assuming the initial margin requirement is 50 percent, construct the equity account balance sheet for this trade. If the maintenance margin is 30 percent, at what price would a margin call result?

28. **Portfolio Margin (LO3, CFA3)** Assume that you have identified three different stocks that you would like to purchase. You decide to buy 100 shares of each stock. Stock A is priced at $30; Stock B is priced at $40; and Stock C is priced at $50. Assuming you deposit $7,200 of your own money and borrow the remainder, construct the equity account balance sheet for this trade. If the maintenance margin is 30 percent, at what portfolio value would a margin call result?

CFA Exam Review by Kaplan Schweser

[CFA1, CFA7, CFA8, CFA9]

Barbara Analee, a registered nurse and businesswoman, recently retired at age 50 to pursue a life as a blues singer. She had been running a successful cosmetics and aesthetics business. She is married to Tom, a retired scientist (age 55). They have saved $3 million in their portfolio and now they want to travel the world. Their three children are all grown and out of college and have begun their own families. Barbara now has two grandchildren. Barbara and Tom feel that they have achieved a comfortable portfolio level to support their family's needs for the foreseeable future.

To meet their basic living expenses, Tom and Barbara feel they need $75,000 per year in today's dollars (before taxes) to live comfortably. As a trained professional, Barbara likes to be actively involved in intensively researching investment opportunities. Barbara and Tom want to be able to provide $10,000 per year (pretax) indexed for inflation to each of their grandchildren over the next 10 years for their college education. They also want to set aside $15,000 each year (pretax) indexed for inflation for traveling for Barbara's musical performances around the United States. They have no debt. Most of their portfolio is currently in large-cap U.S. stocks and Treasury notes.

They have approached Pamela Jaycoo, CFA, for guidance on how to best achieve their financial goals. Inflation is expected to increase at an annual rate of 3 percent into the foreseeable future.

1. What is the Analees' return objective?
   a. 6.67 percent
   b. 6.17 percent
   c. 3.83 percent

2. What is their tolerance for risk?
   a. Average
   b. Below average
   c. Above average

3. What are Barbara's willingness and ability to assume risk?

	Willingness	Ability
a.	Above average	Average
b.	Below average	Average
c.	Above average	Above average

4. Based on the information in the case, which one of the following portfolios should the Analees choose?

	Expected Return	Allocation		
		Portfolio A	Portfolio B	Portfolio C
U.S. large stocks	9%	20%	5%	10%
U.S. small stocks	10	20	15	10
Foreign stocks	12	15	15	10
Corp. bonds	5	15	0	35
Gov. bonds	3	10	0	25
Venture capital	11	5	30	0
Real estate	15	10	30	0
Cash	1	5	5	10
Pretax return		8.8%	11.6%	5.7%
Aftertax return		5.6%	7.4%	3.6%
Aftertax yield		1.9%	1.9%	2.8%

a. Portfolio A
b. Portfolio B
c. Portfolio C

Bloomberg Exercises

1. Identify the top five brokers by volume. (**RANK**)
2. Determine the amount of short interest currently outstanding in Tesla (TSLA) stock. (**SI**)
3. Create a graph of short positions through time in Tesla. (**GF**)
4. Generate a list of the largest short positions in the U.S. by the percentage of shares outstanding. (**SPOS**)

What's on the Web?

1. **Risk Tolerance** As we discussed in the chapter, risk tolerance is based on an individual's personality and investment goals. There are numerous risk tolerance questionnaires on the web. One, provided by Merrill Lynch, is located at www.ml.com. Go to the website, search for Identifying Your Investor Profile, and take the quiz. How conservative or aggressive are you?

2. **Short Interest** You can find the number of short sales on a particular stock at finance.yahoo.com. Go to the site and find the number of shares short sold for ExxonMobil (XOM) under the "Statistics" link. How many shares are sold short in the current month? What about the previous month? What do "Percent of Float" and "Short Ratio" mean?

3. **Broker Call Money Rate** What is the current broker call money rate? To find out, go to www.bankrate.com and look up the call money rate.

4. **Margin Purchases** Suppose you have a margin account with TD Ameritrade. You purchase 1,000 shares of IBM stock on 50 percent margin at today's price. Go to finance.yahoo.com to find your purchase price. Ignoring transaction costs, how much will you borrow? Next, go to www.bankrate.com to find the current broker call money rate. Finally, go to www.TDAmeritrade .com to find out how much above the current broker call money rate you will pay. If you keep your investment for one year, how much will you pay in interest assuming the margin rate stays the same? What does the stock price have to be in one year for you to break even on your investment?

Overview of Security Types

"An investment operation is one which upon thorough analysis promises safety of principal and an adequate return. Operations not meeting these requirements are speculative."

–Benjamin Graham

Learning Objectives

Price quotes for all types of investments are easy to find, but what do they mean? Learn the answers for:

1. Various types of interest-bearing assets.

2. Equity securities.

3. Futures contracts.

4. Option contracts.

You invest $5,000 in Microsoft common stock and just months later sell the shares for $7,500, realizing a 50 percent return. Not bad! At the same time, your neighbor invests $5,000 in Microsoft stock options, which are worth $25,000 at expiration—a 400 percent return. Shazam! Alternatively, your Microsoft shares fall in value to $2,500, and you realize a 50 percent loss. Too bad! But at the same time, your neighbor's Microsoft stock options are now worthless. Clearly, there is a big difference between stock shares and stock options. Security type matters.

Our goal in this chapter is to introduce you to some of the different types of securities that are routinely bought and sold in financial markets around the world. As we mentioned in Chapter 1, we will be focusing on financial assets such as bonds, stocks, futures, and options in this book, so these are the securities we briefly describe here. The securities we discuss are covered in much greater detail in the chapters ahead, so we touch on only some of their most essential features in this chapter.

For each of the securities we examine, we ask three questions. First, what is its basic nature and what are its distinguishing characteristics? Second, what are the potential gains and losses from owning it? Third, how is its price quoted in the financial press?

CFA™ Exam Topics in this Chapter:

1. Time value of money (L1, S1)
2. Overview of equity securities (L1, S12)
3. Fixed-income securities: Defining elements (L1, S13)
4. Derivative markets and instruments (L1, S15)

Go to Connect for a guide that aligns your textbook with CFA readings.

3.1 Classifying Securities

To begin our overview of security types, we first develop a classification scheme for the different securities. As shown in Table 3.1, financial assets can be grouped into three broad categories, and each of these categories can be further subdivided into a few major subtypes. This classification is not exhaustive, but it covers the major types of financial assets. In the sections that follow, we describe these assets in the order in which they appear in Table 3.1.

When we examine some of these security types in more detail, we will see that the distinctions can become a little blurred, particularly with some recently created financial instruments; as a result, some financial assets are hard to classify. The primary reason is that some instruments are hybrids, meaning that they are combinations of the basic types.

As you may have noticed in our discussion, financial assets, such as bonds and stocks, are often called securities. They are often called financial "instruments" as well. In certain contexts, there are distinctions between these terms, but they are used more or less interchangeably in everyday discussion, so we will stick with common usage.

TABLE 3.1	Classification of Financial Assets	
Basic Types		**Major Subtypes**
Interest-bearing		Money market instruments
		Fixed-income securities
Equities		Common stock
		Preferred stock
Derivatives		Futures
		Options

CHECK THIS

3.1a What are the three basic types of financial assets?

3.1b Why are some financial assets hard to classify?

3.2 Interest-Bearing Assets

Related Bloomberg Functions

SRCH Fixed Income Search

MMF Money Market Funds

WB World Bond Markets

TACT TRACE Activity

Broadly speaking, interest-bearing assets (as the name suggests) pay interest. Some pay interest implicitly and some pay it explicitly, but the common denominator is that the value of these assets depends, at least for the most part, on interest rates. The reason that these assets pay interest is that they all begin life as a loan of some sort, so they are all debt obligations of some issuer, most likely a corporation or government.

There are many types of interest-bearing assets. They range from the relatively simple to the astoundingly complex. We discuss some basic types and their features next. The more complex types are discussed in later chapters.

MONEY MARKET INSTRUMENTS

money market instruments
Debt obligations of large corporations and governments with an original maturity of one year or less.

For the most part, **money market instruments** are the simplest form of interest-bearing asset. Money market instruments generally have the following two properties:

1. They are essentially IOUs sold by large corporations or governments to borrow money.

2. They mature in less than one year from the time they are sold, meaning that the loan must be repaid within one year.

WHEN LOSING MONEY MAKES SENSE

An interesting trend developed in European bond markets over the earlier part of this decade: Many investors were increasingly willing to lend money to governments for almost nothing. Why would this be?

To answer this question, consider the eurozone's largest economy. Germany has been a driver of European economic growth and stability, and in unsteady financial markets, its bonds are considered to be among the safest assets available for investors.

In fact, in mid-2012, yields on 2-year German bonds actually turned negative, falling to –.5 percent. What does that mean? Investors ended up receiving less money back than they invested (earning a negative yield) if they held the bonds until their maturity. In the same period, French,

Danish, and Swiss bond yields also turned negative, and Finnish and Dutch bond yields fell to record lows.

This flight to safety reflected a heightened aversion to risk, as other countries struggled to avoid falling into the financial crisis that brought down Greece, Portugal, and Ireland (among others). "It's like putting money under the mattress," Ben Rooney of CNN Money quotes Schwab fixed-income strategist Kathy Jones as saying. "Investors trust the core countries and non-euro countries to return their money, even if it costs them something."

Source: Ben Rooney, "Europe: When Losing Money Makes Sense," *CNN Money,* July 16, 2012.

Most money market instruments trade in very large denominations, and most, but not all, are quite liquid.

The most familiar example of a money market instrument is a Treasury bill, or T-bill for short. Every week, the U.S. Treasury borrows billions of dollars by selling T-bills to the public. Like many (but not all) money market instruments, T-bills are sold on a *discount basis.* This means that T-bills are sold at a price that is less than their stated face value. In other words, an investor buys a T-bill at one price and later, when the bill matures, receives the full face value. The difference is the interest earned.

U.S. Treasury bills are the most liquid type of money market instrument—that is, the type with the largest and most active market. Other types of money market instruments traded in active markets include bank certificates of deposit (or CDs) and corporate and municipal money market instruments.

The potential gain from buying a money market instrument is fixed because the owner is promised a fixed future payment. The most important risk is the risk of default, which is the possibility that the borrower will not repay the loan as promised. With a T-bill, there is (in theory) no possibility of default, so, as we saw in Chapter 1, T-bills are essentially risk-free. In fact, most money market instruments have relatively low risk, but there are exceptions, and a few spectacular defaults have occurred in the past.

Would an investor ever pay more than face value? For a money market instrument, such as a T-bill, that pays a lump sum at maturity, the answer is generally no. There are, however, extreme circumstances when investors might be willing to pay more than face value. Why would investors do so knowing that they are essentially guaranteeing that they will lose money? The answer lies in a situation called a "flight to quality." During the financial crisis of 2008, many investors feared the financial system could collapse. Paying more than face value meant that investors were effectively willing to pay the government to "babysit" their money for a period of time. See the nearby *Investment Updates* box for another example of investors purposely "losing money" in this way.

The financial press quotes prices for different types of money market instruments. These quotes usually appear as interest rates. When they do, some calculations will be necessary to convert the quoted interest rate to a price. The procedures are not complicated, but they involve a fair amount of detail, so we save them for another chapter.

FIXED-INCOME SECURITIES

fixed-income securities
Longer-term debt obligations, often of corporations and governments, that promise to make fixed payments according to a preset schedule.

Fixed-income securities are exactly what the name suggests: securities that promise to make fixed payments according to some preset schedule. The other key characteristic of a fixed-income security is that, like a money market instrument, it begins life as a loan of some sort. Fixed-income securities are therefore debt obligations. They are typically issued by corporations and governments. Unlike money market instruments, fixed-income securities have lives that exceed 12 months at the time they are issued.

The words "note" and "bond" are generic terms for fixed-income securities, but "fixed-income" is more accurate. This term is being used more frequently as securities are increasingly being created that don't fit within traditional note or bond frameworks but are nonetheless fixed-income securities.

EXAMPLES OF FIXED-INCOME SECURITIES To give one particularly simple example of a fixed-income security, near the end of every month, the U.S. Treasury sells over $50 billion of two-year notes to the public. If you buy a two-year note when it is issued, you will receive a check every six months for two years for a fixed amount, called the bond's *coupon,* and in two years you will receive the face amount on the note.

Suppose you buy $1 million in face amount of a 4 percent, two-year note. The 4 percent is called the *coupon rate,* and it tells you that you will receive 4 percent of the $1 million face value each year, or $40,000, in two $20,000 semiannual "coupon" payments. In two years, in addition to your final $20,000 coupon payment, you will receive the $1 million face value. The price you would pay for this note depends on market conditions. U.S. government security prices are discussed in detail in a later chapter.

You must be careful not to confuse the *coupon rate* with the **current yield.** The current yield is the annual coupon divided by the current bond price. For most bonds, the coupon rate never changes, but the current yield fluctuates with the price of the bond.

Check out bond basics at
www.projectinvested.com/category/
markets-explained

current yield
A bond's annual coupon divided by its market price.

| EXAMPLE 3.1 | A "Note-Worthy" Investment? |

Suppose you buy $100,000 in face amount of a just-issued five-year U.S. Treasury note. If the coupon rate is 5 percent, what will you receive over the next five years if you hold on to your investment?

You will receive 5 percent of $100,000, or $5,000, per year, paid in two semiannual coupons of $2,500. In five years, in addition to the final $2,500 coupon payment, you will receive the $100,000 face amount.

To give a slightly different example, suppose you take out a 48-month car loan. Under the terms of the loan, you promise to make 48 payments of $400 per month. It may not look like it to you, but in taking out this loan, you have issued a fixed-income security to your bank. In fact, your bank may even turn around and sell your car loan (perhaps bundled with a large number of other loans) to an investor. This process of *securitization* is most active in the markets for home mortgages and student loans, which are routinely bought and sold in huge quantities.

FIXED-INCOME PRICE QUOTES Corporate bond dealers now report trade information through what is known as the Trade Reporting and Compliance Engine (TRACE). This system is monitored by the Financial Industry Regulatory Authority, or FINRA for short. As this is written, daily transaction prices are reported on thousands of bonds. A nearby *Work the Web* box shows you how to get data from TRACE through FINRA's website.

As shown in Figure 3.1, FINRA provides an online daily snapshot of the data from TRACE by reporting information on the most active investment-grade bonds. Information for the most active high-yield bonds and convertible bonds is available, too. Most of the information is self-explanatory.

To learn more about TRACE, visit
www.finra.org.

Corporate bond quotes have become more available with the rise of the internet. One site where you can find current corporate bond prices is https://finra-markets.morningstar.com/BondCenter/Default.jsp. We went there and searched for bonds issued by 3M Co. (MMM), long known as Minnesota Mining and Manufacturing Company. Here is a look at some of these bonds:

We will focus on the fourth bond in the list. The bond has a coupon rate of 3.875 percent and matures on June 15, 2044. The last sale price of this bond was $113.553 per $100 of face value. At this price, the yield to maturity is 3.036 percent. By clicking on the link for this bond, you can obtain more detailed information such as the issue size, historical pricing, and yields.

Bond Results

⊞ Issuer Name	Symbol	Callable	Sub-Product Type	Coupon	Maturity	Ratings Moody's®	S&P	Last Sale Price	Yield
☐ 3M CO	MMM3869562		Corporate Bond	2.000	06/26/2022	A1	A+	100.582	0.617
☐ 3M CO	MMM4404424	Yes	Corporate Bond	2.250	09/19/2026	A1	A+	101.587	1.873
☐ 3M CO.	MMM4404250	Yes	Corporate Bond	3.125	09/19/2046	A1	A+	101.173	3.056
☐ 3M CO	MMM4131137	Yes	Corporate Bond	3.875	06/15/2044	A1	A+	113.553	3.036
☐ 3M CO	MMM4275877	Yes	Corporate Bond	3.000	08/07/2025	A1	A+	104.478	1.690
☐ 3M CO	MMM4544486	Yes	Corporate Bond	2.250	03/15/2023	A1	A+	101.458	0.863

Source: FINRA, January 2022.

FIGURE 3.1 Corporate Bond Trading

FINRA TRACE Market Aggregate Information

01/20/2022 GO

FINRA TRACE Bond Market Activity

View: **Corporate** | 144A | Agency | Structured Products

	All Issues	Investment Grade	High Yield	Convertible
Total Issues Traded	9381	7020	2125	236
Advances	3854	2916	840	98
Declines	4987	3876	982	129
Unchanged	75	37	36	2
52 Week High	88	14	68	6
52 Week Low	1879	1546	315	18
Dollar Volume*	36980	25144	10282	1552

* Par value in millions

About This Information
End of Day data. Activity as reported to FINRA TRACE (Trade Reporting and Compliance Engine). The Market breadth information represents activity in all TRACE eligible publicly traded securities. The most active information represent the most active fixed-coupon bonds (ranked by par value traded). Inclusion in Investment grade or High Yield tables based on TRACE dissemination criteria. "C" indicates yield is unavailable because of issue's call criteria.

Most Active Investment Grade Bonds

Issuer Name	Symbol	Coupon	Maturity	Moody's®/S&P	High	Low	Last	Change	Yield%
AT&T INC	T5046543	3.500%	09/15/2053	/BBB	95.04900	94.23700	95.01400	0.019000	3.770992
EXXON MOBIL CORP	XOM4976375	3.452%	04/15/2051	Aa1/AA-	104.78800	103.52200	104.78800	1.168000	3.195842
VERIZON COMMUNICATIONS INC	VZ5148413	3.550%	03/22/2051	/BBB+	102.04700	100.82200	101.86300	0.403000	3.446989
CVS HEALTH CORP	CVS4607885	5.050%	03/25/2048	Baa2/BBB	124.47500	123.70000	124.07800	-0.294000	3.603990
AERCAP IRELAND CAP DESIGNATED ACTIVITY C	AER5286241	3.300%	01/30/2032	/	98.19800	97.80300	98.14600	0.355000	3.521258
MERCK & CO INC NEW	MRK5319145	2.150%	12/10/2031	/A+	96.96900	96.46000	96.96900	0.207000	2.498025
ANHEUSER-BUSCH COS LLC / ANHEUSER-BUSCH	BUD4835362	4.900%	02/01/2046	Baa1/	120.41900	119.31900	120.11900	0.193000	3.621806
MICROSOFT CORP	MSFT5152920	2.921%	03/17/2052	/AAA	99.51500	98.84600	99.04000	0.119000	2.969291
BB&T CORP SR MEDIUM TERM NTS BOOK ENTRY	TFC4468102	2.750%	04/01/2022	A3/A-	100.26400	98.99200	100.20900	-0.074000	0.708886
CENOVUS ENERGY INC	CVE3683666	6.750%	11/15/2039	Baa3/	132.66100	131.87900	132.66100	1.314200	4.139015

Source: FINRA, accessed January 21, 2022, https://finra-markets.morningstar.com/BondCenter. FINRA is a registered trademark of the Financial Industry Regulatory Authority, Inc.

EXAMPLE 3.2	Corporate Bond Quotes

In Figure 3.1, which bond has the longest maturity? Assuming a face value of $1,000 each, how much would you have to pay for 100 of these bonds?

The bond with the longest maturity is the first bond in the list, which was issued by AT&T. It has a 3.50 percent coupon and matures in September 2053. Based on the reported last price, the price you would pay is 95.014 percent of face value per bond. Assuming a $1,000 face value, this amount is $950.14 for one bond, or $95,014 for 100 bonds.

The potential gains from owning a fixed-income security come in two forms. First, there are the fixed payments promised and the final payment at maturity. In addition, the prices of most fixed-income securities rise when interest rates fall, so there is the possibility of a gain from a favorable movement in rates. An increase in interest rates will produce a loss.

Another significant risk for many fixed-income securities is the possibility that the issuer will not make the promised payments. This risk depends on the issuer. It doesn't exist for U.S. government bonds, but for many other issuers the possibility is very real. Finally, unlike most money market instruments, fixed-income securities are often quite illiquid, again depending on the issuer and the specific type.

CHECK THIS

3.2a   What are the two basic types of interest-bearing assets?

3.2b   What are the two basic features of a fixed-income security?

3.3 Equities

Equities are probably the most familiar type of security. They come in two basic forms: common stock and preferred stock. Of these, common stock is much more important to most investors, so we discuss it first.

Related Bloomberg Functions

DES	Security Description
MFID	MFID Descriptive Data
SECF	Security Finder
MOST	Most Active Securities
Q	Market Quote
ALLQ	All Quotes
EQS	Equity Screener

Are you a Foolish investor? Go to www.fool.com/how-to-invest/thirteen-steps/index.aspx and find the 13 steps under "How to Invest."

COMMON STOCK

Common stock represents ownership in a corporation. If you own 1,000 shares of IBM, for example, then you own about .00011 percent of IBM (IBM has roughly 900 million shares outstanding). It's really that simple. As a part owner, you are entitled to your pro rata share of anything paid out by IBM. If IBM were to be sold or liquidated, you would receive your share of whatever was left over after all of IBM's debts and other obligations (such as wages) were paid.

As an owner, you also have the right to vote on important matters regarding IBM. Unfortunately, your .00011 percent ownership probably isn't going to carry much weight in any votes. To make matters worse, some companies adopt a dual-class share system. Under this approach, companies issue two (or more) types of shares. The special voting class stock, which is usually retained by the founding owners, carries additional votes relative to the common shares owned by typical investors. A dual-class share system allows the founders of the firm to maintain control without having a majority ownership of the shares.

Table 3.2 provides some examples of well-known companies that have chosen this share structure, along with the number of extra votes that the special share class carries. For example, for every share of the special voting stock that Mark Zuckerberg, Facebook's founder, owns, he receives 10 votes. A recent trend, however, involves adding a *sunset provision* for

TABLE 3.2	Companies with Dual-Class Shares	
Company		**Voting Rights**
Groupon		150
Zynga		70
Facebook		10
Google		10
LinkedIn		10
Zillow		10

these share structures. Under a sunset provision, all share classes revert to a normal one-share, one-vote structure at a specified time, say in five years.

The potential benefits from owning common stock come primarily in two forms. First, many companies (but not all) pay cash dividends to their shareholders. However, neither the timing nor the amount of any dividend is guaranteed. At any time, it can be increased, decreased, or omitted altogether. Dividends are paid strictly at the discretion of a company's board of directors, which is elected by the shareholders.

We typically think dividends come in cash. They do, but there are other forms of dividends. While not common, some firms pay their shareholders a dividend in the form of the actual products the firm produces. These in-kind payouts are called a *whiskey dividend* because the National Distillers Products Corp. was among the first companies to make such a dividend. In 1933, National Distillers provided a coupon to its shareholders: For every five shares owned, an investor received a case of whiskey. We are sure that this dividend attracted a loyal ownership base.

The second potential benefit from owning stock is that the value of your stock may rise because share values overall increase or because the future prospects for your particular company improve (or both). The downside is the reverse: Your shares may lose value if either the economy or your particular company falters. As we saw back in Chapter 1, both the potential rewards and the risks from owning common stock have been substantial, particularly shares of stock in smaller companies.

PREFERRED STOCK

The other type of equity security, preferred stock, differs from common stock in several important ways. First, the dividend on a preferred share is usually fixed at some amount and never changed. Further, in the event of liquidation, preferred shares have a particular face value. The reason that preferred stock (or preference stock, as it is sometimes termed) is called "preferred" is that a company must pay the fixed dividend on its preferred stock before any dividends can be paid to common shareholders. In other words, preferred shareholders must be paid first.

The dividend on preferred stock can be omitted at the discretion of the board of directors, so, unlike a debt obligation, there is no legal requirement that the dividend be paid (as long as the common dividend is also skipped). However, some preferred stock is *cumulative,* meaning that any and all skipped dividends must be paid in full (although without interest) before common shareholders can receive a dividend.

Potential gains from owning preferred stock consist of the promised dividend plus any gains from price increases. The potential losses are the reverse: The dividend may be skipped and the value of your preferred shares may decline from either marketwide decreases in value or diminished prospects for your particular company's future business (or both).

In many ways, preferred stock resembles a fixed-income security; in fact, it is sometimes classified that way. In particular, preferred stocks usually have a fixed payment and a fixed liquidation value (but no fixed maturity date). The main difference is that preferred stock is not a debt obligation. Also, for accounting and tax purposes, preferred stock is treated as equity.

FIGURE 3.2   **NYSE Most Active Stocks**

Volume	Chg Up		Chg Down	Value	Δ AVAT	52Wk Highs	52Wk Lows	
Security			Last	%Chg	Volume↓		Value News (As of 08:30)	↻
1) .... F US		d	21.65	-3.56%	152.01M	3.38B	F-150 Needs Help From Ram for Lightning-Quick High-Grade Climb	
2) .... AAPL US		d	164.51	-1.03%	91.42M	15.25B	Apple Target, Estimates Boosted at Wells Fargo Ahead of Results	
3) ... AMD US		d	121.89	-4.97%	91.16M	11.46B	Xilinx-AMD on Course to Clear China Review Shortly: Dealreporter	
4) ... AAL US		d	16.76	-3.18%	54.89M	938.73M	American Airlines Sues Points Guy Over Rewards Management App	
5) ... BAC US		d	45.75	-1.49%	46.27M	2.14B	Ultra-Rich Americans Ask BofA's Katy Knox Some Unusual Questions (1)	
6) ... NVDA US		d	241.50	-3.66%	43.52M	10.83B	Nvidia Analyst Sees Strong Long-Term Potential for Omniverse	
7) .... T US		d	27.02	-0.95%	42.04M	1.14B	New York Airports Under 5G-Linked Storm Warnings Issued by FAA	
8) ... MSFT US		d	301.60	-0.57%	35.38M	10.86B	'Call of Duty' will stay on Sony's PlayStation console after Activision deal, Xbox ...	
9) .... PFE US		d	54.05	+0.95%	35.11M	1.89B	Focus Taiwan: Taiwan took delivery of its 16th shipment of the Pfizer-BioNTech (...	
10) ... INTC US		d	52.04	-2.95%	28.58M	1.51B	Intel Plans to Spend $20 Billion on Ohio Chipmaking Hub (1)	

Source: Bloomberg Finance L.P.

Preferred stock is a good example of why it is sometimes difficult to neatly and precisely classify every security type. To further complicate matters, some preferred stock issues have dividends that are not fixed. So it seems clear that these securities are not fixed-income securities. However, some bond issues make no fixed payments and allow the issuer to skip payments under certain circumstances. As we mentioned earlier, these are examples of hybrid securities.

To give a more difficult example, consider a *convertible bond.* Such a bond is an ordinary bond in every way except that it can be exchanged for a fixed number of shares of stock at the bondholder's discretion. Whether this is really a debt or equity instrument is difficult (or even impossible) to say. We discuss this particular security in more detail in a later chapter.

COMMON STOCK PRICE QUOTES

Unlike fixed-income securities, the price quotes on common and preferred stock are fairly uniform. The list of the top ten most actively traded stocks on January 20, 2022, is in Figure 3.2. Locate the entry for AT&T (T), which is listed on line 7.

The "Security" column contains the company's ticker symbol. The next column, "Last," is the most recent stock price of $27.02 per share. According to the next column ("%Chg"), this price represents a drop of −.95 percent from the previous day. The "Volume" column reports the actual number of shares traded for the day: 42.04 million. Because investors usually trade stock in multiples of 100 shares, called "round lots," sometimes you will see volume figures reported in multiples of hundreds. For example, if you wanted to report AT&T's volume in round lots, you would report volume as 420,400. Of course, the information reported in Figure 3.2 can also be obtained online from many sources. The nearby *Work the Web* box shows one way.

To interpret this information, you will need to know the company's ticker symbol. The ticker symbol is a unique combination of letters assigned to each company. Nordstrom's ticker symbol, for example, is JWN. Most stocks listed on the New York Stock Exchange (NYSE) have ticker symbols with one to three letters, such as T for AT&T, VZ for Verizon, or WMT for Walmart. Stocks listed on the Nasdaq market generally have ticker symbols with four letters, such as AMZN for Amazon or TSLA for Tesla.

Stock price information is also available all day long on television and on the web. For example, the on-air "ticker tape" is a familiar sight on television, particularly on financially oriented shows and networks. One of the most widely watched financial channels is CNBC. All day long, at the bottom of the screen, two rows of information scroll by. The upper band shows trading on the NYSE and the lower band shows trading on the Nasdaq. A lot of other information (too much, in fact, for us to cover here) will also scroll by.

The display is called a "ticker" because, at one time, information was printed on a thin strip of "ticker tape" (paper) by a "ticker" machine (so named because of the sound it made while printing). In fact, the reason for ticker symbols in the first place was to make

WORK THE WEB

One problem is that prices reported by some sources are sometimes from the previous day. Before you trade, you'll want more up-to-date prices, particularly in fast-moving markets. You can get real-time prices from a premier source like Bloomberg. Suppose you do not have this access. Don't despair. You can get some intraday prices from Yahoo! Finance, a free internet site. Let's get some intraday prices for Nordstrom, Inc., ticker JWN.

Most of the information here is self-explanatory. The abbreviation "Market Cap" is short for "market capitalization," which is the total value of all outstanding shares. Notice that JWN was down 4.22 percent during the previous trading day. The pre-market price was down another .72 percent. We'll discuss other unfamiliar terms, such as "Bid" and "Ask," later on. For now, a good exercise is to select a detailed quote yourself and explore what information is available in the links below the stock quote.

20.90 -0.92 (-4.22%) **20.75** -0.15 (-0.72%)
At close: January 20 04:00PM EST   Pre-Market: 08:31AM EST

Summary   Company Outlook   Chart   Conversations   Statistics   Historical Data   Profile   Financials   Analysis   Options

Previous Close	21.82	Market Cap	3.33B	
Open	21.92	Beta (5Y Monthly)	2.43	
Bid	0.00 x 800	PE Ratio (TTM)	337.10	
Ask	0.00 x 3200	EPS (TTM)	0.06	
Day's Range	20.82 - 22.62	Earnings Date	Feb 28, 2022 - Mar 04, 2022	
52 Week Range	18.95 - 46.45	Forward Dividend & Yield	N/A (N/A)	
Volume	6,100,902	Ex-Dividend Date	Mar 09, 2020	
Avg. Volume	5,938,241	1y Target Est	25.25	

Source: Yahoo! Finance, January 21, 2022.

information quicker and easier to print. Perhaps you have seen old film footage of a "ticker tape parade" in New York. The paper raining down on the celebrities and dignitaries is ticker tape. Ticker machines date to an era before television (if you can imagine such a time). The first one was introduced in 1867 and was later improved upon by none other than Thomas Edison.

Some investors don't necessarily want minute-by-minute price changes. For example, a long-term investor might want a list of companies that pay (high) dividends. A sample of such a list appears in Figure 3.3. This list contains the stocks in the S&P500 with the highest dividend yields.

Locate the entry for Verizon Communications (VZ). The current dividend yield for VZ is 4.8 percent, and its dividend is growing at a rate of about 2.1 percent per year. If we drill down, we would find that Verizon's current stock price is $53.40 per share. Most dividend-paying companies pay their dividends quarterly, and Verizon's most recent dividend was $.64 per share. So note that the 4.8 percent dividend yield reported is actually four times the most recent quarterly dividend (4 × $.64 = $2.56), divided by the current stock price.

The moral of the story is that there are many financial data sources, and they have all sorts of information. So it is becoming easier for investors to find the specific information they desire.

FIGURE 3.3 | Top-Yielding Stocks, S&P500

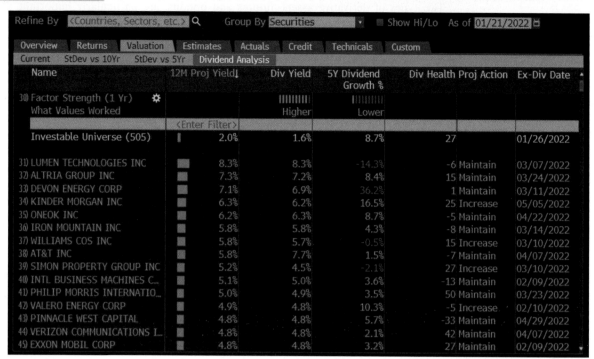

Name	12M Proj Yield↓	Div Yield	5Y Dividend Growth %	Div Health	Proj Action	Ex-Div Date
30) Factor Strength (1 Yr) ✿ What Values Worked		Higher	Lower			
Investable Universe (505)	2.0%	1.6%	8.7%	27		01/26/2022
31) LUMEN TECHNOLOGIES INC	8.3%	8.3%	-14.3%	-6	Maintain	03/07/2022
32) ALTRIA GROUP INC	7.3%	7.2%	8.4%	15	Maintain	03/24/2022
33) DEVON ENERGY CORP	7.1%	6.9%	36.2%	1	Maintain	03/11/2022
34) KINDER MORGAN INC	6.3%	6.2%	16.5%	25	Increase	05/05/2022
35) ONEOK INC	6.2%	6.3%	8.7%	-5	Maintain	04/22/2022
36) IRON MOUNTAIN INC	5.8%	5.8%	4.3%	-8	Maintain	03/14/2022
37) WILLIAMS COS INC	5.8%	5.7%	-0.5%	15	Increase	03/10/2022
38) AT&T INC	5.8%	7.7%	1.5%	-7	Maintain	04/07/2022
39) SIMON PROPERTY GROUP INC	5.2%	4.5%	-2.1%	27	Increase	03/10/2022
40) INTL BUSINESS MACHINES C...	5.1%	5.0%	3.6%	-13	Maintain	02/09/2022
41) PHILIP MORRIS INTERNATIO...	5.0%	4.9%	3.5%	50	Maintain	03/23/2022
42) VALERO ENERGY CORP	4.9%	4.8%	10.3%	-5	Increase	02/10/2022
43) PINNACLE WEST CAPITAL	4.8%	4.8%	5.7%	-33	Maintain	04/29/2022
44) VERIZON COMMUNICATIONS I...	4.8%	4.8%	2.1%	42	Maintain	04/07/2022
45) EXXON MOBIL CORP	4.8%	4.8%	3.2%	27	Maintain	02/09/2022

Source: Bloomberg Finance L.P.

CHECK THIS

3.3a What are the two types of equity securities?

3.3b Why is preferred stock sometimes classified as a fixed-income security?

3.4 Derivatives: Futures Contracts

Related Bloomberg Functions

CT Futures Contract Table

WEIF World Equity Index Futures

CTM Exchange Contracts

primary asset
Security originally sold by a business or government to raise money.

derivative asset
A financial asset that is derived from an existing traded asset rather than issued by a business or government to raise capital. More generally, any financial asset that is not a primary asset.

There is a clear distinction between real assets, which are essentially tangible items, and financial assets, which are pieces of paper describing legal claims. Financial assets can be further subdivided into primary and derivative assets. A **primary asset** (sometimes called a *primitive asset*) is a security that was originally sold by a business or government to raise money; it represents a claim on the assets of the issuer. Thus, stocks and bonds are primary financial assets.

In contrast, as the name suggests, a **derivative asset** is a financial asset that is derived from an existing primary asset rather than issued by a business or government to raise capital. As we will see, derivative assets usually represent claims either on other financial assets, such as shares of stock or even other derivative assets, or on the future price of a real asset such as gold. Beyond this, it is difficult to give a general definition of the term "derivative asset" because there are so many different types, and new ones are created almost every day. On the most basic level, however, any financial asset that is not a primary asset is a derivative asset.

To give a simple example of a derivative asset, imagine that you and a friend buy 1,000 shares of a dividend-paying stock, perhaps the Verizon stock we discussed. You each put up half the money, and you agree to sell your stock in one year. Furthermore, the two of you agree that you will get all the dividends paid while your friend gets all the gains or absorbs all the losses on the 1,000 shares.

This simple arrangement takes a primary asset, shares of Verizon stock, and creates two derivative assets, the dividend-only shares that you hold and the no-dividend shares held by your friend. Derivative assets such as these actually exist, and there are many variations on this basic theme.

Two types of derivative assets, futures and options, are particularly important. Many other types exist, but they can usually be built up from these two basic types, possibly by combining them with other primary assets. Futures are the simpler of the two, so we discuss them first.

FUTURES CONTRACTS

futures contract
An agreement made today regarding the terms of a trade that will take place later.

In many ways, a futures contract is the simplest of all financial assets. A **futures contract** is an agreement made today regarding the terms of a trade that will take place later. Futures contracts are traded at futures exchanges, which are regulated markets that match buyers and sellers. For example, suppose you know that you will want to buy 100 ounces of gold in six months. One thing you could do is strike a deal today with a seller in which you promise to pay, say, $1,800 per ounce in six months for the 100 ounces of gold. In other words, you and the seller, through a futures exchange, agree that six months from now, you will exchange $180,000 for 100 ounces of gold. The agreement that you have created is a futures contract.

With your futures contract, you have locked in the price of gold six months from now. Suppose that gold is actually selling for $1,850 per ounce in six months. You benefit from having entered into the futures contract because you have to pay only $1,800 per ounce. However, if gold is selling for $1,700, you lose because you are forced to pay $1,800 per ounce. Thus, a futures contract is risky because the price of gold in the future can differ from the futures contract price today. Notice that with your futures contract, no money changes hands today.

After entering into the futures contract, what happens if you change your mind in, say, four months and you want out of the contract? The answer is that you can sell your contract to someone else. You would generally have a gain or a loss when you sell. The contract still has two months to run. If market participants generally believe that gold will be worth more than $1,800 when the contract matures in two months, then your contract is valuable and you would have a gain if you sold it. If, on the other hand, market participants think gold will not be worth $1,800, then you would have a loss on the contract if you sold it because you would have to pay someone else to take it off your hands.

You can download lots of basic futures information from the "Education" link at www.cmegroup.com.

Futures contracts are traded all over the world on many types of assets and can be traced back to ancient civilizations. As we discuss in detail in a later chapter, there are two broad categories of futures contracts: *financial futures* and *commodity futures*. The difference is that, with financial futures, the underlying asset is intangible, usually stocks, bonds, currencies, or money market instruments. With commodity futures, the underlying asset is a real asset, typically either an agricultural product (such as cattle or wheat) or a natural resource product (such as gold or oil).

FUTURES PRICE QUOTES

An important feature of exchange-traded futures contracts is that they are *standardized,* meaning that one contract calls for the purchase of a specific quantity of the underlying asset. Further, the contract specifies in detail what the underlying asset is and where it is to be delivered. For example, with a wheat contract, one contract specifies that 5,000 bushels of a particular type of wheat will be delivered at one of a few approved locations on a particular date in exchange for the agreed-upon futures contract price.

In Figure 3.4, futures price quotations for U.S. Treasury bonds (or "T-bonds" for short) are seen as they appear online at cmegroup.com. A nearby *Work the Web* box contains additional information on finding and reading futures price quotes. Looking at Figure 3.4, these are quotes for delivery of T-bonds with a total par, or face, value of $100,000. These contracts are traded on the CBOT, which is the Chicago Board of Trade (part of the CME Group).

The "Month" column in Figure 3.4 tells us the delivery date for the bond specified by the contract. For example, "JUN 2022" indicates that the second contract listed is for T-bond delivery in June 2022. Following the delivery month, we have a series of prices. In order, we have the current (or last) price, the change from the prior close, the prior closing (or settle) price, the open price, the high price, and the low price. The open price is the

FIGURE 3.4   Futures Trading, U.S. 20-Year T-Bond

MONTH	OPTIONS	CHART	LAST	CHANGE	PRIOR SETTLE	OPEN	HIGH	LOW	VOLUME	UPDATED
MAR 2022 ZNH2	OPT	ıl	128'095	+0'190 (+0.46%)	127'225	127'290	128'100	127'280	860,443	08:04:37 CT 21 Jan 2022
JUN 2022 ZNM2	OPT	ıl	128'000	+0'155 (+0.38%)	127'165	127'285	128'035	127'270	1,089	07:45:58 CT 21 Jan 2022
SEP 2022 ZNU2	OPT	ıl	-	-	127'165	-	-	-	0	17:57:58 CT 20 Jan 2022

Source: www.cmegroup.com, March 13, 2022.

price at the start of the trading day; the high and low are the highest and lowest prices for the day. The "Volume" column tells us how many contracts have been traded during the current day.

To see how T-bond futures contracts work, suppose you buy one June 2022 T-bond futures contract at the current settle price, which is the column labeled "Last." What you have done is agree to buy T-bonds with a total par value of $100,000 in June at a price of 128'000 per $100 of par value, where the "000" represents $\frac{0}{32\text{nds}}$ percent of par value. Thus, 128'000 can also be written as $155\frac{0}{32}$, which represents a price of $155,000.00 per $100,000 face value. No money changes hands today. If you take no further action, however, when June rolls around, your T-bonds will be delivered and you must pay for them at that time.

Actually, most futures contracts do not result in delivery. Most buyers and sellers close out their contracts before the delivery date. To close out a contract, you take the opposite side. For example, suppose that with your one T-bond contract, you later decide you no longer wish to be obligated. To get out, you sell one contract, thereby eliminating your position.

GAINS AND LOSSES ON FUTURES CONTRACTS

Futures contracts have the potential for enormous gains and losses. To see why, let's consider again buying T-bond contracts based on the current settle prices in Figure 3.4. To make matters somewhat more interesting, suppose you buy 15 March contracts at the last price of 128'095 per $100 of par value.

One month later, perhaps because of falling inflation, the futures price of T-bonds for March delivery rises five dollars to 133'095. This may not seem like a huge increase, but it generates a substantial profit for you. You have locked in a price of 128'095 per $100 par value. The price has risen to 133'095, so you make a profit of $5 per $100 of par value, or $5,000 per $100,000 face value. With 15 contracts, each of which calls for delivery of $100,000 in face value of T-bonds, you make a tidy profit of 15 × $5,000 = $75,000. Of course, if the price had decreased by five dollars, you would have lost $75,000 on your 15-contract position.

EXAMPLE 3.3   **Future Shock**

Suppose you purchase five December T-bond contracts at the prior settle price of 122'175. How much will you pay today? Suppose in one month you close your position and the December futures price at that time is 117'165. Did you make or lose money? How much?

When you purchase the five contracts, you pay nothing today because the transaction is for September. However, you have agreed to pay 122'175 per $100 par value. If, when you close your position in a month, the futures price is 117'165, you have a loss of 122'175 − 117'165 = $5 \frac{1}{32}$ per $100 par value, or $5 \frac{1}{32}$ × 1,000 = $5,031.25 per contract. Your total loss is thus $5,031.25 × 5 contracts, or $25,156.25 in all (ouch!).

Futures price quotes have also become more available with the rise of the internet. The primary site for finding futures price quotes is www.cmegroup.com.

At the CME Group, futures contracts for agricultural products (e.g., corn, wheat, soybeans), energy (oil, natural gas), interest rates (U.S. Treasury notes and bonds, German bonds), foreign currency (yen, euro), metals (gold, silver), and indexes (Dow Jones, S&P 500) are listed. A complete list of all the contracts traded can be found on the website. Each futures contract has some unique aspects. For example, here is a sample soybean futures screen from the CME Group's website.

MONTH	OPTIONS	CHART	LAST	CHANGE	PRIOR SETTLE	OPEN	HIGH	LOW	VOLUME	UPDATED
MAR 2022 ZSH2	OPT	ⅲ	1419'0	–6'6 (–0.47%)	1425'6	1420'0	1423'6	1405'2	28,772	07:44:54 CT 21 Jan 2022
MAY 2022 ZSK2	OPT	ⅲ	1427'6	–6'6 (–0.47%)	1434'4	1428'4	1432'0	1413'6	5,977	07:44:29 CT 21 Jan 2022
JUL 2022 ZSN2	OPT	ⅲ	1432'4	–6'2 (–0.43%)	1438'6	1432'6	1437'4	1418'2	4,968	07:44:21 CT 21 Jan 2022
AUG 2022 ZSQ2	OPT	ⅲ	1405'2	–5'6 (–0.41%)	1411'0	1402'2	1408'0	1392'6	262	07:42:53 CT 21 Jan 2022
SEP 2022 ZSU2	OPT	ⅲ	1344'4	–7'0 (–0.52%)	1351'4	1344'0	1347'2	1337'0	107	07:36:47 CT 21 Jan 2022
NOV 2022 ZSX2	OPT	ⅲ	1314'4	–5'6 (–0.44%)	1320'2	1315'0	1319'6	1305'4	2,767	07:44:58 CT 21 Jan 2022
JAN 2023 ZSF3	OPT	ⅲ	1316'2	–3'6 (–0.28%)	1320'0	1314'2	1320'4	1306'4	490	07:42:03 CT 21 Jan 2022

Source: www.CMEgroup.com, January 21, 2022.

Locate the line that starts with MAY 2022. This futures contract calls for May 2022 delivery of 5,000 bushels of soybeans. By convention, soybean prices are still quoted in cents and eighths of a cent, even though the minimum price change is one-fourth cent, or two-eighths of a cent. In the "Last" column, you can see an entry of 1427'6, which is 1,427 and 6/8 cents, or $14.2775.

The volume of 5,977 says that there have been 5,977 futures contracts traded today. This volume represents 5,977 × 5,000 = 29,885,000 bushels. The dollar, or notional, value of these contracts is the number of bushels times the per-bushel price. In this case, the May 2022 contracts alone have a dollar value of over $426 million!

Understanding futures markets, their use, and their quoting conventions takes a great deal of study. Your school might even offer a course where you can study futures markets in depth.

3.4a What is a futures contract?

3.4b What are the general types of futures contracts?

3.4c Explain how you make or lose money on a futures contract.

3.5 Derivatives: Option Contracts

Related Bloomberg Functions

OTD Option Descriptions

OMON Option Monitor

An **option contract** is an agreement that gives the owner the right, but not the obligation, to buy or sell (depending on the type of option) a specific asset at a specified price for a set period of time. The most familiar options are stock options. These are options to buy or sell shares of stock, and they are the focus of our discussion here. Options are a very flexible investment tool, and a great deal is known about them. We present some of the most important concepts here; our detailed coverage begins in a later chapter.

OPTION TERMINOLOGY

option contract
An agreement that gives the owner the right, but not the obligation, to buy or sell a specific asset at a specified price for a set period of time.

call option
Grants the holder the right, but not the obligation, to buy the underlying asset at a given strike price.

put option
Grants the holder the right, but not the obligation, to sell the underlying asset at a given strike price.

option premium
The price you pay to buy an option.

strike price
Price specified in an option contract that the holder pays to buy shares (in the case of call options) or receives to sell shares (in the case of put options) if the option is exercised. Also called the *exercise price*.

To learn more about options, visit www.cboe.com and select "Education."

Options come in two flavors, calls and puts. The owner of a **call option** has the right, but not the obligation, to *buy* an underlying asset at a fixed price for a specified time. The owner of a **put option** has the right, but not the obligation, to *sell* an underlying asset at a fixed price for a specified time.

Options occur frequently in everyday life. Suppose that you are interested in buying a used car. You and the seller agree that the price will be $8,000. You give the seller $200 to hold the car for one week, meaning that you have one week to come up with the $8,000 purchase price, or else you lose your $200.

This agreement is a call option. You paid the seller $200 for the right, but not the obligation, to buy the car for $8,000. If you change your mind because, for example, you find a better deal elsewhere, you can walk away. You'll lose your $200, but that is the price you paid for the right, but not the obligation, to buy. The price you pay to purchase an option, the $200 in this example, is called the **option premium.**

A few other definitions will be useful. First, the specified price at which the underlying asset can be bought or sold with an option contract is called the **strike price,** the *striking price,* or the *exercise price.* Using an option to buy or sell an asset is called *exercising* the option.

The *last trading day* for all monthly stock options in the United States is the third Friday of the option's expiration month (except when Friday falls on a holiday, in which case the last trading day is the third Thursday). The *expiration day* for stock options is the Saturday immediately following the last trading day. The expiration day is the last day (in the case of *American-style* options) or the only day (in the case of *European-style* options) on which an option may be *exercised.* More recently, weekly options have become popular. As the name suggests, these options expire at the end of the current week, with the last trading day being either Thursday or Friday, depending on the contract.

OPTIONS VERSUS FUTURES

Our discussion thus far illustrates the two crucial differences between an option contract and a futures contract. The first is that the purchaser of a futures contract is *obligated* to buy the underlying asset at the specified price (and the seller of a futures contract is obligated to sell). The owner of a call option has the right, but not the obligation, to buy.

The second important difference is that when you buy a futures contract, you pay no money at the time of purchase (and you receive none if you sell). However, if you buy an option contract, you pay the premium at the time of the purchase; if you sell an option contract, you receive the premium at the time of the sale.

OPTION PRICE QUOTES

Like futures contracts, most option contracts are standardized. One call option contract, for example, gives the owner the right to buy 100 shares (one round lot) of stock. Similarly, one put option contract gives the owner the right to sell 100 shares. Figure 3.5 presents intraday quotes for call and put options on Nike common stock. The data are from Bloomberg. At the time these quotes were obtained, Nike stock was trading at $144.75.

The left side of Figure 3.5 is a list of call options, while the right side is a list of **put** options. The first column on each side gives the general option characteristics such as the expiration date and strike price. The next few columns provide bid, ask, and last prices (on a per-share basis). The bid price is the price you will receive if you want to sell an option at the prevailing market price; the ask price is the price you will pay if you want to buy an option at the prevailing market price. The column labeled "IVM" stands for implied volatility, which is a difficult concept that we will save for our dedicated chapter on option pricing. The final column on each side reports the trading volume.

Referring to the Nike 150 call options with March expiration, we see that 13 call option contracts have been traded so far in this trading day, and the last transaction price for this option was $4.11 per share. Because each listed option contract actually involves 100 shares, the price per contract was $4.11 × 100 = $411.

The bid and ask prices reflect current market conditions, not the market conditions that prevailed at the time of the last transaction price. Based on the bid and ask prices, what price

FIGURE 3.5   Options Trading

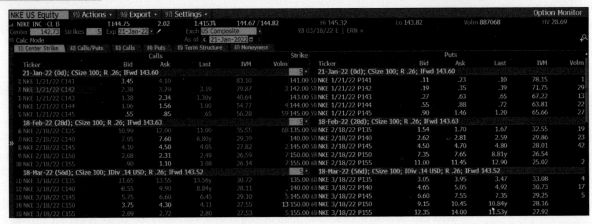

Source: Bloomberg Finance L.P.

would you pay now for one of these call options? Remember, the ask price is the price you pay, so you would pay $4.30 per share, or $430 for the contract. If you were selling, you would sell at the bid price of $3.75 per share, or $375 for the contract. This difference is known as the bid-ask spread, or spread for short.

EXAMPLE 3.4   Put Options

Suppose you want the right to sell 200 shares of Nike sometime before February 18, 2022, at a price of $140. In light of the information in Figure 3.5, what contract should you buy? How much will it cost you?

You want the right to sell stock at a fixed price, so you want to buy put options. Specifically, you want to buy two 140 put contracts with a February expiration. In Figure 3.5, the ask price for this contract is given as $2.81. Recall that each option contract is for 100 shares. So we must multiply the quoted option price by 100. One contract will cost you $281, so two contracts will cost $562.

GAINS AND LOSSES ON OPTION CONTRACTS

As with futures contracts, option contracts have the potential for large gains and losses. Let's consider our previous example in which you paid $430 to purchase one Nike 150 call contract with a March expiration. Suppose you hold on to your contracts until they are about to expire. What are your gains (or losses) if Nike is selling for $170 per share? $130 per share?

If Nike is selling for $170 per share, you will profit handsomely. You have the right to buy 100 shares at a price of $150 per share. Because the stock is worth $170, your options are worth $20 per share, or $2,000 in all. So you invested $430 and ended up with almost five times that amount. Not bad.

If the stock ends up at $130 per share, however, the result is not so pretty. You have the right to buy the stock for $150 when it is selling for $130, so your call options expire worthless. You lose the entire $430 you originally invested. In fact, if the stock price is anything less than $150, you lose the entire $430 premium.

EXAMPLE 3.5

More on Puts

In Example 3.4, you bought two Nike 140 put contracts for $562. Suppose that the expiration date arrives and Nike is selling for $130 per share. How did you do? What's the break-even stock price, that is, the stock price at which you just make enough to cover your $562 cost?

Your put contracts give you the right to sell 200 shares of Nike at a price of $140 per share. If the stock is worth only $130 per share, your put options are worth $10 per share, or $2,000 in all. To determine the break-even stock price, notice that you paid $2.81 per share for the option. The break-even stock price is thus $140 − $2.81 = $137.19. At any price below $137.19, the buyer of the put option makes a profit.

INVESTING IN STOCKS VERSUS OPTIONS

To get a better idea of the potential gains and losses from investing in stocks compared to investing in options, let's suppose you have $15,000 to invest. You're looking at Walmart (WMT), which is currently selling for $150 per share. You also notice that a call option with a $150 strike price and three months to maturity is available. The premium is $10.[1]

You're considering investing all $15,000 either in the stock or in the call options. What is your return from these two investments if, in three months, Walmart is selling for $165 per share? What about $135 per share?

First, if you buy the stock, your $15,000 will purchase one round lot, meaning 100 shares. A call contract costs $1,000 (why?), so you can buy 15 of them. Notice that your 15 contracts give you the right to buy 1,500 shares at $150 per share.

If, in three months, Walmart is selling for $165, your stock will be worth 100 shares × $165 = $16,500. Your dollar gain will be $16,500 less the $15,000 you invested, or $1,500. Because you invested $15,000, your return for the three-month period is $1,500/$15,000 = .10, or 10%. If Walmart is selling for $135 per share, then you lose $1,500 and your return is −10 percent.

If Walmart is selling for $165, your call options are worth $165 − $150 = $15 each, but now you control 1,500 shares, so your options are worth 1,500 shares × $15 = $22,500 total. You invested $15,000, so your dollar return is $22,500 − $15,000 = $7,500 and your percentage return is $7,500/$15,000 = .50, or 50%, compared to 10 percent on the stock investment. If Walmart is selling for $135 when your options mature, however, then you lose everything, and your return is −100 percent.

EXAMPLE 3.6

Put Returns

In our example for Walmart, suppose a put option with a strike price of $150 is also available, with a premium of $7.50. Calculate your percentage return for the three-month holding period if the stock price declines to $141 per share. What is your annualized return?

One put contract costs $750, so you can buy 20 of them. Notice that your 20 contracts give you the right to sell 2,000 shares at $150 per share.

If, in three months, Walmart is selling for $141, your put options are worth $150 − $141 = $9 each. You control 2,000 shares, so your options are worth 2,000 shares × $9 = $18,000 total. You invested $15,000, so your dollar return is $18,000 − $15,000 = $3,000, and your percentage return is $3,000/$15,000 = .20, or 20%.

To annualize your return, we need to compute the effective annual return, recognizing that there are four three-month periods in a year:

$$1 + EAR = 1.20^4$$
$$1 + EAR = 2.0736$$
$$EAR = 1.0736, \text{ or } 107.36\%$$

Your annualized return is about 107 percent.

---

[1] We ignore any dividends paid by Walmart, which would impact the calculation. However, we will return to this impact in a later chapter.

3.5a   What is a call option? A put option?

3.5b   If you buy a call option, what do you hope will happen to the underlying stock? What if you buy a put option?

3.5c   What are the two key differences between a futures contract and an option contract?

3.6 Summary and Conclusions

In this chapter, we examine the basic types of financial assets. We discuss three broad classes: interest-bearing assets, equity securities, and derivative assets (futures and options). For each of the broad classes, we ask three questions. First, what is its basic nature and what are its distinguishing characteristics? Second, what are the potential gains and losses from owning it? Third, how are its prices quoted online and in the financial press? We cover many aspects of these investments. We provide a brief description of these investments broken down by the chapter's important concepts.

1. **Various types of interest-bearing assets.**

    A. Each of these major groups can be further subdivided. Interest-bearing assets include money market instruments and fixed-income securities.

    B. Money market instruments generally have the following two properties: (1) They are essentially IOUs sold by large corporations or governments to borrow money and (2) they mature in less than one year from the time they are sold, meaning that the loan must be repaid within one year.

    C. Fixed-income securities are securities that promise to make fixed payments according to some preset schedule. Another key characteristic of a fixed-income security is that it begins life as a loan of some sort. That is, fixed-income securities are debt obligations. Corporations and governments issue fixed-income securities. Unlike money market instruments, fixed-income securities have lives that exceed 12 months at the time they are issued.

2. **Equity securities.**

    A. The two major equity types are common stock and preferred stock. Common stock represents ownership in a corporation. If you own 1,000 shares of General Electric, then you own a very small percentage of GE's outstanding shares. Nonetheless, you are a part-owner of GE. As a part-owner, you are entitled to your pro rata share of anything paid out by GE, and you have the right to vote on important matters regarding the company.

    B. Preferred stock differs from common stock in several important ways. First, the dividend on a preferred share is usually fixed at some amount and never changed. Second, if the company liquidates, preferred shares have a particular face value. The reason preferred stock is called "preferred" is that a company must pay the fixed dividend on its preferred stock before any dividends can be paid to common shareholders. In other words, preferred shareholders must be paid first.

3. **Futures contracts.**

    A. In many ways, a futures contract is the simplest of all financial assets. A futures contract is an agreement made today regarding the terms of a trade that will take place later.

    B. As an example of a futures contract, suppose you know that you will want to buy 100 ounces of gold in six months. One thing you could do is strike a deal today with a seller in which you promise to pay, say, $1,800 per ounce in six months for the 100 ounces of gold. In other words, you and the seller agree that six months from now, you will exchange $180,000 for 100 ounces of gold. The agreement that you have created is a futures contract.

4. Option contracts.

A. An option contract is an agreement that gives the owner the right, but not the obligation, to buy or sell (depending on the type of option) a specific asset at a specified price for a set period of time.

B. The most familiar options are stock options. These are options to buy or sell shares of stock, and they are the focus of our discussion here. Options are a very flexible investment tool, and a great deal is known about them. We present some of the most important option concepts in this chapter.

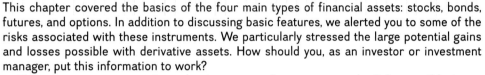

GETTING DOWN TO BUSINESS

This chapter covered the basics of the four main types of financial assets: stocks, bonds, futures, and options. In addition to discussing basic features, we alerted you to some of the risks associated with these instruments. We particularly stressed the large potential gains and losses possible with derivative assets. How should you, as an investor or investment manager, put this information to work?

Following up on our previous chapter, you need to execute each of the possible transaction types suggested by this chapter in a simulated brokerage account. Your goal is to experience some of the large gains (and losses) to understand them on a personal level. Try to do at least the following:

1. Buy a corporate or government bond.
2. Buy agriculture, natural resource, and financial futures contracts.
3. Sell agriculture, natural resource, and financial futures contracts.
4. Buy put and call option contracts.
5. Sell put and call option contracts.

In each case, once you have created the position, be sure to monitor it regularly by checking prices, trading activity, and relevant news using *The Wall Street Journal* or an online information service to understand why it changes in value.

One thing you will discover if you execute these trades is that some of these investments carry relatively low risk and some carry relatively high risk. Which are which? Under what circumstances is each of these investments appropriate? We will have more to say about these investments later, but you'll get a lot more out of our discussion (and have some fun stories to tell) if you already have some personal experience. As always, it's better to become educated about these things with play money before you commit real money.

For the latest information on the real world of investments, visit us at jmdinvestments.blogspot.com.

Key Terms

call option 87
current yield 77
derivative asset 83
fixed-income securities 76
futures contract 84
money market instruments 75

option contract 87
option premium 87
primary asset 83
put option 87
strike price 87

Related Bloomberg Functions

SRCH	Fixed Income Search, 3.2	
MMF	Money Market Funds, 3.2	
WB	World Bond Markets, 3.2	
TACT	TRACE Activity, 3.2	
DES	Security Description, 3.3	
MFID	MFID Descriptive Data, 3.3	
SECF	Security Finder, 3.3	
MOST	Most Active Securities, 3.3	
Q	Market Quote, 3.3	
ALLQ	All Quotes, 3.3	
EQS	Equity Screener, 3.3	
CT	Future Contract Table, 3.4	
WEIF	World Equity Index Futures, 3.4	
CTM	Exchange Contracts, 3.4	
OTD	Option Descriptions, 3.5	
OMON	Option Monitor, 3.5	

Chapter Review Problems and Self-Test

1. **Corporate Bond Quotes (LO1, CFA3)**   Suppose you are planning to purchase a Comcast Corporation bond that matures in 2038 and has a 3.15 percent coupon rate. The last price, as a percentage of face value, is 99.148, or 99.148 percent. Suppose you purchase $100,000 in face value. How much will this bond cost? Assuming semiannual payments, what coupon payments do you receive?

2. **Call Options (LO4, CFA4)**   You plan to purchase Nike call options with a strike price of $140 and a current ask premium of $3.75 per share. If you buy 10 contracts, how much will you pay? Suppose that just as the option is about to expire, Nike is selling for $150 per share. What are your options worth? What is your profit (or loss)?

Answers to Self-Test Problems

1. If you buy $100,000 in face value, you pay $99,148. You will receive 3.15 percent of $100,000, or $3,150, in coupon payments every year, paid in two $1,575 semiannual installments.

2. Because one contract involves 100 shares, the cost of a contract is $375, and 10 contracts would cost $3,750. At expiration, if Nike is selling for $150, then you have the right to buy 10 contracts × 100 shares = 1,000 shares at $140. Your contracts are thus worth $150 − 140 = $10 per share, or $10,000 total. Because they cost you $3,750, your gain is $6,250, which is a return of 166.67 percent.

Test Your Investment Quotient

1. **Money Market Securities (LO1, CFA1)**   Which of the following is not a common characteristic of money market securities?

    a. They are sold on a discount basis.
    b. They mature in less than one year.
    c. The most important risk is default risk.
    d. All of the above are characteristics.

2. **Money Market Securities (LO1, CFA1)** Which of the following money market securities is the most liquid?

   a. U.S. Treasury bills
   b. Bank certificates of deposit
   c. Corporate money market debt
   d. Municipality money market debt

3. **Options (LO4, CFA4)** A European option can be exercised:

   a. Only after American options.
   b. Anytime up to and including the expiration date.
   c. Only on the day before the expiration date.
   d. Only on a European exchange.

4. **Fixed-Income Securities (LO1, CFA3)** Your friend told you she just received her semiannual coupon payment on a U.S. Treasury note with a $100,000 face value that pays a 6 percent annual coupon. How much money did she receive from this coupon payment?

   a. $3,000
   b. $6,000
   c. $30,000
   d. $60,000

5. **Common Stock (LO2, CFA2)** A corporation with common stock issued to the public pays dividends:

   a. At the discretion of management, who are elected by the shareholders.
   b. At the discretion of shareholders since they own the corporation.
   c. At the discretion of the company's board of directors, who are elected by shareholders.
   d. At the discretion of the company's board of directors, who are appointed by management.

6. **Futures Contracts (LO3, CFA4)** You buy (go long) five copper futures contracts at 100 cents per pound, where the contract size is 25,000 pounds. At contract maturity, copper is selling for 102 cents per pound. What is your profit (+) or loss (−) on the transaction?

   a. −$2,500
   b. +$2,500
   c. −$25,000
   d. +$25,000

7. **Futures Contracts (LO3, CFA4)** You sell (go short) 10 gold futures contracts at $400 per ounce, where the contract size is 100 ounces. At contract maturity, gold is selling for $410 per ounce. What is your profit (+) or loss (−) on the transaction?

   a. −$1,000
   b. +$1,000
   c. −$10,000
   d. +$10,000

8. **Option Contracts (LO4, CFA4)** You buy 100 CJC call option contracts with a strike price of $95 at a quoted price of $1. At option expiration, CJC sells for $97. What is your net profit on the transaction?

   a. $2,000
   b. $5,000
   c. $10,000
   d. $20,000

9. **Option Contracts (LO4, CFA4)** You buy 100 CJC put option contracts with a strike price of $92 at a quoted price of $8. At option expiration, CJC sells for $83.80. What is your net profit on the transaction?

   a. $200
   b. $1,000
   c. $2,000
   d. $10,000

10. **Short Sales (LO4, CFA4)** Which of the following statements about short selling is true?

    a. A short position may be hedged by writing call options.
    b. A short position may be hedged by purchasing put options.
    c. Short-sellers may be subject to margin calls if the stock price increases.
    d. Stocks that pay large dividends should be sold short before the ex-dividend date and bought afterward to take advantage of the large price declines in a short time period.

Concept Questions

1. **Money Market Instruments (LO1, CFA1)** What are the distinguishing features of a money market instrument?

2. **Preferred Stock (LO2, CFA2)** Why is preferred stock "preferred"?

3. **WSJ Stock Quotes (LO2, CFA2)** What is the PE ratio reported for stocks in *The Wall Street Journal*? In particular, how is it computed?

4. **Yields (LO1, CFA3)** The current yield on a bond is the coupon rate divided by the price. Thus, it is very similar to what number reported for common and preferred stocks?

5. **Volume Quotations (LO1, LO2, LO3, LO4)** Explain how volume is quoted for stocks, corporate bonds, futures, and options.

6. **Futures Contracts (LO3, CFA4)** Changes in what price lead to gains and/or losses in futures contracts?

7. **Futures Contracts (LO3, CFA4)** What is the open interest on a futures contract? What do you think will usually happen to open interest as maturity approaches?

8. **Futures versus Options (LO3, LO4, CFA4)** What is the difference between a futures contract and an option contract? Do the buyer of a futures contract and the buyer of an option contract have the same rights? What about the seller?

9. **Asset Types (LO1, LO2, LO3, LO4)** What is the distinction between a real asset and a financial asset? What are the two basic types of financial assets, and what does each represent?

10. **Puts versus Calls (LO4, CFA4)** Suppose a share of stock is selling for $100. A put and a call are offered, both with $100 strike prices and nine months to maturity. Intuitively, which do you think is more valuable?

Questions and Problems

Core Questions

1. **Stock Quotations (LO2, CFA2)** You found the following stock quote for DRK Enterprises, Inc., at your favorite website. You also found that the stock paid an annual dividend of $.75, which resulted in a dividend yield of 1.30 percent. What was the closing price for this stock yesterday? How many round lots of stock were traded yesterday?

			DAILY			YTD	52 WEEK		
Company	Symbol	Vol	Close	Chg	%Chg	%Chg	High	Low	%Chg
DRK Enterprises	DRK	18,649,130	??	.26	.45%	8.73%	78.19	51.74	11.0%

2. **Stock Quotations (LO2, CFA2)** In Problem 1, assume the company has 100 million shares of stock outstanding and a PE ratio of 15. What was net income for the most recent four quarters?

3. **Dividend Yields (LO2, CFA2)** You find a stock selling for $74.20 that has a dividend yield of 3.4 percent. What was the last quarterly dividend paid?

4. **Earnings per Share (LO2)** In Problem 3, if the company has a PE ratio of 21.5, what is the earnings per share (EPS) for the company?

5. **Bonds (LO1, CFA3)** You purchase 4,000 bonds with a par value of $1,000 for $978 each. The bonds have a coupon rate of 7.7 percent paid semiannually and mature in 10 years. How much will you receive on the next coupon date? How much will you receive when the bonds mature?

6. **Futures Profits (LO3, CFA4)** The contract size for platinum futures is 50 troy ounces. Suppose you need 300 troy ounces of platinum and the current futures price is $850 per ounce. How many contracts do you need to purchase? How much will you pay for your platinum? What is your dollar profit if platinum sells for $900 a troy ounce when the futures contract expires? What if the price is $800 at expiration?

7. **Option Profits (LO4, CFA4)** You purchase 10 call option contracts with a strike price of $60 and a premium of $1.95. If the stock price at expiration is $72, what is your dollar profit? What if the stock price is $57.95?

8. **Stock Quotations (LO2, CFA2)** You found the following stock quote for Gigantus Corporation in today's newspaper. What was the stock selling for on January 1?

			DAILY			YTD	52 WEEK		
Company	Symbol	Vol	Close	Chg	%Chg	%Chg	High	Low	%Chg
Gigantus	GIG	12,805,325	48.92	.72	1.47%	−1.20%	62.81	45.93	6.5%

Use the following bond quote for Problems 9 and 10:

Company	Symbol	Coupon	Maturity	Moody's/ S&P/Fitch Rating	High	Low	Last	Change	Yield%
Int'l Systems	ISU.GO	6.850%	May 2032	Baa2/BBB/BB−	102.817	91.865	93.231	1.650	7.482%

9. **Bond Quotations (LO1, CFA2)** What is the yield to maturity of the bond? What is the current yield of the bond?

10. **Bond Quotations (LO1, CFA2)** If you currently own 15 of the bonds, how much will you receive on the next coupon date?

Intermediate Questions

Use the following corn futures quotes for Problems 11–13:

Contract Month	Open	High	Low	Settle	Chg	Open Int
			Corn 5,000 bushels			
Mar	455.125	457.000	451.750	452.000	−2.750	597,913
May	467.000	468.000	463.000	463.250	−2.750	137,547
July	477.000	477.500	472.500	473.000	−2.000	153,164
Sep	475.000	475.500	471.750	472.250	−2.000	29,258

11. **Futures Quotations (LO3, CFA4)** How many of the March contracts are currently open? How many of these contracts should you sell if you wish to deliver 225,000 bushels of corn in March? If you actually make delivery, how much will you receive? Assume you locked in the settle price.

12. **Futures Quotations (LO3, CFA4)** Suppose you sell 25 of the May corn futures at the high price of the day. You close your position later when the price is 465.375. Ignoring commission, what is your dollar profit on this transaction?

13. **Using Futures Quotations (LO3, CFA4)** Suppose you buy 15 of the September corn futures contracts at the last price of the day. One month from now, the futures price of this contract is 462.125, and you close out your position. Calculate your dollar profit on this investment.

Use the following quotes for Target stock options for Problems 14–16:

Source: Bloomberg Finance L.P.

14. **Options Quotations (LO4, CFA4)** If you wanted to purchase the right to sell 2,000 shares of Target stock in March 2022 at a strike price of $210 per share, how much would this cost you?

15. **Options Quotations (LO4, CFA4)** Which put contract sells for the lowest price? Which one sells for the highest price? Explain why these respective options trade at such extreme prices.

16. **Using Options Quotations (LO4, CFA4)** In Problem 14, suppose Target stock sells for $200 per share immediately before your options' expiration. What is the rate of return on your investment? What is your rate of return if the stock sells for $220 per share (think about it)? Assume your holding period for this investment is exactly three months.

17. **Options (LO4, CFA4)** You've located the following option quote for Eric-Cartman, Inc. (ECI):

| ECI Stock Price | Strike | Exp. | Call | | Put | |
			Vol.	Last	Vol.	Last
20.25	10	Sep	29	5.50	—	—
20.25	15	Sep	333	7	69	1
20.25	25	Dec	5	2	—	—
20.25	30	Sep	76	2	188	8.75
20.25	35	Oct	89	.50	—	—

Two of the premiums shown can't possibly be correct. Which two? Why?

18. **Annualized Returns (LO2, LO4, CFA1)** Suppose you have $28,000 to invest. You're considering Miller-Moore Equine Enterprises (MMEE), which is currently selling for $40 per share. You also notice that a call option with a $40 strike price and six months to maturity is available. The premium is $4.00. MMEE pays no dividends. What is your annualized return from these two investments if, in six months, MMEE is selling for $48 per share? What about $36 per share?

19. **Annualized Returns (LO2, LO4, CFA1)** In Problem 18, suppose a dividend of $.80 per share is paid. Comment on how the returns would be affected.

20. **Option Returns (LO4, CFA4)** In Problem 18, suppose a put option with a $40 strike is also available with a premium of $2.80. Calculate your percentage return for the six-month holding period if the stock price declines to $36 per share.

Spreadsheet Problem

21. **Option Returns (LO4, CFA4)** You purchase 25 call option contracts with a strike price of $45, a premium of $2.77, and four months until expiration.

   a. If the stock price at expiration is $52, what is your dollar (and percent) profit? What if the stock price is $42?

   b. If you had bought a put contract, how do your answers change?

Bloomberg Exercises

1. Generate a listing of outstanding bonds for McDonald's (MCD). **(SRCH)**
2. Access the description for Nike (NKE) stock and determine the industry in which it is categorized. **(DES)**
3. Find a list of the most active securities for the current trading day. **(MOST)**
4. Screen for stocks that have the highest current dividend yield. **(EQS)**
5. Find a list of available options on Disney (DIS) stock. **(OMON)**

What's on the Web?

1. **Option Prices** You want to find the option prices for Conagra Brands (CAG). Go to finance. yahoo.com, get a stock quote, and follow the "Options" link. What are the option premium and strike price for the highest and lowest strike price options that are nearest to expiring? What are the option premium and strike price for the highest and lowest strike price options expiring next month?

2. **Futures Quotes** Go to www.cmegroup.com and find the contract specifications for corn futures. What is the size of the corn futures contract? On the website, find the settle price for the corn futures contract that will expire the soonest. If you go long 10 contracts, how much will the corn cost at the current price?

3. **LEAPS** Go to www.cboe.com, select the "Products" tab, then select "Stock Index Options (SPX-RUT-MSCI-FTSE)" and "S&P 500® Index Options," and then follow the "SPX LEAPS" link. What are LEAPS? What are the two types of LEAPS? What are the benefits of equity LEAPS? What are the benefits of index LEAPS?

4. **FLEX Options** Go to www.cboe.com, select the "Institutional" tab, and then follow the "Cboe FLEX Options" link. What is a FLEX option? When do FLEX options expire? What is the minimum size of a FLEX option?

PART 1

Mutual Funds, ETFs, and Other Fund Types

"Take calculated risks. That is quite different from being rash."

–General George S. Patton

Learning Objectives

You're probably going to be a mutual fund investor very soon, so you should definitely know the following:

1. The different types of mutual funds.

2. How mutual funds operate.

3. How to find information about mutual fund performance.

4. The workings of exchange-traded funds (ETFs) and hedge funds.

With only $2,000 to invest, you can easily own shares in Microsoft, GM, McDonald's, IBM, Coke, and many more stocks through a mutual fund. Or you can invest in a portfolio of government bonds or other investments. Many thousands of different mutual funds are available to investors. In fact, there are more mutual funds than there are different stocks traded on the Nasdaq and the New York Stock Exchange combined. There are funds for aggressive investors, conservative investors, short-term investors, and long-term investors. There are bond funds, stock funds, international funds, and you-name-it funds. Is there a right fund for you? This chapter will help you find out.

CFA™ Exam Topics in this Chapter:

1. Time value of money (L1, S1)
2. Introduction to corporate governance and other ESG considerations (L1, S9)
3. Introduction to alternative investments (L1, S16)
4. Guidance for standards I–VII (L1, S19)
5. Passive equity investing (L3, S7)
6. Hedge fund strategies (L3, S9)

Go to Connect for a guide that aligns your textbook with CFA readings.

As we discussed in an earlier chapter, if you do not wish to actively buy and sell individual securities on your own, you can invest in stocks, bonds, or other financial assets through a *mutual fund.* Mutual funds are a means of combining or pooling the funds of a large group of investors. The buy and sell decisions for the resulting pool are then made by a fund manager, who is compensated for the service provided.

Mutual funds have become so important that we devote this entire chapter to them and other types of funds. The number of funds and the different fund types available have grown tremendously in recent years. As of January 2022, mutual fund assets in the U.S. totaled about $27 trillion. An estimated 108 million Americans in 62 million households owned mutual funds, up from just 5 million households in 1980.

For mutual fund facts and figures, visit www.ici.org.

One of the reasons for the proliferation of mutual funds is that they have become, on a basic level, consumer products. They are created and marketed to the public in ways that are intended to promote buyer appeal. As every business student knows, product differentiation is a basic marketing tactic, and in recent years mutual funds have become increasingly adept at practicing this common marketing technique.

In fact, if you are not already a mutual fund investor, you very likely will be in the near future. The reason has to do with a fundamental change in the way businesses of all types provide retirement benefits for employees. It used to be that most large employers offered so-called defined benefit pensions. With such a plan, when you retire, your employer pays you a pension, typically based on years of service and salary. The key is that the pension benefit you receive is based on a predefined formula, hence the name.

Defined benefit plans have largely been replaced by "defined contribution" plans. Defined contribution plans are often called 401(k) plans after the section of the tax code that governs them. With a defined contribution plan, your employer will contribute money each pay period to a retirement account on your behalf, but you have to select where the funds go. With this arrangement, the benefit you ultimately receive depends entirely on how your investments do; your employer only makes contributions. Most commonly, you must choose from a group of mutual funds for your investments, so it is important that you understand the different types of mutual funds, as well as their risk and return characteristics.

4.1 Advantages and Drawbacks of Mutual Fund Investing

Related Bloomberg Functions
FUND Mutual Fund Home
MGMT Company Management

ADVANTAGES

Investing in mutual funds offers many advantages. Three of these are diversification, professional management, and the size of the initial investment.

DIVERSIFICATION When you invest in a mutual fund, you are investing in a portfolio, or basket, of securities. As you will learn in detail in later chapters, holding a diversified portfolio helps you reduce risk. How? A mutual fund might invest in hundreds (or thousands) of securities. If the value of one of them falls to zero, this decline will have a small impact on the mutual fund value. Diversification helps you reduce risk, but diversification does not eliminate risk. It is still possible for you to lose money when you invest in a mutual fund. Also note that not all mutual funds are diversified. For example, some intentionally specialize in specific industries or countries.

PROFESSIONAL MANAGEMENT Professional money managers make investment decisions for mutual funds. That is, the mutual fund manager makes the decision of when to add or remove particular securities from the mutual fund. This means that you, as the investor holding the mutual fund, do not have to make these crucial decisions.

MINIMUM INITIAL INVESTMENT Most mutual funds have a minimum initial purchase of $2,500, but some are as low as $1,000 or even $250 in some cases. After your initial purchase, subsequent purchases are sometimes as low as $50. Of course, these amounts vary from fund to fund.

DRAWBACKS

As with any type of investment, mutual funds have some drawbacks, including risk, costs, and taxes.

RISK Let us start with a point that should be obvious. The value of your mutual fund investment, unlike a bank deposit, could fall and be worth less than your initial investment. You should also realize that no government or private agency guarantees the value of a mutual fund.

A not-so-obvious point is that some investors think that there is a cost to diversification. Diversification greatly reduces the risk of loss from holding one (or a few) securities. However, by spreading your investments over many securities, you limit your chances for large returns if one of these securities increases dramatically in value. We happen to think that this is a cost worth bearing.

COSTS Investing in mutual funds entails fees and expenses that do not usually accrue when purchasing individual securities directly. We detail most of these costs later in the chapter.

TAXES When you invest in a mutual fund, you will pay federal income tax (and state and local taxes, if applicable) on:

- Distributions (dividends and capital gains) made by the mutual fund.
- Profits you make when you sell mutual fund shares.

There are some exceptions. A notable one is the receipt of distributions in tax-deferred retirement accounts such as individual retirement accounts (IRAs).

CHECK THIS

4.1a	What are some advantages of investing in mutual funds?
4.1b	What are some drawbacks of investing in mutual funds?

4.2 Investment Companies and Fund Types

Related Bloomberg Functions

IP   Investor Profile

FREP Fund Reporting

NAV   Premium/Discount Analysis

investment company
A business that specializes in pooling funds from individual investors and investing them.

At the most basic level, a company that pools funds obtained from individual investors and invests them is called an **investment company**. In other words, an investment company is a business that specializes in managing financial assets for individual investors. All mutual funds are investment companies, but not all investment companies are mutual funds.

In the sections that follow, we will be discussing various aspects of mutual funds and related entities. Figure 4.1 is a big-picture overview of some of the different types of funds and how they are classified. It will serve as a guide for the next several sections. We will define the various terms that appear as we go along.

OPEN-END VERSUS CLOSED-END FUNDS

open-end fund
An investment company that stands ready to buy and sell shares at any time.

As Figure 4.1 shows, there are two fundamental types of investment companies: *open-end funds* and *closed-end funds*. The difference is important. Whenever you invest in a mutual fund, you do so by buying shares in the fund. However, how shares are bought and sold depends on which type of fund you are considering.

With an **open-end fund**, the fund itself will sell new shares to anyone wishing to buy and will redeem (i.e., buy back) shares from anyone wishing to sell. When an investor wishes to buy open-end fund shares, the fund issues them and then invests the money received. When someone wishes to sell open-end fund shares, the fund sells some of its assets and uses the

FIGURE 4.1   Fund Types

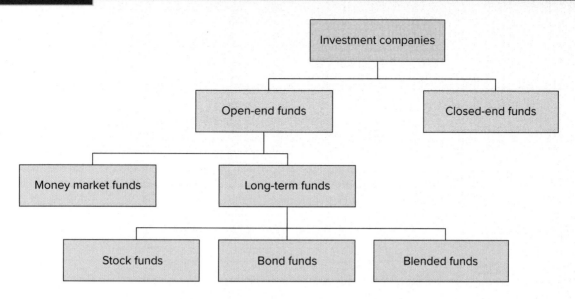

cash to redeem the shares. As a result, with an open-end fund, the number of shares outstanding fluctuates over time.

With a **closed-end fund**, the number of shares is fixed and never changes. If you want to buy shares, you must buy them from another investor. Similarly, if you wish to sell shares that you own, you must sell them to another investor.

Thus, the key difference between an open-end fund and a closed-end fund is that, with a closed-end fund, the fund itself does not buy or sell shares. As we will discuss shares in closed-end funds are listed on stock exchanges just like ordinary shares of stock, and those shares are bought and sold in the same way. Even so, open-end funds are much more popular among individual investors than closed-end funds.

The distinction between open-end funds and closed-end funds is not always as clear-cut as you might think. For example, some open-end funds "close their doors" to new investors. The typical reason for this decision is fund size. If the fund gets too large, exercising effective control over the fund's investments will be difficult for the fund managers. When an open-end fund no longer accepts new investors, existing investors generally can continue to add money to the fund. Of course, existing investors also can withdraw money from the fund.

Strictly speaking, the term "mutual fund" actually refers only to an open-end investment company. Thus, the phrase "closed-end fund" is a bit of an oxymoron, kind of like jumbo shrimp, and the phrase "open-end mutual fund" is a redundancy, an unnecessary repetition, or restatement. Nonetheless, particularly in recent years, the term "investment company" has all but disappeared from common use, and investment companies are now generically called mutual funds. We will stick with this common terminology to avoid confusion.

NET ASSET VALUE

A mutual fund's **net asset value** is an important consideration. Net asset value is calculated by taking the total value of the assets held by the fund less any liabilities and then dividing by the number of outstanding shares. For example, suppose a mutual fund has $105 million in assets and $5 million in liabilities based on current market values and a total of 5 million shares outstanding. Based on the value of net assets held by the fund, $100 million, each share has a value of $100 million/5 million = $20. This $20 is the fund's net asset value, often abbreviated as NAV.

With one important exception, the net asset value of a mutual fund will change essentially every day because the value of the assets held by the fund fluctuates. The one exception concerns money market mutual funds, which we discuss in a later section.

closed-end fund
An investment company with a fixed number of shares that are bought and sold only in the open stock market.

net asset value
The value of assets less liabilities held by a mutual fund, divided by the number of shares outstanding. Abbreviated NAV.

EXAMPLE 4.1 | Net Asset Value

As of mid-2022, the Fidelity Contrafund had over $110 billion in invested assets, making it one of the larger funds in the world. If the fund had 7.45 billion shares outstanding, what is its net asset value?

The net asset value is the asset value per share, or $110 billion/7.45 billion = $14.77.

As we noted, an open-end fund will generally redeem or buy back shares at any time. The price you will receive for shares you sell is the net asset value. Thus, in our example above, you could sell your shares back to the fund and receive $14.77 each. Because the fund stands ready to redeem shares at any time, shares in an open-end fund are always worth their net asset value.

In contrast, because the shares of closed-end funds are bought and sold in the stock markets, their share prices at any point in time may or may not be equal to their net asset values. We examine this issue in more detail in a later section.

CHECK THIS

4.2a What is an investment company?

4.2b What is the difference between an open-end fund and a closed-end fund?

Mutual Fund Operations

In this section, we discuss some essentials of mutual fund operations. We focus on how mutual funds are created, marketed, regulated, and taxed. Our discussion here deals primarily with open-end funds, but much of it applies to closed-end funds as well. Further details on closed-end funds are provided in a later section.

MUTUAL FUND ORGANIZATION AND CREATION

A mutual fund is a corporation. Like a corporation, a mutual fund is owned by its shareholders. The shareholders elect a board of directors; the board of directors is responsible for hiring a manager to oversee the fund's operations. Although mutual funds often belong to a larger "family" of funds, every fund is a separate company owned by its investors.

Most mutual funds are created by investment advisory firms, which are businesses that specialize in managing mutual funds. Investment advisory firms are also called *mutual fund companies.* Increasingly, such firms have additional operations such as discount brokerages and other financial services.

There are hundreds of investment advisory firms in the United States. One of the largest, and probably best known, is Vanguard, with more than 200 mutual funds in the United States, about $7.5 trillion in assets under management, and more than 30 million investors (all figures from 2022). American Funds, Fidelity Investments, and Invesco are some other well-known examples. Many brokerage firms, such as Merrill Lynch and Charles Schwab, also have large investment advisory operations.

Investment advisory firms create mutual funds because they wish to manage them to earn fees. A typical management fee might be .5 percent of the total assets in the fund per year. A fund with $200 million in assets would not be especially large, but it could nonetheless generate management fees of about $1 million per year. Thus, there is a significant economic incentive to create funds and attract investors to them.

For example, a company like Fidelity might one day decide that there is a demand for a fund that buys stock in companies that grow and process citrus fruits. Fidelity could form a mutual fund that specializes in such companies and call it something like the

Fidelity Lemon Fund.[1] A fund manager would be appointed, and shares in the fund would be offered to the public. As shares were sold, the money received would be invested. If the fund was a success, a large amount of money would be attracted and Fidelity would benefit from the fees it earned. If the fund was not a success, the board could vote to liquidate it and return shareholders' money or merge it with another fund.

As our hypothetical example illustrates, an investment advisory firm such as Fidelity can (and often will) create new funds from time to time. Through time, this process leads to a family of funds all managed by the same advisory firm. Each fund in the family will have its own fund manager, but the advisory firm will generally handle the record keeping, marketing, and much of the research that underlies the fund's investment decisions.

In principle, the directors of a mutual fund in a particular family, acting on behalf of the fund shareholders, could vote to fire the investment advisory firm and hire a different one. As a practical matter, this rarely, if ever, occurs. At least part of the reason is that the directors are originally appointed by the fund's founder, and they are routinely reelected. Unhappy shareholders generally "vote with their feet"—that is, they sell their shares and invest elsewhere.

All the major fund families have websites. For example, try www.vanguard.com.

TAXATION OF INVESTMENT COMPANIES

As long as an investment company meets certain rules set by the Internal Revenue Service, it is treated as a "regulated investment company" for tax purposes. This is important because a regulated investment company does not pay taxes on its investment income. Instead, the fund passes through all realized investment income to fund shareholders, who then pay taxes on these distributions as though they owned the securities directly. Essentially, the fund acts as a conduit, funneling gains and losses to fund owners.

To qualify as a regulated investment company, the fund must follow three basic rules: The first rule is that it must in fact be an investment company holding almost all of its assets as investments in stocks, bonds, and other securities. The second rule limits the fund to using no more than five percent of its assets when acquiring a particular security. This is a diversification rule. The third rule is that the fund must pass through all realized investment income to fund shareholders.

THE FUND PROSPECTUS AND ANNUAL REPORT

Mutual funds are required by law to produce a document known as a *prospectus*. The prospectus must be supplied to any investor wishing to purchase shares. Mutual funds must also provide an annual report to their shareholders. The annual report and the prospectus, which are sometimes combined, contain financial statements along with specific information concerning the fund's expenses, gains and losses, holdings, objectives, and management. We discuss many of these items in the next few sections.

MUTUAL FUND TRANSACTIONS

Fund companies have many thousands of individual investors. For closed-end funds, this fact is of little consequence because investor transactions take place in the secondary market. For an open-end fund, however, on any given day, the fund company could receive hundreds (or more) of buy and sell orders for each of its mutual funds.

To reduce the cost and complexity of dealing with so many transactions, fund companies accrue all transactions until the end of the day. That way, they can net out fund inflows and outflows and thereby reduce the number of transactions they have to make in the market on a given day. That is why orders that are entered by an investor at, say, 10:30 AM are still open at the end of the trading day. This clearing process is one reason why mutual funds are not attractive to active investors such as day traders. As we discuss in a later section, this is also one reason why exchange-traded funds (ETFs) have grown in popularity.

Another unique feature of mutual fund investing is how investors would specify the amount they wish to purchase. When you buy and sell stocks, you generally enter the number of shares you wish to purchase or sell, which in turn determines the amount you will pay

---

[1] Fidelity would probably come up with a better name.

or receive. With mutual funds, however, investors enter the dollar amount that they wish to purchase. Based on the NAV at the time, this in turn determines the number of shares the investor will receive. Because investor amounts and fund NAVs are not always nice round numbers, investors often end up holding fractional shares.

CHECK THIS

4.3a   How do mutual funds usually get started?

4.3b   How are mutual funds taxed?

4.3c   How does mutual fund trading differ from stock trading?

 # Mutual Fund Costs and Fees

Related Bloomberg Functions

REQ   Related Equities

All mutual funds have various expenses that are paid by the fund's shareholders. These expenses can vary considerably from fund to fund, and one of the most important considerations in evaluating a fund is its expense structure. All else the same, lower expenses are preferred, of course, but, as we discuss, matters are not quite that cut-and-dried.

TYPES OF EXPENSES AND FEES

Basically, there are four types of expenses or fees associated with buying and owning mutual fund shares:

1. Sales charges or "loads."
2. 12b-1 fees.
3. Management fees.
4. Trading costs.

We discuss each of these in turn.

front-end load
A sales charge levied on purchases of shares in some mutual funds.

SALES CHARGES Many mutual funds charge a fee whenever shares are purchased. These fees are generally called **front-end loads**. Funds that charge loads are called *load funds*. Funds that have no such charges are called *no-load funds*.

When you purchase shares in a load fund, you pay a price in excess of the net asset value, called the *offering price*. The difference between the offering price and the net asset value is the *load*. Shares in no-load funds are sold at net asset value.

Front-end loads can range as high as 8.5 percent, but 5 percent or so would be more typical. Some funds with front-end loads in the 2 percent to 3 percent range are described as *low-load funds*.

Front-end loads are expressed as a percentage of the offering price, not the net asset value. For example, suppose a load fund has an offering price of $100 and a net asset value of $98. The front-end load is $2, which, as a percentage of the $100 offering price, is $2/$100 = .02, or 2 percent. The way front-end loads are calculated understates the load slightly. In our example here, you are paying $100 for something worth only $98, so the load is really $2/$98 = .0204, or 2.04 percent.

EXAMPLE 4.2   Front-End Loads

On a particular day, the Common Sense Growth Fund had a net asset value of $13.91. The offering price was $15.20. Is this a load fund? What is the front-end load?

Because the offering price, which is the price you must pay to purchase shares, exceeds the net asset value, this is definitely a load fund. The load can be calculated by taking the difference between the offering price and the net asset value, $1.29, and dividing by the $15.20 offering price. The result is a hefty front-end load of 8.5 percent.

CDSC
A sales charge levied when investors redeem shares (also called a "back-end" load).

Some funds have "back-end" loads, which are charges levied on redemptions. These loads are often called *contingent deferred sales charges* and abbreviated **CDSC**. The CDSC usually declines through time. It might start out at 6 percent for shares held less than one year, then drop to 3 percent for shares held for two years, and disappear altogether on shares held for three or more years. Some funds offer "level" loads. That is, investors pay an added fee, typically 1 percent, every year they are in the fund.

Different loads are typically designated with letters. For example, front-end loads are often known as A-shares. Back-end loads are designated B-shares, and level loads are called C-shares. You might think that B-shares would be preferred to A-shares because the back-end load would decline over time. You must look at all the fees involved, however. With the back-end and level loads, the fund companies often increase other fees associated with the fund (such as the 12b-1 fee, discussed next). As it happens, B-shares appear to be a dying breed and have mostly disappeared as of 2022. So, two factors that influence your preference for share type are their relative expense structures and your anticipated holding period. But the best choice might be a fund that does not have any load.

12b-1 fees
Named for SEC Rule 12b-1, which allows funds to spend up to 1 percent of fund assets annually to cover distribution and shareholder service costs.

12B-1 FEES So-called **12b-1 fees** are named after the Securities and Exchange Commission (SEC) rule that permits them. Mutual funds are allowed to use a portion of the fund's assets to cover distribution and shareholder service costs. Funds that market directly to the public may use 12b-1 fees to pay for advertising and direct mailing costs. Funds that rely on brokers and other sales force personnel often use 12b-1 fees to provide compensation for their services. The total amount of these fees could be 0 percent to 1 percent of the fund's assets per year. For funds that charge a 12b-1 fee, .25 percent is most common.

Frequently, 12b-1 fees are used in conjunction with a CDSC. Such funds will often have no front-end load, but they effectively make it up through these other costs. Such funds may look like no-load funds, but they are really load funds in disguise. Mutual funds with no front-end or back-end loads and no or minimal 12b-1 fees are often called "pure" no-load funds to distinguish them from the "not-so-pure" funds that may have no loads but still charge hefty 12b-1 fees.

MANAGEMENT FEES As compensation for managing a fund, the fund company receives a management fee. The management fee is generally charged as a percentage of assets held. Management fees typically range from .25 percent to 1.5 percent of total fund assets every year. Sometimes, however, an incentive provision increases the fee if the fund outperforms some benchmark, like the S&P 500 index.

Rather than reporting all the fees separately, fund companies often report their *expense ratio*. The expense ratio is an all-inclusive fee percent that includes both 12b-1 fees and management fees, as well as any other administrative or operating costs.

Some mutual funds are passively managed, meaning they just replicate an index and thus don't really require a fund manager. Management fees can be quite low for such funds. For example, the current expense ratio for the Vanguard 500 Index Fund (VFINX) is .14 percent for its "investor" class. Because VFINX does not have a 12b-1 fee, the expense ratio primarily reflects its management fee. Actively managed funds generally have higher management fees. For example, the American Funds EuroPacific Growth Fund (AEPGX) has an expense ratio of .82 percent, and it also charges a load of 5.75 percent. Obviously, funds have quite different approaches in charging fees.

Fidelity created a stir in the industry in late 2018 when it announced two funds (and later expanded to four funds) with very low fees. How low? Zero!

turnover
A measure of how much trading a fund does, calculated as the lesser of total purchases or sales during a year divided by average daily assets.

TRADING COSTS Mutual funds have brokerage expenses from trading just like individuals do. As a result, mutual funds that do a lot of trading will have relatively high trading costs.

Trading costs can be difficult to get a handle on because they are not reported directly. However, in the prospectus, funds are required to report something known as **turnover**. A fund's turnover is a measure of how much trading a fund does. It is calculated as the lesser of a fund's total purchases or sales during a year, divided by average daily assets.[2]

---

[2] Purchases and sales for a fund are usually different because of purchases and redemptions of fund shares by shareholders. For example, if a fund is growing, purchases will exceed sales.

EXAMPLE 4.3   Turnover

Suppose a fund had average daily assets of $50 million during a particular year. It bought $80 million worth of stock and sold $70 million during the year. What is its turnover?

The lesser of purchases or sales is $70 million, and average daily assets are $50 million. Turnover is thus $70/$50 = 1.4 times.

A fund with a turnover of 1.0 has, in effect, sold off its entire portfolio and replaced it once during the year. Similarly, a turnover of .50 indicates that, loosely speaking, the fund replaced half of its holdings during the year. All else the same, a higher turnover indicates more frequent trading and higher trading costs. You can estimate the average holding period of fund investments using the inverse of the turnover. That is, divide the number one by turnover. For example, if a fund has a turnover of .50, we estimate the fund is holding its investments an average of 2 (= 1/.50) years. Because gains and losses are passed through to investors, these average holding periods can have implications for an investor's tax liability.

While increased trading obviously adds to the amount of commissions paid, it also has some related costs. For example, increased trading will result in gains (and potentially losses) being recognized in the fund. As these gains occur, capital gains will be passed through to the underlying investors. Potentially, these capital gains will increase taxes for the investors.

Another aspect of increased trading relates to the commissions themselves. Typically, an investment manager will have either an in-house or third-party broker who fulfills the trades. This relationship, however, is not always determined by who is the lowest-cost provider. In fact, some fund managers purposefully choose higher-cost providers. Why? The higher cost might provide added research or other materials that the fund manager considers beneficial in managing the fund. This added commission is referred to as *soft dollars*.

Other trading costs result from investor decisions. In particular, mutual funds might charge a *redemption fee* on shares held for less than some minimum time period (also called a "short-term trading fee"). When an investor decides to sell shares, the fund manager must come up with enough cash to buy them (assuming this fund is an open-end fund). If the fund manager does not have enough cash, actual stock shares might have to be sold, and the manager might not want to do that. The redemption fee is designed to encourage investors to remain invested in the mutual fund. Redemption fees are common in funds where the market in shares of the underlying investments is less liquid. We consider a redemption fee a type of trading cost and not a sales charge, or load. It is possible, therefore, for a "no-load" fund to still have a redemption fee.

EXPENSE REPORTING

Mutual funds are required to report expenses in a fairly standardized way in the prospectus. The exact format varies, but the information reported is generally the same. There are three parts to an expense statement. Figure 4.2 shows this information as it was reported for the Fidelity Low-Priced Stock Fund, which is a no-load fund.

The first part of the statement, "Annual operating expenses," includes the management and 12b-1 fees. This fund's management fee was .51 percent of assets. There was no 12b-1 fee. The other expenses include things like legal, accounting, and reporting costs along with director fees. At .14 percent of assets, these costs are not trivial. The sum of these three items is the fund's total operating expense expressed as a percentage of assets, .65 percent in this case. To put the fees in perspective, this fund has about $25.6 billion in assets, so operating costs were about $166.4 million, of which about $131 million was paid for fund management.

The third part of the expense report gives a hypothetical example showing the total expense you would incur over time per $10,000 invested. The example is strictly hypothetical, however, and is only a rough guide. As shown in Figure 4.2, your costs would amount to $810 after 10 years per $10,000 invested, assuming a return of 5 percent per year. This third part of the expense statement is not all that useful, really. What matters for this fund is that expenses appear to run about .65 percent per year, so that is what you pay.

One thing to watch out for is that funds may have 12b-1 fees but may choose not to incur any distribution or shareholder service costs. Similarly, the fund manager can choose to

FIGURE 4.2   Mutual Fund Expenses

Fidelity® Low-Priced Stock Fund

Prospectus
September 29, 2021

Prospectuses are available online. Visit www.fidelity.com to see some examples.

Annual Operating Expenses
(expenses that you pay each year as a % of the value of your investment)

Management fee (fluctuates based on the fund's performance relative to a securities market index)	0.51%
Distribution and/or Service (12b-1) fees	None
Other expenses	0.14%
Total annual operating expenses	0.65%

This **example** helps compare the cost of investing in the fund with the cost of investing in other funds.

Let's say, hypothetically, that the annual return for shares of the fund is 5% and that your shareholder fees and the annual operating expenses for shares of the fund are exactly as described in the fee table. This example illustrates the effect of fees and expenses, but is not meant to suggest actual or expected fees and expenses or returns, all of which may vary. For every $10,000 you invested, here's how much you would pay in total expenses if you sell all of your shares at the end of each time period indicated:

1 year	$ 66
3 years	$ 208
5 years	$ 362
10 years	$ 810

rebate some of the management fee in a particular year (especially if the fund has done poorly). These actions create a low expense figure for a given year, but this does not mean that expenses won't be higher in the future.

WHY PAY LOADS AND FEES?

Because pure no-load funds exist, you might wonder why anyone would buy load funds or funds with substantial CDSC or 12b-1 fees. Finding a good answer to this question is becoming increasingly difficult. At one time, there weren't many no-load funds, and those that existed weren't widely known. Today, there are many good no-load funds, and competition among funds is forcing many funds to lower or do away with loads and other fees.

Having said this, there are basically two reasons that you might want to consider a load fund or a fund with above-average fees. First, you may want a fund run by a particular manager. A good example of this is the Fidelity Magellan Fund. For many years, it was run by Peter Lynch, who is widely regarded as one of the most successful managers in the history of the business. The Magellan Fund was a load fund, leaving you no choice but to pay the load to obtain Lynch's expertise. As we discuss in a later chapter, however, the historical performance of managers might not be a good reason to select a fund.

MONEY MARKET DEPOSIT ACCOUNTS

Most banks offer what are called *money market deposit accounts,* or MMDAs, which are much like money market mutual funds. For example, both money market funds and money market deposit accounts generally have limited check-writing privileges.

There is a very important distinction between such a bank-offered money market account and a money market fund, however. A bank money market account is a bank deposit and offers FDIC protection, whereas a money market fund does not. A money market fund will generally offer SIPC protection, but this is not a perfect substitute. Confusingly, some banks offer both money market accounts and, through a separate, affiliated entity, money market funds.

CHECK THIS

4.5a   What is a money market mutual fund? What are the two types?

4.5b   How do money market mutual funds maintain a constant net asset value?

4.6 Long-Term Funds

Related Bloomberg Functions

HLDS   Holdings Analysis

FSTA   Fund Style Analysis

There are many different types of long-term funds. Historically, mutual funds were classified as stock, bond, or balanced funds. As part of the rapid growth in mutual funds, however, placing all funds into these three categories is becoming increasingly difficult. Also, providers of mutual fund information do not use the same classification schemes.

Mutual funds have different goals, and a fund's objective is the major determinant of the fund type. All mutual funds must state the fund's objective in the prospectus. For example, the Fidelity Contrafund states that it "seeks capital appreciation" and describes its strategy as doing the following:

> Investing in securities of companies whose value Fidelity Management Research believes is not fully recognized by the public. Investing in either "growth" stocks or "value" stocks or both. Normally investing primarily in common stocks.

Thus, this fund invests in different types of stocks with the goal of capital appreciation. This fund is clearly a stock fund, and it might further be classified as a "capital appreciation" fund or "aggressive growth" fund, depending on whose classification scheme is used.

Mutual fund objectives are an important consideration; unfortunately, the truth is they frequently are too vague to provide useful information. For example, a very common objective reads like this: "The Big Bucks Fund seeks capital appreciation, income, and capital preservation." Translation: The fund seeks to (1) increase the value of its shares, (2) generate income for its shareholders, and (3) not lose money. Well, don't we all! More to the point, funds with very similar-sounding objectives can have very different portfolios and, consequently, very different risks. As a result, it is a mistake to look only at a fund's stated objective: Actual portfolio holdings speak louder than prospectus promises.

One of the best mutual fund sites is www.morningstar.com.

STOCK FUNDS

Stock funds exist in great variety. We consider nine separate general types and some subtypes. We also consider some new varieties that don't fit in any category.

CAPITAL APPRECIATION VERSUS INCOME   The first four types of stock funds trade off capital appreciation and dividend income.

1. *Capital appreciation.* As in our example just above, these funds seek maximum capital appreciation. They generally invest in companies that have, in the opinion of the fund manager, the best prospects for share price appreciation without regard to dividends,

company size, or, for some funds, country. Often this means investing in unproven companies or companies perceived to be out of favor.

2. *Growth.* These funds also seek capital appreciation, but they tend to invest in larger, more established companies. Such funds may be somewhat less volatile as a result. Dividends are not an important consideration.

3. *Growth and income.* Capital appreciation is still the main goal, but at least part of the focus is on dividend-paying companies.

4. *Equity income.* These funds focus almost exclusively on stocks with relatively high dividend yields, thereby maximizing the current income of the portfolio.

Among these four fund types, the greater the emphasis on growth, the greater the risk, at least as a general matter. Again, however, these are only rough classifications. Equity income funds, for example, frequently invest heavily in public utility stocks; such stocks had heavy losses in the first part of the 1990s.

COMPANY SIZE–BASED FUNDS These next three fund types focus on companies in a particular size range.

1. *Small company.* As the name suggests, these funds focus on stocks in small companies, where "small" refers to the total market value of the stock. Such funds are often called "small-cap" funds, where "cap" is short for total market value or capitalization. In Chapter 1, we saw that small stocks have traditionally performed very well, at least over the long run, hence the demand for funds that specialize in such stocks. With small-company mutual funds, what constitutes small is variable, ranging from perhaps $10 million up to $1 billion or so in total market value, and some funds specialize in smaller companies than others. Since most small companies don't pay dividends, these funds necessarily emphasize capital appreciation.

2. *Mid-cap.* These funds usually specialize in stocks that are too small to be in the S&P 500 index but too large to be considered small-cap stocks. We now see funds that invest in both small- and mid-cap stocks; such funds are unavoidably called "smid-caps."

3. *Large company.* Large-capitalization, or "large-cap," funds invest in companies with large market values. Most large-cap firms have a market value in excess of $10 billion.

INTERNATIONAL FUNDS Research has shown that diversifying internationally can significantly improve the risk-return trade-off for investors. The number of international funds grew rapidly during the 1980s and early 1990s. However, that growth slowed sharply in the late 1990s. Their numbers shrank in the early 2000s, but they have increased since then. The two fund groups that invest outside the United States are:

1. *Global.* These funds have substantial international holdings but also maintain significant investments in U.S. stocks.

2. *International.* These funds are like global funds, except they focus on non-U.S. equities only.

Among international funds, some specialize in specific regions of the world, such as Europe, the Pacific Rim, or South America. Others specialize in individual countries. Today, there is at least one mutual fund specializing in essentially every country in the world that has a stock market, however small.

International funds that specialize in countries with small or recently established stock markets are often called *emerging markets funds.* Almost all single-country funds, and especially emerging markets funds, are not well diversified and have historically been extremely volatile. *Frontier market funds* specialize in the smallest, and potentially most risky, of emerging countries.

Many funds that are not classified as international funds may actually have substantial overseas investments, so this is one thing to watch out for. It is not unusual for a fund to call itself a "growth" fund and actually invest heavily outside the United States.

SECTOR FUNDS Sector funds specialize in specific sectors of the economy and often focus on particular industries or particular commodities. There are far too many different types to list here. There are funds that only buy software companies, and funds that only buy hardware companies. There are funds that specialize in natural gas producers, oil producers, and precious metals producers. In fact, essentially every major industry in the U.S. economy is covered by at least one fund.

One thing to notice about sector funds is that, like single-country funds, they are obviously not well diversified. Every year, many of the best-performing mutual funds (in terms of total return) are sector funds because whatever sector of the economy is hottest will generally have the largest stock price increases. Funds specializing in that sector will do well. In the same vein, and for the same reason, the worst-performing funds are also almost always some type of sector fund. When it comes to mutual funds, past performance is almost always an unreliable guide to future performance; nowhere is this more true than with sector funds.

OTHER FUND TYPES AND ISSUES Three other types of stock funds that don't fit easily into one of the above categories bear discussing: *index funds, social conscience funds,* and *tax-managed funds.*

To learn more about
social conscience
funds, visit
www.ussif.org
and
www.domini.com.

Is vice nice? Visit
usamutuals.com
to find out about the Vice Fund.

1. *Index funds.* Index funds hold the stocks that make up a particular index in the same relative proportions as the index. The most important index funds are S&P 500 funds, which are intended to track the performance of the S&P 500, the large-stock index we discussed in Chapter 1. By their nature, index funds are passively managed, meaning that the fund manager trades only as necessary to match the index. Such funds are appealing in part because they are generally characterized by low turnover and low operating expenses. Another reason index funds have grown rapidly is that there is considerable debate over whether mutual fund managers can consistently beat the averages. If they can't, the argument runs, why pay loads and management fees when it's cheaper to buy the averages by indexing? To put the importance of index funds into perspective, as of 2022, the largest stock mutual fund in the United States was the Vanguard Total Stock Market Fund, with over $1.2 trillion in assets. This fund, as the name suggests, tracks the entire U.S. stock market. In mid-2022, it had over 4,100 stocks in it. Today, most of the largest stock funds in the United States are index funds.

2. *Social conscience funds.* These funds invest only in companies whose products, policies, or politics are viewed as socially desirable according to some criteria. The specific social objectives range from environmental issues to personnel policies. Such funds are also called *social responsibility funds* or *ESG funds,* where "ESG" stands for environmental, social, and governance. Of course, consensus on what is socially undesirable or irresponsible is hard to find. In fact, there are so-called sin funds (and sector funds) that specialize in these very companies! See the nearby *Investment Updates* box for more information on ESG funds.

3. *Tax-managed funds.* Taxable mutual funds are generally managed without regard for the tax liabilities of fund owners. Fund managers focus on (and are frequently rewarded based on) total pretax returns. However, research has shown that some fairly simple strategies can greatly improve the aftertax returns to shareholders and that focusing just on pretax returns is not a good idea for taxable investors. Tax-managed funds try to hold down turnover to minimize realized capital gains, and they try to match realized gains with realized losses. Such strategies work particularly well for index funds. We predict that funds promoting such strategies will become increasingly common as investors become more aware of the tax consequences of fund ownership.

INVESTMENT UPDATES

SOCIALLY RESPONSIBLE INVESTING: DOING WELL BY DOING GOOD?

Particularly among millennials and gen Z-ers, there is a growing focus on so-called socially responsible investing (SRI) as younger investors seek out ways to do good while also doing well financially. In fact, the U.S. Forum for Sustainable and Responsible Investing reports that assets invested in socially focused funds have grown from about $1.4 trillion in 2012 to over $17.1 trillion at the beginning of 2021. This increase represents a growth rate of over 30 percent per year during this time.

With regard to these SRI funds, there are two key questions: First, what defines socially responsible investing? Second, how well do these funds perform?

In answer to the first question, there has been a relative lack of consistency. In modern times, the start of this investment approach can be traced back to the early 1970s, as investors looked for ways to boycott the Vietnam War. Today, broad definitions of SRI funds range from those that invest in renewable energy to those that focus on improving rights for women or other specific groups. As the interest level has grown, Morningstar has tried to create more

objective tools for evaluating the level of social consciousness that a mutual fund exhibits. Beginning in March 2016, Morningstar began reporting environmental, social, and governance (ESG) scores, which are based on ESG ranks of a fund's holdings (such rankings are widely available; see, as an example, www.msci.com/esg-ratings). Now investors can screen for funds using these metrics just like they would any other performance metric or fund characteristic.

With regard to performance, there is a strong debate on whether social investing helps or hurts returns. Proponents of SRI suggest that high-SRI companies should generate higher returns and/or lower risk, which should improve investment performance. In contrast, opponents suggest that limiting the universe of investments that can be included in a portfolio will result in suboptimal returns. The general consensus is that SRI funds probably earn about the same risk-adjusted return as other funds, at least before management and other fees. So, the good news is that investors with a passion for social causes might be able to invest without seeing a loss in returns.

TAXABLE AND MUNICIPAL BOND FUNDS

Most bond funds invest in domestic corporate and government securities, although some invest in foreign government and non-U.S. corporate bonds as well. As we will see, there are a relatively small number of bond fund types. Basically, five characteristics distinguish bond funds:

1. *Maturity range.* Different funds hold bonds of different maturities, ranging from quite short (2 years) to quite long (25–30 years).

2. *Credit quality.* Some bonds are much safer than others in terms of the possibility of default. U.S. government bonds have no default risk, while so-called high-yield, or "junk," bonds have significant default risk.

3. *Taxability.* Municipal bond funds buy only bonds that are free from federal income tax. Taxable funds buy only taxable issues.

4. *Type of bond.* Some funds specialize in particular types of fixed-income instruments such as mortgages.

5. *Country.* Most bond funds buy only domestic issues, but some buy foreign company and government issues.

SHORT-TERM AND INTERMEDIATE-TERM FUNDS As the names suggest, these two fund types focus on bonds in a specific maturity range. Short-term maturities are generally considered to be less than five years. Intermediate-term would be less than 7–10 years. There are both taxable and municipal bond funds with these maturity targets.

One thing to be careful of with these types of funds is that the credit quality of the issues can vary from fund to fund. One fund could hold very risky intermediate-term bonds, while another might hold only U.S. government issues with similar maturities.

GENERAL FUNDS For both taxable and municipal bonds, this fund category is kind of a catch-all. Funds in this category don't specialize in any particular way. Our warning above concerning varied credit quality applies here. Maturities can differ substantially as well.

HIGH-YIELD FUNDS High-yield, or "junk," municipal and taxable funds specialize in low-credit-quality issues. Such issues have higher promised yields because of their greater risks. As a result, high-yield bond funds can be quite volatile.

MORTGAGE FUNDS A number of funds specialize in so-called mortgage-backed securities such as GNMA (Government National Mortgage Association, referred to as "Ginnie Mae") issues. We discuss this important type of security in detail in a later chapter. There are no municipal mortgage-backed securities (yet), so these are all taxable bond funds.

WORLD FUNDS A relatively limited number of taxable funds invest worldwide. Some specialize in only government issues; others buy a variety of non-U.S. issues. These are all taxable funds.

INSURED FUNDS This is a type of municipal bond fund. Municipal bond issuers frequently purchase insurance that guarantees the bond's payments will be made. Such bonds have very little possibility of default, so some funds specialize in them.

SINGLE-STATE MUNICIPAL FUNDS Earlier we discussed how some money market funds specialize in issues from a single state. The same is true for some bond funds. Such funds are especially important in large states such as California and other high-tax states. Confusingly, this classification refers only to long-term funds. Short-term and intermediate single-state funds are classified with other maturity-based municipal funds.

STOCK AND BOND FUNDS

This last major fund group includes a variety of funds. The only common feature is that these funds don't invest exclusively in either stocks or bonds. For this reason, they are often called "blended" or "hybrid" funds. We discuss a few of the main types.

BALANCED FUNDS Balanced funds maintain a relatively fixed split between stocks and bonds. They emphasize relatively safe, high-quality investments. Such funds provide a kind of "one-stop" shopping for fund investors, particularly smaller investors, because they diversify into both stocks and bonds.

ASSET ALLOCATION FUNDS Two types of funds carry this label. The first is an extended version of a balanced fund. Such a fund holds relatively fixed proportional investments in stocks, bonds, money market instruments, and perhaps real estate or some other investment class. The target proportions may be updated or modified periodically.

The other type of asset allocation fund is often called a *flexible portfolio fund*. Here, the fund manager may hold up to 100 percent in stocks, bonds, or money market instruments, depending on the fund manager's views about the likely performance of these investments. These funds essentially try to time the market, guessing which general type of investment will do well (or least poorly) over the months ahead.

CONVERTIBLE FUNDS Some bonds are convertible, meaning they can be swapped for a fixed number of shares of stock at the option of the bondholder. Some mutual funds specialize in these bonds.

INCOME FUNDS An income fund emphasizes generating dividend and coupon income on its investments, so it would hold a variety of dividend-paying common stocks, as well as preferred stocks and bonds of various maturities.

TARGET DATE FUNDS Also known as life-cycle funds, the asset allocation chosen by target date funds is based on the anticipated retirement date of the investors holding the fund. For example, if a fund company offers a Target Date 2040 fund, the fund is for people planning to retire in or around the year 2040. Because of its long-term investment horizon, this fund will probably hold a portfolio that is heavily allocated to stocks—both domestic and international. As the years pass, the fund manager will increase the asset allocation to fixed income and decrease the equity holdings of the portfolio. This approach is like the equity allocation guideline we discuss elsewhere. Using this guideline, your percentage equity allocation might be something like 100 minus your age (or 120 if you are more aggressive). Target date funds appeal to investors who want a hands-off approach to investing. A potential downside to target date funds is that they sometimes add a layer of management fees—but these extra fees have become less common in recent years.

MUTUAL FUND OBJECTIVES: RECENT DEVELOPMENTS

As we mentioned earlier, a mutual fund's stated objective may not be all that informative. In recent years, there has been a trend toward classifying a mutual fund's objective based on its actual holdings. Figure 4.3 illustrates the classifications used by *The Wall Street Journal*.

FIGURE 4.3 — Mutual Fund Objectives

MUTUAL FUND OBJECTIVES

Investment objectives listed in quarterly closing quote tables are compiled by The Wall Street Journal, based on classifications by Lipper Inc. A fund's investment objective is based on language in the fund's prospectus, and may differ from the Lipper category listed on its snapshot page.

STOCK FUNDS

Emerging Markets (EM): Funds investing in emerging-market equity securities, where the "emerging market" is defined by a country's GNP per capita and other economic measures.

Equity income (EI): Funds seeking high current income and growth of income by investing in equities.

European Region (EU): Funds investing in markets or operations concentrated in the European region.

Global Stock (GL): Funds investing in securities traded outside of the U.S. and may own U.S. securities as well.

Gold Oriented (AU): Funds investing in gold mines, gold-mining finance houses, gold coins or bullion.

Health/Biotech (HB): Funds investing in companies related to health care, medicine and biotechnology.

International Stock (IL): (non-U.S.): Canadian; International; International Small Cap.

Latin American (LT): Funds investing in markets or operations concentrated in Latin American region.

Large-Cap Growth (LG): Funds investing in large companies with long-term earnings that are expected to grow significantly faster than the earnings of stocks in major indexes. Funds normally have above-average price-to-earnings ratios, price-to-book ratios and three-year earnings growth.

Large-Cap Core (LC): Funds investing in large companies, with wide latitude in the type of shares they buy. On average, the price-to-earnings ratios, price-to-book ratios, and three-year earnings growth are in line with those of the U.S. diversified large-cap funds' universe average.

Large-Cap (LV): Funds investing in large companies that are considered undervalued relative to major stock indexes based on price-to-earnings ratios, price-to-book ratios or other factors.

Midcap Growth (MG): Funds investing in midsize companies with long-term earnings that are expected to grow significantly faster than the earnings of stocks in major indexes. Funds normally have above-average price-to-earnings ratios, price-to-book ratios and three-year earnings growth.

Midcap Core (MC): Funds investing in midsize companies, with wide latitude in the type of shares they buy. On average, the price-to-earnings ratios, price-to-book ratios, and three-year earnings growth are in line with those of the U.S. diversified midcap funds' universe average.

Midcap Value (MV): Funds investing in midsize companies that are considered undervalued relative to major stock indexes based on price-to-earnings ratios, price-to-book ratios or other factors.

Multicap Growth (XG): Funds investing in companies of various sizes, with long-term earnings expected to grow significantly faster than the earnings of stocks in major indexes. Funds normally have above-average price-to-earnings ratios, price-to-book ratios, and three-year earnings growth.

Multicap Core (XC): Funds investing in companies of various sizes with average price-to-earnings ratios, price-to-book ratios and earnings growth.

Multicap Value (XV): Funds investing in companies of various size, normally those that are considered undervalued relative to major stock indexes based on price-to-earnings ratios, price-to-book ratios or other factors.

Natural Resources (NR): Funds investing in natural-resource stocks.

Pacific Region (PR): Funds that invest in China Region; Japan; Pacific Ex-Japan; Pacific Region.

Science & Technology (TK): Funds investing in science and technology stocks. Includes telecommunication funds.

Sector (SE): Funds investing in financial services; real estate; specialty & miscellaneous.

S&P 500 Index (SP): Funds that are passively managed and are designed to replicate the performance of the Standard & Poor's 500-stock Index on a reinvested basis.

Small-Cap Growth (SG): Funds investing in small companies with long-term earnings that are expected to grow significantly faster than the earnings of stocks in major indexes. Funds normally have above-average price-to-earnings ratios, price-to-book ratios, and three-year earnings growth.

Small-Cap Core (SC): Funds investing in small companies, with wide latitude in the type of shares they buy. On average, the price-to-earnings ratios, price-to-book ratios, and three-year earnings growth are in line with those of the U.S. diversified small-cap funds' universe average.

Small-Cap Value (SV): Funds investing in small companies that are considered undervalued relative to major stock indexes based on price-to-earnings ratios, price-to-book ratios or other factors.

Specialty Equity (SQ): Funds investing in all market-capitalization ranges, with no restrictions for any one range. May have strategies that are distinctly different from other diversified stock funds.

Utility (UT): Funds investing in utility stocks.

TAXABLE-BOND FUNDS

Short-Term Bond (SB): Ultra-short Obligation; Short Investment Grade Debt; Short-Intermediate Investment Grade Debt.

Short-Term U.S. (SU): Short U.S. Treasury; Short U.S. Government; Short-Intermediate U.S. Government debt.

Intermediate Bond (IB): Funds investing in investment-grade debt issues (rated in the top four grades) with dollar weighted average maturities of five to 10 years.

Intermediate U.S. (IG): Intermediate U.S. Government; Intermediate U.S. Treasury.

Long-Term Bond (AB): Funds investing in corporate- and government-debt issues in the top grades.

Long-Term U.S (LU): General U.S. Government; General U.S. Treasury; Target Maturity.

General U.S. Taxable (GT): Funds investing in general bonds.

High-Yield Taxable (HC): Funds aiming for high current yields from fixed-income securities and tend to invest in lower grade debt.

Mortgage (MT): Adjustable Rate Mortgage; GNMA; U.S. Mortgage.

World Bond (WB): Emerging Markets Debt; Global Income; International Income; Short World MultiMarket Income.

MUNICIPAL-DEBT FUNDS

Short-Term Muni (SM): California Short-Intermediate Muni Debt; Other States Short-Intermediate Muni Debt; Short-Intermediate Muni Debt; Short Muni Debt.

Intermediate Muni (IM): Intermediate-term Muni Debt including single states.

General Muni (GM): Funds investing in muni-debt issues in the top-four credit ratings.

Single-State Municipal (SS): Funds investing in debt of individual states.

High-Yield Municipal (HM): Funds investing in lower-rated muni debt.

Insured Muni (NM): California insured Muni Debt; Florida Insured Muni Debt; Insured Muni Debt; New York Insured Muni Debt.

STOCK & BOND FUNDS

Balanced (BL): Primary objective is to conserve principal, by maintaining a balanced portfolio of both stocks and bonds.

Stock/Bond Blend (MP): Multipurpose funds such as Balanced Target Maturity; Convertible Securities; Flexible Income; Flexible Portfolio; Global Flexible and Income funds, that invest in both stocks and bonds.

Source: *The Wall Street Journal*, 2019, Dow Jones & Company, Inc.

WORK THE WEB

As we have discussed in this chapter, there are thousands of mutual funds. So how do you pick one? One answer is to visit one of the many mutual fund sites on the web and use a fund selector. Here is an example of how they are used. We went to morningstar.com and clicked on "Fund Screener." Note that you might have to register for a free account to have access to this feature. There are many other fund selectors on the web.

For example, wsj.com offers one for subscribers to *The Wall Street Journal*.

Using the Morningstar fund screener, we indicated that we were interested in a domestic stock fund that invests in small-cap growth stocks with relatively low expenses. Out of a database of thousands of funds, here is what was returned:

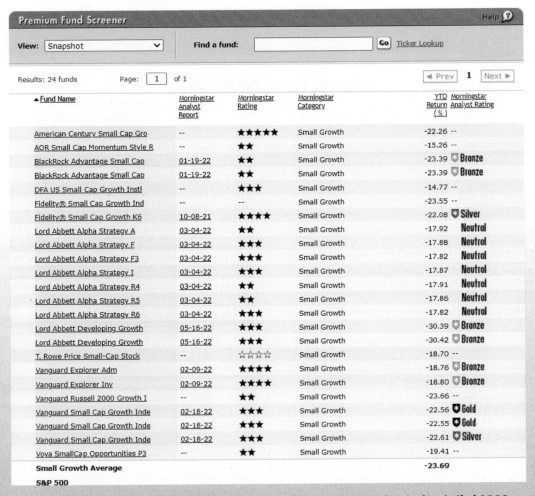

This search narrowed things down in a hurry! Now we have a list of 24 funds. Notice that the first half of 2022 was not a good time to be in small cap growth funds. Clicking on the name of a fund takes you to the Morningstar website, where you can learn more about the fund.

Source: Morningstar.

A key thing to notice in Figure 4.3 is that most general-purpose funds (as opposed to specialized types such as sector funds) are classified based on the market "cap" of the stocks they hold (small, midsize, or large) and also on whether the fund tends to invest in either "growth" or "value" stocks (or both). We will discuss growth versus value stocks in a later chapter; for now, it is enough to know that "growth" stocks are those considered more likely to grow rapidly. "Value" stocks are those that look to be relatively undervalued and thus may be attractive for that reason. Notice that, in this scheme, *all* stocks are growth, value, or a blend of the two, a classic example of the Lake Wobegon effect.[4]

The mutual fund "style" box is a common sight. A style box is a way of visually representing a fund's investment focus by placing the fund into one of nine boxes like this:

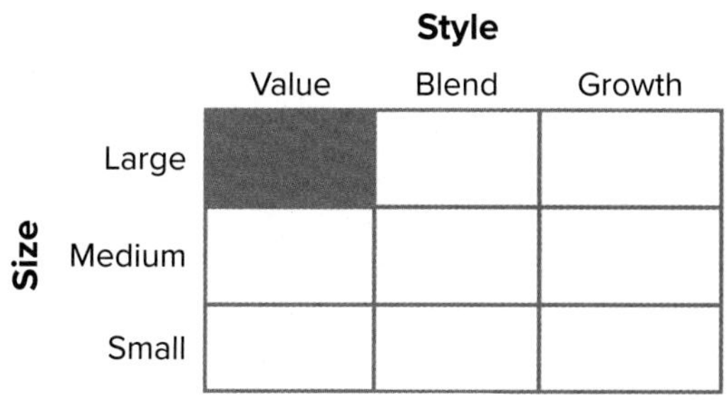

Style

	Value	Blend	Growth
Large	■		
Medium			
Small			

(Size labels on left axis)

As shown, this particular fund focuses on large-cap, value stocks.

These newer mutual fund objectives are also useful for screening mutual funds. As our nearby *Work the Web* box shows, many websites have mutual fund selectors that allow you to find funds with particular characteristics.

CHECK THIS

4.6a What are the three major types of long-term funds? Give several examples of each and describe their investment policies.

4.6b What do single-state municipal funds, single-country stock funds, and sector stock funds have in common?

4.6c What are the distinguishing characteristics of a bond fund?

4.7 Mutual Fund Performance

Related Bloomberg Functions

FSTA	Fund Style Analysis
FSRC	Fund Screening
FSCO	Fund Scoring
FPC	Fund Performance
PORT	Portfolio and Risk Analysis

We close our discussion of open-end mutual funds by looking at some of the performance information reported in the financial press. We then discuss the usefulness of such information for selecting mutual funds.

MUTUAL FUND PERFORMANCE INFORMATION

Mutual fund performance is very closely tracked by a number of organizations. Financial publications of all types periodically provide mutual fund data, and many provide lists of recommended funds. We primarily examine Bloomberg information in this section, but by no means is this source the only one.[5] In fact, we also look at information from sources such as Morningstar and the American Association of Individual Investors (AAII). The information we consider here applies only to open-end funds.

Figure 4.4 reproduces "Performance Benchmarks" from the AAII website (using data from Morningstar). This table compares the recent investment performance of major fund categories, ranked by recent performance. Figure 4.4 includes yardsticks for major fund categories including stocks, taxable bonds, and municipal bonds, among others.

---

[4] In case you aren't familiar with it, Lake Wobegon is a mythical little town in Minnesota where "all the women are strong, all the men are good-looking, and all the children are above average." The "Lake Wobegon effect" is a phrase used to describe the natural tendency of humans to overestimate their abilities and/or attributes.

[5] For more detailed information, publications from companies such as Morningstar, Weisenberger, and Value Line are often available in the library or online. Of course, a mutual fund's prospectus and annual report contain a great deal of information as well.

FIGURE 4.4 | Mutual Fund Performance Benchmarks

PERFORMANCE BENCHMARKS

Returns for the major indexes and the fund categories, updated monthly, to use for comparison.

Ranked by one-month return

Fund Categories   Global Asset Class   **Fund Groups**   Indexes

FUND GROUP	1-MONTH RETURN	YTD RETURN	3-YR ANNUAL RETURN	5-YR ANNUAL RETURN	10-YR ANNUAL RETURN	TOTAL RISK INDEX	YIELD	EXPENSE RATIO
Commodities	3.1%	28.0%	17.5%	10.6%	-0.2%	1.22	23.5%	1.19%
Alternative	-0.6%	0.1%	4.4%	3.5%	2.9%	0.53	1.9%	1.71%
Miscellaneous	-2.3%	-4.7%	-5.3%	-3.5%	-2.7%	1.97	0.1%	2.04%
Municipal Bond	-2.7%	-8.2%	0.2%	1.4%	2.0%	0.33	2.0%	0.78%
Taxable Bond	-2.8%	-7.0%	1.0%	1.6%	2.2%	0.42	2.8%	0.84%
Nontraditional Equity	-3.6%	-5.8%	6.1%	5.1%	5.4%	0.89	1.3%	1.79%
Allocation	-5.9%	-10.8%	6.3%	6.5%	6.7%	0.82	2.6%	0.90%
Sector Equity	-6.7%	-7.0%	9.6%	8.5%	8.6%	1.50	2.0%	1.25%
International Equity	-7.2%	-15.9%	4.8%	5.5%	5.9%	1.24	1.8%	1.13%
U.S. Equity	-8.6%	-14.4%	10.2%	10.6%	11.3%	1.38	0.6%	1.02%

Source: www.aaii.com, May 27, 2022.

Figure 4.5 is a small section of the mutual fund price quotations reported by Bloomberg. All of the funds listed in Figure 4.5 belong to the large family of funds managed by Fidelity Investments. The Blue Chip Value Fund can be found in the row numbered 20. As its name suggests, the Blue Chip Fund has a large-cap focus.[6]

The first piece of information given is the fund's symbol, FBCVX. Following the fund name is the latest net asset value, NAV, for the fund. Next we have the fund's total assets of $628 million. Finally, we have the total return on the fund year-to-date (1.148%) and previous one year return (7.816%).

HOW USEFUL ARE FUND PERFORMANCE RATINGS?

If you look at performance ratings, you might wonder why anyone would buy a fund in a category other than those with the highest returns. Well, the lessons learned in Chapter 1 suggest that these historical returns do not consider the riskiness of the various fund categories. For example, if the market has done well, the best-ranked funds may be the riskiest funds because the riskiest funds normally perform the best in a rising market. In a market downturn, however, these best-ranked funds are most likely to become the worst-ranked funds because the riskiest funds normally perform the worst in a falling market.

These problems with performance measures deal with the evaluation of historical performance. However, there is an even more fundamental criterion. Ultimately, we don't care about historical performance; we care about future performance. Whether historical performance is useful in predicting future performance is the subject of ongoing debate. One thing we can say, however, is that some of the poorest-performing funds are those with very high

---

[6] A blue-chip stock is a well-established, profitable, highly regarded company. A good example might be Microsoft. The term "blue chip" refers to the game of poker, in which chips are used for betting. Traditionally, the blue chips are the most valuable.

FIGURE 4.5 | Mutual Funds: Closing Quotes from Bloomberg

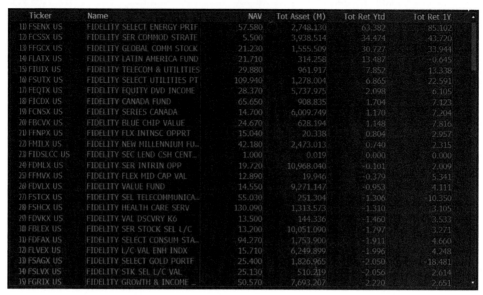

Ticker	Name	NAV	Tot Asset (M)	Tot Ret Ytd	Tot Ret 1Y
11) FSENX US	FIDELITY SELECT ENERGY PRTF	57.580	2,748.130	63.382	85.102
12) FCSSX US	FIDELITY SER COMMOD STRATE	5.500	3,938.514	34.474	43.720
13) FFGCX US	FIDELITY GLOBAL COMM STOCK	21.230	1,555.509	30.727	33.944
14) FLATX US	FIDELITY LATIN AMERICA FUND	21.710	314.258	13.487	-0.645
15) FIUIX US	FIDELITY TELECOM & UTILITIES	29.880	961.917	7.852	13.338
16) FSUTX US	FIDELITY SELECT UTILITIES PT	109.940	1,278.004	6.865	22.591
17) FEQTX US	FIDELITY EQUITY DVD INCOME	28.370	5,737.975	2.098	6.105
18) FICDX US	FIDELITY CANADA FUND	65.650	908.835	1.704	7.123
19) FCNSX US	FIDELITY SERIES CANADA	14.700	6,009.749	1.170	7.204
20) FBCVX US	FIDELITY BLUE CHIP VALUE	24.640	628.194	1.148	7.816
21) FFNPX US	FIDELITY FLX INTNSC OPPRT	15.040	20.338	0.804	2.957
22) FMILX US	FIDELITY NEW MILLENNIUM FU...	42.180	2,473.013	0.740	2.315
23) FIDSLCC US	FIDELITY SEC LEND CSH CENT...	1.000	0.019	0.000	0.000
24) FDMLX US	FIDELITY SER INTRIN OPP	19.720	10,968.040	-0.101	2.009
25) FFMVX US	FIDELITY FLEX MID CAP VAL	12.890	19.946	-0.379	5.341
26) FDVLX US	FIDELITY VALUE FUND	14.550	9,271.147	-0.953	4.111
27) FSTCX US	FIDELITY SEL TELECOMMUNICA...	55.030	251.304	-1.306	-10.350
28) FSHCX US	FIDELITY HEALTH CARE SERV	130.090	1,313.573	-1.310	3.105
29) FDVKX US	FIDELITY VAL DSCVRY K6	13.500	144.336	-1.460	3.533
30) FBLEX US	FIDELITY SER STOCK SEL L/C	13.200	10,051.090	-1.797	3.271
31) FDFAX US	FIDELITY SELECT CONSUM STA...	94.270	1,753.900	-1.911	4.660
32) FLVEX US	FIDELITY L/C VAL ENH INDX	15.710	6,249.899	-1.996	4.248
33) FSAGX US	FIDELITY SELECT GOLD PORTF	25.400	1,826.965	-2.050	-18.481
34) FSLVX US	FIDELITY STK SEL L/C VAL	25.130	510.219	-2.056	2.614
35) FGRIX US	FIDELITY GROWTH & INCOME ...	50.570	7,693.207	-2.220	2.651

Source: Bloomberg Finance L.P. Accessed May 30, 2022.

costs. These costs act as a constant drag on performance, and such funds tend to have persistently poorer returns than otherwise similar funds. In a later chapter, we present more detailed performance measurements.

CHECK THIS

4.7a Which mutual fund in Figure 4.5 had the best year-to-date return? The worst?

4.7b What are some of the problems with comparing historical performance numbers?

4.8 Exchange-Traded Funds

Related Bloomberg Functions
NI ETF Exchange-Traded Funds

For more on ETFs, visit
www.morningstar.com.

For more on ANTs,
visit the Nasdaq:
https://tinyurl.com/y4ewnepd

Relative to mutual funds, exchange-traded funds, or ETFs, are a relatively recent innovation. Although they have been around since 1993, they really began to grow in the late 1990s. As of 2022, almost 2,600 ETFs existed with total net assets of over $7 trillion in the U.S. Over 1,000 ETFs have been created since 2007, and more are in the works.

WHAT IS AN ETF? A typical ETF is a basket of stocks or bonds that investors can buy and sell on a stock exchange. The most common type are indexes, so an ETF provides a way to buy an entire index just like you would buy shares of stock in a single company. For example, the best-known ETF is the "Standard & Poor's Depositary Receipt," or SPDR (pronounced "spider"). This ETF (ticker symbol SPY) is just the S&P 500 index. Two other popular ETFs have catchy nicknames. The "Cubes" (QQQ) is the Nasdaq 100 Index. "Diamonds" (DIA) track the Dow Jones Industrial Average.

If you decide to invest in these three ETFs, you will have plenty of trading partners. In 2022, average daily trading volume for Diamonds was over 5 million shares. For the Cubes, traders exchange more than 80 million shares on a daily basis. Daily trading volume in SPDR, however, routinely tops 100 million shares (that's a lot of spiders).

More specialized ETFs exist. For example, suppose, for some reason, your portfolio has mostly shares in individual large-cap stocks. You can diversify by adding a small piece of many small-cap stocks with the Vanguard Small-Cap ETF (VB). Are you a maven of the Medici? If so, the Italy Index (EWI) might be for you. Have you played enough Monopoly to convince yourself that you are a real estate whiz? Then perhaps you will land on the Vanguard REIT ETF (VNQ). You just cannot decide whether to invest in Europe, Australasia, or the Far East? Why decide, when you can have a portfolio of over 20 country indexes by purchasing shares of the EAFE Index (EFA). Many other ETFs are available.

While stock ETFs are the most numerous type, there are a large number of them that buy bonds, particularly U.S. Treasuries. Other ETFs invest in gold, and in 2022, there are, of course, some that invest in Bitcoin and others that invest in cannabis (marijuana) stocks, with amusing tickers like YOLO and TOKE. In fact, many ETFs have ticker symbols that are intended to be catchy to attract attention, but many seem pretty silly to us.

While most ETFs are indexes of one kind or another, there has been significant growth in actively managed ETFs. These ETFs have been required to publish their holdings every day in the interest of transparency. But the SEC has recently allowed "active non-transparent" ETFs, often called ANTs. The idea is to allow fund managers to conceal their strategies in the hopes of generating superior performance. Such ETFs only disclose their holdings periodically. As of 2022, these represent a small, but rapidly growing, class.

ETF ADVANTAGES As we have seen, unlike mutual funds, ETFs can be bought and sold during the day like shares of stock. They can be sold short, and you can buy and sell options on them. ETFs generally have very low expenses—lower even than index funds—but you must pay a commission when you buy and sell shares. The nearby *Investment Updates* box details these differences.

Figure 4.6 shows a Bloomberg screen with the latest information on large ETFs (as of mid-2022), starting with SPY. Notice that the first half of 2022 was a tough time for the S&P 500. The "YTD Rtn" (year-to-date return) for SPY was −12.30 percent. It was even tougher for the Nasdaq 100; QQQ was down −22.21 percent!

FIGURE 4.6	**Exchange-Traded Funds from Bloomberg**

			1W	YTD	1Y
New Search	Aggregates				
Select Criteria	Flow (USD)		19.25B	165.35B	556.60B
Fund Type: All × Asset Class: Equity × Exchange: United States ×	Flow/Assets		+.37%	+3.16%	+10.63%

2096 matching funds, 2096 matching tickers

Key Metrics | Cost | Performance | Flow | Liquidity | Allocations | Regulatory Structure

Ticker		30D Vol	Class Assets (...	Fund Assets... ↓	YTD Rtn	YTD Class Flow (M USD)		12M Yld	Holdings	Primary	Cross
Median		21.26k	104.84	103.29	-10.74%	+1.13		+1.59%	82		
1) SPY	US	111.54M	380,525.44	380,525.44	-12.30%	-26,218.18		+1.40%	507	Y	N
2) IVV	US	7.05M	302,879.53	302,879.53	-12.24%	+7,355.28		+1.41%	507	Y	N
3) VTI	US	5.44M	267,717.00	267,717.00	-13.55%	+10,660.65		+1.43%	4138	Y	N
4) VOO	US	6.68M	261,969.42	261,969.42	-12.26%	+17,720.35		+1.45%	510	Y	N
5) QQQ	US	91.31M	166,849.89	166,849.89	-22.21%	-666.03		+0.56%	104	Y	N
6) VTV	US	3.30M	102,928.44	102,928.44	-0.73%	+11,368.83		+2.23%	354	Y	N
7) VEA	US	22.59M	102,389.73	102,389.73	-10.30%	+4,282.54		+3.21%	4182	Y	N
8) IEFA	US	19.69M	95,498.13	95,498.13	-11.20%	+3,239.73		+0.17%	3070	Y	N
9) VWO	US	21.16M	73,546.64	73,546.64	-12.73%	+3,234.74		+3.17%	4579	Y	N
10) VUG	US	1.56M	72,817.75	72,817.75	-23.57%	+3,971.07		+0.60%	269	Y	N
11) IEMG	US	20.97M	69,030.84	69,030.84	-13.35%	+2,945.46		+3.53%	2620	Y	N
12) IJR	US	5.40M	66,153.20	66,153.20	-10.44%	-1,296.68		+1.62%	608	Y	N
13) VIG	US	1.66M	64,357.11	64,357.11	-9.48%	+1,325.09		+1.84%	292	Y	N
14) IWF	US	2.75M	62,555.64	62,555.64	-21.52%	+91.16		+0.65%	503	Y	N
15) IJH	US	1.88M	62,540.31	62,540.31	-10.12%	+1,282.74		+1.39%	405	Y	N
16) IWD	US	3.19M	56,222.45	56,222.45	-3.79%	-1,435.60		+1.75%	855	Y	N

Fund List Actions | Advanced Screening | FSRC » | Build Scoring Model | FSCO » | Search for Investors | IS »

Source: Bloomberg Finance L.P. Accessed May 30, 2022.

INVESTMENT UPDATES

MUTUAL FUNDS VS. ETFs

Across a crowded room, index funds and exchange-traded funds (ETFs) are pretty good lookers. Both have low costs, diversification, and approval from Mom and Dad. But it's what's on the inside that counts.

So let's take a deeper look at these two worthy contenders for our investment dollars.

How They Work

Mutual Funds

Traditional, actively managed mutual funds usually begin with a load of cash and a fund management team. Investors send their C-notes to the fund, are issued shares, and the Porsche piloting team of investment managers figures out what to buy. Some of these stock pickers are very good at this. The other 80 percent of them, not so much.

Index mutual funds work similarly to traditional ones except that the managers ride the bus and eat sack lunches. (Actually, there are rarely human managers. Most index funds are computer-driven.) More importantly, index mutual funds put money into stocks that as a whole track a chosen benchmark. Because there's less "research" to pay for—like trips to California to visit that refinery's headquarters (and a little wine tasting . . . I mean, we're in the neighborhood . . .)—index mutual funds generally have lower expenses.

If the fund is popular or its salesmen make it so (yes, funds often have a sales force), it attracts gobs of money. The more money that comes in, the more shares must be created, and the more stocks investment managers (or Hal, the index robot) must go out and buy for the fund.

ETFs

ETFs work almost in reverse. They begin with an idea—tracking an index—and are born of stocks instead of money.

What does that mean? Major investing institutions like Fidelity Investments or the Vanguard Group already control billions of shares. To create an ETF, they simply peel a few million shares off the top of the pile, putting together a basket of stocks to represent the appropriate index. They deposit the shares with a holder and receive a number of creation units in return. (In effect they're trading stocks for creation units, or buying their way into the fund using equities instead of money.)

A creation unit is a large block, perhaps 50,000 shares, of the ETF. These creation units are then split up by the recipients into the individual shares that are traded on the market. More creation units (and more market shares) can be made if institutional investors deposit more shares into the underlying hopper. Similarly, the pool of outstanding ETF shares can be dried up if one of the fat cats swaps back creation units for underlying shares in the basket.

The variation in the fund structures means subtle but important differences at the end of the chain for individual investors.

The Business of Buying

That's the birds and the bees of ETFs and mutual funds. Now let's take 'em for a spin and see how they handle our money.

Timing Trades

With traditional mutual funds, you order your shares and buy them for the NAV (net asset value) at the end of the day. Period. (Unless you're a favored client engaged in illegal, after-hours trading, but that's another story. . . .)

Since ETFs trade like stocks, you can buy and sell them all day long. Though doing that, like any day trading, will likely land you in the gutter searching for loose change, it does have some advantage for the Foolish investor. Limit orders are one. You can tell your broker (or the computerized lackey) to purchase your ETF shares only at a certain price. If the market jumps 3 percent with excitement over some major world event—like a peace pact between Britney and Christina—you can use a limit order to make sure you don't pick up your shares at the top of the soon-to-be-crashing wave of misguided enthusiasm.

Shorting is another possibility. Yes, you black-turtleneck-wearing, world-weary pessimists out there can bet against the index with ETFs, and profit if and when it falls in value.

Making the Minimum

If you've ever visited our table of no-load index funds, you might have sprinted away from the computer shrieking. Under the column titled "account minimum," you see numbers as high as $50,000. That's the price of entry for some index mutual funds. Got less than that? Take your money elsewhere. Or rifle the couch cushions for loose change. Or open an IRA, where minimums are generally much lower.

ETFs, on the other hand, have no minimums. You can purchase as few shares as you like. Want one lonely little share? You can get it. Just make sure that you *choose your broker wisely* so that you don't shell out too much in commissions for your purchases.

Averaging, Joe?

A few years back, it might not have made sense to dollar cost-average into ETFs. If you were trying to buy a few hundred dollars' worth of a fund once a month, the brokerage fees would have taken a big bite of your nest egg and made a no-load index mutual fund a much better bet because mutual funds do not generally charge transaction fees.

But with the advent of ultra low-cost, or even no-cost brokerages, it's now cost-efficient to make small, frequent purchases of ETF shares. Of course, you'll have to put in the buy orders yourself, as you would to purchase a regular stock.

(continued)

Options for Experts

Though we don't recommend them for beginning Fools, ETFs offer advanced trading possibilities. Options are one. These complex little investments give you the right to "call" or "put" (buy or sell) shares of the ETF at some point in the future for some specific price. There's no calling and putting when it comes to mutual funds.

Dividend Differences

Most mutual fund investors take advantage of their fund's automatic dividend reinvestment feature. That saves them the hassle of deciding what to do with the cash that comes their way periodically. If and when the mutual fund pays out a cash dividend, your cut of the dough is automatically reinvested in shares, or partial shares, of the fund.

With dividend-paying ETFs, that moolah winds up in your brokerage account instead, just like the dividend on a regular stock. If you want to reinvest that cash, you have to make another purchase—and you'll get smacked with your usual trading fee unless your broker allows you to reinvest dividends for no extra cost. Many do.

Tax Tales

You hear a lot about tax advantages with ETFs. Treat it like barroom gossip: exciting to hear, but probably an exaggeration.

Inevitable, like death: Don't be fooled by vague talk of ETFs' freedom from Uncle Sam. You still need to pay taxes on your own capital gains—should you be fortunate enough to buy low and sell high—as well as any dividends you receive. Of course, if your funds are in an IRA or employer-sponsored retirement plan, your gains are tax-free until you start collecting. (If they're in a Foolish Roth IRA, everything is tax-free.)

Uncle Sam and the Fund: Beginning investors often do not realize that funds themselves incur capital gains taxes, the cost of which is borne (big shocker) by you, the fund holder, even if you don't sell a single share. The topic is complex and boring enough to spawn entire books, so here are the Cliffs Notes:

- In general, the structure of ETFs tends to avoid the kind of outright selling that would trigger undistributed capital gains and other IRS nightmares. To understand why, think back to the ETF structure. For every ETF seller, there's a buyer.

- On the other hand, if a flood of investors decide to dump a mutual fund, the fund may need to sell the underlying holdings in order to raise the cash to pay out, and that would bring Uncle Sam with hat in hand. ETFs may also have to drop a few schillings into the taxman's cap, for instance, when the underlying index is changed.

- Keep in mind that the traditional fund industry and the ETF industry disagree on the extent of the ETF's advantage. Of course, they're competing for your investment dollar, so you should expect squabbles. Still, according to published reports, the Barclays iShares S&P 500 ETF made capital gains distributions while the Vanguard 500 mutual fund did not.

There you have it: Funds v. ETFs. Which one are you going to put in your little black book? If you think ETFs could put a kick in your portfolio, read on for some investing strategies.

LEVERAGED ETFS The recent growth in the number of types of ETFs has been explosive. A particularly interesting, but potentially dangerous, ETF growth area is in leveraged ETFs. The fund managers of a leveraged ETF create a portfolio designed to provide a return that tracks the underlying index. But by also using derivative contracts, the managers can magnify, or leverage, the return on the underlying index.

Direxion Investments, for example, offers many of these leveraged funds. A couple of examples would be the Daily S&P 500 Bull 3X Shares (symbol SPXL) and the Daily S&P 500 Bear 3X Shares (symbol SPXS). The first fund (SPXL) is designed to provide three times the return of the S&P 500. In other words, if the S&P 500 return on a given day is 1 percent, the SPXL should provide a return of 3 percent. Terrific! What's the danger? Well, leverage works both ways. Losses are also magnified by a factor of 3. The second fund (SPXS) is designed to move in three times the direction *opposite* the return of the S&P 500 index. If the S&P 500 gains 1 percent, then SPXS should lose 3 percent. You can see that SPXS provides a way for investors to go (triple) short on the S&P 500.

These leveraged ETFs seem to track their underlying indexes on a short-term basis, that is, day by day. Over longer periods of time, however, their performance is probably not what you would expect. The Direxion Bull fund, for example, began trading in November 2008.

Over the next two years, the S&P 500 gained about 33 percent. Given its objective, the SPXL fund should have gained 99 percent, which is three times the return of the S&P 500. Over this two-year period, however, the long fund (SPXL) gained only 50 percent. How is this possible?

The answer does not lie with Direxion Investments. Instead, the answer depends on arithmetic versus geometric averages that we discuss elsewhere. Recall that geometric (or compounded) returns are lower than arithmetic returns, with volatility fueling the difference. In the Direxion example, the leveraged fund adds extra volatility to the series of S&P 500 index returns. As a result, returns from any leveraged funds will be less than expected.

As an example, consider a week during which the S&P 500 earns the following daily returns: 1, −2, 2, 1, and 3 percent, respectively. You can check that the arithmetic average is 1 percent, while the geometric average is just slightly less, .986 percent. This difference seems trivial. Consider the returns for a twice-leveraged fund. The arithmetic average is exactly double, 2 percent. The geometric average, however, is only $[(1.02)(.96)(1.04)(1.02)(1.06)]^{(1/5)} - 1 = .0194$, or 1.94 percent.

What is the lesson? The longer you hold these investments and/or the more volatile the underlying index, the less accurate a leveraged fund will be in tracking its stated objective. In fact, in periods of high volatility, it is possible for a leveraged ETF to have a negative return even when the index it is tracking is positive. With this in mind, should you use leveraged ETFs? Maybe, but you should not hold them for long.

EXCHANGE-TRADED NOTES In mid-2006, Barclays Bank introduced exchange-traded notes (ETNs). To investors, ETNs look very similar to ETFs. Like most ETFs, ETNs are designed to allow investors to achieve the same return as a particular index. Also like ETFs, investors can go long or short on an ETN.

Originally, ETNs were created to provide investors with exposure to the risks and returns of commodities, a traditionally volatile arena. However, ETNs now exist for currencies and for many other more exotic investments.

Unlike ETFs, which are baskets of stocks or bonds, ETNs are actually debt securities issued by the respective sponsors, typically banks like JPMorgan and Barclays. Essentially, these ETNs promise to pay investors the return on a commodity index, less a management fee. Deutsche Bank and Goldman Sachs also have ETNs.

There is an important difference between ETFs and ETNs. The holder of an ETF holds a fractional ownership of the shares placed in trust to create the ETF. ETNs, however, are unsecured debt securities. Holders of ETNs are relying on the solvency of the issuing bank when they hold ETNs. Therefore, ETN holders face the risk that the issuing bank might default on the promised payments of the ETN. In addition, ETNs are taxed differently, which complicates matters.

CHECK THIS

4.8a   How does an exchange-traded fund (ETF) differ from a mutual fund?

4.8b   What are some of the advantages of an ETC relative to a mutual fund? Disadvantage?

4.9 Closed-End Funds

Related Bloomberg Functions

NAV   Premium/Discount Analysis

MEMB   Member Weightings

As we described earlier, the major difference between a closed-end fund and an open-end fund is that closed-end funds don't buy and sell shares. Instead, there are a fixed number of shares in the fund, and these shares are bought and sold on the open market. Almost 500 closed-end funds have their shares traded on U.S. stock exchanges, which is far fewer than the roughly 7,500 long-term, open-end mutual funds available to investors.

FIGURE 4.7   Closed-End Fund Analysis from Bloomberg

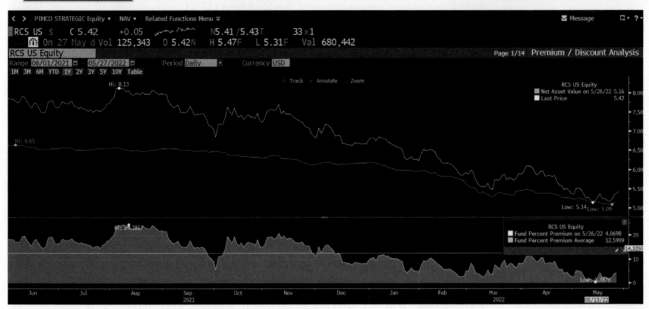

Source: Bloomberg Finance L.P. Accessed May 30, 2022.

Figure 4.7 shows some detailed information from Bloomberg on the PIMCO Strategic Income fund (ticker: RCS).[7] The top graph plots the fund's NAV (blue line) and share price (white line). The difference between the two is known as the closed-end fund (CEF) premium/discount. In this case, the share price is always above the NAV, so this fund sells at a premium relative to its NAV.

The bottom graph plots the CEF premium in greater detail. Notice how much it varies, reaching a high of over 24 percent compared to a low of almost zero. We will say more about this premium in a moment, but you should know that (1) essentially all closed-end funds have either premiums or discounts, (2) the premiums and discounts can be relatively large, and (3) the premiums and discounts fluctuate.

THE CLOSED-END FUND DISCOUNT MYSTERY

Wall Street has many unsolved puzzles, and one of the most famous and enduring has to do with prices of shares in closed-end funds. As we noted earlier, shares in closed-end funds trade in the marketplace. Furthermore, as the Aberdeen Global Income Fund shows, share prices can differ from net asset values. In fact, most closed-end funds sell at a discount or premium relative to their net asset values, and this difference is sometimes substantial.

For example, suppose a closed-end fund owns $100 million worth of stock. It has 10 million shares outstanding, so the NAV is clearly $10. It would not be at all unusual, however, for the share price to be only $9, indicating a 10 percent discount. What is puzzling about this discount is that you can apparently buy $10 worth of stock for only $9!

To make matters even more perplexing, as we have noted, the typical discount fluctuates over time. Sometimes, the discount is very wide; at other times, it almost disappears. Despite a great deal of research, the closed-end fund discount phenomenon remains largely unexplained.

Because of the discount available on closed-end funds, it is often argued that funds with the largest discounts are attractive investments. The problem with this argument is that it assumes that the discount will narrow or disappear. Unfortunately, this may or may not happen; the discount might get even wider.

Sometimes, certain closed-end funds sell at a premium, implying that investors are willing to pay more than the NAV for shares. This case is not quite as perplexing; after all, investors

---

[7] This closed-end fund is a bond fund, but the Bloomberg screen shows it as an equity security. Why? Recall that closed-end fund shares are listed on stock exchanges and trade like stocks, so the shares are treated like equities.

in load funds do the same thing. The reasons for paying loads that we discussed earlier might also apply to these cases. Premiums, however, can become quite exaggerated. For example, when well-known bond investor Bill Gross managed the PIMCO High Income Fund, investors were often willing to pay a premium of over 40 percent. He might have been a good manager, but a 40 percent premium strikes us as both excessive and risky.

We close our discussion with a cautionary note. When a closed-end fund is first created, its shares are offered for sale to the public. For example, a closed-end fund might raise $50 million by selling 5 million shares to the public at $10 per share (the original offer price is almost always $10), which is the fund's NAV.

But there is a catch. If you pay $10, then you are likely to discover two unpleasant facts quite soon. First, the fund promoter will be paid, say, 7 percent of the proceeds right off the top, or about $3.5 million (this will be disclosed in the prospectus). This fee will come out of the fund, leaving a total value of $46.5 million and an NAV of $9.30. Further, as we have seen, the shares could trade at a discount relative to NAV in the market, so you would lose another piece of your investment almost immediately. In short, newly offered closed-end funds are generally very poor investments.

CHECK THIS

4.9a	How does a closed-end fund differ from an open-end fund?
4.9b	What is the closed-end fund discount mystery?

4.10 Hedge Funds

Related Bloomberg Functions

HFS   Hedge Fund Search

hedge fund
An investment company not accessible by the general public.

Extensive information about hedge funds is available on the internet. Try CNBC at www.cnbc.com/hedge-funds.

Hedge funds are a special type of investment company. They are like mutual funds in that a fund manager invests a pool of money obtained from investors. Hedge funds are generally free to pursue almost any investment style they wish. In contrast, as we have discussed, mutual funds are relatively limited in their permitted investment strategies. For example, mutual funds are usually not allowed to do things like sell short or use large degrees of leverage.

When you hear the words "hedge fund," you might think that these funds are low-risk investments (as in the saying "hedging your bets"). Some hedge funds do try to exploit arbitrage opportunities on a low-risk basis. Most hedge funds, however, undertake aggressive, risk-enhancing strategies. We discuss hedge fund investment styles below. First, we compare hedge funds and mutual funds.

Hedge funds are generally not subject to the same disclosure requirements as mutual funds. Further, hedge funds are not required to maintain any particular degree of diversification or liquidity. Unlike mutual funds, for example, hedge funds do not redeem shares on demand. Instead, hedge funds typically designate particular liquidation dates, possibly only once every quarter. Even then, investors need to provide advance notice that they plan to withdraw funds. One reason for such a policy is that the fund might have investments in illiquid assets. As a result, quick redemptions by some investors could damage the investment value for the other investors.

Obviously, investing in hedge funds is not suitable for all investors. To prevent unsophisticated investors from getting involved, hedge funds generally accept only "qualified" (or accredited) investors. To be considered an accredited investor (as an individual), you must be an institution or an individual investor with a net worth of about $1 million or a recurring annual income of more than $200,000 (i.e., you need to be "rich").

HEDGE FUND REGULATION Traditionally, hedge funds were only lightly regulated. There have been attempts to change that in recent years, but hedge funds still face limited disclosure and other regulatory requirements. Very large funds are required to file certain information with the SEC, but much of that information is not available to the public. Smaller funds face very limited regulation.

HEDGE FUND FEES Hedge funds typically have a unique fee structure, where, in addition to a general management fee of 1 to 2 percent of fund assets, the manager is paid a performance fee. This special performance fee is often in the range of 20 to 40 percent of profits realized by the fund's investment strategy. The most common fee structure historically has been 2/20, which is a short way to say that the manager charges an annual 2 percent management fee and also retains 20 percent of the profit earned in the fund. This relatively pricey scheme has been in decline in recent years because investors have become more fee conscious.

One positive aspect of the performance fee is that the hedge fund manager has an incentive to earn as much profit as possible. There are, however, some potentially negative consequences, too. Suppose, for example, the performance bonus is awarded each year. What might the hedge fund manager do if the fund appeared to be certain to lose money this year? One possible strategy is for the manager to have the fund absorb as much loss as possible this year. As a result, the manager would be in a better position to make a large percentage profit for the fund next year (and a healthy performance fee for the manager).

Hedge fund investors are savvy. To prevent the fund from being manipulated by its managers, many fee structures also include constraints (or hurdles) for the manager to meet. A common example is called a *high-water mark*. When a hedge fund fee structure includes a high-water mark, the manager will receive performance fees only when the fund value is higher than its previous highest value. Suppose a manager makes the fund absorb large losses this year. Under this fee structure, the annual 2 percent management fee is still paid. To receive performance fees, however, the manager must bring the hedge fund value to a level above the previous high-water mark. Then, the manager receives a 20 percent bonus of these "new" profits.

Why do hedge fund investors willingly pay high fees? The obvious answer is that the returns earned are high enough to be considered reasonable. Significant debate exists about the issue of hedge fund fees. Many experts opine that when fees are subtracted from hedge fund returns, hedge fund investors are not much better off than investors holding a portfolio that represents the overall stock market.

If these experts are correct, why would anyone invest in a hedge fund instead of a market index fund? The answer relates to the principle of diversification. As you will read elsewhere in this book, investments that appear to have a high level of risk, or those that offer only a nominal return, might turn out to be good additions to a portfolio. In other words, these investments might bring significant diversification benefits to an investment portfolio.

HEDGE FUND STYLES Worldwide there are thousands of hedge funds, and the number keeps growing. Big hedge funds may require a minimum investment of $1 million or more. Small hedge funds may require a minimum investment of $50,000 or less. Whether large or small, each fund develops its own investment style or niche. For example, a hedge fund may focus on a particular sector, like technology, or a particular global region, like Asia or Eastern Europe.

Alternatively, a hedge fund may pursue a particular investment strategy. We highlight some common investment styles below. At the end of each investment style description, we identify its level of expected return volatility.

1. *Market neutral.* The goal of this strategy is to offset risk by holding opposite positions in pairs of securities. These hedge funds are also called *long-short funds.* The managers of these funds take long positions in a set of securities that the managers believe are underpriced. Then, the manager matches these investments with corresponding short positions in overpriced, or even fairly priced, securities. Properly constructed, the resulting portfolio makes money regardless of how the overall market performs, hence the name "market neutral." Be aware that some funds offset all long positions, whereas other funds match only a portion. *Expected volatility: Low.*

2. *Arbitrage.* The goal of the managers of these funds is to identify a mispricing in relationships between securities that theoretically should not exist. Arbitrage fund managers look at pricing relationships for securities offered by the same company, or for investments across time or countries. For example, a hedge fund manager might buy

convertible bonds of a company and short sell the common stock of the same company. *Expected volatility: Low.*

3. *Distressed securities.* The managers of these hedge funds concentrate their investments in securities that are being offered at deep discounts resulting from company-specific or sectorwide distress. For example, a manager of a distressed securities fund might buy securities of firms facing bankruptcy. *Expected volatility: Low to moderate.*

4. *Macro.* These hedge fund managers attempt to profit from changes in global economies brought about by governmental policies that affect interest rates, currencies, or commodity prices. Macro fund managers often use leverage and derivative securities to increase the impact of market moves. *Expected volatility: High.*

5. *Short selling.* In contrast to a long-short fund, a manager of a pure short hedge fund only short sells. In addition, these managers use leverage through the use of margin. *Expected volatility: High.*

6. *Market timing.* Managers of these hedge funds attempt to identify trends in particular sectors or overall global markets. These managers often take concentrated positions and generally use leverage to increase the fund's exposure to predicted movements. *Expected volatility: High.*

As you can see from this list, many approaches are possible, and each has its own risk level. What is the lesson? Even after you make your millions and become a qualified investor, you still have your work cut out trying to identify the best hedge fund for your portfolio. What if you just cannot decide? Well, you might want to use a "fund of funds," which we discuss in the next section.

Information about starting your own hedge fund is available at Turn Key Hedge Funds, www.turnkeyhedgefunds.com.

FUNDS OF FUNDS A significant portion of the money invested in hedge funds is funneled through "funds of funds." A fund of funds is just what the name suggests: an investment company that invests in hedge funds. For an investor, a fund of funds has the advantage that the fund manager may have expertise in selecting hedge funds; moreover, having multiple hedge funds offers a diversification benefit. However, a fund of funds charges fees of its own, on top of the already hefty hedge fund fees, so these advantages come with a cost.

STARTING YOUR OWN HEDGE FUND Ever dream about becoming an investment portfolio manager? You can by starting your own hedge fund. It may be easier than you think. A hedge fund is typically structured as a limited partnership in which the manager is a general partner and the investors are limited partners. Rather than stumble through the legal details, we advise that you will need the services of a lawyer familiar with investment companies, but the bottom line is that it's not difficult to do. Actually, the hardest part about setting up your own hedge fund is finding willing investors. Essentially, you need to find well-to-do individuals who have faith in your investment ideas. Make sure you know all the regulatory requirements that might be imposed on your hedge fund.

CHECK THIS

4.10a   What is a hedge fund? What are the important differences between a hedge fund and a mutual fund?

4.10b   What is a market-neutral investment strategy? Why is this strategy available to hedge funds but not to mutual funds?

4.11 Summary and Conclusions

We covered many aspects of mutual fund investing in this chapter. We saw that there are thousands of mutual funds and dozens of types. We summarize a few of the more important distinctions grouped by the chapter's important concepts.

1. **The different types of mutual funds.**

A. At the most basic level, a company that pools funds obtained from individual investors and invests them is called an investment company. In other words, an investment company is a business that specializes in managing financial assets for individual investors. All mutual funds are investment companies.

B. There are two fundamental types of investment companies: open-end funds and closed-end funds. When an investor wishes to buy open-end fund shares, the fund issues them and then invests the money received. In a closed-end fund, the number of shares is fixed and never changes. If you want to buy shares, you must buy them from another investor.

C. Mutual funds have different investment horizons. Money market mutual funds are an example of funds with a short-term investment horizon. Examples of funds with longer-term investment horizons include:

   • Stock funds that may specialize in things such as capital appreciation, income, company size, international stocks, sector-specific stocks, or indexes.
   • Bond funds that may specialize in short-term bonds, intermediate-term bonds, high-yield bonds, mortgages, or international bonds.
   • Stock and bond funds that may keep a fixed balance among stocks, bonds, and cash or try to outguess the market by moving portfolio weights among stocks, bonds, and cash balances.

2. **How mutual funds operate.**

A. Mutual funds are corporations. Like other corporations, a mutual fund is owned by its shareholders. The shareholders elect a board of directors; the board of directors is responsible for hiring a manager to oversee the fund's operations.

B. Although mutual funds often belong to a larger "family" of funds, every fund is a separate company owned by its shareholders. Most mutual funds are created by investment advisory firms, which are businesses that specialize in managing mutual funds. Investment advisory firms are also called mutual fund companies. Increasingly, such firms have additional operations such as discount brokerages and other financial services.

C. There are hundreds of investment advisory firms in the United States. The largest, and probably best known, is Vanguard. Many brokerage firms, such as Merrill Lynch and Charles Schwab, also have large investment advisory operations.

D. Investment advisory firms create mutual funds because they wish to manage them to earn fees. A typical management fee might be .5 percent of the total assets in the fund per year. A fund with $200 million in assets would not be especially large but could nonetheless generate management fees of about $1 million per year.

3. **How to find information about mutual fund performance.**

A. Funds have very different objectives and, as a result, very different risk and return potentials. Furthermore, funds with similar-sounding objectives can, in fact, be quite different. It is important to consider a fund's actual holdings and investment policies, not just read its stated objective.

B. Mutual fund information is widely available, but performance information should be used with caution. The best-performing funds are often those with the greatest risks or those that happened to be in the right investment at the right time.

4. **The workings of exchange-traded funds (ETFs), closed-end funds, and hedge funds.**

A. An ETF is commonly an index fund that seeks to achieve the same return as a particular market index. Therefore, when you buy an ETF, it is as if you are buying the basket of stocks that make up the index.

B. The most popular ETFs represent well-known indexes like the S&P 500, the Nasdaq 100, or the Dow Jones Industrial Average.

C. Many more specialized ETFs exist. For example, with an ETF, you can get a small piece of many small-cap stocks or mid-cap stocks, or you can invest in country-specific funds or in real estate.

D. Closed-end funds have a fixed number of shares, which are traded like shares of stock. We discussed a significant mystery: The prices of closed-end funds often differ from the value of the assets in the fund.

E. Hedge funds are also investment companies, but they face fewer regulations than a typical mutual fund, in part because they are only sold to qualified investors.

F. Hedge fund strategies vary from low risk (e.g., market neutral, arbitrage) to high risk (e.g., short selling, market timing). No matter the approach, though, the fee structure tends to be similar, with a set management fee as well as a share of profits.

GETTING DOWN TO BUSINESS

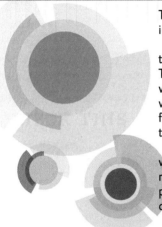

For the latest information on the real world of investments, visit us at jmdinvestments.blogspot.com.

This chapter covered the essentials of mutual funds. How should you, as an investor or investment manager, put this information to work?

The first thing to do is to start looking at mutual fund prospectuses. These are written to be accessible to novice investors (or, at least, they are supposed to be written that way). The best way to begin exploring is to visit websites. Almost any large mutual fund company will have extensive online information available. It is important to look at different funds within a given family and also to look across families. Compare growth funds to growth funds, for example. This adventure will give you some of the real-life background you need to select the types of funds most suitable for you or someone else.

Once you have examined prospectuses on different funds, it's time to invest. Beginning with your simulated account, pick a few funds, invest, and observe the outcomes. Open-end mutual funds are probably the place most of you will begin investing real dollars. An initial purchase can be made with a relatively small amount, perhaps $250, and subsequent purchases can be made in amounts of $50 or less.

Most important of all, the majority of employers now provide employees with retirement plans. The way these work is that, typically, your employer will make a contribution to a mutual fund you select (often from a fairly limited set). Your employer may even match, or more than match, a contribution you make. Such plans may be the only retirement benefit offered, but they can be an extraordinary opportunity for those who take full advantage of them by getting the largest possible match and then investing in a suitable fund. It's an important choice, so the more knowledge you have regarding mutual funds, the better your outcome is likely to be.

Key Terms

12b-1 fees 105
CDSC 105
closed-end fund 101
front-end load 104
hedge fund 125

investment company 100
money market mutual fund 108
net asset value 101
open-end fund 100
turnover 105

Related Bloomberg Functions

FUND   Mutual Fund Home, 4.1

MGMT   Company Management, 4.1

IP   Investor Profile, 4.2

Chapter Review Problems and Self-Test

1. **Front-End Loads (LO2, CFA3)**   The Madura HiGro Fund has a net asset value of $50 per share. It charges a 3 percent load. How much will you pay for 100 shares?

2. **Turnover (LO2, CFA3)**   The Starks Income Fund's average daily total assets were $100 million for the year just completed. Its stock purchases for the year were $20 million, while its sales were $12.5 million. What was its turnover?

Answers to Self-Test Problems

1. You will pay 100 times the offering price. Because the load is computed as a percentage of the offering price, we can compute the offering price as follows:

$$\text{Net asset value} = (1 - \text{Front-end load}) \times \text{Offering price}$$

   In other words, the NAV is 97 percent of the offering price. Because the NAV is $50, the offering price is $50/.97 = $51.55. You will pay $5,155 in all, of which $155 is a load.

2. Turnover is the lesser of purchases or sales divided by average daily assets. In this case, sales are smaller at $12.5, so turnover is $12.5/$100 = .125 times.

Test Your Investment Quotient

1. **Investment Companies (LO2, CFA3)**   Which of the following statements typically does not characterize the structure of an investment company?

   a. An investment company adopts a corporate form of organization.
   b. An investment company invests a pool of funds belonging to many investors in a portfolio of individual investments.
   c. An investment company receives an annual management fee ranging from 3 to 5 percent of the total value of the fund.
   d. The board of directors of an investment company hires a separate investment management company to manage the portfolio of securities and handle other administrative duties.

2. **Expense Statement (LO3)**   Which of the following is *not* part of the expense statement?

   a. Shareholder transaction expenses
   b. Shareholder demographic profile
   c. Annual operating expenses
   d. A hypothetical example of expenses

3. **Mutual Fund Investing (LO2, CFA3)** Which of the following is the least likely advantage of mutual fund investing?

   a. Diversification
   b. Professional management
   c. Convenience
   d. Mutual fund returns are normally higher than market average returns

4. **Open-End Funds (LO2, CFA3)** An open-end mutual fund is owned by which of the following?

   a. An investment company
   b. An investment advisory firm
   c. A "family of funds" mutual fund company
   d. Its shareholders

5. **Closed-End Funds (LO2, CFA3)** Which of the following is most true of a closed-end investment company?

   a. The fund's share price is usually greater than net asset value.
   b. The fund's share price is set equal to net asset value.
   c. Fund shares outstanding vary with purchases and redemptions by shareholders.
   d. Fund shares outstanding are fixed at the issue date.

6. **Closed-End Funds (LO2, CFA3)** A closed-end fund is owned by which of the following?

   a. An investment company
   b. An investment advisory firm
   c. A "family of funds" mutual fund company
   d. Its shareholders

7. **Exchange-Traded Funds (LO4, CFA5)** Which of the following statements regarding ETFs is false?

   a. ETFs are funds that can be traded on a stock market.
   b. ETF investors own shares of the underlying fund sponsor.
   c. ETF shares can be sold short.
   d. ETF shares can be bought on margin.

8. **Closed-End Funds (LO1, CFA3)** Closed-end funds and ETFs have which of the following characteristics in common?

   a. Shares of both closed-end funds and ETFs trade in the secondary market.
   b. Both closed-end funds and ETFs stand ready to redeem shares.
   c. The structures of closed-end funds and ETFs prevent shares from trading at a significant premium or discount to NAV.
   d. Neither ETF nor closed-end fund managers receive a management fee.

9. **Mutual Fund Investing (LO1, CFA3)** Growth, value, large-cap, and small-cap investing are all examples of:

   a. Style investment strategies.
   b. Sector investment strategies.
   c. Index investment strategies.
   d. Lifestyle investment strategies.

10. **Mutual Fund Investing (LO1, CFA6)** One of the main advantages to investing in a fund of funds (FOF) is that FOFs provide:

    a. Improved diversification of assets.
    b. Higher expected returns.
    c. Lower management fees.
    d. Higher volatility of returns.

11. **Fund Types (LO1, CFA5)** Which mutual fund type will most likely incur the smallest tax liability for its investors?

    a. Index fund
    b. Municipal bond fund
    c. Income fund
    d. Growth fund

12. **Fund Types (LO1)** Which mutual fund type will most likely incur the greatest overall risk levels for its investors?
   a. Large-cap index fund
   b. Insured municipal bond fund
   c. Money market mutual fund
   d. Small-cap growth fund

13. **Mutual Fund Fees (LO2, CFA3)** Which of the following mutual fund fees is assessed on an annual basis?
   a. 12b-1 fees
   b. Front-end load
   c. Back-end load
   d. Contingent deferred sales charge (CDSC)

14. **Mutual Fund Fees (LO2, CFA3)** Which of the following mutual fund fees will most likely be the biggest expense for a long-term fund investor?
   a. 12b-1 fees
   b. Front-end load
   c. Back-end load
   d. Contingent deferred sales charge (CDSC)

15. **Mutual Fund Fees (LO2, CFA3)** Which of the following mutual fund fees and expenses is the most difficult for investors to assess?
   a. Sales charges or "loads"
   b. 12b-1 fees
   c. Management fees
   d. Trading costs

Concept Questions

1. **Fund Ownership (LO2)** Who actually owns a mutual fund? Who runs it?

2. **Loads (LO2, CFA5)** Given that no-load funds are widely available, why would a rational investor pay a front-end load? More generally, why don't fund investors always seek out funds with the lowest loads, management fees, and other fees?

3. **Money Market Funds (LO2, CFA1)** Is it true that the NAV of a money market mutual fund never changes? How is this possible?

4. **Money Market Deposit Accounts (LO2, CFA1)** What is the difference between a money market deposit account and a money market mutual fund? Which is riskier?

5. **ETFs versus Index Mutual Funds (LO4, CFA5)** ETFs and index mutual funds hold similar underlying assets. Why might an investor prefer one over the other?

6. **Open-End versus Closed-End Funds (LO2, CFA3)** An open-end mutual fund typically keeps a percentage, often around 5 percent, of its assets in cash or liquid money market assets. How does this affect the fund's return in a year in which the market increases in value? How about during a bad year? Closed-end funds do not typically hold cash. What is it about the structure of open-end and closed-end funds that would influence this difference?

7. **12b-1 Fees (LO2, CFA3)** What are 12b-1 fees? What expenses are 12b-1 fees intended to cover? Many closed-end mutual funds charge a 12b-1 fee. Does this make sense to you? Why or why not?

8. **Open-End versus Closed-End Funds (LO2, CFA3)** If you were concerned about the liquidity of mutual fund shares that you held, would you rather hold shares in a closed-end fund or an open-end fund? Why?

9. **Mutual Fund Performance (LO3, CFA5)** When you look at long-run performance for mutual funds, you typically don't see many poor performers. Why do you suppose they all tend to look so good? *Hint:* Think about the hit TV show *Survivor.*

10. **Hedge Fund Fees (LO4, CFA6)** How does a high-water mark constrain hedge fund managers from earning excess performance management fees?

Questions and Problems

Core Questions

1. **Net Asset Value (LO2, CFA3)** The World Income Appreciation Fund has current assets with a market value of $8.5 billion and has 410 million shares outstanding. What is the net asset value (NAV) for this mutual fund?

2. **Front-End Loads (LO2)** Suppose the mutual fund in Problem 1 has a current market price quotation of $21.89. Is this a load fund? If so, calculate the front-end load.

3. **Calculating NAV (LO2, CFA3)** The Emerging Growth and Equity Fund is a "low-load" fund. The current offer price quotation for this mutual fund is $15.95, and the front-end load is 2.0 percent. What is the NAV? If there are 19.2 million shares outstanding, what is the current market value of assets owned by the fund?

4. **Money Market Funds (LO2, CFA1)** The Aqua Liquid Assets Money Market Mutual Fund has a NAV of $1 per share. During the year, the assets held by this fund appreciated by 1.7 percent. If you had invested $25,000 in this fund at the start of the year, how many shares would you own at the end of the year? What will the NAV of this fund be at the end of the year? Why?

5. **NAV (LO2, CFA3)** An open-end mutual fund has the following stocks:

Stock	Shares	Stock Price
A	6,000	$98
B	33,000	19
C	4,600	89
D	82,500	12

If there are 50,000 shares of the mutual fund, what is the NAV?

6. **NAV (LO2, CFA3)** Suppose the fund in Problem 5 has liabilities of $110,000. What is the NAV of the fund now?

7. **Front-End Load (LO2)** In Problem 6, assume the fund is sold with a 6.25 percent front-end load. What is the offering price of the fund?

8. **Turnover (LO2, CFA4)** A mutual fund sold $36 million of assets during the year and purchased $32 million in assets. If the average daily assets of the fund were $96 million, what was the fund turnover?

9. **Closed-End Funds (LO2, CFA3)** A closed-end fund has total assets of $240 million and liabilities of $110,000. Currently, 11 million shares are outstanding. What is the NAV of the fund? If the shares currently sell for $19.25, what is the premium or discount on the fund?

10. **Mutual Fund Returns (LO2, CFA1)** You invested $10,000 in a mutual fund at the beginning of the year when the NAV was $32.24. At the end of the year, the fund paid $.24 in short-term distributions and $.41 in long-term distributions. If the NAV of the fund at the end of the year was $35.23, what was your return for the year?

Intermediate Questions

11. **Calculating Turnover (LO2, CFA4)** A sector fund specializing in commercial bank stocks had average daily assets of $3.4 billion during the year. This fund sold $1.25 billion worth of stock during the year, and its turnover ratio was .42. How much stock did this mutual fund purchase during the year? What other costs are associated with higher turnover?

12. **Calculating Fees (LO2, CFA1)** In Problem 11, suppose the annual operating expense ratio for the mutual fund is .75 percent and the management fee is .45 percent. How much money did the fund's management earn during the year? If the fund doesn't charge any 12b-1 fees, how much were miscellaneous and administrative expenses during the year?

13. **Calculating Fees (LO2, CFA1)** Suppose you purchased 2,000 shares in the New Pacific Growth Fund on January 2, 2022, at an offering price of $47.10 per share. The front-end load for this fund is 5 percent, and the back-end load for redemptions within one year is 2 percent. The underlying assets in this mutual fund appreciate (including reinvested dividends) by 8 percent during 2022, and you sell back your shares at the end of the year. If the operating expense ratio for the New Pacific Growth Fund is 1.95 percent, what is your total return from this investment? (*Assume that the operating expense is netted against the fund's return.*) What do you conclude about the impact of fees in evaluating mutual fund performance?

Chapter 4 ● Mutual Funds, ETFs, and Other Fund Types 133

14. **Hedge Funds (LO4, CFA6)** You invested $1,250,000 with a market-neutral hedge fund manager. The fee structure is 2/20, and the fund has a high-water mark provision. Suppose the first year the fund manager loses 10 percent and the second year she gains 20 percent. What are the management and performance fees paid each year? Assume management fees are paid at the beginning of each year and performance fees are taken at the end of each year.

15. **ETFs versus Mutual Funds (LO4, CFA5)** Suppose you just inherited $25,000 from your Aunt Louise. You have decided to invest in an S&P index fund, but you haven't decided yet whether to use an ETF or a mutual fund. Suppose the ETF has an annual expense ratio of .09 percent, while the mutual fund charges .21 percent. The mutual fund has no load, but the ETF purchase would carry a $25 commission. Assuming this is a long-term holding and you are not concerned about being able to margin or short sell, which is the better approach?

16. **Expenses and Returns (LO2, CFA1)** The Bruin Stock Fund sells Class A shares that have a front-end load of 5.75 percent, a 12b-1 fee of .23 percent, and other fees of .73 percent. There are also Class B shares with a 5 percent CDSC that declines 1 percent per year, a 12b-1 fee of 1.00 percent, and other fees of .73 percent. If the portfolio return is 10 percent per year and you plan to sell after the third year, should you invest in Class A or Class B shares? What if your investment horizon is 20 years?

17. **Expenses and Returns (LO2, CFA1)** You are going to invest in a stock mutual fund with a 6 percent front-end load and a 1.75 percent expense ratio. You also can invest in a money market mutual fund with a 3.30 percent return and an expense ratio of .10 percent. If you plan to keep your investment for two years, what annual return must the stock mutual fund earn to exceed an investment in the money market fund? What if your investment horizon is 10 years?

18. **Taxes and MMMFs (LO2, CFA1)** Suppose you're evaluating three alternative MMMF investments. The first fund buys a diversified portfolio of municipal securities from across the country and yields 3.2 percent. The second fund buys only taxable, short-term commercial paper and yields 4.9 percent. The third fund specializes in the municipal debt from the state of New Jersey and yields 3.0 percent. If you are a New Jersey resident, your federal tax bracket is 35 percent, and your state tax bracket is 8 percent, which of these three MMMFs offers you the highest aftertax yield?

19. **Taxes and MMMFs (LO2, CFA1)** In Problem 18, which MMMF offers you the highest yield if you are a resident of Texas, which has no state income tax?

20. **Closed-End Funds (LO2, CFA3)** The Argentina Fund has $560 million in assets and sells at a 6.9 percent discount to NAV. If the quoted share price for this closed-end fund is $14.29, how many shares are outstanding? If you purchase 1,000 shares of this fund, what will the total shares outstanding be now?

Spreadsheet Problem

21. **Closed-End Fund Discounts (LO2, CFA3)** Suppose you purchase 5,000 shares of a closed-end mutual fund at its initial public offering; the offer price is $10 per share. The offering prospectus discloses that the fund promoter gets an 8 percent fee from the offering. If this fund sells at a 7 percent discount to NAV the day after the initial public offering, what is the value of your investment?

CFA Exam Review by Kaplan Schweser

[CFA3, CFA6]

Suzanne Harlan has a large, well-diversified stock and bond portfolio. She wants to try some alternative investments, such as hedge funds, and has contacted Lawrence Phillips, CFA, to help assemble a new portfolio.

Before agreeing to make recommendations for Ms. Harlan, Mr. Phillips wants to determine if she is a good candidate for alternative investments. He gives her a standard questionnaire. Here are some of her comments:

- I'm interested in high returns. I'm not afraid of risk, and I'm investing money for the benefit of my heirs.

- I pay a lot of attention to expense and return data from my investments and track their performance closely.

- Investors have told me that assessing the quality of hedge funds is difficult, so I'm interested in purchasing a fund of funds where I can diversify my risk while potentially sharing in some outsized returns.

- I pay several million dollars in taxes every year, and I want any additional investments to be tax-friendly.
- My neighbors founded Kelly Tool and Die 20 years ago. They are declaring bankruptcy, and I am interested in obtaining a partial interest in the business.

Ms. Harlan then tells Mr. Phillips that it is imperative that the returns of any investments he recommends must be in some way comparable to a benchmark.

Mr. Phillips is not excited about the business idea or the fund of funds. However, he does know of several managers of individual hedge funds. He talks her out of a fund of funds and suggests she put her money in the Stillman Fund, which concentrates on spin-offs, generally buying the spun-off company and shorting the parent company.

1. In an attempt to talk Ms. Harlan out of investing in a fund of funds, Mr. Phillips addressed the advantages of investing in individual funds. Which of the following would be his most compelling argument?

   a. The lower expenses of individual funds
   b. The likelihood of style drift in a fund of funds
   c. The lack of a benchmark for a fund of funds

2. What investment approach would be consistent with Ms. Harlan's tolerance for risk?

   a. Distressed security
   b. Arbitrage
   c. Market neutral

3. Which of Ms. Harlan's responses is most likely to make Mr. Phillips consider her a bad candidate for investing in hedge funds?

   a. I pay a lot of attention to expense and return data from my investments and track their performance closely.
   b. I pay several million dollars in taxes every year, and I want any additional investments to be tax-friendly.
   c. I'm interested in high returns. I'm not afraid of risk, and I'm investing money for the benefit of my heirs.

4. If Ms. Harlan is truly concerned about benchmarks, she should avoid which of her suggested investments?

   a. None of them
   b. Kelly Tool and Die
   c. Hedge funds

Bloomberg Exercises

1. Analyze the price and NAV of the ETF with the ticker symbol SPY. Why is the difference so small? **(NAV)**
2. Look up the management team for the Fidelity Magellan (FMAGX) mutual fund. **(MGMT)**
3. Conduct a fund screening to identify the "best" U.S. large-cap value funds. **(FSRC)**
4. Examine the largest positions held by the ETF with the ticker symbol XLY. Is this a diversified set? **(MEMB)**

What's on the Web?

1. **Bond Funds** One of the best internet sites for information on mutual funds is www.morningstar.com. Go to the website and find the ticker symbol for the Harbor Bond Fund. Find all of the following information on the website for this fund: loads, expense ratio, top five holdings, bond quality ratings, the fund's rank in its category for the last seven years, and the Morningstar rating. Next, find out how the Morningstar star ranking system works.

2. **Stock Funds** Go to www.morningstar.com and find the ticker symbol for a domestic stock fund. Enter the ticker symbol and find the following information for the fund: manager and manager start date, year-to-date return, three-year return, five-year return, front-end or back-end loads, actual and maximum 12b-l fees, management fees, expense ratio, the top 25 holdings, and the fund address and phone number.

3. **Morningstar Fund Selector** Find the mutual fund screener on the Morningstar website. How many funds fit the following criteria: domestic stock fund, minimum initial purchase equal to or less than $500, expense ratio less than or equal to category average, and turnover less than 75 percent?

"One of the funny things about the stock market is that every time one man buys, another sells, and both think they are astute."

–William Feather

"If you don't know who you are, the stock market is an expensive place to find out."

–Adam Smith (pseud. for George J. W. Goodman)

Learning Objectives

Take stock in yourself. Make sure you have a good understanding of:

1. The differences between private and public equity, and primary and secondary stock markets.

2. The workings of the New York Stock Exchange.

3. How Nasdaq operates.

4. How to calculate index returns.

On May 17, 1792, a group of commodity brokers met and signed the now famous Buttonwood Tree Agreement, thereby establishing the forerunner of what soon became the New York Stock Exchange (NYSE). While the NYSE structure was relatively stable for decades, there have been many recent changes. In 2007, the NYSE and Euronext completed a merger, forming the NYSE Euronext, which operated large and liquid stock exchanges in Amsterdam, Brussels, Paris, New York, and other cities worldwide. Then, in 2013, NYSE Euronext was acquired by the Intercontinental Exchange (or ICE), which was only 12 years old at the time. This industry is changing rapidly.

Nonetheless, the NYSE is still the world's best-known stock exchange. It's big, too. In early 2022, daily trading volume at the NYSE easily topped 3 billion shares on most days. Established in 1971, and now famous as an arena for "tech" stock investing, daily trading volume at the Nasdaq regularly reached 4 billion shares in 2022. Even though the trading volume suggests the Nasdaq might be larger, the NYSE is still about twice the size of the Nasdaq in terms of underlying market capitalization. Together, the NYSE and Nasdaq account for the vast majority of stock trading in the United States.

CFA™ Exam Topics in this Chapter:

1. Market organization and structure (L1, S11)

2. Security market indexes (L1, S11)

3. Introduction to alternative investments (L1, S16)

4. Private company valuation (L2, S10)

5. Trade strategy and execution (L3, S13)

Go to Connect for a guide that aligns your textbook with CFA readings.

With this chapter, we begin in earnest our study of stock markets. This chapter presents a big-picture overview of how a stock market works and how to read and understand stock market information reported in the financial press.

5.1 Private Equity versus Selling Securities to the Public

PRIVATE EQUITY

Related Bloomberg Functions

PE   Private Equity Overview

IPO   Equity Offerings

LEAG   League Tables

NIM   New Issues Monitor

BAS   Broker Activity Summary

RANK   Broker Rankings

The broad term *private equity* is often used to label the financing for nonpublic companies. For example, one day, you and a friend have a great idea for a new computer software product that helps users communicate using the next-generation Meganet. Filled with entrepreneurial zeal, you christen the product MegaComm and set about bringing it to market.

Working nights and weekends, you are able to create a prototype of your product. It doesn't actually work, but at least you can show it around to illustrate your idea. To develop a working product, you need to hire programmers, buy computers, rent office space, and so on. Unfortunately, because you are both college students, your combined assets are not sufficient to fund a pizza party, much less a start-up company. You need what is often referred to as OPM—other people's money.

Your first thought might be to approach a bank for a loan. You would probably discover, however, that banks are generally not interested in making loans to start-up companies with no assets (other than an idea) run by fledgling entrepreneurs with no track record. Instead, your search for capital would very likely lead you to the **venture capital (VC)** market, an important part of the private equity market.

venture capital (VC)
Financing for new, often high-risk ventures.

Firms other than start-ups might need financing. Thus, in addition to venture capital, other areas of private equity include middle-market firms and large leveraged buyouts. We discuss each of these below, but before we do, we provide a general overview of a typical private equity fund. A private equity fund raises money from investors and invests in private companies.

THE STRUCTURE OF PRIVATE EQUITY FUNDS

Although they have differences, private equity funds and hedge funds share some characteristics. For example, both private equity funds and hedge funds are investment companies set up as limited partnerships that pool money from investors and then invest the money on behalf of those investors.

Of course, investors pay private equity funds a management fee to make investment decisions and, in most cases, the investors also pay a performance fee. Similar to hedge funds, private equity funds typically use a 2/20 fee structure. Under this structure, the private equity fund charges a 2 percent annual management fee and retains 20 percent of all profits earned.

Similar to hedge funds, private equity funds also have built-in constraints to prevent the fund managers from taking excessive compensation. Specifically, private equity funds generally have a *high-water mark* provision, as well as a *clawback* provision. The aim of a clawback provision is to make sure that the manager receives only the agreed-upon performance fee.

Here is how a clawback works. Suppose the private equity fund is set up to have a two-year life. In its first year of operation, the private equity fund earns a 25 percent return. For every $1,000 in the fund, the managers of this private equity fund "receive" a hefty performance fee of $50 (20 percent of the $250 profit). In its second year, the private equity fund investors suffer a 10 percent loss. Under the terms of a typical clawback provision, the managers have to "give back" the first year's performance fee when the fund is liquidated at the end of the second year. At liquidation, the managers earn a fee of $25 for every $1,000 in the fund (20 percent of the accumulated two-year profit of $125). Because the fund managers generally do not take any performance fees until the fund is liquidated, the performance fee for private equity firms is known as *carried interest*.

Like hedge funds, the fees paid to the private equity managers significantly reduce the net return of the fund. The benefit of such investments is frequently debated. Right now, the general thinking is that the average net return to investors in private equity funds is about equal to the return of small-cap stocks. So, is there any benefit to adding this type of investment to a portfolio? The answer depends on whether private equity funds provide significant diversification benefits to investors.

Even if private equity funds do provide diversification benefits, they might not be a reasonable choice for most investors. First, an investor in private equity funds must be an *accredited investor*—that is, he or she must be "rich." Second, the funds are really illiquid, possibly even more illiquid than hedge funds. A typical private equity fund is started by raising money from investors. After the money is raised, the managers invest in private companies, with the intention of improving them and subsequently exiting, preferably through an initial public offering (IPO). This process obviously can take some time. As a result, a typical fund will have a stated life of 7–10 years—which makes for an illiquid investment.

TYPES OF PRIVATE EQUITY FUNDS

VENTURE CAPITAL The term *venture capital* does not have a precise meaning, but it generally refers to financing for new, often high-risk ventures. For example, before it went public, internet auctioneer eBay was venture capital financed. Individual venture capitalists invest their own money, whereas venture capital firms specialize in pooling funds from various sources and investing them.

Venture capitalists and venture capital firms recognize that many or even most new ventures will not fly, but the occasional one will. The potential profits are enormous in such cases. To limit their risk, venture capitalists generally provide financing in stages. At each stage, enough money is invested to reach the next milestone or planning stage. For example, the *first-stage* (or first "round") *financing* might be enough to get a prototype built and a manufacturing plan completed. Based on the results, the *second-stage financing* might be a major investment needed to actually begin manufacturing, marketing, and distribution. There might be many such stages, each of which represents a key step in the process of growing the company.

Venture capital firms often specialize in different stages. Some specialize in very early "seed money," or ground floor, financing. In contrast, financing in the later stages might come from venture capitalists specializing in so-called mezzanine-level financing, where *mezzanine level* refers to the level just above the ground floor. This mezzanine-level financing could come in the form of either debt or equity. In either case, it will likely be structured to limit downside risk and retain upside profit potential. Examples of such securities include preferred stock that is convertible into common stock or a bond that has some attached warrants or call options.

The fact that financing is available in stages and is contingent on specified goals being met is a powerful motivating force for the firm's founders. Often, the founders receive relatively little in the way of salary and have substantial portions of their personal assets tied up in the business. At each stage of financing, the value of the founder's stake grows and the probability of success rises. If goals are not met, the venture capitalist will withhold further financing, thereby limiting future losses.

The internet is a tremendous source of venture capital information for both suppliers and demanders of capital. For example, see nvca.org.

In addition to providing financing, venture capitalists generally will actively participate in running the firm, providing the benefit of experience with previous start-ups as well as general business expertise. This is especially true when the firm's founders have little or no hands-on experience in running a company.

If a start-up succeeds, the big payoff frequently comes when the company is sold to another company or goes public. Either way, investment bankers are often involved in the process.

MIDDLE MARKET When you hear the term *venture capital,* you probably think about investment in start-up companies. There are, however, many examples of private equity investments other than start-up companies. For example, many small, regional private equity funds concentrate their investments in "middle-market" companies. These companies are ongoing concerns (i.e., not start-ups) with a known performance history. Typically, these companies are small, and many are family owned and operated.

Why would an established, middle-market company even be in the market for more capital? Many times these companies need capital if they wish to expand beyond their existing region. Other times, the founders of the firm want to retire from the business. In the latter case, the private equity fund might be interested in purchasing a portion, or all, of the business so that others can take over running the company.

LEVERAGED BUYOUTS You might be familiar with the term *going public,* a process (that we discuss below) where a privately owned company sells ownership shares to the public market. However, what if the opposite happens? What if the company (or someone else) purchases all the shares held by the public at large? This process is called *taking the company private.* Because most publicly traded companies have a large market capitalization, the cost of going private is high. So a manager or investor who wants to take a company private probably needs to borrow a significant amount of money. Taking a company private using borrowed money is called a *leveraged buyout* (LBO). With its need for borrowed money, the activity level in the LBO market depends on credit market conditions.

How big is the typical LBO? Unfortunately, there is no "typical" LBO. We can give you an idea, however, of the potential size of such deals. For example, during the height of the LBO boom around 2007, the Blackstone Group bought Hilton Hotels for $26 billion; Apollo and TPG funds bought Harrah's Entertainment for $31 billion; and a group led by Goldman Sachs bought the energy firm TXU for around $48 billion.

No matter the situation—venture capital, middle market, or LBO—the process and securities used will generally follow the structure we identified in the previous sections. The main difference among the types of private equity funds is really just the types of firms in which the funds are investing.

SELLING SECURITIES TO THE PUBLIC

The goal of the private equity funds we just discussed is to invest in a private company, improve its performance, and then exit the business with a profit. Exiting the firm can be accomplished by selling to another investor. Typically, however, the preferred route is to sell the firm to the general public.

What about private companies that do not have private equity investors? Well, the managers of these companies might decide to raise additional capital by selling shares directly to the general investing public. In either case, shares of stock in the firm would then be listed on a stock exchange.

When we talk about the *stock market,* we are talking about securities that have been sold to the public. The stock market consists of a **primary market** and a **secondary market**. In the primary, or new-issue, market, shares of stock are first brought to the market and sold to investors. In the secondary market, existing shares are traded among investors.

In the primary market, companies issue new securities to raise money. In the secondary market, investors are constantly appraising the values of companies by buying and selling shares previously issued by these companies. We next discuss the operation of the primary market for common stocks, and then we turn our attention to the secondary market for stocks.

THE PRIMARY MARKET FOR COMMON STOCK

The primary market for common stock is how new securities are first brought to market. It is best known as the market for **initial public offerings (IPOs)**. An IPO occurs when a company offers stock for sale to the public for the first time. Typically, the company is small and growing, and it needs to raise capital for further expansion.

An IPO is sometimes called an *unseasoned equity offering* because shares are not available to the public before the IPO. If a company already has shares owned by the public, it can raise equity with a **seasoned equity offering (SEO)**. The terms *secondary* and *follow-on offering* also refer to an SEO. A seasoned equity offering of common stock can be made using a general cash offer or a rights offer. In a **general cash offer**, securities are offered to the general public on a "first-come, first-served" basis. With a **rights offer**, securities are initially offered only to existing owners. Rights offerings are rare in the United States but common in other countries.

primary market
The market in which new securities are originally sold to investors.

secondary market
The market in which previously issued securities trade among investors.

Want to buy shares of companies yet to go public? Check out
www.nasdaqprivatemarket.com.

initial public offering (IPO)
A company's first-time offer of stock for sale to the public.

seasoned equity offering (SEO)
The sale of additional shares of stock by a company whose shares are already publicly traded.

general cash offer
An issue of securities offered for sale to the general public on a cash basis.

rights offer
A public issue of securities in which securities are first offered to existing shareholders (also called a *rights offering*).

For more on IPOs, check out the IPO Center at www.123jump.com.

investment banking firm
A firm specializing in arranging financing for companies.

underwrite
To assume the risk of buying newly issued securities from a company and reselling them to investors.

underwriter spread
Compensation to the underwriter, determined by the difference between the underwriter's buying price and offering price.

syndicate
A group of underwriters formed to share the risk and to help sell an issue.

firm commitment underwriting
The type of underwriting in which the underwriter buys the entire issue, assuming full financial responsibility for any unsold shares.

best efforts underwriting
The type of underwriting in which the underwriter sells as much of the issue as possible but can return any unsold shares to the issuer without financial responsibility.

Obviously, all initial public offerings are cash offers. To illustrate how an IPO occurs, let's look in on the software company that you started several years ago. Suppose your company was initially set up as a privately held corporation with 100,000 shares of stock, all sold for $1 per share. The reason your company is privately held is that shares were not offered for sale to the general public. Instead, you bought 50,000 shares for yourself and sold the remaining 50,000 shares to a few supportive friends and relatives (who assumed the role of venture capitalists).

Fortunately, your company has prospered beyond all expectations. However, company growth is now hampered by a lack of capital. At an informal stockholders' meeting, it is agreed to take the company public. Not really knowing how to do this, you consult your accountant, who recommends an **investment banking firm**. An investment banking firm, among other things, specializes in arranging financing for companies by finding investors to buy newly issued securities.

After lengthy negotiations, including an examination of your company's current financial condition and plans for future growth, your investment banker suggests an issue of 4 million shares of common stock. Two million shares will be distributed to the original stockholders (you and your original investors) in exchange for their old shares. These 2 million shares distributed to the original stockholders ensure that effective control of the corporation will remain in their hands.

After much haggling, your investment banker agrees to **underwrite** the stock issue by purchasing the other 2 million shares from your company for $10 per share. The net effect of this transaction is that you have sold half the company to the underwriter for $20 million. The proceeds from the sale will allow your company to build its own headquarters and double its staff of programmers and sales consultants.

Your investment banker will not keep the 2 million shares but instead will resell them in the primary market, and thinks the stock can probably be sold for $11 per share in an IPO. The difference between the $11 the underwriter sells the stock for and the $10 per share you received is called the **underwriter spread**, or discount. It is the basic compensation received by the underwriter. The typical underwriter spread is in the range of 7 to 10 percent, depending on the size of the offering. Sometimes the underwriter will also get noncash compensation in the form of warrants and stock in addition to the spread.

Underwriters combine to form an underwriting group called a **syndicate** to share the risk and to help sell the issue. In a syndicate, one or more managers arrange the offering. One manager is designated as the lead manager, or principal manager. The lead manager typically has the responsibility of pricing the securities. The other underwriters in the syndicate serve primarily to distribute the issue.

Two basic types of underwriting are typically involved in a cash offer: firm commitment and best efforts. A third, and less common, type of underwriting is Dutch auction underwriting.

FIRM COMMITMENT UNDERWRITING In **firm commitment underwriting**, the issuer sells the entire issue to the underwriters, who then attempt to resell it. This is the most prevalent type of underwriting in the United States. This is really a purchase-resale arrangement, and the underwriter's fee is the spread. For a new issue of seasoned equity, the underwriters can look at the market price to determine what the issue should sell for, and about 95 percent of all such new issues are firm commitments.

If the underwriter cannot sell all of the issue at the agreed-upon offering price, it may have to lower the price on the unsold shares. Nonetheless, with firm commitment underwriting, the issuer receives the agreed-upon amount, and all the risk associated with selling the issue is transferred to the underwriter.

Because the offering price usually isn't set until the underwriters have investigated how receptive the market is to the issue, this risk is usually minimal. Also, because the offering price usually is not set until just before selling commences, the issuer doesn't know precisely what its net proceeds will be until that time.

BEST EFFORTS UNDERWRITING In **best efforts underwriting**, the underwriter is legally bound to use "best efforts" to sell the securities at the agreed-upon offering price. Beyond this, the underwriter does not guarantee any particular amount of money to the issuer. This form of underwriting has become very uncommon in recent years; firm commitments are now the dominant form.

Dutch auction underwriting
The type of underwriting in which the offer price is set based on competitive bidding by investors. Also known as a *uniform price auction.*

DUTCH AUCTION UNDERWRITING With **Dutch auction underwriting**, the underwriter does not set a fixed price at which to sell the shares. Instead, the underwriter conducts an auction in which investors bid for shares. The offer price is determined based on the submitted bids. A Dutch auction is also known by the more descriptive name *uniform price auction.*

This approach to selling securities to the public is relatively new in the IPO market and has not been widely used there, but it is very common in the bond markets. For example, it is the sole procedure used by the U.S. Treasury to sell enormous quantities of notes, bonds, and bills to the public. Dutch auction underwriting was much in the news in 2004 because web search company Google elected to use this approach.

The best way to understand a Dutch, or uniform price, auction is to consider a simple example. Suppose The Roserita Company wants to sell 400 shares to the public. The company receives five bids as follows:

Bidder	Quantity	Price
A	100 shares	$16
B	100 shares	14
C	200 shares	12
D	100 shares	12
E	200 shares	10

Thus, Bidder A is willing to buy 100 shares at $16 each, Bidder B is willing to buy 100 shares at $14, and so on. The Roserita Company examines the bids to determine the highest price that will result in all 400 shares being sold. So, for example, at $14, A and B would buy only 200 shares, so that price is too high. Working our way down, all 400 shares won't be sold until we hit a price of $12, so $12 will be the offer price in the IPO. Bidders A through D will receive shares; Bidder E will not.

Second, notice that at the $12 offer price, there are actually bids for 500 shares, which exceeds the 400 shares Roserita wants to sell. Thus, there has to be some sort of allocation. How this is done varies a bit, but in the IPO market, the approach has been to compute the ratio of shares offered to shares bid at the offer price or better, which, in our example, is 400/500 = .8, and allocate bidders that percentage of their bids. In other words, Bidders A through D would each receive 80 percent of the shares they bid, and each would pay a price of $12 per share.

As is common with an IPO, some restrictions are imposed on you as part of the underwriting contract. Most importantly, you and the other original stockholders agree not to sell any of your personal stockholdings for six months after the underwriting (this is called the "lockup" period). This ties most of your wealth to the company's success and makes selling the stock to investors a more credible undertaking by the underwriter. Essentially, investors are assured that you will be working hard to expand the company and increase its earnings.

Securities and Exchange Commission (SEC)
Federal regulatory agency charged with enforcing U.S. securities laws and regulations.

After the underwriting terms are decided, much of your time will be devoted to the mechanics of the offering. In particular, before shares can be sold to the public, the issue must obtain an approved registration with the **Securities and Exchange Commission (SEC)**. The SEC is the federal regulatory agency charged with regulating U.S. securities markets.

prospectus
Document prepared as part of a security offering detailing information about a company's financial position, its operations, and its investment plans.

SEC regulations governing IPOs are especially strict. To gain SEC approval, you must prepare a **prospectus**, normally with the help of outside accounting, auditing, and legal experts. The prospectus contains a detailed account of your company's financial position, its operations, and its investment plans for the future. Once the prospectus is prepared, it is submitted to the SEC for approval. The SEC makes no judgment about the quality of your company or the value of your stock. Instead, it only checks to make sure that various rules regarding full disclosure and other issues have been satisfied.

red herring
A preliminary prospectus not yet approved by the SEC.

While awaiting SEC approval, your investment banker will circulate a preliminary prospectus among investors to generate interest in the stock offering. This document is commonly called a **red herring** because the cover page is stamped in red ink, indicating that final approval for the stock issue has not yet been obtained. The preliminary prospectus is essentially complete except for the final offering price and a few other pieces of information. These are not set because market conditions might change while SEC approval is being sought. Upon obtaining SEC approval, the prospectus will be updated and completed, and your underwriter can begin selling your company's shares to investors.

To publicize an offering, the underwriter will usually place announcements in newspapers and other outlets. Because of their appearance, these announcements are known as *tombstones,* and they are a familiar sight in the financial press. A sample tombstone as it appeared in *The Wall Street Journal* is shown in Figure 5.1.

As Figure 5.1 shows, a typical tombstone states the name of the company, some information about the stock issue being sold, and the underwriters for the issue. All but very small issues generally involve more than one underwriter, and the names of the participating underwriters are usually listed at the bottom of the tombstone. Those listed first are the "lead" underwriters, who are primarily responsible for managing the issue process.

Initial public stock offerings vary in size a great deal. The 2 million share issue for your hypothetical software company discussed above is a fairly small issue. One of the largest public offerings in the United States was Facebook, which went public in May 2012. The new shares were offered at $38 per share, raised over $16 billion, and created a company market value of over $100 billion. For additional information on the largest IPOs of all time, check out the *Investment Updates* box.

ALTERNATIVE SOURCES OF PUBLIC FUNDING

CROWDFUNDING On April 5, 2012, the Jumpstart Our Business Startups (JOBS) Act was signed into law. A provision of this act allows companies to raise equity through **crowdfunding**, which is the practice of raising small amounts of capital from a large number of people, typically via the internet. Crowdfunding was first used to underwrite the U.S. tour of British rock band Marillion. Originally, the JOBS Act allowed a company to issue up to $1 million in securities in a 12-month period, although this limit was later raised to a maximum of $50 million.

crowdfunding
The practice of raising small amounts of cash from a large number of people, typically via the internet.

We should make an important distinction between two types of crowdfunding—*project* crowdfunding and *equity* crowdfunding. As an example of project crowdfunding, consider the card game Exploding Kittens, which exploded on the crowdfunding website Kickstarter and raised $8.8 million from about 220,000 backers. During the crowdfunding campaign, the company presold card decks. Every backer was shipped a deck of cards for the game, beginning about six months after the campaign ended. In this case, the backers were purchasers, not investors. This type of crowdfunding also has become a popular way to raise money for charitable causes. In contrast, with equity crowdfunding, the backers receive equity in the company.

Check out two of the more well-known project and charitable crowdfunding websites at www.kickstarter.com and www.gofundme.com.

In May 2016, Regulation CF (also known as Title III of the JOBS Act) kicked in, which allows small investors access to new crowdfunding "portals." Previously, investors in crowdfunding had to be "accredited." To qualify as an accredited investor, an individual had to have more than $1 million in net worth or more than $200,000 in income for two of the past three years. Regulation CF, however, allows investors with less than $107,000 in income or assets to invest at least $2,200 per year, up to a maximum of $5,350.

To sell securities through Regulation CF, a company must file a form with the SEC. This filing makes the company eligible to list its securities on a crowdfunding portal that is approved by FINRA (the Financial Industry Regulatory Authority). FINRA also reports bond prices, as we discuss elsewhere in the textbook. With the growth in the market, crowdfunding portals are already specializing in certain areas. For example, there are portals that specialize in only accredited investors, in all investors, or in real estate, to name just a few.

See upcoming ICOs at icodrops.com.

INITIAL COIN OFFERING In addition to sales of traditional debt and equity, a company can raise funds by selling *tokens*. These tokens often grant the holder the right to use the

FIGURE 5.1   IPO Tombstone

This announcement is neither an offer to sell nor a solicitation of an offer to buy any of these securities.
The offering is made only by the Prospectus.

New Issue

11,500,000 Shares

World Wrestling Federation Entertainment, Inc.

Class A Common Stock

Price $17.00 Per Share

Copies of the Prospectus may be obtained in any State in which this announcement
is circulated from only such of the Underwriters, including the undersigned,
as may lawfully offer these securities in such State.

U.S. Offering

9,200,000 Shares

This portion of the underwriting is being offered in the United States and Canada.

Bear, Stearns & Co. Inc.

Credit Suisse First Boston

Merrill Lynch & Co.

Wit Capital Corporation

Allen & Company Incorporated	Banc of America Securities LLC	Deutsche Banc Alex. Brown
Donaldson, Lufkin & Jenrette	A.G. Edwards & Sons, Inc. Hambrecht & Quist	ING Barings
Prudential Securities SG Cowen	Wassertein Perella Securities, Inc.	Advest, Inc.
Axiom Capital Management, Inc.	Blackford Securities Corp.	J.C. Bradford & Co.
Joseph Charles & Assoc., Inc.	Chatsworth Securities LLC	Gabelli & Company, Inc.
Gaines, Berland Inc. Jefferies & Company, Inc.	Josephthal & Co. Inc.	Neuberger Berman, LLC
Raymond James & Associates, Inc.		Sanders Morris Mundy
Tucker Anthony Cleary Gull		Wachovia Securities, Inc.

International Offering

2,300,000 Shares

This portion of the underwriting is being offered outside of the United States and Canada.

Bear, Stearns International Limited

Credit Suisse First Boston

Merrill Lynch International

INVESTMENT UPDATES

TEN LARGEST GLOBAL IPOS IN HISTORY

Saudi Aramco's initial public offering of $25.6 billion in late 2019 shattered records and jumped to the top of the list of biggest global IPOs in history. How does the Aramco number compare to other huge IPOs? The list may surprise you. Only one U.S.-based company made the top five (it wasn't Facebook).

1. Saudi Aramco. $25.6 billion. This Saudi Arabian oil company is one of the world's largest companies. It went public in December 2019, and shares began trading on the Saudi Stock Exchange. The primary IPO was raised to $29.4 billion after the company reportedly sold an additional 450 million shares. Saudi officials decided not to list the shares abroad. So how can you can get a piece of this valuable company? You can invest in it indirectly by purchasing shares of an ETF, such as the iShares MSCI Saudi Arabia ETF (KSA).

2. Alibaba Holdings Group (NYSE: BABA). $21.8 billion. This diversified online e-commerce company, based in China, went public on September 18, 2014. Four days later, underwriters exercised an option to sell more shares, bringing the total IPO to $25 billion. Although technology companies traditionally list on Nasdaq, Alibaba chose the New York Stock Exchange for its debut. Underwriting was handled primarily by Credit Suisse.

3. SoftBank. $21.3 billion. Contrary to what you might think, this Tokyo-based company is not a bank. The company actually provides a range of communication services, including mobile and fixed-line communications, as well as ISP services. Shares began trading on the Tokyo Stock Exchange in December 2008.

4. NTT Mobile Communication Network. $18.1 billion. Also known as NTT DoCoMo, this Tokyo-based telecommunications company went public on October 22, 1998. Underwritten by Goldman Sachs Asia, this IPO launched NTT to the third-largest market cap for a Japanese company. Previously listed on the New York Stock Exchange (NYSE), NTT officially delisted its American Depository Shares (ADS) from the exchange in April 2018.

5. Visa Inc. (NYSE: V). $17.4 billion. This San Francisco–based debit and credit card processing company entered the public market on March 18, 2008—during the global financial crisis. Worldwide, the company has more than 70 million merchants using its services, resulting in more than 200 billion transactions each year.

6. AIA Group (OTC: AAIGF). $17.8 billion. This investment and insurance company, based in Hong Kong, went public on October 21, 2010. Citi underwrote this IPO. The company provides a number of financial services to consumers in 18 different countries in Asia.

7. Enel S.p.A. (OTC: ENLAY). $16.4 billion. This Italian gas and electric company went public on November 1, 1999. The company provides power to consumers in 31 countries in Europe and Asia. It is the only utility company on this IPO list.

8. Meta, formerly Facebook (Nasdaq: FB). $16.0 billion. The company behind the popular social media platform went public on May 1, 2012. This social media technology company's high-profile launch was riddled with trading issues and accusations of inappropriate information sharing. In spite of these issues, Facebook remains the largest technology IPO in U.S. history.

9. General Motors Company (NYSE: GM). $15.8 billion. GM debuted on November 17, 2000, after emerging from a bankruptcy filing one year earlier. The vehicle manufacturer also raised another $4.5 billion in preferred shares, making it the largest IPO for any U.S.-based company.

10. ICBC Bank. $14 billion. The Industrial and Commercial Bank of China (listed on the Shanghai Stock Exchange and the Hong Kong Stock Exchange) went public on October 20, 2006. Merrill Lynch underwrote the IPO.

Source: Kristina Zucchi, Investopedia, March 29, 2022.

company's service in the future. For example, a company building a railroad might issue a token that can be used as a train ticket after the railroad is built.

Token sales occur on digital currency platforms. Tokens can be easily transferred on the platform, or they can be converted to U.S. dollars on specialized token exchanges. This liquidity has made tokens a popular means of funding since their introduction in 2015. Tokens are now purchased by both customers and investors, each of whom might never actually use the token for the service being offered.

The initial sale of a token on a digital currency platform is often called an *initial coin offering,* or ICO (to sound like IPO). Many start-up companies are choosing to raise funds through an ICO rather than the traditional venture capital channels. The most common platform for issuing new tokens is Ethereum, but there are many competitors. In 2017, there were 234 ICOs with a total value of about $3.7 billion.

Token sales are most popular among companies that are building services based on blockchain technology. This technology is at the heart of bitcoin and other cryptocurrencies. A blockchain is a time-stamped ledger of transactions that is kept among a network of users without centralized control. It is similar to a traditional database, except that cryptography is used to make it infeasible to change data once they are added to the chain. Many industries, including finance, are now updating their record-keeping infrastructure with blockchain technology.

Token sales can also serve as an effective marketing tool. This is especially true if the business benefits from network effects as the potential for price appreciation in the tokens attracts new customers. The increase in customers increases the value of the service, which in turn increases the value of the tokens. For example, Civic is building a blockchain-based identity platform, and its currency is used to purchase identity verification services from trusted parties. The company raised $33 million in June 2017 through an ICO of the CVC token. The total value of the tokens increased to over $400 million by early 2018. Unfortunately for investors, this value fell to under $20 million by early 2018. But the market value has rebounded to about $120 million in 2022.

SPACS There is an increasingly popular form of IPOs called SPACs. A special purpose acquisition company (SPAC) is a company formed for the express purpose of raising capital through an IPO in order to acquire an existing company. At the time of their IPOs, SPACs have no existing business operations or even stated targets for acquisition. Investors in SPACs range from well-known private equity funds to celebrities and even the general public. SPACs have two years to complete an acquisition or they must return their funds to investors. Although SPACs as a legal structure have been around for decades, their popularity has recently soared. In 2019, 59 SPACs came to the market, compared to 247 in 2020 and a record 613 SPACs in 2021.

See the market value of tokens at coinmarketcap.com.

THE SECONDARY MARKET FOR COMMON STOCK

In the secondary market for common stock, investors buy and sell shares with other investors. If you think of the primary market as the new-car showroom at an automotive dealer, where cars are first sold to the public, then the secondary market is the used-car lot.

Secondary market stock trading among investors is directed through three channels. An investor may trade:

1. Directly with other investors.
2. Indirectly through a broker who arranges transactions for others.
3. Directly with a dealer who buys and sells securities from inventory.

As we discussed in Chapter 2, for individual investors, almost all common stock transactions are made through a broker. However, large institutional investors, such as pension funds and mutual funds, trade through both brokers and dealers, and they also trade directly with other institutional investors.

DEALERS AND BROKERS

dealer
A trader who buys and sells securities from inventory.

broker
An intermediary who arranges security transactions among investors.

Because most securities transactions involve dealers and brokers, it is important that you understand exactly what these terms mean. A **dealer** maintains an inventory and stands ready to buy and sell at any time. By contrast, a **broker** brings buyers and sellers together but does not maintain an inventory. Thus, when we speak of used-car dealers and real estate brokers, we recognize that the used-car dealer maintains an inventory, whereas the real estate broker normally does not.

In the securities markets, a dealer stands ready to buy securities from investors wishing to sell them and to sell securities to investors wishing to buy them. An important part of the dealer function involves maintaining an inventory to accommodate temporary buy and

146 Part 2 ● Stock Markets

bid price
The price a dealer is willing to pay.

ask price
The price at which a dealer is willing to sell. Also called the offer or offering price.

spread
An option trading strategy involving two or more call options or two or more put options.

sell order imbalances. The price a dealer is willing to pay is called the **bid price**. The price at which a dealer will sell is called the **ask price** (sometimes called the offer or offering price). The difference between the bid and ask prices is called the **spread**. The minimum spread size in U.S. markets is one cent.

A dealer attempts to profit by selling securities at a price higher than the average price paid for them. Of course, this is a goal for all investors, but the distinguishing characteristic of securities dealers is that they hold securities in inventory only until the first opportunity to resell them. Essentially, trading from inventory is their business, and the spread is the compensation they earn.

As you might expect, the spread for all securities is not the same. As a comparison, consider why some companies earn higher margins than others. For example, a grocery store generally has lower margins, but it is able to make up for this through high volume. The same is true for bid-ask spreads. For securities with high trading volume (and therefore increased competition among dealers), the spreads are quite low. For securities that trade in opaque markets, the spreads can be quite high. Either way, the spread is an implicit cost to the investor.

Dealers exist in all areas of the economy, of course, not just in the stock markets. For example, your local university bookstore is both a primary and secondary market textbook dealer. If you buy a new book, then this is a primary market transaction. If you buy a used book, this is a secondary market transaction, and you pay the store's ask price. If you sell the book back, you receive the store's bid price, often half the ask price. The bookstore's spread is the difference between the bid and ask prices.

In contrast, a securities broker arranges transactions between investors, matching investors wishing to buy securities with investors wishing to sell securities. Brokers may match investors with other investors, investors with dealers, and sometimes even dealers with dealers. The distinctive characteristic of securities brokers is that they do not buy or sell securities for their own account. Facilitating trades by others is their business.

Most common stock trading is directed through an organized stock exchange or a trading network. Whether on a stock exchange or through a trading network, the goal is to match investors wishing to buy stocks with investors wishing to sell stocks. The largest, most active organized stock exchange in the United States is the New York Stock Exchange (NYSE). Other well-known stock exchanges include the Chicago Stock Exchange (CHX), the Boston Stock Exchange (BSE), the National Stock Exchange (NSX), and the Philadelphia Stock Exchange (PHLX). The major competitor to the organized stock exchanges is the vast trading network known as Nasdaq. We next discuss the workings of the NYSE, and then we turn to a discussion of Nasdaq.

Want to trade movies or actors? Check out this unique stock exchange, www.hsx.com.

CHECK THIS

5.1a   Is an IPO a primary or a secondary market transaction?

5.1b   Which is bigger, the bid price or the ask price? Why?

5.1c   What is the difference between a securities broker and a securities dealer?

5.2 The New York Stock Exchange

The New York Stock Exchange, or NYSE, popularly known as the Big Board, was founded in 1792. It has occupied its current location on Wall Street since the turn of the twentieth century. Measured in terms of dollar volume of activity and the total value of shares listed, it is the largest stock market in the world.

NYSE exchange member
Before 2006, the NYSE exchange members were the owners of the exchange.

NYSE MEMBERS

The **NYSE exchange members** number 1,366. Before 2006, the exchange members were said to own "seats" on the exchange. Collectively, the members of the exchange were also the owners. For this reason and others, seats were valuable and were bought and sold fairly regularly. Seat prices reached a record $4 million in 2005.

In 2006, the ownership structure changed when the NYSE became a publicly owned corporation. Naturally, its stock is listed on the NYSE. Now, instead of purchasing seats, exchange members must purchase trading licenses, the number of which is still limited to 1,366. In early 2019, a license cost $50,000 per year. Having a license entitles you to buy and sell securities on the floor of the exchange. Different members play different roles in this regard.

On April 4, 2007, the NYSE grew even larger when it merged with Euronext to form NYSE Euronext. Euronext was a stock exchange in Amsterdam, with subsidiaries in Belgium, France, Portugal, and the United Kingdom. With the merger, NYSE Euronext became the world's "first global exchange." Further expansion occurred in 2008 when NYSE Euronext merged with the American Stock Exchange. Then, in November 2013, the acquisition of the NYSE by the Intercontinental Exchange (ICE) was completed. ICE, which was founded in May 2000, was originally a commodities exchange, but its rapid growth gave it the necessary $8.2 billion for the acquisition of the NYSE.

As we briefly describe how the NYSE operates, keep in mind that other markets owned by NYSE Euronext and ICE might function differently. Further, our subsequent discussion in this chapter concerning the NYSE reflects the structure of the exchange as it exists at the time of this writing. How this structure will evolve over time will depend on numerous changes that are being initiated in the global financial markets. For example, before the NYSE's acquisition by ICE, the European Union rejected a proposal to merge the NYSE Euronext and the Deutsche Börse. Had this merger been approved, the discussion in this chapter would have been much different!

What makes the NYSE somewhat unique is that it is a *hybrid market.* In a hybrid market, trading takes place both electronically and face-to-face. With electronic trading, orders to buy and orders to sell are submitted to the exchange. Orders are compared by a computer and whenever there is a match, the orders are executed with no human intervention. Most trades on the NYSE occur this way. For orders that are not handled electronically, the NYSE relies on its license holders. There are three different types of license holders: **designated market makers (DMMs), floor brokers,** and **supplemental liquidity providers (SLPs).**

The DMMs, formerly known as *specialists,* act as dealers in particular stocks. Typically, each stock on the NYSE is assigned to a single DMM. As a dealer, a DMM maintains a two-sided market, meaning that the DMM continually posts and updates bid and ask prices. By doing so, the DMM ensures that there is always a buyer or seller available, thereby promoting market liquidity.

Floor brokers execute trades for customers, trying to get the best price possible. Floor brokers are generally employees of large brokerage firms such as Merrill Lynch, the wealth management division of Bank of America. The interaction between floor brokers and DMMs is the key to nonelectronic trading on the NYSE. We discuss this interaction in detail later in this chapter.

The SLPs are essentially investment firms that agree to be active market participants in the stocks assigned to them. Their job is to make a one-sided market (i.e., offering to either buy or sell). They trade purely for their own accounts (using their own money), so they do not represent customers. They are given a small rebate on their buys and sells, thereby encouraging them to be more aggressive. The NYSE's goal is to generate as much liquidity as possible, which makes it easier for ordinary investors to quickly buy and sell at prevailing prices. Unlike DMMs and floor brokers, SLPs do not operate on the floor of the stock exchange.

In recent years, floor brokers have become less important on the exchange floor because of the efficient Pillar system, which allows orders to be transmitted electronically directly to the DMM. Additionally, the NYSE has an electronic platform called Arca, which accounts for a substantial percentage of all trading on the NYSE, particularly for smaller orders. The average time for a trade to occur on the NYSE Arca is less than 1 second.

Finally, a small number of NYSE members are floor traders who independently trade for their own accounts. Floor traders try to anticipate temporary price fluctuations and profit from them by buying low and selling high. In recent decades, the number of floor traders

designated market maker (DMM)
A new class of market maker at the NYSE; replaced the role of specialists on the exchange floor.

floor brokers
Firms that execute customer orders to buy and sell stock transmitted to the exchange floor.

supplemental liquidity provider (SLP)
A new class of market maker at the NYSE; located off the floor of the exchange.

For up-to-date info on the NYSE, surf to www.nyse.com.

has declined substantially, suggesting that it has become increasingly difficult to profit from short-term trading on the exchange floor.

NYSE-LISTED STOCKS

A company is said to be "listed" on the NYSE Euronext if its stock is traded there. As of March 2021, some 2,529 companies listed on the NYSE represented nearly 25 percent of the world's equity trading. This total includes many large companies so well known that we easily recognize them by their initials—for example, IBM, MMM, and CAT. This total number also includes many companies that are not so readily recognized. For example, relatively few investors would instantly recognize AEP as American Electric Power, but many would recognize AXP as American Express.

U.S. companies that wish to have their stock listed for trading on the "Big Board" must apply for the privilege. Once listed, firms pay an annual fee to the exchange for its services. There are many fees for different services. The maximum total annual fee paid by an issuer is $250,000.

The NYSE has minimum requirements for companies wishing to apply for listing. Although the requirements might change from time to time, examples of minimum requirements in effect in 2022 for U.S. domestic stocks included:

1. The company must have at least 400 shareholders holding 100 or more shares.
2. At least 1.1 million stock shares must be held in public hands.
3. Publicly held shares must have a value of $40 million if they list at the time of their IPO.
4. The company must have aggregate earnings of $10 million before taxes in the previous three years and $2 million pretax earnings in each of the preceding two years.

In practice, most companies with stock listed on the NYSE easily exceed these minimum listing requirements. You can read copious details and minutiae about listing on the NYSE if you surf over to the NYSE Listed Company Manual.

CHECK THIS

5.2a   What are the types of license holders at the New York Stock Exchange?

5.2b   What are the two primary types of market makers at the NYSE? What do they do?

5.3 Operation of the New York Stock Exchange

Now that we have a basic idea of how the NYSE is organized and who the major players are, we turn to the question of how trading actually takes place. Fundamentally, the business of the NYSE is to attract and process order flow—the flow of customer orders to buy and sell stocks. Thus, the NYSE is referred to as an *order-driven market*. Customers of the NYSE are the millions of individual investors and tens of thousands of institutional investors who place their orders to buy and sell NYSE-listed stock shares with member-firm brokers.

About one-third of all NYSE stock trading volume is attributable to individual investors, and almost half (or more) is derived from institutional investors and so-called *high-frequency traders*. In recent years, improved financial technology (i.e., "fintech") has led to an increase in algorithmic trading and machine learning. The remainder represents NYSE member trading, which is largely attributed to DMMs acting as market makers.

Related Bloomberg Functions

NYA   NYSE Composite Index

NYSE FLOOR ACTIVITY

Quite likely you have seen film footage of the NYSE trading floor on television, or you may have visited the NYSE and viewed exchange floor activity from the gallery (when it was open). Either way, you saw a big room, about the size of a small basketball gym. This big room is aptly called "the big room." There are several other, smaller rooms that you normally do not see.

On the floor of the exchange are a number of stations, each with a roughly figure-eight shape. These stations have multiple counters with numerous computer terminal screens above and on the sides. People operate behind and in front of the counters in relatively stationary positions.

Other people move around on the exchange floor, frequently returning to the many telephone banks positioned along the exchange walls. In all, you may have been reminded of worker ants moving around an ant colony. It is natural to wonder: What are all those people doing down there (and why are so many wearing funny-looking coats)?

As an overview of exchange floor activity, here is a quick look at what goes on. Each of the counters at the figure-eight-shaped stations is a **DMM's post**. DMMs normally operate in front of their posts to monitor and manage trading in the stocks assigned to them. Clerical employees working for the DMMs operate behind the counters. Moving around the floor are swarms of floor brokers, many of whom relay customer orders by walking to the posts where these orders can be executed.

Imagine yourself as a floor broker. Your phone clerk has just handed you an order to sell 20,000 shares of KO (the ticker symbol for Coca-Cola common stock) for a customer of the brokerage company that employs you. The order is a **market order**, meaning that the customer wants to sell the stock at the best possible price as soon as possible. You immediately walk (running violates exchange rules) to the post where KO stock is traded.

Upon approaching the post where KO is traded, you check the terminal screen for information on the current market price for KO stock. The screen reveals that the last executed trade for KO was at $64.68 and that the current bid is $64.60 per share. You could immediately sell at $64.60, but that would be too easy.

Instead, as the customer's representative, you are obligated to get the best possible price. It is your job to "work" the order, and your job depends on providing satisfactory order execution service. So you look around for another broker who represents a customer who wants to buy KO stock. Luckily, you quickly find another broker at the post with a market order to buy 20,000 shares of KO. Noticing that the posted asking price is $64.76 per share, you both agree to execute your orders with each other at a price of $64.68. This price, halfway between the posted bid and ask prices, saves each of your customers approximately $.08 × 20,000 = $1,600 compared to the posted prices.

In a trade of this type, in which one floor broker buys from another, the DMM acts only as a broker assisting in matching buy orders and sell orders. On an actively traded stock, many floor brokers can be buying and selling. In such cases, trading is said to occur "in the crowd." Thus, the DMM functions as a broker as long as buyers and sellers are available. The DMM steps in as a dealer when necessary to fill an order that would otherwise go unfilled.

In reality, not all orders are executed so easily. For example, suppose you are unable to find another broker quickly with an order to buy 20,000 shares of KO. Because you have a market order, you may have no choice but to sell at the posted bid price of $64.60. In this case, the need to execute an order quickly takes priority, and the DMM provides the necessary liquidity to allow immediate order execution.

If you think about it, there's no way that the NYSE could trade more than a billion shares a day just using humans. It's physically impossible. What actually happens is that over 99 percent of orders are processed electronically. Human intervention is most important for the NYSE at the opening (9:30 to 9:45 AM ET) and closing (3:35 to 4:00 PM ET) to keep prices stable. During the rest of the trading sessions, nearly all trading is driven by the algorithms of the DMMs and SPLs.

SPECIAL ORDER TYPES

Many orders are transmitted to the NYSE floor as **limit orders**. A limit order is an order to buy or sell stock, where the customer specifies a maximum price he is willing to pay in the case of a buy order, or a minimum price he will accept in the case of a sell order. For example, suppose that as a NYSE floor broker, you receive a limit order to sell 20,000 shares of KO stock at $64.75. This means that the customer is not willing to accept any price below $64.75 per share, even if it means missing the trade.

DMM's post
Fixed place on the exchange floor where the DMM operates.

market order
A customer order to buy or sell securities marked for immediate execution at the current market price.

limit order
Customer order to buy or sell securities with a specified "limit" price. The order can be executed only at the limit price or better.

A **stop order** may appear similar to a limit order, but there is an important difference. With a stop order, the customer specifies a "stop" price. This stop price serves as a trigger point. No trade can occur until the stock price reaches this stop price. When the stock price reaches the stop price, the stop order is immediately converted into a market order. Because the order is now a market order, the customer may get a price that is better or worse than the stop price. Thus, the stop price only serves as a trigger point for conversion into a market order. Unlike a limit price, the stop price places no limit on the price at which a trade can occur. Once converted to a market order, the trade is executed just like any other market order.

The most common type of stop order is a *stop-sell* order, which is an order to sell shares if the stock price falls to a specified stop price below the current stock price. This type of order is generally called a *stop-loss* because it is usually intended to limit losses on a long position. The other type is a *stop-buy* order, which is an order to buy shares if the price rises to a specified stop price above the current stock price. Stop-buy orders are often placed in conjunction with short sales, again as a means of limiting losses.

Placing stop-loss orders is frequently touted as a smart trading strategy, but there are a couple of issues we should mention. For example, suppose you buy 1,000 shares of GoGo Corp. at $20. You simultaneously place a stop-sell order at $15. Thus, you seem to have limited your potential loss to $5 per share.

Unfortunately, after the market closes, a rumor circulates that GoGo has uncovered a significant accounting fraud. The next morning, the stock opens at $8, meaning the first trade occurs at $8 per share. Because this price is below your $15 stop price, a market order to sell your stock will be placed and executed, and you'll lose much more than $5 per share. What you discover is that your stop-loss guarantees only that a market order to sell will be placed as soon as the stock trades at $15 or below.

Adding insult to injury, after your stock is sold, a credible announcement is made indicating that the rumor is false. GoGo shares promptly bounce back to $20, but you were sold out at a big loss. Thus, a second danger in blindly using stop-loss orders is that volatile conditions can lead to an unfavorable stop sale. Table 5.1 summarizes the characteristics of limit and stop orders.

This exact situation happened at the entire market level on May 6, 2010. During the so-called Flash Crash, the Dow Jones Industrial Average suffered its largest and fastest decline ever. Many stocks momentarily lost half their values. The nearby *Investment Updates* box provides some additional detail on this day.

In response to the Flash Crash, regulators updated their approach to **circuit breakers**. At the market level, circuit breakers were designed to calm the market in the event of a steep decline, with the initial levels kicking in with a loss of 10 percent in a given day.

Unfortunately, although there were many stocks with significant losses, the market as a whole never tripped the existing circuit breakers. As a result, regulators lowered the marketwide circuit breaker level to 7 percent and also implemented individual stock circuit breakers. We discuss this issue in more detail in a later chapter.

On August 24, 2015, a similar event occurred, as many stocks saw their prices swing wildly. For example, bellwether stocks such as GE and JPMorgan fell by more than 20 percent, but they quickly recovered. Not only would *stop-loss* orders have been ineffective at preventing

TABLE 5.1	Stock Market Order Types	
Order Type	**Buy**	**Sell**
Market order	Buy at best price available for immediate execution.	Sell at best price available for immediate execution.
Limit order	Buy at best price available, but not more than the preset limit price. Forgo purchase if limit is not met.	Sell at best price available, but not less than the preset limit price. Forgo sale if limit is not met.
Stop order	Convert to a market order to buy when the stock price crosses the stop price from below.	Convert to a market order to sell when the stock price crosses the stop price from above. Also known as a "stop-loss."
Stop-limit order	Convert to a limit order to buy when the stock price crosses the stop price from below.	Convert to a limit order to sell when the stock price crosses the stop price from above.

TRADING PROGRAM SPARKED MAY "FLASH CRASH"

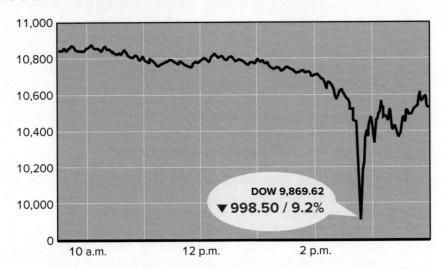

Federal regulators blamed automated trading software for the historic "flash crash" of May 2010. The Securities and Exchange Commission and the Commodity Futures Trading Commission claimed in their report on the incident that a large unnamed investor used a trading algorithm to quickly sell large volumes of orders for futures contracts called E-Minis. Traders use E-Minis to bet on the future performance of stocks in the S&P 500 index.

The selling was initially absorbed by high-frequency traders, but the algorithm responded to a rise in trading volume by increasing the number of E-Mini sell orders it was placing in the market. "What happened next is best described in terms of two liquidity crises—one at the broad index level in the E-Mini, the other with respect to individual stocks," the report said.

What does that mean? The lack of buyers and the rapid selling of E-Mini futures contracts began to affect the value of the underlying stocks and the broader stock indexes. (It certainly didn't help that the market was already under stress due to concerns about the European debt crisis.) Against this backdrop, the Dow Jones industrial average plunged nearly 1,000 points, briefly erasing $1 trillion in market value, before regaining much of the lost ground later that day.

Source: Ben Rooney, "Trading Program Sparked May 'Flash Crash,'" *CNN Money,* October 1, 2010.

losses, but some managers actually blame these order types for much of the volatility. In response, as the nearby *Investment Updates* box illustrates, the NYSE is eliminating some of these order types. Nonetheless, given their popularity and usefulness, brokers will likely continue to offer these special order types to their customers through their own trading programs.

While these new regulations may help to prevent unforeseen losses on stop orders, investors have the ability to add their own level of control. A limit price can be attached to a stop order to create a *stop-limit order.* This is different from a simple stop order in that once the stock price reaches the preset stop price, the order is converted into a limit order. By contrast, a simple stop order is converted into a market order. At this point, the limit order is just like any other limit order.

Notice that with a stop-limit order you must specify two prices, the stop and the limit. The two prices can be the same, or they can be different. In our GoGo Corp. example, you could place a stop-limit sell order at $15 stop, $12 limit. This order converts to a limit order to sell at $12 or better if the price ever hits $15 or below. Thus, you will never sell below $12. Of course, you may never sell at all unless your limit price is reached! Our nearby *Work the Web* box shows how these orders are entered in an actual online brokerage account.

INVESTMENT UPDATES

NYSE ENDS USE OF STOP ORDERS

In 2015, the New York Stock Exchange eliminated stop orders. Why restrict the type of transactions that investors can make? Because other investors, including BlackRock, blame stop orders for escalating extreme share-price swings.

What are stop orders? Stop orders are instructions to immediately trade once a stock hits a certain price, even if the price is far worse than the one specified in the order.

How do stop orders work? Say an investor requests that 1,000 shares of Alpha X get sold once the price falls to $15. If the stock plunges from $20 to $10, without hitting any intermediate prices first, the stop order will be executed at that first stopping point . . . even though it's much lower than the specified $15 target.

Was there a key incident that led investors to call for this ban? You know there was! On August 24, 2015, hundreds of normally stable securities (including blue chips like General Electric and JPMorgan Chase) posted unusual moves,

plunging as much as 21 percent before quickly recovering. BlackRock, the world's biggest asset manager, took a close look at these swings and decided that stop orders were part of the problem.

At least some academics agreed. Annie Massa at Bloomberg quoted James Angel, a Georgetown University professor, as saying that "Stop orders are like land mines; they blow up in ways that are unanticipated by the people who plant them."

Brokerage firms can still program their systems to execute orders achieving the same results as a stop order for their clients. The ban on stop orders, though, should raise awareness of the risks that investors take in making these types of trades.

Source: Annie Massa, "NYSE Kills 'Land Mine' Order Type Some Blame for August Mayhem," *Bloomberg,* November 19, 2015.

CHECK THIS

5.3a   What are the four main types of orders to buy and sell common stocks?

5.3b   What do DMMs do?

5.3c   What is a limit order? How do limit and stop orders differ?

5.4 Nasdaq

Related Bloomberg Functions

CCMP Nasdaq Composite Index

In terms of total dollar volume of trading, the second largest stock market in the United States is Nasdaq (say "Naz-dak"). In terms of the number of companies listed and, on some days, number of shares traded, Nasdaq is actually bigger than the NYSE.

The somewhat odd name is derived from the acronym Nasdaq, which stands for National Association of Securities Dealers Automated Quotations system. But Nasdaq is now a proper name in its own right.

NASDAQ OPERATIONS

Nasdaq's website is www.nasdaq.com. Click on "Our Businesses."

Introduced in 1971, the Nasdaq market is a computer network of securities dealers who disseminate timely security price quotes to Nasdaq subscribers. These dealers act as market makers for securities listed on Nasdaq. As market makers, Nasdaq dealers post bid and ask prices at which they accept sell and buy orders, respectively. For this reason, it is referred to as a *quote-driven market,* as opposed to the NYSE, which is an order-driven market. With each price quote, they also post the number of stock shares that they obligate themselves to trade at their quoted prices.

Like NYSE DMMs, Nasdaq market makers trade on an inventory basis, using their inventory as a buffer to absorb buy and sell order imbalances. Unlike the NYSE DMM system, Nasdaq features multiple market makers for actively traded stocks. Thus, there are two basic differences between the NYSE and Nasdaq:

Chapter 5 ● **The Stock Market** 153

To illustrate the importance of getting order types straight, we captured the actual trading screen from one of the largest discount brokers, E*Trade. On the screen below, the ticker symbol entered is JWN, a purveyor of fine apparel, Nordstrom, Inc. The order is a limit order to buy 200 shares at $26.75. That is, we want to purchase these shares for a price of $26.75 or lower. The limit order is good for the day **only**, but we could also choose for the order to be good until a **specific** date or even good until canceled.

Clicking on the "Preview order" button allows you to **double-check** your order before you submit it for transaction. Here is our preview screen:

NYSE   ↻ Refresh quote
JWN NORDSTROM INC COM

Symbol	Last Price x Size / Exch ⓘ	Bid x size	Ask x size	Volume
JWN	**26.90** +0.3400 (+1.28%)	26.61 x 100	26.93 x 200	10.00M

Action ⓘ   Quantity   Calculate   Snapshot Positions (0) Open Orders (0)
Buy ⌄   200

Price type ⓘ   Limit price ⓘ
Limit ⌄   26.75

Duration ⓘ
Good for day ⌄   ☐ All-or-none ⓘ

Estimated commission   Estimated total cost   [Save for later]   [Preview order]
$0.00 $5,350.00

Source: www.schwab.com.

After checking to make sure we have entered everything correctly, we hit the "Place order" button to submit our order.

NYSE   ↻ Refresh quote
JWN NORDSTROM INC COM

Last Price x Size / Exch ⓘ	Bid x size	Ask x size	Volume
26.90 +0.3400 (+1.28%)	26.61 x 100	26.93 x 200	10.00M

Action	Quantity	Description	Price type	Price	Duration
Buy	200	NORDSTROM INC COM (JWN)	Limit	$26.75	Good for Day

❯ View impact to purchasing power

Estimated commission   Estimated total cost   Change order   Cancel order   [Place order]
$0.00 $5,350.00

Source: www.schwab.com.

---

over-the-counter (OTC) market
Securities market in which trading is almost exclusively done through dealers who buy and sell for their own inventories.

1. Nasdaq is a computer network and has no physical location where trading takes **place**.

2. Nasdaq has a multiple market maker system rather than the DMM/SLP system.

Traditionally, a securities market largely characterized by dealers who buy and sell **securities** for their own inventories is called an **over-the-counter (OTC) market**. Consequently, Nasdaq is often referred to as an OTC market. In their efforts to promote a distinct **image**, Nasdaq officials prefer that the term *OTC* not be used when referring to the Nasdaq **market**. In fact, anyone actively trading today will not refer to Nasdaq as an OTC market.

The Nasdaq is actually made up of three separate markets: the Nasdaq Global Select Market, the Nasdaq Global Market, and the Nasdaq Capital Market. As the market for Nasdaq's larger and more actively traded securities, the Nasdaq Global Select Market lists some well-known companies. The Global Market companies are somewhat smaller in market cap. The smallest companies listed on Nasdaq are in the Nasdaq Capital Market. As you might guess, an important difference among the markets is that the Global Select Market has the most stringent listing requirements. Of course, as Capital Market companies become more established, they can move up to the Global Market or the Global Select Market.

The success of the Nasdaq Global Select Market as a competitor to the NYSE and other organized exchanges can be judged by its ability to attract stock listings by companies that traditionally might have chosen to be listed on the NYSE. Some of the best-known companies in the world such as Microsoft, Apple, Intel, Starbucks, and, of course, Alphabet (aka Google) list their securities on Nasdaq.

NASDAQ PARTICIPANTS

As we mentioned previously, the Nasdaq has historically been a dealer market, characterized by competing market makers. In early 2022, over 3,600 companies were listed on the Nasdaq system. Currently, about 260 Nasdaq member firms act as market makers.

In an important development, in the late 1990s, the Nasdaq system was opened to so-called **electronic communications networks (ECNs)**. ECNs are basically websites that allow investors to trade directly with one another. Investor buy and sell orders placed on ECNs are transmitted to the Nasdaq and displayed along with market maker bid and ask prices. As a result, the ECNs open up the Nasdaq by essentially allowing individual investors to enter orders through their brokers, not just market makers. As a result, the ECNs act to increase liquidity and competition.

If you check prices on the web for both Nasdaq- and NYSE-listed stocks, you'll notice an interesting difference. For Nasdaq stocks, you can actually see the bid and ask prices as well as recent transactions information. The bid and ask prices for the Nasdaq listings you see represent **inside quotes**, that is, the highest bid and the lowest ask prices. For a relatively small fee (or possibly even free from your broker), you can even have access to "Level II" quotes, which show all of the posted bid and ask prices and, frequently, the identity of the market maker. "Level III" quotes provide even more detail and features, and their access is restricted to registered market makers only. Of course, NYSE DMMs post bid and ask prices as well; they are just not disclosed to the general public.

electronic communications network (ECN)
A website that allows investors to trade directly with each other.

inside quotes
The highest bid quotes and the lowest ask quotes offered by dealers for a security.

CHECK THIS

5.4a	How does Nasdaq differ from the NYSE?
5.4b	What are the different levels of access to the Nasdaq network?

5.5 NYSE and Nasdaq Competitors

third market
Off-exchange market for securities listed on an organized exchange.

The NYSE and Nasdaq face strong competition in the market for order execution services from securities trading firms operating in the **third market**. The phrase "third market" refers to trading in exchange-listed securities that occurs off the exchange on which the security is listed. For example, a substantial volume of NYSE-listed stock trading is executed through independent securities trading firms.

This type of market can be attractive to investors who want to make a transaction without that transaction moving the price of the securities they are trading. One specific type of trading portal that allows investors to make these trades is a *crossing network,* which is an electronic trading system that enables the trading of large blocks of shares at prices posted on the actual exchange. Similarly, *dark pools* allow for off-exchange trading without posting the identity of the source making the trade. This system allows large institutional investors to maintain a level of privacy. It also keeps market prices from moving simply based on trading decisions by large institutional investors.

Nasdaq and the NYSE also face substantial competition from the **fourth market**. The term "fourth market" refers to direct trading of exchange-listed securities among investors. A good example of a company engaged in fourth-market trading activity is Instinet, one of the pioneers in ECNs. As we discussed in our previous section, however, these fourth-market ECNs are increasingly becoming integrated into the Nasdaq system or being acquired by other platforms such as BATS Global Markets.

The third and fourth markets are not the only NYSE and Nasdaq competitors. Regional exchanges also attract substantial trading volume away from the NYSE and Nasdaq. For example, thousands of stocks are dually listed on the NYSE and either on Nasdaq or on at least one regional exchange. In a recent move, some large financial firms such as Morgan Stanley and Fidelity have banded together to create the Members Exchange, or MEMX. The idea behind MEMX is to create a trading venue that has lower fees than the NYSE. Similar to how the NYSE was originally created, MEMX is controlled by its members, not by stockholders. We will have to wait to see if this new exchange succeeds.

Some companies do not meet the listing requirements of the NYSE or Nasdaq, so they need to list elsewhere. Even if they do meet these requirements, however, the company's management might still decide to list shares elsewhere. A nearby *Work the Web* box describes an alternative.

fourth market
Market for exchange-listed securities in which investors trade directly with other investors, usually through a computer network.

CHECK THIS

5.5a   What is the third market for securities?

5.5b   What is the fourth market for securities?

5.6 Stock Market Information

Many newspapers publish current price information for a selection of stocks. In the United States, the newspaper best known for reporting stock price information is *The Wall Street Journal* and its online version, wsj.com. Investors interested in an overview of stock market activity refer to daily summaries. Among other things, these summaries contain information regarding several stock market indexes. Immediately below, we describe the most important stock market indexes.

Related Bloomberg Function

INDU   Dow Jones Industrials Average Index

WEI   World Equity Indexes

MEMB   Member Weightings

MRR   Ranked Returns

THE DOW JONES INDUSTRIAL AVERAGE

The most widely followed barometer of day-to-day stock market activity is the Dow Jones Industrial Average (DJIA), often called the "Dow" for short. The DJIA is an index of the stock prices of 30 large companies representative of American industry. There are other, more specialized Dow Jones averages such as a utilities average and a transportation average. We will focus on the industrial average. Figure 5.2 provides a DJIA price chart.

Figure 5.2 shows closing prices and moving averages for the DJIA from November 2022 through late May 2022. We can see that, based on closing prices, the Dow reached a high of about 36,800 during this period compared to a low of about 31,250. Figure 5.3 is a Bloomberg screen showing the 30 well-known companies in the DJIA. Note that the list is sorted by descending prices on January 3, 2022. Why do you think that the weights also descend in value?

Although the Dow is the most familiar stock market index, a number of other indexes are widely followed. In fact, as we begin to discuss next, the Dow is not the most representative index by any means, and the way it is computed presents various problems that can make it difficult to interpret.

What are the Russell indexes? Visit russell.com to find out.

WORK THE WEB

Where do companies trade when they can't (or don't want to) meet the listing requirements of the larger stock markets? Mostly, they trade on the OTCQX®, OTCQB®, and OTC Pink® marketplaces operated by OTC Markets Group. The OTCQX® marketplace includes qualitative and quantitative standards, and the OTCQB® marketplace imposes some requirements as well, though these requirements are less restrictive than those enforced by the larger stock markets. OTC Pink® is called the "Open Marketplace" because there are no filing or financial requirements.

A small portion of companies also continue to trade on the Over-the-Counter Bulletin Board, or OTCBB, operated by the Financial Industry Regulatory Authority, known as FINRA. The OTCBB began as an electronic bulletin board that was created to facilitate OTC trading in nonlisted stocks. It has, however, been effectively replaced by OTC Markets Group's OTCQB® marketplace as the primary marketplace for these types of companies.

Like the OTCQX® and OTCQB®, the OTCBB imposes some requirements, though they are not as restrictive as those of the larger markets. For example, OTCBB only requires that listed firms file financial statements with the SEC (or other relevant agency).

Trading at any of the OTC Markets Group marketplaces, as well as the OTCBB, is conducted under a dealer-driven framework. So, aside from the minimal requirements for inclusion on these marketplaces, all that is necessary for a particular security to begin trading is a registered broker-dealer willing (and being approved) to quote and make a market in the security. Investors can trade OTCQX®, OTCQB®, and OTC Pink® securities in a manner similar to the trading of an exchange-listed stock. Given the ease of trading, these marketplaces (OTCQX®, in particular) are attractive to foreign firms that file with regulators in their home countries but do not have interest in filing with U.S. regulators. These markets are also an option for companies

All Markets

$ VOLUME	SHARE VOLUME
1,548,451,559	**5,177,317,649**
TRADES	ADVANCERS
247,997	**2,285**
DECLINERS	
1,349	

MOST ACTIVE

Price % Change **$ Volume** Share Volume Trades

SYMBOL		PRICE	% CHANGE	$ VOL	SHARE VOL	TRADES
Pink	TCEHY	43.86	-0.39	92,898,901	2,118,078	6,726
QX	GBTC	18.96	-0.42	75,299,109	3,971,472	14,304
QX	ETHE	11.94	-1.89	60,867,768	5,097,803	14,366
QX	RHHBY	43.06	-0.62	58,006,987	1,347,120	3,571
Pink	GLAXF	21.52	-2.71	29,063,255	1,350,523	6
▽	LVMUY	126.38	+3.20	28,880,231	228,519	1,862
Pink	NSRGY	121.58	+1.57	28,058,476	230,782	2,244
Pink	RYLPF	25.226	+0.40	26,802,398	1,062,491	16
Pink	SNYNF	109.40	-0.09	23,658,953	216,261	8
▽	HOCPY	109.385	+0.91	22,020,732	201,314	547

Source: OTCMarkets.com, accessed May 28, 2022.

that have been delisted from the larger markets either by choice or for failure to maintain their listing requirements.

Stocks traded on these markets often have very low prices and are frequently referred to as "penny stocks," "microcaps," or even "nanocaps." Relatively few brokers do research on these companies, so information is often spread through word of mouth or the internet, probably not the most reliable of sources. To get a feel for what trading looks like, we captured information on the most active stocks from www.otcmarkets.com.

At the end of a "typical" day in 2022, total dollar trading volume at the OTC Markets Group surpassed $1.5 billion. By contrast, average daily volume for Microsoft Corp. (MSFT) is about 33 million shares at the Nasdaq. With a stock

price of about $274 per share, this means that total dollar trading volume for Microsoft is about $9 billion, or about 6 times more than the dollar volume of the entire OTC Markets Group.

All in all, the OTCBB and OTC Markets Group can be pretty wild places to trade. Low stock prices allow huge percentage returns on small stock price movements. Be advised, however, that attempts at manipulation and fraud are possible. Also, many stocks on these markets are often very thinly traded, meaning there is little volume. It is not unusual for a stock listed on any of these markets to have zero trades on a given day. Even two or three days in a row without a trade in a particular stock is not uncommon.

FIGURE 5.2 — Dow Jones Industrial Average

Source: finance.yahoo.com, accessed May 27, 2022.

FIGURE 5.3 — The Dow Jones Industrial Average Component Stocks

Source: Bloomberg Finance L.P.

STOCK MARKET INDEXES

The Dow Jones Industrial Average web page is informative, but market watchers might be interested in more detail regarding recent stock market activity. A more comprehensive view of stock market trading is contained in Figure 5.4, which is a Bloomberg screen.

Figure 5.4 reports information about a variety of stock market indexes in addition to the Dow Jones averages. Of the non–Dow Jones indexes shown, by far the best known and most widely followed is Standard & Poor's index of 500 stocks, commonly abbreviated as the S&P 500, or often just the S&P. We have seen this index before. In Chapter 1, we used it as a benchmark to track the performance of large-company common stocks for the last nine decades.

If you were to scrutinize the various indexes in Figure 5.4, you would quickly find essentially four differences between them: (1) the market covered, (2) the types of stocks included, (3) how many stocks are included, and (4) how the index is calculated.

The first three of these differences are straightforward. Some indexes listed in Figure 5.4, such as the Dow Jones, the S&P 500, and Nasdaq, focus on U.S. markets. Other indexes focus on non-U.S. exchanges. For example, the S&P/TXS in the benchmark Canadian market index, containing about 250 companies listed on the Toronto Stock Exchange. The S&P/BMV is an index of the 35 largest and most liquid stocks listed on the Bolsa Mexicana de Valores. The IBVOESPA is the benchmark index of about 84 stocks traded on the B3 (i.e., the Brasil Bolsa Balcão). If you search the internet, you can discover what the indexes are in EMEA and Asia/Pacific.

How stock market indexes are computed is not quite so straightforward, but it is important to understand. There are two major types of stock market indexes: price-weighted and value-weighted. With a **price-weighted index**, stocks are held in the index in proportion to their share prices. With a **value-weighted index**, stocks are held in proportion to the aggregate market value of the companies in the index.

The best way to understand the difference between price and value weighting is to consider an example. To keep things relatively simple, we suppose that there are only two companies in the entire market. We have the following information about their shares outstanding, share prices, and total market values:

price-weighted index
Stock market index in which stocks are held in proportion to their share price.

value-weighted index
Stock market index in which stocks are held in proportion to the aggregate market value of the companies in the index.

		Price per Share		Total Market Value	
	Shares Outstanding	Beginning of Year	End of Year	Beginning of Year	End of Year
Company A	50 million	$10	$14	$500 million	$700 million
Company B	1 million	50	40	50 million	40 million

FIGURE 5.4   Stock Market Major Indexes

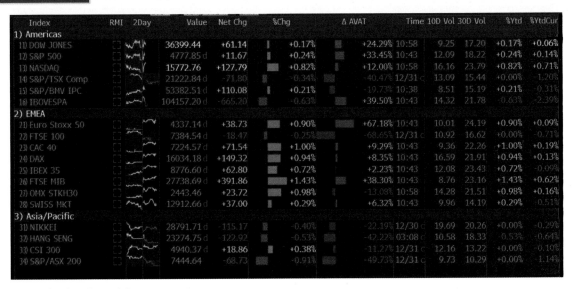

Source: Bloomberg Finance L.P.

As shown, Company A has a lower share price but many more shares outstanding. Ignoring dividends, notice that Company A's stock price rose by 40 percent ($10 to $14) while Company B's stock price fell by 20 percent ($50 to $40).

The question we want to answer here is: How did the market do for the year? There are several ways we could answer this question. We could first focus on what happened to the average share price. The average share price was ($10 + $50)/2 = $30 at the beginning of the year and ($14 + $40)/2 = $27 at the end, so the average share price fell. If we take the average share price as our index, then our index fell from 30 to 27, for a change of −3 points. Because the index began at 30, this is −3/30 = −.10, or a 10 percent decrease. In this case, investors say that the market was "off" by 10 percent.

This is an example of a price-weighted index. Because Company B's stock price is five times bigger than Company A's, it carries five times as much weight in the index. This explains why the index was down even though Company A's stock gained 40 percent whereas Company B's stock only lost 20 percent. The Dow Jones indexes are price weighted.

Alternatively, instead of focusing on the price of a typical share, we could look at what happened to the total value of a typical company. Here we notice that the average total value, in millions, rose from ($500 + $50)/2 = $275 to ($700 + $40)/2 = $370. If we take average total company value as our index, then our index rose from 275 to 370, a 35 percent *increase*.

Read the article "Are growth and value indexes still in style?" to learn more about "value" and "growth" indexes at www.msci.com/www/blog-posts/are-growth-and-value-indexes/02363871894.

This is an example of a value-weighted index. The influence a company has in this case depends on its overall change in total market value, not just its stock price change. Because Company A has a much larger total value, it carries a much larger weight in the index. With the exception of the Dow Jones indexes, most of the other indexes in Figure 5.4, including the Standard & Poor's, are value weighted.

Now we have a problem. One index tells us the market was down by 10 percent, while the other tells us it was up by 35 percent. Which one is correct? The answer seems fairly obvious. The total value of the market as a whole grew from $550 million to $740 million, so the market as a whole increased in value. Put differently, investors as a whole owned stock worth $550 million at the beginning of the year and $740 million at the end of the year. So, on the whole, stock market investors earned 35 percent, even though the average share price went down.

This example shows that a price-weighted index can be misleading as an indicator of total market value. The basic flaw in a price-weighted index is that the effect a company has on the index depends on the price of a single share. However, the price of a single share is only part of the story. Unless the number of shares is also considered, the true impact on the overall market isn't known, and a distorted picture can emerge.

EXAMPLE 5.1 **Caution: Indexes under Construction**

Suppose there are only two stocks in the market and the following information is given:

	Shares Outstanding	Price per Share	
		Beginning of Year	End of Year
Betty Co.	10 million	$10	$11
Gray Bull, Inc.	20 million	20	25

Construct price- and value-weighted indexes and calculate the percentage changes in each.

The average share price rose from $15 to $18, or $3, so the price-weighted index would be up by 3/15 = .20, or 20 percent. Average total market value, in millions, rose from $250 to $305, so the value-weighted index rose by 55/250 = .22, or 22 percent.

MORE ON PRICE-WEIGHTED INDEXES

Earlier we indicated that the Dow Jones averages are price weighted. Given this, you may wonder why the Dow Jones Industrial Average has such a high value when the stock prices used to calculate the average are much smaller. To answer this question, we must explain one last detail about price-weighted indexes.

The extra detail concerns the effects of stock splits on price-weighted indexes. For example, in a 2-for-1 stock split, all current shareholders receive two new shares in exchange for each old share that they own. However, the total value of the company does not change because it is still the same company after the stock split. There are twice as many shares, each worth half as much.

A stock split has no effect on a value-weighted index since the total value of the company does not change. But it can have a dramatic effect on a price-weighted index. To see this, consider what happens to the price-weighted and value-weighted indexes we created above when Company B enacts a 2-for-1 stock split. Based on beginning prices, with a 2-for-1 split, Company B's shares fall to $25. The price-weighted index falls to ($10 + $25)/2 = 17.50 from 30, even though nothing really happened.

For a price-weighted index, the problem of stock splits can be addressed by adjusting the divisor each time a split occurs. Once again, an example is the best way to illustrate. In the case stated just above, suppose we wanted the index value to stay at 30 even though B's price per share fell to $25 as a result of the split. The only way to accomplish this is to add together the new stock prices and divide by something less than 2.

This new number is called the *index divisor,* and it is adjusted as needed to remove the effect of stock splits. To find the new divisor in our case, the stock prices are $25 and $10, and we want the index to equal 30. We solve for the new divisor, d, as follows:

$$\text{Index level} = \frac{\text{Sum of stock prices}}{\text{Divisor}}$$

$$30 = \frac{\$25 + \$10}{d}$$

$$d = \frac{\$35}{30} = 1.16666\ldots$$

The new divisor is thus approximately 1.17.

Adjusting the divisor takes care of the problem in one sense, but it creates another problem. Because we are no longer dividing the sum of the share prices by the number of companies in the index, we can no longer interpret the change in the index as the change in price of an average share.

| EXAMPLE 5.2 | Adjusting the Divisor |

Take a look back at Example 5.1. Suppose that Gray Bull splits 5-for-1. Based on beginning information, what is the new divisor?

Following a 5-for-1 split, Gray Bull's share price will fall from $20 to $4. With no adjustment to the divisor, the price-weighted index would drop from 15 to ($10 + $4)/2 = 7. To keep the index at its old level of 15, we need to solve for a new divisor such that ($10 + $4)/$d$ = 15. In this case, the new divisor would be $14/15 = .93333. This example shows how the divisor can drop below 1.0.

THE DOW JONES DIVISORS

The method we described of adjusting the divisor on a price-weighted index for stock splits is the method used to adjust the Dow Jones averages. Through time, with repeated adjustments for stock splits, the divisor becomes smaller and smaller. As of May 26, 2022, we calculated the DJIA divisor to be a nice, round .1519382795. Because there are 30 stocks in the index, the divisor on the DJIA would be 30 if it were never adjusted, so it has declined substantially. Divisors for the other Dow Jones averages have similarly odd values.

Given their shortcomings, you might wonder why the financial press continues to report the Dow Jones averages. The reason is tradition. The Dow Jones averages have been around for more than 100 years, and each new generation of investors becomes accustomed to its quirks.

MORE ON INDEX FORMATION: BASE-YEAR VALUES

We next discuss one or two more details about indexes. First, to ease interpretation, the starting value of an index is usually set equal to some simple base number, like 100 or 1,000. For example, if you were to create a value-weighted index for the NYSE, the actual value of the index would be very large and cumbersome, so adjusting it makes sense.

To illustrate, suppose we have a value-weighted index with a starting value of 1.4 million. If we want the starting value to be 100, we just divide the starting value, and every subsequent value, by 1.4 million and then multiply by 100. So, if the next value of the index is 1.6 million, the "reindexed" value would be 1.6 million/1.4 million $\times$ 100 = 114.29, which is easily interpreted as a 14.29 percent increase over a base of 100.

EXAMPLE 5.3 **Reindexing**

You've calculated values for an index over a four-year period as follows:

Year 1:	1,687 million
Year 2:	1,789 million
Year 3:	1,800 million
Year 4:	1,700 million

Suppose you wanted the index to start at 1,000. What would the reindexed values be?

To reindex these numbers, we need to (1) divide each of them by the starting value, 1,687 million, and then (2) multiply each by 1,000. Thus, we have:

Year 1:	1,687 million/1,687 million $\times$ 1,000 = 1,000.00
Year 2:	1,789 million/1,687 million $\times$ 1,000 = 1,060.46
Year 3:	1,800 million/1,687 million $\times$ 1,000 = 1,066.98
Year 4:	1,700 million/1,687 million $\times$ 1,000 = 1,007.71

Finally, an important consideration in looking at indexes is whether dividends are included. Most indexes don't include them. As a result, the change in an index measures only the capital gain (or loss) component of your return. When you're trying to evaluate how a particular type of stock market investment has done over time, dividends have to be included to get an accurate picture.

So which index is the best? The most popular alternative to the DJIA is the value-weighted S&P 500. You might further wonder, however, why this popular index limits itself to 500 stocks. The answer is timeliness and accuracy. Almost all stocks in the S&P 500 index trade every day, and therefore accurate daily updates of market prices are available each day. Stocks that do not trade every day can cause **index staleness**. Index staleness occurs when an index does not reflect all current price information because some of the stocks in the index have not traded recently. Also, as a practical matter, the largest 500 companies account for a large portion (about 75 percent) of the value of the overall stock market.

While the value-weighted approach dominates, investors are always in search of a "better mousetrap." So, we have recently seen a surge in the number and types of indexes available. Much of this follows a so-called *fundamental indexing* approach. The most popular are indexes based on fundamental metrics such as earnings or dividend yields, with those stocks having the highest yields receiving the largest weights. As with anything new, however, there is still ongoing debate about whether these approaches actually create a better index.

index staleness
Condition that occurs when an index does not reflect all current price information because some of the stocks in the index have not traded recently.

5.6a What is the difference between price and value weighting in the construction of stock market indexes? Give an example of a well-known index of each type.

5.6b Which is better, price or value weighting? Why?

5.6c Which stock market index is likely to contain the greater degree of index staleness, the DJIA or the NYSE Composite Index? Why?

5.7 Summary and Conclusions

This chapter introduces you to stock markets. We discussed who owns stocks, how the stock exchanges operate, and how stock market indexes are constructed and interpreted. This chapter covers many important aspects of stock markets, including the following items—grouped by the chapter's important concepts.

1. **The differences between private and public equity, and primary and secondary stock markets.**

   A. Private equity funds are investment companies that invest in private companies. These investments range from early-stage financing (i.e., venture capital) to large leveraged buyouts of public companies (i.e., going private).

   B. The stock market is composed of a primary market, where stock shares are first sold, and a secondary market, where investors trade shares among themselves. In the primary market, companies raise money for investment projects. Investment bankers specialize in arranging financing for companies in the primary market. Investment bankers often act as underwriters, buying newly issued stock from the company and then reselling the stock to the public. The primary market is best known as the market for initial public offerings (IPOs).

   C. In the secondary market, investors trade securities with other investors. Secondary market transactions are directed through three channels: directly with other investors, indirectly through a broker, or directly with a dealer. We saw that a broker matches buyers and sellers; a dealer buys and sells out of inventory.

2. **The workings of the New York Stock Exchange.**

   A. Most common stock trading is directed through an organized stock exchange or through a trading network. The most well-known stock exchange in the United States is the New York Stock Exchange (NYSE). Popularly known as the Big Board, the NYSE was once owned by its members. Today, however, the NYSE itself is a publicly traded company (a subsidiary of its parent company Intercontinental Exchange)—so, it is owned by its shareholders.

   B. The three major types of NYSE license holders are designated market makers (DMMs), floor brokers, and supplemental liquidity providers (SLPs). We discussed the role of each in the functioning of the exchange.

3. **How Nasdaq operates.**

   A. The Nasdaq market is a computer network of securities dealers who post timely security price quotes to Nasdaq subscribers. These dealers act as market makers for securities listed on the Nasdaq.

   B. Unlike the NYSE, Nasdaq relies on multiple market makers instead of using a specialist system. Because it is a computer network, the Nasdaq has no physical location.

   C. The Nasdaq network operates with three levels of information access:
   - Level I provides timely and accurate price quotes that are freely available on the internet.

This chapter covered the operations and organization of the major stock markets. It also covered some of the most important order types and the construction of stock market indexes. How should you, as an investor or investment manager, put this information to work?

First, as in some previous chapters, you need to submit as many as possible of the different order types suggested by this chapter in a simulated brokerage account—like Stock-Trak (note that not all simulated brokerage accounts allow all trade types). Your goal is to gain experience with the different order types and what they mean and accomplish for you as an investor or investment manager.

In each case, once you have placed the order, be sure to monitor the price of the stock in question to see if any of your orders should be executed. When an order is executed, compare the result to the stop or limit price to see how you did.

The second thing to do is to start observing the different indexes and learning how they are computed, what's in them, and what they are intended to cover. For example, the Nasdaq 100 is made up of the largest Nasdaq stocks. Is this index broadly representative of big stocks in general? Of Nasdaq stocks in general? Learn about other indexes, like the Russell 2000, at www.russell.com.

For the latest information on the real world of investments, visit us at jmdinvestments.blogspot.com.

- Level II allows users to view price quotes from all Nasdaq market makers. This level allows access to inside quotes. Inside quotes are the highest bid and lowest ask quotes for a Nasdaq-listed security.
- Level III is for use by Nasdaq market makers only. With this access, market makers can change their quotes.

4. How to calculate index returns.

A. Investors interested in an overview of stock market activity refer to the returns on several stock market indexes.

B. The most widely followed barometer of day-to-day stock market activity is the Dow Jones Industrial Average (DJIA), often called the "Dow" for short. The DJIA is an index of the stock prices of 30 large companies representative of American industry. The DJIA is a price-weighted index.

C. Another widely followed index is the Standard & Poor's index of 500 stocks, commonly abbreviated as the S&P 500, or often just the S&P. The S&P 500 index is a value-weighted index.

D. Many newspapers and websites publish current price information for indexes as well as stocks. In the United States, the newspaper best known for reporting stock price information is *The Wall Street Journal*—with its companion website, www.wsj.com.

Key Terms

ask price 147	electronic communications network (ECNs) 155
best efforts underwriting 141	firm commitment underwriting 141
bid price 147	floor brokers 148
broker 148	fourth market 156
circuit breakers 151	general cash offer 140
crowdfunding 143	index staleness 162
dealer 146	initial public offering (IPO) 140
designated market maker (DMM) 148	inside quotes 155
DMM's post 150	investment banking firm 141
Dutch auction underwriting 142	limit order 150

Related Bloomberg Functions

PE	Private Equity Overview, 5.1
IPO	Equity Offerings, 5.1
LEAG	League Tables, 5.1
NIM	New Issues Monitor, 5.1
BAS	Broker Activity Summary, 5.1
RANK	Broker Rankings, 5.1
NYA	NYSE Composite Index, 5.3
CCMP	Nasdaq Composite Index, 5.4
INDU	Dow Jones Industrials Average Index, 5.6
WEI	World Equity Indexes, 5.6
MEMB	Member Weightings, 5.6
MRR	Ranked Returns, 5.6

Chapter Review Problems and Self-Test

1. **Index Construction (LO4, CFA2)** Suppose there are only two stocks in the market and the following information is given:

		Price per Share	
	Shares Outstanding	Beginning of Year	End of Year
Ally Co.	100 million	$60	$66
McBeal, Inc.	400 million	120	100

Construct price- and value-weighted indexes and calculate the percentage changes in each.

2. **Stock Splits (LO4, CFA2)** In Problem 1, suppose that McBeal splits 3-for-1. Based on beginning information, what is the new divisor?

Answers to Self-Test Problems

1. The average share price at the beginning of the year is ($60 + $120)/2 = $90. At the end of the year, the average price is $83. Thus, the average price declined by $7 from $90, a percentage drop of −$7/$90 = −.0778, or −7.78 percent. Total market cap at the beginning of the year is ($60 × 100) + ($120 × 400) = $54 billion. It falls to $46.6 billion, a decline of $7.4 billion. The percentage decline is −$7.4 billion/$54 billion = −.137, or −13.7 percent, or almost twice as much as the price-weighted index.

2. Following a 3-for-1 split, McBeal's share price falls from $120 to $40. To keep the price-weighted index at its old level of 90, we need a new divisor such that $(\$60 + \$40)/d = 90$. In this case, the new divisor would be $\$100/90 = 1.1111$.

Test Your Investment Quotient

1. **New York Stock Exchange (LO2, CFA1)**   Which of the following is false?
   a. DMMs can trade for their own accounts.
   b. DMMs earn income from providing liquidity.
   c. On the NYSE, all buy and sell orders are negotiated through a floor broker.
   d. DMMs stand ready to trade at quoted bid and ask prices.

2. **Private Equity (LO1, CFA3)**   Private equity funds that concentrate in early-stage financing would likely be what type of fund?
   a. Venture capital
   b. Middle market
   c. Leveraged buyouts
   d. Distressed assets

3. **Private Equity (LO1, CFA4)**   The compensation constraint that requires private equity fund managers to "give back" performance fees when subsequent losses occur is a(n) _____ provision.
   a. High-water mark
   b. Clawback
   c. Zenith
   d. Index

4. **Value-Weighted Index (LO4, CFA2)**   An analyst gathered the following data about Stocks J, K, and L, which together form a value-weighted index:

	December 31, Year 1		December 31, Year 2	
Stock	Price	Shares Outstanding	Price	Shares Outstanding
J	$40	10,000	$50	10,000
K	30	6,000	20	12,000*
L	50	9,000	40	9,000

*2-for-1 stock split.

The ending value-weighted index (base index = 100) is closest to:
   a. 92.31
   b. 93.64
   c. 106.80
   d. 108.33

5. **Dow Jones Index (LO4, CFA2)**   The divisor for the Dow Jones Industrial Average (DJIA) is most likely to decrease when a stock in the DJIA:
   a. Has a stock split.
   b. Has a reverse split.
   c. Pays a cash dividend.
   d. Is removed and replaced.

6. **New York Stock Exchange (LO2, CFA1)**   Which of the following activities is not conducted by DMMs on the NYSE?
   a. Acting as dealers for their own accounts
   b. Monitoring compliance with margin requirements
   c. Providing liquidity to the market
   d. Posting bid and ask prices

7. **Stock Markets (LO1, CFA1)** What is a securities market characterized by dealers who buy and sell securities for their own inventories called?

   a. A primary market
   b. A reordered market
   c. An over-the-counter market
   d. An institutional market

8. **Stock Markets (LO1, CFA1)** What is the over-the-counter market for exchange-listed securities called?

   a. Third market
   b. Fourth market
   c. After-market
   d. Block market

9. **Stock Indexes (LO4, CFA2)** If the market price of each of the 30 stocks in the Dow Jones Industrial Average changes by the same percentage amount during a given day, which stock will have the greatest impact on the DJIA?

   a. The one whose stock trades at the highest dollar price per share
   b. The one whose total equity has the highest market value
   c. The one having the greatest amount of equity in its capital structure
   d. The one having the lowest volatility

10. **Stock Indexes (LO4, CFA2)** In calculating the Standard & Poor's stock price indexes, how are adjustments for stock splits made?

    a. By adjusting the divisor
    b. Automatically, due to the manner in which the index is calculated
    c. By adjusting the numerator
    d. Quarterly, on the last trading day of each quarter

11. **Stock Indexes (LO4, CFA2)** Which of the following indexes includes the largest number of actively traded stocks?

    a. The Nasdaq Composite Index
    b. The NYSE Composite Index
    c. The Wilshire 5000 Index
    d. The Value Line Composite Index

12. **Private Equity (LO1, CFA3)** Private equity funds that concentrate in smaller, family-owned companies with established cash flows are typically referred to as:

    a. Venture capital.
    b. Middle market.
    c. Leveraged buyouts.
    d. Distressed assets.

13. **Private Equity (LO1, CFA4)** The compensation constraint that requires private equity fund managers to meet a particular return target before performance fees can be taken is a(n) _____ provision.

    a. High-water mark
    b. Clawback
    c. Zenith
    d. Index

14. **Private Equity (LO1, CFA4)** Private equity funds will often use convertible preferred stock or bonds with attached call options. These types of securities are used because they:

    a. Increase the risk of the transaction.
    b. Shorten the life of the investment.
    c. Allow upside potential associated with a successful venture.
    d. Meet SEC regulations for such investments.

15. **Stock Indexes (LO4, CFA2)** Which one of the following statements regarding the Dow Jones Industrial Average is false?

    a. The DJIA contains 30 well-known large-company stocks.
    b. The DJIA is affected equally by dollar changes in low- and high-priced stocks.
    c. The DJIA is affected equally by percentage changes in low- and high-priced stocks.
    d. The DJIA divisor must be adjusted for stock splits.

Concept Questions

1. **Primary and Secondary Markets (LO1, CFA3)** At your local Chevrolet retailer, both a primary and a secondary market are in action. Explain. Is the Chevy retailer a dealer or a broker?

2. **Brokers (LO1, CFA1)** Why would floor brokers be willing to pay $40,000 per year just for the right to trade on the NYSE?

3. **Market and Limit Orders (LO1, CFA5)** What is the difference between a market order and a limit order? What is the potential downside to each type of order?

4. **Stop That! (LO2, CFA5)** What is a stop-loss order? Why might it be used? Is it sure to stop a loss?

5. **Order Types (LO2, CFA5)** Suppose Intel is currently trading at $50. You want to sell it if it reaches $55. What type of order should you submit?

6. **Order Types (LO2, CFA5)** Suppose Tesla is currently trading at $300. You think that if it reaches $310, it will continue to climb, so you want to buy it if and when it gets there. Should you submit a limit order to buy at $310?

7. **Nasdaq Quotes (LO3, CFA1)** With regard to the Nasdaq, what are inside quotes?

8. **Index Composition (LO4, CFA2)** There are basically four factors that differentiate stock market indexes. What are they? Comment on each.

9. **Index Composition (LO4, CFA2)** Is it necessarily true that, all else the same, an index with more stocks is better? What is the issue here?

10. **Private Equity (LO1, CFA3)** Why would venture capitalists provide financing in stages?

Questions and Problems

Core Questions

1. **Price-Weighted Divisor (LO4, CFA2)** Able, Baker, and Charlie are the only three stocks in an index. The stocks sell for $93, $312, and $78, respectively. If Baker undergoes a 2-for-1 stock split, what is the new divisor for the price-weighted index?

2. **Price-Weighted Divisor (LO4, CFA2)** In Problem 1, assume that Baker undergoes a 4-for-1 stock split. What is the new divisor now?

3. **Order Books (LO2, CFA1)** You find the following order book on a particular stock. The last trade on the stock was at $70.54.

Buy Orders		Sell Orders	
Shares	Price	Shares	Price
250	$70.53	100	$70.56
100	70.52	600	70.57
900	70.51	1,000	70.59
75	70.49	700	70.60
		900	70.61

   a. If you place a market buy order for 100 shares, at what price will it be filled?
   b. If you place a market sell order for 200 shares, at what price will it be filled?
   c. Suppose you place a market order to buy 400 shares. At what price will it be filled?

4. **Price-Weighted Index (LO4, CFA2)** You are given the following information concerning two stocks that make up an index. What is the price-weighted return for the index?

	Shares Outstanding	Price per Share	
		Beginning of Year	End of Year
Kirk, Inc.	35,000	$37	$42
Picard Co.	26,000	84	91

5. **Value-Weighted Index (LO4, CFA2)** Calculate the index return for the information in the previous problem using a value-weighted index.

6. **Reindexing (LO4, CFA2)** In Problem 5, assume that you want to reindex with the index value at the beginning of the year equal to 100. What is the index level at the end of the year?

7. **Index Level (LO4, CFA2)** In Problem 5, assume the value-weighted index level was 408.16 at the beginning of the year. What is the index level at the end of the year?

8. **Reindexing (LO4, CFA2)** Suppose you calculated the total market value of the stocks in an index over a five-year period:

   Year 1: $4,387 million

   Year 2: $4,671 million

   Year 3: $5,032 million

   Year 4: $4,820 million

   Year 5: $5,369 million

   Suppose you wanted the index to start at 1,000. What would the reindexed values be?

Intermediate Questions

9. **Price-Weighted Divisor (LO4, CFA2)** Look back at Problem 1. Assume that Able undergoes a 1-for-2 reverse stock split. What is the new divisor?

10. **DJIA (LO4, CFA2)** On May 31, 2022, the DJIA opened at 33,160.59. The divisor at that time was .15173. Suppose on this day the prices for 29 of the stocks remained unchanged and 1 stock increased $5.00. What would the DJIA level be at the end of the day?

11. **DJIA (LO4, CFA2)** In June 2022, United Healthcare (UNH) was the highest-priced stock in the DJIA and Walgreens (WBA) was the lowest. The opening price for UNH on May 31, 2022, was $496.78, and the closing price for WBA was $43.83. Suppose this day the other 29 stock prices remained unchanged and UNH increased 5 percent. What would the new DJIA level be? Now assume only WBA increased by 5 percent. Find the new DJIA level. Use the information from Problem 10 to answer this question.

12. **DJIA (LO4, CFA2)** Looking back at Problems 10 and 11, what would the new index level be if all stocks on the DJIA increased by $1.00 per share on the next day?

13. **Price-Weighted Divisor (LO4, CFA2)** You construct a price-weighted index of 40 stocks. At the beginning of the day, the index is 8,465.52. During the day, 39 stock prices remain the same, and 1 stock price increases $5.00. At the end of the day, your index value is 8,503.21. What is the divisor on your index?

14. **Price-Weighted Indexes (LO4, CFA2)** Suppose the following three defense stocks are to be combined into a stock index in January 2022 (perhaps a portfolio manager believes these stocks are an appropriate benchmark for their performance):

	Shares (millions)	Price		
		1/1/22	1/1/23	1/1/24
Douglas McDonnell	340	$103	$106	$118
Dynamics General	450	45	39	53
International Rockwell	410	74	63	79

   a. Calculate the initial value of the index if a price-weighting scheme is used.
   b. What is the rate of return on this index for the year ending December 31, 2022? For the year ending December 31, 2023?

15. **Price-Weighted Indexes (LO4, CFA2)** In Problem 14, suppose that Douglas McDonnell shareholders approve a 3-for-1 stock split on January 1, 2023. What is the new divisor for the index? Calculate the rate of return on the index for the year ending December 31, 2023, if Douglas McDonnell's share price on January 1, 2024, is $39.33 per share.

16. **Value-Weighted Indexes (LO4, CFA2)** Repeat Problem 14 if a value-weighted index is used. Assume the index is scaled by a factor of 10 million; that is, if the average firm's market value is $5 billion, the index would be quoted as 500.

17. **Value-Weighted Indexes (LO4, CFA2)** In Problem 16, will your answers change if the Douglas McDonnell stock splits? Why or why not?

18. **Equal-Weighted Indexes (LO4, CFA2)** In addition to price-weighted and value-weighted indexes, an equally weighted index is one in which the index value is computed from the average rate of return of the stocks comprising the index. Equally weighted indexes are frequently used by financial researchers to measure portfolio performance.

   a. Using the information in Problem 14, compute the rate of return on an equally weighted index of the three defense stocks for the year ending December 31, 2022.
   b. If the index value is set to 100 on January 1, 2022, what will the index value be on January 1, 2023? What is the rate of return on the index for 2023?

19. **Dutch Auctions (LO1, CFA1)** Escambia Beach Systems is offering 1,000 shares in a Dutch auction IPO. The following bids have been received:

Bidder	Quantity	Price
A	400	$20
B	400	19
C	300	18
D	200	17

How much will Bidder A have to spend to purchase all of the shares that have been allocated to her?

20. **Equal-Weighted versus Value-Weighted Indexes (LO4, CFA2)** Historically there have been periods where a value-weighted index has a higher return than an equally weighted index and other periods where the opposite has occurred. Why do you suppose this would happen? *Hint:* Look back to Chapter 1.

21. **Geometric Indexes (LO4)** Another type of index is the geometric index. The calculation of a geometric index is similar to the calculation of a geometric return:

$$1 + R_G = \left[\left(1 + R_1\right)\left(1 + R_2\right)\cdots\left(1 + R_N\right)\right]^{1/N}$$

The difference in the geometric index construction is that the returns used are the returns for the different stocks in the index for a particular period, such as a day or year. Construct the geometric index returns for Problem 14 over each of the two years. Assume the beginning index level is 100.

22. **Interpreting Index Values (LO4, CFA2)** Suppose you want to replicate the performance of several stock indexes, some of which are price weighted, others value weighted, and still others equally weighted. Describe the investment strategy you need for each of the index types. Are any of the three strategies passive, in that no portfolio rebalancing need be performed to perfectly replicate the index (assuming no stock splits or cash distributions)? Which of the three strategies do you think is most often followed by small investors? Which strategy is the most difficult to implement?

Spreadsheet Problems

23. **Price-Weighted vs. Value-Weighted Indexes (LO4, CFA2)** Suppose the following four stocks are to be combined into a stock index in January 2022 (perhaps a portfolio manager believes these stocks are an appropriate benchmark for their performance):

		Price		
	Shares (millions)	1/1/22	1/1/23	1/1/24
Brady Corporation	375	$28	$26	$32
Luck Industries	430	39	42	46
Mahomes International	550	50	54	62
Wentz Products	275	21	25	23

a. Calculate the initial value of the index if a price-weighting scheme is used. What is the rate of return on this index for the year ending December 31, 2022? For the year ending December 31, 2023?

b. Now assume that a value-weighted index is used and that it is scaled by a factor of 10 million; that is, if the average firm's market value is $5 billion, the index would be quoted as 500.

CFA Exam Review by Kaplan Schweser

[CFA5]

George White, CFA, and Elizabeth Plain, CFA, manage an account for Briggs and Meyers Securities. In managing the account, White and Plain use a variety of strategies, and they trade in different markets. They use both market and limit orders to execute their trades, which are often based on algorithmic methods. Their supervisor has asked them to compose a summary of their trading records to see how various strategies have worked.

Their supervisor also asks them to assess the costs and risks of the various types of trades. The supervisor specifically asks Mr. White and Ms. Plain to explain the difference in risks associated with market and limit orders. After Mr. White and Ms. Plain explain how limit orders can give a better price, the supervisor asks why they wouldn't always use limit orders.

As part of the discussion, Ms. Plain explains the issue of spread. She uses a recent example where the quoted bid and ask prices of GHT stock were $25.40 and $25.44, respectively.

1. Which of the following statements regarding market orders is most accurate? Market orders:

   a. Have price uncertainty, and limit orders have execution uncertainty.
   b. Have execution uncertainty, and limit orders have price uncertainty.
   c. And limit orders both have execution uncertainty and no price uncertainty.

2. In the example given by Ms. Plain, what was the spread for the GHT stock just prior to execution?

   a. $.06
   b. $.02
   c. $.04

3. Assume that when Mr. White and Ms. Plain entered their buy order for GHT, the price of the stock increased to $25.45. This is the price at which the trade was executed. Given this impact, the effective spread was _____ that in Question 2 above.

   a. Lower than
   b. Higher than
   c. The same as

Bloomberg Exercises

1. Identify companies set to go public in the near future. **(IPO)**
2. Examine the performance of world equity indexes for the last trading day. **(WEI)**
3. Find the current divisor used to calculate the Dow Jones Industrials Average Index (INDU) value. **(DES)**

What's on the Web?

1. **DJIA** As you have seen, in a price-weighted index, a stock with a higher price has a higher weight in the index return. To find out the weight of the stocks in the DJIA, go to www.slickcharts.com/dowjones. Which stock in the DJIA has the highest weight? The lowest weight?

2. **DJIA** You want to find the current divisor for the DJIA. Go to the market data center at www.wsj.com and look up the current divisor.

3. **S&P 500** To find out the most recent changes in the S&P 500, go to www.spglobal.com/ratings. Once at the website, find the 10 most recent additions and deletions to the stocks in the index.

4. **Nikkei 225** The Nikkei 225 Index is a highly followed index that measures the performance of the Japanese stock market. Go to indexes.nikkei.co.jp/en/nkave and find out if the Nikkei 225 is a price-weighted or value-weighted index. What is the divisor for this index? When was the latest reconstitution of the index? Which stocks were added? Which stocks were deleted? *Hint:* Look in the "More Details" section.

Common Stock Valuation

"If a business is worth a dollar and I can buy it for 40 cents, something good may happen to me."

–Warren Buffett

"Prediction is difficult, especially about the future."

–Niels Bohr[1]

Learning Objectives

Separate yourself from the commoners by having a good understanding of these security valuation methods:

1. The basic dividend discount model.

2. The two-stage dividend growth model.

3. The residual income and free cash flow models.

4. Price ratio analysis.

Common stock valuation is one of the most challenging tasks in financial analysis. A fundamental assertion of finance holds that the value of an asset is based on the present value of its future cash flows. Accordingly, common stock valuation attempts the difficult task of predicting the future. Consider that the dividend yield for a typical large-company stock might be about 2 percent. This implies that the present value of dividends to be paid over the next 10 years constitutes only a portion of the current stock price. Thus, much of the value of a typical stock is derived from dividends to be paid more than 10 years away!

CFA™ Exam Topics in this Chapter:

1. Financial reporting quality (L1, S8)
2. Cost of capital—foundational topics (L1, S10)
3. Overview of equity securities (L1, S12)
4. Equity valuation: Concepts and basic tools (L1, S12)
5. Equity valuation: Applications and processes (L2, S8)
6. Discounted dividend valuation (L2, S9)
7. Market-based valuation: Price and enterprise value multiples (L2, S10)
8. Residual income valuation (L2, S10)
9. Free cash flow valuation (L2, S10)

Go to Connect for a guide that aligns your textbook with CFA readings.

---

[1] This quote has also been attributed to Yogi Berra, Samuel Goldwyn, and Mark Twain.

In this chapter, we examine several methods commonly used by financial analysts to assess the economic value of common stocks. These methods are grouped into two categories: discount models and price ratio models. After studying these models, we provide an analysis of a real company to illustrate the use of the methods discussed in this chapter.

6.1 Security Analysis: Be Careful Out There

Related Bloomberg Functions

DES   Security Description

FA   Financial Analysis

It may seem odd that we start our discussion with an admonition to be careful, but in this case, we think it is a good idea. The methods we discuss in this chapter are examples of those used by many investors and security analysts to assist in making buy and sell decisions for individual stocks. The basic idea is to identify both "undervalued" or "cheap" stocks to buy and "overvalued" or "rich" stocks to sell. In practice, however, many stocks that look cheap may in fact be correctly priced for reasons not immediately apparent to the analyst. Indeed, the hallmark of a good analyst is a cautious attitude and a willingness to probe further and deeper before committing to a final investment recommendation.

fundamental analysis
Examination of a firm's accounting statements and other financial and economic information to assess the economic value of a company's stock.

The type of security analysis we describe in this chapter falls under the heading of **fundamental analysis**. Numbers such as a company's earnings per share, cash flow, book equity value, and sales are often called *fundamentals* because they describe, on a basic level, a specific firm's operations and profits (or lack of profits).

Fundamental analysis represents the examination of these and other accounting statement-based company data used to assess the value of a company's stock. Information regarding such things as management quality, products, and product markets is often examined as well.

We urge you to be cautious when you apply these techniques. Further, the simpler the technique, the more cautious you should be. As our later chapter on market efficiency explains, there is good reason to believe that simple techniques that rely on widely available information are not likely to yield systematically superior investment results. In fact, they could lead to unnecessarily risky investment decisions. This is especially true for ordinary investors (like most of us) who do not have timely access to the information that a professional security analyst working for a major securities firm would possess.

Visit the CFA Society New York website at www.cfany.org.

As a result, our goal here is not to teach you how to "pick" stocks with a promise that you will become rich. Certainly, one chapter in an investments text is not likely to be sufficient to acquire that level of investment savvy. Still, an appreciation of the techniques in this chapter is important because buy and sell recommendations made by securities firms are frequently couched in the terms we introduce here. Much of the discussion of individual companies in the financial press relies on these concepts as well, so some background is necessary to interpret commonly presented investment information. In essence, you must learn both the jargon and the concepts of security analysis.

CHECK THIS

6.1a   What is fundamental analysis?

6.1b   What is a "rich" stock? What is a "cheap" stock?

6.1c   Why does valuing a stock necessarily involve predicting the future?

6.2 The Dividend Discount Model

Related Bloomberg Functions

DDM   Dividend Discount Model

DVD   Dividend/Split Summary

BDVD   Bloomberg Dividend Forecast

A fundamental principle of finance says that the value of a security equals the sum of its future cash flows, where the cash flows are adjusted for risk and the time value of money. A popular model used to value common stock is the **dividend discount model**, or **DDM**. The dividend discount model values a share of stock as the sum of all expected future dividend payments, where the dividends are adjusted for risk and the time value of money.

For example, suppose a company pays a dividend at the end of each year. Let D_T denote a dividend to be paid T years from now and let P_0 represent the present value of the future

FA GRO Financial Analysis: Growth

FA ROE Financial Analysis: DuPont Analysis

dividend discount model (DDM)

Method of estimating the value of a share of stock as the present value of all expected future dividend payments.

Check out the American Association of Individual Investors website at www.aaii.com.

dividend stream. Also, let k denote the appropriate risk-adjusted discount rate. Using the dividend discount model, the present value of a share of this company's stock is measured as this sum of discounted future dividends:

$$P_0 = \frac{D_1}{1+k} + \frac{D_2}{(1+k)^2} + \frac{D_3}{(1+k)^3} + \cdots + \frac{D_T}{(1+k)^T} \tag{6.1}$$

In Equation 6.1, we assume that the last dividend is paid T years from now. The value of T depends on the time of the *terminal*, or last, dividend. Thus, if $T = 3$ years and $D_1 = D_2 = D_3 = \$100$, the present value, P_0, is stated as:

$$P_0 = \frac{\$100}{1+k} + \frac{\$100}{(1+k)^2} + \frac{\$100}{(1+k)^3}$$

If the discount rate is $k = 10$ percent, then a quick calculation yields $P_0 = \$248.69$. Thus, the stock price should be about $250 per share.

EXAMPLE 6.1

Using the Dividend Discount Model

Suppose again that a stock pays three annual dividends of $100 per year and the discount rate is $k = 15$ percent. In this case, what is the price of the stock today?

With a 15 percent discount rate, we have:

$$P_0 = \frac{\$100}{1.15} + \frac{\$100}{1.15^2} + \frac{\$100}{1.15^3}$$

Check that the answer is $P_0 = \$228.32$.

EXAMPLE 6.2

Using the Dividend Discount Model Again

Suppose instead that the stock pays three annual dividends of $10, $20, and $30 in Years 1, 2, and 3, respectively, and the discount rate is $k = 10$ percent. What is the price of the stock today?

In this case, we have:

$$P_0 = \frac{\$10}{1.10} + \frac{\$20}{1.10^2} + \frac{\$30}{1.10^3}$$

Check that the answer is $P_0 = \$48.16$.

CONSTANT PERPETUAL GROWTH

constant perpetual growth model

A version of the dividend discount model in which dividends grow forever at a constant rate, and the growth rate is strictly less than the discount rate.

Try surfing to the CFA Institute website at www.cfainstitute.org.

A particularly simple and useful form of the dividend discount model is called the **constant perpetual growth model**. In this case, we assume the firm will pay dividends that grow at the constant rate g forever. In the constant perpetual growth model, stock prices are calculated using this formula:

$$P_0 = \frac{D_0(1+g)}{k-g} \qquad (g < k) \tag{6.2}$$

Because $D_0(1 + g) = D_1$, we can also write the constant perpetual growth model as:

$$P_0 = \frac{D_1}{k-g} \qquad (g < k) \tag{6.3}$$

Either way, we have a very simple, and very widely used, formula for the price of a share of stock based on its future dividend payments.

Notice that the constant perpetual growth model requires that the growth rate be strictly less than the discount rate, that is, $g < k$. It looks as if the share value would be negative if this were not true. Actually, the formula is not valid in this case. The reason is that a perpetual dividend growth rate greater than the discount rate implies an *infinite* value because the present value of the dividends keeps getting bigger and bigger. Because no security can have infinite value, the requirement that $g < k$ makes good economic sense.

To illustrate the constant perpetual growth model, suppose that the growth rate is $g = 4$ percent, the discount rate is $k = 9$ percent, and the current dividend is $D_0 = \$10$. In this case, a simple calculation yields:

$$P_0 = \frac{\$10(1.04)}{.09 - .04} = \$208$$

EXAMPLE 6.3 **Using the Constant Perpetual Growth Model**

Suppose dividends for a particular company are projected to grow at 5 percent forever. If the discount rate is 15 percent and the current dividend is $10, what is the value of the stock?

$$P_0 = \frac{\$10(1.05)}{.15 - .05} = \$105$$

With these inputs, the stock should sell for $105.

HOW DO WE GET THE FORMULA FOR CONSTANT PERPETUAL GROWTH? Good question. Many people wonder how such a simple-looking formula, Equation 6.3, emerges when we add up an infinite number of dividends. Recall that perpetual dividend growth means that dividends will grow forever. This means today's stock price, P_0, equals:

$$P_0 = \frac{D_1}{1+k} + \frac{D_1(1+g)}{(1+k)^2} + \frac{D_1(1+g)^2}{(1+k)^3} + \frac{D_1(1+g)^3}{(1+k)^4} + \cdots \qquad (6.4)$$

Equation 6.4 says that the stock price today is equal to the sum of the discounted amounts of all future dividends. To get the formula for today's stock price when assuming constant perpetual growth, we begin by multiplying both sides of Equation 6.4 by the amount $[(1 + g)/(1 + k)]$. Equation 6.4 then becomes:

$$P_0\left[\frac{1+g}{1+k}\right] = \frac{D_1}{1+k}\left[\frac{1+g}{1+k}\right] + \frac{D_1(1+g)}{(1+k)^2}\left[\frac{1+g}{1+k}\right] \qquad (6.5)$$
$$+ \frac{D_1(1+g)^2}{(1+k)^3}\left[\frac{1+g}{1+k}\right] + \cdots$$
$$= \frac{D_1(1+g)}{(1+k)^2} + \frac{D_1(1+g)^2}{(1+k)^3} + \frac{D_1(1+g)^3}{(1+k)^4} + \cdots$$

Then, we subtract Equation 6.5 from Equation 6.4. If you look closely, you can see that when we do this, we can cancel a lot of terms. In fact, we can cancel all the terms on the right side of Equation 6.5 and all but the first term on the right side of Equation 6.4. Using a little bit of algebra, we show what happens when we subtract Equation 6.5 from Equation 6.4:

$$P_0 - P_0\left[\frac{1+g}{1+k}\right] = \frac{D_1}{1+k} + \frac{D_1(1+g)}{(1+k)^2} - \frac{D_1(1+g)}{(1+k)^2}$$
$$+ \frac{D_1(1+g)^2}{(1+k)^3} - \frac{D_1(1+g)^2}{(1+k)^3} + \cdots$$

$$P_0\left[1 - \frac{1+g}{1+k}\right] = \frac{D_1}{1+k}$$

$$P_0\left[\frac{1+k}{1+k} - \frac{1+g}{1+k}\right] = \frac{D_1}{1+k}$$

$$P_0\left[\frac{k-g}{1+k}\right] = \frac{D_1}{1+k}$$

$$P_0 = \frac{D_1}{1+k} \times \frac{1+k}{k-g}$$

$$P_0 = \frac{D_1}{k-g} \qquad (6.6)$$

Now you know how we get a formula for the price of a share of stock when we assume that dividends grow at a constant rate forever. We apply this formula in the following section.

APPLICATIONS OF THE CONSTANT PERPETUAL GROWTH MODEL In practice, the constant perpetual growth model is the most popular dividend discount model because it is so simple to use. Certainly, the model satisfies Einstein's famous dictum: "Simplify as much as possible, but no more." However, experienced financial analysts are keenly aware that the constant perpetual growth model can be usefully applied only to companies with a history of relatively stable earnings and dividends that are expected to continue to grow into the distant future.

Visit the AEP and DTE websites at www.aep.com and www.dteenergy.com.

A standard example of an industry for which the constant perpetual growth model can often be usefully applied is the electric utility industry. Consider American Electric Power, which is traded on the New York Stock Exchange under the ticker symbol AEP. In early 2022, AEP was paying an annual dividend of $3.00; thus, we set $D_0 = \$3.00$.

To use the constant perpetual growth model, we also need a discount rate and a growth rate. An old quick-and-dirty rule of thumb for a risk-adjusted discount rate for electric utility companies is the yield to maturity on 20-year-maturity U.S. Treasury bonds, plus 2 percent. At the time this example was written, the St. Louis Fed site showed the yield on 20-year-maturity T-bonds was 3.35 percent. Adding 2 percent, we get a discount rate of $k = 5.35$ percent.

Over the past 15 years, AEP has increased its dividend by about 4.4 percent per year. Putting it all together, we have $k = 5.35$ percent, $g = 4.40$ percent, and $D_0 = \$3.00$. Using these numbers, we obtain this estimate for the value of a share of AEP stock:

$$P_0 = \frac{\$3.00(1.044)}{.0535 - .044} = \$329.68$$

This estimate is well above the mid-2022 AEP stock price of $99.65. What is going on? Is it possible that AEP stock is grossly undervalued?

geometric average dividend growth rate
A dividend growth rate based on a geometric average of historical dividends.

Well, it is possible that AEP is undervalued. But recall that we made three important assumptions about the discount rate, the dividend growth rate, and the steady nature of dividend growth in order to estimate AEP's price. A change in any one of these assumptions could easily lead us to a different conclusion. A careful analyst would wonder what happens when these assumptions change. We will return to this point several times in future discussions.

EXAMPLE 6.4 — Valuing DTE Energy Co.

In 2021, the utility company DTE Energy (DTE) paid a $3.56 dividend. Using $D_0 = \$3.56$, $k = 5.35$ percent, and an industry average growth rate of $g = 3$ percent, calculate a present value estimate for DTE. Compare this value with the early 2022 DTE stock price of $129.68.

Plugging in the numbers, we have:

$$P_0 = \frac{\$3.56(1.03)}{.0535 - .03} = \$156.03$$

This estimate is higher than the early 2022 DTE stock price of $129.68, possibly suggesting that DTE stock was undervalued. But again, a careful analyst would test the assumptions made to estimate this price.

HISTORICAL GROWTH RATES

In the constant growth model, a company's historical average dividend growth rate is frequently taken as an estimate of future dividend growth. Sometimes historical growth rates are provided in published information about the company. Other times it is necessary to calculate a historical growth rate yourself. There are two ways to do this: (1) using a **geometric average dividend growth rate** or (2) using an **arithmetic average dividend growth rate**. As we will show, both methods are relatively easy to use.

arithmetic average dividend growth rate
A dividend growth rate based on an arithmetic average of historical dividends.

To show the difference between a geometric average and an arithmetic average of historical dividend growth, suppose that The Broadway Joe Company paid the following dividends at the end of each of these years:

2021:	$2.20	2018:	$1.75
2020:	2.00	2017:	1.70
2019:	1.80	2016:	1.50

We begin with a geometric average growth rate because it is easier to calculate. Notice that five years elapsed between the $1.50 dividend paid at the end of 2016 and the $2.20 dividend paid at the end of 2021. A geometric average growth rate is equivalent to a constant rate of growth over the five-year period that would grow the dividend from $1.50 to $2.20. That is, it is the growth rate that solves this growth equation:

$$\$2.20 = \$1.50(1 + g)^5$$

$$g = \left(\frac{\$2.20}{\$1.50}\right)^{1/5} - 1 = .08, \text{ or } 8\%$$

Thus, in this case, the five-year geometric average dividend growth rate is 8 percent. Notice that this calculation is similar to our calculation of the geometric average return in Chapter 1.

In general, if D_0 is the earliest dividend used and D_N is the latest dividend used to calculate a geometric average dividend growth rate over N years, the general equation used is:

$$g = \left[\frac{D_N}{D_0}\right]^{1/N} - 1 \qquad (6.7)$$

In the above example, $D_0 = \$1.50$, $D_N = \$2.20$, and $N = 5$, which yields $g = 8$ percent.

An arithmetic average growth rate takes a little more effort to calculate because it requires that we first calculate each year's dividend growth rate separately and then calculate an arithmetic average of these annual growth rates. For our Broadway Joe example, the arithmetic average of five years of dividend growth is calculated as follows:

Year	Dividend	Yearly Growth Rate
2021	$2.20	10.00% = ($2.20 − 2.00)/$2.00
2020	2.00	11.11% = (2.00 − 1.80)/1.80
2019	1.80	2.86% = (1.80 − 1.75)/1.75
2018	1.75	2.94% = (1.75 − 1.70)/1.70
2017	1.70	13.33% = (1.70 − 1.50)/1.50
2016	1.50	
		SUM/N = 40.24%/5 = 8.05%

The sum of the five yearly growth rates is 40.24%. Dividing by five yields an arithmetic average growth rate of 40.24%/5 = 8.05%. Notice that this arithmetic average growth rate is close to the geometric average growth rate of 8.0 percent. For dividend growth rates, this close difference between geometric and arithmetic averages is common, but it is not always so.

Remember that geometric averages are always less than or equal to arithmetic averages. The size of the difference depends on the volatility of the returns of the underlying asset. A large difference between the two averages implies that the dividend growth was erratic. An irregular growth pattern calls into question the use of the geometric, or constant growth, formula.

EXAMPLE 6.5 — Erratic Dividend Growth

To illustrate how the geometric average and the arithmetic average of historical dividend growth can differ, consider the following dividends paid by the Joltin' Joe Company:

2021:	$2.20	2018:	$2.00
2020:	2.00	2017:	1.50
2019:	1.80	2016:	1.50

(continued)

Because the starting and ending dividend amounts are the same as they are in the Broadway Joe example, the geometric growth rate is still 8 percent.

For Joltin' Joe's pattern of dividends, the five-year arithmetic average of dividend growth is calculated as follows:

Year	Dividend	Yearly Growth Rate
2021	$2.20	10.00% = ($2.20 − 2.00)/$2.00
2020	2.00	11.11% = (2.00 − 1.80)/1.80
2019	1.80	−10.00% = (1.80 − 2.00)/2.00
2018	2.00	33.33% = (2.00 − 1.50)/1.50
2017	1.50	0.00% = (1.50 − 1.50)/1.50
2016	1.50	
		44.44%/5 = 8.89%

In this case, the sum of the five yearly growth rates is 44.44 percent. Dividing by five yields an arithmetic average growth rate of 44.44%/5 = 8.89%. Notice that this arithmetic average growth rate is somewhat larger than the geometric average growth rate of 8.0 percent, which you can verify using Equation 6.7.

As the Joltin' Joe example shows, sometimes the arithmetic and geometric growth rate averages can yield rather different results. In practice, most analysts prefer to use a geometric average when calculating an average historical dividend growth rate. In any case, a historical average growth rate might or might not be a reasonable estimate of future dividend growth. Many analysts adjust their estimates to reflect other information available to them (for example, whether the growth rate appears to be sustainable).

THE SUSTAINABLE GROWTH RATE

As we have seen, when using the constant perpetual growth model, it is necessary to come up with an estimate of g, the growth rate of dividends. In our previous discussions, we described how to do this using the company's historical average growth rate. We now describe a second way, using the **sustainable growth rate**, which involves using a company's earnings to estimate g.

sustainable growth rate
A dividend growth rate that can be sustained by a company's earnings.

As we have discussed, a limitation of the constant perpetual growth model is that it should be applied only to companies with stable dividend and earnings growth. Essentially, a company's earnings can be paid out as dividends to its stockholders or kept as **retained earnings** within the firm to finance future growth. The proportion of earnings paid to stockholders as dividends is called the **payout ratio**. The proportion of earnings retained for reinvestment is called the **retention ratio**.

retained earnings
Earnings retained within the firm to finance growth.

If we let D stand for dividends and *EPS* stand for earnings per share, then the payout ratio is D/EPS. Because anything not paid out is retained, the retention ratio is just 1 minus the payout ratio. For example, if a company's current dividend is $4 per share and its EPS is currently $10, then the payout ratio is $4/$10 = .40, or 40 percent, and the retention ratio is 1 − .40 = .60, or 60 percent.

payout ratio
Proportion of earnings paid out as dividends.

retention ratio
Proportion of earnings retained for reinvestment.

A firm's sustainable growth rate is equal to its return on equity (ROE) times its retention ratio:[2]

$$\text{Sustainable growth rate} = \text{ROE} \times \text{Retention ratio} \qquad (6.8)$$
$$= \text{ROE} \times (1 - \text{Payout ratio})$$

Return on equity is commonly computed using an accounting-based performance measure and is calculated as a firm's net income divided by shareholders' equity:

$$\text{Return on equity (ROE)} = \text{Net income/Equity} \qquad (6.9)$$

---

[2] Strictly speaking, this formula is correct only if ROE is calculated using beginning-of-period shareholders' equity. If ending figures are used, then the precise formula is ROE × Retention ratio/[1 − (ROE × Retention ratio)]. However, the error from not using the precise formula is usually small, so most analysts might not bother with it.

EXAMPLE 6.6

Calculating Sustainable Growth

In 2021, American Electric Power (AEP) had a return on equity (ROE) of 11.74 percent, had earnings per share (EPS) of $4.97, and paid dividends of $D_0 = \$3.00$. What was AEP's retention rate? Its sustainable growth rate?

AEP's dividend payout was $3.00/$4.97 = .604, or about 60.4 percent. Its retention ratio was thus 1 − .604 = .396, or 39.6 percent. Finally, AEP's sustainable growth rate was .1174 × .396 = .0465, or 4.65 percent.

EXAMPLE 6.7

Valuing American Electric Power (AEP)

Using AEP's rounded sustainable growth rate of 4.65 percent (see Example 6.6) as an estimate of perpetual dividend growth and its current dividend of $3.00, what is the value of AEP's stock assuming a discount rate of 5.5 percent?

Using the constant growth model, we obtain a value of $3.00(1.0465)/(.055 − .0465) = $369.35. Clearly, something is wrong because the actual price was $99.65 in early 2022. Can you identify some reasons for this difference?

EXAMPLE 6.8

Valuing DTE Energy Co. (DTE)

In 2021, DTE had an ROE of 8.15 percent, EPS of $4.69, and a per-share dividend of $D_0 = \$3.56$. Assuming a 5.5 percent discount rate, what is the value of DTE's stock?

Let's get you started. DTE's payout ratio was $3.56/$4.69 = .759, or about 75.9 percent. Thus, DTE's retention ratio was 1 − .759 = .241, or 24.1 percent. DTE's sustainable growth rate is thus 8.15% × .241 = 1.96%.

Using the constant growth model, we obtain a value of $3.56(1.0196)/(.055 − .0196) = $102.65. Here, our estimated price is less that the actual price of $129.68 in early 2022.

Suppose we calculate a sustainable growth rate that is higher than the discount rate. What then? Can we use the constant growth model in this case?

A common problem with sustainable growth rates is that they are sensitive to year-to-year fluctuations in earnings. As a result, security analysts routinely adjust sustainable growth rate estimates to smooth out the effects of earnings variations. Unfortunately, there is no universally standard method to adjust a sustainable growth rate, and analysts depend a great deal on personal experience and their own subjective judgment. Our *Work the Web* box contains more information on analyst-estimated growth rates.

ANALYZING ROE

Two factors are needed to estimate a sustainable growth rate: the dividend payout ratio and ROE. For most firms, dividend policy is relatively stable. Thus, any major changes in the firm's sustainable growth rate likely stem from changes in ROE. Therefore, an understanding of ROE is critical when you are analyzing a stock price.

You might recall from other finance classes that ROE, net income divided by equity, can be broken down into three components. This "decomposition" is so important that it has a name: *the DuPont formula*, because it was first used by the DuPont Company (now DowDuPont). The DuPont formula is:

$$\text{ROE} = \frac{\text{Net income}}{\text{Sales}} \times \frac{\text{Sales}}{\text{Assets}} \times \frac{\text{Assets}}{\text{Equity}} \qquad (6.10)$$

The DuPont formula shows that ROE has three parts. The first part is the firm's *net profit margin*, which measures the amount of net income for each dollar of sales. The second part measures asset efficiency, and it is referred to as *asset turnover*. Asset efficiency measures how much revenue a firm gets from its assets. The third part is called the *equity multiplier*.

WORK THE WEB

We discussed use of the sustainable growth formula to estimate a company's growth rate; however, the formula is not foolproof. Changes in the variables of the model can have a dramatic effect on growth rates. One of the most important tasks of an equity analyst is estimating future growth rates. These estimates require a detailed analysis of the company. One place to find earnings and sales growth rates on the web is Yahoo! Finance at finance.yahoo.com. Here, we pulled up a quote for Coca-Cola (KO) and followed the "Analysis" link. Below you will see an abbreviated look at the results.

As shown, analysts, on average, expect 2022 revenue (sales) to grow from an estimated $41.93 billion to $44.16 billion in 2023, an increase of 5.3 percent.

Earnings Estimate	Current Qtr. (Jun 2022)	Next Qtr. (Sep 2022)	Current Year (2022)	Currency in USD Next Year (2023)
No. of Analysts	19	19	22	22
Avg. Estimate	0.67	0.66	2.47	2.65
Low Estimate	0.61	0.63	2.45	2.54
High Estimate	0.74	0.7	2.54	2.73
Year Ago EPS	0.68	0.65	2.32	2.47

Revenue Estimate	Current Qtr. (Jun 2022)	Next Qtr. (Sep 2022)	Current Year (2022)	Next Year (2023)
No. of Analysts	13	13	17	18
Avg. Estimate	10.56B	10.77B	41.93B	44.16B
Low Estimate	9.17B	10.56B	41.22B	42.77B
High Estimate	11.1B	11.22B	42.42B	45.73B
Year Ago Sales	9.32B	9.75B	38.66B	41.93B
Sales Growth (year/est)	13.30%	10.50%	8.50%	5.30%

Source: Yahoo! Finance, accessed May 2022.

The equity multiplier captures the amount of leverage (or debt) used by the firm. If the equity multiplier equals one, then the firm has no debt.

You can now see the ways that managers of a firm can increase the firm's sustainable growth rate. They can pay out a smaller percentage of the earnings. A lower payout ratio will increase the growth rate. If managers find ways to increase profitability or increase asset efficiency, ROE increases. Finally, managers can increase debt. The resulting increase in the equity multiplier means that ROE increases (assuming a positive profit margin). Looking at the sustainable growth rate formula, you can see that if ROE increases, so does the sustainable growth rate.

Before we move on, it is important to note that valuations are not always just a result of company-specific factors. For example, when Congress passed the Tax Cuts and Jobs Act of 2017, there were many provisions. One key point was the reduction of corporate taxes to a flat rate of 21 percent. How should this change impact stock values? If you consider the sustainable growth formula, you should expect prices to rise. Why? A lower tax rate, all else equal, means higher net income, which will lead to a higher ROE and a higher sustainable growth rate.

6.2a Compare the dividend discount model, the constant growth model, and the constant perpetual growth model. How are they alike? How do they differ?

6.2b What is a geometric average growth rate? How is it calculated?

6.2c What is a sustainable growth rate? How is it calculated?

6.2d What are the components of ROE?

6.3 The Two-Stage Dividend Growth Model

Related Bloomberg Functions

BETA Historical Beta

EQRP Equity Risk Premium

SOVM Sovereign Debt Monitor

two-stage dividend growth model
A dividend discount model that assumes a firm will temporarily grow at a rate different from its long-term growth rate.

In the previous section, the dividend discount model used one growth rate. You might have already thought that a single growth rate is often unrealistic. You might be thinking that companies experience temporary periods of unusually high or low growth, with growth eventually converging to an industry average or an economywide average. In these cases, financial analysts frequently use a **two-stage dividend growth model**.

A two-stage dividend growth model assumes that a firm will initially grow at a rate g_1 during a first stage of growth lasting T years and thereafter grow at a rate g_2 during a perpetual second stage of growth. The formula for the two-stage dividend growth model is stated as follows:

$$P_0 = \frac{D_0(1+g_1)}{k-g_1}\left[1 - \left(\frac{1+g_1}{1+k}\right)^T\right] + \left(\frac{1+g_1}{1+k}\right)^T\left[\frac{D_0(1+g_2)}{k-g_2}\right] \tag{6.11}$$

Equation 6.11 has two parts. The first term on the right-hand side measures the present value of the first T dividends. The second term then measures the present value of all subsequent dividends, assuming that the dividend growth rate changes from g_1 to g_2 at Date T.

Using the formula is mostly a matter of "plug and chug" with a calculator. For example, suppose a firm has a current dividend of $2 and dividends are expected to grow at the rate g_1 = 20 percent for T = 5 years, and thereafter grow at the rate g_2 = 5 percent. With a discount rate of k = 12 percent, the stock price today, P_0, is calculated as:

$$P_0 = \frac{\$2(1.20)}{.12 - .20}\left[1 - \left(\frac{1.20}{1.12}\right)^5\right] + \left(\frac{1.20}{1.12}\right)^5\left[\frac{\$2(1.05)}{.12 - .05}\right]$$

$$= \$12.36 + \$42.36$$

$$= \$54.72$$

In this calculation, the total present value of $54.72 is the sum of a $12.36 present value for the first five dividends plus a $42.36 present value for all subsequent dividends.

EXAMPLE 6.9 | **Using the Two-Stage Model**

Suppose a firm has a current dividend of D_0 = $5, which is expected to "shrink" at the rate g_1 = −10 percent for T = 5 years and thereafter grow at the rate g_2 = 4 percent. With a discount rate of k = 10 percent, what is the value of the stock?

Using the two-stage model, the stock price today, P_0, is calculated as:

$$P_0 = \frac{\$5(.90)}{.10 - (-.10)}\left[1 - \left(\frac{.90}{1.10}\right)^5\right] + \left(\frac{.90}{1.10}\right)^5\left[\frac{\$5(1.04)}{.10 - .04}\right]$$

$$= \$14.25 + \$31.78$$

$$= \$46.03$$

The total present value of $46.03 is the sum of a $14.25 present value of the first five dividends plus a $31.78 present value of all subsequent dividends.

The two-stage growth formula requires that the second-stage growth rate be strictly less than the discount rate, that is, $g_2 < k$. However, the first-stage growth rate g_1 can be greater than, less than, or equal to the discount rate.

EXAMPLE 6.10 | Valuing American Express (AXP)

American Express trades on the New York Stock Exchange under the ticker symbol AXP. In 2021, AXP was paying a dividend of $1.72 and analysts forecasted five-year growth rates of 14 percent for AXP and 6 percent for the overall market. Assume that AXP grows at 14 percent for the next five years, then falls to the market growth rate thereafter. If we use a discount rate of 12 percent, what value would we place on AXP?

$$P_0 = \frac{\$1.72 \times 1.14}{.12 - .14}\left[1 - \left(\frac{1.14}{1.12}\right)^5\right] + \left(\frac{1.14}{1.12}\right)^5\left[\frac{\$1.72 \times 1.06}{.12 - .06}\right]$$
$$= (-\$98.04 \times -.0925) + (1.0925 \times \$30.39)$$
$$= \$9.07 + \$33.20$$
$$= \$42.27$$

This price estimate is much less than AXP's early 2022 share price of $167.15. Is AXP overvalued? What other factors could explain the difference?

EXAMPLE 6.11 | Pepsi! Pepsi! Pepsi! (PEP)

Pepsi shares trade on the Nasdaq under the ticker symbol PEP. In 2021, Pepsi was paying a dividend of $4.25 and analysts forecasted a five-year growth rate of 7.48 percent for Pepsi and a 6 percent growth rate for the overall market. Suppose Pepsi grows at 7.48 percent for five years and then at 6 percent thereafter. Assuming a 12 percent discount rate, what value would we place on PEP?

Plugging this information into the two-stage dividend growth model, we get:

$$P_0 = \frac{\$4.25 \times 1.0748}{.12 - .0748}\left[1 - \left(\frac{1.0748}{1.12}\right)^5\right] + \left(\frac{1.0748}{1.12}\right)^5\left[\frac{\$4.25 \times 1.06}{.12 - .06}\right]$$
$$= (\$101.06 \times .1861) + (.8139 \times \$75.08)$$
$$= \$18.81 + \$61.11$$
$$= \$79.92$$

This estimate is about $90 dollars below PEP's early 2022 share price of $170.41.

Suppose we try a second-stage growth rate of 7.5 percent and a discount rate of 10.25 percent. In this case, we get a price of $165.99 (check this for yourself). This new estimate is much closer to the early 2022 price of PEP. This example illustrates how sensitive stock price estimates using dividend growth models can be to changes in either the estimated growth rate or discount rate.

Visit the AXP and PEP websites at
www.americanexpress.com
and
www.pepsico.com.

NONCONSTANT GROWTH IN THE FIRST STAGE

The last case we consider is nonconstant growth in the first stage. As a simple example of nonconstant growth, consider the case of a company that is currently not paying dividends. You predict that, in five years, the company will pay a dividend for the first time. The dividend will be $.50 per share. You expect that this dividend will then grow at a rate of 10 percent per year indefinitely. The required return on companies such as this one is 20 percent. What is the price of the stock today?

To see what the stock is worth today, we first find out what it will be worth once dividends are paid. We can then calculate the present value of that future price to get today's price. The first dividend will be paid in five years, and the dividend will grow steadily from then on. Using the dividend growth model, we can say that the price in four years will be:

$$P_4 = D_4 \times (1 + g)/(k - g)$$
$$= D_5/(k - g)$$
$$= \$.50/(.20 - .10)$$
$$= \$5$$

FIGURE 6.1 Time Line

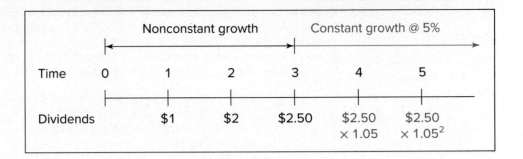

If the stock will be worth $5 in four years, then we can get the current value by discounting this price back four years at 20 percent:

$$P_0 = \$5/1.20^4 = \$5/2.0736 = \$2.41$$

The stock is therefore worth $2.41 today.

The problem of nonconstant growth is only slightly more complicated if the dividends are not zero for the first several years. For example, suppose that you have come up with the following dividend forecasts for the next three years:

Year	Expected Dividend
1	$1.00
2	2.00
3	2.50

After the third year, the dividend will grow at a constant rate of 5 percent per year. The required return is 10 percent. What is the value of the stock today?

In dealing with nonconstant growth, a time line can be very helpful. Figure 6.1 illustrates one for this problem. The important thing to notice is when constant growth starts. As we've shown, for this problem, constant growth starts at Time 3. This means that we can use our constant growth model to determine the stock price at Time 3, P_3. By far the most common mistake in this situation is to incorrectly identify the start of the constant growth phase and, as a result, calculate the future stock price at the wrong time.

The value of the stock is the present value of all future dividends. To calculate this present value, we first have to compute the present value of the stock price three years down the road, just as we did before. We then have to add in the present value of the dividends that will be paid between now and then. So, the price in three years is:

$$P_3 = D_3 \times (1 + g)/(k - g)$$
$$= \$2.50 \times 1.05/(.10 - .05)$$
$$= \$52.50$$

We can now calculate the total value of the stock as the present value of the first three dividends plus the present value of the price at Time 3, P_3:

$$P_0 = \frac{D_1}{(1 + k)^1} + \frac{D_2}{(1 + k)^2} + \frac{D_3}{(1 + k)^3} + \frac{P_3}{(1 + k)^3}$$
$$= \frac{\$1}{1.10} + \frac{\$2}{1.10^2} + \frac{\$2.50}{1.10^3} + \frac{\$52.50}{1.10^3}$$
$$= \$.91 + \$1.65 + \$1.88 + \$39.44$$
$$= \$43.88$$

The value of the stock today is thus $43.88.

EXAMPLE 6.12

"Supernormal" Growth

Chain Reaction, Inc., has been growing at a phenomenal rate of 30 percent per year because of its rapid expansion and explosive sales. You believe that this growth rate will last for three more years and that the rate will then drop to 10 percent per year. If the growth rate then remains at 10 percent indefinitely, what is the total value of the stock? Total dividends just paid were $5 million, and the required return is 20 percent.

Chain Reaction's situation is an example of supernormal growth. It is unlikely that a 30 percent growth rate can be sustained for any extended length of time. To value the equity in this company, we first need to calculate the total dividends over the supernormal growth period:

Year	Total Dividends (in millions)
1	$5.00 × 1.3 = $6.500
2	6.50 × 1.3 = 8.450
3	8.45 × 1.3 = 10.985

The price at Time 3 can be calculated as:

$$P_3 = [D_3 \times (1 + g)]/(k - g)$$

where g is the long-run growth rate. So we have:

$$P_3 = [\$10.985 \times 1.10]/(.20 - .10) = \$120.835 \text{ million}$$

To determine the value today, we need the present value of this amount plus the present value of the total dividends:

$$P_0 = \frac{D_1}{(1 + k)^1} + \frac{D_2}{(1 + k)^2} + \frac{D_3}{(1 + k)^3} + \frac{P_3}{(1 + k)^3}$$

$$= \frac{\$6.50}{1.20} + \frac{\$8.45}{1.20^2} + \frac{\$10.985}{1.20^3} + \frac{\$120.835}{1.20^3}$$

$$= \$5.42 + \$5.87 + \$6.36 + \$69.93$$

$$= \$87.58$$

The total value of the stock today is thus $87.58 million. If there were, for example, 20 million shares, then the stock would be worth $87.58/20 = $4.38 per share.

THE H-MODEL

In Example 6.12, we assumed a supernormal growth rate of 30 percent per year for three years, and then growth at a perpetual 10 percent. For most firms, however, growth does not follow this disjointed path. The growth rate is more likely to start at a high level and then fall over time until reaching its perpetual level.

There are many ways that we can assume the growth rate declines over time. One popular approach is the H-model, which assumes a linear decline in growth. To illustrate this decline, let's look at our example again. Suppose the growth rate begins at 30 percent in Year 1 and reaches 10 percent in Year 4 and beyond. Using the H-model, we would assume that the company's growth rate would decline by 20 percent from the end of Year 1 to the end of Year 4.

If we assume a linear decline, then the growth rate would fall by 6.67 percent per year (= 20 percent/3 years). Using the H-model, our growth estimates would be 30 percent for Year 1, 23.33 percent for Year 2, 16.66 percent for Year 3, and 10 percent for Year 4 and beyond. With these growth estimates, you can repeat Example 6.12. You should find that the firm value is $75.93 million, with a per-share value of $3.80. As we would expect, this value is lower than our initial estimate because we are assuming lower growth rates in Years 2 and 3 compared to the original example.

DISCOUNT RATES FOR DIVIDEND DISCOUNT MODELS

You may wonder where the discount rates used in the preceding examples come from. The answer is that they come from the *capital asset pricing model* (CAPM). Although a detailed discussion of the CAPM is deferred to a later chapter, we can point out here that, based on the CAPM, the discount rate for a stock can be estimated using this formula:

Discount rate = U.S. T-bill rate + (Stock beta × Stock market risk premium)   (6.12)

The components of this formula, as we use it here, are defined as follows:

U.S. T-bill rate:	Return on 90-day U.S. T-bills
Stock beta:	Risk relative to an average stock
Stock market risk premium:	Risk premium for an average stock

The basic intuition for this approach appears in Chapter 1. There we saw that the return we expect to earn on a risky asset had two parts, a "wait" component and a "worry" component. We labeled the wait component as the *time value of money,* and we noted that it can be measured as the return we earn from an essentially riskless investment. Here we use the return on a 90-day Treasury bill as the riskless return.

We called the worry component the *risk premium,* and we noted that the greater the risk, the greater the risk premium. Depending on the exact period studied, the risk premium for the U.S. market as a whole over the past 90 or so years has averaged about 8.3 percent. This 8.3 percent can be interpreted as the risk premium for bearing an average amount of stock market risk. Remember, though, the risk premium has been neither constant through time nor consistent across countries. Based on recent history and global metrics, we proposed that a risk premium around 7 percent might be more applicable over the coming years.

Finally, when we look at a particular stock, we recognize that it may be more or less risky than an average stock. A stock's **beta** is a measure of a single stock's risk relative to an average stock, and we discuss beta at length in a later chapter. For now, it suffices to know that the market average beta is 1.0. A beta of 1.5 indicates that a stock has 50 percent more risk than the average stock, so its risk premium is 50 percent higher. A beta of .50 indicates that a stock is 50 percent less risky than average and has a smaller risk premium.

Over time, T-bill rates have averaged about 4 percent, although they have been much lower in recent years. Taking the concept of stock beta as given for now, a stock beta of .8 yields an estimated discount rate of $4.0\% + (.8 \times 7\%) = 9.6\%$. Similarly, a stock beta of 1.2 yields the discount rate of $4.0\% + (1.2 \times 7\%) = 12.4\%$. For the remainder of this chapter, we will use discount rates calculated according to this CAPM formula.

beta
Measure of a stock's risk relative to the stock market average.

OBSERVATIONS ON DIVIDEND DISCOUNT MODELS

We have examined three dividend discount models: the constant perpetual growth model, the two-stage dividend growth model, and the nonconstant growth model. Each model has advantages and disadvantages. Certainly, the main advantage of the constant perpetual growth model is that it is simple to compute. However, it has several disadvantages: (1) it is not usable for firms not paying dividends, (2) it is not usable when the growth rate is greater than the discount rate, (3) it is sensitive to the choice of growth rate and discount rate, (4) discount rates and growth rates may be difficult to estimate accurately, and (5) constant perpetual growth is often an unrealistic assumption.

The two-stage dividend growth model offers several improvements: (1) it is more realistic since it accounts for low, high, or zero growth in the first stage, followed by constant long-term growth in the second stage; and (2) it is usable when the first-stage growth rate is greater than the discount rate. The two-stage model, however, is also sensitive to the choice of discount rate and growth rates. Also, it is not useful for companies that don't pay dividends, but this limitation applies to dividend models in general.

Financial analysts readily acknowledge the limitations of dividend discount models. Consequently, they also turn to other valuation methods to expand their analyses. In the next few sections, we discuss some popular stock valuation methods based on residual income, free cash flow, and price ratios.

CHECK THIS

6.3a   What are the three parts of a CAPM-determined discount rate?

6.3b   Under what circumstances is a two-stage dividend discount model appropriate?

6.4 The Residual Income Model

To this point, we have been valuing only firms that pay dividends. What about the many companies that don't pay dividends? As it turns out, there is an elegant and simple model that we can use.

RESIDUAL INCOME

At the beginning of any period, we can think of the book, or the accounting, equity in a firm as representing the total amount of money that stockholders have tied up in the company. Let B_{t-1} stand for the book equity per share at the beginning of a period that ends at Time t. Over the period, the stockholders have a required return on that investment of k. Thus, the required return in dollars, or required earnings per share ($REPS$), during the period that ends at Time t is:

$$REPS_t = B_{t-1} \times k$$

The difference between actual earnings, EPS_t, and required earnings, $REPS_t$, during a period is called the *residual income, RI,* and is given by:

$$RI_t = EPS_t - REPS_t = EPS_t - B_{t-1} \times k$$

economic value added (EVA)
A financial performance measure based on the difference between a firm's actual earnings and required earnings.

Residual income is sometimes called **economic value added**, or **EVA** for short. It is also called "abnormal" earnings. Whatever it is called, it is the excess of actual earnings over required earnings. We can also think of it as the value created by a firm in Period t.

Next, we can write the value of a share of stock as the sum of two parts. The first part is the current book value of the firm (i.e., what is currently invested). The second part is the present value of all future residual earnings. That is:

$$P_0 = B_0 + \frac{EPS_1 - B_0 \times k}{(1+k)^1} + \frac{EPS_2 - B_1 \times k}{(1+k)^2} + \frac{EPS_3 - B_2 \times k}{(1+k)^3} + \cdots \qquad (6.13)$$

When we developed the constant perpetual growth model for dividend-paying stocks, we made the simplifying assumption that *dividends* grow at a constant rate of g. Here we make the similar assumption that *earnings* grow at a constant rate of g. With this assumption, we can simplify Equation 6.13 to:

$$P_0 = B_0 + \frac{EPS_0(1+g) - B_0 \times k}{k-g} \qquad (6.14)$$

residual income model (RIM)
A method for valuing stock in a company that does not pay dividends.

Equation 6.14 is known as the **residual income model**, or **RIM**. If we write both terms in Equation 6.14 with a common denominator, we get another way to write the residual income model:

$$P_0 = \frac{EPS_1 - B_0 \times g}{k-g} \qquad (6.15)$$

THE RIM VERSUS THE CONSTANT GROWTH DDM

The RIM is closely related to the constant perpetual growth dividend model. To see the connection, assume that the change in book value per share on a stock is equal to earnings per share minus dividends. This is known as the **clean surplus relationship (CSR)**, written as:

clean surplus relationship (CSR)
An accounting relationship in which earnings minus dividends equals the change in book value per share.

$$EPS_1 - D_1 = B_1 - B_0 \quad or \quad D_1 = EPS_1 + B_0 - B_1$$

Note that in practice the CSR does not exactly hold because various "dirty" surplus changes to book equity are allowed. But it is usually a good approximation, particularly over the long run.

Assuming that earnings and dividends per share grow at rate g, the CSR shows that book value per share must also grow at rate g, so we can write:

$$D_1 = EPS_1 + B_0 - B_1 = EPS_1 + B_0 - B_0(1+g) = EPS_1 - B_0 \times g \qquad (6.16)$$

Plugging the expression for D_1 from Equation 6.16 into Equation 6.15, we see right away that the residual income model is mathematically the same as the constant perpetual growth model:

$$P_0 = \frac{EPS_1 - B_0 \times g}{k-g} = \frac{D_1}{k-g}$$

So these two approaches are really the same, but the RIM is more flexible because we can apply it to any stock, not just dividend payers.

Although we do not present them, there are other forms of the RIM. For example, a two-stage residual income model incorporates two different periods of growth. Also, the case of nonconstant growth for a number of years followed by constant growth can be handled by another form of the residual income model.

As with any model, the RIM is most appropriate for certain types of firms. For example, the focus on book value implies that the RIM might not be appropriate for industries with a large amount of intangible assets that don't show up on the balance sheet, such as a technology company. For insurance and financial firms, however, the RIM might be a good choice because their assets turn over quickly. The quicker the asset turnover, the closer book value is to actual market value.

EXAMPLE 6.13

Just Rocky

Suppose we are evaluating Gibraltar Industries, Inc. (ROCK). In our analysis, we find that ROCK currently pays no dividends, so we conclude that we cannot use a dividend discount model. Thus, we decide to calculate a value using a residual income model, for which we collected the following data:

Share Information	Dec 31, 2021 (Time 0)
EPS_0	$2.30
Dividends	$0
Book value per share, B_0	$25.24

Assume that it is December 31, 2021, and ROCK shares are trading at $66.68 Also assume that $g = 8$ percent and $k = 9$ percent. Using the residual income model:

$$P_0 = B_0 + \frac{EPS_0(1 + g) - B_0 \times k}{k - g}$$

$$= \$25.24 + \frac{\$2.30(1.08) - \$25.24 \times .09}{.09 - .08}$$

$$= \$25.24 + \frac{\$2.484 - \$2.272}{.01}$$

$$= \$46.48$$

Verify this price using Equation 6.15. Be careful to use g, not $(1 + g)$. Is the market price for ROCK shares too low? If you say yes, what are you assuming about the values for g and k?

EXAMPLE 6.14

ROCK On!

Using the relevant data in Example 6.13 and the residual income model, what discount rate, k, results in a price for ROCK of $66.68?

$$P_0 = B_0 + \frac{EPS_0(1 + g) - B_0 \times k}{k - g}$$

$$\$66.68 = \$25.24 + \frac{\$2.30(1.08) - \$25.24 \times k}{k - .08}$$

$$\$41.44 \times (k - .08) = \$2.484 - 25.24k$$

$$41.44k - \$41.44 \times .08 = \$2.484 - 25.24k$$

$$66.68k = \$2.484 + 3.3152$$

$$k = .08697, \text{ or } 8.7\%$$

CHECK THIS

6.4a What does the residual income model do that the perpetual constant growth model cannot do?

6.4b What is the critical assumption that makes the residual income model mathematically equal to the perpetual constant growth model?

6.5 The Free Cash Flow Model

Related Bloomberg Functions

FA CF Financial Analysis: Standardized Cash Flow

XLTP XDCF Excel Template: Discounted Cash Flow

WACC Weighted Average Cost of Capital

The residual income model allows us to value companies that do not pay dividends. But when we used the residual income model, we assumed that the company had positive earnings. Some companies do not pay dividends and have negative earnings. How do we value them? You might think that such companies have little value. Remember that we calculate earnings based on accounting rules that use tax codes. Even though a company has negative earnings, it may have positive cash flows—and a positive value.

The key to understanding how a company can have negative earnings and positive cash flows is how we handle *depreciation*—the writing down of assets. Depreciation reduces earnings, but it impacts cash flow positively because depreciation is counted as an expense. Higher expenses mean lower taxes paid, all else equal. To value companies when we account for depreciation, we turn to a model that examines "free cash flow."

FREE CASH FLOW

Free cash flow (FCF) converts reported earnings into cash flow by adjusting for items that impact earnings and cash flows differently. Formal models can be used to calculate free cash flow (you probably saw some of them in your corporate finance class). Most stock analysts, however, use a relatively simple formula to calculate firm FCF. Specifically, we define FCF as:

$$FCF = EBIT(1 - Tax\ rate) + Depreciation - Capital\ spending \qquad (6.17)$$
$$- Change\ in\ net\ working\ capital$$

From this equation, you can see how it is possible for a company to have negative earnings (i.e., EBIT, earnings before interest and taxes) but have a positive (free) cash flow. Of course, if the company undertakes a large capital expenditure or has a large increase in net working capital, it can have positive earnings and a negative cash flow.

Most analysts agree that in examining a company's financial performance, cash flow can be more informative than net income. To see why, consider the hypothetical example of two identical companies: Twiddle-Dee Co. and Twiddle-Dum Co. Suppose that both companies have the same constant revenues and expenses in each year over a three-year period. Also, suppose each company has no debt (and therefore no interest expense), no capital expenditures (CAPEX), and no change in net working capital (NWC). These constant revenues and cash expenses (excluding depreciation) yield the same constant annual cash flows, and they are stated as follows:

	Twiddle-Dee	Twiddle-Dum
Revenues	$5,000	$5,000
Cash expenses	−3,000	−3,000
Cash flow	$2,000	$2,000

Thus, both companies have the same $2,000 cash flow in each of the three years of this hypothetical example.

Next, suppose that both companies incur total depreciation of $3,000 spread out over the three-year period. Standard accounting practices sometimes allow a manager to choose among several depreciation schedules. Twiddle-Dee Co. chooses straight-line depreciation, and Twiddle-Dum Co. chooses accelerated depreciation. These two depreciation schedules are shown below:

	Twiddle-Dee	Twiddle-Dum
Year 1	$1,000	$1,500
Year 2	1,000	1,000
Year 3	1,000	500
Total	$3,000	$3,000

Note that total depreciation over the three-year period is the same for both companies. However, Twiddle-Dee Co. has the same $1,000 depreciation in each year, while Twiddle-Dum Co. has accelerated depreciation of $1,500 in the first year, $1,000 in the second year, and $500 depreciation in the third year.

Now let's look at the resulting annual cash flows and net income figures for the two companies, recalling that in each year Cash flow = Net income + Depreciation (when capital expenditures, interest expense, and change in NWC all = 0):

	Twiddle-Dee		Twiddle-Dum	
	Cash Flow	Net Income	Cash Flow	Net Income
Year 1	$2,000	$1,000	$2,000	$500
Year 2	2,000	1,000	2,000	1,000
Year 3	2,000	1,000	2,000	1,500
Total	$6,000	$3,000	$6,000	$3,000

Note that Twiddle-Dum Co.'s net income is lower in the first year and higher in the third year than Twiddle-Dee Co.'s net income. This is purely a result of Twiddle-Dum Co.'s accelerated depreciation schedule and has nothing to do with Twiddle-Dum Co.'s actual profitability. However, an inexperienced analyst observing Twiddle-Dum Co.'s rapidly rising annual earnings figures might incorrectly label Twiddle-Dum as a growth company. An experienced analyst would observe that there was no cash flow growth to support this naïve conclusion.

THE FCF MODEL VERSUS THE CONSTANT GROWTH DDM

A basic finance principle is that the price of an asset should equal the present value of its expected future cash flows. The dividend discount model (DDM) assumed that dividends were the relevant cash flow for equity investors, which is a valid approach. What differs when we look at firm FCF? Well, as opposed to dividends, which are paid directly to stockholders, FCF could be used to pay off debt holders and stockholders. Thus, when we use the FCF approach, we are valuing the entire company, not just its equity.

You should remember the basic accounting identity: Assets = Liabilities + Equity. With the DDM, we can value equity directly. With firm FCF, we are actually valuing the overall market value of the company's assets. We can, however, use the FCF approach to value equity, too. The approach has two steps. First, we find the value of the company, and then we subtract the value of the company's debt. We are left with our estimate of the equity value:

$$V_{Equity} = V_{Firm} - V_{Debt} \qquad (6.18)$$

There is another issue to consider. Specifically, when we estimate the required return for the DDM using the CAPM, we use the company's equity beta. If we are valuing the entire company, however, we need to use the "asset" beta.

A beta measures risk. In a later chapter we discuss betas at length, but for now all you need to know about betas is that they measure risk. Asset betas measure the risk of the industry to which the company belongs. Two firms in the same industry should have approximately the same asset betas. Their equity betas, however, could be quite different. Why? As we saw in an earlier chapter, investors can increase portfolio risk by using margin (i.e., borrowing money to buy stock). A business can do the same by using debt in its capital structure. So, when we value the company, we must "convert" reported equity betas into asset betas by adjusting for the amount of leverage being used. The following formula is one way to accomplish this conversion:

$$\beta_{Equity} = \beta_{Asset} \times \left[1 + (1 - t)\frac{Debt}{Equity}\right]$$ (6.19)

Note that when a company has no debt, its equity beta equals its asset beta. Also notice that a higher amount of debt increases the equity beta. This increase makes sense because stockholders face more risk when the company takes on more debt. All else equal, the cash flows to stockholders are more risky when the company has more debt.

Note that we account for the tax rate, t. We do so because the interest cost on the debt is tax deductible. Because the company can deduct interest as an expense, the government effectively subsidizes part of the cost of debt. This subsidy creates a more stable cash flow associated with debt, thereby reducing risk for the equity holders, all else equal. In an extreme example, the government might return money to a company that has a negative taxable income.

Once we have an estimate of FCF, the growth rate of FCF, and the proper discount rate, we can value the company using, for example, a "DDM" formula. We have "DDM" in quotes because we are using firm FCF, not dividends, in the formula. Equation 6.20 summarizes this approach.

$$V_{Firm} = \frac{FCF_1}{k - g} = \frac{FCF_0(1 + g)}{k - g}$$ (6.20)

In Equation 6.20, FCF is the firm-level free cash flow from Equation 6.17. Warning! In Equation 6.20, k and g do represent discount and growth rates, respectively. Note, however, that these two rates are not the same values as those in the formulas where we use dividends. In Equation 6.20, k is the discount rate based on an asset beta and g is the estimate of the growth in FCF. Example 6.15 shows you how to value a company using this approach.

To be consistent in estimating k, we continue to use the CAPM. In this case, however, we use a calculated asset beta, as in Equation 6.19. Note, however, that with the free cash flow approach, we are calculating the overall required return of the firm. You might recall from your corporate finance class that this return is exactly what the weighted average cost of capital (or WACC) represents. So, if you already know the company's WACC, you can use it to calculate the firm value. To be clear, however, the required return we get from inserting an asset beta into the CAPM formula is equivalent to the weighted average cost of capital, or WACC, particularly in the absence of taxes.

EXAMPLE 6.15 **Free Cash Flow Valuation**

Landon Air is a new airline that makes roundtrip flights just between Indianapolis and Boston. It has EBIT of $45 million, interest expense of $6.54 million, no change in net working capital, depreciation expense of $10 million, and capital expenditures of $3 million. Landon Air has an expected constant growth rate in FCF of 3 percent and an average tax rate of 21 percent. Assume that it has a debt-to-equity ratio of .4 (with $100 million of debt); the current equity beta is 1.2; the risk-free rate is 4 percent; and the market risk premium is 7 percent. Landon Air pays no dividends. What is Landon Air's current equity value?

The first step is to calculate Landon Air's asset beta. Using Equation 6.19:

$$1.2 = B_{Asset} \times \left[1 + .4 \times (1 - .21)\right]$$
$$1.2 = B_{Asset} \times 1.32$$
$$B_{Asset} = .912$$

The next step is to use the asset beta to calculate Landon Air's required return, which we can still do using the CAPM:

$$k = .04 + .07(.912) = .1038, \text{ or } 10.38\%$$

(continued)

Next, we need to know Landon Air's free cash flow, which we can calculate using Equation 6.17:

$$FCF \ = \ \$45(1 - .21) + 10 - 3 - 0 \ = \ \$42.55 \text{ million}$$

Now that we have these values, we can use the constant growth model to find the current value for Landon Air (difference due to rounding):

$$\text{Firm value} \ = \ \frac{\$42.55 \times (1 + .03)}{.1038 - .03} \ = \ \$593.62 \text{ million}$$

If Landon Air has $100 million in debt outstanding, then its equity value is $493.62 million. To get the per-share equity value, we would then divide this total equity value by the total number of shares outstanding.

CHECK THIS

6.5a How is it possible for a company to have negative earnings but still have positive free cash flow?

6.5b Why is a firm's equity beta different from its asset beta? When would these two measures of risk be the same?

6.6 Price Ratio Analysis

Related Bloomberg Functions

RV — Relative Valuation

EQRV — Equity Relative Valuation

DES — Security Description

PEBD — Equity Relative Valuation: Price Bands

RVC — Relative Value Correlation

COMP — Comparative Returns

EV — Enterprise Value

price-earnings (PE) ratio
Current stock price divided by annual earnings per share (EPS).

earnings yield (E/P)
Inverse of the P/E ratio: earnings per share divided by price per share.

growth stocks
A term often used to describe high-P/E stocks.

Price ratios are widely used by financial analysts, more so even than dividend discount models. Of course, all valuation methods try to accomplish the same thing, which is to appraise the economic value of a company's stock. However, analysts readily agree that no single method can adequately handle this task on all occasions. In this section, we therefore examine several of the most popular price ratio methods and provide examples of their use in financial analysis.

PRICE-EARNINGS RATIOS

The most popular price ratio used to assess the value of common stock is a company's **price-earnings ratio**, abbreviated as **PE ratio**. In fact, as we saw in Chapter 3, PE ratios are reported in the financial press every day. As we discussed, a price-earnings ratio is calculated as the ratio of a firm's current stock price divided by its annual earnings per share (EPS).

The inverse of a PE ratio is called an **earnings yield**, and it is measured as earnings per share divided by the current stock price (E/P). Clearly, an earnings yield and a price-earnings ratio are two ways to measure the same thing. In practice, earnings yields are less commonly stated and used than PE ratios.

Because most companies report earnings each quarter, annual earnings per share can be calculated either as the most recent quarterly earnings per share times four or as the sum of the last four quarterly earnings per share figures. Many analysts prefer the first method of multiplying the latest quarterly earnings per share value times four. However, some published data sources, including *The Wall Street Journal*, report annual earnings per share as the sum of the last four quarters' figures. Unless a business is seasonal, the difference is usually small, but it can sometimes be a source of confusion.

Financial analysts often refer to high-PE stocks as **growth stocks**. To see why, notice that a PE ratio is measured as the *current* stock price over *current* earnings per share. Now, consider two companies with the same current earnings per share, where one company is a high-growth company and the other is a low-growth company. Which company do you think should have a higher stock price, the high-growth company or the low-growth company?

This question is a no-brainer. All else equal, we would be surprised if the high-growth company did not have a higher stock price, and therefore a higher PE ratio. In general, companies with higher expected earnings growth will have higher PE ratios, which is why high-PE stocks are often referred to as growth stocks.

To give an example, the online retailer Amazon has a history of aggressive sales growth. Its stock trades on Nasdaq under the ticker symbol AMZN. In early 2022, AMZN stock traded at $2,177.18 with earnings per share (EPS) of $64.81, and so Amazon had a PE ratio of $2,177.18/$64.81 = 33.59. This PE ratio is above the 2021 average PE ratio of about 23.6 for the S&P 500 (of which AMZN is a member). Given its growth focus, AMZN has yet to begin paying a dividend. Instead, Amazon reinvests all of its earnings. So far this strategy has been successful, as the firm has grown rapidly.

The reason high-PE stocks are called growth stocks seems obvious enough; however, in a seeming defiance of logic, low-PE stocks are often referred to as **value stocks**. The reason is that low-PE stocks are often viewed as "cheap" relative to *current* earnings. (Notice again the emphasis on "current.") This reasoning suggests that these stocks may represent good investment values, and hence the term "value stocks."

value stocks
A term often used to describe low-P/E stocks.

In mid-2007, shares of the well-known S&P 500 auto company General Motors (GM) were trading at a price of $31.08. With EPS = $3.75, the PE ratio was $31.08/$3.75 = 8.29. This PE ratio was well below the S&P 500 average, so General Motors might have been considered a value stock in mid-2007. But GM went bankrupt in 2009. Maybe GM was not such a value after all.

After all this discussion about growth stocks and value stocks, we want to emphasize, however, that the terms "growth stock" and "value stock" are mostly just commonly used labels. Of course, only time will tell whether a high-PE stock actually turns out to be a high-growth stock, or whether a low-PE stock is really a good value, as the GM example illustrates. What we do know, however, is that over long periods of time, value stocks tend to outperform growth stocks. This outperformance might not be what you expect. Remember, though, the price today of growth stocks reflects high *expected* growth rates. High growth rates do not always occur as predicted. Therefore, the actual returns to growth stocks depend on realized growth rates, not the forecasted growth rates.

Although PE ratios seem quite "easy" to evaluate, you need to be aware that PE ratios are not that stable. To illustrate, consider a company that has a one-time write-off that significantly reduces earnings. If the write-off is truly a one-time event, then the share price should not be impacted too severely. In this case, the price remains stable, but earnings are much lower—resulting in a faux increase in the PE ratio. An unwary investor might even think that this company is a growth stock. The facts about the write-off, however, do not support this conclusion. What would happen if there was a one-time positive impact on earnings? The lesson: A high or low PE ratio is not necessarily bad or good.

Because it is difficult to compare companies that have different PE ratios, investment managers often calculate the PEG ratio. The PEG ratio is calculated by dividing the PE ratio by the expected earnings growth rate. Although not perfect, the PEG ratio provides investors with a better method to compare companies, particularly those with differing growth rates.

For your next investment, would you prefer a low- or high-PEG ratio? All else equal, lower is better because it means that you are paying a small amount relative to the earnings growth you are expecting. Most investment sources label the PEG on a range from 1 (strong buy) to 5 (sell). Amazon has a relatively high PE of 33.59 and also has a relatively low PEG of 1.99. Thus, the market could be expecting that Amazon might continue to sell about as many books and other items as before.

PRICE-CASH FLOW RATIOS

price-cash flow (P/CF) ratio
Current stock price divided by current cash flow per share.

cash flow
In the context of the price-cash flow ratio, usually taken to be net income plus depreciation.

Instead of PE ratios, many analysts prefer to look at price-cash flow ratios. A **price-cash flow (P/CF) ratio** is measured as a company's current stock price divided by its current annual **cash flow** per share. Like earnings, cash flow is normally reported quarterly, and most analysts multiply the last quarterly cash flow figure by four to obtain annual cash flow. Again, like earnings, many published data sources report annual cash flow as a sum of the latest four quarterly cash flows.

Financial analysts typically use both PE ratios and P/CF ratios. They point out that when a company's earnings per share is not significantly larger than its cash flow per share (CFPS), this is a signal, at least potentially, of good-quality earnings. The term "quality" means that the accounting earnings mostly reflect actual cash flow, not just accounting numbers. When earnings are bigger than cash flow, this may be a signal of poor-quality earnings.

Going back to some of our earlier examples, Amazon had CFPS = $69.49, yielding a P/CF ratio of $2,177.18/$69.49 = 31.33. Notice that cash flow per share was about equal to its earnings per share of $64.81. This comparison might suggest good-quality earnings, or it might reflect a high amount of capital expenditures, which was the case for Amazon in 2021. Investigating these different possibilities is a job for a good financial analyst.

PRICE-SALES RATIOS

price-sales (P/S) ratio
Current stock price divided by annual sales per share.

An alternative view of a company's performance is provided by its **price-sales (P/S) ratio**. A price-sales ratio is calculated as the current price of a company's stock divided by its current annual sales revenue per share. A price-sales ratio focuses on a company's ability to generate sales growth. Essentially, a high P/S ratio would suggest high sales growth, while a low P/S ratio might indicate sluggish sales growth.

For example, Amazon had sales per share of $582.13, to yield P/S = $2,177.18/$582.13 = 3.74. We should note that there can be a large variation in price-sales ratios for two companies, particularly if they are in quite different kinds of businesses. Security analysts recognize that price-sales ratios cannot be compared in isolation from other important information.

PRICE-BOOK RATIOS

price-book (P/B) ratio
Market value of a company's common stock divided by its book (or accounting) value of equity.

A very basic price ratio for a company is its **price-book (P/B) ratio**, sometimes called the market-book ratio. A price-book ratio is measured as the market value of a company's outstanding common stock divided by its book value of equity.

Price-book ratios are appealing because book values represent, in principle, historical cost. The stock price is an indicator of current value, so a price-book ratio measures what the equity is worth today relative to what it cost. A ratio bigger than 1.0 indicates that the firm has been successful in creating value for its stockholders. A ratio smaller than 1.0 indicates that the company is actually worth less than it cost.

This interpretation of the price-book ratio seems simple enough, but the truth is that because of varied and changing accounting standards, book values are difficult to interpret. For this reason and others, price-book ratios might not have as much information value as they once did. The exceptions might be for financial and insurance companies, which turn their assets over quickly. The quicker the asset turnover, the closer book value is to actual market value.

APPLICATIONS OF PRICE RATIO ANALYSIS

Price-earnings ratios, price-cash flow ratios, and price-sales ratios are commonly used to calculate estimates of expected future stock prices. This is done by multiplying a historical average price ratio by an expected future value for the price ratio denominator variable. For example, Table 6.1 summarizes such a price ratio analysis for Starbucks Corp. (SBUX) based on information available in early 2022.

In Table 6.1, the five-year average price ratio row contains five-year average PE, P/CF, and P/S ratios. The current value row contains values for earnings per share, cash flow per share, and sales per share; and the growth rate row contains five-year projected growth rates for EPS, CFPS, and SPS.

The expected stock price row contains expected stock prices in one year. The basic idea is this: Because Starbucks had an average PE ratio of 47.76, we will assume that Starbucks' stock

Check out the Starbucks website at www.starbucks.com.

TABLE 6.1	Price Ratio Analysis for Starbucks Corp (SBUX); Early 2022 Stock Price: $71.86		
	Earnings	**Cash Flow**	**Sales**
Five-year average price ratio	47.76 (PE)	27.47 (P/CF)	4.06 (P/S)
Current value per share	$ 3.54 (EPS)	$ 3.10 (CFPS)	$15.06 (SPS)
Growth rate	20.6%	4.0%	11.0%
Expected stock price	$203.90	$88.56	$67.87

price will be 47.76 times its earnings per share one year from now. To estimate Starbucks' earnings one year from now, we note that Starbucks' earnings are projected to grow at a rate of 20.6 percent next year. This growth reflects a rapid bounce back from the effects of the COVID-19 pandemic. If earnings continue to grow at this rate, next year's earnings will be equal to this year's earnings times 1.206. Putting it all together, we have:

$$
\begin{aligned}
\text{Expected price} &= \text{Historical PE ratio} \times \text{Projected EPS} \\
&= \text{Historical PE ratio} \times \text{Current EPS} \\
&\quad \times (1 + \text{Projected EPS growth rate}) \\
&= 47.76 \times \$3.54 \times 1.206 \\
&= \$203.90
\end{aligned}
$$

The same procedure is used to calculate an expected price based on our estimate of a 4.0% growth rate in cash flow per share:

$$
\begin{aligned}
\text{Expected price} &= \text{Historical P/CF ratio} \times \text{Projected CFPS} \\
&= \text{Historical P/CF ratio} \times \text{Current CFPS} \\
&\quad \times (1 + \text{Projected CFPS growth rate}) \\
&= 27.47 \times \$3.10 \times 1.04 \\
&= \$88.56
\end{aligned}
$$

Finally, an expected price based on sales per share is calculated as:

$$
\begin{aligned}
\text{Expected price} &= \text{Historical P/S ratio} \times \text{Projected SPS} \\
&= \text{Historical P/S ratio} \times \text{Current SPS} \\
&\quad \times (1 + \text{Projected SPS growth rate}) \\
&= 4.06 \times \$15.06 \times 1.11 \\
&= \$67.87
\end{aligned}
$$

Learn all about LUV at www.southwest.com.

Notice that in the case of Starbucks, the price ratio methods yield prices ranging from about $68 to about $204. However, when this analysis was made in early 2022, Starbucks' stock price was around $71.86. These estimated price differences might be explained by the fact that historical ratios might be inaccurate for future projections. Analysts must be aware of which ratios tend to be more useful in estimating prices.

EXAMPLE 6.16

All You Need Is Love

Table 6.2 contains information about Southwest Airlines (LUV). Calculate expected share prices using each of the three price ratio approaches.

For example, using the PE approach, we come up with the following estimates of the price of Southwest Airlines stock in one year:

$$
\begin{aligned}
\text{Expected price} &= \text{Historical PE ratio} \times \text{Current EPS} \\
&\quad \times (1 + \text{Projected EPS growth rate}) \\
&= 20.05 \times \$1.61 \times 1.564 \\
&= \$50.49
\end{aligned}
$$

TABLE 6.2

Price Ratio Analysis for Southwest Airlines (LUV); Early 2022 Stock Price: $44.59

	Earnings	Cash Flow	Sales
Five-year average price ratio	20.05 (PE)	13.91 (P/CF)	1.85 (P/S)
Current value per share	$1.61 (EPS)	$2.54 (CFPS)	$21.96 (SPS)
Growth rate	56.4%	6.0%	9.4%
Expected stock price	$50.49	$37.45	$44.44

ENTERPRISE VALUE RATIOS

enterprise value (EV)
The market value of the firm's equity plus the market value of the firm's debt minus cash.

The PE ratio is an equity ratio because the numerator is the price per share of *stock* and the denominator is the earnings per share of *stock*. Practitioners, however, often use ratios involving both debt and equity. Perhaps the most common one is the **enterprise value (EV)** to EBITDA ratio. Enterprise value is equal to the market value of the firm's equity plus the market value of the firm's debt minus cash. EBITDA stands for earnings before interest, taxes, depreciation, and amortization.

For example, imagine Kourtney's Kayaks has equity worth $800 million, debt worth $300 million, and cash of $100 million. The enterprise value is $1 billion (= $800 + $300 − $100). Suppose Kourtney's Kayaks' income statement is:

Revenue	$ 700 million
− Cost of goods sold	−500 million
EBITDA	$ 200 million
− Depreciation and amortization	−100 million
− Interest	−24 million
Pretax income	$76 million
− Taxes (@21%)	−16 million
Net income	$60 million

The EV to EBITDA ratio is 5 (= $1 billion/$200 million). Note that all the items in the income statement below EBITDA are ignored when calculating this ratio.

Analysts often assume that similar firms have similar EV/EBITDA ratios (and similar PE ratios and asset betas, for that matter). For example, suppose the average EV/EBITDA ratio in the industry is 6. If Qwerty Corporation, a firm in the industry with EBITDA of $50 million, is judged to be similar to the rest of the industry, its enterprise value is estimated at $300 million (= 6 × $50 million). Now imagine that Qwerty has $75 million of debt and $25 million of cash. Given our estimate of Qwerty's EV, our estimate of its stock value is $250 million (= $300 − $75 + $25).

Four important questions arise concerning enterprise value ratios.

1. **Does the EV ratio have any advantage over the PE ratio?** Yes. As we have seen in our discussion of asset betas, companies in the same industry may differ by leverage, that is, the ratio of debt to equity. While firms in the same industry may be otherwise comparable, the different degrees of leverage may create variability across firm PE ratios. Because enterprise value includes equity and debt, the impact of leverage on the EV/EBITDA ratio is less than the impact on PE ratios.

2. **Why is EBITDA used in the denominator?** The numerator and denominator of a ratio should be consistent. Because the numerator in the PE ratio is the price of a share of *stock,* it makes sense that the denominator is earnings per share (EPS) of *stock.* That is, interest is specifically subtracted before EPS is calculated because stockholders are residual claimants. By contrast, because EV involves the sum of debt and equity, we need to use a denominator that reflects the flow to both bondholders and stockholders. Thus, we need a denominator that is unaffected by interest payments. We use EBITDA because, as its name implies, EBITDA is calculated before interest payments are subtracted.

3. **Why does the denominator ignore depreciation and amortization?** Many practitioners argue that, because depreciation and amortization are not cash flows, earnings should be calculated before subtracting depreciation and amortization. In other words, depreciation and amortization merely reflect the sunk cost of a previous purchase. Others, however, point out that depreciable assets will eventually be replaced and that depreciation reflects the cost of future replacement.

4. **Why is cash omitted?** Many firms seem to hold considerable amounts of cash. For example, Apple (as of early 2021) holds over $204 billion in cash and investments.

Because an enterprise value ratio attempts to estimate the ability of productive assets to create earnings or cash flow, cash should be omitted. This view, however, is not without criticism because some cash is definitely necessary to run a business.

CHECK THIS

6.6a Why are high-PE stocks sometimes called growth stocks?

6.6b Why might an analyst prefer a price-cash flow ratio to a price-earnings ratio?

6.7 An Analysis of CVS Health Corporation

Related Bloomberg Functions

CP	Company Profile
CN	Individual Company News
CCB	Company Classification Browser
ANR	Analyst Recommendations
DDM	Dividend Discount Model
FA	Financial Analysis
BETA	Historical Beta
FA ROE	Financial Analysis: DuPont Analysis
RVC	Relative Value Correlation
XLTP	Excel Template:
XIDA	Company In-Depth Analysis

Stock market investors have access to many sources of information about the financial performance of companies with publicly traded stock. Indeed, the sheer volume of information available can often be overwhelming. For this reason, several sources publish reference summaries for individual companies. While many of these sources charge hefty fees for access, there are quite a few sources that are available for free, or for a nominal fee.

Two of the most well-known and easy-to-use financial data sources available to all investors are Yahoo! Finance (finance.yahoo.com) and Morningstar (www.morningstar.com). Both provide a mountain of information, much of which we can use for valuing a company's stock. Recently, these two sites have added a section that is only available for pay. But they do grant a trial version for free. To illustrate the process of stock valuation, we are going to consider CVS Health Corporation, which trades on the New York Stock Exchange (NYSE) under the ticker symbol CVS. Figure 6.2 provides a summary quote from Bloomberg, and Table 6.3 provides some key metrics that we collected from Yahoo! and Morningstar.

USING THE DIVIDEND DISCOUNT MODEL

Our first task is to estimate a discount rate for CVS. From Figure 6.2, we can see that CVS's beta is .98. Using a Treasury bill rate of 1.6 percent and a projected stock market risk premium of 8.3 percent, we obtain a CAPM discount rate estimate for CVS of $1.6\% + .98 \times 8.3\% = 9.734\%$.

FIGURE 6.2   **Summary Quote for CVS Health Corporation (CVS), January 3, 2022**

Source: Bloomberg, Finance L.P. Accessed January 2022.

TABLE 6.3

Key Statistics for CVS Health Corporation

Metric	Value	Source
Return on equity	10.5%	Yahoo!
Debt-to-equity ratio	2.09	Yahoo!
Shares outstanding (billions)	1.322	Yahoo!
Sales per share	$220.96	Yahoo!
Earnings per share	$ 5.98	Yahoo!
Cash flow per share	$ 12.25	Estimated via Yahoo!
Book value per share	$ 57.02	Yahoo!
Debt per share	$119.23	Yahoo!
Sales growth estimate	4.30%	Yahoo!
Earnings growth estimate	7.20%	Yahoo!
Cash flow growth estimate	3.50%	Estimated via Morningstar
Five-year average PE	10.21	Morningstar
Five-year average P/CF	7.42	Morningstar
Five-year average P/S	.38	Morningstar

Source: Data as of January 2022.

Our next task is to calculate a sustainable growth rate. From Table 6.3, we can see that CVS's most recent earnings per share (annualized) is $5.98, and the company has annualized dividends per share of $2.00, implying a retention ratio of $1 - \$2.00/\$5.98 = .666$, or 66.6 percent. To finish our estimate of the sustainable growth rate, we need a value for ROE. From the financial highlights provided in Table 6.3, you will note that Yahoo! reports an ROE of 10.5 percent. Putting these together yields a sustainable growth rate of $.666 \times 10.5\% = 6.99\%$.

Finally, with a discount rate and sustainable growth rate, we can calculate a share value for CVS. Using the constant dividend growth rate model with the 2021 dividend of $D_0 = \$2.00$, a discount rate of $k = 9.734$ percent, and a precise growth rate of $g = 6.9883$ percent, we get:

$$P_0 = \frac{\$2.00(1.069883)}{.09734 - .069883} = \$77.93$$

which is not likely true given that this estimated price is extremely low relative to the current, intraday market price of $103.05. As a good analyst would, we'll try something else.

What if we have underestimated the growth rate? As we saw in our *Work the Web* example earlier in the chapter, Yahoo! provides estimates of analysts' forecasted growth rates. Yahoo! includes the low, median, and high estimates across the analysts surveyed. For the next few years, we found that analysts, on average, are actually projecting that CVS will grow earnings at a rate of 7.2 percent (see Table 6.3). So, what if this higher estimate is a more reasonable view of CVS's ongoing dividend growth? If it is, we get:

$$P_0 = \frac{\$2.00(1.072)}{.09734 - .072} = \$84.61$$

which is closer to the market price, but still well below. So, maybe we should consider what growth rate the market is implying by its current price. To find this value, we solve for the growth rate that gives us the current market price:

$$\$103.05 = \frac{\$2.00(1 + g)}{.09734 - g}$$

$$g = .0764, \text{ or } 7.64\%$$

Thus, market participants are pricing CVS to grow dividends at roughly 7.6 percent per year into perpetuity. If we believe the growth rate will be higher, then we should buy the stock. If we do not, then we should sell.

We could stop here, but where is the fun in that? Let's consider a two-stage discount model, where the growth rate stays at 7.2 percent for five years, then drops to a 3 percent growth rate thereafter. This approach assumes that CVS will grow earnings at a rate consistent with analyst estimates for five years, then revert to a more sustainable growth rate thereafter. Using Equation 6.11, we find a price of $36.55:

$$P_0 = \frac{\$2.00(1.072)}{.09734 - .072}\left[1 - \left(\frac{1.072}{1.07934}\right)^5\right] + \left(\frac{1.072}{1.07934}\right)^5\left[\frac{\$2.00(1.03)}{.09734 - .03}\right]$$

$$= \$9.33 + \$27.22$$

$$= \$36.55$$

Our estimate is well below the current market price and further away from the observed price than was the simple dividend growth model. Perhaps the stock is overvalued, or the market's higher implied growth rate is more accurate than our estimates. A good analyst must be able to sort out these issues. One thing an analyst could do is to work in some different assumptions concerning a multistage dividend discount model.

Figure 6.3 is a Bloomberg screen shot showing Bloomberg's multistage dividend discount model assumptions for CVS. Note that Bloomberg estimates earnings for the next two years (i.e., FY2 and FY3), assuming earnings growth of 7.59 percent until the earnings transition to a long-term growth rate of 5.35 percent. Bloomberg assumes a dividend payout ratio of 24.88 percent during the growth years and a payout of 45 percent thereafter. With these assumptions, and perhaps a few more, Bloomberg reports a theoretical CVS price of $80.24. Even Bloomberg's estimate is quite a bit lower than the observed closing price of $103.01. Perhaps the dividend growth model approach is not the best way to estimate today's price of CVS. Let's turn to some other ways.

USING THE RESIDUAL INCOME MODEL

To apply the residual income model, we need to collect the following data: current book value per share, current earnings per share, the discount rate, and the expected growth rate in dividends. We already know that earnings per share is $5.98. From our calculations above, we have estimates of the discount rate ($k = 9.73$ percent) and the sustainable growth rate ($g = 6.99$ percent). Remember, though, we also had analyst-estimated earnings growth of 7.2 percent. So, really, the only additional piece of information we need is the current book value per share, which from Table 6.3 is $57.02.

| FIGURE 6.3 | Multistage Dividend Discount Model Assumptions |

		Dividend Discount Model
		CVS Health Corp
Model Assumptions		
		Risk Premium Country/Region United States
Earnings Per Share FY1	8.034	Bond Rate	1.611 %
Earnings Per Share FY2	8.212	Country/Region Premium	8.266 %
Earnings Per Share FY3	8.869	Beta	0.982
Dividends Per Share FY1	1.999	1) Risk Premium	8.121 %
Growth Years	9	Payout during Growth yrs	24.882 %
Transitional Years	8	Payout at Maturity	45.000 %
Long Term Growth Rate	7.590 %	Growth Rate at Maturity	5.352 %
Closing Price	103.010		
		Currency	USD
Computed Values		
Theoretical Price	80.239		
Percentage Change from Cl...	-22.106 %		
Internal Rate of Return	8.917 %		
Expected Return	-4.144 %		
Implied Growth Rate	10.289 %		

Source: Bloomberg Finance L.P.

With the book value per share of $57.02, we can now apply the residual income model using Equation 6.14. Below you will find two estimates. The first uses the precise sustainable growth rate of 6.9883 percent, while the other uses a growth estimate from analysts of 7.2 percent.

$$P_0 = \$57.02 + \frac{\$5.98(1.069883) - \$57.02(.09734)}{.09734 - .069883} = \$87.89$$

$$P_0 = \$57.02 + \frac{\$5.98(1.072) - \$57.02(.09734)}{.09734 - .072} = \$90.97$$

Note that in both cases that the forecasted EPS is high enough to cover the required earnings based on the book value per share and the required return. Also note that an increase in the growth rate of only 20 basis points has an impact of over $3 on the estimated price.

Remember, under the "clean surplus accounting" relationship, the estimated value from the residual income model should match the estimated value from the dividend growth model. This match does not generally happen in practice, as we can see here. The estimated price for CVS using the sustainable growth rate is $77.93, while it is $87.89 using the RIM.

USING THE FREE CASH FLOW MODEL

From Equation 6.20, we know that we can value a firm on a cash flow basis if we know its free cash flow as well as estimates of the discount rate and growth rate. While we have already estimated discount rates and growth rates, we can't use these estimates because we are focusing on cash flows, not dividends. Remember, free cash flow is available to all investors (both equity and debt holders), so when we use free cash flow, we are valuing the whole firm, not just the equity. Thus, we need a firm-level discount rate, not a discount rate for equity holders.

Using Equation 6.19, we can convert CVS's equity beta of .98 to an asset beta as follows:

$$.98 = B_{Asset} \times [1 + 2.09 \times (1 - .21)]$$
$$.98 = B_{Asset} \times 2.6511$$
$$B_{Asset} = .37 (\text{rounded})$$

The 2.09 used in the formula represents the debt-to-equity ratio, which comes from Table 6.3. The tax rate of .21 is the standard marginal tax rate for most large corporations under the Tax Cuts and Jobs Act of 2017.

Using a Treasury bill rate of 1.6 percent and a projected stock market risk premium of 8.3 percent, we obtain a CAPM discount rate estimate for CVS of $1.6\% + .37 \times 8.3\% = 4.67\%$ (with rounding). As we noted earlier in the chapter, this should be equivalent to the firm's weighted average cost of capital (WACC). So, if you knew the WACC, you could skip the process of unlevering beta and estimating a discount rate. You could then use $k = $ WACC to value the firm.

The most difficult part of using cash flow valuation is coming up with an estimate of cash flow growth. Unfortunately, the free sources don't generally provide this estimate. They do, however, provide historical growth rates, which we have used to estimate a historical average growth rate for CVS's cash flows. Based on our process, Table 6.3 notes a cash flow growth estimate of 3.5 percent, as well as the most recent free cash flow per share of $12.25.

Putting all the information together, we can estimate a firm value using free cash flow as follows (remember to use precise numbers to calculate asset beta and discount rate):

$$V_F = \frac{\$12.25(1.035)}{.0467 - .035} = \$1,085.36$$

Remember, this is the value of the *whole* firm on a per-share basis, but we want to know the per-share equity value. So, we need to subtract out the value of the firm's debt on a per-share basis, which is given in Table 6.3 as $119.23.

Putting all this free cash flow information together, we estimate the per-share equity value for CVS as $V_E = \$1,085.36 - \$119.23 = \$966.13$. Unlike our other estimates, this value is much higher than the current share price. This estimate reflects the importance of the estimate of the current level of free cash flow per share, and the other estimates.

USING PRICE RATIO ANALYSIS

To value a stock using price ratios, we need three pieces of information: (1) the average historical price multiple (PE, P/CF, or P/S), (2) the current value of the underlying metric (earnings per share, cash flow per share, or sales per share), and (3) the forecasted growth rate in earnings, cash flow, or sales. All of this information is included in Table 6.3. For example, CVS had a five-year average PE ratio of 10.21, a P/CF ratio of 7.42, and a P/S ratio of .38.

Putting it all together, we would then estimate share price as:

$$\text{Expected share price} = \text{PE ratio} \times \text{EPS} \times (1 + \text{EPS growth rate})$$
$$\text{Expected share price} = \text{P/CF ratio} \times \text{CFPS} \times (1 + \text{CFPS growth rate})$$
$$\text{Expected share price} = \text{P/S ratio} \times \text{SPS} \times (1 + \text{SPS growth rate})$$

The results of these calculations are found in Table 6.4. You should check these for practice.

We can now summarize our analysis by listing the stock prices obtained by the different ways we have described in this chapter, along with the model used to derive them:

DDM, with calculated sustainable growth rate:	$78.09
DDM, with analyst forecasted growth rate:	$84.74
DDM, two-stage model:	$36.57
Bloomberg's Theoretical Price, using DDM	$80.24
RIM, with calculated sustainable growth rate:	$88.04
RIM, with analyst forecasted growth rate:	$91.11
Price-earnings model:	$65.45
Price-cash flow model:	$94.08
Price-sales model:	$87.58

Notice the wide range of share values we obtained using the various models. This range is not uncommon in security analysis, and it suggests how daunting a task security analysis can be. In this case, the price-cash flow approach yields the closest value to the observed stock price of $103.05. The goal, however, is not to find a model that yields a value closest to the current price. Rather, the goal is to find a model about which we are confident.

Note that all of our estimates lie below the current market price of CVS. What does this comparison mean? Well, it likely means that our approaches estimate the earnings growth prospects for CVS in a manner different than the market does.

So, what is the lesson? A fair amount of subjectivity is entailed in the valuation process, even though we can look at financial data objectively. This subjectivity is why different analysts looking at the same financial information will provide conflicting value estimates. For example, in May 2022 under its premium Stock Analysis section, Morningstar provided a fair value estimate for CVS of $108, but it gave a range of possible values anywhere from $75.60 to $145.80. Even the experts have a hard time determining an exact value! So, don't give up.

TABLE 6.4

Price Ratio Analysis for CVS Health Corporation (CVS)
January 2022 Stock Price: $103.05

	Earnings	Cash Flow	Sales
Five-year average price ratio	10.21 (PE)	7.42 (P/CF)	.38 (P/S)
Current value per share	$ 5.98 (EPS)	$12.25 (CFPS)	$220.96 (SPS)
Growth rate	7.20%	3.50%	4.30%
Expected share price	$65.45	$94.08	$ 87.58

CHECK THIS

6.7a   Can you calculate the growth rate in earnings that would be necessary to provide a RIM valuation equivalent to the market's current price?

 ## Summary and Conclusions

In this chapter, we examined several methods of fundamental analysis used by financial analysts to value common stocks. The methods we examined are the learning objectives for the chapter. We illustrated many of these methods with a detailed analysis of CVS Health Corporation.

1. **The basic dividend discount model.**

   A. Dividend discount models value common stock as the sum of all expected future dividend payments, where the dividends are adjusted for risk and the time value of money.

   B. The dividend discount model is often simplified by assuming that dividends will grow at a constant growth rate. A particularly simple form of the dividend discount model is the case in which dividends grow at a constant perpetual growth rate. The simplicity of the constant perpetual growth model makes it the most popular dividend discount model. However, it should be applied only to companies with stable earnings and dividend growth.

   C. Dividend models require an estimate of future growth. We described the sustainable growth rate, which is measured as a firm's return on equity times its retention ratio, and illustrated its use.

2. **The two-stage dividend growth model.**

   A. Companies often experience temporary periods of unusually high or low growth, where growth eventually converges to an industry average. In such cases, analysts frequently use a two-stage dividend growth model.

   B. The two-stage growth model can be used with two separate growth rates for two distinct time periods, or with growth rates that linearly converge toward the constant growth rate. This latter case is referred to as the H-model.

   C. The two-stage growth model can be used where there is a period with nonconstant dividend growth and a period of constant dividend growth.

3. **The residual income and free cash flow models.**

   A. The difference between actual and required earnings in any period is called residual income. Residual income is sometimes called economic value added.

   B. The residual income model is a method that can be used to value a share of stock in a company that does not pay dividends. To derive the residual income model, a series of constant growth assumptions are made for EPS, assets, liabilities, and equity. Together, these growth assumptions result in a sustainable growth rate.

   C. The clean surplus relationship is an accounting relationship that says earnings minus dividends equals the change in book value per share. The clean surplus relationship might not hold in actual practice. But if the clean surplus relationship is true, then the residual income model is mathematically equivalent to the constant perpetual growth model.

   D. The free cash flow (FCF) model values the entire firm by concentrating on firm FCF.

   E. Because the FCF model values the whole firm, we must use an asset beta rather than an equity beta. We must also use the firm's equity value, which we can get by subtracting the value of the firm's debt from the value of the whole firm.

4. **Price ratio analysis.**

A. Price ratios are widely used by financial analysts. The most popular price ratio is a company's price-earnings ratio. A PE ratio is calculated as the ratio of a firm's stock price divided by its earnings per share (EPS).

B. Financial analysts often refer to high-PE stocks as growth stocks and low-PE stocks as value stocks. In general, companies with high expected earnings growth will have high PE ratios, which is why high-PE stocks are referred to as growth stocks. Low-PE stocks are referred to as value stocks because they are viewed as cheap relative to current earnings.

C. Instead of price-earnings ratios, many analysts prefer to look at price-cash flow (P/CF) ratios. A price-cash flow ratio is measured as a company's stock price divided by its cash flow per share. Most analysts agree that cash flow can provide more information than net income about a company's financial performance.

D. An alternative view of a company's performance is provided by its price-sales (P/S) ratio. A price-sales ratio is calculated as the price of a company's stock divided by its annual sales revenue per share. A price-sales ratio focuses on a company's ability to generate sales growth. A high P/S ratio suggests high sales growth, while a low P/S ratio suggests low sales growth.

E. A basic price ratio for a company is its price-book (P/B) ratio. A price-book ratio is measured as the market value of a company's outstanding common stock divided by its book value of equity. A high P/B ratio suggests that a company is potentially expensive, while a low P/B value suggests that a company may be cheap.

F. A common procedure using price-earnings ratios, price-cash flow ratios, and price-sales ratios is to calculate estimates of expected future stock prices. However, each price ratio method yields a different expected future stock price. Because each method uses different information, each makes a different prediction.

G. An alternative to price ratios is the enterprise value (EV) to EBITDA ratio. Similar to the FCF approach, EV captures both debt and equity.

GETTING DOWN TO BUSINESS

This chapter introduced you to some of the basics of common stock valuation and fundamental analysis. It focused on four important tools used by stock analysts in the real world to assess whether a particular stock is "rich" or "cheap": dividend discount models, residual income models, free cash flow models, and price ratio analysis. How should you, as an investor or investment manager, put this information to use?

The answer is that you need to pick some stocks and get to work! As we discussed in the chapter, experience and judgment are needed to use these models, and the only way to obtain these is through practice. Try to identify a few stocks that look cheap and buy them in a simulated brokerage account such as Stock-Trak. At the same time, find a few that look rich and short them. Start studying PE ratios. Scan *The Wall Street Journal* (or a similar source of market information) and look at the range of PEs. What's a low PE? What's a high one? Do they really correspond to what you would call growth and value stocks?

The internet provides copious information on valuing companies. Try, for example, MarketWatch (marketwatch.com), D&B Hoovers (hoovers.com), and Zacks (zacks.com). Don't forget to check out The Motley Fool (fool.com).

Several trade associations have informative websites that can be helpful. For individual investors, there is the American Association of Individual Investors (aaii.com). The CFA Institute (cfainstitute.org) provides a financial analyst certification (or charter) that is highly respected among security analysts.

For the latest information on the real world of investments, visit us at jmdinvestments.blogspot.com.

Key Terms

arithmetic average dividend growth rate 177
beta 186
cash flow 193
clean surplus relationship (CSR) 187
constant perpetual growth model 175
dividend discount model (DDM) 174
earnings yield (E/P) 192
economic value added (EVA) 187
enterprise value (EV) 196
fundamental analysis 174
geometric average dividend growth rate 177
growth stocks 192

payout ratio 179
price-book (P/B) ratio 194
price-cash flow (P/CF) ratio 193
price-earnings (PE) ratio 192
price-sales (P/S) ratio 194
residual income model (RIM) 187
retained earnings 179
retention ratio 179
sustainable growth rate 179
two-stage dividend growth model 182
value stocks 193

Related Bloomberg Functions

DES	Security Description, 6.1
FA	Financial Analysis, 6.1, 6.7
DDM	Dividend Discount Model, 6.2, 6.7
DVD	Dividend/Split Summary, 6.2
BDVD	Bloomberg Dividend Forecast, 6.2
FA GRO	Financial Analysis: Growth, 6.2
FA ROE	Financial Analysis: DuPont Analysis, 6.2, 6.7
BETA	Historical Beta, 6.3, 6.7
EQRP	Equity Risk Premium, 6.3
SOVM	Sovereign Debt Monitor, 6.3
FA CF	Financial Analysis: Standardized Cash Flow, 6.5
XLTP XDCF	Excel Template: Discounted Cash Flow, 6.5
WACC	Weighted Average Cost of Capital, 6.5
RV	Relative Valuation, 6.6
EQRV	Equity Relative Valuation, 6.6
DES	Security Description, 6.6
PEBD	Equity Relative Valuation: Price Bands, 6.6
RVC	Relative Value Correlation, 6.6
COMP	Comparative Returns, 6.6
EV	Enterprise Value, 6.6
CP	Company Profile, 6.7
CN	Individual Company News, 6.7
CCB	Company Classification Browser, 6.7
ANR	Analyst Recommendations, 6.7
XLTP XIDA	Excel Template: Company In Depth Analysis, 6.7
DDM	Dividend Discount Model, 6.7
FA	Financial Analysis, 6.7
BETA	Historical Beta, 6.7
FA ROE	Financial Analysis: DuPont Analysis, 6.7
RVC	Relative Value Correlation, 6.7

Chapter Review Problems and Self-Test

1. **The Perpetual Growth Model (LO1, CFA6)** Suppose dividends for Layton's Pizza Company are projected to grow at 6 percent forever. If the discount rate is 16 percent and the current dividend is $2, what is the value of the stock?

2. **The Two-Stage Growth Model (LO2, CFA6)** Suppose the Titanic Ice Cube Co.'s dividend grows at a 20 percent rate for the next three years. Thereafter, it grows at a 12 percent rate. What value would we place on Titanic assuming a 15 percent discount rate? Titanic's most recent dividend was $3.

3. **Residual Income Model (LO3, CFA8)** Suppose Al's Infrared Sandwich Company has a current book value of $10.85 per share. The most recent earnings per share (EPS) was $2.96, and earnings are expected to grow at 6 percent forever. The appropriate discount rate is 8.2 percent. Assume the clean surplus relationship is true. Assuming the company maintains a constant retention ratio, what is the value of the company according to the residual income model if there are no dividends?

4. **Price Ratio Analysis (LO4, CFA4)** The table below contains some information about the Jordan Air Co. Provide expected share prices using each of the three price ratio approaches we have discussed.

Price Ratio Analysis for Jordan Air (Current Stock Price: $40)			
	Earnings	**Cash Flow**	**Sales**
Five-year average price ratio	25 (PE)	7 (P/CF)	1.5 (P/S)
Current value per share	$2.00 (EPS)	$6.00 (CFPS)	$30.00 (SPS)
Growth rate	10%	16%	14%

Answers to Self-Test Problems

1. Plugging the relevant numbers into the constant perpetual growth formula results in:

$$P_0 = \frac{\$2(1.06)}{.16 - .06} = \$21.20$$

As shown, the stock should sell for $21.20.

2. Plugging all the relevant numbers into the two-stage formula gets us:

$$P_0 = \frac{\$3(1.20)}{.15 - .20}\left[1 - \left(\frac{1.20}{1.15}\right)^3\right] + \left(\frac{1.20}{1.15}\right)^3\left[\frac{\$3(1.12)}{.15 - .12}\right]$$

$$= \$9.81 + \$127.25$$

$$= \$137.06$$

Thus, the stock should sell for about $137.

3. Recall the formula for the residual income model when the clean surplus relationship is true:

$$P_0 = B_0 + \frac{EPS_0(1 + g) - B_0 \times k}{k - g}$$

Next, make a table of all the information that you need to put into the formula:

Al's Infrared Sandwich Company	Time 0, i.e., Now
Beginning book value, B_0	$10.85
Earnings per share, EPS_0	$2.96
Growth rate, g	6%
Discount rate, k	8.2%

We can now solve the problem.

$$P_0 = \$10.85 + \frac{\$2.96(1 + .06) - \$10.85 \times .082}{.082 - .06}$$

$$P_0 = \$113.03$$

4. Using the PE approach, we come up with the following estimate of the price of Jordan Air in one year:

$$\text{Estimated price} = \text{Average PE} \times \text{Current EPS} \times (1 + \text{Growth rate})$$
$$= 25 \times \$2 \times 1.10$$
$$= \$55$$

Using the P/CF approach, we get:

$$\text{Estimated price} = \text{Average P/CF} \times \text{Current CFPS} \times (1 + \text{Growth rate})$$
$$= 7 \times \$6 \times 1.16$$
$$= \$48.72$$

Finally, using the P/S approach, we get:

$$\text{Estimated price} = \text{Average P/S} \times \text{Current SPS} \times (1 + \text{Growth rate})$$
$$= 1.5 \times \$30 \times 1.14$$
$$= \$51.30$$

Test Your Investment Quotient

1. **Sustainable Growth (LO1, CFA6)** A company has a return on equity (ROE) of 20 percent, and from earnings per share of $5 it pays a $2 dividend. What is the company's sustainable growth rate?
   a. 8 percent
   b. 10 percent
   c. 12 percent
   d. 20 percent

2. **Sustainable Growth (LO1, CFA6)** If the return on equity for a firm is 15 percent and the retention ratio is 40 percent, the sustainable growth rate of earnings and dividends is which of the following?
   a. 6 percent
   b. 9 percent
   c. 15 percent
   d. 40 percent

3. **Dividend Discount Model (LO1, CFA4)** A common stock pays an annual dividend per share of $2.10. The risk-free rate is 7 percent and the risk premium for this stock is 4 percent. If the annual dividend is expected to remain at $2.10, the value of the stock is closest to:
   a. $19.09
   b. $30.00
   c. $52.50
   d. $70.00

4. **Dividend Discount Model (LO1, CFA4)** The constant growth dividend discount model will not produce a finite value if the dividend growth rate is which of the following?
   a. Above its historical average
   b. Above the required rate of return
   c. Below its historical average
   d. Below the required rate of return

5. **Dividend Discount Model (LO1, CFA4)** In applying the constant growth dividend discount model, a stock's intrinsic value will do which of the following when the required rate of return is lowered?
   a. Decrease
   b. Increase
   c. Remain unchanged
   d. Decrease or increase, depending on other factors

6. **Dividend Discount Model (LO1, CFA4)** The constant growth dividend discount model would typically be most appropriate for valuing the stock of which of the following?
   a. A new venture expected to retain all earnings for several years
   b. A rapidly growing company
   c. A moderate growth, mature company
   d. A company with valuable assets not yet generating profits

7. **Dividend Discount Model (LO1, CFA6)** A stock has a required return of 15 percent, a constant growth rate of 10 percent, and a dividend payout ratio of 50 percent. What should the stock's PE ratio be?

    a. 3.0
    b. 4.5
    c. 9.0
    d. 11.0

8. **Dividend Discount Model (LO1, CFA6)** Which of the following assumptions does the constant growth dividend discount model require?

    I. Dividends grow at a constant rate.
    II. The dividend growth rate continues indefinitely.
    III. The required rate of return is less than the dividend growth rate.
    a. I only
    b. III only
    c. I and II only
    d. I, II, and III

9. **Dividend Discount Model (LO2, CFA4)** A stock will not pay dividends until three years from now. The dividend then will be $2.00 per share, the dividend payout ratio will be 40 percent, and return on equity will be 15 percent. If the required rate of return is 12 percent, which of the following is closest to the value of the stock?

    a. $27
    b. $33
    c. $53
    d. $67

10. **Dividend Discount Model (LO1, CFA4)** Assume that at the end of the next year, Company A will pay a $2.00 dividend per share, an increase from the current dividend of $1.50 per share. After that, the dividend is expected to increase at a constant rate of 5 percent. If you require a 12 percent return on the stock, what is the value of the stock?

    a. $28.57
    b. $28.79
    c. $30.00
    d. $31.78

11. **Dividend Discount Model (LO1, CFA6)** A share of stock will pay a dividend of $1.00 one year from now, with dividend growth of 5 percent thereafter. In the context of a dividend discount model, the stock is correctly priced at $10 today. According to the constant dividend growth model, if the required return is 15 percent, what should the value of the stock be two years from now?

    a. $11.03
    b. $12.10
    c. $13.23
    d. $14.40

12. **Free Cash Flow (LO3, CFA9)** A firm has EBIT of $275 million, which is net of $52 million in depreciation. In addition, the firm had $81 million in capital expenditures and an increase in net working capital of $5 million. The firm's tax rate is 21 percent. The firm's FCF is closest (in millions) to:

    a. $280
    b. $101
    c. $231
    d. $183

13. **Free Cash Flow (LO3, CFA9)** A firm had a free cash flow (FCF) in the prior year of $125 million. The FCF is expected to grow at 3 percent per year into perpetuity. The appropriate discount rate is 12 percent. What is the firm's current value (in millions) based on the FCF model?

    a. $1,042
    b. $1,389
    c. $1,555
    d. $1,431

14. **Price Ratios (LO4, CFA5)** Two similar companies acquire substantial new production facilities, which they both will depreciate over a 10-year period. However, Company A uses accelerated depreciation while Company B uses straight-line depreciation. In the first year that the assets are depreciated, which of the following is most likely to occur?

   a. A's P/CF ratio will be higher than B's.
   b. A's P/CF ratio will be lower than B's.
   c. A's PE ratio will be higher than B's.
   d. A's PE ratio will be lower than B's.

15. **Price Ratios (LO4, CFA4)** An analyst estimates the earnings per share and price-to-earnings ratio for a stock market series to be $43.50 and 26 times, respectively. The dividend payout ratio for the series is 65 percent. The value of the stock market series is closest to:

   a. 396
   b. 735
   c. 1,131
   d. 1,866

16. **Enterprise Value Ratio (LO4, CFA7)** Which of the following is an advantage of the enterprise value ratio as compared to price ratios?

   a. The EV ratio excludes interest expense.
   b. The EV ratio adds the value of the firm's cash holding.
   c. The EV ratio captures the value of both firm debt and equity.
   d. The EV ratio controls for the market risk premium while price ratios do not.

17. **PE Ratio (LO4, CFA5)** A company's return on equity is greater than its required return on equity. The earnings multiplier (PE) for that company's stock is most likely to be positively related to the:

   a. Risk-free rate.
   b. Market risk premium.
   c. Earnings retention ratio.
   d. Stock's capital asset pricing model beta.

18. **Residual Income Model (LO3, CFA8)** The residual income model separates the value of the firm into two basic components. What are these two components?

   a. The current book value and the present value of future earnings
   b. The value of earnings per share and the value of cash flow per share
   c. The current value of the firm's shares and the future value of its shares
   d. The time value of money and the value of bearing risk

19. **Residual Income (LO3, CFA8)** Residual income is:

   a. The actual earnings less expected earnings.
   b. Any increase in the value of the firm.
   c. The value of profitable investment projects.
   d. The value added by economical use of assets.

20. **Clean Surplus Relationship (LO3, CFA8)** The clean surplus relationship says that:

   a. Assets minus liabilities minus shareholder's equity equals the change in current assets plus debt payments.
   b. The difference between earnings and dividends equals the change in book value.
   c. Dividends minus earnings equals one minus the payout ratio.
   d. The difference between earnings and dividends equals the change in surplus inventory.

Concept Questions

1. **Dividend Discount Model (LO1, CFA4)** What is the basic principle behind dividend discount models?
2. **PE Ratios (LO4, CFA5)** Why do growth stocks tend to have higher PE ratios than value stocks?
3. **Residual Income Model (LO3, CFA8)** What happens in the residual income model when EPS is negative?
4. **FCF Valuation (LO3, CFA9)** Why do we need to convert the typical equity beta to value a firm using FCF?

5. **Stock Valuation (LO1, CFA5)** Why does the value of a share of stock depend on dividends?

6. **Stock Valuation (LO3, CFA5)** A substantial percentage of the companies listed on the NYSE and the Nasdaq don't pay dividends, but investors are nonetheless willing to buy shares in them. How is this possible given your answer to Question 5?

7. **Taxes (LO1, CFA6)** As a result of the Tax Cuts and Jobs Act of 2017, corporate tax rates were reduced. Under the dividend discount model, how would the tax rate reduction impact stock values?

8. **Constant Perpetual Growth Model (LO1, CFA6)** Under what two assumptions can we use the constant perpetual growth model presented in the chapter to determine the value of a share of stock? How reasonable are these assumptions?

9. **Dividend Growth Models (LO1, CFA4)** Based on the dividend growth models presented in the chapter, what are the two components of the total return of a share of stock? Which do you think is typically larger?

10. **Stock Valuation (LO3, CFA5)** If a firm has no dividends and has negative earnings, which valuation models are appropriate?

Questions and Problems

Core Questions

1. **Dividend Valuation (LO1, CFA6)** JJ Industries will pay a regular dividend of $2.40 per share for each of the next four years. At the end of the four years, the company will also pay out a $40 per share liquidating dividend, and the company will cease operations. If the discount rate is 10 percent, what is the current value of the company's stock?

2. **Dividend Valuation (LO1, CFA6)** In Problem 1, suppose the current share price is $60. If all other information remains the same, what must the liquidating dividend be?

3. **Free Cash Flow Model (LO3, CFA2)** You are going to value Lauryn's Doll Co. using the FCF model. After consulting various sources, you find that Lauryn's has a reported equity beta of 1.4, a debt-to-equity ratio of .3, and a tax rate of 21 percent. Based on this information, what is the asset beta for Lauryn's?

4. **Free Cash Flow Model (LO3, CFA9)** Using your answer to Problem 3, calculate the appropriate discount rate assuming a risk-free rate of 4 percent and a market risk premium of 7 percent.

5. **Free Cash Flow Model (LO3, CFA9)** Lauryn's Doll Co. had EBIT last year of $40 million, which is net of a depreciation expense of $4 million. In addition, Lauryn's made $5 million in capital expenditures and increased net working capital by $3 million. Using the information from Problem 3, what is Lauryn's FCF for the year?

6. **Free Cash Flow Model (LO3, CFA9)** Using your answers from Problems 3 through 5, value Lauryn's Doll Co. assuming the company's FCF is expected to grow at a rate of 3 percent into perpetuity. Is this value the value of the equity?

7. **Enterprise Value (LO4, CFA7)** If a firm has an EV of $750 million and EBITDA of $165 million, what is its EV ratio?

8. **Perpetual Dividend Growth (LO1, CFA6)** Xytex Products just paid a dividend of $1.62 per share, and the stock currently sells for $28. If the discount rate is 10 percent, what is the dividend growth rate?

9. **Perpetual Dividend Growth (LO1, CFA6)** Star Light & Power increases its dividend 3.8 percent per year every year. This utility is valued using a discount rate of 9 percent, and the stock currently sells for $38 per share. If you buy a share of stock today and hold on to it for at least three years, what do you expect the value of your dividend check to be three years from today?

10. **Sustainable Growth (LO1, CFA6)** Rodriquez Products earned $2.80 per share last year and paid a dividend of $1.25 per share. If ROE was 14 percent, what is the sustainable growth rate?

11. **Sustainable Growth (LO4, CFA6)** Joker stock has a sustainable growth rate of 8 percent, ROE of 14 percent, and dividends per share of $1.65. If the PE ratio is 19, what is the value of a share of stock?

12. **Capital Asset Pricing Model (LO1, CFA2)** A certain stock has a beta of 1.3. If the risk-free rate of return is 3.2 percent and the market risk premium is 7.5 percent, what is the expected return of the stock? What is the expected return of a stock with a beta of .75?

13. **Residual Income Model (LO3, CFA8)**   Xin's Bakery expects earnings per share of $2.56 next year. Current book value is $4.70 per share. The appropriate discount rate for Xin's Bakery is 11 percent. Calculate the share price for Xin's Bakery if earnings grow at 3 percent forever.

14. **Residual Income Model (LO3, CFA8)**   For Xin's Bakery described in Problem 13, suppose instead that current earnings per share is $2.56. Calculate the share price for Xin's Bakery.

Intermediate Questions

15. **Two-Stage Dividend Growth Model (LO2, CFA5)**   Could I Industries just paid a dividend of $1.10 per share. The dividends are expected to grow at a 20 percent rate for the next six years and then level off to a 4 percent growth rate indefinitely. If the required return is 12 percent, what is the value of the stock today?

16. **H-Model (LO2, CFA6)**   The dividend for Should I, Inc., is currently $1.25 per share. It is expected to grow at 20 percent next year and then decline linearly to a 5 percent perpetual rate beginning in four years. If you require a 15 percent return on the stock, what is the most you would pay per share?

17. **Multiple Growth Rates (LO2, CFA6)**   Carter Communications does not currently pay a dividend. You expect the company to begin paying a $4 per share dividend in 15 years, and you expect dividends to grow perpetually at 5.5 percent per year thereafter. If the discount rate is 15 percent, how much is the stock currently worth?

18. **Enterprise Value Ratio (LO4, CFA7)**   Jonah's Fishery has EBITDA of $65 million. Jonah's has market value of equity and debt of $420 million and $38 million, respectively. Jonah's has cash on the balance sheet of $12 million. What is Jonah's EV ratio?

19. **Multiple Growth Rates (LO1, CFA6)**   Leisure Lodge Corporation is expected to pay the following dividends over the next four years: $15.00, $10.00, $5.00, and $2.20. Afterwards, the company pledges to maintain a constant 4 percent growth rate in dividends forever. If the required return on the stock is 10 percent, what is the current share price?

20. **Multiple Required Returns (LO1, CFA6)**   Sea Side, Inc., just paid a dividend of $1.68 per share on its stock. The growth rate in dividends is expected to be a constant 5.5 percent per year indefinitely. Investors require an 18 percent return on the stock for the first three years, then a 13 percent return for the next three years, and then an 11 percent return thereafter. What is the current share price?

21. **Price Ratio Analysis (LO4, CFA4)**   Given the information below for Seger Corporation, compute the expected share price at the end of 2022 using price ratio analysis. Assume that the historical (arithmetic) average growth rates will remain the same for 2022.

Year	2016	2017	2018	2019	2020	2021
Price	$94.50	$100.40	$99.10	$97.90	$121.50	$136.80
EPS	4.34	5.05	5.22	6.06	7.00	8.00
CFPS	7.27	8.24	8.71	10.12	11.80	13.10
SPS	52.60	58.52	57.90	60.69	71.60	78.70

22. **Dividend Growth Analysis (LO1, CFA6)**   In Problem 21, suppose the dividends per share over the same period were $1.00, $1.08, $1.17, $1.25, $1.35, and $1.40, respectively. Compute the expected share price at the end of 2022 using the perpetual growth method. Assume the market risk premium is 7.5 percent, Treasury bills yield 3 percent, and the projected beta of the firm is 1.10.

23. **Price Ratio Analysis for Internet Companies (LO4, CFA7)**   Given the information below for HooYah! Corporation, compute the expected share price at the end of 2022 using price ratio analysis. Assume that the historical (arithmetic) average growth rates will remain the same for 2022.

Year	2016	2017	2018	2019	2020	2021
Price	$8.00	$44.50	$116.00	$193.00	$83.00	$13.50
EPS	−4.00	−3.30	−1.80	−.55	.04	.06
CFPS	−9.00	−6.50	−2.80	−.25	.03	.08
SPS	5.00	13.50	18.10	20.30	23.80	21.95

24. **Price Ratio Analysis for Internet Companies (LO4, CFA7)**   Given the information below for StartUp Co., compute the expected share price at the end of 2022 using price ratio analysis.

Year	2018	2019	2020	2021
Price	N/A	$68.12	$95.32	$104.18
EPS	N/A	−7.55	−4.30	−3.68
CFPS	N/A	−11.05	−8.20	−5.18
SPS	N/A	4.10	6.80	8.13

25. **Price Ratio Analysis (LO4, CFA7)**   The current price of Parador Industries stock is $67 per share. Current earnings per share is $3.40, the earnings growth rate is 6 percent, and Parador does not pay a dividend. The expected return on Parador stock is 13 percent. What one-year-ahead PE ratio is consistent with Parador's expected return and earnings growth rate?

26. **Price Ratio Analysis (LO4, CFA7)**   The current price of Parador Industries stock is $67 per share. Current sales per share are $18.75, the sales growth rate is 8 percent, and Parador does not pay a dividend. The expected return on Parador stock is 13 percent. What one-year-ahead P/S ratio is consistent with Parador's expected return and sales growth rate?

Use the following information to answer Problems 27–31.

Beagle Beauties engages in the development, manufacture, and sale of a line of cosmetics designed to make your dog look glamorous. Below you will find selected information necessary to compute some valuation estimates for the firm. Assume the values provided are from year-end 2021. Also assume that the firm's equity beta is 1.40, the risk-free rate is 2.75 percent, and the market risk premium is 7 percent.

Dividends per share	$2.04
Return on equity	9.50%
Book value per share	$17.05

	Earnings	Cash Flow	Sales
2021 value per share	$5.00	$6.60	$25.65
Average price multiple	13.10	9.42	2.36
Forecasted growth rate	13.48%	11.41%	7.34%

27. **Constant Perpetual Growth Model (LO1, CFA6)**   What are the sustainable growth rate and required return for Beagle Beauties? Using these values, estimate the current share price of Beagle Beauties stock according to the constant dividend growth model.

28. **Price Ratios (LO4, CFA7)**   Using the PE, P/CF, and P/S ratios, estimate the 2022 share price for Beagle Beauties.

29. **Residual Income Model (LO3, CFA8)**   Assume the sustainable growth rate and required return you calculated in Problem 27 are valid. Use the clean surplus relationship to calculate the share price for Beagle Beauties with the residual income model.

30. **Clean Surplus Dividend (LO3, CFA8)**   Use the information from Problem 29 and calculate the stock price with the clean surplus dividend. Do you get the same stock price as in Problem 29? Why or why not?

31. **Stock Valuation (LO1, LO3, LO4, CFA5, CFA7, CFA8)**   Given your answers in Problems 27–30, do you feel Beagle Beauties is overvalued or undervalued at its current price of around $82? At what price do you feel the stock should sell?

32. **Residual Income Model and Nonconstant Growth (LO3, CFA8)**   When a stock is going through a period of nonconstant growth for T periods, followed by constant growth forever, the residual income model can be modified as follows:

$$P_0 = \sum_{t=1}^{T} \frac{EPS_t + B_{t-1} - B_t}{(1+k)^t} + \frac{P_T}{(1+k)^T}$$

where:

$$P_T = B_T + \frac{EPS_T(1+g) - B_T \times k}{k-g}$$

Al's Infrared Sandwich Company had a book value of $12.95 at the beginning of the year, and the earnings per share for the past year was $3.41. Molly Miller, a research analyst at Miller, Moore & Associates, estimates that the book value and earnings per share will grow at 12.5 and 11 percent per year for the next four years, respectively. After four years, the growth rate is expected to be 6 percent. Molly believes the required return for the company is 8.2 percent. What is the value per share for Al's Infrared Sandwich Company?

Spreadsheet Problems

33. **Two-Stage Dividend Growth Model (LO2, CFA5)** Hank's Barbecue just paid a dividend of $1.85 per share. The dividends are expected to grow at a 12 percent rate for the next five years and then level off to a 5 percent growth rate indefinitely. If the required return is 10 percent, what is the value of the stock today? What if the required return is 15 percent?

34. **Free Cash Flow Model (LO3, CFA9)** You have been tasked with using the FCF model to value Amara's Jewelry Co. After your initial review, you find that Amara's has a reported equity beta of 1.1, a debt-to-equity ratio of .5, and a tax rate of 21 percent. In addition, market conditions suggest a risk-free rate of 3 percent and a market risk premium of 7 percent. If Amara's had FCF last year of $47.5 million and has current debt outstanding of $120 million, find the value of Amara's equity assuming a 2 percent growth rate in FCF.

CFA Exam Review by Kaplan Schweser

[CFA2, CFA6, CFA9]

Beachwood Builders merged with Country Point Homes on December 31, 2002. Both companies were builders of midscale and luxury homes in their respective markets. In 2019, because of tax considerations and the need to segment the business, Beachwood decided to spin off Country Point, its luxury subsidiary, to its shareholders. Beachwood retained Bernheim Securities to value the spin-off of Country Point as of December 31, 2019.

When the books closed on 2019, Beachwood had $140 million in debt outstanding due in 2028 at a coupon rate of 8 percent, which is a spread of 2 percent above the current risk-free rate. Beachwood also had 5 million common shares outstanding. It pays no dividends, has no preferred shareholders, and faces a total tax rate of 30 percent. Bernheim is assuming a market risk premium of 11 percent.

The common equity allocated to Country Point for the spin-off was $55.6 million as of December 31, 2019. There was no long-term debt allocated from Beachwood.

The managing directors in charge of Bernheim's construction group, Denzel Johnson and Cara Nguyen, are prepping for the valuation presentation. Ms. Nguyen tells Mr. Johnson that Bernheim estimated Country Point's net income at $10 million in 2019, growing $5 million per year through 2023. Based on Ms. Nguyen's calculations, Country Point will be worth $223.7 million in 2023. Ms. Nguyen decided to use a cost of equity for Country Point in the valuation equal to its return on equity at the end of 2019 (rounded to the nearest percentage). Ms. Nguyen also gives Mr. Johnson the table she obtained from Beachwood projecting depreciation and capital expenditures ($ in millions):

	2019	2020	2021	2022	2023
Depreciation	$5	$6	$5	$6	$5
Capital expenditures	7	8	9	10	12

1. What is the estimate of Country Point's free cash flow (FCF) in 2021?
   a. 25
   b. 16
   c. 11

2. What is the cost of capital that Ms. Nguyen used for her valuation of Country Point?
   a. 18 percent
   b. 17 percent
   c. 15 percent

3. Given Ms. Nguyen's estimate of Country Point's terminal value in 2023, what is the growth assumption she must have used for free cash flow after 2023?
   a. 7 percent
   b. 9 percent
   c. 3 percent

4. The value of beta for Country Point is:
  a. 1.09
  b. 1.27
  c. 1.00

5. What is the estimated value of Country Point in a proposed spin-off?
  a. $144.5 million
  b. $162.5 million
  c. $178.3 million

Bloomberg Exercises

1. Identify the forecasted dividend for GE. **(BDVD)**
2. Collect information on the historical growth rate for MMM. **(FA GRO)**
3. Conduct a DuPont analysis of Proctor & Gamble's (PG) return on equity. **(FA ROE)**
4. Find the weighted average cost of capital for Ford (F). **(WACC)**
5. Analyze the PE ratio of Intel (INTC) relative to its peers. **(RV)**
6. Use the dividend discount model to estimate a value for ExxonMobil (XOM). **(DDM)**

What's on the Web?

1. **Sustainable Growth Rate** You can find the home page for Caterpillar, Inc., at www.cat.com. Go to this page and find the most recent annual report for Caterpillar. Calculate the sustainable growth rate for each of the past two years. Are these values the same? Why or why not?

2. **Sustainable Growth Rate** Go to finance.yahoo.com and find the analysts' estimates for Procter & Gamble's (PG) growth rate over the next five years. How does this compare to the industry, sector, and S&P 500 growth rates? Now find the EPS and dividends per share for PG and calculate the sustainable growth rate. How does your number compare to analysts' estimates for the company? Why might these estimates differ?

3. **Perpetual Dividend Growth Model** Go to finance.yahoo.com and find the following information: the beta, the most recent annual dividend, and analysts' estimated growth rate for Johnson & Johnson (JNJ). Next, find the three-month Treasury bill yield on finance.yahoo.com. Assuming the market risk premium is 7 percent, what is the required return for JNJ? What is the value of JNJ stock using the perpetual dividend growth model? Does JNJ appear overpriced, underpriced, or correctly priced? Why might this analysis be inappropriate, or at least misleading?

Stock Price Behavior and Market Efficiency

chapter **7**

"A market is the combined behavior of thousands of people responding to information, misinformation, and whim."

–Kenneth Chang

"If you want to know what's happening in the market, ask the market."

–Japanese proverb

Learning Objectives

You should strive to have your investment knowledge fully reflect:

1. The foundations of market efficiency.

2. The implications of the forms of market efficiency.

3. Market efficiency and the performance of professional money managers.

4. What stock market anomalies, bubbles, and crashes mean for market efficiency.

Controversial, intriguing, and baffling issues are at the heart of this chapter. We begin by investigating a very basic question: Can you, as an investor, consistently "beat the market?" You may be surprised to learn that evidence strongly suggests that the answer to this question is probably not. We show that even professional money managers have trouble beating the market. At the end of the chapter, we describe some market phenomena that sound more like carnival sideshows, such as the "amazing January effect."

CFA™ Exam Topics in This Chapter:

1. Market efficiency (L1, S11)
2. Overview of equity portfolio management (L3, S7)
3. Passive equity investing (L3, S7)

Go to Connect for a guide that aligns your textbook with CFA readings.

7.1 Introduction to Market Efficiency

efficient markets hypothesis (EMH)
The hypothesis stating that, as a practical matter, investors cannot consistently "beat the market."

For more on market efficiency, go to www.e-m-h.org.

Market efficiency is probably the most controversial and intriguing issue in investments. The debate that has raged around market efficiency for decades shows few signs of abating. The central issue in the market efficiency debate is: Can you (or anyone else) consistently "beat the market?"

If the answer to this question is no, then the market is said to be efficient. The **efficient markets hypothesis (EMH)** asserts that, as a practical matter, organized financial markets like the New York Stock Exchange are efficient. The controversy surrounding the EMH centers on this assertion.

In the sections that follow, we discuss many issues surrounding the EMH. You will notice that we focus our discussion on stock markets. The reason is that the debate on the EMH and the associated research have largely centered on these markets. However, the same principles and arguments would also apply to any organized financial market, such as the markets for government bonds, corporate bonds, commodity futures, and options.

CHECK THIS

7.1a What is the central issue in the market efficiency debate?

7.1b How would you state the efficient markets hypothesis?

7.2 What Does "Beat the Market" Mean?

Good question. As we discussed in Chapter 1, and elsewhere, there is a risk-return trade-off. On average, at least, we expect riskier investments to have larger returns than less risky assets. So, the fact that an investment appears to have a high or low return doesn't tell us much. We need to know if the return was high or low relative to the risk involved.

abnormal return
A return in excess of that earned by other investments having the same risk.

Instead, to determine if an investment is superior to another, we need to compare abnormal returns. The **abnormal return** on an investment is the difference between what that investment earned and what other investments with the same risk earned. A positive abnormal return means that an investment has outperformed other investments of the same risk. Thus, *consistently earning a positive abnormal return* is what we mean by "beating the market."

CHECK THIS

7.2a What is an abnormal return?

7.2b What does it mean to "beat the market"?

7.3 Foundations of Market Efficiency

Three economic forces can lead to market efficiency: (1) investor rationality, (2) independent deviations from rationality, and (3) arbitrage. These conditions are so powerful that any one of them can result in market efficiency. We discuss aspects of these conditions in detail throughout this chapter. Given their importance, however, we briefly introduce each of them here. In our discussions, we use the term "rational" to mean only that investors do not systematically overvalue or undervalue financial assets in light of the information that they possess.

If every investor always made perfectly rational investment decisions, earning an abnormal return would be difficult, if not impossible. The reason is simple: If everyone is fully rational, equivalent risk assets would all have the same expected returns. Put differently, no bargains would be available because relative prices would all be correct.

Even if the investor rationality condition does not hold, however, the market could still be efficient. Suppose that many investors are irrational, and a company makes a relevant announcement about a new product. Some investors will be overly optimistic, some will be overly pessimistic, but the net effect might be that these investors cancel each other out. In a sense, the irrationality is noise that is diversified away. As a result, the market could still be efficient (or nearly efficient). What is important here is that irrational investors don't all (or mostly all) have similar beliefs. Even under this condition, called "independent deviations from rationality," the market might still be efficient.

Let us now think of a market with many irrational traders and further suppose that their collective irrationality does not balance out. In this case, observed market prices can be too high or too low relative to their risk. Now suppose there are some well-capitalized, intelligent, and rational investors. This group of traders would see these high or low market prices as a profit opportunity and engage in arbitrage—buying relatively inexpensive stocks and selling relatively expensive stocks.

If these rational arbitrage traders dominate irrational traders, the market will still be efficient. We sometimes hear the expression "Market efficiency doesn't require that everybody be rational, just that somebody is." In our next section, we look more closely at market efficiency and discuss several different forms.

CHECK THIS

7.3a   What three economic conditions cause market efficiency?

7.3b   How would well-capitalized, intelligent, and rational investors profit from market inefficiency?

7.4 Forms of Market Efficiency

Now that we have a little more precise notion of what beating the market means, we can be a little more precise about market efficiency. A market is efficient *with respect to some particular information* if that information is not useful in earning a positive abnormal return. Notice the emphasis we place on "with respect to some particular information."

For example, it seems unlikely that knowledge of Dwight Howard's free-throw shooting percentage (low) would be of any use in beating the market. If so, we would say that the market is efficient with respect to the information in Dwight's free-throw percentage. On the other hand, if you have prior knowledge concerning impending takeover offers, you could most definitely use that information to earn a positive abnormal return. Thus, the market is not efficient with regard to this information. We hasten to add that such information is probably "insider" information, and insider trading is generally, though not always, illegal (in the United States, at least). As we discuss later in the chapter, using insider information illegally might well earn you a stay in a jail cell and a stiff financial penalty.

Thus, the question of whether a market is efficient is meaningful only relative to some type of information. Put differently, if you are asked whether a particular market is efficient, you should always reply, "With respect to what information?" Three general types of information are particularly interesting in this context, and it is traditional to define three forms of market efficiency: weak, semistrong, and strong.

The particular sets of information used in the three forms of market efficiency are *nested*. That is, the information set in the strong form includes the information set in the semistrong form, which in turn includes the information set in the weak form. Figure 7.1 shows the relationships among the information sets.

A weak form efficient market is one in which the information reflected in past prices and volume figures is of no value in beating the market. As we discuss in our next chapter, one form of stock market analysis, called "technical analysis," is based on using past prices and volume to predict future prices. If a market is weak form efficient, however, then technical

FIGURE 7.1   Information Sets for Market Efficiency

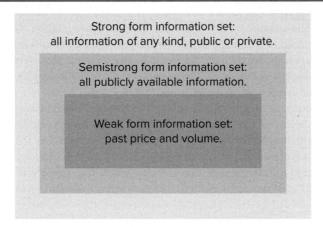

analysis is of no use whatsoever. You might as well read tea leaves as stock price charts if the market is weak form efficient.

In a semistrong form efficient market, publicly available information of any and all kinds is of no use in beating the market. If a market is semistrong form efficient, then the fundamental analysis techniques we described in a previous chapter are useless. Also, notice that past prices and volume data are publicly available information, so if a market is semistrong form efficient, it is also weak form efficient.

The implications of semistrong form efficiency are, at a minimum, semistaggering. What it literally means is that nothing in the library, for example, is of any value in earning a positive abnormal return. How about a firm's financial statements? Useless. How about information in the financial press? Worthless. This book? Sad to say, if the market is semistrong form efficient, nothing in this book will be of any use in beating the market. You can imagine that this form of market efficiency is hotly disputed.

Finally, in a strong form efficient market, no information of any kind, public or private, is useful in beating the market. Notice that if a market is strong form efficient, it is necessarily weak and semistrong form efficient as well. Ignoring the issue of legality, possession of nonpublic inside information of many types clearly would enable you to earn essentially unlimited returns, so this case is not particularly interesting. Instead, the market efficiency debate focuses on the first two forms.

CHECK THIS

7.4a   What role does information play in determining whether markets are efficient?

7.4b   What are the forms of market efficiency?

7.5 Why Would a Market Be Efficient?

The driving force toward market efficiency is competition and the profit motive. Investors constantly try to identify superior-performing investments. Using the most advanced information-processing tools available, investors and security analysts constantly appraise stock values, buying those stocks that look even slightly undervalued and selling those that look even slightly overvalued. This constant appraisal and subsequent trading activity (as well as all the research behind these activities) act to ensure that prices never differ much from their efficient market price.

To give you an idea of how strong the incentive is to identify superior investments, consider a large mutual fund such as the Fidelity Magellan Fund, which has about $23 billion under management (as of mid-2022). Suppose Fidelity was able through its research to improve the performance of this fund by 20 basis points for one year only (recall that a basis point is 1 percent of 1 percent, i.e., .0001). How much would this one-time 20 basis point improvement be worth?

The answer is .0020 times $23 billion, or $46 million. Thus, Fidelity would be willing to spend up to $46 million to boost the performance of this one fund by as little as one-fifth of one percent for a single year only. As this example shows, even relatively small performance enhancements are worth tremendous amounts of money and thereby create the incentive to unearth relevant information and use it.

Because of this incentive, the fundamental characteristic of an efficient market is that prices are correct in the sense that they fully reflect relevant information. If and when new information comes to light, prices may change, and they may change by a lot. It depends on the nature of the new information. However, in an efficient market, right here, right now, price is a consensus opinion of value, where that consensus is based on the information and intellect of hundreds of thousands, or even millions, of investors around the world.

CHECK THIS

7.5a What is the driving force behind market efficiency?

7.5b Why does this driving force work?

7.6 Some Implications of Market Efficiency

DOES OLD INFORMATION HELP PREDICT FUTURE STOCK PRICES?

Related Bloomberg Functions

NH	News Headlines
EVT	Company Events
EE SURP	Price Reaction and Surprise

In its weakest form, the efficient markets hypothesis is the simple statement that stock prices fully reflect all past information. If this is true, this means that studying past price movements in the hopes of predicting future stock price movements is really a waste of time.

In addition, a very subtle prediction is at work here. That is, no matter how often a particular stock price path has related to subsequent stock price changes in the past, there is no assurance that this relationship will occur again in the future.

Researchers have used sophisticated statistical techniques to test whether past stock price movements are of any value in predicting future stock price movements. This turns out to be a surprisingly difficult question to answer clearly and without qualification.

In short, although some researchers have been able to show that future returns are partly predictable from past returns, the predicted returns are not *economically* important, which means that predictability is not sufficient to earn an abnormal return. In addition, trading costs generally swamp attempts to build a profitable trading system on the basis of past returns. Researchers have been unable to provide evidence of a superior trading strategy that uses only past returns. That is, trading costs matter, and buy-and-hold strategies involving broad market indexes are extremely difficult to outperform. (If you know how to outperform a broad market index after accounting for trading costs, please share it with us.)

RANDOM WALKS AND STOCK PRICES

If you were to ask people you know whether stock market prices are predictable, many of them would say yes. To their surprise, and perhaps yours, it is very difficult to predict stock market prices. In fact, considerable research has shown that stock prices change through time as if they are random. That is, stock price increases are about as likely as stock price decreases. When the path that a stock price follows shows no discernible pattern, then the stock's price behavior is largely consistent with the notion of a **random walk**. A random walk is related to the weak form version of the efficient markets hypothesis because past knowledge of the stock price is not useful in predicting future stock prices.

Figure 7.2 illustrates daily price changes for Tesla stock from May 18, 2021, through May 13, 2022. To qualify as a true random walk, Tesla stock price changes would have to

random walk
No discernible pattern to the path that a stock price follows through time.

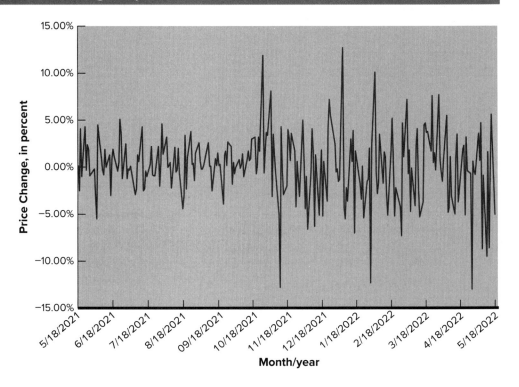

be truly independent from day to day. In addition, the distribution of possible stock prices each day must be the same. Even so, the graph of daily price changes for Tesla stock is essentially what a random walk looks like. It is certainly hard to see any pattern in the daily price changes of Tesla.

HOW DO STOCK PRICES REACT TO NEW INFORMATION?

In its semistrong form, the efficient markets hypothesis is the simple statement that stock prices fully reflect publicly available information. Stock prices change when traders buy and sell shares based on their view of the future prospects for the stock. The future prospects for the stock are influenced by unexpected news announcements. Examples of unexpected news announcements might include an increase or decrease in the dividend paid by a stock, an increase or decrease in the forecast for future earnings, lawsuits over company practices, or changes in the leadership team. As shown in Figure 7.3, prices could adjust to a positive news announcement in three basic ways.

- *Efficient market reaction.* The price instantaneously adjusts to, and fully reflects, new information. There is no tendency for subsequent increases or decreases to occur.

- *Delayed reaction.* The price partially adjusts to the new information, but days elapse before the price completely reflects new information.

- *Overreaction and correction.* The price overadjusts to the new information; it overshoots the appropriate new price but eventually falls to the appropriate price.

EVENT STUDIES

Although the following example is a bit old, it is a classic case study of how researchers use the event study method to investigate how news affects stock prices. In an event study, researchers identify news, i.e., an event, and see how the news affects stock prices.

A news event occurred on Friday, May 25, 2007, when executives of Advanced Medical Optics, Inc. (EYE), recalled a contact lens solution called Complete MoisturePlus Multi-Purpose

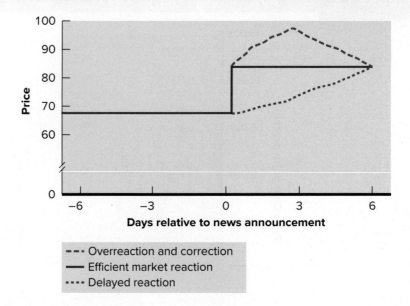

Solution. Advanced Medical Optics took this voluntary action after the Centers for Disease Control and Prevention (CDC) found a link between the solution and a rare corneal infection. The medical name for this infection is *Acanthamoeba* keratitis, or AK for short.

About two out of every million contact lens users in the United States each year are afflicted with AK. Although instances of AK are rare, AK is serious—this infection can lead to vision loss, and sometimes it can lead to the need for a cornea transplant. The CDC determined that the risk of developing AK is about seven times greater for consumers using the Complete MoisturePlus contact lens solution than for those consumers using other contact lens solutions.

Executives at Advanced Medical Optics chose to recall their product even though they did not find evidence their manufacturing process introduced the parasite that can lead to AK. Further, company officials believed that the occurrences of AK were most likely the result of end users who failed to follow safe procedures when installing contact lenses.

Nevertheless, the recall was announced following the market close on Friday, May 25, 2007. Following the long weekend, EYE shares opened on Tuesday, May 29, 2007, at $34.37, down $5.83 from the Friday close of $40.20. Figure 7.4 is a plot of the price per share of Advanced Medical Optics in the days surrounding this news announcement.

event study
A research method designed to help study the effects of news on stock prices.

Researchers use a technique known as an **event study** to test the effects of news announcements on stock prices. When researchers look for effects of news on stock prices, however, they must make sure that overall market news is accounted for in their analysis. The reason is simple. Suppose the whole market had fallen drastically on May 29, 2007. How would researchers be able to separate the overall market decline from the isolated news concerning Advanced Medical Optics?

To answer this question, researchers calculate abnormal returns. The equation to calculate an abnormal return is:

$$\text{Abnormal return} = \text{Observed return} - \text{Expected return} \qquad (7.1)$$

The expected return can be calculated using a market index (like the Nasdaq 100 index or the S&P 500 index) or by using a long-term average return on the stock. As we discussed earlier in the chapter, this expected return should be based on assets that have a similar expected level of risk. If we use market returns, we must adjust these returns to reflect any differences in risk relative to the asset being evaluated.

Researchers then align the abnormal return on a stock to the days relative to the news announcement. Usually, researchers assign the value of zero to the day a news announcement

FIGURE 7.4

The Price of Shares for Advanced Medical Optics, May 14, 2007, through June 15, 2007

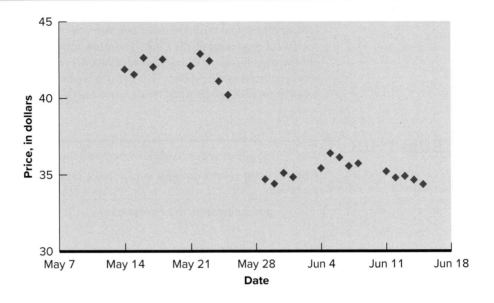

FIGURE 7.5

Cumulative Abnormal Returns for Advanced Medical Optics, March 30, 2007, through July 25, 2007

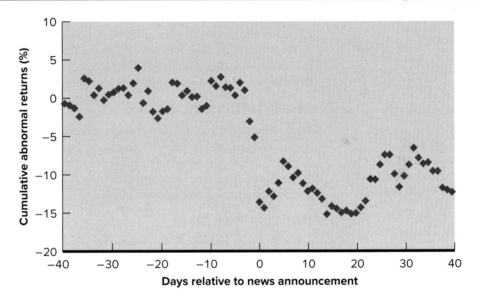

is made. One day after the news announcement is assigned a value of +1, two days after the news announcement is assigned a value of +2, and so on. Similarly, one day before the news announcement is assigned a value of −1.

According to the efficient markets hypothesis, the abnormal return today should relate only to information released on that day. Any previously released information should have no effect on abnormal returns because this information has been available to all traders. Also, the return today cannot be influenced by information that traders do not yet know.

To evaluate abnormal returns, researchers usually accumulate them over some period. Figure 7.5 is a plot of the cumulative abnormal returns for Advanced Medical Optics beginning 40 days before the announcement. The first cumulative abnormal return, or CAR, is equal to the abnormal return on Day −40. The CAR on Day −39 is the sum of the first two abnormal returns, the CAR on Day −38 is the sum of the first three, and so on. By examining CARs, we can see if there was an over- or underreaction to an announcement.

As you can see in Figure 7.5, Advanced Medical's cumulative abnormal return hovered around zero before the announcement. After the news was released, there was a large, sharp downward movement in the CAR. The stock price gyrated as additional news was released, but the overall pattern of cumulative abnormal returns is essentially what the efficient markets hypothesis would predict. That is, there is a band of cumulative abnormal returns, a sharp break in cumulative abnormal returns, and another band of cumulative abnormal returns.

CHECK THIS

7.6a	How is a random walk affiliated with the efficient markets hypothesis?
7.6b	What are the possible market price reactions to a news announcement?
7.6c	How do researchers use event studies to examine the effects of news announcements on stock prices?

7.7 Informed Traders and Insider Trading

Recall that if a market is strong form efficient, no information of any kind, public or private, is useful in beating the market. However, inside information of many types clearly would enable you to earn essentially unlimited returns. This fact generates an interesting question: Should any of us be able to earn returns based on information that is not known to the public?

In the United States (and in many other countries), making profits on nonpublic information is illegal. This ban is said to be necessary if investors are to have trust in U.S. stock markets. The U.S. Securities and Exchange Commission (SEC) is charged with enforcing laws concerning illegal trading activities. As a result, it is important for you to be able to distinguish between informed trading, insider trading, and legal insider trading.

Related Bloomberg Functions

INSD Insider and Shareholder Activity

INFORMED TRADING

informed trader
An investor who makes a buy or sell decision based on public information and analysis.

When an investor makes a decision to buy or sell a stock based on publicly available information and analysis, this investor is said to be an **informed trader**. The information that an informed trader possesses might come from reading *The Wall Street Journal,* reading quarterly reports issued by a company, gathering financial information from the internet, talking to other traders, or a host of other sources.

INSIDER TRADING

Some informed traders are also insider traders. When you hear the term *insider trading,* you most likely think that such activity is illegal. However, as you will see at the end of this section, not all insider trading is illegal.

material nonpublic information
Any information that could reasonably be expected to affect the price of a security.

WHO IS AN INSIDER? For the purposes of defining illegal insider trading, an insider is someone who has **material nonpublic information**. Not only is such information not known to the public, but if it were known, it would impact the stock price. A person can be charged with insider trading when that person acts on such information in an attempt to make a profit.

Frequently, when an illegal insider trade occurs, there is a *tipper* and a *tippee.* The tipper is the person who has, on purpose, divulged material nonpublic information. The tippee is the person who has knowingly used such information in an attempt to make a profit. For example, a tipper could be a CEO who spills some inside information to a friend who does not work for the company. If the friend then knowingly uses this inside information to make a trade, this tippee is guilty of insider trading.

Proving that a trader is a tippee is difficult for the SEC because keeping track of insider information flows and subsequent trades is difficult. For example, suppose a person makes a trade based on the advice of a stockbroker. Even if the broker based this advice on material nonpublic information, the trader might not have been aware of the broker's knowledge. The SEC must prove that the trader was, in fact, aware that the broker's information was based on material nonpublic information.

Sometimes, people accused of insider trading claim that they just "overheard" someone talking. Suppose, for example, you are at a restaurant and overhear a conversation between Bill Gates and his CFO concerning some potentially explosive news regarding Microsoft Corp. If you then go out and make a trade in an attempt to profit from what you overheard, you would be violating the law (even though the information was "innocently obtained"). When you take possession of material nonpublic information, you become an insider and are bound to obey insider trading laws. Note that in this case, Bill Gates and his CFO, although careless, are not necessarily in violation of insider trading laws.

LEGAL INSIDER TRADING A company's corporate insiders can make perfectly legal trades in the stock of their company. To do so, they must comply with the reporting rules made by the U.S. Securities and Exchange Commission. When they make a trade and report it to the SEC, these trades are reported to the public and are available on many investment websites. In addition, corporate insiders must declare that trades that they made were based on public information about the company, rather than "inside" information. Most public companies also have guidelines that must be followed. For example, companies commonly allow insiders to trade only during certain windows throughout the year, often sometime after earnings have been announced.

To see recent insider trades for a company of your choice, check out the "Executive" tab of a stock quote at www.morningstar.com.

IT'S NOT A GOOD THING: WHAT DID MARTHA DO? Martha Stewart became one of America's most successful entrepreneurs by telling people how to entertain, cook, and decorate their homes. She built her superhomemaker personality into a far-flung international enterprise. In fact, her company, Martha Stewart Living Omnimedia, went public in 1999, raising $873 million in the initial public offering.

Ms. Stewart was in the legal news because the U.S. Securities and Exchange Commission believed that she was told by her friend Sam Waksal, who founded a company called ImClone, that a cancer drug being developed by ImClone had been rejected by the Food and Drug Administration. This development was bad news for ImClone. Martha Stewart sold her 3,928 shares in ImClone on December 27, 2001. On that day, ImClone traded below $60 per share, a level that Ms. Stewart claimed triggered an existing stop-loss order. However, the SEC believed that Ms. Stewart illegally sold her shares because she had information concerning FDA rejection before it became public.

The FDA rejection was announced after the market closed on Friday, December 28, 2001. This news was a huge blow to ImClone shares, which closed at about $46 per share on the following Monday (the first trading day after the information became public). Shares in ImClone subsequently fell to under $10 per share about six months later, in mid-2002. Ironically, shares of ImClone rallied to sell for more than $80 per share in mid-2004.

In June 2003, Martha Stewart and her stockbroker, Peter Bacanovic, were indicted on nine federal counts. They both pleaded not guilty, and Ms. Stewart's trial began in January 2004. Just days before the jury began to deliberate, however, Judge Miriam Cedarbaum dismissed the most serious charge—securities fraud. Ms. Stewart, however, was convicted on all four counts of obstructing justice and lying to investigators.

Judge Cedarbaum fined Martha Stewart $30,000 and sentenced her to five months in prison, two years of probation, and five months of home confinement after her release. The fine was the maximum allowed under federal rules; the sentence was the minimum the judge could impose. Peter Bacanovic was fined $4,000 and sentenced to five months in prison and two years of probation.

To summarize, Martha Stewart was accused, but not convicted, of insider trading. The same can be said of Phil Mickelson, who was recently investigated for insider trading in Dean Foods. Unlike Mickelson, however, Martha Stewart was also accused, and convicted, of obstructing justice and misleading investigators, leading to a short time in prison.

Although her conviction barred her from taking on the duties of an executive officer, Martha still earned a hefty salary for other roles in her company. In fact, she earned about $5.5 million per year before Sequential Brands Group acquired her company in 2015.

7.7a   What makes a stock trader an informed trader?

7.7b   What traders are considered to be insiders?

7.7c   What is the difference between legal insider trading and illegal insider trading?

 7.8 How Efficient Are Markets?

ARE FINANCIAL MARKETS EFFICIENT?

Financial markets are one of the most extensively documented human endeavors. Colossal amounts of financial market data are collected and reported every day. These data, particularly stock market data, have been exhaustively analyzed to test market efficiency.

You would think that with all this analysis going on, we would know whether markets are efficient, but really we don't. Instead, what we seem to have, at least in the minds of many researchers, is a growing realization that beyond a point, we just can't tell.

For example, it is not difficult to program a computer to test trading strategies that are based solely on historic prices and volume figures. Many such strategies have been tested, and the bulk of the evidence indicates that such strategies are not useful.

More generally, market efficiency is difficult to test for four basic reasons:

1. The risk adjustment problem.

2. The relevant information problem.

3. The dumb luck problem.

4. The data snooping problem.

We briefly discuss each in turn.

The first issue, the risk adjustment problem, is the easiest to understand. Earlier, we noted that beating the market means consistently earning a positive abnormal return. To determine whether an investment has a positive abnormal return, we have to adjust for its risk. As we discuss elsewhere in this book, the truth is that we are not even certain exactly what we mean by risk, much less how to measure it precisely and then adjust for it. Thus, what appears to be a positive abnormal return may be the result of a faulty risk adjustment procedure.

The second issue, the relevant information problem, is even more troublesome. Remember that the concept of market efficiency is meaningful only relative to some particular information. As we look back in time and try to assess whether a particular market behavior was inefficient, we have to recognize that we cannot possibly know all the information that may have been underlying that market behavior.

For example, suppose we see that 10 years ago the price of a stock shot up by 100 percent over a short period of time, and then subsequently collapsed. We dig through all the historical information we can find, but we can find no reason for this behavior. What can we conclude? Nothing, really. For all we know, an undocumented rumor existed of a takeover that never materialized, and relative to this information, the price behavior was perfectly efficient.

In general, there is no way to tell whether we have all the relevant information. Without all the relevant information, we cannot tell if some observed price behavior is inefficient. Put differently, any price behavior, no matter how bizarre, might be efficient, and therefore explainable, with respect to some information.

The third problem has to do with evaluating investors and money managers. One type of evidence frequently cited to prove that markets can be beaten is the enviable track record of certain legendary investors. A prime example is Warren Buffett, whose firm Berkshire Hathaway has compounded an annual return of over 20 percent per year since 1951. This compares to an approximate 10 percent return on the S&P 500 over the same period.

The argument goes that the existence of a successful investor such as Warren Buffett proves market inefficiency. Is this correct? Maybe yes, maybe no. You may be familiar with the following expression: "If you put an immortal monkey in front of a typewriter, this monkey will eventually produce *Hamlet*." In a similar manner, suppose we have thousands of monkeys who are tasked with picking stocks for a portfolio. We would find that some of these monkeys would appear to be amazingly talented and rack up extraordinary gains. As you surely recognize, however, this is caused by random chance.

Similarly, if we track the performance of thousands of money managers over some period of time, some managers will accumulate remarkable track records and a lot of publicity. Are they good or are they lucky? If we could track them for many decades, we might be able to tell, but for the most part, money managers are not around long enough for us to accumulate sufficient data. We discuss the performance of money managers as a group later in the chapter.

Our final problem has to do with what is known as "data snooping." Instead of monkeys at typewriters, think of what can happen if thousands of finance researchers with thousands of computers are all studying the same data and are looking for inefficiencies. Apparent patterns, or anomalies, will surely be found.

In fact, researchers have discovered extremely simple patterns that, at least historically, have been both highly successful and very hard to explain. We discuss some of these later in the chapter. These discoveries raise another problem: ghosts in the data. If we look long enough and hard enough at any data, we are bound to find some apparent patterns by sheer chance. But are these patterns real? Only time will tell.

Notwithstanding the four problems we have discussed, based on the last 30+ years of scientific research, three generalities about market efficiency seem in order. First, short-term stock price and market movements appear to be very difficult, or even impossible, to predict with any accuracy (at least with any objective method of which we are aware). Second, the market reacts quickly and sharply to new (i.e., unanticipated) information, and the vast majority of studies of the impact of new information find little or no evidence that the market underreacts or overreacts to new information in a way that can be profitably exploited. Third, if the stock market can be beaten, the way to do it is at least not obvious, so the implication is that the market is not grossly inefficient.

SOME IMPLICATIONS OF MARKET EFFICIENCY

To the extent that you think a market is efficient, there are some important investment implications. Going back to Chapter 2, we saw that the investment process can be viewed as having two parts: asset allocation and security selection. Even if all markets are efficient, asset allocation is still important because the way you divide your money among the various types of investments will strongly influence your overall risk-return relation.

If markets are efficient, however, then security selection is less important. Market efficiency means you do not have to worry too much about overpaying or underpaying for any particular security. In fact, if markets are efficient, you would probably be better off buying a large basket of stocks and following a passive investment strategy. Your main goal would be to hold your costs to a minimum while maintaining a broadly diversified portfolio.

In broader terms, if markets are efficient, then little role exists for professional money managers. You should not pay load fees to buy mutual fund shares, and you should shop for low management fees. You should not work with full-service brokers, and so on.

Recent investor decisions echo this transition. Over the past decade, the proportion of investment dollars flowing to low-cost, passively managed funds has increased significantly. As of early 2019, passively managed funds represented about 48 percent of all managed assets. In fact, Bloomberg recently forecasted that by the end of 2019, passively managed investments will represent more than half of all fund investments.

If markets are efficient, there is one other thing that you should not do: You should not try to time the market. Recall that market timing amounts to moving money in and out of the market based on your expectations of future market direction. By trying to time the market, all you will accomplish is to guarantee that you will, on average, underperform the market.

In fact, market efficiency aside, market timing is hard to recommend. Historically, most of the gains earned in the stock market have tended to occur over relatively short periods of time. If you miss even a single one of these short market run-ups, you will likely never catch up. Put differently, successful market timing requires phenomenal accuracy to be of any benefit, and anything less than that will, based on the historical record, result in underperforming the market.

CHECK THIS

7.8a What are the four basic reasons market efficiency is difficult to test?

7.8b What are the implications to investors if markets are efficient?

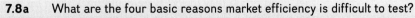

7.9 Market Efficiency and the Performance of Professional Money Managers

Related Bloomberg Functions

FUND Mutual Funds Home

PORT Portfolio and Risk Analysis

Let's have a stock market investment contest in which you are going to take on professional money managers. Of course, the professional money managers have at their disposal their skill, banks of computers, and scores of analysts to help pick their stocks. Does this sound like an unfair match? Well, it is—you have a terrific advantage!

It's true. You can become an expert investor by using the following investment strategy: Hold a broad-based market index. One such index that you can easily buy is a mutual fund called the Vanguard 500 Index Fund (there are other market index mutual funds, too). This low-fee mutual fund is designed to produce investment results that correspond to the price and yield performance of the S&P 500 index. The fund tracks the performance of the S&P 500 index by investing its assets in the stocks that make up the S&P 500 index. By the way, this fund is popular—as of June 2022, the Vanguard 500 Index Fund was one of the largest stock mutual funds in the United States, with over $360 billion in assets.

As discussed in a previous chapter, a general equity mutual fund (GEF) is a pool of money invested in stocks that is overseen by a professional money manager. Figure 7.6 shows the growth in the number of actively managed GEFs in the United States from 1989 through 2021. The solid blue line shows the total number of funds that have existed for at least one year, while the solid red line shows the number of funds that have existed for at least 10 years.

From Figure 7.6, you can see that it is difficult for professional money managers to keep their funds in existence for 10 years (if it were easy, there would not be much difference between the solid blue line and the solid red line). The figure also illustrates the growing impact of passive investing strategies. In particular, the number of GEFs grew quickly during the 1990s and early 2000s. Since 2008, however, the number of actively managed mutual funds has declined, mostly due to a shift to passive investments (e.g., index funds).

Figure 7.6 also shows the number of these funds that beat the performance of the Vanguard 500 Index Fund. You can see that there is much more variation in the dashed blue line than in the dashed red line. What this means is that in any given year, it is hard to predict how many professional money managers will beat the Vanguard 500 Index Fund. But the low level and low variation of the dashed red line mean that the percentage of professional money managers who can beat the Vanguard 500 Index Fund over a 10-year investment period is low and stable. This lack of performance by active managers is a primary reason investors have shifted away from these higher-cost actively managed funds.

Figures 7.7 and 7.8 are bar charts that show the percentage of managed equity funds that beat the Vanguard 500 Index Fund. Figure 7.7 uses return data for the previous year only, while Figure 7.8 uses return data for the previous 10 years. As you can see from Figure 7.7, in only 12 of the 33 years spanning 1989 through 2021 did more than half the professional money managers beat the Vanguard 500 Index Fund. The performance is almost as bad

FIGURE 7.6

The Growth of Actively Managed Equity Funds, 1989–2021

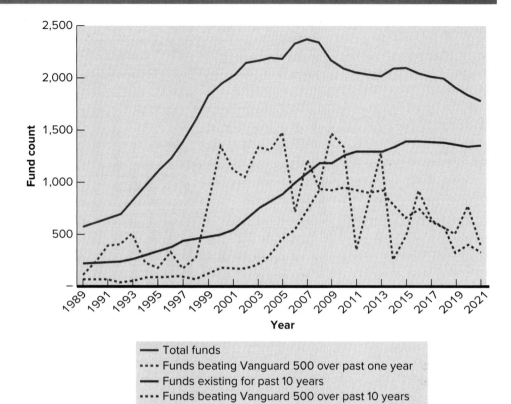

Total funds
Funds beating Vanguard 500 over past one year
Funds existing for past 10 years
Funds beating Vanguard 500 over past 10 years

Source: Author calculations.

FIGURE 7.7

Percentage of Managed Equity Funds Beating the Vanguard 500 Index Fund, One-Year Returns

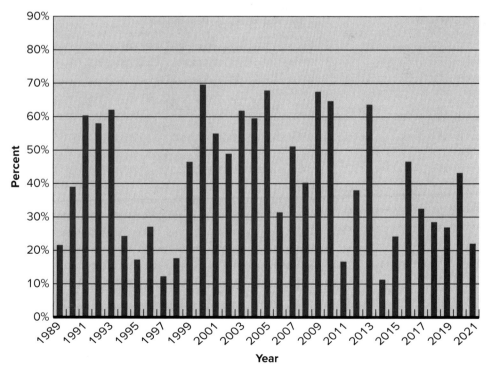

Source: Author calculations.

Chapter 7 ● Stock Price Behavior and Market Efficiency 227

FIGURE 7.8

Percentage of Managed Equity Funds Beating the Vanguard 500 Index Fund, 10-Year Returns

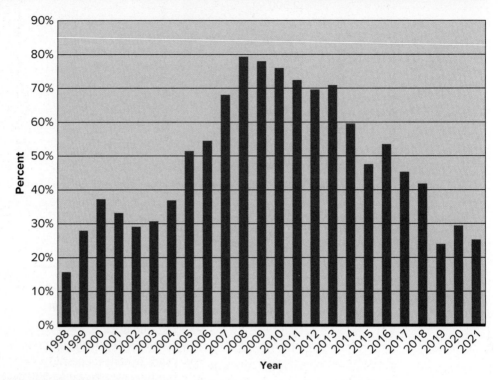

Source: Author calculations.

TABLE 7.1 — **The Performance of Professional Money Managers versus the Vanguard 500 Index Fund**

Length of Each Investment Period (Years)	Span	Number of Investment Periods	Number of Investment Periods Half the Funds Beat Vanguard	Percent	Number of Investment Periods Three-Fourths of the Funds Beat Vanguard	Percent
1	1989–2021	33	12	36.4%	0	0.0%
3	1991–2021	31	13	41.9	1	3.2
5	1993–2021	29	13	44.8	1	3.4
10	1998–2021	24	11	45.8	3	12.5

Source: Author calculations.

when it comes to 10-year investment periods (1989–1998 through 2012–2021). As shown in Figure 7.8, in only 11 of these 24 investment periods did more than half the professional money managers beat the Vanguard 500 Index Fund.

Table 7.1 presents more evidence concerning the performance of professional money managers. Using data from 1989 through 2021, we divide this time period into 1-year investment periods, rolling 3-year investment periods, rolling 5-year investment periods, and rolling 10-year investment periods. Then, after we calculate the number of investment periods, we ask two questions: (1) What percentage of the time did half the professionally managed funds beat the Vanguard 500 Index Fund? and (2) What percentage of the time did three-fourths of the professionally managed funds beat the Vanguard 500 Index Fund?

As you see in Table 7.1, the performance of professional money managers is generally quite poor relative to the Vanguard 500 Index Fund.

The figures and table in this section raise some difficult and uncomfortable questions for securities analysts and other investment professionals. If markets are inefficient, and tools like fundamental analysis are valuable, why don't mutual fund managers do better? Why can't mutual fund managers even beat a broad market index?

The performance of professional money managers is especially troublesome when we consider the enormous resources at their disposal and the substantial survivorship bias that exists. The survivorship bias comes into being because managers and funds that do especially poorly disappear. If beating the market was possible, then this Darwinian process of elimination should lead to a situation in which the survivors, as a group, are capable of doing so. The fact that professional money managers seem to lack the ability to outperform a broad market index is consistent with the notion that, overall, the equity market is efficient.

So if the market is this efficient, what is the role for portfolio managers? The role of a portfolio manager in an efficient market is to build a portfolio to meet the specific needs of individual investors. You have learned that a basic principle of investing is to hold a well-diversified portfolio. However, exactly which diversified portfolio is optimal varies by investor.

Some factors that influence portfolio choice include the investor's age, tax bracket, risk aversion, and even employer. Employer? Sure. Suppose you work for Starbucks and part of your compensation is stock options. Like many companies, Starbucks offers its employees the opportunity to purchase company stock at less than market value. Of course, you would take advantage of this opportunity. You can imagine that you could wind up with a lot of Starbucks stock in your portfolio, which means you are not holding a diversified portfolio. The role of your portfolio manager would be to help you add other assets to your portfolio so that it is once again well diversified.

CHECK THIS

7.9a How well do professional money managers perform, on average, against a broad market index?

7.9b What are the implications of this performance for investors?

7.10 Anomalies

In this section, we discuss some aspects of stock price behavior that are both baffling and potentially hard to reconcile with market efficiency. Researchers call these *market anomalies.* Keep three facts in mind as you read about market anomalies. First, anomalies are generally "small," in that they do not involve many dollars relative to the overall size of the stock market. Second, many anomalies are fleeting and tend to disappear when discovered. Finally, anomalies are not easily used as the basis for a trading strategy because transaction costs render many of them unprofitable.

Related Bloomberg Functions

TRA	Total Returns Analysis
EVTS	Events Calendar
EE	Earnings and Estimates

THE DAY-OF-THE-WEEK EFFECT

In the stock market, which day of the week has, on average, the biggest return? The question might strike you as silly; after all, what would make one day different from any other on average? On further reflection, though, you might realize that one day is different: Monday.

When we calculate a daily return for the stock market, we take the percentage change in closing prices from one trading day to the next. For every day except Monday, this is a 24-hour period. However, because the markets are closed on weekends, the average return on Monday is based on the percentage change from Friday's close to Monday's close, a 72-hour period. Thus, the average Monday return would be computed over a three-day period, not just a one-day period. Because of this longer time period, we would predict that Monday should have the highest return; in fact, Monday's average return should be three times as large.

day-of-the-week effect
The tendency for Monday to have a negative average return.

Given this reasoning, it may come as a surprise to you to learn that Monday has the lowest average return. In fact, Monday is the only day with a negative average return. This is the **day-of-the-week effect**. Table 7.2 shows the average return by day of the week for the S&P 500 for the period January 1950 through December 2021.

TABLE 7.2

Average Daily S&P 500 Returns, by Day of the Week (Dividends Included)

Time Period	Weekday				
	Monday	Tuesday	Wednesday	Thursday	Friday
1950–2021	−.065%	.050%	.095%	.058%	.092%
1950–1980	−.138	.027	.125	.069	.136
1981–2021	.009	.066	.073	.049	.058

Source: Author calculations, using value-weighted returns.

In the 71 years spanning 1950 to 2021, the negative return on Monday is significant, both in a statistical sense and in an economic sense. This day-of-the-week effect does not appear to be a fluke; it exists in other markets, such as the bond market, and it exists in stock markets outside the United States. It has defied explanation since it was first documented in the early 1980s. As you can see in Table 7.2, the effect is strong in the 1950–1980 time period. The effect, however, is not apparent in the 1981–2021 time period, suggesting that it might have disappeared.

Still, critics of the efficient markets hypothesis point to this strange return behavior as evidence of market inefficiency. While this return behavior is odd, exploiting it presents a problem. That is, how this return behavior can be used to earn a positive abnormal return is not clear. This murkiness is especially true in the 1981–2021 time period (i.e., in the period following the time when the effect was first documented). So whether this strange return behavior points to inefficiency is hard to say.

THE AMAZING JANUARY EFFECT

We saw in Chapter 1 that returns from small-cap common stocks have significantly outdistanced the returns from large-cap common stocks. Beginning in the early 1980s, researchers reported that the difference was too large even to be explained by differences in risk. In other words, small stocks appeared to earn positive abnormal returns.

Further research found that, in fact, a substantial percentage of the return on small stocks has historically occurred early in the month of January, particularly in the few days surrounding the turn of the year. Even closer research documents that this peculiar phenomenon is more pronounced for stocks that have experienced significant declines in value, or "losers."

Thus, we have the famous "small-stock-in-January-especially-around-the-turn-of-the-year-for-losers effect," or SSIJEATTOTYFLE for short. For obvious reasons, this phenomenon is usually just dubbed the **January effect**. To give you an idea of how big this effect is, we first plotted average returns by month going back to 1926 for large stocks in Figure 7.9A. As shown, the average return per month has been just under 1 percent.

In Figure 7.9A, there is nothing remarkable about January; the largest average monthly return for large stocks occurred in July (followed closely by December); and the lowest average monthly return occurred in September. From a statistical standpoint, there is nothing too exceptional about these large-stock returns. After all, some month has to be the highest, and some month has to be the lowest.

Figure 7.9B, however, shows average returns by month for small stocks (notice the difference in vertical axis scaling between Figures 7.9A and 7.9B). The month of January definitely jumps out. Over the 96 years covered, small stocks gained, on average, about 5.8 percent in the month of January alone! Comparing Figures 7.9A and 7.9B, we see, outside the month of January, small stocks have not done especially well relative to large stocks. To a lesser extent, we see that small stocks have done better than large stocks in February, but large stocks have done better than small stocks by a similar amount in October.

The January effect appears to exist in many major markets around the world, so it's not unique to the United States (it's actually more pronounced in some other markets). It also exists in some markets other than stock markets. Critics of market efficiency point to enormous gains to be had from investing in January and ask: How can an efficient market have

January effect
Tendency for small stocks to have large returns in January.

FIGURE 7.9A

Large Stocks' Average Monthly Returns, 1926–2021, Dividends Included

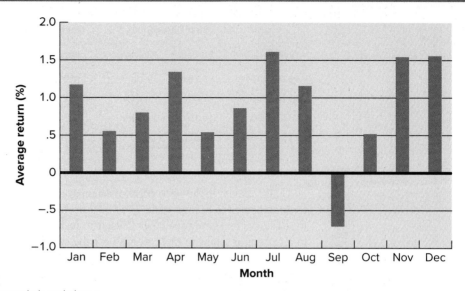

Source: Author calculations.

FIGURE 7.9B

Small Stocks' Average Monthly Returns, 1926–2021, Dividends Included

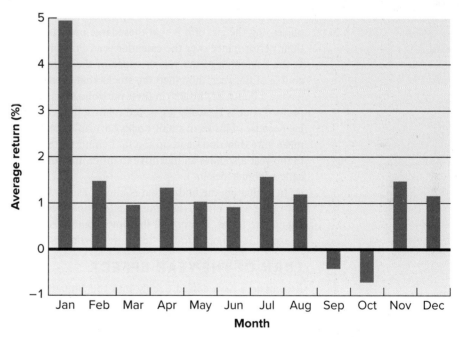

Source: Author calculations.

such unusual behavior? Why don't investors take advantage of this opportunity and thereby drive it out of existence?

In Table 7.3, you can see that, on average, small stock returns were 3.78 percent higher than large stock returns in the 1926–2021 time period. The next-best month in this period (February) is more than canceled out by the worst month (October). When we break the 1926–2021 time period into smaller time intervals, you can see that the January effect has diminished over time. In fact, in the 1988–2021 time period, the best monthly difference of 1.52 percent actually occurs in June, and even this difference is more than canceled out by the worst monthly difference of −1.65 percent (July).

TABLE 7.3

Monthly Returns of Small Stocks Minus Monthly Returns of Large Stocks, by Various Time Periods, 1926–2021

Time Period	Best Difference		Next-Best Difference		Worst Difference	
	Percent	Month	Percent	Month	Percent	Month
1926–2021	3.78%	January	.99%	February	−1.19%	October
1926–1956	5.30	January	1.37	May	−1.71	December
1957–1987	5.15	January	.92	February	−2.02	October
1988–2021	1.52	June	1.18	January	−1.65	July

Source: Author calculations.

Unlike the day-of-the-week effect, the January effect is at least partially understood. Two factors are thought to be important. The first is tax-loss selling. Investors have a strong tax incentive to sell stocks that have gone down in value to realize the loss for tax purposes. This trading leads to a pattern of selling in these stocks near the end of the year and buying after the turn of the year. In large stocks, this activity wouldn't have much effect, but in the smaller stocks, it could.

The tax-loss selling argument is plausible because researchers have looked to see whether the January effect existed in the United States before there was an income tax—and they found no January effect. However, the January effect has been found in other countries that didn't (or don't) have calendar tax years or didn't (or don't) have capital gains taxes. However, foreign investors in those markets (such as U.S. investors) did (or do). So, debate continues about the tax-loss selling explanation.

The second factor has to do with institutional investors. The argument here has several pieces, but the gist of it is that these large investors compensate portfolio managers based on their performance over the calendar year. Portfolio managers therefore pile into small stocks at the beginning of the year because of their growth potential, bidding up prices. Over the course of the year, they shed the stocks that do poorly because they don't want to be seen as having a bunch of "losers" in their portfolio (this is called "window dressing"). Also, because performance is typically measured relative to the S&P 500, portfolio managers who begin to lag because of losses in small stocks have an incentive to sell them and buy S&P 500 stocks to make sure they don't end up too far behind the S&P 500. Managers who are well ahead late in the year also have an incentive to move into S&P 500 stocks to preserve their leads (this is called "bonus lock-in").

In evaluating the oddity that is known as the January effect, keep in mind that, unlike the day-of-the-week effect, the January effect does not even exist for the market as a whole, so, in big-picture terms, it is not all that important. Also, it doesn't happen every year, so attempts to exploit it will occasionally result in substantial losses.

TURN-OF-THE-YEAR EFFECT

Researchers have delved deeply into the January effect to see whether the effect is due to returns during the whole month of January or to returns bracketing the end of the year. Researchers look at returns over a specific three-week period and compare them to the returns for the rest of the year. In Table 7.4, we calculated daily market returns from 1962

TABLE 7.4

The Turn-of-the-Year Effect

Time Period	Market Return on the:		
	Turn-of-the-Month Days (%)	Rest of the Days (%)	Difference (%)
1962–2021	.120%	.039%	.081%
1962–1990	.161	.031	.130
1991–2021	.082	.046	.036

Source: Author calculations.

through 2021. The specific three-week period we call "Turn-of-the-Year Days" is the last week of daily returns in a calendar year and the first two weeks of daily returns in the next calendar year. Any daily return that does not fall into this three-week period is put into the "Rest of the Days" category.

As you can see in Table 7.4, the returns in the "Turn-of-the-Year Days" category are higher than returns in the "Rest of the Days" category. Further, the difference is also apparent (albeit very small) in the more recent 1991–2021 period. The difference, however, was much higher in the 1962–1990 period. Again, we see that, once identified, these anomalies tend to fade with time.

TURN-OF-THE-MONTH EFFECT

Financial market researchers have also investigated whether a turn-of-the-month effect exists. In Table 7.5, we took daily stock market returns and separated them into two categories. If the daily return is from the last day of any month or the first three days of the following month, it is put into the "Turn-of-the-Month Days" category. All other daily returns are put into the "Rest of the Days" category.

As you can see in Table 7.5, the returns in the "Turn-of-the-Month Days" category are higher than the returns in the "Rest of the Days" category. As with the turn-of-the-year anomaly, the turn-of-the-month effect is apparent in each of the three time periods we report. While the effect is still pronounced in the 1991–2021 time period, it is lower than in the 1962–1990 time period. Again, the fact that this effect exists is puzzling to proponents of the EMH.

The day-of-the-week, turn-of-the-month, turn-of-the-year, and January effects are examples of calendar anomalies. There are noncalendar anomalies as well. Two well-known noncalendar anomalies have to do with earnings announcements and price-earnings ratios.

THE EARNINGS ANNOUNCEMENT PUZZLE

As you saw earlier in this chapter, unexpected news releases can have a dramatic impact on the price of a stock. One news item that is particularly important to investors is an earnings announcement. These announcements contain information about past earnings and future earnings potential.

Researchers have shown that substantial price adjustments do occur in anticipation of actual earnings. According to the EMH, stock prices should then respond very quickly to unanticipated news, or the earnings "surprise." However, researchers have found that it takes days (or even longer) for the market price to adjust fully.

Bloomberg has a page where you can look up earnings surprises. Figure 7.10 shows the earnings surprises for Under Armour, Inc. Notice that Under Armour had three consecutive quarters of positive earnings surprises. Can you use that fact to make profits? Proponents of the EMH would say, "No." But some researchers have found that buying stocks after positive earnings surprises is a profitable investment strategy.

THE PRICE-EARNINGS (PE) PUZZLE

As we have discussed elsewhere, the PE ratio is widely followed by investors and is used in stock valuation. Researchers have found that, on average, stocks with relatively low PE ratios (i.e., value stocks) outperform stocks with relatively high PE ratios (i.e., growth stocks), even after adjusting for other factors like risk. Because a PE ratio is publicly available

TABLE 7.5	The Turn-of-the-Month Effect		
	Market Return on the:		
Time Period	**Turn-of-the-Year Days (%)**	**Rest of the Days (%)**	**Difference (%)**
1962–2021	.120%	.028%	.092%
1962–1990	.162	.014	.148
1991–2021	.080	.041	.039

Source: Author calculations.

FIGURE 7.10   Earnings Surprises for Under Armour, Inc.

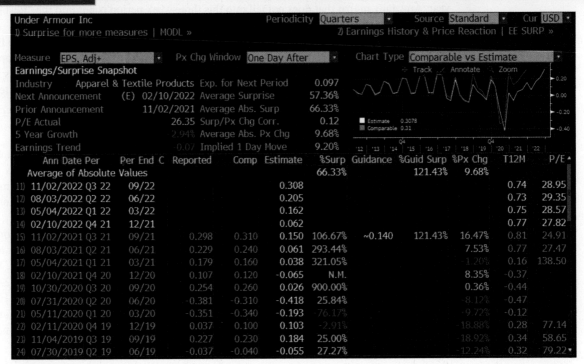

Under Armour Inc												
Periodicity: Quarters Source: Standard Cur: USD												

Measure EPS, Adj+   Px Chg Window One Day After   Chart Type Comparable vs Estimate

Earnings/Surprise Snapshot

Industry Apparel & Textile Products	Exp. for Next Period	0.097
Next Announcement (E) 02/10/2022	Average Surprise	57.36%
Prior Announcement 11/02/2021	Average Abs. Surp	66.33%
P/E Actual 26.35	Surp/Px Chg Corr.	0.12
5 Year Growth 2.94%	Average Abs. Px Chg	9.68%
Earnings Trend 0.07	Implied 1 Day Move	9.20%

	Ann Date	Per	Per End	C	Reported	Comp	Estimate	%Surp	Guidance	%Guid Surp	%Px Chg	T12M	P/E
	Average of Absolute Values							66.33%		121.43%	9.68%		
11)	11/02/2022	Q3 22	09/22				0.308					0.74	28.95
12)	08/03/2022	Q2 22	06/22				0.205					0.73	29.35
13)	05/04/2022	Q1 22	03/22				0.162					0.75	28.57
14)	02/10/2022	Q4 21	12/21				0.062					0.77	27.82
15)	11/02/2021	Q3 21	09/21		0.298	0.310	0.150	106.67%	~0.140	121.43%	16.47%	0.81	24.91
16)	08/03/2021	Q2 21	06/21		0.229	0.240	0.061	293.44%			7.53%	0.77	27.47
17)	05/04/2021	Q1 21	03/21		0.179	0.160	0.038	321.05%			-1.20%	0.16	138.50
18)	02/10/2021	Q4 20	12/20		0.107	0.120	-0.065	N.M.			8.35%	-0.37	
19)	10/30/2020	Q3 20	09/20		0.254	0.260	0.026	900.00%			0.36%	-0.44	
20)	07/31/2020	Q2 20	06/20		-0.381	-0.310	-0.418	25.84%			-8.12%	-0.47	
21)	05/11/2020	Q1 20	03/20		-0.351	-0.340	-0.193	-76.17%			-9.72%	-0.12	
22)	02/11/2020	Q4 19	12/19		0.037	0.100	0.103	-2.91%			-18.88%	0.28	77.14
23)	11/04/2019	Q3 19	09/19		0.227	0.230	0.184	25.00%			-18.92%	0.34	58.65
24)	07/30/2019	Q2 19	06/19		-0.037	-0.040	-0.055	27.27%			-12.24%	0.32	79.22

Source: Bloomberg Finance L.P.

information, according to the EMH, it should already be reflected in stock prices. However, purchasing stocks with relatively low PE ratios appears to be a potentially profitable investment strategy.

There are many other noncalendar anomalies. For example, the market appears to do worse on cloudy days than sunny days. But rather than continuing with a laundry list of anomalies—however much fun they might provide—we will instead turn to some spectacular events in market history.

CHECK THIS

7.10a What is the day-of-the-week effect?

7.10b What is the amazing January effect?

7.10c What is the turn-of-the-year effect?

7.11 Bubbles and Crashes

As a famous philosopher once said, "Those who do not remember the past are condemned to repeat it."[1] Nowhere is this statement seemingly more appropriate in finance than in a discussion of bubbles and crashes.

A **bubble** occurs when market prices soar far in excess of what normal and rational analysis would suggest. Investment bubbles eventually pop because they are not based on fundamental values. When a bubble does pop, investors find themselves holding assets with plummeting values.

bubble
A situation where observed prices soar far higher than fundamentals and rational analysis would suggest.

---

[1] George Santayana is credited with this statement.

crash
A situation where market prices collapse significantly and suddenly.

A **crash** is a significant and sudden drop in marketwide values. Crashes are generally associated with a bubble. Typically, a bubble lasts much longer than a crash. A bubble can form over weeks, months, or even years. Crashes, on the other hand, are sudden, generally lasting less than a week. However, the disastrous financial aftermath of a crash can last for years.

THE CRASH OF 1929

During the Roaring Twenties, the stock market was supposed to be the place where everyone could get rich. The market was widely believed to be a no-risk situation. Many people invested their life savings without learning about the potential pitfalls of investing. At the time, investors could purchase stocks by putting up 10 percent of the purchase price and borrowing the remainder from a broker. This level of leverage was one factor that led to the sudden market downdraft in October 1929.

As you can see in Figure 7.11, on Friday, October 25, the Dow Jones Industrial Average closed up about one point, at 301.22. On Monday, October 28, it closed at 260.64, down 13.5 percent. On Tuesday, October 29, the Dow closed at 230.07, with an intraday low of 212.33, which is about 30 percent lower than the closing level on the previous Friday. On this day, known as "Black Tuesday," NYSE volume of 16.4 million shares was more than four times normal levels.

Although the Crash of 1929 was a large decline, it pales with respect to the ensuing bear market. As shown in Figure 7.12, the DJIA rebounded about 20 percent following the October 1929 crash. However, the DJIA then began a protracted fall, reaching the bottom at 40.56 on July 8, 1932. This level represents about a 90 percent decline from the record high level of 386.10 on September 3, 1929. By the way, the DJIA did not surpass its previous high level until November 24, 1954, more than 25 years later.

THE CRASH OF OCTOBER 1987

Once, when we spoke of *The* Crash, we meant October 29, 1929. That was until October 1987. The Crash of 1987 began on Friday, October 16. On huge volume (at the time) of about 338 million shares, the DJIA fell 108 points to close at 2,246.73. It was the first time in history that the DJIA fell by more than 100 points in one day.

October 19, 1987, now wears the mantle of "Black Monday." This day was indeed a dark and stormy one on Wall Street; the market lost about 22.6 percent of its value on a new record volume of about 600 million shares traded. The DJIA plummeted 508.32 points to close at 1,738.74.

FIGURE 7.11 Dow Jones Industrial Average, October 21, 1929, to October 31, 1929

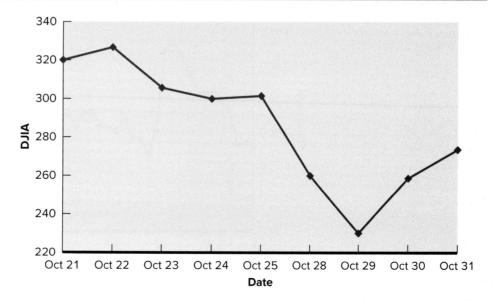

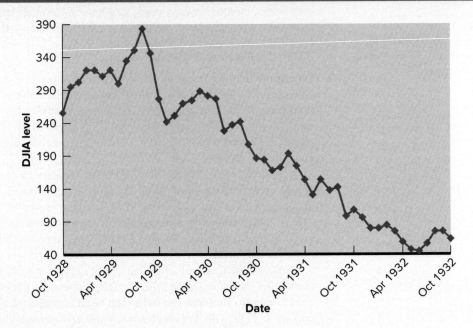

During the day on Tuesday, October 20, the DJIA continued to plunge in value, reaching an intraday low of 1,616.21. But the market rallied and closed at 1,841.01, up 102 points. From the then-market high on August 25, 1987, of 2,746.65 to the intraday low on October 20, 1987, the market had fallen over 40 percent.

After the Crash of 1987, however, there was no protracted depression. In fact, as you can see in Figure 7.13, the DJIA took only two years to surpass its previous market high made in August 1987.

What happened? It's not exactly ancient history, but, here again, debate rages. One faction says that irrational investors had bid up stock prices to ridiculous levels until Black Monday, when the bubble burst, leading to panic selling as investors dumped their stocks. The other

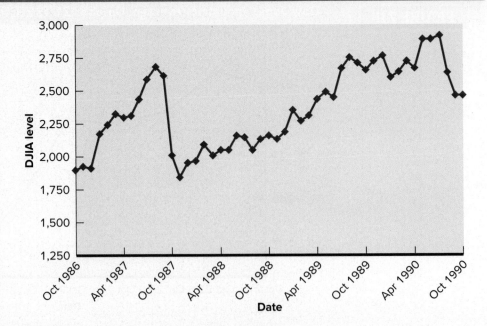

faction says that before Black Monday, markets were volatile, volume was heavy, and some ominous signs about the economy were filtering in. From the close on October 13 to the close on October 16, 1987, for example, the market fell by over 10 percent, the largest three-day drop since May 1940 (when German troops broke through French lines near the start of World War II). To top it all off, market values had risen sharply because of a dramatic increase in takeover activity, but Congress was in session and was actively considering antitakeover legislation.

Another factor is that beginning a few years before the Crash of 1987, large investors had developed techniques known as *program trading* designed for very rapid selling of enormous quantities of shares of stock following a market decline. These techniques were still largely untested because the market had been strong for years. However, following the huge sell-off on October 16, 1987, sell orders came pouring in on Monday at a pace never before seen. In fact, these program trades were (and are) blamed by some for much of what happened.

One of the few things we know for certain about the Crash of 1987 is that the stock exchanges suffered a meltdown. The NYSE could not handle the volume. Posting of prices was delayed by hours, so investors had no idea what their positions were worth. The specialists couldn't handle the flow of orders, and some specialists actually began selling. Nasdaq went offline when it became impossible to get through to market makers. It has even been alleged that many stopped answering the phone.

On the two days following the crash, prices rose by about 14 percent, one of the biggest short-term gains ever. Prices remained volatile for some time, but as antitakeover talk in Congress died down, the market recovered.

The Crash of 1987 led to some significant infrastructure changes that make it possible for the NYSE to handle much heavier trading volume. One of the most interesting changes was the introduction of **NYSE circuit breakers**. Different circuit breakers are triggered if the S&P 500 index level drops by 7, 13, or 20 percent. Specifically, the Level 1 and Level 2 circuit breakers kick in if the S&P 500 index falls 7 percent or 13 percent, respectively, before 3:25 P.M. Trading halts in all stocks for 15 minutes when the decline triggers a Level 1 or Level 2 circuit breaker. If the S&P 500 index falls 20 percent at any time during the day, this decline triggers a Level 3 circuit breaker, which means trading is halted for the remainder of the day.

Circuit breaker trigger limits were originally implemented in 1998, but they were modified to the 7, 13, and 20 percent triggers in April 2013. Point drops that trigger the circuit breakers are recalculated each day based on the daily level of the S&P 500 index. Because circuit breakers are designed to slow a market decline, they are often called "speed bumps."

Naturally, how well circuit breakers work is a matter of debate. In fact, in another chapter we discussed the "Flash Crash" that occurred on May 6, 2010. Even though many stocks and exchange-traded funds fell over 50 percent during the course of the day, the entire market never dropped far enough to trigger the circuit breakers. In response, regulators imposed individual stock circuit breakers to help control undue volatility in individual stocks. For more on individual stock circuit breakers, take a look at the nearby *Investment Updates* box.

One of the most remarkable things about the Crash of 1987 is how little impact it seems to have had. If you look back at the data in Chapter 1, you will see that the market was actually up slightly in 1987. The postcrash period was one of the better times to be in the market, and the Crash of 1987 increasingly looks like a blip in one of the most spectacular market increases that U.S. investors have ever seen. One thing is clearly true: October is the cruelest month for market investors. Indeed, two years after the Crash of 1987, a minicrash occurred on October 13, 1989, as the DJIA fell 190 points in the afternoon (following the collapse of a proposed buyout of United Airlines).

NYSE circuit breakers
Rules that kick in to slow or stop trading when the DJIA declines by more than a preset amount in a trading session.

THE ASIAN CRASH

The crash of the Nikkei index, which began in 1990, lengthened into a particularly long bear market. It is quite like the Crash of 1929 in that respect.

The Asian crash started with a booming bull market in the 1980s. Japan and emerging Asian economies seemed to be forming a powerful economic force. The "Asian economy" became an investor outlet for those wary of the U.S. market after the Crash of 1987.

INVESTMENT UPDATES

STOCK CIRCUIT BREAKERS

In 2012, the Securities and Exchange Commission updated the system-wide circuit breaker system and also added individual stock circuit breakers to better control market activity during times of stress.

How these circuit breakers work varies in accordance with the stock price and timing of the declines. They are designed so that trading on individual stocks with a price above $3 will be halted for five minutes when a price decline of more than 5 percent below the stock's average price occurs over the previous five-minute interval. The same cutoff will be in place for stocks with a jump in price

of more than 5 percent under the same circumstances. This is designed to address volatility.

Different constraints are placed around trading during the 15-minute opening and closing periods, allowing for a slightly greater price change (10 percent, versus 5) in either direction before triggering the breakers.

Source: Bob Pisani, "Here's a Brief Review of the Stock Circuit Breakers," *CNBC,* August 24, 2015.

To give you some idea of the bubble that was forming in Japan between 1955 and 1989, real estate prices in Japan increased by 70 times, and stock prices increased 100 times over. In 1989, price-earnings ratios of Japanese stocks climbed to unheard-of levels as the Nikkei index soared past 39,000. In retrospect, there were numerous warning signals about the Japanese market. At the time, however, optimism about the continued growth in the Japanese market remained high. Crashes never seem to occur when the outlook is poor, so, as with other crashes, many people did not foresee the impending Nikkei crash.

As you can see in Figure 7.14, in the three years from December 1986 to the peak in December 1989, the Nikkei 225 index rose from under 15,000 to about 39,000. Over the next three years, the index fell to about the 15,000 level. In April 2003, the Nikkei Index stood at a level that was 80 percent off its peak in December 1989. Even 25 years later, in 2009, the Nikkei was at about the same level as it stood in 1984.

THE "DOT-COM" BUBBLE AND CRASH

The growth of the World Wide Web is documented at www.zakon.org/robert/internet/timeline.

How many websites do you think existed at the end of 1994? Would you believe only about 10,000? By the end of 1999 the number of active websites stood at about 9,500,000, and at the beginning of 2019 there were almost 2 billion active websites worldwide.

FIGURE 7.14   Nikkei 225 Index, January 1984 to January 2010

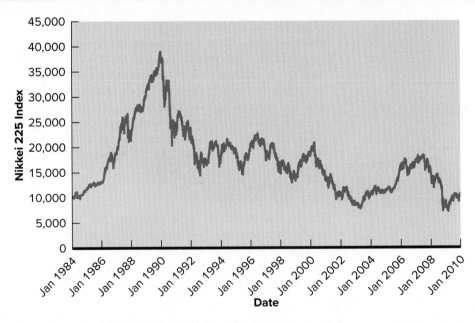

TABLE 7.6	Values of the Amex Internet Index and the S&P 500 Index					
Date	Amex Internet Index Value	Gain to Peak from Oct. 1, 1998 (%)	Loss from Peak to Trough (%)	S&P 500 Index Value	Gain to Peak from Oct. 1, 1998 (%)	Loss from Peak to Trough (%)
October 1, 1998	114.68			986.39		
Late March 2000 (peak)	688.52	500%		1,293.72	31%	
Early October 2002 (trough)	58.59		−91%	776.76		−40%

Source: Author calculations.

By the mid-1990s, the rise in internet use and its international growth potential fueled widespread excitement over the "new economy." Investors did not seem to care about solid business plans—only big ideas. Investor euphoria led to a surge in internet IPOs, which were commonly referred to as "dot-coms" because so many of their names ended in ".com." Of course, the lack of solid business models doomed many of the newly formed companies. Many of them suffered huge losses, and some folded relatively shortly after their IPOs.

The extent of the dot-com bubble and subsequent crash is presented in Table 7.6 and Figure 7.15, which compare the Amex Internet index and the S&P 500 index. As shown in Table 7.6, the Amex Internet index soared from a level of 114.68 on October 1, 1998, to its peak of 688.52 in late March 2000, an increase of 500 percent. The Amex Internet index then fell to a level of 58.59 in early October 2002, a drop of 91 percent. By contrast, the S&P 500 index rallied about 31 percent in the same 1998–2000 time period and fell 40 percent during the 2000–2002 time period.

THE CRASH OF OCTOBER 2008

Elsewhere, we detail the stock market crash of 2008, where many market indexes fell more than 40 percent. Given the recent nature of these events, debate as to the fundamental cause is ongoing. Much of the preceding bubble (and crash), however, appears to have been a function of "easy money." Unqualified borrowers frequently received large, so-called subprime home loans at low "teaser" rates, which, after a certain amount of time, were reset at more reasonable levels, meaning that required monthly payments increased. If real estate prices were still rising, owners could easily refinance. When prices began to level off and fall, however, the number of bankruptcies increased significantly. These bankruptcies set off a downward spiral effect in securities related to real estate, which we discuss in more detail in another chapter.

FIGURE 7.15	Values of the Amex Internet Index and the S&P 500 Index, October 1995 through December 2012

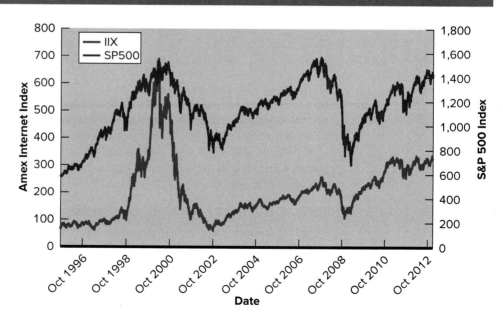

FIGURE 7.16

Dow Jones Industrial Average, January 2008 through January 2013

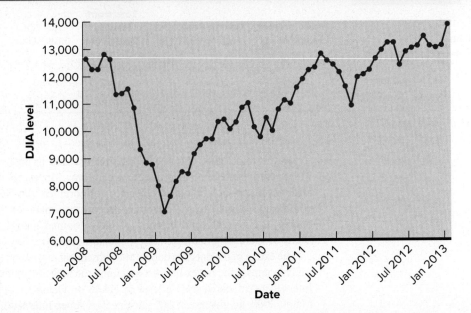

FIGURE 7.17

Dow Jones Industrial Average, October 3, 2008, to October 17, 2008

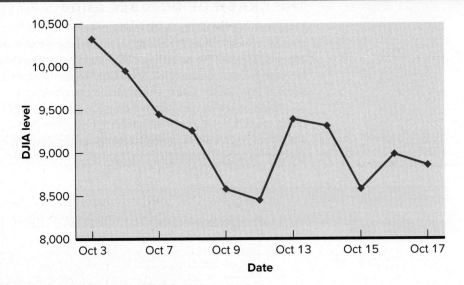

To get a clearer picture of the progression of 2008, take a close look at Figure 7.16. This figure details the monthly closing price of the Dow Jones Industrial Average (DJIA). You can see that it declined steeply over almost the entire year. The months of October and November were particularly severe. Recall that this was the time during which investment banks such as Lehman Brothers and Bear Stearns (which had taken highly leveraged positions in real estate) went under or were acquired. Figure 7.17 shows the daily values for the DJIA from October 3 through October 17, 2008.

THE "COVID-19" CRASH OF 2020

Figure 7.18 shows the dramatic effects of the onset of the lock-downs in response to the COVID-19 pandemic. The DJIA fell from about 29,000 in mid-February 2020 to about 19,000 in only five weeks. Then, in only about eight months, the DJIA level was back at its level before the dramatic sell-off in the spring of 2020.

FIGURE 7.18

Dow Jones Industrial Average, March 2019 to December 2020

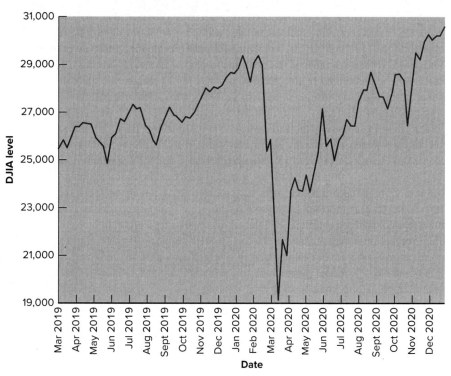

Source: Author Calculations and finance.yahoo.com.

CHECK THIS

7.11a What is a stock market bubble? A stock market crash?

7.11b What are NYSE circuit breakers? What are they intended to do?

7.11c What is a major difference between the Crash of October 1929 and the Crash of October 1987?

7.11d Do you think the Crash of October 2008 resembles the Crash of October 1929 or the Crash of October 1987? Why?

7.12 Summary and Conclusions

In this chapter, we examined market price behavior and market efficiency. Market efficiency is probably the most controversial and intriguing issue in investments. We cover many aspects of market efficiency in this chapter—which we summarize by the chapter's important concepts.

1. **The foundations of market efficiency.**

   A. The efficient markets hypothesis (EMH) asserts that, as a practical matter, organized financial markets like the New York Stock Exchange are efficient.

   B. Researchers who study efficient markets often ask whether it is possible to "beat the market." We say that you beat the market if you can consistently earn returns above those earned by other investments having the same risk. We refer to this as an abnormal return.

   C. If a market is efficient, earning these abnormal returns is not possible, except by luck. The controversy surrounding the EMH centers on this assertion.

2. **The implications of the forms of market efficiency.**

   A. The EMH states that the market is efficient with respect to some particular information if that information is not useful in earning a positive abnormal return.

   B. The forms of market efficiency and their information sets are:
   - *Weak form:* Past price and volume information.
   - *Semistrong form:* All publicly available information.
   - *Strong form:* All information of any kind, public or private.

   C. We discuss how information affects market prices by influencing traders to act on the arrival of information. We show you how to distinguish among informed trading, illegal insider trading, and legal insider trading.

3. **Market efficiency and the performance of professional money managers.**

   A. Testing market efficiency is difficult. We discussed four reasons for this: (1) the risk adjustment problem, (2) the relevant information problem, (3) the dumb luck problem, and (4) the data snooping problem.

   B. We then presented evidence concerning tests of market efficiency. One lesson we demonstrate is that professional money managers have been unable to beat the market consistently—despite their tremendous resources, experience, opportunities, and incentives. Also, this fact is true despite patterns and other oddities that have occurred historically in the stock market.

   C. The fact that professional money managers have been unable to beat the market supports the notion that markets are generally rather efficient.

4. **What stock market anomalies, bubbles, and crashes mean for market efficiency.**

   A. We discuss some aspects of stock price behavior that are both baffling and hard to reconcile with market efficiency.

   B. We discuss the day-of-the-week effect, the amazing January effect, the turn-of-the-year effect, the turn-of-the-month effect, the earnings announcement puzzle, and the price-earnings (PE) puzzle.

   C. We present some market history concerning some famous bubbles and crashes, including the Crash of October 1929, the Crash of October 1987, the Asian crisis, the dot-com bubble and crash, the Crash of 2008, and the COVID-19 Crash of 2020.

GETTING DOWN TO BUSINESS

This chapter covered market efficiency. In it, we raised a significant question: Can you, or indeed anyone, consistently beat the market? In other words, is the market efficient? This is a question that every investor needs to think about because it has direct, practical implications for investing and portfolio management.

If you think the market is relatively efficient, then your investment strategy should focus on minimizing costs and taxes. Asset allocation is your primary concern, and you will still need to establish the risk level you are comfortable with. But beyond this, you should be a buy-and-hold investor, transacting only when absolutely necessary. Investments such as low-cost, low-turnover mutual funds make a lot of sense. Tools for analyzing the market are irrelevant at best. Thus, in some ways, the appropriate investment strategy is kind of boring, but it's the one that will pay off over the long haul in an efficient market.

In contrast, if you think the market is not particularly efficient, then you've got to be a security picker. You also have to decide what market analyzing tools to use. This is also true if you are in the money management business; you have to decide which specific stocks or bonds to hold.

In the end, the only way to find out if you've got what it takes to beat the market is to try, and the best way to try is with a simulated brokerage account. Be honest with yourself: You think you can beat the market; most novice investors do. Some change their minds and some don't. As to which tools to use, you will have to find out which ones work (or don't work) for you.

For the latest information on the real world of investments, visit us at jmdinvestments.blogspot.com.

Key Terms

abnormal return 215
bubble 234
crash 235
day-of-the-week effect 229
efficient markets hypothesis (EMH) 215
event study 220

informed trader 222
January effect 230
material nonpublic information 222
NYSE circuit breakers 237
random walk 218

Related Bloomberg Functions

NH	News Headlines, 7.6
EVT	Company Events, 7.6
EE SURP	Price Reaction and Surprise, 7.6
INSD	Insider and Shareholder Activity, 7.7
FUND	Mutual Funds Home, 7.9
PORT	Portfolio and Risk Analysis, 7.9
TRA	Total Return Analysis, 7.10
EVTS	Events Calendar, 7.10
EE	Earnings and Estimates, 7.10

Chapter Review Problems and Self-Test

1. **Market Research (LO3, CFA1)** Smolira Investment Trust (SIT) runs a retirement account for college professors, with a current market value of $2 billion. Alchemy, Inc., offers to conduct market research in an attempt to sift through the market data to find a way to increase the return to SIT's portfolio by 30 basis points this year. Alchemy is offering to conduct the research for the sum of $9 million. Is this price too high or too low?

2. **Picking a Money Manager (LO3, CFA1)** You are helping your very rich aunt Molly decide where to invest her portfolio. She is planning to take a 10-year world tour after she invests the bulk of her portfolio. She thinks that picking a money manager is unimportant because she believes any professional money manager must be able to beat the market. She's just planning to pick a professional money manager at random. What do you tell her?

Answers to Self-Test Problems

1. Assuming that Alchemy, Inc., actually can conduct research that allows Smolira Investment Trust (SIT) to increase its portfolio return by 30 basis points this year, SIT would be willing to pay up to $2,000,000,000 times .0030 = $6,000,000 for this research. So the price of $9 million is too high.

2. You could show her Figure 7.8. In this figure, it is clear that picking a professional manager at random gives her about a 25 to 30 percent chance of beating a market fund like the Vanguard 500 Index Fund. If she invests her sizable portfolio in the Vanguard 500 Index Fund, she has about a 70 to 75 percent chance of beating a professional money manager picked at random.

Test Your Investment Quotient

1. **Efficient Markets Hypothesis (LO4, CFA1)** A market anomaly refers to:
   a. An exogenous shock to the market that is sharp but not persistent.
   b. A price or volume event that is inconsistent with historical price or volume trends.
   c. A trading or pricing structure that interferes with efficient buying or selling of securities.
   d. Price behavior that differs from the behavior predicted by the efficient markets hypothesis.

2. **Efficient Markets Hypothesis (LO1, CFA1)** Which of the following assumptions does not imply an informationally efficient market?

   a. Security prices adjust rapidly to reflect new information.
   b. The timing of one news announcement is independent of other news announcements.
   c. The risk-free rate exists, and investors can borrow and lend unlimited amounts at the risk-free rate.
   d. Many profit-maximizing participants, each acting independently of the others, analyze and value securities.

3. **Efficient Markets Hypothesis (LO2, CFA1)** After lengthy trial and error, you discover a trading system that would have doubled the value of your investment every six months if applied over the last three years. Which of the following problems makes it difficult to conclude that this is an example of market inefficiency?

   a. Risk adjustment problem
   b. Relevant information problem
   c. Dumb luck problem
   d. Data snooping problem

4. **Efficient Markets Hypothesis (LO2, CFA1)** In discussions of financial market efficiency, which of the following is not one of the stylized forms of market efficiency?

   a. Strong form
   b. Semistrong form
   c. Weak form
   d. Economic form

5. **Beating the Market (LO3, CFA2)** Which of the following is not considered a problem when evaluating the ability of a trading system to "beat the market"?

   a. Risk adjustment problem
   b. Relevant information problem
   c. Data measurement problem
   d. Data snooping problem

6. **Calendar Anomalies (LO4, CFA2)** Which month of the year, on average, has had the highest stock market returns as measured by a small-stock portfolio?

   a. January
   b. March
   c. June
   d. December

7. **NYSE Circuit Breakers (LO4)** Which of the following intraday changes in the Dow Jones Industrial Average (DJIA) will trigger a Level 1 circuit breaker?

   a. 7 percent drop before 3:25 P.M.
   b. 7 percent drop after 3:25 P.M.
   c. 7 percent rise before 3:25 P.M.
   d. 7 percent rise after 3:25 P.M.

8. **Efficient Markets Hypothesis (LO2, CFA1)** The SEC has regulations that prohibit trading on inside information. If the market is _____ form efficient, such regulation is not needed.

   a. Weak
   b. Semistrong
   c. Technical
   d. Strong

9. **The January Effect (LO4, CFA2)** Which of the following is a possible explanation of the January effect?

   i. Institutional window dressing
   ii. Bonus demand
   iii. Tax-loss selling
       a. I only
       b. I and II only
       c. I and III only
       d. I, II, and III

10. **NYSE Circuit Breakers (LO4)** Circuit breakers implemented by the NYSE were designed to:
    a. Reduce the January effect.
    b. Reduce the effect of technical trading.
    c. Eliminate program trading.
    d. Slow a market decline.

11. **Market Efficiency Implications (LO2, CFA2)** Assume the market is semistrong form efficient. The best investment strategy is to:
    a. Examine the past prices of a stock to determine the trend.
    b. Invest in an actively managed mutual fund whose manager searches for underpriced stocks.
    c. Invest in an index fund.
    d. Examine financial statements to find stocks that are not selling at intrinsic value.

12. **Market Efficiency Implications (LO2, CFA2)** Assume the market is weak form efficient. If this is true, technical analysts _____ earn abnormal returns and fundamental analysts _____ earn abnormal returns.
    a. Could; could
    b. Could; could not
    c. Could not; could not
    d. Could not; could

13. **Efficient Markets Hypothesis (LO1, CFA1)** Which of the following is *not* true concerning the efficient markets hypothesis?
    a. Markets that are less organized are not as likely to be efficient.
    b. Markets with wide fluctuations in prices cannot be efficient.
    c. The efficient markets hypothesis deals only with the stock market.
    d. Prices in an efficient market are fair on average.

14. **Efficient Markets Hypothesis (LO2, CFA1)** You purchase a stock that you expect to increase in value over the next year. One year later, after the discovery that the CEO embezzled funds and the company is close to bankruptcy, the stock has fallen in price. Which of the following statements is true?
    a. This is a violation of weak form efficiency.
    b. This is a violation of semistrong form efficiency.
    c. This is a violation of all forms of market efficiency.
    d. This is not a violation of market efficiency.

15. **Efficient Markets Hypothesis (LO2, CFA1)** Which of the following statements concerning market efficiency is true?
    a. If the market is weak form efficient, it is also semistrong form efficient.
    b. If the market is semistrong form efficient, it is also strong form efficient.
    c. If the market is weak form efficient, it is also strong form efficient.
    d. If the market is semistrong form efficient, it is also weak form efficient.

Concept Questions

1. **Efficient Markets (LO2, CFA1)** A stock market analyst is able to identify mispriced stocks by comparing the average price for the last 10 days to the average price for the last 60 days. If this is true, what do you know about the market?

2. **Efficient Markets (LO2, CFA1)** Critically evaluate the following statement: "Playing the stock market is like gambling. Such speculative investing has no social value, other than the pleasure people get from this form of gambling."

3. **Misconceptions about Efficient Markets (LO3, CFA2)** Several celebrated investors and stock pickers have recorded huge returns on their investments over the past two decades. Is the success of these particular investors an invalidation of an efficient stock market? Explain.

4. **Interpreting Efficient Markets (LO2, CFA2)** For each of the following scenarios, discuss whether profit opportunities exist from trading in the stock of the firm under the conditions that

(1) the market is not weak form efficient, (2) the market is weak form but not semistrong form efficient, (3) the market is semistrong form but not strong form efficient, and (4) the market is strong form efficient.

    a. The stock price has risen steadily each day for the past 30 days.

    b. The financial statements for a company were released three days ago, and you believe you've uncovered some anomalies in the company's inventory and cost control reporting techniques that are understating the firm's true liquidity strength.

    c. You observe that the senior management of a company has been buying a lot of the company's stock on the open market over the past week.

    d. Your next-door neighbor, who happens to be a computer analyst at the local steel plant, casually mentions that a German steel conglomerate hinted yesterday that it might try to acquire the local firm in a hostile takeover.

5. **Performance of the Pros (LO3, CFA3)**   In the mid- to late-1990s, the performance of the pros was unusually poor—on the order of 90 percent of all equity mutual funds underperformed a passively managed index fund. How does this bear on the issue of market efficiency?

6. **Efficient Markets (LO1, CFA1)**   A hundred years ago or so, companies did not compile annual reports. Even if you owned stock in a particular company, you were unlikely to be allowed to see the balance sheet and income statement for the company. Assuming the market is semistrong form efficient, what does this say about market efficiency then compared to now?

7. **Efficient Markets Hypothesis (LO2, CFA1)**   You invest $10,000 in the market at the beginning of the year, and by the end of the year your account is worth $15,000. During the year the market return was 10 percent. Does this mean that the market is inefficient?

8. **Efficient Markets Hypothesis (LO1, CFA1)**   Which of the following statements are true about the efficient markets hypothesis?

    a. It implies perfect forecasting ability.

    b. It implies that prices reflect all available information.

    c. It implies an irrational market.

    d. It implies that prices do not fluctuate.

    e. It results from keen competition among investors.

9. **Semistrong Efficiency (LO2, CFA2)**   If a market is semistrong form efficient, is it also weak form efficient? Explain.

10. **Efficient Markets Hypothesis (LO2, CFA1)**   What are the implications of the efficient markets hypothesis for investors who buy and sell stocks in an attempt to "beat the market"?

11. **Efficient Markets Hypothesis (LO2, CFA1)**   Aerotech, an aerospace technology research firm, announced this morning that it hired the world's most knowledgeable and prolific space researchers. Before today, Aerotech's stock had been selling for $100. Assume that no other information is received over the next week and the stock market as a whole does not move.

    a. What do you expect will happen to Aerotech's stock?

    b. Consider the following scenarios:

        i. The stock price jumps to $118 on the day of the announcement. In subsequent days it floats up to $123, and then falls back to $116.

        ii. The stock price jumps to $116 and remains at that level.

        iii. The stock price gradually climbs to $116 over the next week.

    Which scenario(s) indicate market efficiency? Which do not? Why?

12. **Efficient Markets Hypothesis (LO2, CFA1)**   When the 56-year-old founder of Gulf & Western, Inc., died of a heart attack, the stock price immediately jumped from $18.00 a share to $20.25, a 12.5 percent increase. This is evidence of market inefficiency because an efficient stock market would have anticipated his death and adjusted the price beforehand. Assume that no other information is received and the stock market as a whole does not move. Is this statement about market efficiency true or false? Explain.

13. **Efficient Markets Hypothesis (LO2, CFA1)**   Today, the following announcement was made: "Early today the Justice Department reached a decision in the Universal Product Care (UPC) case. UPC has been found guilty of discriminatory practices in hiring. For the next five years, UPC must pay $2 million each year to a fund representing victims of UPC's policies." Assuming the market is efficient, should investors not buy UPC stock after the announcement because the litigation will cause an abnormally low rate of return? Explain.

14. **Efficient Markets Hypothesis (LO2, CFA1)**   Newtech Corp. is going to adopt a new chip-testing device that can greatly improve its production efficiency. Do you think the lead engineer can profit from purchasing the firm's stock before the news release on the device? After reading the announcement in *The Wall Street Journal,* should you be able to earn an abnormal return from purchasing the stock if the market is efficient?

15. **Efficient Markets Hypothesis (LO2, CFA1)**   TransTrust Corp. has changed how it accounts for inventory. Taxes are unaffected, although the resulting earnings report released this quarter is 20 percent higher than it would have been under the old accounting system. There is no other surprise in the earnings report, and the change in the accounting treatment was publicly announced. If the market is efficient, will the stock price be higher when the market learns that the reported earnings are higher?

16. **Efficient Markets Hypothesis (LO3, CFA1)**   The Durkin Investing Agency has been the best stock picker in the country for the past two years. Before this rise to fame occurred, the Durkin newsletter had 200 subscribers. Those subscribers beat the market consistently, earning substantially higher returns after adjustment for risk and transaction costs. Subscriptions have skyrocketed to 10,000. Now, when the Durkin Investing Agency recommends a stock, the price instantly rises several points. The subscribers currently earn only a normal return when they buy recommended stock because the price rises before anybody can act on the information. Briefly explain this phenomenon. Is Durkin's ability to pick stocks consistent with market efficiency?

17. **Efficient Markets Hypothesis (LO2, CFA1)**   Your broker commented that well-managed firms are better investments than poorly managed firms. As evidence, your broker cited a recent study examining 100 small manufacturing firms that eight years earlier had been listed in an industry magazine as the best-managed small manufacturers in the country. In the ensuing eight years, the 100 firms listed have not earned more than the normal market return. Your broker continued to say that if the firms were well managed, they should have produced better-than-average returns. If the market is efficient, do you agree with your broker?

18. **Efficient Markets Hypothesis (LO2, CFA1)**   A famous economist just announced in *The Wall Street Journal* his findings that the recession is over and the economy is again entering an expansion. Assume market efficiency. Can you profit from investing in the stock market after you read this announcement?

19. **Efficient Markets Hypothesis (LO2, CFA1)**   Suppose the market is semistrong form efficient. Can you expect to earn abnormal returns if you make trades based on:
    a. Your broker's information about record earnings for a stock?
    b. Rumors about a merger of a firm?
    c. Yesterday's announcement of a successful new product test?

20. **Efficient Markets Hypothesis (LO2, CFA1)**   The efficient markets hypothesis implies that all mutual funds should obtain the same expected risk-adjusted returns. Therefore, we can pick mutual funds at random. Is this statement true or false? Explain.

21. **Efficient Markets Hypothesis (LO2, CFA1)**   Assume that markets are efficient. During a trading day, American Golf, Inc., announces that it has lost a contract for a large golfing project that, prior to the news, it was widely believed to have secured. If the market is efficient, how should the stock price react to this information if no additional information is released?

22. **Efficient Markets Hypothesis (LO2, CFA2)**   Prospectors, Inc., is a publicly traded gold prospecting company in Alaska. Although the firm's searches for gold usually fail, the prospectors occasionally find a rich vein of ore. What pattern would you expect to observe for Prospectors's cumulative abnormal returns if the market is efficient?

Questions and Problems

Core Questions

1. **Cumulative Abnormal Returns (LO2, CFA2)**   On November 14, Thorogood Enterprises announced that the public and acrimonious battle with its current CEO had been resolved. Under the terms of the deal, the CEO would step down from his position immediately. In exchange, he was given a generous severance package. Given the information below, calculate the cumulative abnormal return (CAR) around this announcement. Assume the company has an expected return equal to the market return. Graph and interpret your results. Do your results support market efficiency?

Date	Market Return (%)	Company Return (%)
Nov 7	.5	.4
Nov 8	.3	.4
Nov 9	−.2	−.3
Nov 10	−.6	−.5
Nov 11	1.3	1.1
Nov 14	−.1	1.8
Nov 15	.1	.1
Nov 16	.9	.7
Nov 17	.2	.3
Nov 18	−.2	.0
Nov 21	.3	.2

2. **Cumulative Abnormal Returns (LO2, CFA2)**   The following diagram shows the cumulative abnormal returns (CAR) for oil exploration companies announcing oil discoveries over a 30-year period. Month 0 in the diagram is the announcement month. Assume that no other information is received and the stock market as a whole does not move. Is the diagram consistent with market efficiency? Why or why not?

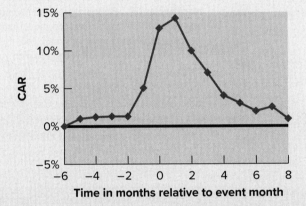

3. **Cumulative Abnormal Returns (LO2, CFA2)**   The following figures present the results of four cumulative abnormal returns (CAR) studies. Indicate whether the results of each study support, reject, or are inconclusive about the semistrong form of the efficient markets hypothesis. In each figure, Time 0 is the date of an event.

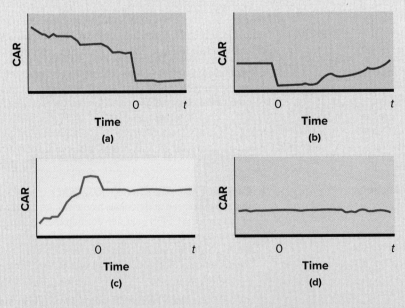

4. **Cumulative Abnormal Returns (LO2, CFA2)** A study analyzed the behavior of the stock prices of firms that had lost antitrust cases. Included in the diagram are all firms that lost the initial court decision, even if the decision was later overturned on appeal. The event at Time 0 is the initial, pre-appeal court decision. Assume no other information was released, aside from that disclosed in the initial trial. The stock prices all have a beta of 1. Is the diagram consistent with market efficiency? Why or why not?

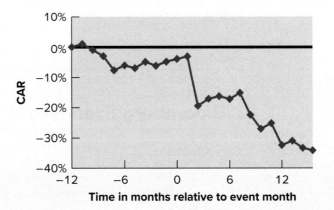

Time in months relative to event month

Intermediate Questions

5. **Cumulative Abnormal Returns (LO2, CFA2)** Ross Co.; Westerfield, Inc.; and Jordan Company announced a new agreement to market their respective products in China on July 18, February 12, and October 7, respectively. Given the information below, calculate the cumulative abnormal return (CAR) for these stocks as a group. Assume all companies have an expected return equal to the market return. Graph and interpret your results. Do your results support market efficiency?

	Ross Co.			Westerfield, Inc.			Jordan Company	
Date	Market Return	Company Return	Date	Market Return	Company Return	Date	Market Return	Company Return
July 12	−.2	−.4	Feb 8	−.7	−.9	Oct 1	.3	.5
July 13	.1	.3	Feb 9	−.8	−.9	Oct 2	.2	.8
July 16	.6	.8	Feb 10	.6	.4	Oct 3	.9	1.3
July 17	−.4	−.2	Feb 11	.8	1.0	Oct 6	−.1	−.5
July 18	1.9	1.3	Feb 12	−.1	.1	Oct 7	−2.4	−.5
July 19	−.8	−.6	Feb 15	1.3	1.4	Oct 8	.3	.3
July 20	−.9	−1.0	Feb 16	.7	.7	Oct 9	−.5	−.4
July 23	.6	.4	Feb 17	−.1	.0	Oct 10	.1	−.1
July 24	.1	.0	Feb 18	.5	.4	Oct 13	−.2	−.6

Spreadsheet Problems

6. **Event Study (LO2, CFA2)** Assume that on March 15, Trenten Medical received approval for a new drug. Using the data below from February 15 through February 28 as the measurement period, calculate the cumulative abnormal return (CAR) in the +/−3 days surrounding the announcement date.

Measurement Window			Event Window		
Date	Trenten Return	Market Return	Date	Trenten Return	Company Return
Feb 15	1.18	.19	Mar 12	−.61	−.12
Feb 18	2.03	−.03	Mar 13	2.66	.85
Feb 19	1.60	.53	Mar 14	3.98	.13
Feb 20	2.20	1.92	Mar 15	20.69	−2.48
Feb 21	−.10	−2.08	Mar 18	5.56	3.43

	Measurement Window			Event Window	
Date	Trenten Return	Market Return	Date	Trenten Return	Company Return
Feb 22	.45	.08	Mar 19	3.01	.70
Feb 25	−1.58	−1.54	Mar 20	.07	.97
Feb 26	−1.62	−1.58			
Feb 27	3.58	2.06			
Feb 28	−2.81	−2.71			

Bloomberg Exercises

Core Questions

1. Review the news headlines for today's market. **(NH)**

2. Examine Walgreens' (WBA) recent earnings and the impact of any surprises on its stock price. **(SURP)**

3. Identify any transactions recently made by insiders in **PayPal (PYPL)**. **(INSD)**

Behavioral Finance and the Psychology of Investing

"The investor's chief problem, and even his worst enemy, is likely to be himself."

–Benjamin Graham

"There are three factors that influence the market: Fear, Greed, and Greed."

–Market folklore

Learning Objectives

Psych yourself up and get a good understanding of:

1. Prospect theory.

2. The implications of investor overconfidence and misperceptions of randomness.

3. Sentiment-based risk and limits to arbitrage.

4. The wide array of technical analysis methods used by investors.

Be honest: Do you think of yourself as a better-than-average driver? If you do, you are not alone. About 80 percent of people who are asked this question will say yes. Evidently, we tend to overestimate our abilities behind the wheel. Does the same bias exist when it comes to making investment decisions?

You will probably not be surprised when we say that human beings sometimes make errors in judgment. How these errors, and other aspects of human behavior, affect investors and asset prices falls under the general heading of "behavioral finance." In the first part of this chapter, our goal is to acquaint you with some common types of mistakes investors make and their financial implications. As you will see, researchers have identified a wide variety of potentially damaging behaviors. In the second part of the chapter, we describe a trading strategy known as "technical analysis." Some investors use technical analysis as a tool to try to exploit patterns in prices. These patterns are thought to exist (by advocates of technical analysis) because of predictable behavior by investors.

CFA™ Exam Topics in This Chapter:

1. Market efficiency (L1, S11)
2. The behavioral biases of individuals (L1, S18)
3. Technical analysis (L1, S18)
4. The behavioral biases of individuals (L3, S1)
5. Behavioral finance and the investment process (L3, S1)

Go to Connect for a guide that aligns your textbook with CFA readings.

8.1 Introduction to Behavioral Finance

behavioral finance
The area of finance dealing with the implications of investor reasoning errors on investment decisions and market prices.

Sooner or later, you are going to make an investment decision that winds up costing you a lot of money. Why is this going to happen? You already know the answer. Sometimes you make sound decisions, but you get unlucky when something happens that you could not have reasonably anticipated. At other times (and painful to admit), you make a bad decision, one that could have (and should have) been avoided. The beginning of investment wisdom is to recognize the circumstances that lead to poor decisions and thereby cut down on the damage done by investment blunders.

As we previously noted, the area of research known as **behavioral finance** attempts to understand and explain how reasoning errors influence investor decisions and market prices. Much of the research done in the area of behavioral finance stems from work in the area of cognitive psychology, which is the study of how people—including investors—think, reason, and make decisions. Errors in reasoning are often called *cognitive errors* or *cognitive biases*.

Some proponents of behavioral finance believe that cognitive errors by investors will cause market inefficiencies. Recall that in a previous chapter we identified three economic conditions that lead to market efficiency: (1) investor rationality, (2) independent deviations from rationality, and (3) arbitrage. For a market to be inefficient, all three of these conditions must be absent. That is, a substantial portion of investors must make irrational investment decisions, and the collective irrationality of these investors then must lead to an overly optimistic or pessimistic market situation that cannot be corrected via arbitrage by rational, well-capitalized investors. Do irrational investor decisions or investor biases affect financial markets? This question is the subject of a raging debate, and we are not going to take sides. Instead, our goal is to introduce you to the ideas and issues.

CHECK THIS

8.1a What is behavioral finance?

8.1b What three conditions must be absent for a market to be inefficient?

8.2 Prospect Theory

prospect theory
An alternative theory to classical, rational economic decision making, which emphasizes, among other things, that investors tend to behave differently when they face prospective gains and losses.

Prospect theory, developed in the late 1970s, is a collection of ideas that provides an alternative to classical, rational economic decision making. The foundation of prospect theory rests on the idea that investors are much more distressed by prospective losses than they are happy about prospective gains. Researchers have found that a typical investor considers the pain of a $1 loss to be about twice as great as the pleasure received from a $1 gain. Also, researchers have found that investors respond in different ways to identical situations. The difference depends on whether the situation is presented in terms of losses or in terms of gains.

Investors seem to be willing to take more risk to avoid the loss of a dollar than they are to make a dollar profit. Also, if an investor has the choice between a sure gain and a gamble that could increase or decrease the sure gain, the investor is likely to choose the sure gain. Choosing a sure gain over a gamble is called *risk-averse behavior*. If the same investor is faced with a sure loss and a gamble that could increase or decrease the sure loss, the investor is likely to take the gamble. Choosing the gamble over the sure loss is called *risk-taking behavior*.

This focus on gains and losses and the tendency of investors to be risk-averse with regard to gains, but risk-taking when it comes to losses, is the essence of prospect theory. In contrast, fully rational investors (in an economic sense) are presumed to care only about their overall wealth, not the gains and losses associated with individual pieces of that wealth.

To give a simple example, suppose you own just two stocks (which is, of course, a bad idea from a diversification standpoint). On a particular day, one stock goes up sharply, but the other goes down so that your total wealth is unchanged. On another day, neither stock changes price at all. In both cases, your total wealth was unaffected, but in the first case you would probably be upset that your big gain was canceled out. If you are, you are focusing on the individual pieces, not the big picture. As we will see in the next few subsections, this kind of thinking can lead to potentially damaging errors in judgment.

A NOTE ON INVESTOR BIASES

Prospect theory has many parts, and we only present some of the main ones. The predictions of prospect theory help us think about the many psychological biases of investors. Being human, we like to group items together to help us learn more about them. The biases of human investors can be put into two main groups.

One main group of errors is called *cognitive errors*. Investors can deal with the effects of these errors by learning about how they affect investment decisions. Cognitive errors can be split into two subgroups. One subgroup deals with how stubborn people are when they get new information. The more this news clashes with current beliefs, the less likely it is to influence decisions. This subgroup of cognitive errors is called *belief perseverance biases*. The other subgroup of cognitive errors looks at whether investors deal with new information in an irrational way. This subgroup of cognitive errors is called *information processing biases*.

The other main group of errors is called *behavioral biases*. Importantly, it is much more difficult for investors to deal with the effects of behavioral biases on investment decisions. Why? Behavioral biases are deeply ingrained in the feelings and views of investors. As a result, learning about these biases will likely not reduce their effects.

What biases do you have?

FRAME DEPENDENCE

An important aspect of prospect theory is the notion that people focus on changes in wealth versus levels of wealth. **Frame dependence**, a belief perseverance cognitive bias, is a result of this phenomenon.

If an investment problem is presented in two different (but really equivalent) ways, investors often make inconsistent choices. That is, how a problem is described, or framed, seems to matter to people. Some people believe that frames are transparent; that is, investors should be able to see through the way the question is asked. Do they? Do you? Try this: Jot down your answers in the following two scenarios.

> **Scenario One.** Suppose we give you $1,000. You have the following choices:
>
> **a.** You can receive another $500 for sure.
>
> **b.** You can flip a fair coin. If the coin flip comes up heads, you get another $1,000, but if it comes up tails, you get nothing.
>
> **Scenario Two.** Suppose we give you $2,000. You have the following choices:
>
> **a.** You can lose $500 for sure.
>
> **b.** You can flip a fair coin. If the coin flip comes up heads, you lose $1,000, but if it comes up tails, you lose nothing.

What were your answers? Did you choose Option A in the first scenario and Option B in the second? If that's what you did, you are guilty of focusing on gains and losses, and not paying attention to what really matters, namely, the impact on your wealth. However, you are not alone. About 85 percent of the people who are presented with the first scenario choose Option A, and about 70 percent of the people who are presented with the second scenario choose Option B.

If you look closely at the two scenarios, you will see that they are actually identical. You end up with $1,500 for sure if you pick Option A, or else you end up with a 50-50 chance of either $1,000 or $2,000 if you pick Option B. So you should pick the same option in both scenarios. Which option you prefer is up to you, but the point is that you should never pick Option A in one scenario and Option B in the other. But people do so because the phrasing, or framing, of the question leads them to answer the questions differently. This scenario is an example of frame dependence.

frame dependence
The theory that how a problem is described—that is, framed—matters to people.

Similar behavior has been documented among participants of company-sponsored retirement plans, such as 401(k) plans. Historically, participants were required to "opt into" the plans—meaning they were required to sign up to participate. Under this approach, less than half of all eligible employees chose to enroll. More recently, however, companies have been allowed to enroll employees automatically, while offering them the choice to "opt out" of the plan. Although the choices are identical, the outcomes have been much different. After the "opt out" change, the percentage of workers who participated in the plans significantly increased. After framing the decision differently (opting out versus opting in), the behavior of participants changed.

Our frame dependence examples offer several important investment lessons. First, an investor can always frame a decision problem in broad terms (like wealth) or in narrow terms (like gains and losses). Second, broad and narrow frames often lead the investor to make different choices. Although using a narrow frame (like gains and losses) is human nature, doing so can lead to irrational decisions. Therefore, using broad frames, like overall wealth, generally results in better investment decisions.

MENTAL ACCOUNTING AND HOUSE MONEY

mental accounting
The tendency to segment money into mental "buckets."

When people engage in **mental accounting**, they tend to segment their money into mental "buckets." Mental accounting is an information processing cognitive bias. Spending regular income differently from bonuses and investing prudently in one's retirement account while taking wild risks with a separate stock account are two examples of mental accounting.

Casinos in Las Vegas (and elsewhere) know all about a concept called "playing with house money." The casinos have found that gamblers are far more likely to take big risks with money that they have won from the casino (i.e., "house money"). Also, casinos have found that gamblers are not as upset about losing house money as they are about losing the money they brought with them to gamble. As you can see, the house money effect is a result of mental accounting.

It may seem natural for you to feel that some money is precious because you earned it through hard work, sweat, and sacrifice, whereas other money is less precious because it came to you as a windfall. But these feelings are plainly irrational because any dollar you have buys the same amount of goods and services no matter how you obtained that dollar.

- **Lesson One.** There are no "paper profits." Your profits are yours.

- **Lesson Two.** All your money is your money. That is, you should not separate your money into bundles labeled "house money" and "my money."

A year ago, you bought shares in Fama Enterprises for $40 per share, and you bought shares in French Company for $5 per share. Yesterday, Fama Enterprises and French Company shares were both selling for $30 per share. Today, shares in both companies are selling for $15 per share. You might feel very differently about the decline depending on which stock you looked at. With Fama Enterprises, the decline makes a bad situation even worse. Now you are down $25 per share on your investment. On the other hand, with French Company, you only "give back" some of your "paper profit." You are still way ahead. This kind of thinking is playing with house money. Whether you lose from your original investment or from your investment gains is irrelevant.

Frame dependence, mental accounting, and the house money effect are all consistent with the predictions of prospect theory. Many other types of judgment errors have been documented. One important class of these judgment errors is known as behavioral biases.

LOSS AVERSION

loss aversion
A reluctance to sell investments after they have fallen in value. Also known as the *break-even* or *disposition effect.*

A phenomenon known as **loss aversion** is a complex behavioral bias. Loss aversion is a key element of prospect theory. We are all familiar with risk-averse behavior. People buy insurance to reduce the financial risks of a car wreck. Risk-averse investors tend to seek certainty over risk. Risk-averse investors seek to diversify portfolios, thereby reducing portfolio risk. Loss aversion goes beyond merely looking to reduce risk. Loss aversion is a sheer desire to avoid loss. Loss-averse investors shun losses. We do not know the exact cause of loss aversion, but we can describe its effects.

When you add a new stock to your portfolio, it is human nature for you to associate the stock with its purchase price. As the price of the stock changes through time, you will have unrealized gains or losses when you compare the current price to the purchase price. Through time, you will mentally account for these gains and losses, and how you feel about the investment depends on whether you are ahead or behind.

When you add stocks to your portfolio, you unknowingly create a personal relationship with each of your stocks. As a result, selling one of them becomes more difficult. It is as if you have to "break up" with this stock, or "fire" it from your portfolio. As with personal relationships, these "stock relationships" can be complicated and, believe it or not, make selling stocks difficult at times. This is often referred to as the *status quo bias,* or the *endowment effect.*

In fact, you might have particular difficulty selling a stock at a price lower than your purchase price. If you sell a stock at a loss, you may have a hard time thinking that purchasing the stock in the first place was correct. You might feel this way even if the decision to buy was actually a very good decision. A further complication is that you will also think that if you can somehow "get even," you will be able to sell the stock without any hard feelings. Loss aversion leads to the reluctance to sell investments, such as shares of stock, after they have fallen in value. This aspect of loss aversion, often a function of **anchoring**, is also called the *break-even* or *disposition effect.* Those suffering from it are sometimes said to have "get-evenitis." Legendary investor Warren Buffett offers the following advice: "The stock doesn't know you own it. You have feelings about it, but it has no feelings about you. The stock doesn't know what you paid. People shouldn't get emotionally involved with their stocks."

To see if you are likely to suffer from loss aversion, consider the following two investments:

Investment One. A year ago, you bought shares in Fama Enterprises for $40 per share. Today, these shares are worth $20 each.

Investment Two. A year ago, you bought shares in French Company for $5 per share. Today, these shares are worth $20 each.

What will you do? Will you (1) sell one of these stocks and hold the other, (2) sell both of these stocks, or (3) hold both of these stocks?

Because you are reading about loss aversion, you will undoubtedly recognize that if you choose to keep the shares in Fama Enterprises, you might be suffering from loss aversion. Why do we say might? Suppose you are considering a new investment in Fama Enterprises. Does your rational analysis say that it is reasonable to purchase shares at $20? If the rational answer is no, then you should sell. If the rational answer is yes, then you do not suffer from loss aversion. However, if you blindly argued to yourself that if shares in Fama Enterprises were a good buy at $40, then they must be a steal at $20, you might have a raging case of loss aversion. There are two important lessons from this example:

- **Lesson One.** The market says that shares in Fama Enterprises are currently worth $20. The market does not care that you paid $40 a year ago.

- **Lesson Two.** You should not care about your purchase price of Fama Enterprises either. You must evaluate your shares at their current price.

How about the shares in French Company? Do you sell them and take the profit? Once again, the lessons are the same. The market says that shares in French Company are worth $20 per share today. The fact that you paid $5 a year ago is not relevant. Note that selling either of these stocks has tax consequences. Your careful analysis should acknowledge the existence of taxes and transaction fees, as well as their impact on the net proceeds available to you after you sell a security.

How destructive is loss aversion? Perhaps the most famous case of loss aversion, or "get-evenitis," occurred in 1995, when 28-year-old Nicholas Leeson caused the collapse of his employer, the 233-year-old Barings Bank. At the end of 1992, Leeson had lost about £2 million, which he hid in a secret account. By the end of 1993, his losses were about £23 million, and they mushroomed to £208 million at the end of 1994. Instead of admitting to these losses, Leeson gambled more of the bank's money in an attempt to "double-up and catch-up." On February 23,

1995, Leeson's losses were about £827 million ($1.3 billion at the time) and his trading irregularities were uncovered. Although he attempted to flee prosecution, he was caught, arrested, tried, convicted, and imprisoned. Also, his wife divorced him.

It is unlikely that you will suffer from a case of loss aversion as severe as Nicholas Leeson's, but loss aversion does affect everyday investors. For example, we know that individual investors sell "winners" more frequently than they sell "losers." If a typical individual investor had 100 stocks with unrealized gains, the investor might sell 15 of them and keep 85. If the same investor had 100 stocks with unrealized losses, the investor would tend to sell 10 of them and keep 90. That is, individual investors are typically about 1.5 times more likely to sell a stock that has gone up in price than they are to sell a stock that has fallen in price.

This effect is worse when investors hold mutual funds. With mutual funds, when investors choose to sell, they are more than 2.5 times as likely to sell a winning fund than a losing fund. How about professional money managers who manage the mutual funds? They also suffer from loss aversion.

Recall that behavioral biases are deeply rooted in the beliefs and views of investors. As a result, behavioral biases are difficult to correct. Loss aversion is a prime example of a behavioral bias. There are many other behavioral biases. For example, here are a few:

- **Myopic loss aversion.** This behavior is the tendency to focus on avoiding short-term losses, even at the expense of long-term gains. For example, you might fail to invest "retirement" money in stocks because you have a fear of loss in the near term.

- **Regret aversion.** This aversion is the tendency to avoid making a decision because you fear that, in hindsight, the decision will have been less than optimal. Regret aversion relates to myopic loss aversion.

- **Sunk cost fallacy.** This mistake is the tendency to "throw good money after bad." An example is to keep buying a stock or mutual fund in the face of unfavorable developments.

- **Endowment effect.** This effect is the tendency to consider something that you own to be worth more than it would be if you did not own it. Because of the endowment effect, people sometimes demand more money to give up something than they would be willing to pay to acquire it.

CHECK THIS

8.2a   What is the basic prediction of prospect theory?

8.2b   What is frame dependence?

8.2c   How does loss aversion affect investment decisions?

8.3 Overconfidence

We are all overconfident about our abilities in many areas (recall our question about your driving ability at the beginning of the chapter). Here is another example. Ask yourself: What grade will I receive in this course (in spite of the arbitrary and capricious nature of the professor)? In our experience, almost everyone will either say A or, at worst, B. Sadly, when we ask our students this question, we always feel confident (but not overconfident) that at least some of our students are going to be disappointed.

Being overconfident is a serious problem for you as an investor. Overconfidence is a behavioral bias, meaning it is difficult to change. Like many behavioral biases, investors have to learn to adapt to the effects of these biases.

Concerning investment behavior, overconfidence appears in several ways. The classic example is diversification, or the lack of it. Investors tend to invest too heavily in the company for which they work. When you think about it, this loyalty can be very bad financially because both your earning power (your income) and your retirement nest egg depend on one company.

Other examples of the lack of diversification include investing too heavily in the stocks of local companies. You might do this because you read about them in the local news or you know someone who works there. That is, you might be unduly confident that you have a high degree of knowledge about local companies versus distant companies.

OVERCONFIDENCE AND TRADING FREQUENCY

If you are overconfident about your investment skill, you are likely to trade too much. You should know that researchers have found that investors who make relatively more trades have lower returns than investors who trade less frequently. Based on brokerage account activity over a particular period, researchers found that the average household earned an annual return of 16.4 percent (a very good time period). However, those households that traded the most earned an annual return of only 11.4 percent. The moral is clear: Excessive trading is hazardous to your wealth.

OVERTRADING AND GENDER: "IT'S (BASICALLY) A GUY THING"

In a study published in 2001, Professors Brad Barber and Terrance Odean examined the effects of overconfidence. As identified above, two possible effects of overconfidence are that it leads to more trading and more trading leads to lower returns. If investors could be divided into groups that differed in overconfidence, then these effects could be examined in greater detail.

Barber and Odean began with the fact that psychologists have found that men are more overconfident than women in the area of finance. So, do men trade more than women? Do portfolios of men underperform the portfolios of women? Barber and Odean show that the answer to both questions is yes.

Barber and Odean examined the trading accounts of men and women and found that men trade about 50 percent more than women. They found that both men and women reduce their portfolio returns through excessive trading. However, men did so by 94 basis points more per year than women. The difference is even bigger between single men and single women. Single men traded 67 percent more than single women, and single men reduced their return by 144 basis points compared to single women.

Using four risk measures, and accounting for the effects of marital status, age, and income, Barber and Odean also found that men invested in riskier positions than women. Young and single people held portfolios that displayed more return volatility and contained a higher percentage of stocks in small companies. Investors with higher incomes also accepted more market risk. These results are comforting because it seems to make sense that the relatively young and the relatively wealthy should be willing to take more investment risk, particularly if they do not have dependents.

WHAT IS A DIVERSIFIED PORTFOLIO TO THE EVERYDAY INVESTOR?

It is clear to researchers that most investors have a poor understanding of what constitutes a well-diversified portfolio. Researchers have discovered that the average number of stocks in a household portfolio is about four, and the median is about three.

Ask yourself: What percentage of these households beat the market? If you are like most people, your answer is too low. Researchers have found, however, that even when accounting for trading costs, about 43 percent of the households outperformed the market. Surprised? The lack of diversification is the source of your surprise.

Think about it like this. Suppose all investors held just one stock in their account. If there are many stocks, about half the individual stock returns outperform the market average. Therefore, about half the investors will beat the market. Quickly: Did you think that you would certainly be in that half that would beat the market? If you did, this should show you that you might be prone to overconfidence. To measure your level of overconfidence, see the nearby *Work the Web* box.

As we noted, overconfidence is a common behavioral bias. When we compare ourselves to others, we tend to consider ourselves better, whether it be as a driver, an investor, or a leader. While some people are more overconfident than others, it is safe to say that we have probably all exhibited overconfidence at some point.

To see how overconfident you are, take the following test from www.messymatters.com/calibration. An excerpt of the quiz is included below.

Are you overconfident? For each of the 10 questions given in the quiz, you will provide a low and high guess such that you are 90 percent sure the correct answer falls between the two. Your challenge is to be neither too narrow (i.e., overconfident) nor too wide (i.e., underconfident).

In particular, if you have "no idea," then give a very wide range; and if you happen to be quite certain, then give a narrow range. If your "overconfidence" is perfectly calibrated, then 90 percent of your intervals (no more, no less) should contain the right answers.

1. What was Martin Luther King, Jr.'s age at death?

[ ] - [ ]

2. What is the length of the Nile River, in miles?

[ ] - [ ]

3. How many countries belong to OPEC?

[ ] - [ ]

4. How many books are there in the Old Testament?

[ ] - [ ]

5. What is the diameter of the moon, in miles?

[ ] - [ ]

6. What is the weight of an empty Boeing 747, in pounds?

[ ] - [ ]

7. In what year was Mozart born?

[ ] - [ ]

[Submit]

To complete the quiz, go to www.messymatters.com/calibration and enter your answers. Are you average or above average when it comes to being overconfident?

Source: www.messymatters.com/calibration. Accessed January 13, 2022.

ILLUSION OF KNOWLEDGE

Overconfident investors tend to underestimate the risk of individual stocks and their overall portfolios. This aspect of overconfidence typically stems from a belief that information you hold is superior to information held by other investors. You believe, therefore, that you are able to make better judgments. This belief is referred to as the *illusion of knowledge.*

A possible example of this behavior was observed in 2009 following the bankruptcy of General Motors. As part of the reorganization process, GM's management announced that existing shares were worthless (i.e., had a value of $0 per share). Nonetheless, these existing shares continued to trade, albeit at low, but positive, value. If management stated the shares were worthless, why would anyone continue to buy them? No one knows for sure. A possible explanation, however, is that this "noise trading" was driven by investors with an illusion of knowledge. These investors thought that they knew more about the prospects of GM's common stock than did the managers of GM.

A recent winner of the Spanish lottery exhibited illusion of knowledge (and control). When asked why he chose the number 48, he replied, "Well, I dreamed of the number seven for seven nights in a row, and since seven times seven is 48 . . ."[1] While this gentleman probably would not do very well in an investments class, his luck saved him.

SNAKEBITE EFFECT

Are you an avid skateboarder? If not, maybe you never tried it, or maybe it has never appealed to you. Or you might have tried skateboarding but gave it up because of a bad experience (say, a broken leg, arm, both, or worse). If you fall into the latter category, you could well have experienced the snakebite effect concerning skateboarding.

As it relates to investing, the snakebite effect refers to the unwillingness of investors to take a risk following a loss. This behavioral bias is sometimes considered to have the opposite influence of overconfidence. The snakebite effect, also known as a regret-aversion bias, makes people less confident in the investment process following a loss. This particular phenomenon has been well documented in fund flows to mutual funds. More money tends to be liquidated from mutual funds following some significant market declines. In other market declines, less money than "normal" tends to flow toward mutual funds. Unfortunately, this action is the opposite of what rational investors do—that is, "buy low, sell high."

CHECK THIS

8.3a   How does overconfidence appear in investment behavior?

8.3b   What are the effects of trading frequency on portfolio performance?

8.3c   How does the snakebite effect impact investors?

 ## 8.4 Misperceiving Randomness and Overreacting to Chance Events

Cognitive psychologists have discovered that the human mind is a pattern-seeking device. As a result, we conclude that causal factors or patterns are at work behind sequences of events even when the events are truly random. In behavioral finance, this tendency, known as the **representativeness heuristic**, can lead to cognitive errors. For example, if something is random, it should look random. But what does random look like?

representativeness heuristic
Concluding that causal factors are at work behind random sequences.

Suppose we flip a coin 20 times and write down whether we get a head or a tail. Then we do it again. The results of our two sets of 20 flips are:

First 20: T T T H T T T H T T H H H T H H T H H H

Second 20: T H T H H T T H T H T H T T H T H T H H

Do these sequences of heads and tails both look random to you? Most people would say that the first 20 and the second 20 somehow look "different," even though both are random sequences and both have 10 heads and 10 tails.

[1] Penguin Random House LLC.

Let's look at this a bit differently by graphing the results. We'll start at zero. If a head occurs, we will subtract one; if a tail occurs, we will add one. Table 8.1 lists the results. Suppose we graph the two sets of 20 flips in Figure 8.1. Do the two series look different to you? Do you think the line labeled First 20 has a pattern to it, but the line labeled Second 20 appears to be random? If you do, your mind saw a pattern in a random sequence of coin flips, even though both patterns are the result of random coin flips with 10 heads and 10 tails.

The representativeness heuristic assumes that people tend to ignore base rates. In a well-known research study by Professors Daniel Kahneman and Amos Tversky, subjects were shown personality descriptions and asked to estimate the probability that the person described was a lawyer. One group was told that the description was drawn from a sample of 30 lawyers and 70 engineers. The second group was told that the description was drawn from a sample of 70 lawyers and 30 engineers. Both groups, however, produced a similar probability that the personality sketch was that of a lawyer. You might conclude that people often find what they are looking for in the data.

Although making fun of lawyers is, for some, a happy pastime, representativeness has a major impact on investors. As an example, consider what you would do if someone asked you to choose between investing in Microsoft or Cal-Maine Foods. You might attempt to do some detailed research and choose the "better" company. Most investors, however, are prone to choose Microsoft because it is well known. This example shows the common error of confusing a good company with a good investment.

TABLE 8.1 — The Results of Two Sets of 20 Coin Flips

	First 20 Flips			Second 20 Flips		
Flip Number	Result	+1/−1	Accumulated Sum	Result	+1/−1	Accumulated Sum
			0			0
1	T	1	1	T	1	1
2	T	1	2	H	−1	0
3	T	1	3	T	1	1
4	H	−1	2	H	−1	0
5	T	1	3	H	−1	−1
6	T	1	4	T	1	0
7	T	1	5	T	1	1
8	H	−1	4	H	−1	0
9	T	1	5	T	1	1
10	T	1	6	H	−1	0
11	H	−1	5	T	1	1
12	H	−1	4	H	−1	0
13	H	−1	3	T	1	1
14	T	1	4	T	1	2
15	H	−1	3	H	−1	1
16	H	−1	2	T	1	2
17	T	1	3	H	−1	1
18	H	−1	2	T	1	2
19	H	−1	1	H	−1	1
20	H	−1	0	H	−1	0
Number of heads	10			10		
Number of tails	10			10		

FIGURE 8.1

The Pattern of Two Different Sets of 20 Coin Flips

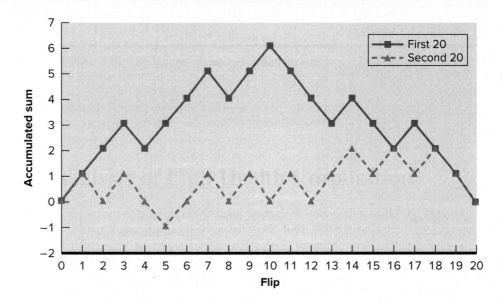

THE "HOT-HAND" FALLACY

Basketball fans generally believe that success breeds success. Suppose we look at the recent performance of two basketball players named LeBron and Nikola. Both of these players make half of their shots. But LeBron just made two shots in a row, while Nikola just missed two shots in a row. Researchers have found that if they ask 100 basketball fans which player has the better chance of making the next shot, 91 of them will say LeBron because he has a "hot hand." Further, 84 of these fans believe that it is important for teammates to pass the ball to LeBron after he has made two or three shots in a row.

But—and the sports fans among you will have a hard time with this—researchers have found that the hot hand might be an illusion. That is, players really do not deviate much from their long-run shooting averages, although fans, players, announcers, and coaches think they do. Cognitive psychologists actually studied the shooting percentage of one professional basketball team for a season. The findings are presented in Table 8.2. Detailed analysis of shooting data failed to show that players make or miss shots more or less frequently than what would be expected by chance. That is, statistically speaking, all the shooting percentages in Table 8.2 are the "same."

The shooting percentages in Table 8.2 may suggest that teams tried harder to defend a shooter who had made the last two or three shots. To take this possibility into account, researchers have also studied percentages for undefended shots—free throws. Researchers

TABLE 8.2 **Shooting Percentages and the History of Previous Attempts**

Shooting Percentage on Next Shot	History of Previous Attempts
46%	Made 3 in a row
50	Made 2 in a row
51	Made 1
52	First shot of the game
54	Missed 1
53	Missed 2 in a row
56	Missed 3 in a row

told fans that a certain player was a 70 percent free-throw shooter and was about to shoot two foul shots. They asked fans to predict what would happen on the second shot if the player:

1. Made the first free throw.

2. Missed the first free throw.

Fans thought that this 70 percent free-throw shooter would make 74 percent of the second free throws after making the first free throw but would only make 66 percent of the second free throws after missing the first free throw. Researchers studied free-throw data from a professional basketball team over two seasons. They found that the result of the first free throw does not matter when it comes to making or missing the second free throw. On average, the shooting percentage on the second free throw was 75 percent when the player made the first free throw. On average, the shooting percentage on the second free throw was also 75 percent when the player missed the first free throw.

It is true that basketball players shoot in streaks. But these streaks are within the bounds of long-run shooting percentages. So it is an illusion that players are either "hot" or "cold." If you are a believer in the "hot hand," however, you are likely to reject these facts because you "know better" from watching your favorite teams over the years. You are being fooled by randomness because randomness often appears in clusters.

The **clustering illusion** is our human belief that random events that occur in clusters are not really random. For example, it strikes most people as very unusual if heads comes up four times in a row during a series of coin flips. However, if a fair coin is flipped 20 times, there is about a 50 percent chance of getting four heads in a row. Ask yourself, if you flip four heads in a row, do you think you have a "hot hand" at coin flipping?

Mutual fund investing is one area where investors seem to fall prey to the clustering illusion. Every year, funds that have had exceptionally good performance receive large inflows of investor money. Despite the universal disclaimer that "past performance is no guarantee of future results," investors nonetheless clearly chase past returns.

THE GAMBLER'S FALLACY

People commit the gambler's fallacy when they assume that a departure from what occurs on average, or in the long run, will be corrected in the short run. Another way to think about the gambler's fallacy is that because an event has not happened recently, it has become "overdue" and is more likely to occur. People sometimes refer (wrongly) to the "law of averages" in such cases.

Roulette is a random game where gamblers can make various bets on the spin of the wheel. There are 38 numbers on an American roulette table: 2 green ones, 18 red ones, and 18 black ones. One possible bet is whether the spin will result in a red number or in a black number. Suppose a red number has appeared five times in a row. Gamblers will often become confident that the next spin will be black, when the true chance remains at about 50 percent (of course, it is exactly 18 in 38).

The misconception arises from the human intuition that the overall odds of the wheel must be reflected in a small number of spins. That is, gamblers often become convinced that the wheel is "due" to hit a black number after a series of red numbers. Gamblers do know that the odds of a black number appearing are always unchanged: 18 in 38. But gamblers cannot help but feel that after a long series of red numbers, a black one must appear to restore the "balance" between red and black numbers over time. Thousands of betting systems exist that claim to be able to generate money by betting opposite to recent outcomes. One simple example in roulette is to wait until four red numbers in a row appear—then bet on black. Internet hucksters sell "guaranteed" betting systems that are essentially based on the gambler's fallacy. None of them work. Think about it. If these betting systems actually worked, why would they be for sale?

The hot-hand fallacy and the gambler's fallacy can be thought of as forecasting errors. Professors Kahneman and Tversky discovered that people place too much weight on recent experiences. Overweighting what recently happened can help explain both of these fallacies. The difference between them lies in the belief that future events will resemble past events (hot-hand fallacy) or that a turnaround is due (gambler's fallacy).

Of course, there are many other investor errors and biases. Here is a partial list. Which ones do you think are difficult for investors to change?

- **Law of small numbers.** If you believe in the law of small numbers, you believe that a small sample of outcomes always resembles the long-run distribution of outcomes. If your investment guru has been right five out of seven times recently, you might believe that his long-run average of being correct is also five out of seven. The law of small numbers is related to recency bias and to the gambler's fallacy.

- **Recency bias.** Humans tend to give recent events more importance than less recent events. For example, during the great bull market that occurred from 1995 to 1999, many investors thought the market would continue its big gains for a long time—forgetting that bear markets also occur (which happened from 2000 to 2002 and again in 2008 to 2009). Recency bias is related to the law of small numbers.

- **Availability bias.** You suffer from availability bias when you put too much weight on information that is easily available and place too little weight on information that is hard to obtain. Your financial decisions will suffer if you consider only information that is easy to obtain.

- **Self-attribution bias.** This bias occurs when you attribute good outcomes to your own skill but blame bad outcomes on luck.

- **Wishful thinking bias.** You suffer from wishful thinking bias when you believe what you want to believe. Wishful thinking bias relates to self-attribution bias.

- **False consensus.** This is the tendency to think that other people are thinking the same thing about a stock you own (or are going to buy). False consensus relates to overconfidence.

CHECK THIS

8.4a   What is the representativeness heuristic?

8.4b   What is the hot-hand fallacy? How could it affect investor decisions?

8.4c   What is the gambler's fallacy? How could it affect investor decisions?

8.5 More on Behavioral Finance

HEURISTICS

You probably have had to evaluate some stocks, and maybe you even had to pick the ones you thought were best. In doing so, you surely found that a large amount of information is available—stock reports, analyst estimates, financial statements, and the list goes on. How can you, or any investor, possibly evaluate all this information correctly? Sadly, the truth is one cannot do so. So, how do most investors make decisions? Most likely, investment decisions are made by using rules of thumb, or heuristics (fancy name).

A heuristic simplifies the decision-making process by identifying a defined set of criteria to evaluate. Unfortunately, investors often choose inappropriate criteria. For example, investors might choose criteria that identify good companies, but not necessarily good investments.

Another example involves 401(k) plans. Researchers have found that most investors allocate among their investment choices equally. This choice presents some serious implications. For retirement plans that offer more bond funds than stock funds, participants will choose a conservative portfolio (i.e., more bonds than stocks). For retirement plans that offer more stock funds than bond funds, participants will choose a more aggressive portfolio (i.e., more stocks than bonds). This behavior is referred to as the "1/n

phenomenon," as investors allocate $1/n$ percent to each of the n funds available. This heuristic-based allocation simplifies the decision process, but it is definitely not optimal for many investors.

HERDING

Have you ever watched a nature documentary that shows schools of fish? If you have, recall how the fish move if a danger is detected. Do the fish scatter? No. They tend to move together in a quick and pronounced manner. This behavior is known as *herding.*

While we are well aware of such behavior among animals, this behavior is also common among investors. For example, many academic studies conclude that stock analysts tend to exhibit herding behavior in their earnings forecasts and stock ratings. Where one analyst goes, others follow—presumably from the fear of being left behind. This might be a preservation behavior similar to that exhibited by fish. For example, if an analyst rates a stock a strong buy, while everyone else is saying sell or hold, the lone analyst faces risk. If he is right, he will be considered a genius. If he is incorrect, however, he will probably lose his job. Does avoiding this "survival of the fittest" outcome motivate analysts to herd? Analysts would probably say no, but the evidence seems to point to herding.

This behavior is also common among individual investors. Among many factors, one prominent trigger seems to be media interaction. After a stock is highlighted in an investment periodical or on a television show, volume tends to increase, as does stock price. Many of you are probably familiar with Jim Cramer, the host of the TV show *Mad Money.* When Mr. Cramer recommends a stock, it typically experiences a significant uptick on the following day. Why is this? Maybe Mr. Cramer has added new information to the market, or maybe investors are herding by following his recommendation.

Taken together with other biases, herding behavior might represent the most significant challenge to market efficiency. If herding occurs, then we would expect trends in the market to continue and strengthen, at least for a period of time. Thus, if we could identify a trend in prices, then we should be able to earn an abnormal return by trading on this information. Price trends are the focus of our upcoming section on technical analysis. If the market is efficient, however, knowing these trends will not help investors predict future price changes.

What do we find in practice? Well, many researchers have addressed this topic, with most of the evidence pointing in favor of a so-called *momentum effect.* How would an investor take advantage of a momentum effect? The investor looks at stock returns over the last six months. Then, the investor buys a set of stocks that had the highest returns over the last six months and sells a set of stocks that had the lowest returns. If there is a momentum effect, the investor would, on average, earn a positive abnormal return by holding these positions over the next six months. If this strategy works, we might need to change the golden rule of investing from "buy low, sell high" to "buy high, sell higher."

HOW DO WE OVERCOME BIAS?

Proponents of behavioral finance generally contend that most behavioral biases are difficult, if not impossible, to change. By contrast, they argue that, in many cases, cognitive errors can be corrected through learning about them. While these distinctions are likely debatable, we can generally agree on things we can do to help overcome, or at least reduce, the negative impact of any bias on our investment decisions.

The most important thing is to know about potential biases; hence, by reading this chapter, you are better prepared than most investors. By understanding what errors you could make, you might be less likely to make them. To help you even more, take a look at the nearby *Investment Updates* box, where we provide a few lists of the most common mistakes made by investors. Notice the overlap to the topics we have covered in this chapter.

Other actions you can take to reduce bias include diversifying your portfolio, avoiding situations (or media) that you know will unduly influence you, and creating objective investment criteria. Although these actions are not guaranteed to completely eliminate biases, they should at least give you an advantage over other investors who have not taken such precautions.

MOST COMMON INVESTMENT MISTAKES ACCORDING TO VARIOUS FINANCIAL SOURCES

A. According to *Forbes* (September 27, 2021)

1. Availability bias
2. Status quo bias
3. Egocentric bias
4. Affect heuristic bias
5. Overconfidence

B. According to *Business Insider* (April 6, 2021)

1. Mental accounting
2. Loss aversion
3. Overconfidence
4. Anchoring
5. Herd behavior

C. According to *Investopedia* (July 2021)

1. Overconfidence
2. Regret
3. Limited attention span
4. Chasing trends

D. According to *CNBC* (August 2018)

1. Overconfidence
2. Anchoring to purchase price
3. Learning the wrong lessons

CHECK THIS

8.5a What is the "1/n phenomenon"?

8.5b Explain herding behavior by investors.

8.5c What potential biases might affect how you invest?

8.6 Sentiment-Based Risk and Limits to Arbitrage

It is important to realize that the efficient markets hypothesis does not require every investor to be rational. As we have noted, all that is required for a market to be efficient is that at least some investors are smart and well financed. These investors are prepared to buy and sell to take advantage of any mispricing in the marketplace. This activity is what keeps markets efficient. Sometimes, however, a problem arises in this context.

LIMITS TO ARBITRAGE

limits to arbitrage
The notion that the price of an asset may not equal its correct value because of barriers to arbitrage.

The term **limits to arbitrage** refers to the notion that under certain circumstances, rational, well-capitalized traders may be unable to correct a mispricing, at least not quickly. The reason is that strategies designed to eliminate mispricings are often risky, costly, or somehow restricted. Three important impediments are:

- *Firm-specific risk.* This is the most obvious risk facing a would-be arbitrageur. Suppose that you believe that the observed price on Ford stock is too low, so you purchase many, many shares. Then, some unanticipated negative news drives the price of Ford stock even lower. Of course, you could try to hedge some firm-specific risk by shorting shares in another stock, say, Honda. But there is no guarantee that the price of Honda will fall if some firm-specific event triggers a decline in the price of Ford. It might even rise, leaving you even worse off. Furthermore, in many, if not most, cases, there might not even be a stock that could be considered a close substitute.

noise trader
A trader whose trades are not based on information or meaningful financial analysis.

sentiment-based risk
A source of risk to investors above and beyond firm-specific risk and overall market risk.

- *Noise trader risk.* A **noise trader** is someone whose trades are not based on information or financially meaningful analysis. Noise traders could, in principle, act together to worsen a mispricing in the short run. Noise trader risk is important because the worsening of a mispricing could force the arbitrageur to liquidate early and sustain steep losses. As the economist John Maynard Keynes once famously observed, "Markets can remain irrational longer than you can remain solvent."[2]

  Noise trader risk is also called **sentiment-based risk**, meaning the risk that an asset's price is being influenced by sentiment (or irrational belief such as illusion of knowledge) rather than fact-based financial analysis. If sentiment-based risk exists, then it is another source of risk beyond the systematic and unsystematic risks we discussed in an earlier chapter.

- *Implementation costs.* These include transaction costs such as bid-ask spreads, brokerage commissions, and margin interest. In addition, there might be some short-sale constraints. One short-sale constraint arises when there are not enough shares of the security to borrow so that the arbitrageur can take a large short position. Another short-sale constraint stems from legal restrictions. Many money managers, especially pension fund and mutual fund managers, are not allowed to sell short.

When these or other risks and costs are present, a mispricing may persist because arbitrage is too risky or too costly. Collectively, these risks and costs create barriers or limits to arbitrage. How important these limits are is difficult to say, but we do know that mispricings occur, at least on occasion. To illustrate, we consider two well-known examples.

THE 3COM/PALM MISPRICING

On March 2, 2000, a profitable provider of computer networking products and services, 3Com, sold 5 percent of one of its subsidiaries to the public via an initial public offering (IPO). At the time, the subsidiary was known as Palm (the Palm trademark is now owned by TCL).

3Com planned to distribute the remaining Palm shares to 3Com shareholders at a later date. Under the plan, if you owned 1 share of 3Com, you would receive 1.5 shares of Palm. So, after 3Com sold part of Palm via the IPO, investors could buy Palm shares directly, or they could buy them indirectly by purchasing shares of 3Com.

What makes this case interesting is what happened in the days that followed the Palm IPO. If you owned 1 share of 3Com, you would be entitled, eventually, to 1.5 shares of Palm. Therefore, each 3Com share should be worth at least 1.5 times the value of each Palm share. We say "at least" because the other parts of 3Com were profitable. As a result, each 3Com share should have been worth much more than 1.5 times the value of one Palm share. But, as you might guess, things did not work out this way.

The day before the Palm IPO, shares in 3Com sold for $104.13. After the first day of trading, Palm closed at $95.06 per share. Multiplying $95.06 by 1.5 results in $142.59, which is the minimum value one would expect to pay for 3Com. But the day Palm closed at $95.06, 3Com shares closed at $81.81, more than $60 lower than the price implied by Palm. It gets stranger.

A 3Com price of $81.81 when Palm is selling for $95.06 implies that the market values the rest of 3Com's businesses (per share) at $81.81 − $142.59 = −$60.78. Given the number of 3Com shares outstanding at the time, this means the market placed a negative value of about −$22 billion for the rest of 3Com's businesses. Of course, a stock price cannot be negative. This means, then, that the price of Palm relative to 3Com was much too high.

To profit from this mispricing, investors would purchase shares of 3Com and short shares of Palm. In a well-functioning market, this action would quickly force the prices into alignment. What happened?

As you can see in Figure 8.2, the market valued 3Com and Palm shares in such a way that the non-Palm part of 3Com had a negative value for about two months, from March 2, 2000, until May 8, 2000. Even then, it took approval by the IRS for 3Com to proceed with the planned distribution of Palm shares before the non-Palm part of 3Com once again had a positive value.

---

[2] This remark is generally attributed to Keynes, but whether he actually said it is unknown.

FIGURE 8.2

The Percentage Difference between 1 Share of 3Com and 1.5 Shares of Palm, March 2, 2000, to July 27, 2000

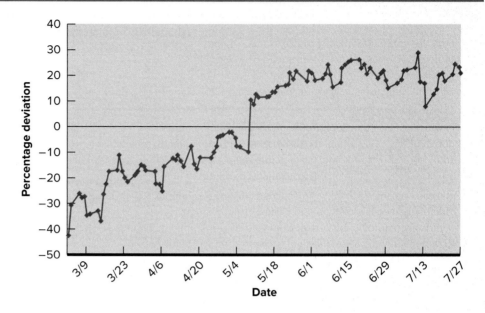

THE ROYAL DUTCH/SHELL PRICE RATIO

Another fairly well-known example of a mispricing involves two large oil companies. In 1907, Royal Dutch of the Netherlands and Shell of the United Kingdom agreed to merge their business enterprises and split profits on a 60–40 basis. So, whenever the stock prices of Royal Dutch and Shell were not in a 60–40 ratio, there was a potential opportunity to make an arbitrage profit. If, for example, the ratio were 50-50, you would buy Royal Dutch and short sell Shell.

Figure 8.3 plots the daily deviations from the 60–40 ratio of the Royal Dutch price to the Shell price. If the prices of Royal Dutch and Shell are in a 60–40 ratio, there is a zero

FIGURE 8.3   Royal Dutch and Shell 60–40 Price Ratio Deviations, 1962 to 2005

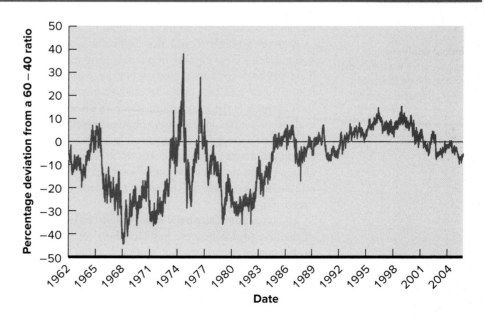

percentage deviation. If the price of Royal Dutch is too high compared to the Shell price, there is a positive deviation. If the price of Royal Dutch is too low compared to the price of Shell, there is a negative deviation. As you can see in Figure 8.3, there have been large and persistent deviations from the 60–40 ratio. In fact, the ratio was seldom at 60–40 for most of the time from 1962 through mid-2005 (when the companies merged).

CHECK THIS

8.6a What does the term "limits to arbitrage" mean?

8.6b If there were no limits to arbitrage, what would have been the relationship between 1 share of 3Com and 1.5 shares of Palm?

8.6c If there were no limits to arbitrage, what would have been the relationship between the prices of Royal Dutch and Shell?

8.7 Technical Analysis

Many investors try to predict future stock price movements based on investor sentiment, errors in judgment, and/or historical price movements. These investors are using **technical analysis**. Unlike fundamental analysis, technical analysis does not rely on traditional valuation techniques like those presented in our earlier chapters.

Related Bloomberg Functions

GP	Graph Price
TECH	Technical Analysis
GF	Graph Fundamentals
BTST	Basic Backtesting
RSI	Relative Strength Index
GPMA	Multi Moving Average Chart
BOLL	Bollinger Bands
MACD	Moving Avg Convergence/ Divergence
GPF	Fibonacci Retracements

technical analysis
Using past price data and other nonfinancial data to identify future trading opportunities.

WHY DOES TECHNICAL ANALYSIS CONTINUE TO THRIVE?

Proponents of the efficient markets hypothesis do not believe that technical analysis can assist investors in predicting future stock price movements. If that is the case, why is technical analysis still used? In fact, in this internet and computer age, technical analysis is actually thriving. Why?

One possible reason that technical analysis still exists is that an investor can derive thousands of potentially successful technical analysis systems by using historical security prices. Past movements of security prices are easy to fit into a wide variety of technical analysis systems. As a result, proponents of technical analysis can continuously tinker with their systems and find methods that fit historical prices. This process is known as "backtesting." Alas, though, successful investment is all about future prices.

Another possible reason that technical analysis still exists is that it sometimes works. Again, given a large number of possible technical analysis systems, it is possible that many of them will work (or appear to work) in the short run. It is also possible that the market is not fully efficient and that technical analysis actually helps to identify these inefficiencies. One such example is the momentum effect we discussed earlier. You should know, however, that evidence of market inefficiency is hotly contested.

To give an example of a technical analysis tool, or a technical "indicator," consider trying to analyze market sentiment. The term "market sentiment" refers to the prevailing mood among investors about the future outlook of an individual security or the market. Market sentiment is generally classified as optimistic (bullish), neutral (undecided), or pessimistic (bearish).

Market sentiment usually takes time to change. That is, it takes time for, say, 80 percent of the investors to become bullish if only 50 percent of the investors are currently bullish. Investors who rely on market sentiment often believe that once 80 percent of the investors are bullish or bearish, a consensus has been reached. Further, once a consensus is reached, investors take this as a sign of an impending turn in the direction of the market. One way to measure market sentiment is to ask investors whether they think the market is going up or down. Suppose you ask 50 investors whether they are "bullish" or "bearish" on the market over the next month. Twenty say that they are bearish. The market sentiment index (MSI) can then be calculated as:

$$MSI = \frac{\text{Number of bearish investors}}{\text{Number of bullish investors} + \text{Number of bearish investors}}$$

$$MSI = \frac{20}{30 + 20} = .40$$

The MSI has a maximum value of 1.00, which occurs when every investor you ask is bearish on the market. The MSI has a minimum value of 0, which occurs when every investor you ask is bullish on the market. Note that if you are constructing a sentiment index, you will have to decide how many investors to ask, the identity of these investors, and their investment time frame, that is, daily, weekly, monthly, quarterly, or longer. You can construct a sentiment index for any financial asset for any investment time interval you choose.

People who calculate and use sentiment indexes often view them as "contrarian indicators." This means that if most other investors are bearish, perhaps the market is "oversold" and prices are due to rebound. Or if most other investors are bullish, perhaps the market is "overbought" and prices will be heading down.

The following saying is useful when you are trying to remember how to interpret the MSI: "When the MSI is high, it is time to buy; when the MSI is low, it is time to go." Note that there is no theory to guide investors as to what level of the MSI is "high" and what level is "low." This lack of precise guidance is a common problem with a technical indicator like the MSI.

Technical analysis techniques are centuries old, and their number is enormous. Many, many books on the subject have been written. For this reason, we only touch on the subject and introduce some of its key ideas in the next few sections. Although we focus on the use of technical analysis in the stock market, you should be aware that it is very widely used in commodity markets, and most comments herein apply to those markets as well.

Recall that investors with a positive outlook on the market are often called "bulls," and their outlook is characterized as "bullish." A rising market is called a "bull market." In contrast, pessimistic investors are called "bears," and their dismal outlook is characterized as "bearish." A falling market is called a "bear market." Technical analysts essentially search for bullish or bearish signals, meaning positive or negative indicators about stock prices or market direction.

DOW THEORY

Learn more about Dow theory at thedowtheory.com.

Dow theory
A method for predicting market direction that relies on the Dow Industrial and the Dow Transportation averages.

Dow theory is a method of analyzing and interpreting stock market movements that dates back to the turn of the twentieth century. The theory is named after Charles Dow, a cofounder of the Dow Jones Company and an editor of the Dow Jones–owned newspaper, *The Wall Street Journal.*

The essence of Dow theory is that there are, at all times, three forces at work in the stock market: (1) a primary direction or trend, (2) a secondary reaction or trend, and (3) daily fluctuations. According to the theory, the primary direction is either bullish (up) or bearish (down), and it reflects the long-run direction of the market.

However, the market can, for limited periods of time, depart from its primary direction. These departures are called *secondary reactions* or *trends* and may last for several weeks or months. These are eliminated by *corrections*, which are reversions to the primary direction. Daily fluctuations are essentially noise and are of no real importance.

The basic purpose of the Dow theory is to signal changes in the primary direction. To do this, two stock market averages, the Dow Jones Industrial Average (DJIA) and the Dow Jones Transportation Average (DJTA), are monitored. If one of these departs from the primary trend, the movement is viewed as secondary. However, if a departure in one is followed by a departure in the other, then this is viewed as a *confirmation* that the primary trend has changed. The Dow theory was, at one time, very well known and widely followed. It is less popular today, but its basic principles underlie more contemporary approaches to technical analysis.

ELLIOTT WAVES

Elliott wave theory
A method for predicting market direction that relies on a series of past market price swings (i.e., waves).

Learn more about the Elliott wave at www.elliottwave.com.

In the early 1930s, an accountant named Ralph Nelson Elliott developed the **Elliott wave theory**. While recuperating from life-threatening anemia (as well as his disastrous losses in the Crash of October 1929), Elliott read a book on Dow theory and began to study patterns of market price movements. Elliott discovered what he believed to be a persistent and recurring pattern that operated between market tops and bottoms. His theory was that these patterns, which he called "waves," collectively expressed investor sentiment. Through use of sophisticated measurements that he called "wave counting," a wave theorist could forecast market turns with a high degree of accuracy.

In 1935, Elliott published his theory in his book *The Wave Principle*. His main theory was that there was a repeating eight-wave sequence. The first five waves, which he called "impulsive," were followed by a three-wave "corrective" sequence. Figure 8.4 shows the basic Elliott wave pattern. The impulse waves are labeled numerically, 1 through 5, while the corrective waves are labeled A, B, and C.

The basic Elliott wave theory gets very complicated because, under the theory, each wave can subdivide into finer wave patterns that are classified into a multitude of structures. Notwithstanding the complex nature of the Elliott wave theory, it is still a widely followed indicator.

SUPPORT AND RESISTANCE LEVELS

support level
Price or level below which a stock or the market as a whole is unlikely to fall.

resistance level
Price or level above which a stock or the market as a whole is unlikely to rise.

A key concept in technical analysis is the identification of support and resistance levels. A **support level** is a price or level below which a stock or the market as a whole is unlikely to fall. A **resistance level** is a price or level above which a stock or the market as a whole is unlikely to rise.

The idea behind these levels is straightforward. As a stock's price (or the market as a whole) falls, it reaches a point where investors increasingly believe that it can fall no further—the point at which it "bottoms out." Essentially, purchases by bargain-hungry investors ("bottom-feeders") pick up at that point, thereby "supporting" the price. A resistance level is formed by reverse logic. As a stock's price (or the market as a whole) rises, it reaches a point where investors increasingly believe that it can go no higher—the point at which it "tops out." Once it does, sales by profit-hungry investors ("profit takers") pick up, thereby "resisting" further advances.

Resistance and support areas are usually viewed as psychological barriers. As the DJIA approaches levels with three zeros, such as 35,000, increased talk of "psychologically important" prices appears in the financial press. A "breakout" occurs when a stock (or the market

| **FIGURE 8.4** | Basic Elliott Wave Pattern |

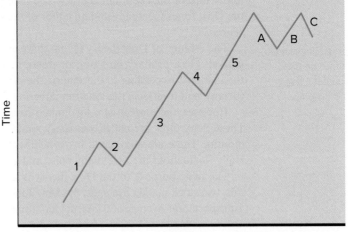

as a whole) closes below a support level or above a resistance level. A breakout is usually interpreted to mean that the price move will continue in that direction.

As this discussion illustrates, much colorful language is used under the heading of technical analysis. We will see many more examples just ahead.

TECHNICAL INDICATORS

Technical analysts rely on a variety of technical indicators to forecast the direction of the market. Every day, *The Wall Street Journal* publishes a variety of such indicators. An excerpt of the "Diaries" section (from www.wsj.com) appears in Figure 8.5.

Much, but not all, of the information presented is self-explanatory. The first item listed in Figure 8.5 is the number of issues, i.e., stocks, traded. This number fluctuates because, on any given day, there may be zero trading volume in some stocks listed on the NYSE. In the rows that follow, we see the number of price advances, the number of price declines, and the number of unchanged prices. The number of stock prices reaching new highs and new lows as of that day is also listed.

FIGURE 8.5 **Market Diaries**

Markets Diary: Closing Snapshot

DIARIES

GO TO: Volume by Market | Breakdown of Volume | Crossing Session | Weekly Totals

Tuesday, January 11, 2022   Find Historical Data 🖼 | WHAT'S THIS?

Notice to readers: As of 3/3/11, Closing Arms Index (TRIN) calculation is based on composite data. Click here for historical data prior to 3/3/11.

NYSE	Latest close	Previous close	Week ago
Issues traded	3,494	3,529	3,479
Advances	2,461	1,218	1,739
Declines	892	2,133	1,639
Unchanged	141	178	101
New highs	96	95	132
New lows	57	205	49
Adv. volume*	688,827,985	387,371,991	619,437,859
Decl. volume*	156,703,958	607,953,004	323,273,950
Total volume*	825,624,837	1,006,704,339	948,953,023
Closing Arms (TRIN)†	0.53	0.89	0.60
Block trades*	3,761	4,142	4,317
Adv. volume	3,417,259,349	1,742,691,675	2,985,020,118
Decl. volume	659,202,809	2,715,390,686	1,690,865,342
Total volume	4,112,072,779	4,518,123,909	4,705,184,417

Nasdaq	Latest close	Previous close	Week ago
Issues traded	4,911	4,990	4,825
Advances	3,204	1,597	1,902
Declines	1,444	3,126	2,730
Unchanged	263	267	193
New highs	45	87	148
New lows	172	740	146
Closing Arms (TRIN)†	0.66	0.58	0.88
Block trades*	24,657	29,179	29,912
Adv. volume	3,354,742,056	2,403,015,985	2,248,198,332
Decl. volume	992,125,147	2,708,861,648	2,836,115,674
Total volume	4,389,184,900	5,284,763,916	5,284,763,916

*Primary market NYSE, NYSE American or NYSE Arca only.
†Compares the ratio of advancing to declining issues with the ratio of volume of shares rising and falling. Arms Index or
TRIN = (advancing issues/declining issues)/(composite volume of advancing issues/composite volume of declining issues).
Generally, an Arms of less than 1.00 indicates buying demand; above 1.00 indicates selling pressure.

Source: *The Wall Street Journal*, 2022. Dow Jones & Company, Inc.

TABLE 8.3

Advance/Decline Line Calculation

Weekday	Stocks Advancing	Stocks Declining	Difference	Cumulative Difference
Monday	2,593	882	1,711	1,711
Tuesday	1,331	2,095	−764	947
Wednesday	660	2,779	−2,119	−1,172
Thursday	1,681	1,748	−67	−1,239
Friday	1,394	1,996	−602	−1,841

One popular technical indicator is called the *advance/decline line*. This indicator shows, for some given period, the cumulative difference between advancing stocks and declining stocks. For example, Table 8.3 contains advance and decline information for the Nasdaq Composite for the January 3, 2022, to January 7, 2022, trading week.

In Table 8.3, notice how we take the difference between the number of stocks advancing and declining on each day and then accumulate the difference through time. For example, on Monday, 1,711 more stocks advanced than declined. On Tuesday, 764 fewer stocks advanced than declined. Over the two days, the cumulative advance/decline is thus $1,711 − 764 = 947$.

This cumulative advance/decline number, once plotted, is the advance/decline line. A downward-sloping advance/decline line would be considered a bearish signal, whereas an upward-sloping advance/decline line is a bullish signal. The advance/decline line is often used to measure market "breadth." If the market is going up, for example, then technical analysts view it as a good sign if there is market breadth. That is, the signal is more bullish if the advance is accompanied by a steeply upward-sloping advance/decline line.

The next few rows in Figure 8.5 deal with trading volume. These rows represent trading volume for advancing stocks, declining stocks, and unchanged stocks (which is calculated by subtracting advancing volume and declining volume from volume traded). For a technical analyst, heavy advancing volume is generally viewed as a bullish signal of buyer interest. This is particularly true if more stocks are up than down and if a lot of new highs appear as well.

The entry labeled "Closing Arms (TRIN)" is the ratio of average trading volume in declining stocks to average trading volume in advancing stocks. It is calculated as follows:

$$\text{Arms} = \frac{\text{Declining volume/Declining stocks}}{\text{Advancing volume/Advancing stocks}} \tag{8.1}$$

The ratio is named after its inventor, Richard Arms; it is often called the "TRIN," which is an acronym for "TR(ading) IN(dex)." Notice that the numerator in this ratio is the average volume for stocks that declined on that day. The denominator is the average volume for advancing stocks. Values greater than 1.00 are considered bearish because the indication is that declining shares had heavier volume. Using the numbers from Figure 8.5 for the Nasdaq, we can calculate the Arms value as follows:

$$\text{Arms} = \frac{992,125,147/1,444}{3,354,742,056/3,204} = \frac{687,067}{1,047,048} = .6562$$

which rounds to the value shown in Figure 8.5. A caveat: Some sources reverse the numerator and the denominator when they calculate this ratio.

The final piece of information in Figure 8.5, "Block trades," refers to trades in excess of 10,000 shares. At one time, these trades were taken to be indicators of buying or selling by large institutional investors. Today these trades are routine, and it is difficult to see how this information is particularly useful.

RELATIVE STRENGTH CHARTS

relative strength
A measure of the performance of one investment relative to another.

Relative strength charts illustrate the performance of one company, industry, or market relative to another. Very commonly, such plots are created to analyze how a stock has done relative to its industry or the market as a whole.

To illustrate how such plots are constructed, suppose that on some particular day, we invest equal amounts, say $100, in both Coke and Pepsi (the amount does not matter; what matters is that the original investment is the same for both). On every subsequent day, we take the ratio of the value of our Coke investment to the value of our Pepsi investment, and we plot it. A ratio bigger than 1.0 indicates that, on a relative basis, Coke has outperformed Pepsi, and vice versa. Thus, a value of 1.20 indicates that Coke has done 20 percent better than Pepsi over the period studied. Notice that if both stocks are down, a ratio bigger than 1.0 indicates that Coke is down by less than Pepsi.

EXAMPLE 8.1   **Relative Strength**

Consider the following series of monthly stock prices for two hypothetical companies:

Month	Susan, Inc.	Carolyn Co.
1	$25	$50
2	24	48
3	22	45
4	22	40
5	20	39
6	19	38

On a relative basis, how has Susan, Inc., done compared to Carolyn Co.?

To answer, suppose we had purchased four shares of Susan, Inc., and two shares of Carolyn Co. for an investment of $100 in each. We can calculate the value of our investment in each month and then take the ratio of Susan, Inc., to Carolyn Co. as follows:

	Investment Value		
Month	Susan, Inc. (4 shares)	Carolyn Co. (2 shares)	Relative Strength
1	$100	$100	1.00
2	96	96	1.00
3	88	90	.98
4	88	80	1.10
5	80	78	1.03
6	76	76	1.00

What we see is that over the first four months, both stocks were down, but Susan, Inc., outperformed Carolyn Co. by 10 percent. However, after six months the two had done equally well (or equally poorly).

CHARTING

Learn more about charting at www.stockcharts.com. Select "ChartSchool."

Technical analysts rely heavily on charts showing recent market activity in terms of either prices or, less frequently, volume. In fact, technical analysis is sometimes called "charting," and technical analysts are often called "chartists." There are many types of charts, but the basic idea is that by studying charts of past market prices (or other information), the chartist identifies particular patterns that signal the direction of a stock or the market as a whole. We briefly describe some charting techniques next.

OPEN-HIGH-LOW-CLOSE CHARTS (OHLC) Perhaps the most popular charting method is the bar chart. The most basic bar chart uses the stock's opening, high, low, and closing prices for the period covered by each bar. If the technician is constructing a daily bar chart, the technician will use the daily opening, high, low, and closing prices of the stock. The high and low prices are represented by the top and bottom of the vertical bar, and the opening and closing prices are shown by short horizontal lines crossing the vertical bar. The example of a bar chart for Amazon in Figure 8.6 is from stockcharts.com.

FIGURE 8.6 Bar Chart for Amazon

Source: StockCharts.com.

An extension of the open-high-low-close chart is the candlestick chart. This chart identifies, by color, whether the daily stock price closed up or down. To capture this movement, the chartist draws a box connecting the opening and closing prices. If the stock trades up on the day, the body of the candlestick is clear. If the price trades down on the day, the candlestick is darkened.

PRICE CHANNEL A price channel is a chart pattern using OHLC data that can slope upward, downward, or sideways. Price channels belong to the group of price patterns known as *continuation patterns*. In a continuation pattern, the price of the stock is expected to continue along its main direction. A price channel has two boundaries, an upper trendline and a lower trendline. The upper trendline marks resistance and the lower trendline marks support. If the overall price movement of the stock is downward, the upper trendline is called the main trendline, and the lower trendline is called the channel line. The example of a price channel for Apple in Figure 8.7 is from Bloomberg.

HEAD AND SHOULDERS A head and shoulders chart pattern belongs to a group of price charts known as *reversal patterns*. Reversal pattern charts also use OHLC data. These chart patterns signal that a reversal from the main trendline is possibly going to occur. Because it belongs to the reversal pattern group, a head and shoulders pattern is identified as either a *head and shoulders top* or a *head and shoulders bottom*. The example of a head and shoulders top for CNET Networks in Figure 8.8 is also from the website stockcharts.com.

FIGURE 8.7 Price Channel Chart for Apple

Source: Bloomberg Finance L.P.

FIGURE 8.8   Head and Shoulders Chart for CNET Networks, Inc.

CNET Networks, Inc. (CNET) Nasdaq Nat. Mkt.   © StockCharts.com
9-Jun-2000   Open 34.62 High 35.00 Low 33.75 Close 34.50 Volume 610.5K Chg +0.75 (+2.22%) ▲

Source: StockCharts.com.

For more technical analysis charts
and explanations, visit
bigcharts.marketwatch.com.

As you can see, the head and shoulders top formation has three components: the *left shoulder,* the *head,* and the *right shoulder.* To qualify as a head and shoulders top pattern, the shoulders must be lower than the head. Then, a *neckline support* is drawn between the valleys formed by the left and right shoulders. The reversal signal is generated when the neckline is *pierced.* In the case of CNET, once the stock price fell below $45, the stock plunged to $25. Of course, there are *false piercings,* which do not result in a sudden downdraft of the stock.

MOVING AVERAGES Moving averages are used to generate price reversal signals. As the name implies, a moving average is the average closing price of a stock over a fixed length of time, say 20 days. Each day, the new closing price is added to the calculation, and the oldest closing price is dropped from the calculation.

Moving averages are either simple or exponential. In a *simple moving average,* all days are given equal weighting. In an *exponential moving average,* more weight is given to the most recently observed price. Market technicians, like many investors, often believe that the latest price observed for a stock is the most important piece of information about the stock. In Example 8.2, we present data for a three-day simple moving average and data for a three-day exponential moving average, where two-thirds of the average weight is placed on the most recent price.

EXAMPLE 8.2   **Three-Day Simple Moving Average and Three-Day Exponential Moving Average**

Day	Closing Price	Three-Day Simple Moving Average	Three-Day Exponential Moving Average
1	$89.00	—	—
2	88.44	—	$88.72
3	87.60	$88.35	87.97
4	86.20	87.41	86.79
5	85.75	86.52	86.10

(Continued)

Day	Closing Price	Three-Day Simple Moving Average	Three-Day Exponential Moving Average
6	84.57	85.51	85.08
7	83.64	84.65	84.12
8	76.70	81.64	79.17
9	76.65	79.00	77.49
10	75.48	76.28	76.15

To calculate the first three-day simple moving average, we need three closing prices. The first simple moving average entry is:

$$(\$89.00 + \$88.44 + \$87.60)/3 = \$88.35$$

The second simple moving average entry is:

$$(\$88.44 + \$87.60 + \$86.20)/3 = \$87.41$$

To calculate a three-day exponential moving average, we begin by averaging the first two days:

$$(\$89.00 + \$88.44)/2 = \$88.72$$

This number appears first in the exponential moving average column. To obtain the next one, you must decide how much weight is placed on the latest price. As noted above, we selected a 2/3, or .667, weight. To calculate the next exponential moving average entry, we multiply the latest closing price by .667 and the average of the first two days by .333:

$$(.667)(\$87.60) + (.333)(\$88.72) = \$87.97$$

The next exponential moving average entry is:

$$(.667)(\$86.20) + (.333)(\$87.97) = \$86.79$$

You can see that the simple moving average and the exponential moving average generate different numbers. The exponential moving average responds more quickly to the latest price information than does the simple moving average.

In practice, 50-day moving averages are frequently compared to 200-day moving averages. The 200-day moving average might be thought of as an indicator of the long-run trend, while the 50-day average might be thought of as a short-run trend. If the 200-day average was rising while the 50-day average was falling, the indication might be that price declines are expected in the short term, but the long-term outlook is favorable. Alternatively, the indication might be that there is a danger of a change in the long-term trend.

Most technical analysts focus on points where the moving averages cross. If the shorter-term moving average crosses the longer-term moving average from below, this movement is referred to as a *golden cross*. Technicians regard the golden cross to be a strong bullish indicator. A *death cross* occurs when the shorter-term moving average crosses the longer-term average from above. Given its name, you can probably guess that this occurrence is a bearish indicator. Our nearby *Work the Web* box gives an additional example.

PUTTING IT ALL TOGETHER Quite often, a market technician will use multiple chart indicators to help in making trading decisions. Let's examine the collection of technical information available from the website bigcharts.marketwatch.com. We set the website controls starting with "Advanced Chart" to give us one year of daily data for Microsoft (MSFT). In addition, we asked the website to provide us with 9-day and 18-day exponential moving averages (EMAs), Bollinger bands, volume, MACD, and money flow. The results appear in Figure 8.9.

WORK THE WEB

Charts are easy to draw online. Two of the best sites are stockcharts.com and bigcharts.marketwatch.com. Another really good site is finance.yahoo.com. We provide an example using Yahoo!'s basic technical analysis, but the menu presents many technical analysis options.

As illustrated, we have drawn a moving average chart for Procter & Gamble (PG). The jagged line tracks PG's daily stock price over the past year. The two smoother lines are the 50-day and 200-day moving averages. Notice the 50-day average crosses the 200-day average in mid-July 2021 from below. Such a crossing, known as a golden cross, is sometimes interpreted as a signal to buy. In this case, the signal has been true so far. Notice that the stock price rose from about $135 to about $160 in about six months.

Source: Yahoo! Finance.

BOLLINGER BANDS John Bollinger created Bollinger bands in the early 1980s. The purpose of Bollinger bands is to provide relative levels of high and low prices. Bollinger bands represent a 2-standard-deviation bound calculated from the moving average (this is why Bollinger bands do not remain constant). In Figure 8.9, the Bollinger bands surround a 20-day moving average. The Bollinger bands are the maroon bands that appear in the top chart. Bollinger bands have been interpreted in many ways by their users. For example, when the stock price is relatively quiet, the Bollinger bands are tight, which indicates a possible pent-up tension that must be released by a subsequent price movement.

MACD MACD stands for moving average convergence divergence. The MACD indicator is a trading indicator that uses data from three moving averages to form two lines, a fast line and a slow line. The fast line, called the *MACD line,* is the 12-day moving average minus the 26-day moving average. The slow line, called the *signal line,* is a 9-day exponential moving average. The convergence/divergence of these three averages is represented by the solid black bars in the third chart of Figure 8.9. The basic MACD trading rule is to sell when the MACD falls below its signal line and to buy when the MACD rises above its signal line.

MONEY FLOW The idea behind money flow is to identify whether buyers are more eager to buy the stock than sellers are to sell it. In its purest form, money flow looks at each trade. To calculate the money flow indicator, the technician multiplies price and volume for the trades that occur at a price higher than the previous trade price. The technician then sums this money flow. From this sum, the technician subtracts another money flow: the accumulated total of price times volume for trades that occur at prices lower than the previous trade. Example 8.3 shows how to calculate money flow using hypothetical data.

FIGURE 8.9

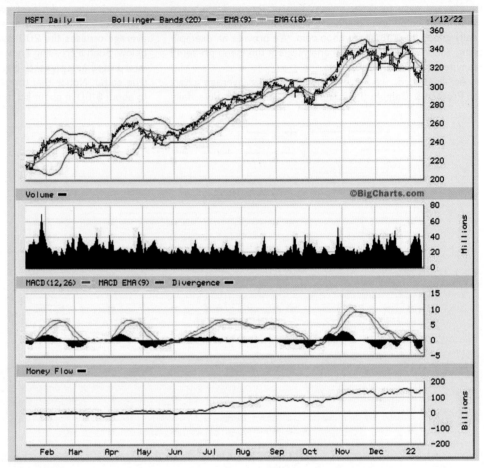

Source: Yahoo! Finance.

| EXAMPLE 8.3 | Calculating Money Flow |

Price	Up (+); Down (−); Unchanged (0)	Volume	Price × Volume	Money Flow (+)	Money Flow (−)	Net Money Flow
10						
11	+	1,000	11,000	11,000		
12	+	100	1,200	12,200		
12	0	500	6,000			
11	−	500	5,500		5,500	
10	−	50	500		6,000	
At the end of the day:						6,200

Traders using money flow look for a divergence between money flow and price. If price remains stable but money flow becomes highly positive, this is taken as an indicator that the stock price will soon increase. Similarly, if the stock price remains stable but the money flow becomes quite negative, this is taken as an indicator that the stock price will soon decrease.

FIBONACCI NUMBERS

Traders using technical analysis are interested in timing their purchase or sale of a stock. As you know by now, these traders look for support or resistance stock price levels. As strange as it may seem, one source that traders use is known as the *golden mean*. The golden mean is sometimes abbreviated by the Greek letter phi (φ). The golden mean, φ, is approximately equal to 1.618 (it is precisely equal to $(\sqrt{5} + 1)/2$). The golden mean is mathematically interesting because, among other things, $\varphi^2 = \varphi + 1$.

The golden mean also results from a series of numbers known as *Fibonacci numbers*. The infinite Fibonacci series grows as follows:

$$1, 1, 2, 3, 5, 8, 13, 21, 34, 55, 89, 144, 233, 377, 610, 987. . .$$

Note that the series begins with 1, 1 and grows by adding the two previous numbers together (for example, $21 + 34 = 55$). Let's look at the ratio of some numbers to their predecessor in the series:

$$21/13 = 1.6154$$
$$34/21 = 1.6190$$
$$55/34 = 1.6176$$
$$89/55 = 1.6182$$

The ratio converges to 1.618, or φ. Market technicians are interested in φ because:

$$(\phi - 1)/\phi = .618/1.618 = .382$$
$$1/\phi = 1.000/1.618 = .618 = \phi - 1$$

Market technicians use these numbers to predict support and resistance levels. For example, as a stock increases in value over time, it will occasionally pull back in value. Suppose a stock has increased from \$40 to \$60 and has recently begun to fall a bit in value. Using the $(\varphi - 1)/\varphi$ ratio, market technicians would predict the primary support area would occur at \$52.36 (\$60 − \$40 = \$20; \$20 × .382 = \$7.64; \$60 − \$7.64 = \$52.36). A similar calculation that uses the $1/\varphi$ ratio of .618 instead of .382 results in the secondary support area of \$47.64. If the stock were to pierce this secondary support level and close below it, the rally would be declared over. Market technicians would then begin to look for opportunities to sell the stock short if it subsequently rallied.

Nature provides many instances involving Fibonacci numbers. The number of petals on a flower is often a Fibonacci number. For example, black-eyed Susans have 13 petals and ordinary daisies have 34. Also, pinecones and pineapples have spirals containing 8 or 13 scales. There are so many other examples that some observers classify Fibonacci numbers as a "law of nature." Because of this "law," some market technicians believe that the Fibonacci numbers should also apply to market prices.

OTHER TECHNICAL INDICATORS

We close our discussion of technical analysis by describing a few additional technical indicators. The "odd-lot" indicator looks at whether odd-lot purchases (purchases of fewer than 100 shares) are up or down. One argument is that odd-lot purchases represent the activities of smaller, unsophisticated investors, so when they start buying, it's time to sell. This is a good example of a "contrarian" indicator. In contrast, some argue that because short selling is a fairly sophisticated tactic, increases in short selling are a negative signal.

Some indicators can seem (more than) a little silly, but they are a fun diversion. For example, there is the "hemline" indicator, which is also known as the "bull markets and bare knees" indicator. Through much of the nineteenth century, long skirts dominated women's fashion and the stock market experienced many bear markets. In the 1920s, flappers revealed their knees and the stock market boomed. Even the stock market crash of October 1987 was predicted by hemlines. During the 1980s, miniskirts flourished, but by October 1987, a fashion shift had women wearing longer skirts.

One of the more famous (or fatuous, depending on how you look at it) indicators is the **Super Bowl** indicator, which forecasts the direction of the market based on whether the National Football Conference or the American Football Conference wins. A Super Bowl win by a National Football Conference team or an American Football Conference team that used to be in the old National Football League (i.e., Pittsburgh Steelers, Baltimore Colts) is bullish. This probably strikes you as absurd, so you might be surprised to learn that through February 2021, the Super Bowl indicator forecast the direction of the stock market with about 80 percent accuracy.

If you want a more recent indicator of stock market performance from the world of sports, consider horse racing's Triple Crown. In 2015, American Pharoah won the Triple Crown, becoming the first horse to do so since Affirmed did it in 1978. Before American Pharoah, only 11 horses accomplished this feat. Why does this matter for the stock market? Well, in 8 of those 11 years, the Dow finished down for the year. More recently, Justify won the Triple Crown in 2018, and the market fell. So, the indicator is now 9 for 13, although there might be an inquiry into the effect on the indicator by the "dividend-aided" positive market performance in 2015.

There are many other technical trading rules. How seriously should you take them? That's up to you, but our advice is to keep in mind that life is full of odd coincidences. Just because a bizarre stock market predictor seems to have worked well in the past doesn't mean that it is going to work in the future.

CHECK THIS

8.7a	What is technical analysis?
8.7b	What is the purpose of charting a stock's past price?
8.7c	What is the purpose of using technical indicators?

 8.8 ## Summary and Conclusions

The topic of this chapter is behavioral finance and technical analysis. In this chapter, we cover many aspects of this evolving area in finance. We summarize these aspects of the chapter's important concepts.

1. **Prospect theory.**

   A. Prospect theory is a collection of ideas that provides an alternative to classical, rational economic decision making. The foundation of prospect theory rests on the idea that investors are much more distressed by prospective losses than they are happy about prospective gains.

   B. Researchers have found that a typical investor considers the pain of a $1 loss to be about twice as great as the pleasure received from the gain of $1. Also, researchers have found that investors respond in different ways to identical situations. The difference depends on whether the situation is presented in terms of losses or in terms of gains.

   C. Researchers have identified other befuddling examples of investor behavior. Three of them are:

   - *Frame dependence.* If an investment problem is presented in two seemingly different (but actually equivalent) ways, investors often make inconsistent choices. That is, how a problem is described, or framed, seems to matter to people.

   - *Mental accounting.* Through time, you will mentally account for gains and losses in your investments. How you feel about the investment depends on whether you are ahead or behind. This behavior is known as mental accounting.

   - *House money.* Casinos in Las Vegas (and elsewhere) know all about a concept called "playing with house money." The casinos have found that gamblers are far more likely to take big risks with money won from the casino (i.e., the "house money") than with their "hard-earned cash." Casinos also know that gamblers are not as upset about losing house money as they are about losing the money they brought with them to gamble. This is puzzling because all your money is your money.

2. The implications of investor overconfidence and misperceptions of randomness.

A. One key to becoming a wise investor is to avoid certain types of behavior. By studying behavioral finance, you can see the potential damage to your (or your client's) portfolio from overconfidence and psychologically induced errors.

B. The evidence is relatively clear on one point: Investors probably make mistakes. A much more difficult question, and one where the evidence is not at all clear, is whether risks stemming from errors in judgment by investors can influence market prices and lead to market inefficiencies. An important point is that market efficiency does not require that all investors behave in a rational fashion. It just requires that some do.

3. Sentiment-based risk and limits to arbitrage.

A. "Limits to arbitrage" is a term that refers to the notion that under certain circumstances, rational, well-capitalized traders may be unable to correct a mispricing, at least not quickly. The reason is that strategies designed to eliminate mispricings are often risky, costly, or somehow restricted. Three important such problems are firm-specific risk, noise trader risk, and implementation costs.

B. When these or other risks and costs are present, a mispricing may persist because arbitrage is too risky or too costly. Collectively, these risks and costs create barriers or limits to arbitrage. How important these limits are is difficult to say, but we do know that mispricings occur, at least on occasion. Two well-known examples are 3Com/Palm and Royal Dutch/Shell.

4. The wide array of technical analysis methods used by investors.

A. Many investors try to predict future stock price movements based on investor sentiment, errors in judgment, or historical price movements. Such investors rely on the tools of technical analysis, and we present numerous specific methods used by technical analysts.

B. Whether these tools or methods work is much debated. We close this chapter by noting the possibility that market prices are influenced by factors like errors in judgment by investors, sentiment, emotion, and irrationality. If they are, however, we are unaware of any scientifically proven method investors like you can use to profit from these influences.

GETTING DOWN TO BUSINESS

This chapter deals with various aspects of behavioral finance. How do you go about incorporating these concepts into the management of your portfolio? First, recall that one of the major lessons from this chapter is that, at times, you may be your own worst enemy when you are investing.

But suppose that you are able to harness your own psychological flaws that unduly influence your investment decisions. To profit from insights from behavioral finance, you might try to shift your portfolio to take advantage of situations where you perceive other market participants have incorrectly valued certain stocks, bonds, derivatives, market sectors, or even countries. Shifting portfolio weights to take advantage of these opportunities is called a "dynamic" trading strategy.

Here is one example of using a dynamic trading strategy: Consider a typical value/growth portfolio weight-shifting scheme. When there is a great deal of market overreaction, perhaps signaled by high market volatility, you would increase, or tilt, your relative portfolio weight toward value stocks. When there is a great deal of market underreaction, perhaps

(continued)

signaled by low market volatility, you would increase your relative weighting in growth stocks. The problem, of course, is knowing when and how to tilt your portfolio to take advantage of what you perceive to be market overreactions and underreactions. At times, you can do very well when you tilt your portfolio. Other times, to use an old commodity market saying, "you get your head handed to you."

A great amount of information is available on the internet about behavioral finance and building portfolios. One interesting place to start is the "Research" section at psychonomics.com. Make sure that the money that you are using to test any trading scheme is only a small portion of your investment portfolio.

For the latest information on the real world of investments, visit us at jmdinvestments.blogspot.com.

Key Terms

anchoring 255
behavioral finance 252
clustering illusion 262
Dow theory 269
Elliott wave theory 270
frame dependence 253
limits to arbitrage 265
loss aversion 254
mental accounting 254

noise trader 266
prospect theory 252
relative strength 272
representativeness heuristic 259
resistance level 270
sentiment-based risk 266
support level 270
technical analysis 268

Related Bloomberg Functions

GP	Graph Price, 8.7
TECH	Technical Analysis, 8.7
GF	Graph Fundamentals, 8.7
BTST	Basic Backtesting, 8.7
RSI	Relative Strength Index, 8.7
GPMA	Multi Moving Average Chart, 8.7
BOLL	Bollinger Bands, 8.7
MACD	Mov Avg Convergence/Divergence, 8.7
GPF	Fibonacci Retracements, 8.7

Chapter Review Problems and Self-Test

1. **It's All Relative (LO4, CFA3)** Consider the following series of weekly stock prices for two companies:

Week	Cats Co.	Dog Power
1	$10	$80
2	12	82
3	16	80
4	15	84
5	14	85
6	12	88

On a relative basis, how has Cats Co. done compared to Dog Power?

2. **Simple Moving Averages (LO4, CFA3)**   Using the prices from Problem 1, calculate the three-week simple moving average prices for both companies.

Answers to Self-Test Problems

1. Suppose we had purchased eight shares of Cats Co. and one share of Dog Power. We can calculate the value of our investment in each week and then take the ratio of Cats Co. to Dog Power as follows:

	Investment Value		
Week	Cats Co. (8 shares)	Dog Power (1 share)	Relative Strength
1	$80	$80	1.00
2	96	82	1.17
3	128	80	1.60
4	120	84	1.43
5	112	85	1.32
6	96	88	1.09

Cats Co. has significantly outperformed Dog Power over much of this period; however, after six weeks, the margin has fallen to about 9 percent from as high as 60 percent.

2. The moving averages must be calculated relative to the share price; also note that results cannot be computed for the first two weeks because of insufficient data.

Week	Cats Co.	Cats Co. Moving Average	Dog Power	Dog Power Moving Average
1	$10	—	$80	—
2	12	—	82	—
3	16	$12.67	80	$80.67
4	15	14.33	84	82.00
5	14	15.00	85	83.00
6	12	13.67	88	85.67

Test Your Investment Quotient

1. **Technical Analysis (LO4, CFA3)**   Which of the following is a basic assumption of technical analysis in contrast to fundamental analysis?

   a. Financial statements provide information crucial in valuing a stock.
   b. A stock's market price will approach its intrinsic value over time.
   c. Aggregate supply and demand for goods and services are key determinants of stock value.
   d. Security prices move in patterns, which repeat over long periods.

2. **Technical Analysis (LO4, CFA3)**   Which of the following is least likely to be of interest to a technical analyst?

   a. A 15-day moving average of trading volume
   b. A relative strength analysis of stock price momentum
   c. Company earnings and cash flow growth
   d. A daily history of the ratio of advancing stocks over declining stocks

3. **Dow Theory (LO4, CFA3)**   Dow theory asserts that three forces are at work in the stock market at any time. Which of the following is *not* one of these Dow theory forces?

   a. Daily price fluctuations
   b. A secondary reaction or trend
   c. A primary direction or trend
   d. Reversals or overreactions

4. **Technical Indicators (LO4, CFA3)**   The advance/decline line is typically used to:

   a. Measure psychological barriers.
   b. Measure market breadth.
   c. Assess bull market sentiment.
   d. Assess bear market sentiment.

5. **Technical Indicators (LO4, CFA3)**   The closing Arms (TRIN) ratio is the ratio of:

   a. Average trading volume in declining stocks to advancing stocks.
   b. Average trading volume in NYSE stocks to Nasdaq stocks.
   c. The number of advancing stocks to the number of declining stocks.
   d. The number of declining stocks to the number of advancing stocks.

6. **Technical Indicators (LO4, CFA3)**   Resistance and support areas for a stock market index are viewed as technical indicators of:

   a. Economic barriers.
   b. Psychological barriers.
   c. Circuit breakers.
   d. Holding patterns.

7. **Behavioral Finance Concepts (LO1, CFA5)**   When companies changed the structure of 401(k) plans to allow employees to opt out rather than in, the participation rates significantly increased. This is an example of:

   a. Representativeness.
   b. The house money effect.
   c. Frame dependence.
   d. A heuristic.

8. **Behavioral Finance Concepts (LO1, CFA4)**   When someone who wins money is more willing to lose the gains, this is referred to as:

   a. Representativeness.
   b. The house money effect.
   c. Frame dependence.
   d. A heuristic.

9. **Behavioral Finance Concepts (LO2, CFA1)**   Investors are generally more likely to choose a well-known company when faced with a choice between two firms. This is an example of:

   a. Representativeness.
   b. The house money effect.
   c. Frame dependence.
   d. A heuristic.

10. **Behavioral Finance Concepts (LO2, CFA4)**   Many investors try to simplify the investment process by using rules of thumb to make decisions. This is an example of:

    a. Representativeness.
    b. The house money effect.
    c. Frame dependence.
    d. A heuristic.

11. **Behavioral Finance Concepts (LO2, CFA5)**   All of the following are ways to help reduce behavioral biases except:

    a. Learning about the biases.
    b. Diversifying your portfolio.
    c. Watching more financial news programs.
    d. Creating objective investment criteria.

12. **Behavioral Finance Concepts (LO1, CFA1)**   Which of the following topics related to behavioral finance deals with the idea that investors experience more pain from a loss than pleasure from a comparable gain?

    a. Frame dependence
    b. Prospect theory
    c. Loss aversion
    d. Mental accounting

13. **Limits to Arbitrage (LO3, CFA1)**   Which of the following is not a reason that rational, well-capitalized investors can correct a mispricing, at least not immediately?

    a. Firm-specific risk
    b. Implementation costs
    c. Aversion risk
    d. Noise trader risk

14. **Technical Indicators (LO4, CFA3)**   Which of the following techniques deals with the breadth of the market?

    a. Price channels
    b. Advance/decline lines
    c. Bollinger bands
    d. Support and resistance lines

15. **Technical Indicators (LO4, CFA3)**   Which of the following techniques does not assume there are psychologically important barriers in stock prices?

    a. Price channels
    b. Advance/decline lines
    c. Bollinger bands
    d. Support and resistance lines

Concept Questions

1. **Dow Theory (LO4, CFA3)**   In the context of Dow theory, what are the three forces at work at all times? Which is the most important?

2. **Technical Analysis (LO4, CFA3)**   To a technical analyst, what are support and resistance areas?

3. **Mental Accounting (LO1, CFA4)**   Briefly explain mental accounting and identify the potential negative effect of this bias.

4. **Heuristics (LO2, CFA1)**   Why do 401(k) plans with more bond choices tend to have participants with portfolios more heavily allocated to fixed income?

5. **Overconfidence (LO2, CFA5)**   In the context of behavioral finance, why do men tend to underperform women with regard to the returns in their portfolios?

6. **Overconfidence (LO2, CFA4)**   What is the "illusion of knowledge" and how does it impact investment performance?

7. **Dow Theory (LO4, CFA3)**   Why do you think the industrial and transportation averages are the two that underlie Dow theory?

8. **Limits to Arbitrage (LO3)**   In the chapter, we discussed the 3Com/Palm and Royal Dutch/Shell mispricings. Which of the limits to arbitrage would least likely be the main reason for these mispricings? Explain.

9. **Contrarian Investing (LO4, CFA3)**   What does it mean to be a contrarian investor? How would a contrarian investor use technical analysis?

10. **Technical Analysis (LO4, CFA3)**   A frequent argument against the usefulness of technical analysis is that trading on a pattern has the effect of destroying the pattern. Explain what this means.

11. **Gaps (LO4, CFA3)**   Gaps are another technical analysis tool used in conjunction with open-high-low-close charts. A gap occurs when either the low price for a particular day is higher than the high price from the previous day or the high price for a day is lower than the low price from the previous day. Do you think gaps are a bullish or bearish signal? Why?

12. **Probabilities (LO2, CFA2)**   Suppose you are flipping a fair coin in a coin-flipping contest and have flipped eight heads in a row. What is the probability of flipping a head on your next coin flip? Suppose you flipped a head on your ninth toss. What is the probability of flipping a head on your tenth toss?

13. **Prospect Theory (LO1, CFA1)**   How do prospect theory and the concept of a rational investor differ?

14. **Frame Dependence (LO1, CFA4)**   How can frame dependence lead to irrational investment decisions?

15. **Noise Trader Risk (LO3, CFA2)**   What is noise trader risk? How can noise trader risk lead to market inefficiencies?

Questions and Problems

Core Questions

1. **Advance/Decline Lines (LO4, CFA3)**   Use the data below to construct the advance/decline line for the stock market. Volume figures are in thousands of shares.

	Stocks Advancing	Advancing Volume	Stocks Declining	Declining Volume
Monday	1,634	825,503	1,402	684,997
Tuesday	1,876	928,360	1,171	440,665
Wednesday	1,640	623,369	1,410	719,592
Thursday	2,495	1,101,332	537	173,003
Friday	1,532	508,790	1,459	498,585

2. **Calculating Arms Ratio (LO4, CFA3)**   Using the data in Problem 1, construct the Arms ratio on each of the five trading days.

3. **Simple Moving Averages (LO4, CFA3)**   The table below shows the closing monthly stock prices for Penn Co. and Teller, Inc. Calculate the simple three-month moving average for each month for both companies.

Penn	Teller
$169.64	$600.36
173.29	613.40
180.13	586.76
195.81	544.10
196.69	529.02
204.49	506.38
222.52	603.69
215.23	540.96
216.23	515.04
213.51	592.64
192.29	599.39
173.10	645.90

4. **Exponential Moving Averages (LO4, CFA3)**   Using the stock prices in Problem 3, calculate the exponential three-month moving average for both stocks where two-thirds of the average weight is placed on the most recent price.

5. **Exponential Moving Averages (LO4, CFA3)**   Using the stock prices in Problem 3, calculate the exponential three-month moving average for Penn and Teller. Place 50 percent of the average weight on the most recent price. How does this exponential moving average compare to your result from Problem 4?

6. **Market Sentiment Index (LO4, CFA3)**   A group of investors was polled each week for the last five weeks about whether they were bullish or bearish concerning the market. Construct the market sentiment index for each week based on these polls. Assuming the market sentiment index is being used as a contrarian indicator, which direction would you say the market is headed?

Week	Bulls	Bears
1	58	63
2	53	68
3	47	74
4	50	71
5	43	78

7. **Money Flow (LO4, CFA3)** You are given the following information concerning the trades made on a particular stock. Calculate the money flow for the stock based on these trades. Is the money flow a positive or negative signal in this case?

Price	Volume
$70.12	
70.14	1,900
70.13	1,400
70.09	1,800
70.05	2,100
70.07	2,700
70.03	3,000

8. **Moving Averages (LO4, CFA3)** Suppose you are given the following information on a broad equity market index:

Date	Close
4/1/2022	2,867.19
4/2/2022	2,867.24
4/3/2022	2,873.40
4/4/2022	2,879.39
4/5/2022	2,892.74
4/8/2022	2,895.77
4/9/2022	2,878.20
4/10/2022	2,888.21
4/11/2022	2,888.32
4/12/2022	2,907.41

Calculate the simple three-day moving average for the index and the exponential three-day moving average where two-thirds of the weight is placed on the most recent close. Why would you want to know the moving average for an index? If the close on April 12, 2022, was below the three-day moving average, would it be a buy or sell signal?

9. **Support and Resistance Levels (LO4, CFA3)** Below you will see a stock price chart for Cisco Systems from finance.yahoo.com. Do you see any resistance or support levels? What do support and resistance levels mean for the stock price?

Source: Yahoo! Finance.

10. **Advance/Decline Lines and Arms Ratio (LO4, CFA3)** Use the data below to construct the advance/decline line and Arms ratio for the market. Volume is in thousands of shares.

	Stocks Advancing	Advancing Volume	Stocks Declining	Declining Volume
Monday	2,530	995,111	519	111,203
Tuesday	2,429	934,531	639	205,567
Wednesday	1,579	517,007	1,407	498,094
Thursday	2,198	925,424	823	313,095
Friday	1,829	592,335	1,188	384,078

11. **Money Flow (LO4, CFA3)** A stock had the following trades during a particular period. What was the money flow for the stock? Is the money flow a positive or negative signal in this case?

Week	Day	Price	Volume
1	Monday	$61.85	
	Tuesday	61.81	1,000
	Wednesday	61.82	1,400
	Thursday	61.85	1,300
	Friday	61.84	800
2	Monday	61.87	1,100
	Tuesday	61.88	1,400
	Wednesday	61.92	600
	Thursday	61.91	1,200
	Friday	61.93	1,600

Intermediate Questions

12. **Fibonacci Numbers (LO4, CFA3)** A stock recently increased in price from $32 to $45. Using φ, what are the primary and secondary support areas for the stock?

13. **Simple Moving Averages (LO4, CFA3)** Below you will find the closing stock prices for Auction Makers over a three-week period. Calculate the simple three-day and five-day moving averages for the stock and graph your results. Are there any technical indications of the future direction of the stock price?

Week	Day	Close
1	Monday	$39.65
	Tuesday	39.30
	Wednesday	39.86
	Thursday	41.05
	Friday	41.23
2	Monday	41.02
	Tuesday	40.75
	Wednesday	41.16
	Thursday	40.38
	Friday	39.44
3	Monday	40.07
	Tuesday	40.19
	Wednesday	40.56
	Thursday	41.21
	Friday	40.74

14. **Exponential Moving Averages (LO4, CFA3)** Use the information from Problem 13 to calculate the three-day and five-day exponential moving averages for Auction Makers and graph your results. Place two-thirds of the average weight on the most recent stock price. Are there any technical indications of the future direction of the stock price?

15. **Put/Call Ratio (LO4, CFA3)** Another technical indicator is the put/call ratio. The put/call ratio is the number of put options traded divided by the number of call options traded. The put/call ratio can be constructed on the market or on an individual stock. Below you will find the number of puts and calls traded over a four-week period for all stocks:

Week	Puts	Calls
1	1,874,986	1,631,846
2	1,991,650	1,772,815
3	2,187,450	1,976,277
4	2,392,751	2,182,270

How would you interpret the put/call ratio? Calculate the put/call ratio for each week. From this analysis, does it appear the market is expected to be upward trending or downward trending?

Spreadsheet Problems

16. **Moving Averages (LO4, CFA3)** From the data below for the Dow Jones Industrial Average, calculate the three-day simple moving average. Fill in the "Buy/Sell Signal" column for this trading indicator. Then, calculate the three-day exponential moving average and fill in the "Buy/Sell Signal" column for this trading indicator. Assume that the current closing price will receive 4/5 of the weight in the exponential moving average. Finally, fill in the "Signal Comparison" column. On which days do the signals disagree?

Date	Adj Close	3-Day Simple Moving Average	Buy/Sell Signal	3-Day Exponential Moving Average	Buy/Sell Signal	Signal Comparison
1/24/22	34,070.61					
1/25/22	34,186.64					
1/26/22	34,520.82					
1/27/22	34,261.75					
1/28/22	34,135.24					
1/31/22	34,691.17					
2/1/22	35,151.47					
2/2/22	35,378.19					
2/3/22	35,520.08					
2/4/22	35,095.74					
2/7/22	35,108.38					
2/8/22	35,160.68					
2/9/22	35,614.90					
2/10/22	35,630.81					
2/11/22	35,267.89					

17. **Bollinger Bands (LO4, CFA3)** From the data below, calculate the upper and lower Bollinger bands, which represent plus (or minus) two standard deviations of the 20-day simple moving average added (subtracted) from the 20-day simple moving average. If the daily price approaches or exceeds the upper Bollinger band, traders will look for a continued upward movement in the stock price. Graph the 20-day simple moving average, the upper and lower Bollinger bands, and the price of the stock. Does the graph tell you that traders expect continued strength or weakness in the stock price?

Date	Close	20-Day Simple Moving Average	Standard Deviation of 20-Day Moving Average	Lower Bollinger Band	Upper Bollinger Band
3/26/2022	186.79	180.88	3.40		
3/27/2022	188.47	181.50	3.60		
3/28/2022	188.72	182.18	3.80		
3/29/2022	189.95	182.96	4.00		
4/1/2022	191.24	183.71	4.20		
4/2/2022	194.02	184.48	4.39		
4/3/2022	195.35	185.40	4.57		
4/4/2022	195.69	186.45	4.72		
4/5/2022	197.00	187.61	4.86		
4/8/2022	200.10	188.81	4.99		
4/9/2022	199.50	189.87	5.10		
4/10/2022	200.62	190.80	5.19		
4/11/2022	198.95	191.74	5.25		
4/12/2022	198.87	192.51	5.27		

CFA Exam Review by Kaplan Schweser

[CFA1, CFA2, CFA4, CFA5]

Terry Shriver and Mary Trickett are portfolio managers for High End Investment Managers. As part of their annual review of their client portfolios, they consider the appropriateness of their client portfolios given their clients' investment policies. Their boss, Jill Castillo, is concerned that Shriver and Trickett allow the clients' behavioral biases to enter into the asset allocation decision, so she has asked them to review their notes from meetings with clients. The information below is excerpted from their notes regarding the clients named.

Tom Higgins: "In the past five years, I have consistently outperformed the market averages in my stock portfolio. It really does not take a genius to beat a market average, but I am proud to say that I have beaten the market averages by at least 2 percent each year and have not once lost money. I would continue managing my portfolio myself, but with a new baby and a promotion, I just don't have time."

Joanne McHale: "The last three quarters were bad for my portfolio. I have lost about a third of my value, primarily because I invested heavily in two aggressive growth mutual funds that had bad quarters. I need to get back one-third of my portfolio's value because I am only 15 years away from retirement and I don't have a defined-benefit pension plan. Because of this, I am directing Mary Trickett to invest my savings in technology mutual funds. Their potential return is much higher, and I believe I can recover my losses with them."

Jack Sims: "I enjoy bird-watching and hiking. I am an avid environmental advocate and will only invest in firms that share my concern for the environment. My latest investment was in Washington Materials, which was recently featured in an environmental magazine for its outstanding dedication to environmental protection."

1. Which of the following best describes Tom Higgins's behavioral characteristic in investment decisions?
   a. Tom is overconfident.
   b. Tom uses frame dependence.
   c. Tom uses anchoring.

2. Which of the following best describes the potential problem with Mr. Higgins's investment strategy?
   a. He will underestimate the risk of his portfolio and underestimate the impact of an event on stocks.
   b. He will overestimate the risk of his portfolio and overestimate the impact of an event on stocks.
   c. He will underestimate the risk of his portfolio and overestimate the impact of an event on stocks.

3. Which of the following best describes Joanne McHale's behavioral characteristic in investment decisions?

   a. Joanne is loss-averse.
   b. Joanne uses the *ceteris paribus* heuristic.
   c. Joanne is experiencing the snakebite effect.

4. Which of the following best describes Jack Sims's behavioral characteristic in investment decisions?

   a. Jack is overconfident.
   b. Jack uses frame dependence.
   c. Jack uses representativeness.

5. Which of the following would Mr. Higgins, Ms. McHale, and Mr. Sims be least likely to use when making investment decisions?

   a. Heuristics
   b. Their personal experiences
   c. Fundamental analysis

Bloomberg Exercises

1. Construct a basic price chart for Caterpillar (CAT). **(GP)**
2. Review the list of technical factors that can be added to a chart. **(TECH)**
3. Identify which technical indicator has been most profitable for trading Cisco (CSCO). **(BTST)**
4. Generate an RSI chart for CVS. **(RSI)**

What's on the Web?

1. **Bollinger Bands** You can learn more about Bollinger bands at www.chartsmart.com. What does the site say about using Bollinger bands in technical analysis? Now go to finance.yahoo.com and enter your favorite stock. Find the technical analysis section and view the Bollinger bands for your stock. What does the chart tell you about this stock?

2. **Relative Strength** Relative strength measures the performance of a stock against a "bogey," which is either another stock or suitable index. Pick your favorite stock and go to the technical analysis area of finance.yahoo.com. Compare the relative strength of your stock against a close competitor and the S&P 500 index. How is this stock performing relative to these bogeys?

3. **Triangles** Go back to school! Check out the "ChartSchool" link at stockcharts.com. How many different types of triangles are listed on the site? What does each type of triangle mean to a technical analyst?

4. **Market Volume** An important tool for most technical traders is market volume. Go to www.marketvolume.com to discover the reasons market volume is considered important.

Interest Rates

"We reckon hours and minutes to be dollars and cents."

—Thomas Chandler Haliburton (from *The Clockmaker*)

Learning Objectives

It will be worth your time to increase your rate of interest in these topics:

1. Money market prices and rates.

2. Rates and yields on fixed-income securities.

3. Treasury STRIPS and the term structure of interest rates.

4. Nominal versus real interest rates.

Benjamin Franklin stated a fundamental truth of commerce when he sagely advised young tradesmen to "remember that time is money." In finance, we call this opportunity cost, which is the foundation of the time value of money. But how much time corresponds to how much money? Interest constitutes a rental payment for money, and an interest rate tells us how much money for how much time. But there are many interest rates, each corresponding to a particular money market. Interest rates state money prices in each of these markets.

CFA™ Exam Topics in This Chapter:

1. The time value of money (L1, S1)

2. Aggregate output, prices, and economic growth (L1, S3)

3. Understanding business cycles (L1, S3)

4. Fixed-income securities: Defining elements (L1, S13)

5. Introduction to fixed-income valuation (L1, S13)

6. Understanding fixed-income risk and return (L1, S14)

7. Fundamentals of credit analysis (L1, S14)

8. The term structure and interest rate dynamics (L2, S11)

9. Economics and investment markets (L2, S16)

Go to Connect for a guide that aligns your textbook with CFA readings.

This chapter is the first dealing specifically with interest-bearing assets. As we discussed in a previous chapter, there are two basic types of interest-bearing assets: money market instruments and fixed-income securities. For both types of asset, interest rates are a key determinant of asset values. Furthermore, because trillions of dollars in interest-bearing assets are outstanding, interest rates play a pivotal role in financial markets and the economy.

Because interest rates are one of the most closely watched financial market indicators, we devote this entire chapter to them. We first discuss the many different interest rates that are commonly reported in the financial press, along with some of the different ways interest rates are calculated and quoted. We then go on to describe the basic determinants and separable components of interest rates.

9.1 Interest Rate History and Money Market Rates

Recall from Chapter 3 that money market instruments are debt obligations that have a maturity of less than one year at the time they are originally issued. Each business day, *The Wall Street Journal* publishes a list of current interest rates for several categories of money market securities in its "Money Rates" report. We will discuss these interest rates and the securities they represent following a quick look at the history of interest rates.

INTEREST RATE HISTORY

In Chapter 1, we saw how looking back at the history of returns on various types of investments gave us a useful perspective on rates of return. Similar insights are available from interest rate history. For example, in May 2022, interest rates on short-term government securities were about 1.1 percent and long-term rates were about 3.1 percent. We might ask, "Are these rates unusually high or low?" To find out, we examine Figure 9.1, which graphically illustrates 222 years of interest rates in the United States.

Two interest rates are plotted in Figure 9.1, one for bills and one for bonds. Both rates are based on U.S. Treasury securities, or close substitutes. We discuss bills and bonds in detail in this chapter and the next chapter. For now, it is enough to know that bills are short term and bonds are long term, so what is plotted in Figure 9.1 are short- and long-term interest rates.

FIGURE 9.1   **Interest Rate History (U.S. Interest Rates, 1800–2021)**

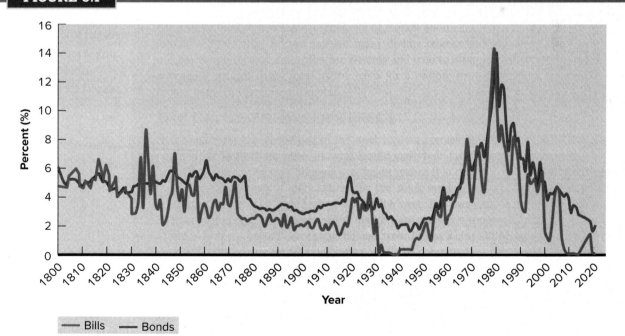

Source: Adapted from Jeremy J. Siegel, *Stocks for the Long Run*, 3rd ed., © McGraw-Hill, 2002; and the Federal Reserve Bank of St. Louis.

EXAMPLE 9.1

A Quick Review of the Time Value of Money

Undoubtedly, your instincts tell you that $1,000 received in three years is not the same as $1,000 received today. But if you are going to receive $1,000 today, what is an equivalent amount of money received in three years?

Fortunately, an equation tells us exactly what this is:

$$\text{Future value} = \text{Present value} \times (1 + r)^N \tag{9.1}$$

In this equation, the r represents a periodic interest rate (expressed as a decimal) and the N represents the number of periods (expressed as an integer). Although the periods could be weeks, months, or years, the important thing to remember is that the interest rate must be expressed as an interest rate *per period*.

Suppose you have $1,000 to invest and you can invest at an annual rate of 3.5 percent per year. In Equation 9.1, the per-period interest rate is .035. If you invest for three years ($N = 3$), the amount you will have in three years is:

$$\$1,108.718 = \$1,000 \times (1 + .035)^3$$

which would be rounded to $1,108.72.

You can also use Equation 9.1 to tell you how much a future amount is worth today. If we divide both sides of Equation 9.1 by $(1 + r)^N$ and rearrange terms, we get:

$$\text{Present value} = \frac{\text{Future value}}{(1 + r)^N} \tag{9.2}$$

which, by the rules of exponents, can be written as:

$$\text{Present value} = \text{Future value} \times (1 + r)^{-N} \tag{9.3}$$

That is, $(1 + r)^{-N}$ is just another way to write $1/(1 + r)^N$.

If you remember the relationship between Equations 9.1 and 9.3, you will soon become very comfortable with *compounding*, which is Equation 9.1, and *discounting*, which is Equation 9.3.

To continue with our numerical example, first note that $(1 + .035)^3 = 1.108718$. Therefore, using Equation 9.2:

$$\text{Present value} = \frac{\text{Future value}}{(1 + r)^N}$$

$$\$1,000 = \frac{\$1,108.718}{1.108718}$$

Suppose you invest $500 at 4 percent for six years. How much money will you have at the end of six years?

$$\text{Future value} = \text{Present value} \times (1 + r)^N$$

$$\$632.66 = \$500 \times (1 + .04)^6$$

Now suppose you will be getting $800 in four years. What is an equivalent amount today if you discount at 3.7 percent?

$$\text{Present value} = \text{Future value} \times (1 + r)^{-N}$$

$$\$691.79 = \$800 \times (1 + .037)^{-4}$$

Probably the most striking feature in Figure 9.1 is the fact that the highest interest rates in U.S. history occurred in the not-too-distant past. Rates began rising sharply in the 1970s and then peaked at extraordinary levels in the early 1980s. They have generally declined since then. The other striking aspect of U.S. interest rate history is the low short-term interest rate levels that prevailed from the 1930s to the 1960s, as well as in recent years. These rate levels have been the result, in large part, of deliberate actions by the Federal Reserve Board to keep short-term rates low—a policy that ultimately proved unsustainable and even disastrous in the years following the 1960s. Much was learned by the experience, and now the Federal Reserve is generally more concerned with controlling inflation.

THE FLIGHT TO QUALITY

Attentive bond investors may have noticed that bad news regarding current events, like the exit of Britain from the European Union or Russia invading Crimea, is almost always positive for U.S. Treasuries. They may also wonder why this is—wouldn't it make sense for geopolitical instability to also be harmful to financial market performance?

Sometimes it is; stocks and other high-risk assets typically exhibit more volatility and declines when headlines are unfavorable. However, U.S. Treasuries, due to their status as one of the lowest-risk investments in the world (if held until maturity), actually benefit when the investment backdrop becomes unstable. This phenomenon is known as the "flight to quality" or "flight to safety."

This dynamic unfolds in the markets when investors are more concerned about protecting themselves from potential losses than they are with making gains. During turbulent times in the market, investors often move toward investments where they are not likely to experience a loss of principal. These "safe havens" typically include the government bonds of the largest industrialized countries, especially the United States.

As Thomas Kenny at thebalance.com puts it, "At the simplest level, the flight to quality is an investor saying to him- or herself, 'Do I feel comfortable taking risk, or am I better keeping my money safe right now?' If enough people opt for the latter, the result is typically a rally in U.S. Treasuries."

The Flight to Quality in Action

Back in mid-2011, the European debt crisis took center stage as the key driver of financial market performance. It seemed increasingly likely that Greece or one of the smaller members of the bloc might default, or even that the euro's value might collapse. Investors were understandably worried.

As a result, investors sold stocks, commodities, and high-risk bonds, moving cash out of the assets most likely to suffer losses on account of the crisis situation. As this happened, U.S. Treasury prices surged and yields fell to record low levels. For example, one-year U.S. Treasuries spent much of the last six months of 2011 trading with a yield below .20 percent. This yield even fell as low as .09 percent.

What does this tell us? This shows that investors were willing to hold a one-year investment that paid almost nothing—and was far below the rate of inflation—just for the privilege of keeping their principal investments safe from turmoil in the global economy. This is the flight to quality as it happens in practice.

Source: Thomas Kenny, "What Is the Flight to Quality?," *The Balance.*

With long-term rates around 3 percent as this chapter was written, many market observers have commented that these interest rate levels are extraordinarily low. Based on the history of interest rates illustrated in Figure 9.1, however, 3 percent may be low relative to the last 30 years, but it is not at all low compared to rates during the 171-year period from 1800 to 1970. Indeed, long-term rates would have to fall well below 3 percent to be considered low by historical standards. Example 9.1 shows how investors use interest rates.

Why have interest rates been at such low levels over the last few years? We noted that the low rates may be attributable to the actions of the Federal Reserve, but other factors are at play as well. With the Crash of 2008, many investors undertook a "flight to quality," selling risky assets and moving into safe ones. See our *Investment Updates* box for more on this issue.

This flight to quality increases the demand for Treasury securities, particularly short-term bills. Based on the formulas in Example 9.1, you will see that as prices rise due to increased demand, the interest rates will fall. So, the reduction in rates could really be primarily a result of the crash. After the crash, market participants increased their purchases of extremely safe assets like U.S. Treasury bills.

MONEY MARKET RATES

Figure 9.2 is a Bloomberg screen shot of money rates. A commonly quoted interest rate is the **prime rate**. The prime rate is a key short-term interest rate because it is the basis for interest rates that large commercial banks charge on short-term loans (rates are quoted as prime plus or minus a spread). The prime rate is well known as a **bellwether rate** of bank lending to business. The prime rate shown is for the United States. Other countries, i.e., Canada, the European Central Bank, Japan, Switzerland, Great Britain, Australia, and Hong Kong, also have a prime rate.

The **federal funds rate** (or just "Fed funds") is a fundamental interest rate for commercial bank activity. The Fed funds rate is the interest rate that banks charge each other for overnight loans of $1 million or more. This interbank rate is set by continuous bidding among

prime rate
The basic interest rate on short-term loans that the largest commercial banks charge their most creditworthy corporate customers.

bellwether rate
Interest rate that serves as a leader or as a leading indicator of future trends, e.g., interest rates as a bellwether of inflation.

federal funds rate
Interest rate that banks charge each other for overnight loans of $1 million or more.

FIGURE 9.2   Money Rates

Fed Funds | FOMC »			Fed O/N Repo		US T-Bill						USD Deposit Rates			Rev Repo (Bid/Ask)		
FDFD	0.0700	0.0900	SOFR	0.05	4W	0.05	+0.03	0.05	0.05		O/N	0.0600	0.2100	O/N	0.06	0.03
OBFR01		0.07	TGCR	0.05	2M	0.05	+0.02	0.05	0.05		1W	0.0600	0.2000	1W	0.07	0.04
Commercial Paper			BGCR	0.05	3M	0.06	+0.03	0.06	0.06		2W	0.0700	0.2200	2W	0.08	0.04
30D		0.080	AFX O/N Rate		6M	0.19	+0.02	0.20	0.19		1M	0.1100	0.2600	1M	0.09	0.04
90D		0.190	AMERIBOR	0.15	1Y	0.39	+0.01	0.39	0.38							

Dow Jones			S&P 500 E-Mini Future			NASDAQ Composite Index			CRB Commodity Index		
DJIA	36365.78	+27.48	SPX Fut	4762.75	+4.25	CCMP	15745.57	+100.60	CRB	232.37	-1.59

US Bonds | FIT »						90D EUR$ FUT		SOFR FUT		LIBOR Fix		BSBY Fix	SOFR Fix
T 0 $\frac{3}{4}$ 12/31/23	0.780	99-30	99-30$\frac{1}{8}$	-.03		MAR	99.6500	SFR1	99.940	O/N	0.06438	0.10919	
T 1 12/15/24	1.024	99-29+	99-29$\frac{3}{4}$	-.06$\frac{1}{4}$		JUN	99.3950	SFR2	99.755	1W	0.07638		
T 1 $\frac{1}{4}$ 12/31/26	1.354	99-15$\frac{3}{4}$	99-16	-.14		SEP	99.1750	SFR3	99.520	1M	0.10125	0.07482	0.05573
T 1 $\frac{3}{8}$ 12/31/28	1.536	98-29+	98-30	-.21		DEC	98.9150	SFR4	99.325	2M	0.15250		
T 1 $\frac{3}{8}$ 11/15/31	1.611	97-27	97-27+	-.29		MAR	98.7300	SFR5	99.150	3M	0.20913	0.17919	0.09110
T 2 11/15/41	2.026	99-17	99-18+	-1-16+		JUN	98.5450	SFR6	98.955	6M	0.33875	0.28719	0.19336
T 1 $\frac{7}{8}$ 11/15/51	1.997	97-07+	97-08+	-2-03						1Y	0.58313	0.48165	

Spot FX | FXC »		Key Rates		Swaps		10Y Note Future			Funds Future	
JPY	115.3100	Prime	3.25	3Y	1.2221	CBT	129-19+	-27+	JAN	99.918
EUR	1.1292	BLR	2.00	5Y	1.4465	Commodities			30Y MBS | BBTM »	
GBP	1.3452	FDTR	0.25	10Y	1.6668	NYM WTI	75.86	+0.65	FNCL 2.5	101-22+101-23+ -.12
CAD	1.2760	Discount	0.25	30Y	1.8098	GOLD	1800.38	-28.82	G2SF 2.5	102-03 102-04+ -.12
									Current Coupon	2.159

Source: Bloomberg Finance L.P.

discount rate
The interest rate the Fed charges its member banks on loans.

For the latest on money market rates, visit
www.money-rates.com.

call money rate
The interest rate brokers pay to borrow bank funds for lending to customer margin accounts.

commercial paper
Short-term, unsecured debt issued by large corporations.

banks, where banks wishing to lend funds quote "offer rates" (rates at which they are willing to lend), and banks wishing to borrow funds quote "bid rates" (rates they are willing to pay).

The Federal Reserve's **discount rate** is another pivotal interest rate for commercial banks. The discount rate is the interest rate that the Fed offers to commercial banks for overnight reserve loans. You might recall from your Money and Banking class that banks are required to maintain reserves equal to some fraction of their deposit liabilities. When a bank cannot supply sufficient reserves from internal sources, it must borrow reserves from other banks through the federal funds market. Therefore, the Fed discount rate and the Fed funds rate are usually closely linked.

The Federal Reserve Bank is the central bank of the United States. As we discuss in more detail in a later chapter, the "Fed" has the responsibility to manage interest rates and the money supply to control inflation and promote stable economic growth. The discount rate is a basic tool of monetary policy for the Federal Reserve Bank. An announced change in the discount rate is often interpreted as a signal of the Federal Reserve's intentions regarding future monetary policy.

For example, by increasing the discount rate, the Federal Reserve may be signaling that it intends to pursue a tight-money policy, most likely to control budding inflationary pressures. Similarly, by decreasing the discount rate, the Federal Reserve may be signaling an intent to pursue a loose-money policy to stimulate economic activity. Of course, many times a discount rate change is simply a case of the Federal Reserve catching up to financial market conditions rather than leading them. Indeed, the Federal Reserve often acts like the lead goose, who, upon looking back and seeing the flock heading in another direction, quickly flies over to resume its position as "leader" of the flock.

Another important interest rate reported is the **call money rate**, or the call rate. "Call money" refers to loans from banks to security brokerage firms, and the call rate is the interest rate that brokerage firms pay on call money loans. As we discussed in Chapter 2, brokers use funds raised through call money loans to make margin loans to customers to finance leveraged stock and bond purchases. The call money rate is the basic rate that brokers use to set interest rates on customer call money loans. Brokers typically charge their customers the call money rate plus a premium (or spread), where the broker and the customer may negotiate the premium. For example, a broker may charge a customer the basic call money rate plus 1 percent for a margin loan to purchase common stock.

Commercial paper is short-term, unsecured debt issued by large corporations. The commercial paper market is dominated by financial corporations, such as banks and insurance companies, or financial subsidiaries of large corporations. A leading commercial paper rate is the rate that JP Morgan pays on short-term debt issues. This commercial paper rate is a benchmark for this market because JP Morgan is one of the largest single issuers of commercial paper. Most other corporations issuing commercial paper will pay a slightly higher interest rate than this benchmark rate. Commercial paper is a popular investment vehicle for portfolio managers and corporate treasurers with excess funds on hand that they wish to invest on a short-term basis. Euro commercial paper refers to commercial paper denominated in euros rather than dollars.

The **London Interbank Offered Rate (LIBOR)** is the rate that most international banks charge one another for loans of Eurodollars overnight in the London market. LIBOR is a cornerstone in the pricing of money market issues and other short-term debt issues by both government and corporate borrowers. Interest rates are frequently quoted as some spread over LIBOR, and they then float with the LIBOR rate. For example, a corporation may be quoted a loan rate from a London bank at LIBOR plus 2 percent.

Because of scandals in the LIBOR market, LIBOR is being replaced by another reference interest rate. According to the United Kingdom's Financial Conduct Authority, it will be phased out as early as the end of 2021. In the United States, the Secured Overnight Financing Rate (SOFR) is the successor. In October 2020, the reference rate on about $80 trillion in swaps was converted from LIBOR to SOFR. SOFR is the rate on repurchased Treasury securities and is published daily by the New York Federal Reserve.

There are other reference rates quoted around the world. For example, Euro LIBOR refers to deposits denominated in euros–the common currency of 19 European Union countries. Like LIBOR, the Euro LIBOR rate is calculated by the British Bankers' Association (BBA) from quotes provided by London banks. The EURIBOR is an interest rate that also refers to deposits denominated in euros. The EURIBOR, however, is based largely on interest rates from banks in the European Union interbank market. HIBOR is an interest rate based on Hong Kong dollars. HIBOR is the interest rate between banks in the Hong Kong interbank market.

Eurodollars are U.S. dollar–denominated deposits at foreign banks or foreign branches of U.S. banks. Eurodollar rates are interest rates paid for large-denomination Eurodollar certificates of deposit. Eurodollar CDs are negotiable and are traded in a large, active Eurodollar money market.

U.S. Treasury bills, or just **T-bills,** represent short-term U.S. government debt issued through the U.S. Treasury. The Treasury bill market is the world's largest market for new debt securities with one year or less to maturity. As such, the Treasury bill market leads all other credit markets in determining the general level of short-term interest rates. Figure 9.2 reports Treasury bill interest rates for different maturities–from four weeks (4W) to a year (1Y). The interest rates determined at each Treasury bill auction are closely watched by professional money managers throughout the world. The overnight repurchase, or "repo," rate is essentially the rate charged on overnight loans that are collateralized by U.S. Treasury securities.

There are other important money rates that are not reported in Figure 9.2. One key rate is that which is paid on **certificates of deposit**, or **CDs.** Certificates of deposit represent large-denomination deposits of $100,000 or more at commercial banks for a specified length of time. The interest rate paid on CDs usually varies according to the time length of the deposit. For example, a six-month CD might pay a higher interest rate than a three-month CD, which in turn might pay a higher interest rate than a one-month CD.

Large-denomination certificates of deposit are generally negotiable instruments, meaning that they can be bought and sold among investors through a broker. This fact means that they are often called *negotiable certificates of deposit,* or *negotiable CDs.* The large-denomination CDs described here should not be confused with the small-denomination CDs that banks offer retail customers. These small-denomination CDs are bank time deposits. They normally pay a lower interest rate than large-denomination CDs and are not negotiable instruments.

Another important rate is called a **banker's acceptance**, which is essentially a postdated check upon which a commercial bank has guaranteed payment. Banker's acceptances are normally used to finance international trade transactions. For example, as an importer, you wish to purchase computer components from a company in Singapore and pay for the goods three months after delivery. You write the exporter a postdated check. You and the exporter agree, however, that once the goods are shipped, your bank will guarantee payment on the date specified on the check. After your goods are shipped, the exporter presents the relevant

London Interbank Offered Rate (LIBOR)
Interest rate that international banks charge one another for overnight Eurodollar loans.

Visit JP Morgan at www.jpmorgan.com.

For more on LIBOR, visit www.theice.com/iba.
For more on SOFR, visit www.sofrrate.com.

Eurodollars
U.S. dollar–denominated deposits at foreign banks or foreign branches of U.S. banks.

U.S. Treasury bill (T-bill)
A short-term U.S. government debt instrument issued by the U.S. Treasury.

certificates of deposit (CDs)
Large-denomination deposits of $100,000 or more at commercial banks for a specified term.

banker's acceptance
A postdated check on which a bank has guaranteed payment; commonly used to finance international trade transactions.

documentation, and if all is in order, your bank stamps the word "*ACCEPTED*" on your check. At this point, your bank has created an acceptance, which means it has promised to pay the acceptance's face value (the amount of the check) at maturity (the date on the check). The exporter can then keep the acceptance or sell it in the money market.

Finally, the Federal Home Loan Mortgage Corporation (FHLMC), commonly called "Freddie Mac," and the Federal National Mortgage Association (FNMA), commonly called "Fannie Mae," are government-sponsored agencies that purchase large blocks of home mortgages. Then, they combine them into mortgage pools, where each pool can represent several tens of millions of dollars of home mortgages. Because home mortgages are long-term obligations, these are not actually money market rates. With several trillion dollars of mortgages outstanding, however, the mortgage market has a considerable influence on money market activity.

CHECK THIS

9.1a Which money market interest rates are most important to commercial banks?

9.1b Which money market interest rates are most important to nonbank corporations?

9.2
Money Market Prices and Rates

Related Bloomberg Functions

MMR Money Rate Monitors

Money market securities typically make a single payment of face value at maturity and make no payments before maturity. Such securities are called **pure discount securities** because they sell at a discount relative to their face value. In this section, we discuss the relationship between the price of a money market instrument and the interest rate quoted on it.

One of the things you will notice in this section is that market participants quote interest rates in several different ways. This inconsistent treatment presents a problem when we wish to compare rates on different investments. Therefore, we must put rates on a common footing before we can compare them.

pure discount security
An interest-bearing asset that makes a single payment of face value at maturity with no payments before maturity.

After going through the various interest rate conventions and conversions needed to compare them, you might wonder why everybody doesn't just agree to compute interest rates and prices in some uniform way. Well, perhaps they should, but they definitely do not. As a result, we must review some of the various procedures actually used in money markets. We hope you come to recognize that the calculations are neither mysterious nor even especially difficult, although they are rooted in centuries-old procedures and may sometimes be tedious. However, given the billions of dollars of securities traded every day based on these numbers, it is important to understand them.

Another thing to notice is that the word "yield" appears frequently. For now, you can take it as given that the yield on an interest-bearing asset is a measure of the interest rate being offered by the asset. We discuss the topic of yields in greater detail in another chapter.

basis point
Regarding interest rates or bond yields, one basis point is 1 percent of 1 percent.

Bond yields and many interest rates are quoted as a percentage with two decimal places, such as 5.82 percent. With this quote, the smallest possible change would be .01 percent, or .0001. This amount, which is 1 percent of 1 percent, is called a **basis point**. So, if an interest rate of 5.82 percent rose to 5.94 percent, we would say this rate rose by $94 - 82 = 12$ **basis points**. The quantity to the left of the decimal point (i.e., the "5") is called the "handle." Traders frequently omit the handle when quoting or discussing rates since, presumably, anyone actively trading would already know it.

BANK DISCOUNT RATE QUOTES

bank discount basis
A method for quoting interest rates on money market instruments.

Interest rates for some key money market securities, including Treasury bills and banker's acceptances, are quoted on a **bank discount basis**, or simply discount basis. An interest rate quoted on a discount basis is often called a *discount yield*. If we are given an interest rate quoted on a bank discount basis for a particular money market instrument, then we calculate the price of that instrument as follows:

$$\text{Current price} = \text{Face value} \times \left(1 - \frac{\textbf{Days to maturity}}{\textbf{360}} \times \text{Discount yield}\right) \qquad (9.4)$$

The term "discount yield" here refers to the quoted interest rate. It should not be confused with the Federal Reserve's discount rate discussed earlier.

To give an example, suppose a banker's acceptance has a face value of $1 million that will be paid in 90 days. If the interest rate, quoted on a discount basis, is 5 percent, what is the current price of the acceptance?

As the following calculation shows, a discount yield of 5 percent and maturity of 90 days gives a current price of $987,500.

$$\$987{,}500 = \$1{,}000{,}000 \times \left(1 - \frac{90}{360} \times .05\right)$$

The difference between the face value of $1 million and the price of $987,500 is $12,500 and is called the "discount." This discount is the interest earned over the 90-day period until the acceptance matures.

Notice that the formula used to calculate the acceptance price assumes a 360-day business year. This practice dates back to a time when calculations were performed manually. Assuming a 360-day business year, with exactly four 90-day quarters, rather than a true 365-day calendar year, made manual discount calculations simpler and less subject to error. Consequently, if $1 million is discounted over a full calendar year of 365 days using a bank discount yield of 5 percent and an assumed 360-day business year, the resulting price of $949,305.56 is calculated as follows:

$$\$949{,}305.56 = \$1{,}000{,}000 \times \left(1 - \frac{365}{360} \times .05\right)$$

EXAMPLE 9.2	Money Market Prices

The rate on a particular money market instrument, quoted on a discount basis, is 4 percent. The instrument has a face value of $100,000 and will mature in 71 days. What is its price? What if it has 51 days to maturity?

Using the bank discount basis formula, we have:

$$\text{Current price} = \text{Face value} \times \left(1 - \frac{\textbf{Days to maturity}}{\textbf{360}} \times \text{Discount yield}\right)$$

$$\$99{,}211.11 = \$100{,}000 \times \left(1 - \frac{71}{360} \times .04\right)$$

Check for yourself that the price in the second case of a 51-day maturity is $99,433.33.

TREASURY BILL QUOTES

For price and yield data on U.S. Treasury securities, visit www.cnbc.com and select the "Bonds" link under the "Markets" tab.

Figure 9.3 is a Bloomberg screen that reports quotes for some Treasury bills. The maturity of each bill issue is shown in the left-most column. The two columns following the maturity give the discount yield on a bid and ask basis for each bill. The bid discount is used to calculate the dollar amount that Treasury bill dealers are willing to pay for that Treasury bill. The ask discount is used to calculate the dollar amount that dealers will accept to sell a Treasury bill. The column immediately left of the graph shows the change in the ask discount yield from the previous day.

For example, consider the bill that matures on June 30, 2022. This bill has a bid discount rate of .202 percent and an ask discount rate of .190 percent. The Bloomberg screen is from January 24, 2022. Thus, this bill matures in 157 days. For a $1 million face value Treasury bill, the corresponding bid and ask prices can be calculated by using the discount yields shown, along with our bank discount basis pricing formula. For example, the bid price would be:

FIGURE 9.3

U.S. Treasury Bills

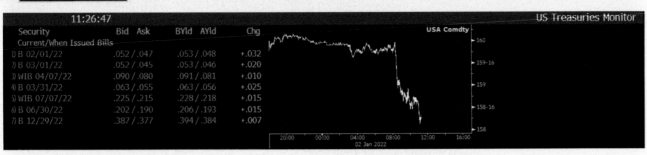

Security	Bid Ask	BYld AYld	Chg
Current/When Issued Bills			
1) B 02/01/22	.052 / .047	.053 / .048	+.032
2) B 03/01/22	.052 / .045	.053 / .046	+.020
3) WIB 04/07/22	.090 / .080	.091 / .081	+.010
4) B 03/31/22	.063 / .055	.063 / .056	+.025
5) WIB 07/07/22	.225 / .215	.228 / .218	+.015
6) B 06/30/22	.202 / .190	.206 / .193	+.015
7) B 12/29/22	.387 / .377	.394 / .384	+.007

Source: Bloomberg Finance L.P.

$$\text{Bid price} = \$999,119.06 = \$1,000,000 \times \left(1 - \frac{157}{360} \times .00202\right)$$

Check that the ask price would be \$999,171.39. As we would expect, the ask price is greater than the bid price. This difference, or spread, is the compensation dealers make for a "round-trip" transaction. Dealers sell at the ask price and buy at the bid price.

EXAMPLE 9.3

T-Bill Prices

Suppose you wanted to buy a T-bill with 85 days to maturity and a face value of \$5,000,000. How much would you have to pay if the ask discount is 3.41 percent?

Because you are buying, you must pay the ask price. To calculate the ask price, we use the ask discount in the bank discount basis formula:

$$\text{Ask price} = \$4,959,743.06 = \$5,000,000 \times \left(1 - \frac{85}{360} \times .0341\right)$$

Treasury bill prices may be calculated using a built-in spreadsheet function. An example of how to use an Excel™ spreadsheet to calculate a Treasury bill price is shown in the nearby *Spreadsheet Analysis* box.

SPREADSHEET ANALYSIS

	A	B	C	D	E	F	G	H
1								
2			**Treasury Bill Price and Yield Calculations**					
3								
4	A Treasury bill traded on May 16, 2022, pays \$100 on August 15, 2022. Assuming							
5	a discount rate of 2.65 percent, what are its price and bond equivalent yield?							
6	*Hint:* Use the Excel functions TBILLPRICE and TBILLEQ.							
7								
8		\$99.3301	=TBILLPRICE("5/16/2022","8/15/2022",0.0265)					
9								
10		2.705%	=TBILLEQ("5/16/2022","8/15/2022",0.0265)					
11								
12								
13	A credit card charges a nominal annual interest rate of 15 percent. With interest							
14	charged monthly, what is the effective annual rate (EAR) on this credit card?							
15	*Hint:* Use the Excel function EFFECT							
16								
17		16.075%	=EFFECT(0.15,12)					
18								

Source: Microsoft.

There are two columns in Figure 9.3 that list the corresponding bid and ask bond equivalent yields. It is important to realize that the ask yield is not quoted on a discount basis. Unlike a discount rate, a bond equivalent yield assumes a 365-day calendar year. Bond equivalent yields are principally used to compare yields on Treasury bills with yields on other money market instruments as well as Treasury bonds and other bonds (we discuss these long-term yields in another chapter).

BANK DISCOUNT YIELDS VERSUS BOND EQUIVALENT YIELDS

A bank discount yield is converted to a bond equivalent yield using the following formula:

$$\text{Bond equivalent yield} = \frac{365 \times \text{Discount yield}}{360 - \text{Days to maturity} \times \text{Discount yield}} \qquad (9.5)$$

This conversion formula is correct for maturities of six months or less. Calculation of bond equivalent yields for maturities greater than six months is a little more complicated, and we will not discuss it here, particularly because T-bills with maturities greater than six months are less common.

For example, suppose the ask discount rate on a T-bill with 170 days to maturity is 3.22 percent. What is the bond equivalent yield? Plugging into the conversion formula, a 3.22 percent discount is converted into a bond equivalent yield as follows:

$$.03315 = \frac{365 \times .0322}{360 - 170 \times .0322}$$

The bond equivalent yield is thus 3.315 percent.

EXAMPLE 9.4 | **Bond Equivalent Yields**

Suppose a T-bill has 45 days to maturity and an ask discount of 5 percent. What is the bond equivalent yield?

Using the bond equivalent yield conversion formula, we have:

$$.05101 = \frac{365 \times .05}{360 - 45 \times .05}$$

The bond equivalent yield is thus 5.101 percent.

Bond equivalent yields may be calculated using a built-in spreadsheet function. An example of how to use an Excel™ spreadsheet to calculate a bond equivalent yield is shown in the nearby *Spreadsheet Analysis* box.

One common cause of confusion about bond equivalent yield calculations is the way that leap years are handled. The rule is that we must use 366 days if February 29 occurs within the next 12 months. For example, 2024 is a leap year. So, beginning on March 1, 2023, we must use 366 days in the numerator of Equation 9.6. Then, beginning on March 1, 2024, we must revert to using 365 days.

EXAMPLE 9.5 | **Back to the Future: Leap Year Bond Equivalent Yields**

Calculate the ask yield (bond equivalent yield) for a T-bill price quoted in December 2023 with 119 days to maturity and an ask discount of 5.41 percent.

Because the 12-month period following the date of the price quote includes February 29, 2024, we must use 366 days. Plugging this into the conversion formula, we get:

$$.0560 = \frac{366 \times .0541}{360 - 119 \times .0541}$$

Therefore, 5.60 percent is the ask yield stated as a bond equivalent yield.

We can calculate a Treasury bill ask price using the ask(ed) yield, which is a bond equivalent yield, as follows:

$$\text{Bill price} = \frac{\text{Face value}}{1 + \text{Bond equivalent yield} \times \text{Days to maturity}/365} \qquad (9.6)$$

For example, we have calculated the 3.315 percent bond equivalent yield on a T-bill with 170 days to maturity and a 3.22 percent ask discount rate. If we calculate its price using this bond equivalent yield, we get:

$$\$984,794 = \frac{\$1,000,000}{1 + .03315 \times 170/365}$$

Check that, ignoring a small rounding error, you get the same price using the bank discount formula.

BOND EQUIVALENT YIELDS, APRs, AND EARs

Money market rates not quoted on a discount basis are generally quoted on a "simple" interest basis. Simple interest rates are calculated just like the annual percentage rate (APR) on a consumer loan. So, for the most part, money market rates are either bank discount rates or APRs. For example, CD rates are APRs.

In fact, the bond equivalent yield on a T-bill with less than six months to maturity is also an APR. As a result, like any APR, it understates the true interest rate, which is usually called the *effective annual rate,* or EAR. In the context of the money market, EARs are sometimes referred to as effective annual yields, effective yields, or annualized yields. Whatever it is called, to find out what a T-bill, or any other money market instrument, is really going to pay you, yet another conversion is needed. We will get to the needed conversion in a moment.

First, however, recall that an APR is equal to the interest rate per period multiplied by the number of periods in a year. For example, if the rate on a car loan is 1 percent per month, then the APR is 1 percent × 12 = 12 percent. In general, if we let *m* be the number of periods in a year, an APR is converted to an EAR as follows:

$$1 + EAR = \left(1 + \frac{APR}{m}\right)^m \qquad (9.7)$$

For example, on our 12 percent APR car loan, the EAR can be determined by:

$$1 + EAR = \left(1 + \frac{.12}{12}\right)^{12}$$
$$= 1.01^{12}$$
$$= 1.126825$$
$$EAR = .126825, \text{ or } 12.6825\%$$

Thus, the rate on the car loan is really 12.6825 percent per year.

EXAMPLE 9.6 | **APRs and EARs**

A typical credit card may quote an APR of 18 percent. On closer inspection, you will find that the rate is actually 1.5 percent per month. What annual interest rate are you really paying on such a credit card?

With 12 periods in a year, an APR of 18 percent is converted to an EAR as follows:

$$1 + EAR = \left(1 + \frac{.18}{12}\right)^{12}$$
$$= 1.015^{12}$$
$$= 1.1956$$
$$EAR = .1956, \text{ or } 19.56\%$$

Thus, the rate on this credit card is really 19.56 percent per year.

Effective annual rates may be calculated using a built-in spreadsheet function. An example of how to use an Excel™ spreadsheet to calculate an effective annual rate is shown in the previous *Spreadsheet Analysis* box.

Now, to see that the bond equivalent yield on a T-bill is just an APR, we can first calculate the price on the bill we considered earlier (3.22 percent ask discount, 170 days to maturity). Using the bank discount formula, the ask price for $1 million in face value is:

$$\text{Ask price} = \$984{,}794 = \$1{,}000{,}000 \times \left(1 - \frac{170}{360} \times .0322 \right)$$

The discount is $15,206. Thus, on this 170-day investment, you earn $15,206 in interest on an investment of $984,794. On a percentage basis, you earned:

$$\frac{\$15{,}206}{\$984{,}794} = .01544, \text{ or } 1.544\%$$

In a 365-day year, there are $365/170 = 2.147$ periods of 170-day length. So, if we multiply what you earned over the 170-day period by the number of 170-day periods in a year, we get:

$$2.147 \times 1.544\% = .03315, \text{ or } 3.315\%$$

This is the bond equivalent yield we calculated earlier.

Finally, for this T-bill, we can calculate the EAR using this 3.315 percent:

$$1 + EAR = \left(1 + \frac{.03315}{2.147} \right)^{2.147}$$
$$= 1.03345$$
$$EAR = .03345, \text{ or } 3.345\%$$

In the end, we have three different rates for this simple T-bill. The last one, the EAR, finally tells us what we really want to know: What rate are we actually going to earn on a compounded basis?

EXAMPLE 9.7 | **Discounts, APRs, and EARs**

A money market instrument with 60 days to maturity has a quoted ask price of 99, meaning $99 per $100 face value. What are the banker's discount yield, the bond equivalent yield, and the effective annual return?

First, to get the discount yield, we have to use the bank discount formula and solve for the discount yield:

$$\$99 = \$100 \times \left(1 - \frac{60}{360} \times \text{Discount yield} \right)$$

With a little algebra, we see that the discount yield is 6 percent.

We convert this to a bond equivalent yield as follows:

$$\frac{365 \times .06}{360 - 60 \times .06} = .06145, \text{ or } 6.145\%$$

The bond equivalent yield is thus 6.145 percent.

Finally, to get the EAR, note that there are $365/60 = 6.0833$ sixty-day periods in a year, so:

$$1 + EAR = \left(1 + \frac{.06145}{6.0833} \right)^{6.0833}$$

$$= 1.06305$$

$$EAR = .06305, \text{ or } 6.305\%$$

This example illustrates the general result that the discount yield is lower than the bond equivalent yield, which in turn is less than the EAR.

9.2a What are the three different types of interest rate quotes that are important for money market instruments?

9.2b How are T-bill rates quoted? How are CD rates quoted?

9.2c Of the three different types of interest rate quotes, which is the largest? Which is the smallest? Which is the most relevant?

9.3 Rates and Yields on Fixed-Income Securities

Related Bloomberg Functions

GC3D	Graph Curve Surface
GIY	Intraday Yield Curve
YAS	Yield and Spread Analysis
XLTP XYAS	Excel Template: Price/Yield/Spread Calculator

For more information on fixed-income securities, visit www.sifma.org.

For the latest U.S. Treasury rates, check www.bloomberg.com.

Treasury yield curve
A graph of Treasury yields plotted against maturities.

Thus far, we have focused on short-term interest rates, where "short term" means one year or less. Of course, these are not the only interest rates we are interested in, so we now begin to discuss longer-term rates by looking at fixed-income securities. To keep this discussion to a manageable length, we defer the details of how some longer-term rates are computed to another chapter.

Fixed-income securities include long-term debt contracts from a wide variety of issuers. The largest single category of fixed-income securities is debt issued by the U.S. government. The second largest category of fixed-income securities is mortgage debt issued to finance real estate purchases. The two other large categories of fixed-income securities are debt issued by corporations and debt issued by municipal governments. Each of these categories represents several trillion dollars of outstanding debt. Corporate bonds and municipal government bonds are covered in a later chapter.

Because of its sheer size, the leading world market for debt securities is the market for U.S. Treasury securities. Interest rates for U.S. Treasury debt are closely watched throughout the world, and daily reports can be found in most major newspapers.

THE TREASURY YIELD CURVE

The **Treasury yield curve** is a plot of Treasury yields against maturities. Yields are measured along the vertical axis, and maturities are measured along the horizontal axis. The Treasury yield curve is fundamental to bond market analysis because it represents the interest rates that financial markets are charging to the world's largest debtor with the world's highest credit rating—the U.S. government. In essence, the Treasury yield curve represents interest rates for default-free lending across the maturity spectrum. As such, almost all other domestic interest rates are determined with respect to U.S. Treasury interest rates. A *Work the Web* box in this section shows what a yield curve looks like.

The yield curve is also considered by some to have predictive power. In particular, if the yield curve is upward sloping, the expectation is that yields will be higher in the future. If the yield curve is downward sloping, the expectation is that yields will be lower in the future. A downward-sloping yield curve is also called an *inverted yield curve*. Because lower interest rates are generally associated with recessionary conditions, some market watchers view an inverted curve as a negative signal. The nearby *Investment Updates* box provides some historical examples of various yield curve shapes.

The difference in yields across various maturities is also important for investors in certain industries. For example, the 2-10 spread, which is the difference in yield between 2-year and 10-year notes, is critically important for investors in banking firms. Banks typically borrow money at shorter-term rates and lend at longer-term rates. So, a larger spread is generally good for bank profit margins and, therefore, good for the prices of banking stocks.

RATES ON GLOBAL FIXED-INCOME INVESTMENTS

Figure 9.4 is a Bloomberg screen that shows interest rates on government bonds that all mature in about 10 years. Current interest rates and the highest and lowest interest rates over the previous 52-week period are reported. Note that the current interest rates range from a low of .013 percent in the Netherlands to 4.504 percent in Brazil.

WORK THE WEB

What does the current Treasury yield curve look like? You can find the answer on the web in many different places, including treasury.gov, where you can get daily data for yield curves. Here is a Bloomberg screen showing the U.S. Treasury yield curve, along with what the yield curve looked like one week ago and one month ago. Despite its appearance, this yield curve would be considered relatively flat compared to historic yield curves. Note that the shortest-term rates are close to zero percent, and the six-month rate is only about 1.50 percent. Here's a question for you: What is the yield premium for the 20-year over the 5-year?

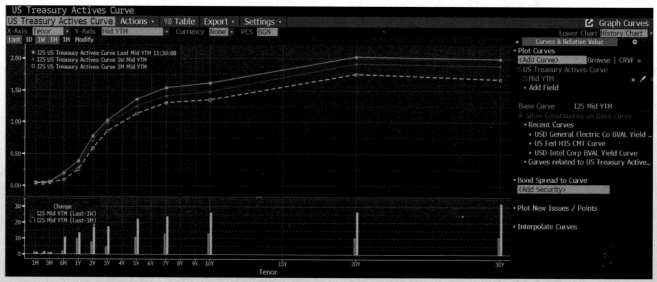

Source: Bloomberg Finance L.P.

FIGURE 9.4

Tracking Bond Benchmarks

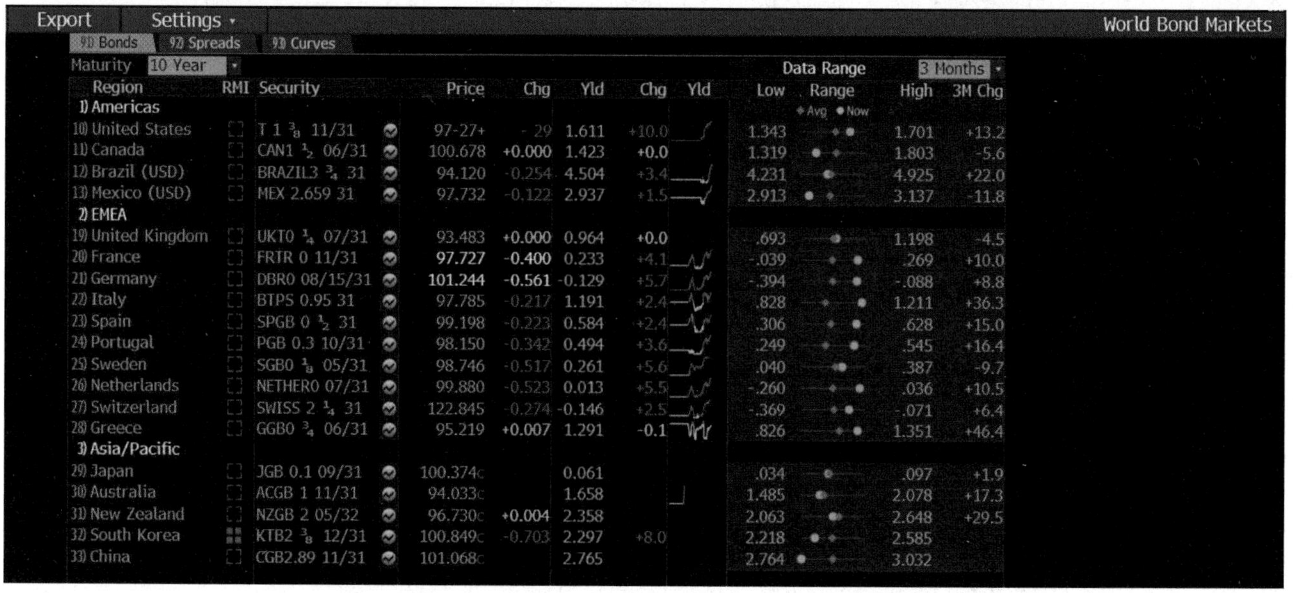

Region	RMI	Security	Price	Chg	Yld	Chg Yld	Low	Range Avg ◆ Now	High	3M Chg
1) Americas										
10) United States		T 1 ⅜ 11/31	97-27+	- 29	1.611	+10.0	1.343		1.701	+13.2
11) Canada		CAN1 ½ 06/31	100.678	+0.000	1.423	+0.0	1.319		1.803	-5.6
12) Brazil (USD)		BRAZIL3 ¾ 31	94.120	-0.254	4.504	+3.4	4.231		4.925	+22.0
13) Mexico (USD)		MEX 2.659 31	97.732	-0.122	2.937	+1.5	2.913		3.137	-11.8
2) EMEA										
19) United Kingdom		UKTO ¼ 07/31	93.483	+0.000	0.964	+0.0	.693		1.198	-4.5
20) France		FRTR 0 11/31	97.727	-0.400	0.233	+4.1	.039		.269	+10.0
21) Germany		DBR0 08/15/31	101.244	-0.561	-0.129	+5.7	-.394		-.088	+8.8
22) Italy		BTPS 0.95 31	97.785	-0.217	1.191	+2.4	.828		1.211	+36.3
23) Spain		SPGB 0 ½ 31	99.198	-0.223	0.584	+2.4	.306		.628	+15.0
24) Portugal		PGB 0.3 10/31	98.150	-0.342	0.494	+3.6	.249		.545	+16.4
25) Sweden		SGB0 ⅛ 05/31	98.746	-0.517	0.261	+5.6	.040		.387	-9.7
26) Netherlands		NETHER0 07/31	99.880	-0.523	0.013	+5.5	-.260		.036	+10.5
27) Switzerland		SWISS 2 ¼ 31	122.845	-0.274	-0.146	+2.5	-.369		.071	+6.4
28) Greece		GGB0 ¾ 06/31	95.219	+0.007	1.291	-0.1	.826		1.351	+46.4
3) Asia/Pacific										
29) Japan		JGB 0.1 09/31	100.374c		0.061		.034		.097	+1.9
30) Australia		ACGB 1 11/31	94.033c		1.658		1.485		2.078	+17.3
31) New Zealand		NZGB 2 05/32	96.730c	+0.004	2.358		2.063		2.648	+29.5
32) South Korea		KTB2 ⅜ 12/31	100.849c	-0.703	2.297	+8.0	2.218		2.585	
33) China		CGB2.89 11/31	101.068c		2.765		2.764		3.032	

Export   Settings ▾

9) Bonds   92) Spreads   93) Curves

Maturity 10 Year ▾

Data Range 3 Months ▾

World Bond Markets

Source: Bloomberg Finance L.P.

The yield range above omits the negative yields in Germany and Switzerland. Why? Well, generally, when you buy a bond, you expect to get back more money in the future than you invested today. Recently, however, some government bonds have had a negative yield to maturity. For example, in August 2019, the German government sold 30-year bonds that had a

YIELD CURVES 101

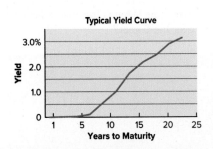

Typical Yield Curve

The yield curve illustrates the prevailing yields on Treasury securities across different maturities. The maturities span from shorter term debt in the range of 1 to 3 months, to longer term debt with a 30 year maturity. In a typical yield curve, longer term rates are higher than shorter term rates. This curve is associated with a generally optimistic view of the economy.

Other Yield Curve Shapes

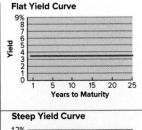

Flat Yield Curve

A flat yield curve indicates that yields are about the same for bonds of all maturities. Some investors view this as a "goldilocks" scenario, while others see it as signifying uncertainty.

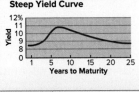

Steep Yield Curve

A steep yield curve indicates that longer term yields are significantly higher than shorter term yields. This shape is often associated with a perceived recovery from a recession.

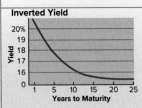

Inverted Yield

An inverted yield curve indicates that longer term yields are lower than shorter term yields. This unusual situation is viewed as a sign of a potential recession.

Source: Ben Levisohn, *The Wall Street Journal*, November 27, 2010, Dow Jones & Company, Inc.

yield of negative .11 percent. Investors bought €824 million of these bonds, yet would only get back €795 million in 2050.

Note that a negative yield does not mean that the investor has to pay money to the borrower. A negative yield means that the bond price today is so high that even with coupon payments over the life of the bond, investors will not make a profit when they get their principal back at maturity. Will we see negative yields in the U.S. bond markets? Time will tell.

Although Figure 9.4 does not show yields for them, a variety of government agencies borrow money in financial markets. The Tennessee Valley Authority (TVA) is an example of such an agency. In recent years, U.S. government agencies have issued debt with maturities as long as 50 years. U.S. government agency debt does not carry the same credit guarantee as U.S. Treasury debt, and therefore interest rates on agency debt reflect a premium over interest rates on Treasury debt. Also, agency securities are often subject to state taxes, whereas Treasury securities are not.

As we discussed earlier in the chapter, the Federal Home Loan Mortgage Corporation (FHLMC), or Freddie Mac, and the Federal National Mortgage Association (FNMA), or Fannie Mae, are government-sponsored agencies that repackage home mortgages into mortgage pools, where each pool represents several tens of millions of dollars of home mortgages. A third agency, the Government National Mortgage Association (GNMA), better known as "Ginnie Mae," is also an active mortgage repackager.

"Tax-exempts" are bonds issued by municipal governments. Coupon interest payments on most municipal bonds are exempt from federal income taxes, and they are often exempt from state income taxes too.

Municipal bonds are generally classified as either general obligation bonds or revenue bonds. General obligation bonds are secured by the general taxing power of the issuing municipality. Revenue bonds are secured by revenues generated from specific projects, such as toll roads, airports, or user fees for services. Because of their tax-exempt status, interest rates on high-quality municipal bonds are generally lower than interest rates on comparable

U.S. Treasury securities. Exceptions, however, can occur. Municipal governments can declare bankruptcy. So, in cases of distress, the yields on municipals will likely exceed the yields of comparable U.S. Treasury securities.

CHECK THIS

9.3a What is the yield curve? Why is it important?

9.3b Why are corporate bond yields higher than Treasury bond yields?

9.3c Why are municipal bond yields lower than Treasury bond yields?

9.4 The Term Structure of Interest Rates

Related Bloomberg Functions

BYFC Bond Yield Forecast

USD U.S. Treasuries Monitor

term structure of interest rates
Relationship between time to maturity and interest rates for default-free, pure discount instruments.

The yield curve tells us the relationship between Treasury bond yields and time to maturity. The **term structure of interest rates** (or just "term structure") is a similar, but not identical, relationship. Recall that a pure discount instrument has a single payment of face value at maturity with no other payments until then. Treasury bonds are not pure discount instruments because they pay coupons every six months. Pure discount instruments with more than a year to maturity are often called "zero coupon bonds," or just "zeroes," because they are, in effect, bonds with a zero coupon rate.

The term structure of interest rates is the relationship between time to maturity and interest rates for default-free, pure discount instruments. So, the difference between the yield curve and the term structure is that the yield curve is based on coupon bonds, whereas the term structure is based on pure discount instruments. The term structure is sometimes called the "zero coupon yield curve" to distinguish it from the Treasury yield curve.

TREASURY STRIPS

U.S. Treasury STRIPS
Pure discount securities created by stripping coupons and principal payments of Treasury notes and bonds. *STRIPS* stands for Separate Trading of Registered Interest and Principal of Securities.

Until about 1987, the term structure of interest rates was not directly observable because default-free, pure discount instruments with maturities greater than one year did not exist or reliable data on them were not available. Today, however, the term structure of interest rates can be easily seen by examining yields on **U.S. Treasury STRIPS**.

STRIPS are pure discount instruments created by "stripping" the coupons and principal payments of U.S. Treasury notes and bonds into separate parts and then selling the parts separately. The term *STRIPS* stands for Separate Trading of Registered Interest and Principal of Securities. For example, a Treasury note with 10 years to maturity will make 20 semiannual coupon payments during its life and will also make a principal payment at maturity. This note can therefore be separated, or stripped, into 21 separate parts, and each part can be bought and sold separately. The Treasury originally allowed notes and bonds with 10 years or more to maturity (at the time they were issued) to be stripped. Today, any note or bond is strippable.

Read more about STRIPS at www.treasurydirect.gov by selecting "Financial Institutions," then "Treasury Marketable Securities."

Figure 9.5 is a sample U.S. Treasury STRIPS intraday price report of individual STRIPS bid and ask yields from Bloomberg. STRIPS can be created from a coupon payment, a Treasury bond principal payment, or a Treasury note principal payment. Figure 9.5 shows some STRIPS quotes for coupons and one quote from Treasury bond principal payment. Of course, Figure 9.5 contains only a partial list of all available STRIPS.

The first column of Figure 9.5 gives the maturity of each STRIPS listed. The next two columns contain bid and ask yield to maturity for each STRIPS. Given a maturity and these yields, you can calculate bid and ask prices. As always, the bid price is the price dealers will pay to buy the STRIPS, and the ask price is the price dealers will accept to sell the STRIPS. The fourth column in Figure 9.5 reports the change in the ask yield from the previous day.

STRIPS prices are stated as a price per $100 of face value. In the very recent past, STRIPS prices were quoted in dollars and thirty-seconds of a dollar. That is, a quote of, say, 84:08 stood for 84 and 8/32 of a dollar, or $84.25. Today, however, STRIPS prices are quoted to three decimal points. For example, suppose a coupon interest STRIPS has an ask price quote

FIGURE 9.5   Treasury STRIPS

11:32	Outright	Switch	Bfly									

4) Actives	5) Bills	6) Notes	7) TIPS	8) Strips	9) Sprds	10) Curves	11) FRN	12) Bfly	13) WI

21) S/0-5	22) S/5-10	23) S/10-15	24) S/15-20	25) S/20-25	26) S/25-30

Coupon Strips				Principal Strips		
31) S 8/31	1.756 / 1.701	+0.102		52)	/	
32) S N/31	1.773 / 1.718	+0.102		53)	/	
33) S 2/32	1.786 / 1.737	+0.101		54)	/	
34) S 5/32	1.797 / 1.749	+0.101		55)	/	
35) S 8/32	1.816 / 1.767	+0.103		56)	/	
36) S N/32	1.830 / 1.780	+0.100		57)	/	
37) S 2/33	1.848 / 1.796	+0.103		58)	/	
38) S 5/33	1.859 / 1.808	+0.105		59)	/	
39) S 8/33	1.874 / 1.824	+0.105		60)	/	
40) S N/33	1.890 / 1.837	+0.106		61)	/	
41) S 2/34	1.903 / 1.852	+0.101		62)	/	
42) S 5/34	**1.914** / **1.865**	+0.107		63)	/	
43) S 8/34	1.926 / 1.877	+0.104		64)	/	
44) S 5/35	1.947 / 1.895	+0.109		65)	/	
45) S 2/35	1.956 / 1.906	+0.104		66)	/	
46) S 5/35	1.970 / 1.916	+0.107		67)	/	
47) S 8/35	1.981 / 1.929	+0.106		68)	/	
48) S N/35	1.986 / 1.931	+0.104		69)	/	
49) S 2/36	1.999 / 1.948	+0.105		70) SP 2/36	1.648 / 1.602	+0.089
50) S 2/36	1.648 / 1.602	+0.089		71)	/	
51) S 5/36	2.011 / 1.956	+0.106		72)	/	

of 93.668. This means that the price per $100 face value is $93.668. Thus, the skill of being able to divide by 32 is no longer highly valued, at least in STRIPS trading.

YIELDS FOR U.S. TREASURY STRIPS

An ask yield for a U.S. Treasury STRIPS is an APR (APRs were discussed earlier in this chapter). It is calculated as two times the true semiannual rate. Calculation of the yield on a STRIPS is a standard time value of money calculation. The price today of the STRIPS is the *present value;* the face value received at maturity is the *future value.* As shown in Example 9.1, the relationship between present value and future value is:

$$\text{Present value} = \frac{\text{Future value}}{(1 + r)^N}$$

In this equation, r is the rate per period and N is the number of periods. Notice that a period is not necessarily one year long. For Treasury STRIPS, the number of periods is two times the number of years to maturity, here denoted by $2M$, and the interest rate is the "yield to maturity" (*YTM*) divided by 2:

$$\text{STRIPS price} = \frac{\text{Face value}}{(1 + YTM/2)^{2M}} \tag{9.8}$$

Consider the 5/34 STRIPS that has an ask yield quote of 1.865. Another Bloomberg screen confirms that this STRIPS matures on 5/15/2034. At the time of the ask yield quote, assume that there are 12.5 years to maturity. The semiannual rate is 1.865%/2 = .9325%. Also, 12.5 years to maturity converts to 2 × 12.5 = 25 semiannual periods. To calculate the ask price, we plug in the future value, the rate per period, and the number of periods:

$$\text{STRIPS price} = \frac{\$100}{(1 + .009325)^{25}}$$
$$= 79.29$$

In this case, the purchaser pays $79.29 per $100 of face value for the STRIPS. You should verify that the bid price of this same STRIPS is $78.81 which, of course, is lower than the ask price.

If we need to go the other way and calculate the ask yield on a STRIPS given its price, we can rearrange the basic present value equation to solve it for r:

$$r = \left(\frac{\text{Future value}}{\text{Present value}}\right)^{1/N} - 1$$

For STRIPS, $N = 2M$ is the number of semiannual periods and $r = YTM/2$ is the semiannual interest rate, so the formula is:

$$YTM = 2 \times \left[\left(\frac{\text{Face value}}{\text{STRIPS price}}\right)^{1/2M} - 1\right] \qquad (9.9)$$

Consider a STRIPS maturing in six years with an ask price of 73.031. Its yield to maturity of 5.3072 percent is calculated immediately below and would be reported as 5.31 percent.

$$.053073 = 2 \times \left[\left(\frac{100}{73.031}\right)^{1/12} - 1\right]$$

As another example, consider a STRIPS maturing in 20 years with an ask price of 26.188. As calculated immediately below, its yield to maturity of 6.8128 percent would be reported as 6.81 percent.

$$.068128 = 2 \times \left[\left(\frac{100}{26.188}\right)^{1/40} - 1\right]$$

Of course, if you know how to use a financial calculator, finding the price or yield for a STRIPS bond is much easier than doing all these calculations by hand. Make sure you remember to set the payment to zero.

CHECK THIS

9.4a   What is the yield to maturity (YTM) on a STRIPS maturing in five years if its ask price quote is 77.75?

9.4b   What is the YTM of a STRIPS maturing in 15 years if its ask price quote is 36.813?

9.4c   What is the YTM of a STRIPS maturing in 25 years if its ask price quote is 18.656?

9.5 Nominal versus Real Interest Rates

Related Bloomberg Functions

WBI   World Inflation Bonds

There is a fundamental distinction between *nominal* and *real* interest rates. **Nominal interest rates** are interest rates as we ordinarily observe them; for example, as they are reported in *The Wall Street Journal* and elsewhere. All the money market rates we discussed earlier in this chapter, as well as the STRIPS yields, are nominal rates.

REAL INTEREST RATES

nominal interest rates
Interest rates as they are normally observed and quoted, with no adjustment for inflation.

real interest rates
Interest rates adjusted for the effect of inflation, calculated as the nominal rate less the rate of inflation.

Real interest rates are nominal rates adjusted for the effects of price inflation. To obtain a real interest rate, subtract an inflation rate from a nominal interest rate:

$$\text{Real interest rate} = \text{Nominal interest rate} - \text{Inflation rate} \qquad (9.10)$$

The real interest rate is thus named because it measures the real change in the purchasing power of an investment. For example, if the nominal interest rate for a one-year certificate of deposit is 7 percent, then a one-year deposit of $100,000 will grow to $107,000. But if the inflation rate over the same year is 4 percent, you would need $104,000 after one year passes

FIGURE 9.6

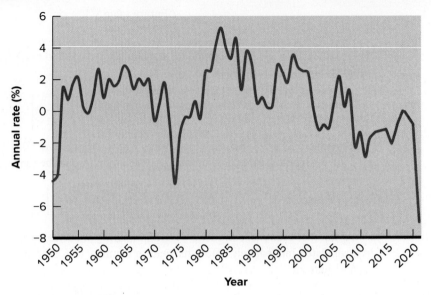

Source: Federal Reserve Bank of St. Louis, *SBBI Yearbook* 2022 (Kroll LLC), and author calculations.

to buy what costs $100,000 today. Thus, the real increase in purchasing power for your investment is only $3,000, and, therefore, the real interest rate is only 3 percent.

Figure 9.6 displays real interest rates based on the annual rates of return on U.S. Treasury bills and the inflation rates over the 72-year period 1950 through 2021. As shown in Figure 9.6, following a negative spike at the beginning of the Korean War in 1950, real interest rates for Treasury bills were generally positive until the oil embargo by the Organization of the Petroleum Exporting Countries (OPEC) in 1973. After this, real rates were generally negative until the Federal Reserve Board initiated a tight-money policy to fight an inflationary spiral in the late 1970s. The tight-money policy caused the 1980s to begin with historically high real interest rates. Throughout the 1980s, real Treasury bill rates were falling as inflation subsided. Real rates most recently went negative following the Crash of 2008 and the "flight to quality" that followed. Real rates, however, have been negative since the onset of the COVID-19 pandemic. During this 72-year period, the average real Treasury bill interest rate was slightly less than 1 percent.

THE FISHER HYPOTHESIS

Fisher hypothesis
Assertion that the general level of nominal interest rates follows the general level of inflation.

The relationship between nominal interest rates and the rate of inflation is often couched in terms of the *Fisher hypothesis,* which is named for economist Irving Fisher, who formally proposed it in 1930. The **Fisher hypothesis** asserts that the general level of nominal interest rates follows the general level of inflation.

According to the Fisher hypothesis, interest rates are on average higher than the rate of inflation. Therefore, it logically follows that short-term interest rates reflect current inflation, whereas long-term interest rates reflect investor expectations of future inflation. Figure 9.7 graphs nominal interest rates and inflation rates used to create Figure 9.6. Notice that when inflation rates were high, Treasury bill returns tended to be high also, as predicted by the Fisher hypothesis. Recently, you can see how inflation has greatly outpaced the nominal T-bill rate.

INFLATION-INDEXED TREASURY SECURITIES

In recent years, the U.S. Treasury has issued securities that guarantee a fixed rate of return in excess of realized inflation rates. These inflation-indexed Treasury securities (TIPS) pay a fixed coupon rate on their current principal and adjust their principal semiannually according

INVESTMENT UPDATES

SHOULD I PUT ALL MY BOND MONEY INTO TIPS?

William Baldwin, Senior Contributor
Jan 15, 2022, 06:00am EST
© 2021 BLOOMBERG FINANCE LP

A reader asked "Last year I moved some of my 401(k) into the Vanguard Inflation Protected Securities fund and it earned 5.7% in 2021. The amount I have in Fidelity's U.S. Bond Index lost 1.8% last year. Do you think I should move all my bond money into the TIPS fund?"

Mr. William Baldwin answers that it's conceivable that 2022 will be another good year for TIPs. Conceivable, but not likely. He does not think it's a good idea to go whole hog into these bonds.

To make his case, he points out two things central to any portfolio decision. One is diversification: You need to diversify your inflation bets. The other thing is expected return.

Diversification comes naturally to equity investors. They know it's unwise to put all their money in one stock. Not so obvious is the diversification that should go into a portfolio of very high-grade bonds, that is, bonds that are extremely unlikely to go into default.

Many bond funds hold a heavy dose of U.S. government-guaranteed bonds. The big difference is in what inflation does to the returns from these funds. Unless the fund hold TIPS bonds, there is no inflation protection.

So TIPS must be the better bonds to own? Not so fast. Take a look at the interest coupons. The yield on the unprotected bond portfolio is a nominal yield and it comes to 1.7 percent. The yield on the TIPS is a real yield, which is nice, but it's a ridiculously low number: minus .9 percent.

Putting both numbers in nominal terms for comparison, we get the following. The average bond in the Fidelity portfolio, if held to maturity, will deliver 1.7 percent a year in interest. The average bond in the Vanguard TIPS portfolio, if held to maturity, will deliver interest of minus .9 percent plus the inflation adjustment. If inflation averages 2 percent, the TIPS bonds will deliver 1.1 percent in nominal terms.

If inflation averages more than 2.6 percent, the TIPS come out ahead. If inflation averages less than 2.6 percent, you'll wish you went for the unprotected bonds. You don't know what's going to happen to inflation. The wise course of action is to diversify your inflation bets.

With interest yields so low, why would anyone buy bonds? Not to make money. Bonds usually preserve capital during stock market crashes. They are like fire insurance. You don't expect to profit from fire insurance, but it makes sense to buy it.

To sum up: Move some, but not too much, of your unprotected bond fund into a TIPS fund, and don't expect wealth from bonds.

Source: William Baldwin, "Should I Put All My Bond Money into TIPS?," www.forbes.com, January 15, 2021.

| FIGURE 9.7 | Inflation Rates and T-Bill Rates, 1950 through 2021 |

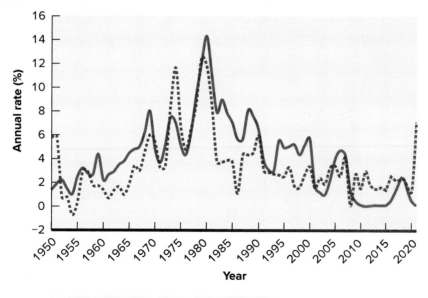

Source: Federal Reserve Bank of St. Louis and *SBBI Yearbook* 2022 (Kroll LLC).

to the most recent inflation rate. For investors wanting long-term protection against inflation along with the safety of U.S. Treasury bonds, inflation-indexed Treasury securities are perhaps the perfect investment.

For example, suppose an inflation-indexed note is issued with a coupon rate of 2 percent and an initial principal of $1,000. Six months later, the note will make a coupon payment based on the annual coupon rate of 2 percent. Before the coupon payment is determined, however, the principal is adjusted for inflation. Suppose the six-month inflation rate was 1.5 percent. To account for inflation, the note's principal is increased to $1,000 × 1.015 = $1,015. Thus, the coupon payment is $1,015 × 2%/2 = $10.15. Notice the inflation-adjusted coupon payment is $.15 higher than the coupon payment without an inflation adjustment. This inflation adjustment process continues throughout the note's life. At maturity, the investor receives the final adjusted (or accrued) principal amount. The investor, therefore, receives inflation-adjusted coupon payments throughout the life of the note and also receives an inflation-adjusted principal at maturity.

Figure 9.8 is a Bloomberg screen shot taken in May 2022 that shows details for one particular TIPS bond. This bond has a coupon rate of 2.375 percent and matures on January 15, 2025. In Figure 9.8, you can see the price of this bond is $108.59, with a bid price of 108-15 and an ask price of 108-22. The bid and ask quotes are in points and 32nds of a point. So, the bid price is 108 plus 15/32nds, which is $108.47.

The yield to maturity of this TIPS bond is quoted as 282.16 basis points below the yield of an ordinary bond that matures in about a year, May 18, 2023. The yield of that bond is 1.988, or 198.8 basis points. So, the yield of this TIPS bond is quoted as 198.8 − 282.16 = −83.36. The yield shown, −0.8335, is calculated without rounding.

We cover bond pricing in detail in another chapter. But to approximate the quoted yield, you can use the coupon rate of 2.375 percent and a face value of $100 to compute the semiannual coupon payments. The tricky part is calculating the time to maturity, which is about 967 days.

FIGURE 9.8 — Inflation-Indexed Treasury Securities

108-15+/108-22	-0.797/-0.870	BGN @ 12:15	⬚No Notes	95) Buy	96) Sell
1) Yield & Spread	2) Graphs	3) Pricing	4) Description	5) Custom	6) Yields

TII 2 ⅜ 01/15/25 (912810FR4)

				Economic Factors		
Spread	-282.16 bp	vs	1y B 0 05/18/23 ▾	Base CPI Value	07/15/2004	188.49677
Price	108.585938	⟳	1.9325 12:23:48	Reference CPI Value	05/25/2022	286.64865
Yield	-0.833541 Wst ▾		1.988044 Conv ▾	CPURNSA <INDEX>	03/22	287.50400
Wkout	01/15/2025 @ 100.00	Duration	Yld 6 6	CPURNSA <INDEX>	02/22	283.71600
Settle	05/25/22 ▣		05/25/22 ▣	CPI @ Last CPN Date		277.20274
				Flat Index Ratio		1.47060
				Accrued Ratio Growth		0.05011
Street Real Yield			-0.833541	Index Ratio		1.52071
Treasury Yield Equivalent			-0.833610	**Invoice**		
				Index Ratio		1.52071000
Inflation Assumption | SWIL »			8.3917 %	Face		1,000 M
Yield w/Inflation Assumption			7.364164	Principal		1,651,277.21
				Accrued (130 Days)		12,970.14
Real Cpn Accrued Int			0.852901	Total (USD)		1,664,247.35

Sensitivity Analysis

Yield-Beta Assumption	0.500	1.000
Effective Duration	1.282	2.565
Risk	2.134	4.269
Convexity	0.020	0.080

That number of days is about 2.65 years, or about 5.3 six-month periods. These inputs results in a yield to maturity of −.8231, which is pretty close to what is shown in Figure 9.8.

If you are a careful reader, however, you will say, "Hold your horses! That face value is incorrect and so are the semiannual coupon payments." The careful reader is correct. From the screen shot, notice that the principal is $166.42 per $100. This value will change with inflation until the bond matures. At that time, the bond holder receives the final accrued principal amount. As we discuss above, the periodic coupon payments also vary as inflation changes over time.

CHECK THIS

9.5a What is the difference between a nominal interest rate and a real interest rate?

9.5b What does the Fisher hypothesis assert?

9.5c What is the distinguishing feature of inflation-indexed Treasury securities?

(9.6) Traditional Theories of the Term Structure

Yield curves have been studied by financial economists for well over a century. During this period, a number of different theories have been proposed to explain why yield curves may be upward sloping at one point in time and then downward sloping or flat at another. We discuss three of the most popular traditional theories of the term structure in this section. We then present a modern perspective on the term structure in the following section.

Related Bloomberg Functions

ILBE World Inflation Breakeven Rates

EXPECTATIONS THEORY

expectations theory
The term structure of interest rates is a reflection of financial market beliefs regarding future interest rates.

According to the **expectations theory** of the term structure of interest rates, the shape of a yield curve expresses financial market expectations regarding future interest rates. Essentially, an upward-sloping yield curve predicts an increase in interest rates, and a downward-sloping yield curve predicts a decrease in interest rates. A flat yield curve expresses the sentiment that interest rates are not expected to change in the near future.

EXPECTATIONS AND FORWARD RATES The basic principles of the expectations theory can be explained with a two-period example. Let r_1 stand for the current market interest rate on a one-year investment and let r_2 be the current market interest rate on a two-year investment. Also, let $r_{1,1}$ be the market interest rate on a one-year investment that will be available in one year. Of course, this rate is not known today.

For a two-year investment, you have two strategies available. First, you can invest for two years at the rate r_2. In this case, $1 invested today will become $(1 + r_2)^2$ in two years. For example, if $r_2 = 10$ percent, you would have $1 \times (1 + .10)^2 = 1.21 in two years for every dollar you invest.

Alternatively, you can invest for one year at the rate r_1, and at the end of one year, you can reinvest the proceeds at the rate $r_{1,1}$. In this case, $1 invested today will become $(1 + r_1)(1 + r_{1,1})$ in two years. For example, suppose $r_1 = 10$ percent, and after a year passes, it turns out that $r_{1,1} = 8$ percent. Then you would end up with $1 \times 1.10 \times 1.08 = 1.19. Alternatively, suppose that after a year passes, it turns out that $r_{1,1} = 12$ percent; then you would have $1 \times 1.10 \times 1.12 = 1.23. Notice that this second strategy entails some uncertainty since the next year's interest rate, $r_{1,1}$, is not known when you originally select your investment strategy.

forward rate
An expected future interest rate implied by current interest rates.

The expectations theory of the term structure of interest rates asserts that, on average, the two-year investment proceeds, $(1 + r_2)^2$ and $(1 + r_1)(1 + r_{1,1})$, will be equal. In fact, we can obtain what is known as the implied **forward rate**, $f_{1,1}$, by setting the two total proceeds equal to each other:

$$\left(1 + r_2\right)^2 = \left(1 + r_1\right)\left(1 + f_{1,1}\right)$$

Solving for the forward rate, $f_{1,1}$, we see that:

$$f_{1,1} = \frac{(1 + r_2)^2}{1 + r_1} - 1$$

Notice that this forward interest rate is a future interest rate implied by current interest rates.

According to expectations theory, the forward rate $f_{1,1}$ is an accurate predictor of the rate $r_{1,1}$ to be realized one year in the future. Thus, if $r_2 = 10$ percent and $r_1 = 8$ percent, then $f_{1,1} = 12$ percent, approximately. This forward rate predicts that the one-year interest rate one year from now will increase (from the current one-year rate of 8 percent to a higher one-year rate of 12 percent). Alternatively, if $r_2 = 10$ percent and $r_1 = 12$ percent, then $f_{1,1} = 8$ percent, approximately. This forward rate predicts that the one-year interest rate one year from now will decrease.

In general, if $r_2 > r_1$, such that the term structure is upward sloping, then expectations theory predicts an interest rate increase. Similarly, if $r_2 < r_1$, indicating a downward-sloping term structure, then expectations theory predicts an interest rate decrease. Thus, the slope of the term structure points in the predicted direction of future interest rate changes.

EXAMPLE 9.8

Looking Forward

Suppose the yield on a two-year STRIPS is 7 percent and the yield on a one-year STRIPS is 6 percent. Based on the expectations theory, what will the yield on a one-year STRIPS be one year from now?

According to the expectations theory, the implied forward rate is an accurate predictor of what the interest rate will be. Thus, solving for the forward rate, we have:

$$(1 + r_2)^2 = (1 + r_1)(1 + f_{1,1})$$
$$(1 + .07)^2 = (1 + .06)(1 + f_{1,1})$$

and the forward rate is:

$$f_{1,1} = \frac{1.07^2}{1.06} - 1 = .0800943, \text{ or } 8.00943\%$$

Based on the expectations theory, the rate next year will be about 8 percent. Notice that this is higher than the current rate, as we would predict since the term structure is upward sloping.

EXPECTATIONS THEORY AND THE FISHER HYPOTHESIS The expectations theory is closely related to the Fisher hypothesis we discussed earlier. The relationship between the expectations theory of interest rates and the Fisher hypothesis is stated as follows: If expected future inflation is higher than current inflation, then we are likely to see an upward-sloping term structure where long-term interest rates are higher than short-term interest rates. Similarly, if future inflation is expected to be lower than its current level, we would then be likely to see a downward-sloping term structure where long-term interest rates are lower than short-term interest rates.

In other words, taken together, the expectations theory and the Fisher hypothesis assert that an upward-sloping term structure tells us that the market expects that nominal interest rates and inflation are likely to be higher in the future.

MATURITY PREFERENCE THEORY

Another traditional theory of the term structure asserts that lenders prefer to lend short term to avoid tying up funds for long periods of time. In other words, they have a preference for shorter maturities. At the same time, borrowers prefer to borrow long term to lock in secure financing for long periods of time.

maturity preference theory
Long-term interest rates contain a maturity premium necessary to induce lenders into making longer-term loans.

According to the **maturity preference theory**, then, borrowers have to pay a higher rate to borrow long term rather than short term to essentially bribe lenders into loaning funds for longer maturities. The extra interest is called a *maturity premium.*[1]

The Fisher hypothesis, maturity preference theory, and expectations theory can coexist without problem. For example, suppose the shape of a yield curve is basically determined by expected future interest rates according to expectations theory. But where do expected future interest rates come from? According to the Fisher hypothesis, expectations regarding future interest rates are based on expected future rates of inflation. Thus, expectations theory and the Fisher hypothesis mesh quite nicely.

Furthermore, a basic yield curve determined by inflationary expectations could also accommodate maturity preference theory. All we need to do is add a maturity premium to longer-term interest rates. In this view, long-term, default-free interest rates have three components: a real rate, an anticipated future inflation rate, and a maturity premium.

MARKET SEGMENTATION THEORY

market segmentation theory
Debt markets are segmented by maturity, with the result that interest rates for various maturities are determined separately in each segment.

An alternative theory of the term structure of interest rates is the **market segmentation theory**, which asserts that debt markets are segmented according to the various maturities of debt instruments available for investment. By this theory, each maturity represents a separate, distinct market. For example, one group of lenders and borrowers may prefer to lend and borrow using securities with a maturity of 10 years, while another group may prefer to lend and borrow using securities with a maturity of 5 years. Segmentation theory states that interest rates corresponding to each maturity are determined separately by supply and demand conditions in each market segment.

Another theory of the term structure, known as the *preferred habitat theory,* is essentially a compromise between market segmentation and maturity preference. In the preferred habitat theory, as in the market segmentation theory, different investors have different preferred maturities. The difference is that they can be induced to move to less preferred maturities by a higher interest rate. In the maturity preference theory, the preferred habitat is always toward shorter maturities rather than longer maturities.

CHECK THIS

9.6a   According to the expectations theory, what does an upward-sloping term structure indicate?

9.6b   What basic assertion does maturity preference theory make about investor preferences? If this assertion is correct, how does it affect the term structure of interest rates?

9.6c   What is a maturity premium?

9.7 Determinants of Nominal Interest Rates: A Modern Perspective

Related Bloomberg Functions

CRPR   Credit Profile
DRSK   Bloomberg Default Risk
LQA   Liquidity Assessment
IFMO   Inflation Monitor

Our understanding of the term structure of interest rates has increased significantly in the last few decades. Also, the evolution of fixed-income markets has shown us that, at least to some extent, traditional theories discussed in our previous section may be inadequate to explain the term structure. We discuss some problems with these theories next and then move on to a modern perspective.

---

[1] Traditionally, maturity preference theory has been known as "liquidity" preference theory, and the maturity premium was termed a "liquidity" premium. However, as we discussed in a previous chapter, the term "liquidity" is universally used to indicate the relative ease with which an asset can be sold. Also, the term "liquidity premium" now has a different meaning. To avoid confusion and to make this theory more consistent with modern views of liquidity, interest rates, and the term structure, we have adopted the more descriptive name of *maturity premium.*

PROBLEMS WITH TRADITIONAL THEORIES

To illustrate some problems with traditional theories, we could examine the behavior of the term structure in the last two decades. What we would find is that the term structure is almost always upward sloping. But contrary to the expectations hypothesis, interest rates have not always risen. Furthermore, as we saw with the STRIPS term structure, it is often the case that the term structure turns down at very long maturities. According to the expectations hypothesis, market participants apparently expect rates to rise for 20 or so years and then decline. This seems to be stretching things a bit.

In terms of maturity preference, the world's biggest borrower, the U.S. government, borrows much more heavily in the short term than the long term. Furthermore, many of the biggest buyers of fixed-income securities, such as pension funds, have a strong preference for long maturities. It is hard to square these facts with the behavioral assumptions underlying the maturity preference theory.

Finally, in terms of market segmentation, the U.S. government borrows at all maturities. Many institutional investors, such as mutual funds, are more than willing to move among maturities to obtain more favorable rates. At the same time, some bond trading operations do nothing other than buy and sell various maturity issues to exploit even very small perceived premiums. In short, in the modern fixed-income market, market segmentation does not seem to be a powerful force.

MODERN TERM STRUCTURE THEORY

Going back to Chapter 1, we saw that long-term government bonds had higher returns, on average, than short-term T-bills. They had substantially more risk as well. In other words, there appears to be a risk-return trade-off for default-free bonds as well, and long-term bonds appear to have a risk premium.

Notice that this risk premium doesn't result from the possibility of default since the premium exists on default-free U.S. government debt. Instead, it exists because longer-term bond prices are more volatile than shorter-term prices. As we discuss in detail in the next chapter, the reason is that, for a given change in interest rates, long-term bond prices change more than short-term bonds. Put differently, long-term bond prices are much more sensitive to interest rate changes than short-term bonds. This is called *interest rate risk,* and the risk premium on longer-term bonds is called the *interest rate risk premium.*

The interest rate risk premium carried by long-term bonds leads us to a modern reinterpretation of the maturity preference hypothesis. All else equal, investors do prefer short-term bonds to long-term bonds. The reason is that short-term bonds are less risky. As a result, long-term bonds have to offer higher yields to compensate investors for the extra interest rate risk.

Putting it together, the modern view of the term structure suggests that nominal interest rates on default-free securities can be stated as follows:

$$NI = RI + IP + RP \tag{9.11}$$

where:

NI = Nominal interest rate

RI = Real interest rate

IP = Inflation premium

RP = Interest rate risk premium

In Equation 9.11, the real rate of interest is assumed to be the same for all securities, and on average, the real interest rate (RI) is positive, as predicted by the Fisher hypothesis.

As we discussed above, the inflation premium (IP) reflects investor expectations of future price inflation. The inflation premium may be different for securities with different maturities because expected inflation may be different over different future horizons. For example, the expected average rate of inflation over the next two years may be different from the expected average rate of inflation over the next five years.

In addition to the real rate and the inflation premium, nominal rates reflect an interest rate risk premium (RP) that increases with the maturity of the security being considered. As a result, if interest rates are expected to remain constant through time, the term structure would have a positive slope. This is consistent with maturity preference theory. Indeed, for zero coupon bonds, the interest rate risk premium and the maturity premium are the same thing.

The separate effects of the inflation premium and the interest rate risk premium are difficult to distinguish. For example, the yields for U.S. Treasury STRIPS in Figure 9.5 reveal a substantial yield premium for long-maturity STRIPS over short-term STRIPS. This yield premium for long-maturity STRIPS reflects the combined effects of the inflation premium and the risk premium. However, it is unclear how much of the total premium is caused by an inflation premium and how much is caused by a risk premium. Figure 9.9 shows how nominal interest rates can be separated into the real interest rate, the inflation premium, and the interest rate risk premium.

LIQUIDITY AND DEFAULT RISK

Thus far we have examined the components of interest rates on default-free, highly liquid securities such as Treasury STRIPS. We now expand our coverage to securities that are less liquid, not default-free, or both, to present a more detailed decomposition of nominal interest rates. When we are finished, what we will see is that nominal interest rates for individual securities can be decomposed into five basic components as follows:

$$NI = RI + IP + RP + LP + DP \qquad (9.12)$$

FIGURE 9.9   **The Term Structure of Interest Rates**

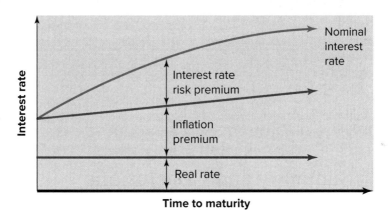

(a) Upward-sloping term structure

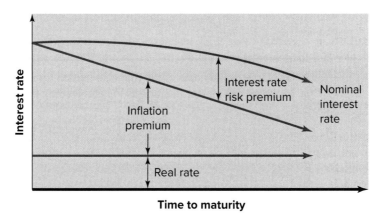

(b) Downward-sloping term structure

where:

NI = Nominal interest rate

RI = Real interest rate

IP = Inflation premium

RP = Interest rate risk premium

LP = Liquidity premium

DP = Default premium

We have already discussed the first three components of the nominal interest rate. We now consider the two new ones on our list, the default and liquidity premiums.

The *liquidity premium* (LP) is a reflection of the fact that two otherwise identical securities may have very different degrees of liquidity. All else the same, the one with less liquidity would have to offer a higher yield as compensation. For Treasury securities, "on-the-run issues" are the most actively traded (i.e., liquid) bonds. The on-the-run issue is the most recently issued Treasury note or bond of a given maturity.

The fifth, and final, component of a nominal interest rate is a *default premium* (DP). Investors demand a default premium to assume the risk of holding a security that might default on its promised payments. Naturally, the greater the risk of default for a particular bond issue, the larger the default premium required by investors. The topic of default risk is discussed in detail for corporate bonds and municipal bonds in another chapter.

In addition to the five basic components we have discussed, another important determinant of nominal interest rates is tax status. As we briefly discussed in an earlier chapter, municipal bonds are not taxed at the federal level, but all other bonds are (including Treasury bonds). All else the same, taxable bonds must pay higher rates than nontaxable bonds. As a result, the rate on a high-quality municipal issue will normally be less than the rate on a Treasury issue, even though the Treasury is more liquid and has no default risk.

CHECK THIS

9.7a   What are the major risk premiums that impact the nominal interest rate?

9.8 Summary and Conclusions

The time value of money is arguably the most important principle of finance. Interest rates are a convenient way to measure and state the time value of money. Furthermore, understanding interest rates is essential for understanding money market and fixed-income securities. This chapter covers many topics relating to interest rates. They are grouped here by the learning objectives of the chapter.

1. **Money market prices and rates.**

   A. Money market is the name of the financial market for short-term borrowing and lending. In the money market, the borrowing and lending period is generally less than a year.

   B. Important short-term money market rates include the prime rate, the federal funds rate, and the Federal Reserve's discount rate. The prime rate is a bellwether of bank lending to business, while the federal funds rate and the Federal Reserve's discount rate are indicators of the availability of money and credit within the banking system.

2. **Rates and yields on fixed-income securities.**

   A. Fixed-income securities promise a regular payment during the life of the security. In addition, most fixed-income securities also promise a lump-sum payment at the end of

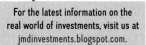
the life of the security. Generally, when they are issued, fixed-income securities have a life ranging from 2 to 30 years.

B. The Treasury yield curve plots the relationship between yields on U.S. Treasury securities and their maturities. The Treasury yield curve is fundamental to bond market analysis because it represents the interest rates that financial markets are charging to the world's largest debtor with the world's highest credit rating—the U.S. government.

3. Treasury STRIPS and the term structure of interest rates.

A. The term structure of interest rates is the fundamental relationship between time to maturity and interest rates for default-free, pure discount instruments such as U.S. Treasury STRIPS.

B. A number of different theories—including the expectations theory, the maturity preference theory, and the market segmentation theory—have been proposed to explain why the term structure of interest rates and yield curves may be upward sloping at one point in time and then downward sloping or flat at another time. In a modern view of the term structure, yields on default-free, pure discount bonds are determined by the real rate of interest, expectations of future inflation, and an interest rate risk premium.

4. Nominal versus real interest rates.

A. Nominal interest rates are interest rates that we ordinarily observe. Nominal interest rates have five basic components: the real rate, an inflation premium, an interest rate risk premium, a liquidity premium, and a default premium. The real interest rate is the nominal interest rate adjusted for the effects of inflation.

B. U.S. Treasury securities are free of default risk and are generally free from liquidity risk. For other debt issues, however, these two nominal interest rate components are very important.

C. When nominal interest rates change, long-term bond prices change more than short-term bonds. Put differently, long-term bond prices are much more sensitive to interest rate changes than are short-term bonds. This difference in price changes is called interest rate risk.

D. The liquidity premium reflects the fact that two otherwise identical securities could have starkly different degrees of liquidity. All else the same, the one with less liquidity would have to offer a higher yield as compensation. The fifth component of a nominal interest rate, the default premium, reflects the extra yield that investors demand to assume the risk of holding a security that might default on its promised payments.

Key Terms

bank discount basis 298
banker's acceptance 297
basis point 298
bellwether rate 295
call money rate 296
certificates of deposit (CDs) 297
commercial paper 296
discount rate 296
Eurodollars 297
expectations theory 313
federal funds rate 295
Fisher hypothesis 310

forward rate 313
London Interbank Offered Rate (LIBOR) 297
market segmentation theory 315
maturity preference theory 315
nominal interest rates 309
prime rate 295
pure discount security 298
real interest rates 309
term structure of interest rates 307
Treasury yield curve 304
U.S. Treasury bill (T-bill) 297
U.S. Treasury STRIPS 307

Related Bloomberg Functions

CBRT	Central Bank Rate Analysis, 9.1
GC	Graph Curves, 9.1
BTMM	Treasury & Money Markets, 9.1
BOOM	Money Market Offerings, 9.1
LOIS	LIBOR-OIS 3-Month Spread, 9.1
MMR	Money Rate Monitors, 9.2
GC3D	Graph Curve Surface, 9.3
GIY	Intraday Yield Curve, 9.3
YAS	Yield and Spread Analysis, 9.3
XLTP XYAS	Excel Template: Price/Yield/Spread Calculator, 9.3
BYFC	Bond Yield Forecast, 9.4
USD	US Treasuries Monitor, 9.4
WBI	World Inflation Bonds, 9.5
ILBE	World Inflation Breakeven Rates, 9.6
CRPR	Credit Profile, 9.7
DRSK	Bloomberg Default Risk, 9.7
LQA	Liquidity Assessment, 9.7
IFMO	Inflation Monitor, 9.7

Chapter Review Problems and Self-Test

1. **Money Market Prices (LO1, CFA1)** The rate on a particular money market instrument, quoted on a discount basis, is 5 percent. The instrument has a face value of $100,000 and will mature in 40 days. What is its price?

2. **Bond Equivalent Yields (LO1, CFA1)** Suppose a T-bill has 75 days to maturity and an ask discount of 4 percent. What is the bond equivalent yield?

Answers to Self-Test Problems

1. Using the bank discount basis formula, we have:

$$\text{Current price} = \text{Face value} \times \left(1 - \frac{\text{Days to maturity}}{360} \times \text{Discount yield}\right)$$

$$\$99,444.44 = \$100,000 \times \left(1 - \frac{40}{360} \times .05\right)$$

You would pay $99,444.44.

2. Using the bond equivalent yield conversion formula, we have:

$$\frac{365 \times .04}{360 - 75 \times .04} = .0409, \text{ or } 4.09\%$$

The bond equivalent yield is thus 4.09 percent.

Test Your Investment Quotient

1. **Interest Rates (LO2, CFA1)**   Which of the following interest rates is a bellwether (leading indicator) rate of bank lending to business?

   a. Unsecured business loan rate
   b. Prime rate
   c. Commercial paper rate
   d. Banker's acceptance rate

2. **Interest Rates (LO2, CFA1)**   Among the following interest rates, which is normally the highest rate?

   a. Commercial paper rate
   b. U.S. Treasury bill rate
   c. Federal funds rate
   d. Federal Reserve discount rate

3. **T-Bill Yields (LO1, CFA1)**   A U.S. Treasury bill with 180 days to maturity has a discount yield of 5 percent and a face value of $100,000. What is its current price?

   a. $97,500
   b. $95,000
   c. $92,500
   d. $90,000

4. **T-Bill Yields (LO1, CFA1)**   A U.S. Treasury bill with 90 days to maturity has a price of $95,000. What is its discount yield?

   a. 5 percent
   b. 10 percent
   c. 15 percent
   d. 20 percent

5. **T-Bill Yields (LO1, CFA1)**   A 30-day U.S. Treasury bill is selling at a 12 percent yield on a discount basis. Which of the following is the approximate bond equivalent yield?

   a. 6.0 percent
   b. 11.7 percent
   c. 12.0 percent
   d. 12.3 percent

6. **Effective Annual Rates (LO2, CFA1)**   A credit card company states an annual percentage rate (APR) of 12 percent, which is actually a rate of 1 percent per month. What is the EAR?

   a. 12 percent
   b. 12.68 percent
   c. 13.08 percent
   d. 13.76 percent

7. **STRIPS Yields (LO3, CFA5)**   A U.S. Treasury STRIPS maturing in 10 years has a current price of $502.57 for $1,000 of face value. What is the yield to maturity of this STRIPS?

   a. 7.0 percent
   b. 7.12 percent
   c. 8.0 percent
   d. 8.12 percent

8. **STRIPS Yields (LO3, CFA5)**   A U.S. Treasury STRIPS with a $1,000 face value maturing in five years has a yield to maturity of 7 percent. What is the current price of this STRIPS?

   a. $930
   b. $712.99
   c. $708.92
   d. $650

9. **Bond Yields (LO2, CFA1)**   An analyst finds that the semiannual interest rate that equates the present value of the bond's cash flow to its current market price is 3.85 percent. Consider the following possible alternatives:

   I. The bond equivalent yield on this security is 7.70 percent.
   II. The effective annual yield on the bond is 7.85 percent.
   III. The bond's yield to maturity is 7.70 percent.
   IV. The bond's horizon return is 8.35 percent.
   Which of these alternatives are true?

   a. I and II only
   b. II, III, and IV only
   c. I, II, and III only
   d. III only

10. **Forward Rates (LO3, CFA7)**   An analyst gathered the following spot rates:

Time (years)	Annual Spot Rate
1	15.0%
2	12.5
3	10.0
4	7.5

   The one-year forward rate two years from now is closest to:

   a. −4.91 percent
   b. 5.17 percent
   c. 10.05 percent
   d. 7.5 percent

11. **Zeroes (LO2, CFA5)**   If an investor's required return is 12 percent, the value of a 10-year maturity zero coupon bond with a maturity value of $1,000 is closest to:

   a. $312
   b. $688
   c. $1,000
   d. $1,312

12. **Fisher Hypothesis (LO4, CFA3)**   The Fisher hypothesis essentially asserts which of the following?

   a. Nominal interest rates follow inflation.
   b. Real interest rates follow inflation.
   c. Inflation follows real interest rates.
   d. Inflation follows nominal interest rates.

13. **Term Structure Theory (LO3, CFA9)**   Which one of the following statements about the term structure of interest rates is true?

   a. The expectations hypothesis indicates a flat yield curve if anticipated future short-term rates exceed current short-term rates.
   b. The expectations hypothesis contends that the long-term rate is equal to the anticipated short-term rate.

    c. The liquidity premium theory indicates that, all else being equal, longer maturities will have lower yields.

    d. The market segmentation theory contends that borrowers and lenders prefer particular segments of the yield curve.

14. **Term Structure Theory (LO3, CFA9)** Which one of the following is *not* an explanation of the relationship between a bond's interest rate and its term to maturity?

    a. Default (credit) risk hypothesis

    b. Expectations hypothesis

    c. Liquidity preference hypothesis

    d. Segmentation hypothesis

15. **Term Structure Theory (LO3, CFA2)** Which theory explains the shape of the yield curve by considering the relative demands for various maturities?

    a. Relative strength theory

    b. Segmentation theory

    c. Unbiased expectations theory

    d. Liquidity premium theory

16. **Term Structure Theory (LO3, CFA2)** The concepts of spot and forward rates are most closely associated with which one of the following explanations of the term structure of interest rates?

    a. Expectations hypothesis

    b. Liquidity premium theory

    c. Preferred habitat hypothesis

    d. Segmented market theory

17. **Forward Rates (LO3, CFA7)** The current one-year interest rate is 6 percent and the current two-year interest rate is 7 percent. What is the implied forward rate for next year's one-year rate?

    a. 9 percent

    b. 8 percent

    c. 7 percent

    d. 6 percent

18. **Forward Rates (LO3, CFA7)** The current one-year interest rate is 7 percent and the current two-year interest rate is 6 percent. What is the implied forward rate for next year's one-year rate?

    a. 7 percent

    b. 6 percent

    c. 5 percent

    d. 4 percent

19. **Forward Rates (LO3, CFA7)** The six-month Treasury bill spot rate is 4 percent, and the one-year Treasury bill spot rate is 5 percent. The implied six-month forward rate six months from now is which of the following?

    a. 3.0 percent

    b. 4.5 percent

    c. 5.5 percent

    d. 5.9 percent

20. **Forward Rates (LO3, CFA7)** An analyst gathers the following information:

Years to Maturity	Spot Rate
1	5.00%
2	6.00
3	6.50

Based on the data above, the one-year implied forward rate two years from now is closest to:

    a. 6.25 percent

    b. 7.01 percent

    c. 7.26 percent

    d. 7.51 percent

Concept Questions

1. **Interest Rate History (LO2, CFA5)** Based on the history of interest rates, what is the range of short-term rates that has occurred in the United States? The range of long-term rates? What is a typical value for each?

2. **Discount Securities (LO1, CFA1)** What are pure discount securities? Give two examples.

3. **Fed Funds versus the Discount Rate (LO1, CFA4)** Compare and contrast the Fed funds rate and the discount rate. Which do you think is more volatile? Which market do you think is more active? Why?

4. **Commercial Paper (LO1, CFA1)** Compare and contrast commercial paper and Treasury bills. Which would typically offer a higher interest rate? Why?

5. **SOFR (LO1, CFA5)** What is SOFR? Why is it important?

6. **Bank Discount Rates (LO1, CFA1)** Why do you suppose rates on some money market instruments are quoted on a bank discount basis? (*Hint:* Why use a 360-day year?)

7. **STRIPS (LO3, CFA5)** What are the three different types of Treasury STRIPS that are publicly traded?

8. **Nominal and Real Rates (LO4, CFA3)** When we observe interest rates in the financial press, do we see nominal or real rates? Which are more relevant to investors?

9. **TIPS (LO4, CFA2)** Evaluate the following statement: "Treasury inflation protected securities (TIPS) pay a fixed coupon."

10. **Term Structure (LO4, CFA4)** Discuss how each of the following theories for the term structure of interest rates could account for a downward-sloping term structure of interest rates:

    a. Pure expectations
    b. Maturity preference
    c. Market segmentation

Questions and Problems

Core Questions

1. **STRIPS (LO3, CFA6)** What is the price of a Treasury STRIPS with a face value of $100 that matures in 10 years and has a yield to maturity of 3.5 percent?

2. **STRIPS (LO3, CFA6)** A Treasury STRIPS matures in 7 years and has a yield to maturity of 4.4 percent. If the par value is $100,000, what is the price of the STRIPS? What is the quoted price?

3. **STRIPS (LO3, CFA6)** A Treasury STRIPS is quoted at 90.875 and has 5 years until maturity. What is the yield to maturity?

4. **STRIPS (LO3, CFA1)** What is the yield to maturity on a Treasury STRIPS with 4 years to maturity and a quoted price of 70.485?

5. **Fisher Effect (LO4, CFA3)** A stock had a return of 8.9 percent last year. If the inflation rate was 2.1 percent, what was the approximate real return?

6. **Fisher Effect (LO4, CFA3)** Your investments increased in value by 11.6 percent last year, but your purchasing power increased by only 7.6 percent. What was the approximate inflation rate?

7. **Treasury Bill Prices (LO1, CFA1)** What is the price of a U.S. Treasury bill with 56 days to maturity quoted at a discount yield of 1.15 percent? Assume a $1 million face value.

8. **Treasury Bill Prices (LO1, CFA1)** In Problem 7, what is the bond equivalent yield?

9. **Treasury Bill Prices (LO1, CFA1)** How much would you pay for a U.S. Treasury bill with 112 days to maturity quoted at a discount yield of 2.18 percent? Assume a $1 million face value.

10. **Treasury Bill Prices (LO1, CFA1)** In Problem 9, what is the bond equivalent yield?

Intermediate Questions

11. **Treasury Bills (LO1, CFA1)** A Treasury bill with 64 days to maturity is quoted at 99.012. What are the bank discount yield, the bond equivalent yield, and the effective annual return?

12. **Treasury Bills (LO1, CFA1)** A Treasury bill purchased in January 2024 has 55 days until maturity and a bank discount yield of 2.48 percent. What is the price of the bill as a percentage of face value? What is the bond equivalent yield?

13. **Money Market Prices (LO1, CFA1)** The treasurer of a large corporation wants to invest $20 million in excess short-term cash in a particular money market investment. The prospectus quotes the instrument at a true yield of 3.15 percent; that is, the EAR for this investment is 3.15 percent. However, the treasurer wants to know the money market yield on this instrument to make it comparable to the T-bills and CDs she has already bought. If the term of the instrument is 90 days, what are the bond equivalent and discount yields on this investment?

Use the following information to answer Problems 14–18:

U.S. Treasury STRIPS, close of business February 15, 2022:

Maturity	Price	Maturity	Price
Feb 2023	97.123	Feb 2026	90.066
Feb 2024	94.770	Feb 2027	87.528
Feb 2025	92.424	Feb 2028	85.410

14. **Treasury STRIPS (LO3, CFA1)** Calculate the quoted yield for each of the STRIPS given in the table above. Does the market expect interest rates to go up or down in the future?

15. **Treasury STRIPS (LO3, CFA1)** What is the yield of the February 2024 STRIPS expressed as an EAR?

16. **Forward Interest Rates (LO3, CFA2)** According to the pure expectations theory of interest rates, how much do you expect to pay for a one-year STRIPS on February 15, 2023? What is the corresponding implied forward rate? How does your answer compare to the current yield on a one-year STRIPS? What does this tell you about the relationship between implied forward rates, the shape of the zero coupon yield curve, and market expectations about future spot interest rates?

17. **Forward Interest Rates (LO3, CFA7)** According to the pure expectations theory of interest rates, how much do you expect to pay for a five-year STRIPS on February 15, 2023? How much do you expect to pay for a two-year STRIPS on February 15, 2025?

18. **Bond Price Changes (LO3, CFA6)** Suppose the (quoted) yield on each of the six STRIPS increases by .05 percent. Calculate the percentage change in price for the one-year, three-year, and six-year STRIPS. Which one has the largest price change? Now suppose that the quoted price on each STRIPS decreases by .500. Calculate the percentage change in (quoted) yield for the one-year, three-year, and six-year STRIPS. Which one has the largest yield change? What do your answers tell you about the relationship between prices, yields, and maturities for discount bonds?

19. **TIPS (LO4, CFA2)** Suppose you purchase a $1,000 TIPS on January 1, 2024. The bond carries a fixed coupon of 1 percent. Over the first two years, semiannual inflation is 2 percent, 3 percent, 1 percent, and 2 percent, respectively. For each six-month period, calculate the accrued principal and coupon payment.

20. **Inflation and Returns (LO3, CFA1)** You observe that the current interest rate on short-term U.S. Treasury bills is 1.64 percent. You also read in the newspaper that the GDP deflator, which is a common macroeconomic indicator used by market analysts to gauge the inflation rate, currently implies that inflation is .7 percent. Given this information, what is the approximate real rate of interest on short-term Treasury bills? Is it likely that your answer would change if you used some alternative measure for the inflation rate, such as the CPI? What does this tell you about the observability and accuracy of real interest rates compared to nominal interest rates?

21. **Forward Interest Rates (LO3, CFA7)** Consider the following spot interest rates for maturities of one, two, three, and four years.

$$r_1 = 4.3\% \quad r_2 = 4.9\% \quad r_3 = 5.6\% \quad r_4 = 6.4\%$$

What are the following forward rates, where $f_{1,k}$ refers to a forward rate for the period beginning in one year and extending for k years?

$$f_{1,1} = \quad ; \quad f_{1,2} = \quad ; \quad f_{1,3} =$$

Hint: Use the equation $(1 + r_1)(1+f_{1,k})^k = (1 + r_{k+1})^{k+1}$ to solve for $f_{1,k}$.

22. **Forward Interest Rates (LO3, CFA9)** Based on the spot interest rates in the previous question, what are the following forward rates, where $f_{k,1}$ refers to a forward rate beginning in k years and extending for 1 year?

$$f_{2,1} = \quad ; \quad f_{3,1} =$$

Hint: Use the equation $(1 + r_k)^k(1 + f_{k,1}) = (1 + r_{k+1})^{k+1}$ to solve for $f_{k,1}$.

23. **Expected Inflation Rates (LO4, CFA3)** Based on the spot rates in Problem 21, and assuming a constant real interest rate of 2 percent, what are the expected inflation rates for the next four years?

Hint: Use the Fisher hypothesis and the unbiased expectations theory.

Spreadsheet Problems

24. **Treasury Bills (LO1, CFA1)** A Treasury bill that settles on May 18, 2022, pays $100,000 on August 21, 2022. Assuming a discount rate of .44 percent, what are the price and bond equivalent yield?

25. **Effective Annual Rate (LO2, CFA1)** You have a car loan with a nominal rate of 5.99 percent. With interest charged monthly, what is the effective annual rate (EAR) on this loan?

26. **STRIPS (LO3, CFA6)** What is the price of a Treasury STRIPS with a face value of $100 that matures in five years and has a yield to maturity of 3.3 percent?

CFA Exam Review by Kaplan Schweser

[CFA2, CFA7, CFA9]

James Wallace, CFA, is a fixed-income fund manager at a large investment firm. Each year the firm recruits a group of new college graduates. Recently, Mr. Wallace was asked to teach the fixed-income portion of the firm's training program. Mr. Wallace wants to start by teaching the various theories of the term structure of interest rates and the implications of each theory for the shape of the Treasury yield curve. To evaluate the trainees' understanding of the subject, he creates a series of questions.

The following interest rate scenario is used to derive examples on the different theories used to explain the shape of the term structure and for all computational problems in Mr. Wallace's lecture. He assumes a rounded day count of .5 year for each semiannual period.

To read the Period column, let's look at the 12×18 line. The "12" stands for 12 months from now and the "18" stands for 18 months from now. So, the 12×18 forward rate is a 6-month rate that begins 12 months from now.

Period (months)	LIBOR Forward Rates	Implied Spot Rates
0 × 6	5.00%	5.00%
6 × 12	5.50	5.25
12 × 18	6.00	5.50
18 × 24	6.50	5.75
24 × 30	6.75	5.95
30 × 36	7.00	6.12

1. Mr. Wallace asks the trainees which of the following explains an upward-sloping yield curve according to the pure expectations theory.

   a. The market expects short-term rates to rise through the relevant future.
   b. There is greater demand for short-term securities than for long-term securities.
   c. There is a risk premium associated with more distant maturities.

2. Mr. Wallace asks the trainees which of the following explains an upward-sloping yield curve according to the market segmentation theory.

   a. The market expects short-term rates to rise through the relevant future.
   b. There is greater demand for short-term securities than for long-term securities.
   c. There is a risk premium associated with more distant maturities.

3. According to the expectations theory, which of the following is closest to the one-year implied forward rate one year from now?

   a. 6.58 percent
   b. 5.75 percent
   c. 6.25 percent

4. Mr. Wallace is particularly interested in the effects of a steepening yield curve. Which of the following is most accurate for a steepening curve?

   a. The price of short-term Treasuries increases relative to long-term Treasuries.
   b. The price of long-term Treasuries increases relative to short-term Treasuries.
   c. The price of short-term Treasury securities increases.

Bloomberg Exercises

1. Compare benchmark interest rates across countries. **(CBRT)**
2. Review current money market rates. **(BTMM)**
3. Download a pricing calculator for bonds and explore the primary inputs. **(XLTP XYAS)**
4. Examine the current yield curve and identify whether it is a traditional upward-sloping pattern. **(GC)**

What's on the Web?

1. **Yield Curve** What is the shape of the Treasury yield curve today? Go to www.bloomberg.com and find out. Is the yield curve upward sloping or downward sloping? According to the expectations theory, are interest rates in the future expected to be higher or lower than they are today?

2. **STRIPS** Go to www.treasurydirect.gov and search the site to find information on Treasury STRIPS. Answer the following questions: Which Treasury securities are eligible to be stripped? What are minimum par amounts for stripping? How do I buy STRIPS? Why do investors hold STRIPS?

Bond Prices and Yields

"More money has been lost reaching for yield than at the point of a gun."

–Raymond DeVoe

Learning Objectives

Bonds can be an important part of portfolios. You will learn:

1. How to calculate bond prices and yields.

2. The importance of yield to maturity.

3. Interest rate risk and Malkiel's theorems.

4. How to measure the impact of interest rate changes on bond prices.

Interest rates go up and bond prices go down. But which bonds go down the most and which go down the least? Interest rates go down and bond prices go up. But which bonds go up the most and which go up the least? For bond portfolio managers, these are important questions about interest rate risk. For anyone managing a bond portfolio, an understanding of interest rate risk rests on an understanding of the relationship between bond prices and yields.

In the preceding chapter on interest rates, we introduced the subject of bond yields. As we promised there, we now return to this subject and discuss bond prices and yields in greater detail. We first describe how bond yields are determined and how they are interpreted. We then go on to examine what happens to bond prices as yields change. Finally, once we have a good understanding of the relation between bond prices and yields, we examine some of the fundamental tools of bond risk analysis used by fixed-income portfolio managers.

CFA™ Exam Topics in This Chapter:

1. Noncurrent (long-term) liabilities (L1, S7)
2. Fixed-income securities: Defining elements (L1, S13)
3. Fixed-income markets: Issuance, trading, and funding (L1, S13)
4. Introduction to fixed-income valuation (L1, S13)
5. Understanding fixed-income risk and return (L1, S14)
6. Fundamentals of credit analysis (L1, S14)

Go to Connect for a guide that aligns your textbook with CFA readings.

10.1 Bond Basics

A bond is essentially a security that offers the investor a series of fixed interest payments during its life, along with a fixed payment of principal when it matures. So long as the bond issuer does not default, the schedule of payments does not change. When originally issued, bonds normally have maturities ranging from 2 years to 30 years, but bonds with maturities of 50 or 100 years also exist. Bonds issued with maturities of less than 10 years are usually called *notes*. A very small number of bond issues with no stated maturity are referred to as *perpetuities* or *consols*.

STRAIGHT BONDS

The most common type of bond is the so-called straight bond. By definition, a straight bond is an IOU that obligates the issuer to pay the bondholder a fixed sum of money at the bond's maturity along with constant, periodic interest payments during the life of the bond. The fixed sum paid at maturity is referred to as *bond principal, par value, stated value,* or *face value*. The periodic interest payments are called *coupons*. Perhaps the best example of straight bonds is U.S. Treasury bonds issued by the federal government to finance the national debt. However, corporations and municipal governments also routinely issue debt in the form of straight bonds.

In addition to a straight bond component, many bonds have special features. These features are sometimes designed to enhance a bond's appeal to investors. For example, convertible bonds have a conversion feature that grants bondholders the right to convert their bonds into shares of common stock of the issuing corporation. As another example, "putable" bonds have a put feature that grants bondholders the right to sell their bonds back to the issuer at a predetermined price.

These and other special features are attached to many bond issues, but we defer discussion of special bond features until a later chapter. For now, it is only important to know that when a bond is issued with one or more special features, strictly speaking, it is no longer a straight bond. However, bonds with attached special features will normally have a straight bond component, namely, the periodic coupon payments and fixed principal payment at maturity. For this reason, straight bonds are important as the basic unit of bond analysis.

The prototypical example of a straight bond pays a series of constant semiannual coupons, along with a face value of $1,000 payable at maturity. This example is used in this chapter because it is common and realistic. For example, most corporate bonds are sold with a face value of $1,000 per bond, and most bonds (in the United States at least) pay constant semiannual coupons.

COUPON RATE AND CURRENT YIELD

A familiarity with bond yield measures is important for understanding the financial characteristics of bonds. As we briefly discussed in a previous chapter, two basic yield measures for a bond are its coupon rate and current yield.

A bond's **coupon rate** is defined as its annual coupon amount divided by its par value, or, in other words, its annual coupon expressed as a percentage of face value:

coupon rate
A bond's annual coupon divided by its par value. Also called *coupon yield* or *nominal yield*.

$$\text{Coupon rate} = \frac{\text{Annual coupon}}{\text{Par value}} \qquad (10.1)$$

For example, suppose a $1,000 par value bond pays semiannual coupons of $40. The annual coupon is then $80; stated as a percentage of par value, the bond's coupon rate is $80/$1,000 = .08, or 8%. A coupon rate is often referred to as the *coupon yield* or the *nominal yield*. Notice that the word "nominal" here has nothing to do with inflation.

A bond's **current yield** is its annual coupon payment divided by its current market price:

current yield
A bond's annual coupon divided by its market price.

$$\text{Current yield} = \frac{\text{Annual coupon}}{\text{Bond price}} \qquad (10.2)$$

For example, suppose a $1,000 par value bond paying an $80 annual coupon has a price of $1,032.25. The current yield is $80/$1,032.25 = .0775, or 7.75%. Similarly, a price of $969.75

implies a current yield of $80/$969.75 = .0825, or 8.25%. Notice that whenever there is a change in the bond's price, the coupon rate remains constant. However, a bond's current yield is inversely related to its price, and it changes whenever the bond's price changes.

CHECK THIS

10.1a   What is a straight bond?

10.1b   What is a bond's coupon rate? Its current yield?

10.2 Straight Bond Prices and Yield to Maturity

The single most important yield measure for a bond is its **yield to maturity**, commonly abbreviated as **YTM**. By definition, a bond's yield to maturity is the discount rate that equates the bond's price with the computed present value of its future cash flows. A bond's yield to maturity is sometimes called its *promised yield,* but more commonly the yield to maturity of a bond is referred to as its *yield.* In general, if the term "yield" is being used with no qualification, it means yield to maturity.

STRAIGHT BOND PRICES

For straight bonds, the following standard formula is used to calculate a bond's price given its yield:

$$\text{Bond price} = \frac{C/2}{YTM/2}\left[1 - \frac{1}{(1 + YTM/2)^{2M}}\right] + \frac{FV}{(1 + YTM/2)^{2M}}$$

This formula can be simplified just a bit as follows:

$$\text{Bond price} = \frac{C}{YTM}\left[1 - \frac{1}{(1 + YTM/2)^{2M}}\right] + \frac{FV}{(1 + YTM/2)^{2M}} \tag{10.3}$$

where: C = Annual coupon, the sum of two semiannual coupons

FV = Face value

M = Maturity in years

YTM = Yield to maturity

In this formula, the coupon used is the annual coupon, which is the sum of the two semi-annual coupons. As discussed in our previous chapter for U.S. Treasury STRIPS, the yield on a bond is an annual percentage rate (APR), calculated as twice the true semiannual yield. As a result, the yield on a bond somewhat understates its effective annual rate (EAR).

The straight bond pricing formula has two separate components. The first component is the present value of all the coupon payments. Because the coupons are fixed and paid on a regular basis, you may recognize that they form an ordinary annuity, and the first piece of the bond pricing formula is a standard calculation for the present value of an annuity. The other component represents the present value of the principal payment at maturity, and it is a standard calculation for the present value of a single lump sum.

Calculating bond prices is mostly "plug and chug" with a calculator. In fact, a good financial calculator or spreadsheet should have this formula built into it. In any case, we will work through a few examples the long way to illustrate the calculations.

Suppose a bond has a $1,000 face value, 20 years to maturity, an 8 percent coupon rate, and a yield of 9 percent. What's the price? Using the straight bond pricing formula, the price of this bond is calculated as follows:

1. Present value of semiannual coupons:

$$\frac{\$80}{.09}\left[1 - \frac{1}{1.045^{40}}\right] = \$736.06338$$

Related Bloomberg Functions

BVAL   Bloomberg Valuation

FIPX   Fixed Income Price Discovery

XLTC XFIC   Excel Template: Fixed Income Comparables Analysis

yield to maturity (YTM)
The discount rate that equates a bond's price with the present value of its future cash flows. Also called *promised yield* or just *yield.*

2. Present value of $1,000 principal:

$$\frac{\$1{,}000}{1.045^{40}} = \$171.92870$$

The price of the bond is the sum of the present values of coupons and principal:

$$\text{Bond price} = \$736.06 + \$171.93 = \$907.99$$

So, this bond sells for $907.99.

EXAMPLE 10.1

Calculating Straight Bond Prices

Suppose a bond has 20 years to maturity and a coupon rate of 8 percent. The bond's yield to maturity is 7 percent. What's the price?

In this case, the coupon rate is 8 percent and the face value is $1,000, so the annual coupon is $80. The bond's price is calculated as follows:

1. Present value of semiannual coupons:

$$\frac{\$80}{.07}\left[1 - \frac{1}{1.035^{40}}\right] = \$854.20289$$

2. Present value of $1,000 principal:

$$\frac{\$1{,}000}{1.035^{40}} = \$252.57247$$

The bond's price is the sum of coupon and principal present values:

$$\text{Bond price} = \$854.20 + \$252.57 = \$1{,}106.78$$

This bond sells for $1,106.78.

Straight bond prices may be calculated using a built-in spreadsheet function. An example of how to use an Excel™ spreadsheet to calculate a bond price is shown in the nearby *Spreadsheet Analysis* box.

SPREADSHEET ANALYSIS

	A	B	C	D	E	F	G	H
1								
2			**Calculating the Price of a Coupon Bond**					
3								
4	A Treasury bond traded on March 30, 2022 matures in 20 years on March 30, 2042.							
5	Assuming an 2 percent coupon rate and a 4 percent yield to maturity, what is the							
6	price of this bond?							
7	Hint: Use the Excel function PRICE.							
8								
9		$ 72.6445	=PRICE("3/30/2022","3/30/2042",0.02,0.05,100,2,3)					
10								
11	For a bond with $1,000 face value, multiply the price by 10 to get $726.44.							
12								
13	This function uses the following arguments:							
14								
15			=PRICE("Now","Maturity",Coupon,Yield,100,2,3)					
16								
17	The 100 indicates redemption value as a percent of face value.							
18	The 2 indicates semi-annual coupons.							
19	The 3 specifies an actual day count with 365 days per year.							
20								

Source: Microsoft.

PREMIUM AND DISCOUNT BONDS

Bonds are commonly distinguished according to whether they are selling at par value or at a discount or premium relative to par value. These three relative price descriptions—premium, discount, and par bonds—are defined as follows:

1. *Premium bonds.* Bonds with a price greater than par value are said to be selling at a premium. The yield to maturity of a premium bond is less than its coupon rate.

2. *Discount bonds.* Bonds with a price less than par value are said to be selling at a discount. The yield to maturity of a discount bond is greater than its coupon rate.

3. *Par bonds.* Bonds with a price equal to par value are said to be selling at par. The yield to maturity of a par bond is equal to its coupon rate.

The important thing to notice is that whether a bond sells at a premium or at a discount depends on the relation between its coupon rate and its yield. If the coupon rate exceeds the yield, the bond will sell at a premium. If the coupon is less than the yield, the bond will sell at a discount.

EXAMPLE 10.2 | **Premium and Discount Bonds**

Consider two bonds, both with eight years to maturity and a 7 percent coupon. One bond has a yield to maturity of 5 percent, while the other has a yield to maturity of 9 percent. Which of these bonds is selling at a premium and which is selling at a discount? Verify your answer by calculating each bond's price.

For the bond with a 9 percent yield to maturity, the coupon rate of 7 percent is less than the yield, indicating a discount bond. The bond's price is calculated as follows:

$$\frac{\$70}{.09}\left[1 - \frac{1}{1.045^{16}}\right] + \frac{\$1,000}{1.045^{16}} = \$887.66$$

For the bond with a 5 percent yield to maturity, the coupon rate of 7 percent is greater than the yield, indicating a premium bond. The bond's price is calculated as follows:

$$\frac{\$70}{.05}\left[1 - \frac{1}{1.025^{16}}\right] + \frac{\$1,000}{1.025^{16}} = \$1,130.55$$

The relationship between bond prices and bond maturities for premium and discount bonds is graphically illustrated in Figure 10.1 for bonds with an 8 percent coupon rate. The vertical axis measures bond prices, and the horizontal axis measures bond maturities.

FIGURE 10.1 | **Premium, Par, and Discount Bond Prices**

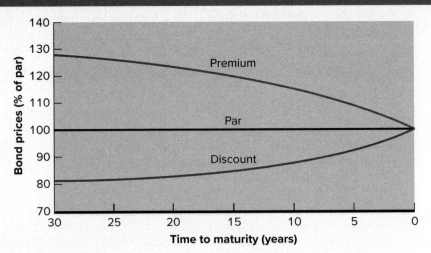

Figure 10.1 also describes the paths of premium and discount bond prices as their maturities shorten with the passage of time, assuming no changes in yield to maturity. As shown, the time paths of premium and discount bond prices follow smooth curves. Over time, the price of a premium bond declines and the price of a discount bond rises. At maturity, the price of each bond converges to its par value.

Figure 10.1 illustrates the general expectation that, for discount bonds, holding the coupon rate and yield to maturity constant, the longer the term to maturity of the bond, the greater is the discount from par value. For premium bonds, holding the coupon rate and yield to maturity constant, the longer the term to maturity of the bond, the greater is the premium over par value.

Even though bond prices change (almost constantly) with interest rates, most bonds are actually issued at par. When a company issues a bond at par, the company is picking a coupon rate that matches the required return on the bond when the bond is issued. The company could change the number of bonds it issues to generate a desired level of proceeds. Therefore, why would it matter whether bonds are issued at par? The answer relates to accounting rules that require companies to amortize premiums and discounts to par over the life of the bonds. So, pricing at par allows companies to avoid the unnecessary burden associated with accounting for these rules.

EXAMPLE 10.3 | **Premium Bonds**

Consider two bonds, both with a 9 percent coupon rate and the same yield to maturity of 7 percent, but with different maturities of 5 and 10 years. Which has the higher price? Verify your answer by calculating the prices.

First, because both bonds have a 9 percent coupon and a 7 percent yield, both bonds sell at a premium. Based on what we know, the one with the longer maturity will have a higher price. We can check these conclusions by calculating the prices as follows:

5-year maturity, premium bond price:

$$\frac{\$90}{.07}\left[1 - \frac{1}{1.035^{10}}\right] + \frac{\$1,000}{1.035^{10}} = \$1,083.17$$

10-year maturity, premium bond price:

$$\frac{\$90}{.07}\left[1 - \frac{1}{1.035^{20}}\right] + \frac{\$1,000}{1.035^{20}} = \$1,142.12$$

Notice that the longer-maturity premium bond has a higher price, as we predicted.

EXAMPLE 10.4 | **Discount Bonds**

Now consider two bonds, both with a 9 percent coupon rate and the same yield to maturity of 11 percent, but with different maturities of 5 and 10 years. Which has the higher price? Verify your answer by calculating the prices.

These are both discount bonds. (Why?) The one with the shorter maturity will have a higher price. To check, the prices can be calculated as follows:

5-year maturity, discount bond price:

$$\frac{\$90}{.11}\left[1 - \frac{1}{1.055^{10}}\right] + \frac{\$1,000}{1.055^{10}} = \$924.62$$

10-year maturity, discount bond price:

$$\frac{\$90}{.11}\left[1 - \frac{1}{1.055^{20}}\right] + \frac{\$1,000}{1.055^{20}} = \$880.50$$

In this case, the shorter-maturity discount bond has the higher price.

RELATIONSHIPS AMONG YIELD MEASURES

We have discussed three different bond rates or yields in this chapter: the coupon rate, the current yield, and the yield to maturity. We've seen the relationship between coupon rates and yields for discount and premium bonds. We can extend this to include current yields by noting that the current yield is between the coupon rate and the yield to maturity (unless the bond is selling at par, in which case all three are equal).

Putting together our observations about yield measures, we have the following:

Premium bonds (Price > Par): Coupon rate > Current yield > Yield to maturity

Discount bonds (Price < Par): Coupon rate < Current yield < Yield to maturity

Par value bonds (Price = Par): Coupon rate = Current yield = Yield to maturity

Thus, when a premium bond and a discount bond both have the same yield to maturity, the premium bond has a higher current yield than the discount bond. However, as shown in Figure 10.1, the advantage of a high current yield for a premium bond is offset by the fact that the price of a premium bond must ultimately fall to its face value when the bond matures. Similarly, the disadvantage of a low current yield for a discount bond is offset by the fact that the price of a discount bond must ultimately rise to its face value at maturity. For these reasons, current yield is not a reliable guide to what an actual yield (i.e., YTM) will be.

If you wish to get current price and yield information for Treasury note and bond issues, try the internet. The nearby *Work the Web* box displays a typical search query and the search results from a popular website.

A NOTE ON BOND PRICE QUOTES

If you buy a bond between coupon payment dates, the price you pay will usually be more than the price you are quoted. The reason is that standard convention in the bond market is to quote prices net of "accrued interest," meaning that accrued interest is deducted to arrive at the quoted price. This quoted price is called the **clean price**. The price you actually pay, however, includes the accrued interest. This price is the **dirty price**, also known as the *full* or *invoice price*.

An example is the easiest way to understand these prices. Suppose you buy a bond with a 12 percent annual coupon, payable semiannually. You actually pay $1,080 for this bond, so $1,080 is the dirty, or invoice, price. Further, on the day you buy it, the next coupon is due in four months, so you are between coupon dates. Notice that the next coupon will be $60.

The accrued interest on a bond is calculated by taking the fraction of the coupon period that has passed, in this case two months out of six, and multiplying this fraction by the next coupon, $60. So, the accrued interest in this example is $2/6 \times \$60 = \$20$. The bond's quoted price (i.e., its clean price) would be $1,080 − $20 = $1,060.[1]

Keep in mind that clean prices and accrued interest are purely quoting conventions. The price that matters to you is the invoice price because that is what you will actually pay for the bond. The only thing that's important about accrued interest on a bond is that it may impact the taxes you owe on the first coupon you receive.

clean price
The price of a bond net of accrued interest; this is the price that is typically quoted.

dirty price
The price of a bond including accrued interest, also known as the *full or invoice price*. This is the price the buyer actually pays.

CHECK THIS

10.2a A straight bond's price has two components. What are they?

10.2b What do you call a bond that sells for more than its face value?

10.2c What is the relationship between a bond's price and its term to maturity when the bond's coupon rate is equal to its yield to maturity?

10.2d Does current yield more strongly overstate yield to maturity for long-maturity or short-maturity premium bonds?

---

[1] The way accrued interest is calculated actually depends on the type of bond being quoted, for example, Treasury or corporate. The difference has to do with exactly how the fractional coupon period is calculated. In our example just above, we implicitly treated the months as having exactly the same length (i.e., 30 days each, 360 days in a year), which is consistent with the way corporate bonds are quoted. In contrast, for Treasury bonds, actual day counts are used. If you look back at our *Spreadsheet Analysis* exhibit, you'll see that we had to specify this treatment to value our Treasury bond.

Current information on Treasury bond prices and yields is available on many websites. As an example, we accessed the "Research" link at www.bloomberg.com. In the markets area of the site, you can find the "rates and bonds" link. Then you can search for U.S. government bonds. Also on the page, you will find TIPS bonds, Federal Reserve rates, and municipal bonds.

Treasury Yields

NAME	COUPON	PRICE	YIELD	1 MONTH	1 YEAR	TIME (EDT)
GB3:GOV 3 Month	0.00	1.03	1.05%	+25	+105	11:06 AM
GB6:GOV 6 Month	0.00	1.44	1.47%	+19	+146	11:06 AM
GB12:GOV 12 Month	0.00	1.91	1.96%	-3	+194	11:06 AM
GT2:GOV 2 Year	2.50	100.01	2.50%	-13	+235	11:06 AM
GT5:GOV 5 Year	2.75	100.12	2.73%	-13	+195	11:06 AM
GT10:GOV 10 Year	2.88	101.11	2.75%	-7	+119	11:06 AM
GT30:GOV 30 Year	2.88	98.20	2.97%	+8	-72	11:06 AM

Source: www.bloomberg.com, accessed May 2022.

10.3 More on Yields

Related Bloomberg Functions

BYFC Bond Yield Forecasts

YAS CALLS Yield and Spread Analysis: Yield to Call

In the previous section, we focused on finding a straight bond's price given its yield. In this section, we reverse direction to find a bond's yield given its price. We then discuss the relationship among the various yield measures we have seen. We finish the section with some additional yield calculations.

Before we begin the process of calculating yields, you should be aware of an important assumption made when yield is calculated. This assumption is that an investor will be able to reinvest the coupon interest payments at a rate equal to the yield to maturity of the bond. Therefore, an investor will earn the bond's yield to maturity only if the investor holds the bond to maturity and if all the coupon interest payments received are reinvested at a rate equal to the bond's yield to maturity.

The actual, or realized, rate earned on the bond can be lower or higher than the yield to maturity—it depends on how long the investor holds the bond and the rate at which the coupon payments are reinvested. Think about the difference like this: The yield to maturity is an expectation (or a forecast) of what the return would be from holding the bond if interest rates do not change, if the investor reinvests the coupons, and if the investor holds the bond to maturity. Because interest rates do change and because investors might not hold the bond to maturity, the actual return could be quite different.

For example, suppose interest rates change but the investor reinvests the coupons and holds the bond to maturity. In this case, the actual return differs from the yield to maturity because the bondholder reinvests the coupons at different interest rates. Suppose interest rates change, the investor reinvests the coupons, but the bondholder sells the bond before maturity. In this case, the actual return differs from the yield to maturity because the bondholder reinvests the coupons at different interest rates and because the selling price of the bond might be different from the face value of the bond. We revisit this issue in more detail in a later section.

CALCULATING YIELDS

To calculate a bond's yield given its price, we use the same straight bond formula used previously. The only way to find the yield is by trial and error. Financial calculators and spreadsheets do it this way at very high speed (and likely with more accuracy).

To illustrate, suppose we have a 6 percent bond with 10 years to maturity. Its price is 90, meaning 90 percent of face value. Assuming a $1,000 face value, the price is $900 and the coupon is $60 per year. What's the yield?

To find out, all we can do is try different yields until we come across the one that produces a price of $900. However, we can speed things up quite a bit by making an educated guess using what we know about bond prices and yields. We know the yield on this bond is greater than its 6 percent coupon rate because it is a discount bond. So let's first try 8 percent in the straight bond pricing formula:

$$\frac{\$60}{.08}\left[1 - \frac{1}{1.04^{20}}\right] + \frac{\$1,000}{1.04^{20}} = \$864.10$$

The price with an 8 percent yield is $864.10, which is somewhat less than the $900 price, but not too far off.

To finish, we need to ask whether the 8 percent we used was too high or too low. We know that the higher the yield, the lower is the price. Thus, 8 percent is a little too high, so let's try 7.5 percent:

$$\frac{\$60}{.075}\left[1 - \frac{1}{1.0375^{20}}\right] + \frac{\$1,000}{1.0375^{20}} = \$895.78$$

Now we're very close. We're still a little too high on the yield (since the price is a little low). If you try 7.4 percent, you'll see that the resulting price is $902.29, so the yield is between 7.4 and 7.5 percent (it's actually 7.435 percent). You should be thinking that a financial calculator is definitely a more efficient way to solve these problems!

EXAMPLE 10.5 **Calculating YTM**

Suppose a bond has eight years to maturity, a price of 110, and a coupon rate of 8 percent. What is its yield?

This is a premium bond, so its yield is less than the 8 percent coupon. If we try 6 percent, we get (check this) $1,125.61. The yield is therefore a little bigger than 6 percent. If we try 6.5 percent, we get (check this) $1,092.43, so the answer is slightly less than 6.5 percent. Check that 6.4 percent is almost exact (the exact yield is 6.3843 percent).

Yields to maturity may be calculated using a built-in spreadsheet function. An example of how to use an Excel™ spreadsheet to calculate the yield to maturity of a coupon bond is shown in the nearby *Spreadsheet Analysis* box.

YIELD TO CALL

The discussion in this chapter so far has assumed that a bond will have an actual maturity equal to its originally stated maturity. However, this is not always so because most bonds are **callable bonds**. When a bond issue is callable, the issuer can buy back outstanding bonds before the bonds mature. In exchange, bondholders receive a special **call price**, which is often equal to face value, although it may be slightly higher. When a call price is equal to face value, the bond is said to be *callable at par*.

When a bond is called, the bondholder does not receive any more coupon payments. Therefore, some callable bonds are issued with a provision known as a **make-whole call price**. The make-whole call price is calculated as the present value of the bond's remaining cash flows. The discount rate used to calculate the present value is often the yield of a comparable-maturity Treasury bond plus a prespecified premium. The first bonds issued to the investment public with a make-whole call provision were the Quaker State Corporation bonds issued in 1995. Since then, callable bond issues with make-whole call provisions have become common.

callable bond
A bond is callable if the issuer can buy it back before it matures.

call price
The price the issuer of a callable bond must pay to buy it back.

make-whole call price
The present value of the bond's remaining cash flows.

SPREADSHEET ANALYSIS

	A	B	C	D	E	F	G	H
1								
2		**Calculating the Yield to Maturity of a Coupon Bond**						
3								
4	A Treasury bond traded on March 30, 2022 matures in 8 years on March 30, 2030.							
5	Assuming an 4 percent coupon rate and a price of 110, what is this bond's yield							
6	to maturity?							
7	Hint: Use the Excel function YIELD.							
8								
9		2.6070%		=YIELD("3/30/2022","3/30/2030",0.04,110,100,2,3)				
10								
11	This function uses the following arguments:							
12								
13			=YIELD("Now","Maturity",Coupon,Price,100,2,3)					
14								
15	Price is entered as a percent of face value.							
16	The 100 indicates redemption value as a percent of face value.							
17	The 2 indicates semi-annual coupons.							
18	The 3 specifies an actual day count with 365 days per year.							
19								

Source: Microsoft.

Bonds are called at the convenience of the issuer, and a call usually occurs after a fall in market interest rates allows issuers to refinance outstanding debt with new bonds paying lower coupons, a process known as *bond refunding*. However, an issuer's call privilege is often restricted so that outstanding bonds cannot be called until the end of a specified **call protection period**, also termed a *call deferment period*. As a typical example, a bond issued with a 20-year maturity may be sold to investors subject to the restriction that it is callable anytime after an initial 5-year call protection period.

> **call protection period**
> The period during which a callable bond cannot be called. Also called a *call deferment period*.

> **yield to call (YTC)**
> Measure of return that assumes a bond will be redeemed at the earliest call date.

If a bond is callable, its yield to maturity may no longer be a useful number. Instead, the **yield to call**, commonly abbreviated **YTC**, may be more meaningful. Yield to call is a yield measure that assumes a bond issue will be called at its earliest possible call date.

We calculate a bond's yield to call using the straight bond pricing formula we have been using with two changes. First, instead of time to maturity, we use time to the first possible call date. Second, instead of face value, we use the call price. The resulting formula is thus:

$$\text{Callable bond price} = \frac{C}{YTC}\left[1 - \frac{1}{(1 + YTC/2)^{2T}}\right] + \frac{CP}{(1 + YTC/2)^{2T}} \quad \text{(10.4)}$$

where: C = Constant annual coupon

CP = Call price of the bond

T = Time in years until earliest possible call date

YTC = Yield to call assuming semiannual coupons

Calculating a yield to call requires the same trial-and-error procedure as calculating a yield to maturity. Most financial calculators either will handle the calculation directly or can be tricked into it by just changing the face value to the call price and the time to maturity to time to call.

To give a trial-and-error example, suppose a 20-year bond has a coupon of 8 percent, has a price of 98, and is callable in 10 years. The call price is 105. What are its yield to maturity and yield to call?

Based on our earlier discussion, we know the yield to maturity is slightly bigger than the coupon rate. (Why?) After some calculation, we find it to be 8.2 percent.

To find the bond's yield to call, we pretend it has a face value of 105 instead of 100 ($1,050 versus $1,000) and will mature in 10 years. With these two changes, the procedure is exactly the same. We can try 8.5 percent, for example:

$$\frac{\$80}{.085}\left[1 - \frac{1}{1.0425^{20}}\right] + \frac{\$1,050}{1.0425^{20}} = \$988.51$$

Because $988.51 is a little too high, the yield to call is slightly bigger than 8.5 percent. If we try 8.6, we find that the price is $981.83, so the yield to call is about 8.6 percent (it's 8.6276 percent).

A natural question comes up in this context. Which is bigger, the yield to maturity or the yield to call? The answer depends on the call price. If the bond is callable at par (as many are), then for a premium bond, the yield to maturity is greater. For a discount bond, the reverse is true.

Many financial data sources will provide both the yield to maturity and the yield to call. What if, however, the data source gives you only a single yield value? Which one does it give you? Well, the answer is: It depends. Generally speaking, the lower of the two yields is reported, and the data provider will often refer to this yield as the *yield to worst*. If so, this fact implies that the yield to maturity is typically reported for discount bonds, while the yield to call is given for premium bonds.

EXAMPLE 10.6　　**Yield to Call**

An 8.5 percent coupon bond maturing in 15 years is callable at 105 in 5 years. If the price is 100, which is bigger, the yield to call or the yield to maturity?

Since this is a par bond callable at a premium, the yield to call is bigger. We can verify this by calculating both yields. Check that the yield to maturity is 8.50 percent, whereas the yield to call is 9.308 percent.

Yield to call can be calculated using a built-in spreadsheet function. An example of how to use an Excel™ spreadsheet to calculate a yield to call is shown in the nearby *Spreadsheet Analysis* box.

SPREADSHEET ANALYSIS

	A	B	C	D	E	F	G	H
1								
2				**Calculating Yield to Call**				
3								
4	A bond traded on March 30, 2022 matures in 15 years on March 30, 2037 and may							
5	be called anytime after March 30, 2027 at a call price of 105. The bond pays an							
6	3.5 percent coupon and currently trades at par. What are the yield to maturity							
7	and yield to call for this bond?							
8								
9	Yield to maturity is based on the 2037 maturity and the current price of 100.							
10								
11		3.5000%	=YIELD("3/30/2022","3/30/2037",0.035,100,100,2,3)					
12								
13	Yield to call is based on the 2027 call date and the call price of 105.							
14								
15		4.4048%	=YIELD("3/30/2022","3/30/2027",0.035,100,105,2,3)					
16								

Source: Microsoft.

USING A FINANCIAL CALCULATOR

Calculating a bond price is relatively easy using the formulas you have seen. But you are probably thinking (and rightfully so) that you will never use the formulas to calculate a bond price if you have a financial calculator or spreadsheet available. This thinking is even more true for calculating yield because the trial-and-error process requires using formulas and is both long and frustrating.

Our Spreadsheet Analysis boxes have illustrated how to use spreadsheets. When you take your next finance test, however, you might not have access to a spreadsheet. Or, if you plan to take a professional exam such as the one sponsored by the CFA™ Institute, you are only allowed to use a financial calculator. Moreover, these test providers limit which calculators you can use. One calculator approved for the CFA™ Exam is the Texas Instruments BAII Plus. Many of you will already have one of these calculators because it is often required for finance courses.

You might have learned how to use your financial calculator in a prerequisite corporate finance class. If so, great! But just in case you did not, or if you need a refresher, we will provide a few basic instructions on how to calculate a bond price and a bond yield. Figure 10.2 shows a replica of the TI BAII Plus financial calculator.

Let's rework Example 10.1, where we calculated a bond price. In that example, we have a bond with 20 years to maturity, a coupon rate of 8 percent, and a yield to maturity of 7 percent. We need to enter this information into the calculator and then ask it to compute the bond price. We have highlighted the row of time value buttons that we use for data entry and calculations.

FIGURE 10.2   Texas Instruments BAII Plus Financial Calculator

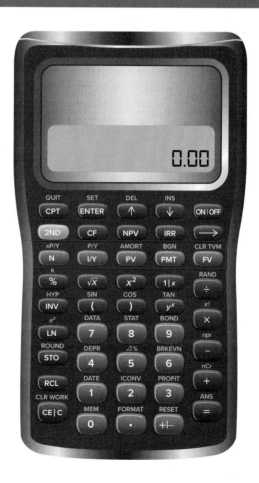

Fortunately, the button labels closely match what we have already talked about. For example, N is the number of periods. In our example, N = 40 since we have 20 years of semiannual payments. To enter this number, we type in 40, then hit the N button. You should notice that when you do so, the "=" sign pops on the screen. This indicates the calculator has accepted your input. We then move on to the remaining values.

We have a coupon rate of 8 percent, which means there is an annual coupon payment of $80 (assuming a $1,000 face value bond). Because the bond pays its coupon semiannually, we type in $40, then hit the PMT button. Again, the "=" sign should pop up. Let's enter the yield to maturity next, which is the button labeled "I/Y". The calculator already assumes that the yield is in percentage terms. So, we would enter 3.5 for the coupon (why not 7?). Finally, we input the face value (button labeled "FV") of $1,000.

With these values input into the calculator, we then ask it to calculate the bond price. We do so by tapping the CPT button in the upper left corner, then tapping the PV key. This should provide a price of $1,106.78, which matches our calculation (with a 1 cent rounding error) in Example 10.1.

Suppose we want to calculate the yield to maturity instead. The process is about the same. We enter the number of periods, the coupon payment, the current price of the bond, and the face value of the bond. Tap the CPT button, and solve for the yield to maturity by tapping the I/Y key.

CAUTION! When you input the bond price, you need to enter it as a negative number. In this way, you tell the calculator that the value is the price you are paying (i.e., a cash outflow). Because you are receiving the coupon payment and the face value as cash inflows, you enter them as positive numbers. If you do not keep track of the cash outflows and inflows correctly, your calculator will display the dreaded ERROR 5 message. You will think there is something wrong with your calculator. Sadly, however, it is simply pilot error.

Finally, remember that we have entered semiannual data. Thus, when we compute the yield, the calculator gives us a semiannual interest rate. To find the commonly reported annual yield to maturity, we need to multiply this semiannual interest rate by two.[2]

CHECK THIS

10.3a   What does it mean for a bond to be callable?

10.3b   What is the difference between yield to maturity and yield to call?

10.3c   Yield to call is calculated just like yield to maturity except for two changes. What are the changes?

10.4 Interest Rate Risk and Malkiel's Theorems

Bond yields are essentially interest rates, and, like interest rates, they fluctuate over time. When interest rates change, bond prices change. This is called **interest rate risk**. The term *interest rate risk* refers to the possibility of losses on a bond from changes in interest rates.

PROMISED YIELD AND REALIZED YIELD

The terms *yield to maturity* and *promised yield* both seem to imply that the yield originally stated when a bond is purchased is what you will actually earn if you hold the bond until it matures. Actually, this is not generally correct. The return or yield you actually earn on a bond is called the **realized yield**, and an originally stated yield to maturity is almost never exactly equal to the realized yield.

Related Bloomberg Functions

DUR   Duration Risk Factors

interest rate risk
The possibility that changes in interest rates will result in losses in a bond's value.

realized yield
The yield actually earned or "realized" on a bond.

---

[2] There is an alternative way to find the yield to maturity such that you do not need to make the final adjustment of multiplying by two. However, it requires you to change the payments per year (P/Y) in the calculator. We find that doing this leads to more errors, as students forget to change this assumption when moving from one problem to another.

As we discussed in a previous section, the reason a realized yield will almost always differ from a promised yield is that interest rates fluctuate. This fact means that coupons are reinvested at different rates and, maybe more importantly, bond prices also rise or fall as a result. One consequence is that if a bond is sold before maturity, its price might be higher or lower than originally anticipated. As a result, the realized yield will be different from the promised yield.

In an earlier section, we concluded that the realized and promised yields would be equal if you reinvested coupons at the yield to maturity and if you held the bond to maturity. That is, a bond's realized yield will equal its promised yield, for the most part, only if its yield doesn't change at all over the life of the bond—an unlikely event. As we will find over the next few sections, we can make more precise conclusions on the ways a bond price changes.

INTEREST RATE RISK AND MATURITY

While changing interest rates systematically affect all bond prices, it is important to realize that the impact of changing interest rates is not the same for all bonds. Some bonds are more sensitive to interest rate changes than others. To illustrate, Figure 10.3 shows how two bonds with different maturities can have different price sensitivities to changes in bond yields.

In Figure 10.3, bond prices are measured on the vertical axis and bond yields are measured on the horizontal axis. Both bonds have the same 8 percent coupon rate, but one bond has a 5-year maturity while the other bond has a 20-year maturity. Both bonds display the inverse relationship between bond prices and bond yields. Since both bonds have the same 8 percent coupon rate and both sell for par, their yields are 8 percent.

However, when bond yields are greater than 8 percent, the 20-year-maturity bond has a lower price than the 5-year-maturity bond. In contrast, when bond yields are less than 8 percent, the 20-year-maturity bond has a higher price than the 5-year-maturity bond. Essentially, falling yields cause both bond prices to rise, but the longer-maturity bond experiences a larger price increase than the shorter-maturity bond. Similarly, rising yields cause both bond prices to fall, but the price of the longer-maturity bond falls by more than the price of the shorter-maturity bond.

MALKIEL'S THEOREMS

The effect illustrated in Figure 10.3, along with some other important relationships among bond prices, maturities, coupon rates, and yields, is succinctly described by Burton Malkiel's five bond price theorems.[3] These five theorems are:

1. Bond prices and bond yields move in opposite directions. As a bond's yield increases, its price decreases. Conversely, as a bond's yield decreases, its price increases.

FIGURE 10.3 **Bond Prices and Yields**

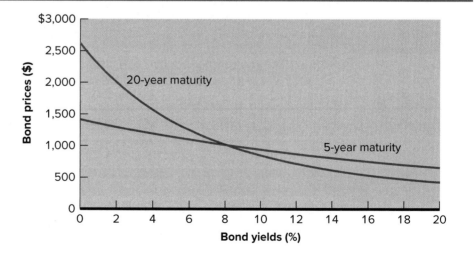

[3] Burton G. Malkiel, "Expectations, Bond Prices, and the Term Structure of Interest Rates," *Quarterly Journal of Economics* (May 1962), pp. 197–218.

2. For a given change in a bond's yield to maturity, the longer the term to maturity of the bond, the greater will be the magnitude of the change in the bond's price.

3. For a given change in a bond's yield to maturity, the size of the change in the bond's price increases at a diminishing rate as the bond's term to maturity lengthens.

4. For a given change in a bond's yield to maturity, the resulting percentage change in the bond's price is inversely related to the bond's coupon rate.

5. For a given absolute change in a bond's yield to maturity, the magnitude of the price increase caused by a decrease in yield is greater than the price decrease caused by an increase in yield.

The first, second, and fourth of these theorems are the simplest and most important. The first one says that bond prices and yields move in opposite directions. The second one says that longer-term bonds are more sensitive to changes in yields than shorter-term bonds. The fourth one says that lower-coupon bonds are more sensitive to changes in yields than higher-coupon bonds.

The other two theorems require more calculations. The third theorem says that a bond's sensitivity to interest rate changes increases as its maturity grows, but at a diminishing rate. In other words, a 10-year bond is much more sensitive to changes in yield than a 1-year bond. However, a 30-year bond is only slightly more sensitive than a 20-year bond. Finally, the fifth theorem says essentially that the loss you would suffer from, say, a 1 percent increase in yields is less than the gain you would enjoy from a 1 percent decrease in yields.

Table 10.1 illustrates the first three of these theorems by providing prices for 8 percent coupon bonds with maturities of 5, 10, and 20 years and yields to maturity of 7 percent and 9 percent. Be sure to check these for practice. As the first theorem says, bond prices are lower when yields are higher (9 percent versus 7 percent). As the second theorem indicates, the differences in bond prices between yields of 7 percent and 9 percent are greater for bonds with a longer term to maturity. However, as the third theorem states, the effect increases at a diminishing rate as the maturity lengthens. To see this, notice that $136.10 is 67.7 percent larger than $81.14, while $198.79 is only 46.1 percent larger than $136.10.

To illustrate the last two theorems, we present prices for 20-year-maturity bonds with coupon rates and yields to maturity of 6 percent, 8 percent, and 10 percent (again, calculate these for practice) in Table 10.2. To illustrate the fourth theorem, compare the loss on the 6 percent and the 8 percent bonds as yields move from 8 percent to 10 percent. The 6 percent bond loses ($656.82 − $802.07)/$802.07 = −.181, or −18.1%. The 8 percent bond loses ($828.41 − $1,000)/$1,000 = −.172, or −17.2%, showing that the bond with the lower coupon is more sensitive to a change in yields. You can (and should) verify that the same is true for a yield increase.

TABLE 10.1

Bond Prices and Yields

	Time to Maturity		
Yields	5 Years	10 Years	20 Years
7%	$1,041.58	$1,071.06	$1,106.78
9%	960.44	934.96	907.99
Price difference	$ 81.14	$ 136.10	$ 198.79

TABLE 10.2

Twenty-Year Bond Prices and Yields

	Coupon Rates		
Yields	6%	8%	10%
6%	$1,000.00	$1,231.15	$1,462.30
8%	802.07	1,000.00	1,197.93
10%	656.82	828.41	1,000.00

Finally, to illustrate the fifth theorem, take a look at the 8 percent coupon bond in Table 10.2. As yields decrease by 2 percent from 8 percent to 6 percent, the bond's price climbs by $231.15. As yields rise by 2 percent, the bond's price falls by $171.59.

As we have discussed, bond maturity is an important factor determining the sensitivity of a bond's price to changes in interest rates. However, bond maturity is an incomplete measure of bond price sensitivity to yield changes. For example, we have seen that a bond's coupon rate is also important. An improved measure of interest rate risk for bonds that accounts for both differences in maturity and differences in coupon rates is our next subject.

CHECK THIS

10.4a   True or false: A bond price's sensitivity to interest rate changes increases at an increasing rate as maturity lengthens.

10.4b   Which is more sensitive to an interest rate shift: a low-coupon bond or a high-coupon bond?

10.5 Duration

To account for differences in interest rate risk across bonds with different coupon rates and maturities, the concept of **duration** is widely applied. As we will explore in some detail, duration measures a bond's sensitivity to interest rate changes. The idea behind duration was first presented by Frederick Macaulay in an early study of U.S. financial markets.[4] Today, duration is a very widely used measure of a bond's price sensitivity to changes in bond yields.

Related Bloomberg Functions

FISA   Fixed Income Scenario Analysis

DURA   Duration Analysis

PDA   Position Duration Analysis

duration
A widely used measure of a bond's sensitivity to changes in bond yields.

MACAULAY DURATION

There are several duration measures. The original version is called *Macaulay duration.* The usefulness of Macaulay duration stems from the fact that it satisfies the following approximate relationship between percentage changes in bond prices and changes in bond yields:

$$\text{Percentage change in bond price} \approx -\text{Duration} \times \frac{\text{Change in } YTM}{(1 + YTM/2)} \qquad (10.5)$$

As a consequence, two bonds with the same duration, but not necessarily the same maturity, have approximately the same price sensitivity to a change in bond yields. This approximation is quite accurate for relatively small changes in yields, but it becomes less accurate when large changes are considered.

To see how we use this result, suppose a bond has a Macaulay duration of six years and its yield decreases from 10 percent to 9.5 percent. The resulting percentage change in the price of the bond is calculated as follows:

$$-6 \times \frac{.095 - .10}{1.05} = .0286, \text{ or } 2.86\%$$

Thus, the bond's price rises by 2.86 percent in response to a yield decrease of 50 basis points.

MODIFIED DURATION

Some analysts prefer to use a variation of Macaulay duration called *modified duration.* The relationship between Macaulay duration and modified duration for bonds paying semiannual coupons is:

$$\text{Modified duration} = \frac{\text{Macaulay duration}}{(1 + YTM/2)} \qquad (10.6)$$

---

[4] Frederick Macaulay, *Some Theoretical Problems Suggested by the Movements of Interest Rates, Bond Yields, and Stock Prices in the United States since 1856* (New York: National Bureau of Economic Research, 1938).

EXAMPLE 10.7

Macaulay Duration

A bond has a Macaulay duration of 11 years and its yield increases from 8 percent to 8.5 percent. What will happen to the price of the bond?

The resulting percentage change in the price of the bond can be calculated as follows:

$$-11 \times \frac{.085 - .08}{1.04} = -.0529, \text{ or } -5.29\%$$

The bond's price declines by approximately 5.29 percent in response to a 50 basis point increase in yield.

As a result, based on modified duration, the approximate relationship between percentage changes in bond prices and changes in bond yields is:

$$\text{Percentage change in bond price} \approx -\text{Modified duration} \times \text{Change in } YTM \qquad (10.7)$$

In other words, to calculate the percentage change in the bond's price, we multiply the modified duration by the change in yields.

EXAMPLE 10.8

Modified Duration

A bond has a Macaulay duration of 8.5 years and a yield to maturity of 9 percent. What is its modified duration?

The bond's modified duration is calculated as follows:

$$\frac{8.5}{1.045} = 8.134$$

Notice that we divided the yield by 2 to get the semiannual yield.

EXAMPLE 10.9

Modified Duration

A bond has a modified duration of seven years. Suppose its yield increases from 8 percent to 8.5 percent. What happens to its price?

We can very easily determine the resulting percentage change in the price of the bond using its modified duration:

$$-7 \times (.085 - .08) = -.035, \text{ or } -3.5\%$$

The bond's price declines by about 3.5 percent.

CALCULATING MACAULAY DURATION

Macaulay duration is often described as a bond's *effective maturity*. For this reason, duration values are conventionally stated in years. The first fundamental principle for calculating the duration of a bond concerns the duration of a zero coupon bond. Specifically, the duration of a zero coupon bond is equal to its maturity. Thus, on a pure discount instrument, such as the U.S. Treasury STRIPS, no calculation is necessary to come up with Macaulay duration.

The second fundamental principle for calculating duration concerns the duration of a coupon bond with multiple cash flows. The duration of a coupon bond is a weighted average of individual maturities of all the bond's separate cash flows. The weights attached to the maturity of each cash flow are proportionate to the present values of each cash flow.

A sample duration calculation for a bond with three years until maturity is illustrated in Table 10.3. The bond sells at par value. It has an 8 percent coupon rate and an 8 percent yield to maturity.

TABLE 10.3

Calculating Bond Duration

Years	Cash Flow	Discount Factor	Present Value	Years × Present Value ÷ Bond Price
.5	$ 40	.96154	$ 38.4615	.0192 years
1.0	40	.92456	36.9822	.0370
1.5	40	.88900	35.5599	.0533
2.0	40	.85480	34.1922	.0684
2.5	40	.82193	32.8771	.0822
3.0	1,040	.79031	821.9271	2.4658
			$ 1,000.00	2.7259 years
			Bond Price	Bond Duration

As shown in Table 10.3, calculating a bond's duration can be laborious—especially if the bond has a large number of separate cash flows. Fortunately, relatively simple formulas are available for many of the important cases. For example, if a bond is selling for par value, its duration can be calculated easily using the following formula:

$$\text{Par value bond duration} = \left[1 - \frac{1}{(1 + YTM/2)^{2M}} \right] \frac{(1 + YTM/2)}{YTM} \qquad (10.8)$$

where: M = Bond maturity in years

YTM = Yield to maturity assuming semiannual coupons

For example, using $YTM = 8\%$ and $M = 3$ years, we obtain the same duration value (2.7259 years) computed in Table 10.3.

EXAMPLE 10.10

Duration for a Par Value Bond

Suppose a par value bond has a 6 percent coupon and 10 years to maturity. What is its duration?

Because the bond sells for par, its yield is equal to its coupon rate, 6 percent. Plugging this into the par value bond duration formula, we have:

$$\text{Par value bond duration} = \frac{(1 + .06/2)}{.06} \left[1 - \frac{1}{(1 + .06/2)^{20}} \right]$$

After a little work on a calculator, we find that the duration is 7.66 years.

The par value bond duration formula (Equation 10.8) is useful for calculating the duration of a bond that is actually selling at par value. Unfortunately, the general formula for bonds not necessarily selling at par value is somewhat more complicated. The general duration formula for a bond paying constant semiannual coupons is:

$$\text{Duration} = \frac{1 + YTM/2}{YTM} - \frac{(1 + YTM/2) + M(CPR - YTM)}{YTM + CPR[(1 + YTM/2)^{2M} - 1]} \qquad (10.9)$$

where: CPR = Constant annual coupon rate

M = Bond maturity in years

YTM = Yield to maturity assuming semiannual coupons

Although somewhat tedious for manual calculations, this formula is used in many computer programs that calculate bond duration. Some popular personal computer spreadsheet packages and financial calculators have built-in functions to help you perform this calculation. An example of how to use an Excel™ spreadsheet to calculate a Macaulay duration and modified duration is shown in the nearby *Spreadsheet Analysis* box.

EXAMPLE 10.11

Duration for a Discount Bond

A bond has a yield to maturity of 7 percent. It matures in 12 years, and its coupon rate is 6 percent. What is its modified duration?

We first must calculate the Macaulay duration using the unpleasant-looking formula just above. We finish by converting the Macaulay duration to modified duration. Plugging into the duration formula, we have:

$$\text{Duration} = \frac{1 + .07/2}{.07} - \frac{(1 + .07/2) + 12(.06 - .07)}{.07 + .06[(1 + .07/2)^{24} - 1]}$$

$$= \frac{1.035}{.07} - \frac{1.035 + 12(-.01)}{.07 + .06(1.035^{24} - 1)}$$

After a little button pushing, we find that the duration is 8.56 years. Finally, converting to modified duration, we find that the modified duration is equal to 8.56/1.035 = 8.27 years.

PROPERTIES OF DURATION

Macaulay duration has a number of important properties. For straight bonds, the basic properties of Macaulay duration can be summarized as follows:

1. All else the same, the longer a bond's maturity, the longer is its duration.

2. All else the same, a bond's duration increases at a decreasing rate as maturity lengthens.

3. All else the same, the higher a bond's coupon, the shorter is its duration.

4. All else the same, a higher yield to maturity implies a shorter duration.

SPREADSHEET ANALYSIS

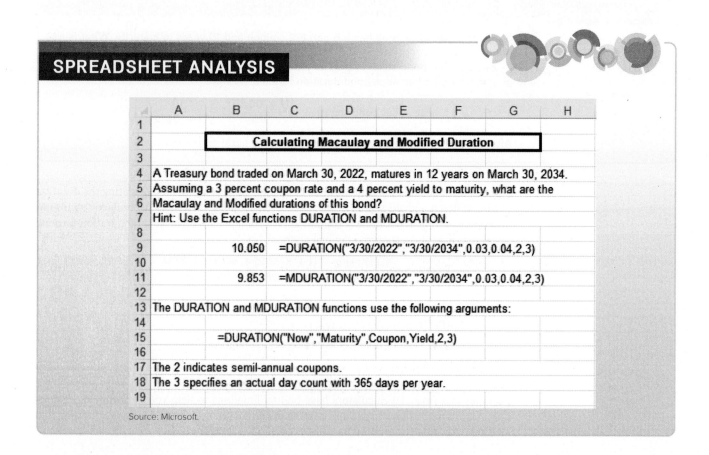

	A	B	C	D	E	F	G	H
1								
2			**Calculating Macaulay and Modified Duration**					
3								
4	A Treasury bond traded on March 30, 2022, matures in 12 years on March 30, 2034.							
5	Assuming a 3 percent coupon rate and a 4 percent yield to maturity, what are the							
6	Macaulay and Modified durations of this bond?							
7	Hint: Use the Excel functions DURATION and MDURATION.							
8								
9		10.050	=DURATION("3/30/2022","3/30/2034",0.03,0.04,2,3)					
10								
11		9.853	=MDURATION("3/30/2022","3/30/2034",0.03,0.04,2,3)					
12								
13	The DURATION and MDURATION functions use the following arguments:							
14								
15			=DURATION("Now","Maturity",Coupon,Yield,2,3)					
16								
17	The 2 indicates semil-annual coupons.							
18	The 3 specifies an actual day count with 365 days per year.							
19								

Source: Microsoft.

FIGURE 10.4   Bond Duration and Maturity

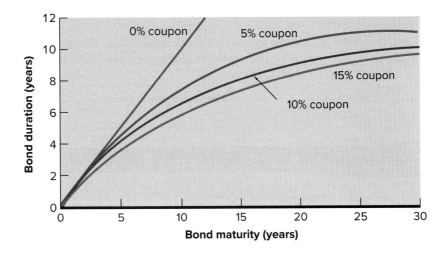

As we saw earlier, a zero coupon bond has a duration equal to its maturity. The duration on a bond with coupons is always less than its maturity. Because of the second principle, durations much longer than 10 or 15 years are rarely seen. An exception to some of these principles involves very long maturity bonds selling at a very steep discount. This exception rarely occurs in practice, so these principles are generally correct.

A graphical illustration of the relationship between duration and maturity is presented in Figure 10.4, where duration is measured on the vertical axis and maturity is measured on the horizontal axis. In Figure 10.4, the yield to maturity for all bonds is 10 percent. Bonds with coupon rates of 0 percent, 5 percent, 10 percent, and 15 percent are presented. As the figure shows, the duration of a zero coupon bond rises step for step with maturity. For the coupon bonds, however, the duration initially moves closely with maturity, as our first duration principle suggests, but, consistent with the second principle, the lines begin to flatten out after four or five years. Also, consistent with our third principle, the lower-coupon bonds have higher durations.

CHECK THIS

10.5a   What does duration measure?

10.5b   What is the duration of a zero coupon bond?

10.5c   What happens to a bond's duration as its maturity grows?

 # Bond Risk Measures Based on Duration

In this section, we examine some risk measures that are either based on duration or closely related to it. These measures are commonly used by bond traders and other fixed-income professionals.

DOLLAR VALUE OF AN 01

dollar value of an 01
Change in bond price resulting from a change in yield to maturity of one basis point.

A popular measure of interest rate risk among bond professionals is the **dollar value of an 01** (say "dollar value of an oh-one"), which measures the change in bond price resulting from a one basis point change in yield to maturity, where one basis point is 1 percent of 1 percent, that is, .01 percent, or .0001. The dollar value of an 01 is also known as the *value of a basis point.* The dollar value of an 01 can be stated through the modified duration of a bond as follows:

$$\text{Dollar value of an } 01 \approx \text{Modified duration} \times \text{Bond price} \times .0001 \qquad (10.10)$$

YIELD VALUE OF A 32ND

yield value of a 32nd
Change in yield to maturity that would lead to a 1/32 change in bond price.

When bond prices are quoted in 1/32's of a point, as is the historical convention, for example, with U.S. Treasury notes and bonds, the **yield value of a 32nd** is often used by bond professionals as an additional or alternative measure of interest rate risk. The yield value of a 32nd is the change in yield to maturity that would lead to a 1/32 change in bond price. A simple way to obtain the yield value of a 32nd is to multiply the dollar value of an 01 by 32 and then invert the result:

$$\text{Yield value of a 32nd} \approx \frac{1}{32 \times \text{Dollar value of an 01}} \qquad (10.11)$$

EXAMPLE 10.12 | **Bond Risk Measures Based on Duration**

The bond in Example 10.11 has a modified duration of 8.27 years. What is its dollar value of an 01? What is its yield value of a 32nd?

We must first calculate the price of this bond using the bond pricing formula provided earlier in this chapter (or with your financial calculator):

$$\text{Bond price} = \frac{6}{.07}\left[1 - \frac{1}{(1 + .035)^{24}}\right] + \frac{100}{(1 + .035)^{24}}$$
$$= \$91.971$$

Then, plugging the modified duration of 8.27 years and the bond price as a percentage of par value, 91.971, into Equation 10.10, we obtain the dollar value of an 01:

$$\text{Dollar value of an 01} \approx 8.27 \times 91.971 \times .0001 = .076$$

Thus, a one basis point change in yield will change the bond price by about $.076, or 7.6 cents per $100 of face value (in the opposite direction). For a $1,000 face value bond, this would be 76 cents.

Next, we multiply by 32 and invert to obtain the yield value of a 32nd:

$$\text{Yield value of a 32nd} \approx \frac{1}{32 \times .076} = .41086$$

Now we see that a change in yield of .41 basis point, or .0041 percent, would lead to a change in bond price of about 1/32. As a check, we calculate a bond price obtained by changing the yield from 7 percent to 7.0041 percent:

$$\text{Bond price} = \frac{6}{.070041}\left[1 - \frac{1}{(1 + .03500205)^{24}}\right] + \frac{100}{(1 + .03500205)^{24}}$$
$$= \$91.94$$

The resulting price change is $.03 ≈ $91.97 − $91.94. Because 1/32 of a point corresponds to $.03125, we see that our computed yield value of a 32nd is quite accurate.

CHECK THIS

10.6a What is the relationship between modified duration and the dollar value of an 01?

10.6b What is the relationship between the dollar value of an 01 and the yield value of a 32nd?

10.7 Dedicated Portfolios and Reinvestment Risk

Duration has another property that makes it a vital tool in bond portfolio management. To explore this subject, we first need to introduce two important concepts: dedicated portfolios and reinvestment risk.

DEDICATED PORTFOLIOS

dedicated portfolio
A bond portfolio created to prepare for a future cash outlay.

For a practical view of bond portfolio management, visit
www.financialpipeline.com.

A firm can invest in coupon bonds when it is preparing to meet a future liability or other cash outlay. A bond portfolio formed for such a specific purpose is called a **dedicated portfolio.** When the future liability payment of a dedicated portfolio is due on a known date, this date is commonly called the portfolio's *target date.*

Pension funds provide a good example of dedicated portfolio management. A pension fund normally knows years in advance the amount of benefit payments it must make to its beneficiaries. The fund can then purchase coupon bonds today to prepare for these future payments.

Let's work through an example. Suppose the Safety First pension fund estimates that it must pay benefits of about $100 million in five years. Safety First then decides to buy coupon bonds yielding 8 percent. These coupon bonds pay semiannual coupons, mature in five years, and are currently selling at par. If interest rates *do not change over the next five years,* how much money does Safety First need to invest today in these coupon bonds to have $100 million in five years?

Fortunately, we can use Equation 10.3—and some ingenuity—to answer this question. Recall that Equation 10.3 says that today's bond price, P, is the present value of the coupons plus the present value of the promised face value. However, in the case of Safety First, we want to solve for a future value. So let's make Equation 10.3 into an equation for future value by multiplying by the amount $(1 + YTM/2)^{2M}$:

$$P = \frac{C}{YTM}\left[1 - \frac{1}{(1 + YTM/2)^{2M}}\right] + \frac{\text{Face value}}{(1 + YTM/2)^{2M}}$$

$$P(1 + YTM/2)^{2M} = \frac{C}{YTM}[(1 + YTM/2)^{2M} - 1] + \text{Face value} \qquad (10.12)$$

Equation 10.12 shows us that the future value of all the payments made on a bond over its life is the current value, P, multiplied by $(1 + YTM/2)^{2M}$. In the case of Safety First, we know the future value is $100,000,000, so we have:

$$\text{Future value} = \$100{,}000{,}000 = P(1 + YTM/2)^{2M}$$

We can rearrange this equation to solve for the present value:

$$\text{Present value} = P = \$100{,}000{,}000/(1 + YTM/2)^{2M}$$

The bonds being considered by Safety First have a yield to maturity of 8 percent and mature in five years, so:

$$\text{Present value} = P = \$100{,}000{,}000/(1 + .08/2)^{2\times5}$$
$$= \$100{,}000{,}000/(1 + .04)^{10}$$
$$= \$67{,}556{,}417$$

Thus, Safety First needs to invest about $67.5 million today. Because the bonds in question sell for par, this $67.5 million is also the total face value of the bonds.

With this face value, the coupon payment every six months is $67,556,417 × .08/2 = $2,702,257. When Safety First invests each of these coupons at 8 percent (i.e., the YTM), the total future value of the coupons is $32,443,583. Safety First will also receive the face value of the coupon bonds in five years, or $67,556,417. In five years, Safety First will have $32,443,583 + $67,556,417 = $100,000,000.

Therefore, Safety First needs about $67.5 million to construct a dedicated bond portfolio to fund a future liability of $100 million. However, consider another important fact: We calculated this amount assuming that Safety First can invest each coupon amount at 8 percent over the next five years. If the assumption is true (i.e., interest rates do not change over the next five years), Safety First's bond fund will grow to the amount needed.

REINVESTMENT RISK

As we have seen, the bond investment strategy of the Safety First pension fund will be successful if all coupons received during the life of the investment *can be reinvested at a constant 8 percent YTM.* However, in reality, yields at which coupons can be reinvested are uncertain, and a target date surplus or shortfall is therefore likely to occur.

			Reinvestment YTM:	7.00%	8.00%	9.00%
			Coupon Rate:	8.00%	8.00%	8.00%
Year	Six-Month Period	Payment		Payment Value, End of Year 5	Payment Value, End of Year 5	Payment Value, End of Year 5
1	1	$2,702,257		$ 3,682,898	$ 3,846,154	$ 4,015,811
	2	2,702,257		3,558,356	3,698,225	3,842,881
2	3	2,702,257		3,438,025	3,555,985	3,677,398
	4	2,702,257		3,321,763	3,419,217	3,519,041
3	5	2,702,257		3,209,433	3,287,708	3,367,503
	6	2,702,257		3,100,902	3,161,258	3,222,491
4	7	2,702,257		2,996,040	3,039,671	3,083,724
	8	2,702,257		2,894,725	2,922,761	2,950,932
5	9	2,702,257		2,796,836	2,810,347	2,823,858
	10	2,702,257		2,702,257	2,702,257	2,702,257
		Future value of coupons		$31,701,235	$ 32,443,583	$ 33,205,896
		Face value received (at end of Year 5)		$67,556,417	$ 67,556,417	$ 67,556,417
		Target date portfolio value		$99,257,652	$100,000,000	$100,762,313

TABLE 10.4 — Reinvestment Rate Risk

reinvestment rate risk
The uncertainty about the future or target date portfolio value that results from the need to reinvest bond coupons at yields not known in advance.

The uncertainty about the future or target date portfolio value that results from the need to reinvest bond coupons at yields that cannot be predicted in advance is called **reinvestment rate risk**. Thus, the uncertain portfolio value on the target date represents reinvestment risk. In general, more distant target dates entail greater uncertainty and reinvestment risk.

To examine the impact of reinvestment risk, we continue with the example of the Safety First pension fund's dedicated bond portfolio. We will add one small wrinkle. We assume that Safety First buys 8 percent coupon bonds that are selling at par. However, we will not assume that interest rates stay constant at 8 percent.

Instead, consider two cases, one in which all bond coupons are reinvested at a 7 percent YTM and one in which all coupons are reinvested at a 9 percent YTM. The value of the portfolio on the target date will be the payment of the fixed $67.5 million principal plus the future value of the 10 semiannual coupons compounded at either 7 percent or 9 percent. Note that the coupon rate is 8 percent in both cases.

As shown in Table 10.4, a value of $99.258 million is realized by a 7 percent reinvestment YTM, and a target date portfolio value of $100.762 million is realized through a 9 percent reinvestment YTM. The difference between these two amounts, about $1.5 million, illustrates reinvestment risk.

As this example illustrates, a maturity matching strategy for a dedicated bond portfolio has reinvestment risk. Further, we changed interest rates by only 1 percent. Reinvestment risk can be much greater than what we have shown. Our example also understates a pension fund's total reinvestment risk because it considers only a single target date. In reality, pension funds have a series of target dates, and a shortfall at one target date typically coincides with shortfalls at other target dates, too.

A simple solution for reinvestment risk is to purchase zero coupon bonds that pay a fixed principal at a maturity chosen to match a dedicated portfolio's target date. Because there are no coupons to reinvest, there is no reinvestment risk. However, a zero coupon bond strategy has its drawbacks, too. As a practical matter, U.S. Treasury STRIPS are the only zero coupon bonds issued in sufficient quantity to even begin to satisfy the dedicated portfolio needs of pension funds, insurance companies, and other institutional investors.

However, U.S. Treasury securities have lower yields than even the highest-quality corporate bonds. A yield difference of only .25 percent between Treasury securities and corporate bonds can make a substantial difference in the initial cost of a dedicated bond portfolio.

For example, suppose that Treasury STRIPS have a yield of 7.75 percent. Using semiannual compounding, the present value of these zero coupon bonds providing a principal payment of $100 million at a five-year maturity is calculated as follows:

$$\text{STRIPS price} = \frac{\$100,000,000}{(1 + .0775/2)^{2 \times 5}}$$

$$= \frac{\$100,000,000}{(1 + .03875)^{10}}$$

$$= \$68,373,787$$

This cost of $68.374 million based on a 7.75 percent yield is significantly higher than the previously stated cost of $67.556 million based on an 8 percent yield. From the perspective of the Safety First pension fund, this represents a hefty premium to pay to eliminate reinvestment risk. Fortunately, as we discuss in the next section, other methods are available at lower cost.

CHECK THIS

10.7a What is a dedicated portfolio?

10.7b What is reinvestment rate risk?

10.8 Immunization

immunization
Constructing a portfolio to minimize the uncertainty surrounding its target date value.

Constructing a dedicated portfolio to minimize the uncertainty in its target date value is called **immunization**. In this section, we show how duration can be used to immunize a bond portfolio against reinvestment risk.

PRICE RISK VERSUS REINVESTMENT RATE RISK

To understand how immunization is accomplished, suppose you own a bond with eight years to maturity. However, your target date is actually just six years from now. If interest rates rise, are you happy or unhappy?

Your initial reaction is probably "unhappy" because you know that as interest rates rise, bond values fall. However, things are not so simple. Clearly, if interest rates rise, then, in six years, your bond will be worth less than it would have been at a lower rate. This is called **price risk**. However, it is also true that you will be able to reinvest the coupons you receive at a higher interest rate. As a result, your reinvested coupons will be worth more. In fact, the net effect of an interest rate increase might be to make you better off.

price risk
The risk that bond prices will decrease, which arises in dedicated portfolios when the target date value of a bond or bond portfolio is not known with certainty.

As our simple example illustrates, for a dedicated portfolio, interest rate changes have two effects. Interest rate increases act to decrease bond prices (price risk) but increase the future value of reinvested coupons (reinvestment rate risk). In the other direction, interest rate decreases act to increase bond values but decrease the future value of reinvested coupons. The key observation is that these two effects—price risk and reinvestment rate risk—tend to offset each other.

You might wonder if it is possible to engineer a portfolio in which these two effects offset each other more or less precisely. As we illustrate next, the answer is most definitely yes.

IMMUNIZATION BY DURATION MATCHING

The key to immunizing a dedicated portfolio is to match its duration to its target date. If this is done, then the impacts of price and reinvestment rate risk will almost exactly offset, and interest rate changes will have a minimal impact on the target date value of the portfolio. In fact, immunization is often referred to as *duration matching*.

To see how a duration matching strategy can be applied to reduce target date uncertainty, suppose the Safety First pension fund initially purchases $67.5 million of par value bonds paying 8 percent coupons with a maturity of 6.2 years instead of 5 years. Why 6.2 years? From the par value duration formula, Equation 10.8, a maturity of 6.2 years corresponds to a duration of 5 years. Thus, the duration of Safety First's dedicated bond portfolio is now matched to its five-year portfolio target date.

Suppose that immediately after the bonds are purchased, a one-time shock causes bond yields to either jump up to 10 percent or jump down to 6 percent. As a result, all coupons are reinvested at either a 10 percent yield or a 6 percent yield, depending on which way rates jump.

This example is illustrated in Figure 10.5, where the left vertical axis measures initial bond portfolio values and the right vertical axis measures bond portfolio values realized by holding the portfolio until the bonds mature in 6.2 years. The horizontal axis measures the passage of time from initial investment to bond maturity. The positively sloped lines plot bond portfolio values through time for bond yields that have jumped to either 10 percent or 6 percent immediately after the initial investment of $67.5 million in par value 8 percent coupon bonds. This example assumes that after their initial jump, bond yields remain unchanged.

As shown in Figure 10.5, the initial jump in yields causes the value of Safety First's bond portfolio to jump in the opposite direction. If yields increase, bond prices fall, but coupons are reinvested at a higher interest rate, thereby leading to a higher portfolio value at maturity. In contrast, if yields decrease, bond prices rise, but a lower reinvestment rate reduces the value of the portfolio at maturity.

However, what is remarkable is that regardless of whether yields rise or fall, there is almost no difference in Safety First's portfolio value at the duration-matched five-year target date. Thus, the immunization strategy of matching the duration of Safety First's dedicated portfolio to its portfolio target date has almost entirely eliminated reinvestment risk.

DYNAMIC IMMUNIZATION

The example of the Safety First pension fund immunizing a dedicated bond portfolio using a duration matching strategy assumed that the bond portfolio was subject to a single yield shock. In reality, bond yields change constantly. Therefore, successful immunization requires that a dedicated portfolio be rebalanced frequently to maintain a portfolio duration equal to the portfolio's target date.

For example, by purchasing bonds with a maturity of 6.2 years, the Safety First pension fund had matched the duration of the dedicated portfolio to the fund's 5-year target date. One year later, however, the target date is four years away, and bonds with a duration of four years are required to maintain a duration matching strategy. Assuming interest rates haven't changed, the par value duration formula shows that a maturity of 4.7 years corresponds to a duration of 4 years. Thus, to maintain a duration-matched target date, the Safety First fund must sell its originally purchased bonds now with a maturity of 5.2 years and replace them with bonds having a maturity of 4.7 years.

dynamic immunization
Periodic rebalancing of a dedicated bond portfolio to maintain a duration that matches the target maturity date.

The strategy of periodically rebalancing a dedicated bond portfolio to maintain a portfolio duration matched to a specific target date is called **dynamic immunization**. The advantage of

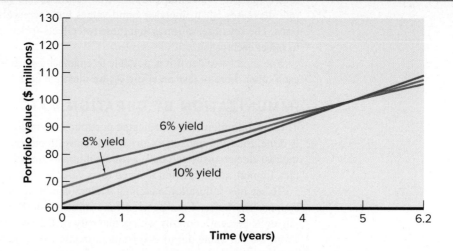

FIGURE 10.5   Bond Price and Reinvestment Rate Risk

dynamic immunization is that reinvestment risk caused by continually changing bond yields is greatly reduced. The drawback of dynamic immunization is that each portfolio rebalancing incurs management and transaction costs. Therefore, portfolios should not be rebalanced too frequently. In practice, rebalancing on an intermittent basis, say, each quarter, is a reasonable compromise between the costs of rebalancing and the benefits of dynamic immunization.

CHECK THIS

10.8a What are the two effects on the target date value of a dedicated portfolio of a shift in yields? Explain why they tend to offset.

10.8b How can a dedicated portfolio be immunized against shifts in yields?

10.8c Why is rebalancing necessary to maintain immunization?

10.9 Summary and Conclusions

This chapter covers the basics of bonds, bond yields, duration, and immunization. Among other items, we covered the following topics—grouped by the chapter's important concepts.

1. **How to calculate bond prices and yields.**

   A. The straight bond pricing formula has two separate components. The first component is the present value of all the coupon payments. Because the coupons are fixed and paid on a regular basis, you may recognize that they form an ordinary annuity, and the first piece of the bond pricing formula is a standard calculation for the present value of an annuity. The other component represents the present value of the principal payment at maturity, and it is a standard calculation for the present value of a single lump sum.

   B. Calculating bond prices is mostly "plug and chug" with a calculator. In fact, a good financial calculator or spreadsheet should have this formula built into it. However, it is important to be able to work bond calculations the "long way" so that you know how the formulas work.

   C. Coupon bonds are generally distinguished according to whether they are selling at par value or at a discount or premium relative to par value. Bonds with a price greater than par value are said to be selling at a premium, which occurs when the coupon rate is greater than the yield to maturity. Bonds with a price less than par value are said to be selling at a discount, which occurs when the coupon rate is less than the yield to maturity.

2. **The importance of yield to maturity.**

   A. There are three different yield measures: coupon yield or rate, current yield, and yield to maturity. Each is calculated using a specific equation, and which is the biggest or smallest depends on whether the bond is selling at a discount or a premium.

   B. Important relationships among bond prices, maturities, coupon rates, and yields are described by Malkiel's five bond price theorems.

   C. A stated yield to maturity is almost never equal to an actually realized yield because yields are subject to bond price risk and coupon reinvestment rate risk.

3. **Interest rate risk and Malkiel's theorems.**

   A. Bond prices and bond yields move in opposite directions. As a bond's yield increases, its price decreases. Conversely, as a bond's yield decreases, its price increases.

   B. For a given change in a bond's yield to maturity, the longer the term to maturity of the bond, the greater will be the magnitude of the change in the bond's price.

   C. For a given change in a bond's yield to maturity, the size of the change in the bond's price increases at a diminishing rate as the bond's term to maturity lengthens.

   D. For a given change in a bond's yield to maturity, the absolute magnitude of the resulting change in the bond's price is inversely related to the bond's coupon rate.

E. For a given absolute change in a bond's yield to maturity, the magnitude of the price increase caused by a decrease in yield is greater than the price decrease caused by an increase in yield.

4. How to measure the impact of interest rate changes on bond prices.

A. Bond price risk is the risk that a bond sold before maturity must be sold at a price different from the price predicted by an originally stated yield to maturity. Coupon reinvestment risk is the risk that bond coupons must be reinvested at yields different from an originally stated yield to maturity.

B. To account for differences in interest rate risk across bonds with different coupon rates and maturities, the concept of duration is widely applied. Duration is a direct measure of a bond's price sensitivity to changes in bond yields.

C. Bond portfolios are often created for the purpose of preparing for a future liability payment. Portfolios formed for such a specific purpose are called dedicated portfolios. When the future liability payment of a dedicated portfolio is due on a known date, that date is called the portfolio's target date.

D. Minimizing the uncertainty of the value of a dedicated portfolio's future target date value is called immunization. A strategy of matching a bond portfolio's duration to the target maturity date accomplishes this goal.

GETTING DOWN TO BUSINESS

This chapter covered bond basics. How should you, as an investor or investment manager, put this information to work?

Now that you've been exposed to basic facts about bonds, their prices, and their yields, you might try applying the various principles we have discussed. Do this by buying some bonds, perhaps in a simulated brokerage account, and then observing the behavior of their prices and yields. Buying Treasury bonds is the best place to start.

With a simulated brokerage account, buy two Treasury bonds with the same maturity but different coupons. This will let you see the impact of coupon rates on price volatility. Similarly, buy two bonds with very different maturities but similar coupon rates. You'll see firsthand how maturity determines the risk of a bond.

While you're at it, calculate the durations of the bonds you buy. As their yields fluctuate, check that the percentage change in price is very close to what your calculated duration suggests it should be.

To learn more about bond prices and yields, visit some interesting websites such as Investing in Bonds (www.investinginbonds.com).

For the latest information on the real world of investments, visit us at jmdinvestments.blogspot.com.

Key Terms

call price 336
call protection period 337
callable bond 336
clean price 334
coupon rate 329
current yield 329
dedicated portfolio 349
dirty price 334
dollar value of an 01 347
duration 343

dynamic immunization 352
immunization 351
interest rate risk 340
make-whole call price 336
price risk 351
realized yield 340
reinvestment rate risk 350
yield to call (YTC) 337
yield to maturity (YTM) 330
yield value of a 32nd 348

Related Bloomberg Functions

YAS	Yield and Spread Analysis, 10.1
BVAL	Bloomberg Valuation, 10.2
FIPX	Fixed Income Price Discovery, 10.2
XLTC XFIC	Excel Template: Fixed Income Comparables Analysis, 10.2
BYFC	Bond Yield Forecasts, 10.3
YAS CALLS	Yield and Spread Analysis: Yield to Call, 10.3
DUR	Duration Risk Factors, 10.4
FISA	Fixed Income Scenario Analysis, 10.5
DURA	Duration Analysis, 10.5
PDA	Position Duration Analysis, 10.5

Chapter Review Problems and Self-Test

1. **Straight Bond Prices (LO1, CFA5)**   Suppose a bond has 10 years to maturity and a coupon rate of 6 percent. The bond's yield to maturity is 8 percent. What's the price?

2. **Premium Bonds (LO1, CFA3)**   Suppose we have two bonds, both with a 6 percent coupon rate and the same yield to maturity of 4 percent, but with different maturities of 5 and 15 years. Which has the higher price? Verify your answer by calculating the prices.

3. **Macaulay Duration (LO4, CFA6)**   A bond has a Macaulay duration of nine years, and its yield increases from 6 percent to 6.25 percent. What will happen to the price of the bond?

Answers to Self-Test Problems

1. Here, the coupon rate is 6 percent and the face value is $1,000, so the annual coupon is $60. The bond's price is calculated as follows:

   Present value of semiannual coupons:

   $$\frac{\$60}{.08}\left[1 - \frac{1}{1.04^{20}}\right] = \$407.70979$$

   Present value of $1,000 principal:

   $$\frac{\$1,000}{1.04^{20}} = \$456.38695$$

   The bond's price is the sum of coupon and principal present values:

   $$\text{Bond price} = \$407.71 + \$456.39 = \$864.10$$

2. Because both bonds have a 6 percent coupon and a 4 percent yield, both bonds sell at a premium, and the one with the longer maturity will have a higher price. We can verify these conclusions by calculating the prices as follows:

   5-year-maturity premium bond price:

   $$\frac{\$60}{.04}\left[1 - \frac{1}{1.02^{10}}\right] + \frac{\$1,000}{1.02^{10}} = \$1,089.83$$

   15-year-maturity premium bond price:

   $$\frac{\$60}{.04}\left[1 - \frac{1}{1.02^{30}}\right] + \frac{\$1,000}{1.02^{30}} = \$1,223.96$$

   Notice that the longer-maturity premium bond has a higher price, just as we thought.

3. The resulting percentage change in the price of the bond can be calculated as follows:

   $$-9 \times \frac{.0625 - .06}{1.03} = -.0218, \text{or} -2.18\%$$

   The bond's price declines by approximately 2.18 percent in response to a 25 basis point increase in yields.

1. **Yield to Maturity (LO2, CFA3)**   The yield to maturity on a bond is:

   a. Below the coupon rate when the bond sells at a discount and above the coupon rate when the bond sells at a premium.
   b. The interest rate that makes the present value of the payments equal to the bond price.
   c. Based on the assumption that all future payments received are reinvested at the coupon rate.
   d. Based on the assumption that all future payments received are reinvested at future market rates.

2. **Bond Yields (LO1, CFA5)**   In which one of the following cases is the bond selling at a discount?

   a. Coupon rate is greater than current yield, which is greater than yield to maturity.
   b. Coupon rate, current yield, and yield to maturity are all the same.
   c. Coupon rate is less than current yield, which is less than yield to maturity.
   d. Coupon rate is less than current yield, which is greater than yield to maturity.

3. **Bond Yields (LO1, CFA3)**   When are yield to maturity and current yield on a bond equal?

   a. When market interest rates begin to level off
   b. If the bond sells at a price in excess of its par value
   c. When the expected holding period is greater than one year
   d. If the coupon and market interest rate are equal

4. **Bond Yields (LO1, CFA5)**   Which of the following states the correct relationship among yield measures for discount bonds?

   a. Coupon rate < Current yield < Yield to maturity
   b. Current yield < Coupon rate < Yield to maturity
   c. Coupon rate < Yield to maturity < Current yield
   d. Yield to maturity < Coupon rate < Current yield

5. **Bond Yields (LO1, CFA5)**   Which of the following states the correct relationship among yield measures for premium bonds?

   a. Coupon rate > Current yield > Yield to maturity
   b. Current yield > Coupon rate > Yield to maturity
   c. Coupon rate > Yield to maturity > Current yield
   d. Yield to maturity > Coupon rate > Current yield

6. **Bond Prices (LO1, CFA3)**   Consider a five-year bond with a 10 percent coupon that is presently trading at a yield to maturity of 8 percent. If market interest rates do not change, one year from now the price of this bond:

   a. Will be higher.
   b. Will be lower.
   c. Will be the same.
   d. Cannot be determined.

7. **Bond Prices (LO1, CFA2)**   Using semiannual compounding, what would be the price of a 15-year, zero coupon bond that has a par value of $1,000 and a required return of 8 percent?

   a. $308
   b. $315
   c. $464
   d. $555

8. **Bond Prices (LO1, CFA2)**   If an investor's required return is 12 percent, the value of a 10-year-maturity zero coupon bond with a maturity value of $1,000 is closest to:

   a. $312
   b. $688
   c. $1,000
   d. $1,312

9. **Duration (LO4, CFA3)**   Another term for bond duration is:

   a. Actual maturity.
   b. Effective maturity.
   c. Calculated maturity.
   d. Near-term maturity.

10. **Duration (LO4, CFA6)** Which of the following is not a property of duration?

   a. A longer maturity generally yields a longer duration.
   b. Duration generally increases at a decreasing rate as maturity lengthens.
   c. A bigger coupon generally yields a longer duration.
   d. A higher yield to maturity generally yields a shorter duration.

11. **Duration (LO4, CFA4)** Which statement is true for the Macaulay duration of a zero coupon bond?

   a. It is equal to the bond's maturity in years.
   b. It is equal to one-half the bond's maturity in years.
   c. It is equal to the bond's maturity in years divided by its yield to maturity.
   d. It cannot be calculated because of the lack of coupons.

12. **Duration (LO4, CFA6)** Which of the following states the correct relationship between Macaulay duration and modified duration?

   a. Modified duration = Macaulay duration/$(1 + YTM/2)$
   b. Modified duration = Macaulay duration $\times (1 + YTM/2)$
   c. Modified duration = Macaulay duration/YTM
   d. Modified duration = Macaulay duration $\times YTM$

13. **Duration (LO4, CFA6)** Which one of the following bonds has the shortest duration?

   a. Zero coupon, 10-year maturity
   b. Zero coupon, 13-year maturity
   c. 8 percent coupon, 10-year maturity
   d. 8 percent coupon, 13-year maturity

14. **Duration (LO4, CFA6)** Identify the bond that has the longest duration (no calculations necessary).

   a. 20-year maturity with an 8 percent coupon
   b. 20-year maturity with a 12 percent coupon
   c. 15-year maturity with a 0 percent coupon
   d. 10-year maturity with a 15 percent coupon

15. **Duration (LO4, CFA3)** Which bond has the longest duration?

   a. 8-year maturity, 6 percent coupon
   b. 8-year maturity, 11 percent coupon
   c. 15-year maturity, 6 percent coupon
   d. 15-year maturity, 11 percent coupon

16. **Duration (LO4, CFA3)** The duration of a bond normally increases with an increase in:

   a. Term to maturity.
   b. Yield to maturity.
   c. Coupon rate.
   d. All of the above.

17. **Duration (LO4, CFA6)** When interest rates decline, what happens to the duration of a 30-year bond selling at a premium?

   a. It increases.
   b. It decreases.
   c. It remains the same.
   d. It increases at first, then declines.

18. **Duration (LO4, CFA6)** An 8 percent, 20-year corporate bond is priced to yield 9 percent. The Macaulay duration for this bond is 8.85 years. Given this information, how many years is the bond's modified duration?

   a. 8.12
   b. 8.47
   c. 8.51
   d. 9.25

19. **Using Duration (LO4, CFA2)** A 9-year bond has a yield to maturity of 10 percent and a modified duration of 6.54 years. If the market yield changes by 50 basis points, what is the change in the bond's price?

   a. 3.27 percent
   b. 3.66 percent
   c. 6.54 percent
   d. 7.21 percent

20. **Using Duration (LO4, CFA3)**   A 6 percent coupon bond paying interest semiannually has a modified duration of 10 years, sells for $800, and is priced at a yield to maturity (YTM) of 8 percent. If the YTM increases to 9 percent, the predicted change in price, using the duration concept, is which of the following amounts?

   a. $76.56
   b. $76.92
   c. $77.67
   d. $80.00

21. **Immunization (LO4, CFA5)**   Which of the following strategies is most likely to yield the best interest rate risk immunization results for a bond portfolio?

   a. Maturity matching
   b. Duration matching
   c. Buy and hold
   d. Investing in interest rate–sensitive stocks

22. **Immunization (LO4, CFA5)**   Consider two dedicated bond portfolios, both with the same 10-year target dates. One is managed using a buy-and-hold strategy with reinvested coupons. The other is managed using a dynamic immunization strategy. The buy-and-hold portfolio is most likely to outperform the immunized portfolio under what kind of interest rate environment?

   a. Steadily rising interest rates.
   b. Steadily falling interest rates.
   c. Constant interest rates.
   d. Performance will be the same under any environment.

23. **Bond Yields (LO1, CFA5)**   A zero coupon bond paying $100 at maturity 10 years from now has a current price of $50. Its yield to maturity is closest to which of the following?

   a. 5 percent
   b. 6 percent
   c. 7 percent
   d. 8 percent

24. **Bond Price (LO1, CFA5)**   A newly issued 10-year option-free bond is valued at par on June 1, 2018. The bond has an annual coupon of 8.0 percent. On June 1, 2021, the bond has a yield to maturity of 7.1 percent. The price of the bond on June 1, 2023, is closest to:

   a. 100.0 percent of par.
   b. 102.5 percent of par.
   c. 104.3 percent of par.
   d. 105.4 percent of par.

25. **Interest Rate Risk (LO3, CFA6)**   The interest rate risk of a noncallable bond is most likely to be positively related to the:

   a. Risk-free rate.
   b. Bond's coupon rate.
   c. Bond's time to maturity.
   d. Bond's yield to maturity.

Concept Questions

1. **Bond Prices (LO1, CFA3)**   What are premium, discount, and par bonds?

2. **Bond Features (LO1, CFA2)**   In the United States, what is the normal face value for corporate and U.S. government bonds? How are coupons calculated? How often are coupons paid?

3. **Coupon Rates and Current Yields (LO1, CFA3)**   What are the coupon rate and current yield on a bond? What happens to these if a bond's price rises?

4. **Interest Rate Risk (LO3, CFA4)**   What is interest rate risk? What are the roles of a bond's coupon and maturity in determining its level of interest rate risk?

5. **Bond Yields (LO1, CFA2)**   For a premium bond, which is greater: the coupon rate or the yield to maturity? Why? For a discount bond? Why?

6. **Bond Yields (LO2, CFA4)** What is the difference between a bond's promised yield and its realized yield? Which is more relevant? When we calculate a bond's yield to maturity, which of these are we calculating?

7. **Interpreting Bond Yields (LO2, CFA3)** Is the yield to maturity (YTM) on a bond the same thing as the required return? Is YTM the same thing as the coupon rate? Suppose that today a 10 percent coupon bond sells at par. Two years from now, the required return on the same bond is 8 percent. What is the coupon rate on the bond now? The YTM?

8. **Interpreting Bond Yields (LO2, CFA3)** Suppose you buy a 9 percent coupon, 15-year bond today when it is first issued. If interest rates suddenly rise to 15 percent, what happens to the value of your bond? Why?

9. **Bond Prices versus Yields (LO1, CFA3)** (a) What is the relationship between the price of a bond and its YTM? (b) Explain why some bonds sell at a premium to par value and other bonds sell at a discount. What do you know about the relationship between the coupon rate and the YTM for premium bonds? What about discount bonds? For bonds selling at par value? (c) What is the relationship between the current yield and YTM for premium bonds? For discount bonds? For bonds selling at par value?

10. **Yield to Call (LO1, CFA5)** For callable bonds, the financial press generally reports either the yield to maturity or the yield to call. Often yield to call is reported for premium bonds, and yield to maturity is reported for discount bonds. What is the reasoning behind this convention?

Questions and Problems

Core Questions

1. **Bond Prices (LO1, CFA5)** Aloha, Inc., has 7 percent coupon bonds on the market that have 12 years left to maturity. If the YTM on these bonds is 9.1 percent, what is the current bond price?

2. **Bond Yields (LO1, CFA2)** Rolling Company bonds have a coupon rate of 4 percent, 14 years to maturity, and a current price of $1,086. What is the YTM? The current yield?

3. **Bond Prices (LO1, CFA3)** A bond has a coupon rate of 8.2 percent and 9 years until maturity. If the yield to maturity is 7.4 percent, what is the price of the bond?

4. **Bond Prices (LO1, CFA3)** A bond with 25 years until maturity has a coupon rate of 7.2 percent and a yield to maturity of 6 percent. What is the price of the bond?

5. **Yield to Maturity (LO1, CFA5)** A bond sells for $902.30 and has a coupon rate of 6 percent. If the bond has 12 years until maturity, what is the yield to maturity of the bond?

6. **Yield to Maturity (LO1, CFA5)** A bond with a maturity of 12 years sells for $1,047. If the coupon rate is 8.2 percent, what is the yield to maturity of the bond?

7. **Yield to Maturity (LO1, CFA5)** May Industries has a bond outstanding that sells for $928. The bond has a coupon rate of 7.5 percent and nine years until maturity. What is the yield to maturity of the bond?

8. **Yield to Maturity (LO1, CFA5)** Atlantis Fisheries issues zero coupon bonds on the market at a price of $417 per bond. Each bond has a face value of $1,000 payable at maturity in 20 years. What is the yield to maturity for these bonds?

9. **Yield to Call (LO1, CFA5)** The Atlantis Fisheries zero coupon bonds referred to in Problem 8 are callable in 10 years at a call price of $500. Using semiannual compounding, what is the yield to call for these bonds?

10. **Yield to Call (LO1, CFA5)** If, instead, the Atlantis Fisheries zero coupon bonds referred to in Problems 8 and 9 are callable in 10 years at a call price of $550, what is their yield to call?

Intermediate Questions

11. **Coupon Rates (LO1, CFA2)** Ghost Rider Corporation has bonds on the market with 10 years to maturity, a YTM of 7.5 percent, and a current price of $938. What must the coupon rate be on the company's bonds?

12. **Bond Prices (LO1, CFA5)** Great Wall Pizzeria issued 10-year bonds one year ago at a coupon rate of 6.20 percent. If the YTM on these bonds is 7.4 percent, what is the current bond price?

13. **Bond Yields (LO1, CFA3)** Soprano's Spaghetti Factory issued 25-year bonds two years ago at a coupon rate of 7.5 percent. If these bonds currently sell for 108 percent of par value, what is the YTM?

14. **Bond Price Movements (LO1, CFA3)**   A zero coupon bond with a 6 percent YTM has 20 years to maturity. Two years later, the price of the bond remains the same. What's going on here?

15. **Realized Yield (LO2, CFA6)**   For the bond referred to in Problem 14, what would be the realized yield if it were held to maturity?

16. **Bond Price Movements (LO1, CFA5)**   Bond P is a premium bond with an 8 percent coupon, a YTM of 6 percent, and 15 years to maturity. Bond D is a discount bond with an 8 percent coupon and a YTM of 10 percent, and also has 15 years to maturity. If interest rates remain unchanged, what do you expect the price of these bonds to be 1 year from now? In 5 years? In 10 years? In 14 years? In 15 years? What's going on here?

17. **Interest Rate Risk (LO3, CFA4)**   Both Bond A and Bond B have 6 percent coupons and are priced at par value. Bond A has 5 years to maturity, while Bond B has 15 years to maturity. If interest rates suddenly rise by 2 percent, what is the percentage change in price of Bond A? Of Bond B? If rates were to suddenly fall by 2 percent instead, what would the percentage change in price of Bond A be now? Of Bond B? Illustrate your answers by graphing bond prices versus YTM. What does this problem tell you about the interest rate risk of longer-term bonds?

18. **Interest Rate Risk (LO3, CFA4)**   Bond J is a 4 percent coupon bond. Bond K is an 8 percent coupon bond. Both bonds have 10 years to maturity and a YTM of 7 percent. If interest rates suddenly rise by 2 percent, what is the percentage price change of these bonds? What if rates suddenly fall by 2 percent instead? What does this problem tell you about the interest rate risk of lower-coupon bonds?

19. **Finding the Bond Maturity (LO1, CFA2)**   LKD Co. has 8 percent coupon bonds with a YTM of 6.8 percent. The current yield on these bonds is 7.4 percent. How many years do these bonds have left until they mature?

20. **Finding the Bond Maturity (LO1, CFA2)**   You've just found a 10 percent coupon bond on the market that sells for par value. What is the maturity on this bond?

21. **Realized Yields (LO2, CFA6)**   Suppose you buy a 6 percent coupon bond today for $1,080. The bond has 10 years to maturity. What rate of return do you expect to earn on your investment? Two years from now, the YTM on your bond has increased by 2 percent, and you decide to sell. What price will your bond sell for? What is the realized yield on your investment? Compare this yield to the YTM when you first bought the bond. Why are they different? Assume interest payments are reinvested at the original YTM.

22. **Yield to Call (LO1, CFA3)**   Fooling Company has a 10 percent callable bond outstanding on the market with 25 years to maturity, call protection for the next 10 years, and a call premium of $100. What is the yield to call (YTC) for this bond if the current price is 108 percent of par value?

23. **Calculating Duration (LO4, CFA6)**   What is the Macaulay duration of a 7 percent coupon bond with five years to maturity and a current price of $1,025.30? What is the modified duration?

24. **Using Duration (LO4, CFA6)**   In Problem 23, suppose the yield on the bond suddenly increases by 2 percent. Use duration to estimate the new price of the bond. Compare your answer to the new bond price calculated from the usual bond pricing formula. What do your results tell you about the accuracy of duration?

25. **Dollar Value of an 01 (LO4, CFA2)**   What is the dollar value of an 01 for the bond in Problem 23?

26. **Yield Value of a 32nd (LO4, CFA2)**   A Treasury bond with 8 years to maturity is currently quoted at 106:16. The bond has a coupon rate of 7.5 percent. What is the yield value of a 32nd for this bond?

27. **Calculating Duration (LO4, CFA6)**   A bond with a coupon rate of 8 percent sells at a yield to maturity of 9 percent. If the bond matures in 10 years, what is the Macaulay duration of the bond? What is the modified duration?

28. **Calculating Duration (LO4, CFA6)**   Assume the bond in Problem 27 has a yield to maturity of 7 percent. What is the Macaulay duration now? What does this tell you about the relationship between duration and yield to maturity?

29. **Calculating Duration (LO4, CFA6)**   You find a bond with 19 years until maturity that has a coupon rate of 8 percent and a yield to maturity of 7 percent. What is the Macaulay duration? The modified duration?

30. **Using Duration (LO4, CFA3)**   Suppose the yield to maturity on the bond in Problem 29 increases by .25 percent. What is the new price of the bond using duration? What is the new price of the bond using the bond pricing formula? What if the yield to maturity increases by 1 percent? By 2 percent? By 5 percent? What does this tell you about using duration to estimate bond price changes for large interest rate changes?

31. **Bootstrapping (LO1)** One method used to obtain an estimate of the term structure of interest rates is called *bootstrapping*. Suppose you have a one-year zero coupon bond with a rate of $r1$ and a two-year bond with an annual coupon payment of C. To bootstrap the two-year rate, you can set up the following equation for the price (P) of the coupon bond:

$$P = \frac{C_1}{1 + r_1} + \frac{C_2 + \text{Par value}}{(1 + r_2)^2}$$

Because you can observe all of the variables except r_2, the spot rate for two years, you can solve for this interest rate. Suppose there is a zero coupon bond with one year to maturity that sells for $949 and a two-year bond with a 7.5 percent coupon paid annually that sells for $1,020. What is the interest rate for two years? Suppose a bond with three years until maturity and an 8.5 percent annual coupon sells for $1,029. What is the interest rate for three years?

32. **Bootstrapping (LO1)** You find that the one-, two-, three-, and four-year interest rates are 4.2 percent, 4.5 percent, 4.9 percent, and 5.1 percent, respectively. What is the yield to maturity of a four-year bond with an annual coupon rate of 6.5 percent? *Hint:* Use the bootstrapping technique in Problem 31 to find the price of the bond.

Spreadsheet Problems

33. **Yield to Maturity (LO1, CFA3)** A Treasury bond that settles on August 10, 2022, matures on April 15, 2027. The coupon rate is 4.5 percent and the quoted price is 106:17. What is the bond's yield to maturity?

34. **Bond Yields (LO1, CFA3)** A bond that settles on June 7, 2022, matures on July 1, 2042, and may be called at any time after July 1, 2032, at a price of 105. The coupon rate on the bond is 6 percent and the price is 115.00. What are the yield to maturity and yield to call on this bond?

35. **Duration (LO4, CFA6)** A Treasury bond that settles on October 18, 2022, matures on March 30, 2041. The coupon rate is 5.30 percent, and the bond has a 4.45 percent yield to maturity. What are the Macaulay duration and modified duration?

36. **Realized Yields (LO2, CFA6)** Assume you purchase (at par) a 10-year bond with a 6 percent coupon and a $1,000 face value. Suppose you are only able to reinvest the coupons at a rate of 4 percent. If you sell the bond after five years when the yield to maturity is 7 percent, what is your realized yield?

CFA Exam Review by Kaplan Schweser

[CFA3, CFA5, CFA6]

Frank Myers, CFA, is a fixed-income portfolio manager for a large pension fund. A member of the Investment Committee, Fred Spice, is very interested in learning about the management of fixed-income portfolios. Mr. Spice has approached Mr. Myers with several questions.

Mr. Myers has decided to illustrate fixed-income trading strategies using a fixed-rate bond and note. Both bonds have semiannual coupons. Unless otherwise stated, all interest rate changes are parallel. The characteristics of these securities are shown in the table below.

	Fixed-Rate Bond	Fixed-Rate Note
Price	107.18	100.00
Yield to maturity	5.00%	5.00%
Periods to maturity	18	8
Modified duration	6.9848	3.5851

1. Mr. Spice asks Mr. Myers how a fixed-income manager would position his portfolio to capitalize on his expectations of increasing interest rates. Which of the following would be the most appropriate strategy?

    a. Lengthen the portfolio duration.
    b. Buy fixed-rate bonds.
    c. Shorten the portfolio duration.

2. Mr. Spice asks Mr. Myers to quantify the value changes from changes in interest rates. To illustrate, Mr. Myers computes the value change for the fixed-rate note. He assumes an increase in interest rates of 100 basis points. Which of the following is the best estimate of the change in value for the fixed-rate note?

   a. −$7.17
   b. −$3.59
   c. $3.59

3. For an increase of 100 basis points in the yield to maturity, by what amount would the fixed-rate bond's price change?

   a. −$7.49
   b. −$5.73
   c. −$4.63

4. Mr. Spice wonders how a fixed-income manager would position his portfolio to capitalize on the expectation of an upward-shifting and twisting term structure. For the twist, interest rates on long-term bonds increase by more than those on shorter-term notes.

   a. Sell bonds and buy notes.
   b. Buy bonds and sell notes.
   c. Buy both bonds and notes.

Bloomberg Exercises

1. Identify a McDonald's (MCD) corporate bond and examine its valuation metrics. **(BVAL)**

2. Download an Excel template for comparing fixed-income products. **(XLTC XFIC)**

3. Explore the duration characteristics for a Home Depot (HD) corporate bond. **(DURA)**

What's on the Web?

1. **Bond Markets** Go to the Market Data tab at finra-markets.morningstar.com and find the section for Bonds. What is the outlook for the bond market today? What are the major news items today that are expected to influence the bond market?

2. **Government Bonds** Go to www.bloomberg.com and look up the yields for U.S. government bonds using the "Rates & Bonds" link. You should also find a listing for foreign government bonds. Are the yields on all government bonds the same? Why or why not?

Diversification and Risky Asset Allocation

"It is the part of a wise man not to venture all his eggs in one basket."

—Miguel de Cervantes

Learning Objectives

To get the most out of this chapter, diversify your study time across:

1. How to calculate expected returns and variances for a security.

2. How to calculate expected returns and variances for a portfolio.

3. The importance of portfolio diversification.

4. The efficient frontier and the importance of asset allocation.

Intuitively, we all know that diversification is important for managing investment risk. But how exactly does diversification work, and how can we be sure we have an efficiently diversified portfolio? Insightful answers can be gleaned from the modern theory of diversification and asset allocation.

In this chapter, we examine the role of diversification and asset allocation in investing. Most of us have a strong sense that diversification is important. After all, Cervantes's advice against "putting all your eggs in one basket" has become a bit of folk wisdom that seems to have stood the test of time quite well. Even so, the importance of diversification has not always been well understood. Diversification is important because portfolios with many investments usually produce a more consistent and stable total return than portfolios with just one investment. When you own many stocks, even if some of them decline in price, others are likely to increase in price (or at least stay at the same price).

CFA™ Exam Topics in This Chapter:

1. Time value of money (L1, S1)
2. Probability concepts (L1, S1)
3. Portfolio management: An overview (L1, S17)
4. Portfolio risk and return: Part I (L1, S17)
5. Basics of portfolio planning and construction (L1, S18)
6. Overview of asset allocation (L3, S3)

Go to Connect for a guide that aligns your textbook with CFA readings.

You might be thinking that a portfolio with only one investment could do very well if you pick the right solitary investment. Indeed, had you decided to hold only Dell (DELL) stock during the 1990s or shares of Apple (AAPL) in the 2000s, your portfolio would have been very profitable. As an investor, though, you do not get to look backwards in time—you must look forward and ask which single investment today will be very profitable in the future. That's the problem. If you pick the wrong one, you could get wiped out. In fact, had you held DELL in the 2000s, that would have been a mistake. Its price fell from a high of $57 in March 2000 to under $14 in 2013, before restructuring and performing positively during the last decade. Knowing which investment will perform best in the future is impossible. Obviously, if we knew, then there would be no risk. Therefore, investment risk plays an important role in portfolio diversification.

The role and impact of diversification on portfolio risk and return were first formally explained in the early 1950s by financial pioneer Harry Markowitz. These aspects of portfolio diversification were an important discovery—Professor Markowitz shared the 1986 Nobel Prize in Economics for his insights on the value of diversification. His pioneering work has become known as *modern portfolio theory,* or MPT for short.

Surprisingly, Professor Markowitz's insights are not related to how investors care about risk or return. In fact, we can talk about the benefits of diversification without having to know how investors feel about risk. Realistically, however, it is investors who care about the benefits of diversification. Therefore, to help you understand Professor Markowitz's insights, we make two assumptions. First, we assume that investors prefer more return to less return; and second, we assume that investors prefer less risk to more risk. In this chapter, we focus on variance and standard deviation as key measures of risk, although we expand on this in an upcoming chapter.

11.1 Expected Returns and Variances

In Chapter 1, we discussed how to calculate average returns and variances using historical data. We begin this chapter with a discussion of how to analyze returns and variances when the information we have concerns future returns and their probabilities. We start here because the notion of diversification involves future returns and variances of future returns.

EXPECTED RETURNS

Related Bloomberg Functions

HVG Historical Volatility Graph

GV Graph Volatility

See how traders attempt to profit from expected returns at

www.earningswhispers.com.

We start with a straightforward case. Consider a period of time such as a year. We have two stocks, say, Starcents and Jpod. Starcents is expected to have a return of 25 percent in the coming year; Jpod is expected to have a return of 20 percent during the same period.

In a situation such as this, if all investors agreed on these expected return values, why would anyone want to hold Jpod? After all, why invest in one stock when the expectation is that another will do better? Clearly, the answer must depend on the different risks of the two investments. The return on Starcents, although *expected* to be 25 percent, could turn out to be significantly higher or lower. Similarly, Jpod's *realized* return could be significantly higher or lower than expected.

For example, suppose the economy booms. In this case, we think Starcents will have a 70 percent return. But if the economy tanks and enters a recession, we think the return will be −20 percent. In this case, we say that there are *two states of the economy,* which means that there are two possible outcomes. This scenario is oversimplified, of course, but it allows us to illustrate some key ideas without a lot of computational complexity.

Suppose we think boom and recession are equally likely to happen, meaning there is a 50-50 chance of each outcome. Table 11.1 illustrates the basic information we have described and some additional information about Jpod. Notice that Jpod earns 30 percent if there is a recession and 10 percent if there is a boom.

Obviously, if you buy one of these stocks, say, Jpod, what you earn in any particular year depends on what the economy does during that year. Suppose these probabilities stay the same through time. If you hold Jpod for a number of years, you'll earn 30 percent about half the time and 10 percent the other half. In this case, we say your **expected return** on Jpod, $E(R_J)$, is 20 percent:

expected return
Average return on a risky asset expected in the future.

$$E(R_J) = .50 \times 30\% + .50 \times 10\% = 20\%$$

TABLE 11.1 — States of the Economy and Stock Returns

State of Economy	Probability of State of Economy	Security Returns if State Occurs	
		Starcents	Jpod
Recession	.50	−20%	30%
Boom	.50	70	10
	1.00		

TABLE 11.2 — Calculating Expected Returns

(1) State of Economy	(2) Probability of State of Economy	Starcents		Jpod	
		(3) Return if State Occurs	(4) Product (2) × (3)	(5) Return if State Occurs	(6) Product (2) × (5)
Recession	.50	−20%	−10%	30%	15%
Boom	.50	70	35	10	5
	1.00		$E(R_S) = 25\%$		$E(R_J) = 20\%$

In other words, you should expect to earn 20 percent from this stock, on average. Note, however, that you might not ever earn exactly 20 percent.

For Starcents, the probabilities are the same, but the possible returns are different. Here we lose 20 percent half the time and we gain 70 percent the other half. The expected return on Starcents, $E(R_S)$, is thus 25 percent:

$$E(R_S) = .50 \times -20\% + .50 \times 70\% = 25\%$$

Table 11.2 illustrates these calculations.

In Chapter 1, we defined a risk premium as the difference between the returns on a risky investment and a risk-free investment, and we calculated the historical risk premiums on some different investments. Using our projected returns, we can calculate the *projected* or *expected risk premium* as the difference between the expected return on a risky investment and the certain return on a risk-free investment.

For example, suppose risk-free investments are currently offering an 8 percent return. We will say that the risk-free rate, which we label R_f, is 8 percent. Given this, what is the projected risk premium on Jpod? On Starcents? Because the expected return on Jpod, $E(R_J)$, is 20 percent, the projected risk premium is:

$$
\begin{aligned}
\text{Risk premium} &= \text{Expected return} - \text{Risk-free rate} \\
&= E(R_J) - R_f \\
&= 20\% - 8\% \\
&= 12\%
\end{aligned}
$$
(11.1)

Similarly, the risk premium on Starcents is $25\% - 8\% = 17\%$.

In general, the expected return on a security or other asset is equal to the sum of the possible returns multiplied by their probabilities. So, if we have 100 possible returns, we would multiply each one by its probability and then add up the results. The sum would be the expected return. The risk premium would then be the difference between this expected return and the risk-free rate.

EXAMPLE 11.1 — Unequal Probabilities

Look again at Tables 11.1 and 11.2. Suppose you thought a boom would occur 20 percent of the time instead of 50 percent. What are the expected returns on Starcents and Jpod in this case? If the risk-free rate is 10 percent, what are the risk premiums?

The first thing to notice is that a recession must occur 80 percent of the time (1 − .20 = .80) because there are only two possibilities. With this in mind, Jpod has a 30 percent

TABLE 11.3

Calculating Expected Returns

		Starcents		Jpod	
(1) **State of** **Economy**	**(2)** **Probability of** **State of Economy**	**(3)** **Return if** **State Occurs**	**(4)** **Product** **(2) × (3)**	**(5)** **Return if** **State Occurs**	**(6)** **Product** **(2) × (5)**
Recession	.80	−20%	−16%	30%	24%
Boom	.20	70	14	10	2
	1.00		$E(R_s) = -2\%$		$E(R_J) = 26\%$

return in 80 percent of the years and a 10 percent return in 20 percent of the years. To calculate the expected return, we multiply the possibilities by the probabilities and add up the results:

$$E(R_J) = .80 \times 30\% + .20 \times 10\% = 26\%$$

Written as decimals, the returns are:

$$E(R_J) = .80 \times .30 + .20 \times .10 = .26$$

Table 11.3 summarizes the calculations for both stocks. Notice that the expected return on Starcents is −2 percent.

The risk premium for Jpod is 26% − 10% = 16% in this case. The risk premium for Starcents is negative: −2% − 10% = −12%. This is a little unusual, but, as we will see, it's not impossible.

CALCULATING THE VARIANCE OF EXPECTED RETURNS

There's more on risk measures at www.investopedia.com and teachmefinance.com.

To calculate the variances of the expected returns on our two stocks, we first determine the squared deviations from the expected return. We then multiply each possible squared deviation by its probability. Next we add these up, and the result is the variance.

To illustrate, one of our stocks in Table 11.2, Jpod, has an expected return of 20 percent. In a given year, the return will actually be either 30 percent or 10 percent. The possible deviations are thus 30% − 20% = 10% or 10% − 20% = −10%. In this case, the variance is:

$$\text{Variance} = \sigma^2 = .50 \times (10\%)^2 + .50 \times (-10\%)^2$$
$$= .50 \times (.10)^2 + .50 \times (-.10)^2 = .01$$

Notice that we used decimals to calculate the variance. The standard deviation is then just the square root of the variance:

$$\text{Standard deviation} = \sigma = \sqrt{.01} = .10 = 10\%$$

Table 11.4 contains the expected return and variance for both stocks. Notice that Starcents has a much larger variance. Starcents has the higher expected return, but Jpod has less risk. You could get a 70 percent return on your investment in Starcents, but you could also lose 20 percent. However, an investment in Jpod will always pay at least 10 percent.

Which of these stocks should you buy? We can't really say; it depends on your personal preferences regarding risk and return. We can be reasonably sure, however, that some investors would prefer one and some would prefer the other.

TABLE 11.4

Expected Returns and Variances

	Starcents	Jpod
Expected return, $E(R)$	.25, or 25%	.20, or 20%
Variance of expected return, σ^2	.2025	.0100
Standard deviation of expected return, σ	.45, or 45%	.10, or 10%

You've probably noticed that the way we calculated expected returns and variances of expected returns here is somewhat different from the way we calculated returns and variances in Chapter 1 (and probably different from the way you learned it in your statistics course). The reason is that we were examining historical returns in Chapter 1, so we estimated the average return and variance based on some actual events. Here, we have projected future returns and their associated probabilities. Therefore, we must calculate expected returns and variances of these expected returns.

EXAMPLE 11.2 | **More Unequal Probabilities**

Going back to Table 11.3 in Example 11.1, what are the variances on our two stocks once we have unequal probabilities? What are the standard deviations?

Converting all returns to decimals, we can summarize the needed calculations as follows:

(1) State of Economy	(2) Probability of State of Economy	(3) Return Deviation from Expected Return	(4) Squared Return Deviation	(5) Product (2) × (4)
Starcents				
Recession	.80	$-.20 - (-.02) = -.18$	.0324	.02592
Boom	.20	$.70 - (-.02) = .72$	.5184	.10368
				$\sigma_S^2 = .12960$
Jpod				
Recession	.80	$.30 - .26 = .04$	.0016	.00128
Boom	.20	$.10 - .26 = -.16$	.0256	.00512
				$\sigma_J^2 = .00640$

Based on these calculations, the standard deviation for Starcents is:

$$\sigma_S = \sqrt{.1296} = .36, \text{ or } 36\%$$

The standard deviation for Jpod is much smaller:

$$\sigma_J = \sqrt{.0064} = .08, \text{ or } 8\%$$

CHECK THIS

11.1a How do we calculate the expected return on a security?

11.1b In words, how do we calculate the variance of an expected return?

11.2 Portfolios

Related Bloomberg Functions

PRTU Portfolio Administration

PORT Portfolio and Risk Analytics

Thus far in this chapter, we have concentrated on individual assets considered separately. However, most investors actually hold a **portfolio** of assets. All we mean by this is that investors tend to own more than just a single stock, bond, or other asset. Given that this is true, portfolio return and portfolio risk are obviously relevant. Accordingly, we now discuss portfolio expected returns and variances.

TABLE 11.5	Expected Portfolio Return			
	(1) State of Economy	**(2)** Probability of State of Economy	**(3)** Portfolio Return if State Occurs	**(4)** Product (2) × (3)
	Recession	.50	.50 × −20% + .50 × 30% = 5%	2.5%
	Boom	.50	.50 × 70% + .50 × 10% = 40%	20.0%
				$E(R_p)$ = 22.5%

portfolio
Group of assets such as stocks and bonds held by an investor.

portfolio weight
Percentage of a portfolio's total value invested in a particular asset.

PORTFOLIO WEIGHTS

There are many equivalent ways of describing a portfolio. The most convenient approach is to list the percentages of the total portfolio's value that are invested in each portfolio asset. We call these percentages the **portfolio weights**.

For example, if we have $50 in one asset and $150 in another, then our total portfolio is worth $200. The percentage of our portfolio invested in the first asset is $50/$200 = .25, or 25%. The percentage of our portfolio invested in the second asset is $150/$200 = .75, or 75%. Notice that the weights sum up to 1.00 (100%) because all of our money is invested somewhere.[1]

PORTFOLIO EXPECTED RETURNS

Let's go back to Starcents and Jpod. You put half your money in each. The portfolio weights are obviously .50 and .50. What is the pattern of returns on this portfolio? The expected return?

To answer these questions, suppose the economy actually enters a recession. In this case, half your money (the half in Starcents) loses 20 percent. The other half (the half in Jpod) gains 30 percent. Your portfolio return, R_p, in a recession will thus be:

$$R_p = .50 \times -20\% + .50 \times 30\% = 5\%$$

Table 11.5 summarizes the remaining calculations. Notice that when a boom occurs, your portfolio would return 40 percent:

$$R_p = .50 \times 70\% + .50 \times 10\% = 40\%$$

As indicated in Table 11.5, the expected return on your portfolio, $E(R_p)$, is 22.5 percent.

We can save ourselves some work by calculating the expected return more directly. Given these portfolio weights, we could have reasoned that we expect half of our money to earn 25 percent (the half in Starcents) and half of our money to earn 20 percent (the half in Jpod). Our portfolio expected return is thus:

$$E(R_p) = .50 \times E(R_S) + .50 \times E(R_J)$$
$$= .50 \times 25\% + .50 \times 20\%$$
$$= .225, \text{ or } 22.5\%$$

This is the same portfolio return that we calculated in Table 11.5.

This method of calculating the expected return on a portfolio works no matter how many assets are in the portfolio. Suppose we had n assets in our portfolio, where n is any number at all. If we let x_i stand for the percentage of our money in Asset i, then the expected return is:

$$E(R_p) = x_1 \times E(R_1) + x_2 \times E(R_2) + \cdots + x_n \times E(R_n) \tag{11.2}$$

Equation 11.2 says that the expected return on a portfolio is a straightforward combination of the expected returns on the assets in that portfolio. In fact, the portfolio expected return is a simple weighted average of the expected returns of the assets that comprise the portfolio. This result seems somewhat obvious, but, as we will examine next, the obvious approach is not always the right one.

---

[1] Some of it could be in cash, of course, but we would then consider cash to be another of the portfolio assets. In fact, as we learned in an earlier chapter, we could even have a negative weight in an asset if we had a short position.

EXAMPLE 11.3

More Unequal Probabilities

Suppose we had the following projections on three stocks:

State of Economy	Probability of State of Economy	Returns		
		Stock A	Stock B	Stock C
Boom	.50	10%	15%	20%
Bust	.50	8	4	0

We want to calculate portfolio expected returns in two cases. First, what would be the expected return on a portfolio with equal amounts invested in each of the three stocks? Second, what would be the expected return if half of the portfolio were in A, with the remainder equally divided between B and C?

From our earlier discussion, the expected returns on the individual stocks are:

$$E(R_A) = 9.0\% \quad E(R_B) = 9.5\% \quad E(R_C) = 10.0\%$$

(Check these for practice.) If a portfolio has equal investments in each asset, the portfolio weights are all the same. Such a portfolio is said to be *equally weighted*. Because there are three stocks in this case, the weights are all equal to 1/3. The portfolio expected return is thus:

$$E(R_p) = 1/3 \times 9.0\% + 1/3 \times 9.5\% + 1/3 \times 10.0\% = 9.5\%$$

In the second case, check that the portfolio expected return is 9.375 percent.

PORTFOLIO VARIANCE OF EXPECTED RETURNS

From the preceding discussion, the expected return on a portfolio that contains equal investments in Starcents and Jpod is 22.5 percent. What is the standard deviation of return on this portfolio? Simple intuition might suggest that half of our money has a standard deviation of 45 percent and the other half has a standard deviation of 10 percent, so the portfolio's standard deviation might be calculated as follows:

$$\sigma_p = .50 \times 45\% + .50 \times 10\% = 27.5\%$$

Unfortunately, this approach is *completely incorrect!*

Let's see what the standard deviation really is. Table 11.6 summarizes the relevant calculations. As we see, the portfolio's standard deviation is much less than 27.5 percent—it's only 17.5 percent. What is illustrated here is that the variance on a portfolio is not generally a simple combination (or weighted average) of the variances of the assets in the portfolio.

We can illustrate this point a little more dramatically by considering a slightly different set of portfolio weights. Suppose we put 2/11 (about 18 percent) in Starcents and the other 9/11 (about 82 percent) in Jpod. If a recession occurs, this portfolio will have a return of:

$$R_p = 2/11 \times -20\% + 9/11 \times 30\% = 20.91\%$$

TABLE 11.6

Calculating Portfolio Variance and Standard Deviation

(1) State of Economy	(2) Probability of State of Economy	(3) Portfolio Returns if State Occurs	(4) Squared Deviation from Expected Return*	(5) Product (2) × (4)
Recession	.50	5%	$(5 - 22.5)^2 = 306.25$	153.125
Boom	.50	40	$(40 - 22.5)^2 = 306.25$	153.125
			Variance, $\sigma_p^2 = 306.25$	
			Standard deviation, $\sigma_p = \sqrt{306.25} = 17.5\%$	

*Notice that we used percents for all returns. Verify that if we wrote returns as decimals, we would get a variance of .030625 and a standard deviation of .175.

If a boom occurs, this portfolio will have a return of:

$$R_p = 2/11 \times 70\% + 9/11 \times 10\% = 20.91\%$$

Notice that the return is the same no matter what happens. No further calculation is needed: This portfolio has a zero variance and, theoretically, no risk!

This portfolio is a nice bit of financial alchemy. We take two quite risky assets and, by mixing them just right, we create a riskless portfolio. It seems very clear that combining assets into portfolios can substantially alter the risks faced by an investor. This observation is crucial. We will begin to explore its implications in the next section.[2]

EXAMPLE 11.4

Portfolio Variance and Standard Deviations

In Example 11.3, what are the standard deviations of the two portfolios?

State of Economy	Probability of State of Economy	Returns			
		Stock A	Stock B	Stock C	Portfolio
Boom	.50	10%	15%	20%	13.75%
Bust	.50	8	4	0	5.00

To answer, we first have to calculate the portfolio returns in the two states. We will work with the second portfolio, which has 50 percent in Stock A and 25 percent in each of Stocks B and C. The relevant calculations are summarized as follows.

The portfolio return when the economy booms is calculated as:

$$R_p = .50 \times 10\% + .25 \times 15\% + .25 \times 20\% = 13.75\%$$

The return when the economy goes bust is calculated the same way. Check that it's 5 percent, and also check that the expected return on the portfolio is 9.375 percent. Expressing returns in decimals, the variance is thus:

$$\sigma_p^2 = .50 \times (.1375 - .09375)^2 + .50 \times (.05 - .09375)^2 = .0019141$$

The standard deviation is:

$$\sigma_p = \sqrt{.0019141} = .04375, \text{ or } 4.375\%$$

Check: Using equal weights, verify that the portfolio standard deviation is 5.5 percent.

Note: If the standard deviation is 4.375 percent, the variance should be somewhere between 16 and 25 (the squares of 4 and 5, respectively). If we square 4.375, we get 19.141. To express a variance in percentage, we must move the decimal four places to the right. That is, we must multiply .0019141 by 10,000—which is the square of 100.

CHECK THIS

11.2a What is a portfolio weight?

11.2b How do we calculate the variance of an expected return?

 Diversification and Portfolio Risk

Our discussion to this point has focused on some hypothetical securities. We've seen that portfolio risks can, in principle, be quite different from the risks of the assets that make up the portfolio. We now look more closely at the risk of an individual asset versus the risk of a

---

[2] Earlier, we had a risk-free rate of 8 percent. Now we have, in effect, a 20.91 percent risk-free rate. If this situation actually existed, there would be a very profitable opportunity! In reality, we expect that all riskless investments would have the same return.

portfolio of many different assets. As we did in Chapter 1, we will examine some stock market history to get an idea of what happens with actual investments in U.S. capital markets.

THE EFFECT OF DIVERSIFICATION: ANOTHER LESSON FROM MARKET HISTORY

In Chapter 1, we saw that the standard deviation of the annual return on a portfolio of large-company common stocks was about 20 percent per year. Does this mean that the standard deviation of the annual return on a typical stock in that group is about 20 percent? As you might suspect by now, the answer is no. This observation is extremely important.

To examine the relationship between portfolio size and portfolio risk, Table 11.7 illustrates typical average annual standard deviations for equally weighted portfolios that contain different numbers of randomly selected NYSE securities.

In column 2 of Table 11.7, we see that the standard deviation, or total risk, for a "portfolio" of one security is just under 50 percent per year—49.24 percent, to be precise. What this means is that if you randomly select a single NYSE stock and put all your money into it, your standard deviation of return would typically have been about 50 percent per year. Obviously, such a strategy has significant risk! If you were to randomly select two NYSE securities and put half your money in each, your average annual standard deviation would have been about 37 percent.

The important thing to notice in Table 11.7 is that the standard deviation declines as the number of securities is increased. By the time we have 100 randomly chosen stocks (and 1 percent invested in each), the portfolio's volatility has declined by 60 percent, from 50 percent per year to 20 percent per year. With 500 securities, the standard deviation is 19.27 percent per year, similar to the approximately 20 percent per year we saw in Chapter 1 for our group of large-company common stocks. The small difference exists because the portfolio securities, portfolio weights, and the time periods covered are not identical.

An important foundation of the diversification effect is the random selection of stocks. When stocks are chosen at random, the resulting portfolio represents different sectors, market caps, and other features. Consider what would happen, however, if you formed a portfolio of 30 stocks, but all were technology companies. In this case, you might think you have a

TABLE 11.7 — Portfolio Standard Deviations

(1) Number of Stocks in Portfolio	(2) Average Standard Deviation of Annual Portfolio Returns	(3) Ratio of Portfolio Standard Deviation to Standard Deviation of a Single Stock
1	49.24%	1.00
2	37.36	.76
4	29.69	.60
6	26.64	.54
8	24.98	.51
10	23.93	.49
20	21.68	.44
30	20.87	.42
40	20.46	.42
50	20.20	.41
100	19.69	.40
200	19.42	.39
300	19.34	.39
400	19.29	.39
500	19.27	.39
1,000	19.21	.39

Source: Table 1, Meir Statman. (September 1987). "How Many Stocks Make a Diversified Portfolio?" *Journal of Financial and Quantitative Analysis* 22, 353–64. Derived from E. J. Elton and M. J. Gruber. (October 1977). "Risk Reduction and Portfolio Size: An Analytic Solution." *Journal of Business* 50, 415–37.

diversified portfolio, but because all these stocks have similar characteristics, you are actually closer to having "all your eggs in one basket."

Similarly, during times of extreme market stress, such as the Crash of 2008, many seemingly unrelated asset categories tend to move together—down. Thus, diversification, although generally a good thing, doesn't always work as we might hope.

THE PRINCIPLE OF DIVERSIFICATION

Figure 11.1 illustrates the point we've been discussing. What we have plotted is the standard deviation of the return versus the number of stocks in the portfolio. Notice in Figure 11.1 that the benefit in terms of risk reduction from adding securities drops off as we add more and more. By the time we have 10 securities, most of the diversification effect is already realized, and by the time we get to 30 or so, there is very little remaining benefit.

The diversification benefit does depend on the time period over which returns and variances are calculated. For example, the data in Table 11.7 precede 1987. Scholars revisited diversification benefits by looking at more recent stock returns and variances and found that 50 stocks were needed to build a highly diversified portfolio in this time period. The point is that investors should be thinking in terms of 30 to 50 individual stocks when they are building a diversified portfolio.

principle of diversification
Spreading an investment across a number of assets will eliminate some, but not all, of the risk.

Figure 11.1 illustrates two key points. First, some of the riskiness associated with individual assets can be eliminated by forming portfolios. The process of spreading an investment across assets (and thereby forming a portfolio) is called *diversification*. The **principle of diversification** tells us that spreading an investment across many assets will eliminate some of the risk. Not surprisingly, risks that can be eliminated by diversification are called "diversifiable" risks.

The second point is equally important. There is a minimum level of risk that cannot be eliminated by diversifying. This minimum level is labeled "nondiversifiable risk" in Figure 11.1. Taken together, these two points are another important lesson from financial market history: Diversification reduces risk, but only up to a point. Put another way, some risk is diversifiable and some is not.

THE FALLACY OF TIME DIVERSIFICATION

Has anyone ever told you, "You're young. You should have a large amount of equity (or other risky assets) in your portfolio"? While this advice could be true, the argument frequently used to support this strategy is incorrect. In particular, the common argument goes something like this: Although stocks are more volatile in any given year, over time this volatility cancels itself out. Although this argument sounds logical, it is only partially correct. Investment professionals refer to this argument as the *time diversification fallacy*.

| FIGURE 11.1 | Portfolio Diversification |

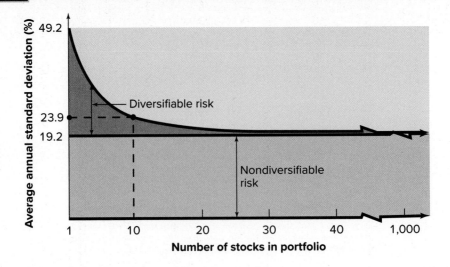

How can such logical-sounding advice be so faulty? Well, let's begin with what is true about this piece of advice. Recall from the very first chapter that the average yearly return of large-cap stocks over the last 96 individual years is about 12 percent, and the standard deviation is about 20.0 percent. For most investors, however, time horizons are much longer than a single year, so let's look at the average returns of longer investment horizon periods.

Let's use a five-year investment period to start. If you use the data in Table 1.1 from 1926 through 1930, the geometric average return for large-cap stocks was 8.26 percent. You can confirm this average using the method to calculate a geometric, or compounded, average return that we present in Chapter 1. After this calculation, we only have the average for one historical five-year period. Instead, suppose we calculate all possible five-year geometric average returns using the data in Table 1.1. That is, we would calculate the geometric average return using data from 1927 to 1931, then 1928 to 1932, and so on.

When we finish all this work, we have a series of five-year geometric average returns. If we wanted, we could compute the simple average and standard deviation of these five-year geometric, or compounded, averages. Then, we could repeat the whole process using a rolling 10-year period or using a rolling 15-year period (or whatever period we might want to use).

We have made these calculations for nine different holding periods, ranging from 1 year to 40 years. Our calculations appear in Table 11.8. What do you notice about the averages and standard deviations?

As the time periods get longer, the average geometric return generally falls. This pattern is consistent with our discussion of arithmetic and geometric averages in Chapter 1. What is more important for our discussion here, however, is the pattern of the standard deviation of the average returns. Notice that as the time period increases, the standard deviation of the geometric averages falls and actually approaches zero. The fact that it does is the true impact of time diversification.

So, at this point do you think time diversification is true or a fallacy? Well, the problem is that even though the standard deviation of the geometric *return* tends to zero as the time horizon grows, the standard deviation of your *wealth* does not. As investors, we care about wealth levels and the standard deviation of wealth levels over time.

Let's make the following calculation. Suppose someone invested a lump sum of $1,000 at the beginning of 1926. Using the return data from Table 1.1, you can verify that this $1,000 has grown to $1,486.97 five years later. Next, we suppose someone invests $1,000 in 1927 and see what it grows to at the end of 1931. We make this calculation for all possible five-year investment periods and seven other longer periods. Our calculations appear in Table 11.9, where we provide wealth averages and standard deviations.

What do you notice about the wealth averages and standard deviations in Table 11.9? Well, the average ending wealth amount is larger over longer time periods. This result makes sense—after all, we are investing for longer time periods. What is important for our discussion, however, is the standard deviation of wealth. Notice that this risk measure increases with the time horizon.

TABLE 11.8	Average Geometric Returns by Investment Holding Period (1926–2021)								
	Investment Holding Period (in years)								
	1	5	10	15	20	25	30	35	40
Average return	12.2%	10.2%	10.4%	9.7%	9.5%	9.5%	9.5%	9.4%	9.3%
Standard deviation of return	19.6%	8.4%	5.5%	4.4%	3.4%	2.6%	1.7%	1.1%	.7%

TABLE 11.9	Average Ending Wealth by Investment Holding Period (1926–2021)								
	Investment Holding Period (in years)								
	1	5	10	15	20	25	30	35	40
Average wealth	$1,121	$1,713	$2,988	$4,676	$7,375	$11,397	$17,122	$24,970	$44,430
Standard deviation of wealth	$196	$596	$1,376	$2,654	$4,512	$6,937	$8,654	$9,218	$11,630

Now you know about the time diversification fallacy: Time diversifies returns but not wealth. As investors, we are more concerned about how much money we have (i.e., our wealth) than we are about our exact percentage return over the life of our investment accounts.

So, should younger investors put more money in equity? The answer is probably still yes—but for logically sound reasons that differ from the reasoning underlying the fallacy of time diversification. If you are young and your portfolio suffers a steep decline in a particular year, what could you do? You could make up for this loss by changing your work habits (e.g., your type of job, hours, second job). People approaching retirement have little future earning power, so a major loss in their portfolio will have a much greater impact on their wealth. Thus, the portfolios of young people should contain relatively more equity (i.e., risk).

CHECK THIS

11.3a What happens to the standard deviation of return for a portfolio if we increase the number of securities in the portfolio?

11.3b What is the principle of diversification?

11.3c What is the time diversification fallacy?

11.4 Correlation and Diversification

We've seen that diversification is important. What we haven't discussed is how to get the most out of diversification. For example, in our previous section, we investigated what happens if we spread our money evenly across randomly chosen stocks. We saw that significant risk reduction resulted from this strategy, but you might wonder whether even larger gains could be achieved using a more sophisticated approach. As we begin to examine that question here, the answer is yes.

WHY DIVERSIFICATION WORKS

correlation
The tendency of the returns on two assets to move together.

Why diversification reduces portfolio risk as measured by the portfolio's standard deviation is important and worth exploring in some detail. The key concept is **correlation**, which is the extent to which the returns on two assets move together. If the returns on two assets tend to move up and down together, we say they are *positively* correlated. If they tend to move in opposite directions, we say they are *negatively* correlated. If there is no particular relationship between the two assets, we say they are *uncorrelated.*

The *correlation coefficient,* which we use to measure correlation, ranges from −1 to +1, and we will denote the correlation between the returns on two assets, say A and B, as $Corr(R_A, R_B)$. The Greek letter ρ (rho) is often used to designate correlation as well. A correlation of +1 indicates that the two assets have a *perfect* positive correlation. For example, suppose that whatever return Asset A realizes, either up or down, Asset B does the same thing by exactly twice as much. In this case, they are perfectly correlated because the movement on one is completely predictable from the movement on the other. Notice, however, that perfect correlation does not necessarily mean they move by the same amount.

A zero correlation means that the two assets are uncorrelated. If we know that one asset is up, then we have no idea what the other one is likely to do; there is no relation between them. Perfect negative correlation [$Corr(R_A, R_B) = -1$] indicates that they always move in opposite directions. Figure 11.2 illustrates the three benchmark cases of perfect positive, perfect negative, and zero correlation.

Diversification works because security returns are generally not perfectly correlated. We will be more precise about the impact of correlation on portfolio risk in just a moment. For now, it is useful to think about combining two assets into a portfolio. If the two assets are highly positively correlated (the correlation is near +1), then they have a strong tendency to move up and down together. As a result, they offer limited diversification benefit.

FIGURE 11.2   Correlations

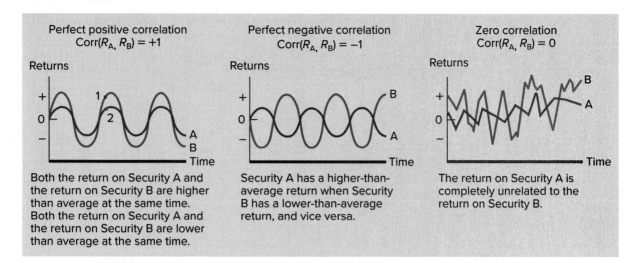

Perfect positive correlation
$\text{Corr}(R_A, R_B) = +1$

Both the return on Security A and the return on Security B are higher than average at the same time. Both the return on Security A and the return on Security B are lower than average at the same time.

Perfect negative correlation
$\text{Corr}(R_A, R_B) = -1$

Security A has a higher-than-average return when Security B has a lower-than-average return, and vice versa.

Zero correlation
$\text{Corr}(R_A, R_B) = 0$

The return on Security A is completely unrelated to the return on Security B.

For example, two stocks from the same industry, say, General Motors and Ford, will tend to be relatively highly correlated because the companies are in essentially the same business, and a portfolio of two such stocks is not likely to be very diversified.

In contrast, if the two assets are negatively correlated, then they tend to move in opposite directions; whenever one zigs, the other tends to zag. In such a case, the diversification benefit will be substantial because variation in the return on one asset tends to be offset by variation in the opposite direction from the other. In fact, if two assets have a perfect negative correlation [$\text{Corr}(R_A, R_B) = -1$], then it is possible to combine them such that all risk is eliminated. Looking back at our example involving Jpod and Starcents in which we were able to eliminate all of the risk, what we now see is that they must be perfectly, or almost perfectly, negatively correlated.

To illustrate the impact of diversification on portfolio risk further, suppose we observed the actual annual returns on two stocks, A and B, for the years 2018–2022. We summarize these returns in Table 11.10. In addition to actual returns on Stocks A and B, we also calculated the returns on an equally weighted portfolio of A and B in Table 11.10. We label this portfolio as AB. In 2018, for example, Stock A returned 10 percent and Stock B returned 15 percent. Because Portfolio AB is half invested in each, its return for the year was:

$$1/2 \times 10\% + 1/2 \times 15\% = 12.5\%$$

The returns for the other years are calculated similarly.

At the bottom of Table 11.10, we calculated the average returns and standard deviations on the two stocks and the equally weighted portfolio. These averages and standard deviations are calculated just as they were in Chapter 1 (check a couple just to refresh your memory).

TABLE 11.10   **Annual Returns on Stocks A and B**

Year	Stock A	Stock B	Portfolio AB
2018	10%	15%	12.5%
2019	30	−10	10.0
2020	−10	25	7.5
2021	5	20	12.5
2022	10	15	12.5
Average returns	9%	13%	11.0%
Standard deviations	14.3%	13.5%	2.2%

FIGURE 11.3   Impact of Diversification

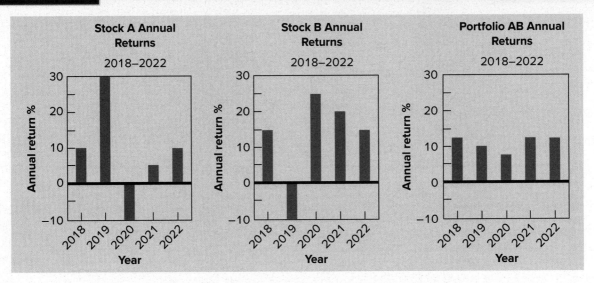

The impact of diversification is apparent. The two stocks have standard deviations in the 13 percent to 14 percent per year range, but the portfolio's volatility is only 2.2 percent. In fact, if we compare the portfolio to Stock A, it has both a higher return (11 percent vs. 9 percent) and much less risk.

Figure 11.3 illustrates in more detail what is occurring with our example. Here we have three bar graphs showing the year-by-year returns on Stocks A and B and Portfolio AB. Examining the graphs, we see that in 2019, for example, Stock A earned 30 percent while Stock B lost 10 percent. The following year, Stock B earned 25 percent, while Stock A lost 10 percent. These ups and downs tend to cancel out in Portfolio AB, however, with the result that there is much less variation in return from year to year. In other words, the correlation between the returns on Stocks A and B is relatively low.

Calculating the correlation between Stocks A and B is not difficult, but it would require us to digress a bit. Instead, we will explain the needed calculation in the next chapter, where we build on the principles developed here.

CALCULATING PORTFOLIO RISK

We've seen that correlation is an important determinant of portfolio risk. To further pursue this issue, we need to know how to calculate portfolio variances directly. For a portfolio of two assets, A and B, the variance of the return on the portfolio, σ_p^2, is given by Equation 11.3:

$$\sigma_p^2 = x_A^2 \sigma_A^2 + x_B^2 \sigma_B^2 + 2x_A x_B \sigma_A \sigma_B \text{Corr}(R_A, R_B) \qquad (11.3)$$

In this equation, x_A and x_B are the percentages invested in Assets A and B. Notice that $x_A + x_B = 1$. (Why?)

For a portfolio of three assets, the variance of the return on the portfolio, σ_p^2, is given by Equation 11.4:

$$\sigma_p^2 = x_A^2 \sigma_A^2 + x_B^2 \sigma_B^2 + x_C^2 \sigma_C^2 + 2x_A x_B \sigma_A \sigma_B \text{Corr}(R_A, R_B)$$
$$+ 2x_A x_C \sigma_A \sigma_C \text{Corr}(R_A, R_C) + 2x_B x_C \sigma_B \sigma_C \text{Corr}(R_B, R_C) \qquad (11.4)$$

Note that six terms appear in Equation 11.4. There is a term involving the squared weight and the variance of the return for each of the three assets (A, B, and C), as well as a *cross-term* for each pair of assets. The cross-term involves pairs of weights, pairs of standard deviations of returns for each asset, and the correlation between the returns of the asset pair. If you had a portfolio of six assets, you would have an equation with 21 terms. (Can you write this equation?) If you had a portfolio of 50 assets, the equation for the variance of this portfolio would have 1,275 terms! Let's return to Equation 11.3.

Equation 11.3 looks a little involved, but its use is straightforward. For example, suppose Stock A has a standard deviation of 40 percent per year and Stock B has a standard deviation of 60 percent per year. The correlation between them is .15. If you put half your money in each, what is your portfolio standard deviation?

To answer, we just plug the numbers into Equation 11.3. Note that x_A and x_B are each equal to .50, while σ_A and σ_B are .40 and .60, respectively. Taking $\text{Corr}(R_A, R_B) = .15$, we have:

$$\begin{aligned} \sigma_p^2 &= .50^2 \times .40^2 + .50^2 \times .60^2 + 2 \times .50 \times .50 \times .40 \times .60 \times .15 \\ &= .25 \times .16 + .25 \times .36 + .018 \\ &= .148 \end{aligned}$$

Thus, the portfolio variance is .148. As always, variances are not easy to interpret because they are based on squared returns, so we calculate the standard deviation by taking the square root:

$$\sigma_p = \sqrt{.148} = .3847, \text{or } 38.47\%$$

Once again, we see the impact of diversification. This portfolio has a standard deviation of 38.47 percent, which is less than either of the standard deviations on the two assets that are in the portfolio.

EXAMPLE 11.5

Portfolio Variance and Standard Deviation

In the example we just examined, Stock A has a standard deviation of 40 percent per year and Stock B has a standard deviation of 60 percent per year. Suppose now that the correlation between them is .35. Also suppose you put one-fourth of your money in Stock A. What is your portfolio standard deviation?

If you put 1/4 (or .25) in Stock A, you must have 3/4 (or .75) in Stock B, so $x_A = .25$ and $x_B = .75$. Making use of Equation 11.3 to find portfolio variance, we have:

$$\begin{aligned} \sigma_p^2 &= .25^2 \times .40^2 + .75^2 \times .60^2 + 2 \times .25 \times .75 \times .40 \times .60 \times .35 \\ &= .0625 \times .16 + .5625 \times .36 + .0315 \\ &= .244 \end{aligned}$$

Thus, the portfolio variance is .244. Taking the square root, we get:

$$\sigma_p = \sqrt{.244} = .49396 \approx 49\%$$

This portfolio has a standard deviation of 49 percent, which is between the individual standard deviations. This shows that a portfolio's standard deviation isn't necessarily less than the individual standard deviations.

The impact of correlation in determining the overall risk of a portfolio has significant implications. For example, consider an investment in international equity. Historically, this sector has had slightly lower returns than large-cap U.S. equity, but the international equity volatility has been much higher.

If investors prefer more return to less return, and less risk to more risk, why would anyone allocate funds to international equity? The answer lies in the fact that the correlation of international equity to U.S. equity is much less than +1. Although international equity is quite risky by itself, adding international equity to an existing portfolio of U.S. investments can reduce risk. In fact, as we discuss in the next section, adding international equity could actually give our portfolio a better return-to-risk (or more efficient) profile.

Another important point about international equity and correlations is that correlations are not constant over time. Investors expect to receive significant diversification benefits from international equity, but if correlations increase, much of the benefit will be lost. When does this happen? Well, in the Crash of 2008, correlations across markets increased significantly, as almost all asset classes declined in value (an exception was short-term government debt). As investors, we must be mindful of the differences between expected and actual outcomes—particularly during crashes and bear markets.

THE IMPORTANCE OF ASSET ALLOCATION, PART 1

asset allocation
How an investor spreads portfolio dollars among broad asset classes.

Why are correlation and **asset allocation** important, practical, real-world considerations? Well, suppose that as a very conservative, risk-averse investor, you decide to invest all of your money in a bond mutual fund. Based on your analysis, you think this fund has an expected return of 6 percent with a standard deviation of 10 percent per year. A stock fund is available, however, with an expected return of 12 percent, but the standard deviation of 15 percent is too high for your taste. Also, the correlation between the returns on the two funds is about .10.

Is the decision to invest 100 percent in the bond fund a wise one, even for a very risk-averse investor? The answer is no; in fact, it is a bad decision for any investor. To see why, Table 11.11 shows expected returns and standard deviations available from different combinations of the two mutual funds. In constructing the table, we begin with 100 percent in the stock fund and work our way down to 100 percent in the bond fund by reducing the percentage in the stock fund in increments of .05. These calculations are all done just like our examples above; you should check some (or all) of them for practice.

Beginning in the first row in Table 11.11, we have 100 percent in the stock fund, so our expected return is 12 percent and our standard deviation is 15 percent. As we begin to move out of the stock fund and into the bond fund, we are not surprised to see both the expected return and the standard deviation decline. However, what might surprise you is the fact that

TABLE 11.11	Risk and Return with Stocks and Bonds		
Portfolio Weights			
Stocks	**Bonds**	**Expected Return**	**Standard Deviation (Risk)**
1.00	.00	12.00%	15.00%
.95	.05	11.70	14.31
.90	.10	11.40	13.64
.85	.15	11.10	12.99
.80	.20	10.80	12.36
.75	.25	10.50	11.77
.70	.30	10.20	11.20
.65	.35	9.90	10.68
.60	.40	9.60	10.21
.55	.45	9.30	9.78
.50	.50	9.00	9.42
.45	.55	8.70	9.12
.40	.60	8.40	8.90
.35	.65	8.10	8.75
.30	.70	7.80	8.69
.25	.75	7.50	8.71
.20	.80	7.20	8.82
.15	.85	6.90	9.01
.10	.90	6.60	9.27
.05	.95	6.30	9.60
.00	1.00	6.00	10.00

FIGURE 11.4 — Risk and Return with Stocks and Bonds

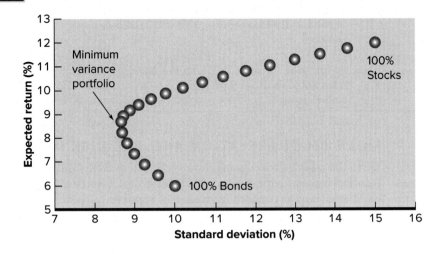

the standard deviation falls only so far and then begins to rise again. In other words, beyond a point, adding more of the lower-risk bond fund actually increases your risk!

The best way to see what is going on is to plot the various combinations of expected returns and standard deviations calculated in Table 11.11, as we do in Figure 11.4. We placed the standard deviations from Table 11.11 on the horizontal axis and the corresponding expected returns on the vertical axis.

Examining the plot in Figure 11.4, we see that the various combinations of risk and return available all fall on a smooth curve (in fact, for the geometrically inclined, it's a hyperbola). This curve is called an **investment opportunity set** because it shows the possible combinations of risk and return available from portfolios of these two assets. One important thing to notice is that, as we have shown, there is a portfolio that has the smallest standard deviation (or variance—same thing) of all. It is labeled "minimum variance portfolio" in Figure 11.4. What are its approximate expected return and standard deviation?

Now we see clearly why a 100 percent bonds strategy is a poor one. With a 10 percent standard deviation, the bond fund offers an expected return of 6 percent. However, Table 11.11 shows us that a combination of about 60 percent stocks and 40 percent bonds has almost the same standard deviation, but a return of about 9.6 percent. Comparing 9.6 percent to 6 percent, we see that this portfolio has a return that is fully 60 percent greater (6% × 1.6 = 9.6%) with the same risk. Our conclusion? Asset allocation matters.

Going back to Figure 11.4, notice that any portfolio that plots below the minimum variance portfolio is a poor choice because, no matter which one you pick, there is another portfolio with the same risk and a much better return. In the jargon of finance, we say that these undesirable portfolios are *dominated* and/or *inefficient*. Either way, we mean that given their level of risk, the expected return is inadequate compared to some other portfolio of equivalent risk. A portfolio that offers the highest return for its level of risk is said to be an **efficient portfolio**. In Figure 11.4, the minimum variance portfolio and all portfolios that plot above it are therefore efficient.

Review modern portfolio theory at www.moneychimp.com.

investment opportunity set
Collection of possible risk-return combinations available from portfolios of individual assets.

efficient portfolio
A portfolio that offers the highest return for its level of risk.

EXAMPLE 11.6 — More Portfolio Variance and Standard Deviation

Looking at Table 11.11, suppose you put 57.627 percent in the stock fund. What is your expected return? Your standard deviation? How does this compare with the bond fund?

If you put 57.627 percent in stocks, you must have 42.373 percent in bonds, so $x_A = .57627$ and $x_B = .42373$. From Table 11.11, you can see that the standard deviation for stocks and bonds is 15 percent and 10 percent, respectively. Also, the correlation

(continued)

between stocks and bonds is .10. Making use of Equation 11.3 for portfolio variance, we have:

$$\sigma_p^2 = .57627^2 \times .15^2 + .42373^2 \times .10^2 + 2 \times .57627 \times .42373 \times .15 \times .10 \times .10$$
$$= .332 \times .0225 + .180 \times .01 + .0007325$$
$$= .01$$

Thus, the portfolio variance is .01, so the standard deviation is .1, or 10 percent. Check that the expected return is 9.46 percent. Compared to the bond fund, the standard deviation is now identical, but the expected return is almost 350 basis points higher.

MORE ON CORRELATION AND THE RISK-RETURN TRADE-OFF

Given the expected returns and standard deviations on the two assets, the shape of the investment opportunity set in Figure 11.4 depends on the correlation. The lower the correlation, the more bowed to the left the investment opportunity set will be. To illustrate, Figure 11.5 shows the investment opportunity for correlations of -1, 0, and $+1$ for two stocks, A and B. Notice that Stock A has an expected return of 12 percent and a standard deviation of 15 percent, while Stock B has an expected return of 6 percent and a standard deviation of 10 percent. These are the same expected returns and standard deviations we used to build Figure 11.4, and the calculations are all done the same way; just the correlations are different. Notice also that we use the symbol ρ to stand for the correlation coefficient.

In Figure 11.5, when the correlation is $+1$, the investment opportunity set is a straight line connecting the two stocks, so, as expected, there is little or no diversification benefit. As the correlation declines to zero, the bend to the left becomes pronounced. For correlations between $+1$ and zero, there would be a less pronounced bend.

Finally, as the correlation becomes negative, the bend becomes quite pronounced, and the investment opportunity set actually becomes two straight-line segments when the correlation hits -1. Notice that the minimum variance portfolio has a zero variance in this case.

It is sometimes desirable to be able to calculate the percentage investments needed to create the minimum variance portfolio. For a two-asset portfolio, Equation 11.5 shows the weight in Asset A, x_A^*, that achieves the minimum variance.

$$x_A^* = \frac{\sigma_B^2 - \sigma_A \sigma_B \text{Corr}(R_A, R_B)}{\sigma_A^2 + \sigma_B^2 - 2\sigma_A \sigma_B \text{Corr}(R_A, R_B)} \tag{11.5}$$

A question at the end of the chapter asks you to prove that Equation 11.5 is correct.

EXAMPLE 11.7 | Finding the Minimum Variance Portfolio

Looking back at Table 11.11, what combination of the stock fund and the bond fund has the lowest possible standard deviation? What is the minimum possible standard deviation?

Recalling that the standard deviations for the stock fund and bond fund were .15 and .10, respectively, and noting that the correlation was .1, we have:

$$x_A^* = \frac{.10^2 - .15 \times .10 \times .10}{.15^2 + .10^2 - 2 \times .15 \times .10 \times .10}$$
$$= .288136$$
$$\approx 28.8\%$$

Thus, the minimum variance portfolio has 28.8 percent in stocks and the balance, 71.2 percent, in bonds. Plugging these into our formula for portfolio variance, we have:

$$\sigma_p^2 = .288^2 \times .15^2 + .712^2 \times .10^2 + 2 \times .288 \times .712 \times .15 \times .10 \times .10$$
$$= .007551$$

The standard deviation is the square root of .007551, or about 8.7 percent. Notice that this is where the minimum occurs in Figure 11.4.

FIGURE 11.5   Risk and Return with Two Assets

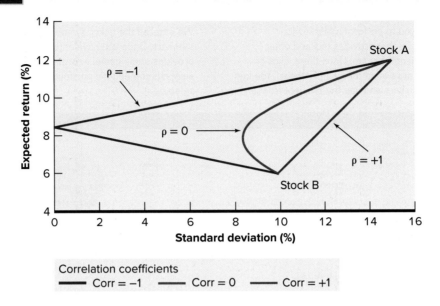

Correlation coefficients
—— Corr = −1   —— Corr = 0   —— Corr = +1

CHECK THIS

11.4a Fundamentally, why does diversification work?

11.4b If two stocks have positive correlation, what does this mean?

11.4c What is an efficient portfolio?

11.5 The Markowitz Efficient Frontier

In the previous section, we looked closely at the risk-return possibilities available when we consider combining two risky assets. Now we are left with an obvious question: What happens when we consider combining three or more risky assets? As we will see, at least on a conceptual level, the answer turns out to be a straightforward extension of our previous examples that use two risky assets.

Related Bloomberg Functions

PORT OP   Portfolio Optimization

XLTP XAAO Excel Template: Asset Allocation Optimizer

THE IMPORTANCE OF ASSET ALLOCATION, PART 2

As you saw in Equation 11.4, the formula to compute a portfolio variance with three assets is a bit cumbersome. Indeed, the amount of calculation increases greatly as the number of assets in the portfolio grows. The calculations are not difficult, but using a computer is highly recommended for portfolios consisting of more than three assets!

We can, however, illustrate the importance of asset allocation using only three assets. How? Well, a mutual fund that holds a broadly diversified portfolio of securities counts as only one asset. So, with three mutual funds that hold diversified portfolios, we can construct a diversified portfolio with these three assets. Suppose we invest in three index funds—one that represents U.S. stocks, one that represents U.S. bonds, and one that represents foreign stocks. Then we can see how the allocation among these three diversified portfolios matters. (Our *Getting Down to Business* box at the end of the chapter presents a more detailed discussion of mutual funds and diversification.)

Figure 11.6 shows the result of calculating the expected returns and portfolio standard deviations when there are three assets. To illustrate the importance of asset allocation, we calculated expected returns and standard deviations from portfolios composed of three key investment types: U.S. stocks, foreign (non-U.S.) stocks, and U.S. bonds. These asset classes

Several websites allow you to perform a Markowitz-type analysis. One free site that provides this and other information is portfoliovisualizer.com. Once there, click on "Examples" and find the area titled "Efficient Frontier." You can select asset classes or tickers and see the efficient frontier.

We entered the ticker symbols for Wells Fargo, Nike, and Walmart. Once you have entered the data, the website provides some useful information. In particular, the output suggests the optimal portfolio allocation for the stocks we selected.

Source: Portfolio Visualizer, 2022.

are not highly correlated in general; therefore, we assume a zero correlation in all cases. When we assume that all correlations are zero, the return to this portfolio is still:

$$R_p = x_F R_F + x_S R_S + x_B R_B \qquad (11.6)$$

But when all correlations are zero, the variance of the portfolio becomes:

$$\sigma_p^2 = x_F^2 \sigma_F^2 + x_S^2 \sigma_S^2 + x_B^2 \sigma_B^2 \qquad (11.7)$$

Suppose the expected returns and standard deviations are as follows:

	Expected Returns	Standard Deviations
Foreign stocks, F	18%	35%
U.S. stocks, S	12	22
U.S. bonds, B	8	14

Check out the online journal at www.efficientfrontier.com.

We can now compute risk-return combinations as we did in our two-asset case. We create tables similar to Table 11.11, and then we can plot the risk-return combinations.

FIGURE 11.6   Markowitz Efficient Portfolio

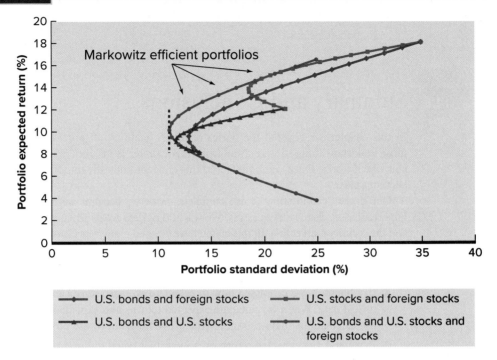

Markowitz efficient portfolios

U.S. bonds and foreign stocks   U.S. stocks and foreign stocks

U.S. bonds and U.S. stocks   U.S. bonds and U.S. stocks and foreign stocks

Markowitz efficient frontier

The set of portfolios with the maximum return for a given standard deviation.

In Figure 11.6, each point plotted is a possible risk-return combination. Comparing the result with our two-asset case in Figure 11.4, we see that now not only do some assets plot below the minimum variance portfolio on a smooth curve, but we have portfolios plotting inside as well. Only combinations that plot on the upper left-hand boundary are efficient; all the rest are inefficient. This upper left-hand boundary is called the **Markowitz efficient frontier**, and it represents the set of risky portfolios with the maximum return for a given standard deviation.

Figure 11.6 makes it clear that asset allocation matters. For example, a portfolio of 100 percent U.S. stocks is highly inefficient. For the same standard deviation, there is a portfolio with an expected return almost 400 basis points, or 4 percent, higher. Or, for the same expected return, there is a portfolio with about half as much risk! Our nearby *Work the Web* box shows you how an efficient frontier can be created online.

The analysis in this section can be extended to any number of assets or asset classes. In principle, it is possible to compute efficient frontiers using thousands of assets. As a practical matter, however, this analysis is most widely used with a relatively small number of asset classes. For example, most investment banks maintain so-called model portfolios. These are recommended asset allocation strategies typically involving three to six asset categories.

A primary reason that the Markowitz analysis is not usually extended to large collections of individual assets has to do with data requirements. The inputs into the analysis are (1) expected returns on all assets, (2) standard deviations on all assets, and (3) correlations between every pair of assets. Moreover, these inputs have to be measured with some precision or we just end up with a garbage-in, garbage-out (GIGO) system.

Suppose we just look at 2,000 NYSE stocks. We need 2,000 expected returns and standard deviations. We already have a problem because returns on individual stocks cannot be predicted with precision at all. To make matters worse, however, we need to know the correlation between every *pair* of stocks. With 2,000 stocks, there are $2{,}000 \times 1{,}999/2 = 1{,}999{,}000$, or almost 2 million, unique pairs![3] Also, as with expected returns, correlations between individual stocks are very difficult to predict accurately. We will return to this issue in our next chapter, where we show that there may be an extremely elegant way around the problem.

---

[3] With 2,000 stocks, there are $2{,}000^2 = 4{,}000{,}000$ possible pairs. Of these, 2,000 involve pairing a stock with itself. Further, we recognize that the correlation between A and B is the same as the correlation between B and A, so we only need to actually calculate half of the remaining 3,998,000 correlations.

CHECK THIS

11.5a   What is the Markowitz efficient frontier?

11.5b   Why is Markowitz portfolio analysis most commonly used to make asset allocation decisions?

11.6 Summary and Conclusions

In this chapter, we covered the basics of diversification and portfolio risk and return. The most important thing to take away from this chapter is an understanding of diversification and why it works. Once you understand this concept, then the importance of asset allocation becomes clear.

Our diversification story is not complete, however, because we have not considered one important asset class: riskless assets. We will add riskless assets when we talk about risk, return, and the security market line. In this chapter, we covered many aspects of diversification and risky assets. We recap some of these aspects, grouped below by the learning objectives of the chapter.

1. **How to calculate expected returns and variances for a security.**

   A. In Chapter 1, we discussed how to calculate average returns and variances using historical data. When we calculate expected returns and expected variances, we have to use calculations that account for the probabilities of future possible returns.

   B. In general, the expected return on a security is equal to the sum of the possible returns multiplied by their probabilities. So, if we have 100 possible returns, we would multiply each one by its probability and then add up the results. The sum is the expected return.

   C. To calculate the variances, we first determine the squared deviations from the expected return. We then multiply each possible squared deviation by its probability. Next we add these, and the result is the variance. The standard deviation is the square root of the variance.

2. **How to calculate expected returns and variances for a portfolio.**

   A. A portfolio's expected return is a simple weighted combination of the expected returns on the assets in the portfolio. This method of calculating the expected return on a portfolio works no matter how many assets are in the portfolio.

   B. The variance of a portfolio is generally not a simple combination of the variances of the assets in the portfolio. Review Equations 11.3 and 11.4 to verify this fact.

3. **The importance of portfolio diversification.**

   A. Diversification is a very important consideration. The principle of diversification tells us that spreading an investment across many assets can reduce some, but not all, of the risk. Based on U.S. stock market history, for example, about 60 percent of the risk associated with owning individual stocks can be eliminated by naive diversification.

   B. Diversification works because asset returns are not perfectly correlated. All else the same, the lower the correlation, the greater is the gain from diversification.

   C. It is even possible to combine some risky assets in such a way that the resulting portfolio has zero risk. This is a nice bit of financial alchemy.

4. **The efficient frontier and the importance of asset allocation.**

   A. When we consider the possible combinations of risk and return available from portfolios of assets, we find that some are inefficient (or dominated) portfolios. An inefficient portfolio is one that offers too little return for its risk.

   B. For any group of assets, there is a set that is efficient. That set is known as the Markowitz efficient frontier. The Markowitz efficient frontier simultaneously represents (1) the set of risky portfolios with the maximum return for a given standard deviation and (2) the set of risky portfolios with the minimum standard deviation for a given return.

GETTING DOWN TO BUSINESS

This chapter explained diversification, a very important consideration for real-world investors and money managers. The chapter also explored the Markowitz efficient portfolio concept, which shows how (and why) asset allocation affects portfolio risk and return.

Building a diversified portfolio is not a trivial task. Of course, as we discussed many chapters ago, mutual funds provide one way for investors to build diversified portfolios, but there are some significant caveats concerning mutual funds as a diversification tool. First of all, investors sometimes assume a fund is diversified because it holds a relatively large number of stocks. However, with the exception of some index funds, most mutual funds will reflect a particular style of investing, either explicitly, as stated in the fund's objective, or implicitly, as favored by the fund manager. For example, in the mid- to late-1990s, stocks as a whole did very well, but mutual funds that concentrated on smaller stocks generally did not do well at all.

It is tempting to buy a number of mutual funds to ensure broad diversification, but even this may not work. Within a given fund family, the same manager may actually be responsible for multiple funds. In addition, managers within a large fund family frequently have similar views about the market and individual companies.

Thinking just about stocks for the moment, what does an investor need to consider to build a well-diversified portfolio? At a minimum, such a portfolio probably needs to be diversified across industries, with no undue concentrations in particular sectors of the economy; it needs to be diversified by company size (small, mid-cap, and large); and it needs to be diversified across "growth" (i.e., high-PE) and "value" (i.e., low-PE) stocks. Perhaps the most controversial diversification issue concerns international diversification. The correlation between international stock exchanges is surprisingly low, suggesting large benefits from diversifying globally.

Perhaps the most disconcerting fact about diversification is that it leads to the following paradox: A well-diversified portfolio will always be invested in something that does not do well! Put differently, such a portfolio will almost always have both winners and losers. In many ways, that's the whole idea. Even so, it requires a lot of financial discipline to stay diversified when some portion of your portfolio seems to be doing poorly. The payoff is that, over the long run, a well-diversified portfolio should provide much steadier returns and be much less prone to abrupt changes in value.

For the latest information on the real world of investments, visit us at jmdinvestments.blogspot.com.

Key Terms

asset allocation 378
correlation 374
efficient portfolio 379
expected return 364
investment opportunity set 379

Markowitz efficient frontier 383
portfolio 367
portfolio weight 368
principle of diversification 372

Related Bloomberg Functions

HVC	Historical Volatility Graph, 11.1
GV	Graph Volatility, 11.1
PRTU	Portfolio Administration, 11.2
PORT	Portfolio and Risk Analytics, 11.2
PC	Peer Correlation, 11.4
CORR	My Correlation Matrices, 11.4
CFND	Correlation Finder, 11.4
PORT OP	Portfolio Optimization, 11.5
XLTP XAAO	Excel Template: Asset Allocation Optimizer, 11.5

Chapter Review Problems and Self-Test

Use the following table of states of the economy and stock returns to answer the review problems:

State of Economy	Probability of State of Economy	Security Returns if State Occurs	
		Roten	Bradley
Bust	.40	−10%	30%
Boom	.60	40	10
	1.00		

1. **Expected Returns (LO1, CFA1)** Calculate the expected returns for Roten and Bradley.
2. **Standard Deviations (LO1, CFA1)** Calculate the standard deviations for Roten and Bradley.
3. **Portfolio Expected Returns (LO2, CFA2)** Calculate the expected return on a portfolio of 50 percent Roten and 50 percent Bradley.
4. **Portfolio Volatility (LO2, CFA4)** Calculate the variance and standard deviation of a portfolio of 50 percent Roten and 50 percent Bradley.

Answers to Self-Test Problems

1. We calculate the expected returns as follows:

		Roten		Bradley	
(1) State of Economy	(2) Probability of State of Economy	(3) Return if State Occurs	(4) Product (2) × (3)	(5) Return if State Occurs	(6) Product (2) × (5)
Bust	.40	−10%	−.04	30%	.12
Boom	.60	40	.24	10	.06
			$E(R) = 20\%$		$E(R) = 18\%$

2. We calculate the standard deviations as follows:

(1) State of Economy	(2) Probability of State of Economy	(3) Return Deviation from Expected Return	(4) Squared Return Deviation	(5) Product (2) × (4)
Roten				
Bust	.40	−.30	.09	.036
Boom	.60	.20	.04	.024
				$\sigma^2 = .06$
Bradley				
Bust	.40	.12	.0144	.00576
Boom	.60	−.08	.0064	.00384
				$\sigma^2 = .0096$

Taking square roots, the standard deviations are 24.495 percent for Roten and 9.798 percent for Bradley.

3. We calculate the expected return on a portfolio of 50 percent Roten and 50 percent Bradley as follows:

(1) State of Economy	(2) Probability of State of Economy	(3) Portfolio Return if State Occurs	(4) Product (2) × (3)
Bust	.40	10%	.04
Boom	.60	25	.15
			$E(R_p) = 19\%$

4. We calculate the variance and standard deviation of a portfolio of 50 percent Roten and 50 percent Bradley as follows:

(1) State of Economy	(2) Probability of State of Economy	(3) Portfolio Return if State Occurs	(4) Squared Deviation from Expected Return	(5) Product (2) × (4)
Bust	.40	.10	.0081	.00324
Boom	.60	.25	.0036	.00216

$$\sigma_p^2 = .00540$$
$$\sigma_p = 7.3485\%$$

Test Your Investment Quotient

1. **Diversification (LO3, CFA6)** Starcents has an expected return of 25 percent and Jpod has an expected return of 20 percent. What is the likely investment decision for a risk-averse investor?

   a. Invest all funds in Starcents.
   b. Invest all funds in Jpod.
   c. Do not invest any funds in Starcents and Jpod.
   d. Invest funds partly in Starcents and partly in Jpod.

2. **Return Standard Deviation (LO1, CFA1)** Starcents experiences returns of 5 percent or 45 percent, each with an equal probability. What is the return standard deviation for Starcents?

   a. 30 percent
   b. 25 percent
   c. 20 percent
   d. 10 percent

3. **Return Standard Deviation (LO1, CFA1)** Jpod experiences returns of 0 percent, 25 percent, or 50 percent, each with a one-third probability. What is the approximate return standard deviation for Jpod?

   a. 30 percent
   b. 25 percent
   c. 20 percent
   d. 10 percent

4. **Expected Return (LO1, CFA1)** An analyst estimates that a stock has the following return probabilities and returns depending on the state of the economy:

State of Economy	Probability	Return
Good	.1	15%
Normal	.6	13
Poor	.3	7

   What is the expected return of the stock?

   a. 7.8 percent
   b. 11.4 percent
   c. 11.7 percent
   d. 13.0 percent

5. **Risk Aversion (LO3, CFA3)** Which of the following statements best reflects the importance of the asset allocation decision to the investment process? The asset allocation decision:

   a. Helps the investor decide on realistic investment goals.
   b. Identifies the specific securities to include in a portfolio.
   c. Determines most of the portfolio's returns and volatility over time.
   d. Creates a standard by which to establish the appropriate investment time horizon.

6. **Optimal Portfolios (LO4, CFA4)** The best portfolios would be those that are described as having:

 a. The minimum risk for every level of return.
 b. Proportionally equal units of risk and return.
 c. The maximum excess rate of return for every given level of risk.
 d. The highest return for each level of beta using the capital asset pricing model.

7. **Diversification (LO3, CFA2)** An investor is considering adding another investment to a portfolio. To achieve the maximum diversification benefits, the investor should add an investment that has a correlation coefficient with the existing portfolio closest to:

 a. −1.0
 b. −.5
 c. 0
 d. +1.0

8. **Risk Premium (LO2, CFA1)** Starcents has an expected return of 25 percent, Jpod has an expected return of 20 percent, and the risk-free rate is 5 percent. You invest half your funds in Starcents and the other half in Jpod. What is the risk premium for your portfolio?

 a. 20 percent
 b. 17.5 percent
 c. 15 percent
 d. 12.5 percent

9. **Return Standard Deviation (LO2, CFA4)** Both Starcents and Jpod have the same return standard deviation of 20 percent, and Starcents and Jpod returns have zero correlation. You invest half your funds in Starcents and the other half in Jpod. What is the return standard deviation for your portfolio?

 a. 20 percent
 b. 14.14 percent
 c. 10 percent
 d. 0 percent

10. **Return Standard Deviation (LO2, CFA4)** Both Starcents and Jpod have the same return standard deviation of 20 percent, and Starcents and Jpod returns have a correlation of +1. You invest half your funds in Starcents and the other half in Jpod. What is the return standard deviation for your portfolio?

 a. 20 percent
 b. 14.14 percent
 c. 10 percent
 d. 0 percent

11. **Return Standard Deviation (LO2, CFA4)** Both Starcents and Jpod have the same return standard deviation of 20 percent, and Starcents and Jpod returns have a correlation of −1. You invest half your funds in Starcents and the other half in Jpod. What is the return standard deviation for your portfolio?

 a. 20 percent
 b. 14.14 percent
 c. 10 percent
 d. 0 percent

12. **Minimum Variance Portfolio (LO2, CFA3)** Both Starcents and Jpod have the same return standard deviation of 20 percent, and Starcents and Jpod returns have zero correlation. What is the minimum attainable standard deviation for a portfolio of Starcents and Jpod?

 a. 20 percent
 b. 14.14 percent
 c. 10 percent
 d. 0 percent

13. **Minimum Variance Portfolio (LO2, CFA3)** Both Starcents and Jpod have the same return standard deviation of 20 percent, and Starcents and Jpod returns have a correlation of −1. What is the minimum attainable return deviation for a portfolio of Starcents and Jpod?

 a. 20 percent
 b. 14.14 percent
 c. 10 percent
 d. 0 percent

14. **Minimum Variance Portfolio (LO2, CFA3)**   Stocks A, B, and C each has the same expected return and standard deviation. The following shows the correlations between returns on these stocks:

	Stock A	Stock B	Stock C
Stock A	+1.0		
Stock B	+.9	+1.0	
Stock C	+.1	−.4	+1.0

Given these correlations, which of the following portfolios constructed from these stocks would have the lowest risk?

a. One equally invested in Stocks A and B
b. One equally invested in Stocks A and C
c. One equally invested in Stocks B and C
d. One totally invested in Stock C

15. **Markowitz Efficient Frontier (LO4, CFA4)**   Which of the following portfolios cannot lie on the efficient frontier as described by Markowitz?

	Portfolio	Expected Return	Standard Deviation
a.	W	9%	21%
b.	X	5	7
c.	Y	15	36
d.	Z	12	15

Concept Questions

1. **Diversification and Market History (LO3, CFA6)**   Based on market history, what is the average annual standard deviation of return for a single, randomly chosen stock? What is the average annual standard deviation for an equally weighted portfolio of many stocks?

2. **Interpreting Correlations (LO2, CFA2)**   If the returns on two stocks are highly correlated, what does this mean? If they have no correlation? If they are negatively correlated?

3. **Efficient Portfolios (LO4, CFA4)**   What is an efficient portfolio?

4. **Expected Returns (LO2, CFA2)**   True or false: If two stocks have the same expected return of 12 percent, then any portfolio of the two stocks will also have an expected return of 12 percent.

5. **Portfolio Volatility (LO2, CFA4)**   True or false: If two stocks have the same standard deviation of 45 percent, then any portfolio of the two stocks will also have a standard deviation of 45 percent.

6. **Time Diversification (LO3, CFA6)**   Why should younger investors be willing to hold a larger amount of equity in their portfolios?

7. **Asset Allocation (LO4, CFA6)**   Assume you are a very risk-averse investor. Why might you still be willing to add an investment with high volatility to your portfolio?

8. **Minimum Variance Portfolio (LO2, CFA3)**   Why is the minimum variance portfolio important in regard to the Markowitz efficient frontier?

9. **Markowitz Efficient Frontier (LO4, CFA4)**   True or false: It is impossible for a single asset to lie on the Markowitz efficient frontier.

10. **Portfolio Variance (LO2, CFA4)**   Suppose two assets have zero correlation and the same standard deviation. What is true about the minimum variance portfolio?

Questions and Problems

Core Questions

1. **Expected Returns (LO1, CFA1)**   Use the following information on states of the economy and stock returns to calculate the expected return for Dingaling Telephone:

State of Economy	Probability of State of Economy	Security Return if State Occurs
Recession	.25	−8%
Normal	.50	13
Boom	.25	23

2. **Standard Deviations (LO1, CFA1)** Using the information in Question 1, calculate the standard deviation of returns.

3. **Expected Returns and Deviations (LO1, CFA1)** Repeat Questions 1 and 2 assuming that all three states are equally likely.

Use the following information on states of the economy and stock returns to answer Questions 4–7:

State of Economy	Probability of State of Economy	Security Returns if State Occurs	
		Roll	Ross
Bust	.40	−10%	21%
Boom	.60	28	8

4. **Expected Returns (LO1, CFA1)** Calculate the expected returns for Roll and Ross by filling in the following table (verify your answer by expressing returns as percentages as well as decimals):

		Roll		Ross	
(1) State of Economy	(2) Probability of State of Economy	(3) Return if State Occurs	(4) Product (2) × (3)	(5) Return if State Occurs	(6) Product (2) × (5)
Bust					
Boom					

5. **Standard Deviations (LO1, CFA1)** Calculate the standard deviations for Roll and Ross by filling in the following table (verify your answer using returns expressed in percentages as well as decimals):

(1) State of Economy	(2) Probability of State of Economy	(3) Return Deviation from Expected Return	(4) Squared Return Deviation	(5) Product (2) × (4)
Roll				
Bust				
Boom				
Ross				
Bust				
Boom				

6. **Portfolio Expected Returns (LO2, CFA2)** Calculate the expected return on a portfolio of 55 percent Roll and 45 percent Ross by filling in the following table:

(1) State of Economy	(2) Probability of State of Economy	(3) Portfolio Return if State Occurs	(4) Product (2) × (3)
Bust			
Boom			

7. **Portfolio Volatility (LO2, CFA4)** Calculate the volatility of a portfolio of 35 percent Roll and 65 percent Ross by filling in the following table:

(1) State of Economy	(2) Probability of State of Economy	(3) Portfolio Return if State Occurs	(4) Squared Deviation from Expected Return	(5) Product (2) × (4)
Bust				
Boom				
$\sigma_p^2 =$				
$\sigma_p =$				

8. **Calculating Returns and Standard Deviations (LO1, CFA1)** Based on the following information, calculate the expected return and standard deviation for the two stocks:

State of Economy	Probability of State of Economy	Rate of Return if State Occurs	
		Stock A	Stock B
Recession	.3	.04	−.20
Normal	.4	.09	.13
Boom	.3	.12	.33

9. **Returns and Standard Deviations (LO2, CFA4)** Consider the following information:

State of Economy	Probability of State of Economy	Rate of Return if State Occurs		
		Stock A	Stock B	Stock C
Boom	.10	.18	.48	.33
Good	.30	.11	.18	.15
Poor	.40	.05	−.09	−.05
Bust	.20	−.03	−.32	−.09

a. Your portfolio is invested 25 percent each in Stocks A and C and 50 percent in Stock B. What is the expected return of the portfolio?
b. What is the variance of this portfolio? The standard deviation?

10. **Portfolio Returns and Volatilities (LO2, CFA4)** Fill in the missing information in the following table. Assume that Portfolio AB is 40 percent invested in Stock A.

Year	Stock A	Stock B	Portfolio AB
2018	11%	21%	
2019	37	−38	
2020	−21	48	
2021	26	16	
2022	13	24	
Average return			
Standard deviation			

11. **Portfolio Returns and Volatilities (LO2, CFA4)** Given the following information, calculate the expected return and standard deviation for a portfolio that has 35 percent invested in Stock A, 45 percent in Stock B, and the balance in Stock C:

State of Economy	Probability of State of Economy	Returns		
		Stock A	Stock B	Stock C
Boom	.40	15%	18%	20%
Bust	.60	10	0	−10

12. **Portfolio Variance (LO2, CFA4)** Use the following information to calculate the expected return and standard deviation of a portfolio that is 50 percent invested in 3 Doors, Inc., and 50 percent invested in Down Co.:

	3 Doors, Inc.	Down Co.
Expected return, $E(R)$	14%	10%
Standard deviation, σ	42	31
Correlation		.10

13. **More Portfolio Variance (LO4, CFA2)** In Problem 12, what is the standard deviation if the correlation is +1? 0? −1? As the correlation declines from +1 to −1 here, what do you see happening to portfolio volatility? Why?

14. **Minimum Variance Portfolio (LO4, CFA3)** In Problem 12, what are the expected return and standard deviation on the minimum variance portfolio?

15. **Asset Allocation (LO4, CFA3)** Fill in the missing information assuming a correlation of .30:

Portfolio Weights			
Stocks	Bonds	Expected Return	Standard Deviation
1.00		12%	21%
.80			
.60			
.40			
.20			
.00		7%	12%

16. **Minimum Variance Portfolio (LO4, CFA3)** Consider two stocks, Stock D, with an expected return of 13 percent and a standard deviation of 31 percent, and Stock I, an international company, with an expected return of 16 percent and a standard deviation of 42 percent. The correlation between the two stocks is −.10. What is the weight of each stock in the minimum variance portfolio?

17. **Minimum Variance Portfolio (LO2, CFA3)** What are the expected return and standard deviation of the minimum variance portfolio in Problem 16?

18. **Minimum Variance Portfolio (LO4, CFA3)** Asset K has an expected return of 10 percent and a standard deviation of 28 percent. Asset L has an expected return of 7 percent and a standard deviation of 18 percent. The correlation between the assets is .40. What are the expected return and standard deviation of the minimum variance portfolio?

19. **Minimum Variance Portfolio (LO4, CFA3)** The stock of Bruin, Inc., has an expected return of 14 percent and a standard deviation of 42 percent. The stock of Wildcat Co. has an expected return of 12 percent and a standard deviation of 57 percent. The correlation between the two stocks is .25. Is it possible for there to be a minimum variance portfolio since the highest-return stock has the lowest standard deviation? If so, calculate the expected return and standard deviation of the minimum variance portfolio.

20. **Portfolio Variance (LO2, CFA2)** You have a three-stock portfolio. Stock A has an expected return of 12 percent and a standard deviation of 41 percent, Stock B has an expected return of 16 percent and a standard deviation of 58 percent, and Stock C has an expected return of 13 percent and a standard deviation of 48 percent. The correlation between Stocks A and B is .30, between Stocks A and C is .20, and between Stocks B and C is .05. Your portfolio consists of 45 percent Stock A, 25 percent Stock B, and 30 percent Stock C. Calculate the expected return and standard deviation of your portfolio. The formula for calculating the variance of a three-stock portfolio is:

$$\sigma_p^2 = x_A^2 \sigma_A^2 + x_B^2 \sigma_B^2 + x_C^2 \sigma_C^2 + 2 x_A x_B \sigma_A \sigma_B \text{Corr}(R_A, R_B)$$
$$+ 2 x_A x_C \sigma_A \sigma_C \text{Corr}(R_A, R_C) + 2 x_B x_C \sigma_B \sigma_C \text{Corr}(R_B, R_C)$$

21. **Minimum Variance Portfolio (LO4, CFA3)** You are going to invest in Asset J and Asset S. Asset J has an expected return of 13 percent and a standard deviation of 54 percent. Asset S has an

expected return of 10 percent and a standard deviation of 19 percent. The correlation between the two assets is .50. What are the standard deviation and expected return of the minimum variance portfolio? What is going on here?

22. **Portfolio Variance (LO2, CFA2)** Suppose two assets have perfect positive correlation. Show that the standard deviation on a portfolio of the two assets is:

$$\sigma_p = x_A \times \sigma_A + x_B \times \sigma_B$$

(*Hint:* Look at the expression for the variance of a two-asset portfolio. If the correlation is +1, the expression is a perfect square.)

23. **Portfolio Variance (LO2, CFA4)** Suppose two assets have perfect negative correlation. Show that the standard deviation on a portfolio of the two assets is:

$$\sigma_p = \pm \left(x_A \times \sigma_A - x_B \times \sigma_B \right)$$

(*Hint:* See previous problem.)

24. **Portfolio Variance (LO2, CFA4)** Using the result in Problem 23, show that whenever two assets have perfect negative correlation, it is possible to find a portfolio with a zero standard deviation. What are the portfolio weights? (*Hint:* Let x be the percentage in the first asset and $(1 - x)$ be the percentage in the second. Set the standard deviation to zero and solve for x.)

25. **Portfolio Variance (LO2, CFA3)** Derive our expression in the chapter for the portfolio weight in the minimum variance portfolio. (Danger! Calculus required!) (*Hint:* Let x be the percentage in the first asset and $(1 - x)$ the percentage in the second. Take the derivative with respect to x and set it to zero. Solve for x.)

Spreadsheet Problems

26. **Markowitz Efficient Frontier (LO4, CFA4)** Assume you are evaluating two stocks, Stock A and Stock B. Stock A has an expected return and standard deviation of 10 percent and 25 percent, respectively. Stock B has an expected return and standard deviation of 15 percent and 40 percent, respectively. Assuming their correlation is .2, create a graph of the investment opportunity set.

CFA Exam Review by Kaplan Schweser

[CFA2, CFA4, CFA6]
Andy Green, CFA, and Sue Hutchinson, CFA, are considering adding alternative investments to the portfolio they manage for a private client. After much discussion, they have decided to add a hedge fund to the portfolio. In their research, Mr. Green focuses on hedge funds that have the highest returns, while Ms. Hutchinson focuses on finding hedge funds that can reduce portfolio risk while maintaining the same level of return.

After completing their research, Mr. Green proposes two funds: the New Horizon Emerging Market Fund (NH), which takes long-term positions in emerging markets, and the Hi Rise Real Estate Fund (HR), which holds a highly leveraged real estate portfolio. Ms. Hutchinson proposes two hedge funds: the Quality Commodity Fund (QC), which takes conservative positions in commodities, and the Beta Naught Fund (BN), which manages an equity long/short portfolio that targets a market risk of zero. The table below details the statistics for the existing portfolio, as well as for the four potential funds. The standard deviation of the market's return is 18 percent.

	Existing	NH	HR	QC	BN
Average return	10%	20%	10%	6%	4%
Standard deviation	16%	50%	16%	16%	25%
Beta	.8	.9	.4	−.2	0
Correlation with existing portfolio		.32	.45	−.23	.00

Mr. Green and Ms. Hutchinson have agreed to select the fund that will provide a portfolio with the highest return-to-risk ratio (i.e., average return relative to standard deviation). They have decided to invest 10 percent of the portfolio in the selected fund.

As an alternative to one fund, Mr. Green and Ms. Hutchinson have discussed investing 5 percent in the Beta Naught Fund (BN) and 5 percent in one of the other three funds. This new 50/50 hedge fund would then serve as the 10 percent allocation in the portfolio.

1. Mr. Green and Ms. Hutchinson divided up their research into return enhancement and diversification benefits. Based on the stated goals of their research, which of the two approaches is more likely to lead to an appropriate choice?

   a. Green's research
   b. Hutchinson's research
   c. Neither is appropriate.

2. Which of the following is closest to the expected return of the client's portfolio if 10 percent of the portfolio is invested in the New Horizon (NH) Emerging Market Fund?

   a. 11 percent
   b. 10.2 percent
   c. 11.8 percent

3. Which of the following is closest to the expected standard deviation of the client's portfolio if 10 percent of the portfolio is invested in the Quality Commodity (QC) Fund?

   a. 9.6 percent
   b. 14.1 percent
   c. 16.0 percent

4. Which of the following is closest to the expected return of a portfolio that consists of 90 percent of the original portfolio, 5 percent of the Hi Rise (HR) Real Estate Fund, and 5 percent of the Beta Naught (BN) Fund?

   a. 9.0 percent
   b. 10.4 percent
   c. 9.7 percent

5. When combined with Beta Naught in a 50/50 portfolio, which of the other three funds will produce a portfolio that has the lowest standard deviation?

   a. New Horizon only
   b. Quality Commodity only
   c. Either Hi Rise or Quality Commodity

Bloomberg Exercises

1. Examine the historical volatility of Pfizer (PFE) stock. **(HVG)**
2. Review the correlation of Walmart (WMT) relative to its peers. **(PC)**
3. Download the asset allocation optimizer into Excel and explore its capabilities. **(XLTP XAAO)**

PART 4

Return, Risk, and the Security Market Line

"To win, you have to risk loss."

—Franz Klammer

Learning Objectives

Studying some topics will yield an expected reward. For example, make sure you know:

1. The difference between expected and unexpected returns.

2. The difference between systematic risk and unsystematic risk.

3. The security market line and the capital asset pricing model.

4. The importance of beta.

An important insight of modern financial theory is that some investment risks yield an expected reward, while other investment risks do not. Essentially, risks that can be eliminated by diversification do not yield an expected reward, and risks that cannot be eliminated by diversification do yield an expected reward. Thus, financial markets are somewhat fussy regarding which risks are rewarded and which risks are not.

Chapter 1 presented some important lessons from capital market history. The most noteworthy, perhaps, is that there is a reward, on average, for bearing risk. We called this reward a *risk premium.* The second lesson is that this risk premium is positively correlated with an investment's risk.

In this chapter, we return to an examination of the reward for bearing risk. Specifically, we have two tasks to accomplish. First, we have to define risk more precisely and then discuss how to measure it. Second, once we have a better understanding of what we mean by "risk," we will go on to quantify the relation between risk and return in financial markets.

When we examine the risks associated with individual assets, we find two types of risk: systematic and unsystematic. This distinction is crucial because, as we will see, systematic risk affects almost all assets in the economy, at least to some degree, whereas unsystematic risk affects at most only a small number of assets. This observation allows us to say a great deal about the risks and returns on individual assets. In particular, it is the basis for a famous relationship between risk and return called the *security market line,* or SML. To develop the SML, we introduce the equally famous beta coefficient, one of the centerpieces of modern finance. Beta and the SML are key concepts because they supply us with at least part of the answer to the question of how to go about determining the expected return on a risky investment.

CFA™ Exam Topics in This Chapter:

1. Cost of capital—foundational topics (L1, S10)
2. Introduction to industry and company analysis (L1, S12)
3. Portfolio risk and return: Part II (L1, S17)
4. Return concepts (L2, S8)

Go to Connect for a guide that aligns your textbook with CFA readings.

Announcements, Surprises, and Expected Returns

In our previous chapter, we discussed how to construct portfolios and evaluate their returns. We now begin to describe more carefully the risks and returns associated with individual securities. Thus far, we have measured volatility by looking at the difference between the actual return on an asset or portfolio, R, and the expected return, $E(R)$. We now look at why those deviations exist.

Related Bloomberg Functions

EE SURP	Price Reaction and Surprise
EA	Earnings Analysis
CN	Company News

EXPECTED AND UNEXPECTED RETURNS

To begin, consider the return on the stock of a hypothetical company called Flyers. What will determine this stock's return in, say, the coming year?

The return on any stock traded in a financial market is composed of two parts. First, the normal, or expected, return from the stock is the part of the return that investors predict or expect. This return depends on the information investors have about the stock, and it is based on the market's understanding today of the important factors that will influence the stock in the coming year.

The second part of the return on the stock is the uncertain, or risky, part. This is the portion that comes from unexpected information revealed during the year. A list of all possible sources of such information would be endless, but here are a few basic examples:

News about Flyers's product research

Government figures released on gross domestic product

The latest news about exchange rates

The news that Flyers's sales figures are higher than expected

A sudden, unexpected drop in interest rates

Based on this discussion, one way to express the return on Flyers stock in the coming year would be:

$$\text{Total return} - \text{Expected return} = \text{Unexpected return} \qquad (12.1)$$

or

$$R - E(R) = U$$

where R stands for the actual total return in the year, $E(R)$ stands for the expected part of the return, and U stands for the unexpected part of the return. What this says is that the actual return, R, differs from the expected return, $E(R)$, because of surprises that occur during the year. In any given year, the unexpected return will be positive or negative, but, through time, the average value of U will be zero. This means that, on average, the actual return equals the expected return.

ANNOUNCEMENTS AND NEWS

Visit the earnings calendar in the free services section at www.earningswhispers.com.

We need to be careful when we talk about the effect of news items on stock returns. For example, suppose Flyers's business is such that the company prospers when gross domestic product (GDP) grows at a relatively high rate and suffers when GDP is relatively stagnant. In this case, in deciding what return to expect this year from owning stock in Flyers, investors either implicitly or explicitly must think about what GDP is likely to be for the coming year.

When the government actually announces GDP figures for the year, what will happen to the value of Flyers stock? Obviously, the answer depends on what figure is released. More to the point, however, the impact depends on how much of that figure actually represents new information.

At the beginning of the year, market participants will have some idea or forecast of what the yearly GDP figure will be. To the extent that shareholders have predicted GDP, that prediction will already be factored into the expected part of the return on the stock, $E(R)$.

On the other hand, if the announced GDP is a surprise, then the effect will be part of U, the unanticipated portion of the return.

As an example, suppose shareholders in the market had forecast that the GDP increase this year would be .5 percent. If the actual announcement this year is exactly .5 percent, the same as the forecast, then the shareholders don't really learn anything, and the announcement isn't news. There should be no impact on the stock price as a result. This is like receiving redundant confirmation about something that you suspected all along; it reveals nothing new.

To give a more concrete example, Nabisco once announced it was taking a massive $300 million charge against earnings for the second quarter in a sweeping restructuring plan. The company also announced plans to cut its workforce sharply by 7.8 percent, eliminate some package sizes and small brands, and relocate some of its operations. This all seems like bad news, but the stock price didn't even budge. Why? Because it was already fully expected that Nabisco would take such actions, and the stock price already reflected the bad news.

A common way of saying that an announcement isn't news is to say that the market has already discounted the announcement. The use of the word "discount" here is different from the use of the term in computing present values, but the spirit is the same. When we discount a dollar to be received in the future, we say it is worth less to us today because of the time value of money. When an announcement or a news item is discounted into a stock price, we say that its impact is already a part of the stock price because the market already knew about it.

Going back to Flyers, suppose the government announces that the actual GDP increase during the year has been 1.5 percent. Now shareholders have learned something, namely, that the increase is one percentage point higher than they had forecast. This difference between the actual result and the forecast—one percentage point in this example—is sometimes called the *innovation* or the *surprise*.

This distinction explains why what seems to be bad news can actually be good news. For example, Gymboree, a retailer of children's apparel, had a 3 percent decline in same-store sales for a particular month, yet its stock price shot up 13 percent on the news. In the retail business, same-store sales, which are sales by existing stores in operation at least a year, are a crucial barometer, so why was this decline good news? Analysts had been expecting significantly sharper declines, so the situation was not as bad as previously thought.

A key fact to keep in mind about news and price changes is that news about the future is what matters. For example, Crocs, Inc. (CROX), once announced quarterly earnings that grew more than 25 percent year-over-year. That seems like good news, but Crocs's stock price promptly dropped because the market was expecting a much higher growth rate. Similarly, Microsoft once reported a 50 percent jump in profits, exceeding projections. That seems like really good news, but Microsoft's stock price proceeded to decline sharply. Why? Because Microsoft warned that its phenomenal growth could not be sustained indefinitely. Its 50 percent increase in current earnings was not a good predictor of future earnings growth.

To summarize, an announcement can be broken into two parts, the anticipated, or expected, part plus the surprise, or innovation:

$$\text{Announcement} = \text{Expected part} + \text{Surprise} \qquad (12.2)$$

See recent earnings surprises at finance.yahoo.com/calendar.

The expected part of any announcement is the part of the information that the market uses to form the expectation, $E(R)$, of the return on the stock. The surprise is the news that influences the unanticipated return on the stock, U.

Our discussion of market efficiency in a previous chapter bears on this discussion. We are assuming that relevant information known today is already reflected in the expected return. This assumption is identical to saying that the current price reflects relevant publicly available information. We are thus implicitly assuming that markets are at least reasonably efficient in the semistrong form sense. Henceforth, when we speak of news, we will mean the surprise part of an announcement and not the portion that the market had expected and therefore already discounted.

Suppose Intel were to announce that earnings for the quarter just ending were up by 20 percent relative to a year ago. Do you expect that the stock price would rise or fall on the announcement?

The answer is that you can't really tell. Suppose the market was expecting a 40 percent increase. In this case, the 20 percent increase would be a negative surprise, and we would expect the stock price to fall. On the other hand, if the market was expecting only a 10 percent increase, there would be a positive surprise, and we would expect the stock to rise on the news.

TRACKING SURPRISES

As you can see, surprises of all kinds have a significant impact on prices. One particularly important surprise is whether or not a company meets, or fails to meet, its expected earnings number. So, as you might expect, analysts track how often companies meet their targets, to what extent they surprise, and the associated stock price reaction when a surprise occurs. For an example of tracking earnings and surprises for Nike, check out Figure 12.1.

FIGURE 12.1   Earnings Surprises

Source: Bloomberg Finance L.P.

CHECK THIS

12.1a   What are the two basic parts of a return on common stock?

12.1b   Under what conditions will an announcement have no effect on common stock prices?

Risk: Systematic and Unsystematic

It is important to distinguish between expected and unexpected returns because the unanticipated part of the return, that portion resulting from surprises, is the significant risk of any investment. After all, if we always receive exactly what we expect, then the investment is perfectly predictable and, by definition, risk-free. In other words, the risk of owning an asset comes from surprises—unanticipated events.

There are important differences, though, among various sources of risk. Look back at our previous list of news stories. Some of these stories are directed specifically at Flyers, and some are more general. Which of the news items are of specific importance to Flyers?

Announcements about interest rates or GDP are clearly important for nearly all companies, whereas the news about Flyers's product research or its sales is of specific interest to Flyers investors only. We distinguish between these two types of events because, as we will see, they have very different implications.

SYSTEMATIC AND UNSYSTEMATIC RISK

The first type of surprise, the one that affects most assets, we label **systematic risk**. A systematic risk is one that influences a large number of assets, each to a greater or lesser extent. Because systematic risks have marketwide effects, they are sometimes called *market risks*.

The second type of surprise we call **unsystematic risk**. An unsystematic risk is one that affects a single asset, or possibly a small group of assets. Because these risks are unique to individual companies or assets, they are sometimes called *unique* or *asset-specific risks*. We use these terms interchangeably.

As we have seen, uncertainties about general economic conditions (such as GDP, interest rates, or inflation) are examples of systematic risks. These conditions affect nearly all companies to some degree. An unanticipated increase, or surprise, in inflation, for example, affects wages and the costs of supplies that companies buy. This surprise affects the value of the assets that companies own, and it affects the prices at which companies sell their products. Forces such as uncertainties about general economic conditions are the essence of systematic risk because all companies are susceptible to these forces.

In contrast, the announcement of a labor strike by a particular company will primarily affect that company and, perhaps, a few others (such as primary competitors and suppliers). It is unlikely to have much of an effect on the broad market, however, or on the affairs of companies not in the same business, so this is an unsystematic event.

SYSTEMATIC AND UNSYSTEMATIC COMPONENTS OF RETURN

The distinction between a systematic risk and an unsystematic risk is never really as exact as we would like it to be. Even the most narrow and peculiar bit of news about a company ripples through the economy. This ripple effect happens because every enterprise, no matter how tiny, is a part of the economy. It's like the proverb about a kingdom that was lost because one horse lost a horseshoe nail. However, not all ripple effects are equal—some risks have much broader effects than others.

The distinction between the two types of risk allows us to break down the surprise portion, U, of the return on the Flyers stock into two parts. Earlier, we broke down the actual return into its expected and surprise components: $R - E(R) = U$. We now recognize that the total surprise component for Flyers, U, has a systematic and an unsystematic component, so:

$$R - E(R) = U = \text{Systematic portion} + \text{Unsystematic portion} \qquad (12.3)$$

Because it is traditional, we will use the Greek letter epsilon, ε, to stand for the unsystematic portion. Because systematic risks are often called "market" risks, we use the letter m to stand for the systematic part of the surprise. With these symbols, we can rewrite the formula for the total return:

$$R - E(R) = U = m + \varepsilon \qquad (12.4)$$

The important thing about the way we have broken down the total surprise, U, is that the unsystematic portion, ε, is unique to Flyers. For this reason, it is unrelated to the unsystematic

---

Related Bloomberg Functions

ECSU Economics Surprises Monitor

WECO Economic Calendars by Country

---

systematic risk
Risk that influences a large number of assets. Also called *market risk*.

unsystematic risk
Risk that influences a single company or a small group of companies. Also called *unique* or *asset-specific risk*.

Analyze risk at
www.portfolioscience.com.

portion of return on most other assets. To see why this is important, we need to return to the subject of portfolio risk.

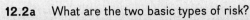

EXAMPLE 12.2 **Systematic versus Unsystematic Events**

Suppose Intel were to unexpectedly announce that its latest computer chip contains a significant flaw in its floating point unit that makes it unable to handle numbers bigger than a couple of gigatrillion (meaning that, among other things, the chip cannot calculate Intel's quarterly profits). Is this a systematic or unsystematic event?

Obviously, this event is for the most part unsystematic. However, it would also benefit Intel's competitors to some degree and, at least potentially, harm some users of Intel products, such as personal computer makers. Thus, as with most unsystematic events, there is some spillover, but the effect is mostly confined to a relatively small number of companies.

A similar example occurred with Merck and Moderna. Merck announced some positive results for its antiviral drug in treating the coronavirus. As a result, vaccine makers such as Moderna experienced a significant price decline.

CHECK THIS

12.2a What are the two basic types of risk?

12.2b What is the distinction between the two types of risk?

12.3 Diversification, Systematic Risk, and Unsystematic Risk

In the previous chapter, we introduced the principle of diversification. What we saw was that some of the risk associated with individual assets can be diversified away and some cannot. We are left with an obvious question: Why is this so? The answer hinges on the distinction between systematic and unsystematic risk.

DIVERSIFICATION AND UNSYSTEMATIC RISK

By definition, an unsystematic risk is one that is particular to a single asset or, at most, a small group of assets. For example, if the asset under consideration is stock in a single company, such things as successful new products and innovative cost savings will tend to increase the value of the stock. Unanticipated lawsuits, industrial accidents, strikes, and similar events will tend to decrease future cash flows and thereby reduce share value.

Here is the important observation: If we hold only a single stock, then the value of our investment will fluctuate because of company-specific events. If we hold a large portfolio, on the other hand, some of the stocks in the portfolio will go up in value because of positive company-specific events and some will go down in value because of negative events. The net effect on the overall value of the portfolio will be relatively small, however, because these effects will tend to cancel each other out.

Now we see why some of the variability associated with individual assets is eliminated by diversification. When we combine assets into portfolios, the unique, or unsystematic, events—both positive and negative—tend to "wash out" once we have more than just a few assets. This is an important point that bears repeating:

Unsystematic risk is essentially eliminated by diversification, so a portfolio with many assets has almost no unsystematic risk.

In fact, the terms *diversifiable risk* and *unsystematic risk* are often used interchangeably.

DIVERSIFICATION AND SYSTEMATIC RISK

We've seen that unsystematic risk can be eliminated by diversification. What about systematic risk? Can it also be eliminated by diversification? The answer is no because, by definition, a systematic risk affects almost all assets. As a result, no matter how many assets we put into a portfolio, systematic risk doesn't go away. Thus, for obvious reasons, the terms *systematic risk* and *nondiversifiable risk* are used interchangeably.

Because we have introduced so many different terms, it is useful to summarize our discussion before moving on. What we have seen is that the total risk of an investment can be written as:

$$\text{Total risk} = \text{Systematic risk} + \text{Unsystematic risk} \qquad (12.5)$$

Systematic risk is also called *nondiversifiable risk* or *market risk*. Unsystematic risk is also called *diversifiable risk, unique risk,* or *asset-specific risk*. Most important, for a well-diversified portfolio, unsystematic risk is negligible. For such a portfolio, essentially all risk is systematic.

From our discussion in other chapters, you should remember that we defined risk as variability, and we used standard deviation (or variance) to estimate the level of risk. Now that you know about different types of risk, you must know that standard deviation is a measure of total risk. An asset that has a high standard deviation might not compensate investors with high returns. Why? Suppose most of the asset's total risk comes from unsystematic risk. Investors are not compensated for bearing unsystematic risk. Assets with high systematic risk, however, do (in theory) compensate investors with high returns. What we need, therefore, is a measure that captures systematic risk. Enter *beta*.

CHECK THIS

12.3a Why is some risk diversifiable? Why is some risk not diversifiable?

12.3b Why can't systematic risk be diversified away?

12.4 Systematic Risk and Beta

Related Bloomberg Functions

BETA Historical Beta

PORT Portfolio & Risk Analysis

We now begin to address another question: What determines the size of the risk premium on a risky asset? Put another way, why do some assets have a larger risk premium than others? The answer, as we discuss next, is also based on the distinction between systematic and unsystematic risk.

THE SYSTEMATIC RISK PRINCIPLE

Thus far, we've seen that the total risk associated with an asset can be decomposed into two components: systematic and unsystematic risk. We have also seen that unsystematic risk can be essentially eliminated by diversification. The systematic risk present in an asset, on the other hand, cannot be eliminated by diversification.

Based on our study of capital market history in Chapter 1, we know that there is a reward, on average, for bearing risk. However, we now need to be more precise about what we mean by risk. The **systematic risk principle** states that the reward for bearing risk depends only on the systematic risk of an investment.

systematic risk principle
The reward for bearing risk depends only on the systematic risk of an investment.

The underlying rationale for this principle is straightforward: Because unsystematic risk can be eliminated at virtually no cost (by diversifying), there is no reward for bearing it. In other words, the market does not reward risks that are borne unnecessarily.

The systematic risk principle has a remarkable and very important implication:

The expected return on an asset depends only on that asset's systematic risk.

This principle has an obvious corollary: No matter how much total risk an asset has (i.e., no matter how high its standard deviation), only the systematic portion is relevant in determining the expected return (and the risk premium) on that asset. This observation is consistent with our previous discussion on portfolio diversification. For example, recall that we noted that purchasing a security with high volatility could actually reduce total portfolio risk. How is this possible? Well, in the current context, if this high volatility is primarily a result of unsystematic risk, then much of the volatility is diversified away. In other words, this stock, although highly volatile, had low systematic, or market, risk.

MEASURING SYSTEMATIC RISK

Because systematic risk is the crucial determinant of an asset's expected return, we need some way of measuring the level of systematic risk for different investments. The specific measure we will use is called the **beta coefficient**, designated by the Greek letter β. A beta coefficient, or just beta for short, tells us how much systematic risk a particular asset has relative to an average asset. By definition, an average asset has a beta of 1.0. An asset with a beta of .50, therefore, has half as much systematic risk as an average asset. Likewise, an asset with a beta of 2.0 has twice as much systematic risk.

Table 12.1 presents the estimated beta coefficients for the stocks of some well-known companies. These estimates come from two sources: MarketWatch and Yahoo! Finance. The range of betas in Table 12.1 is typical for stocks of large U.S. corporations. You should realize, however, that betas outside this range occur.

The important thing to remember is that the expected return, and thus the risk premium, on an asset depends only on its systematic risk. Because assets with larger betas have greater systematic risks, they will have greater expected returns. Thus, from Table 12.1, an investor who buys stock in Walmart, with a beta of .52, should expect to earn less and lose less, on average, than an investor who buys stock in Harley-Davidson, with a beta of about 1.47.

One cautionary note is in order: Not all betas are created equal. For example, in Table 12.1, MarketWatch reports a beta for Microsoft of 1.19. At the same time, however, Yahoo! Finance puts Microsoft's beta substantially lower at .87. The difference results from the different assumptions used to calculate beta coefficients. We will have more to say on this subject when we explain how betas are calculated in a later section, but for now we point out that it is due to a couple of possible issues.

First, betas are calculated relative to a chosen index or benchmark, such as the S&P 500. Second, betas are calculated over a defined time period. Thus, the differences in the beta coefficients in Table 12.1 likely stem from differences in the benchmark index and/or differences in the defined time period. Our nearby *Work the Web* box shows one way to find betas online.

Find betas at finance.yahoo.com and www.marketwatch.com.

beta coefficient (β)
Measure of the relative systematic risk of an asset. Assets with betas larger (smaller) than 1 have more (less) systematic risk than average.

TABLE 12.1	Beta Coefficients	

| | Beta, β | |
Company	MarketWatch	Yahoo!
ExxonMobil	1.03	1.35
IBM	.94	1.10
Starbucks	1.01	.82
Walmart	.53	.52
Microsoft	1.19	.87
Harley-Davidson	1.31	1.47
Tesla	1.38	2.04
Southwest Airlines	1.05	1.12
Nike	.97	.94

Sources: finance.yahoo.com and www.marketwatch.com. Accessed January 2022.

WORK THE WEB

Suppose you want to find the beta for a company like Southwest Airlines. One way is to go to the web. We went to finance.yahoo.com, looked up Southwest Airlines Co. (LUV), and followed the "Statistics" link. This is part of what we found:

The reported beta for Southwest Airlines is 1.12, which means that Southwest Airlines has about 1.12 times the systematic risk of a typical stock. Thus, it is above average.

Trading Information

Stock Price History

Beta (5Y Monthly)	1.12
52-Week Change	-7.06%
S&P500 52-Week Change	23.58%
52 Week High	64.75
52 Week Low	38.66
50-Day Moving Average	45.23
200-Day Moving Average	52.54

Source: Yahoo! Finance.

EXAMPLE 12.3

Total Risk versus Beta

Consider the following information on two securities. Which has greater total risk? Which has greater systematic risk? Greater unsystematic risk? Which asset will have a higher risk premium?

	Standard Deviation	Beta
Security A	40%	.50
Security B	20	1.50

From our discussion, recall that standard deviation measures total risk and beta measures systematic risk. Therefore, Security A has greater total risk, but it has substantially less systematic risk. Because total risk is the sum of systematic and unsystematic risk, Security A must have greater unsystematic risk. Finally, from the systematic risk principle, Security B will have a higher risk premium and a greater expected return, despite the fact that it has less total risk.

PORTFOLIO BETAS

Earlier, we saw that the riskiness of a portfolio has no simple relation to the risks of the assets in the portfolio. By contrast, a portfolio beta can be calculated just like a portfolio expected return. For example, looking again at Table 12.1, suppose you put half of your money in Starbucks and half in Nike. Using MarketWatch betas, what would the beta of this combination be? Because Starbucks has a beta of 1.01 and Nike has a beta of .97, the portfolio's beta, β_p, would be

$$\beta_p = .50 \times \beta_{Starbucks} + .50 \times \beta_{Nike}$$
$$= .50 \times 1.01 + .50 \times .97$$
$$= .99$$

In general, if we had a large number of assets in a portfolio, we would multiply each asset's beta by its portfolio weight and then add the results to get the portfolio's beta.[1]

EXAMPLE 12.4 **Portfolio Betas**

Suppose we have the following information:

Security	Amount Invested	Expected Return	Beta
Stock A	$1,000	8%	.80
Stock B	2,000	12	.95
Stock C	3,000	15	1.10
Stock D	4,000	18	1.40

What is the expected return on this portfolio? What is the beta of this portfolio? Does this portfolio have more or less systematic risk than an average asset?

To answer, we first have to calculate the portfolio weights. Notice that the total amount invested is $10,000. Of this, $1,000/$10,000 = .10, or 10%, is invested in Stock A. Similarly, 20 percent is invested in Stock B, 30 percent is invested in Stock C, and 40 percent is invested in Stock D. The expected return, $E(R_p)$, is thus:

$$E(R_p) = .10 \times E(R_A) + .20 \times E(R_B) + .30 \times E(R_C) + .40 \times E(R_D)$$
$$= .10 \times 8\% + .20 \times 12\% + .30 \times 15\% + .40 \times 18\%$$
$$= 14.9\%$$

Similarly, the portfolio beta, β_p, is:

$$\beta_p = .10 \times \beta_A + .20 \times \beta_B + .30 \times \beta_C + .40 \times \beta_D$$
$$= .10 \times .80 + .20 \times .95 + .30 \times 1.10 + .40 \times 1.40$$
$$= 1.16$$

This portfolio thus has an expected return of 14.9 percent and a beta of 1.16. Because the beta is larger than 1, this portfolio has greater systematic risk than an average asset.

CHECK THIS

12.4a   What is the systematic risk principle?

12.4b   What does a beta coefficient measure?

12.4c   How do you calculate a portfolio beta?

12.4d   True or false: The expected return on a risky asset depends on that asset's total risk. Explain.

---

[1] When combining individual asset betas into a portfolio beta, each beta must be calculated relative to the same index. For example, you could not calculate a weighted average portfolio beta from a bond beta calculated relative to the Barclay's Aggregate Bond Index and a stock beta calculated relative to the S&P 500 index.

The Security Market Line

Related Bloomberg Functions

WACC Weighted Average Cost of Capital

CRP Country Risk Premium

EQRP Equity Risk Premium

We're now in a position to see how risk is rewarded in the marketplace. To begin, suppose that Asset A has an expected return of $E(R_A) = 16\%$ and a beta of $\beta_A = 1.6$. Further suppose that the risk-free rate is $R_f = 4\%$. Notice that a risk-free asset, by definition, has no systematic risk (or unsystematic risk), so a risk-free asset has a beta of zero.

For more information on risk management, visit www.fenews.co.uk.

BETA AND THE RISK PREMIUM

Consider a portfolio made up of Asset A and a risk-free asset. We can calculate some different possible portfolio expected returns and betas by varying the percentages invested in these two assets. For example, if 25 percent of the portfolio is invested in Asset A, then the expected return is:

$$E(R_p) = .25 \times E(R_A) + (1 - .25) \times R_f$$
$$= .25 \times 16\% + .75 \times 4\%$$
$$= 7\%$$

Similarly, the beta on the portfolio, β_p, would be:

$$\beta_p = .25 \times \beta_A + (1 - .25) \times 0$$
$$= .25 \times 1.6$$
$$= .40$$

Notice that, because the weights must add up to 1, the percentage invested in the risk-free asset is equal to 1 minus the percentage invested in Asset A.

One thing that you might wonder is whether the percentage invested in Asset A can exceed 100 percent. The answer is yes. This can happen if the investor borrows at the risk-free rate and invests the proceeds in stocks. For example, suppose an investor has $100 and borrows an additional $50 at 4 percent, the risk-free rate. The total investment in Asset A would be $150, or 150 percent of the investor's wealth. This process would be similar to buying on margin, which we discussed in an earlier chapter. The expected return in this case would be:

$$E(R_p) = 1.50 \times E(R_A) + (1 - 1.50) \times R_f$$
$$= 1.50 \times 16\% - .50 \times 4\%$$
$$= 22\%$$

The beta on the portfolio would be:

$$\beta_p = 1.50 \times \beta_A + (1 - 1.50) \times 0$$
$$= 1.50 \times 1.6$$
$$= 2.4$$

We can calculate some other possibilities as follows:

Percentage of Portfolio in Asset A	Portfolio Expected Return	Portfolio Beta
0%	4%	.0
25	7	.4
50	10	.8
75	13	1.2
100	16	1.6
125	19	2.0
150	22	2.4

In Figure 12.2A, we plot these portfolio expected returns against portfolio betas. Notice that all the combinations fall on a straight line.

THE REWARD-TO-RISK RATIO

What is the slope of the straight line in Figure 12.2A? As always, the slope of a straight line is equal to the rise over the run. In this case, as we move out of the risk-free asset into Asset A, the expected return goes from 4 percent to 16 percent, a rise of 12 percent. At the same time, the beta increases from zero to 1.6, a run of 1.6. The slope of the line is thus 12%/1.6 = 7.5%.

Notice that the slope of our line is the risk premium on Asset A, $E(R_A) - R_f$, divided by Asset A's beta, β_A:

$$\text{Slope} = \frac{E(R_A) - R_f}{\beta_A}$$
$$= \frac{16\% - 4\%}{1.6}$$
$$= 7.50\%$$

What this tells us is that Asset A offers a *reward-to-risk* ratio of 7.5 percent.[2] In other words, Asset A has a risk premium of 7.50 percent per "unit" of systematic risk.

THE BASIC ARGUMENT

Now suppose we consider a second asset, Asset B. This asset has a beta of 1.2 and an expected return of 12 percent. Which investment is better, Asset A or Asset B? You might think that we really cannot say—some investors might prefer A and some investors might prefer B. Actually, however, we can say: A is better because, as we will demonstrate, B offers inadequate compensation for its level of systematic risk, at least relative to A.

To begin, we calculate different combinations of expected returns and betas for portfolios of Asset B and a risk-free asset, just as we did for Asset A. For example, if we put 25 percent in Asset B and the remaining 75 percent in the risk-free asset, the portfolio's expected return will be:

$$E(R_p) = .25 \times E(R_B) + (1 - .25) \times R_f$$
$$= .25 \times 12\% + .75 \times 4\%$$
$$= 6\%$$

Similarly, the beta on the portfolio, β_p, would be:

$$\beta_p = .25 \times \beta_B + (1 - .25) \times 0$$
$$= .25 \times 1.2$$
$$= .30$$

Some other possibilities are as follows:

Percentage of Portfolio in Asset B	Portfolio Expected Return	Portfolio Beta
0%	4%	.0
25	6	.3
50	8	.6
75	10	.9
100	12	1.2
125	14	1.5
150	16	1.8

When we plot these combinations of portfolio expected returns and portfolio betas in Figure 12.2B, we get a straight line, just as we did for Asset A.

The key thing to notice is that when we compare the results for Assets A and B, as in Figure 12.2C, the line describing the combinations of expected returns and betas for Asset

---

[2] This ratio is sometimes called the *Treynor index*, after one of its originators. We discuss the Treynor index and other risk-adjusted portfolio performance measures in another chapter.

FIGURE 12.2   Betas and Portfolio Returns

A. Portfolio expected returns and betas for Asset A

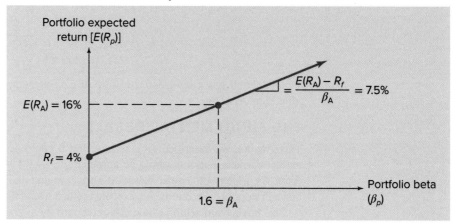

B. Portfolio expected returns and betas for Asset B

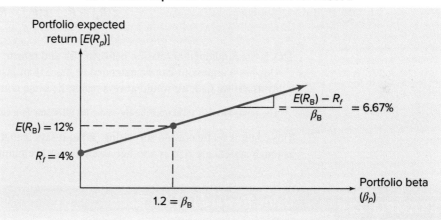

C. Portfolio expected returns and betas for both assets

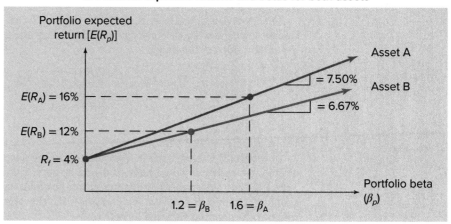

A is higher than the one for Asset B. What this result tells us is that for any given level of systematic risk (as measured by beta), some combination of Asset A and the risk-free asset always offers a larger return. Therefore, we can state that Asset A is a better investment than Asset B.

Another way of seeing that Asset A offers a superior return for its level of risk is to note that the slope of our line for Asset B is:

$$\text{Slope} = \frac{E(R_B) - R_f}{\beta_B}$$

$$= \frac{12\% - 4\%}{1.2}$$

$$= 6.67\%$$

Thus, Asset B has a reward-to-risk ratio of 6.67 percent, which is less than the 7.5 percent offered by Asset A.

THE FUNDAMENTAL RESULT

The situation we described for Assets A and B could not persist in a well-organized, active market because investors would be attracted to Asset A and away from Asset B. As a result, Asset A's price would rise and Asset B's price would fall. Because prices and expected returns move in opposite directions, A's expected return would decline and B's would rise.

This buying and selling would continue until the two assets plot on exactly the same line, which means they would offer the same reward for bearing risk. In other words, in an active, competitive market, it must be true that:

$$\frac{E(R_A) - R_f}{\beta_A} = \frac{E(R_B) - R_f}{\beta_B} \qquad (12.6)$$

This is the fundamental relation between risk and return.

Our basic argument can be extended to more than just two assets. In fact, no matter how many assets we had, we would always reach the same conclusion:

The reward-to-risk ratio must be the same for all assets in a competitive financial market.

This result is really not too surprising. What it says is that, for example, if one asset has twice as much systematic risk as another asset, its risk premium should be twice as large.

EXAMPLE 12.5 | **Using Reward-to-Risk Ratios**

Suppose we see that the reward-to-risk ratio for all assets equals 7.2. If the risk-free rate is 4 percent, what is the required return for an arbitrary Asset i with (1) a beta of 1? (2) a beta of 0?

To answer Question (1), write down the reward-to-risk equation and set it equal to 7.2. Because we know the risk-free rate and the beta of the asset, we can easily solve for the expected return of the asset:

$$\frac{E(R_i) - R_f}{\beta_i} = 7.2$$

$$\frac{E(R_i) - 4.0}{1} = 7.2$$

Therefore, $E(R_i) = 11.2$ percent.

Question (2) is a bit trickier. We cannot use the same approach used in Question (1) directly because we would have to divide by zero. But let's think. Beta is the measure of risk in the reward-to-risk equation. If the portfolio has zero risk, its expected return should not reflect a premium for carrying risk. Therefore, the answer is 4 percent, the rate of return on the risk-free asset.

Because all assets in the market must have the same reward-to-risk ratio, they all must plot on the same line. This argument is illustrated in Figure 12.3. As shown, Assets A and B plot directly on the line and thus have the same reward-to-risk ratio.

If an asset is plotted above the line, such as C in Figure 12.3, its reward-to-risk ratio is too high because its expected return is too high. An expected return has two inputs: the expected

FIGURE 12.3   Expected Returns and Systematic Risk

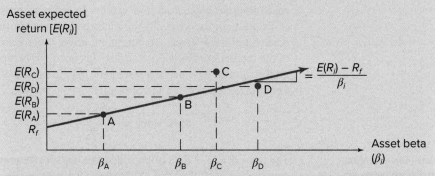

The fundamental relationship between beta and expected return is that all assets must have the same reward-to-risk ratio, $[E(R_i) - R_f]/\beta_i$. This means that they would all plot on the same straight line. Assets A and B are examples of this behavior. Asset C's expected return is too high; Asset D's is too low.

price and the price today. The expected return is calculated as $E(R) = [E(P) - P_{today}]/P_{today}$, or $[E(P)/P_{today}] - 1$. To *lower* the expected return for Asset C, its price today must *increase* until the reward-to-risk ratio for Asset C plots exactly on the line. Similarly, if an asset is plotted below the line, such as D in Figure 12.3, its reward-to-risk ratio is too low because its expected return is too low. To *increase* the expected return for Asset D, its price today must *fall* until the reward-to-risk ratio for Asset D also plots exactly on the line.

The arguments we have presented apply to active, competitive, well-functioning markets. Active financial markets, such as the NYSE, best meet these criteria. Other markets, such as real asset markets, may or may not. For this reason, these concepts are most useful in examining active, and largely efficient, financial markets.

EXAMPLE 12.6   Buy Low, Sell High

A security is said to be *overvalued* relative to another security if its price today is too high given its expected return and risk. Suppose you observe the following:

Security	Beta	Expected Return
Melan Co.	1.3	14.0%
Choly Co.	.8	10.0
Baby Co.	1.0	11.5

The risk-free rate is currently 6 percent. Is one of the securities overvalued relative to the others?

To answer, we compute the reward-to-risk ratios. For Melan, this ratio is (14% − 6%)/1.3 = 6.15%; for Choly, this ratio is 5 percent; and for Baby, it is 5.5 percent. What we conclude is that Choly offers an insufficient expected return for its level of risk, at least relative to Melan and Baby. Because its expected return is too low, its price is too high. In other words, Choly is overvalued relative to Melan and Baby, and we would expect to see its price fall relative to Melan and Baby. Notice that we could also say Melan and Baby are *undervalued* relative to Choly. What can you say about the relative pricing of Melan and Baby?

---

security market line (SML)
Graphical representation of the linear relationship between systematic risk and expected return in financial markets.

THE SECURITY MARKET LINE

The line that results when we plot expected returns and beta coefficients is obviously of some importance, so it's time we gave it a name. This line, which we use to describe the relationship between systematic risk and expected return in financial markets, is usually called the **security market line** (**SML**), and it is one of the most important concepts in modern finance.

MARKET PORTFOLIOS We will find it very useful to know the equation of the SML. Although there are many different ways we could write it, we will discuss the most frequently seen version. Suppose we consider a portfolio made up of all of the assets in the market. Such a portfolio is called a *market portfolio,* and we express the expected return on this market portfolio as $E(R_M)$.

Because all the assets in the market must plot on the SML, so must a market portfolio made up of those assets. To determine where it plots on the SML, we need to know the beta of the market portfolio, β_M. Because this portfolio is representative of all of the assets in the market, it must have average systematic risk. In other words, it has a beta of 1. We could therefore express the slope of the SML as:

$$\text{SML slope} = \frac{E(R_M) - R_f}{\beta_M} = \frac{E(R_M) - R_f}{1} = E(R_M) - R_f$$

market risk premium
The risk premium on a market portfolio, i.e., a portfolio made of all assets in the market.

The term $E(R_M) - R_f$ is often called the **market risk premium** because it is the risk premium on a market portfolio.

THE CAPITAL ASSET PRICING MODEL To finish up, if we let $E(R_i)$ and β_i stand for the expected return and beta, respectively, on any asset in the market, then we know that the asset must plot on the SML. As a result, we know that its reward-to-risk ratio is the same as that of the overall market:

$$\frac{E(R_i) - R_f}{\beta_i} = E(R_M) - R_f$$

If we rearrange this, we can write the equation for the SML as:

$$E(R_i) = R_f + [E(R_M) - R_f] \times \beta_i \qquad (12.7)$$

capital asset pricing model (CAPM)
A theory of risk and return for securities in a competitive capital market.

There's a CAPM calculator (if you really need it!) at moneychimp.com.

Equation 12.7 is the famous **capital asset pricing model (CAPM).**[3] What the CAPM shows is that the expected return for an asset depends on three things:

1. *The pure time value of money.* As measured by the risk-free rate, R_f, this is the reward for merely waiting for your money, without taking any risk.

2. *The reward for bearing systematic risk.* As measured by the market risk premium, $E(R_M) - R_f$, this component is the reward the market offers for bearing an average amount of systematic risk.

3. *The amount of systematic risk.* As measured by β_i, this is the amount of systematic risk present in a particular asset relative to that in an average asset.

EXAMPLE 12.7 | **Risk and Return**

Suppose the risk-free rate is 4 percent, the market risk premium is 8.6 percent, and a particular stock has a beta of 1.3. Based on the CAPM, what is the expected return on this stock? What would the expected return be if the beta were to double?

With a beta of 1.3, the risk premium for the stock is 1.3 × 8.6%, or 11.18 percent. The risk-free rate is 4 percent, so the expected return is 15.18 percent. If the beta were to double to 2.6, the risk premium would double to 22.36 percent, so the expected return would be 26.36 percent.

By the way, the CAPM works for portfolios of assets just as it does for individual assets. In an earlier section, we saw how to calculate a portfolio's beta in the CAPM equation.

Figure 12.4 summarizes our discussion of the SML and the CAPM. As before, we plot expected return against beta. Now we recognize that, based on the CAPM, the slope of the SML is equal to the market risk premium, $E(R_M) - R_f$.

---

[3] Our discussion of the CAPM is actually closely related to the more recent development, arbitrage pricing theory (APT). The theory underlying the CAPM is more complex than we have indicated here, and it has implications beyond the scope of this discussion. As we present it here, the CAPM has essentially identical implications to those of the APT, so we don't distinguish between them.

FIGURE 12.4 Security Market Line (SML)

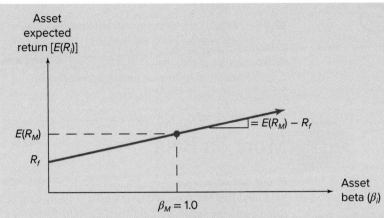

The slope of the security market line is equal to the market risk premium, i.e., the reward for bearing an average amount of systematic risk. The equation describing the SML can be written as:

$$E(R_i) = R_f + [E(R_M) - R_f] \times \beta_i$$

This is the capital asset pricing model (CAPM).

The concepts presented so far in this chapter are important, and it is worth repeating some of the major points. Table 12.2 summarizes these concepts in the order in which they appear in this chapter.

TABLE 12.2 Risk and Return Summary

1. **Total risk.** The *total risk* of an investment is measured by the variance or, more commonly, the standard deviation of its return.

2. **Total return.** The *total return* on an investment has two components: the expected return and the unexpected return. The unexpected return comes about because of unanticipated events. The risk from investing stems from the possibility of an unanticipated event.

3. **Systematic and unsystematic risks.** *Systematic risks* (also called *market risks*) are unanticipated events that affect almost all assets to some degree because the effects are economywide. *Unsystematic risks* are unanticipated events that affect single assets or small groups of assets. Unsystematic risks are also called *unique* or *asset-specific risks*.

4. **The effect of diversification.** Some, but not all, of the risk associated with a risky investment can be eliminated by *diversification*. The reason is that unsystematic risks, which are unique to individual assets, tend to wash out in a large portfolio, but systematic risks, which affect all of the assets in a portfolio to some extent, do not.

5. **The systematic risk principle and beta.** Because unsystematic risk can be freely eliminated by diversification, the *systematic risk principle* states that the reward for bearing risk depends only on the level of systematic risk. The level of systematic risk in a particular asset, relative to the average, is given by the *beta* of that asset.

6. **The reward-to-risk ratio and the security market line.** The *reward-to-risk ratio* for Asset *i* is the ratio of its risk premium, $E(R_i) - R_f$, to its beta, β_i:

$$\frac{E(R_i) - R_f}{\beta_i}$$

In a well-functioning market, this ratio is the same for every asset. As a result, when asset expected returns are plotted against asset betas, all assets plot on the same straight line, called the *security market line* (SML).

7. **The capital asset pricing model.** From the SML, the expected return on Asset *i* can be written:

$$E(R_i) = R_f + [E(R_M) - R_f] \times \beta_i$$

This is the *capital asset pricing model* (CAPM). The expected return on a risky asset thus has three components: The first is the pure time value of money (R_f); the second is the market risk premium, $E(R_M) - R_f$; and the third is the beta for the asset (β_i).

12.5a What is the fundamental relationship between risk and return in active markets?

12.5b What is the security market line (SML)? Why must all assets plot directly on it in a well-functioning market?

12.5c What is the capital asset pricing model (CAPM)? What does it tell us about the required return on a risky investment?

12.6 More on Beta

In our last several sections, we discussed the basic economic principles of risk and return. We found that the expected return on a security depends on its systematic risk, which is measured using the security's beta coefficient, β. In this section, we examine beta in more detail. We first illustrate more closely what it is that beta measures. We then show how betas can be estimated for individual securities, and we discuss why different sources report different betas for the same security.

Related Bloomberg Functions

HRA Regression Analysis

A CLOSER LOOK AT BETA

Going back to the beginning of the chapter, we discussed how the actual return on a security, R, could be written as follows:

$$R - E(R) = m + \epsilon \tag{12.8}$$

Recall that in Equation 12.8, m stands for the systematic or marketwide portion of the unexpected return. Based on our discussion of the CAPM, we can now be a little more precise about this component.

Specifically, the systematic portion of an unexpected return depends on two things. First, it depends on the size of the systematic effect. We will measure this as $R_M - E(R_M)$, which is the difference between the actual return on the overall market and the expected return. Second, as we have discussed, some securities have greater systematic risk than others, and we measure this risk using beta. Putting it together, we have:

$$m = [R_M - E(R_M)] \times \beta \tag{12.9}$$

In other words, the marketwide, or systematic, portion of the return on a security depends on both the size of the marketwide surprise, $R_M - E(R_M)$, and the sensitivity of the security to such surprises, β.

Now, if we combine Equations 12.8 and 12.9, we have:

$$\begin{aligned} R - E(R) &= m + \epsilon \\ &= [R_M - E(R_M)] \times \beta + \epsilon \end{aligned} \tag{12.10}$$

Equation 12.10 gives us some additional insight into beta by telling us why some securities have higher betas than others. A high-beta security is one that is relatively sensitive to overall market movements, whereas a low-beta security is one that is relatively insensitive. In other words, the systematic risk of a security is just a reflection of its sensitivity to overall market movements.

A hypothetical example is useful for illustrating the main point of Equation 12.10. Suppose a particular security has a beta of 1.2, the risk-free rate is 5 percent, and the expected return on the market is 12 percent. From the CAPM, we know that the expected return on the security is:

$$\begin{aligned} E(R) &= R_f + [E(R_M) - R_f] \times \beta \\ &= .05 + (.12 - .05) \times 1.2 \\ &= .134 \end{aligned}$$

Thus, the expected return on this security is 13.4 percent. However, we know that in any year the actual return on this security will be more or less than 13.4 percent because of unanticipated systematic and unsystematic events.

TABLE 12.3   Decomposing Total Returns

| Year | Actual Returns | | Unexpected Returns | | Systematic Portion | Unsystematic Portion (ε) |
	R (1)	R_M (2)	$R - E(R)$ (3)	$R_M - E(R_M)$ (4)	$[R_M - E(R_M)] \times \beta$ (5)	$[R - E(R)] - [R_M - E(R_M)] \times \beta$ (6)
1	20.0%	15%	6.6%	3%	3.6%	3%
2	−24.6	−3	−38.0	−15	−18.0	−20
3	23.0	10	9.6	−2	−2.4	12
4	36.8	24	23.4	12	14.4	9
5	3.4	7	−10.0	−5	−6.0	−4

Columns 1 and 2 of Table 12.3 list the actual returns on our security, R, for a five-year period along with the actual returns for the market as a whole, R_M, for the same period. Given these actual returns and the expected returns on the security (13.4 percent) and the market as a whole (12 percent), we can calculate the unexpected returns on the security, $R - E(R)$, along with the unexpected return on the market as a whole, $R_M - E(R_M)$. The results are shown in columns 3 and 4 of Table 12.3.

Next we decompose the unexpected returns on the security—that is, we break them down into their systematic and unsystematic components in columns 5 and 6. From Equation 12.9, we calculate the systematic portion of the unexpected return by taking the security's beta, 1.2, and multiplying it by the market's unexpected return:

$$\text{Systematic portion} = m = [R_M - E(R_M)] \times \beta$$

Finally, we calculate the unsystematic portion by subtracting the systematic portion from the total unexpected return:

$$\text{Unsystematic portion} = \varepsilon = [R - E(R)] - [R_M - E(R_M)] \times \beta$$

Notice that the unsystematic portion is essentially whatever is left over after we account for the systematic portion. For this reason, it is sometimes called the "residual" portion of the unexpected return.

Figure 12.5 illustrates the main points of this discussion by plotting the unexpected returns on the security in Table 12.3 against the unexpected return on the market as a whole. These are the individual points in the graph, each labeled by year. We also plot the systematic portions of the

FIGURE 12.5   Unexpected Returns and Beta

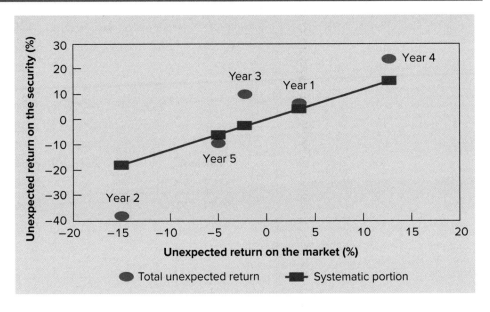

unexpected returns in Table 12.3 and connect them with a straight line. Notice that the slope of the straight line is equal to 1.2, the beta of the security. As indicated, the distance from the straight line to an individual point is the unsystematic portion of the return, ε, for a particular year.

WHERE DO BETAS COME FROM?

As our discussion to this point shows, beta is a useful concept. It allows us to estimate the expected return on a security, it tells how sensitive a security's return is to unexpected market events, and it lets us separate out the systematic and unsystematic portions of a security's return. In our example above, we were given that the beta was 1.2, so the required calculations were all pretty straightforward. Suppose, however, that we didn't have the beta ahead of time. In that case, we would have to estimate it.

A security's beta is a measure of how sensitive the security's return is to overall market movements. That sensitivity depends on two things: (1) how closely correlated the security's return is with the overall market's return and (2) how volatile the security is relative to the market. Specifically, going back to our previous chapter, let $\text{Corr}(R_i, R_M)$ stand for the correlation between the return on a particular Security i and the overall market. As in prior chapters, let σ_i and σ_M be the standard deviations on the security and the market, respectively. Given these numbers, the beta for the security, β_i, is:

$$\beta_i = \text{Corr }(R_i,\ R_M) \times \sigma_i/\sigma_M \tag{12.11}$$

In other words, the beta is equal to the correlation multiplied by the ratio of the standard deviations.

From previous chapters, we know how to calculate the standard deviations in Equation 12.11. However, we have not yet discussed how to calculate correlations. While the simplest way is to use a spreadsheet or calculator, a straightforward way to proceed is to construct a worksheet like Table 12.4.

The first six columns of Table 12.4 are familiar from Chapter 1. The first two contain five years of returns on a particular security and the overall market. We add these up and divide by 5 to get the average returns of 10 percent and 12 percent for the security and the market, respectively, as shown in the table. In the third and fourth columns, we calculate the return deviations by taking each individual return and subtracting out the average return. In columns 5 and 6, we square these return deviations. To calculate the variances, we total these squared deviations and divide by $5 - 1 = 4$. We calculate the standard deviations by taking the square root of the variances, and we find that the standard deviations for the security and the market are 18.87 percent and 15.03 percent, respectively.

TABLE 12.4	Calculating Beta					
	Returns		**Return Deviations**		**Squared Deviations**	
Year	Security (1)	Market (2)	Security (3)	Market (4)	Security (5)	Market (6)	Product of Deviations (7)
1	.10	.08	.00	−.04	.0000	.0016	.0000
2	−.08	−.12	−.18	−.24	.0324	.0576	.0432
3	−.04	.16	−.14	.04	.0196	.0016	−.0056
4	.40	.26	.30	.14	.0900	.0196	.0420
5	.12	.22	.02	.10	.0004	.0100	.0020
Totals	.50	.60	0	0	.1424	.0904	.0816

	Average Returns	**Variances**	**Standard Deviations**
Security	.50/5 = .10, or 10%	.1424/4 = .0356	$\sqrt{.0356}$ = .1887, or 18.87%
Market	.60/5 = .12, or 12%	.0904/4 = .0226	$\sqrt{.0226}$ = .1503, or 15.03%

Covariance = Cov(R_i, R_M) = .0816/4 = .0204

Correlation = Corr(R_i, R_M) = .0204/(.1887 × .1503) = .72

Beta = β = .72 × (.1887/.1503) = .903 ≈ .9

covariance
A measure of the tendency of two things to move or vary together.

Now we come to the part that's new. In the last column of Table 12.4, we have calculated the product of the return deviations by multiplying columns 3 and 4. When we total these products and divide by $5 - 1 = 4$, the result is called the **covariance**.

Covariance, as the name suggests, is a measure of the tendency of two things to vary together. If the covariance is positive, then the tendency is to move in the same direction, and vice versa for a negative covariance. A zero covariance means there is no particular relation. For our security in Table 12.4, the covariance is +.0204, so the security tends to move in the same direction as the market.

A problem with covariances is that, like variances, the actual numbers are hard to interpret (the sign, of course, is not). For example, our covariance is .0204, but just from this number, we can't really say if the security has a strong or weak tendency to move with the market. To fix this problem, we divide the covariance by the product of the two standard deviations. The result is the correlation coefficient, introduced in the previous chapter.

From Table 12.4, the correlation between our security and the overall market is .72. Recalling that correlations range from -1 to $+1$, this .72 tells us that the security has a fairly strong tendency to move with the overall market, but that tendency is not perfect.

Now we have reached our goal of calculating the beta coefficient. As shown in the last row of Table 12.4, from Equation 12.11 we have:

$$\beta_i = \text{Corr}\,(R_i, R_M) \times \sigma_i/\sigma_M$$
$$= .72 \times (.1887/.1503)$$
$$= .90$$

We find that this security has a beta of .9, so it has slightly less than average systematic risk. As our nearby *Spreadsheet Analysis* box shows, these calculations can be done easily with a spreadsheet.

SPREADSHEET ANALYSIS

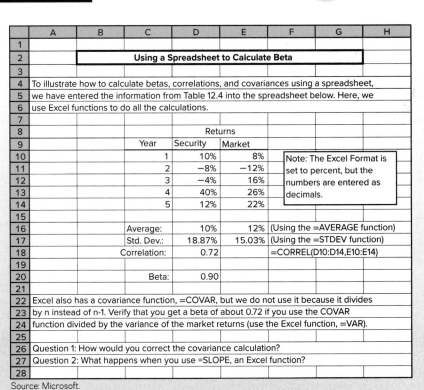

	A	B	C	D	E	F	G	H
1								
2			Using a Spreadsheet to Calculate Beta					
3								
4	To illustrate how to calculate betas, correlations, and covariances using a spreadsheet,							
5	we have entered the information from Table 12.4 into the spreadsheet below. Here, we							
6	use Excel functions to do all the calculations.							
7								
8				Returns				
9			Year	Security	Market			
10			1	10%	8%	Note: The Excel Format is		
11			2	−8%	−12%	set to percent, but the		
12			3	−4%	16%	numbers are entered as		
13			4	40%	26%	decimals.		
14			5	12%	22%			
15								
16			Average:	10%	12%	(Using the =AVERAGE function)		
17			Std. Dev.:	18.87%	15.03%	(Using the =STDEV function)		
18			Correlation:	0.72		=CORREL(D10:D14,E10:E14)		
19								
20			Beta:	0.90				
21								
22	Excel also has a covariance function, =COVAR, but we do not use it because it divides							
23	by n instead of n-1. Verify that you get a beta of about 0.72 if you use the COVAR							
24	function divided by the variance of the market returns (use the Excel function, =VAR).							
25								
26	Question 1: How would you correct the covariance calculation?							
27	Question 2: What happens when you use =SLOPE, an Excel function?							
28								

Source: Microsoft.

ANOTHER WAY TO CALCULATE BETA

At the bottom of the previous *Spreadsheet Analysis* box, you will notice Question 2, which suggests using the built-in slope function in Excel. If you use this function, be sure to select the market returns as the "*x* data" and the security returns as the "*y* data." When you do, you will find that the result is the security's beta of .90.

To understand why the slope function gives us the beta, consider Figure 12.6A, which is a simple scatter plot of the market and security returns. Notice that we plotted the market returns on the *x* axis and the security returns on the *y* axis. Looking at the plot, we see that the security has a positive relationship with the market.

To capture the nature of this relationship, consider Figure 12.6B, which adds a simple trend line to the data. We refer to this as the *characteristic line.* Notice that the line almost crosses at the origin.

Recall that beta measures relative movement. For example, a security with a beta of 1 is expected to move, on average, with the market. In this case, what would the characteristic line look like? It would be a line with a 45-degree angle, or a slope of 1. This slope indicates that as the market goes up 1 percent, we would expect the stock to do the same. In mathematical terms, the measure of rise over run is slope. So, if we define the market as the *x* data and the stock as the *y* data, the slope is effectively the beta of the security.

FIGURE 12.6   Graphical Representation of Calculating Beta

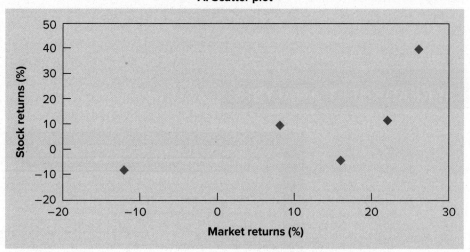

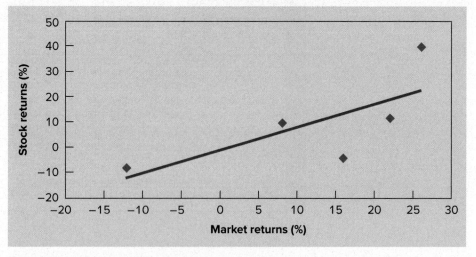

SPREADSHEET ANALYSIS

	A	B	C	D	E	F
1						
2		**Using a Regression in Excel to Calculate Beta**				
3						
4						
5	*Regression Statistics*					
6	Multiple R	0.7192				
7	R Square	0.5173				
8	Adjusted R Square	0.3563				
9	Standard Error	15.1375				
10	Observations	5				
11						
12	ANOVA					
13		*df*	*SS*	*MS*	*F*	*Significance F*
14	Regression	1	736.5663	736.5664	3.214418126	1.1709
15	Residual	3	687.4336	229.1445428		
16	Total	4	1424			
17						
18		*Coefficients*	*Standard Error*	*t Stat*	*P-value*	
19	Intercept	−0.8319	9.0736	−0.0917	0.9327	
20	Market Returns	0.9027	0.5035	1.7929	0.1709	

Source: Microsoft.

Applying this method to Figure 12.6B, what do you think the beta is? Notice that when the market has a return of 10 percent, the security is expected to have a return slightly less than 10 percent. The characteristic line thus suggests that the beta for this security is less than 1 because the stock return is less than a corresponding market return. Because comovements in returns seem to be rather close, however, our answer of .90 seems appropriate.

You might recall from your statistics class an alternative method for estimating a "line of best fit." Hopefully you remember this as a simple linear regression. In this case, we are going to "regress" the returns of the security (*y* data) on the returns of the market (*x* data). Fortunately, Excel also has a built-in regression function. If you look at the next *Spreadsheet Analysis* box, you can see a portion of the output from this process.

You will notice that the output provides an estimate of the intercept, as well as a coefficient (or slope) on the *x* data (i.e., the market returns). You should see that the estimated value is .90, which is consistent with our earlier calculations.

You might wonder why this approach is necessary if we can go to the internet and look up the data. Well, the ability to calculate your own beta is important for several reasons. For example, as we showed earlier in this chapter, internet sites will report different betas for a stock. Being able to understand which is the best estimate can be helpful. In addition, what if you are trying to evaluate a fund manager or an investment that is not publicly traded? In that case, you would have to "build" a beta yourself.

WHY DO BETAS DIFFER?

Based on what we've studied so far, you can see that beta is a pretty important topic. You might wonder, then, are all published betas calculated in the same way? Well, as we pointed out earlier in Table 12.1, different data providers such as Yahoo! Finance and MarketWatch provide different estimates of beta. There are a few lessons to be learned from these differences. The important thing to remember is that analysts estimate betas from actual data. Different analysts use different methods, and it is possible that they use different data. Let's discuss some of the key ways beta estimates can differ.

First, there are two issues concerning data. Betas can be calculated using daily, weekly, monthly, quarterly, or annual returns. In principle, it does not matter which is chosen, but with real data, different estimates will result. Second, betas can be estimated over relatively short periods, such as a few weeks, or over long periods of 5 to 10 years (or even more).

The trade-off here is not hard to understand. Betas obtained from high-frequency returns, such as daily returns, are less stable than those obtained from less frequent returns, such as monthly returns. This argues for using monthly or longer returns. On the other hand, any time we estimate something, we would like to have a large number of recent observations. This argues for using weekly or daily returns. There is no ideal balance; the most common choices are three to five years of monthly data or a single year of weekly data. The betas we get from a year of weekly data are more current in the sense that they reflect only the previous year, but they tend to be less stable than those obtained from longer periods.

Another issue has to do with choice of a market index. All along, we have discussed the return on the "overall market," but we have not been very precise about how to measure this. By far the most common choice is to use the S&P 500 stock market index to measure the overall market, but this is not the only alternative. Different sources use different indexes to capture the overall market, and different indexes will lead to different beta estimates.

You might wonder whether some index is the "correct" one. The answer is yes, but a problem comes up. In principle, when we speak of the overall market in the CAPM, what we really mean is the market for every risky asset of every type. In other words, what we would need is an index that included all the stocks, bonds, real estate, precious metals, and everything else in the entire world (not just the United States). Obviously, no such index exists, so instead we must choose some smaller index to proxy for this much larger one.

A few sources calculate betas the way we described in Table 12.4, but then they go on to adjust them for statistical reasons. One common adjustment is for "reversion to the mean," which you may remember from your statistics class. Under such an adjustment, betas above 1 are adjusted downward and betas below 1 are adjusted upward. A more detailed discussion of the possible adjustments goes beyond our discussion, but such proprietary adjustments are another reason why betas differ across sources.

Figure 12.7 shows in detail how Bloomberg calculates the beta for Microsoft. Bloomberg has regressed the returns of Microsoft versus the returns of the SPX (or S&P 500) index. They have used two years' worth of weekly data, and the result is a beta of .848. Note, however, that the system allows the user to change all of these assumptions. You can look at daily (or other) time periods, use a different index, or change the length of time. In the end, though, the regression process remains the same.

The bottom line is that we are interested in knowing what the beta of the stock will be in the future, but we have to estimate betas using historical data. Anytime we use the past to predict the future, the possibility of a poor estimate exists—even if the calculation process is sound. Unlike some forecasts, you should be able to understand how to estimate betas. Perhaps you can even recreate some of the published betas.

FIGURE 12.7 Beta Calculation

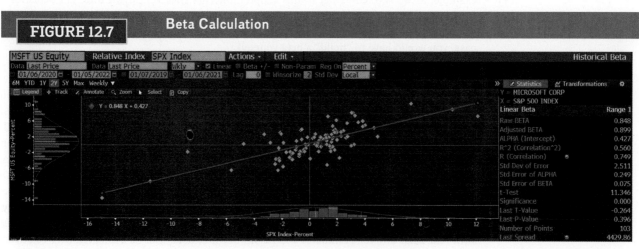

Source: Bloomberg Finance L.P.

12.6a How is beta similar to a slope coefficient?

12.6b Within the context of correlation, how is it possible for a stock to have a high variance but still have a low beta?

12.7 Extending CAPM

The previous two sections introduced you to the famous capital asset pricing model, or CAPM for short. For investors, the CAPM has a stunning implication: What you earn on your portfolio over time depends only on the level of systematic risk you bear. The corollary is equally striking: As a diversified investor, you do not need to be concerned with the total risk or volatility of any individual asset in your portfolio—it is irrelevant.

Of course, we should note that the CAPM is a theory, and, as with any theory, whether it is correct is a question for the data. So, does the CAPM work or not? Put more directly, does expected return depend on beta, and beta alone, or do other factors come into play? There are few more hotly debated questions in all of finance.

In this section, we first present a short history of attempts to test the CAPM. Then we discuss one of the most important extensions of the CAPM, the so-called Fama-French three-factor model. We conclude with a more general discussion of factor analysis.

A (VERY) BRIEF HISTORY OF TESTING CAPM

The CAPM was introduced in the mid-1960s (but, perhaps surprisingly, tests of this model began to appear only in the early 1970s). When researchers test the CAPM, they essentially look to see whether average returns are linearly related to beta. That is, they want to know if asset returns and beta line up as shown in Figure 12.4. The earliest tests of the CAPM suggested that return and risk (as measured by beta) showed a reasonable relationship. However, the relationship was not so strong that financial researchers were content to move on and test other theories.

To summarize years of testing, the relationship between returns and beta appeared to vary depending on the time period that was studied. Over some periods, the relationship was strong. In others, it was apparent but not strong. In still others, it was seemingly nonexistent, or even negative.

Over the years, researchers refined their techniques to measure betas. In addition, the question was raised whether researchers could calculate betas at all. The basic argument was that betas could not be calculated relative to the overall market portfolio because we cannot observe the true market portfolio. Nonetheless, despite this insightful critique, researchers continue to test the CAPM and debate the findings of CAPM research to this day.

Despite the debate between CAPM critics and CAPM champions, some important ideas have emerged. Few researchers question these general principles:

- Investing has two dimensions: risk and return.
- It is inappropriate to look at the risk of an individual security. What is appropriate is how the individual security contributes to the risk of a diversified portfolio.
- Risk can be decomposed into systematic risk and unsystematic risk.
- Investors will be compensated only for taking systematic risk.

THE FAMA-FRENCH THREE-FACTOR MODEL

To illustrate some aspects of the debate surrounding CAPM, we now briefly explore the Fama-French three-factor model, which gets its name from its creators, Professors Eugene Fama and Kenneth French. Table 12.5 illustrates an important finding from years of research into stock market returns. As shown, two groups of stocks have tended to do noticeably better than the market as a whole: (1) stocks with a small market capitalization (small-cap stocks)

TABLE 12.5 — Average Annual Value-Weighted Percentage Returns from 25 Portfolios Formed on Size (Cap) and Book-to-Market, 1927–2021

	(Lowest B/M) 1	2	3	4	(Highest B/M) 5
1 (smallest cap)	9.07	13.47	16.45	19.52	21.39
2	12.14	15.63	16.02	17.53	19.25
3	12.74	15.02	15.36	16.42	17.58
4	12.59	13.36	14.37	15.92	16.72
5 (largest cap)	11.46	11.05	12.46	11.83	14.67

Source: Author calculations using data from the website of Ken French.

and (2) stocks that have a higher-than-average ratio of book (or accounting) value to market value of equity (so-called value stocks).

Table 12.5 is formed as follows. First, for each year of historical data, each of a large number of stocks is ranked on the basis of its market cap, or size. The smallest 20 percent of the stocks are placed into the market cap Quintile 1, the next smallest 20 percent are placed into market cap Quintile 2, and so on. Then, the same stocks are ranked on the basis of their book-to-market (B/M) ratio. The smallest 20 percent are placed into B/M Quintile 1, the next smallest 20 percent are placed into B/M Quintile 2, and so on.

Let's look at the cell with an average annual return of 9.07 percent. This number is calculated as follows: After the sorting described above, we put stocks into portfolios according to both of their quintile scores, for a total of 25 ($= 5 \times 5$) portfolios. So, for example, the stocks with both the smallest cap and the lowest B/M end up in the Quintile 1-1 portfolio. As shown in Table 12.5, over the time period 1927 to 2021, the average annual return for stocks in the Quintile 1-1 portfolio is 9.07 percent.

Three things should jump out at you in Table 12.5. Notice that the cell 1-5, which contains stocks with the smallest cap and highest B/M, has had the highest returns (21.39 percent). Looking down each column, you can see that in three columns, the highest return belongs to the smallest cap quintile (we see this pattern in columns 3, 4, and 5). Looking across each row, you can see that in every row, the highest return belongs to the highest B/M quintile.

Based on further analysis of these data, Professors Fama and French concluded that differences in beta were not sufficient to explain the differences in returns in Table 12.5. Consequently, they argue that two additional factors beyond beta must be considered to understand differences in expected returns on stocks, namely, market cap and B/M. Thus, their model of stock returns has a total of three factors.

At this point, you probably understand two of the factors—beta and market cap. But what does the B/M (or book-to-market) ratio represent? When a stock has a low B/M ratio, the market is paying a higher price per share relative to the firm's book value per share. Companies with low B/M ratios, therefore, are typically referred to as growth companies. Thus, the interpretation of this ratio is similar to that of a company with a high PE ratio. Firms with high B/M ratios would generally be considered value companies.

Using this description of the B/M ratio, it is clear from the data in Table 12.5 that value companies, all else equal, generally outperform growth companies. This is obviously not true each year, but over this long period of time, value has definitely outperformed. This result stands in stark contrast to what most investors think. But the data in Table 12.5 are quite clear.

FACTOR ANALYSIS AND STYLE PORTFOLIOS

Investors are always looking for ways to increase their returns. Because of Fama and French's findings, researchers have increased their search for other potential factors that underlie asset returns. The process of modeling the relationship between asset returns and their potential systematic drivers, or factors, is called *factor analysis*.

While there is no limit on the type of factors chosen, potential factors generally fall into two categories. Macroeconomic factors include items such as inflation or GDP growth, which we discuss in another chapter. Fundamental factors would be such things as a stock's dividend yield or earnings growth rate, which we also discuss in other chapters.

Investors use statistical models (such as a linear regression) to try to estimate how sensitive an asset's return is to a set of factors. This sensitivity is referred to as the *factor beta,* or *factor loading.* If the sensitivity to a factor is high, there is an important implication: Potentially, investors could form portfolios using this factor to generate higher returns. For example, the Fama-French three-factor model identifies two important factors, size and book-to-market value, that drive asset returns. Portfolios created based on factors are often referred to as *factor portfolios,* or *style portfolios.*

Factor analysis has given rise to many different investment approaches. For example, a growing number of funds focus on allocating capital based on fundamental factors, such as growth in cash flow. Other funds focus on allocating capital based on market factors, such as a stock's price momentum. There are even a growing number of passively managed index funds that follow a *fundamental indexing* approach. In this approach, asset weights are determined according to the asset's sensitivity to a prespecified factor rather than to a security's market value.

There are a large number of factors that could be considered. Of course, investors want to identify opportunities to generate excess returns. As a result, we think it is safe to say that factor analysis is here to stay.

CHECK THIS

12.7a   What are the three factors in the basic Fama-French model?

12.7b   Explain how factor analysis is used to create style portfolios.

12.8 Summary and Conclusions

This chapter covers the essentials of risk and return. Along the way, we introduced a number of definitions and concepts. The most important of these is the security market line, or SML. The SML is important because it tells us the reward offered in financial markets for bearing risk. Because we covered quite a bit of ground, it's useful to summarize the basic economic logic underlying the SML as follows.

1. **The difference between expected and unexpected returns.**

   A. The return on any stock traded in a financial market is composed of two parts. The expected return from the stock is the part of the return that investors predict or expect. This return depends on the information investors have about the stock, and it is based on the market's understanding today of the important factors that will influence the stock in the coming year.

   B. The second part of the return on the stock is the uncertain, or risky, part. This is the portion that comes from unexpected information revealed during the year.

2. **The difference between systematic risk and unsystematic risk.**

   A. Based on capital market history, there is a reward for bearing risk. This reward is the risk premium on an asset.

   B. The total risk associated with an asset has two parts: systematic risk and unsystematic risk. Unsystematic risk can be freely eliminated by diversification (this is the principle of diversification), so only systematic risk is rewarded. As a result, the risk premium on an asset is determined by its systematic risk. This is the systematic risk principle.

3. **The security market line and the capital asset pricing model.**

A. An asset's systematic risk, relative to the average, can be measured by its beta coefficient, β_i. The risk premium on an asset is then given by the market risk premium multiplied by the asset's beta coefficient, $[E(R_M) - R_f] \times \beta_i$.

B. The expected return on an asset, $E(R_i)$, is equal to the risk-free rate, R_f, plus the asset's risk premium: $E(R_i) = R_f + [E(R_M) - R_f] \times \beta_i$. This is the equation of the SML, and it is often called the capital asset pricing model (CAPM).

4. **The importance of beta.**

A. Systematic risk is the crucial determinant of an asset's expected return. Therefore, we need some way to measure the level of systematic risk for different investments.

B. The specific measure we use is called the beta coefficient, designated by the Greek letter β. A beta coefficient, or beta for short, tells us how much systematic risk a particular asset has relative to an average asset.

C. By definition, an average asset has a beta of 1.0 relative to itself. An asset with a beta of .50, therefore, has half as much systematic risk as an average asset.

D. Toward the end of the chapter, we showed how betas are calculated and we discussed some of the main reasons different sources report different beta coefficients. We closed the chapter by presenting a discussion of factor models, an important extension to the basic CAPM.

GETTING DOWN TO BUSINESS

An immediate implication of the CAPM is that you, as an investor, need to be aware of the level of systematic risk you are carrying. Look up the betas of the stocks you hold in your simulated brokerage account and compute your portfolio's systematic risk. Is it bigger or smaller than 1.0? More important, is the portfolio's beta consistent with your desired level of portfolio risk?

Betas are particularly useful for understanding mutual fund risk and return. Because most mutual funds are at least somewhat diversified (the exceptions being sector funds and other specialized funds), they have relatively little unsystematic risk, and their betas can be measured with some precision. Look at the funds you own and identify their betas (www.morningstar.com is a good source). Are the risk levels what you intended? As you study mutual fund risk, you will find some other measures exist, most of which are closely related to the measures discussed in this chapter. Take a few minutes to understand these as well.

Does expected return depend on beta, and beta alone, or do other factors come into play? There is no more hotly debated question in all of finance, and the research that exists to date is inconclusive. (Some researchers would dispute this!) At a minimum, beta appears to be a useful measure of market-related volatility, that is, risk. Whether beta is a useful measure of expected return (much less a comprehensive one) awaits more research. Lots more research.

For the latest information on the real world of investments, visit us at jmdinvestments.blogspot.com.

Key Terms

beta coefficient (β) 402
capital asset pricing model (CAPM) 410
covariance 415
market risk premium 410

security market line (SML) 409
systematic risk 399
systematic risk principle 401
unsystematic risk 399

Related Bloomberg Functions

EE SURP	Price Reaction and Surprise, 12.1
EA	Earnings Analysis, 12.1
CN	Company News, 12.1
ECSU	Economics Surprises Monitor, 12.2
WECO	Economics Calendars by Country, 12.2
BETA	Historical Beta, 12.4
PORT	Portfolio & Risk Analytics, 12.4
WACC	Weighted Average Cost of Capital, 12.5
CRP	Country Risk Premiums, 12.5
EQRP	Equity Risk Premiums, 12.5
HRA	Regression Analysis, 12.6
FTW	Factors to Watch, 12.7
FTST	Factor Backtester, 12.7

Chapter Review Problems and Self-Test

1. **Risk and Return (LO3, CFA3)**   Suppose you observe the following situation:

Security	Beta	Expected Return
Sanders	1.8	22.00%
Janicek	1.6	20.44

   If the risk-free rate is 7 percent, are these two stocks correctly priced relative to each other? What must the risk-free rate be if they are correctly priced?

2. **CAPM (LO3, CFA1)**   Suppose the risk-free rate is 8 percent. The expected return on the market is 16 percent. If a particular stock has a beta of .7, what is its expected return based on the CAPM? If another stock has an expected return of 24 percent, what must its beta be?

Answers to Self-Test Problems

1. If we compute the reward-to-risk ratios, we get $(22\% - 7\%)/1.8 = 8.33\%$ for Sanders versus 8.4% for Janicek. Relative to Sanders, Janicek's expected return is too high, so its price is too low.

   If they are correctly priced, then they must offer the same reward-to-risk ratio. The risk-free rate would be:

   $$\frac{22\% - R_f}{1.8} = \frac{20.44\% - R_f}{1.6}$$

   With a little algebra, we find that the risk-free rate must be 8 percent:

   $$22\% - R_f = (20.44\% - R_f)(1.8/1.6)$$
   $$22\% - 20.44\% \times 1.125 = R_f - R_f \times 1.125$$
   $$R_f = .0796, \text{ or } 7.96\%$$

2. Because the expected return on the market is 16 percent, the market risk premium is $16\% - 8\% = 8\%$ (the risk-free rate is also 8 percent). The first stock has a beta of .7, so its expected return is $8\% + 8\% \times .7 = 13.6\%$.

For the second stock, notice that the risk premium is 24% − 8% = 16%. Because this is twice as large as the market risk premium, the beta must be exactly equal to 2. We can verify this using the CAPM:

$$E(R_i) = R_f + [E(R_M) - R_f] \times \beta_i$$
$$24\% = 8\% + (16\% - 8\%) \times \beta_i$$
$$\beta_i = 16\%/8\% = 2.0$$

Test Your Investment Quotient

1. **Portfolio Return (LO3, CFA1)**   According to the CAPM, what is the rate of return of a portfolio with a beta of 1?

   a. Between R_M and R_f
   b. The risk-free rate, R_f
   c. Beta $\times (R_M - R_f)$
   d. The return on the market, R_M

2. **Stock Return (LO1, CFA4)**   The return on a stock is said to have which two of the following basic parts?

   a. An expected return and an unexpected return
   b. A measurable return and an unmeasurable return
   c. A predicted return and a forecast return
   d. A total return and a partial return

3. **News Components (LO1, CFA4)**   A news announcement about a stock is said to have which two of the following parts?

   a. An expected part and a surprise
   b. Public information and private information
   c. Financial information and product information
   d. A good part and a bad part

4. **News Effects (LO1, CFA4)**   A company announces that its earnings have increased 50 percent over the previous year, which matches analysts' expectations. What is the likely effect on the stock price?

   a. The stock price will increase.
   b. The stock price will decrease.
   c. The stock price will rise and then fall after an overreaction.
   d. The stock price will not be affected.

5. **News Effects (LO1, CFA4)**   A company announces that its earnings have decreased 25 percent from the previous year, but analysts expected a small increase. What is the likely effect on the stock price?

   a. The stock price will increase.
   b. The stock price will decrease.
   c. The stock price will rise and then fall after an overreaction.
   d. The stock price will not be affected.

6. **News Effects (LO1, CFA4)**   A company announces that its earnings have increased 25 percent from the previous year, but analysts actually expected a 50 percent increase. What is the likely effect on the stock price?

   a. The stock price will increase.
   b. The stock price will decrease.
   c. The stock price will rise and then fall after an overreaction.
   d. The stock price will not be affected.

7. **Factor Analysis (LO1, CFA4)**   An investor completed a factor analysis to evaluate the impact of earnings growth and cash flow yield on stock price performance. The factor analysis model provides estimates of the impacts of these factors. We refer to these estimated impacts as:

   a. Relational boundaries.
   b. Factor loadings.
   c. Factor efficiencies.
   d. Contradictory anomalies.

8. **Security Risk (LO2, CFA3)**   The systematic risk of a security is also called its:

   a. Perceived risk.
   b. Unique or asset-specific risk.
   c. Market risk.
   d. Fundamental risk.

9. **Security Risk (LO2, CFA3)**   Which type of risk is essentially eliminated by diversification?

   a. Perceived risk
   b. Market risk
   c. Systematic risk
   d. Unsystematic risk

10. **Security Risk (LO2, CFA3)**   The systematic risk principle states that:

    a. Systematic risk doesn't matter to investors.
    b. Systematic risk can be essentially eliminated by diversification.
    c. The reward for bearing risk is independent of the systematic risk of an investment.
    d. The reward for bearing risk depends only on the systematic risk of an investment.

11. **Security Risk (LO2, CFA3)**   The systematic risk principle has an important implication, which is:

    a. Systematic risk is preferred to unsystematic risk.
    b. Systematic risk is the only risk that can be reduced by diversification.
    c. The expected return on an asset is independent of its systematic risk.
    d. The expected return on an asset depends only on its systematic risk.

12. **CAPM (LO3, CFA1)**   A financial market's security market line (SML) describes:

    a. The relationship between systematic risk and expected returns.
    b. The relationship between unsystematic risk and expected returns.
    c. The relationship between systematic risk and unexpected returns.
    d. The relationship between unsystematic risk and unexpected returns.

13. **Risk Aversion (LO3, CFA3)**   Which of the following is not an implication of risk aversion for the investment process?

    a. The security market line is upward sloping.
    b. The promised yield on AAA-rated bonds is higher than on A-rated bonds.
    c. Investors expect a positive relationship between expected return and risk.
    d. Investors prefer portfolios that lie on the efficient frontier to other portfolios with equal rates of return.

14. **Unsystematic Risk (LO2, CFA3)**   In the context of capital market theory, unsystematic risk:

    a. Is described as unique risk.
    b. Refers to nondiversifiable risk.
    c. Remains in the market portfolio.
    d. Refers to the variability in all risky assets caused by macroeconomic factors and other aggregate market-related variables.

15. **Security Market Line (LO3, CFA1)**   Which of the following statements about the security market line (SML) is false?

    a. Properly valued assets plot exactly on the SML.
    b. The SML leads all investors to invest in the same portfolio of risky assets.
    c. The SML provides a benchmark for evaluating expected investment performance.
    d. The SML is a graphic representation of the relationship between expected return and beta.

Concept Questions

1. **Diversifiable Risk (LO2, CFA3)**   In broad terms, why is some risk diversifiable? Why are some risks nondiversifiable? Does it follow that an investor can control the level of unsystematic risk in a portfolio but not the level of systematic risk?

2. **Announcements and Prices (LO1, CFA4)**   Suppose the government announces that, based on a just-completed survey, the growth rate in the economy is likely to be 2 percent in the coming year, compared to 5 percent for the year just completed. Will security prices increase, decrease, or stay the same following this announcement? Does it make any difference whether the 2 percent figure was anticipated by the market? Explain.

3. **Announcements and Risk (LO2, CFA4)** Classify the following events as mostly systematic or mostly unsystematic. Is the distinction clear in every case?

a. Short-term interest rates increase unexpectedly.
b. The interest rate a company pays on its short-term debt borrowing is increased by its bank.
c. Oil prices unexpectedly decline.
d. An oil tanker ruptures, creating a large oil spill.
e. A manufacturer loses a multimillion-dollar product liability suit.
f. A Supreme Court decision substantially broadens producer liability for injuries suffered by product users.

4. **Announcements and Risk (LO2, CFA4)** Indicate whether the following events might cause stocks in general to change price, and whether they might cause Big Widget Corp.'s stock to change price.

a. The government announces that inflation unexpectedly jumped by 2 percent last month.
b. Big Widget's quarterly earnings report, just issued, generally fell in line with analysts' expectations.
c. The government reports that economic growth last year was at 3 percent, which generally agreed with most economists' forecasts.
d. The directors of Big Widget die in a plane crash.
e. Congress approves changes to the tax code that will increase the top marginal corporate tax rate. The legislation had been debated for the previous six months.

5. **Diversification and Risk (LO2, CFA3)** True or false: The most important characteristic in determining the expected return of a well-diversified portfolio is the standard deviations of the individual assets in the portfolio. Explain.

6. **Announcements (LO1, CFA4)** As indicated by examples in this chapter, earnings announcements by companies are closely followed by, and frequently result in, share price revisions. Two issues should come to mind. First, earnings announcements concern past periods. If the market values stocks based on expectations of the future, why are numbers summarizing past performance relevant? Second, these announcements concern accounting earnings. Such earnings may have little to do with cash flow, so, again, why are they relevant?

7. **Beta (LO4, CFA3)** Is it possible that a risky asset could have a beta of zero? Explain. Based on the CAPM, what is the expected return on such an asset? Is it possible that a risky asset could have a negative beta? What does the CAPM predict about the expected return on such an asset? Can you give an explanation for your answer?

8. **Relative Valuation (LO3, CFA3)** Suppose you identify a situation in which one security is overvalued relative to another. How would you go about exploiting this opportunity? Does it matter if the two securities are both overvalued relative to some third security? Are your profits certain in this case?

9. **Reward-to-Risk Ratio (LO3, CFA3)** Explain what it means for all assets to have the same reward-to-risk ratio. How can you increase your return if this holds true? Why would we expect that all assets have the same reward-to-risk ratio in liquid, well-functioning markets?

10. **Systematic versus Firm-Specific Risk (LO2, CFA3)** Dudley Trudy, CFA, recently met with one of his clients. Trudy typically invests in a master list of 30 securities drawn from several industries. After the meeting concluded, the client made the following statement: "I trust your stock-picking ability and believe that you should invest my funds in your five best ideas. Why invest in 30 companies when you obviously have stronger opinions on a few of them?" Trudy plans to respond to his client within the context of modern portfolio theory.

a. Contrast the concepts of systematic and firm-specific risk and give one example of each.
b. Critique the client's suggestion. Discuss the impact of systematic risk and firm-specific risk on portfolio risk as the number of securities in a portfolio is increased.

Questions and Problems

Core Questions

1. **Stock Betas (LO3, CFA3)** A stock has an expected return of 13.2 percent, the risk-free rate is 3.5 percent, and the market risk premium is 7.5 percent. What must the beta of this stock be?

2. **Market Returns (LO3, CFA1)** A stock has an expected return of 8.0 percent, its beta is .60, and the risk-free rate is 3 percent. What must the expected return on the market be?

3. **Risk-Free Rates (LO3, CFA1)** A stock has an expected return of 12 percent and a beta of 1.4, and the expected return on the market is 10 percent. What must the risk-free rate be?

4. **Market Risk Premium (LO3, CFA1)** A stock has a beta of .8 and an expected return of 11 percent. If the risk-free rate is 4.5 percent, what is the market risk premium?

5. **Portfolio Betas (LO4, CFA3)** You own a stock portfolio invested 10 percent in Stock Q, 25 percent in Stock R, 50 percent in Stock S, and 15 percent in Stock T. The betas for these four stocks are 1.4, .6, 1.5, and .9, respectively. What is the portfolio beta?

6. **Portfolio Betas (LO4, CFA1)** You own 400 shares of Stock A at a price of $60 per share, 500 shares of Stock B at $85 per share, and 900 shares of Stock C at $25 per share. The betas for the stocks are .8, 1.2, and .7, respectively. What is the beta of your portfolio?

7. **Stock Betas (LO4, CFA1)** You own a portfolio equally invested in a risk-free asset and two stocks. If one of the stocks has a beta of 1.20 and the total portfolio is exactly as risky as the market, what must the beta be for the other stock in your portfolio?

8. **Expected Returns (LO3, CFA3)** A stock has a beta of .85, the expected return on the market is 11 percent, and the risk-free rate is 3 percent. What must the expected return on this stock be?

9. **CAPM and Stock Price (LO3, CFA4)** A share of stock sells for $35 today. The beta of the stock is 1.2 and the expected return on the market is 12 percent. The stock is expected to pay a dividend of $.80 in one year. If the risk-free rate is 5.5 percent, what should the share price be in one year?

10. **Portfolio Weights (LO4, CFA3)** A stock has a beta of .9 and an expected return of 9 percent. A risk-free asset currently earns 4 percent.

    a. What is the expected return on a portfolio that is equally invested in the two assets?
    b. If a portfolio of the two assets has a beta of .5, what are the portfolio weights?
    c. If a portfolio of the two assets has an expected return of 8 percent, what is its beta?
    d. If a portfolio of the two assets has a beta of 1.80, what are the portfolio weights? How do you interpret the weights for the two assets in this case? Explain.

Intermediate Questions

11. **Portfolio Risk and Return (LO3, CFA1)** Asset W has an expected return of 12.0 percent and a beta of 1.1. If the risk-free rate is 4 percent, complete the following table for portfolios of Asset W and a risk-free asset. Illustrate the relationship between portfolio expected return and portfolio beta by plotting the expected returns against the betas. What is the slope of the line that results?

Percentage of Portfolio in Asset W	Portfolio Expected Return	Portfolio Beta
0%		
25		
50		
75		
100		
125		
150		

12. **Relative Valuation (LO3, CFA3)** Stock Y has a beta of 1.05 and an expected return of 13 percent. Stock Z has a beta of .70 and an expected return of 9 percent. If the risk-free rate is 5 percent and the market risk premium is 7 percent, are these stocks correctly priced?

13. **Relative Valuation (LO3, CFA3)** In Problem 12, what would the risk-free rate have to be for the two stocks to be correctly priced relative to each other?

14. **CAPM (LO3, CFA1)** Using the CAPM, show that the ratio of the risk premiums on two assets is equal to the ratio of their betas.

15. **Relative Valuation (LO3, CFA3)** Suppose you observe the following situation:

Security	Beta	Expected Return
Peat Co.	1.05	12.3
Re-Peat Co.	.90	11.8

Assume these securities are correctly priced. Based on the CAPM, what is the expected return on the market? What is the risk-free rate?

16. **Calculating Beta (LO3, CFA3)** Show that another way to calculate beta is to take the covariance between the security and the market and divide by the variance of the market's return.

17. **Calculating Beta (LO4, CFA3)** Fill in the following table, supplying all the missing information. Use this information to calculate the security's beta.

Year	Returns Security	Returns Market	Return Deviations Security	Return Deviations Market	Squared Deviations Security	Squared Deviations Market	Product of Deviations
2018	8	5					
2019	−18	−14					
2020	21	15					
2021	38	21					
2022	16	7					

18. **Analyzing a Portfolio (LO4, CFA3)** You have $100,000 to invest in a portfolio containing Stock X, Stock Y, and a risk-free asset. You must invest all of your money. Your goal is to create a portfolio that has an expected return of 13 percent and that has only 70 percent of the risk of the overall market. If X has an expected return of 31 percent and a beta of 1.8, Y has an expected return of 20 percent and a beta of 1.3, and the risk-free rate is 7 percent, how much money will you invest in Stock Y? How do you explain your answer?

19. **Systematic versus Unsystematic Risk (LO2, CFA4)** Consider the following information on Stocks I and II:

State of Economy	Probability of State of Economy	Rate of Return if State Occurs Stock I	Rate of Return if State Occurs Stock II
Recession	.30	.05	−.18
Normal	.40	.19	.14
Irrational exuberance	.30	.13	.29

The market risk premium is 8 percent and the risk-free rate is 5 percent. Which stock has the most systematic risk? Which one has the most unsystematic risk? Which stock is "riskier"? Explain.

20. **Systematic and Unsystematic Risk (LO2, CFA4)** The beta for a certain stock is 1.15, the risk-free rate is 5 percent, and the expected return on the market is 13 percent. Complete the following table to decompose the stock's return into the systematic return and the unsystematic return.

Year	Actual Returns R	Actual Returns R_M	Unexpected Returns $R - E(R)$	Unexpected Returns $R_M - E(R_M)$	Systematic Portion $[R_M - E(R_M)] \times \beta$	Unsystematic Portion (ε) $[R - E(R)] - [R_M - E(R_M)] \times \beta$
2018	10	12				
2019	11	8				
2020	−8	−11				
2021	−6	14				
2022	28	7				

21. **CAPM (LO3, CFA3)** Landon Stevens is evaluating the expected performance of two common stocks, Furhman Labs, Inc., and Garten Testing, Inc. The risk-free rate is 4 percent, the expected return on the market is 11.5 percent, and the betas of the two stocks are 1.2 and .9, respectively. Landon's own forecasts of the returns on the two stocks are 13.75 percent for Furhman Labs and 10.50 percent for Garten. Calculate the required return for each stock. Is each stock undervalued, fairly valued, or overvalued?

Spreadsheet Problems

22. Calculating Beta (LO4, CFA1) You are given the following information concerning a stock and the market:

	Returns	
Year	Market	Stock
2017	18%	34%
2018	11	27
2019	12	3
2020	−14	−21
2021	37	16
2022	15	22

Calculate the average return and standard deviation for the market and the stock. Next, calculate the correlation between the stock and the market, as well as the stock's beta. Use a spreadsheet to calculate your answers.

CFA Exam Review by Kaplan Schweser

[CFA1, CFA3]

Janet Bellows, a portfolio manager, is attempting to explain asset valuation to a junior colleague, Bill Clay. Ms. Bellows's explanation focuses on the capital asset pricing model (CAPM). Of particular interest is her discussion of the security market line (SML) and its use in security selection. After a short review of the CAPM and SML, Ms. Bellows decides to test Mr. Clay's knowledge of valuation using the CAPM. Ms. Bellows provides the following information for Mr. Clay:

- The risk-free rate is 7 percent.
- The market risk premium during the previous year was 5.5 percent.
- The standard deviation of market returns is 35 percent.
- This year, the market risk premium is estimated to be 7 percent.
- Stock A has a beta of 1.30 and is expected to generate a 15.5 percent return.
- The correlation of Stock B with the market is .88.
- The standard deviation of Stock B's returns is 58 percent.

Then Ms. Bellows provides Mr. Clay with the following information about Ohio Manufacturing, Texas Energy, and Montana Mining:

	Ohio	Texas	Montana
Beta	.50		1.50
Required return	10.5%	11.0%	
Expected return	12.0%	10.0%	15.0%
S&P 500 expected return		14.0%	

1. Based on the stock and market data provided above, which of the following data regarding Stock A is most accurate?

	Required Return	Recommendation
a.	16.1%	Sell
b.	16.1%	Buy
c.	14.15%	Sell

2. The beta of Stock B is closest to:
   a. .51
   b. 1.07
   c. 1.46

3. Which of the following represents the best investment advice?

    a. Avoid Texas because its expected return is lower than its required return.

    b. Buy Montana and Texas because their required returns are lower than their expected returns.

    c. Buy Montana because it is expected to return more than Texas, Ohio, and the market.

4. If the market risk premium decreases by 1 percent while the risk-free rate remains the same, the security market line:

    a. Becomes steeper.

    b. Becomes flatter.

    c. Parallel shifts downward.

Bloomberg Exercises

1. Review the impact of recent earnings surprises on Coca-Cola (KO) stock. (**EE SURP**)

2. Read recent news headlines for Best Buy (BBY). (**CN**)

3. Find the beta for Travelers (TRV) stock. (**BETA**)

4. Identify the equity risk premium for General Electric (GE). (**EQRP**)

What's on the Web?

1. **Expected Return** You want to find the expected return for The Home Depot using CAPM. First you need the risk-free rate. Go to www.bloomberg.com and find the current interest rate for three-month Treasury bills. Use the average large-company stock risk premium from Chapter 1 as the market risk premium. Next, go to finance.yahoo.com, enter the ticker symbol HD for The Home Depot, and find the beta for The Home Depot. What is the expected return for The Home Depot using CAPM? What assumptions have you made to arrive at this number?

2. **Portfolio Beta** You have decided to invest in an equally weighted portfolio consisting of American Express, Procter & Gamble, Johnson & Johnson, and United Technologies and need to find the beta of your portfolio. Go to finance.yahoo.com and find the beta for each of the companies. What is the beta for your portfolio?

3. **Beta** Which stocks have the highest and lowest betas? Go to finance.yahoo.com and find the stock screener. Enter 0 as the maximum beta. How many stocks currently have a beta less than 0? Which stock has the lowest beta? Go back to the stock screener and enter 3 as the minimum value. How many stocks have a beta greater than 3? What about 4? Which stock has the highest beta?

4. **Security Market Line** Go to finance.yahoo.com and enter the ticker symbol GE for General Electric. Find the beta for this company and the target stock price in one year. Using the current share price and the target stock price, compute the expected return for this stock. Don't forget to include the expected dividend payments over the next year. Now go to www.bloomberg.com and find the current interest rate for three-month Treasury bills. Using this information, calculate the expected return of the market using the reward-to-risk ratio. Does this number make sense? Why or why not?

Performance Evaluation and Risk Management

"It is not the return on my investment that I am concerned about; it is the return of my investment!"

—Will Rogers

"The stock market will fluctuate!"

—J. P. Morgan

Humorist Will Rogers expressed concern about "the return *of* [his] investment." Famed financier J. P. Morgan, when asked by a reporter what he thought the stock market would do, replied with his well-known quote. Both Will Rogers and J. P. Morgan understood a basic fact of investing—investors holding risky assets ask worrisome questions like: How well are my investments doing? How much money am I making (or losing)? and What are my chances of incurring a significant loss?

This chapter examines methods to deal with two related problems faced by investors in risky assets. These are (1) evaluating risk-adjusted investment performance and (2) assessing and managing the risks involved with specific investment strategies. Both subjects have come up previously in this book, but we have deferred a detailed discussion of them until now.

CFA™ Exam Topics in This Chapter:

1. Organizing, visualizing, and describing data (L1, S1)
2. Introduction to risk management (L1, S18)
3. Introduction to the Global Investment Performance Standards (GIPS) (L1, S19)
4. Analysis of active portfolio management (L2, S16)
5. Portfolio performance evaluation (L3, S13)
6. Overview of the Global Investment Performance Standards (L3, S16)

Go to Connect for a guide that aligns your textbook with CFA readings.

We first consider the problem of performance evaluation. Specifically, suppose we have investment returns data for several portfolios covering a recent period, and we wish to evaluate how well these portfolios have performed relative to other portfolios or some investment benchmark. The need for this form of scrutiny arises in a number of situations, including:

- An investor wants to compare the investment performance of several dozen candidate funds before choosing a mutual fund.
- A pension fund administrator wants to select a money manager and thus needs to compare the investment performance of a group of money managers.
- An employer wants to compare the performance of several investment companies before selecting one for inclusion in the company-sponsored 401(k) retirement plan.

In the first section of this chapter, we examine several useful evaluation measures of portfolio performance and discuss how they might be applied to these and similar situations.

In the second part of the chapter, we discuss the important problem of risk management from the perspective of an investor or money manager concerned with the possibility of a large loss. Specifically, we examine methods to assess the probabilities and magnitudes of losses we might expect to experience during a set future time period. These risk assessment techniques are commonly employed in a number of situations, including:

- A New York Stock Exchange designated market maker (DMM) wants to know how much of a loss is possible with a 5 percent probability during the coming day's trading from the DMM firm's inventory.
- The foreign currency manager of a commercial bank wants to know how much of a loss is possible with a 2 percent probability on the bank's foreign currency portfolio during the coming week.
- A futures exchange clearinghouse wants to know what amount of margin funds should be deposited by exchange members to cover extreme losses that might occur with a "once in a century" probability.

Methods used to assess risk in these and similar scenarios fall into the category commonly referred to as "Value-at-Risk." Value-at-Risk techniques are widely applied by commercial banks, securities firms, and other financial institutions to assess and understand the risk exposure of portfolios under their management.

13.1 Performance Evaluation

performance evaluation
The assessment of how well a money manager achieves a balance between high returns and acceptable risks.

Investors have a natural (and very rational) interest in how well particular investments have done. This is true whether the investors manage their own portfolio or have money managed by a professional. Concern with investment performance motivates the topic of **performance evaluation**. In general terms, performance evaluation focuses on assessing how well a money manager achieves high returns balanced with acceptable risks.

Going back to our discussion of efficient markets in an earlier chapter, we raised the question of risk-adjusted performance and whether anyone can consistently earn an "abnormal" return, thereby "beating the market." The standard example is an evaluation of investment performance achieved by the manager of a mutual fund. Such a performance evaluation is more than an academic exercise because its purpose is to help investors decide whether they should entrust investment funds to the fund manager. Our goal here is to introduce you to the primary tools used to make this assessment.

PERFORMANCE EVALUATION MEASURES

A variety of measures are used to evaluate investment performance. Here, we examine some of the best-known and most popular measures: the Sharpe ratio, the Treynor ratio, Jensen's alpha, the information ratio, and R-squared. But before we do so, let us first briefly discuss a naïve measure of performance evaluation—the **raw return** on a portfolio.

The raw return on an investment portfolio, here denoted by R_p, is the total percentage return on the portfolio with no adjustment for risk or comparison to any benchmark. Calculating percentage returns was discussed in Chapter 1. The fact that a raw portfolio return does not reflect any consideration of risk suggests that its usefulness is limited when making investment decisions. After all, risk is important to almost every investor.

THE SHARPE RATIO

A basic measure of investment performance that includes an adjustment for risk is the Sharpe ratio, originally proposed by Nobel laureate William F. Sharpe. The **Sharpe ratio** is computed as a portfolio's risk premium divided by the standard deviation of the portfolio's return:

$$\text{Sharpe ratio} = \frac{R_p - R_f}{\sigma_p} \tag{13.1}$$

In this case, the portfolio risk premium is the raw portfolio return less a risk-free return, that is, $R_p - R_f$, which we know is the basic reward for bearing risk. In Chapter 1, we also referred to the risk premium as the *excess return*. Do not confuse the term *excess return* with the term *abnormal return*. *Abnormal return* is a measure of returns earned compared to other investments having similar risk. In this chapter, we explain how analysts attempt to convert excess return (or the risk premium) into measures of (risk-adjusted) abnormal return. Abnormal returns allow for a better comparison between investment choices.

The return standard deviation, σ_p, is a measure of risk, which we have discussed in previous chapters. More precisely, return standard deviation is a measure of the *total* risk (as opposed to systematic risk) for a security or a portfolio. Thus, the Sharpe ratio is a reward-to-risk ratio that focuses on total risk. Because total risk is used to make the adjustment, the Sharpe ratio is probably most appropriate for evaluating relatively diversified portfolios or for evaluating investments that will be purchased on a stand-alone basis.

EXAMPLE 13.1 **Look Sharpe**

Over a recent three-year period, the average annual return on a portfolio was 20 percent and the annual return standard deviation for the portfolio was 25 percent. During the same period, the average return on 90-day Treasury bills was 5 percent. What is the Sharpe ratio for this portfolio during this three-year period?

Referring to Equation 13.1, we calculate:

$$\text{Sharpe ratio} = \frac{.20 - .05}{.25} = .6$$

This indicates that the Sharpe ratio of portfolio excess return to total risk is .6.

Recall that standard deviation measures the movement away from an investment's average, or mean, return. As you might suspect, investors might not really be concerned with positive deviations from the mean. After all, who would fret over a higher-than-expected return on an investment? Investors are, however, greatly concerned with lower-than-expected returns. That is, investors are troubled by negative deviations from the mean.

Using the Sharpe ratio to measure performance could unduly penalize an investment manager that has generated positive abnormal returns. Positive abnormal returns generate volatility, but it is "good" volatility. Thus, many investors have turned to the Sortino ratio as another measure of performance.

The purpose of the Sortino ratio is to penalize the investment manager for having undesirable volatility caused by negative abnormal returns, i.e., downside risk. You calculate the Sortino ratio the same way you calculate the Sharpe ratio—with one important exception. In the Sortino ratio, you calculate the standard deviation using only returns that lie below the mean.

EXAMPLE 13.2

Sort It Out

Assume an investment fund had the following returns (in percent) over the last six years: 6, 12, −3, 8, 2, and 5. What is the Sortino ratio for this investment fund? How does it compare to the Sharpe ratio?

The first step is to calculate the mean return and deviations. The mean return is the arithmetic average, which is 5 percent (check this). To calculate the variance, recall that it is the sum of the squared differences divided by $(N-1)$. Remember, to get the standard deviation, we take the square root of the variance. However, for the Sortino ratio, we only include differences for returns below the mean, which in this case would be Year 3 and Year 5.

	Squared Differences	
	Sharpe	Sortino
Year 1	1	0
Year 2	49	0
Year 3	64	64
Year 4	9	0
Year 5	9	9
Year 6	0	0
Sum	132	73

For example, in Year 2, the return difference is $12 - 5 = 7$, so the squared difference is 49. Because the return is higher than average, however, it is not included in the Sortino ratio.

The variance used in the Sharpe ratio is $132/(6-1) = 26.4$, and the standard deviation is the square root, which is 5.14 percent. For the Sortino ratio, the variance is $73/(6-1) = 14.60$, and the standard deviation is 3.82. With these values, we can then calculate the Sharpe and Sortino ratios (assuming a risk-free rate of 3 percent):

$$\text{Sharpe ratio} = \frac{.05 - .03}{.0514} = .39$$

$$\text{Sortino ratio} = \frac{.05 - .03}{.0382} = .52$$

THE TREYNOR RATIO

Treynor ratio
Measures investment performance as the ratio of portfolio risk premium over portfolio beta.

Another standard measure of investment performance that includes an adjustment for systematic risk is the Treynor ratio (or index), originally suggested by Jack L. Treynor. The **Treynor ratio** is computed as a portfolio's risk premium divided by the portfolio's beta coefficient:

$$\text{Treynor ratio} = \frac{R_p - R_f}{\beta_p} \qquad (13.2)$$

As with the Sharpe ratio, the Treynor ratio is a reward-to-risk ratio. The key difference is that the Treynor ratio looks at systematic risk only, not total risk.

EXAMPLE 13.3

The Treynor Ratio

Over a three-year period, the average return on a portfolio was 20 percent and the beta for the portfolio was 1.25. During the same period, the average return on 90-day Treasury bills was 5 percent. What is the Treynor ratio for this portfolio during this period?

Referring to the Treynor ratio equation, we calculate:

$$\text{Treynor ratio} = \frac{.20 - .05}{1.25} = .12$$

This reveals that the Treynor ratio of portfolio excess return to portfolio beta is .12.

You may recall that we saw the Treynor ratio in a previous chapter when we discussed the security market line. There we said that in an active, competitive market, a strong argument can be made that all assets (and portfolios of those assets) should have the same Treynor ratio, that is, the same reward-to-risk ratio, where "risk" refers to systematic risk. To the extent that they don't, there is evidence that at least some portfolios have earned positive abnormal returns.

Both the Sharpe and Treynor ratios are relative measures. A relative measure means that no absolute number represents a "good" or "bad" performance. Rather, to evaluate the performance, the ratios must be compared to those of other managers—or to a benchmark index. So, it is possible for a manager to have negative Sharpe and Treynor ratios and still be considered "good." This odd result occurs if the benchmark also experiences a negative return for the period under review. In relative terms, the negative ratios of the manager could still outperform the benchmark. In evaluating these ratios, higher is better. We can compare funds relative to one another, as well as relative to the ratio for the fund's benchmark index.

JENSEN'S ALPHA

Jensen's alpha
Measures investment performance as the raw portfolio return less the return predicted by the capital asset pricing model.

Another common measure of investment performance that draws on capital asset pricing theory for its formulation is Jensen's alpha, proposed by Professor Michael C. Jensen. **Jensen's alpha** is computed as the raw portfolio return less the expected portfolio return predicted by the capital asset pricing model (CAPM).

Recall from a previous chapter that, according to the CAPM, a portfolio expected return, $E(R_p)$, can be written as:

$$E(R_p) = R_f + \left[E(R_M) - R_f\right] \times \beta_p \tag{13.3}$$

To compute Jensen's alpha, we compare the actual return, R_p, to the predicted return. The difference is the alpha, denoted α_p:

$$\text{Jensen's alpha} = \alpha_p = R_p - E(R_p)$$
$$= R_p - \left\{R_f + \left[E(R_M) - R_f\right] \times \beta_p\right\} \tag{13.4}$$

Jensen's alpha is easy to understand. It is the return above or below the security market line, and, in this sense, it can be interpreted as a measure of the amount by which the portfolio "beat the market." Alpha is therefore a measure of abnormal return. This interpretation is illustrated in Figure 13.1, which shows a portfolio with a positive (*A*), zero (*B*), and negative (*C*) alpha, respectively. As shown, a positive alpha is a good thing because the portfolio has a relatively high return given its level of systematic risk. Unlike the Sharpe and Treynor ratios, alphas can be compared in an absolute (as opposed to relative) sense. A Jensen's alpha of zero means the portfolio earned no abnormal return.

FIGURE 13.1   Jensen's Alpha

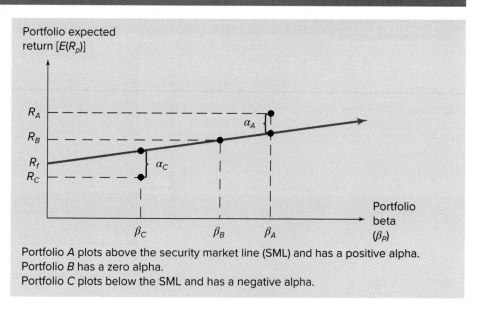

Portfolio *A* plots above the security market line (SML) and has a positive alpha.
Portfolio *B* has a zero alpha.
Portfolio *C* plots below the SML and has a negative alpha.

EXAMPLE 13.4	Jensen's Alpha

Over a three-year period, the average annual return on a portfolio was 20 percent and the beta for the portfolio was 1.25. During the same period, the average annual return on 90-day Treasury bills was 5 percent and the average return on the market portfolio was 15 percent. What is Jensen's alpha for this portfolio during this period?

Referring to the Jensen's alpha equation above, we calculate:

$$.20 - [.05 + 1.25(.15 - .05)] = .025$$

This shows that the portfolio had an alpha measure of portfolio abnormal return of 2.5 percent.

ANOTHER METHOD TO CALCULATE ALPHA

In an earlier chapter where we examined beta, we discussed the characteristic line, which graphs the relationship between the return of an investment (on the *y*-axis) and the return of the market or benchmark (on the *x*-axis). Recall that the slope of this line represents the investment's beta. Beta gives us the predicted movement in the return of the stock for a given movement in the market or benchmark. With only a slight modification, we can extend this approach to calculate an investment's alpha.

Consider the following equation, which rearranges Equation 13.3:

$$E(R_p) - R_f = \left[E(R_m) - R_f \right] \times \beta_p \tag{13.5}$$

If you compare this equation to the equation for the characteristic line, the only difference is that a risk-free rate appears. In fact, we could define the returns of the portfolio and the market as excess returns—meaning we subtract the risk-free rate from the returns of the portfolio. Doing so provides the following equation, which is similar to that of the characteristic line:

$$E(R_{p,RP}) = E(R_{m,RP}) \times \beta_p \tag{13.6}$$

As an example, consider the outcome when we evaluate an S&P 500 index fund. We expect that the returns on the fund (excluding any expenses) will match the returns of the market. In this case, the resulting graph of the returns of the fund versus the market would look something like Figure 13.2. The slope of this line is 1. This slope makes sense because the fund is exactly tracking the market (i.e., its beta is 1). Further, the alpha would be zero because the fund is earning no positive (or negative) abnormal return. Instead, it is returning exactly what the market does (and at the same level of risk).

FIGURE 13.2	Index Fund Excess Returns versus Market Excess Returns

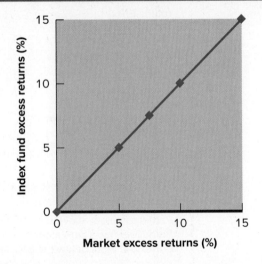

FIGURE 13.3   **Security Returns versus Market Returns**

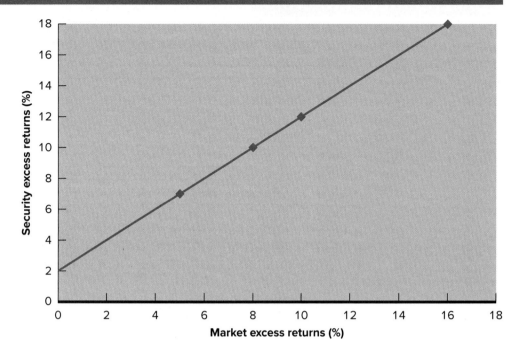

What would happen, though, if an actively managed fund took on the same amount of risk as the market (i.e., a beta of 1), but the fund earned exactly 2 percent more than the market every period? Well, if we graphed this hypothetical situation, it would look something like Figure 13.3. Notice that the slope (i.e., beta) is still 1, but the x-intercept is now 2. This is actually the fund's alpha, which we could verify using Equation 13.4.

Suppose that we have a fund whose returns are not consistently higher (or lower) than the market by a fixed amount. How could we estimate this fund's alpha? Well, similar to our previous beta calculation, we can apply a simple linear regression. In this case, we would regress the excess return of the investment on the excess return of the market. The intercept of this estimated equation is the fund's alpha. As an example of this approach, consider the nearby *Spreadsheet Analysis* box.

In the spreadsheet example, the intercept estimate is $-.0167$. This estimate is given in the same units as the original data, so the alpha is estimated to be -1.67 percent per year. We can verify this number using Equation 13.4. The average return of the security over the five-year period was 10 percent, while the average market return was 12 percent and the average risk-free rate was 2.6 percent. The beta of this security is .96, which is the coefficient estimate on the x variable. With these numbers:

$$\text{Alpha} = 10 - [2.6 + .96(12.0 - 2.6)] = -.0162, \text{ or } -1.62\%$$

You will notice that the regression method and Equation 13.4 produce similar, but not exact, alphas and betas. Part of the difference stems from using an average risk-free rate (as in Equation 13.4) versus using each year's risk-free rate (as in the regression technique). For example, if you use a risk-free rate of 2.6 percent for each year and run a new regression, the beta is .90. Inserting this beta into the equation above results in an alpha of -1.06 percent, which is about equal to the alpha estimate from this new regression, -1.08 percent.

Although Equation 13.4 is easy to use, the regression approach has some potential advantages over Equation 13.4. For example, the output of the regression will include a significance level for the alpha estimate. Having a significance level allows us to decide whether the alpha is statistically significantly different from zero. Using the t-statistic and p-value from our *Spreadsheet Analysis* box, we conclude that we are only 15 percent confident (1 minus the p-value) that this estimated alpha value is different from zero. The information ratio we discuss below provides a similar analysis.

SPREADSHEET ANALYSIS

	A	B	C	D	E	F
1						
2			**Using a Spreadsheet to Calculate Alpha**			
3						
4	To illustrate how to calculate alpha, we have replicated the returns of a security and the market					
5	over a five-year period. In addition, we have listed the risk-free rate. From these, we have					
6	calculated the excess return for the security and the market, which is simply the return over					
7	and above the risk-free rate.					
8						
9			Returns			Excess Returns	
10	Year	Security	Market	Risk-free	Security	Market
11	1	10%	8%	3%	7%	5%
12	2	−8%	−12%	2%	−10%	−14%
13	3	−4%	16%	4%	−8%	12%
14	4	40%	26%	1%	39%	25%
15	5	12%	22%	3%	9%	19%
16						
17	We then choose the regression function under the data analysis tab. We enter cells E11:E15 as					
18	the y-data and cells F11:F15 as the x-data. The resulting output is:					
19						
20	SUMMARY OUTPUT					
21						
22	*Regression Statistics*					
23	Multiple R	0.741036				
24	R Square	0.549135				
25	Adjusted R Square	0.398846				
26	Standard Error	0.152192				
27	Observations	5				
28						
29		*Coefficients*	*Standard Error*	*t Stat*	*p-value*	
30	Intercept	−0.016692	0.08296698	−0.20118	0.853423	
31	X Variable 1	0.964804	0.504734054	1.91151	0.1519	
32						

Source: Microsoft.

Another advantage of the regression approach is that you can pick the most relevant benchmark for the comparison. Data providers such as Morningstar report an alpha for most mutual funds, but they decide which index to use for comparison. For example, consider evaluating a value-oriented mutual fund. Most sources will quote alphas relative to the S&P 500 index. To be more specific, however, you might want to evaluate the fund versus a subset of the S&P 500, such as the S&P 500 Value index. Knowing how to calculate your own alpha is helpful in this case.

INFORMATION RATIO

Consider a mutual fund that reports a positive alpha. How do we know whether this alpha is statistically significantly different from zero or simply represents a result of random chance? We have discussed evaluating the significance level of the alpha estimate that comes from the regression. An alternative is to calculate the fund's **information ratio**.

information ratio
Alpha divided by tracking error.

tracking error
A measure of how volatile a portfolio is relative to its benchmark.

The information ratio is calculated as the difference between a fund's return and its benchmark, divided by its tracking error. The **tracking error** measures the volatility of the fund's returns relative to its benchmark. As an example, consider the fund we evaluated in the *Spreadsheet Analysis* box in the previous section. In the first year, the fund earned an excess return (return above the risk-free rate) of 7 percent and the market had an excess return of 5 percent. The difference between these two values is 2 percent. Over the five years, the differences between the excess returns are 2 percent, 4 percent, −20 percent, 14 percent, and −10 percent, respectively.

The average of these differences is −2.0 percent. The tracking error is the standard deviation of these return differences, which in this case is 13.2 percent (check this number for practice). So, this fund's information ratio is −2.0 percent divided by 13.2 percent, which is −.15. Because the standard deviation is always positive, the information ratio will always have the same sign as the difference in returns.

Consider two firms that have the same alpha. The information ratio provides a "tiebreaker" in the sense that we would prefer the one with the greatest chance of continued outperformance. For example, if two funds both have alphas of 1.5 percent, we would prefer the one with the higher information ratio because less risk (or volatility) is associated with this fund. For this fund, it would be more likely that the ability to generate positive abnormal return is repeatable, and not a result of random volatility.

EXAMPLE 13.5 | **Information Ratio**

A fund has a return difference of .8 percent and a tracking error of 5.9 percent. What is the fund's information ratio?

$$\text{Information ratio} = .8/5.9 = .14$$

R-SQUARED

R-squared
A portfolio's or security's squared correlation to the market or benchmark.

Elsewhere, we discussed the importance of an investment's correlation to other securities. Recall that correlation measures how returns for a particular security move relative to returns for another security. Correlation also plays a key role in performance measurement.

Suppose a particular fund has had a large alpha over the past three years. All else equal, we might say that this fund is a good choice. However, what if the fund is a sector-based fund that invests only in gold? Well, it is possible that the large alpha is due to a run-up in gold prices over the period and is not reflective of good management or future potential.

To evaluate this type of risk, we can calculate **R-squared**, which is the squared correlation of the fund to the market. For example, if this fund's correlation with the market is .6, then the R-squared value is $.6^2 = .36$. R-squared represents the percentage of the fund's movement that can be explained by movements in the market. Because correlation ranges only from −1 to +1, R-squared values will range from 0 to 100 percent. An R-squared of 100 indicates that all movements in the security are driven by the market, indicating a correlation of −1 or +1. This would be true for an index fund.

EXAMPLE 13.6 | **R-Squared**

A portfolio has a correlation to the market of .9. What is the R-squared? What percentage of the portfolio's return is driven by the market? What percentage comes from asset-specific risk?

$$R\text{-squared} = .9^2 = .81$$

This value implies that 81 percent of the portfolio's return is driven by the market. Thus, 19 percent (i.e., 100 − 81 percent) is driven by risk specific to the portfolio's individual holdings.

FINDING PERFORMANCE MEASURES

We have discussed a number of helpful performance metrics, so you might be wondering whether you have to calculate these for every fund or manager you want to evaluate. Thankfully, the answer is no. Given their importance, many data providers actually report the metrics for publicly traded funds. A good, free source for information on publicly traded funds is Morningstar (www.morningstar.com). Check out the Work the Web example in the next section.

Source: Bloomberg Finance L.P.

But what if you are trying to evaluate the performance of a privately managed portfolio. In this case, you might turn to a source such as Bloomberg, which has the ability to calculate performance on almost any custom portfolio. As an example, we evaluated the performance of the student-managed investment fund at Butler University over the last five years. Check out the results in Figure 13.4.

Looking at Figure 13.4, how would you judge the performance? Well, over the last three months, the fund has struggled, exhibiting a positive alpha and a Sharpe ratio that is lower than the market benchmark, which is the S&P 500 in this case. This performance is understandable. The end of 2021 saw the onslaught of the Omicron variant of the coronavirus. Most of the time, however, investors are more concerned about long-term performance. Through a long-term lens, the fund looks quite good. It had a positive alpha over the last two years, as well as a higher Sharpe ratio.

CHECK THIS

13.1a What is the Sharpe ratio of portfolio performance?

13.1b What is the difference between the Sharpe and Sortino ratios?

13.1c What is the Treynor ratio of portfolio performance?

13.1d What is Jensen's alpha?

13.1e Why can Jensen's alpha be interpreted as measuring by how much an investment portfolio beat the market?

13.1f What is the information ratio?

13.1g What is R-squared?

13.2 Comparing Performance Measures

Related Bloomberg Functions

XLTP XMFP   Excel Template:
Fund Holdings
Comparison Model

Table 13.1 presents investment performance data for three risky portfolios, A, B, and C, along with return data for the market portfolio and a risk-free portfolio, denoted by M and F, respectively. Based on the performance data in Table 13.1, Table 13.2 provides computed performance measures for Portfolios A, B, and C and the market portfolio, M. The market portfolio is a benchmark of investment performance. Often the familiar S&P 500 index is the adopted proxy for the market portfolio.

TABLE 13.1

Investment Performance Data

Portfolio	R_p	σ_p	β_p
A	12%	40%	.5
B	15	30	.75
C	20	22	1.4
M	15	15	1.0
F	5	0	.0

TABLE 13.2

Portfolio Performance Measurement

Portfolio	Sharpe Ratio	Treynor Ratio	Jensen's Alpha
A	.175	.14	2%
B	.333	.133	2.5
C	.682	.107	1
M	.667	.10	0

As shown in Table 13.2, the Sharpe ratio ranks the three risky portfolios in ascending order of performance: A, B, and C. By contrast, the Treynor ratio ranks these three risky portfolios in reverse order of performance: C, B, and A. Jensen's alpha yields another portfolio ranking altogether, with the ascending order of performance: C, A, and B.

The example above illustrates that the three performance measures can yield substantially different performance rankings. The fact that each of the three performance measures can produce such different results leaves us with the burning question: "Which performance measure should we use to evaluate portfolio performance?"

Well, the simple answer is: "It depends." If you wish to select a performance measure to evaluate an entire portfolio held by an investor, then the Sharpe ratio is appropriate. But if you wish to choose a performance measure to individually evaluate securities or portfolios for possible inclusion in a broader (or "master") portfolio, then either the Treynor ratio or Jensen's alpha is appropriate.

In broader terms, all three measures have strengths and weaknesses. As we have seen, Jensen's alpha is easy to interpret. Comparing Jensen's alpha and the Treynor ratio, we see that they are really very similar. The only difference is that the Treynor ratio standardizes everything, including any excess return, relative to beta. If you were to take Jensen's alpha and divide it by beta, then you would have a Jensen-Treynor alpha, which measures excess return relative to beta. The result would be similar to the information ratio.

A common weakness of the Jensen and Treynor measures is that both require a beta estimate. As we discussed in our last chapter, betas from different sources can differ substantially; as a result, what appears to be a positive alpha might just be due to a mismeasured beta.

The Sharpe ratio has the advantage that no beta is necessary, and standard deviations can be calculated unambiguously. The drawback is that total risk is frequently not what really matters. However, for a relatively well-diversified portfolio, most of the risk is systematic, so there's not much difference between total risk and systematic risk. For this reason, when we evaluate mutual funds, the Sharpe ratio is probably the most frequently used. Furthermore, if a mutual fund is not very diversified, then its standard deviation would be larger, resulting in a smaller Sharpe ratio. Thus, in effect, the Sharpe ratio penalizes a portfolio for being undiversified.

To see how these performance measures are used in practice, have a look at our nearby *Work the Web* box, which shows some actual numbers for a mutual fund.

The various performance measures we have discussed are frequently used to evaluate mutual funds or, more accurately, mutual fund managers. For example, the information below concerns the Fidelity Low-Priced Stock Fund, which is a small cap value fund. We obtained the numbers from www.morningstar.com by entering the fund's ticker symbol (FLPSX) and following the "Risk" tab.

For this fund, the beta is .99, so the degree of market risk is about average. The fund's alpha is −4.37 percent, which could indicate lagging past performance. The fund's standard deviation is 16.51 percent. Of course, we cannot judge these values in isolation.

The fund's R-squared is 84.56, which means that about 85 percent of its returns are driven by the market's return. This example illustrates the importance of being able to understand how to compute all these measures.

Risk & Volatility Measures ⓘ

Trailing	Investment	Category	Index
Alpha	-4.37	-9.00	—
Beta	0.99	1.17	—
R^2	84.56	81.46	—
Sharpe Ratio	0.76	0.56	0.62
Standard Deviation	16.51	20.07	19.00

USD | Investment as of Dec 31, 2021 | Category: Mid-Cap Value as of Dec 31, 2021 | Index: Morningstar US Mid Cap Brd Val TR USD as of Dec 31, 2021 | Calculation Benchmark: S&P 500 TR USD

Market Volatility Measures ⓘ

Capture Ratios	Investment	Category	Index
Upside	88	90	—
Downside	108	128	—

Drawdown	Investment %	Category %	Index %
Maximum	-28.04	-32.58	-32.82

Drawdown Peak Date	Drawdown Valley Date	Max Drawdown Duration
Jan 01, 2020	Mar 31, 2020	3 Months

USD | As of Dec 31, 2021 | Category: Mid-Cap Value | Index: Morningstar US Mid Cap Brd Val TR USD | Calculation Benchmark: S&P 500 TR USD | Drawdown as of Dec 31, 2021

Source: Morningstar, accessed January 2022.

EXAMPLE 13.7 — Picking Portfolios

Suppose you must invest all of your money in only one portfolio from choices A, B, or C as presented in Table 13.1. Which portfolio should you choose?

Because you can select only one portfolio, the Sharpe ratio measure of portfolio performance should be used. Referring to Table 13.2, we see that Portfolio C has the highest Sharpe ratio of excess return per unit of total risk. Therefore, Portfolio C should be chosen.

| EXAMPLE 13.8 | Picking Portfolios Again |

Suppose you are considering whether Portfolios A, B, and C presented in Table 13.1 should be included in a broader master portfolio. Should you select one, two, or all three of these portfolios to include in your master portfolio?

Because you are selecting portfolios for inclusion in a master portfolio, either the Treynor ratio or Jensen's alpha should be used. Suppose you decide to consider any portfolio that outperforms the market portfolio, M, based on either the Treynor ratio or Jensen's alpha. Referring to Table 13.2, we see that all three portfolios have Treynor ratios and Jensen's alphas greater than the market portfolio. Therefore, you should decide to include all three portfolios in your master portfolio.

For some specifics on the actual standards, check out www.gipsstandards.org.

GLOBAL INVESTMENT PERFORMANCE STANDARDS

As the previous example illustrates, comparing investments is sometimes difficult because the various performance metrics can provide different rankings. In the previous example, this difference was caused purely by the nature of the returns. Even if the various metrics provided a similar ranking, however, we could still make an incorrect choice in selecting an investment manager.

How so? Well, remember the adage "garbage in, garbage out." Sadly, this principle applies to the performance measurement process. In particular, our metrics are often based on returns (and other inputs) that are self-reported by the firms we are evaluating. This issue is particularly true for managers who do not offer a publicly traded portfolio.

To provide a measure of consistency in reported performance, the CFA™ Institute developed the Global Investment Performance Standards (GIPS). These standards provide investment firms with guidance for calculating and reporting their performance results to prospective (and current) clients. By standardizing the process, GIPS provide investors with the ability to make comparisons across managers.

Firms are not required by law to comply with GIPS. Rather, compliance with these standards is voluntary. Firms that do comply, however, are recognized by the CFA Institute, which might give these firms more credibility among potential investors.

SHARPE-OPTIMAL PORTFOLIOS

In this section, we show how to obtain a funds allocation with the highest possible Sharpe ratio. Such a portfolio is said to be "Sharpe optimal." The method is closely related to the procedure of obtaining a Markowitz efficient frontier discussed in a previous chapter. This comes as no surprise because both methods are used to achieve an optimal balance of risk and return for investment portfolios.

To illustrate the connection, have a look at Figure 13.5, which shows the investment opportunity set of risk-return possibilities for a portfolio of two assets, a stock fund and a bond fund. Now the question is: "Of all of these possible portfolios, which one is Sharpe optimal?" To find out, consider the portfolio labeled A in the figure. Notice that we have drawn a straight line from the risk-free rate running through this point.

What is the slope of this straight line? As always, the slope of a straight line is the "rise over the run." In this case, the return rises from the risk-free rate, R_f to the expected return on Portfolio A, so the rise is $E(R_A) - R_f$. At the same time, risk moves from zero for a risk-free asset up to the standard deviation on Portfolio A, so the run is $\sigma_A - 0 = \sigma_A$. Thus, the slope is $[E(R_A) - R_f]/\sigma_A$, which is just the Sharpe ratio for Portfolio A.

So, the slope of a straight line drawn from the risk-free rate to a portfolio in Figure 13.5 tells us the Sharpe ratio for that portfolio. This is always the case, even if there are many

FIGURE 13.5   The Sharpe-Optimal Portfolio

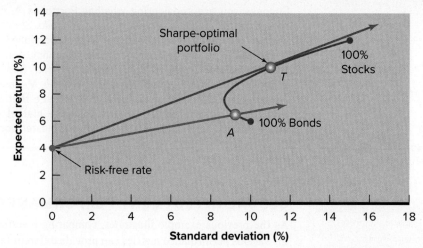

Portfolio T has the highest Sharpe ratio of any possible combination of these two assets, so it is Sharpe optimal.

assets, not just two. Finding the Sharpe-optimal portfolio thus boils down to finding the line with the steepest slope. Looking again at Figure 13.5, we quickly figure out that the line with the steepest slope is always going to be the one that just touches (i.e., is tangent to) the investment opportunity set. We have labeled this Portfolio T (for tangent).

We now have an interesting and important result. The Markowitz efficient frontier tells us which portfolios are efficient, but it does not tell us which of the efficient portfolios is the best. What Figure 13.5 shows is that, of those efficient portfolios, one is the very best, at least in the sense of being Sharpe optimal.

To illustrate how to find the Sharpe-optimal portfolio, consider stock and bond funds with returns of 12 percent and 6 percent, respectively. The standard deviations are 15 percent and 10 percent, respectively, and the correlation is .10. From our discussion in another chapter, we know that the expected return on a portfolio of two assets is given by:

$$E(R_p) = x_S E(R_S) + x_B E(R_B)$$

where x_S and x_B are the percentages invested in the stock and bond funds, respectively. Also from another chapter, the variance on a portfolio of these two assets is:

$$\sigma_P^2 = x_S^2 \sigma_S^2 + x_B^2 \sigma_B^2 + 2 x_S x_B \sigma_S \sigma_B \text{Corr}(R_S, R_B)$$

Putting it all together, the Sharpe ratio for our two-asset portfolio looks like this:

$$\frac{E(R_p) - R_f}{\sigma_P} = \frac{x_S E(R_S) + x_B E(R_B) - R_f}{\sqrt{x_S^2 \sigma_S^2 + x_B^2 \sigma_B^2 + 2 x_S x_B \sigma_S \sigma_B \text{Corr}(R_S, R_B)}} \tag{13.7}$$

Our task is to find the values of x_S and x_B that make this ratio as large as possible. This looks like a tough job, but, as our nearby *Spreadsheet Analysis* box shows, it can be done relatively easily. As shown there, assuming a risk-free interest rate of 4 percent, the highest possible Sharpe ratio is .553 based on a 70–30 mix between stocks and bonds.

Once the formulas are entered for the portfolio return, standard deviation, and Sharpe ratio, we can solve for the portfolio weights that give us the highest possible Sharpe ratio. We do not have to worry about the weight in bonds because the weight in bonds is equal to 1 minus the weight in stocks. You can use the Solver tool for this task.

You can see in the *Spreadsheet Analysis* box that we ask Solver to change the portfolio weight in stocks so that the maximum Sharpe ratio is obtained. Note that we also required

	A	B	C	D	E	F	G	H
1								
2			Optimal Sharpe Ratio with Two Risky Assets--Stocks and Bonds					
3								
4		Expected Returns:						
5		Stocks =	0.12					
6		Bonds =	0.06			Portfolio Return, E(Rp) =		0.102
7								
8		Risk-Free Rate =	0.04			Portfolio Standard Deviation, SD(Rp) =		0.112
9								
10		Standard Deviations:					Sharpe Ratio =	0.553
11		Stocks =	0.15					
12		Bonds =	0.10					
13						Portfolio Weights to Maximize Sharpe Ratio:		
14		Correlation between					Stocks =	0.7000
15		Stocks and Bonds =	0.10				Bonds =	0.3000
16							(= 1 – H14)	
17								
18	Formulas for Portfolio Return, Portfolio Standard Deviation, and Sharpe Ratio:							
19								
20		E(Rp) =	H14*C5+H15*C6					
21								
22		SD(Rp) =	SQRT(H14*H14*C11*C11+H15*H15*C12*C12+2*H14*H15*C15*C11*C12)					
23								
24	Sharpe Ratio = (E(Rp) - RF) / SD(Rp) = (H6-C8)/H8							
25								
26	Using SOLVER® to compute portfolio weights that maximize the Sharpe Ratio:							

Solver Parameters [?] [X]

Set Target Cell: H10

Equal To: ⦿ Max ⃝ Min ⃝ Value of: 0

By Changing Cells:
H14

Subject to the Constraints:
H14 >= 0
H15 >= 0

[Solve] [Close] [Guess] [Options] [Add] [Change] [Delete] [Reset All] [Help]

Source: Microsoft.

that the weights in stocks and bonds both be equal to or greater than zero, although this requirement isn't needed if we are able to go short. If any of the returns, standard deviations, or correlations are changed, the Solver tool must be rerun. Build this spreadsheet yourself and see if you get the same answer we did. Then, change the correlation between stocks and bonds to .20. Does the Sharpe ratio increase or decrease? What happens to the weights? For those of you who are "old school," Example 13.9 shows the formula that can be used to calculate the Sharpe-optimal weights.

EXAMPLE 13.9

Sharpe-Optimal Portfolio Calculations

Suppose you have the following expected return and risk information for stocks and bonds that will be used to form a Sharpe-optimal portfolio.

$$E(R_S) = .12$$
$$\sigma_S = .15$$
$$E(R_B) = .06$$
$$\sigma_B = .10$$
$$\text{Corr } (R_S, R_B) = .10$$
$$R_F = .04$$

In the case of just two risky assets (stocks and bonds), the formulas for the portfolio weights for the optimal Sharpe portfolio are:

$$x_S = \frac{\sigma_B^2 \times [E(R_S) - R_F] - \text{Corr } (R_S, R_B) \times \sigma_S \times \sigma_B \times [E(R_B) - R_F]}{\sigma_B^2 \times [E(R_S) - R_F] + \sigma_S^2 \times [E(R_B) - R_F] - [E(R_S) + E(R_B) - 2 \times R_F] \times \text{Corr } (R_S, R_B) \times \sigma_S \times \sigma_B}$$

and:

$$x_B = 1 - x_S$$

Calculate the Sharpe-optimal portfolio weights and the expected return and standard deviation for the Sharpe-optimal portfolio.

Inserting the expected return and risk information into these formulas yields the following optimal Sharpe portfolio weights for stocks and bonds:

$$x_S = \frac{.10^2 \times [.12 - .04] - .10 \times .15 \times .10 \times [.06 - .04]}{.10^2 \times [.12 - .04] + .15^2 \times [.06 - .04] - [.12 + .06 - 2 \times .04] \times .10 \times .15 \times .10}$$
$$= .70$$

and:

$$x_B = 1 - x_S = 1 - .70 = .30$$

With these results, we now have all the information needed to calculate the expected return and standard deviation for the Sharpe-optimal portfolio:

$$\begin{aligned} E(R_p) &= x_S E(R_S) + x_B E(R_B) \\ &= .70 \times .12 + .30 \times .06 \\ &= .102, \text{ or } 10.2\% \end{aligned}$$

$$\begin{aligned} \sigma_p &= \sqrt{x_S^2 \sigma_S^2 + x_B^2 \sigma_B^2 + 2 x_S x_B \sigma_S \sigma_B \text{Corr } (R_S, R_B)} \\ &= \sqrt{.70^2 \times .15^2 + .30^2 \times .10^2 + 2 \times .70 \times .30 \times .15 \times .10 \times .10} \\ &= .112, \text{ or } 11.2\% \end{aligned}$$

CHECK THIS

13.2a Explain the difference between systematic risk measured by beta and total risk measured by standard deviation. When are they essentially the same?

13.2b What is a Sharpe-optimal portfolio?

13.2c Among the many Markowitz efficient portfolios, which one is Sharpe optimal?

Investment Risk Management

Related Bloomberg Functions

PORT VR Portfolio and Risk
Analysis: Portfolio
Value at Risk (VaR)

**investment risk
management**
Concerns a money manager's
control over investment risks,
usually with respect to potential short-run losses.

Value-at-Risk (VaR)
Assesses risk by stating the
probability of a loss a portfolio
might experience within a fixed
time horizon with a specified
probability.

In the first part of this chapter, we discussed performance evaluation within a framework of optimizing the trade-off between risk and return for an investment portfolio.
In the remainder of this chapter, we examine **investment risk management** within the
framework of a money manager's concern over potential losses for an investment portfolio within a specific time horizon. We focus on what is known as the Value-at-Risk
approach.

VALUE-AT-RISK

An important goal of this chapter is to learn how to assess portfolio risk using **Value-at-Risk**. In
essence, the Value-at-Risk (usually abbreviated **VaR**) method involves evaluating the probability of a significant loss. The basic approach we describe here is widely used by many different
financial institutions.

The VaR measure of investment risk is closely related to something we discussed way back
in Chapter 1. There we said that if the returns on an investment follow a normal distribution,
then we can state the probability that a portfolio's return will be within a certain range.
Because a normal distribution is completely specified by its mean and standard deviation,
these are all that we need to state this probability.

For example, suppose you own an S&P 500 index fund. What is the probability of a return
of −8 percent or worse in a particular year? As we saw in Chapter 1, since 1926, the return
on the S&P 500 index has averaged about 12 percent per year with a standard deviation of
about 20 percent per year. A return of −8 percent is approximately one standard deviation
below the average $(.12 − .20 = −.08)$. We know from Chapter 1 (and basic statistics) that the
odds of being within one standard deviation are about 2/3, or .67. Being within one standard
deviation of the mean of .12 is defined as being between $.12 + .20$ and $.12 − .20$, i.e., between
$−.08$ and $+ .32$.

If the odds of being within this range are 2/3, then the odds of being outside this range are
about 1/3. Finally, if we are outside this range, then half of the time we'll be above this range
and half of the time we'll be below. Half of 1/3 is 1/6, so we'll experience a return of −.08 or
worse 1/6, or about 17 percent, of the time.

Putting it together, if you own an S&P 500 index fund, this risk assessment can be stated:

$$\text{Prob } (R_p \leq −.08) = 17\%$$

Your VaR statistic is thus a return of −.08 or worse with a probability of 17 percent. By the
way, here is an important note: When we say a loss of −.08 or worse, we mean that *one year
from now* your portfolio value is down by 8 percent or more.

EXAMPLE 13.10 | **VaR Risk Statistic**

You agree with J. P. Morgan that the stock market will fluctuate and have become concerned with how these fluctuations might affect your stock portfolio. Having read about
the VaR method for measuring investment risk, you decide to apply it to your portfolio.

Suppose you believe that there is a 5 percent chance of a return of −18 percent or
worse in the coming week. Mathematically, this risk assessment can be stated as:

$$\text{Prob } (R_p \leq −18\%) = 5\%$$

Taken together, this −18 percent (or worse) expected loss and 5 percent probability form
a VaR "statistic" for your stock portfolio.

13.3a What is the probability of realizing a portfolio return one or more standard deviations below the expected mean return?

13.3b What is the probability of realizing a portfolio return two or more standard deviations below the expected mean return?

13.3c Your portfolio has a mean return of 15 percent and a return standard deviation of 25 percent. What portfolio return is two standard deviations below the mean?

13.4 More on Computing Value-at-Risk

In this section we extend our discussion of computing VaR. Our main goal is to examine how to evaluate horizons that are shorter or longer than one year. The easiest way to do this is to take our earlier example concerning the S&P 500 and extend it a bit.

Once again, suppose you own an S&P 500 index fund. What is the probability of a loss of 30 percent or more over the next two years? To answer, we need to know the average two-year return and the average two-year return standard deviation. Getting the average two-year return is easy enough; we double the one-year average, so the two-year average return is $2 \times .12 = .24$, or 24 percent.

The two-year standard deviation is a little trickier. The two-year variance is double the one-year variance. In our case, the one-year variance is $.20^2 = .04$, and the two-year variance is thus .08. As always, to get the two-year standard deviation, we take the square root of this, which is .28, or 28 percent. The main thing to notice is that the two-year standard deviation is not double the one-year number. In fact, if you look at it, the two-year number is equal to the one-year number multiplied by the square root of 2, or 1.414.

Now we can answer our question. A two-year loss of 30 percent is roughly equal to the two-year average return of 24 percent less two standard deviations: $.24 - 2 \times .28 = -.32$. From Chapter 1, we know that the odds of being within two standard deviations are 95 percent, so the odds of being outside this range are 5 percent. The odds of being on the bad side (the loss side) are half that, namely, 2.5 percent.

In general, if we let T stand for the number of years, then the expected return on a portfolio over T years, $E(R_{p,T})$, can be written as:

$$E(R_{p,T}) = E(R_p) \times T \qquad (13.8)$$

Similarly, the standard deviation can be written as:

$$\sigma_{p,T} = \sigma_p \times \sqrt{T} \qquad (13.9)$$

If the time period is less than one year, T is a fraction of a year.

When you do a VaR analysis, you have to pick the time horizon and loss level probability. You can pick any probability you want, of course, but the most common are 1, 2.5, and 5 percent. We know that 2.5 percent, which is half of 5 percent, corresponds to two standard deviations (actually 1.96 to be more precise) below the expected return. To get the 1 percent and 5 percent numbers, you would need to find an ordinary z table to tell you the number of standard deviations. We'll save you the trouble. The 1 percent level is 2.326 standard deviations below the average and the 5 percent level is 1.645 "sigmas" below.

Wrapping up our discussion, the VaR statistics for these three levels can be summarized as follows:

$$\text{Prob}\left[R_{p,T} \le E(R_p) \times T - 2.326 \times \sigma_p \sqrt{T}\right] = 1\%$$
$$\text{Prob}\left[R_{p,T} \le E(R_p) \times T - 1.96 \times \sigma_p \sqrt{T}\right] = 2.5\% \qquad (13.10)$$
$$\text{Prob}\left[R_{p,T} \le E(R_p) \times T - 1.645 \times \sigma_p \sqrt{T}\right] = 5\%$$

Notice that if T, the number of years, is equal to 1, the 1 percent level corresponds to once in a century. Similarly, 5 percent is once every 20 years and 2.5 percent is once every 40 years. Examples 13.11 through 13.14 show you how to use VaR statistics.

EXAMPLE 13.11 **VaR Risk Statistic**

The Ned Kelley Hedge Fund focuses on investing in bank and transportation companies in Australia with above-average risk. The average annual return is 15 percent with an annual return standard deviation of 50 percent. What loss level can we expect over a two-year investment horizon with a probability of .17?

We assume a two-year expected return of 30 percent. The one-year variance is $.50^2 = .25$, so the two-year variance is .50. Taking the square root, we get a two-year standard deviation of .7071, or 70.71 percent. A loss probability of .17 corresponds to one standard deviation below the mean, so the answer to our question is $.30 - .7071 = -.4071$, a substantial loss. We can write this succinctly as:

$$\text{Prob } (R_p \le -40.71\%) = 17\%$$

Notice that there is a 17 percent chance of a 40.71 percent loss or worse over the next two years.

EXAMPLE 13.12 **VaR Risk Statistic**

Going back to the Ned Kelley Hedge Fund in our previous example, what loss level might we expect over six months with a probability of .17?

The six-month expected return is half of 15 percent, or 7.5 percent. The six-month standard deviation is $.5 \times \sqrt{1/2} = .3536$. So the answer to our question is $.075 - .3536 = -.2786$. Again, we can write this succinctly as:

$$\text{Prob } (R_p \le -27.86\%) = 17\%$$

Thus, there is a 17 percent chance of a 27.86 percent loss or worse over the next six months.

EXAMPLE 13.13 **A One-in-Twenty Loss**

For the Ned Kelley Hedge Fund specified in our previous examples, what is the expected loss for the coming year with a probability of 5 percent?

In this case, with an annual return mean of 15 percent and an annual return standard deviation of 50 percent, set $T = 1$ for a one-year time horizon and calculate this VaR statistic:

$$\text{Prob}\left[R_{p,1} \le E(R_p) \times 1 - 1.645\,\sigma_p \times \sqrt{1}\right] = \text{Prob } (R_{p,1} \le 15\% - 1.645 \times 50\%)$$
$$= \text{Prob } (R_{p,1} \le -67.25\%) = 5\%$$

Thus, we can expect a loss of 67.25 percent or worse over the next year with a 5 percent probability.

EXAMPLE 13.14

A One-in-a-Hundred Loss

For the Ned Kelley Hedge Fund specified in our previous examples, what is the expected loss for the coming month with a 1 percent probability?

Setting $T = 1/12$ for a one-month time horizon, we calculate this VaR statistic:

$$\text{Prob}\left[R_{p,T} \leq E(R_p) \times 1/12 - 2.326\sigma_p \times \sqrt{1/12}\right]$$
$$= \text{Prob}\left(R_{p,T} \leq 1.25\% - 2.326 \times 50\% \times .2887\right)$$
$$= \text{Prob}\left(R_{p,T} \leq -32.32\%\right) = 1\%$$

Thus, we can expect a loss of 32.32 percent or more with a 1 percent probability over the next month.

As an application of Value-at-Risk, consider the problem of determining VaR statistics for a Sharpe-optimal stock and bond portfolio. As with any VaR problem for a portfolio, remember that the key to the problem is to first determine the expected return and standard deviation for the portfolio. From our discussion in Chapter 11 and earlier in this chapter, we know that the expected return and standard deviation of a stock and bond portfolio are specified by these two equations:

$$E(R_p) = x_S E(R_S) + x_B E(R_B)$$
$$\sigma_p = \sqrt{x_S^2 \sigma_S^2 + x_B^2 \sigma_B^2 + 2 x_S x_B \sigma_S \sigma_B \text{Corr}(R_S, R_B)}$$

Thus, the problem of calculating VaR statistics for a Sharpe-optimal portfolio is the same for any portfolio once the appropriate portfolio weights are determined.

CHECK THIS

13.4a   Your portfolio allocates 40 percent of funds to ABC stock and 60 percent to XYZ stock. ABC has a return mean and standard deviation of 15 percent and 20 percent, respectively. XYZ stock has a return mean and standard deviation of 25 percent and 30 percent, respectively. What is the portfolio return standard deviation if the return correlation between ABC and XYZ is zero?

13.4b   Based on your answer to the previous question, what is the smallest expected loss for your portfolio in the coming year with a probability of 1 percent? What is the smallest expected loss for your portfolio in the coming month with a probability of 5 percent?

13.5 Summary and Conclusions

In this chapter, we covered the related topics of performance measurement and risk management.

1. **How to calculate the best-known portfolio evaluation measures.**

A. Our goal with performance measurement is essentially to rank investments based on their risk-adjusted, or abnormal, returns. We introduced and discussed the most frequently used tools to do this: the Sharpe ratio (and the related Sortino ratio), the Treynor ratio, Jensen's alpha, the information ratio, and R-squared.

B. As we saw, each has a somewhat different interpretation. Also, which one is the most suitable depends on the specific question to be answered.

2. **The strengths and weaknesses of these portfolio evaluation measures.**

A. Sharpe ratio. *Strength:* No beta estimate is necessary, and standard deviations can be calculated unambiguously. *Weakness:* Total risk is frequently not what really matters.

However, for a relatively well-diversified portfolio, most of the risk is systematic, so there's not much difference between total risk and systematic risk.

B. Treynor ratio. *Strength:* The Treynor ratio standardizes everything, including any excess return, relative to beta. *Weakness:* The Treynor measure requires a beta estimate.

C. Jensen's alpha. *Strength:* Jensen's alpha is easy to interpret. *Weakness:* The Jensen measure requires a beta estimate. Betas from different sources can differ substantially, and, as a result, what appears to be a positive alpha might just be due to a mismeasured beta.

D. The information ratio and *R*-squared help to determine the accuracy of the other metrics, particularly alpha.

3. How to calculate a Sharpe-optimal portfolio.

A. The slope of a straight line drawn from the risk-free rate to a portfolio on a return–standard deviation graph tells us the Sharpe ratio for that portfolio. This is always the case, even with many assets, not just two. The portfolio with the highest slope is called Sharpe optimal.

B. Finding the Sharpe-optimal portfolio boils down to finding the portfolio with the steepest slope. The line with the steepest slope is always going to be the one that just touches (i.e., is tangent to) the investment opportunity set. That portfolio is sometimes labeled Portfolio T (for tangent).

C. The Markowitz efficient frontier tells us which portfolios are efficient; it does not tell us which one of the efficient portfolios is the best. Given a risk-free rate, the Sharpe-optimal portfolio is the best portfolio, at least as measured by the Sharpe ratio.

4. How to calculate and interpret Value-at-Risk.

A. We introduce the popular and widely used method to assess portfolio risk called "Value-at-Risk," or VaR. Here the goal is usually to assess the probability of a large loss within a fixed time frame.

B. Investors use this tool both to better understand the risks of their existing portfolios and to assess the risks of potential investments. The VaR measure is closely related to something we discussed way back in Chapter 1.

C. If the returns on an investment follow a normal distribution, then we can state the probability that a portfolio's return will be within a certain range. Because a normal distribution is completely specified by its mean and standard deviation, these two statistics are all that we need to state the probability of a loss of a certain size.

GETTING DOWN TO BUSINESS

This chapter covered the essentials of performance evaluation and investment risk management. With thousands of mutual funds and investment companies competing for performance while trying to control risk, these topics are especially important. If you wish to learn more about these subjects, a good place to start is the internet.

A useful and informative website on investment performance analysis is that of Professor William F. Sharpe (stanford.edu/~wfsharpe), the Nobel laureate who, among his other notable accomplishments, created the Sharpe ratio. You can also consult www.garp.org, which is the website of the Global Association of Risk Professionals (GARP), an independent organization of financial risk management practitioners and researchers.

Because financial institutions generally prefer that their risk profiles be kept private, a large part of the world of financial risk management is hidden from public view. Nevertheless, the field of risk management is large and growing. If you want to know more about this fascinating subject, an interesting website that provides a wealth of information is the Society of Risk Management Consultants (srmcsociety.org).

For the latest information on the real world of investments, visit us at jmdinvestments.blogspot.com.

Key Terms

information ratio 438

investment risk management 447

Jensen's alpha 435

performance evaluation 432

raw return 432

R-squared 439

Sharpe ratio 433

tracking error 438

Treynor ratio 434

Value-at-Risk (VaR) 447

Related Bloomberg Functions

PORT	Portfolio and Risk Analytics, 13.1
HFA	Historical Fund Analysis, 13.1
FREP	Fund Reporting, 13.1
FPC	Fund Performance, 13.1
BETA	Historical Beta, 13.1
EQRP	Equity Risk Premium, 13.1
HRA	Historical Regression Analysis, 13.1
CORR	My Correlation Matrices, 13.1
XLTP XMFP	Excel Template: Fund Holdings Comparison Model, 13.2
PORT VR	Portfolio and Risk Analysis: Portfolio Value at Risk (VaR), 13.3

Chapter Review Problems and Self-Test

1. **Performance Measures (LO1, CFA5)**   Compute Sharpe ratios, Treynor ratios, and Jensen's alphas for Portfolios A, B, and C based on the following returns data, where M and F stand for the market portfolio and risk-free rate, respectively:

Portfolio	R_p	σ_p	β_p
A	10%	30%	.75
B	15	25	1.00
C	20	40	1.50
M	15	15	1.00
F	5	0	.00

2. **Value-at-Risk (VaR) (LO4, CFA2)**   A portfolio manager believes her $100 million stock portfolio will have a 10 percent return standard deviation during the coming week and that her portfolio's returns are normally distributed. What is the probability of her losing $10 million or more? What is the dollar loss expected with a 5 percent probability? What is the dollar loss expected with a 1 percent probability?

Answers to Self-Test Problems

1. Using Equations 13.1, 13.2, and 13.4 yields these performance measurement values:

Portfolio	Sharpe Ratio	Treynor Ratio	Jensen's Alpha
A	.167	.0667	−2.5%
B	.400	.10	0
C	.375	.10	0
M	.667	.10	0

2. Because a mean is not given, but the time horizon is only one week, we can assume a mean of zero. Thus, the probability of a $10 million or greater loss is the probability of a loss of one or more return standard deviations. For a normal distribution, a realization 1.645 or more standard deviations below the mean occurs with about a 5 percent probability, yielding a potential loss of at least 1.645 × $10 million = $16.45 million. For a normal distribution, a realization 2.326 or more standard deviations below the mean occurs with about a 1 percent probability, yielding a potential loss of at least 2.326 × $10 million = $23.26 million.

Test Your Investment Quotient

IQ

1. **Beta and Standard Deviation (LO2, CFA1)**   Beta and standard deviation differ as risk measures in that beta measures:
   a. Only unsystematic risk, whereas standard deviation measures total risk.
   b. Only systematic risk, whereas standard deviation measures total risk.
   c. Both systematic and unsystematic risk, whereas standard deviation measures only unsystematic risk.
   d. Both systematic and unsystematic risk, whereas standard deviation measures only systematic risk.

Answer Questions 2 through 7 based on the following information:

Risk and Return Data			
Portfolio	Average Return	Standard Deviation	Beta
P	17%	20%	1.1
Q	24	18	2.1
R	11	10	.5
S	16	14	1.5
S&P 500	14	12	1.0

A pension fund administrator wants to evaluate the performance of four portfolio managers. Each manager invests only in U.S. common stocks. During the most recent five-year period, the average annual total return on the S&P 500 was 14 percent and the average annual rate on Treasury bills was 8 percent. The table above shows risk and return measures for each portfolio.

2. **Treynor Ratio (LO1, CFA5)**   The Treynor portfolio performance measure for Portfolio P is:
   a. 8.18.
   b. 7.62.
   c. 6.00.
   d. 5.33.

3. **Sharpe Ratio (LO1, CFA5)**   The Sharpe portfolio performance measure for Portfolio Q is:
   a. .45.
   b. .89.
   c. .30.
   d. .57.

4. **Jensen's Alpha (LO1, CFA5)**   The Jensen's alpha portfolio performance measure for Portfolio R is:
   a. 2.4 percent.
   b. 3.4 percent.
   c. 0 percent.
   d. −1 percent.

5. **Treynor Ratio (LO1, CFA5)**   Which portfolio has the highest Treynor ratio?
   a. P
   b. Q
   c. R
   d. S

6. **Sharpe Ratio (LO1, CFA5)** Which portfolio has the highest Sharpe ratio?
   a. P
   b. Q
   c. R
   d. S

7. **Jensen's Alpha (LO1, CFA5)** Which portfolio has the highest Jensen's alpha?
   a. P
   b. Q
   c. R
   d. S

8. **Sortino Ratio (LO1, CFA5)** The primary difference between the Sharpe ratio and the Sortino ratio is that the Sortino ratio considers:
   a. Total volatility.
   b. Only systematic risk.
   c. Only upside volatility.
   d. Only downside volatility.

9. **Normal Distribution (LO4, CFA1)** Given a data series that is normally distributed with a mean of 100 and a standard deviation of 10, about 95 percent of the numbers in the series will fall within:
   a. 60 to 140.
   b. 70 to 130.
   c. 80 to 120.
   d. 90 to 110.

10. **Normal Distribution (LO4, CFA1)** Given a data series that is normally distributed with a mean of 100 and a standard deviation of 10, about 99 percent of the numbers in the series will fall within:
    a. 60 to 140.
    b. 80 to 120.
    c. 70 to 130.
    d. 90 to 110.

11. **Normal Distribution (LO4, CFA1)** A normal distribution is completely specified by its:
    a. Mean and correlation.
    b. Variance and correlation.
    c. Variance and standard deviation.
    d. Mean and standard deviation.

12. **Standard Normal Distribution (LO4, CFA4)** A normal random variable is transformed into a standard normal random variable by:
    a. Subtracting its mean and dividing by its standard deviation.
    b. Adding its mean and dividing by its standard deviation.
    c. Subtracting its mean and dividing by its variance.
    d. Adding its mean and multiplying by its standard deviation.

13. **Standard Normal Distribution (LO4, CFA4)** The probability that a standard normal random variable is either less than -1 or greater than $+1$ is:
    a. 2 percent.
    b. 5 percent.
    c. 10 percent.
    d. 31.74 percent.

14. **Standard Normal Distribution (LO4, CFA4)** The probability that a standard normal random variable is either less than -1.96 or greater than $+1.96$ is approximately:
    a. 2 percent.
    b. 5 percent.
    c. 10 percent.
    d. 31.74 percent.

15. **Value-at-Risk (VaR) (LO4, CFA4)** The Value-at-Risk statistic for an investment portfolio states:
    a. The probability of an investment loss.
    b. The value of the risky portion of an investment portfolio.
    c. The smallest investment loss expected with a specified probability.
    d. The largest investment loss expected with a specified probability.

Concept Questions

1. **Performance Evaluation Ratios (LO2, CFA5)** Explain the difference between the Sharpe ratio and the Treynor ratio.
2. **Performance Evaluation Measures (LO2, CFA5)** What is a common weakness of Jensen's alpha and the Treynor ratio?
3. **Jensen's Alpha (LO2, CFA5)** Explain the relationship between Jensen's alpha and the security market line (SML) of the capital asset pricing model (CAPM).
4. **Sharpe Ratio (LO2, CFA5)** What are one advantage and one disadvantage of the Sharpe ratio?
5. **Comparing Alphas (LO2, CFA5)** Suppose that two investments have the same alpha. What things might you consider to help you determine which investment to choose?
6. **Optimal Sharpe Ratio (LO3, CFA5)** What is meant by a Sharpe-optimal portfolio?
7. **Sortino Ratio (LO1, CFA5)** What is the difference between the Sharpe ratio and the Sortino ratio?
8. **Value-at-Risk (VaR) Statistic (LO4, CFA2)** Explain the meaning of a Value-at-Risk statistic in terms of a smallest expected loss and the probability of such a loss.
9. **Value-at-Risk (VaR) Statistic (LO4, CFA2)** The largest expected loss for a portfolio is −20 percent with a probability of 95 percent. Relate this statement to the Value-at-Risk statistic.
10. **Performance Measures (LO2, CFA5)** Most sources report alphas and other metrics relative to a standard benchmark, such as the S&P 500. When might this method be an inappropriate comparison?

Questions and Problems

Core Questions

1. **Standard Deviation (LO4, CFA2)** You find a particular stock has an annual standard deviation of 54 percent. What is the standard deviation for a two-month period?
2. **Standard Deviation (LO4, CFA2)** You find the monthly standard deviation of a stock is 8.60 percent. What is the annual standard deviation of the stock?
3. **Performance Evaluation (LO1, CFA5)** You are given the following information concerning three portfolios, the market portfolio, and the risk-free asset:

Portfolio	R_p	σ_p	β_p
X	12%	29%	1.25
Y	11	24	1.10
Z	8	14	.75
Market	10	19	1.00
Risk-free	4	0	0

What are the Sharpe ratio, Treynor ratio, and Jensen's alpha for each portfolio?

4. **Information Ratio (LO1, CFA5)** Assume that the tracking error of Portfolio X in Problem 3 is 9.2 percent. What is the information ratio for Portfolio X?
5. **R-Squared (LO1, CFA5)** In Problem 3, assume that the correlation of returns on Portfolio Y to returns on the market is .75. What percentage of Portfolio Y's return is driven by the market?
6. **Information Ratio (LO1, CFA5)** The Layton Growth Fund has an average return that is 2.1 percent higher than the market benchmark. You have determined that Layton's information ratio is .5. What must Layton's tracking error be relative to its benchmark?
7. **Value-at-Risk (VaR) Statistic (LO4, CFA2)** DW Co. stock has an annual return mean and standard deviation of 12 percent and 30 percent, respectively. What is the smallest expected loss in the coming year with a probability of 5 percent?
8. **Value-at-Risk (VaR) Statistic (LO4, CFA2)** Woodpecker, Inc., stock has an annual return mean and standard deviation of 18 percent and 44 percent, respectively. What is the smallest expected loss in the coming month with a probability of 2.5 percent?

9. **Value-at-Risk (VaR) Statistic (LO4, CFA2)** Your portfolio allocates equal funds to the DW Co. and Woodpecker, Inc., stocks referred to in Problems 7 and 8. The return correlation between DW Co. and Woodpecker, Inc., is zero. What is the smallest expected loss for your portfolio in the coming month with a probability of 2.5 percent?

10. **Sharpe Ratio (LO1, CFA5)** What is the formula for the Sharpe ratio for a stock and bond portfolio with a zero correlation between stock and bond returns?

11. **Sharpe Ratio (LO1, CFA5)** What is the formula for the Sharpe ratio for an equally weighted portfolio of stocks and bonds?

12. **Sharpe Ratio (LO1, CFA5)** What is the formula for the Sharpe ratio for a portfolio of stocks and bonds with equal expected returns, i.e., $E(R_S) = E(R_B)$, and a zero return correlation?

13. **Value-at-Risk (VaR) Statistic (LO4, CFA2)** A stock has an annual return of 11 percent and a standard deviation of 54 percent. What is the smallest expected loss over the next year with a probability of 1 percent? Does this number make sense?

14. **Value-at-Risk (VaR) Statistic (LO4, CFA2)** For the stock in Problem 13, what is the smallest expected gain over the next year with a probability of 1 percent? Does this number make sense? What does this tell you about stock return distributions?

15. **Value-at-Risk (VaR) Statistic (LO4, CFA2)** Tyler Trucks stock has an annual return mean and standard deviation of 10 percent and 26 percent, respectively. Michael Moped Manufacturing stock has an annual return mean and standard deviation of 18 percent and 62 percent, respectively. Your portfolio allocates equal funds to Tyler Trucks stock and Michael Moped Manufacturing stock. The return correlation between Tyler Trucks and Michael Moped Manufacturing is .5. What is the smallest expected loss for your portfolio in the coming month with a probability of 5 percent?

16. **Value-at-Risk (VaR) Statistic (LO4, CFA2)** Using the same return means and standard deviations as in Problem 15 for Tyler Trucks and Michael Moped Manufacturing stocks, but assuming a return correlation of −.5, what is the smallest expected loss for your portfolio in the coming month with a probability of 5 percent?

17. **Value-at-Risk (VaR) Statistic (LO4, CFA2)** Your portfolio allocates equal amounts to three stocks. All three stocks have the same mean annual return of 14 percent. Annual return standard deviations for these three stocks are 30 percent, 40 percent, and 50 percent. The return correlations among all three stocks are zero. What is the smallest expected loss for your portfolio in the coming year with a probability of 1 percent?

18. **Optimal Sharpe Portfolio Value-at-Risk (LO3, CFA2)** You are constructing a portfolio of two assets, Asset A and Asset B. The expected returns of the assets are 12 percent and 15 percent, respectively. The standard deviations of the assets are 29 percent and 48 percent, respectively. The correlation between the two assets is .25 and the risk-free rate is 5 percent. What is the optimal Sharpe ratio in a portfolio of the two assets? What is the smallest expected loss for this portfolio over the coming year with a probability of 2.5 percent?

Answer Problems 19 through 21 based on the following information.

You have been given the following return information for a mutual fund, the market index, and the risk-free rate. You also know that the return correlation between the fund and the market is .97.

Year	Fund	Market	Risk-Free
2018	−15.2%	−24.5%	1%
2019	25.1	19.5	3
2020	12.4	9.4	2
2021	6.2	7.6	4
2022	−1.2	−2.2	2

19. **Performance Metrics (LO1, CFA5)** What are the Sharpe and Treynor ratios for the fund?

20. **Jensen's Alpha (LO1, CFA5)** Calculate Jensen's alpha for the fund, as well as its information ratio.

21. **Sortino Ratio (LO1, CFA5)** What is the Sortino ratio for the fund and the market?

Spreadsheet Problems

22. **Optimal Sharpe Ratio (LO3, CFA4)** You are constructing a portfolio of two assets. Asset A has an expected return of 12 percent and a standard deviation of 24 percent. Asset B has an expected return of 18 percent and a standard deviation of 54 percent. The correlation between the two assets is .20 and the risk-free rate is 4 percent. To achieve the highest possible Sharpe ratio, what should be the weight of each asset in the portfolio?

23. **Performance Metrics (LO1, CFA1)** You have been given the following return information for two mutual funds (Papa and Mama), the market index, and the risk-free rate.

Year	Papa Fund	Mama Fund	Market	Risk-Free
2018	−12.6%	−22.6%	−24.5%	1%
2019	25.4	18.5	19.5	3
2020	8.5	9.2	9.4	2
2021	15.5	8.5	7.6	4
2022	2.6	−1.2	−2.2	2

Calculate the Sharpe ratio, Treynor ratio, Jensen's alpha, information ratio, and R-squared for both funds and determine which is the best choice for your portfolio.

CFA Exam Review by Kaplan Schweser

[CFA1, CFA5]
Kelli Blakely is a portfolio manager for the Miranda Fund, a core large-cap equity fund. The market proxy and benchmark for performance measurement is the S&P 500. Although the Miranda portfolio generally mirrors the S&P sector weightings, Ms. Blakely is allowed a significant amount of flexibility.

Ms. Blakely was able to produce exceptional returns last year (as outlined in the table below). Much of this performance is attributable to her pessimistic outlook, which caused her to change her asset class exposure to 50 percent stocks and 50 percent cash. The S&P's allocation was 97 percent stocks and 3 percent cash. The risk-free rate of cash returns was 2 percent.

	Miranda	S&P 500
Return	10.2%	−22.5%
Standard deviation	37%	44%
Beta	1.10	

1. What are the Sharpe ratios for the Miranda Fund and the S&P 500?

	Miranda	S&P 500
a.	.2216	−.5568
b.	.3515	−.2227
c.	.0745	−.2450

2. What are the Treynor measures for the Miranda Fund and the S&P 500?

	Miranda	S&P 500
a.	.2216	−.5568
b.	.3515	−.2227
c.	.0745	−.2450

3. What is the Jensen alpha for the Miranda Fund?
   a. .2216
   b. .3515
   c. .0745

Bloomberg Exercises

1. Find the beta and risk premium for the Vanguard International Value Fund (VTRIX). **(BETA, EQRP)**

2. Conduct a regression analysis for the returns of the Fidelity Large Cap Stock Fund (FLCSX) on the S&P 500. **(HRA)**

3. Initiate a performance analysis of the Templeton Global Bond Fund (TPINX). **(PORT)**

4. Download a mutual fund performance model into Excel. **(XLTP XMFP)**

What's on the Web?

1. **Morningstar Ratings** Go to www.morningstar.com and find out how to interpret the "Bear Market Percentile Rank." While you are at the website, also learn more about the best-fit index numbers. What do the best-fit index numbers mean?

2. **Morningstar Risk** Go to www.morningstar.com and find out how Morningstar calculates the "Morningstar Rating" category. What percentage of funds are rated as Below Average by Morningstar? What percentage are rated Average?

3. **Modified VaR** Go to www.alternativesoft.com and learn about modified VaR proposed at the website. Why would you want to use a modified VaR?

4. **VaR Data** You can calculate your own VaR statistics by downloading recent security price data off the web. Go to finance.yahoo.com and enter the ticker symbol ^GSPC (don't forget the caret when entering ticker symbols for stock indexes). Now click on the link for "Historical Data." There you will see that you can get daily, weekly, or monthly price data for any period by setting the beginning and ending dates as indicated under "Historical Prices." You can also download the price data into a spreadsheet. Go to the bottom of the page and click on the "Download Data" link. With the downloaded price data, you will need to calculate returns and then return averages and standard deviations. Using these, calculate the VaR statistics for your data as discussed and illustrated in this chapter.

Futures Contracts

"There are two times in a man's life when he should not speculate: when he can't afford it and when he can."

–Mark Twain

"When you bet on a sure thing—hedge!"

–Robert Half

Learning Objectives

You will derive many future benefits if you have a good understanding of:

1. The basics of futures markets and how to obtain price quotes for futures contracts.

2. The risks involved in futures market speculation.

3. How cash prices and futures prices are linked.

4. How futures contracts can be used to transfer price risk.

Futures contracts can be used for speculation or for risk management. For would-be speculators, Mark Twain's advice is well worth considering. In addition to their risk dimension, trading in futures contracts adds a time dimension to commodity markets. A futures contract separates the date of the agreement—when a delivery price is specified—from the date when delivery and payment actually occur. Both buyers and sellers can manage risk effectively when these dates are separated. This fundamental feature of futures contracts is one of the reasons that futures contracts have withstood the test of time.

This chapter covers modern-day futures contracts. The first sections discuss the basics of futures contracts and how their prices are quoted in the financial press. From there, we move into a general discussion of how futures contracts are used for speculation and risk management. We also present the theoretical relationship between current cash prices and futures prices.

CFA™ Exam Topics in This Chapter:

1. Derivative markets and instruments (L1, S15)
2. Basics of derivatives pricing and valuation (L1, S15)
3. Introduction to alternative investments (L1, S16)
4. Pricing and valuation of forward commitments (L2, S13)
5. Swaps, forwards, and futures strategies (L3, S4)

Go to Connect for a guide that aligns your textbook with CFA readings.

14.1 Futures Contract Basics

forward contract
Agreement between a buyer and a seller, who both commit to a transaction at a future date at a price set by negotiation today.

futures contract
Contract between a seller and a buyer specifying a commodity or financial instrument to be delivered and price paid at contract maturity. Futures contracts are managed through an organized futures exchange.

futures price
Price negotiated by buyer and seller at which the underlying commodity or financial instrument will be delivered and paid for to fulfill the obligations of a futures contract.

By definition, a **forward contract** is a formal agreement between a buyer and a seller who both commit to a commodity transaction at a future date at a price set by negotiation today. The genius of forward contracting is that it allows a producer to sell a product to a willing buyer before it is actually produced. By setting a price today, both buyer and seller remove price uncertainty as a source of risk. With less risk, buyers and sellers mutually benefit and commerce is stimulated. This principle has been understood and practiced for centuries.

Futures contracts represent a step beyond forward contracts. Futures contracts and forward contracts accomplish the same economic task, which is to specify a price today for future delivery. This specified price is called the **futures price**, or *settle price*. However, while a forward contract can be struck between any two parties, futures contracts are managed through organized futures exchanges. Sponsorship through a futures exchange is a major distinction between a futures contract and a forward contract.

As we discuss later, because futures contracts are listed on exchanges, they come with many standardized features, such as the size of the contract and the delivery date. This standardization comes with trade-offs relative to forward contracts. For example, on the negative side, the fixed size of the futures contract means that buyers and sellers might not be able to match a particular position exactly.

On the positive side, the standardization of futures contracts facilitates the trading of contracts after they are created—thereby increasing liquidity. Further, because the exchange ensures that both sides of the trade can cover any potential losses they might incur, futures contracts have little counterparty risk. For most investors, the advantages of futures contracts well outweigh the disadvantages.

MODERN HISTORY OF FUTURES TRADING

The Chicago Board of Trade (CBOT) was the first organized futures exchange in the United States. The CBOT was established in 1848 and grew with the westward expansion of American ranching and agriculture. The CBOT became the largest, most active futures exchange in the world. Other early American futures exchanges include the MidAmerica Commodity Exchange (founded in 1868), New York Cotton Exchange (1870), New York Mercantile Exchange (1872), Chicago Mercantile Exchange (1874), Minneapolis Grain Exchange (1881), New York Coffee Exchange (1882), and Kansas City Board of Trade (1882).

For more than 100 years, American futures exchanges devoted their activities exclusively to commodity futures. However, a revolution began in the 1970s with the introduction of financial futures. Unlike commodity futures, which call for delivery of a physical commodity, financial futures require delivery of a financial instrument. The first financial futures were foreign currency contracts introduced in 1972 at the International Monetary Market (IMM), a division of the Chicago Mercantile Exchange (CME).

Next came interest rate futures, introduced at the CBOT in 1975. An interest rate futures contract specifies delivery of a fixed-income security. For example, an interest rate futures contract might specify a U.S. Treasury bill, note, or bond as the underlying instrument. Two of the most actively traded futures contracts are based on interest rates: Eurodollars (traded at the CME) and Treasury notes (traded at the CBOT).

Stock index futures were introduced in 1982 at the Kansas City Board of Trade (KBT), the Chicago Mercantile Exchange, and the New York Futures Exchange (NYFE). A stock index futures contract specifies a particular stock market index as its underlying instrument.

Financial futures have been so successful that they now constitute the bulk of all futures trading. This success is largely attributed to the fact that financial futures have become an indispensable tool for financial risk management by corporations and portfolio managers. As we will see, futures contracts can be used to reduce risk through hedging strategies or to increase risk through speculative strategies. In this chapter, we discuss futures contracts generally, but, because this text deals with financial markets, we will ultimately focus on financial futures.

During 2007, several important commodity exchanges merged. For example, in January 2007, the Intercontinental Exchange (ICE), which listed mainly energy contracts, purchased the New York Board of Trade (NYBOT) for about $1 billion. The NYBOT listed "soft" commodities such as coffee, sugar, cocoa, and cotton. The NYBOT was once the New York Cotton Exchange (NYCE). Through previous mergers the NYBOT had acquired the Coffee, Sugar, and Cocoa Exchange (CSCE) as well as the New York Futures Exchange (NYFE).

On July 9, 2007, the Chicago Mercantile Exchange finalized its merger with its long-time rival, the Chicago Board of Trade. In this whopper of a deal, the CME bought the CBOT for about $8 billion. The book value of the new company, The CME Group, Inc., was about $26 billion. Then, in 2008, the newly formed CME Group acquired the New York Mercantile Exchange (NYMEX), giving it greater exposure to metals and petroleum-based futures. On December 3, 2012, the CME Group announced it had completed its acquisition of the Kansas City Board of Trade.

FUTURES CONTRACT FEATURES

Futures contracts are a type of derivative security because the value of the contract is derived from the value of an underlying instrument. For example, the value of a futures contract to buy or sell gold is derived from the market price of gold. However, because a futures contract represents a zero-sum game between a buyer and a seller, the net value of a futures contract is always zero. That is, any gain realized by the buyer is exactly equal to a loss realized by the seller, and vice versa.

Futures are contracts and, in practice, exchange-traded futures contracts are standardized to facilitate convenience in trading and price reporting. Standardized futures contracts have a set contract size specified according to the particular underlying instrument. For example, a standard gold futures contract specifies a contract size of 100 troy ounces. This means that a single gold futures contract obligates the seller to deliver 100 troy ounces of gold to the buyer at contract maturity. In turn, the contract also obligates the buyer to accept the gold delivery and pay the negotiated futures price for the delivered gold.

To properly understand a futures contract, we must know the specific terms of the contract. In general, futures contracts must stipulate at least the following five contract terms:

1. The identity of the underlying commodity or financial instrument.
2. The futures contract size.
3. The futures maturity date, also called the expiration date.
4. The delivery or settlement procedure.
5. The futures price.

First, a futures contract requires that the underlying commodity or financial instrument be clearly identified. This is stating the obvious, but it is important that the obvious is clearly understood in financial transactions.

Second, the size of the contract must be specified. As stated earlier, the standard contract size for gold futures is 100 troy ounces. For U.S. Treasury note and bond futures, the standard contract size is $100,000 in par value notes or bonds, respectively.

The third contract term that must be stated is the maturity date. Contract maturity is the date on which the seller is obligated to make delivery and the buyer is obligated to make payment.

Fourth, the delivery process must be specified. For commodity futures, delivery normally entails sending a warehouse receipt for the appropriate quantity of the underlying commodity. After delivery, the buyer pays warehouse storage costs until the commodity is sold or otherwise disposed.

Finally, the futures price must be mutually agreed on by the buyer and seller. The futures price (or contract settlement price) is quite important because it is the price that the buyer will pay and the seller will receive for delivery at expiration of the contract.

For financial futures, delivery is often accomplished by a transfer of registered ownership. For example, ownership of U.S. Treasury bills, notes, and bonds is registered at the Federal Reserve in computerized book-entry form. Futures delivery is accomplished by a notification to the Fed to make a change of registered ownership.

One problem with futures quotes from newspapers is that the prices are from the previous trading day. If you want to know the latest quotes, one place to find intraday quotes is the website of the futures exchange. We wanted to find current prices for futures contracts on the 30 blue-chip companies in the Dow Jones Industrial Average. We went to www.cme-group.com, surfed around, and found these (delayed) intraday quotes:

Quotes are delayed about 10 minutes because access to real-time quotes is not free! As you can see, the website reports information on different stock index futures contracts.

We pulled information on the E-mini Dow Futures contract. This futures contract trades in a standard size of $5 times the level of the index. You can see information for three futures contracts that are set to expire in 2022. Like many futures contracts, trading volume is much higher in the near-term contract. You will notice that you can get quoted prices for Globex Futures (which we report here) and Globex Options (which we cover in another chapter). The Globex platform is a global electronic trading system. Through Globex, traders have around-the-clock access to a variety of interest rate and index futures contracts.

E-MINI DOW ($5) FUTURES - QUOTES

VENUE: GLOBEX

🔒 ⬤ AUTO-REFRESH IS OFF   *Last Updated 07 Jun 2022 02:56:20 PM CT. Market data is delayed by at least 10 minutes.*

MONTH	OPTIONS	CHART	LAST	CHANGE	PRIOR SETTLE	OPEN	HIGH	LOW	VOLUME	UPDATED
JUN 2022 YMM2	OPT	📊	33170	+258 (+0.78%)	32912	32903	33178	32603	143,014	14:46:19 CT 07 Jun 2022
SEP 2022 YMU2	OPT	📊	33152	+264 (+0.80%)	32888	32825	33152	32590	1,699	14:43:35 CT 07 Jun 2022
DEC 2022 YMZ2	OPT	📊	-	-	33102	-	-	-	0	14:24:59 CT 07 Jun 2022

Source: CME Group, www.cmegroup.com.

Other financial futures feature cash settlement, which means that the buyer and seller settle up in cash with no actual delivery. We discuss cash settlement in more detail when we discuss stock index futures. The important thing to remember for now is that delivery procedures are selected for convenience and low cost. Specific delivery procedures are set by the futures exchange and may change slightly from time to time.

FUTURES PRICES

For futures markets information for many more contracts, visit
www.cmegroup.com
and
www.ice.com.

The largest volume of futures trading in the United States takes place in Chicago. However, futures trading is also quite active at futures exchanges in New York, Kansas City, and Minneapolis. Current futures prices for contracts traded at the major futures exchanges are reported each day in the print version of *The Wall Street Journal*. Our nearby *Work the Web* box shows how to get prices online, and Figure 14.1 provides a snapshot of some of the most actively traded futures contracts from the various exchanges.

In our snapshot of futures prices, the information is divided into sections according to categories of the underlying commodities or financial instruments. For example, the section "Metal & Petroleum Futures" reports price information for commodities such as copper, gold, and petroleum products. The "Agriculture Futures" section lists futures price information for corn, wheat, soybeans, live cattle, lean hogs, coffee, sugar, and cocoa, among others. Separate sections report financial futures, which include "Interest Rate," "Currency," and "Index" categories.

Each section states the contract name, futures exchange, and contract size, along with price information for various contract maturities. For example, under "Metal & Petroleum Futures" we find the Copper contract traded at the Commodities Exchange (CMX), i.e., the COMEX (which is one of four CME Group futures exchanges). The standard contract size for copper is 25,000 pounds per contract. The futures price is quoted in dollars per pound.

FIGURE 14.1   Futures Prices (June 3, 2022)

Futures Contracts

Metal & Petroleum Futures

	Open	Contract High hi lo	Low	Settle	Chg	Open Interest
Copper-High (CMX)-25,000 lbs.; $ per lb.						
June	4.5500	4.5675	4.4725	4.4775	-0.0765	2,990
July	4.5550	4.5770	4.4580	4.4720	-0.0805	97,721
Gold (CMX)-100 troy oz.; $ per troy oz.						
June	1867.60	1871.90	1846.10	1845.40	-21.10	11,542
July	1869.80	1875.00	1847.20	1847.30	-21.10	2,128
Aug	1872.60	1878.60	1849.70	1850.20	-21.20	434,414
Oct	1880.90	1886.40	1858.00	1858.30	-21.10	11,843
Dec	1890.10	1895.40	1867.00	1867.40	-21.10	38,667
Feb'23	1899.60	1905.00	1877.00	1877.30	-21.00	7,139
Palladium (NYM)-50 troy oz.; $ per troy oz.						
June	2045.00	2045.00	1959.00	1975.40	-61.10	53
Sept	2048.50	2065.00	1953.50	1985.90	-61.60	6,629
Platinum (NYM)-50 troy oz.; $ per troy oz.						
June				1017.20	-12.00	5
July	1023.30	1037.10	1011.40	1016.40	-12.00	45,551
Silver (CMX)-5,000 troy oz.; $ per troy oz.						
June	22.405	22.410	21.925	21.890	-0.364	134
July	22.355	22.525	21.860	21.908	-0.367	104,614
Crude Oil, Light Sweet (NYM)-1,000 bbls.; $ per bbl.						
July	117.55	120.46 ▲	115.23	118.87	2.00	280,459
Aug	114.90	117.77 ▲	112.73	116.23	1.93	167,815
Sept	112.22	114.90 ▲	110.08	113.47	1.89	155,493
Dec	104.62	107.19 ▲	102.93	105.91	1.70	250,065
June'23	94.78	96.88 ▲	93.62	95.82	1.15	138,031
Dec	88.40	90.26	87.59	89.30	0.69	134,440
NY Harbor ULSD (NYM)-42,000 gal.; $ per gal.						
July	4.2696	4.3504 ▲	4.1969	4.2803	.0719	74,119
Aug	4.1397	4.2200 ▲	4.0740	4.1549	.0532	41,436
Gasoline-NY RBOB (NYM)-42,000 gal.; $ per gal.						
July	4.2495	4.3096 ▲	4.1550	4.2522	.0613	105,474
Aug	4.0083	4.0810 ▲	3.9452	4.0278	.0552	52,089
Natural Gas (NYM)-10,000 MMBtu.; $ per MMBtu.						
July	8.412	8.693	8.267	8.523	.038	205,638
Aug	8.406	8.677	8.257	8.510	.036	72,260
Sept	8.334	8.634	8.223	8.473	.036	108,172
Oct	8.417	8.600	8.200	8.446	.037	95,142
Jan'23	8.525	8.742	8.405	8.635	.055	66,258
May	5.178	5.309 ▲	5.084	5.296	.107	62,207

Agriculture Futures

	Open	High hi lo	Low	Settle	Chg	Open Interest
Corn (CBT)-5,000 bu.; cents per bu.						
July	730.25	736.00	725.75	727.00	-3.25	528,973
Dec	693.25	697.75	688.50	690.00	-4.25	485,270
Oats (CBT)-5,000 bu.; cents per bu.						
July	655.00	692.50	654.00	690.50	37.00	1,410
Sept	631.50	640.50	627.25	636.75	5.50	840
Soybeans (CBT)-5,000 bu.; cents per bu.						
July	1728.75	1730.50	1694.00	1697.75	-31.50	275,089
Nov	1539.75	1542.50	1521.75	1527.00	-14.75	268,869
Soybean Meal (CBT)-100 tons; $ per ton.						
July	414.90	418.00	407.30	407.90	-7.00	121,121
Dec	397.80	399.50	390.30	390.90	-8.10	121,304
Soybean Oil (CBT)-60,000 lbs.; cents per lb.						
July	81.58	82.53	80.25	81.85	.41	119,990
Dec	77.24	77.73	75.98	77.07	-.17	121,678
Rough Rice (CBT)-2,000 cwt.; $ per cwt.						
July	16.97	17.05	16.78	16.80	-.18	7,130
Sept	17.25	17.30	17.05	17.06	-.20	3,649
Wheat (CBT)-5,000 bu.; cents per bu.						
July	1061.50	1069.25	1036.25	1040.00	-18.25	140,791
Sept	1073.00	1080.50	1048.00	1051.75	-18.00	74,587
Wheat (KC)-5,000 bu.; cents per bu.						
July	1146.00	1157.50	1119.00	1121.00	-22.50	78,262
Sept	1153.50	1164.00	1126.25	1128.25	-22.00	45,459
Cattle-Feeder (CME)-50,000 lbs.; cents per lb.						
Aug	173.000	174.275	172.150	173.875	.925	28,565
Sept	175.475	176.650	174.700	176.300	.825	8,217
Cattle-Live (CME)-40,000 lbs.; cents per lb.						
June	133.475	133.925	133.200	133.600	-.025	20,912
Aug	134.200	134.575	133.625	133.850	-.275	138,471
Hogs-Lean (CME)-40,000 lbs.; cents per lb.						
June	110.500	110.700	109.875	110.200	.150	16,376
July	111.825	113.200	110.350	110.750	-1.425	49,222
Lumber (CME)-110,000 bd. ft.; $ per 1,000 bd. ft.						
July	605.00	630.00	595.60	623.30	24.80	1,354
Sept	612.00	639.70	612.00	632.00	14.30	696
Milk (CME)-200,000 lbs.; cents per lb.						
June	24.40	24.45	24.29	24.33	.01	5,015
July	24.73	24.73	24.50	24.60	-.13	4,952
Cocoa (ICE-US)-10 metric tons; $ per ton.						
July	2,497	2,535	2,456	2,469	-16	92,373
Sept	2,513	2,557	2,489	2,505	-5	75,249
Coffee (ICE-US)-37,500 lbs.; cents per lb.						
July	236.15	240.00	231.45	232.40	-5.85	75,230
Sept	236.00	239.90	231.60	232.55	-5.70	62,573
Sugar-World (ICE-US)-112,000 lbs.; cents per lb.						
July	19.35	19.42	19.25	19.29	-.06	302,857
Oct	19.61	19.61	19.43	19.47	-.06	232,430
Sugar-Domestic (ICE-US)-112,000 lbs.; cents per lb.						
July	35.80	35.80	35.75	35.80	-.02	375
Sept	36.40	36.50	36.40	36.42	.12	2,155

	Open	Contract High hi lo	Low	Settle	Chg	Open Interest
Cotton (ICE-US)-50,000 lbs.; cents per lb.						
July	139.14	140.70	136.06	138.18	-.93	68,270
Dec	120.10	120.38	116.92	117.90	-2.20	98,243
Orange Juice (ICE-US)-15,000 lbs.; cents per lb.						
July	180.55	183.30	179.85	180.70	.45	8,432
Sept	175.30	176.00	174.90	175.95	.70	3,209

Interest Rate Futures

	Open	High hi lo	Low	Settle	Chg	Open Interest
Ultra Treasury Bonds (CBT) - $100,000; pts 32nds of 100%						
June				154-220	-1-02.0	18,884
Sept	155-030	155-130	152-280	154-080	-1-02.0	1,267,557
Treasury Bonds (CBT) - $100,000; pts 32nds of 100%						
June				139-060	-18.0	23,598
Sept	138-230	138-280	137-130	138-040	-19.0	1,176,025
Treasury Notes (CBT) - $100,000; pts 32nds of 100%						
June	119-085	119-115		118-270	119-015	-7.5	24,007
Sept	118-270	118-300	118-115	118-175	-10.0	3,445,466
5 Yr. Treasury Notes (CBT) - $100,000; pts 32nds of 100%						
June				112-237	-5.2	49,484
Sept	112-140	112-155	112-042	112-085	-6.0	3,744,012
2 Yr. Treasury Notes (CBT) - $200,000; pts 32nds of 100%						
June	105-271	105-281	105-247	105-258	-1.1	37,870
Sept	105-119	105-136	105-090	105-105	-1.2	2,093,872
30 Day Federal Funds (CBT) - $5,000,000; 100 - daily avg.						
June	98.9175	98.9175	98.9150	98.9150	.0000	164,209
July	98.6000	98.6000	98.5900	98.5950	.0000	339,890
10 Yr. Del. Int. Rate Swaps (CBT) - $100,000; pts 32nds of 100%						
June				86-170	-12.0	11,962
Three-Month SOFR (CME) - $1,000,000; 100 - daily avg.						
March	99.4925	99.4925	99.4900	99.4925	.0000	463,198
June'23	96.8650	96.8750	96.7900	96.8150	-.0450	725,382
Eurodollar (CME) - $1,000,000; pts of 100%						
June	98.2375	98.2400	98.2300	98.2375	.0025	1,118,887
Sept	97.3650	97.3850	97.3400	97.3500	-.0050	946,327
Dec	96.8050	96.8300	96.7550	96.7750	-.0200	1,381,195
Dec'23	96.8000	96.8150	96.7250	96.7450	-.0550	1,163,706

Currency Futures

	Open	High hi lo	Low	Settle	Chg	Open Interest
Japanese Yen (CME) - ¥12,500,000; $ per 100¥						
June	.7702	.7713	.7637	.7645	-.0058	229,461
Sept				.7685	-.0058	6,879
Canadian Dollar (CME) - CAD 100,000; $ per CAD						
June	.7954	.7967	.7937	.7945	-.0005	119,361
Sept				.7941	-.0005	14,468
British Pound (CME) - £62,500; $ per £						
June	1.2575	1.2590	1.2484	1.2500	-.0067	240,844
Sept				1.2510	-.0067	13,207
Swiss Franc (CME) - CHF 125,000; $ per CHF						
June	1.0446	1.0467	1.0373	1.0393	-.0048	46,735
Sept	1.0508	1.0532	1.0439	1.0457	-.0049	3,169
Australian Dollar (CME) - AUD 100,000; $ per AUD						
June	.7266	.7283	.7202	.7214	-.0041	150,572
Sept				.7222	-.0042	3,853
Mexican Peso (CME) - MXN 500,000; $ per MXN						
June	.05112	.05122 ▲	.05093	.05103	-.00001	212,434
Sept	.05013	.05027 ▲	.04999	.05008	...	1,667
Euro (CME) - €125,000; $ per €						
June	1.0752	1.0768	1.0707	1.0725	-.0019	662,811
Sept				1.0786	-.0019	38,292

Index Futures

	Open	High hi lo	Low	Settle	Chg	Open Interest
Mini DJ Industrial Average (CBT) - $5 x Index						
June	33250	33317	32824	32888	-335	80,283
Sept				32865	-333	1,463
Mini S&P 500 (CME) - $50 x Index						
June	4177.75	4189.00	4096.75	4107.00	-68.25	2,188,296
Sept	4182.00	4191.00	4098.00	4109.50	-68.50	54,812
Mini S&P Midcap 400 (CME) - $100 x Index						
June				2519.40	-29.20	54,917
Sept				2521.40	-29.30	11
Mini Nasdaq 100 (CME) - $20 x Index						
June	12896.00	12945.25	12503.00	12551.00	-342.75	260,187
Sept	12935.00	12973.75	12532.50	12580.50	-343.75	6,845
Mini Russell 2000 (CME) - $50 x Index						
June	1896.90	1902.70	1863.40	1881.30	-15.60	536,956
Sept				1881.80	-15.80	1,560
Mini Russell 1000 (CME) - $50 x Index						
June				2258.00	-37.10	17,284
U.S. Dollar Index (ICE-US) - $1,000 x Index						
June	101.78	102.25	101.66	102.16	.33	60,546
Sept	101.57	102.10	101.45	101.95	.33	1,629

Sources: *The Wall Street Journal*, June 3, 2022, Dow Jones & Company, Inc., and SIX Financial Information.

EXAMPLE 14.1

Futures Quotes

In Figure 14.1, locate the gold and wheat contracts. Where are they traded? What are the contract sizes for the gold and wheat contracts and how are their futures prices specified?

The gold contract trades on the CMX, the COMEX division of the CME Group. One gold contract calls for delivery of 100 troy ounces. The gold futures price is quoted in dollars per troy ounce.

Wheat contracts are traded on the Chicago Board of Trade (CBT) and the Kansas City Board of Trade (KC). One wheat contract calls for delivery of 5,000 bushels of wheat, and wheat futures prices are quoted in cents per bushel. Why do you think there are different wheat prices at these exchanges? Is all wheat the same?

For futures prices and price charts, visit these websites: futures.tradingcharts.com and www.barchart.com.

The reporting format for each futures contract is similar. For example, the first column of a price listing gives the contract delivery/maturity month. For each maturity month, the next six columns report futures information observed during the previous day: the price at opening of trade ("Open"); the highest intraday price ("High"); an area to signal a life-of-contract high or low; the lowest intraday price ("Low"); the price at close of trading ("Settle," often referred to as the "Last" price); and the change in settle price from the previous day ("Chg"). The last column reports open interest for each contract maturity, which is the number of contracts outstanding at the end of that day's trading.

By now, we see that four of the contract terms for futures contracts are stated in the futures price listing. These are:

1. The identity of the underlying commodity or financial instrument.

2. The futures contract size.

3. The futures maturity date.

4. The futures price.

Exact contract terms for the delivery process are available from the appropriate futures exchange on request.

EXAMPLE 14.2

Futures Prices

In Figure 14.1, locate the soybean contract with the greatest open interest. Explain the information provided.

The soybean (or just "bean") contract with the greatest open interest is specified by the contract maturity with the greatest number of contracts outstanding, so the July contract is the one we seek. One contract calls for delivery of 5,000 bushels of beans (a bushel, of course, is four pecks and weighs about 60 pounds). The closing price for delivery at maturity is quoted in cents per bushel. Because there are 5,000 bushels in a single contract, the total contract value is the settle price per bushel of 1,697.75 cents times 5,000, or $84,887.50, for the July contract.

To get an idea of the magnitude of financial futures trading, take a look at the fourth entry under "Interest Rate Futures" in Figure 14.1, the CBT Treasury note contract. This entry is for 10-year T-note futures (note the next three entries are for the 5-year and the 2-year T-note, and the third for 30-day federal funds.) One T-note contract calls for the delivery of $100,000 in par value notes. The total open interest in these contracts often exceeds a million contracts. In fact, as we see from the quote, the September contract has an open interest of about 1.3 million contracts. Thus, the total face value represented by the outstanding June contracts is about $130 billion.

You might notice there is a quote for an Ultra T-Bond. By design, these new bond futures contracts are for traders who are interested in the long end of the yield curve. When they expire, T-Bond futures are settled by delivering actual T-Bonds. The bonds that are deliverable on the

Ultra T-Bond futures contracts must have at least 25 years remaining to maturity. By comparison, deliverable bonds on the existing T-Bond futures contract must have a maturity of at least 15 years.

Who does all this trading? The orders originate from money managers around the world and are sent to the various exchanges' trading floors and electronic systems for execution. On the floor, the orders are executed by professional traders who are quite vocal in trying to get the best prices. In the next section, we will discuss how and why futures contracts are used for speculation and hedging.

CHECK THIS

14.1a What is a forward contract?

14.1b What is a futures contract, and why is it different from a forward contract?

14.1c What is a futures price?

14.2 Why Futures?

The major economic purpose of futures contracts is to allow hedgers to transfer risk to speculators. Therefore, a viable futures market cannot exist without participation by both hedgers and speculators. We begin to help you understand the use of futures markets by describing how speculators use futures markets. We then turn to a discussion about how hedgers use futures contracts.

SPECULATING WITH FUTURES

Suppose you are thinking about speculating on commodity prices because you believe that you can accurately forecast future prices. The most convenient way to speculate is to use futures contracts. If you believe that gold prices will increase, then you can speculate on this belief by buying gold futures. Alternatively, if you think gold prices will decrease, you can speculate by selling gold futures.

Buying a futures contract is often referred to as "going long," or establishing a **long position**. Selling a futures contract is often called "going short," or establishing a **short position**. A **speculator** accepts price risk in an attempt to profit on the direction of prices. Speculators can go long or short in futures contracts. A speculator who is long benefits from price increases and loses from price decreases. The opposite is true for a speculator who is short.

To illustrate the basics of speculating, suppose you believe the price of gold will go up. In particular, suppose the current price for delivery in three months is $1,850 per ounce (this $1,850 is called the "futures" price, or settle price). You think that gold will be selling for much more than $1,850 three months from now, so you go long 100 gold contracts that expire in three months. When you do, you are obligated to take delivery of gold and pay the agreed-upon price, $1,850 per ounce. Each gold contract represents 100 troy ounces, so 100 contracts represents 10,000 troy ounces of gold with a total contract value of 10,000 × $1,850 = $18,500,000. In futures jargon, you have an $18.5 million long gold position.

Suppose your belief turns out to be correct, and three months later, the market price of gold is $1,870 per ounce. Your three-month futures contracts have just expired. So, to fulfill the terms of your long futures position, you accept delivery of 10,000 troy ounces of gold, pay $1,850 per ounce, and immediately sell the gold at the market price of $1,870 per ounce. Your profit is $20 per ounce, or 10,000 × $20 = $200,000. Of course, you will pay some brokerage commissions and taxes out of this profit.

Suppose your belief turns out to be incorrect and gold prices fall. You will lose money in this case because you are obligated to buy the 10,000 troy ounces at the agreed-upon price of $1,850 per ounce. If gold prices fell to, say, $1,825 per ounce, you would lose $25 per ounce, or 10,000 × $25 = $250,000. In addition, you will pay some brokerage commissions.

As this gold example shows, futures speculation can lead to substantial gains and losses. An important point is that your gains from futures speculation depend on accurate forecasts of the direction of future prices. You must ask yourself: Is it easy to forecast price changes?

Related Bloomberg Functions

FRD   FX Forward
          Calculator

XLTP XDVO Excel Template:
           Futures Contract
           Value Calculator

To learn more about futures, visit the
CME Institute at
www.cmegroup.com.

long position
A market position where the holder benefits from price increases and loses from price decreases.

short position
A market position where the holder benefits from price decreases and loses from price increases.

speculator
A person or firm that takes the risk of loss for the chance for profit.

Consider another example of commodity speculation. Suppose you analyze weather patterns and you are convinced that the coming winter months will be colder than usual. You believe that this will cause heating oil prices to rise. (Heating oil is labeled as NY Harbor ULSD in Figure 14.1.)

You can speculate on this belief by going long heating oil futures. The standard contract size for heating oil is 42,000 gallons. Suppose you go long 10 contracts at a futures price of $4.30 per gallon. Your long position has a total contract value of $10 \times 42,000 \times \$4.30 = \$1,806,000$.

If the price of heating oil at contract maturity is, say, $4.10 per gallon, your loss before commissions would be 20 cents per gallon, or $10 \times 42,000 \times \$.20 = \$84,000$. Of course, if heating oil prices rose by 20 cents per gallon, you would gain $84,000 (less applicable commissions) instead.

Once again, futures speculation can lead to substantial gains and losses. The important point from this example is that your gains from futures speculation depend on you making more accurate weather forecasts than other traders. So ask yourself: How easy is it to out-forecast other traders?

EXAMPLE 14.3 **What Would Juan Valdez Do?**

After an extensive analysis of political currents in Central and South America, you conclude that the political situation will stabilize. As a result, you believe that coffee prices in the future will be lower than currently indicated by futures prices. Would you go long or short? Analyze the impact of a swing in coffee prices of 20 cents per pound in either direction if you have a 10-contract position, where each contract calls for delivery of 37,500 pounds of coffee.

You would go short because you expect prices to decline. Because you are short 10 contracts, you must deliver $10 \times 37,500 = 375,000$ pounds of coffee to fulfill your contract. If coffee prices fall to 20 cents below your originally contracted futures price, then you make 20 cents per pound, or $\$.20 \times 37,500 \times 10 = \$75,000$. Of course, if you are wrong and the political situation destabilizes, the resulting $.20 increase in coffee prices would generate a $75,000 loss in your short futures position.

HEDGING WITH FUTURES

PRICE RISK Many businesses face price risk when their activities require them to hold a working inventory. By a working inventory, we mean that firms purchase and store goods for later resale at market prices. Price risk is the risk that the firm will not be able to sell its goods at a price sufficiently higher than the acquisition cost.

For example, suppose you own a regional heating oil distributorship and must keep a large pre–heating season inventory of heating oil of, say, 2.1 million gallons. In futures market jargon, this heating oil inventory represents a long position in the underlying commodity. If heating oil prices go up, the value of the heating oil you have in inventory goes up, but if heating oil prices fall, the value of the heating oil you have to sell goes down. Your risk is not trivial because even a 15-cent-per-gallon fluctuation in the price of heating oil will cause your inventory to change in value by $315,000. Because you are in the business of distributing heating oil, and not in the business of speculating on heating oil prices, you decide to remove this price risk from your business operations.

Investors face similar risks. For example, consider a U.S. investor who buys stock in Australia. The investor now has the risk of the investment itself and the risk of the currency exchange rate between Australia and the United States. For example, if the investment goes up in value, but the Australian dollar depreciates sufficiently relative to the U.S. dollar, then the net result could be a loss for the investor. To shed the "price" (or currency) risk, the investor could use currency futures to "lock in" an Australian/U.S. dollar exchange rate. In this case, the investor would hedge by selling (i.e., take a short position) in Australian dollar futures contracts.

Whether the investor chooses to shift this risk depends on many factors. For example, when we discussed diversification, we saw that the lower the correlation, the higher the diversification benefit from combining securities. So, to the extent that an investor desires diversification, the investor might choose to pass on hedging currency. Further, the investor might not know the planned holding period of the investment, making it difficult to place a precise hedge.

THE MECHANICS OF SHIFTING PRICE RISK An important function of futures markets is that they allow firms that have price risk to shift it to others who want price risk. A person or company that wants to shift price risk to others is called a **hedger**. Hedgers transfer price risk by taking a futures market position that is the opposite of their existing position in the **underlying asset**. You can think about this using a portfolio approach. Hedgers look to add a futures market position to their position in the underlying asset that will provide cash to the hedgers when their position in the underlying asset declines in value. However, the cost of adding a futures position is that the futures position draws down cash when the position in the underlying asset generates value.

In the case of your heating oil enterprise, the heating oil you have in inventory represents a long position in the underlying asset. Therefore, the value of this heating oil inventory can be protected by taking a short position in heating oil futures contracts. Hedgers often say they are "selling" futures contracts when they are initiating a short position. Because you are using this short position for hedging purposes, you have created a **short hedge**.

With a short hedge in place, changes in the value of your long position in the underlying asset are offset by an approximately equal, but opposite, change in value of your short futures position.

A CLASSIC EXAMPLE OF A SHORT HEDGE One of the first questions a hedger has to answer is how many futures contracts are needed to shift risk. This question has many answers, and most can be found in a course devoted to futures contracts and other derivatives. However, a reasonable hedging strategy is known as a **full hedge**. When a hedger has an equal, but opposite, futures position to the position in the underlying asset, the hedger is said to have a full hedge.

Heating oil futures contracts are traded on the New York Mercantile Exchange (NYM), a division of the CME Group. The standard contract size for heating oil futures is 42,000 gallons per contract. Because you wish to full hedge 2.1 million gallons, you need to sell 2,100,000/42,000 = 50 heating oil contracts.

Suppose the average acquisition price of your 2.1 million gallons of heating oil is $1.40 per gallon and that today's futures price for delivery during your heating season is $1.50. In the past, market conditions in your distribution area were such that you could sell your heating oil to your customers at a price 20 cents higher than the prevailing futures price. To help finance your inventory purchases, you borrowed money. During the heating season, you have to make an interest payment of $200,000.

Given these numbers, you can forecast your pretax profit per gallon of heating oil. Revenues are 2,100,000 × $1.70 = $3,570,000. The cost of the heating oil is 2,100,000 × $1.40 = $2,940,000. Subtracting this cost and the debt payment of $200,000 from revenue results in a pretax profit of $430,000, or $430,000/2,100,000 = $.205 per gallon.

However, if heating oil prices decrease by $.20, your pretax profit per gallon of heating oil will only be $.005. You view this risk as unacceptable and decide to hedge by selling 50 heating oil futures contracts at a price of $1.50 per gallon. Table 14.1 summarizes three possible outcomes: heating oil prices remain steady, they increase by $.20, and they decrease by $.20.

As you can see in Table 14.1, with the short hedge, your pretax profit will be $.205 per gallon in all three cases. To see why, suppose heating oil prices fall by $.20. In this case, revenues are 2,100,000 × $1.50 = $3,150,000. The cost of the heating oil is 2,100,000 × $1.40 = $2,940,000. Subtracting this cost and the debt payment of $200,000 from revenues results in an unhedged pretax profit of $10,000, or $10,000/2,100,000 = $.005 per gallon. However, if you had a short hedge in place, your pretax futures profit is $420,000 because ($1.50 − $1.30) × 42,000 × 50 = $420,000. Adding $420,000 to the unhedged pretax profit of $10,000 results in a hedged pretax profit of $430,000, which is $430,000/2,100,000 = $.205 per gallon.

In fact, your pretax profit will remain steady for a wide range of prices. We illustrate this result in Figure 14.2. In Figure 14.2, the blue line represents your pretax profit per gallon of heating oil for a wide range of possible heating oil selling prices. The red line represents your futures market gains or losses. Note that heating oil futures prices and futures contract gains (losses) appear across the top and on the right side of the graph. If futures prices remain unchanged at $1.50, you have no futures gain or loss. If futures prices fall to $1.30, your futures gain is $.20.

In Figure 14.2, the purple line remains steady at a value of $.205. This means that for a wide range of heating oil selling prices, your pretax profit remains unchanged if you employ the short hedge.

	Base Case: No Change in Heating Oil Price	Heating Oil Price Decrease	Heating Oil Price Increase
Heating oil inventory (gal.)	2,100,000	2,100,000	2,100,000
Selling price, per gallon	$ 1.70	$ 1.50	$ 1.90
Average purchase price, per gallon	$ 1.40	$ 1.40	$ 1.40
Futures price	$ 1.50	$ 1.30	$ 1.70
Without a Hedge			
Revenue	$3,570,000	$3,150,000	$3,990,000
Cost of inventory sold	$2,940,000	$2,940,000	$2,940,000
Interest expense	$ 200,000	$ 200,000	$ 200,000
Pretax profit	$ 430,000	$ 10,000	$ 850,000
Pretax profit, per gallon	$ .205	$ .005	$ .405
With Short Hedge (short futures at $1.50)			
Revenue	$3,570,000	$3,150,000	$3,990,000
Cost of inventory sold	$2,940,000	$2,940,000	$2,940,000
Interest expense	$ 200,000	$ 200,000	$ 200,000
Futures gain (loss)	$ 0	$ 420,000	($ 420,000)
Pretax profit	$ 430,000	$ 430,000	$ 430,000
Hedge effect (constant pretax profit)	$ .205	$ .205	$ .205
Futures gain (loss), per gallon	$ .00	$ .20	($ .20)

Your business activities may also include distributing other petroleum products like gasoline and natural gas. Futures contracts are also available for gasoline and natural gas, and therefore they may be used for hedging purposes. In fact, your business activities might dictate you use another common hedge, known as a **long hedge**.

long hedge
Adding a long futures position to a short position in the underlying asset.

Firms that use a long hedge do not currently own the underlying asset but plan to acquire it in the future. In this case, it is as if the firm is "short" the underlying asset because if the price increases between now and the time at which the firm actually purchases the underlying asset, the firm will pay more than it thought. Note that the firm does not go into the market and establish a short position in the underlying asset. That would be speculating. Rather, its planned business activities create situations where the firm is exposed to price increases in the underlying asset. This exposure is what gives rise to the saying that the firm is effectively "short the underlying."

FINAL THOUGHTS ABOUT HEDGING In real hedging applications, many factors influence the exact profit recognized. But this example provides you with an overview of how hedging works. The important thing to remember is this: *If you want to shed risk, do not take risk.* That is, if you are long the underlying asset, do not buy futures too!

There is an easy way to remember which position to take in the futures market. In the heating oil example above, pretax profits per gallon change penny by penny with heating oil price changes. That is, the slope of the blue line in Figure 14.2 is one. To eliminate price risk, the hedger needs to add a futures position to the underlying position that results in a slope of zero. What number do we have to add to one to get zero? Obviously, the answer is negative one, which is the slope of the red line in Figure 14.2.

Figure 14.2 is sometimes called "the X" or "the cross" in that it shows how the risk of the futures position offsets the risk of the underlying position. If you can remember Figure 14.2, you will remember which futures position to take when you want to hedge.

Hedging greatly reduces and, in some cases, eliminates the possibility of a loss from a decline in the price of the underlying asset. However, by hedging with futures, the firm also eliminates the possibility of a gain from a price increase in the underlying asset. This is an important point. If the price of the underlying asset rises, you will incur a loss on your futures position.

Forgone opportunities for increases in the value of the underlying asset, however, represent the bulk of hedging costs. Failure to shift price risk through hedging means that the firm

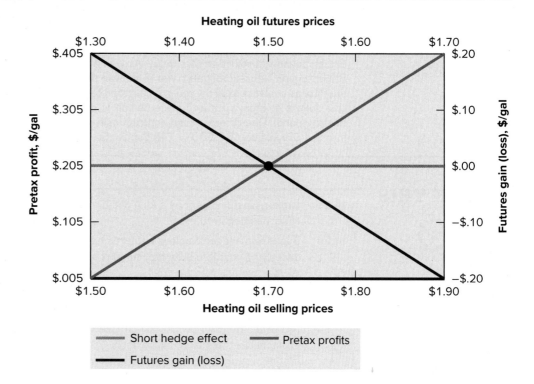

is actually holding price risk. Some people think that holding price risk that could be shifted is the same as taking price risk. The owners of the firm must decide whether they are price risk shifters or price risk holders.

EXAMPLE 14.4   **Short Hedging**

Suppose you have an inventory of 1.8 million pounds of soybean oil. Describe how you would hedge this position.

Because you are long in the underlying commodity, soybean oil, you need to go short in futures (i.e., sell). A single soybean oil contract calls for delivery of 60,000 pounds of soybean oil. To hedge your position, you need to sell 1.8 million/60,000 = 30 futures contracts.

EXAMPLE 14.5   **More Hedging**

You need to buy 360,000 pounds of orange juice concentrate in three months. How can you hedge the price risk associated with this planned purchase? One orange juice contract calls for delivery of 15,000 pounds of orange juice concentrate.

In this example, if the price of concentrate increases between now and when you actually purchase the orange juice concentrate, you will pay more than you thought. So, effectively, you have a "short" position in the underlying asset because you do not currently own it (but you do plan to buy it later). To offset the risk of higher orange juice concentrate prices when you actually buy, you need to establish a long futures position today (this hedge is known as a long hedge). You should buy 360,000/15,000 = 24 contracts.

EXAMPLE 14.6   **Even More Hedging**

Suppose your company will receive payment of £15 million in three months, at which time your company will convert the British pounds to U.S. dollars. What is the standard futures contract size for British pounds? Describe how you could use futures contracts to lock in an exchange rate from British pounds to U.S. dollars for your planned receipt of £15 million, including how many contracts are required.

Your company will be receiving £15 million, so you are effectively long British pounds. So, if the British pound per U.S. dollar exchange rate falls, the British pounds you will receive will decline in terms of their value in U.S. dollars.

To hedge these British pounds, you can use a short hedge. That is, you short (or sell) British pound futures contracts today. As with any short position, your short position in British pound futures obligates you to deliver the underlying asset. In this case, when the futures contract expires, you are obligated to deliver British pounds. You will receive U.S. dollars at today's futures price (which is quoted as the U.S. dollar price for one British pound). One British pound contract calls for delivery of £62,500. You will therefore sell £15 million/£62,500 = 240 contracts.

CHECK THIS

14.2a Explain what is meant by a long position in futures and what is meant by a short position in futures.

14.2b Suppose a hedger employs a futures hedge that is two-thirds the size of the underlying position. Why do you think this is called a "partial" hedge?

14.2c You have a short position in the underlying asset. How would you modify Figure 14.2 in this case?

14.2d Suppose a firm has a long position in the underlying asset. What happens if this firm buys futures contracts instead of selling futures contracts? Create an example like the one shown in Table 14.1 to help explain the consequences. (By the way, this activity is jokingly referred to as a "Texas hedge.")

14.3 Futures Trading Accounts

For a list of online futures brokers, see www.nerdwallet.com.

A futures exchange, like a stock exchange, allows only exchange members to trade on the exchange. Exchange members may be firms or individuals trading for their own accounts, or they may be brokerage firms handling trades for customers. Some firms conduct both trading and brokerage operations on the exchange. In this section, we discuss the mechanics of a futures trading account as it pertains to a customer with a trading account at a brokerage firm.

The biggest customer trading accounts are those of corporations that use futures to manage their business risks and money managers who hedge or speculate with clients' funds. Many individual investors also have futures trading accounts of their own, although speculation by individual investors is not recommended without a full understanding of all risks involved. Whether a futures trading account is large or small, the mechanics of account trading are essentially the same.

There are several essential things to know about futures trading accounts. The first thing is that margin is required. In this way, futures accounts resemble the stock margin accounts we discussed in a previous chapter; however, the specifics are quite different. **Futures margin** is a deposit of funds in a futures trading account dedicated to covering potential losses from an outstanding futures position. An **initial margin** is required when a futures position is first established. The amount varies according to contract type and size, but margin requirements for futures contracts usually range between 5 percent and 15 percent of total contract value. Initial margin is the same for both long and short futures positions.

The second thing to know about a futures trading account is that contract values in outstanding futures positions are marked to market on a daily basis. **Marking to market** is a process whereby gains and losses on outstanding futures positions are recognized at the end of each trading day.

For example, suppose one morning you call your broker and instruct her to go long five U.S. Treasury note contracts for your account. A few minutes later, she calls back to confirm order execution at a futures price of 125. Because the Treasury note contract size is $100,000 par value, contract value is 125% × $100,000 = $125,000 per contract. Thus, the total position value for your order is $625,000, for which your broker requires $35,000 initial margin. In addition,

futures margin
Deposit of funds in a futures trading account dedicated to covering potential losses from an outstanding futures position.

initial margin
The minimum margin that must be supplied on a securities purchase.

marking to market
In futures trading accounts, the process whereby gains and losses on outstanding futures positions are recognized on a daily basis.

maintenance margin
The minimum margin that must be present at all times in a margin account.

your broker requires that at least $27,500 in **maintenance margin** be present at all times. The necessary margin funds are immediately wired from a bank account to your futures account.

Now, at the end of trading that day, Treasury note futures close at a price of 123. Overnight, all accounts are marked to market. Your Treasury note futures position is marked to $123,000 per contract, or a $615,000 total position value. This value means you have lost $10,000. This loss is deducted from your initial margin, leaving you with only $25,000 in your futures account.

margin call
Notification to increase the margin level in a trading account.

Because the maintenance margin level on your account is $27,500, your broker will issue a **margin call** on your account. Essentially, your broker will notify you that you must immediately restore your margin level to the initial margin level of $35,000, or else she will close out your Treasury note futures position at whatever trading price is available at the exchange.

This example illustrates what happens when a futures trading account is marked to market and the resulting margin funds fall below the maintenance margin level. The alternative, and more pleasant, experience occurs when a futures price moves in your favor, and the marking-to-market process adds funds to your account. In this case, marking-to-market gains can be withdrawn from your account so long as remaining margin funds are not less than the initial margin level.

The third thing to know about a futures trading account is that a futures position can be closed out at any time; you do not have to hold a contract until maturity. A futures position is closed out by instructing your broker to close out your position. To close out a position, your broker will enter a **reverse trade** for your account.

reverse trade
A trade that closes out a previously established futures position by taking the opposite position.

A reverse trade works like this: Suppose you are currently short five Treasury note contracts, and you instruct your broker to close out the position. Your broker responds by going long five Treasury note contracts for your account. In this case, going long five contracts is a reverse trade because it exactly cancels your previous five-contract short position. At the end of the day in which you make your reverse trade, your account will be marked to market at the futures price realized by the reverse trade. From then on, your position is closed out, and no more gains or losses will be realized.

This example illustrates that closing out a futures position is no more difficult than initially entering into a position. There are two basic reasons to close out a futures position before contract maturity. The first is to capture a current gain or loss, without realizing further price risk. The second is to avoid the delivery requirement that comes from holding a futures contract until it matures. In fact, over 98 percent of all futures contracts are closed out before contract maturity, which indicates that less than 2 percent of all futures contracts result in delivery of the underlying commodity or financial instrument.

Before closing this section, let's briefly list the three essential things to know about a futures trading account as discussed above:

1. Margin is required.
2. Futures accounts are marked to market daily.
3. A futures position can be closed out at any time by a reverse trade.

Understanding the items in this list is important to anyone planning to use a futures trading account.

CHECK THIS

14.3a What are the three essential things you should know about a futures trading account?

14.3b What is meant by initial margin for a futures position? What is meant by maintenance margin for a futures position?

14.3c Explain the process of marking to market a futures trading account. What is a margin call, and when is one issued?

14.3d How is a futures position closed out by a reverse trade? What proportion of all futures positions are closed out by reverse trades rather than by delivery at contract maturity?

14.4 Cash Prices versus Futures Prices

We now turn to the relationship between today's price of some commodity or financial instrument and its futures price. We begin by examining current cash prices.

Related Bloomberg Functions

CARC Commodity Arbitrage Calculator

FES Covered Interest Arbitrage Calculator

cash price
Price of a commodity or financial instrument quoted for current delivery. Also called the *spot price.*

cash market
Market in which commodities or financial instruments are traded for immediate delivery. Also called the *spot market.*

CASH PRICES

The **cash price** of a commodity or financial instrument is the price quoted for current delivery. The cash price is also called the *spot price,* as in "on the spot." In futures jargon, terms like "spot gold" or "cash wheat" are used to refer to commodities being sold for current delivery in what is called the **cash market** or the *spot market.*

Figure 14.3 is a Bloomberg screen for "Cash" or "Spot" prices in early January 2022. The data are divided into sections according to commodity categories. Each section gives commodity names along with cash market prices for the day of trading and the year to date (YTD) percent change in prices. For example, at the beginning of January, West Texas Intermediate (WTI) Crude oil had a spot price of $76.09 per barrel. Gold had a spot price of $1,800.11 per ounce. Corn had a spot price of 587.75 cents per bushel, or about $5.88.

CASH-FUTURES ARBITRAGE

Intuitively, you might think that the cash price of a commodity is closely related to its futures price. If you do, then your intuition is quite correct. In fact, your intuition is backed up by strong economic argument and more than a century of experience observing the simultaneous operation of cash and futures markets.

As a routine matter, cash and futures prices are closely watched by market professionals. To understand why, suppose you notice that spot gold is trading for $1,800 per ounce while the two-month futures price is $1,850 per ounce. Do you see a profit opportunity?

You should, because buying spot gold today at $1,800 per ounce while simultaneously selling gold futures at $1,850 per ounce locks in a $50 per ounce profit. True, gold has storage costs (you have to put it somewhere) and a spot gold purchase ties up capital that could be earning interest. These costs, however, are small relative to the $50 per ounce gross profit, which is $50/$1,800 = .0278, or 2.78% per two months, or about 16.7 percent per year. Furthermore, this profit is risk-free! Alas, in reality, such easy profit opportunities are the stuff of dreams.

FIGURE 14.3 — Commodity Cash Prices

Commodity	2Day	Price	Norm Chg	%Chg	Δ AVAT	Time	%YTD	%YTDCur
1) Energy								
2) NYM WTI Crude		76.09	+0.88	+1.17%	+17.00%	11:55	+1.17%	+1.17%
3) ICE Brent Crude		78.95	+1.17	+1.50%	+9.57%	11:55	+1.50%	+1.50%
4) ICE ARA Gasoil		677.00	+10.00	+1.50%	-38.95%	11:54	+1.50%	+1.50%
5) NYM NYH Gasoline		226.30	+3.84	+1.73%	-9.04%	11:55	+1.55%	+1.55%
6) NYM NYH Heating Oil		236.32	+3.79	+1.63%	-10.20%	11:55	+1.42%	+1.42%
7) NYM HH Nat Gas		3.71	-0.02	-0.46%	+19.66%	11:55	-0.46%	-0.46%
8) ICE NBP Nat Gas		170.64	-46.12	-21.28%	+34.22%	12/31/22	+202.55%	+201.27%
9) Metals								
10) LME Aluminum		2,807.50	-10.50	-0.37%	--	12/31/22	+41.83%	+41.83%
11) LME Copper		9,720.50	+29.00	+0.30%	--	12/31/22	+25.17%	+25.17%
12) Spot Gold		**1,800.11**	-29.08	-1.59%	--	12:05	-1.59%	-1.59%
13) DCE Iron Ore		674.00	+0.00	+0.00%	-33.93%	12/31/22	-36.61%	-36.61%
14) LME Nickel		20,757.00	+170.00	+0.83%	--	12/31/22	+24.94%	+24.94%
15) Spot Silver		22.84	-0.47	-2.00%	--	12:05	-2.00%	-2.00%
16) SHF Steel Rebar		4,301.00	-19.00	-0.44%	-22.21%	12/31/22	+7.77%	+7.77%
17) Agriculture								
18) CME Live Cattle		139.25	-0.45	-0.32%	+25.44%	11:55	+0.25%	+0.25%
19) ICE Coffee		223.15	-2.95	-1.30%	+51.73%	11:55	-1.30%	-1.30%
20) CBT Corn		587.75	-5.50	-0.93%	+53.21%	11:55	-0.93%	-0.93%
21) ICE Cotton		113.37	+0.77	+0.68%	-0.02%	11:55	+0.68%	+0.68%
22) CBT Soybeans		1,347.50	+8.25	+0.62%	-90.23%	11:55	+0.24%	+0.24%
23) ICE Sugar		18.73	-0.15	-0.79%	-25.66%	11:55	-0.79%	-0.79%
24) CBT SRW Wheat		755.75	-15.00	-1.95%	+26.89%	11:55	-1.95%	-1.95%

Source: Bloomberg Finance L.P. Accessed January 3, 2022.

CONTANGO AND ITS EFFECT ON YOUR COMMODITY ETF/ETN

As exchange traded funds (ETFs) have grown, so have investments and interest in a couple of related investment types: commodity based ETFs and exchange traded notes (ETNs). While they share some similarities with standard ETFs, many commodity-based ETFs and ETNs are subject to a phenomenon called contango, which arises when front-month futures contracts are cheaper than second-month futures contracts. Put more simply, contango occurs when the price of a commodity for future delivery is higher than the spot price. An opposite phenomenon, backwardation, can also occur.

This affects all ETFs and ETNs that are futures based or track commodity indexes (or both), which typically invest in the front month futures contracts of the tracked commodities. Contango generates what is known as a negative roll yield. This negative roll yield can negatively affect the returns of the ETF and cause tracking errors. The wider the spread, or "contango effect," the higher the risk that said negative roll yield will also negatively affect the net asset value of the full

ETF. According to Kevin Grewal at Smartstops, "When markets are in contango, which some argue is a normal price relationship which reflects the costs of carrying the commodity, the relative ETF will underperform its underlying commodity."

Many commonly traded ETFs have been influenced by contango, including the US Oil Fund (NYSE:USO), the United States Natural Gas Fund (NYSE:UNG), and the iPath S&P GSCI Crude Oil Total Return Index ETN (NYSE:OIL). For (NYSE:USO) and (NYSE:UNG), their investment goals are to follow the percentage change in the price of their respective commodities' front month contract, so their performance doesn't always follow the performance of their respective underlying indexes. Many experts recommend utilizing an exit strategy to help mitigate risk when investing in these funds.

Source: http://etfdailynews.com/2010/06/08/is-your-commodity-etfetn-influenced-by-contango-ung-uso-oil/, June 8, 2010.

---

cash-futures arbitrage
Strategy for earning risk-free profits from an unusual difference between cash and futures prices.

basis
The difference between the cash price and the futures price for a commodity, i.e., Basis = Cash price − Futures price.

carrying-charge market
The case where the futures price is greater than the cash price; i.e., the basis is negative.

inverted market
The case where the futures price is less than the cash price; i.e., the basis is positive.

Earning risk-free profits from an unusual difference between cash and futures prices is called **cash-futures arbitrage**. In a competitive market, cash-futures arbitrage has very slim profit margins. In fact, the profit margins are almost imperceptible when they exist at all.

If you compare cash and futures prices quoted at the same time, you will see that cash prices and futures prices are seldom equal. In futures jargon, the difference between a cash price and a futures price is called the **basis**.[1]

For commodities with storage costs, the cash price is usually less than the futures price. This is referred to as a **carrying-charge market**, or *contango*. Sometimes, however, the cash price is greater than the futures price, and this is referred to as an **inverted market**, or *backwardation*. We can summarize this discussion of carrying-charge markets, inverted markets, and basis as follows:

$$\text{Carrying charge market: Basis} = \text{Cash price} - \text{Futures price} < 0$$
$$\text{Inverted market:} \qquad \text{Basis} = \text{Cash price} - \text{Futures price} > 0 \qquad (14.1)$$

A variety of factors can lead to an economically justifiable difference between a commodity's cash price and its futures price, including availability of storage facilities, transportation costs, and seasonal price fluctuations. The primary determinants of the cash-futures basis, however, are storage costs and interest costs. Storage cost is the cost of holding the commodity in a storage facility, and interest cost refers to interest income forgone on funds used to buy and hold the commodity.

If a futures price rises far enough above a cash price to more than cover storage costs and interest expense, commodity traders will undertake cash-futures arbitrage by buying in the cash market and selling in the futures market. This trading drives down the futures price and drives up the cash price until the basis is restored to an economically justifiable level.

Similarly, if a futures price falls far enough relative to a cash price, traders will undertake cash-futures arbitrage by short selling in the cash market and buying in the futures market. This trading drives down the cash price and drives up the futures price until an economically justifiable basis is restored. In both cases, arbitrage ensures that the basis is kept at an economically appropriate level.

As we discussed in another chapter, many investors use exchange-traded funds (ETFs) or notes (ETNs) to gain exposure to areas that have traditionally been off limits to smaller

---

[1] The official Commodity Trading Manual of the CME Group defines "basis" as the difference between the cash price and the futures price, i.e., Basis = Cash price − Futures price. We will be consistent with the CME Group definition. For nonagricultural futures, however, the basis is nearly always defined as the futures price minus the cash price.

investors. In particular, commodity-based investments have become quite popular. Some of the largest such funds are SLV (silver), GLD (gold), USO (oil), UNG (natural gas), and UUP (the U.S. dollar). These funds allow for diversification—but they come with unusual risks. As the nearby *Investment Updates* box discusses, these risks are associated with two curiously named price structures: contango and backwardation.

BASIC SPOT-FUTURES PARITY

Let's build on our gold example from above to show the theoretical relationship between spot and futures prices. Recall that the spot price was $1,800 an ounce. Suppose that 12-month T-bills are yielding 2 percent. What should the one-year gold futures price be, assuming storage costs are zero?

To answer, notice that you can buy 100 ounces of gold for $1,800 per ounce, or $180,000 total. You can eliminate the price risk associated with this purchase by selling one gold futures contract, which covers 100 ounces. The net effect of this transaction is that you have created a risk-free asset. Because the risk-free rate is 2 percent, your investment must have a future value of $180,000 × 1.02 = $183,600. The futures price today should be $1,836 per ounce.

Suppose the gold futures price is actually $1,825. What would you do? To make money, you would sell 100 ounces of gold in the cash market for $1,800 an ounce. You might have some gold, or you might have to borrow it from your friend (who does not charge you to borrow gold—what a good friend!). You would then invest the $180,000 at 2% and simultaneously buy one futures contract.

At the end of the year, your investment grows to $183,600. You would use $182,500 to buy gold to fulfill your futures contract obligation. Also, you return the gold to your inventory (or deliver it to your good friend). You pocket $1,100. This trading is another example of cash-futures arbitrage.

More generally, if we let F be the futures price, S be the spot price, and r be the risk-free rate, then our example illustrates that:

$$F = S(1 + r) \qquad (14.2)$$

In other words, the futures price is the future value of the spot price, calculated at the risk-free rate. This is the famous **spot-futures parity** condition. This condition must hold in the absence of cash-futures arbitrage opportunities.

spot-futures parity
The relationship between spot prices and futures prices that holds in the absence of arbitrage opportunities.

More generally, if r is the risk-free rate per period and the futures contract matures in T periods, then the spot-futures parity condition is:

$$F_T = S(1 + r)^T \qquad (14.3)$$

Notice that T could be a fraction of one period. For example, if we have the risk-free rate per year, but the futures contract matures in six months, T would be 1/2.

EXAMPLE 14.7   **Parity Check**

Suppose we see silver spot prices are $23 per ounce. The risk-free rate is 4 percent per year. If a silver futures contract matures in three months, what should the futures price be?
From our spot-futures parity condition, we have:

$$F_T = S(1 + r)^T$$
$$= \$23(1.04)^{1/4}$$
$$= \$23.23$$

The futures price should be $23.23. Notice that r is expressed as an annual rate and T is expressed in terms of years for this example. Therefore, we set $r = .04$ and $T = 1/4$.

SPOT-FUTURES PARITY WITH STORAGE COSTS

In our spot-futures parity example above, we assumed that we could store the commodity at a zero cost. But if there are storage costs, then we need to modify the spot-futures parity equation.

For a commodity, let Y stand for the storage cost and assume that we pay the storage cost at or near the end of the futures contract's life. In this case, the spot-futures parity condition becomes:

$$F = S(1 + r) + Y \qquad (14.4)$$

Notice that we have added the amount of the storage cost to the future value of the spot gold price. The reason is that the futures contract must reflect the future value of the spot gold and the storage cost.

An alternative, and useful, way to write the storage cost-adjusted spot-futures parity result in Equation 14.4 is to define y as the storage cost as a percentage of the spot price. That is, we divide the upcoming storage cost by the current spot price. That is, $y = Y/S$. With this fraction in mind, we can write the storage cost-adjusted parity result as:

$$
\begin{aligned}
F &= S(1 + r) + Y(S/S) \\
&= S(1 + r) + S(Y/S) \\
&= S(1 + r) + Sy \\
&= S(1 + r + y)
\end{aligned}
\tag{14.5}
$$

Finally, as above, if there is something other than a single period involved, we would write:

$$
F_T = S(1 + r + y)^T \tag{14.6}
$$

where T is the number of periods (or fraction of a period) and r is the interest rate per period.

For example, suppose there is a crude oil futures contract that matures in six months. The current spot crude oil price is $80. The risk-free rate is 4 percent per year and the storage cost is 3 percent per year. What should the futures price be?

Plugging in the values to our storage cost-adjusted parity equation, we have:

$$
\begin{aligned}
F_T &= S(1 + r + y)^T \\
&= \$80(1 + .04 + .03)^{1/2} \\
&= \$82.75
\end{aligned}
$$

Notice that we set T equal to $1/2$ because the futures contract matures in six months.

CHECK THIS

14.4a What is the spot price for a commodity?

14.4b With regard to futures contracts, what is the basis?

14.4c What is an inverted market?

14.4d What is the spot-futures parity condition?

14.5 Stock Index Futures

Related Bloomberg Functions

FV World Equity Index Fair Value

FAIR Fair Value Monitor

EIRV Equity Index Relative Value

WIRP World Interest Rate Probability

DLV Cheapest-to-Deliver

For information on stock index futures, visit the website at CME Group, www.cmegroup.com.

There are a number of futures contracts on stock market indexes. Because these contracts are particularly important, we devote this entire section to them. We first describe the contracts and then discuss some trading and hedging strategies involving their use.

BASICS OF STOCK INDEX FUTURES

Locate the section labeled "Index Futures" in Figure 14.1. Here we see various stock index futures contracts. The second contract listed, the Mini S&P 500, has the highest open interest (by far). With this contract, actual delivery would be difficult or impossible because the seller of the contract would have to buy all 500 stocks in exactly the right proportions to deliver. Clearly, this portfolio formation is not practical. While index funds are available, they will generally not match the actual index weights precisely. For these reasons, stock index futures contracts feature cash settlement.

To understand how stock index futures work, suppose you bought one Mini S&P 500 contract at a futures price of 4,100. The contract size is $50 times the level of the index. What this means is that, at maturity, the buyer of the contract will pay the seller $50 times the difference between today's futures price of 4,100 and the level of the S&P 500 index at contract maturity.

For example, suppose that at maturity the S&P had actually fallen to 4,070. In this case, the buyer of the contract must pay $50 × (4,100 − 4,070) = $1,500 to the seller of the contract. In effect, the buyer of the contract has agreed to purchase 50 "units" of the index at a price of $4,100 per unit. If the index is below 4,100, the buyer will lose money. If the index is above that, then the seller will lose money.

EXAMPLE 14.8 **Index Futures**

Suppose you are convinced that the Dow stocks are going to skyrocket in value. Consequently, you buy 20 Mini-DJIA futures contracts maturing in six months at a price of 32,900. Suppose that the Dow Jones Industrial Average is at 33,220 when the contracts mature. How much will you make or lose?

The futures price is 32,900, and this Mini-DJIA has a contract size of $5 times the level of the index. At maturity, if the index is at 33,220, you make $5 × (33,220 − 32,900) = $1,600 per contract. With 20 contracts, your total profit is $32,000.

INDEX ARBITRAGE

In our spot-futures parity example above, we accounted for storage costs. Financial assets do not have storage costs, but they can pay dividends.

For a stock, we let D stand for the dividend and we assume that the dividend is paid in one period, at or near the end of the futures contract's life. A useful way to think of dividends is in terms of dividend yield. In our notation, the dividend yield is $d = D/S$. Notice that we must subtract the dividend from the future value of the stock price. The reason is that if you buy the futures contract, you will not receive the dividend, but the dividend payment will reduce the stock price.

Following the approach above:

$$
\begin{aligned}
F &= S(1 + r) - D(S/S) \\
&= S(1 + r) - S(D/S) \\
&= S(1 + r) - Sd \\
&= S(1 + r - d)
\end{aligned}
\tag{14.7}
$$

Finally, as above, if there is something other than a single period involved, we would write:

$$
F_T = S(1 + r - d)^T
\tag{14.8}
$$

index arbitrage
Strategy of monitoring the futures price on a stock index and the level of the underlying index to exploit deviations from parity.

where T is the number of periods (or fraction of a period) and r is the interest rate per period.

The spot-futures parity relation we developed above is the basis for a common trading strategy known as **index arbitrage**. Index arbitrage refers to monitoring the futures price on a stock index along with the level of the underlying index. The trader looks for violations of parity and trades as appropriate.

For example, suppose the Mini S&P 500 futures price for delivery in one year is 4,100. The current S&P 500 index level is 4,000. The dividend yield on the S&P is projected to be 3 percent per year and the risk-free rate is 5 percent. Is there a trading opportunity here?

From our dividend-adjusted parity Equation 14.8, the futures price should be:

$$
\begin{aligned}
F_T &= S(1 + r - d)^T \\
&= 4,000(1 + .05 - .03)^1 \\
&= 4,080
\end{aligned}
$$

For information on program trading, visit
www.programtrading.com.
For information on stock index arbitrage, visit
www.indexarb.com.

Thus, based on our parity calculation, the futures price is too high. We want to buy low, sell high, so we buy the index and simultaneously sell the futures contract.

Index arbitrage is often implemented as a **program trading** strategy. While this term covers a lot of ground, it generally refers to the monitoring of relative prices by computer to more quickly spot opportunities. In some cases, it includes submitting the needed buy and sell orders using a computer to speed up the process.

program trading
Computer-assisted monitoring of relative prices of financial assets; it sometimes includes computer submission of buy and sell orders to exploit perceived arbitrage opportunities.

Whether a computer is used in program trading is not really the issue; instead, a program trading strategy is any coordinated, systematic procedure for exploiting (or trying to exploit) violations of parity or other arbitrage opportunities. Such a procedure is a trading "program" in the sense that whenever certain conditions exist, certain trades are made. Thus, the process is sufficiently mechanical that it can be automated, at least in principle.

Technically, the NYSE defines program trading as the simultaneous purchase or sale of at least 15 different stocks with a total value of $1 million or more. Program trading can account for over half the total trading volume on the NYSE, but not all program trading involves stock index arbitrage.

HEDGING STOCK MARKET RISK WITH FUTURES

Earlier, in our classic hedging example, we discussed hedging using futures contracts in the context of a business protecting the value of its inventory. We now discuss some hedging strategies available to portfolio managers based on financial futures. An investment portfolio is an inventory of securities, and financial futures can be used to reduce the risk of holding a securities portfolio.

We consider the specific problem of an equity portfolio manager wishing to protect the value of a stock portfolio from the risk of an adverse movement of the overall stock market. Here, the portfolio manager wishes to establish a short hedge position to reduce risk and must determine the number of futures contracts required to properly hedge a portfolio.

In this hedging example, you are responsible for managing a broadly diversified stock portfolio with a current value of $185 million. Analysis of market conditions leads you to believe that the stock market is unusually susceptible to a price decline during the next few months. Of course, nothing is certain regarding stock market fluctuations, but you are still sufficiently concerned to believe that action is required.

A fundamental problem exists for you, however, in that no futures contract exactly matches your particular portfolio. As a result, you decide to protect your stock portfolio from a fall in value caused by a falling stock market using stock index futures. This is an example of a **cross-hedge**, where a futures contract on a related, but not identical, commodity or financial instrument is used to hedge a particular spot position.

cross-hedge
Hedging a particular spot position with futures contracts on a related, but not identical, commodity or financial instrument.

Thus, to hedge your portfolio, you wish to establish a short hedge using stock index futures. To do this, you need to know how many index futures contracts are required to form an effective hedge. Four basic inputs are needed to calculate the number of stock index futures contracts required to hedge a stock portfolio:

1. The current value of your stock portfolio.
2. The beta of your stock portfolio.
3. The contract value of the index futures contract used for hedging.
4. The beta of the futures contract.

Based on previous chapters, you are familiar with the concept of beta as a measure of market risk for a stock portfolio. Essentially, beta measures portfolio risk relative to the overall stock market. We will assume that you have maintained a beta of 1.25 for your $185 million stock portfolio.

You believe that the market (and your portfolio) will fall in value over the next three months and you decide to eliminate market risk from your portfolio. Because you hold a stock portfolio, you know that you will need to establish a short hedge using futures contracts. You decide to use futures contracts on the S&P 500 index because you used this index to calculate the beta for your portfolio.

From *The Wall Street Journal,* you find that the Mini S&P 500 futures price for contracts that mature in three months is currently 4,100. Because the contract size for the Mini S&P 500 futures is 50 times the index level, the current value of a single S&P 500 index futures contract is $50 \times 4,100 = \$205,000$.

You now have all the information you need to calculate the number of Mini S&P 500 index futures contracts needed to hedge your $185 million stock portfolio. The number of stock index futures contracts needed to hedge the portfolio fully is:

$$\text{Number of contracts} = \frac{V_P}{V_F} \times \frac{\beta_P}{\beta_F} \qquad (14.9)$$

where: V_P = Value of the stock portfolio

V_F = Value of one stock index futures contract

β_P = Current beta of the stock portfolio

β_F = Current beta of the futures contract

For your particular hedging problem, $\beta_P = 1.25$, $V_P = \$185$ million, and $V_F = \$205,000$. We are not given the beta of the futures contract, but because we are using S&P 500 futures, the beta should be close to that of the S&P 500, which is 1. The only time β_F would be different from 1 is if the futures contract being used is different from the index being used to calculate the beta of the underlying portfolio. For example, if we calculate the beta of the underlying portfolio using the S&P 500, but we use Dow futures contracts to hedge, then we would also have to calculate the beta of the Dow futures contracts relative to the S&P 500 index.

Given the information in our example, the following calculation results:

$$\text{Number of contracts} = \frac{\$185,000,000}{\$205,000} \times \frac{1.25}{1} = 1,128.05$$

Thus, you can establish an effective short hedge by going short 1,128 S&P 500 index futures contracts. This short hedge will protect your stock portfolio against the risk of a general fall in the stock market during the remaining three-month life of the futures contract.

EXAMPLE 14.9

Hedging with Stock Index Futures

How many stock index futures contracts are required to completely hedge a $250 million stock portfolio, assuming a portfolio beta of .75 and a Mini S&P 500 index futures level of 4,200?

Using Equation 14.9:

$$\text{Number of contracts} = \frac{250,000,000}{210,000} \times \frac{.75}{1} = 892.86$$

Therefore, you need to short 893 stock index futures contracts to hedge this $250 million portfolio. In this example, note that the value of one futures contract is given by $50 × 4,200 = $210,000.

HEDGING INTEREST RATE RISK WITH FUTURES

Having discussed hedging a stock portfolio, we now turn to hedging a bond portfolio. As we will see, the bond portfolio hedging problem is similar to the stock portfolio hedging problem. Once again, we will be cross-hedging, but this time using futures contracts on U.S. Treasury notes. Here, our goal is to protect the bond portfolio against changing interest rates.

In this example, you are responsible for managing a bond portfolio with a current value of $100 million. Recently, rising interest rates have caused your portfolio to fall in value slightly, and you are concerned that interest rates may continue to trend upward for the next several months. You decide to establish a short hedge based on 10-year Treasury note futures.

The formula for the number of U.S. Treasury note futures contracts needed to hedge a bond portfolio is similar to Equation 14.9:

$$\text{Number of contracts} = \frac{D_P \times V_P}{D_F \times V_F} \qquad (14.10)$$

where: D_p = Duration of the bond portfolio

V_p = Value of the bond portfolio

D_F = Duration of the futures contract

V_F = Value of a single futures contract

We already know the value of the bond portfolio, which is $100 million. Also, suppose that the duration of the portfolio is given as eight years. Next, we must calculate the duration of the futures contract and the value of the futures contract.

As a useful rule of thumb, the duration of an interest rate futures contract is equal to the duration of the underlying instrument plus the time remaining until contract maturity:

$$D_F = D_U + M_F \qquad (14.11)$$

where: D_F = Duration of the futures contract

D_U = Duration of the underlying instrument

M_F = Time remaining until contract maturity

For simplicity, let us suppose that the duration of the underlying U.S. Treasury note is 6½ years and the futures contract has a maturity of ½ year, yielding a futures contract duration of 7 years.

The value of a single futures contract is the current futures price times the futures contract size. The standard contract size for U.S. Treasury note futures contracts is $100,000 par value. Now suppose that the futures price is 118, or 118 percent of par value. This yields a futures contract value of $100,000 × 1.18 = $118,000.

You now have all inputs required to calculate the number of futures contracts needed to hedge your bond portfolio. The number of U.S. Treasury note futures contracts needed to hedge the bond portfolio is calculated as follows:

$$\text{Number of contracts} = \frac{8 \times \$100,000,000}{7 \times \$118,000} = 968.52$$

Thus, you can establish an effective short hedge by going short 968 or 969 futures contracts for 10-year U.S. Treasury notes. This short hedge will protect your bond portfolio against the risk of a general rise in interest rates during the life of the futures contracts.

EXAMPLE 14.10 **Hedging with U.S. Treasury Note Futures**

How many futures contracts are required to hedge a $250 million bond portfolio with a portfolio duration of 5 years using 10-year U.S. Treasury note futures with a duration of 7.5 years and a futures price of 115?

Using the formula for the number of contracts, we have:

$$\text{Number of contracts} = \frac{5 \times \$250,000,000}{7.5 \times \$115,000} = 1,449.28$$

You therefore need to sell 1,449 contracts to hedge this $250 million portfolio.

FUTURES CONTRACT DELIVERY OPTIONS

cheapest-to-deliver option
Seller's option to deliver the cheapest instrument when a futures contract allows several instruments for delivery. For example, U.S. Treasury note futures allow delivery of any Treasury note with a maturity between 6½ and 10 years.

Many futures contracts have a delivery option whereby the seller can choose among several different "grades" of the underlying commodity or instrument when fulfilling delivery requirements. Naturally, we expect the seller to deliver the cheapest among available options. In futures jargon, this is called the **cheapest-to-deliver option.** The cheapest-to-deliver option is an example of a broader feature of many futures contracts, known as a "quality" option. Of course, futures buyers know about the delivery option, and therefore the futures prices reflect the value of the cheapest-to-deliver instrument.

As a specific example of a cheapest-to-deliver option, the 10-year Treasury note contract allows delivery of any Treasury note with a maturity between 6½ and 10 years. This complicates the bond portfolio hedging problem. For the portfolio manager trying to hedge a bond portfolio with U.S. Treasury note futures, the cheapest-to-deliver feature means that a note can be hedged only based on an assumption about which note will actually be delivered. Furthermore, through time the cheapest-to-deliver note may vary, and, consequently, the hedge will have to be monitored regularly to make sure that it correctly reflects the note issue that is most likely to be delivered. Fortunately, because this is a common problem, many commercial advisory services provide this information to portfolio managers and other investors.

CHECK THIS

14.5a What is a cross-hedge?

14.5b What are the basic inputs required to calculate the number of stock index futures contracts needed to hedge an equity portfolio?

14.5c What are the basic inputs required to calculate the number of U.S. Treasury note futures contracts needed to hedge a bond portfolio?

14.5d What is the cheapest-to-deliver option?

 14.6 Summary and Conclusions

The topic of this chapter is futures markets. In this chapter, we surveyed the basics of futures markets and contracts—which we summarize by the chapter's important concepts.

1. **The basics of futures markets and how to obtain price quotes for futures contracts.**

A. A futures contract is an agreement between a buyer and a seller for a future transaction at a price set today. Futures contracts are managed through organized futures exchanges. The existence of a futures exchange virtually eliminates default risk. Four major terms for standardized futures contracts are (1) the identity of the underlying commodity or financial instrument, (2) the futures contract size, (3) the futures maturity date, and (4) the future price at which the contract will be fulfilled.

B. Most commodity futures contracts call for delivery of a physical commodity. Financial futures require delivery of a financial instrument or, in many cases, cash. Futures contracts are a type of derivative security because the value of the contract is derived from the value of an underlying instrument.

C. Quotes for futures prices are available through the financial press. These days, however, delayed intraday quotes for futures prices are available at the websites of many futures exchanges.

2. **The risks involved in futures market speculation.**

A. Speculators accept price risk in an attempt to profit on the direction of prices. Speculators can go long or short futures contracts. Speculators buy futures contracts if they think prices are going to go higher. Buying futures is often referred to as "going long," or establishing a long position. Speculators sell futures contracts if they think prices are going lower. Selling futures is often called "going short," or establishing a short position.

B. Futures speculation can lead to substantial gains and losses. An important point is that your gains from futures speculation depend on accurate forecasts of the direction of future prices. You must ask yourself: Is it easy to forecast price changes?

C. You can sustain losses in futures markets far in excess of your original margin deposit. As futures market prices move against your position, you could be asked to deposit more money into your futures trading account.

3. **How cash prices and futures prices are linked.**

A. The cash price of a commodity or financial instrument is the price quoted for current delivery. The cash price is also called the spot price.

GETTING DOWN TO BUSINESS

This chapter covered the essentials of what many consider to be a complex subject, futures contracts. We hope you realize that futures contracts per se are not complicated at all; in fact, they are, for the most part, quite simple. This doesn't mean that they're for everybody, of course. Because of the tremendous leverage possible, very large gains and losses can (and do) occur with great speed.

To experience some of the gains and losses from outright speculation, you should buy and sell a variety of contracts in a simulated brokerage account such as Stock-Trak. Be sure to go both long and short and pick a few of each major type of contract.

The internet is a rich resource for more information on trading futures. Probably the best place to begin is by visiting the websites of the major futures exchanges: the CME Group (www.cmegroup.com), the Intercontinental Exchange (www.theice.com), and the London Metals Exchange (www.lme.com). You might also visit the websites of some other international futures exchanges. Wikipedia has a list of worldwide futures exchanges. Bear in mind that the list changes frequently.

For information on futures markets regulation, the federal agency charged with regulating U.S. futures markets is the Commodity Futures Trading Commission (www.cftc.gov). The professional organization charged with self-regulation is the National Futures Association (www.nfa.futures.org). General information on futures markets and trading can be found at the Futures Industry Association (fia.org).

For the latest information on the real world of investments, visit us at jmdinvestments.blogspot.com.

B. The futures price is the future value of the spot price, calculated at the risk-free rate. This statement is the famous spot-futures parity condition. This condition must hold in the absence of cash-futures arbitrage opportunities.

4. How futures contracts can be used to transfer price risk.

A. Hedging is the major economic reason for the existence of futures markets. However, a viable futures market requires participation by both hedgers and speculators.

B. Hedgers transfer price risk to speculators, and speculators absorb price risk. Therefore, hedging and speculating are complementary activities.

C. Hedgers transfer price risk by taking a futures position opposite to their position in the spot market. For example, if the hedger has an inventory of some commodity, the hedger is said to be long in the spot market. Therefore, the hedger will offset price risk in the spot market by taking a short position in the futures market.

Key Terms

basis 473
carrying-charge market 473
cash market 472
cash price 472
cash-futures arbitrage 473
cheapest-to-deliver option 479
cross-hedge 477
forward contract 460
full hedge 467
futures contract 460
futures margin 470
futures price 460
hedger 467
index arbitrage 476

initial margin 470
inverted market 473
long hedge 468
long position 465
maintenance margin 471
margin call 471
marking to market 470
program trading 476
reverse trade 471
short hedge 467
short position 465
speculator 465
spot-futures parity 474
underlying asset 467

Related Bloomberg Functions

CTM	Contracts Table Menu, 14.1
DES	Security Description, 14.1
SSI	Standing Settlement Instructions, 14.1
FRD	FX Forward Calculator, 14.2
XLTP XDVO	Excel Template: Futures Contract Value Calculator, 14.2
CARC	Commodity Arbitrage Calculator, 14.4
FES	Covered Interest Arbitrage Calculator, 14.4
FV	World Equity Index Fair Value, 14.5
FAIR	Fair Value Monitor, 14.5
EIRV	Equity Index Relative Value, 14.5
WIRP	World Interest Rate Probability, 14.5
DLV	Cheapest-to-Deliver, 14.5

Chapter Review Problems and Self-Test

1. **Futures Gains and Losses (LO1, CFA2)** Suppose you purchase 10 orange juice contracts today at the settle price of $1 per pound. How much do these 10 contracts cost you? If the settle price is lower tomorrow by 2 cents per pound, how much do you make or lose? The contract size is 15,000 pounds.

2. **Spot-Futures Parity (LO3, CFA1)** There is a futures contract on a stock index, which is currently selling at $200 per share. The contract matures in two months; the risk-free rate is 5 percent annually. The stocks in the index do not pay dividends. What does the parity relationship imply the futures price should be?

Answers to Self-Test Problems

1. If you go long (purchase) 10 contracts, you pay nothing today (you will be required to post margin, but a futures contract is an agreement to exchange cash for goods later, not today). If the settle price drops by 2 cents per pound, you lose $.02 × 15,000 pounds (the contract size) = $300 per contract. With 10 contracts, you lose $3,000.

2. The spot-futures parity condition is:

$$F_T = S(1 + r - d)^T$$

where S is the spot price, r is the risk-free rate, d is the dividend yield, F is the futures price, and T is the time to expiration measured in years.

Plugging in the numbers, with zero for the dividend yield and 1/6 for the number of years (2 months out of 12), we have:

$$F_{1/6} = \$200(1 + .05)^{1/6} = \$201.63$$

Test Your Investment Quotient

1. **Futures versus Forward Contracts (LO1, CFA2)** Which of the following statements is true regarding the distinction between futures contracts and forward contracts?

    a. Futures contracts are exchange-traded, whereas forward contracts are OTC-traded.
    b. All else equal, forward prices are higher than futures prices.
    c. Forward contracts are created from baskets of futures contracts.
    d. Futures contracts are cash-settled at maturity, whereas forward contracts result in delivery.

2. **Futures versus Forward Contracts (LO1, CFA2)**   In which of the following ways do futures contracts differ from forward contracts?

   I. Futures contracts are standardized.
   II. For futures, performance of each party is guaranteed by a clearinghouse.
   III. Futures contracts require a daily settling of any gains or losses.
      a. I and II only
      b. I and III only
      c. II and III only
      d. I, II, and III

3. **Futures Contracts (LO1, CFA2)**   The open interest on a futures contract at any given time is the total number of outstanding:

   a. Contracts.
   b. Unhedged positions.
   c. Clearinghouse positions.
   d. Long and short positions.

4. **Futures Margin (LO2, CFA2)**   Initial margin for a futures contract is usually:

   a. Regulated by the Federal Reserve.
   b. Less than 2 percent of contract value.
   c. In the range between 2 percent and 5 percent of contract value.
   d. In the range between 5 percent and 15 percent of contract value.

5. **Futures Margin (LO2, CFA2)**   In futures trading, the minimum level to which an equity position may fall before requiring additional margin is most accurately termed the:

   a. Initial margin.
   b. Variation margin.
   c. Cash flow margin.
   d. Maintenance margin.

6. **Futures Margin (LO2, CFA2)**   A silver futures contract requires the seller to deliver 5,000 troy ounces of silver. An investor sells one April silver futures contract at a price of $15 per ounce, posting an $8,400 initial margin. If the required maintenance margin is $6,900, the price per ounce at which the investor would first receive a maintenance margin call is closest to:

   a. $13.62.
   b. $14.70.
   c. $15.30.
   d. $16.38.

7. **Futures Margin (LO2, CFA2)**   Which of the following statements is false about futures account margin?

   a. Initial margin is higher than maintenance margin.
   b. A margin call results when account margin falls below maintenance margin.
   c. Marking to market of account margin occurs at least daily.
   d. A margin call results when account margin falls below initial margin.

8. **Futures Contracts (LO1, CFA2)**   Which of the following contract terms changes daily during the life of a futures contract?

   a. Futures price
   b. Futures contract size
   c. Futures maturity date
   d. Underlying commodity

9. **Futures Delivery (LO1, CFA2)**   On the maturity date, stock index futures contracts require delivery of:

   a. Common stock.
   b. Common stock plus accrued dividends.
   c. Treasury bills.
   d. Cash.

10. **Spot-Futures Parity (LO3, CFA1)**   A Treasury note futures contract has a quoted price of 100. The underlying bond has a coupon rate of 7 percent and the current market interest rate is 7 percent. Spot-futures parity then implies a cash bond price of:

    a. 93.
    b. 100.

    c. 107.

    d. 114.

11. **Spot-Futures Parity (LO3, CFA1)**   A stock index futures contract maturing in one year has a currently traded price of $1,000. The cash index has a dividend yield of 2 percent and the interest rate is 5 percent. Spot-futures parity then implies a cash index level of:

    a. $933.33.

    b. $970.87.

    c. $1,071.

    d. $1,029.

12. **Spot-Futures Parity (LO3, CFA1)**   A stock index futures contract matures in one year. The cash index currently has a level of $1,000 with a dividend yield of 2 percent. If the interest rate is 5 percent, then spot-futures parity implies a futures price of:

    a. $943.40.

    b. $970.87.

    c. $1,060.

    d. $1,030.

13. **Futures Hedging (LO3, CFA2)**   You manage a $100 million stock portfolio with a beta of .8. Given a contract size of $100,000 for a stock index futures contract, how many contracts are needed to hedge your portfolio? Assume the beta of the futures contract is 1.

    a. 8

    b. 80

    c. 800

    d. 8,000

14. **Futures Hedging (LO4, CFA2)**   You manage a $100 million bond portfolio with a duration of 9 years. You wish to hedge this portfolio against interest rate risk using T-bond futures with a contract size of $100,000 and a duration of 12 years. How many contracts are required?

    a. 750

    b. 1,000

    c. 133

    d. 1,333

15. **Futures Hedging (LO4, CFA2)**   Which of the following is not an input needed to calculate the number of stock index futures contracts required to hedge a stock portfolio?

    a. The value of the stock portfolio

    b. The beta of the stock portfolio

    c. The contract value of the index futures contract

    d. The initial margin required for each futures contract

Concept Questions

1. **Understanding Futures Quotations (LO1, CFA2)**   Using Figure 14.1, answer the following questions:

    a. How many exchanges trade wheat futures contracts?

    b. If you have a position in 10 gold futures, what quantity of gold underlies your position?

    c. If you are short 20 corn futures contracts and you opt to make delivery, what quantity of corn must you supply?

    d. Which maturity of the gasoline contract has the largest open interest? Which one has the smallest open interest?

2. **Hedging with Futures (LO4, CFA2)**   Kellogg's uses large quantities of corn in its breakfast cereal operations. Suppose the near-term weather forecast for the corn-producing states is droughtlike conditions, so corn prices are expected to rise. To hedge its costs, Kellogg's decides to use the Chicago Board of Trade corn futures contracts. Should the company be a short hedger or a long hedger in corn futures?

3. **Hedging with Futures (LO4, CFA2)**   Suppose one of Fidelity's mutual funds closely mimics the S&P 500 index. The fund has done very well during the year, and, in November, the fund manager wants to lock in the gains he has made using stock index futures. Should he take a long or short position in S&P 500 index futures?

4. **Hedging with Futures (LO4, CFA2)** A mutual fund that predominantly holds long-term Treasury bonds plans to liquidate the portfolio in three months. However, the fund manager is concerned that interest rates may rise from current levels and wants to hedge the price risk of the portfolio. Should she buy or sell Treasury bond futures contracts?

5. **Hedging with Futures (LO4, CFA2)** An American electronics firm imports its completed circuit boards from Japan. The company signed a contract today to pay for the boards in Japanese yen upon delivery in four months; the price per board in yen was fixed in the contract. Should the importer buy or sell Japanese yen futures contracts?

6. **Hedging with Futures (LO4, CFA2)** Jed Clampett just dug another oil well, and, as usual, it's a gusher. Jed estimates that in two months, he'll have 2 million barrels of crude oil to bring to market. However, Jed would like to lock in the value of this oil at today's prices because the oil market has been skyrocketing recently. Should Jed buy or sell crude oil futures contracts?

7. **Hedging with Futures (LO4, CFA2)** The town of South Park is planning a bond issue in six months and Kenny, the town treasurer, is worried that interest rates may rise, thereby reducing the value of the bond issue. Should Kenny buy or sell Treasury bond futures contracts to hedge the impending bond issue?

8. **Futures Markets (LO1, CFA2)** Is it true that a futures contract represents a zero-sum game, meaning that the only way for a buyer to win is for a seller to lose, and vice versa?

9. **Program Trading (LO1) Program traders closely monitor relative futures and cash market prices, but program trades are not actually made on a fully mechanical basis. What are some of the complications that might make program trading using, for example, the S&P 500 contract more difficult than the spot-futures parity formula indicates?**

10. **Short Selling (LO1, CFA2)** What are the similarities and differences in taking the short side of a futures contract and short selling a stock? How do the cash flows differ?

Questions and Problems

Core Questions

1. **Understanding Futures Quotations (LO1, LO2, CFA2)** Using Figure 14.1, answer the following questions:
   a. What was the settle price for July 2022 coffee futures on this date? What is the total dollar value of this contract at the close of trading for the day?
   b. What was the settle price for July 2022 gasoline futures on this date? If you held 10 contracts, what is the total dollar value of your futures position?
   c. Suppose you held an open position of 25 June 2022 Mini Dow Jones Industrial Average futures on this day. What is the change in the total dollar value of your position for this day's trading? If you held a long position, would this represent a profit or a loss to you?
   d. Suppose you are short 10 July 2022 soybean oil futures contracts. Would you have made a profit or a loss on this day?

2. **Futures Profits and Losses (LO2, CFA2)** You are long 20 July 2022 soybean futures contracts. (Grain traders would say you are "long 100," i.e., 100,000 bushels.) Calculate your dollar profit or loss from this trading day using Figure 14.1.

3. **Futures Profits and Losses (LO2, CFA2)** You are short 15 July 2022 corn futures contracts. (Grain traders would say that you are "short 75," i.e., 75,000 bushels.) Calculate your dollar profit or loss from this trading day using Figure 14.1.

4. **Futures Profits and Losses (LO2, CFA2)** You are short 30 June 2022 five-year Treasury note futures contracts. Calculate your profit or loss from this trading day using Figure 14.1.

5. **Open Interest (LO1, CFA2)** Referring to Figure 14.1, what is the total open interest on the June 2022 Japanese yen contract? Does it represent long positions, short positions, or both? Based on the settle price on the contract, what is the dollar value of the open interest?

6. **Spot-Futures Parity (LO3, CFA1)** A non-dividend-paying stock is currently priced at $16.40. The risk-free rate is 3 percent and a futures contract on the stock matures in six months. What price should the futures be?

7. **Spot-Futures Parity (LO3, CFA1)** A non-dividend-paying stock has a futures contract with a price of $94.90 and a maturity of two months. If the risk-free rate is 4.5 percent, what is the price of the stock?

8. **Spot-Futures Parity (LO3, CFA1)** A non-dividend-paying stock has a current share price of $42.60 and a futures price of $42.95. If the maturity of the futures contract is four months, what is the risk-free rate?

9. **Spot-Futures Parity (LO3, CFA1)** A stock has a current share price of $49.24 and a dividend yield of 1.5 percent. If the risk-free rate is 5.4 percent, what is the futures price if the maturity is four months?

10. **Spot-Futures Parity (LO3, CFA1)** A single-stock futures contract is priced at $27.18. The stock has a dividend yield of 1.25 percent and the risk-free rate is 2.5 percent. If the futures contract matures in six months, what is the current stock price?

Intermediate Questions

11. **Margin Call (LO2, CFA2)** Suppose the initial margin on heating oil futures is $8,400, the maintenance margin is $7,200 per contract, and you establish a long position of 10 contracts today, where each contract represents 42,000 gallons. Tomorrow, the contract settles down $.04 from the previous day's price. Are you subject to a margin call? What is the maximum price decline on the contract that you can sustain without getting a margin call?

12. **Marking to Market (LO2, CFA2)** You are long 10 gold futures contracts, established at an initial settle price of $1,300 per ounce, where each contract represents 100 troy ounces. Your initial margin to establish the position is $12,000 per contract and the maintenance margin is $11,200 per contract. Over the subsequent four trading days, gold settles at $1,295, $1,290, $1,305, and $1,315, respectively. Compute the balance in your margin account at the end of each of the four trading days, and compute your total profit or loss at the end of the trading period. Assume that a margin call requires you to fund your account back to the initial margin requirement.

13. **Marking to Market (LO2, CFA2)** You are short 15 gasoline futures contracts, established at an initial settle price of $2.085 per gallon, where each contract represents 42,000 gallons. Your initial margin to establish the position is $7,425 per contract and the maintenance margin is $6,500 per contract. Over the subsequent four trading days, gasoline settles at $2.071, $2.099, $2.118, and $2.146, respectively. Compute the balance in your margin account at the end of each of the four trading days, and compute your total profit or loss at the end of the trading period. Assume that a margin call requires you to fund your account back to the initial margin requirement.

14. **Futures Profits (LO2, CFA2)** You went long 20 July 2022 crude oil futures contracts at a price of $116.50. Looking back at Figure 14.1, if you closed your position at the settle price on this day, what was your profit?

15. **Futures Profits (LO2, CFA2)** You shorted 15 June 2022 British pound futures contracts at the high price for the day. Looking back at Figure 14.1, if you closed your position at the settle price on this day, what was your profit?

16. **Index Arbitrage (LO3, CFA1)** Suppose the CAC-40 Index (a widely followed index of French stock prices) is currently at 4,920, the expected dividend yield on the index is 2 percent per year, and the risk-free rate in France is 6 percent annually. If CAC-40 futures contracts that expire in six months are currently trading at 4,952, what program trading strategy would you recommend?

17. **Cross-Hedging (LO4, CFA2)** You have been assigned to implement a three-month hedge for a stock mutual fund portfolio that primarily invests in medium-sized companies. The mutual fund has a beta of 1.15 measured relative to the S&P Midcap 400, and the net asset value of the fund is $175 million. Should you be long or short in the Midcap 400 futures contracts? Assuming the Midcap 400 Index is at 1,450 and its futures contract size is 500 times the index, determine the appropriate number of contracts to use in designing your cross-hedge strategy.

18. **Spot-Futures Parity (LO3, CFA3)** Suppose the 6-month Mini S&P 500 futures price is 2,281.55, while the cash price is 2,270.42. What is the *implied difference* between the risk-free interest rate and the dividend yield on the S&P 500?

19. **Spot-Futures Parity (LO3, CFA3)** Suppose the 6-month Mini S&P 500 futures price is 2,399.25, while the cash price is 2,370.48. What is the *implied dividend yield* on the S&P 500 if the risk-free interest rate is 5 percent?

20. **Hedging Interest Rate Risk (LO4, CFA2)** Suppose you want to hedge a $500 million bond portfolio with a duration of 5.1 years using 10-year Treasury note futures with a duration of 6.7 years, a futures price of 102, and 3 months to expiration. The multiplier on Treasury note futures is $100,000. How many contracts do you buy or sell?

21. **Hedging Interest Rate Risk (LO4, CFA2)** Suppose you want to hedge a $400 million bond portfolio with a duration of 8.4 years using 10-year Treasury note futures with a duration of 6.2

years, a futures price of 102, and 85 days to expiration. The multiplier on Treasury note futures is $100,000. How many contracts do you buy or sell?

22. **Futures Arbitrage (LO3, CFA4)** A non-dividend-paying stock is currently priced at $48.15 per share. A futures contract maturing in five months has a price of $48.56 and the risk-free rate is 4 percent. Describe how you could make an arbitrage profit from this situation. How much could you make on a per-share basis?

23. **Futures Arbitrage (LO3, CFA4)** A stock is currently priced at $53.87 and the futures on the stock that expire in six months have a price of $55.94. The risk-free rate is 5 percent and the stock is not expected to pay a dividend. Is there an arbitrage opportunity here? How would you exploit it? What is the arbitrage opportunity per share of stock?

Spreadsheet Problems

24. **Hedging Heating Oil with Futures (LO4, CFA5)** Heating oil futures contracts are traded on the New York Mercantile Exchange (NYM), a division of the CME Group. The standard contract size for heating oil futures is 42,000 gallons per contract. You have an inventory of 1.68 million gallons, and you want to construct a full hedge. Suppose the average acquisition price of your 1.68 million gallons of heating oil is $1.75 per gallon and that today's futures price for delivery during your heating season is $2.05. In the past, market conditions in your distribution area were such that you could sell your heating oil to your customers at a price 25 cents higher than the prevailing futures price. To help finance your inventory purchases, you borrowed money. During the heating season, you have to make an interest payment of $600,000. Calculate the pretax profit for your enterprise in the cases shown in the spreadsheet without a hedge in place and with a hedge in place.

	Base Case: No Change in Heating Oil Price	Heating Oil Price Decrease	Heating Oil Price Increase
Heating oil inventory (gal.)	16,800,000	16,800,000	16,800,000
Selling price, per gallon	$2.30	$1.90	$2.70
Avg. purchase price, per gallon	$1.75	$1.75	$1.75
Futures price	$2.05	$1.65	$2.45
Without a Hedge			
Revenue	_____	_____	_____
Cost of inventory sold			
Interest expense	_____	_____	_____
Pretax profit	_____	_____	_____
Pretax profit, per gallon			
With Short Hedge (short futures at $2.05)			
Contracts needed			
Revenue	_____	_____	_____
Cost of inventory sold			
Interest expense	_____	_____	_____
Futures gain (loss)	_____	_____	_____
Pretax profit	_____	_____	_____
Pretax profit, per gallon			
Futures gain (loss), per gallon			

CFA Exam Review by Kaplan Schweser

[CFA2, CFA4, CFA5]

Jackson, Inc., is a multinational company based in West Point, Mississippi, that makes freight cars. One-third of Jackson's sales occur in the Netherlands. To manufacture the cars, the firm must import approximately half of the raw materials from Canada.

Two months from now, Jackson plans to sell freight cars to a Dutch firm for €15 million. To protect the company from any adverse moves in exchange rates, Jackson enters into a €15 million futures contract due in 60 days. Jackson also enters into a 60-day futures contract to lock in C$8.5 million, which will be used to purchase steel from a supplier.

The current euro to U.S. dollar exchange rate is €.79/$1 while the Canadian dollar to U.S. dollar exchange rate is C$1.30/$1. The 60-day euro to U.S. dollar rate is €.80/$1, while the Canadian dollar to U.S. dollar rate is C$1.33/$1. At the end of the two months, the actual euro to U.S. dollar exchange rate is €.90/$1 and the actual Canadian dollar to U.S. dollar rate is C$1.20/$1.

To help understand the relationships, Jackson's chief risk officer, Dr. Charles Miles, has put together the following table on hedging currency positions:

Currency Exposure	Position	Action
Receiving foreign currency	Long	Buy forward contracts
Paying foreign currency	Short	Sell forward contracts

1. **When hedging its exchange rate risk on the freight car sale, Jackson used a futures contract to:**
   a. Sell €15 million in exchange for $18.75 million.
   b. Buy €15 million in exchange for $18.75 million.
   c. Sell €15 million in exchange for $16.67 million.

2. **To hedge the foreign exchange risk relative to the Canadian dollar, Jackson should:**
   a. Buy a futures contract to exchange $7,083,333 for C$8.5 million.
   b. Buy a futures contract to exchange $6,390,977 for C$8.5 million.
   c. Sell a futures contract to exchange $6,390,977 for C$8.5 million.

3. **In regard to the table that Dr. Miles constructed, which of the following is true?**
   a. The receiving foreign currency position is correct; the action is incorrect.
   b. The receiving foreign currency position is incorrect; the action is also incorrect.
   c. The paying foreign currency position is correct; the action is also correct.

Bloomberg Exercises

1. Review the list of futures contracts traded on the exchanges. **(CTM)**
2. Examine the current fair value of major world equity indexes. **(FV)**
3. Pick a commodity futures contract and identify its cheapest-to-deliver option. **(DLV)**

What's on the Web?

1. **Single Stock Futures** Go to www.theice.com. How many single-stock futures are traded on this exchange? What is the contract size of a single-stock future? What are the minimum tick size, contract month, and contract expiration? What is the margin requirement?

2. **Spot-Futures Parity** Go to www.theice.com and find the futures quotes for Barclays. Now go to www.londonstockexchange.com and find the current stock price for Barclays. What is the implied risk-free rate using these prices? Does each different maturity give you the same interest rate? Why or why not?

3. **Contract Specifications** You want to find the contract specifications for futures contracts. Go to the CME Group at www.cmegroup.com and find the contract specifications for corn, rough rice, butter, and lean hogs. What are the contract sizes for each of these contracts?

4. **The Juice** Go to the Intercontinental Exchange website at www.theice.com. What contracts are traded on the Intercontinental Exchange? What does "FCOJ" stand for? What are the trading months for FCOJ futures contracts? What are the position limits for FCOJ futures contracts? What is the last trading day of the expiration month for FCOJ futures? What are the trading months and last trading day for FCOJ options contracts? What is the FCOJ Differential contract?

5. **Hedging with Futures** You are working for a company that processes beef and will take delivery of 720,000 pounds of cattle in August. You would like to lock in your costs today because you are concerned about an increase in cattle prices. Go to the CME Group at www.cmegroup.com and find the contract size for live cattle. How many futures contracts will you need to hedge your exposure? Will you go long or short on these contracts? Now find the most recent price quote for live cattle futures on the CME Group website. What price are you effectively locking in if you traded at the last price? Suppose cattle prices increase 5 percent before the expiration. What is your profit or loss on the futures position? What if the price decreases by 5 percent? Explain how your futures position has eliminated your exposure to price risk in the live cattle market.

Stock Options

"I have no objection to the granting of options. Companies should use whatever form of compensation best motivates employees—whether this be cash bonuses, trips to Hawaii, restricted stock grants or stock options."

—Warren Buffett

Learning Objectives

Give yourself some in-the-money academic and professional options by understanding:

1. The basics of option contracts and how to obtain price quotes.

2. The difference between option payoffs and option profits.

3. The workings of some basic option trading strategies.

4. The logic behind the put-call parity condition.

Options have fascinated investors for centuries. The option concept is simple. Instead of buying stock shares today, you buy an option to buy the stock at a later date at a price specified in the option contract. You are not obligated to exercise the option, but if doing so benefits you, of course you will. Moreover, the most you can lose is the original price of the option, which is normally only a fraction of the stock price. Sounds good, doesn't it?

Options on common stocks have traded in financial markets for about as long as common stocks have been traded. However, it was not until 1973, when the Chicago Board Options Exchange (CBOE) was established, that options trading became a large and important part of the financial landscape. Since then, the success of options trading has been phenomenal.

Much of the success of options trading is attributable to the tremendous flexibility that options offer investors in designing investment strategies. For example, options can be used to reduce risk through hedging strategies or to increase risk through speculative strategies. As a result, when properly understood and applied, options are appealing both to conservative investors and to aggressive speculators.

In this chapter, we discuss options generally, but our primary focus is on options on individual common stocks. We also discuss options on stock market indexes, which are options on portfolios of common stocks. We begin by reviewing some of the ideas we touched on in an earlier chapter, where we very briefly discussed options.

CFA™ Exam Topics in This Chapter:

1. Derivative markets and instruments (L1, S15)
2. Basics of derivatives pricing and valuation (L1, S15)
3. Valuation of contingent claims (L2, S13)
4. Option strategies (L3, S4)

Go to Connect for a guide that aligns your textbook with CFA readings.

15.1 Options on Common Stocks

OPTION BASICS

Related Bloomberg Functions

OMON Option Monitor

OTD Option Description

MOSO Most Active Options

derivative security
Security whose value is derived from the value of another security. Options are a type of derivative security.

call option
Grants the holder the right, but not the obligation, to buy the underlying asset at a given strike price.

put option
Grants the holder the right, but not the obligation, to sell the underlying asset at a given strike price.

strike price
Price specified in an option contract that the holder pays to buy shares (in the case of call options) or receives to sell shares (in the case of put options) if the option is exercised. Also called the *exercise price.*

American option
An option that can be exercised any time before expiration.

European option
An option that can be exercised only at expiration.

Visit these options exchanges:
www.cboe.com
and
www.nyse.com.

As we have discussed, options on common stock are a type of **derivative security** because the value of a stock option is "derived" from the value of the underlying common stock. For example, the value of an option to buy or sell IBM stock is derived from the value of IBM stock. However, the relationship between the value of a particular stock option and the value of the underlying stock depends on the specific type of option.

Recall that there are two basic option types: **call options** and **put options**. Call options are options to buy and put options are options to sell. Thus, a call option on IBM stock is an option to buy IBM shares and a put option on IBM stock is an option to sell IBM shares. More specifically, a call option on common stock grants the holder the right, but not the obligation, to buy the underlying stock at a given **strike price** before the option expiration date. Similarly, a put option on common stock grants the holder the right, but not the obligation, to sell the underlying stock at a given strike price before the option expiration date. The strike price, also called the *exercise price,* is the price at which stock shares are bought or sold to fulfill the obligations of the option contract.

Options are contracts, and, in practice, option contracts are standardized to facilitate convenience in trading and price reporting. Standardized stock options have a contract size of 100 shares of common stock per option contract. This means that a single call option contract involves an option to buy 100 shares of stock. Likewise, a single put option contract involves an option to sell 100 shares of stock.

Because options are contracts, an understanding of stock options requires that we know the specific contract terms. In general, options on common stock must stipulate at least the following six contract terms:

1. The identity of the underlying stock.
2. The strike price, also called the striking or exercise price.
3. The option contract size.
4. The option expiration date, also called the option maturity.
5. The option exercise style.
6. The delivery or settlement procedure.

First, a stock option contract requires that the specific stock issue be clearly identified. While this may seem to be stating the obvious, in financial transactions it is important that the "obvious" is in fact clearly and unambiguously understood by all concerned parties.

Second, the strike price, also called the exercise price, must be stipulated. The strike price is quite important because it is the price that an option holder will pay (in the case of a call option) or receive (in the case of a put option) if the option is exercised.

Third, the size of the contract must be specified. As stated earlier, the standard contract size for stock options is 100 stock shares per option.

The fourth contract term that must be stated is the option expiration date. An option cannot be exercised after its expiration date. If an option is unexercised and its expiration date has passed, the option becomes worthless.

Fifth, the option's exercise style determines when the option can be exercised. There are two basic exercise styles: American and European. **American options** can be exercised any time before option expiration, but **European options** can be exercised only at expiration. Options on individual stocks are normally American style and stock index options are usually European style.

Finally, in the event that a stock option is exercised, the settlement process must be stipulated. For stock options, standard settlement requires delivery of the underlying stock shares several business days after a notice of exercise is made by the option holder.

Like a stock exchange, or, for that matter, any securities exchange, an options exchange is a marketplace where buy and sell orders from customers are matched up with each other. Stock options are traded in financial markets in a manner similar to the way that common stocks are traded. For example, there are organized options exchanges, and there are over-the-counter (OTC) options markets. The largest volume of stock options trading in the United States takes place at the Chicago Board Options Exchange (CBOE).

OPTION PRICE QUOTES

Stock option prices are available on the websites of the exchanges on which the options trade. For example, Figure 15.1 reproduces part of a page from the Chicago Board Options Exchange (www.cboe.com) website. The quote is for some options traded on Tesla, Inc.

For the Tesla options listed in Figure 15.1, options are separated by expiration date. We have provided only a small sample of the large number of Tesla options that are available. Historically, standardized option contracts were offered only by month. These so-called monthly options expire on the third Friday of the expiration month. For the Tesla options quoted in Figure 15.1, a July 15th expiration represents the standard monthly contract. Although quotes for this option do not appear in Figure 15.1, you can easily find them on www.cboe.com.

More recently, weekly options have become widely available. By convention, weekly stock options are created on a Thursday and expire the following Friday (or the Friday of the designated expiration week). The exception is that there are no weekly options listed the week when a monthly option will expire.

The notable difference between a monthly and a weekly option is their time to expiration. That is, their other features are the same. Weekly options are only available in the short term, generally, but not always, within the current month. For investors who want an option position six months out, the available contract is the standard monthly option contract. Thus, the only expiration date available that far out is the third Friday of the designated month.

Back to Figure 15.1. These first three contract terms—the identity of the underlying stock, the strike price, and the expiration date—will not change during the life of the option. Because the price of a stock option depends in part on the price of the underlying stock, however, the price of an option changes as the stock price changes.

Current option prices for both calls and puts are reported in Figure 15.1 in the columns labeled "Last." The quote also provides bid and ask prices, which would be relevant depending on whether you are buying or selling the options. The option prices are stated on a per-share

---

FIGURE 15.1   **Listed Options Quotations**

Tesla Inc

2022-06-09 15:59:59 ET (Delayed)   Bid: 718.56   Ask: 719.12   Vol: 17,906,371   Last: 718.56   Change: -6.48 (+-0.8931%)

Filters By:

Volume:	Expiration Type:	Options Range:	Size:	Expiration:	
All	All	Near the Money	3	2022 July	View Chain

Options Chain   Total Records: 30

Calls   Fri Jul 01 2022   **Puts**

Last	Net	Bid	Ask	Vol	IV	Delta	Gamma	Int	Strike	Last	Net	Bid	Ask	Vol	IV	Delta	Gamma	Int
59.01	-0.74	54.25	57.8	5	0.69	0.5811	0.0032	52	TSLA 705.000	40.86	+4.11	40.75	41.9	24	0.69	-0.4195	0.0032	229
54.5	-2.3	52.65	54.1	5	0.69	0.5648	0.0032	145	TSLA 710.000	43.04	+4.265	43.05	44.1	57	0.69	-0.4358	0.0032	375
50.85	-3.1	49.8	51.55	37	0.69	0.5485	0.0033	67	TSLA 715.000	43.1	+2.125	45.3	46.45	65	0.69	-0.4521	0.0033	297
48.65	-2.575	47.75	48.6	41	0.69	0.532	0.0033	375	TSLA 720.000	47.78	+4.53	47.8	48.9	69	0.68	-0.4686	0.0033	215
46.1	-2.5	45.25	46.05	71	0.68	0.5154	0.0033	136	TSLA 725.000	48.66	+3.035	50.3	51.35	46	0.68	-0.4852	0.0033	60
43.19	-2.835	42.85	43.65	59	0.68	0.4988	0.0033	104	TSLA 730.000	53.55	+5.575	52.95	54	460	0.68	-0.5018	0.0033	108

Calls   Fri Jul 08 2022   **Puts**

Last	Net	Bid	Ask	Vol	IV	Delta	Gamma	Int	Strike	Last	Net	Bid	Ask	Vol	IV	Delta	Gamma	Int
89	+21.575	61.8	66.85	2	0.71	0.581	0.0027	53	TSLA 705.000	48.6	+4.225	48.55	49.65	16	0.7	-0.4198	0.0027	141
62.1	-2.5	59.1	64.05	23	0.7	0.567	0.0028	47	TSLA 710.000	47.7	+1.175	50.65	52	30	0.7	-0.4338	0.0028	107
58.75	-3.05	57.4	59.5	9	0.69	0.553	0.0028	26	TSLA 715.000	53.2	+4.475	52.7	54.3	19	0.69	-0.4479	0.0028	83
56.7	-2.225	55.05	56.9	25	0.69	0.5388	0.0028	33	TSLA 720.000	56.23	+5.205	55.6	56.8	30	0.69	-0.4621	0.0028	43
54.1	-2.375	53.05	54.4	20	0.69	0.5246	0.0028	49	TSLA 725.000	57.35	+4.275	58.05	59.15	34	0.69	-0.4764	0.0028	37
51.8	-2.15	50.35	52	85	0.69	0.5103	0.0028	64	TSLA 730.000	57.24	+1.69	60.65	62	77	0.69	-0.4906	0.0029	58

Source: www.cboe.com. Accessed June 9, 2022.

Here is a stock quote and an option chain for FedEx (FDX) from Yahoo! Finance (finance.yahoo.com).

Let's take a look at one of the option symbols to see what it means. Look at the symbol FDX220610C00210000 at the beginning of the list of call options. The first three characters, "FDX," represent the ticker symbol for FedEx Corp. The next six digits tell us the expiration year (22), the expiration month (06), and the expiration day (10), respectively. So these options expire on June 10, 2022. The next character, "C," tells us whether this option is a call (C) or a put (P). The next five digits (00210) tell us the integer of strike price, in dollars, or $210. The final three digits (000) tell us the fraction of strike price, in dollar decimals, in this case $.000. The strike price, therefore, is $210.00. Of course, one can easily find the strike price by looking in the third column (labeled "Strike").

The fourth column ("Last Price") reports the option price for the last trade. The next two columns ("Bid" and "Ask") contain representative bid and ask price quotes from dealers. The next column ("Change") states the change in price from the previous day's last trade, where a zero indicates either no change in price or no trade that day. The percentage change from the previous day's close appears in the following column. "Volume" reports trading volume as the number of contracts traded that day, and "Open Interest" states open interest as the total number of contracts outstanding. The final column provides an estimate of implied volatility, which is a topic for another chapter.

FedEx Corporation (FDX)
NYSE - Nasdaq Real Time Price. Currency in USD

218.64 +1.47 (+0.68%)
As of 03:30PM EDT. Market open.

Summary | Company Outlook | Chart | Conversations | Statistics | Historical Data | Profile | Financials | Analysis | Options

Previous Close	217.17	Market Cap	56.268B
Open	217.20	Beta (5Y Monthly)	1.32
Bid	218.29 x 900	PE Ratio (TTM)	11.44
Ask	218.65 x 900	EPS (TTM)	19.09
Day's Range	215.46 - 221.36	Earnings Date	Jun 23, 2022
52 Week Range	192.82 - 304.59	Forward Dividend & Yield	3.00 (1.38%)
Volume	1,828,789	Ex-Dividend Date	Mar 04, 2022
Avg. Volume	2,417,668	1y Target Est	288.54

Calls for June 10, 2022

Contract Name	Last Trade Date	Strike	Last Price	Bid	Ask	Change	% Change	Volume	Open Interest	Implied Volatility
FDX220610C00210000	2022-06-09 10:15AM EDT	210.00	7.90	7.50	8.45	-1.35	-14.59%	4	635	53.66%
FDX220610C00212500	2022-06-09 12:44PM EDT	212.50	8.50	5.25	6.00	+2.90	+51.79%	3	61	51.56%
FDX220610C00215000	2022-06-09 3:47PM EDT	215.00	4.37	3.55	4.15	+0.72	+19.73%	43	194	47.75%
FDX220610C00217500	2022-06-09 3:32PM EDT	217.50	3.06	2.00	2.78	+0.81	+36.00%	41	79	47.12%
FDX220610C00220000	2022-06-09 3:31PM EDT	220.00	1.65	1.06	1.44	+0.35	+26.92%	428	388	41.48%
FDX220610C00222500	2022-06-09 3:44PM EDT	222.50	0.80	0.46	0.67	+0.17	+26.98%	604	424	38.87%

Puts for June 10, 2022

Contract Name	Last Trade Date	Strike	Last Price	Bid	Ask	Change	% Change	Volume	Open Interest	Implied Volatility
FDX220610P00210000	2022-06-09 3:31PM EDT	210.00	0.40	0.34	0.47	-0.30	-42.86%	258	937	41.21%
FDX220610P00212500	2022-06-09 3:52PM EDT	212.50	0.67	0.65	0.94	-0.48	-41.74%	66	459	40.87%
FDX220610P00215000	2022-06-09 3:59PM EDT	215.00	1.51	1.35	1.53	-0.47	-23.74%	182	490	37.60%
FDX220610P00217500	2022-06-09 3:05PM EDT	217.50	1.68	1.85	2.63	-1.54	-47.83%	94	290	36.96%
FDX220610P00220000	2022-06-09 3:10PM EDT	220.00	2.80	2.86	4.05	-0.80	-22.22%	245	147	34.67%
FDX220610P00222500	2022-06-09 1:39PM EDT	222.50	3.65	5.20	6.00	-2.80	-43.41%	86	71	34.86%

Source: Yahoo! Finance.

basis, but the actual price of an option contract is 100 times the per-share price. Each option contract represents an option on 100 shares of stock. Following the Bid and Ask columns is a column showing the volume of each contract traded so far on this particular day. The final column is the current open interest outstanding in each contract.

option chain
A list of available option contracts and their prices for a particular security arrayed by strike price and maturity.

Aside from the exchanges, option prices are widely available online. One easy-to-use source is Yahoo! Finance (finance.yahoo.com). The nearby *Work the Web* box contains an **option chain** for FedEx (FDX) stock options. The top box reports the time and price for the last trade in FedEx stock, along with the change in price from the previous day and the trading volume so far for the current day. The bottom boxes contain the FedEx option chain, one for call options and one for put options.

CHECK THIS

15.1a What is a call option? What is a put option?

15.1b What are the six basic contract terms that an option contract must specify?

15.1c What is an option chain?

15.2 The Options Clearing Corporation

Visit the OCC at
www.theocc.com.

Suppose that you order a new car through a local dealer and pay a $2,000 deposit. Further suppose that, two weeks later, you receive a letter informing you that your dealer has entered bankruptcy. No doubt, you would be quite upset at the prospect of losing your $2,000 deposit.

Now consider a similar situation where you pay $2,000 for several call options through a broker. On the day before expiration, you tell your broker to exercise the options because they would produce, say, a $5,000 payoff. Then, a few days later, your broker tells you that the call writer entered bankruptcy proceedings and that your $2,000 call premium and $5,000 payoff were lost. No doubt, this default would upset you. However, this situation cannot occur if your option trade was made on a registered options exchange. In effect, the exchange eliminates counterparty risk.

Option traders who transact on options exchanges have an important ally. The **Options Clearing Corporation (OCC)**, founded in 1973, is the clearing agency for these options exchanges: the BATS Options Market, the Chicago Board Options Exchange, the International Securities Exchange, NYSE Arca, and the Nasdaq Options Market, among others.

Options Clearing Corporation (OCC)
Private agency that guarantees that the terms of an option contract will be fulfilled if the option is exercised; issues and clears all option contracts trading on U.S. exchanges.

Once an option trade is made on an options exchange, the Options Clearing Corporation steps in and becomes a party to both sides of the trade. In other words, the option buyer effectively purchases the option from the OCC and the seller effectively sells the option to the OCC. In this way, each investor is free from the worry that the other party will default. Each option investor looks to the OCC.

Most option investors are unaware of the OCC because only member firms of an options exchange deal directly with it. However, in fact, all option contracts traded on U.S. options exchanges are originally issued, guaranteed, and cleared by the OCC. Brokerage firms merely act as intermediaries between investors and the OCC.

The OCC is an agency consisting of brokerage firms that are called "clearing members." The OCC's clearing members represent more than 100 of the largest U.S. broker-dealers, futures commission merchants, and non-U.S. securities firms. To guarantee the performance of all trades, the OCC has capital contributed by clearing members. If existing capital were to prove insufficient, the OCC could draw additional funds from its members. This structure ensures the integrity of the options markets.

The OCC began life as the clearinghouse for listed equity options. Today, however, the OCC clears many products. The OCC is regulated by both the Securities and Exchange Commission (SEC) and the Commodities Futures Trading Commission (CFTC). Under the watchful eye of the SEC, the OCC clears trades for put and call options on common stocks, stock indexes, foreign currencies, and single-stock futures. With CFTC oversight, the OCC clears and settles trades in futures contracts and options on futures contracts.

Visit the OIC at
www.optionseducation.org.

The OCC also sponsors the Options Industry Council (OIC). Founded in 1992, the OIC was created to educate investors about the benefits and risks of exchange-traded equity options. The OIC conducts hundreds of seminars and webcasts and distributes thousands of interactive CDs and brochures each year. In addition, the OIC has an extensive website for investors to explore.

CHECK THIS

15.2a Who makes up the OCC? Who regulates the OCC?

15.2b How does the OCC protect option traders?

15.2c What is the OIC, and what does it do?

Why Options?

As a stock market investor, a basic question you might ask is "Why buy stock options instead of buying shares of stock directly?" Good question! To answer it properly, we need to compare the possible outcomes from two investment strategies. The first investment strategy is buying stock. The second strategy involves buying a call option that allows the holder to buy stock any time before option expiration.

To learn more about options, visit the "Education" tab at www.cboe.com.

For example, suppose you buy 100 shares of 3M (MMM) stock at a price of $140 per share, representing an investment of $14,000. Afterwards, three things could happen to the stock price: It could go up, go down, or remain the same. If the stock price goes up, you make money; if it goes down, you lose money. Of course, if the stock price remains the same, you break even.

Now, consider the alternative strategy of buying a call option with a strike price of $140 expiring in three months at a per-share price of $5. This corresponds to a contract price of $500 because the standard option contract size is 100 shares. The first thing to notice about this strategy is that you have invested $500; therefore, the most that you can lose is $500.

To compare the two investment strategies just described, let's examine three possible cases for MMM's stock price at the close of trading on the third Friday of the option's expiration month. In Case 1, the stock price goes up to $150. In Case 2, the stock price goes down to $130. In Case 3, the stock price remains the same at $140.

Case 1: If the stock price goes up to $150, and you originally bought 100 shares at $140 per share, then your profit is $100 \times (\$150 - \$140) = \$1,000$. As a percentage of your original investment amount of $14,000, this represents a return on investment of $\$1,000/\$14,000 = .0714$, or 7.14%.

Alternatively, if you originally bought the call option, you can exercise the option and buy 100 shares at the strike price of $140 and sell the stock at the $150 market price. After accounting for the original cost of the option contract, your profit is $100 \times (\$150 - \$140) - \$500 = \$500$. As a percentage of your original investment of $500, this represents a return on investment of $\$500/\$500 = 1.00$, or 100%.

Case 2: If the stock price goes down to $130, and you originally bought 100 shares at $140 per share, then your loss is $100 \times (\$130 - \$140) = -\$1,000$. As a percentage of your original investment, this represents a return of $-\$1,000/\$14,000 = -.0714$, or −7.14%.

If instead you originally bought the call option, exercising the option would not pay and it would expire worthless. You would then realize a total loss of your $500 investment, and your return is −100 percent.

Case 3: If the stock price remains the same at $140, and you bought 100 shares, you break even and your return is zero percent.

However, if you bought the call option, exercising the option would not pay and it would expire worthless. Once again, you would lose your entire $500 investment.

As these three cases illustrate, the outcomes of the two investment strategies differ significantly, depending on subsequent stock price changes. Whether one strategy is preferred over another is a matter for each individual investor to decide. What is important is the fact that options offer an alternative means of formulating investment strategies.

EXAMPLE 15.1

Stock Returns

Suppose you bought 100 shares of stock at $50 per share. If the stock price goes up to $60 per share, what is the percentage return on your investment? If, instead, the stock price falls to $40 per share, what is the percentage return on your investment?

If the stock goes up to $60 per share, you make $10/$50 = .20, or 20%. If it falls to $40 per share, you lose −$10/$50 = −.20, or −20%.

EXAMPLE 15.2

Call Option Returns

In Example 15.1, suppose that you bought one call option contract for $200. The strike price is $50. If the stock price is $60 just before the option expires, should you exercise the option? If you exercise the option, what is the percentage return on your investment? If you don't exercise the option, what is the percentage return on your investment?

If the stock price is $60, you should definitely exercise. If you do, you will make $10 per share, or $1,000, from exercising. Once we deduct the $200 original cost of the option, your net profit is $800. Your percentage return is $800/$200 = 4.00, or 400%. If you don't exercise, you lose your entire $200 investment, so your loss is 100 percent.

EXAMPLE 15.3

More Call Option Returns

In Example 15.2, if the stock price is $40 just before the option expires, should you exercise the option? If you exercise the option, what is the percentage return on your investment? If you don't exercise the option, what is the percentage return on your investment?

If the stock price is $40, you shouldn't exercise because, by exercising, you will be paying $50 per share. If you did exercise, you would lose $10 per share, or $1,000, plus the $200 cost of the option, or $1,200 total. This would amount to a $1,200/$200 = 6.00, or 600% loss! If you don't exercise, you lose the $200 you invested, for a loss of 100 percent.

Of course, we can also calculate percentage gains and losses from a put option purchase. Here we make money if the stock price declines. So, suppose you buy a put option with a strike price of $20 for $.50. If you exercise your put when the stock price is $18, what is your percentage gain?

You make $2 per share because you are selling at $20 when the stock is worth $18. Your put contract cost $50, so your net profit is $200 − $50 = $150. As a percentage of your original $50 investment, you made $150/$50 = 3.00, or 300%.

CHECK THIS

15.3a If you buy 100 shares of stock at $10 and sell out at $12, what is your percentage return?

15.3b If you buy one call contract with a strike price of $10 for $100 and exercise it when the stock is selling for $12, what is your percentage return?

Stock Index Options

Related Bloomberg Functions

SSI   Standing Settlement
          Instructions

Learn more about trading
index options at
www.cboe.com.

stock index option
An option on a stock market
index. The most popular stock
index options are options on
the S&P 100 index, S&P 500
index, and Dow Jones Industrial Average.

cash-settled option
An option contract settled by a
cash payment from the option
writer to the option holder
when the option is exercised.

Following the tremendous success of stock options trading on the Chicago Board Options Exchange, the exchange looked for other new financial products to offer to investors and portfolio managers. In 1982, the CBOE created stock index options, which represented a new type of option contract at the time.

INDEX OPTIONS: FEATURES AND SETTLEMENT

A **stock index option** is an option on a stock market index. The first stock index options were contracts on the Standard & Poor's index of 100 large companies representative of American industry. This index is often called the "S&P 100." S&P 100 index options trade under the ticker symbol OEX, and S&P 100 index options are referred to as "OEX options." The second stock index options introduced by the CBOE were contracts on the Standard & Poor's index of 500 companies, the "S&P 500." S&P 500 index options trade under the ticker symbol SPX and are referred to as "SPX options." In 1997, the CBOE introduced options on the Dow Jones Industrial Average (DJIA), which trade under the ticker symbol DJX.

Besides the different underlying indexes, the major difference between SPX, DJX, and OEX contracts is that OEX options are American style, whereas SPX and DJX options are European style. The CBOE also lists the "XEO option," which is based on the S&P 100 index. The XEO option has European-style exercise. American-style options can be exercised any time before expiration, whereas European-style options can be exercised only on the last day before option expiration.

Before stock index options could be introduced, one very important detail that had to be worked out was what to do when an index option is exercised. Exchange officials saw that settlement by delivery was obviously impractical because of the number of stocks comprising an index. Instead, a cash settlement procedure was adopted for index options. For this reason, all stock index options are **cash-settled options**. With cash settlement, when a stock index option is exercised, the option writer pays a cash amount to the option buyer based on the difference between the exercise date index level and the option's strike price. For example, suppose you had purchased an SPX call option with a strike price of $4,000, and the S&P 500 index was $4,020 on the day of exercise. The difference between the index level and the strike price is $4,020 − $4,000 = $20. Because the contract size for SPX options is 100 times the S&P 500 index, the option writer must pay $100 × $20 = $2,000 to the option holder exercising the option.

In the example above, the contract size for SPX options was stated to be 100 times the S&P 500 index. In fact, the contract size for almost all standardized stock index options is 100 times the underlying index. Thus, the actual price of a stock index option is 100 times the price stated on an index-level basis. There are only a few exceptions to this rule. For example, the CBOE offers so-called Reduced Value (or "mini") index options with a contract size that is one-tenth the size of standard index options. Reduced Value index options are appealing to some individual investors, but they represent a small share of all index options trading.

INDEX OPTION PRICE QUOTES

As with individual stock options, quotes for index options are readily available online. As you might expect, the process of finding and interpreting the information is similar. Figure 15.2 is a from www.cboe.com for S&P 500 options. You can see that the data is laid out in the same way as the data in Figure 15.1.

EXAMPLE 15.4   **Index Options**

Suppose you bought 10 July 3900 SPX call contracts at a quoted price of $130. How much did you pay in total? At option expiration, suppose the S&P 500 index is at 3950. What would you receive? What is your profit, if any?

The price per SPX contract is 100 times the quoted price. Because you bought 10 contracts, you paid a total of $130 × 100 × 10 = $130,000. If the S&P 500 is at 3950 at expiration, you would receive $100 × (3950 − 3900) = $5,000 per contract, or $50,000 in all. This $50,000 would be paid to you in cash because index options feature cash settlement. Your loss, however, is $50,000 − $130,000, or −$80,000.

FIGURE 15.2   **S&P 500 Index Options Quote**

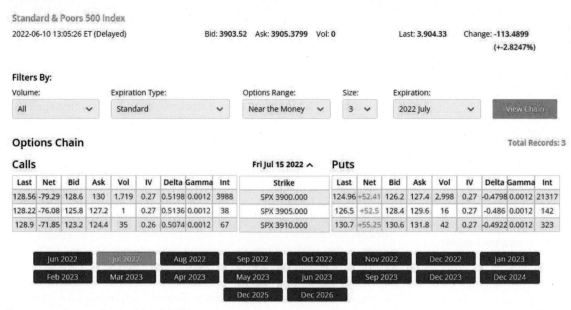

Standard & Poors 500 index

2022-06-10 13:05:26 ET (Delayed)   Bid: 3903.52   Ask: 3905.3799   Vol: 0   Last: 3,904.33   Change: -113.4899
(+-2.8247%)

Filters By:

Volume:	Expiration Type:	Options Range:	Size:	Expiration:	
All ∨	Standard ∨	Near the Money ∨	3 ∨	2022 July ∨	View Chain

Options Chain   Total Records: 3

Calls   Fri Jul 15 2022 ∧   **Puts**

Last	Net	Bid	Ask	Vol	IV	Delta	Gamma	Int	Strike	Last	Net	Bid	Ask	Vol	IV	Delta	Gamma	Int
128.56	-79.29	128.6	130	1,719	0.27	0.5198	0.0012	3988	SPX 3900.000	124.96	+52.41	126.2	127.4	2,998	0.27	-0.4798	0.0012	21317
128.22	-76.08	125.8	127.2	1	0.27	0.5136	0.0012	38	SPX 3905.000	126.5	+52.5	128.4	129.6	16	0.27	-0.486	0.0012	142
128.9	-71.85	123.2	124.4	35	0.26	0.5074	0.0012	67	SPX 3910.000	130.7	+55.25	130.6	131.8	42	0.27	-0.4922	0.0012	323

Jun 2022	Jul 2022	Aug 2022	Sep 2022	Oct 2022	Nov 2022	Dec 2022	Jan 2023
Feb 2023	Mar 2023	Apr 2023	May 2023	Jun 2023	Sep 2023	Dec 2023	Dec 2024
			Dec 2025	Dec 2026			

Source: www.cboe.com. Accessed June 9, 2022.

15.5 Option Intrinsic Value and "Moneyness"

Related Bloomberg Functions
OMON Option Monitor

intrinsic value
The payoff that an option holder receives assuming the underlying stock price remains unchanged from its current value.

To understand option payoffs and profits, we need to know some important concepts related to option value. The first important concept is called **intrinsic value**. The intrinsic value of an option is what the option would be worth if it were expiring immediately. Equivalently, the intrinsic value of an option is the payoff to an option holder if the underlying stock price does not change from its current value.

Computing the intrinsic value of an option is easy—all you need to know is whether the option is a call or a put, the strike price of the option, and the price of the underlying stock. The intrinsic value calculation, however, depends on whether the option is a call or a put.

You can calculate the intrinsic value of an option at any time, whether the option is dead or alive. For ease, we begin with examples where the option is just about to expire, and then show formulas that can be used at any time to calculate intrinsic value.

INTRINSIC VALUE FOR CALL OPTIONS

The first step to calculate the intrinsic value of a call option is to compare the underlying stock price to the strike price. Suppose a call option contract specifies a strike price of $50, and the underlying stock price is $45. Also, suppose this option was just minutes from expiring. With the stock price at $45 and a strike price of $50, this call option would have no value. Why would you pay anything to buy the stock at $50 when you can buy it for $45? In this situation, the value of this call option is zero.

Alternatively, suppose the underlying stock price is $55. If the call option with a strike of $50 was minutes from expiration, it would be worth about $5. Why? This option grants the holder the right to buy the stock for $50 when everyone else would have to pay the going market price of $55.

Let's look at call options that are not about to expire. If the underlying stock price is less than the strike price, the intrinsic value for a call option is set to zero. If, however, the underlying stock price, S, is greater than the strike price, K, the intrinsic value for a call option is the value $S - K$. Equation 15.1 shows how to calculate the intrinsic value of a call option.

$$\text{Call option intrinsic value} = \text{MAX}(S - K, 0) \tag{15.1}$$

In Equation 15.1, MAX stands for maximum and the comma stands for the word "or." You read Equation 15.1 as follows: The **call option intrinsic value** is the maximum of the stock price minus the strike price or zero.

call option intrinsic value
The maximum of (*a*) the stock price minus the strike price or (*b*) zero.

We assume that call option investors are rational and will prefer to exercise only call options that have a positive intrinsic value. For call options, rational exercise implies that the call option holder is able to purchase the stock for less than its current market price.

INTRINSIC VALUE FOR PUT OPTIONS

The first step to calculate the intrinsic value of a put option is also to compare the underlying stock price to the strike price. Suppose a put option contract specifies a strike price of $50, and the underlying stock price is $55. Also, suppose this option was minutes from expiring. With the stock price at $55 and a strike price of $50, this put option would have no value. Why would you pay anything to be able to sell the stock at $50 when you can sell shares for $55? In this situation, the value of the put option is zero.

Alternatively, suppose the underlying stock price is $45. If the put option with a strike price of $50 was minutes from expiration, it would be worth about $5. Why? This put option grants the holder the right to sell the stock for $50 when everyone else would have to sell at the going market price of $45.

Let's look at put options that are not just about to expire. If the underlying stock price is greater than the strike price, the intrinsic value for a put option is set to zero. If, however, the underlying stock price is less than the strike price, the intrinsic value for a put option is the value $K - S$. Equation 15.2 shows how to calculate the intrinsic value of a put option.

$$\text{Put option intrinsic value} = \text{MAX}(K - S, 0) \tag{15.2}$$

In Equation 15.2, MAX stands for maximum and the comma stands for the word "or." You read Equation 15.2 as follows: The **put option intrinsic value** is the maximum of the strike price minus the stock price or zero.

put option intrinsic value
The maximum of (*a*) the strike price minus the stock price or (*b*) zero.

We assume that put option investors are rational and will prefer to exercise only put options that have a positive intrinsic value. For put options, rational exercise implies that the put option holder is able to sell the stock for more than its current market price.

TIME VALUE

Now that you know how to calculate the intrinsic value of an option, you can think of intrinsic value as the amount of money an investor receives if exercising the option is rational. Note, however, that being rational and being smart are not the same thing. For example, in most cases the investor would be better off to sell the option rather than exercise it because the price of the option will be greater than its intrinsic value.

The difference between the price of the option and the intrinsic value of the option is known as **option time value**. At expiration, the time value of an option is zero. Before expiration, the time value for options with American-style exercise is at least zero, but it is almost always positive. Because options with American-style exercise can be exercised at any time, arbitrageurs will ensure that the price of these options remains at least as high as their intrinsic value. For options with European-style exercise, however, deep in-the-money put option prices that are less than intrinsic value are possible.

option time value
The difference between the price of an option and its intrinsic value.

A full discussion of why investors exercise options is a topic generally covered in a derivatives course. Calculating option prices, including time value, is the topic of a whole other chapter in this textbook.

THREE LESSONS ABOUT INTRINSIC VALUE

There are three important lessons about intrinsic value. First, investors can calculate intrinsic value whether the option is "dead" (at expiration) or "alive" (before expiration). Second, at expiration, the value of an option equals its intrinsic value because no time value is left at expiration. Third, before expiration, the value of an option equals its intrinsic value plus its time value.

SHOW ME THE MONEY

Option investors have developed shortcuts in the way they talk about the intrinsic value of options. Three important terms in this lingo are **in-the-money options**, **at-the-money options**, and **out-of-the-money options**.

Essentially, in-the-money options are those call options or put options with a positive intrinsic value. For an at-the-money call or put option, the strike price is exactly equal to the underlying stock price. For an out-of-the-money call option, the stock price is less than the strike price. For an out-of-the-money put option, the strike price is less than the stock price. Exercising an out-of-the-money option does not result in a positive payoff.

Once you get the hang of all this "moneyness" and intrinsic value language, you will see that it is not difficult. Examples 15.5 through 15.10 give you some practice. Also, the chart immediately below summarizes the relationship between the stock price and the strike price for in-the-money, out-of-the-money, and at-the-money call and put options.

in-the-money option
Any option with a positive intrinsic value.

at-the-money option
Any option with a strike price exactly equal to the underlying price.

out-of-the-money option
An option that would not yield a positive payoff if the stock price remained unchanged until expiration.

	In the Money	Out of the Money	At the Money
Call option	$S > K$	$S < K$	$S = K$
Put option	$S < K$	$S > K$	$S = K$

EXAMPLE 15.5 | **In-the-Money Call Option**

Walmart (WMT) stock is currently $120 per share. Let's look at a call option to buy WMT stock at $118 ($118 is the strike price). The stock price is greater than the strike price. If the call option were exercised immediately, there would be a positive payoff of $2 = $120 − $118. Because the option has a positive payoff if it is exercised immediately, this option is known as an in-the-money option.

EXAMPLE 15.6 | **Out-of-the-Money Call Option**

Walmart (WMT) stock is currently $120 per share. Let's look at a call option to buy WMT stock at $123 ($123 is the strike price). Because the stock price is less than the strike price, immediate exercise would not benefit the option holder. Because option exercise would not yield a positive payoff, this option is called an out-of-the-money option.

EXAMPLE 15.7 | **Intrinsic Value for Calls**

Suppose a call option exists with 20 days to expiration. It is selling for $1.65. The underlying stock price is $41.15. Calculate the intrinsic value and time value of (1) a call with a strike price of $40 and (2) a call with a strike price of $45.

A call with a strike price of $40 has an intrinsic value of MAX($S − K$, 0) = MAX($41.15 − $40, 0) = $1.15. The time value of this call option equals the option price minus the intrinsic value, $1.65 − $1.15 = $.50.

A call with a strike price of $45 has an intrinsic value of MAX($S − K$, 0) = MAX($41.15 − $45, 0) = $0. The time value of this call option equals the option price minus the intrinsic value, $1.65 − $0 = $1.65.

| EXAMPLE 15.8 | In-the-Money Put Option |

AT&T (T) stock is selling at $21. Let's look at a put option to sell T at a price of $23 per share ($23 is the strike price). Notice that the stock price is less than the strike price. If the put option were exercised immediately, it would yield a payoff of $2 = $23 − $21. Because the option has a positive payoff if exercised immediately, it is known as an in-the-money option.

| EXAMPLE 15.9 | Out-of-the-Money Put Option |

AT&T (T) stock is selling at $21. Let's look at a put option to sell T at a price of $18 per share ($18 is the strike price). Because the stock price is greater than the strike price, immediate exercise would not benefit the option holder. Because option exercise would not yield a positive payoff, this option is called an out-of-the-money option.

| EXAMPLE 15.10 | Intrinsic Value for Puts |

Suppose a put option exists with 15 days to expiration. It is selling for $5.70. The underlying asset price is $42.35. Calculate the intrinsic value and time value of (1) a put with a strike price of $40 and (2) a put with a strike price of $45.

A put with a strike price of $40 has an intrinsic value of MAX($K − S$, 0) = MAX($40 − $42.35, 0) = $0. The time value of this put option equals the option price minus the intrinsic value, $5.70 − $0 = $5.70.

A put with a strike price of $45 has an intrinsic value of MAX($K − S$, 0) = MAX($45 − $42.35, 0) = $2.65. The time value of this put option equals the option price minus the intrinsic value, $5.70 − $2.65 = $3.05.

CHECK THIS

15.5a All else equal, would an in-the-money option or an out-of-the-money option have a higher price? Why?

15.5b Does an out-of-the-money option ever have value? Why?

15.5c What is the intrinsic value of a call option? A put option?

15.5d Suppose the stock price is $35. Is there a strike price for which a call option and a put option have the same intrinsic value?

15.6 Option Payoffs and Profits

Options are appealing because they offer investors a wide variety of investment strategies. In fact, there is essentially no limit to the number of different investment strategies available using options. However, fortunately for us, only a small number of basic strategies are available, and more complicated strategies are built from these. We discuss the payoffs from these basic strategies here and in the next section.

Related Bloomberg Functions

XLTP XOSA Excel Template: Option Portfolio P/L

OPTION WRITING

Thus far, we have discussed options from the standpoint of the buyer only. However, options are contracts, and every contract must link at least two parties. The two parties to an option

option writing
Taking the seller's side of an option contract.

call writer
One who has the obligation to sell stock at the option's strike price if the option is exercised.

put writer
One who has the obligation to buy stock at the option's strike price if the option is exercised.

To learn more about options, see www.optionseducation.org.

contract are the buyer and the seller. The seller of an option is called the "writer," and the act of selling an option is referred to as **option writing**.

By buying an option, you buy the right, but not the obligation, to exercise the option before the option's expiration date. By selling or writing an option, you take the seller's side of the option contract. As a result, option writing involves receiving the option price and, in exchange, assuming the obligation to satisfy the buyer's exercise rights if the option is exercised.

For example, a **call writer** is obligated to sell stock at the option's strike price if the buyer decides to exercise the call option (to buy the stock). Similarly, a **put writer** is obligated to buy stock at the option's strike price if the buyer decides to exercise the put option (to sell the stock).

OPTION PAYOFFS

It is useful to think about option investment strategies in terms of their initial cash flows and terminal cash flows. The initial cash flow of an option is the price of the option, also called the option *premium*. To the option buyer, the option price (or premium) is a cash outflow. To the option writer, the option price (or premium) is a cash inflow. The terminal cash flow of an option is the option's payoff that could be realized from the exercise privilege. To the option buyer, a payoff entails a cash inflow. To the writer, a payoff entails a cash outflow.

For example, suppose the current price of ExxonMobil (XOM) stock is $80 per share. You buy a call option on XOM with a strike price of $80. The premium is $4 per share. Thus, the initial cash flow is −$400 for you and +$400 for the option writer. What are the terminal cash flows for you and the option writer if XOM has a price of $90 when the option expires? What are the terminal cash flows if XOM has a price of $70 when the option expires?

If XOM is at $90, then you experience a cash inflow of $10 per share, whereas the writer experiences an outflow of $10 per share. If XOM is at $70, you both have a zero cash flow when the option expires because it is worthless. Notice that in both cases the buyer and the seller have the same cash flows, just with opposite signs. This shows that options are a "zero-sum game," meaning that any gains to the buyer must come at the expense of the seller and vice versa.

OPTION PAYOFF DIAGRAMS

When investors buy options, the price that they are willing to pay depends on their assessment of the likely payoffs (cash inflows) from the exercise privilege. Likewise, when investors write options, an acceptable selling price depends on their assessment of the likely payoffs (cash outflows) resulting from the buyers' exercise privilege. Given this, a general understanding of option payoffs is critical for understanding how option prices are determined.

A payoff diagram is a very useful graphical device for understanding option payoffs. The payoffs from buying a call option and the payoffs from selling (or writing) a call option are seen in the payoff diagram in Figure 15.3. The vertical axis of Figure 15.3 measures option payoffs, and the horizontal axis measures the possible stock prices on the option expiration date. These examples assume that the call option has a strike price of $50 and that the option will be exercised only on its expiration date.

In Figure 15.3, notice that the call option payoffs are zero for all stock prices below the $50 strike price. This is because the call option holder will not exercise the option to buy stock at the $50 strike price when the stock is available in the stock market at a lower price. In this case, the option expires worthless.

In contrast, if the stock price is higher than the $50 strike price, the call option payoff is equal to the difference between the market price of the stock and the strike price of the option. For example, if the stock price is $60, the call option payoff is equal to $10, which is the difference between the $60 stock price and the $50 strike price. This payoff is a cash inflow to the buyer because the option buyer can buy the stock at the $50 strike price and sell the stock at the $60 market price. However, this payoff is a cash outflow to the writer because the option writer must sell the stock at the $50 strike price when the stock's market price is $60.

FIGURE 15.3   Call Option Payoffs

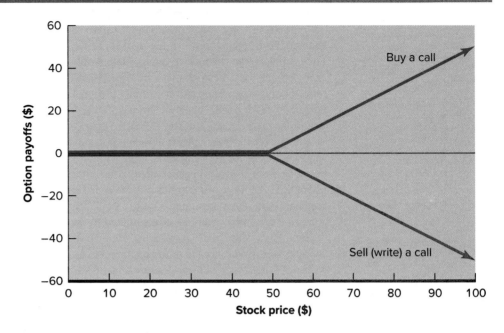

FIGURE 15.4   Put Option Payoffs

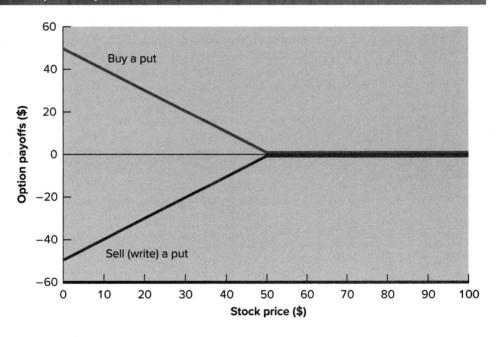

Putting it all together, the distinctive "hockey stick" shape of the call option payoffs shows that the payoff is zero if the stock price is below the strike price. Above the strike price, however, the buyer of the call option gains $1 for every $1 increase in the stock price. Of course, as shown, the call option writer loses $1 for every $1 increase in the stock price above the strike price.

Figure 15.4 is an example of a payoff diagram illustrating the payoffs from buying a put option and from selling (or writing) a put option. As with our call option payoffs, the vertical axis measures option payoffs and the horizontal axis measures the possible stock prices on the option expiration date. Once again, these examples assume that the put has a strike price of $50 and that the option will be exercised only on its expiration date.

In Figure 15.4, the put option payoffs are zero for all stock prices above the $50 strike price. This is because a put option holder will not exercise the option to sell stock at the $50 strike price when the stock can be sold in the stock market at a higher price. In this case, the option expires worthless.

In contrast, if the stock price is lower than the $50 strike price, the put option payoff is equal to the difference between the market price of the stock and the strike price of the option. For example, if the stock price is $40, the put option payoff is equal to $10, which is the difference between the $40 stock price and the $50 strike price. This payoff is a cash inflow to the buyer because the option buyer can buy the stock at the $40 market price and sell the stock at the $50 strike price. However, this payoff is a cash outflow to the writer because the option writer must buy the stock at the $50 strike price when the stock's market price is $40.

Our payoff diagrams illustrate an important difference between the maximum possible gains and losses for puts and calls. Notice that if you buy a call option, there is no upper limit to your potential profit because there is no upper limit to the stock price. However, with a put option, the most you can make is the strike price. In other words, the best thing that can happen to you if you buy a put is for the stock price to go to zero. Of course, whether you buy a put or a call, your potential loss is limited to the option premium you pay.

Similarly, as shown in Figure 15.3, if you write a call, there is no limit to your possible loss, but your potential gain is limited to the option premium you receive. As shown in Figure 15.4, if you write a put, both your gain and loss are limited, although the potential loss could be substantial.

OPTION PROFIT DIAGRAMS

Between them, Figures 15.3 and 15.4 tell us essentially everything we need to know about the payoffs from the four basic strategies involving options: buying and writing puts and calls. However, these figures give the payoffs at expiration only and so do not consider the original cash inflow or outflow. Option profit diagrams are an extension of payoff diagrams that do take into account the initial cash flow.

As we have seen, the profit from an option strategy is the difference between the option's terminal cash flow (the option payoff) and the option's initial cash flow (the option price, or premium). An option profit diagram adjusts option payoffs for the original price of the option. This means that the option premium is subtracted from the payoffs from buying options and added to payoffs from writing options.

To illustrate, Figures 15.5 and 15.6 are profit diagrams corresponding to the four basic investment strategies for options. In each diagram, the vertical axis measures option profits

| FIGURE 15.5 | Call Option Profits |

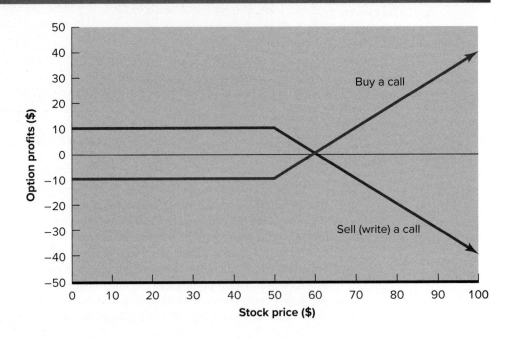

FIGURE 15.6   Put Option Profits

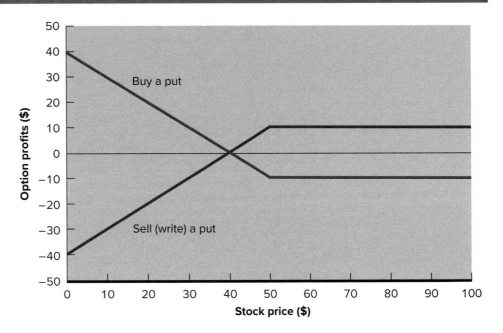

and the horizontal axis measures possible stock prices. Each profit diagram assumes that the option's strike price is $50 and that the put and call option prices are both $10. Notice that in each case the characteristic hockey stick shape is maintained; the "stick" is just shifted up or down.

CHECK THIS

15.6a   What is option writing?

15.6b   What are the payoffs and profits from writing call options?

15.6c   What are the payoffs and profits from writing put options?

15.6d   Explain how a payoff diagram that shows option value at expiration can be thought of as a diagram that shows the intrinsic value of the option at expiration.

15.7   Using Options to Manage Risk

Thus far, we have considered the payoffs and profits from buying and writing individual calls and puts. In this section, we consider what happens when we start to combine puts, calls, and shares of stock. We could examine any of numerous combinations, but we will stick to a few of the most basic and important strategies. Note that in the following discussion, the diagrams represent pretax outcomes.

Related Bloomberg Functions

SOVR   Sovereign CDS Monitor

CDS   CDS Landing Page

THE PROTECTIVE PUT STRATEGY

Suppose you own a share of Nordstrom, Inc. (JWN), stock currently worth $45. Suppose you also purchase a put option with a strike price of $45 for $2. What is the net effect of this purchase?

To answer, we can compare what happens if Nordstrom stock stays at or above $45 to what happens if it drops below $45. If Nordstrom stock stays at or above $45, your put will expire worthless because you would choose not to exercise it. You would lose the $2 you paid

FIGURE 15.7   Protective Put on a Share of Nordstrom Stock

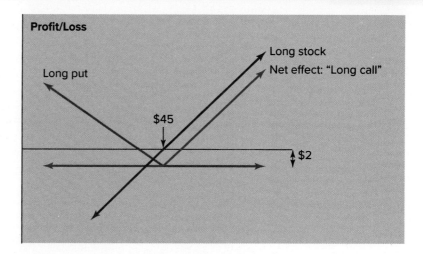

for the put option. However, if Nordstrom stock falls below $45, you would exercise your put and the put writer would pay you $45 for your stock. No matter how far below $45 the price falls, you have guaranteed that you will receive $45 for your Nordstrom share of stock.

Thus, by purchasing a put option, you have protected yourself against a price decline. In the jargon of Wall Street, you have paid $2 to eliminate the "downside risk." For this reason, the strategy of buying a put option on a stock you already own is called a **protective put** strategy. Figure 15.7 shows the net effect of the protective put strategy. Notice that the net effect resembles the profit diagram of a long call. That is, when an investor who owns stock buys a put, the profit diagram of this new portfolio resembles the profit diagram of a long call.

The protective put strategy reduces the overall risk faced by an investor, so it is a conservative strategy. This is a good example of how options, or any derivative asset, can be used to decrease risk rather than increase it. Stated differently, options can be used to hedge as well as speculate, so they do not inherently increase risk.

protective put
Strategy of buying a put option on a stock already owned. This strategy protects against a decline in value.

CREDIT DEFAULT SWAPS

If you own a car, you surely have car insurance. Insurance is effectively a put option. You pay a premium to the insurance company. If you get into an accident (we hope not), then you have the right to "put" your car to the insurance company in exchange for a cash payout. This situation is not unique to cars or stocks—investors have the ability to buy "insurance" on many assets.

One type of put option that received quite a bit of attention during the recent financial crisis was a credit default swap (CDS). A CDS is essentially a portfolio of put options on a fixed-income asset (i.e., a bond). For example, consider an investor who buys a bond of a distressed company. To hedge the risk of default, the investor might be able to purchase a CDS on the bond. If the bond issuer defaults, then the holder of a CDS is compensated according to the terms of the CDS contract.

While the example we provided is for a single bond, most CDS contracts are sold on baskets of fixed-income securities known as *collateralized debt obligations,* or CDOs. We discuss these securities in detail in a later chapter. But no matter how complex the underlying security, the CDS works pretty much the same: The CDS acts like a protective put option.

So, why were CDS contracts so important in the financial crisis following the Crash of 2008? Well, two factors played key roles. First, at the height of the crisis, analysts estimated that about $55 *trillion* in securities were being hedged using credit default swaps. To put this dollar amount into perspective, at the same time the estimated net wealth of all U.S. citizens was $56 trillion. This comparison illustrates the importance of CDS contracts to the financial markets.

Second, historically most CDS contracts were not traded on an exchange. Rather, these specialized contracts were bought and sold directly between buyers and sellers. This type of trading means that counterparty risk is prevalent. In fact, you might recall the fall of two investment banking stalwarts, Bear Stearns and Lehman Brothers, as well as the insurance giant AIG. These firms were active players in the CDS market, and each firm was undercapitalized relative to its position. As with any type of leverage, positions work well when asset prices move in the "right" direction. Disastrous ruin can occur, however, when prices move in the "wrong" direction. Such is the hard lesson about leverage learned time and again.

Because CDS contracts act like insurance contracts, the costs of the contracts can tell us something about the perceived risk of default for the underlying firm. In fact, many investors (both bond and stock) pay great attention to CDS spreads. For example, each month Citigroup screens stocks based on both dividend yields and CDS spreads. The goal is to provide a list of stocks that pay a high dividend and also have low credit risk. Citigroup refers to this approach as its "CDS-adjusted dividend stock screen."

THE PROTECTIVE PUT STRATEGY AND CORPORATE RISK MANAGEMENT

Suppose you own and operate a gold mine. Your revenue stream is risky because it will change as world gold prices change. However, your costs, which mostly consist of moving around tons of dirt and boulders, do not change as world gold prices change. Therefore, your profits change as world gold prices change.

This "underlying risk exposure" is the blue line in Figure 15.8. Suppose you decide to protect your operation from the possibility of low gold prices with the purchase of a put option. The put option profit is the red line in Figure 15.8. Your "net exposure" is the green line in Figure 15.8.

To construct your net exposure, you combine the blue line and the red line. Once you do, you see that to the left of the vertical axis, the result is that if gold prices fall, the decrease in profits reflects only the cost of purchasing the put option; decreases in the price of gold will not adversely affect your profits.

To the right of the vertical axis, if gold prices increase, your profits will increase too. However, they will be smaller than if you had not purchased the put option.

USING CALL OPTIONS IN CORPORATE RISK MANAGEMENT

Suppose you own and operate an airline that uses jet aircraft. Assume that you and your employees are skilled at competitively pricing seats on your flights. This skill results in a relatively stable revenue stream. Your operating costs, however, will vary with world prices for jet fuel because, after labor, jet fuel is the second largest operating expense for an airline.

FIGURE 15.8   Using Puts to Manage Risk

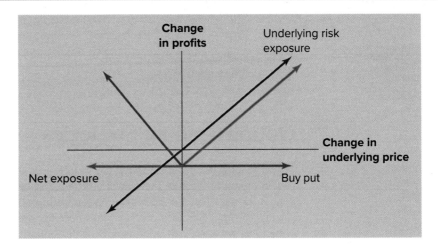

FIGURE 15.9   Using Calls to Manage Risk

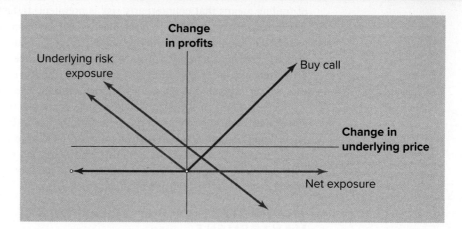

The competitive nature of the airline industry means that you cannot easily pass higher fuel prices on to passengers by raising fares. Changes in jet fuel prices could thus affect your profits. Fortunately, you can protect your profits using call options.

The red line in Figure 15.9 represents your underlying exposure to increases in jet fuel prices. Suppose you decide to protect your profits from the possibility of high jet fuel prices with the purchase of a call option. The call option profit is the blue line in Figure 15.9. Your net exposure is the green line in Figure 15.9.

To construct your net exposure, you combine the blue line and the red line. Once you do, you see that to the left of the vertical axis, the result is that if jet fuel prices fall, your profits will increase. However, because you purchased call options, your profits will decrease by the amount of the cost of purchasing the call options. Decreases in the price of jet fuel thus will increase your profits.

To the right of the vertical axis, if the price of jet fuel increases, the decrease in your profits reflects only the cost of purchasing the call option. That is, the increase in jet fuel prices will not adversely affect your profits.

Futures contracts are also available on jet fuel (although they are thinly traded). What is the big difference between using futures contracts or option contracts to hedge? Well, remember that with futures contracts, whether you buy or sell, you have an obligation. If jet fuel prices fall, you will still have to buy the fuel at the agreed-upon settle price. You have no obligation with a long option position. In this case, you can abandon your option position and buy the jet fuel at prevailing market prices.

CHECK THIS

15.7a   What is a protective put strategy, and how does it work?

15.7b   What is a credit default swap?

15.7c   Explain how a company can use options today to protect itself from higher future input prices.

 Option Trading Strategies

For ideas on option trading strategies, see www.commodityworld.com.

In this section, we present three types of option trading strategies. In the first type, traders add an option position to their stock position. Strategies in this category help traders modify their stock risk. The second type of option trading strategy is called a *spread*. A spread strategy involves taking a position on two or more options of the same type at the same time. By same type, we mean call options only or put options only. The third type of option trading

Related Bloomberg Functions

XLTP XSTR   Excel Template:
Option Strategy
Worksheet

strategy is called a *combination*. In a combination, the trader takes a position in a mixture of call and put options. Note that the effects of these strategies are pretax effects. Nonetheless, learning about these pretax effects is important for option traders.

THE COVERED CALL STRATEGY

Suppose you own a share of Nordstrom, Inc. (JWN), stock that is currently worth $45. Now, instead of buying a put, consider selling a call option for, say, $3, with an exercise price of $45. What is the net effect of this strategy?

To answer, we can compare what happens if Nordstrom stock stays below $45 (the exercise price on the option you sold) to what happens if Nordstrom's stock price rises above $45. If Nordstrom stock stays below $45, the option will expire worthless, and you pocket the $3 premium you received from selling the call option. If Nordstrom stock rises above $45, the call option holder will exercise the call option against you, and you must deliver the Nordstrom stock in exchange for $45.

Thus, when you sell a call option on stock you already own, you keep the option premium no matter what. The worst thing that can happen to you is that you will have to sell your stock at the exercise price. Because you already own the stock, you are said to be "covered," which is why this is known as the **covered call** strategy.

Let's examine your covered call strategy further. Nordstrom stock is currently selling for $45. Because the strike price on the call option is $45, the net effect of this strategy is to give up the possibility of profits on the stock in exchange for the certain option premium of $3. Figure 15.10 shows the covered call option position on Nordstrom stock. Notice that the net effect resembles the profit diagram of a short put. That is, when an investor who owns stock sells a call, the profit diagram of this new portfolio resembles the profit diagram of a short put.

In Wall Street jargon, a covered call exchanges uncertain future "upside" potential for certain cash today, thereby reducing risk and potential reward. In contrast, a strategy of selling call options on stock you do not own is known as a "naked" call strategy, which, as we saw earlier, has unlimited potential losses. Thus, selling call options either is highly risky or else acts to reduce risk, depending on whether you are covered or naked. This distinction is important to understand.

SPREADS

A **spread** strategy involves taking a position on two or more options of the same type. By same type, we mean call options only or put options only.

covered call
Strategy of selling a call option on stock already owned.

spread
An option trading strategy involving two or more call options or two or more put options.

FIGURE 15.10   Covered Call Option on Nordstrom Stock

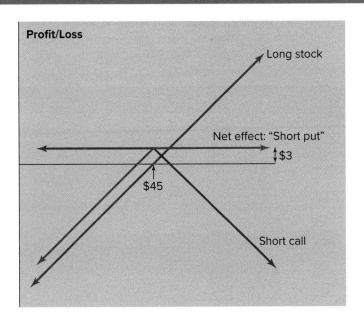

Three examples of spreads are:

- *Bull call spreads.* This spread is formed by buying a call and also selling a call with a higher strike price. This spread is known as a "bull" spread because traders make a profit from this strategy if the underlying stock price increases in value.

- *Bear call spreads.* This spread is formed by buying a call and also selling a call with a lower strike price. This spread is known as a "bear" spread because traders make a profit from this strategy if the underlying stock price decreases in value.

- *Butterfly spreads.* Using call options with equally spaced strikes, a "long" butterfly spread is formed by three option positions. To create a long butterfly spread, the trader buys one call option with the lowest strike price and buys one call option with the highest strike price while also selling two options with the middle strike. Traders profit from a long butterfly spread if the underlying stock price hovers around the strike price of the middle options.

There are many more examples of option spreads. For example, traders can form bull put spreads, bear put spreads, and short butterfly spreads. Traders can also form butterfly spreads using put options. These are just a few of the vast number of option spread strategies. You can learn more about these trading strategies in a derivatives course or online. For starters, see the terrific set of tutorials at www.cboe.com/Education.

COMBINATIONS

For more information on trading options, see www.ino.com.

combination
An option trading strategy involving two or more call and put options.

In a **combination**, the trader takes a position in a mixture of call and put options. Perhaps the best-known combination is called a *straddle.* Here is how a straddle works: Suppose a share of stock is currently selling at $50. You think the price is going to make a major move, but you are uncertain about the direction. What could you do? One answer is buy a call and buy a put, each with a $50 exercise price. That way, if the stock goes up sharply, your call will pay off; if it goes down sharply, your put will pay off. This combination is an example of a long straddle.

This strategy is called a straddle because you have, in effect, "straddled" the current $50 stock price. It is a long straddle because you bought both options. Figure 15.11 shows the profit from a long straddle. Note that the stock must make a major move for the trader to profit from this strategy. In fact, the stock price must either climb to a price equal to the option strike price plus the cost of both options or it must fall to a price equal to the option strike price minus the cost of both options.

If you thought the stock price was not going to make a major move in either direction, you might sell a put and a call, thereby generating income today. This combination is an example of a short straddle. In this case, your income would be maximized if the stock price at option expiration equals the option strike price, $50 in this example. If the stock price is $50 at option expiration, both options would expire worthless.

There are many other combination strategies, with colorful names such as strips, straps, strangles, collars, and box "spreads" (which, for no known reason, are called spreads but are really combinations).

FIGURE 15.11	**Long Straddle Using a Long Call and a Long Put**

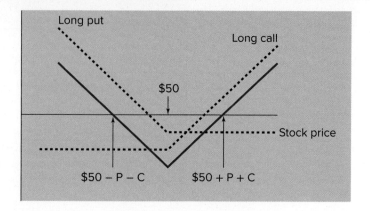

EXAMPLE 15.11

Another Option Strategy

You own a share of stock worth $80. Suppose you sell a call option with a strike price of $80 and also buy a put with a strike price of $80. What is the net effect of these transactions on the risk of owning the stock?

Notice that what you have done is combine a protective put and a covered call strategy. To see the effect of doing this, suppose that, at option expiration, the stock is selling for more than $80. In this case, the put is worthless. The call will be exercised against you, and you will receive $80 for your stock. If the stock is selling for less than $80, the call is worthless. You would exercise your put and sell the stock for $80. In other words, the net effect is that you have guaranteed that you will exchange the stock for $80 no matter what happens, so you have created a riskless asset.

Although option trading strategies are captivating, we really should move on. Up to now, we have mostly focused our attention on what options are worth when they expire. In our closing sections, we will put down the foundation we need to calculate option prices before expiration.

CHECK THIS

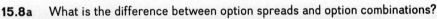

15.8a   What is the difference between option spreads and option combinations?

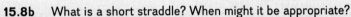

15.8b   What is a short straddle? When might it be appropriate?

15.9 Arbitrage and Option Pricing Bounds

The "hockey stick" diagrams that show option payoffs can help you learn an extremely important concept: intrinsic value. The payoff diagrams, however, show what happens only at option expiration. Investors are also quite interested in option prices before expiration.

In our next chapter, we will calculate option prices before expiration. In this section and the next one, we will explore how arbitrage forces set some price limits on option prices before expiration. An arbitrage is a trading opportunity that (1) requires no net investment on your part, (2) has no possibility of loss, and (3) has at least the potential for a gain.

In general, option price limits depend on (1) whether the option in question is American or European and (2) whether a dividend is paid between today and the option expiration day. Dividends make discussing option price limits much more complicated. Therefore, in this section, we assume that the stock pays no dividends over the life of the option.

THE UPPER BOUND FOR CALL OPTION PRICES

What is the most a call option could sell for before expiration? Suppose we have a call option on a share of stock. The current stock price is $60 and the stock pays no dividends. Without more information, we cannot say a lot about the price of the call option, but we do know one thing: The price of the option must be less than $60. How do we know this?

If you think about it, the right to buy a share of stock cannot be worth more than the share itself. To illustrate, suppose the call option was actually selling for $65 when the stock was selling at $60. What would you do?

What you would do is get very rich, very fast. You would sell call options at $65 and buy stock at $60. You pocket the $5 difference. The worst thing that can happen to you is that the options are exercised and you receive the exercise price. In this case, it is theoretically possible for you to make an unlimited amount of money at no risk. This trading strategy will work for options with either American- or European-style exercise.

This situation is an example of a true arbitrage opportunity. Unfortunately, such simple money machines don't exist very often (if at all) in the real world, so we know that a call option can't sell for more than the underlying stock.

THE UPPER BOUND FOR PUT OPTION PRICES

At expiration, we know that the value of a put option equals its intrinsic value. If the stock price is zero, then the intrinsic value is equal to the strike price of the put option. Therefore, at expiration, the most a put option can sell for is the strike price. What is the most that a put option can sell for before expiration? The answer is the present value of the strike price.

To begin to see this bound, suppose we have a put option with an exercise price of $50 and the put option price is $60. This situation is an arbitrage opportunity. What would you do? You would sell puts for $60 and deposit the proceeds in the bank. The worst thing that could happen to you at expiration is that you would have to buy the stock for $50 a share. However, you would also have $10 per share in cash (the difference between the $60 you received and the $50 you paid for the stock) and the interest on the proceeds.

Now suppose we have a put option with an exercise price of $50 and the put option price is also $50. This situation is also an arbitrage opportunity. You would sell puts for $50 and deposit the proceeds in the bank. Again, the worst thing that could happen to you at expiration is that you would have to buy the stock for $50 a share. However, you keep the interest on the proceeds from the sale of the put.

So, the upper bound on a European put's price is less than the strike price. How much less? The answer depends on the going interest rate on risk-free investments. We will have an arbitrage if the price of the put plus the interest you could earn over the life of the option is greater than the stock price. For example, suppose the risk-free rate is 3 percent per quarter. We have a put option selling for $49 with an exercise price of $50 and 90 days to maturity. Is there an arbitrage opportunity?

Yes, there is. You would sell the put and invest the $49 for 90 days at 3 percent to get $49 × 1.03 = $50.47. You will make at least $.47 guaranteed. At this point, you probably see where this is going. What is the maximum put value that does not result in an arbitrage opportunity? This value is:

$$\text{Maximum put price} \times 1.03 = \$50$$
$$\text{Maximum put price} = \$50/1.03 = \$48.54$$

Notice that our answer, $48.54, is the present value of the strike price computed at the risk-free rate. This result is the general answer: The maximum price for a European put option is the present value of the strike price computed at the risk-free rate.

The most put options with American-style exercise can sell for before expiration is the strike price. If an American put option had a price higher than the strike price, traders would sell these puts and invest the proceeds. The worst that could happen is that the stock price falls to zero and the holder of the American put exercises the put. The American put seller must buy the stock at the strike price—which is lower than the price of the put. The trader keeps the difference between the put price and the strike price, plus any interest earned before the put buyer exercised the put.

THE LOWER BOUNDS FOR CALL AND PUT OPTION PRICES

What is the lowest price possible for call and put options? Can an option have a negative value? A negative value means that holders would pay someone to take the option off their hands. However, option holders can let the option expire, so there would be no need to pay someone to haul away options. Thus, we conclude that options cannot have a negative value, which is true for European- and American-style options.

AMERICAN CALLS We can set a "higher" lower bound by answering this question: Is it possible for an American call option to sell for less than its intrinsic value? The answer is no. We know that sometimes the intrinsic value of an option is zero and that the value of an option cannot be less than zero, but it can be zero. However, what about the cases in which the intrinsic value of an option is greater than zero? Why does the option have to sell for at least as much as its intrinsic value?

To see this result, suppose a current stock price is $S = \$60$ and a call option with a strike price of $K = \$50$ has a price of $C = \$5$. Clearly, this call option is in the money, and the $5 call price is less than the intrinsic value of $S - K = \$10$.

If you are presented with these actual stock and option prices, you have an arbitrage opportunity. That is, you have a way to obtain a riskless profit by following a simple three-step strategy.

First, buy the call option at its price of $C = \$5$. Second, immediately exercise the call option and buy the stock from the call writer at the strike price of $K = \$50$. At this point, you have acquired the stock for $55, which is the sum of the call price plus the strike price.

As a third and final step, sell the stock at the current market price of $S = \$60$. Because you acquired the stock for $55 and sold the stock for $60, you have earned an arbitrage profit of $5. Clearly, if such an opportunity continued to exist, you would repeat these three steps over and over until you became bored with making easy money. But realistically, such easy arbitrage opportunities do not exist, and it therefore follows that an American call option price is never less than its intrinsic value (even when dividends are paid). That is:

$$\text{American call option price} \geq \text{MAX}(S - K, \ 0) \tag{15.3}$$

AMERICAN PUTS A similar arbitrage argument applies to American put options. For example, suppose a current stock price is $S = \$40$ and a put option with a strike price of $K = \$50$ has a price of $P = \$5$. This $5 put price is less than the option's intrinsic value of $K - S = \$10$. To exploit this profit opportunity, you first buy the put option at its price of $P = \$5$ and then buy the stock at its current price of $S = \$40$. At this point, you have acquired the stock for $45, which is the sum of the put price plus the stock price.

Now you immediately exercise the put option, thereby selling the stock to the option writer at the strike price of $S = \$50$. Because you acquired the stock for $45 and sold the stock for $50, you have earned an arbitrage profit of $5. Again, you would not realistically expect such an easy arbitrage opportunity to exist. Therefore, we conclude that the price of an American put option price is never less than its intrinsic value:

$$\text{American put option price} \geq \text{MAX}(K - S, 0) \tag{15.4}$$

EUROPEAN CALLS Because European options cannot be exercised before expiration, we cannot use the arbitrage strategies that we used to set lower bounds for American options. We must use a different approach (which can be found in many textbooks that focus on options). It turns out that the lower bound for a European call option is greater than its intrinsic value.

$$\text{European call option price} \geq \text{MAX}[S - K/(1 + r)^T, 0] \tag{15.5}$$

EUROPEAN PUTS The lower bound for a European put option price is less than its intrinsic value. In fact, in-the-money European puts will frequently sell for less than their intrinsic value. How much less? Using an arbitrage strategy that accounts for the fact that European put options cannot be exercised before expiration, the lower bound for a European put option is:

$$\text{European put option price} \geq \text{MAX}[K/(1 + r)^T - S, 0] \tag{15.6}$$

To give you some intuition, let's look at an extreme case. Suppose the stock price falls to zero before expiration and there is absolutely no chance that the stock price will recover before expiration. American put holders would immediately exercise their puts because it is impossible for the puts to get further into the money. European put holders also would like to exercise their puts immediately for the same reason. However, they cannot. In this example, you can see that European put holders have a riskless asset that will be worth $K at expiration. Therefore, it is worth the present value of $K. Looking at Equation 15.6, you can see that the lower bound increases as the option gets closer to expiration.

A STRONGER BOUND When no dividends are paid, Equation 15.5 also becomes the lower bound for American call option prices. Equation 15.5 is a "stronger" lower bound than Equation 15.3. To illustrate why Equation 15.5 is stronger, consider an example where $S = \$44$, $K = \$40$, $r = 10$ percent, and $T = 1$ year. Equation 15.5 says that for an American (or European) call option on a non-dividend-paying stock: $C \geq S - K/(1 + r)^T$, i.e., $C \geq \$44 - \$40/1.1 = \$7.64$. Equation 15.3, however, says that for American (not European) calls: $C \geq S - K$, or $C \geq \$44 - \$40 = \$4$. So, Equation 15.5 is a stronger (i.e., higher) lower bound than Equation 15.3. That is, stating that the American call price must exceed $7.64 is stronger than saying the American call price must exceed $4.

15.10 Put-Call Parity

Suppose an investor has a long stock position and then decides to buy a protective put and sell a covered call at the same time. What happens in this case? That is, what kind of portfolio has this investor formed (assume both options have European-style exercise)? We will be creative and name the set of positions in these three risky assets "Portfolio A."

Table 15.1 presents the value of each position in Portfolio A when the options expire. For the put and the call, we calculate the intrinsic value of the option and then determine whether the investor receives or pays the intrinsic value.

For example, if the expiration date stock price is less than the strike price, that is, if $S_T < K$, then the call option expires worthless and the put option has an intrinsic value of $K - S_T$. Because you bought the put option, you receive the intrinsic value.

If the stock price on option expiration day exactly equals the strike price, both the call and the put expire worthless. However, if the expiration day stock price is greater than the strike price, that is, $S_T > K$, the put option expires worthless and the call option intrinsic value is $S_T - K$. Because you sold the call, however, you must pay the call option holder the intrinsic value. So, to you, the value of the call option is $-(S_T - K)$.

In Table 15.1, notice that whether the expiration date stock price is less than, equal to, or greater than the strike price, the payoff to Portfolio A is always equal to the strike price, K. This means that this portfolio, which contains three risky assets, has a risk-free payoff at option expiration.

Because Portfolio A is risk-free, the cost of acquiring Portfolio A today should be equal to the cost of acquiring any other risk-free investment that will be worth K in one year. One such risk-free investment is a U.S. Treasury bill. The discounted amount, $K/(1 + r_f)^T$, is the cost of a U.S. Treasury bill paying K dollars at option expiration.[1]

TABLE 15.1 — **Two Portfolios with the Same Value at Option Expiration**

		Value at Option Expiration in One Year if:		
Portfolio A	**(cost today is)**	$S_T < K$	$S_T = K$	$S_T > K$
Long stock	S	S_T	S_T	S_T
Long put	P	$K - S_T$	0	0
Short call	$-C$	0	0	$-(S_T - K)$
Total	$S + P - C$	K	K	K

Portfolio B	**(cost today is)**			
Long T-bill	$K/(1 + r_f)^T$	K	K	K

---

[1] In this discounted amount, r_f is the risk-free interest rate for one year and T represents the time to maturity. In this case, the time to maturity is one year, so $T = 1$. If the time to maturity is, say, six months, then $T = \frac{1}{2}$. In other words, in the discounted amount $K/(1 + r_f)^T$, the risk-free rate, r_f, is entered as an annual rate and the time to maturity, T, is entered in years (or a fraction of a year).

We now use the fundamental principle of finance that states that two investments with the same risk and the same payoff on the same future date must have the same price today. If this fundamental principle were not true, then investors could create unlimited amounts of risk-free profits.

From Table 15.1, we see that Portfolio A and Portfolio B have the same payoff, K, at the option expiration date. The cost today of acquiring Portfolio A is $S + P - C$. The cost today of acquiring Portfolio B is $K/(1 + r_f)^T$. Setting these costs equal to one another yields this equation:

$$S + P - C = K/(1 + r_f)^T \qquad (15.7)$$

Equation 15.7 says something important about the relationship among the stock price, a put option, a call option, and a riskless asset. If we have any three prices, we can figure out the price of the fourth. Also, note that we have three assets on one side of Equation 15.7 and one on the other. By reading the signs of the terms in Equation 15.7, we know what position to take in the three assets that have the same payoff as the fourth asset.

EXAMPLE 15.12

Option Alchemy

Miss Molly, your eccentric (and very wealthy) aunt, wants you to explain something to her. Recently, at the Stable Club, she heard something fantastic. Her friend Rita said that there is a very interesting way to combine shares, puts, calls, and T-bills. Rita claims that having a share of stock and a put is the same as having a call and a T-bill. Miss Molly cannot believe it. Using the following information for Blue Northern Enterprises, show her that Rita is correct.

Stock price	$110
Put price	$5
Call price	$15
Strike price for both options	$105
Options expire in	1 year
One-year interest rate	5%

For $115, an investor can buy one share of stock and one put.[2] An investor can also take this $115, buy one call for $15, and invest $100. What happens in one year? We know the investment will grow to $105 in one year ($100 × 1.05 = $105). We know the options will be worth their intrinsic value in one year. However, we do not know what the stock price per share will be in one year. Therefore, we have listed some possible values below.

Gains and Losses from Investing $115 in Two Ways			
First Way: Stock and Put			
Stock Price in One Year	Value of Put Option ($K = 105)	Combined Value	Gain or Loss (from $115)
$125	$0	$125	$10
120	0	120	5
115	0	115	0
110	0	110	−5
105	0	105	−10
100	5	105	−10
95	10	105	−10
90	25	105	−10

(continued)

---

[2] This example uses prices per share. You know that exchange-traded option contracts are on 100 shares. An investor would have to buy 100 shares for $11,000 and one put for 100 × $5 = $500. This total outlay is $11,500 (or $115 per share).

Stock Price in One Year	Value of Call Option (K = $105)	Value of T-Bill	Combined Value	Gain or Loss (from $115)
$125	$20	$105	$125	$10
120	15	105	120	5
115	10	105	115	0
110	5	105	110	−5
105	0	105	105	−10
100	0	105	105	−10
95	0	105	105	−10
90	0	105	105	−10

What happens? We see that in both ways, you will have the same gain or loss for each stock price. That is, in one year, the combined value of a stock and a put is the same as the combined value of a call and a T-bill.

Therefore, the value today of a share of stock and a put is the same as today's value of a call and a T-bill (with a price equal to the strike price). It looks like Rita is correct.

Rearranging Equation 15.7 a bit yields the **put-call parity** relationship, which is generally written as:

$$C - P = S - K/(1 + r_f)^T \tag{15.8}$$

put-call parity
The no-arbitrage relationship between put and call prices for European-style options with the same strike price and expiration date.

Put-call parity is the most basic relationship between two European option prices. Put-call parity states that the difference between a call option price and a put option price for options with the same strike price and expiration date is equal to the difference between the underlying stock price and the discounted strike price.

PUT-CALL PARITY WITH DIVIDENDS

The put-call parity argument stated above assumes that the underlying stock paid no dividends before option expiration. But what happens if the stock does pay a dividend before option expiration? To begin, we will rewrite the put-call parity relationship as:

$$S = C - P + K/(1 + r_f)^T \tag{15.9}$$

Equation 15.9 says that holding a long stock position has the same payoff at option expiration as the portfolio consisting of a long call, a short put, and a long T-bill. However, will these payoffs be identical if the stock pays a dividend? The answer is no. The holder of the stock will receive a dividend at some time before option expiration. To get the same payoff, the holder of the portfolio needs an extra amount today. Because the dividend occurs at a later date, this extra amount is the *present value* of the dividend.

If the stock does pay a dividend before option expiration, then we adjust the put-call parity equation to:

$$C - P = S - \text{Div} - K/(1 + r_f)^T \tag{15.10}$$

In Equation 15.10, "Div" represents the present value of any dividend paid before option expiration.

EXAMPLE 15.13 | Implied Put Option Prices

A current stock price is $50, and a call option with a strike price of $55 maturing in two months has a price of $8. The stock will pay a $1 dividend in one month. If the interest rate is 6 percent, what is the price implied by put-call parity for a put option with a $50 strike price that matures in two months?

Rearranging the put-call parity equation yields the following price for a put option:

$$P = C - S + \text{Div} + K/(1 + r_f)^T$$
$$\$13.46 = \$8 - \$50 + \$1/1.06^{1/12} + \$55/1.06^{2/12}$$

WHAT CAN WE DO WITH PUT-CALL PARITY?

Put-call parity allows us to calculate the price of a call option before it expires. However, to calculate the call option price using put-call parity, you have to know the price of a put option with the same strike. No problem, you say. Put-call parity allows us to calculate the price of a put option. However, to calculate the put option price using put-call parity, you have to know the price of a call option with the same strike price. Uh-oh.

Do we abandon the notion of put-call parity? No. If you use an option pricing model to calculate a call option price, you can use put-call parity to calculate a put price. Option pricing models are the topic of the next chapter. As you can see in the following examples, put-call parity is also useful for arbitrageurs to align call and put option prices.

| EXAMPLE 15.14 | Identifying an Arbitrage Opportunity with Put-Call Parity |

Suppose you observe the following market prices:

$$S = \$40$$
$$C = \$\ 3$$
$$P = \$\ 2$$

The strike price for the call and the put is $40. The riskless interest rate is 6 percent per year, and the options expire in three months. The stock does not pay dividends. Is there an arbitrage opportunity?

To answer this question, use put-call parity (PCP) to calculate the "PCP-implied put price." Then compare this calculated price to the market price of puts. This difference, if any, is the potential arbitrage profit.

$$\text{PCP-implied put price} = C - S + K/(1 + r_f)^T$$
$$\$2.42 = \$3 - \$40 + \$40/1.06^{3/12}$$
$$\text{Potential arbitrage profit} = \text{PCP-implied put price} - \text{Market price of puts}$$
$$\$.42 = \$2.42 - 2.00$$

| EXAMPLE 15.15 | Taking Advantage of an Arbitrage Opportunity |

In Example 15.14, we calculated a $.42 potential arbitrage profit. How would an arbitrageur take advantage of this opportunity? How much profit will the arbitrageur make?

In Example 15.14, buying a call, selling stock, and investing the discounted strike together have a value of $2.42. If an arbitrageur has these three positions, this portfolio is called a long "synthetic put." However, the arbitrageur can buy actual puts for $2.00. Arbitrageurs make money when they buy low and sell high. Therefore, the arbitrageur will buy a put for $2.00 and sell a synthetic put. That is, the investor will sell a call, buy stock, and borrow the difference. The arbitrageur can spend $2.00 to purchase an actual put and receive $2.42 for the sale of a synthetic put. This results in a potential profit of $.42. However, traders incur costs of trading. The realized pretax profit will be the potential profit minus trading costs.

This approach is used quite often by arbitrageurs. A recent example is provided in the nearby *Investment Updates* box.

ONE-WAY VOL BETS SEEN AS "FOOL'S ERRAND" BY 6,000% WINNER

Heads you lose, tails you lose. This year for the first time, trading strategies betting on a jump in equity market volatility and those wagering for calm are both losing.

The reason? February's "volmageddon" blow out, which did enough to sink short-volatility strategies but not enough to protect long-vol trades from the tranquility that's enveloped stocks on their way to new peaks.

"Winning trades are quite hard to come by," said Lincoln Edwards, founder of Houndstooth Capital Management LLC, a $7.5 million hedge fund in Austin, Texas, that reaped 6,000 percent in February's meltdown. These days his bets seek to ride volatility on the way down as well as up; trying to time the crests is "a fool's errand," he reckons.

Edwards at Houndstooth says he likes puts on short-VIX positions just as the gauge spikes. While risky, the trade pays off in a market that reliably returns to calm.

"We like VIX options that trade a couple months out," he said. "Since February, we've seen some sort of VIX spike almost every single month. Selling option spreads a couple months out allows you enough time for the VIX to calm back down and erode the options' value."

Source: Dani Burger and Yakob Peterseil, "One-Way Vol Bets Seen as 'Fool's Errand' by 6,000% Winner," *Bloomberg*, August 29, 2018, www.bloomberg.com/news/articles/2018-08-29/volatility-traders-damned-either-way-as-february-bets-washed-out.

CHECK THIS

15.10a Your friend Kristen claims that forming a portfolio today of long call, short put, and short stock has a value at option expiration equal to $-K$. Does it? (*Hint:* Create a table similar to Table 15.1.)

15.10b If a dividend payment occurs before option expiration, investors lower today's stock price to an "effective stock price." Why does this adjustment reduce call values and increase put values?

15.10c Exchange-traded options on individual stocks have American-style exercise. Therefore, put-call parity does not hold exactly for these options. Using option chain data from finance.yahoo.com or from the online version of *The Wall Street Journal* (www.wsj.com), compare the differences between selected call and put option prices with the differences between stock prices and discounted strike prices. You can find a short-term, riskless T-bill rate at www.reuters.com. How closely does put-call parity appear to hold for these equity options with American-style exercise?

15.11 Summary and Conclusions

In 1973, organized stock options trading began when the Chicago Board Options Exchange (CBOE) was established. Since then, options trading has grown enormously. In this chapter, we examined a number of concepts and issues surrounding stock options—which we have grouped by the chapter's important concepts.

1. **The basics of option contracts and how to obtain price quotes.**

A. Options are contracts. Standardized stock options represent a contract size of 100 shares of common stock per option contract. We saw how standardized option prices are quoted online.

B. Options on common stock are derivative securities because the value of a stock option is derived from the value of the underlying common stock. The two basic types of options are call options and put options. Holders of call options have the right, but not the obligation, to buy the underlying asset at the strike, or exercise, price. Holders of put options have the right, but not the obligation, to sell the underlying asset at the strike, or exercise, price.

C. A stock index option is an option on a stock market index such as the S&P 500. All stock index options use a cash settlement procedure when they are exercised. With a cash settlement procedure, when a stock index option is exercised, the option writer pays a cash amount to the option buyer.

D. The Options Clearing Corporation (OCC) is the clearing agency for major options exchanges in the United States. It guarantees that the terms of an option contract are fulfilled if the option is exercised.

2. The difference between option payoffs and option profits.

A. The initial cash flow of an option is the price of the option, also called the option premium. To the option buyer, the option price (or premium) is a cash outflow. To the option writer, the option price (or premium) is a cash inflow. The terminal cash flow of an option is the option's payoff realized from the exercise privilege.

B. At expiration, the value of the option is its intrinsic value. For call options, this value is the maximum of zero or the stock price minus the strike price. For put options, this value is the maximum of zero or the strike price minus the stock price.

C. The profit from an option strategy is the difference between the option's terminal cash flow (the option payoff) and the option's initial cash flow (the option price, or premium). An option profit diagram adjusts option payoffs for the original price of the option. This means that the option premium is subtracted from the payoffs from buying options and added to payoffs from writing options. Note that these profits are pretax.

3. The workings of some basic option trading strategies.

A. There are many option trading strategies. In one strategy type, traders add an option position to their stock position. Examples of this strategy include protective puts and covered calls.

B. A spread is another type of option trading strategy. A spread strategy involves taking a position on two or more options of the same type at the same time. By same type, we mean call options only or put options only. A "butterfly" is a well-known example of a spread.

C. A combination is the third type of option trading strategy. In a combination, the trader takes a position in a mixture of call and put options. A straddle is the best-known combination.

D. Option prices have boundaries enforced by arbitrage. A call option cannot sell for more than the underlying asset, and a put option cannot sell for more than the strike price on the option.

4. The logic behind the put-call parity condition.

A. Put-call parity is perhaps the most fundamental relationship between two option prices. Put-call parity states that the difference between a call price and a put price for European-style options with the same strike price and expiration date is equal to the difference between the stock price and the discounted strike price.

B. The logic behind put-call parity is based on the fundamental principle of finance stating that two securities with the same riskless payoff on the same future date must have the same price.

GETTING DOWN TO BUSINESS

This chapter added to your understanding of put and call options by covering the rights, obligations, and potential gains and losses involved in trading options. How should you put this information to work? You need to buy and sell options to experience the gains and losses that options can provide. So, with a simulated brokerage account (such as Stock-Trak), you should first execute each of the basic option transactions: buy a call, sell a call, buy a put, and sell a put.

For help getting started, you can find an enormous amount of information about options on the internet. A useful place to start is the Chicago Board Options Exchange (www.cboe.com). Excellent websites devoted to options education are the Options Industry Council (www.optionseducation.org) and the Options Clearing Corporation (www.theocc.com).

For information on option trading strategies, try entering the strategy name into an internet search engine. For example, enter the search phrases "covered calls" or "protective puts" for online information about those strategies.

If you're having trouble understanding options ticker symbols, don't feel alone because almost everyone has trouble at first. For help on the net, try the search phrases "option symbols" or "options symbols." Of course, the options exchanges listed above also provide complete information on the option ticker symbols they use.

For the latest information on the real world of investments, visit us at jmdinvestments.blogspot.com.

Key Terms

American option 491
at-the-money option 500
call option 491
call option intrinsic value 499
call writer 502
cash-settled option 497
combination 510
covered call 509
derivative security 491
European option 491
in-the-money option 500
intrinsic value 498
option chain 494

option time value 499
option writing 502
Options Clearing Corporation (OCC) 494
out-of-the-money option 500
protective put 506
put option 491
put option intrinsic value 499
put writer 502
put-call parity 516
spread 509
stock index option 497
strike price 491

Related Bloomberg Functions

OMON	Option Monitor, 15.1 and 15.5
OTD	Option Description, 15.1
MOSO	Most Active Options, 15.1
SSI	Standing Settlement Instructions, 15.4
XLTP XOSA	Excel Template: Option Portfolio P/L, 15.6
SOVR	Sovereign CDS Monitor, 15.7
CDS	CDS Landing Page, 15.7
XLTP XSTR	Excel Template: Option Strategy Worksheet, 15.8

Chapter Review Problems and Self-Test

1. **Call Option Payoffs (LO2, CFA2)** You purchase 25 call option contracts on Blue Ox stock. The strike price is $22 and the premium is $1. If the stock is selling for $24 per share at expiration, what are your call options worth? What is your net profit? What if the stock were selling for $23? $22?

2. **Stock versus Options (LO1, CFA1)** Stock in Bunyan Brewery is currently priced at $20 per share. A call option with a $20 strike price and 60 days to maturity is quoted at $2. Compare the percentage gains and losses from a $2,000 investment in the stock versus the option in 60 days for stock prices of $26, $20, and $18.

3. **Put-Call Parity (LO4, CFA1)** A call option sells for $8. It has a strike price of $80 and six months until expiration. If the underlying stock sells for $60 per share, what is the price of a put option with an $80 strike price and six months until expiration? The risk-free interest rate is 6 percent per year.

Answers to Self-Test Problems

1. Blue Ox stock is selling for $24. You own 25 contracts, each of which gives you the right to buy 100 shares at $22. Your options are thus worth $2 per share on 2,500 shares, or $5,000. The option premium was $1, so you paid $100 per contract, or $2,500 total. Your net profit is $2,500. If the stock is selling for $23, your options are worth $2,500, so your net profit is exactly zero. If the stock is selling for $22, your options are worthless, and you lose the entire $2,500 you paid.

2. Bunyan stock costs $20 per share, so if you invest $2,000, you'll get 100 shares. The option premium is $2, so an option contract costs $200. If you invest $2,000, you'll get $2,000/$200 = 10 contracts. If the stock is selling for $26 in 60 days, your profit on the stock is $6 per share, or $600 total. The percentage gain is $600/$2,000 = .30, or 30%.

   In this case, your options are worth $6 per share, or $600 per contract. You have 10 contracts, so your options are worth $6,000 in all. Since you paid $2,000 for the 10 contracts, your profit is $4,000. Your percentage gain is a whopping $4,000/$2,000 = 2.00, or 200%.

   If the stock is selling for $20, your profit is $0 on the stock, so your percentage return is 0 percent. Your options are worthless (why?), so the percentage loss is −100 percent. If the stock is selling for $18, verify that your percentage loss on the stock is −10 percent and your loss on the options is again −100 percent.

3. Using the put-call parity formula, we have:

$$C - P = S - K/(1 + r)^T$$

Rearranging to solve for P, the put price, and plugging in the other numbers gets us:

$$P = C - S + K/(1 + r)^T$$
$$= \$8 - \$60 + \$80/1.06^{1/2}$$
$$= \$25.70$$

Test Your Investment Quotient

1. **Option Contracts (LO1, CFA1)** Which of the following is not specified by a stock option contract?
   a. The underlying stock's price
   b. The size of the contract
   c. Exercise style—European or American
   d. Contract settlement procedure—cash or delivery

2. **Option Payoffs (LO2, CFA2)** All of the following statements about the value of a call option at expiration are true, except that the:
   a. Short position in the same call option can result in a loss if the stock price exceeds the exercise price.
   b. Value of the long position equals zero or the stock price minus the exercise price, whichever is higher.

c. Value of the long position equals zero or the exercise price minus the stock price, whichever is higher.

d. Short position in the same call option has a zero value for all stock prices equal to or less than the exercise price.

3. **Option Strategies (LO3, CFA2)**   Which of the following stock option strategies has the greatest potential for large losses?

   a. Writing a covered call
   b. Writing a covered put
   c. Writing a naked call
   d. Writing a naked put

4. **Option Strategies (LO3, CFA4)**   Which statement does not describe an at-the-money protective put position (comprised of owning the stock and the put)?

   a. It protects against loss at any stock price below the strike price of the put.
   b. It has limited profit potential when the stock price rises.
   c. It returns any increase in the stock's value, dollar for dollar, less the cost of the put.
   d. It provides a pattern of returns similar to a stop-loss order at the current stock price.

5. **Put-Call Parity (LO4, CFA1)**   Which of the following is not included in the put-call parity condition?

   a. Price of the underlying stock
   b. Strike price of the underlying call and put option contracts
   c. Expiration dates of the underlying call and put option contracts
   d. Volatility of the underlying stock

6. **Put-Call Parity (LO4, CFA1)**   According to the put-call parity condition, a risk-free portfolio can be created by buying 100 shares of stock and:

   a. Writing one call option contract and buying one put option contract.
   b. Buying one call option contract and writing one put option contract.
   c. Buying one call option contract and buying one put option contract.
   d. Writing one call option contract and writing one put option contract.

7. **Option Strategies (LO3, CFA4)**   Investor A uses options for defensive and income reasons. Investor B uses options as an aggressive investment strategy. What is an appropriate use of options for investors A and B, respectively?

   a. Writing covered calls/buying puts on stock not owned
   b. Buying out-of-the-money calls/buying puts on stock owned
   c. Writing naked calls/buying in-the-money calls
   d. Selling puts on stock owned/buying puts on stock not owned

8. **Option Strategies (LO3, CFA3)**   Which one of the following option combinations best describes a straddle? Buy both a call and a put on the same stock with:

   a. Different exercise prices and the same expiration date.
   b. The same exercise price and different expiration dates.
   c. The same exercise price and the same expiration date.
   d. Different exercise prices and different expiration dates.

9. **Option Strategies (LO3, CFA3)**   Which of the following strategies is the riskiest options transaction if the underlying stock price is expected to increase substantially?

   a. Writing a naked call option
   b. Writing a naked put option
   c. Buying a call option
   d. Buying a put option

10. **Option Gains and Losses (LO2, CFA3)**   You create a "strap" by buying two calls and one put on ABC stock, all with a strike price of $45. The calls cost $5 each and the put costs $4. If you close your position when ABC stock is priced at $55, what is your per-share gain or loss?

   a. $4 loss
   b. $6 gain
   c. $10 gain
   d. $20 gain

11. **Option Gains and Losses (LO2, CFA3)**   A put on XYZ stock with a strike price of $40 is priced at $2.00 per share, while a call with a strike price of $40 is priced at $3.50. What is the maximum

per-share loss to the writer of the uncovered put and the maximum per-share gain to the writer of the uncovered call?

	Maximum Loss to Put Writer	Maximum Gain to Call Writer
a.	$38.00	$3.50
b.	$38.00	$36.50
c.	$40.00	$3.50
d.	$40.00	$40.00

12. **Option Pricing (LO2, CFA3)** If a stock is selling for $25, the exercise price of a put option on that stock is $20, and the time to expiration of the option is 90 days, what are the minimum and maximum prices for the put today?

   a. $0 and $5
   b. $0 and $20
   c. $5 and $20
   d. $5 and $25

13. **Option Strategies (LO3, CFA4)** Which of the following strategies is most suitable for an investor wishing to eliminate "downside" risk from a long position in stock?

   a. A long straddle position
   b. A short straddle position
   c. Writing a covered call option
   d. Buying a protective put option

14. **Covered Calls (LO3, CFA1)** The current price of an asset is $75. A three-month, at-the-money American call option on the asset has a current value of $5. At what value of the asset will a covered call writer break even at expiration?

   a. $70
   b. $75
   c. $80
   d. $85

15. **Option Strategies (LO3, CFA2)** The current price of an asset is $100. An out-of-the-money American put option with an exercise price of $90 is purchased along with the asset. If the break-even point for this hedge is at an asset price of $114 at expiration, then the value of the American put at the time of purchase must have been:

   a. $0
   b. $4
   c. $10
   d. $14

Concept Questions

1. **Basic Properties of Options (LO1, CFA1)** What is a call option? A put option? Under what circumstances might you want to buy each? Which one has greater potential profit? Why?

2. **Calls versus Puts (LO1, CFA1)** Complete the following sentence for each of these investors:

   a. A buyer of call options
   b. A buyer of put options
   c. A seller (writer) of call options
   d. A seller (writer) of put options

   The (buyer/seller) of a (put/call) option (pays/receives) money for the (right/obligation) to (buy/sell) a specified asset at a fixed price for a fixed length of time.

3. **Option Break-Even (LO2, CFA2)** In general, if you buy a call option, what stock price is needed for you to break even on the transaction ignoring taxes and commissions? If you buy a put option?

4. **Protective Puts (LO3, CFA4)** Buying a put option on a stock you own is sometimes called "stock price insurance." Why?

5. **Defining Intrinsic Value (LO2, CFA1)** What is the intrinsic value of a call option? How do we interpret this value?

6. **Defining Intrinsic Value (LO2, CFA1)** What is the intrinsic value of a put option? How do we interpret this value?

7. **Arbitrage and Options (LO2, CFA3)** You notice that shares of stock in the Patel Corporation are going for $50 per share. Call options with an exercise price of $35 per share are selling for $10. What's wrong here? Describe how you could take advantage of this mispricing if the option expires today.

Use the following options quotations to answer Questions 8 through 11:

Option & N.Y. Close	Strike Price	Expiration	Calls Vol.	Calls Last	Puts Vol.	Puts Last
Milson						
59	55	Mar	98	3.50	66	1.06
59	55	Apr	54	6.25	40	1.94
59	55	Jul	25	8.63	17	3.63
59	55	Oct	10	10.25	5	3.25

8. **Interpreting Options Quotes (LO1, CFA2)** How many option contracts on Milson stock were traded with an expiration date of July? How many underlying shares of stock do these option contracts represent?

9. **Interpreting Options Quotes (LO1, LO2, CFA1)** Are the call options in the money? What is the intrinsic value of a Milson Corp. call option?

10. **Interpreting Options Quotes (LO1, LO2, CFA1)** Are the put options in the money? What is the intrinsic value of a Milson Corp. put option?

11. **Interpreting Options Quotes (LO1, LO2, CFA3)** Two of the options are clearly mispriced. Which ones? At a minimum, what should the mispriced options sell for? Explain how you could profit from the mispricing in each case.

12. **Option Strategies (LO3, CFA4)** Recall the option strategies of a protective put and covered call discussed in the text. Suppose you have sold short some shares of stock. Discuss analogous option strategies and how you would implement them. (*Hint:* They're called protective calls and covered puts.)

13. **Put-Call Parity (LO4, CFA1)** A put and a call option have the same maturity and strike price. If both are at the money, which is worth more? Prove your answer and then provide an intuitive explanation.

14. **Put-Call Parity (LO4, CFA1)** A put and a call option have the same maturity and strike price. If they also have the same price, which one is in the money?

15. **Put-Call Parity (LO4, CFA2)** One thing the put-call parity equation tells us is that given any three of a stock—a call, a put, and a T-bill—the fourth can be synthesized or replicated using the other three. For example, how can we replicate a share of stock using a put, a call, and a T-bill?

Questions and Problems

Core Questions

1. **Call Option Payoffs (LO2, CFA2)** Suppose you purchase eight call contracts on Macron Technology stock. The strike price is $60 and the premium is $3. If, at expiration, the stock is selling for $64 per share, what are your call options worth? What is your net profit?

2. **Put Option Payoffs (LO2, CFA2)** Suppose you purchase five put contracts on Testaburger Co. The strike price is $45 and the premium is $3. If, at expiration, the stock is selling for $39 per share, what are your put options worth? What is your net profit?

3. **Stock versus Options (LO2, CFA1)** Stock in Cheezy-Poofs Manufacturing is currently priced at $50 per share. A call option with a $50 strike and 90 days to maturity is quoted at $1.95. Compare the percentage gains and losses from a $97,500 investment in the stock versus the option in 90 days for stock prices of $40, $50, and $60.

Use the following options quotations to answer Problems 4 through 7:

Close	Strike Price	Expiration	Calls Vol.	Calls Last	Puts Vol.	Puts Last
Hendreeks						
103	100	Feb	72	5.20	50	2.40
103	100	Mar	41	8.40	29	4.90
103	100	Apr	16	10.68	10	6.60
103	100	Jul	8	14.30	2	10.10

4. **Options Quotes (LO1)** Suppose you buy 50 April 100 call option contracts. How much will you pay, ignoring commissions?

5. **Calculating Option Payoffs (LO2, CFA2)** In Problem 4, suppose that Hendreeks stock is selling for $105.70 per share on the expiration date. How much is your options investment worth? What if the stock price is $101.60 on the expiration date?

6. **Calculating Option Payoffs (LO2, CFA2)** Suppose you buy 30 March 100 put option contracts. What is your maximum gain? On the expiration date, Hendreeks is selling for $84.60 per share. How much is your options investment worth? What is your net gain?

7. **Calculating Option Payoffs (LO2, CFA2)** Suppose you write 30 of the July 100 put contracts. What is your net gain or loss if Hendreeks is selling for $90 at expiration? For $110? What is the break-even price, that is, the terminal stock price that results in a zero profit?

8. **Put-Call Parity (LO4, CFA1)** A call option is currently selling for $3. It has a strike price of $65 and six months to maturity. What is the price of a put option with a $65 strike price and six months to maturity? The current stock price is $66 and the risk-free interest rate is 5 percent.

9. **Put-Call Parity (LO4, CFA1)** A call option currently sells for $8. It has a strike price of $80 and five months to maturity. A put with the same strike and expiration date sells for $6. If the risk-free interest rate is 4 percent, what is the current stock price?

10. **Put-Call Parity (LO4, CFA1)** A put option with a strike price of $50 sells for $3.20. The option expires in two months and the current stock price is $51. If the risk-free interest rate is 5 percent, what is the price of a call option with the same strike price?

11. **Put-Call Parity (LO4, CFA1)** A call option is currently selling for $3.90. It has a strike price of $45 and five months to maturity. The current stock price is $47 and the risk-free rate is 4 percent. The stock will pay a dividend of $1.45 in two months. What is the price of a put option with the same exercise price?

12. **Put-Call Parity (LO4, CFA1)** A call option is currently selling for $4.60. It has a strike price of $60 and three months to maturity. A put option with the same strike price sells for $7.20. The risk-free rate is 6 percent and the stock will pay a dividend of $2.10 in three months. What is the current stock price?

13. **Put-Call Parity (LO4, CFA1)** A put option is currently selling for $8.30. It has a strike price of $80 and seven months to maturity. The current stock price is $83. The risk-free rate is 5 percent and the stock will pay a $1.40 dividend in two months. What is the price of a call option with the same strike price?

14. **Call Option Writing (LO2, CFA3)** Suppose you write 10 call option contracts with a $50 strike. The premium is $2.75. Evaluate your potential gains and losses at option expiration for stock prices of $40, $50, and $60.

15. **Put Option Writing (LO2, CFA3)** Suppose you write 15 put option contracts with a $45 strike. The premium is $2.40. Evaluate your potential gains and losses at option expiration for stock prices of $35, $45, and $55.

16. **Index Options (LO2, CFA1)** Suppose you buy one SPX call option contract with a strike of 4200. At maturity, the S&P 500 index is at 4218. What is your net gain or loss if the premium you paid was $14?

17. **Option Strategies (LO3, CFA4)** You write a put with a strike price of $60 on stock that you have shorted at $60 (this is a "covered put"). What are the expiration date profits to this position for stock prices of $50, $55, $60, $65, and $70 if the put premium is $1.80?

18. **Option Strategies (LO3, CFA4)** You buy a call with a strike price of $70 on stock that you have shorted at $70 (this is a "protective call"). What are the expiration date profits to this position for stock prices of $60, $65, $70, $75, and $80 if the call premium is $3.40?

19. **Option Strategies (LO3, CFA4)** You simultaneously write a covered put and buy a protective call, both with strike prices of $80, on stock that you have shorted at $80. What are the expiration date payoffs to this position for stock prices of $70, $75, $80, $85, and $90?

20. **Option Strategies (LO3, CFA4)** You simultaneously write a put and buy a call, both with strike prices of $80, naked, i.e., without any position in the underlying stock. What are the expiration date payoffs to this position for stock prices of $70, $75, $80, $85, and $90?

21. **Option Strategies (LO3, CFA4)** You buy a straddle, which means you purchase a put and a call with the same strike price. The put price is $2.80 and the call price is $4.20. Assume the strike price is $75. What are the expiration date profits to this position for stock prices of $65, $70, $75, $80, and $85? What are the expiration date profits for these same stock prices? What are the break-even stock prices?

22. **Index Option Positions (LO3, CFA3)** Suppose you buy one SPX call option with a strike of 4125 and write one SPX call option with a strike of 4150. What are the payoffs at maturity to this position for S&P 500 index levels of 4050, 4100, 4150, 4200, and 4250?

23. **Index Option Positions (LO3, CFA3)** Suppose you buy one SPX put option with a strike of 4100 and write one SPX put option with a strike of 4125. What are the payoffs at maturity to this position for S&P 500 index levels of 4000, 4050, 4100, 4150, and 4200?

24. **Index Option Positions (LO3, CFA3)** Suppose you buy one SPX call option with a strike of 4100 and write one SPX put option with a strike of 4100. What are the payoffs at maturity to this position for S&P 500 index levels of 4000, 4050, 4100, 4150, and 4200?

25. **Index Option Positions (LO3, CFA3)** Suppose you buy one each of SPX call options with strikes of 4000 and 4200 and write two SPX call options with a strike of 4100. What are the payoffs at maturity to this position for S&P 500 index levels of 3900, 3950, 4000, 4050, 4100, 4150, and 4200?

26. **Strangles (CFA4)** A strangle is created by buying a put and buying a call on the same stock with a higher strike price and the same expiration. A put with a strike price of $100 sells for $6.75 and a call with a strike price of $110 sells for $8.60. Draw a graph showing the payoff and profit for a straddle using these options.

27. **Bull Spread with Calls (CFA4)** You create a bull spread using calls by buying a call and simultaneously selling a call on the same stock with the same expiration at a higher strike price. A call option with a strike price of $20 sells for $4.55 and a call with a strike price of $25 sells for $1.24. Draw a graph showing the payoff and profit for a bull spread using these options.

28. **Bull Spread with Puts (CFA4)** You can also create a bull spread using put options. To do so, you buy a put and simultaneously sell a put at a higher strike price on the same stock with the same expiration. A put with a strike price of $20 is available for $.45 and a put with a strike price of $25 is available for $1.64. Draw a graph showing the payoff and profit for a bull spread using these options.

Spreadsheet Problems

29. **Butterfly Spread with Calls (CFA4)** You create a butterfly spread using calls by buying a call at K_1, buying a call at K_3, and selling two calls at K_2. All of the calls are on the same stock and have the same expiration date. Additionally, butterfly spreads assume that $K_2 = \frac{1}{2}(K_1 + K_3)$. Calls on a stock with strike prices of $35, $40, and $45 are available for $7.00, $3.59, and $1.31, respectively. Draw a graph showing the payoff and profit for a butterfly spread using these options.

30. **Butterfly Spread with Puts (CFA4)** You can also create a butterfly spread using puts by buying a put at K_1, buying a put at K_3, and selling two puts at K_2. All of the puts are on the same stock and have the same expiration date, and the assumption that $K_2 = \frac{1}{2}(K_1 + K_3)$ still holds. Puts on a stock with strike prices of $35, $40, and $45 are available for $.90, $2.35, and $5.10, respectively. Draw a graph showing the payoff and profit for a butterfly spread using these options.

[CFA1, CFA2]

Rachel Barlow is a recent finance graduate from Columbia University. She has accepted a position at a large investment bank but must first complete an intensive training program. Currently she is spending three months at her firm's Derivatives Trading Desk. To prepare for her assignment, Ms. Barlow decides to review her notes on option relationships, concentrating particularly on put-call parity. The data she will be using in her review are provided below. She also decides to assume continuous compounding.

	Option 1	Option 2
Stock price	$100	$110
Strike price	$100	$100
Interest rate	7%	7%
Dividend yield	0%	0%
Time to maturity (years)	.5	.5
Standard deviation of stock	20%	20%
Call option price	$7.38	$14.84

1. She would like to compute the value of the corresponding put option for Option 1. Which of the following is closest to Ms. Barlow's answer?

   a. $3.79
   b. $3.94
   c. $4.41

2. Ms. Barlow notices that the stock in the table above does not pay dividends. If the stock begins to pay a dividend, how will the price of the call option be affected?

   a. It will decrease.
   b. It will increase.
   c. It will not change.

3. She would like to compute the value of the corresponding put option for Option 2. Which of the following is closest to Ms. Barlow's answer?

   a. $.98
   b. $1.41
   c. $4.84

Bloomberg Exercises

1. Identify the most active options traded on Microsoft (MFST). **(OMON)**
2. Review contract characteristics for an option of your choice on Verizon (VZ). **(OTD)**
3. Collect a list of the most actively traded options. **(MOSO)**

What's on the Web?

1. **Option Prices** You want to find the option prices for Intel (INTC). Go to finance.yahoo.com and find the option price quotes for Intel. What are the option premium and strike price for the highest and lowest strike price options that are nearest to expiring? What are the option premium and strike price for the highest and lowest strike price options expiring next month?

2. **Option Symbol Construction** What is the option symbol for a call option on Cisco Systems (CSCO) with a strike price of $25 that expires in July? Go to www.cboe.com and find the links for the option ticker symbol construction. Find the basic ticker symbol for Cisco Systems options

and the codes for the expiration month and strike price. Use these codes to construct the call option ticker symbol. Now construct the ticker symbol for a put option with the same strike price and expiration.

3. **Option Expiration**   Go to www.cboe.com and find the expiration calendar for options traded on the CBOE. On what day do equity options expire in the current month? On what day do they expire next month?

4. **LEAPS**   Go to www.cboe.com and find the link for "LEAPS." What are LEAPS? What are the two types of LEAPS? What are the benefits of equity LEAPS? What are the benefits of index LEAPS?

5. **FLEX Options**   Go to www.cboe.com and find the link for "FLEX Options." What is a FLEX option? When do FLEX options expire? What is the minimum size of a FLEX option?

Option Valuation

"I have compared the results of observation with those of theory . . . to show that the market, unwittingly, obeys a law which governs it, the law of probability."

–Louis Bachelier

Learning Objectives

Make sure the price is right by making sure that you have a good understanding of:

1. How to price options using the one-period and two-period binomial models.

2. How to price options using the Black-Scholes model.

3. How to hedge a stock portfolio using options.

4. The workings of employee stock options.

What is an option worth? Actually, this is one of the more difficult questions in finance. Option valuation is an esoteric area of finance because it often involves complex mathematics. Fortunately, just like most options professionals, you can learn quite a bit about option valuation with only modest mathematical tools. But no matter how far you might wish to delve into this topic, you must begin with the Black-Scholes option pricing model. This model is the core from which most other option pricing models trace their ancestry.

The previous chapter introduced the basics of stock options. From an economic standpoint, perhaps the most important subject was the expiration date payoffs of stock options. Bear in mind that when investors buy options today, they are buying risky future payoffs. Likewise, when investors write options today, they become obligated to make risky future payments. In a competitive financial marketplace, option prices observed each day are collectively agreed on by buyers and writers assessing the likelihood of all possible future payoffs and payments. Option prices are set accordingly.

In this chapter, we spend a lot of time showing you how to calculate stock option prices. We begin with a simple way to calculate stock option prices and then discuss the binomial option pricing model. The discussion ends with the Black-Scholes option pricing model, which is widely regarded by finance professionals as the premier model of stock option valuation.

CFA™ Exam Topics in This Chapter:

1. Basics of derivatives pricing and valuation (L1, S15)
2. Valuation of contingent claims (L2, S13)
3. Option strategies (L3, S4)

Go to Connect for a guide that aligns your textbook with CFA readings.

16.1 A Simple Model to Value Options Before Expiration

Calculating the value of an option before it expires can be complex. However, we can illustrate many of the key insights to this problem using a simple example. Suppose we are looking at a call option with one year to maturity and a $110 exercise price. The current stock price is $108 and the one-year risk-free rate, r, is 10 percent.

We know that an option is worth its intrinsic value at expiration. To calculate the intrinsic value, we need the strike price and the stock price at option expiration. We know the strike price today and at option expiration. We know the stock price today, but we do not know what the stock price will be in one year. A method frequently used to forge on and calculate option prices today is to assume that today we "know" the range of possible values for the underlying asset at option expiration.

We start with an uncomplicated example. Assume we know (somehow) that the stock price will be either $130 or $115 in one year. Keep in mind, though, that the stock price in one year is still uncertain. We do know that the stock price is going to be either $130 or $115 (but no other values). We do not know the odds associated with these two prices. In other words, we know the possible values of the stock, but not the probabilities associated with these two values.[1]

Because the strike price is $110, we know the call option value at expiration will be either $130 - $110 = $20 or $115 - $110 = $5. Once again, we do not know which one. We do know one very important thing: The call option is certain to finish in the money.

What about puts with a strike price of $110? In both cases, the put will finish out of the money. That is, the value of this put at expiration is zero regardless of the stock price. What is this put worth today? Think about it by answering this question: How much are you willing to pay today for a riskless asset that will have a zero value in one year? You are right, zero.

If you know the price of a put with the same strike, you can use put-call parity to price a call option before it expires. An expiration day stock price of either $130 or $115 means that a put option with a $110 strike price has a value of zero today and at expiration. Therefore, in this case, we can use put-call parity to calculate the value of a call with a strike price of $110:

$$C - P = S_0 - K/(1 + r)^T$$
$$C - 0 = \$108 - \$110/1.10$$
$$C = \$108 - \$100 = \$8$$

Many other pairs of stock prices also result in a zero value for the put. Therefore, the fact that we selected these two particular stock prices is not what allowed us to calculate the call option price. What allowed us to calculate the call option price were these two facts: (1) the chosen pair of stock prices guarantees that the call option will finish in the money and (2) the chosen pair of stock prices also guarantees that a put option with the same strike price will finish out of the money.[2]

We conclude that pricing a call option when we are certain that the call option will finish somewhere in the money is easy. We use a put option value of zero and the put-call parity equation to obtain the value of the call option before it expires.

---

[1] If we knew these probabilities, we could calculate the expected value of the stock price at expiration.

[2] You might be wondering what would happen if the stock price were less than the present value of the exercise price. In this event, the call price would be negative. But this cannot happen in this example because we are certain that the stock price will be at least K in one year because we know the call option will finish in the money. If the current price of the stock is less than $K/(1 + r)^T$, then the return on the stock is certain to be greater than the risk-free rate—which creates an arbitrage opportunity. For example, if the stock is currently selling for $80, then the minimum return will be ($115 − $80)/$80 = .4375, or 43.75%. Because we can borrow at 10 percent, we can earn a certain minimum return of 33.75 percent per dollar borrowed. This, of course, is an arbitrage opportunity.

16.1a Rework the example in this section to price a call option today that expires in one year if $K = \$105$, $S = \$100$, $r = 10\%$, and the stock price will be either $120 or $110 in one year.

16.2 The One-Period Binomial Option Pricing Model

Related Bloomberg Functions
OVME Option Price Equity/IR

In the previous section, we made good use of the fact that the call option would always expire in the money. Suppose we want to allow the call option to expire in the money or out of the money.[3] How do we proceed in this case? Well, we need a different option pricing model. We will start our tour of option pricing models by looking at the one-period binomial option pricing model (BOPM).

THE ONE-PERIOD BINOMIAL OPTION PRICING MODEL—THE ASSUMPTIONS

Suppose the stock price today is S and the stock pays no dividends. We will assume that the stock price in one period is either $S \times u$ or $S \times d$, where u (for "up" factor) is bigger than 1 and d (for "down" factor) is less than 1.[4] For example, suppose the stock price today is $100 and u and d are 1.10 and .95, respectively. With these numbers, the stock price in one period will be either $\$100 \times 1.10 = \$110$ or $\$100 \times .95 = \$95$.

THE ONE-PERIOD BINOMIAL OPTION PRICING MODEL—THE SETUP

Suppose we start with the values given in Table 16.1. To begin to calculate the call price today, suppose an investor:

- Buys one share of stock and
- Sells one call option.

A key question to ask is "What is the value of this portfolio today and in one period when the option expires?" To answer this question, we first write down all the prices that we know today and all the prices we know at expiration. We show these prices on two "trees" in Figure 16.1. In the world of option pricing models, a collection of stock or option prices is known as a tree.

As shown in Figure 16.1, we know the stock price today ($100), but we do not know the call price today (we are trying to calculate this). In one period when the option expires, we know that the stock price will either increase to $110 (which is $S \times u = \$100 \times 1.10$) or decrease to $95 (which is $S \times d = \$100 \times .95$).

At expiration, we know that the call option is worth its intrinsic value. If the stock price increases to $110, the intrinsic value of the call option, C_u, is MAX[110 − 100, 0], or $10. Similarly, if the stock price decreases to $95, the call option intrinsic value, C_d, is MAX[95 − 100, 0], or $0.

TABLE 16.1	Inputs for the One-Period BOPM	
S	= $100	Current stock price
u	= 1.10	Up factor
d	= .95	Down factor
r	= 3%	Risk-free interest rate
K	= $100	Strike price
T	= 1 period	Periods to option expiration

[3] We limit our discussion here to call options. Of course, we can make parallel statements for put options.
[4] Note that we are assuming that d is less than 1.0, but d does not necessarily have to be less than 1.0, as was the case in Section 16.1.

FIGURE 16.1   Stock Price Tree and Option Priced Tree

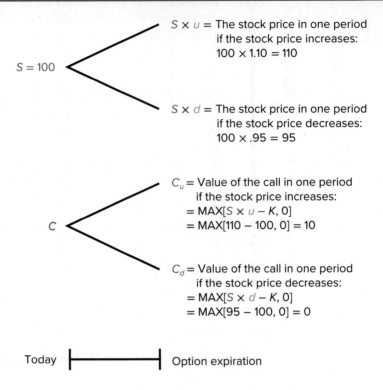

Today |———————| Option expiration

What is the value of the portfolio of one share of stock and short one call option? If the stock price increases to $110, the call finishes in the money–with an intrinsic value equal to $10. Because the investor sold the call option, the investor owes the intrinsic value. Therefore, the portfolio value is $110 − $10, or $100. If the stock price decreases to $95, the call finishes out of the money, so it has an intrinsic value equal to $0. Therefore, the portfolio value is $95 + $0 = $95.

THE ONE-PERIOD BINOMIAL OPTION PRICING MODEL—THE FORMULA

Is there a way to form a portfolio of stock and options that is worth the same amount regardless of the price of the stock in one period? It turns out that there is, and this way is a truly brilliant insight. Instead of buying one share, suppose the investor buys a "fractional" share of stock (which we will represent by the Greek letter *delta,* Δ). What happens in this case?

In Figure 16.2, we know all values at expiration except Δ. The key to the solution hinges on the fact that the investor can choose the size of the fractional share, Δ. That is, the investor

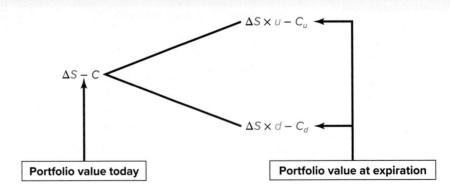

can choose a value for Δ where the portfolio has the same value at expiration for both stock prices. In other words, the investor can choose Δ so that $\Delta S \times u - C_u = \Delta S \times d - C_d$.

For simplicity, we will drop the multiplication sign when we calculate Δ as follows:

$$\Delta Su - \Delta Sd = C_u - C_d$$
$$\Delta(Su - Sd) = C_u - C_d$$
$$\Delta = \frac{C_u - C_d}{Su - Sd}$$

Using the numbers in our example:

$$\Delta = \frac{C_u - C_d}{Su - Sd} = \frac{10 - 0}{110 - 95} = \frac{10}{15} = \frac{2}{3}$$

Have we succeeded in making the portfolio riskless? Yes:

$$(\Delta S \times u) - C_u = (\Delta S \times d) - C_d$$
$$(2/3)(100)(1.10) - 10 = (2/3)(100)(.95) - 0$$
$$73.33 - 10 = 63.33$$

We now have what we need to calculate the call price today, C. We choose Δ so that the portfolio has the same value for both possible stock prices. That is, the portfolio of long Δ shares and short one call option is riskless (for the right value of Δ). Therefore, a riskless portfolio today should be worth $(\Delta S - C)(1 + r)$ in one period. So:

$$(\Delta S - C)(1 + r) = \Delta S \times u - C_u \qquad (16.1)$$

The only unknown value in Equation 16.1 is C. Rearranging the values in Equation 16.1 results in:

$$C = \frac{\Delta S(1 + r - u) + C_u}{1 + r} \qquad (16.2)$$

We can calculate the call price today using Equation 16.2:

$$
\begin{aligned}
C &= \frac{\Delta S(1 + r - u) + C_u}{1 + r} \\
&= \frac{(2/3)(100)(1 + .03 - 1.10) + 10}{1.03} \\
&= \frac{(200/3)(-.07) + 10}{1.03} \\
&= \frac{5.33}{1.03} = \$5.18
\end{aligned}
$$

Equation 16.2 is one way to write the formula for the one-period binomial option pricing model. Now that we know the price of the call, we can use put-call parity to calculate the price of a put with a strike of $100:

$$
\begin{aligned}
P + S &= C + K/(1 + r_f) \\
P + 100 &= 5.18 + 100/1.03 \\
P &= 5.18 + 100/1.03 - 100 \\
&= \$2.27
\end{aligned}
$$

EXAMPLE 16.1 **Using the One-Period BOPM**

A stock is currently selling for $25 per share. In one period, it will be worth either $20 or $30. The riskless interest rate is 5 percent per period. There are no dividends. What is today's price of a call option with a strike price of $27?

To answer this question, we can use the one-period binomial option pricing model:

$$C = \frac{\Delta S(1 + r - u) + C_u}{1 + r}$$

(continued)

To calculate Δ:

$$\Delta = \frac{C_u - C_d}{Su - Sd} = \frac{3 - 0}{30 - 20} = \frac{3}{10}$$

We also have to calculate u, which is $30/$25 = 1.20. We can now calculate the price of the call option:

$$
\begin{aligned}
C &= \frac{\Delta S(1 + r - u) + C_u}{1 + r} \\
&= \frac{(3/10)(\$25)(1 + .05 - 1.20) + \$3}{1.05} \\
&= \frac{(\$75/10)(-.15) + \$3}{1.05} \\
&= \frac{\$1.875}{1.05} = \$1.79
\end{aligned}
$$

WHAT IS DELTA?

Delta, Δ, is an important proportion. We will use delta later in the chapter when we are talking about hedging the risk of adverse stock price movements using options.

An easy way to think about delta is to recall that delta is a proportion of shares to calls that is needed to form a risk-free portfolio, that is, a portfolio of shares and calls that does not change in value when the stock price changes. Remember, the investor can choose many values for delta. However, there is only one delta that helps the investor form a risk-free portfolio.

Therefore, a delta of 2/3 means that we need two shares and three calls to form a risk-free portfolio. The portfolio is risk-free because losses (gains) in the call options are offset by gains (losses) in the stock. So you can think of delta as the fractional share amount needed to offset, or hedge, changes in the price of one call.

In our detailed example, we calculated a delta of 2/3, or .67. This means that the number of shares to hedge one call is .67. Similarly, the number of calls to hedge one share is $1/\Delta$, or 3/2. That is, we need three call options to hedge two shares.

CHECK THIS

16.2a Suppose the stock price today is $95, not $100 as shown in Figure 16.1. Nothing else changes in the detailed example that follows Figure 16.1. Does delta still equal .67? What is the call price?

16.2b You calculate a delta of .8. How many shares and calls are needed to form a risk-free portfolio? What positions (i.e., long or short) does the investor have in shares and calls?

16.3 The Two-Period Binomial Option Pricing Model

In the previous section, we could price an option one period before it expires. Suppose there are two periods to expiration. What do we do in this case? It turns out that we repeat much of the process we used in the previous section.

In this section, we calculate the price of a European call option. However, we can use this method to calculate the price of a European put option, too. Using a slight modification to allow for early exercise, this technique can also be used to calculate prices for American calls and puts. In fact, this basic technique is so powerful that, with the right modifications, it can be used to price an exotic array of options.

TABLE 16.2	Inputs for the Two-Period BOPM		
S_0	=	$50	Stock price today
u	=	1.20	Up factor ($u > 1$) per period
d	=	.85	Down factor ($d < 1$) per period
r_f	=	8%	Risk-free interest rate per period
K	=	$55	Strike price
T	=	2	Periods to option expiration

The best way to learn this technique is to work a detailed example. Suppose we have the set of inputs given in Table 16.2.

We need to point out one more important assumption. That is, in our detailed example, we assume that u, d, and r_f do not change in the two periods until option expiration. With this additional assumption and the inputs in Table 16.2, we will show that the call option is worth $6.29 today.

STEP 1: BUILD A PRICE TREE FOR STOCK PRICES THROUGH TIME

The upper part of Figure 16.3 shows the stock prices through time. Because there are more than two dates, we denote the stock price today as S_0. Starting at $S_0 = 50, S_1 (the stock price at Time 1) is:

$$S_0 \times u = $50 \times 1.20 = $60 \quad \text{if the stock price increases}$$

$$S_0 \times d = $50 \times .85 = $42.50 \quad \text{if the stock price decreases}$$

Next, if the stock price in one period is $60, then the price in two periods will be either $60 × 1.20 = $72 or $60 × .85 = $51. Similarly, if the price in one period is $42.50, then the price in two periods will be either $42.50 × 1.20 = $51 or $42.50 × .85 = $36.13.

Thus, there are three stock prices in two periods, corresponding to a sequence of (1) two up moves, (2) two down moves, or (3) one up move and one down move. Notice that it doesn't matter if we go up, then down or down, then up. We end up at $51 either way. In symbols, the three possible S_2 stock prices are:

1. $S_2 = S_{uu} = S_0 \times u \times u = S_0 \times u^2$ (two up moves).
2. $S_2 = S_{dd} = S_0 \times d \times d = S_0 \times d^2$ (two down moves).
3. $S_2 = S_{ud} = S_0 \times u \times d = S_0 \times u \times d$ (one up move and one down move).

STEP 2: USE THE INTRINSIC VALUE FORMULA TO CALCULATE THE POSSIBLE OPTION PRICES AT EXPIRATION

As we calculated, the three possible stock prices at expiration are $72, $51, and $36.13. We plug each of these stock prices into the intrinsic value formula. Because the strike price is $K = 55, the possible values for the call option at expiration are:

$$\text{MAX}[S_T - K, 0] = \text{MAX}[$72 - $55, $0] = $17$$

$$\text{MAX}[S_T - K, 0] = \text{MAX}[$51 - $55, $0] = $0$$

$$\text{MAX}[S_T - K, 0] = \text{MAX}[$36.13 - $55, $0] = $0$$

Notice that in two of the possible cases, the call has zero value at expiration.

STEP 3: CALCULATE THE FRACTIONAL SHARE NEEDED TO FORM EACH RISK-FREE PORTFOLIO AT THE NEXT-TO-LAST DATE

To form the risk-free portfolio, we need to calculate the possible values for Δ in the next-to-last period. Recall that the portfolio is risk-free when the investor sells one call and buys a fraction, Δ, of one share.

Let us begin by looking at the point where the stock price is $60. You can see that the two possible stock prices from that point are $72 and $51. In addition, because the strike price is $55,

FIGURE 16.3

Stock Price Tree

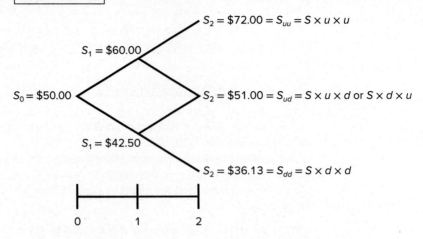

$S_2 = \$72.00 = S_{uu} = S \times u \times u$

$S_1 = \$60.00$

$S_0 = \$50.00$

$S_2 = \$51.00 = S_{ud} = S \times u \times d \text{ or } S \times d \times u$

$S_1 = \$42.50$

$S_2 = \$36.13 = S_{dd} = S \times d \times d$

0   1   2

Call Price Tree

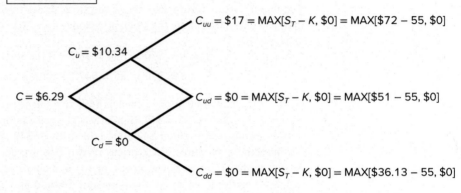

$C_{uu} = \$17 = MAX[S_T - K, \$0] = MAX[\$72 - 55, \$0]$

$C_u = \$10.34$

$C = \$6.29$

$C_{ud} = \$0 = MAX[S_T - K, \$0] = MAX[\$51 - 55, \$0]$

$C_d = \$0$

$C_{dd} = \$0 = MAX[S_T - K, \$0] = MAX[\$36.13 - 55, \$0]$

Delta Values

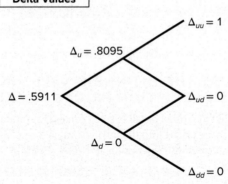

$\Delta_{uu} = 1$

$\Delta_u = .8095$

$\Delta = .5911$

$\Delta_{ud} = 0$

$\Delta_d = 0$

$\Delta_{dd} = 0$

two call option values, $17 and $0, are possible. You can see that it is as if we have an option with one period to expiration. Therefore, we can use the notation from the one-period binomial option pricing model to calculate Δ:

$$\Delta = \frac{C_u - C_d}{Su - Sd} = \frac{\$17 - \$0}{\$72 - \$51} = \frac{\$17}{\$21} = .8095$$

Likewise, from the point where the stock price is $42.50, the two possible stock prices are $51 and $36.13. Note, however, that because the strike price is $55, the option is worth $0 regardless of the stock price in one period. In this case, the Δ is:

$$\Delta = \frac{C_u - C_d}{Su - Sd} = \frac{\$0 - \$0}{\$51 - \$36.13} = \frac{\$0}{\$14.88} = 0$$

STEP 4: CALCULATE ALL POSSIBLE OPTION PRICES AT THE NEXT-TO-LAST DATE

We can now use these values for Δ to calculate the call prices when the stock price is $60 or when it is $42.50. When the stock price is $60, we use $\Delta = .8095$, $C_u = \$17$, $r = 8\%$, and $u = 1.20$ to calculate the call price:

$$C = \frac{\Delta S(1 + r - u) + C_u}{1 + r} = \frac{(.8095 \times \$60)(1 + .08 - 1.20) + \$17}{1.08} = \$10.34$$

When the stock price is $42.50, we use $\Delta = 0$, $C_u = \$0$, $r = 8\%$, and $u = 1.20$ to calculate the call price:

$$C = \frac{\Delta S(1 + r - u) + C_u}{1 + r} = \frac{(0 \times \$42.50)(1 + .08 - 1.20) + \$0}{1.08} = \$0$$

The intuition for a call with zero value is simple. Ask yourself: What price am I willing to pay today for a call option that will always have a value of zero in one period? Or think of it like this: This call option gives you the right to buy shares for $55 next period. However, the stock price will always be lower than $55 next period. How much are you willing to pay today for this call option? We are sure that you said zero (aren't we?).

STEP 5: REPEAT THIS PROCESS BY WORKING BACK TO TODAY

From the point where the stock price is $50, there are two possible stock prices, $60 and $42.50. If the stock price is $60, we know the call option is worth $10.34. When the stock price is $42.50, we know that the call option is worth $0. In this case, Δ is:

$$\Delta = \frac{C_u - C_d}{Su - Sd} = \frac{\$10.34 - \$0}{\$60 - \$42.50} = \frac{\$10.34}{\$17.50} = .5911$$

Using $\Delta = .5911$, $C_u = \$10.34$, $r = 8\%$, and $u = 1.20$, we calculate the call price as:

$$C = \frac{\Delta S(1 + r - u) + C_u}{1 + r} = \frac{(.5911 \times 50)(1 + .08 - 1.20) + 10.34}{1.08} = \$6.29$$

Using put-call parity, the price of the put with a $55 strike is:

$$P = C - S + \frac{K}{1 + r} = \$6.29 - \$50 + \frac{\$55}{1.08} = \$7.22$$

We summarize these calculations in Figure 16.3. Note that, over time, as S increases, so do Δ and C.

16.4 The Binomial Option Pricing Model with Many Periods

When we have more than two periods, nothing really changes. We still work backwards one period at a time. Figure 16.4 shows a binomial tree with five periods to option expiration. Now there are six option values at expiration. To calculate today's option price, you would have to calculate 14 intermediate option prices, which would be fairly tedious and explains why computers come in handy to calculate option prices.

FIGURE 16.4   A Five-Period Stock Price Tree

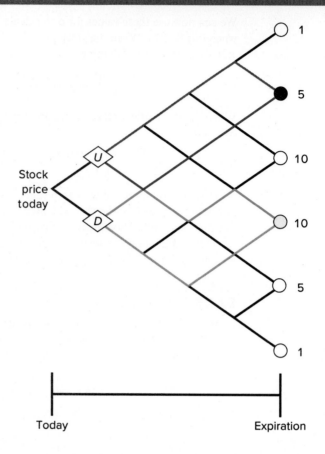

Looking at Figure 16.4, note the various paths that the stock can follow after the stock has increased or decreased in price. There are five ways that the stock could wind up at the black dot. For example, from the diamond marked U, the stock could follow the blue or red path to the black dot at the end of the tree. The collection of possible stock price paths is also called the "lattice."

As another example, from the diamond marked D, the stock could follow the orange or turquoise path to the yellow dot at the end of the tree. The stock price today can wind up at the yellow dot following 10 paths. In Figure 16.4, we show the number of ways that the stock can follow to the end points of the tree. As you can see, the stock can follow only one path to reach the highest and lowest possible prices. Also, you will notice that the way the numbers increase from 1 to 10 and then decrease back to 1 is symmetric.

Let's get crazy. Figure 16.5 shows a lattice with 18 periods to expiration. We have super-imposed a two-period binomial option pricing lattice over it. In this way, you can see that two periods can be subdivided into many periods.

There are many possible stock paths in Figure 16.5. In fact, there are 2^{18} (or 262,144) of them. Yikes! We have written down the possible ways that the stock price can wander to its ending prices at the option expiration date. As before, there is only one way to get to the highest possible stock price. However, there are 18 paths to the next highest stock price. You can see a symmetry to the way the paths increase in number from 1 to 48,620 and then decrease back to 1.

If you wanted to calculate today's option price, you don't have to worry about the number of paths. However, you do have to worry about the number of intersections at which the stock price can increase or decrease. With 18 periods to expiration, you would need to calculate 19 expira-tion day stock prices and 170 intermediate option prices (that should seem like a lot to you).

What happens when the number of periods gets *really* big? The answer is that we could always use a computer to handle the calculations, but we can use a more elegant method. As it happens, when the number of periods gets huge, the price calculated using our binomial approach converges to the price from the famous Black-Scholes option pricing model, which we study in the next section.

FIGURE 16.5 An 18-Period Stock Price Tree

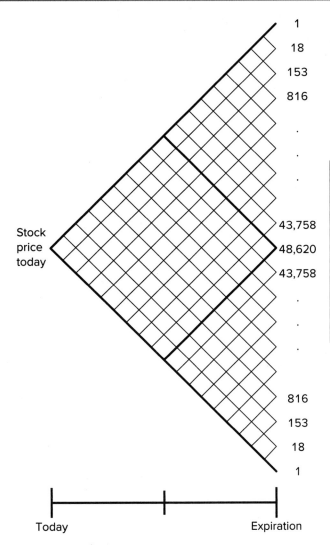

1

18

153

816

·

·

43,758

48,620

43,758

·

·

·

816

153

18

1

Stock price today

Today   Expiration

The range of possible stock prices at option expiration widens as the values for *U* and *D* grow farther apart. However, the number of ways to get to the end do not depend on *U* and *D*.

CHECK THIS

16.4a   Why is it that nothing really changes when there are more than two periods to expiration?

16.4b   Why don't you have to worry about the number of paths the stock price can take before expiration? What do you have to worry about?

 # 16.5 The Black-Scholes Option Pricing Model

Related Bloomberg Functions

OVML Option Valuation FX/ Commodity

Option pricing theory made a great leap forward in the early 1970s with the development of the Black-Scholes option pricing model by Fischer Black and Myron Scholes. Recognizing the important theoretical contributions by Robert Merton, many finance professionals knowledgeable in the history of option pricing theory refer to an extended version of the Black-Scholes model as the Black-Scholes-Merton option pricing model. In 1997, Myron Scholes and Robert Merton were awarded the Nobel Prize in Economics for their pioneering work in option pricing theory. Unfortunately, Fischer Black had died two years earlier and thus did not share the Nobel Prize, which cannot be awarded posthumously.

Our focus is on the basic Black-Scholes model. The Black-Scholes option pricing model states the value of a European option on a non–dividend-paying stock as a function of these five input factors:

1. The current price of the underlying stock.
2. The strike price specified in the option contract.
3. The risk-free interest rate over the life of the option contract.

expiry
A shortened way of saying "time to maturity."

4. The time remaining until the option contract expires, sometimes called **expiry**.
5. The price volatility of the underlying stock (i.e., the distribution of possible stock prices at expiration).

In the model, the five inputs are defined as follows:

S = Current stock price

K = Option strike price

r = Risk-free interest rate

T = Time remaining until option expiration

σ = Sigma, representing stock price volatility

The CBOE has a free options calculator that will do most of the calculations in this chapter at www.cboe.com.

In terms of these five inputs, the Black-Scholes formula for the price of a European call option on a single share of common stock is:

$$C = SN(d_1) - Ke^{-rT} N(d_2) \qquad (16.3)$$

The Black-Scholes formula for the price of a European put option on a share of common stock is:

$$P = Ke^{-rT} N(-d_2) - SN(-d_1) \qquad (16.4)$$

In these call and put option formulas, the numbers d_1 and d_2 are calculated as:

$$d_1 = \frac{\ln(S/K) + (r + \sigma^2/2)T}{\sigma\sqrt{T}} \text{ and } d_2 = d_1 - \sigma\sqrt{T}$$

For many links to option-related topics, see www.theocc.com.

In the formulas above, call and put option prices are algebraically represented by C and P, respectively. In addition to the five input factors S, K, r, T, and σ, the following three mathematical functions are used in the call and put option pricing formulas:

1. e^x, or $\exp(x)$, denoting the natural exponent of the value of x.
2. $\ln(x)$, denoting the natural logarithm of the value of x.
3. $N(x)$, denoting the standard normal probability of the value of x.

EXAMPLE 16.2   Computing Black-Scholes Option Prices

Calculate call and put option prices, given the following inputs to the Black-Scholes option pricing formula:

Stock price	S =	$50
Strike price	K =	$45
Time to maturity	T =	3 months
Stock volatility	σ =	25%
Interest rate	r =	6%

Referring to Equations 16.3 and 16.4, first we compute values for d_1 and d_2:

$$d_1 = \frac{\ln(50/45) + (.06 + .25^2/2) \times .25}{.25 \times \sqrt{.25}}$$

$$= \frac{.10536 + .09125 \times .25}{.125}$$

$$= 1.02538$$

$$d_2 = d_1 - .25 \times \sqrt{.25}$$

$$= .90038$$

The following standard normal probabilities are provided:

$$N(d_1) = N(1.02538) = .84741 \qquad N(-d_1) = 1 - N(d_1) = .15259$$
$$N(d_2) = N(.90038) = .81604 \qquad N(-d_2) = 1 - N(d_2) = .18396$$

We can now calculate the price of the call option as:

$$C = \$50 \times .84741 - \$45 \times e^{-.06 \times .25} \times .81604$$

$$= \$50 \times .84741 - \$45 \times .98511 \times .81604$$

$$= \$6.195$$

and the price of the put option as:

$$P = \$45 \times e^{-.06 \times .25} \times .18396 - \$50 \times .15259$$

$$= \$45 \times .98511 \times .18396 - \$50 \times .15259$$

$$= \$.525$$

Exact standard normal probabilities provided in this example are obtained from Excel using the function NORMSDIST(x). A detailed example of how to use an Excel spreadsheet to calculate Black-Scholes option prices is shown in a *Spreadsheet Analysis* box later in this chapter.

EXAMPLE 16.3 — Using a Web-Based Option Calculator

The purpose of Example 16.2 was to show you that the Black-Scholes formula is not hard to use—even if at first it looks imposing. If you are in a hurry to price an option or if you want to verify the price of an option that you have calculated, a number of option calculators are available on the web. Let's check our previous answers by using the option calculator we found at option-price.com.

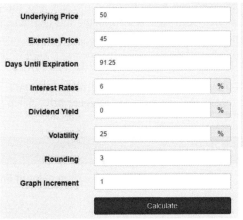

	Underlying Price	50
Exercise Price	45
Days Until Expiration	91.25
Interest Rates	6 %
Dividend Yield	0 %
Volatility	25 %
Rounding	3
Graph Increment	1

Calculate

	Call Option	Put Option
Theoretical Price	6.195	0.525
Delta	0.847	-0.153
Gamma	0.038	0.038
Vega	0.059	0.059
Theta	-0.014	-0.007
Rho	0.09	-0.02

Source: option-price.com.

Note that we use 91.25 days to expiration and set rounding to 3 in the option calculator. Our answers match the numbers in Example 16.2. If you use 91 days to expiration and set the rounding to 2, you'll get slightly different answers.

16.5a Consider the following inputs to the Black-Scholes option pricing model:

$S = \$65$

$K = \$60$

$T = .25$ year

$r = 5\%$

$\sigma = 25\%$

These input values yield a call option price of $6.78 and a put option price of $1.03. Verify these prices from your own calculations.

 # Varying the Option Price Input Values

Related Bloomberg Functions

OTD   Option Description

An important goal of this chapter is to provide an understanding of how option prices change as a result of varying each of the five input values. Table 16.3 summarizes the sign effects of the five inputs on call and put option prices. A plus sign indicates a positive effect and a minus sign indicates a negative effect on the price of the option. For example, if the stock price increases, the call option price increases and the put option price decreases.

The two most important inputs determining stock option prices are the stock price and the strike price. However, the other input factors are also important determinants of option value. We next discuss each input factor separately.

VARYING THE UNDERLYING STOCK PRICE

Certainly, the price of the underlying stock is one of the most important determinants of the price of a stock option. As the stock price increases, the call option price increases and the put option price decreases. This is not surprising because a call option grants the right to buy stock shares and a put option grants the right to sell stock shares at a fixed strike price. Consequently, a higher stock price at option expiration increases the payoff of a call option. Likewise, a lower stock price at option expiration increases the payoff of a put option.

For a given set of input values, the relationship between call and put option prices and an underlying stock price is illustrated in Figure 16.6. In Figure 16.6, stock prices are measured on the horizontal axis and option prices are measured on the vertical axis. Notice that the curves describing the relationships between call and put option prices and the underlying stock price have a convex (bowed) shape. Convexity is a fundamental characteristic of the relationship between option prices and stock prices.

VARYING THE OPTION'S STRIKE PRICE

As the strike price increases, the call price decreases and the put price increases. This is reasonable because a higher strike price means that we must pay a higher price when we exercise

TABLE 16.3	Five Inputs Affecting Option Prices		
		Sign of Input Effect	
Input		**Call**	**Put**
Underlying stock price (S)		+	−
Strike price of the option contract (K)		−	+
Time remaining until option expiration (T)		+	+
Volatility of the underlying stock price (σ)		+	+
Risk-free interest rate (r)		+	−

FIGURE 16.6

Put and Call Option Prices

Input values:

$K = \$100$

$T = 1/4$ year

$r = 5\%$

$\sigma = 25\%$

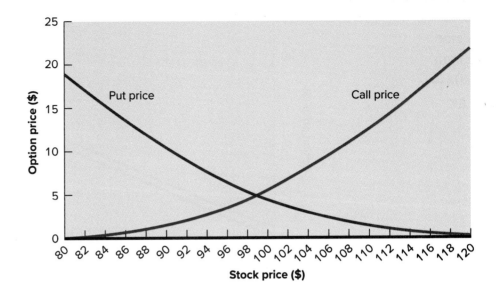

a call option to buy the underlying stock, thereby reducing the call option's value. Similarly, a higher strike price means that we will receive a higher price when we exercise a put option to sell the underlying stock, thereby increasing the put option's value. Of course, this logic works in reverse also; as the strike price decreases, the call price increases and the put price decreases.

VARYING THE TIME REMAINING UNTIL OPTION EXPIRATION

Time remaining until option expiration is an important determinant of option value. As time remaining until option expiration lengthens, both call and put option prices normally increase. This is expected because a longer time remaining until option expiration allows more time for the stock price to move away from a strike price and increase the option's payoff, thereby making the option more valuable. The relationship between call and put option prices and time remaining until option expiration is illustrated in Figure 16.7, where time remaining until option expiration is measured on the horizontal axis and option prices are measured on the vertical axis.

FIGURE 16.7

Option Prices and Time to Expiration

Input values:

$S = \$100$

$K = \$100$

$r = 5\%$

$\sigma = 25\%$

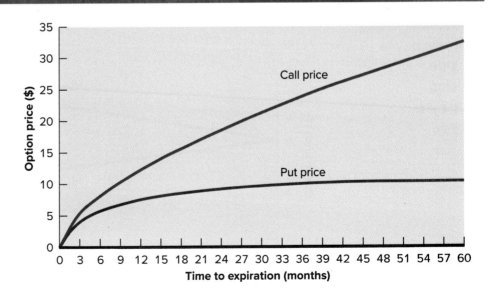

FIGURE 16.8

Option Prices and Sigma

Input values:

$S = \$100$

$K = \$100$

$T = 1/4$ year

$r = 5\%$

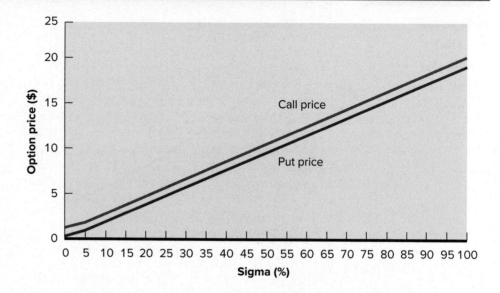

VARYING THE VOLATILITY OF THE STOCK PRICE

Stock price volatility (sigma, σ) plays an important role in determining option value. As stock price volatility increases, both call and put option prices increase. This is as expected because the more volatile the stock price, the greater is the likelihood that the stock price will move farther away from a strike price and increase the option's payoff, thereby making the option more valuable. Remember, option payoffs are asymmetric. That is, the downside is limited to a value of zero. So, any increase in volatility can only make the range of possible payoffs bigger (and better). The relationship between call and put option prices and stock price volatility is graphed in Figure 16.8, where volatility is measured on the horizontal axis and option prices are measured on the vertical axis.

VARYING THE INTEREST RATE

Although seemingly not as important as the other inputs, the interest rate still noticeably affects option values. As the interest rate increases, the call price increases and the put price decreases. This is explained by the time value of money. A higher interest rate implies a greater discount, which lowers the present value of the strike price that we pay when we exercise a call option or receive when we exercise a put option. Figure 16.9 graphs the relationship

FIGURE 16.9

Option Prices and Interest Rates

Input values:

$S = \$100$

$K = \$100$

$T = 1/4$ year

$\sigma = 25\%$

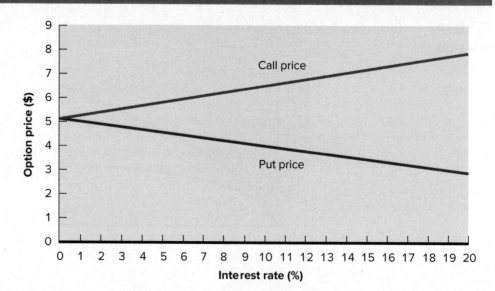

between call and put option prices and interest rates, where the interest rate is measured on the horizontal axis and option prices are measured on the vertical axis.

CHECK THIS

16.6a   Using put-call parity and the data in Figure 16.6, at what stock price will the call and the put have the same value?

16.6b   In Figure 16.7, why do the call and the put both have a value of zero at expiration?

 ## 16.7 Measuring the Impact of Stock Price Changes on Option Prices

delta
Measure of the dollar impact of a change in the underlying stock price on the value of a stock option. Delta is positive for a call option and negative for a put option.

Investment professionals using options in their investment strategies have standard methods to state the impact of changes in input values on option prices. The two inputs that most affect stock option prices over a short period, say a few days, are the stock price and the stock price volatility. The approximate impact of a stock price change on an option price is stated by the option's **delta**.

We introduced the concept of delta, Δ, when we discussed the binomial model earlier in this chapter. The difference between deltas in the binomial model and the Black-Scholes model is simple. Delta in the binomial model is calculated over discrete time periods, which can be very short. In the Black-Scholes model, time periods are infinitesimally short. In the Black-Scholes model, therefore, we measure delta as an instantaneous change in the option price when the stock price changes. In the Black-Scholes option pricing model, expressions for call and put option deltas are stated as follows, where the mathematical function and $N(x)$ were previously defined:

$$\text{Call option delta} = N(d_1) > 0$$
$$\text{Put option delta} = -N(-d_1) < 0$$

As shown above, a call option delta is always positive and a put option delta is always negative. This can be seen in Table 16.3, where the "+" indicates a positive change for a call option price and the "−" indicates a negative change for a put option price resulting from an increase in the underlying stock price.

EXAMPLE 16.4   **Computing Call and Put Option Deltas**

Given the inputs to the Black-Scholes option pricing formula provided in Example 16.2, calculate call and put option deltas. The necessary values for d_1, $N(d_1)$, and $N(-d_1)$ were provided in Example 16.2.

$$N(d_1) = N(1.02538) = .84741 \qquad\qquad N(-d_1) = 1 - N(d_1) = .15259$$

Therefore:

$$\text{Call option delta} = N(d_1) = .84741$$
$$\text{Put option delta} = -N(-d_1) = -.15259$$

Notice that $N(d_1) - 1 = .84741 - 1 = -.15259 = -N(-d_1)$.

Refer to the nearby *Spreadsheet Analysis* box for examples of using a spreadsheet to calculate Black-Scholes call and put option prices, as well as deltas.

SPREADSHEET ANALYSIS

	A	B	C	D	E	F	G
1							
2			Calculating Black-Scholes Option Prices				
3							
4	XYZ stock has a price of $50 and an annual return volatility of 25 percent. The riskless						
5	interest rate is 6 percent. Calculate call and put option prices with a strike price of $45						
6	and a 3-month time to expiration (0.25 year).						
7							
8	Stock =	50		d1 =	1.0254	N(d1) =	0.84741
9	Strike =	45				N(-d1) =	0.15259
10	Volatility =	0.25		d2 =	0.9004	N(d2) =	0.81604
11	Time =	0.25				N(-d2) =	0.18396
12	Rate =	0.06					
13						exp(-Rate x Time) =	0.98511
14							
15	Call Price =	Stock x N(d1) - Strike x exp(-Rate x Time) x N(d2) =					6.195
16	Put Price =	Strike x exp(-Rate x Time) x N(-d2) - Stock x N(-d1) =					0.525
17							
18							
19	Formula entered in E8 is =(LN(B8/B9)+(B12+0.5*B10^2)*B11)/(B10*SQRT(B11))						
20	Formula entered in E10 is =E8-B10*SQRT(B11)						
21	Formulas entered in G8 and G9 are =NORMSDIST(E8) and =NORMSDIST(-E8)						
22	Formulas entered in G10 and G11 are =NORMSDIST(E10) and =NORMSDIST(-E10)						
23							
24							
25			Calculating Black-Scholes Deltas				
26							
27	Call Delta =	N(d1) =					0.84741
28	Put Delta =	N(d1) - 1 = -N(-d1) =					-0.15259
29							

Source: Microsoft.

INTERPRETING OPTION DELTAS

Interpreting the meaning of an option delta is relatively straightforward. Delta measures the impact of a change in the stock price on an option price, where a $1 change in the stock price causes an option price to change by approximately delta dollars. For example, using the input values stated immediately below, we obtain a call option price (rounded) of $6.20 and a put option price (rounded) of $.52. These input values yield a call option delta of +.85 and a put option delta of −.15.

$$S = \$50$$
$$K = \$45$$
$$T = .25$$
$$r = 6\%$$
$$\sigma = 25\%$$

If we change the stock price from $50 to $51, we get a call option price of $7.06 and a put option price of $.39. Thus, a +$1 stock price change increased the call option price by $.86 and decreased the put option price by $.13. These price changes are close to, but not exactly equal to, the call option delta value of +.85 and put option delta value of −.15.

CHECK THIS

16.7a Why do investors care about option deltas?

16.7b Why do you think deltas for call options are positive but deltas for put options are negative?

Hedging Stock with Stock Options

Related Bloomberg Functions

OSA   Option Scenario Analysis

Now that we know how to calculate option prices and option deltas, we turn our attention to an important way investors use options. Options provide investors with the opportunity to protect themselves against losses. Taking advantage of this opportunity is known as hedging.

Suppose you own 1,000 shares of XYZ stock, the stock we analyzed in the *Spreadsheet Analysis* earlier in the chapter. From the assumptions used in the *Spreadsheet Analysis,* we calculated prices and deltas for call and put options. If we had used all the same assumptions but used a stock price of $49 instead of $50, we would get a different set of prices and deltas for call and put options. Table 16.4 provides a convenient summary (notice we have rounded the change in option prices to two decimal places). In Table 16.4, all option prices use these inputs: a strike of $45, volatility of 25 percent, a risk-free rate of 6 percent, and three months to maturity.

Further, suppose that you want to protect yourself against declines in the XYZ stock price. That is, you want to hedge: You want a portfolio that does not change in value if the stock price changes. To form this portfolio, you must add some options to your portfolio. How many options to add and whether you should be buying or selling options are two important questions that we answer. To begin, let us write down our goal:

$$\text{Change in value of stock portfolio} + \text{Change in value of options} = 0 \qquad (16.5)$$

The change in the value of the stock portfolio equals the change in the stock price times the number of shares. Similarly, the change in the value of options held is the change in the option price times the number of options. The one point to remember, however, is that the change in the option price depends on the change in the price of the stock.

From earlier in the chapter, we know that the delta of an option is a prediction of how the option price will change when the stock price changes by one dollar. If a call option has a delta of .58, the option price will change $.58 when the stock price changes by one dollar. If the stock price increases by only $.50, then the option delta predicts that the call option price will increase by $.29. We generally assume that the stock price changes by one dollar when we are talking about hedging, but the stock price can change by other amounts. The lesson is that the change in the option price is equal to the option delta times the change in the stock price, which we denote as ΔS. So, if we multiply the change in the option price by the number of options held, we have the change in the value of options held. Knowing how to calculate these changes in value, we can write:

$$\Delta S \times \text{Shares held} + \text{Option delta} \times \Delta S \times \text{Number of options} = 0 \qquad (16.6)$$

You can see that the change in the stock price, ΔS, can be eliminated from the equation. We know the number of shares we have, and we can calculate an option delta using our favorite option pricing model. All we need to do is calculate the number of options that we need to add, which is:

$$\begin{aligned} \text{Number of options} &= -\text{Shares held} \times (1/\text{Option delta}) \\ &= -\text{Shares held}/\text{Option delta} \end{aligned} \qquad (16.7)$$

Equation 16.7 offers two important lessons. First, recall that an option delta tells us how many shares you need to hedge one call. The number of options that you need to hedge one share, therefore, is one divided by the option delta. Second, notice the minus sign out front. You can figure out whether to buy options depending on whether you get a positive number or a negative number in Equation 16.7. We saw that deltas for call options are

TABLE 16.4	Using the Black-Scholes Option Model for Hedging				
XYZ Stock Price	**Call Price**	**Call Delta**	**Put Price**	**Put Delta**
$50	$6.195	.8474	$.525	−.1526
$49	$5.368	.8061	$.698	−.1939
Change in option price:	−$.83		$.17	

positive (but between zero and one) and deltas for put options are negative (but between minus one and zero). So, if we are hedging shares using call options, we need to sell call options. If we are hedging shares using put options, we need to purchase put options. An example will help you use these formulas.

HEDGING USING CALL OPTIONS—THE PREDICTION

As shown in Table 16.3, stock prices and call option prices are directly related. When the stock price increases, so do prices of call options on these shares. From Table 16.4, the call option delta is .8474 when the XYZ stock price is $50. The call option delta is a prediction that the call option price will increase (decrease) by about $.85 if the stock price increases (decreases) by $1.00.

So, to hedge declines in XYZ share prices using call options, you need to write, or sell, call options to protect against a price decline. But notice that if the price of XYZ stock fell by $1.00 and you had 1,000 options, you would gain only $847.40. This would partially, but not fully, offset your loss of $1,000. You can do better by writing more options. Fortunately, you can use Equation 16.7 to tell you how many call options to write:

$$\text{Number of options} = -\text{Shares} \times (1/\text{Option delta})$$
$$= -1{,}000/.8474 = -1{,}180.07$$

The minus sign confirms that you should write, or sell, call options. Because traded call options have 100 options per contract, you would need to write:

$$-1{,}180.07/100 \approx -12$$

call option contracts to create a hedge using call options with a strike of $45.

HEDGING USING CALL OPTIONS—THE RESULTS

Suppose you write 12 call option contracts at a price of $6.20 (rounded) per option, or $620 per contract. Further, just as you feared, XYZ stock fell in value by $1.00, so you suffered a $1,000 loss in the value of your shares. But what happened to the value of the call options you wrote? At the new XYZ stock price of $49, each call option is now worth $5.37 (rounded), a decrease of $.83 for each call, or $83 per contract. Because you wrote 12 call option contracts, your call option gain was $996.

Your gain in the call options nearly offsets your loss of $1,000 in XYZ shares. Why isn't it exact? You can see from Table 16.4 that delta also fell when the stock price fell. This means that you did not sell quite enough options. But because option contracts consist of 100 shares, you really did about as well as you could with this simple hedge.

HEDGING USING PUT OPTIONS—THE PREDICTION

As shown in Table 16.3, stock prices and put option prices are inversely related. When the stock price increases, put option prices on these shares decrease. From Table 16.4, the put option delta is −.1526 when the stock price is $50. The put option delta is a prediction that the put option price will decrease (increase) by about $.15 if the stock price increases (decreases) by $1.00.

Therefore, you want to purchase put options to profit from their price increase if the stock price decreases. But notice that if the price of XYZ stock fell by $1.00 and you had 1,000 put options, you would gain only $152.60. This is insignificant when compared to your $1,000 loss in XYZ shares. You will have to purchase more put options if you are going to have a better hedge. Fortunately, Equation 16.7 also tells you how many put options to purchase:

$$\text{Number of options} = -\text{Shares} \times (1/\text{Option delta})$$
$$= -1{,}000/-.1526 = 6{,}553.47$$

Because this number is positive, this confirms that you want to purchase put options. Because traded put options have 100 options per contract, you would need to purchase:

$$6{,}553.47/100 \approx 66$$

put option contracts to create a hedge using put options with a strike of $45.

HEDGING USING PUT OPTIONS—THE RESULTS

Suppose you purchase 66 put option contracts at a price of $.53 (rounded) per option, or $53 per contract. Again, as you feared, XYZ stock fell in value by $1.00, so you suffered a $1,000 loss in the value of your shares. But what happened to the value of the put options? At the new XYZ stock price of $49, each put option is now worth $.70, an increase of $.17 for each put option, or $17 per contract. Because you purchased 66 put option contracts, your put option gain was $1,122.

Your gain in the put options more than offsets your loss of $1,000 in XYZ shares. Why isn't it exact? You can see from Table 16.4 that the put delta also fell when the stock price fell (but it increased in absolute value). This means that you purchased too many put options. If you had purchased 59 put option contracts, you would have offset your share loss more closely.

How would you have known that 59 put options make a better hedge than 66 options? By constructing a table similar to Table 16.4 in advance, you would know that these put options increase in value by $.17 when the stock falls in value by $1. Therefore, each put option contract increases by about $17. Dividing $1,000 by $17 yields 58.82, telling us that 59 put contracts will provide a good hedge.

CHECK THIS

16.8a What happens to call and put prices when the price of the underlying stock changes?

16.8b What is the goal of a hedger who uses options?

16.9 Hedging a Stock Portfolio with Stock Index Options

Portfolio managers can hedge their entire equity portfolio by using stock index options. In this section, we examine how an equity portfolio manager might hedge a diversified stock portfolio using stock index options.

To begin, suppose that you manage a $10 million diversified portfolio of large-company stocks and that you maintain a portfolio beta of 1.00 for this portfolio. With a beta of 1.00, changes in the value of your portfolio closely follow changes in the Standard & Poor's 500 index. Therefore, you decide to use options on the S&P 500 index as a hedging vehicle. S&P 500 index options trade on the Chicago Board Options Exchange (CBOE) under the ticker symbol SPX. Each SPX option has a contract value of 100 times the current level of the S&P 500 index.

SPX options are a convenient hedging vehicle for an equity portfolio manager because they are European style and because they settle in cash at expiration. For example, suppose you hold one SPX call option with a strike price of 4,100 and at option expiration, the S&P 500 index stands at 4,107. In this case, your cash payoff is $100 times the difference between the index level and the strike price, or $100 × (4,107 − 4,100) = $700. Of course, if the expiration date index level falls below the strike price, your SPX call option expires worthless.

Hedging a stock portfolio with index options requires first calculating the number of option contracts needed to form an effective hedge. While you can use either put options or call options to construct an effective hedge, we assume that you decide to use call options to hedge your $10 million equity portfolio. Using stock index call options to hedge an equity portfolio involves writing a certain number of option contracts. In general, the number of stock index option contracts needed to hedge an equity portfolio is stated by the equation:

$$\text{Number of option contracts} = -\frac{\text{Portfolio beta} \times \text{Portfolio value}}{\text{Option delta} \times \text{Option contract value}} \qquad (16.8)$$

In your case, you have a portfolio beta of 1.00 and a portfolio value of $10 million. You now need to calculate an option delta and option contract value.

The option contract value for an SPX option is 100 times the current level of the S&P 500 index. Checking the CBOE website, you see that the S&P 500 index has a value of 4,046, which means that each SPX option has a current contract value of $404,600.

To calculate an option delta, you must decide which particular contract to use. You decide to use options with a March expiration and a strike price of 4,050, that is, the March 4050 SPX contract. From the internet you find that the price for these options is $98.84 and their delta is .533.

You now have sufficient information to calculate the number of option contracts needed to construct an effective hedge for your equity portfolio. By using Equation 16.8, we can calculate the number of March 4050 SPX options that you should write to form an effective hedge:

$$-\frac{1.00 \times \$10,000,000}{.533 \times \$404,600} \approx -46 \text{ contracts}$$

Furthermore, by writing 43 March 4050 call options, you receive $46 \times 100 \times \$98.84 = \$454,664$.

To assess the effectiveness of this hedge, suppose the S&P 500 index and your stock portfolio both immediately fall in value by 1 percent. This is a loss of $100,000 on your stock portfolio. After the S&P 500 index falls by 1 percent, its level is 4,005.54. Suppose the call option price is now $C = \$78.68$. If you were to buy back the 46 contracts, you would pay $46 \times 100 \times \$78.68 = \$361,928$. Because you originally received $454,664 for the options, this represents a gain of $\$454,664 - \$361,928 = \$92,736$, which cancels most, but not all, of the $100,000 loss on your equity portfolio. Your final net loss is $7,264, which is much less than what you would have lost if you were unhedged. As you keep studying options, you will learn how to improve your hedge.

To maintain an effective hedge over time, you will need to rebalance your options hedge on, say, a weekly basis. Rebalancing requires calculating anew the number of option contracts needed to hedge your equity portfolio, and then buying or selling options in the amount necessary to maintain an effective hedge. The nearby *Investment Updates* box contains a brief comparison of various index option products used to hedge equity portfolios.

EXAMPLE 16.5

The Option Hedge Ratio for a Stock Portfolio

You are managing a $15 million stock portfolio with a beta of 1.1, which you decide to hedge by buying index put options with a contract value of $125,000 per contract and a delta of −.40. How many option contracts are required?

Plugging our information into Equation 16.8 yields this calculation:

$$-\frac{1.1 \times \$15,000,000}{-.40 \times \$125,000} = 330 \text{ contracts}$$

Thus, you would need to buy 330 put option contracts.

WHAT'S A BETTER HEDGE—VIX OR SPX?

Equity investors who want a broad-based hedge have essentially three vehicles from which to choose: equity index options (SPY, SPX, ES, etc.), CBOE Volatility Index (VIX) futures (or their ETF permutations), and VIX options. Which is best?

One argument in favor of using VIX-linked products is that they are independent of any price level in the underlying equity index. If you enter a one-year at-the-money SPX hedge today using the at-the-money strike price, the puts you bought won't do you much good if the market rallies sharply for six months and then slips dramatically thereafter. Using a strike-dependent price-based hedge, it is entirely possible to lose money on both the hedge and the core portfolio if the hedged asset(s) don't follow a favorable path over the life of the hedge.

The big advantage of volatility-based products is that they are linked not to some absolute price level, but to an absolute volatility level. In my experience, many equity investors are more concerned about hedging against volatility than about protecting against declines below some specific price level. Gradual, orderly bear markets can be managed as easily as steady bull markets; it's the sudden shocks that concern people.

I'm not as favorably inclined toward VIX options, though. For one thing, outright VIX option buyers seem to be paying

for their optionality two times over: VIX futures already have option-like properties in that they tend to carry a premium to current IV levels, especially in further months. That premium "decays" as a given contract nears expiration, such that a "buy and hold" VIX futures trader isn't gaining long exposure to volatility explosions for free: Most of the time, she is paying each month for the privilege of watching volatility not explode. That volatility risk premium is not so large that hedging becomes prohibitive—not at all—but in my opinion the added costs of VIX options are only worthwhile if those option hedges are actively and carefully managed.

That last point suggests the rejoinder available to any proponent of conventional equity index hedges: Strike dependence is only a major problem for investors who insist on passive, long-dated hedges. An investor who is willing to roll their option hedges more frequently can avoid the problem of strike dependence and therefore can trade the more easily understood S&P 500 products. So my own order of preference for hedging an equity portfolio runs: VIX futures, SPX options, and then VIX options.

CHECK THIS

16.9a In the hedging example in the text, suppose that your equity portfolio had a beta of 1.50 instead of 1.00. What number of SPX call options would be required to form an effective hedge?

16.9b Alternatively, suppose that your equity portfolio had a beta of .50. What number of SPX call options would then be required to form an effective hedge?

16.10 Implied Standard Deviations

Related Bloomberg Functions

WVOL FX Implied Volatility Matrix

OVDV Volatility Surface

The Black-Scholes option pricing model is based on five inputs: a stock price, a strike price, an interest rate, the time remaining until option expiration, and the stock price volatility. Of these five factors, only the stock price volatility is not directly observable and must be estimated somehow. A popular method to estimate stock price volatility is to use an implied value from an option price. A stock price volatility estimated from an option price is called an **implied standard deviation** or **implied volatility**, often abbreviated as **ISD** or **IVOL,** respectively. Implied volatility and implied standard deviation are two terms for the same thing.

Solving for an ISD using the other option price inputs (and the option price) can be tedious. Fortunately, many option calculators will do the work for you. Suppose you have a call option with a strike price of $45 that expires in three months. The stock currently sells for $50, the option sells for $7, and the interest rate is 6 percent per year. What is the ISD? To find out, we went to the "Implied Volatility" tab of the options calculator at www.option-price.com. After entering this information, here is what we got.

Notice the calculator uses time to maturity in days, so we input 91 (which is about 3 months, or .25 of a year). Based on the input data, the underlying stock has an ISD of 36.82 percent per year.

Option Type	Call Option
Underlying Price	50
Exercise Price	45
Days Until Expiration	91
Interest Rate	6
Dividend Yield	0
Market Price	7
Implied Volatility	36.82%

Calculate

Source: www.option-price.com.

implied standard deviation (ISD)
An estimate of stock price volatility obtained from an option price.

implied volatility (IVOL)
Another term for implied standard deviation.

VIX
An implied volatility calculated from options on the S&P 500 Index.

VXN
An implied volatility calculated from options on the Nasdaq 100 index.

VXO
An implied volatility calculated from options on the S&P 100 index. (Discontinued in August 2021)

Calculating an implied volatility requires that all input factors have known values, except sigma, and that a call or put option price be known. For example, consider the following option price input values, absent a value for sigma:

$S = \$50$

$K = \$45$

$T = .25$

$r = 6\%$

Suppose we also have a call price of $C = \$6.195$. Based on this call price, what is the implied volatility? In other words, in combination with the input values stated above, what sigma value yields a call price of $C = \$6.195$? The answer comes from Example 16.2, which shows that a sigma value of .25, or 25 percent, yields a call option price of $6.195.

Now suppose we wish to know what volatility value is implied by a call price of $C = \$7$. To obtain this implied volatility value, we must find the value for sigma that yields this call price. By trial and error, you can try various sigma values until a call option price of $7 is obtained. This occurs with a sigma value of 36.77 percent, which is the ISD corresponding to a call option price of $7. Our nearby *Work the Web* box shows how to get ISDs the easy way.

CBOE IMPLIED VOLATILITIES FOR STOCK INDEXES

The Chicago Board Options Exchange (CBOE) publishes two implied volatility indexes: the S&P 500 Volatility Index (**VIX**) and the Nasdaq 100 Volatility Index (**VXN**). The CBOE used to have another volatility index on the S&P 100, with a ticker symbol of **VXO**. The CBOE decommissioned the VXO in August 2021.

VIX is an implied volatility calculated from options on the S&P 500 Index. VXN is an implied volatility calculated from options on the Nasdaq 100 index. These indexes are two of the most popular measures of investor expectations of future stock market volatility. They are based on options traded on two major stock market indexes: the S&P 500 and the Nasdaq 100. The ticker symbols for these volatility indexes and the underlying stock indexes are summarized as follows:

Volatility Index Ticker	Stock Index	Stock Index Ticker
VIX	S&P 500	SPX
VXN	Nasdaq 100	NDX

Current and historic levels for these volatility indexes are available at the CBOE website (cboe.com). You can also check them at Yahoo! Finance (finance.yahoo.com), along with the levels of their underlying stock indexes, using their ticker symbols. Note that the ticker symbols for these indexes do not correspond to traded securities and so must be preceded by a caret sign, that is, ^VIX and ^VXN.

The VIX and VXN implied volatility indexes are reported as annualized standard deviations. These volatility indexes provide investors with current estimates of expected market volatility in the month ahead. In fact, another name for the VIX is the "investor fear gauge." This name stems from the belief that the VIX reflects investors' collective prediction of near-term market volatility, or risk. Generally, the VIX increases during times of high financial stress and decreases during times of low financial stress.

Some investors use the VIX as a buy-sell indicator. This is because low levels of the VIX have, in many instances, preceded market sell-offs. The market saying is: "When the VIX is high, it's time to buy; when the VIX is low, it's time to go!"

CHECK THIS

16.10a Using the option calculator and the data in the nearby Work the Web, what is the implied standard deviation when the call option market price is $8 instead of $7? $6 instead of $7? What do you observe?

16.10b Using the option calculator and the data in the nearby Work the Web, what is the implied standard deviation of a similar put option?

16.11 Employee Stock Options

employee stock option (ESO)
An option granted to an employee by a company that gives the employee the right to buy shares of stock in the company at a fixed price for a fixed time.

In this section, we take a brief look at **employee stock options (ESOs)**. An ESO is, in essence, a call option that a firm gives to employees giving them the right to buy shares of stock in the company. The practice of granting options to employees has become widespread. It is almost universal for upper management, but some companies, like The Gap and Starbucks, have granted options to almost every employee. Thus, an understanding of ESOs is important. Why? Because you may very soon be an ESO holder!

ESO FEATURES

Because ESOs are basically call options, we have already covered most of the important aspects. However, ESOs have a few features that make them different from regular stock options. The details differ from company to company, but a typical ESO has a 10-year life, which is much longer than most ordinary options. Unlike traded options, ESOs cannot be sold. They also have what is known as a "vesting" period. Often, for up to three years or so, an ESO cannot be exercised and also must be forfeited if an employee leaves the company. After this period, the options "vest," which means they can be exercised. Sometimes employees who resign with vested options are given a limited time to exercise their options.

Why are ESOs granted? There are basically two reasons. First, the owners of a corporation (the shareholders) face the basic problem of aligning shareholder and management interests and also of providing incentives for employees to focus on corporate goals. ESOs are a powerful motivator because, as we have seen, the payoffs on options can be very large. High-level executives in particular stand to gain enormous wealth if they are successful in creating value for stockholders.

The second reason some companies rely heavily on ESOs is that an ESO has no immediate, up-front, out-of-pocket cost to the corporation. In smaller, possibly cash-strapped, companies, ESOs are a substitute for ordinary wages. Employees are willing to accept them instead of cash, hoping for big payoffs in the future. In fact, ESOs are a major recruiting tool, allowing businesses to attract talent that they otherwise could not afford.

ESO REPRICING

ESOs are almost always "at the money" when they are issued, meaning that the stock price is equal to the strike price. Notice that, in this case, the intrinsic value is zero, so there is no value from immediate exercise. Of course, even though the intrinsic value is zero, an ESO is still quite valuable because of, among other things, its very long life.

If the stock falls significantly after an ESO is granted, then the option is said to be "underwater." On occasion, a company will decide to lower the strike price on underwater options. Such options are said to be "restruck" or "repriced."

The practice of repricing ESOs is very controversial. Companies that do it argue that once an ESO becomes deeply out of the money, it loses its incentive value because employees recognize there is only a small chance that the option will finish in the money. In fact, employees may leave and join other companies where they receive a fresh options grant.

Critics of repricing point out that a lowered strike price is, in essence, a reward for failing. They also point out that if employees know that options will be repriced, then much of the incentive effect is lost. Today, many companies award options on a regular basis, perhaps annually or even quarterly. That way, an employee will always have at least some options that are near the money even if others are underwater. Also, regular grants ensure that employees always have unvested options, which gives them an added incentive to stay with their current employer rather than forfeit the potentially valuable options.

ESOS AT THE GAP, INC.

The Gap, Inc., is a large, well-known company whose stock trades under the ticker symbol GPS (GAP is the ticker symbol for Great Atlantic & Pacific Tea Co., which you probably know as A&P). The Gap grants employee stock options that are fairly standard. This description of The Gap's ESOs is taken from its annual report:

> Under our stock option plans, options to purchase common stock are granted to officers, directors, eligible employees and consultants at exercise prices equal to the fair market value of the stock at the date of grant. Stock options generally expire 10 years from the grant date, three months after termination, or one year after the date of retirement or death, if earlier. Stock options generally vest over a four-year period, with shares becoming exercisable in equal annual installments of 25 percent.[5]

The Gap's ESOs are not European-style options because they vest in equal increments over a four-year period. By "vest," we mean the holders can exercise these options. If you were granted options on 500 shares of GPS stock, you could exercise options on 125 shares one year after the grant date, another 125 shares two years after the grant date, another 125 shares three years after the grant date, and the last 125 shares four years after the grant date. Of course, you wouldn't have to exercise your options this quickly. As long as you stay with the company, you could wait 10 years to exercise your options just before they expire.

VALUING EMPLOYEE STOCK OPTIONS

The Financial Accounting Standards Board issued FASB 123 to tell companies how to calculate the fair value of employee stock options. Basically, FASB 123 states that the fair value of ESOs should be determined using an option pricing model that takes into account the:

- Stock price at the grant date.
- Exercise price.
- Expected life of the option.
- Volatility of the underlying stock.

---

[5] The Gap, Inc.

TABLE 16.5

Coca-Cola Employee Stock Options

Inputs	Input Value Assumptions	
Stock price	$44.55	$44.55
Exercise price	$44.655	$44.655
Time horizon	15 years	6 years
Volatility	25.53%	30.20%
Risk-free interest rate	5.65%	3.40%
Dividend yield	1.59%	1.70%
Black-Scholes-Merton option value	$19.92	$13.06

- Risk-free interest rate over the expected life of the option.
- Expected dividends.

As a practical matter, many companies calculate ESO prices using the Black-Scholes-Merton option pricing model. The Black-Scholes-Merton model is very similar to the Black-Scholes model. The difference between the two models is that expected dividends are an input for the Black-Scholes-Merton model.

In terms of its six inputs, the Black-Scholes-Merton call option formula is:[6]

$$C = Se^{-yT}\,N(d_1) - Ke^{-rT}\,N(d_2)$$ (16.9)

One piece of Equation 16.9 that is different from the Black-Scholes formula is that the stock price is discounted by the term e^{-yT}. In this discounting term, y represents the stock's dividend yield. In addition, the numbers d_1 and d_2 are calculated as:

$$d_1 = \frac{\ln(S/K) + (r - y + \sigma^2/2)\,T}{\sigma\sqrt{T}} \text{ and } d_2 = d_1 - \sigma\sqrt{T}$$

How do companies use the Black-Scholes-Merton formula to calculate ESO values? As an example, in December 2002, The Coca-Cola Company granted to several executives employee stock options representing more than half a million shares of Coke stock. The options had a stated term of 15 years, but to allow for the fact that employee stock options are often exercised before maturity, Coca-Cola used two time horizon assumptions to value the options: the longest possible term of 15 years and an expected term of 6 years. The company then adjusted the interest rate, dividend yield, and volatility assumptions to each of these terms.

The different input values assumed and the resulting Black-Scholes option values are summarized in Table 16.5. Notice that Coca-Cola assumed a higher volatility and dividend yield but a lower riskless interest rate for the six-year time horizon assumption. These assumptions seem reasonable because stock market volatility was relatively high and interest rates were relatively low in 2002.

Visit the Coca-Cola website at www.coca-cola.com for more investor information.

CHECK THIS

16.11a What are the key differences between a traded stock option and an ESO?

16.11b What is ESO repricing? Why is it controversial?

16.11c If you terminate your employment at The Gap, Inc., how long do you have to decide whether you will exercise your employee stock options?

---

[6] Strictly speaking, the Black-Scholes-Merton formula is used for European options. ESOs are a hybrid between European options and American options. Before vesting, ESO holders cannot exercise these options, so ESOs are like European options in the vesting period. After vesting, ESO holders can exercise their ESOs before the ESO expires, so ESOs are like American options after the vesting period.

16.12 Summary and Conclusions

In this chapter, we examined stock option prices. Many important concepts and details of option pricing were covered. We summarize some of these aspects below. However, be warned: The following summary does not include important details of how to calculate option prices. You will need to study the body of the chapter to become proficient in these important details.

1. **How to price options using the one-period and two-period binomial models.**

A. We show the details for a method to price European call options using the one-period and two-period binomial models. With a slight modification to allow for early exercise, this technique can also be used to calculate prices for American calls and puts. In fact, this basic technique is so powerful that, with the right modifications, it can be used to price an exotic array of options.

B. The details of this method are:
   - *Step 1:* Build a price tree for stock prices through time.
   - *Step 2:* Use the intrinsic value formula to calculate the possible option prices at expiration.
   - *Step 3:* Calculate the fractional share needed to form each risk-free portfolio at the next-to-last date.
   - *Step 4:* Calculate all the possible option prices at the next-to-last date.
   - *Step 5:* Repeat this process by working back to today.

2. **How to price options using the Black-Scholes model.**

A. The Black-Scholes option pricing formula states that the value of a stock option is a function of the current stock price, option strike price, risk-free interest rate, time remaining until option expiration, and the stock price volatility.

B. The two most important determinants of the price of a stock option are the price of the underlying stock and the strike price of the option. As the stock price increases, call prices increase and put prices decrease. Conversely, as the strike price increases, call prices decrease and put prices increase.

C. Time remaining until option expiration is an important determinant of option value. As time remaining until option expiration lengthens, both call and put option prices normally increase. Stock price volatility also plays an important role in determining option value. As stock price volatility increases, both call and put option prices increase.

D. Of the five input factors to the Black-Scholes option pricing model, only the stock price volatility is not directly observable and must be estimated somehow. A stock price volatility estimated from an option price is called an implied volatility or an implied standard deviation, which are two terms for the same thing.

E. The two input factors that most affect stock option prices over a short period, say, a few days, are the stock price and the stock price volatility. The impact of a stock price change on an option price is measured by the option's delta.

3. **How to hedge a stock portfolio using options.**

A. Call option deltas are always positive and put option deltas are always negative. Delta measures the impact of a stock price change on an option price, where a one-dollar change in the stock price causes an option price to change by approximately delta dollars.

B. Options on the underlying stock can be used by investors to protect themselves from price declines in shares that they own. Option deltas can be used to calculate the number of options needed to hedge shares that are owned. Investors can write call options or purchase put options to provide protection from decreases in share prices.

C. Options on the S&P 500 index are a convenient hedging vehicle for an equity portfolio because they are European style and because they settle for cash at option expiration. Hedging a stock portfolio with index options requires calculating the number of option contracts needed to form an effective hedge.

D. To maintain an effective hedge over time, hedgers should rebalance their hedge on a regular basis. Rebalancing requires (1) recalculating the number of option contracts needed to hedge an equity portfolio and then (2) buying or selling options in the amount necessary to maintain an effective hedge.

4. The workings of employee stock options.

A. An employee stock option (ESO) is, in essence, a call option that a firm gives to employees giving them the right to buy shares of stock in the company. The practice of granting options to employees has become widespread. ESOs provide an incentive for employees to work to increase the firm's stock price.

B. ESOs have a few features that make them different from regular stock options. The details differ from company to company, but a typical ESO has a 10-year life, which is much longer than most ordinary options. Unlike traded options, ESOs cannot be sold. They also have what is known as a "vesting" period. Often, for up to three years or so, an ESO cannot be exercised and also must be forfeited if an employee leaves the company. After this period, the options vest, which means they can be exercised.

C. The Financial Accounting Standards Board issued FASB 123 to tell companies how to calculate the fair value of employee stock options. As a practical matter, many companies calculate ESO prices using the Black-Scholes-Merton option pricing model. The Black-Scholes-Merton model is very similar to the Black-Scholes model. The difference between the two models is that expected dividends are an input for the Black-Scholes-Merton model.

GETTING DOWN TO BUSINESS

For the latest information on the real world of investments, visit us at jmdinvestments.blogspot.com.

In this chapter we introduced you to the Nobel Prize–winning Black-Scholes option pricing formula. We saw that the formula and its associated concepts are fairly complex, but, despite that complexity, the formula is widely used by traders and money managers. You can find out more about the Black-Scholes option pricing model on the internet. Enter "Black-Scholes" into an internet search engine for links to hundreds of websites.

To put into practice some real-world uses for the concepts we discussed, you should gather options trading information from the web and then use the information to trade options through Stock-Trak. Some suggested websites are the Web Center for Futures and Options (www.ino.com), www.option-price.com, and PMpublishing (www.pmpublishing.com). Of course, don't forget the most extensive website for options, the Chicago Board Options Exchange (www.cboe.com).

Another important use for option pricing theory is to gain some insight into stock market volatility. Recall that in Chapter 1 we discussed the probabilities associated with returns equal to the average plus or minus a particular number of standard deviations. Implied standard deviations (ISDs) provide a means of broadening this analysis to anything with traded options. You can learn a lot about implied volatilities and how they are used by options professionals on the internet. Enter the search phrase "implied volatility" or "implied standard deviation" into your favorite internet search engine for links to dozens of websites, like IVolatility (www.ivolatility.com).

Key Terms

delta 545
employee stock option (ESO) 555
expiry 540
implied standard deviation (ISD) 552

implied volatility (IVOL) 552
VIX 552
VXN 552
VXO 552

Related Bloomberg Functions

OVME Option Price Equity/IR, 16.2

OVML Option Valuation FX/Commodity, 16.5

OTD Option Description, 16.6

OSA Option Scenario Analysis, 16.8

WVOL FX Implied Volatility Matrix, 16.10

OVDV Volatility Surface, 16.10

Chapter Review Problems and Self-Test

1. **Black-Scholes Formula (LO2, CFA2)** What is the value of a call option if the underlying stock price is $100, the strike price is $90, the underlying stock volatility is 40 percent, and the risk-free rate is 4 percent? Assume the option has 60 days to expiration.

2. **Black-Scholes Formula (LO2, CFA2)** What is the value of a put option using the assumptions from Problem 1?

Answers to Self-Test Problems

1. We will use these input values to calculate the price of the call option:

   S = current stock price = $100

   K = option strike price = $90

   r = risk-free interest rate = .04

   σ = stock volatility = .40

   T = time to expiration = 60 days

   We first compute values for d_1 and d_2:

$$d_1 = \frac{\ln(100/90) + (.04 + .4^2/2) \times 60/365}{.4\sqrt{60/365}}$$

$$= \frac{.10536 + .12 \times .16438}{.16218}$$

$$= .77130$$

$$d_2 = d_1 - .16218 = .77130 - .16218$$

$$= .60912$$

The following standard normal probabilities are given:

$$N(d_1) = N(.77130) = .77973 \quad N(d_2) = N(.60912) = .72878$$

We can now calculate the price of the call option as:

$$C = \$100 \times .77973 - \$90 \times e^{-.04 \times 60/365} \times .72878$$

$$= \$100 \times .77973 - \$90 \times .99345 \times .72878$$

$$= \$12.81$$

2. Since we already know the values for d_1 and d_2, we can solve for $N(-d_1)$ and $N(-d_2)$ as follows:

$$N(-d_1) = 1 - N(d_1) = 1 - .77973 = .22027$$
$$N(-d_2) = 1 - N(d_2) = 1 - .72878 = .27122$$

We can now calculate the price of the put option as:

$$P = \$90 \times e^{-.04 \times 60/365} \times .27122 - \$100 \times .22027$$
$$= \$90 \times .99345 \times .27122 - \$100 \times .22027$$
$$= \$2.22$$

Alternatively, using put-call parity (from the previous chapter):

$$P = C + Ke^{-rT} - S$$
$$= \$12.81 + \$90 \times e^{-.04 \times 60/365} - \$100$$
$$= \$12.81 + \$90 \times .99345 - \$100$$
$$= \$2.22$$

Test Your Investment Quotient

1. **Black-Scholes Model (LO2, CFA2)**   The only variable in the Black-Scholes option pricing model that cannot be directly observed is the:

   a. Stock price volatility.
   b. Time to expiration.
   c. Stock price.
   d. Risk-free rate.

2. **Delta (LO2, CFA2)**   You purchase a call option with a delta of .34. If the stock price decreases by $2.00, the price of the option will approximately:

   a. Increase by $.34.
   b. Decrease by $.34.
   c. Increase by $.68.
   d. Decrease by $.68.

3. **Black-Scholes Model (LO2, CFA2)**   In the Black-Scholes option pricing model, the value of an option contract is a function of five inputs. Which of the following is not one of these inputs?

   a. The price of the underlying stock
   b. The strike price of the option contract
   c. The expected return on the underlying stock
   d. The time remaining until option expiration

4. **Black-Scholes Formula (LO2, CFA2)**   In the Black-Scholes option valuation formula, an increase in a stock's volatility:

   a. Increases the associated call option value.
   b. Decreases the associated put option value.
   c. Increases or decreases the option value, depending on the level of interest rates.
   d. Does not change either the put or call option value because put-call parity holds.

5. **Option Prices (LO2, CFA2)**   Which one of the following will increase the value of a call option?

   a. An increase in interest rates
   b. A decrease in time to expiration of the call
   c. A decrease in the volatility of the underlying stock
   d. A decrease in the price of the underlying stock

6. **Option Prices (LO2, CFA2)**   Which one of the following would tend to result in a high value of a call option?

   a. Interest rates are low.
   b. The variability of the underlying stock is high.
   c. There is little time remaining until the option expires.
   d. The exercise price is high relative to the stock price.

7. **Option Price Factors (LO2, CFA2)** Which of the following incorrectly states the signs of the impact of an increase in the indicated input factor on call and put option prices?

   a. Strike price of the option contract
   b. Time remaining until option expiration
   c. Underlying stock price
   d. Volatility of the underlying stock price

Call	Put
+	−
+	+
+	−
+	+

8. **Option Prices (LO2, CFA2)** Increasing the time to maturity of a call option will _____ the price of the option at a(n) _____ rate.

   a. Increase; increasing
   b. Decrease; decreasing
   c. Increase; decreasing
   d. Decrease; decreasing

9. **Option Prices (LO2, CFA2)** All else the same, an increase in which of the following will decrease the price of a call option?

   a. The strike price
   b. The price of the underlying stock
   c. The standard deviation of the underlying stock
   d. The risk-free rate

10. **Hedging with Options (LO3, CFA3)** All else the same, as the value of an option used to hedge an equity portfolio increases, the number of options needed to hedge the portfolio:

    a. Increases.
    b. Decreases.
    c. Will not change.
    d. Increases only if the beta of the portfolio is less than 1.

11. **Hedging with Options (LO3, CFA3)** You wish to hedge a $5 million stock portfolio with a portfolio beta equal to 1. The hedging index call option has a delta equal to .5 and a contract value equal to $100,000. Which of the following hedging transactions is required to hedge the stock portfolio?

    a. Write 200 index call option contracts.
    b. Write 100 index call option contracts.
    c. Buy 200 index call option contracts.
    d. Buy 100 index call option contracts.

12. **Hedging with Options (LO3, CFA3)** You wish to hedge a $10 million stock portfolio with a portfolio beta equal to 1. The hedging index put option has a delta equal to −.5 and a contract value of $200,000. Which of the following hedging transactions is required to hedge the stock portfolio?

    a. Write 200 put option contracts.
    b. Write 100 put option contracts.
    c. Buy 200 put option contracts.
    d. Buy 100 put option contracts.

13. **Implied Volatility (LO4, CFA2)** Which of the following provides the best economic interpretation of implied volatility for an underlying stock?

    a. Implied volatility predicts the stock's future volatility.
    b. Implied volatility states the stock's historical volatility.
    c. Implied volatility is unrelated to the underlying stock.
    d. Implied volatility is an accurate measure of interest rate risk.

14. **Employee Stock Options (LO4, CFA3)** You are an employee at L^3 Corporation and have just been awarded stock options. The options have a vesting period of five years and an exercise price of $50. L^3 stock has an implied volatility of 22 percent and does not pay a dividend. If the

current stock price is $48 and the risk-free rate is 4 percent, the per-share value of your options is closest to:

a. $5.85
b. $9.62
c. $12.61
d. $15.27

15. **Implied Volatility (LO4, CFA2)**   The implied volatility for an at-the-money call option suddenly jumps from 25 percent to 50 percent. This most likely means that:

a. The underlying stock has just paid a dividend.
b. The volatility jump is temporary.
c. The option has a short time to expiration.
d. An unforeseen event has increased the risk of the underlying stock.

Concept Questions

1. **Option Prices (LO2, CFA1)**   What are the six factors that determine an option's price?

2. **Options and Expiration Dates (LO2, CFA2)**   What is the impact of lengthening the time to expiration on an option's value? Explain.

3. **Options and Stock Price Volatility (LO2, CFA2)**   What is the impact of an increase in the volatility of the underlying stock on an option's value? Explain.

4. **Options and Dividend Yields (LO2, CFA2)**   What happens to the stock price when the stock pays a dividend? What impact does a dividend have on the prices of call and put options?

5. **Options and Interest Rates (LO2, CFA2)**   How do interest rates affect option prices? Explain.

6. **Time Value (LO2, CFA2)**   What is the time value of a call option? Of a put option? What happens to the time value of a call option as the maturity increases? What about a put option?

7. **Delta (LO2, CFA2)**   What does an option's delta tell us? Suppose a call option with a delta of .60 sells for $5.00. If the stock price rises by $1, what will happen to the call's value?

8. **Employee Stock Options (LO4)**   What is vesting in regard to employee stock options? Why would a company use a vesting schedule with employee stock options?

9. **Employee Stock Options (LO4)**   You own stock in a company that has just initiated employee stock options. How do the employee stock options benefit you as a shareholder?

10. **Employee Stock Options (LO4)**   In general, employee stock options cannot be sold to another party. How do you think this affects the value of an employee stock option compared to a market-traded option?

Questions and Problems

Core Questions

1. **Black-Scholes Model (LO2, CFA2)**   What is the value of a call option if the underlying stock price is $84, the strike price is $80, the underlying stock volatility is 42 percent, and the risk-free rate is 4 percent? Assume the option has 135 days to expiration.

2. **Black-Scholes Model (LO2, CFA2)**   What is the value of a call option if the underlying stock price is $81, the strike price is $90, the underlying stock volatility is 50 percent, and the risk-free rate is 3 percent? Assume the option has 60 days to expiration.

3. **Black-Scholes Model (LO2, CFA2)**   What is the value of a call option if the underlying stock price is $73, the strike price is $75, the underlying stock volatility is 37 percent, and the risk-free rate is 5 percent? Assume the option has 100 days to expiration.

4. **Black-Scholes-Merton Model (LO2, CFA2)**   A stock is currently priced at $63 and has an annual standard deviation of 43 percent. The dividend yield of the stock is 2 percent and the risk-free rate is 4 percent. What is the value of a call option on the stock with a strike price of $60 and 45 days to expiration?

5. **Black-Scholes-Merton Model (LO2, CFA2)**   The stock of Nugents Nougats currently sells for $44 and has an annual standard deviation of 45 percent. The stock has a dividend yield of 2.5 percent and the risk-free rate is 4.1 percent. What is the value of a call option on the stock with a strike price of $40 and 65 days to expiration?

6. **Black-Scholes Model (LO2, CFA2)** The stock of Lead Zeppelin, a metal manufacturer, currently sells for $68 and has an annual standard deviation of 41 percent. The risk-free rate is 6 percent. What is the value of a put option with a strike price of $70 and 45 days to expiration?

7. **Black-Scholes Model (LO2, CFA2)** What is the value of a put option if the underlying stock price is $42, the strike price is $35, the underlying stock volatility is 47 percent, and the risk-free rate is 5 percent? Assume the option has 140 days to expiration.

8. **Black-Scholes Model (LO2, CFA2)** A stock with an annual standard deviation of 30 percent currently sells for $67. The risk-free rate is 3 percent. What is the value of a put option with a strike price of $80 and 60 days to expiration?

9. **Hedging with Options (LO3, CFA3)** You are managing a pension fund with a value of $300 million and a beta of 1.07. You are concerned about a market decline and wish to hedge the portfolio. You have decided to use SPX calls. How many contracts do you need if the delta of the call option is .62 and the S&P index is currently at 4,030?

10. **Hedging with Options (LO3, CFA3)** Suppose you have a stock market portfolio with a beta of 1.15 that is currently worth $300 million. You wish to hedge against a decline using index options. Describe how you might do so with puts and calls. Suppose you decide to use SPX calls. Calculate the number of contracts needed if the call option you pick has a delta of .50 and the S&P 500 index is at 4,050.

11. **One-Period Binomial Option Pricing (LO1, CFA2)** A stock is currently selling for $45. In one period, the stock will move up by a factor of 1.15 or down by a factor of .87. A call option with a strike price of $50 is available. If the risk-free rate of interest is 2.5 percent for this period, what is the value of the call option?

12. **One-Period Binomial Option Pricing (LO1, CFA2)** A stock is currently priced at $74 and will move up by a factor of 1.20 or down by a factor of .80 over the next period. The risk-free rate of interest is 4.2 percent. What is the value of a call option with a strike price of $75?

13. **One-Period Binomial Option Pricing (LO1, CFA2)** A stock with a current price of $58 has a put option available with a strike price of $55. The stock will move up by a factor of 1.13 or down by a factor of .88 over the next period and the risk-free rate is 3 percent. What is the price of the put option?

14. **Black-Scholes Model (LO2, CFA2)** A call option matures in six months. The underlying stock price is $70 and the stock's return has a standard deviation of 20 percent per year. The risk-free rate is 4 percent per year, compounded continuously. If the exercise price is $0, what is the price of the call option?

15. **Black-Scholes Model (LO2, CFA2)** A call option has an exercise price of $60 and matures in six months. The current stock price is $68 and the risk-free rate is 5 percent per year, compounded continuously. What is the price of the call if the standard deviation of the stock is 0 percent per year?

16. **Black-Scholes Model (LO2, CFA2)** A stock is currently priced at $55. A call option with an expiration of one year has an exercise price of $60. The risk-free rate is 12 percent per year, compounded continuously, and the standard deviation of the stock's return is infinitely large. What is the price of the call option?

17. **Employee Stock Options (LO4, CFA2)** In its 10Q dated February 4, 2022, LLL, Inc., had outstanding employee stock options representing over 272 million shares of its stock. LLL accountants estimated the value of these options using the Black-Scholes-Merton formula and the following assumptions:

S = current stock price = $20.72

K = option strike price = $23.15

r = risk-free interest rate = .043

σ = stock volatility = .29

T = time to expiration = 3.5 years

What was the estimated value of these employee stock options per share of stock? (*Note:* LLL pays no dividends.)

18. **Hedging Employee Stock Options (LO4, CFA3)** Suppose you hold LLL employee stock options representing options to buy 10,000 shares of LLL stock. You wish to hedge your position by

buying put options with three-month expirations and a $22.50 strike price. How many put option contracts are required? Use the same assumptions specified in Problem 17. (Note that such a trade may not be permitted by the covenants of many ESO plans. Even if the trade were permitted, it could be considered unethical.)

19. **Employee Stock Options (LO4, CFA3)** Immediately after establishing your put options hedge, volatility for LLL stock suddenly jumps to 45 percent. This changes the number of put options required to hedge your employee stock options. How many put option contracts are now required? (Except for the new volatility, use the same assumptions specified in Problem 18.)

20. **Two-Period Binomial Option Pricing (CFA2)** A stock is currently selling for $60. Over the next two periods, the stock will move up by a factor of 1.15 or down by a factor of .87 each period. A call option with a strike price of $60 is available. If the risk-free rate of interest is 3.2 percent per period, what is the value of the call option?

21. **Two-Period Binomial Option Pricing (CFA2)** A stock is currently priced at $35 and will move up by a factor of 1.18 or down by a factor of .85 each period over each of the next two periods. The risk-free rate of interest is 3 percent. What is the value of a put option with a strike price of $40?

22. **Two-Period Binomial Option Pricing (CFA2)** A stock with a current price of $78 has a call option available with a strike price of $80. The stock will move up by a factor of .95 or down by a factor of .80 each period for the next two periods and the risk-free rate is 3.5 percent. What is the price of the call option today?

Spreadsheet Problems

23. **Black-Scholes Model (LO2, CFA2)** A stock has a price of $32 and an annual return volatility of 45 percent. The risk-free rate is 3.0 percent. Using a computer spreadsheet program, calculate the call and put option prices with a strike price of $31.50 and a 90-day expiration. Also calculate the deltas of the call and put.

CFA Exam Review by Kaplan Schweser

[CFA1, CFA2]

Ronald Franklin, CFA, is responsible for developing a new investment strategy for his firm. Given recent poor performance, the firm wants all of its equity portfolio managers to overlay options on all positions.

Mr. Franklin gained experience with basic option strategies at his previous job. As an exercise, he decides to review the fundamentals of option valuation using a simple example. Mr. Franklin recognizes that the behavior of an option's value is dependent on many variables and decides to spend some time closely analyzing this behavior, particularly in the context of the Black-Scholes option pricing model (and assuming continuous compounding). His analysis resulted in the information shown below:

Exhibit 1: Input for Option Pricing	
Stock price	$100
Strike price	$100
Interest rate	7%
Dividend yield	0%
Time to maturity (years)	1.0
Standard deviation of stock	.20

Exhibit 2: Option Sensitivities		
	Call	Put
Delta	.6736	−.3264

1. Mr. Franklin wants to compute the value of the call option using the information in Exhibit 1. Which of the following is closest to his answer?
   a. $4.78
   b. $5.55
   c. $11.54

2. Mr. Franklin wants to compute the value of the put option that corresponds to the call value calculated in the previous question. Which of the following is the closest to his answer?

   a. $4.78

   b. $5.55

   c. $11.54

3. Mr. Franklin is interested in the sensitivity of the put option to changes in the volatility of the underlying equity's returns. If the volatility of the underlying equity's returns increases, the value of the put option:

   a. Decreases.

   b. Increases.

   c. Does not change.

4. Mr. Franklin wants to know how the put option in Exhibit 1 behaves when all the parameters are held constant except delta. Which of the following is the best estimate of the change in the put option's price when the underlying equity increases by $1?

   a. $.33

   b. −$.33

   c. −$3.61

Bloomberg Exercises

1. Explore the calculator used to price equity options. **(OVME)**

2. Review the implied volatility attached to options on Lowe's (LOW) stock. **(OVDV)**

3. Find the option "Greeks" for an option on General Mills (GIS). **(OTD)**

What's on the Web?

1. Black-Scholes Model Go to www.option-price.com and find the option pricing calculator. There are a call and a put option on a stock that expire in 30 days. The strike price is $55 and the current stock price is $58.70. The standard deviation of the stock is 45 percent per year and the risk-free rate is 4.8 percent per year, compounded continuously. What are the prices of the call and the put? What are the deltas for the call and the put?

2. Black-Scholes Model Go to www.cboe.com and find the option pricing calculator. A stock is currently priced at $98 per share and has a standard deviation of 58 percent per year. Options are available with an exercise price of $95 and the risk-free rate of interest is 5.2 percent per year, compounded continuously. What are the prices of the call and the put that expire next month? What are the deltas of the call and the put? How do you interpret these numbers? How do your answers change for an exercise price of $100?

3. Implied Standard Deviation Go to www.option-price.com and find the option pricing calculator. You purchased a call option for $11.50 that matures in 55 days. The strike price is $95 and the underlying stock has a price of $99.50. If the risk-free rate is 5.4 percent, compounded continuously, what is the implied standard deviation of the stock? Using this implied standard deviation, what is the price of a put option with the same characteristics?

4. Black-Scholes-Merton Model Recalculate Problems 1 and 2 assuming a dividend yield of 2 percent per year. How does this change your answers?

Alternative Investments

"Buy land. They ain't making any more of the stuff."

—American humorist Will Rogers

Learning Objectives

To get an alternative view of your investments, make sure you:

1. Understand the benefits and risks of alternative investments.

2. Identify the styles and structure of hedge funds and private equity funds.

3. Understand how commodities can be used within an investment portfolio.

4. Identify the forms of investment and valuation alternatives for real estate.

Are you into alternative music? For many of you, the answer is probably yes. But just what constitutes "alternative" music? It's hard to say in an objective way, and the same is true for alternative investments. Loosely speaking, the term "alternative investments" refers to investment strategies and assets that lie outside the more common, everyday approaches to asset selection and portfolio management.

Our goal in this chapter is to provide you with a basic understanding of some common types of alternative investments. To accomplish this goal, we begin with a general discussion of the benefits and risks of alternative investments as compared to more traditional assets like stocks, bonds, or mutual funds. Then we examine two subcategories of alternative investments: alternative *strategies* and alternative *assets.*

Within the strategies category, we explore two primary investment companies: hedge funds and private equity funds, which include venture capital. We discussed hedge funds briefly in an earlier chapter, but we will provide greater depth here. For alternative assets, we concentrate on the two most widely held: commodities and real estate. We also examine cryptocurrency. This newer area of alternative assets has attracted much attention. With an understanding of these common alternative investments, you should be able to build a much more diversified (and hopefully more efficient) investment portfolio.

CFA™ Exam Topics in This Chapter:

1. Introduction to alternative investments (L1, S16)
2. Fintech (L1, S18)
3. Real estate investments (L2, S14)
4. Private equity investments (L2, S14)
5. Introduction to commodities and commodity derivatives (L2, S14)
6. Hedge fund strategies (L3, S9)
7. Asset allocation to alternative investments (L3, S9)

Go to Connect for a guide that aligns your textbook with CFA readings.

17.1 Benefits and Risks

As with any traditional investment, there are benefits and risks to alternative investments as well. We explore some of the most common in this section.

Related Bloomberg Functions

RICH Bloomberg Billionaires Index

ENDO U.S. College Endowments

BENEFITS OF ALTERNATIVE INVESTMENTS

If you wanted to invest in large-cap stocks, you could choose to purchase a typical index mutual fund or an exchange-traded fund (ETF), such as SPY (the SPDR S&P 500 ETF Trust). If you do, you have a long position in this asset: You want its value to increase. In contrast, an investor with a bearish market outlook could use an inverse ETF (such as SH, the ProShares Short S&P 500 fund). Even though this investor buys the inverse ETF, she has a short position: She wants the value of the market to fall. If the market falls, the value of the inverse ETF goes up.

Now, consider what would happen if you created an equally weighted portfolio that contained a long position in both SPY and SH. Effectively, you have formed an almost risk-free portfolio. If the market had a positive return day, your long position (SPY) would benefit, but the negative return on your inverse ETF (SH) would offset this gain. The opposite occurs if the market experiences a down day. So, you might be asking, "What is the point of this whole example?" Well, this extreme example illustrates the principle of diversification that we talked about in a previous chapter.

Investors often avoid asset classes that are considered too risky, such as alternative investments, when considered in isolation. Our example, however, shows that we were able to add another risky investment (SH) to an existing risky asset (SPY) in such a way that we actually reduced the overall portfolio risk.

As we explained in an earlier chapter, investors are not rewarded on the basis of the total risk on an individual investment. The relative (or systematic) risk matters. That is, how does the potential investment move in relation to the current portfolio held? The same concept applies to alternative investments. Adding an alternative investment will likely not completely eliminate the risk of a portfolio. It is possible, however, that adding an extremely "risky" alternative asset can actually reduce the risk of the overall portfolio.

You might recall that diversification benefits depend on the correlation among asset returns. If an asset's return does not have a high positive correlation with the returns of the assets already in the portfolio, then risk can be reduced. As a result, the portfolio can have lower risk and still have the same, or even better, return. That is, the portfolio is more efficient.

Let's use gold as an example. Many investors flocked to this alternative asset in the wake of the 2008 financial crisis. As a result, the price of gold doubled from about $800 per ounce in early 2008 to over $1,600 per ounce in mid-2011. Over this time, the correlation of gold with the S&P 500 index was almost zero. Thus, adding gold to a portfolio effectively lowered risk (and, in this case, increased return), even though gold prices in isolation might be just as volatile as the portfolio of stocks in the S&P 500.

A REAL-WORLD EXAMPLE INPRS is a state government entity that oversees the pension and retirement fund management for state employees in Indiana. One of INPRS's main responsibilities is to decide on an asset allocation for its $30+ billion portfolio. Obviously, this important decision will ultimately impact thousands of people, from the plan participants to the taxpayers that provide the source of funds. Wouldn't it be interesting to get INPRS's view on alternative investments and the potential benefits they bring?

To illustrate the potential benefits, take a look at Figure 17.1. This figure compares a traditionally diversified portfolio that INPRS held about 30 years ago to its more recent portfolio, which includes a broader range of investments. In Figure 17.1A, you can see the "traditional" portfolio made up of large-cap domestic stocks (S&P 500), bonds (Barclay's Aggregate), and international equity (MSCI EAFE). With this allocation, INPRS earned a historical average return of about 6.86 percent and had a standard deviation of about 11.12 percent. Let's look, however, at the benefit INPRS experienced by adding alternative investments to its portfolio.

FIGURE 17.1A | Traditional Portfolio

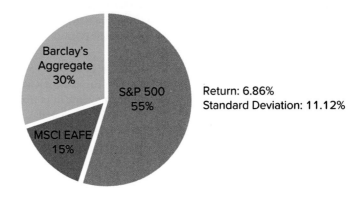

Return: 6.86%
Standard Deviation: 11.12%

FIGURE 17.1B | More Diversified Portfolio

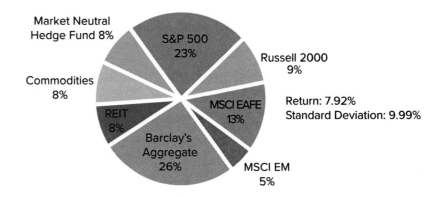

Return: 7.92%
Standard Deviation: 9.99%

In Figure 17.1B, the portfolio now has the same three assets as before, plus a small-cap stock index (Russell 2000) and an international emerging markets index (MSCI EM). Notice that the portfolio also contains three alternative investments: real estate (which is the REIT component), commodities, and a market neutral hedge fund. What is the impact of these changes?

Each category added is individually more volatile than the assets that were already in the portfolio. The new portfolio, however, has a lower standard deviation (9.99 percent, down from 11.12 percent). In addition, the return increased (7.92 percent, up from 6.86 percent). This result is the best of both worlds—lower risk and higher return. Thus, the primary benefit of these alternative investments is a better all-around (i.e., more efficient) portfolio. Results like these are the reason why entities such as INPRS include alternative investments in their portfolios.

RISKS OF ALTERNATIVE INVESTMENTS

Given the benefits discussed above, you might be completely ready to add alternative investments to your portfolio. Before you do, however, you also need to be aware of the added difficulties (and risks) of alternative investments.

STRUCTURE AND TRANSPARENCY The Securities and Exchange Commission (SEC) is the federal agency responsible for enforcing securities laws. Investment advisors must register with the SEC once they reach a certain size. Many alternative investment funds, however, have historically been structured to avoid registering with the SEC.

To avoid having to register, funds are often structured as limited partnerships. The manager serves as the general partner, and the underlying investors are limited partners.

Besides having this basic structure, the funds also limit the number of limited partners to fewer than 100 and do not offer shares for sale to the general public. These distinctive features circumvent many registration requirements. They also enable the funds to use strategies not generally available to the managers of more traditional funds. These strategies include things like having highly concentrated positions, being extremely leveraged, short selling, and holding illiquid securities.

This overall structure creates at least two possible issues. First, if the fund is limited to fewer than 100 people, then to create a large fund, the minimum investment amounts are generally large, preventing many investors from gaining access. For example, most successful, well-known funds, such as AQR Capital, have minimum investments of at least $1 million (or more). Second, the lack of registration means that the fund itself is less transparent because it faces fewer reporting requirements. The lack of information reporting adds risk, particularly considering that the underlying investments might even be less transparent. As a result, the lack of transparency at these two levels makes it more difficult for investors to value the investment opportunity.

LIQUIDITY Alternative investments are generally less liquid than traditional investments. For example, alternative fund managers will often limit investor access to their money. Hedge funds, which we describe in detail below, often impose *lockup periods.* A lockup period means that investors commit to a minimum time period, say two years, before they can withdraw any of their money. Even after the lockup period, investor redemptions might be limited to particular windows of time, say, once per quarter. And, even with this permitted access, investors often must provide notice of at least 30 days.

Similarly, private equity funds, which we discuss later in this chapter, are also less liquid than traditional investments. Most private equity funds have a set life, typically 10 years. After investors commit to investing, the fund will "call" the capital when the managers are ready to invest it. Thus, not only do investors have a long time commitment, but there is also some uncertainty about when they will have to provide money to the fund. While these constraints allow private equity funds to take longer-term positions, they definitely reduce liquidity for investors. This issue is sometimes offset with the use of a *takedown schedule,* which is a predetermined time frame over which capital will be called.

TAXES When you buy a stock, the tax implications are straightforward—potentially, there will be dividend income each year, as well as a capital gain (or loss) when you sell the stock. For alternative investments, the tax implications are not always so clear-cut. As an example, if you invest in a fund that is structured as a limited partnership, then each year you will receive a statement called a Schedule K-1.

Tax treatment of this partnership income (or loss) is more complicated than traditional income taxes. Further, partnership income can trigger the alternative minimum tax—another complicated calculation. What does different tax treatment mean for investors in alternative assets? Often, it means that these investors will need to hire specialists to help them calculate their tax bills. Paying for this help is an implicit cost to investors who add alternative investments to their portfolio.

COMPENSATION AND COSTS For a typical mutual fund, an investor is charged a management fee, maybe around 1 percent (though often less). For alternative investment funds, the standard management fee is much higher. A typical hedge or private equity fund uses a 2/20 fee structure. This fee structure means that the investor is charged an annual management fee of 2 percent. In addition, the investor leaves behind 20 percent of the annual profits for the fund managers. While these funds might produce high gross returns, the net returns (after taxes and fees) might not be so attractive.

In addition, directly investing in alternative assets such as gold or real estate is typically more costly. Trading costs are higher, and with physical assets, the investor pays for storage and insurance. These costs, all else equal, reduce the net return investors earn from these assets. We discuss these issues in greater detail later in the chapter.

QUALIFIED INVESTORS Given all the potential risks and costs, you might be having second thoughts about alternative investments. If so, you are not alone. Even the U.S. government recognizes that these investments are complex, so it limits who is able to invest in them. The U.S. government classifies some investors as **accredited investors**. Only accredited investors are allowed (by the U.S. government) to employ certain investment strategies, particularly pertaining to hedge funds and private equity funds.

An accredited investor is defined generally as someone who is "rich." Obviously, this term is vague. Specifically, to be classified as an accredited investor, a person must have at least $1 million in net assets to invest, or have an income of at least $200,000 ($300,000 if married) in each of the last two years. In addition, institutional investors, like those managing pensions and endowments, could also be considered accredited. Thus, while alternative assets might be beneficial, not all investors will be able to take advantage of every asset or strategy.

accredited investors
In the United States, an investor who has assets or income that exceed a minimum level set by the federal government and qualifies to invest in more aggressive alternative investments and strategies.

CHECK THIS

17.1a	How is it possible to add a volatile asset to a portfolio yet actually lower overall risk?
17.1b	What are some of the primary risks associated with alternative investments?

 17.2 Hedge Funds

When you hear the name "hedge fund," you might think that these funds are actually low-risk investments (as in the saying "hedging your bets"). Some hedge funds do try to exploit arbitrage opportunities on a low-risk basis. Most hedge funds, however, actually undertake aggressive, risk-enhancing strategies—thus, only accredited investors may participate.

While hedge funds are considered an alternative investment strategy, most hedge funds primarily invest in publicly available underlying securities like stocks, bonds, futures, and options. For hedge funds, it is not the actual investments that are classified as alternative. Instead, the alternative classification stems from the strategies that hedge funds use in these securities. For example, hedge funds might use extensive leverage, short sell, or use some combination of these approaches.

HEDGE FUND REGULATION

Historically, hedge funds have not been subject to much regulation. In the past 20+ years, however, some events have triggered a renewed effort by the federal government to increase hedge fund regulation. In 1998, a hedge fund named Long-Term Capital Management collapsed. The Federal Reserve stepped in and helped bail out the firm in order to avoid a systemic financial crisis.

In response to this event and others, beginning in 2006, the Securities and Exchange Commission (SEC) required larger hedge funds (those with assets under management over $100 million) to register as investment advisors. Hedge fund managers do not have to register each of the funds they manage. Instead, managers must provide some basic information to the SEC and have a person on staff whose duties include helping the hedge fund comply with SEC rules. To ensure compliance, the SEC can randomly examine registered hedge fund managers.

The role of hedge funds in the most recent financial crisis of 2008 is still being hotly debated. As such, Congress is considering even stricter regulations. As would be expected, the hedge fund industry is defending itself and resisting these efforts. See the nearby *Investment Updates* box for more on this issue.

Related Bloomberg Functions

HFND	Overview of Hedge Fund Solutions
HFS	Hedge Fund Search
MARB	M&A Arbitrage
HFA	Historical Fund Analysis
COMP	Comparative Returns
FSTA	Fund Style Analysis

Find information on hedge funds at
www.barclayhedge.com.

INVESTMENT UPDATES

ARE HEDGE FUNDS "TOO SAFE TO FAIL"?

A global hedge fund association, seeking to deflect efforts to increase regulation of the investment vehicles, said today hedge funds aren't "systemically important financial institutions" that would require special government oversight.

While more than 1,400 hedge funds closed during the recent financial crisis, the Alternative Investment Management Association said, they did so in "an orderly manner."

"The 2008 experience shows that hedge funds are 'safe to fail,' even if they are not fail-safe," said Todd Groome, chairman of the association, in a statement. "This difficult period provided a very up-to-date and significant stress test concerning hedge fund risk to markets."

AIMA's argument comes as regulators continue to mull which organizations should be deemed systemically important, in a bid to better devise rules to rein in financial companies that are "too big to fail."

The Dodd-Frank financial-overhaul law automatically designates banks with $50 billion or more in assets as systemically important, but gives regulators authority to decide which nonbank financial firms pose systemic risks.

Some regulators have told Congress they want a larger number of non-bank firms, such as hedge funds, to provide data to regulators even if they escape the systemic designation.

One often-cited example in the argument to boost regulation of hedge funds is the 1998 rescue of Long-Term Capital Management L.P. organized by the Federal Reserve, which had feared its failure might cause a chain reaction in markets and among counterparties on Wall Street.

Source: Amy Or, "Are Hedge Funds 'Too Safe to Fail'?," *The Wall Street Journal,* July 7, 2011.

HEDGE FUND FEES

As we noted in the previous section, most hedge funds have traditionally charged a 2/20 fee. This means that the investor pays a management fee of 2 percent and gives 20 percent of the profits earned to the fund manager on an annual basis. Although this approach has been common, there are many different fee structures—and some can be quite elaborate. In almost every case, however, the performance fee (in this case, the 20 percent) is the main feature of the compensation structure.

One positive aspect of the performance fee is that the hedge fund manager has an incentive to earn as much profit as possible. There are, however, some potentially negative consequences. Suppose the performance bonus is awarded each year. What might the hedge fund manager do if he knew that the fund was going to lose money this year? One possible strategy to maximize the fund's bonus is for the manager to write off as much loss as possible in the current year. As a result, the manager would be in a better position to make a large percentage profit for the fund next year (and a healthy performance fee for the manager).

high-water mark
A provision that ensures performance fees are not earned when the value of the fund regains previous levels. The value of the fund must exceed the previous high value of the fund before new performance fees are paid to the manager.

Hedge fund investors are savvy. To prevent this type of manipulation, many fee structures also include constraints (or hurdles) that the manager must meet. One of the more common is a **high-water mark**. When a hedge fund has a high-water mark, the manager will only receive performance fees when the fund's value is higher than its previous highest value. Should the value of the investment drop in a given period, then the manager must make the value of the investment exceed the previous high-water mark before performance fees are paid. For a more detailed illustration of a high-water mark provision, take a look at Example 17.1.

EXAMPLE 17.1 | High-Water Mark

You invested $1,000,000 with a hedge fund that has a standard 2/20 fee structure and a high-water mark provision. Suppose the returns over the first two years are −5 percent and 25 percent, respectively. What are the management and performance fees paid each year? Assume the management fees are paid at the beginning of each year and performance fees, when relevant, are paid at the end of each year.

(continued)

Management fees are paid on the invested amount, so the first-year management fee is $20,000 (= $1,000,000 × .02). Because this fee is paid at the beginning of the year, the remaining $980,000 is invested. With a −5% loss, the end-of-year balance is $931,000 (= $980,000 × .95). No performance fee is paid.

At the beginning of Year 2, the 2 percent management fee is applied, which is $18,620 (= $931,000 × .02). The manager has $912,380 to invest in Year 2. The second-year return is 25 percent, meaning the ending balance is $1,140,475 (= $912,380 × 1.25). A performance fee will be paid, but only on the amount above the maximum portfolio value since inception, which in this case is the initial investment of $1,000,000.

The fund manager receives a performance fee of ($1,140,475 − $1,000,000) × .20 = $28,095. The investor's net balance is $1,112,380. This ending balance represents a geometric average return of 5.47 percent over the two-year period, which is much less than the average of the actual yearly returns. This example shows that fees have a big impact on these investments.

Why are investors willing to pay these high fees? The obvious answer is that the returns earned may still be high enough to provide the investor a reasonable net return. However, there is significant debate surrounding this issue. Many experts believe that the returns offered by hedge funds are not much better than the overall stock market, particularly after fees are subtracted.

If hedge fund returns are not higher than, say, a simple market index fund, is there any reason to invest with a hedge fund? Yes. As we concluded earlier, the answer depends on the principle of diversification. That is, investments should be judged on how their returns move with the assets already in the portfolio.

HEDGE FUND STYLES

Worldwide there are thousands of hedge funds. Whether large or small, each fund has its own investment style or niche. For example, a hedge fund might focus on a particular sector, like technology, or a particular global region, like Asia or Eastern Europe. Alternatively, a hedge fund might pursue a particular investment strategy. In this section, we highlight some common investment styles. After we describe each style, we identify its level of expected return volatility.

1. *Market neutral.* The goal of this strategy is to offset risk by holding opposite positions in pairs of securities. These funds are also called *long-short funds.* The managers of these funds take long positions in a set of securities that the managers believe are underpriced. Then, the manager matches these investments with corresponding short positions in securities that are perceived to be overpriced. Properly constructed, the resulting portfolio makes money regardless of the direction of the overall market, hence the name "market neutral." Be aware that some funds might offset all long positions, whereas other funds match only a portion of them. *Expected volatility: Low to moderate.*

2. *Arbitrage.* With this strategy, fund managers attempt to identify a mispricing in relationships between securities that, theoretically, should not exist. Arbitrage fund managers look at pricing relationships for securities offered by the same company or for investments across time or countries. For example, a hedge fund manager might buy convertible bonds of a company and short sell the common stock of the same company. This strategy is called *convertible arbitrage.* Another common arbitrage strategy is buying the stock of an acquisition target and short selling the stock of the acquiring firm. This strategy is called *M&A (merger and acquisition) arbitrage.* Example 17.2 illustrates this strategy. *Expected volatility: Low.*

EXAMPLE 17.2

M&A Arbitrage

Tango Corp. has made an offer to acquire Cash Corp. The deal specifies that one share of Tango will be exchanged for two shares of Cash. Tango is currently trading at $50 per share, and, after a run-up following the acquisition announcement, Cash is currently priced at $24 per share. The deal has been approved by the board and is awaiting approval by the stockholders and federal agencies, both of which seem likely. What trades would an arbitrage hedge fund manager make in this situation?

The hedge fund manager should short one share of Tango and purchase two shares of Cash. The net cash flow is a $2 inflow. If the acquisition goes through as planned, the two shares of Cash will be converted into one share of Tango, which can then be used to cover the short position. The risk is that the acquisition may not be approved or may not occur for some other reason.

3. *Distressed securities.* The managers of these hedge funds concentrate their investments in securities that are being offered at deep discounts, which typically result from company-specific or sectorwide distress. For example, a manager of a distressed securities fund might buy shares in firms that are facing bankruptcy. This particular approach falls into the category of "event-driven" funds. *Expected volatility: Low to moderate.*

4. *Macro.* These hedge fund managers attempt to profit from changes in global economies brought about by government policy changes that affect such things as interest rates, currencies, or commodity prices. Macro fund managers will often use leverage and derivatives to increase the impact of market movements. *Expected volatility: High.*

5. *Short selling.* In contrast to a long-short fund, a pure short hedge fund manager only short sells. *Expected volatility: High.*

6. *Market timing.* Managers of these hedge funds attempt to identify trends in particular sectors or overall global markets. Often, these managers take concentrated positions, i.e., they "put a lot of eggs into one basket." Also, they generally use leverage to increase the fund's exposure to predicted movements. *Expected volatility: High.*

As you can see, there are many hedge fund styles, and we did not list them all. Note that each style has its own level of risk. Once you make your millions and become a qualified investor, you still have your work cut out trying to identify the best hedge fund for your portfolio. What if you cannot decide? Maybe you will invest in a fund of funds.

FUNDS OF FUNDS A significant portion of the money invested in hedge funds is funneled through *funds of funds*. A fund of funds is just what the name suggests: An investment company that invests in hedge funds. For investors, a fund of funds has advantages and disadvantages.

A specific advantage of funds of funds is diversification. Remember, most hedge funds have high minimum investment requirements. Thus, an investor might not have enough money to invest in multiple strategies, or even enough to enter a particular fund. A fund of funds enables investors to hold positions in many hedge funds. In spirit, a fund of funds works like an equity mutual fund. If investors buy a mutual fund, they have a position in many stocks. Another advantage is the potential expertise that fund of funds managers might have in selecting the "best" hedge funds. The due diligence they provide might enable the creation of a better portfolio of hedge funds than an individual could build.

Funds of funds, however, have disadvantages, too. A big drawback is the added layer of fees that are charged by the fund of funds. When you consider two layers of management and performance fees, these fees can be quite hefty. Another potential disadvantage could be the effect on one's overall portfolio diversification. Diversification, as noted above, is generally considered to be a good thing when investing. In this context, though, it is important to note that a fund of funds might blend funds to reduce the overall risk of the hedge portfolio; thus, adding this component to an investment portfolio might result in lower returns if diversification on the hedge fund side offsets the benefits of diversification in the investor's portfolio.

PERFORMANCE COMPARISON

For a traditional mutual fund, we typically judge performance relative to a benchmark. For example, we would compare the performance of a large-cap fund to the S&P 500. If we compare a fund to the correct benchmark on the basis of both risk and return, we can calculate the fund's alpha. Most hedge fund strategies, however, do not correspond to typical market segments such as large-cap equity, small-cap equity, corporate bonds, or government bonds. As a result, it is difficult to judge performance. In fact, hedge funds sometimes refer to themselves as *absolute return* funds, which implies that there is no relative benchmark. While this lack of correlation benefits portfolio diversification, it makes performance evaluation much more difficult.

So, how do we separate "good" hedge funds from "bad" hedge funds? Well, we still rely on performance comparisons, but the comparison is made relative to composite style category indexes. For example, several data vendors provide average returns for the various investment styles we discussed: market neutral, arbitrage, distressed securities, etc. With this information, we can at least see whether a particular hedge fund performed above the average of the hedge funds in its style category.

This comparison provides some objective information, but the composites often have their own problems. The composites might not reflect all underlying hedge funds, particularly because hedge fund managers get to decide whether to report their performance. Similarly, because hedge fund styles are not standardized, even comparing hedge funds to the performance of others in a given style category might not be meaningful.

Another significant issue is survivorship bias. Many unsuccessful hedge funds close their doors, so only successful hedge funds survive to report performance results. Investors do not know in advance if the hedge fund they use will survive. Thus, the style benchmark return is higher than it would be if we adjusted the benchmark returns for shuttered hedge funds. Of course, you should conduct some research before you invest; however, you should understand that comparing hedge funds is much less objective than comparing mutual funds.

CHECK THIS

17.2a	Explain the workings of a 2/20 fee structure with a high-water mark provision.
17.2b	Identify some common hedge fund strategies.

Private Equity Funds

In the previous section, you learned that hedge funds primarily invest in publicly available securities, so it is not really the underlying assets that are "alternative." What is alternative about hedge funds is the strategies that they use. Private equity funds are alternative investments because they invest in companies that are not publicly traded. Thus, private equity funds provide a way for investors to diversify into privately held companies.

PRIVATE EQUITY AND VENTURE CAPITAL

In his dorm room in 1984, Michael Dell started PC's Limited (now called Dell Technologies). Today, the company has a market capitalization of over $45 billion. What happened to allow for this dramatic growth? A significant portion of the growth can be traced to investments by private equity and venture capital funds.

A business goes through various stages in its development. When an entrepreneur begins a company, it is likely just an idea—i.e., the company is in the *seed* stage. The entrepreneur then develops the idea through the early, or *start-up,* stage until it reaches the *formative* stage. In this stage, the company begins to sell products and/or services. If successful, the business enters the *late* stage as it continues to grow.

Related Bloomberg Functions

PE	Private Equity Overview
PEFR	Private Equity Fundraising Environment
MA	Mergers and Acquisitions
PEBM	Private Equity Return Analysis
PFRV	Private Equity Fund Relative Value

At each stage, the existing owners might need additional funding. They also might need outside expertise. Enter private equity and venture capital funds. Both types of investment funds provide funding and industry knowledge in exchange for ownership in the business. The main difference involves the stage in which the participation occurs. Venture capitalists typically provide seed and early-stage financing. Private equity funds offer formative and late-stage capital.

While the process is similar, there are obvious differences in the risk profiles of venture capital and private equity funds. Venture capital is a much riskier type of investment fund because the business failure rates in the early stages can be quite high. As you learned early in the book, however, there is a potential trade-off between risk and return. Thus, venture capitalists will demand a larger potential return (and ownership percentage) in exchange for their investment.

Venture capital and private equity funds will usually concentrate in specific areas. For example, some venture capital and private equity funds might be industry specific, focusing on technology or energy. Others might work only with distressed companies. The largest area, however, is diversified private equity because funds in this category span multiple areas looking for the best investment opportunities. To give some perspective on the size and distribution of private equity funds, check out Table 17.1. The table lists the top 10 fund managers as of early 2022. The rankings are based on the total amount of capital raised during the previous five years.

PRIVATE PLACEMENT MEMORANDUM

Before a private equity fund makes any investments, it must raise capital. Like hedge funds, private equity and venture capital funds are primarily structured as limited partnerships. Unlike hedge funds, however, these funds have stated lives, typically 10 years. Thus, private equity funds are constantly being created (and liquidated). To raise enough money, managers must have a successful track record in their previous funds. If they do not, they will likely need to reduce their fee structure and settle for a smaller fund size. To raise capital, fund managers create a **private placement memorandum (PPM)** that provides details on the proposed fund. These details include the fund's expected life, its target size, and the strategies the fund manager intends to use. The PPM also includes details on the fund's fee structure and any restrictions to which it will subject itself.

The fee structure is similar to those of hedge funds in that many use a standard 2/20 approach, with a 2 percent management fee per year and a 20 percent performance fee. There are, however, significant differences. For example, the management fee is charged on the *total amount* that has been committed for investment, called **committed capital**, not just that which has been called and invested.

Check out
www.pwcmoneytree.com
for details on current activity in the
venture capital industry.

private placement memorandum (PPM)
A memorandum that details the characteristics of a proposed private equity fund and is distributed to potential investors.

committed capital
The total amount of capital that an investor has committed to invest in a fund over its entire life.

TABLE 17.1	Top 10 Private Equity Firms by Funds Raised over the Last 5 Years	
Rank	Firm Name	Funds Raised ($ billion)
1	The Blackstone Group	$93.2
2	Kohlberg Kravis Roberts	$79.9
3	CVC Capital Partners	$60.4
4	The Carlyle Group	$50.8
5	Thomas Bravo	$46.7
6	EQT	$44.2
7	Vista Equity Partners	$40.4
8	TPG	$40.3
9	Warburg Pincus	$37.6
10	Neuberger Berman	$37.5

Source: Private Equity International.

carried interest

The performance fee earned by the private equity manager. It is typically *carried* until near the end of the fund's life, when it is paid.

hurdle rate

The minimum return the private equity manager must generate before any carried interest is awarded.

clawback provision

A provision that forces private equity fund managers to return carried interest in the case of subsequent poor performance.

For private equity and venture capital funds, the performance fee is typically referred to as **carried interest**. This carried interest is most often subject to a **hurdle rate**. A hurdle rate is a minimum return that must be achieved before any carried interest is paid. A hurdle rate acts as an additional incentive for managers to perform as well as they can.

To prevent fund managers from taking performance distributions too early, most funds also contain a **clawback provision**. This provision requires the general partner (i.e., fund manager) to return capital in a case where an early investment generates high returns, but subsequent investments perform poorly. What happens to the carried interest generated by the returns to the early investment? Investors should not have to pay for one successful investment that is followed by a series of poor investments. Effectively, the clawback provision does not allow the payout of carried interest to the general partners until the fund is liquidated or near liquidation.

Importantly, the PPM spells out how the fund can use leverage to enhance returns. When managers identify an investment, they can enhance returns by using a combination of committed capital and borrowed funds. As expected, however, the use of leverage increases the risk of the fund. By setting maximum leverage levels, the risk level of the fund is reduced. The risk is not eliminated because managers can still make poor investment decisions.

While it isn't an official PPM, check out Figure 17.2, which is a summary of the Warburg Pincus Private Equity XIV fund. The fund is seeking to raise $16 billion and will have a base management fee of 1.50 percent. Once the firm begins to invest, its performance, which is typically measured using an internal rate of return, or IRR, will be reported.

THE INVESTMENT PROCESS

After the manager distributes the PPM to accredited investors, investors will decide whether to invest in the fund. When the fund manager has enough capital commitments, the fund manager proceeds to the actual investment process. Private equity funds and venture capital funds tend to follow this five-step investment process: deal flow, valuation, deal structure, value creation, and exit. Let's look at some aspects of each of these steps.

FIGURE 17.2 **Warburg Pincus Private Equity XIV Fund**

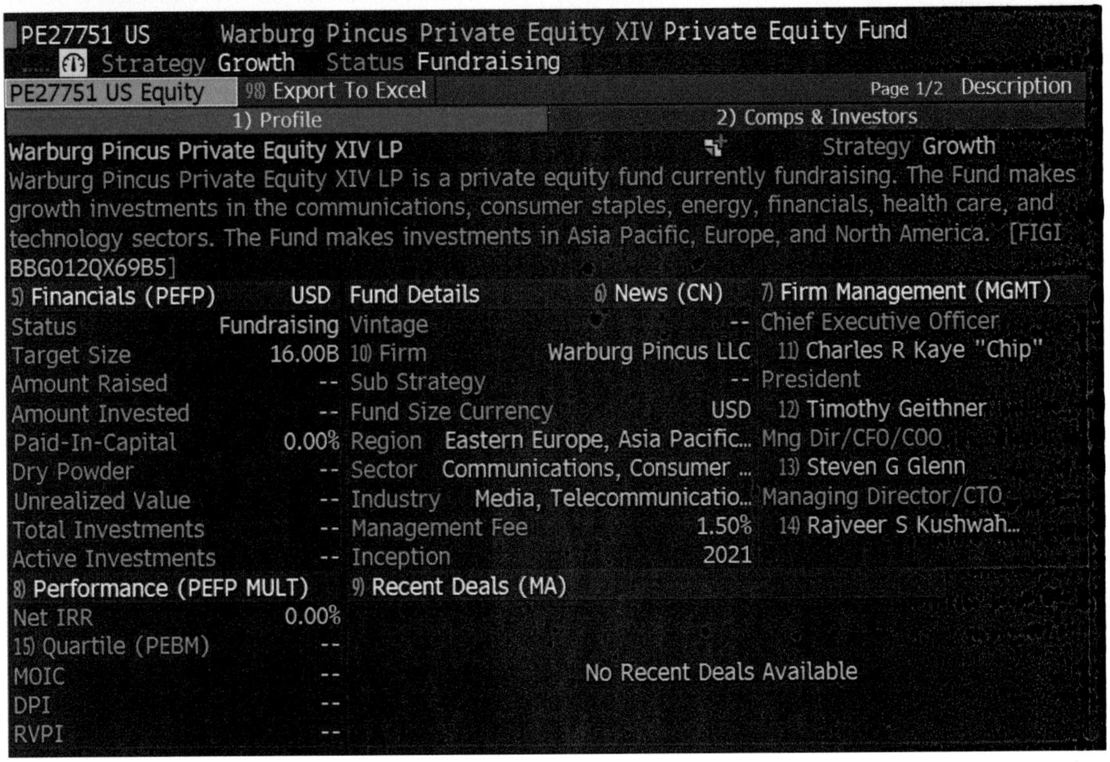

Source: Bloomberg Finance L.P.

DEAL FLOW The phrase "garbage in, garbage out" is particularly applicable for private equity firms. Much of a fund's success will be based on the quality of the deals from which to choose. Well-known, prestigious funds will receive many unsolicited offers that they can evaluate. Even lesser-known, smaller fund managers receive unsolicited offers, particularly if they have developed a strong network within the industry and investor community.

An average private equity fund might evaluate about 500 potential investments in a year. From this investment set, the fund manager applies some basic filters to pare down the investment set to a manageable number. These filters might include the investment size (minimum and maximum), the industry, or standard financial ratios. This filtering might result in a subset of 20 to 50 deals that are evaluated at a deeper level.

With further scrutiny of existing company management, the company's product line, and other items, the fund managers decide to offer preliminary deals—maybe to five or six companies. A proposed deal is formalized in a **letter of intent (LOI)**, which contains details of the preliminary structure of the investment and the dollar amount that the fund offers to invest. Even after agreement is made on the LOI, however, there is more due diligence to do. As such, not all LOIs are officially accepted; the fund manager or the target company might pull out of the deal. In the end, an average private equity firm might close only one or two deals per year. While this number might seem small, there is a large amount of work required to manage even one private equity transaction.

letter of intent (LOI)
Document that provides details of a proposed deal between the private equity fund and the firm selling equity or debt.

VALUATION Unlike investing in publicly traded companies, there is no transparent market to help investors see the market value of a target firm. Thus, fund managers rely on their own valuation models. These models might include the various traditional discounted present value models of cash flows. The dominant approach used by these funds, however, appears to be based on a multiple of current cash flows, with a focus on EBITDA (earnings before interest, taxes, depreciation, and amortization).

With an EBITDA number, fund managers can evaluate historical deals in the industry to determine an appropriate multiple, say five to seven times EBITDA. When this multiple is applied to the target firm's EBITDA, the fund manager can estimate a value for the target firm. Refer to Example 17.3 to see how to make calculations associated with a sample deal.

EXAMPLE 17.3 **Multiples Valuation**

Centerwire Capital Partners is considering an investment in Glass Technologies. Glass has an EBITDA of $12.2 million, and Centerwire determines that similar deals have recently closed at a 5.5 times multiple. With this multiple in mind, what is the valuation estimate for Glass Technologies?

The valuation estimate is the EBITDA times the average industry multiple, which in this case is $12.2 million × 5.5 = $67.1 million. As we discussed in a prior chapter, when EBITDA is used, the valuation is for the entire firm, not just for equity. Centerwire and Glass Technologies will negotiate this valuation and the percentage of the firm that Centerwire will own.

Unfortunately, price multiples are not stable, and they will vary depending on both firm size and industry. Multiples also vary through time because of changing economic conditions. For this reason, much of the analysis of private equity funds is done according to the funds vintage year, which is the year it began.

DEAL STRUCTURE Once the firm and the fund settle on a valuation, the next step is to agree on the terms of the deal. The major term of the deal is the fund's dollar investment and the percentage of the company the fund owns. The ownership percentage can range from only, say, 5 percent to as much as 100 percent. In many cases, however, the fund will require its ownership to be above 50 percent, which gives operating control to the fund. In addition, the fund manager might require that the fund get a specified number of seats on the company's board of directors—which, again, helps the fund maintain operational control of the firm. The value of the company drives the percentage ownership the fund receives for its investment.

In addition, particularly for venture capital funds, the ownership required is related to the expected value of the firm when the fund exits its investment. One valuation approach often used is called the *venture capital method.* There are three basic steps to this valuation method:

Step 1: *Estimate the post-money (exit) valuation.* Private equity and venture capital funds profit by investing in companies so that the companies can grow in value. These funds then sell their ownership and move on to search for new deals. Before investing, the fund manager forecasts the value of the investment when the fund exits the deal. Estimating this value means that the fund manager has to specify how long the fund anticipates holding this ownership, and, potentially, how the fund will exit the deal. Both of these factors will impact the exit valuation.

Step 2: *Determine the pre-money valuation.* After negotiations, the fund manager and target company agree on an amount the fund will invest. Using the venture capital fund's required rate of return, this amount will be compounded forward to the exit date. For most funds, the required return is quite high, often 50 percent or more. This return might seem excessive, but consider the high risk involved with investing in young companies, many of which fail.

Step 3: *Determine the ownership fraction.* Once the required future value of the fund's initial investment and the exit value of the company are estimated, the ratio of these two values determines the fund's required ownership percentage.

Example 17.4 walks you through an example of the venture capital valuation method.

EXAMPLE 17.4 — **Venture Capital Method**

Scenic Ventures is considering an investment in a start-up firm offering ecotourism excursions in Costa Rica. Scenic Ventures estimates that, if the venture is successful, the ecotourism company will have a value of $25 million in four years, the time of the exit. Scenic has agreed to an initial investment of $3 million and requires a return of 50 percent on these types of investments. What ownership fraction will Scenic demand in exchange for its investment?

Step 1: Post-money (exit) valuation = $25 million

Step 2: Pre-money valuation = $3 million, with a future value of $3 million $\times 1.50^4 =$ $15.1875 million

Step 3: Ownership fraction = $15.1875/$25 = .6075, or 60.75%

In addition to straight equity, there are other possible deal structures. Venture capital funds often use preferred stock that is convertible into shares of common stock. With convertible preferred stock, the fund might be able to specify the payment of an annual dividend. This dividend reduces the investment's risk because it provides some cash flow to the fund before the exit date. Many companies that need venture capital, however, do not have the cash flow to make dividend payments. Even without a dividend, convertible preferred stock might still be used—to provide some protection to the fund in case the company goes bankrupt. The most critical aspect of convertible preferred stock, however, is the conversion feature. This feature enables the venture capital fund to retain the potential of an upside return if the company succeeds. Thus, convertible preferred stock is a way to enhance downside protection without forgoing upside return—the best of both worlds.

Some private equity funds make debt-based investments. These firms are often called *mezzanine funds* because they are between the debt and equity levels on the balance sheet. These "mez" funds provide debt financing to firms that might be able to borrow more from traditional lenders. Obviously, this investment is higher risk than typical debt. As a result, the interest rates on these debts are generally higher than rates on other debts. Mez funds might also demand *warrants* as part of the agreement. A warrant is really just a call option on a specified number of shares in the firm, so owning warrants is another way to be compensated for risk. Thus, if the firm is successful, the private equity fund makes a return on the mez debt, as well as through equity it is able to collect by exercising the warrants.

INVESTMENT UPDATES

TV STINT PUTS CITIKITTY NEAR $1 MILLION MARK

How might an appearance on national TV impact a young business with just one product?

For CitiKitty, Inc., a recent stint on ABC's *Shark Tank* has put the six-year-old enterprise on track to hit the $1 million mark in sales this year. Founder Rebecca Rescate says the company received more orders for its cat toilet-training kit during the week after the reality show aired in mid-May than it did for all of 2010, when revenue totaled just $350,000. *Shark Tank* invites entrepreneurs to pitch investors for financing. Rescate went on the show seeking $100,000 in exchange for a 15 percent equity stake in her company. She landed two offers in that range and accepted one from Kevin Harrington, chairman and founder of TVGoods, Inc., a Clearwater, FL, marketing company that specializes in producing infomercials. Rescate says she went with Harrington, even though he requested a slightly larger equity stake than the other investor, real-estate mogul Barbara Corcoran, because she saw him as a better fit for her business. CitiKitty has produced one standard TV commercial and its kits are in As Seen on TV stores across the nation.

Harrington says he opted to invest in CitiKitty mainly because it has a proven track record. "In our business, having something that has been tested already is a very positive thing," he explains. Harrington says he also likes that the company's kits offer consumers an opportunity to save by no longer having to invest in litter or litter boxes. Plus, the effect of the product is amusing to watch in action, as demonstrated through a number of videos the company created that show cats using the toilet. "It's the kind of product that we look for, something that has a wow factor to it," he says.

Through her new partnership with Harrington and TVGoods, Rescate says she's so far secured a deal for shelf space at several Walgreens outlets. They're now working together on getting CitiKitty into more retail locations.

Source: Sarah E. Needleman, "TV Stint Puts CitiKitty Near $1 Million Mark," *The Wall Street Journal*, July 6, 2011.

The structures we have addressed are only a small sampling of what is possible. Because private equity investments are an agreement between two parties, there is really no limit to the range and complexity of the deal structure. As long as both sides agree, any term can be written into the contract.

VALUE CREATION Once a deal is in place, the real work begins. In addition to their capital investment, a good private equity or venture capital fund will bring expertise and industry contacts to their acquisition. These resources are valuable to the company because they did not have access to them before the deal. Fund managers will often take board seats and might even be involved in day-to-day operations. In an extreme case, the fund managers might even replace the management of the acquired firm. The overall ownership goal is to restructure and grow the business to increase cash flow (i.e., EBITDA). Increasing cash flow comes from improving the business—improving margins, expanding product lines, and making other operational refinements.

Although the multiple of cash flow paid for the business often depends on the industry, there is variation. Firms with more stable cash flows receive higher multiples, particularly at higher levels of EBITDA. The goals of the fund manager are to increase the cash flow and to expand the multiple.

To give you an idea of value creation, take a look at the nearby *Investment Updates* box featuring ABC's *Shark Tank,* which debuted in 2009. In this show, entrepreneurs present their businesses to a panel of venture capitalists, all of whom have the opportunity to assess the business and make an offer. As a result of the show, many entrepreneurs, like the one in the article, have received both capital and expertise to help them grow their businesses.

For more on *Shark Tank*, visit abc.go.com/shows/shark-tank.

EXIT Recall that private equity and venture capital funds have defined lives—mostly in the range of 10 years. As a result, defining an exit strategy is important. There are three basic ways for the fund to exit. The worst-case scenario is the company fails and the fund managers lose their investment.

Obviously, a much more desirable outcome is to sell the business at a profit. This sale could be to another private equity fund (i.e., financial buyer) or to another company in the industry (i.e., strategic buyer). Another type of sale is an initial public offering (IPO), where the company sells equity to the general public. An IPO often generates the highest return for the fund.

PERFORMANCE MEASUREMENT

As with hedge funds, there is not a defined benchmark for comparing the performance of private equity and venture capital funds. Thus, it becomes a "beauty contest" of sorts, where one fund is compared to the others that are available, often based on subjective assessments. This comparison is even more difficult when performance data for funds are based on assets yet to be liquidated.

Some academic studies have examined overall industry returns over longer periods of time. The most interesting result is that the total return of private equity funds seems to be in line with the overall stock market. Given that these funds are more risky, we might expect a higher return. The high fees paid, however, might be the reason behind the lower-than-expected returns. Remember, though, the greatest benefit of these funds might not be a higher return, but rather the potential diversification benefits they bring.

CHECK THIS

17.3a What restricts a private equity manager from taking too much carried interest?

17.3b What are the basic steps of the private equity or venture capital investment process?

17.4 Commodities

Related Bloomberg Functions

BCOM	Bloomberg Commodity Index
MTL	Precious Metals Prices
COMM	Commodity Product Catalog
CTM	Exchange Contracts
CFMX	Cash Future Matrix
FXFA	FX-Interest Rate Arbitrage
ETF	Exchange Traded Funds
ETFL	ETF Implied Volatility

By definition, a commodity is a basic good that is nearly identical to other goods of the same type. That is, there is not much variation in a given commodity, even if it is provided by two different producers. For example, an ounce of gold in the United States is equivalent to an ounce of gold in China. Commodity exchanges are marketplaces where commodities trade. Trading commodities can involve spot price, or immediate, transactions or futures trading. Traditionally, commodities were primarily physical goods, such as gold, oil, or corn. More recently, however, commodity futures exchanges have also added contracts on financial assets, such as currencies, fixed income products, equity indexes, and other indexes.

Commodities have two basic roles. First, producers of goods use commodities as inputs. For example, jewelers use gold, textile mills use cotton, oil refineries use crude oil, and flour mills use wheat. Second, investors can trade commodities—either to shift risk or to take risk.

Investors can use commodities to diversify their portfolio risk further. Investors can also trade commodities to help protect their portfolios from general price increases in the economy. Finally, nonagricultural commodities like copper, silver, and gold are not perishable. These commodities can act as a store of value—similar to one of the roles of money. Particularly for U.S. investors, commodities can also help protect against inflation, or a loss in purchasing power, because many commodities are priced worldwide in dollars.

A prime example of this is oil. No matter where in the world it is traded, oil typically changes hands in dollars. Because it is traded in many world markets, oil prices reflect the supply and demand in many markets—which is one reason oil prices are so volatile. Being priced in dollars also plays a part in the volatility of oil prices. If the value of the dollar declines versus other currencies, oil becomes cheaper around the world. Foreign buyers can convert their currencies into a larger number of dollars and buy more oil for the same amount of their home currency. This buying pressure pushes demand (and price) up. In this situation, for U.S. investors holding oil, the oil price increase resulting from the dollar's decline protects their portfolio in real terms—i.e., oil prices provide an inflation hedge. Thus, once again, while the return to alternative assets might not be higher over time than traditional assets, the diversification they provide can be quite valuable.

How do investors diversify into commodities? Basically, individual investors have three choices: spot market transactions, futures contracts, and third-party managers (commodity-based funds). In the following sections, we discuss some aspects of each of these three approaches.

SPOT MARKET TRANSACTIONS

If you wanted to own gold, you could visit your local coin dealer and purchase a U.S. Liberty Gold Eagle or South African Krugerrand. Both of these coins contain one troy ounce of gold. By the way, one pound contains 14.58333 troy ounces. As of early 2022, one of these coins was worth over $1,800. By purchasing these coins, the investor is making a spot market transaction, which means buying (or selling) the actual commodity today. Spot market transactions result in an actual physical exchange of the commodity.

For small spot market transactions like buying gold coins, local dealers are the primary suppliers. As in any dealer market, dealers make money from the spread on each transaction. That is, the asking prices investors pay exceed the bid prices investors receive for the commodity. Remember, the size of the spread depends on the liquidity and competition in a particular spot market. For small transactions, the spread is relatively high. For example, if the spot price of gold were $1,800 per troy ounce, you might pay $1,850, or more, to purchase a gold coin from a dealer. Moreover, this price does not include the premium that is charged for some gold coins that are more collectible than others.

For large transactions, investors do not visit the local coin shop. Imagine walking in and asking to purchase 5,000 troy ounces of gold, which represents over 340 pounds and $9 million. Obviously, these large transactions are conducted in a different way. In most cases, these transactions take place through the exchange of a storage receipt. A seller who owns a large amount of gold will likely store it in a central repository. The seller signs over the gold to the buyer—there is no physical exchange of gold. If the buyer keeps the gold in the same location, this process really simplifies the transaction. Further, because these purchases are large, the bid-ask spread per ounce will be much lower.

Regardless of the size of the spot transaction, there are other costs. For example, physical commodities must be stored and insured. Storage and insurance are inexpensive for a small number of gold coins if you own a safe and have them covered on your homeowners insurance policy. On a large scale, however, storing gold in a depository will be much more costly.

FUTURES CONTRACTS

Futures contracts allow investors to benefit from commodity price changes without actually owning the physical commodity. Recall from our discussion of futures markets in another chapter that investors can benefit from price increases or price decreases. For example, investors who agree to take delivery of the commodity in the future are locking in a price today that they will pay. If the commodity's price rises, these investors earn a profit because they have a contract that allows them to buy the commodity at less than the current price. Similarly, investors who agree to make delivery of the commodity in the future benefit from price declines.

Compared to spot market trades, futures contracts have benefits and disadvantages. Being able to use margin is one potential advantage of using futures contracts. Investors may purchase one gold futures contract, giving them a position consisting of 100 troy ounces. In the spot market, 100 ounces of gold at a price of $1,800 costs $180,000, plus a commission. In the futures markets, however, the initial margin on a gold futures contract is much less, say $6,500. Thus, for a much smaller investment, futures contracts enable investors to take the same size position as spot market investors. For the same investment amount, futures contracts enable investors to take a much larger position than spot market investors.

Recall, however, that using margin brings additional risk. The leverage created by using margin means that small movements in the commodity's price will have a large impact on the investor's return. In our example, the margin in the futures account is $6,500/$180,000 = .0361, or 3.61%. Using this value, we can calculate a leverage factor, which tells us the percentage movement in the futures position for a given movement in the underlying commodity. The leverage factor is calculated as:

$$\text{Leverage factor} = 1/\text{Margin percentage} \qquad (17.1)$$

For this example, the leverage factor is 1/.0361 = 27.69 times. So, for every one percent change in the price of gold, the equity in this account changes by 27.69 percent. Obviously, this price change greatly benefits the investor if the price change is in a favorable direction. This leverage, however, can be quite damaging if the price change is unfavorable.

Investors can hold physical commodities as long as they want to pay the storage and insurance costs. Futures contracts, however, are short-term positions, generally lasting only a few months. If investors want to hold an ongoing futures market position, they must "roll" the contracts before they expire. Investors roll over their futures contract position by closing out the contract they hold and replacing it with (i.e., rolling into) a contract with a longer time to expiration. Rolling contracts come with a cost in addition to the small trading commission, and the roll cost can be substantial.

In our chapter on futures contracts, we discussed spot-futures parity. This parity equation identifies the expected relationship between spot and futures prices:

$$F = S \times (1 + r)^T \tag{17.2}$$

In Equation 17.2, F is the futures price; S is the spot price; r is the annual interest rate; and T is the time to futures contract settlement, measured in fractions of a year. For example, if the spot price of gold is $1,800 per ounce, the interest rate is 4 percent per year, and the contract lasts three months, then, ignoring storage costs, the futures contract price should be:

$$F = \$1,800 \times 1.04^{3/12} = \$1,817.74$$

contango
In the futures market, a term to indicate that the futures price is higher than the spot price.

Equation 17.2 shows that the futures price is higher than the spot price, and this difference increases with the contract's length. This relationship is known as **contango**. When traders roll a long futures contract position, a market in contango means that they close out the current contract at a lower price than what they pay to roll into the longer contract. Thus, each time traders roll a contract in a contango market, they incur a loss, which is the roll cost. It is even possible that investors lose money when the spot price of the commodity remains unchanged.

backwardation
In the futures market, a term that indicates that the futures price is lower than the spot price.

The opposite of roll cost is roll yield. Roll yields are possible when the futures contracts for a commodity are in "backwardation." **Backwardation** means that futures prices are lower than spot prices. In this case, when investors roll a long position, they sell at a price higher than the price they pay to replace the long futures position with a new contract. This relationship is unusual across most commodities, with the exception of crude oil and related products such as unleaded gasoline and heating oil.

ARBITRAGE IN FUTURES CONTRACTS Why should we expect the spot-futures parity relationship to hold? If it did not hold, then active traders would engage in arbitrage trades and earn excess returns. This monitoring aligns spot prices and futures prices. For example, suppose the futures price was $1,850 per ounce—higher than Equation 17.2 predicts. In this case, a trader buys 100 ounces of gold in the spot market and sells one gold futures contract (which covers 100 ounces). This is called a *cash and carry trade* because the trader buys in the cash (i.e., spot) market and carries the gold to the time when the gold can be delivered to settle the terms of the futures contract. In addition, the trader uses borrowed money to buy gold in the spot market. In this manner, the trader has no investment but makes a profit—the definition of an arbitrage. How big is the trader's profit?

In our example, the trader borrows $1,800 for three months at a 4 percent interest rate and buys gold in the spot market. The trader holds, or carries, the gold until futures contract settlement. Because the trader sold a gold futures contract, the trader is agreeing to deliver 100 ounces of gold when the contract expires and receive $1,850 per ounce. Based on the interest rate, the trader needs $1,817.74 to repay the loan in three months. So, these trades today result in a profit of $32.26 (per ounce) in three months. Traders looking for arbitrage opportunities keep the spot-futures relationship in, or close to, parity.

You might be wondering whether the trader has to pay for storage and insurance in the example above. The answer is yes. Thus, we must adjust the spot-futures parity equation to include storage and insurance costs. That is:

$$F = (S + PVSC) \times (1 + r)^T \tag{17.3}$$

Notice that the spot price includes the term *PVSC*, which is the present value of the storage and insurance costs. The present value of the storage and insurance costs is added to today's spot price because the trader will also borrow this amount of money to store and insure the gold for three months.

Suppose storage and insurance costs are $1.25 per ounce per month. We calculate the present value of these cash outflows as follows:

$$PVSC = \frac{\$1.25}{\left(1 + \frac{.04}{12}\right)} + \frac{\$1.25}{\left(1 + \frac{.04}{12}\right)^2} + \frac{\$1.25}{\left(1 + \frac{.04}{12}\right)^3} = \$3.725$$

Thus, the expected futures price would be:

$$F = (\$1,800 + \$3.725) \times 1.04^{3/12} = \$1,821.50$$

The storage and insurance costs reduce the arbitrage profits. By how much? The arbitrage profit without any storage and insurance costs is $1,850 − $1,817.74 = $32.26. With storage costs, the arbitrage profit is $1,850 − $1,821.50 = $28.50.

Why should investors using commodity futures in their portfolio care about all this parity stuff? When the spot-futures parity relationship holds, it means that futures prices reflect fair value. If futures prices did not reflect fair value, then investors using commodity futures in their portfolios would be taking additional risk.

THIRD-PARTY MANAGERS

Spot market transactions require storage facilities, and trading futures contracts yourself can be quite hazardous to your wealth. Fortunately, market participants have created two products to trade commodities in an easier way: (1) commodity-based exchange-traded funds (ETFs) or notes (ETNs) and (2) hedge funds that offer managed futures strategies.

EXCHANGE-TRADED FUNDS AND NOTES We discussed ETFs in detail in an earlier chapter. Here we will concentrate on some key issues for exchange-traded funds that deal in commodities. To give you an idea of the products available, take a look at Table 17.2. The table provides a sampling of some of the most popular exchange-traded products. You will see from this small sample that there are products available that are diversified across all commodities (such as PDBC and GSG). There are also funds that concentrate in specific commodities (such as GLD, SLV, and USO). Investors have many choices.

One thing you might notice is that some funds are specifically labeled ETFs, while others might be considered ETNs. An ETF is a traditional exchange-traded fund, where an investor owns a proportional share of the underlying assets held by the fund. For example, GLD is a traditional ETF. This fund receives dollars from investors and purchases physical gold. Investors then effectively own their proportion of the actual gold held by the fund. The value of an ETF should move in direct relation to the market price of the asset it holds. When the price of gold increases, so does the value of GLD.

Exchange-traded notes have two main differences from ETFs. Effectively, an ETN is a debt instrument created by an issuer. Unlike bonds, however, the promised return is based on the

TABLE 17.2	Commodity ETFs and ETNs	
Ticker	**Name**	**Assets ($ billions)**
GLD	SPDR Gold Shares ETF	$57.07
IAU	iShares Gold Trust	$28.72
SLV	iShares Silver Trust	$12.25
PDBC	Invesco Optimum Yield Commodity Strategy	$ 4.84
DBC	Invesco DB Commodity Index Tracking Fund	$ 2.82
USO	United States Oil Fund	$ 2.54
GSG	iShares S&P GSCI Commodity-Indexed Trust	$ 1.47

FIGURE 17.3   Return of UNG versus Natural Gas Index

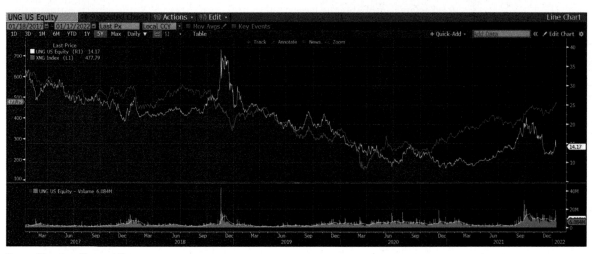

Source: Bloomberg Finance L.P.

movement of some underlying asset (such as oil). So, investors in ETNs do not own assets. Instead, they own a variable-rate debtlike instrument. For most people, this difference is irrelevant. In fact, most ETN investors probably do not know this fact. One related issue, however, is taxes. ETNs are taxed differently than ETFs. ETNs are treated like partnerships. Thus, as we discussed with hedge funds and private equity funds, there might be unique tax issues with ETNs (such as partnership income being reported on a Schedule K-1 tax form).

A second difference is that ETNs, rather than holding physical assets, attempt to mimic price movements in the underlying commodity using futures contracts. Thus, the same potential disadvantages we discussed above, in particular the roll cost, apply to ETNs, too. As an example, take a look at Figure 17.3. The graph charts the return of UNG (a natural gas fund) versus the actual natural gas index price (^XNG). You should notice that natural gas prices experienced a decline over the past five years, dropping roughly 23 percent. The ETF, however, actually lost over 50 percent over the same period. Much of this difference is from the impact of contango on the roll cost. So, buyer beware! Exchange-traded commodity products are not all equal.

MANAGED FUTURES One particular hedge fund investment style is called *managed futures*. These funds trade futures contracts. Some might be diversified across multiple commodities, while others concentrate on currencies, metals, energy, Treasury bonds or other interest rate futures contracts, stock index futures, or some other area. In all cases, the goal of these funds is to attempt to exploit trading opportunities, such as the carry trade we discussed.

Another common trading example is known as the *crack spread*. For example, after crude oil is extracted from the ground, it can be refined (cracked) into multiple petroleum-related products, such as gasoline, heating oil, and kerosene. If the prices of the refined products move too far away from the crude oil prices, traders can try to arbitrage the crack spread by buying crude oil futures and selling the futures for gasoline and heating oil, or vice versa. A similar trade can be made in soybeans, soybean meal, and soybean oil. This trade is called the *crush spread* because soybeans are crushed to make the products.

CHECK THIS

17.4a What are some basic ways to invest in commodities?

17.4b Why does the rolling of futures contracts create a cost when a futures market is in contango?

Real Estate

17.5

Real estate is probably the largest alternative asset category. Some experts estimate that about one-third of all assets in U.S. portfolios are in real estate. If you look at investor accounts held at brokerages and other institutions, real estate does not appear. Consider, however, that home ownership is one type of real estate investment. For many people, their home is their most valuable asset.

When we consider real estate as an alternative asset, this class is broad. For example, we could invest in assets such as raw land, residential apartments, houses to rent, or commercial buildings (offices, warehouses, retail space, and hotels). In every case, real estate returns come from two sources: (1) rental income, net of operating costs, generated by the property and (2) capital gains (or losses) associated with sale at a higher (lower) price than the purchase price.

FORMS OF REAL ESTATE INVESTMENT

The simplest form of real estate investment is an all-cash deal, in which the asset is financed by 100 percent equity. Obviously, this type of investment requires a large cash outlay, which limits the size of the investments that can be made. A much more likely scenario is called *leveraged equity,* that is, using debt and equity. For example, most people who buy a home make an equity down payment (say 20 percent) and borrow the rest. In this form, we say the investment is leveraged.

The leveraged equity approach is also the most commonly used approach for commercial real estate investments. The benefit of using leverage is that a larger investment can be made than would otherwise be possible in an all-equity deal. The risk, however, is that leverage will exaggerate the gains and losses associated with movement in the price of the underlying real estate. This impact of leverage is familiar: We saw it when we discussed margin trading earlier in this chapter.

The mortgage loans that result from leveraged equity deals are also forms of real estate investment. Given the size and importance of this particular market, we devote an entire subsequent chapter to this specific topic. For now, understand that a bank will package together a set of mortgage loans (i.e., create a "mortgage-backed security") and sell this bundle to investors. The resulting investment is a form of fixed income security, in that there are promised repayments at designated future dates. As we saw with the subprime crisis in 2008, however, these assets can get much more complicated.

For individual investors, the most feasible way to invest in real estate is probably through real estate investment trusts, or REITs. Most of these trusts are publicly traded securities that purchase a diversified portfolio of real estate properties. The portfolio could be shopping malls around the country, office buildings, condos, or other real estate properties. The goal of the trust is to generate income from the underlying properties, which is then passed through to investors.

A similar investment is commingled real estate funds, or CREFs. These funds work much like REITs, with the exception that they are private funds. Many of these funds, in fact, could be considered private equity funds. Thus, many of the same aspects we discussed earlier in the chapter about private equity funds apply to CREFs.

REAL ESTATE VALUATION

When we value any asset, we can apply some basic principles. For example, we might ask, "What is the price of a similar asset?" Or we might try to calculate the cost to replace the asset if we had to. We can also apply these approaches to valuing real estate if we can find comparable assets. There are three common approaches used to value real estate assets.

COST APPROACH The cost approach asks the question "What would it cost to replace the building in its current form?" Obviously, we must include the cost of the land and the building costs. The approach to building costs is straightforward. We would obtain estimates from builders on what they would charge to rebuild the asset—i.e., the current construction costs.

While this approach is easy, it has some drawbacks. One issue is the difference between market value and construction costs. In the wake of the most recent recession, the values of existing properties fell significantly. In fact, many fell below what it would cost to rebuild a similar structure. In contrast, a building might be more valuable than the cost to rebuild it if it has a stable tenant base or has some features that are not easily replaced.

SALES COMPARISON The sales comparison approach is commonly used to value homes. This valuation method is similar to a price multiple comparison. For example, within a given area, many houses (and other buildings) will sell at a given price per square foot. We can evaluate historical transactions to calculate an average price multiple, then apply it to the number of square feet in the building under consideration.

There are, however, limitations to this approach. One limitation is that prices are not stable through time. So, if we are using historical averages over long periods, current pricing trends might be significantly different. For example, there was a huge drop in home prices following the housing crisis and recession in 2008. Thus, using comparable sales from 2006 and 2007 would not have been accurate in 2008.

Another limitation of the comparison approach is that total square footage is not the only variable that determines property values. For a house, characteristics such as the number of bedrooms or bathrooms also play a role. To create a more formal comparison, there are two options. First, we could include only assets that are virtually identical, but this method severely limits the size of our comparison set. Second, we could conduct a regression analysis (remember your stats class), where we evaluate the impact of each underlying attribute on sales prices. This analysis helps us estimate the value that the market places on a set of individual features of the property. As an example, we might be able to calculate that a swimming pool adds, on average, $17,500 to the value of a home, while each additional bedroom adds $28,000 to the value. While this approach involves a statistical approach, it can provide greater accuracy for property values.

net operating income (NOI)
The income after expenses generated by a property.

INCOME APPROACH The primary goal of most real estate investment, particularly commercial real estate, is to generate rental income. Using the income approach to valuation is consistent with this goal. This approach can be used to calculate the present value of the **net operating income (NOI)** generated by the property. The NOI is gross potential income, less expenses, which includes items such as expected vacancy rates, utilities, and repairs. Investment in real estate often provides tax write-offs, so we definitely want the model to capture any relevant tax benefits, too.

When we use the income approach, we assume that the NOI is a perpetual payment, so we can use a simple perpetuity formula to estimate the value:

$$\text{Estimate of property value} = \frac{\text{NOI}}{\text{Market capitalization rate}} \qquad (17.4)$$

You recall that the present value of a perpetuity is the cash flow divided by the discount rate. In Equation 17.4, the market capitalization rate (or cap rate) is the discount rate. The cap rate represents the required rate of return on similar real estate properties. To estimate this rate, most investors will use historic transactions on similar properties. For a detailed calculation, check out Example 17.5.

EXAMPLE 17.5 | **The Income Approach**

You are considering a rental property investment. You estimate gross potential income of $100,000 per year. You expect, however, an average vacancy rate of 5 percent. Operating costs will average $45,000 per year. A similar property with an estimated NOI of $60,000 recently sold for $480,000. Based on this information, what is the estimated value of the rental property that you are considering?

1.   NOI = $100,000 × (1 − .05) − $45,000 = $50,000

2. Find the market capitalization rate using the comparable sale:

$480,000 = $60,000/Cap rate

Cap rate = .125, or 12.5%

3. Thus, the estimated value for the rental property is

$50,000/.125 = $400,000

CHECK THIS

17.5a What are the primary approaches to valuing real estate?

17.5b How might the recent cap on mortgage interest deductions affect real estate values?

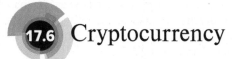

17.6 Cryptocurrency

AN OVERVIEW

The "crypto" world emerged in 2008 with the online posting of a white paper written under the pseudonym Nakamoto Satoshi. That paper described a novel approach to transferring value electronically. The new approach was built on bitcoin, which is today the most well-known cryptocurrency.

Perhaps you are asking, "Why do we need a new approach?" Well, when you use traditional institutions (i.e., banks) to transfer money, there are time lags. That is, if you are transferring money to someone using a different institution, the money does not arrive instantly. New transaction providers, like Venmo, can solve this problem, but only if you are transferring funds to someone else who has a Venmo account. The goal of cryptocurrency is to simplify, accelerate, and securitize online transfers without the need for a dedicated financial intermediary. Thus, cryptocurrency is part of a larger movement known as decentralized finance, or "DeFi."

CREATION OF A BITCOIN

A bitcoin is created and awarded when an individual or a team, called a bitcoin "miner," is the first one to solve a math problem. You probably expect that the problem is quite complex, but it isn't. Rather, it is more like having to guess the right answer when there is a huge number of possible answers. Miners use large arrays of computers to do the guessing as rapidly as possible. In fact, these arrays are so big that bitcoin mining has become controversial in some circles due to its power consumption and the associated greenhouse gases.

Through this process, new bitcoins are mined and added to the overall supply. To retain value, though, the supply of bitcoin is limited to 21 million coins. This limit is one reason why some investors like cryptocurrency. They believe there is less chance for loss in value due to added supply (think about the impact of inflation on purchasing power).

Are you wondering how many bitcoins have been issued? As of early 2022, more than 90 percent of the supply has been awarded. Market participants estimate that the last bitcoin will be mined around February 2140.

BLOCKCHAIN TECHNOLOGY

Each bitcoin is unique. Keeping track of who owns which one is obviously important. The solution proposed by Satoshi is a distributed ledger called the blockchain. A distributed ledger is a record of transactions and ownership that is maintained in many duplicate locations as opposed to being controlled by one entity.

The blockchain is a permanent record of who owns bitcoins. The blockchain is updated whenever bitcoins change hands, thereby making it possible to verify the rightful owner. A primary benefit of the blockchain technology is it is less expensive and has faster transaction settlements. What might have taken days can now take place in a matter of minutes, all in a secure, private transaction. The fact that the transaction is private puts the "crypto" in cryptocurrency. All details of bitcoin ownership are encrypted, so owners, buyers, and sellers are all anonymous. This anonymity is appealing to people wishing to protect their privacy for legitimate reasons. Of course, it is also appealing to people who wish to hide money from, say, tax collectors.

Blockchain technology can be used for more than just transferring value. The ability to document ownership has led to whole new classes of assets. For example, suppose I was a famous photographer. If I tried to sell you a photograph I had taken, you probably wouldn't give me very much, knowing that I could sell copies to thousands of people. So, your copy wouldn't be unique. Suppose, however, I somehow added ownership to the photograph so that you were the only one with a documented claim. That documented claim would add significant value (because no one could use the photograph without your permission). As a result, you would be willing to pay me a lot more money. Well, blockchain allows digital assets to have documented ownership. So, for example, many athletes have begun to issue and sell their own digital "cards." Such an asset is known as a nonfungible token, or NFT. Almost anything that can be created and displayed on a screen is a candidate to become an NFT.

CRYPTOCURRENCY AS AN INVESTMENT

You can see how blockchain adds potential benefits for users. But what about cryptocurrency as an investment? You are probably wondering how big the crypto market is and whether it is even worth talking about. Well, it is. As of January 2022, the cryptocurrency market had a combined value of roughly $2 trillion. Bitcoin, because it was the first cryptocurrency and is now the most popular, represents about half of this value. You might be surprised to learn that as many as 6,000 different cryptocurrencies exist.

You might be wondering how to value a crypto asset. Is it like gold and act as a store of value? If so, then we could compare their values. For example, the current above-ground gold stock is worth about $13 trillion. If bitcoin fully replaces gold, then that would imply a value of about $620,000 per bitcoin. Is there a good reason, however, to assume bitcoin fully replaces gold, and aren't there other stores of value that bitcoin could replace? These questions make it difficult to value bitcoin in this way. Some bitcoin proponents, however, still suggest that these extreme values are long-term price targets.

Another choice is to view bitcoin like a house. We could then estimate bitcoin value based on replacement cost. Under this approach, we could determine value based on the actual cost to mine a bitcoin. This approach, however, is circular. The bitcoin price also causes miners to enter and exit the market. Another approach is to treat bitcoin like a collectible (like a trading card or work of art). Under this approach, an asset only has as much value as someone is willing to pay for it. So, the value is really more emotional, and demand driven, rather than having any underlying foundation. Maybe this viewpoint is why Jamie Dimon, the CEO of JP Morgan, has said, "bitcoin is worthless." While he is correct that a bitcoin has no tangible value, couldn't the same be said for the $10 bill in your pocket?

As you can see, there is much uncertainty surrounding how to value cryptocurrency, whether it is a reasonable investment, and what are its long-term prospects. This uncertainty mirrors the volatility in cryptocurrency prices. For example, in 2020 bitcoin had a return of 302.8 percent. But, in 2018, the return was −72.8 percent. Given this volatility, crypto really isn't suitable for most investors, and particularly not as a large portion of a portfolio.

So, what conclusions might we make? If someone is going to invest in bitcoin, or an alternative cryptocurrency, it is most logical to treat it as an alternative investment. In this context, adding a small allocation can provide diversification due to its low correlations with traditional asset markets. Also, an investment in crypto can potentially enhance returns, but its volatility can also have a significant downside impact. Just like any other volatile, alternative asset, you want to hold enough to gain some benefit, but not so much to create too much asset-specific risk.

One additional challenge is custody. With stocks, your broker holds them for you. With currency, banks fulfill this role. But how do you actually "hold" a bitcoin? The answer is through a private key (i.e., password) that unlocks the bitcoin in the distributed ledger and allows you to transfer bitcoin to others. Unfortunately, if a person loses their key, the bitcoin is lost forever. So, holding the password in one file on a computer is risky—the computer could crash or be hacked. This risk is where bitcoin wallets come into play. Electronic bitcoin wallets store private keys and bitcoin information. But now bitcoin wallets need to be stored, adding another complexity. Bitcoin wallets can also be lost. In fact, a British man allegedly threw his private key for 7,500 bitcoins in the trash. These bitcoins were valued in the hundreds of millions of dollars. To this day, he is trying to get his city to scour the dump to find the digital wallet.

Moving forward, we expect tradeable securities (or trusts) like ETFs to become popular. One such example is Grayscale Bitcoin Trust (GBTC), which allows investors to buy and

FIGURE 17.4   Benefits and Risks of the Cryptocurrency Market

	Benefits	Risks
Cryptocurrency Investing	**Potential for appreciation** Some investors are attracted to the volatile price swings as a potential for profit. **Portfolio diversification** Some investors believe that if the lack of correlation with other asset classes continues, cryptocurrency could add diversification to a portfolio.	**Potential for financial loss** Cryptocurrency prices historically have been highly volatile, and fluctuations could result in significant financial losses regardless of whether you have direct or indirect exposure.
Direct Investing (spot market) Considerations	**Transaction transparency** The use of blockchain records transactions between parties in a verifiable and permanent way visible to all. **24/7 access** Unlike traditional exchange-traded products, cryptocurrency can be bought or sold at any time. **Control** With no ties to banks, regulators, or governmental policies, cryptocurrency theoretically provides user autonomy.	**Potential for fraud** <u>According to the Federal Trade Commission,</u> "Many people have reported being lured to websites that look like opportunities for investing in or mining cryptocurrencies, but are bogus." **Lack of recoverability** Cryptocurrency assets are accessed using a key that's not retrievable if lost. Similarly, if you lose access to the place where you store your key, you will effectively lose possession of your cryptocurrency.
Indirect Investing Considerations	**Regulation** The investment products offered at Schwab provide an element of regulation and consumer protections that spot trading lacks. **Recoverability** Access to conventional investment accounts can usually be recovered if your credentials are misplaced.	**High expenses for trusts and funds** Cryptocurrency trusts and mutual funds can involve high expenses, with fees exceeding 2% or more of the investment. **Leverage risk for futures** Cryptocurrency futures are leveraged products, meaning you could lose more than you initially invested.

Source: Schwab, www.schwab.com/cryptocurrency.

sell bitcoin much like an ETF. Unfortunately, the market isn't yet well developed, so such funds have a $50,000 minimum and 2 percent fee, both of which are high. Some brokers such as Robinhood are also starting to custody some cryptocurrencies. We expect more mainstream brokers to do the same as the market develops.

For a quick summary of our discussion, check out Figure 17.4, which is an overview from Schwab regarding some key benefits and risks of the cryptocurrency market.

CHECK THIS

17.6a Beyond serving as an investment, how does cryptocurrency add value to transaction markets?

17.6b What is a big risk with holding bitcoin on a digital wallet?

 17.7 Summary and Conclusions

1. **Understand the benefits and risks of alternative investments.**

A. Alternative investments might provide a higher return than traditional investments. Their main benefit, however, is how their returns can help further diversify a portfolio.

B. Risks include reduced pricing transparency, limited liquidity, and added tax complications. The most practical disadvantages, however, are the high costs and the potential requirement that investors must be classified as qualified, or accredited.

2. Identify the styles and structure of hedge funds and private equity funds.

A. Both hedge funds and private equity funds are structured as limited partnerships, with the manager serving as the general partner and investors serving as limited partners.

B. To compensate the general partners, a 2/20 fee structure is customary. This implies a 2 percent yearly management fee and a performance fee of 20 percent of the profits. The performance fee is controlled through provisions such as a high-water mark, hurdle rate, or clawback provision.

C. Hedge funds have their own unique investment styles, but common categories include market neutral, arbitrage, distressed, macro, short selling, and market timing. Funds of funds are also popular, as they provide diversification across investment styles, but at a steep cost.

D. Private equity funds purchase an ownership stake in private companies and bring expertise to the business. Venture capital is a type of private equity that concentrates on seed and early-stage financing.

3. Understand how commodities can be used within an investment portfolio.

A. Commodities as a whole have a low correlation to traditional markets. Thus, investment in commodities can add diversification benefits and act as a potential hedge against inflation.

B. Positions in commodities can be taken in the spot or futures markets. Investors can also use commodity ETFs, ETNs, or managed futures hedge funds.

C. Spot commodity transactions require direct storage costs, whereas futures contracts often have an indirect storage cost due to rollover. Futures market prices in contango contain these costs.

4. Identify the forms of investment and valuation alternatives for real estate.

A. Real estate can be purchased outright using 100 percent equity, or it can be purchased using leverage via a mortgage loan. Mortgage loans are often packaged and sold as mortgage-backed securities. The most common publicly traded real estate investment is a REIT, or real estate investment trust.

B. Methods to value real estate include using replacement cost, using comparable transactions, or calculating the present value of net operating income using the perpetuity formula.

GETTING DOWN TO BUSINESS

While alternative investments can be quite risky individually, they can be valuable additions to an investment portfolio. As we discussed, you can easily purchase assets such as commodities and real estate, particularly because exchange-traded funds (ETFs) and REITs are readily available. What about hedge funds and private equity funds, however, that require investors to be qualified? For most young investors, investing in hedge funds or private equity funds is likely just an investment goal. Do they have any investment options today?

Direct investment in these funds is not possible for investors who are not qualified. For private equity, however, one alternative is to consider Warren Buffett's company, Berkshire Hathaway. Berkshire Hathaway is similar to a private equity fund because it takes large ownership positions (often 100 percent) in companies. Some of these companies are private, while others are publicly traded and then are "taken private." Because Berkshire Hathaway is publicly traded, investors can easily buy shares in Berkshire Hathaway—just as they can with any other publicly traded equity. The underlying businesses held by Berkshire Hathaway, however, might provide some of the diversification benefits of private equity.

For the latest information on the real world of investments, visit us at jmdinvestments.blogspot.com.

Key Terms

accredited investor 569
backwardation 581
carried interest 575
clawback provision 575
committed capital 574
contango 581

high-water mark 570
hurdle rate 575
letter of intent (LOI) 576
net operating income (NOI) 585
private placement memorandum (PPM) 574

Related Bloomberg Functions

RICH	Bloomberg Billionaires Index, 17.1
ENDO	U.S. College Endowments, 17.1
HFND	Overview of Hedge Fund Solutions, 17.2
HFS	Hedge Fund Search, 17.2
MARB	M&A Arbitrage, 17.2
HFA	Historical Fund Analysis, 17.2
COMP	Comparative Returns, 17.2
FSTA	Fund Style Analysis, 17.2
PE	Private Equity Overview, 17.3
PEFR	Private Equity Fundraising Environment, 17.3
MA	Mergers and Acquisitions, 17.3
PEBM	Private Equity Return Analysis, 17.3
PFRV	Private Equity Fund Relative Value, 17.3
BCOM	Bloomberg Commodity Index, 17.4
MTL	Precious Metals Prices, 17.4
COMM	Commodity Product Catalog, 17.4
CTM	Exchange Contracts, 17.4
CFMX	Cash Future Matrix, 17.4
FXFA	FX-Interest Rate Arbitrage, 17.4
ETF	Exchange Traded Funds, 17.4
ETFL	ETF Implied Volatility, 17.4
REIT	Real Estate Investment Trusts, 17.5
CPRT	Real Estate Cap Rates, 17.5

Chapter Review Problems and Self-Test

1. **Private Equity Valuation (LO2, CFA4)**   FRS Capital Advisors, a private equity firm, is considering purchasing Tom's Auto, a private company. Tom's EBITDA is $4.1 million, and FRS has collected information on two similar transactions. Information on these comparable purchases follows:

Company	EBITDA	Valuation
Tiga's Auto Nation	$2.5 million	$14.50 million
Benicio's Imports	$5.4 million	$30.24 million

   What value should FRS assign to Tom's Auto?

2. **Spot-Futures Arbitrage (LO3, CFA6)**   Suppose silver is currently trading at $17 per troy ounce. You are evaluating a four-month carry trade opportunity using silver. The appropriate interest rate is 3 percent, and the carrying cost is $.55 per ounce per month. If the current market price of a four-month futures contract on silver is $21 per troy ounce, calculate the potential carry trade profit per ounce.

Answers to Self-Test

1. The EBITDA multiples for the comparable transactions are:

   Tiga's Auto Nation: $14.50/$2.5 = 5.8$ times

   Benicio's Imports: $30.24/$5.4 = 5.6$ times

   The average multiple is 5.7 times. Thus, an appropriate valuation for Tom's Auto would be $4.1 million $\times$ 5.7 = $23.37 million.

2. Using spot-futures parity, we can determine what the price of a futures contract should be:

$$F = (S + PVSC) \times (1 + r)^T$$

   The present value of the storage costs (*PVSC*) is:

$$PVSC = \frac{\$.55}{\left(1 + \frac{.03}{12}\right)} + \frac{\$.55}{\left(1 + \frac{.03}{12}\right)^2} + \frac{\$.55}{\left(1 + \frac{.03}{12}\right)^3} + \frac{\$.55}{\left(1 + \frac{.03}{12}\right)^4} = \$2.186$$

   Thus, $F = (\$17 + \$2.186) \times 1.03^{4/12} = \$19.38$

   Because the actual futures price of $21 is greater than $19.38, we can accomplish a carry trade. We will borrow $19.186, which will enable us to purchase silver in the spot market and pay the storage costs. We will simultaneously sell the futures contract at a settle price of $21. At expiration, we will deliver the silver to settle the futures contract and pay back our loan, which will net $21 − $19.38 = $1.62 per troy ounce.

Test Your Investment Quotient

1. **Risks of Alternative Investments (LO1, CFA1)** All of the following are limitations of alternative investments except:

   a. Low volatility.
   b. Limited liquidity.
   c. High costs.
   d. Limited transparency.

2. **Fee Limitations (LO1, CFA1)** All of the following prevent alternative investment managers from generating excessive performance fees except a:

   a. High-water mark provision.
   b. Clawback provision.
   c. Contango provision.
   d. Hurdle rate.

3. **Fee Structure (LO2, CFA1)** A hedge fund has a 2/20 fee structure. If the fund has $12 million of assets under management, what is the yearly management fee?

   a. $24,000
   b. $240,000
   c. $1,320,000
   d. $2,400,000

4. **Performance Comparison (LO2, CFA7)** You are attempting to compare the performance of a particular hedge fund to a reported composite benchmark. If there is a survivorship bias in the composite benchmark, its return is:

   a. Understated.
   b. Overstated.
   c. Accurate.
   d. None of the above.

5. **Investment Styles (LO2, CFA1)** Which of the following is not a common investing style of hedge funds?

   a. Market neutral
   b. Short selling
   c. Market timing
   d. Buy and hold

6. **Venture Capital (LO2, CFA1)** A venture capital fund will typically invest in which stage of a business's development?

   a. Early stage
   b. Middle stage
   c. Late stage
   d. None of the above

7. **Raising Money (LO2, CFA4)** A private placement memorandum (PPM) will typically address all of the following items except:

   a. Planned acquisitions.
   b. The fund's anticipated life.
   c. The fund's target size.
   d. Leverage limits.

8. **Private Equity Process (LO2, CFA4)** Which of the following choices correctly identifies the order of steps that a private equity firm goes through in its investing process?

   a. Deal flow, valuation, deal structure, value creation, exit
   b. Deal flow, deal structure, value creation, valuation, exit
   c. Deal structure, deal flow, valuation, value creation, exit
   d. Value creation, deal flow, valuation, deal structure, exit

9. **Commodity Futures (LO3, CFA5)** A commodity ETF that uses futures contracts to mimic the return of an underlying commodity will experience a roll yield if the market is in:

   a. Contango.
   b. Convexity.
   c. Backwardation.
   d. Parity.

10. **ETN vs. ETF (LO3, CFA1)** Which of the following choices is a distinguishing characteristic of a commodity-based ETN, as compared to an ETF?

   a. An ETN typically holds spot positions.
   b. An ETF is taxed like a partnership.
   c. An ETN is a debt instrument.
   d. An ETF will often experience roll yield.

11. **Hedge Fund Styles (LO3, CFA6)** A style of hedge fund that primarily invests in commodity-related securities is:

   a. Distressed security.
   b. M&A arbitrage.
   c. Short selling.
   d. Managed futures.

12. **Real Estate Investment Styles (LO4, CFA3)** A form of real estate investment that typically involves a fund manager issuing ownership shares that are publicly traded on the stock market is called a:

   a. REIT.
   b. CREF.
   c. TIAA.
   d. PVSC.

13. **Cryptocurrency (CFA2)** Which of the following is not a risk of investing in cryptocurrency?

   a. Losing the digital wallet on which the cryptocurrency is stored
   b. Higher volatility that traditional assets
   c. Uncertainty in determining underlying value
   d. All of the above are risks of investing in cryptocurrency.

14. **Real Estate Valuation (LO4, CFA3)** Which of the following real estate valuation approaches finds the present value of a perpetuity of a property's net operating income (NOI)?

   a. Cost approach
   b. Sales comparison
   c. Income approach
   d. Net margin approach

15. **Real Estate Valuation (LO4, CFA3)** You have identified a rental property that you would like to purchase. If your cap rate is 12 percent and you estimate the property's NOI to be $190,000, what is the maximum price you would pay?

   a. $22,800
   b. $190,000
   c. $1.58 million
   d. $15.8 million

Concept Questions

1. **Benefits of Alternative Investments (LO1, CFA1)** In isolation, alternative investments are extremely volatile. So, why might even a moderately conservative investor consider these investments for her portfolio?

2. **Accredited Investors (LO1, CFA1)** Define what is meant by an "accredited" investor. Why do you think the federal government limits some investments to only these investors?

3. **Performance Comparison (LO2, CFA7)** Discuss why evaluating the performance of hedge funds and private equity funds is difficult.

4. **Fee Limitations (LO2, CFA1)** Briefly explain how a high-water mark prevents hedge fund managers from manipulating their performance fee.

5. **Funds of Funds (LO2, CFA1)** What are the advantages and disadvantages of a funds of funds approach to investing in hedge funds?

6. **Fee Limitations (LO2, CFA4)** Briefly explain why investors in private equity funds will often demand a clawback provision with respect to carried interest.

7. **Security Types (LO2, CFA4)** Why do venture capital funds often use convertible preferred stock in their investments?

8. **Futures Contract Pricing (LO3, CFA1)** Define contango in futures markets and discuss how it creates a potential roll cost.

9. **Commodity Investments (LO3, CFA1)** Describe the relative disadvantages of spot positions versus futures contracts for investing in commodities.

10. **ETNs vs. ETFs (LO3, CFA1)** What are the disadvantages of investing in exchange-traded notes (ETNs) as compared to exchange-traded funds (ETFs)?

11. **Cryptocurrency (CFA2)** What are the benefits of blockchain technology?

12. **Cryptocurrency (CFA2)** What are the risks of investing in cryptocurrency?

Questions and Problems

Core Questions

1. **Performance Fee (LO2, CFA1)** High Rollers Hedge Fund has a standard 20 percent performance fee. If High Rollers were able to raise $10 million and generate a 25 percent return in its first year of operation, what would be the dollar amount of its performance fee?

2. **Arbitrage (LO2, CFA1)** Arm Technologies has offered to purchase Hammer Group by exchanging one share of Arm for three shares of Hammer. Arm is currently trading at $50 per share and Hammer is currently selling for $15 per share. What is the potential arbitrage profit per share of Arm Technologies?

3. **Performance Fee (LO2, CFA4)** Private Partner Ventures is a private equity fund that just formed a new $1 billion fund. It recently made its first capital call for $300 million. If it uses a standard 2/20 fee structure, what is its management fee in the first year?

4. **Performance Fee (LO2, CFA4)** Assume Cambridge Ventures raises $10,000,000 for a private equity fund with a one-year life. The fund has a hurdle rate of 6 percent, above which it earns a carried interest of 20 percent. If Cambridge generates a return of 18 percent, what is the firm's carried interest for the year?

5. **Private Equity Valuation (LO2, CFA4)** A company with an EBITDA of $2.9 million was recently acquired for $18.6 million. What is the valuation multiple implied in this price?

6. **Futures Margin (LO3, CFA1)**   You have decided to use futures contracts to invest in silver at a settle price of $15 per ounce. Each futures contract has a standard size of 5,000 troy ounces and an initial margin requirement of $4,500. If you purchase 25 contracts, what is the total margin (in dollars) you will need to provide?

7. **Leverage Factor (LO3, CFA1)**   Given the information in the previous problem, what is the leverage factor associated with these contracts. If silver rises to $17 per ounce, what is your total percentage return?

8. **Spot-Futures Parity (LO3, CFA5)**   Assume the spot price of wheat is $3.17 per bushel. The appropriate interest rate is 3 percent, and there are no storage costs. Under spot-futures parity, calculate the price for a six-month wheat futures contract?

9. **Real Estate Valuation (LO4, CFA3)**   A potential investment property has an NOI of $425,000 and a capitalization rate of 15 percent. Using the income approach, calculate the value of this investment property.

10. **Real Estate Valuation (LO4, CFA3)**   A real estate investment company just bought an office building. The company estimates that the building will generate $945,000 in net operating income annually. If the building was purchased for $5.25 million, what is the implied capitalization rate?

Intermediate Questions

11. **Performance Fee (LO2, CFA1)**   A hedge fund with $25 million of assets under management has a standard 2/20 fee structure and earns 14 percent this year. Assume that management fees are paid at the beginning of each year and performance fees are paid at the end of each year. Assume that the fund's fee structure also contains a high-water mark provision.

    a. What is the management fee collected by the fund managers?
    b. What is the performance fee collected by the fund managers?
    c. What is the investor's net return?

12. **Performance Fee (LO2, CFA6)**   Two years ago, you invested $750,000 with a market-neutral hedge fund manager. The fee structure is 2/20, and the fund has a high-water mark provision. Suppose the first year the fund manager lost 10 percent, and the second year she gained 20 percent. Assume management fees are paid at the beginning of each year and performance fees are paid at the end of each year. Under the terms of the high-water mark provision:

    a. What are the management and performance fees paid in Year 1?
    b. What are the management and performance fees paid in Year 2?

13. **Private Equity Valuation (LO2, CFA4)**   Robbin Partners, a private equity fund, has identified Nest Corp. as a potential acquisition target. Nest has an EBITDA of $28 million. Robbin knows that these similar deals have recently closed:

Company	EBITDA	Valuation
Shell Technologies	$20 million	$ 96 million
Layer Company	$36 million	$165.6 million
Case Partners	$30 million	$ 150 million

Based on the above transactions:

    a. What is the average price multiple?
    b. Using the valuation multiple from part (a), what is the estimated value of Nest Corp.?

14. **Venture Capital Pricing (LO2, CFA4)**   Vista Venture Partners is considering an investment in a start-up firm that has developed a new technology for streaming data. If the venture is successful, Vista estimates it will be able to grow the business to an exit value of $380 million in five years. Vista has agreed to an initial investment of $12 million to fund the early-stage development. If Vista has a 45 percent required return, what ownership percentage will it demand in exchange for its investment?

15. **Leverage Factor (LO3, CFA1)**   You have decided to purchase 25 oil futures contracts at a settle price of $55 per barrel. Each futures contract has a standard size of 1,000 barrels and an initial margin requirement of $5,500.

    a. What is the leverage factor associated with these contracts?
    b. If oil rises to $56.25 per barrel, what is the total percentage return on your futures position?
    c. What is the total percentage return on your futures position if oil falls to $54 per barrel?

16. **Real Estate Valuation (LO4, CFA3)** Sky High Partners is evaluating a high-rise office building to add to its investment portfolio. To calculate a value, Sky High plans to use the income approach, based on the following estimates:

Gross potential yearly rental income	$894,000
Estimated vacancy rate	3.5%
Yearly operating costs	$426,000
Market capitalization rate	16%

    a. Compute the net operating income (NOI) for the building.
    b. Using the income approach, calculate the value for the office building.

17. **Real Estate Valuation (LO4, CFA3)** Using price data from several recent housing transactions in a particular area, Polaris Real Estate Group has identified the main characteristics that affect prices. The estimated value impact of each characteristic, as well as a standard base price, is as follows:

Characteristic	Units	Impact
Base price		$125,000
Living area	Square feet	$35/square foot
Number of bathrooms	Number	$8,000/bathroom
Age of home	Years	−$6,000/year

Using the above values, estimate a price for a five-year-old home that has a living area of 1,500 square feet and two bathrooms.

18. **Real Estate Valuation (LO4, CFA3)** Centerland Partners has collected information on the recent purchases of three small shopping centers. Centerland is considering the purchase of a similar property with an NOI of $3.1 million.

Shopping Center	NOI	Valuation
Castleton Round	$2.2 million	$13.75 million
Fashion Commons	$3.6 million	$22.22 million
Belden Square	$2.7 million	$16.46 million

    a. What is the market capitalization rate?
    b. What valuation should Centerland assign to the target property?

Spreadsheet Problems

19. **Spot-Futures Arbitrage (LO3, CFA5)** Suppose unleaded gasoline is currently trading at $3 per gallon. You face an interest rate of 4 percent and a carrying cost of $.07 per gallon per month. The current market price of a four-month futures contract on gasoline is $3.50 per gallon. You are evaluating a three-month carry trade opportunity.

    a. Determine the present value of the storage costs (*PVSC*).
    b. Identify what the futures price should be under spot-futures parity.
    c. Explain the trades necessary to conduct the carry trade and calculate the potential profit per gallon.

20. **Spot-Futures Arbitrage (LO3, CFA5)** Given the information in the previous problem, how would the trade change if instead the futures price for gasoline were $2.95 per gallon?

CFA Exam Review by Kaplan Schweser

(CFA6, CFA7)
Suzanne Harlan has a large, well-diversified stock and bond portfolio. She wants to try some alternative investments, such as hedge funds, and has contacted Lawrence Phillips, CFA, to help her assemble a new portfolio.

Before agreeing to make recommendations for Ms. Harlan, Phillips wants to determine whether she is a good candidate for alternative investments. He gives her a standard questionnaire. Here are some of her comments:

- I'm interested in high returns. I'm not afraid of risk, and I'm investing money for the benefit of my heirs.

- I pay a lot of attention to expense and return data from my investments, and track their performance closely.

- Investors have told me that it is difficult to assess the quality of hedge funds, so I'm interested in purchasing a fund of funds so that I can diversify my risk while potentially sharing in some outsized returns.

- I pay several million dollars in taxes every year, and I want any additional investments to be tax-friendly.

- My neighbors founded Kelly Tool and Die 20 years ago. They are declaring bankruptcy, and I am interested in obtaining a partial interest in the business.

- It is imperative that the returns of any investments you recommend must be in some way comparable to a benchmark.

Mr. Phillips is not excited about the idea of acquiring an interest in the business, and does not, in general, recommend funds of funds. He does know, however, several managers of individual hedge funds. Mr. Phillips steers Ms. Harlan to the Stillman Fund, which concentrates on spin-offs. Its strategy is to buy the spun-off company and short the parent company.

1. In an attempt to persuade Ms. Harlan away from investing in a fund of funds, Mr. Phillips addressed the advantages of investing in individual funds. Which of the following would be his most compelling argument?

   a. The lower expenses of individual funds
   b. The likelihood of style drift in a fund of funds
   c. The lack of a benchmark for a fund of funds

2. What investment approach would be consistent with Ms. Harlan's tolerance for risk?

   a. Distressed security
   b. Arbitrage
   c. Market neutral

3. Which of Ms. Harlan's responses is most likely to make Mr. Philips consider her a bad candidate for investing in hedge funds?

   a. I pay a lot of attention to expense and return data from my investments and track their performance closely.
   b. I pay several million dollars in taxes every year, and I want any additional investments to be tax-friendly.
   c. I'm interested in high returns. I'm not afraid of risk, and I'm investing money for the benefit of my heirs.

4. If Ms. Harlan is truly concerned about benchmarks, she should avoid which of her suggested investments?

   a. None of them
   b. Kelly Tool and Die
   c. Hedge funds

Bloomberg Exercises

1. Check to see if your college is on the list of the largest endowments. (**ENDO**)
2. Review the homepage for hedge funds in Bloomberg. (**HFND**)
3. Identify upcoming mergers and acquisitions. (**MA**)
4. Review the cap rate for different types of real estate investments over time. (**CPRT**)

What's on the Web?

1. **Futures Exchange** The primary website for information on futures markets in the United States is www.cmegroup.com. Visit this site and examine the prices of some commodities. Take a specific look at corn futures and determine if the market is in contango or in backwardation.

2. **Real Estate Investment Trusts** Visit www.reit.com and use the REIT market data section to identify which sectors have had the best recent performance.

Corporate and Government Bonds

"Creditors have better memories than debtors."

—Benjamin Franklin

Learning Objectives

Conform to your fixed-income knowledge covenants by learning:

1. The basic types of corporate bonds.

2. How callable and convertible bonds function.

3. The different types of government bonds.

4. The basics of bond ratings.

Corporations and governments issue bonds intending to meet all obligations of interest and repayment of principal. Investors buy bonds believing that the corporation or government intends to fulfill its debt obligation in a timely manner. Although defaults can and do occur, the market for bonds exists only because borrowers are able to convince investors of their original intent to avoid default. Reaching this state of trust is not easy—it normally requires elaborate contractual arrangements.

Almost all corporations issue notes and bonds to raise money to finance investment projects. Indeed, for many corporations, the value of notes and bonds outstanding can exceed the value of common stock shares outstanding. Nevertheless, many investors do not think of corporate bonds when they think about investing. Most investors, however, are well aware that sovereign governments, particularly the U.S. federal government, issue substantial amounts of debt. Investors might not immediately think about the corporate bond market because the largest and most important debt market is that for debt issued by the U.S. government. This market is truly global because a large share of federal debt is sold to foreign investors. As a result, the U.S. government debt market sets the tone for debt markets around the world. In this chapter, we examine securities issued by corporations, as well as by federal, state, and local governments. These securities represent a combined value of many trillions of dollars.

CFA™ Exam Topics in This Chapter:

1. Fixed-income securities: Defining elements (L1, S13)
2. Fixed-income markets: Issuance, trading, and funding (L1, S13)
3. Understanding fixed-income risk and return (L1, S14)
4. Fundamentals of credit analysis (L1, S14)
5. Valuation and analysis of bonds with embedded options (L2, S12)

Go to Connect for a guide that aligns your textbook with CFA readings.

18.1 Corporate Bond Basics

Related Bloomberg Functions

SRCH Fixed Income Search

FIW Fixed Income Worksheet

DDIS Debt Distribution

For more information on corporate bonds, visit www.investinginbonds.com.

Corporate bonds represent the debt of a corporation owed to its bondholders. More specifically, a corporate bond is a security issued by a corporation that represents a promise to pay to its bondholders a fixed sum of money at a future maturity date, along with periodic payments of interest. The fixed sum paid at maturity is the bond's *principal,* also called its *par* or *face value.* The periodic interest payments are called *coupons.*

From an investor's point of view, corporate bonds represent an investment distinct from common stock. The three most fundamental differences are:

1. Common stock represents an ownership claim on the corporation, whereas bonds represent a creditor's claim on the corporation.

2. Promised cash flows—that is, coupons and principal—to be paid to bondholders are stated in advance when the bond is issued. By contrast, the amount and timing of dividends paid to common stockholders may change at any time.

3. Most corporate bonds are issued as callable bonds, which means that the bond issuer has the right to buy back outstanding bonds before the maturity date of the bond issue. When a bond issue is called, coupon payments stop and the bondholders are forced to surrender their bonds to the issuer in exchange for the cash payment of a specified call price. By contrast, common stock is almost never callable.

The corporate bond market is large, with several trillion dollars of corporate bonds outstanding in the United States. The sheer size of the corporate bond market prompts an important inquiry: Who owns corporate bonds and why? The answer is that most corporate bond investors belong to only a few distinct categories. The single largest group of corporate bond investors is life insurance companies, which hold about 20 percent of all outstanding corporate bonds. Remaining ownership is spread among individual investors, pension funds, banks, and foreign investors.

The pattern of corporate bond ownership is largely explained by the fact that corporate bonds provide a source of predictable cash flows. While individual bonds occasionally default on their promised cash payments, large institutional investors can diversify away most default risk by including a large number of different bond issues in their portfolios. Thus, life insurance companies and pension funds find that corporate bonds are a natural investment vehicle to provide for future payments of retirement and death benefits because both the timing and amount of these benefit payments can be matched with bond cash flows. These institutions can eliminate much of their financial risk by matching the timing of cash flows received from a bond portfolio to the timing of cash flows needed to make benefit payments—a strategy called *cash flow matching.* For this reason, life insurance companies and pension funds together own more than half of all outstanding corporate bonds. For similar reasons, individual investors might own corporate bonds as a source of steady cash income. However, since individual investors cannot easily diversify default risk, they should normally invest only in bonds with higher credit quality or in a bond mutual fund.

Every corporate bond issue has a specific set of issue terms associated with it. The issue terms associated with any particular bond can range from a relatively simple arrangement, where the bond is little more than an IOU of the corporation, to a complex contract specifying in great detail what the issuer can and cannot do with respect to its obligations to bondholders. Bonds issued with a standard, relatively simple set of features are popularly called **plain vanilla bonds** or "bullet" bonds.

plain vanilla bonds
Bonds issued with a relatively standard set of features. Also known as *bullet bonds.*

As an illustration of a plain vanilla corporate debt issue, Table 18.1 summarizes the issue terms for a note issue by Jack Russell Corp. Referring to Table 18.1, we see that the Jack Russell Corp. notes were issued in December 2021 and mature five years later in December 2026. Each individual note has a face value denomination of $1,000. Because the total issue amount is $20 million, the entire issue contains 20,000 notes. Each note pays a $100 annual coupon, which is equal to 10 percent of its face value. The annual coupon is split between two semiannual $50 payments made each June and December. Based on the original offer price of 100, which means 100 percent of the $1,000 face value, the notes have a yield to maturity

TABLE 18.1

Jack Russell Corp. Five-Year Note Issue

Issue amount	$20 million	Note issue total face value is $20 million
Issue date	12/15/2021	Notes offered to the public in December 2021
Maturity date	12/31/2026	Remaining principal due December 31, 2026
Face value	$1,000	Face value denomination is $1,000 per note
Coupon interest	$100 per annum	Annual coupons are $100 per note
Coupon dates	6/30, 12/31	Coupons are paid semiannually
Offering price	100	Offer price is 100 percent of face value
Yield to maturity	10%	Based on stated offer price
Call provision	Not callable	Notes may not be paid off before maturity
Security	None	Notes are unsecured
Rating	Not rated	Privately placed note issue

of 10 percent. The notes are not callable, which means that the debt may not be paid off before maturity.

unsecured debt
Bonds, notes, or other debt issued with no specific collateral pledged as security for the bond issue. Also called *debentures*.

The Jack Russell Corp. notes are **unsecured debt,** which means that no specific collateral has been pledged as security for the notes. Unsecured debt is often referred to as *debentures*. In the event that the issuer defaults on its promised payments, the note holders may take legal action to acquire sufficient assets of the company to settle their claims as creditors. They might, however, have to share this claim with other creditors who have an equal legal claim or yield to creditors with a higher legal claim.

When issued, the Jack Russell Corp. notes were not reviewed by a rating agency like Moody's or Standard & Poor's. Thus, the notes are unrated. If the notes were to be assigned a credit rating, they would probably be rated as "junk grade." The term "junk," commonly used for high-risk debt issues, is unduly pejorative. After all, the company must repay the debt. If the company is in a high-risk industry, however, the probability is high that the company might have difficulty paying off the debt in a timely manner.

Reflecting their below-average credit quality, the Jack Russell Corp. notes were not issued to the general public. Instead, the notes were privately placed with two insurance companies. Such private placements are common among relatively small debt issues. Private placements will be discussed in greater detail later in this chapter.

CHECK THIS

18.1a   What are the fundamental differences between corporate bonds and stock?

18.1b   Why do corporate bonds represent an attractive investment for insurance companies?

18.2 Corporate Bond Indentures

Related Bloomberg Functions

CAST   Capital Structure

NI EQL   Equity-Linked Securities

OVCV   Convertible Valuation

CSCH   Convertible Search

CVM   Convertible Table

A bond indenture is a formal written agreement between the corporation and the bondholders. It is an important legal document that spells out in detail the mutual rights and obligations of the corporation and the bondholders with respect to the bond issue. Indenture contracts are often quite long, sometimes several hundred pages, and make for very tedious reading. In fact, very few bond investors ever read the original indenture, but instead might refer to an **indenture summary** provided in the **prospectus** that was circulated when the bond issue was originally sold to the public. Alternatively, a summary of the most important features of an indenture is published by debt rating agencies.

The Trust Indenture Act of 1939 requires that any bond issue subject to regulation by the Securities and Exchange Commission (SEC), which includes most corporate bond and note issues sold to the general public, must have a trustee appointed to represent the interests of the bondholders. Also, all responsibilities of a duly appointed trustee must be specified in detail in the indenture. Some corporations maintain a blanket or open-ended indenture that applies to all currently outstanding bonds and any new bonds that are issued, while other corporations write a new indenture contract for each new bond issue sold to the public.

The Trust Indenture Act of 1939 does not require an indenture when a bond issue is not sold to the general public. For example, the bonds might be sold only to one or more financial institutions in what is called a **private placement.** Private placements are exempt from registration requirements with the SEC. Nevertheless, even privately placed debt issues often have a formal indenture contract. Next, we present some of the most important provisions frequently specified in a bond indenture agreement.

BOND SENIORITY PROVISIONS

A corporation may have several different bond issues outstanding; these issues normally can be differentiated according to the seniority of their claims on the firm's assets. Seniority usually is specified in the indenture contract.

Consider a corporation with two outstanding bond issues: (1) a mortgage bond issue with certain real estate assets pledged as security and (2) a debenture bond issue with no specific assets pledged as security. In this case, the mortgage bond issue has a senior claim on the pledged assets but no specific claim on other corporate assets. The debenture bond has a claim on all corporate assets not specifically pledged as security for the mortgage bond, but it would have only a residual claim on assets pledged as security for the mortgage bond issue. This residual claim would apply only after all obligations to the mortgage bondholders have been satisfied.

As another example, suppose a corporation has two outstanding debenture issues. In this case, seniority is normally assigned to the bonds first issued by the corporation. The bonds issued earliest have a senior claim on the pledged assets and are called **senior debentures.** The bonds issued later have a junior or subordinate claim and are called **subordinated debentures.**

The seniority of an existing debt issue is usually protected by a **negative pledge clause** in the bond indenture. A negative pledge clause prohibits a new issue of debt with seniority over a currently outstanding issue. However, it may allow a new debt issue to share equally in the seniority of an existing issue. A negative pledge clause is part of the indenture agreement of most senior debenture bonds.

CALL PROVISIONS

Most corporate bond issues have a call provision allowing the issuer to buy back all or part of its outstanding bonds at a specified call price sometime before the bonds mature. The most frequent motive for a corporation to call outstanding bonds is to take advantage of a general fall in market interest rates. Lower interest rates allow the corporation to replace currently outstanding high-coupon bonds with a new issue of bonds paying lower coupons. Replacing existing bonds with new bonds is called **bond refunding.**

TRADITIONAL FIXED-PRICE CALL PROVISIONS There are two major types of call provisions, *traditional fixed-price* and *make-whole.* From an investor's point of view, a fixed-price call provision has a distinct disadvantage. For example, suppose an investor is currently holding bonds paying 10 percent coupons. Further suppose that, after a fall in market interest rates, the corporation is able to issue new bonds that only pay 8 percent coupons. By calling existing 10 percent coupon bonds, the issuer forces bondholders to surrender their bonds in exchange for the fixed call price, which happens at a time when the bondholders can reinvest funds only at lower interest rates. If instead the bonds were noncallable, the bondholders would continue to receive the original 10 percent coupons.

For this reason, callable bonds are less attractive to investors than noncallable bonds. Consequently, a callable bond will sell at a lower price (or, equivalently, a higher yield) than a comparable noncallable bond. Despite their lower prices, corporations generally prefer to issue fixed-price callable bonds. However, to reduce the price gap between callable and noncallable bonds, issuers typically allow the indenture contract to specify certain restrictions on their ability to call an outstanding bond issue. Three features are commonly used to restrict an issuer's call privilege:

1. Callable bonds usually have a *deferred call provision* that provides a *call protection period* during which a bond issue cannot be called. For example, a bond may be call-protected for a period of five years after its issue date.

2. A call price often includes a *call premium* over par value. A standard arrangement stipulates a call premium equal to one year's coupon payments for a call occurring at the earliest possible call date. Over time, the call premium is gradually reduced until it is eliminated entirely. After some future date, the bonds become callable at par value.

3. Some indentures specifically prohibit an issuer from calling outstanding bonds for the purpose of refunding at a lower coupon rate but still allow a call for other reasons. This *refunding provision* prevents the corporation from calling an outstanding bond issue solely as a response to falling market interest rates. However, the corporation can still pay off its bond debt ahead of schedule by using funds acquired from, say, earnings, or funds obtained from the sale of newly issued common stock.

After a bond's call protection period has elapsed, a rational investor would be unwilling to pay much more than the call price for the bond because the issuer might call the bond at any time and pay only the call price for the bond. Consequently, a bond's call price serves as an effective ceiling on its market price. It is important for bond investors to understand how the existence of a price ceiling for callable bonds alters the standard price-yield relationship for bonds. Recall our discussion of yield to call versus yield to maturity in a previous chapter.

The relationship between interest rates and prices for comparable callable and noncallable bonds is illustrated in Figure 18.1. In this example, the vertical axis measures bond prices and the horizontal axis measures bond yields. In this two-bond example, both bonds pay the same coupon and are alike in all respects except that one of the bonds is callable any time at par value.

As shown in Figure 18.1, the noncallable bond has the standard *convex price-yield relationship,* where the price-yield curve is bowed toward the origin. When the price-yield curve is bowed to the origin, this is called *positive convexity.* In contrast, the fixed-price callable bond has a convex or bowed price-yield relationship in the region of high yields, but it is bowed away from the origin in the region of low yields. This is called *negative convexity.* The important lesson here is that no matter how low market interest rates might fall, the maximum price of an unprotected fixed-price callable bond is generally bounded above by its call price.

| **FIGURE 18.1** | **Noncallable Bonds and Fixed-Price Callable Bonds** |

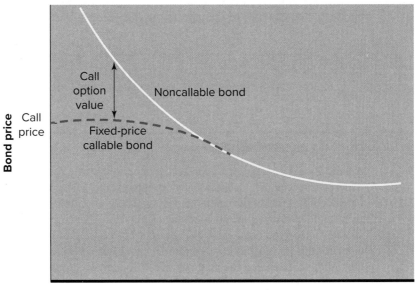

Yield to maturity

CHECK THIS

18.2a What is the purpose of bond seniority provisions?

18.2b After a call protection period has elapsed, why is the call price an effective ceiling on the market price of a callable bond with a fixed-price call provision?

MAKE-WHOLE CALL PROVISION In just the last few years, a new type of call provision, a "make-whole" call, has become common in the corporate bond market. If a callable bond has a make-whole call provision, bondholders receive approximately what the bond is worth if the bond is called. This call provision gets its name because the bondholder does not suffer a loss in the event of a call; that is, the bondholder is "made whole" when the bond is called.

Like a fixed-price call provision, a make-whole call provision allows the borrower to pay off the remaining debt early. Unlike a fixed-price call provision, however, a make-whole call provision requires the borrower to make a lump-sum payment representing the present value of all payments that will not be made because of the call. The discount rate used to calculate the present value is usually equal to the yield on a comparable-maturity U.S. Treasury security plus a fixed, predetermined *make-whole premium*.

Because the yield of a comparable U.S. Treasury security changes over time, the call price paid to bondholders changes over time. As interest rates decrease, the make-whole call price increases because the discount rate used to calculate the present value decreases. As interest rates increase, the make-whole call price decreases. In addition, make-whole call provisions typically specify that the minimum amount received by a bondholder is the par value of the bond.

As interest rates decline, even in the region of low yields, the price of bonds with a make-whole call provision will increase. That is, these bonds exhibit the standard convex price-yield relationship in all yield regions. In contrast, recall that bond prices with a fixed-price call provision exhibit negative convexity in the region of low yields.

CALLABLE BONDS AND DURATION In an earlier chapter, we discussed the concept of the duration of a bond. Recall that duration is a weighted average measure of when cash flows are received. We use duration to estimate how sensitive bond prices are to changes in interest rates.

To determine the duration of plain vanilla bonds, either the Macaulay or the modified duration measure we discussed in another chapter is appropriate. For bonds with embedded options, such as callable bonds, these standard duration measures will not correctly estimate the price and interest rate relationship. For callable bonds, we must calculate the *effective* duration of the bond. We can also use effective duration to estimate how sensitive bond prices are to changes in interest rates. When we calculate effective duration, however, we use option pricing methods to account for the embedded option to call the bond.

CHECK THIS

18.2c Suppose you hold a bond with a make-whole call provision. The coupon rate on this bond is 5.90 percent. At what yield to maturity will this bond sell for par?

PUT PROVISIONS

A bond issue with a put provision grants bondholders the right to sell their bonds back to the issuer at a special *put price,* normally set at par value. These so-called **put bonds** are "putable" on each of a series of designated *put dates.* These are often scheduled to occur annually, but they sometimes occur at more frequent intervals. At each put date, the bondholder decides whether to sell the bond back to the issuer or continue to hold the bond until the next put date. For this reason, put bonds are often called *extendible bonds* because the bondholder has the option of extending the maturity of the bond at each put date.

Notice that by granting bondholders an option to sell their bonds back to the corporation at par value, the put feature provides an effective floor on the market price of the bond.

put bonds
Bonds that can be sold back to the issuer at a prespecified price on any of a sequence of prespecified dates. Also called *extendible bonds.*

EXAMPLE 18.1

Calculating the Make-Whole Call Premium

Assume that LKD Energy, Inc., sold a total of $1.25 billion worth of notes and bonds, and the first tranche issue of $300 million in notes has the following terms:

Settlement date:	7/16/2021
First payment:	2/1/2022
Maturity:	8/1/2026
Coupon:	5.90%
Price:	99.864
Yield:	5.931%
Spread:	90 basis points above U.S. Treasury notes
Make-whole call:	15 basis points above U.S. Treasury notes
Ratings:	Baa2 (Moody's); BBB (S&P)

If these notes were called immediately, what price would LKD Energy have to pay to these note holders? To calculate the make-whole call premium of these notes, we need to add 15 basis points to the yield of comparable-maturity U.S. Treasury notes.

We find the yield of comparable-maturity U.S. Treasury notes by subtracting the 90 basis point spread from the yield of the LKD notes, 5.931% − .90% = 5.031%. Then we add the 15 basis point make-whole premium: 5.031% + .15% = 5.181%. Discounting the remaining cash flows of the note at 5.181 percent, we get a make-whole call price of about $103.15—which is about $3.29 more than the current price of the notes ($99.864). You must remember to use the standard bond pricing formula to discount these cash flows.

You can verify this price using Excel. Using the information above, enter =PRICE("7/16/2021", "8/1/2026", .059, .05181, 100, 2) into an Excel cell and you will get a price of $103.15.

Thus, the put feature offers protection to bondholders from rising interest rates and the associated fall in bond prices.

A put feature also helps protect bondholders from acts of the corporation that might cause a deterioration of the bond's credit quality. However, this protection is not granted without a cost to bond investors because a putable bond will command a higher market price (and thus a lower yield) than a comparable nonputable bond.

CHECK THIS

18.2d Using Figure 18.1 as a guide, what would the price-yield relationship look like for a noncallable bond putable at par value?

18.2e Under what conditions would a put feature not yield an effective floor for the market price of a put bond? (*Hint:* Think about default risk.)

BOND-TO-STOCK CONVERSION PROVISIONS

convertible bonds
Bonds that holders can exchange for common stock according to a prespecified conversion ratio.

Some bonds have a valuable bond-to-stock conversion feature. These bonds are called convertible bonds. **Convertible bonds** grant bondholders the right to exchange each bond for a designated number of common stock shares of the issuing firm. To avoid confusion in a discussion of convertible bonds, it is important to understand some basic terminology.

1. The number of common stock shares acquired in exchange for each converted bond is called the *conversion ratio:*

   Conversion ratio = Number of stock shares acquired by conversion

2. The par value of a convertible bond divided by its conversion ratio is called the bond's *conversion price:*

$$\text{Conversion price} = \frac{\text{Bond par value}}{\text{Conversion ratio}}$$

3. The market price per share of common stock acquired by conversion times the bond's conversion ratio is called the bond's *conversion value:*

$$\text{Conversion value} = \text{Price per share of stock} \times \text{Conversion ratio}$$

For example, suppose a convertible bond with a par value of $1,000 can be converted into 20 shares of the issuing firm's common stock. In this case, the conversion price is $1,000/20 = $50. Continuing this example, suppose the firm's common stock has a market price of $40 per share; then the conversion value of a single bond is 20 × $40 = $800.

From an investor's perspective, the conversion privilege of convertible bonds has the distinct advantage that bondholders can receive a share of any increase in common stock value. However, the conversion option has a price. A corporation can sell par value convertible bonds with a coupon rate substantially less than the coupon rate of comparable nonconvertible bonds. This forgone coupon interest represents the price of the bond's conversion option.

When convertible bonds are originally issued, their conversion ratio is customarily set to yield a conversion value of 10 percent to 20 percent less than par value. For example, suppose the common stock of a company has a price of $30 per share and the company issues convertible bonds with a par value of $1,000 per bond. To set the original conversion value at $900 per bond, the company would set a conversion ratio of 30 stock shares per bond. Thereafter, the conversion ratio is fixed, but each bond's conversion value becomes linked to the firm's stock price, which may rise or fall in value. The price of a convertible bond reflects the conversion value of the bond. In general, the higher the conversion value, the higher the bond price, and vice versa.

Investing in convertible bonds is more complicated than owning nonconvertible bonds because the conversion privilege presents convertible bondholders with an important timing decision. When is the best time to exercise a bond's conversion option and exchange the bond for shares of common stock? The answer is that investors should normally postpone conversion as long as possible because while they hold the bonds, they continue to receive coupon payments. After converting to common stock, they lose all subsequent coupons. In general, unless the total dividend payments on stock acquired by conversion are somewhat greater than the forgone bond coupon payments, investors should hold on to their convertible bonds to continue to receive coupon payments.

The rational decision of convertible bondholders to postpone conversion as long as possible is limited, however, because convertible bonds are almost always callable. Firms customarily call outstanding convertible bonds when their conversion value has risen by 10 percent to 15 percent above bond par value, although there are many exceptions to this rule. When a convertible bond issue is called by the issuer, bondholders are forced to make an immediate decision whether to convert to common stock shares or accept a cash payment of the call price. Fortunately, the decision is simple—convertible bondholders should choose whichever is more valuable, the call price or the conversion value.

CHECK THIS

18.2f Describe the conversion decision that convertible bondholders must make when the bonds mature.

GRAPHICAL ANALYSIS OF CONVERTIBLE BOND PRICES

The price of a convertible bond is closely linked to the value of the underlying common stock shares that can be acquired by conversion. A higher stock price implies a higher bond price, and, conversely, a lower stock price yields a lower bond price.

The relationship between the price of a convertible bond and the price of the firm's common stock is depicted in Figure 18.2. In this example, the convertible bond's price is measured on the vertical axis and the stock price is measured along the horizontal axis. The straight, upward-sloping line is the bond's conversion value; the slope of the line is the conversion ratio. The horizontal line represents the price of a comparable nonconvertible bond with the same coupon rate, maturity, and credit quality.

A convertible bond is said to be an **in-the-money bond** when its conversion value is greater than its call price. If an in-the-money convertible bond is called, rational bondholders will

in-the-money bond
A convertible bond whose conversion value is greater than its call price.

FIGURE 18.2 | Convertible Bond Prices

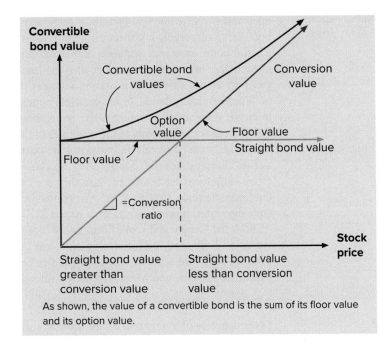

As shown, the value of a convertible bond is the sum of its floor value and its option value.

convert their bonds into common stock. When the conversion value is less than the call price, a convertible bond is said to be *out of the money.* If an out-of-the-money bond is called, rational bondholders will accept the call price and forgo the conversion option. In practice, however, convertible bonds are seldom called when they are out of the money.

The curved line in Figure 18.2 shows the relationship between a convertible bond's price and the underlying stock price. As shown, there are two lower bounds on the value of a convertible bond. First, a convertible bond's price can never fall below its **intrinsic bond value,** also commonly called its *investment value* or *straight bond value.* This value is what the bond would be worth if it were not convertible, but otherwise identical in terms of coupon, maturity, and credit quality. Second, a convertible bond can never sell for less than its *conversion value* because, if it did, investors could buy the bond and convert, thereby realizing an immediate, riskless profit.

Thus, the *floor value* of a convertible bond is its intrinsic bond value or its conversion value, whichever is larger. As shown in Figure 18.2, however, a convertible bond will generally sell for more than this floor value. This extra is the amount that investors are willing to pay for the right, but not the obligation, to convert the bond at a future date at a potentially much higher stock price. We refer to this extra amount as the *option value* of the bond.

An interesting variation of a bond-to-stock conversion feature occurs when the company issuing the bonds is different from the company whose stock is acquired by the conversion. In this case, the bonds are called **exchangeable bonds.** While not unusual, exchangeable bonds are less common than convertible bonds.

intrinsic bond value
The price below which a convertible bond cannot fall, equal to the value of a comparable nonconvertible bond. Also called *investment value or straight bond value.*

exchangeable bonds
Bonds that can be converted into common stock shares of a company other than the issuer.

CHECK THIS

18.2g For nonconvertible bonds, the call price is a ceiling on the market price of the bond. Why might the call price not be an effective ceiling on the price of a convertible bond?

BOND MATURITY AND PRINCIPAL PAYMENT PROVISIONS

term bonds
Bonds issued with a single maturity date.

Term bonds represent the most common corporate bond maturity structure. A term bond issue has a single maturity date. On this date, all outstanding bond principal must be paid off. The indenture contract for a term bond issue normally stipulates the creation of a *sinking fund.* As we discuss below, a sinking fund is an account established to repay bondholders

serial bonds
Bonds issued with a regular sequence of maturity dates.

through a series of fractional redemptions before the bond reaches maturity. Thus, at maturity, only a fraction of the original bond issue will still be outstanding.

An alternative maturity structure is provided by **serial bonds,** where a fraction of an entire bond issue is scheduled to mature in each year over a specified period. Essentially, a serial bond issue represents a collection of sub-issues with sequential maturities. As an example, a serial bond issue may stipulate that one-tenth of an entire bond issue must be redeemed in each year over a 10-year period, with the last fraction redeemed at maturity. Serial bonds generally do not have a call provision, whereas term bonds usually do have a call provision.

When originally issued, most corporate bonds have maturities of 30 years or less. However, in recent years some companies have issued bonds with 40- and 50-year maturities. In 1993, The Walt Disney Company made headlines in the financial press when it sold 100-year-maturity bonds, sometimes referred to as *century bonds.* This bond issue became popularly known as the "Sleeping Beauty" bonds, after the classic Disney movie. However, the prince might arrive early for these bonds because they are callable after 30 years. Nevertheless, this was the first time since 1954 that 100-year bonds were sold by any borrower in the United States. Only days later, however, Coca-Cola issued $150 million of 100-year-maturity bonds.

Both the Disney and Coke bond issues locked in the unusually low interest rates prevailing in 1993. You may be wondering if the low interest rates that have existed in recent years have enticed more borrowers to issue century bonds. The answer is yes. The governments of Argentina, Austria, and Mexico have recently issued 100-year bonds.

SINKING FUND PROVISIONS

sinking fund
An account used to provide for scheduled redemptions of outstanding bonds.

The indentures of many term bonds include a **sinking fund** provision that requires the corporation to make periodic payments into a trustee-managed account. Account reserves are then used to provide for scheduled redemptions of outstanding bonds. The existence of a sinking fund is an important consideration for bond investors mainly for two reasons:

1. A sinking fund provides a degree of security to bondholders because payments into the sinking fund can be used only to pay outstanding obligations to bondholders.

2. A sinking fund provision requires fractional bond issue redemptions according to a preset schedule. Therefore, some bondholders will be repaid their invested principal before the stated maturity for their bonds whether they want repayment or not.

As part of a *scheduled sinking fund redemption,* some bondholders may be forced to surrender their bonds in exchange for cash payment of a special *sinking fund call price.* For this reason, not all bondholders may be able to hold their bonds until maturity, even though the entire bond issue has not been called according to a general call provision. For example, the indenture for a 25-year-maturity bond issue may require that one-twentieth of the bond issue be retired annually, beginning immediately after an initial five-year call protection period.

Typically, when a redemption is due, the sinking fund trustee will select bonds by lottery. Selected bonds are then called, and the affected bondholders receive the call price, which for sinking fund redemptions is usually par value. However, the issuer normally has a valuable option to buy back the required number of bonds in the open market and deliver them to the sinking fund trustee instead of delivering the cash required for a par value redemption. Issuers naturally prefer to exercise this option when bonds can be repurchased in the open market at less than par value.

CHECK THIS

18.2h   For bond investors, what are some of the advantages and disadvantages of a sinking fund provision?

COUPON PAYMENT PROVISIONS

Coupon rates are stated on an annual basis. For example, an 8 percent coupon rate indicates that the issuer promises to pay 8 percent of a bond's face value to the bondholder each year. However, splitting an annual coupon into two semiannual payments is an almost universal practice in the United States. An exact schedule of coupon payment dates is specified in the bond indenture when the bonds are originally issued.

If a company suspends payment of coupon interest, it is said to be in default. Default is a serious matter. In general, bondholders have an unconditional right to the timely payment of interest and principal. They also have a right to bring legal action to enforce such payments. Upon suspension of coupon payments, the bondholders could, for example, demand an acceleration of principal repayment along with all past-due interest. However, a corporation in financial distress has a right to seek protection in bankruptcy court from inflexible demands by bondholders. As a practical matter, it is often in the best interests of both the bondholders and the corporation to negotiate a new debt contract. Indeed, bankruptcy courts normally encourage a settlement that minimizes any intervention on their part.

PROTECTIVE COVENANTS

protective covenants
Restrictions in a bond indenture designed to protect bondholders.

In addition to the provisions already discussed, a bond indenture is likely to contain a number of **protective covenants**. These agreements are designed to protect bondholders by restricting the actions of a corporation that might cause a deterioration in the credit quality of a bond issue. Protective covenants can be classified into two types: negative covenants and positive, or affirmative, covenants.

A *negative covenant* is a "thou shalt not" for the corporation. Here are some examples of negative covenants that might be found in an indenture agreement:

1. The firm cannot pay dividends to stockholders in excess of what is allowed by a formula based on the firm's earnings.
2. The firm cannot issue new bonds that are senior to currently outstanding bonds. Also, the amount of a new bond issue cannot exceed an amount specified by a formula based on the firm's net worth.
3. The firm cannot refund an existing bond issue with new bonds paying a lower coupon rate than the currently outstanding bond issue it would replace.
4. The firm cannot buy bonds issued by other companies, nor can it guarantee the debt of any other company.

A *positive covenant* is a "thou shalt." It specifies things that a corporation must do, or conditions that it must abide by. Here are some common examples of positive covenants:

1. Proceeds from the sale of assets must be used either to acquire other assets of equal value or to redeem outstanding bonds.
2. In the event of a merger, acquisition, or spin-off, the firm must give bondholders the right to redeem their bonds at par value.
3. The firm must maintain the good condition of all assets pledged as security for an outstanding bond issue.
4. The firm must periodically supply audited financial information to bondholders.

CHECK THIS

18.2i   Why would a corporation voluntarily include protective covenants in its bond indenture contract?

ADJUSTABLE-RATE BONDS

adjustable-rate bonds
Securities that pay coupons that change according to a prespecified rule. Also called *floating-rate bonds*, or *floaters*.

Many bond, note, and preferred stock issues allow the issuer to adjust the annual coupon according to a rule or formula based on current market interest rates. These securities are called **adjustable-rate bonds**; they are also sometimes called *floating-rate bonds* or *floaters*.

For example, a typical adjustment rule might specify that the coupon rate be reset annually to be equal to the current rate on 180-day-maturity U.S. Treasury bills plus 2 percent. Alternatively, a more flexible rule might specify that the coupon rate on a bond issue cannot be set below 105 percent of the yield to maturity of newly issued five-year Treasury notes. Thus, if five-year Treasury notes have recently been sold to yield 2 percent, the minimum allowable coupon rate is $1.05 \times 2\% = 2.1\%$.

Adjustable-rate bonds and notes are often putable at par value. For this reason, an issuer may set a coupon rate above an allowable minimum to discourage bondholders from selling their bonds back to the corporation.

Most adjustable-rate bonds have coupon rates that rise and fall with market interest rates. The coupon rates of some adjustable-rate bonds, however, move opposite to market interest rates. These bonds are called *inverse floaters.* A fall in the benchmark interest rate results in an increase in the coupon rate of an inverse floater. This relationship magnifies bond price fluctuations. For example, if interest rates fall, bond prices rise. Further, the higher coupon rate that results will cause the inverse floater bond price to rise even more. The opposite is true if rates rise. Thus, prices of inverse floaters can be extremely volatile.

CHECK THIS

18.2j How does an adjustable coupon rate feature affect the interest rate risk of a bond?

18.2k How might bondholders respond if the coupon rate on an adjustable-rate putable bond was set below market interest rates?

18.3 # Government Bond Basics

Related Bloomberg Functions

DEBT Sovereign Debt Monitor

The value of the outstanding U.S. federal government debt can be found at www.treasurydirect.gov.

The U.S. federal government is the largest single borrower in the world. As of August 2022, the national debt of the U.S. was about $31 trillion, up about $10 trillion since January 2019. Responsibility for managing outstanding government debt belongs to the U.S. Treasury, which acts as the financial agent of the federal government.

The U.S. Treasury finances government debt by issuing marketable securities and nonmarketable securities. Most of the gross public debt is financed by the sale of marketable securities at regularly scheduled Treasury auctions. Marketable securities include Treasury bills, Treasury notes, and Treasury bonds, often called T-bills, T-notes, and T-bonds, respectively. Outstanding marketable securities trade among investors in a large, active financial market called the Treasury market. Nonmarketable securities include U.S. Savings Bonds, Government Account Series, and State and Local Government Series. Many individuals are familiar with U.S. Savings Bonds because they are sold only to individual investors. Government Account Series are issued to federal government agencies and trust funds, in particular, the Social Security Administration trust fund. State and Local Government Series are purchased by municipal governments.

Visit www.investinginbonds.com for more information on U.S. Treasury securities.

Treasury security ownership is registered with the U.S. Treasury. When an investor sells a U.S. Treasury security to another investor, registered ownership is officially transferred by notifying the U.S. Treasury of the transaction. However, only marketable securities allow registered ownership to be transferred. Nonmarketable securities do not allow a change of registered ownership and therefore cannot be traded among investors. For example, a U.S. Savings Bond is a nonmarketable security. If an investor wishes to sell a U.S. Savings Bond, it must be redeemed by the U.S. Treasury. This is normally a simple procedure.

Another large market for government debt is the market for municipal government debt. There are more than 89,000 state and local governments in the United States, most of which have issued outstanding debt obligations. In a typical year, well over 11,000 new municipal debt issues are brought to market. Total municipal debt outstanding in the United States is estimated to be over $4 trillion. Of this total, individual investors hold over half, either through direct purchase or indirectly through mutual funds. The remainder is split between holdings of property and casualty insurance companies and commercial banks.

face value
The value of a bill, note, or bond at its maturity when a payment of principal is made. Also called *redemption value.*

18.4 # U.S. Treasury Bills, Notes, Bonds, and STRIPS

Treasury bills are short-term obligations that mature in six months or less. They are originally issued with maturities of 4, 13, or 26 weeks. A T-bill entitles its owner to receive a single payment at the bill's maturity, called the bill's **face value** or *redemption value.*

Related Bloomberg Functions

SOVM	Sovereign Debt Monitor
USD	U.S. Treasuries Monitor
ILBE	World Inflation Breakeven Rates
FIT TIPS	Fixed Income Trading: U.S. TIPS
ILB	Inflation-Linked Bonds

discount basis
Method of selling a Treasury bill at a discount from face value.

imputed interest
The interest paid on a Treasury bill determined by the size of its discount from face value.

STRIPS
Treasury program allowing investors to buy individual coupon and principal payments from a whole Treasury note or bond. Acronym for *Separate Trading of Registered Interest and Principal of Securities.*

zero coupon bond
A note or bond paying a single cash flow at maturity. Also called *zeroes.*

Visit the U.S. Treasury at
www.treasury.gov.

The smallest-denomination T-bill has a face value of $1,000. T-bills are sold on a **discount basis**, where a price is set at a discount from face value. For example, if a $10,000 bill is sold for $9,500, then it is sold at a discount of $500, or 5 percent. The discount represents the **imputed interest** on the bill.

Treasury notes are medium-term obligations with original maturities of 10 years or less, but more than 1 year. They are normally issued with original maturities of 2, 5, or 10 years, and they have face value denominations as small as $1,000. Besides a payment of face value at maturity, T-notes also pay semiannual coupons.

Treasury bonds are long-term obligations with much longer original-issue maturities. Since 1985, the Treasury has only issued T-bonds with a maturity of 30 years in its regular bond offerings. Like T-notes, T-bonds pay their face value at maturity, pay semiannual coupons, and have face value denominations as small as $1,000.

The coupon rate for T-notes and T-bonds is set according to interest rates prevailing at the time of issuance. For example, if the prevailing interest rate for a Treasury note of a certain maturity is 4 percent, then the coupon rate—that is, the annual coupon as a percentage of par value—for a new issue with that maturity is set at or near 4 percent. Thus, a $10,000 par value T-note paying a 4 percent coupon would pay two $200 coupons each year. Coupon payments normally begin six months after issuance and continue to be paid every six months until the last coupon is paid along with the face value at maturity. Once set, the coupon rate remains constant throughout the life of a U.S. Treasury note or bond.

Treasury STRIPS are derived from Treasury notes originally issued with maturities of 10 years, as well as from Treasury bonds. Since 1985, the U.S. Treasury has sponsored the **STRIPS** program, an acronym for *Separate Trading of Registered Interest and Principal of Securities.* This program allows brokers to divide Treasury bonds and notes into *coupon strips* and *principal strips,* thereby allowing investors to buy and sell the strips of their choice. Principal strips represent face value payments, and coupon strips represent coupon payments. For example, a 30-year-maturity T-bond can be separated into 61 strips, representing 60 semiannual coupon payments and a single face value payment. Under the Treasury STRIPS program, each of these strips can be separately registered to different owners.

The terms "STRIPS" and "strips" can sometimes cause confusion. The acronym STRIPS is used when speaking specifically about the Treasury STRIPS program. The term *strips,* however, now popularly refers to any note or bond issue broken down into its component parts. In this generic form, the term *strips* is acceptable.

Because each strip created under the STRIPS program represents a single future payment, STRIPS securities effectively become **zero coupon bonds** and are commonly called *zeroes.* The unique characteristics of Treasury zeroes make them an interesting investment choice.

The yield to maturity of a zero coupon bond is the interest rate that an investor will receive if the bond is held until it matures. Table 18.2 lists bond prices for zero coupon bonds with a face value of $10,000; maturities of 5, 10, 20, and 30 years; and yields from 3 percent to 15 percent. As shown, a $10,000 face-value zero coupon bond with a term to maturity of 20 years and an 8 percent yield has a price of $2,082.89.

Figure 18.3 graphs prices of zero coupon bonds with a face value of $10,000. The vertical axis measures bond prices, and the horizontal axis measures bond maturities. Bond prices for yields of 4, 8, and 12 percent are illustrated.

CHECK THIS

18.4a What are some possible reasons why individual investors might prefer to buy Treasury STRIPS rather than common stocks?

18.4b What are some possible reasons why individual investors might prefer to buy individual Treasury STRIPS rather than whole T-notes or T-bonds?

18.4c For zero coupon bonds with the same face value and yield to maturity, is the price of a zero with a 15-year maturity larger or smaller than the average price of two zeroes with maturities of 10 years and 20 years? Why?

		TABLE 18.2	Zero Coupon Bond Prices, $10,000 Face Value	

Yield to Maturity		Bond Maturity		
	5 Years	**10 Years**	**20 Years**	**30 Years**
3.0%	$8,616.67	$7,424.70	$5,512.62	$4,092.96
3.5	8,407.29	7,068.25	4,996.01	3,531.30
4.0	8,203.48	6,729.71	4,528.90	3,047.82
4.5	8,005.10	6,408.16	4,106.46	2,631.49
5.0	7,811.98	6,102.71	3,724.31	2,272.84
5.5	7,623.98	5,812.51	3,378.52	1,963.77
6.0	7,440.94	5,536.76	3,065.57	1,697.33
6.5	7,262.72	5,274.71	2,782.26	1,467.56
7.0	7,089.19	5,025.66	2,525.72	1,269.34
7.5	6,920.20	4,788.92	2,293.38	1,098.28
8.0	6,755.64	4,563.87	2,082.89	950.60
8.5	6,595.37	4,349.89	1,892.16	823.07
9.0	6,439.28	4,146.43	1,719.29	712.89
9.5	6,287.23	3,952.93	1,562.57	617.67
10.0	6,139.13	3,768.89	1,420.46	535.36
10.5	5,994.86	3,593.83	1,291.56	464.17
11.0	5,854.31	3,427.29	1,174.63	402.58
11.5	5,717.37	3,268.83	1,068.53	349.28
12.0	5,583.95	3,118.05	972.22	303.14
12.5	5,453.94	2,974.55	884.79	263.19
13.0	5,327.26	2,837.97	805.41	228.57
13.5	5,203.81	2,707.96	733.31	198.58
14.0	5,083.49	2,584.19	667.80	172.57
14.5	4,966.23	2,466.35	608.29	150.02
15.0	4,851.94	2,354.13	554.19	130.46

EXAMPLE 18.2

Calculating a STRIPS Price

What is the price of a STRIPS maturing in 20 years with a face value of $10,000 and a yield to maturity of 7.5 percent?

The STRIPS price is calculated as the present value of a single cash flow as follows:

$$\text{STRIPS price} = \frac{\$10,000}{(1 + .075/2)^{40}}$$

$$= \$2,293.38$$

You can also calculate a STRIPS price using a built-in spreadsheet function. For example, the nearby *Spreadsheet Analysis* box contains this STRIPS price calculation using an Excel spreadsheet.

EXAMPLE 18.3

Calculating a STRIPS Yield

What is the yield to maturity of a STRIPS maturing in 10 years with a face value of $10,000 and a price of $5,200?

The STRIPS yield is calculated as a yield to maturity of a single cash flow as follows:

$$\text{STRIPS yield} = 2 \times \left[\left(\frac{\$10,000}{\$5,200} \right)^{1/20} - 1 \right]$$

$$= .0665, \text{ or } 6.65\%$$

The nearby *Spreadsheet Analysis* box contains an example of this STRIPS yield calculation using an Excel spreadsheet.

FIGURE 18.3

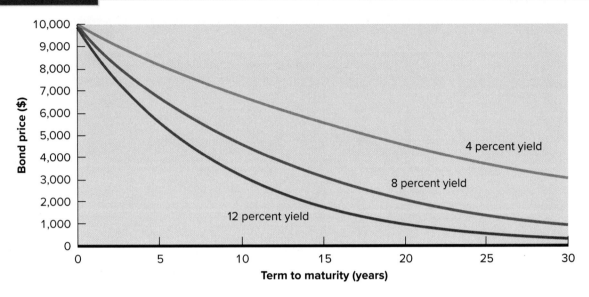

Zero Coupon Bond Prices ($10,000 Face Value)

TREASURY BOND AND NOTE PRICES

Figure 18.4 displays a Bloomberg screen listing prices and other relevant information for Treasury notes. Treasury note price quotes on Bloomberg are stated in points, 32nds of a point, and eighths of a 32nd of a point of par basis. For example, the first bid of 100-01 7/8 is 100 plus 1 and 7/8th of a 32nd, or 100 plus .054688 or 100.054688. Notice that the fourth quote is 100-02+. For whatever reason, the plus sign represents a half, or 4/8ths. So, the bid price of this note is 100.078125.

Because Treasury bonds and notes pay semiannual coupons, bond yields are stated on a semiannual basis. The relationship between the price of a note or bond and its yield to

SPREADSHEET ANALYSIS

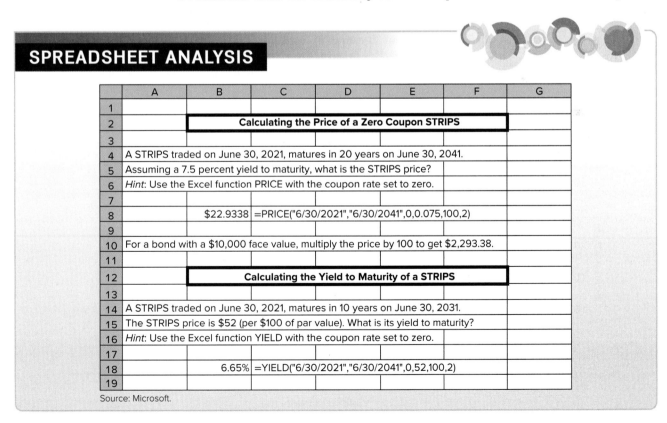

	A	B	C	D	E	F	G
1							
2			Calculating the Price of a Zero Coupon STRIPS				
3							
4	A STRIPS traded on June 30, 2021, matures in 20 years on June 30, 2041.						
5	Assuming a 7.5 percent yield to maturity, what is the STRIPS price?						
6	*Hint:* Use the Excel function PRICE with the coupon rate set to zero.						
7							
8		$22.9338	=PRICE("6/30/2021","6/30/2041",0,0.075,100,2)				
9							
10	For a bond with a $10,000 face value, multiply the price by 100 to get $2,293.38.						
11							
12			Calculating the Yield to Maturity of a STRIPS				
13							
14	A STRIPS traded on June 30, 2021, matures in 10 years on June 30, 2031.						
15	The STRIPS price is $52 (per $100 of par value). What is its yield to maturity?						
16	*Hint:* Use the Excel function YIELD with the coupon rate set to zero.						
17							
18		6.65%	=YIELD("6/30/2021","6/30/2041",0,52,100,2)				
19							

Source: Microsoft.

FIGURE 18.4 U.S. Treasury Quotes

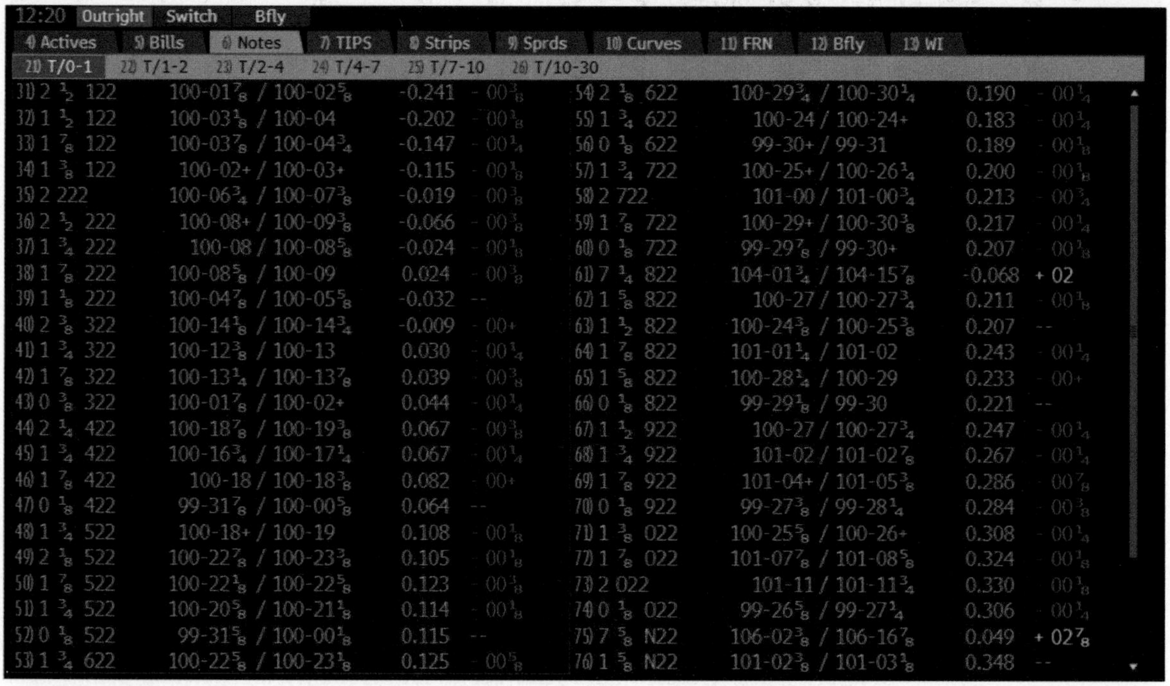

12:20 Outright Switch Bfly
4) Actives 5) Bills 6) Notes 7) TIPS 8) Strips 9) Sprds 10) Curves 11) FRN 12) Bfly 13) WI
21) T/0-1 22) T/1-2 23) T/2-4 24) T/4-7 25) T/7-10 26) T/10-30

31) 2 1/2 122	100-01 7/8 / 100-02 5/8	-0.241	- 00 3/8	54) 2 1/8 622	100-29 3/4 / 100-30 1/4	0.190	- 00 1/4
32) 1 1/2 122	100-03 1/8 / 100-04	-0.202	- 00 1/8	55) 1 3/4 622	100-24 / 100-24+	0.183	- 00 1/4
33) 1 7/8 122	100-03 7/8 / 100-04 3/4	-0.147	- 00 1/4	56) 0 1/8 622	99-30+ / 99-31	0.189	- 00 1/8
34) 1 3/8 122	100-02+ / 100-03+	-0.115	- 00 1/8	57) 1 3/4 722	100-25+ / 100-26 1/4	0.200	- 00 1/8
35) 2 222	100-06 3/4 / 100-07 3/8	-0.019	00 3/8	58) 2 722	101-00 / 101-00 3/4	0.213	- 00 3/4
36) 2 1/2 222	100-08+ / 100-09 3/8	-0.066	- 00 3/8	59) 1 7/8 722	100-29+ / 100-30 3/8	0.217	- 00 1/4
37) 1 3/4 222	100-08 / 100-08 5/8	-0.024	- 00 1/8	60) 0 1/8 722	99-29 7/8 / 99-30+	0.207	- 00 1/8
38) 1 7/8 222	100-08 5/8 / 100-09	0.024	- 00 3/8	61) 7 1/4 822	104-01 3/4 / 104-15 7/8	-0.068	+ 02
39) 1 1/8 222	100-04 7/8 / 100-05 5/8	-0.032	--	62) 1 5/8 822	100-27 / 100-27 3/4	0.211	- 00 1/8
40) 2 3/8 322	100-14 1/8 / 100-14 3/4	-0.009	- 00+	63) 1 1/2 822	100-24 3/8 / 100-25 3/8	0.207	--
41) 1 3/4 322	100-12 3/8 / 100-13	0.030	- 00 1/4	64) 1 7/8 822	101-01 1/4 / 101-02	0.243	- 00 1/4
42) 1 7/8 322	100-13 1/4 / 100-13 7/8	0.039	- 00 3/8	65) 1 5/8 822	100-28 1/4 / 100-29	0.233	- 00+
43) 0 3/8 322	100-01 7/8 / 100-02+	0.044	- 00 1/4	66) 0 1/8 822	99-29 1/8 / 99-30	0.221	--
44) 2 1/4 422	100-18 7/8 / 100-19 3/8	0.067	- 00 3/8	67) 1 1/2 922	100-27 / 100-27 3/4	0.247	- 00 1/4
45) 1 3/4 422	100-16 3/4 / 100-17 1/4	0.067	- 00 1/4	68) 1 3/4 922	101-02 / 101-02 7/8	0.267	- 00 1/4
46) 1 7/8 422	100-18 / 100-18 3/8	0.082	- 00+	69) 1 7/8 922	101-04+ / 101-05 3/8	0.286	- 00 7/8
47) 0 1/8 422	99-31 7/8 / 100-00 5/8	0.064	--	70) 0 1/8 922	99-27 3/8 / 99-28 1/4	0.284	- 00 3/8
48) 1 3/4 522	100-18+ / 100-19	0.108	- 00 1/8	71) 1 3/8 022	100-25 5/8 / 100-26+	0.308	- 00 1/4
49) 2 1/8 522	100-22 7/8 / 100-23 3/8	0.105	- 00 1/8	72) 1 7/8 022	101-07 7/8 / 101-08 5/8	0.324	- 00 1/8
50) 1 7/8 522	100-22 1/8 / 100-22 5/8	0.123	- 00 1/8	73) 2 022	101-11 / 101-11 3/4	0.330	00 1/8
51) 1 3/4 522	100-20 5/8 / 100-21 1/8	0.114	- 00 1/8	74) 0 1/8 022	99-26 5/8 / 99-27 1/4	0.306	- 00 1/4
52) 0 1/8 522	99-31 5/8 / 100-00 1/8	0.115	--	75) 7 5/8 N22	106-02 3/8 / 106-16 7/8	0.049	+ 02 7/8
53) 1 3/4 622	100-22 5/8 / 100-23 1/8	0.125	- 00 5/8	76) 1 5/8 N22	101-02 3/8 / 101-03 1/8	0.348	--

Source: Bloomberg Finance L.P.

maturity was discussed in an earlier chapter. For convenience, the bond price formula from that chapter is restated here:

$$\text{Bond price} = \frac{\text{Annual coupon}}{YTM} \times \left[1 - \frac{1}{(1 + YTM/2)^{2M}}\right] + \frac{\text{Face value}}{(1 + YTM/2)^{2M}}$$

Figure 18.5 illustrates the relationship between the price of a bond and its yield to maturity for 2-year, 7-year, and 30-year terms to maturity. Notice that each bond has a price of 100 when its yield is 8 percent. This price indicates that each bond has an 8 percent coupon rate because when a bond's coupon rate is equal to its yield to maturity, its price is equal to its par value.

FIGURE 18.5 Bond Prices ($100 Face Value)

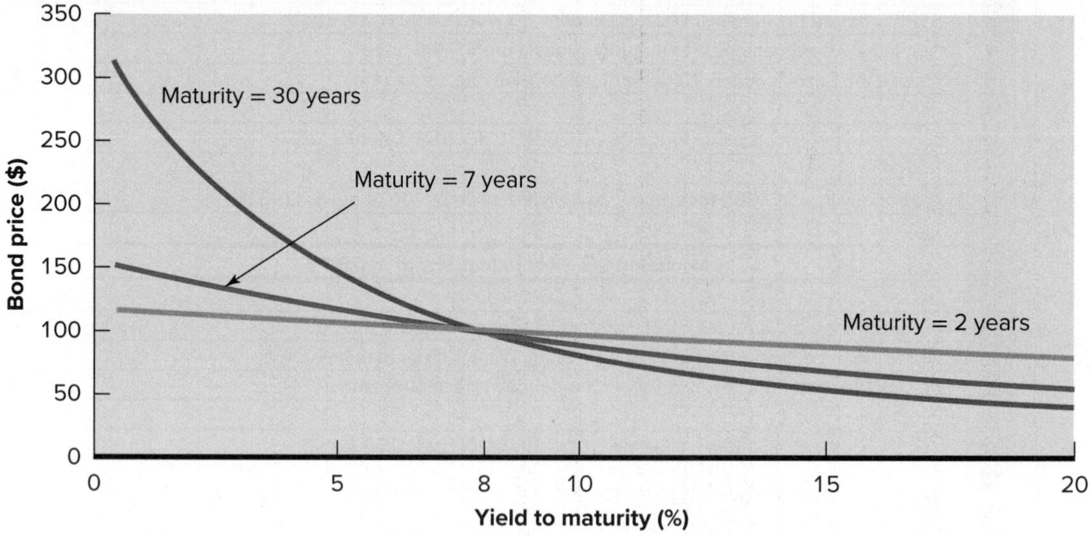

Bond price ($)
350
300
250
200
150
100
50
0
Maturity = 30 years
Maturity = 7 years
Maturity = 2 years
0
5
8
10
15
20
Yield to maturity (%)

bid-ask spread
The difference between a dealer's ask price and bid price.

The difference between a dealer's ask and bid prices is called the **bid-ask spread.** The bid-ask spread measures the dealer's gross profit from a single round-trip transaction of buying a security at the bid price and then selling it at the ask price.

CHECK THIS

18.4d What would Figure 18.5 look like if the three bonds all had coupon rates of 6 percent? What about 10 percent?

18.4e In Figure 18.4, which Treasury issues have the narrowest spreads? Why do you think this is so?

18.4f Examine the spreads between bid and ask prices for Treasury notes and bonds listed online at www.wsj.com.

18.5 U.S. Treasury Auctions

Related Bloomberg Functions

ECO Economic Calendars

AUCR Auction Results

For recent information on Treasury auctions, visit www.treasurydirect.gov.

stop-out bid
The lowest competitive bid in a U.S. Treasury auction that is accepted.

The Federal Reserve Bank conducts regularly scheduled auctions for Treasury securities. At each Treasury auction, the Federal Reserve accepts sealed bids of two types: competitive bids and noncompetitive bids. Competitive bids for T-bills specify a bid price and a bid quantity. The bid price is what the bidder is willing to pay, and the bid quantity is the face value amount that the bidder will purchase if the bid is accepted. Noncompetitive bids specify only a bid quantity because the price charged to noncompetitive bidders will be determined by the results of the competitive auction process. Individual investors can submit noncompetitive bids, but only Treasury securities dealers can submit competitive bids.

At the close of bidding, all sealed bids are forwarded to the U.S. Treasury for processing. As a first step, all noncompetitive bids are accepted automatically and are subtracted from the total issue amount. Then a **stop-out bid** is determined; this is the price at which all competitive bids are sufficient to finance the remaining issue amount. Competitive bids at or above the stop-out bid are accepted, and bids below the stop-out bid are rejected.

Since 1998, all U.S. Treasury auctions have been single-price auctions in which all accepted competitive bids pay the stop-out bid. The stop-out bid is also the price paid by noncompetitive bidders. For example, suppose an auction for T-bills with $20 billion of face value receives $28 billion of competitive bids and $4 billion of noncompetitive bids. Noncompetitive bids are automatically accepted, leaving $16 billion for competitive bidders. Now suppose the stop-out bid for this $16 billion amount is $9,700 for a $10,000 face-value T-bill. Accepted competitive bidders and all noncompetitive bidders pay this price of $9,700.

The process is similar for T-bond and T-note issues, except that bids are made on a yield basis, where competitive bids state yields instead of prices. A coupon rate for the entire issue is then set according to the average competitive-bid yield.

CHECK THIS

18.5a The Federal Reserve announces an offering of Treasury bills with a face value amount of $25 billion. The response is $5 billion of noncompetitive bids, along with the following competitive bids:

Bidder	Price Bid	Quantity Bid
A	$9,500	$5 billion
B	9,550	5 billion
C	9,600	5 billion
D	9,650	5 billion
E	9,700	5 billion

In a single-price auction, which bids are accepted and what prices are paid by each bidder? How much money is raised by the entire offering?

18.5b What is a stop-out bid?

18.6 Federal Government Agency Securities

Visit
www.investinginbonds.com
for more information on agency
securities.

Most U.S. government agencies consolidate their borrowing through the Federal Financing Bank, which obtains funds directly from the U.S. Treasury. However, several federal agencies are authorized to issue securities directly to the public. For example, the World Bank and the Tennessee Valley Authority issue notes and bonds directly to investors.

Bonds issued by U.S. government agencies share an almost equal credit quality with U.S. Treasury issues. Most agency debt does not carry an explicit guarantee of the U.S. government. A federal agency on the verge of default, however, would probably receive government support to ensure timely payment of interest and principal on outstanding debt. This perception is supported by historical experience and the political reality that Congress would likely feel compelled to rescue an agency that it created if it became financially distressed.

This conjecture was confirmed in September 2008. The Federal Housing Finance Agency (FHFA) placed two government-sponsored enterprises (GSEs), Fannie Mae and Freddie Mac, into conservatorship. This decision was supported by the U.S. Treasury and the Federal Reserve Bank. The U.S. Treasury pledged taxpayer money to keep these GSEs solvent. Thus, government agency notes and bonds are attractive to many investors because they offer higher yields than comparable U.S. Treasury securities but carry the implied backing of the government.

If you compare bid and ask dealer price quotes for agency bonds, you will find that agency bonds have a higher bid-ask spread than Treasury bonds. The reason for the higher bid-ask spread is that agency bond trading volume is much lower than Treasury bond trading volume. To compensate for the lower volume, dealers charge higher spreads. Thus, trading agency bonds is costlier than trading Treasury bonds. Consequently, agency bonds are usually purchased by institutional investors planning to hold the bonds until they mature. As a result, price quotes are not as readily available—an inherent risk of holding less liquid securities and an additional reason for higher yields. Another reason for the higher yields on agency bonds compared to Treasury bonds is that interest income from agency bonds is subject to federal, state, and local taxation, whereas Treasury interest payments are subject only to federal taxation.

CHECK THIS

18.6a   Why do agency bonds carry a higher yield than comparable U.S. Treasury bonds?

18.7 Municipal Bonds

Related Bloomberg Functions

MSRC   Muni Bond Search
PICK   Muni Offerings
GBY   Municipal Bond Monitor

Visit
www.investinginbonds.com
for more about municipal bonds.

Municipal notes and bonds are intermediate- to long-term interest-bearing obligations of state and local governments or agencies of those governments. The defining characteristic of municipal notes and bonds, often called "munis," is that coupon interest is usually exempt from federal income tax. Consequently, the market for municipal debt is commonly called the *tax-exempt market.* Most of the 50 states also have an income tax, but their tax treatment of municipal debt interest varies. Only a few states exempt coupon interest on out-of-state municipal bonds from in-state income tax, but most states do allow in-state municipal debt interest to be an exemption from in-state income tax. In any case, state income tax rates are normally much lower than federal income tax rates, and state taxes can be used as an itemized deduction from federal taxable income. Consequently, state taxes are usually a secondary consideration for municipal bond investors.

The federal income tax exemption makes municipal bonds attractive to investors in the highest income tax brackets. This includes many individual investors, commercial banks, and property and casualty insurance companies—precisely those investors who actually hold almost all municipal debt. However, yields on municipal debt are less than on corporate debt with similar features and credit quality. This eliminates much, but not all, of the advantage of the tax exemption. Therefore, tax-exempt investors, including pension funds and retirement accounts of individuals, nonprofit institutions, and some life insurance companies, normally do not invest in municipal bonds. Instead, they prefer to invest in higher-yielding corporate bonds.

Municipal bonds are typically less complicated investments than corporate bonds. However, while municipal debt often carries a high credit rating, **default risk** does exist. Thus, investing in municipal debt requires more care than investing in U.S. Treasury securities.

To illustrate some standard features of a municipal bond issue, Table 18.3 summarizes the issue terms for a hypothetical bond issued by the city of Bedford Falls. We see that the bonds were issued in December 2021 and mature 30 years later in December 2051. Each bond has a face value denomination of $5,000 (typical for municipal bonds) and pays an annual coupon equal to 6 percent of face value. The annual coupon is split between two semiannual payments each June and December. Based on the original offer price of 100, or 100 percent of par value, the bonds have a yield to maturity of 6 percent. The Bedford Falls bonds are call-protected for 10 years, until January 2032. Thereafter, the bonds are callable any time at par value.

The Bedford Falls bonds are **general obligation bonds (GOs),** which means that the bonds are secured by the full faith and credit of the city of Bedford Falls. "Full faith and credit" means the power of the municipality to collect taxes. The trustee for the bond issue is Potters Bank of Bedford Falls. A trustee is appointed to represent the financial interests of bondholders and administer the sinking fund for the bond issue. A sinking fund requires a bond issuer to redeem for cash a fraction of an outstanding bond issue on a periodic basis. The sinking fund in this example requires that, beginning 10 years after issuance, the city must redeem at par value $2.5 million of the bond issue each year. At each annual redemption, a fraction of the bond issue is called and the affected bondholders receive the par value call price.

MUNICIPAL BOND FEATURES

Municipal bonds are typically callable, pay semiannual coupons, and often have a par value denomination of $5,000. Municipal bond prices are stated as a percentage of par value. Thus, a price of 102 indicates that a bond with a par value of $5,000 has a price of $5,100. By convention, however, municipal bond dealers commonly use yield quotes rather than price quotes in their trading procedures. For example, a dealer might quote a bid yield of 6.25 percent for a 5 percent coupon bond with seven years to maturity, indicating a willingness to buy at a price

---

TABLE 18.3 — **City of Bedford Falls General Obligation Bonds**

Issue amount	$50 million	Bond issue represents a total face value amount of $50 million
Issue date	12/15/21	Bonds were offered to the public on December 15, 2021
Maturity date	12/31/51	All remaining principal must be paid at maturity on December 31, 2051
Par value	$5,000	Each bond has a face value of $5,000
Coupon rate	6%	Annual coupons of $300 per bond
Coupon dates	12/31, 6/30	Semiannual coupons of $150
Offering price	100	Offer price is 100% of par value
Yield to maturity	6%	Based on stated offer price
Call provision	Callable after 12/31/31	Bonds are call-protected for 10 years
Call price	100	Bonds are callable at par value
Trustee	Potters Bank of Bedford Falls	The trustee is appointed to represent the bondholders and administer the sinking fund
Sinking fund	$2.5 million annual par redemptions after 12/31/31	City must redeem at par value $2.5 million of the bond issue each year beginning in 2032

determined by that yield. The actual dollar bid price in this example is \$4,649.99, as shown in the following bond price calculation:

$$\frac{\$250}{.0625} \times \left[1 - \frac{1}{1.03125^{14}}\right] + \frac{\$5,000}{1.03125^{14}} = \$4,649.99$$

Because many thousands of different municipal bond issues are outstanding, only a few large issues trade with sufficient frequency to justify having their prices reported in the financial press.

Municipal bonds are commonly issued with a serial maturity structure. In a serial bond issue, a fraction of the total issue amount is scheduled to mature in each year over a multiple-year period. A call provision is another standard feature of most municipal bond issues. You should remember that a call provision allows an issuer to retire outstanding bonds before they mature, usually to refund with new bonds after a fall in market interest rates. When the bond is called, each bondholder receives the bond's call price in exchange for the bond.

Some municipal bonds are putable, and these are called *put bonds*. The holder of a put bond, also called a *tender offer bond,* has the option of selling the bond back to the issuer, normally at par value. Some put bonds can be tendered at any time, whereas others can be tendered only on regularly scheduled dates.

TYPES OF MUNICIPAL BONDS

There are two basic types of municipal bonds: general obligation bonds, often referred to as GOs, and revenue bonds. General obligation bonds are issued by all levels of municipal governments, including states, counties, cities, towns, school districts, and water districts. They are secured by the general taxing powers of the municipalities issuing the bonds. For state governments and large city governments, tax revenue is collected from a diverse base of income taxes on corporations and individuals, sales taxes, and property taxes. In contrast, tax revenues for smaller municipalities are largely derived from property taxes, although sales taxes have become increasingly important. Because of their large, diverse tax bases, general obligation bonds issued by states and large cities are often called *unlimited tax bonds* or *full faith and credit bonds.*

However, some general obligation bonds are called *limited tax bonds.* The distinction between limited and unlimited tax bonds arises when a constitutional limit or other statutory limit is placed on the power of a municipality to assess taxes. For example, an amendment to the California state constitution, popularly known as Proposition 13 when it was enacted, placed rigid limits on the ability of California municipalities to assess taxes on real estate.

revenue bonds
Municipal bonds secured by revenues collected from a specific project or projects.

Revenue bonds constitute the bulk of all outstanding municipal bonds. **Revenue bonds** are bonds secured by proceeds collected from the projects they finance. Thus, the credit quality of a revenue bond issue is largely determined by the ability of a project to generate revenue. A few examples of the many different kinds of projects financed by revenue bonds are listed below.

Airport and seaport bonds. Used to finance development of airport and seaport facilities. Secured by user fees and lease revenues.

College dormitory bonds. Used to finance construction and renovation of dormitory facilities. Secured by rental fees.

Industrial development bonds. Used to finance development of projects ranging from factories to shopping centers. Secured by rental and leasing fees.

Multifamily housing bonds. Used to finance construction of housing projects for senior citizens or low-income families. Secured by rental fees.

Highway and road gas tax bonds. Used to finance highway construction. May be secured by specific toll revenues or general gas tax revenues.

Student loan bonds. Used to purchase higher education student loans. Secured by loan repayments and federal guarantees.

hybrid bonds
Municipal bonds secured by project revenues with some form of general obligation credit guarantees.

Many municipal bonds possess aspects of both general obligation and revenue bonds; these are called **hybrid bonds.** Typically, a hybrid is a revenue bond secured by project-specific cash flows, but with additional credit guarantees. A common form of hybrid is the *moral obligation bond.* This is a state-issued revenue bond with provisions for obtaining general revenues when project-specific resources are inadequate. Usually, extra funds can be obtained only with approval of a state legislature, which is said to be "morally obligated" to assist a financially distressed state-sponsored project. However, a moral obligation is not a guarantee, and the likelihood of state assistance varies. Municipal bond credit analysts consider each state's history of assistance, as well as current state financial conditions, when evaluating the credit-quality enhancement of the moral obligation. In general, experienced municipal bond investors agree that a state will first service its own general obligation debt before providing service assistance to moral obligation debt. This is typically evidenced by the higher yields on moral obligation debt compared to general obligation debt.

Since 1983, all newly issued municipal bonds have had to be registered—that is, the identity of all bondholders must be registered with the issuer. With registered bonds, the issuer sends coupon interest and principal payments only to the registered owner of a bond. Additionally, it is now standard practice for registered bonds to be issued in book entry form; bondholders are not issued printed bond certificates, but instead receive notification that their ownership is officially registered. The actual registration record is maintained by the issuer in computer files. This contrasts with the now defunct practice (in the United States) of issuing bearer bonds, where coupon interest and principal were paid to anyone who presented the bond certificates.

MUNICIPAL BOND INSURANCE

insured municipal bonds
Bonds secured by an insurance policy that guarantees bond interest and principal payments should the issuer default.

In the last few decades, it has become increasingly common for municipalities to obtain bond insurance for new bond issues. **Insured municipal bonds,** besides being secured by the issuer's resources, are also backed by an insurance policy written by a commercial insurance company. The policy provides for prompt payment of coupon interest and principal to municipal bondholders in the event of a default by the issuer. The cost of the insurance policy is paid by the issuer at the time of issuance. The policy cannot be canceled while any bonds are outstanding. With bond insurance, the credit quality of the bond issue is determined by the financial strength of the insurance company, not the municipality alone. Credit rating agencies are certainly aware of this fact. Consequently, a bond issue with insurance can obtain a higher credit rating than would be possible without insurance, and therefore sells at a higher price.

Visit the websites of these municipal bond insurers:
www.mbia.com and www.ambac.com.

Municipal bond insurance companies manage default risk in three ways. First, they insure bond issues only from municipalities that have a good credit rating on their own. Second, municipal bond insurers diversify default risk by writing insurance policies for municipalities spread across a wide geographic area. Third, and perhaps most important, to compete in the municipal bond insurance business, insurers must maintain substantial investment portfolios as a source of financial reserves. Without sizable reserves, a company's insurance policies are not credible and municipalities will avoid purchasing insurance from them.

EQUIVALENT TAXABLE YIELD

Consider an individual investor who must decide whether to invest in a corporate bond paying annual coupon interest of 8 percent or a municipal bond paying annual coupon interest of 5 percent. Both bonds are new issues with a triple-A credit rating, both bonds sell at par value, and the investor plans to hold the bonds until they mature. Since both bonds are purchased at par value, their coupon rates are equal to their originally stated yields to maturity. For the municipal bond, this is a tax-exempt yield; for the corporate bond, this is a taxable yield.

Clearly, if the investment is for a tax-exempt retirement account, corporate debt is preferred because the coupon interest is higher and tax effects are not a consideration. But if the investment is not tax-exempt, the decision should be made on an aftertax basis. Essentially, the investor must decide which investment provides the highest return after accounting for income tax on corporate debt interest. This is done by comparing the tax-exempt yield of 5 percent on municipal bonds with an equivalent taxable yield. An equivalent taxable yield depends on the investor's marginal tax rate and is computed as follows:

$$\text{Equivalent taxable yield} = \frac{\text{Tax-exempt yield}}{1 - \text{Marginal tax rate}}$$

For example, suppose the investor is in a 35 percent marginal tax bracket. Then a tax-exempt yield of 5 percent is shown to correspond to an equivalent taxable yield of 7.69 percent as follows:

$$\text{Equivalent taxable yield} = \frac{.05}{1 - .35} = .0769, \text{ or } 7.69\%$$

In this case, the investor would prefer the taxable yield of 8 percent on the corporate bond to the equivalent taxable yield of 7.69 percent on the municipal bond.

Alternatively, the investor could compare the aftertax yield on the corporate bond with the tax-exempt yield on the municipal bond. An aftertax yield is computed as follows:

$$\text{Aftertax yield} = \text{Taxable yield} \times (1 - \text{Marginal tax rate})$$

To change the example, suppose that the investor is in a 40 percent marginal tax bracket. This results in an aftertax yield of 4.8 percent, as shown below:

$$\text{Aftertax yield} = .08 \times (1 - .40) = .048, \text{ or } 4.8\%$$

In this case, the tax-exempt yield of 5 percent on the municipal bond is preferred to the aftertax yield of 4.8 percent on the corporate bond.

Another approach is to compute the critical marginal tax rate that would leave an investor indifferent between a given tax-exempt yield on a municipal bond and a given taxable yield on a corporate bond. A critical marginal tax rate is found as follows:

$$\text{Critical marginal tax rate} = 1 - \frac{\text{Tax-exempt yield}}{\text{Taxable yield}}$$

For the example considered here, the critical marginal tax rate is 37.5 percent, determined as follows:

$$\text{Critical marginal tax rate} = 1 - \frac{5\%}{8\%} = 37.5\%$$

Investors with a marginal tax rate higher than the critical marginal rate would prefer the municipal bond, whereas investors in a lower tax bracket would prefer the corporate bond.

TAXABLE MUNICIPAL BONDS

private activity bonds
Taxable municipal bonds used to finance facilities used by private businesses.

The Tax Reform Act of 1986 imposed notable restrictions on the types of municipal bonds that qualify for federal tax exemption of interest payments. In particular, the 1986 act expanded the definition of **private activity bonds.** Private activity bonds include any municipal security where 10 percent or more of the issue finances facilities used by private entities and is secured by payments from private entities.

Interest on private activity bonds is tax-exempt only if the bond issue falls into a so-called qualified category. Qualified private activity bonds that still enjoy a tax-exempt interest privilege include public airport bonds, multifamily housing bonds, nonvehicular mass commuting bonds, and various other project bonds. The major types of private activity bonds that do not qualify for tax-exempt interest are those used to finance sports stadiums, convention facilities, parking facilities, and industrial parks. However, these taxable private activity bonds may still enjoy exemption from state and local income tax.

In any case, as a result of the 1986 act and the continuing need to finance private activity projects, new issues of taxable municipal revenue bonds are frequently sold with yields similar to corporate bond yields. In addition, the Tax Cuts and Jobs Act of 2017 reduced both individual and corporate income tax rates, making municipal bonds generally less attractive.

CHECK THIS

18.7a An investor with a marginal tax rate of 30 percent is interested in a tax-exempt bond with a yield of 6 percent. What is the equivalent taxable yield of this bond?

18.7b A taxable bond has a yield of 10 percent, and a tax-exempt bond has a yield of 7 percent. What is the critical marginal tax rate for these two bonds?

18.8 Bond Credit Ratings

Related Bloomberg Functions

DES	Security Description
RATD	Ratings Definitions
CSDR	Sovereign Ratings
CRPR	Credit Profile
YAS	Yield and Spread Analysis
SOVR	Sovereign CDS Monitor
DIS	Distressed Bonds

credit rating
An assessment of the credit quality of a bond issue based on the issuer's financial condition.

Visit these rating agency websites: Kroll at www.kroll.com, Fitch at www.fitchratings.com, Moody's at www.moodys.com, and S&P at www.spglobal.com/ratings.

When a corporation or municipality sells a new bond issue to investors, it usually subscribes to several bond rating agencies for a credit evaluation of the bond issue. Each contracted rating agency then provides a **credit rating**—an assessment of the credit quality of the bond issue based on the issuer's financial condition. Rating agencies charge a fee for this service. As part of the contractual arrangement between the bond issuer and the rating agency, the issuer agrees to allow a continuing review of its credit rating even if the rating deteriorates. Without a credit rating, a new bond issue would be quite difficult to sell to the public, which is why almost all non-Treasury bond issues originally sold to the general public have a credit rating assigned at the time of issuance. Also, most of those bond issues have ratings assigned by several rating agencies.

Established rating agencies in the United States include Kroll, LLC (Kroll); Fitch Ratings (Fitch); Moody's Investors Service (Moody's); and Standard & Poor's Corporation (S&P). Of these, the two best-known rating agencies are Moody's and Standard & Poor's. These companies publish regularly updated credit ratings for thousands of domestic and international bond issues.

It is important to realize that bond ratings are assigned to particular bond issues and not to the issuer of those bonds. For example, a senior corporate bond issue is likely to have a higher credit rating than a subordinated corporate issue even if both are issued by the same corporation. Similarly, a corporation with two bond issues outstanding may have a higher credit rating assigned to one issue because that issue has stronger covenant protection specified in the bond's indenture contract.

Seniority and covenant protection are not the only things that affect bond ratings. Bond rating agencies consider a number of factors before assigning a credit rating, including an appraisal of the financial strength of the issuer, the caliber of the issuer's management, the issuer's position in an industry, and the industry's position in the economy.

Table 18.4 summarizes corporate bond rating symbols and definitions used by Moody's (first column) and Standard & Poor's (second column). Fitch and Kroll use a similar scale to Standard & Poor's. As shown, bond credit ratings fall into three broad categories: investment-grade, speculative-grade, and extremely speculative-grade.

In general, a bond rating is intended to be a comparative indicator of overall credit quality for a particular bond issue. The rating in itself, however, is not a recommendation to buy or sell a bond. In fact, few investors realize that the ratings themselves are not guaranteed by the rating agencies. Moreover, the ratings are subject to an upgrade or a downgrade at any time. The rating agencies design their rating systems to provide an independent review of the bond. Bond ratings, like any analyst recommendation, are subject to error.

The system to rate bonds attracted considerable attention during the Crash of 2008. Many real estate loans had been packaged together and sold as a type of fixed-income investment known as mortgage-backed securities (MBS), which we discuss in detail in a later chapter. The rating agencies provided ratings on many of these investments, and most were rated as "triple A," the highest investment grade possible. After the underlying mortgages began to default, however, many of these securities lost significant value. The rating agencies subsequently received considerable criticism for being inaccurate in their assessment and rating of these securities.

WHY BOND RATINGS ARE IMPORTANT

Even with the errors discussed above, bond credit ratings assigned by independent rating agencies remain quite important to bond market participants. Only a few institutional investors have the resources and expertise necessary to properly evaluate a bond's credit quality on their own. Bond ratings provide investors with reliable, professional evaluations of bond issues at a reasonable cost. This information is indispensable for assessing the economic value of a bond.

prudent investment guidelines
Restrictions on investment portfolios stipulating that securities purchased must meet a certain level of safety.

Furthermore, many financial institutions have **prudent investment guidelines** stipulating that only securities with a certain level of investment safety may be included in their portfolios. For example, bond investments for many pension funds are limited to investment-grade

TABLE 18.4

Corporate Bond Credit Rating Symbols

Rating Agency		
Moody's	Standard & Poor's	Credit Rating Description
Investment-Grade Bond Ratings		
Aaa	AAA	Highest credit rating, maximum safety
Aa1	AA1	
Aa2	AA	High credit quality, investment-grade bonds
Aa3	AA–	
A1	A1	
A2	A	Upper-medium quality, investment-grade bonds
A3	A–	
Baa1	BBB1	
Baa2	BBB	Lower-medium quality, investment-grade bonds
Baa3	BBB–	
Speculative-Grade Bond Ratings		
Ba1	BB1	Low credit quality, speculative-grade bonds
Ba2	BB	
Ba3	BB–	
B1	B1	Very low credit quality, speculative-grade bonds
B2	B	
B3	B–	
Extremely Speculative-Grade Bond Ratings		
Caa	CCC1	Extremely low credit standing, high-risk bonds
	CCC	
	CCC–	
Ca	CC	Extremely speculative
C	C	
	D	Bonds in default

bonds rated at least Baa by Moody's or at least BBB by Standard & Poor's. Bond ratings provide a convenient measure to monitor implementation of these guidelines.

Individuals who invest in bonds also find published bond ratings useful. Individual investors generally do not have the ability to diversify as extensively as do large institutions. With limited diversification opportunities, an individual should invest only in bonds with higher credit ratings.

AN ALTERNATIVE TO BOND RATINGS

Bond ratings are not the only way to evaluate the credit quality of a bond. One particularly important measure is a bond's credit spread. The credit spread is an estimate of the difference in yield between the bond in question and a comparable-maturity Treasury security. The higher the credit spread, the higher the level of perceived default risk.

Credit spreads and credit ratings should show a strong correlation. High-grade bonds should have a lower spread than low-grade bonds. The potential benefit of using credit spreads instead of bond ratings, however, is that credit spreads are updated nearly continuously through the trading activities of many bond market participants. By way of contrast, credit ratings tend to be more stable and therefore could be a lagging indicator of the bond's quality.

For more insight on this issue, check out Figure 18.6, which provides a graph of corporate yield spreads over time. Note that average credit spreads are not constant through time. These spreads clearly widen during recessions, such as the one associated with the Crash of 2008.

FIGURE 18.6 | Corporate Yield Spreads through Time

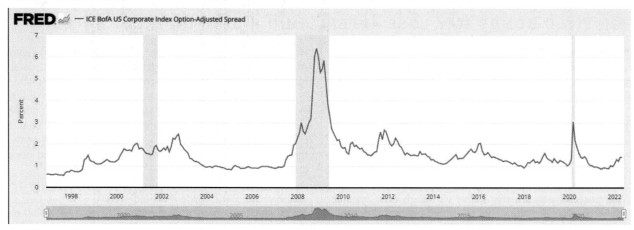

Shaded areas indicate U.S. recessions. Source: ICE Benchmark Administration Limited (IBA). fred.stlouisfed.org.

CHECK THIS

18.8a Does a low credit rating necessarily imply that a bond is a bad investment?

18.8b What factors besides the credit rating might be important in deciding whether a particular bond is a worthwhile investment?

JUNK BONDS

high-yield bonds
Bonds with a speculative credit rating that is offset by a yield premium offered to compensate for higher credit risk. Also called *junk bonds*.

Bonds with a speculative or lower grade rating—that is, those rated Ba or lower by Moody's or BB or lower by Standard & Poor's—are commonly called **high-yield bonds**, or, more colorfully, *junk bonds.* The designation "junk" is somewhat misleading and often unduly pejorative because junk bonds have economic value. Junk bonds represent debt with a higher-than-average credit risk. To put the term in perspective, one should realize that most consumer debt and small-business debt represent higher-than-average credit risk. Yet it is generally considered desirable from an economic and social perspective that credit be available to consumers and small businesses.

Junk bonds that were originally issued with an investment-grade credit rating that subsequently fell to speculative grade because of unforeseen economic events are called *fallen angels.* Another type, *original-issue junk,* is defined as bonds originally issued with a speculative-grade rating.

Junk bonds are attractive investments for many institutional investors with well-diversified portfolios. The logic of junk bond investing revolves around the possibility that the *yield premium* for junk bonds might be high enough to justify accepting the higher default rates of junk bonds. As an example of this logic, consider the following back-of-the-envelope calculations.

Suppose that the average yield on junk bonds is 10 percent when U.S. Treasury bonds yield 7 percent. In this case, the yield premium of junk bonds over default-free Treasury bonds is 3 percent. Further suppose that an investor expects about 4 percent of all outstanding junk bonds to default each year, and experience suggests that when junk bonds default, bondholders on average receive 50 cents for each dollar of bond face value. Based on these rough assumptions, diversified junk bond investors expect to lose 2 percent (= .04 × .50) of their portfolio value each year through defaults. But with a junk bond yield premium of 3 percent, the junk bond portfolio is expected to outperform U.S. Treasury bonds by 1 percent per year.

It is true that a junk bond portfolio is much more expensive to manage than a Treasury bond portfolio. For a $1 billion bond portfolio, however, a junk bond yield premium of 1 percent represents $10 million of additional interest income per year.

HIGH-YIELD BONDS MAY LOSE APPEAL AMID RISING INTEREST RATES

If you're looking to add more return to your portfolio, by now you know that you need to take on more (systematic) risk. Some people reach for more bond yield, however, using so called "high-yield bonds," which used to be called "junk bonds."

You should also know well that bond yields and bond prices move in opposite directions. Recently, these high-yield bonds' prices have fallen quite a bit. According to the ICE Bank of America U.S. High-Yield Index, the yield on these bonds is about 7.5 percent as of May 17, 2022, as compared to 4.42 percent at the beginning of January.

You should be aware that high-yield bonds have greater default risk than investment-grade bonds. What does this difference mean? It means that the issuers of these bonds are less likely to make the scheduled coupon payments and perhaps pay the face value at maturity. So you, the bond holder, might not be compensated for your investment.

Some market observers believe that the risk of default is correctly reflected in the price and, hence, yield of these bonds. Mr. Charles Sachs, chief investment officer at Kaufman Rossin Wealth in Miami, however, says that the prices of these bonds generally have more downside potential than predicted by traditional risk versus reward measures.

Since March 2022, the Federal Reserve has taken aggressive action to combat a 40-year high in inflation, raising its benchmark interest rate several times. It likely will continue to do so.

The central bank's continued tightening could present risks for high-yield bonds, according to Mr. Matthew Gelfand, a CFP and executive director of Tricolor Capital Advisors in Bethesda, Maryland. He states that default rates tend to increase as economic growth slows down.

So how do you judge the potential performance of high-yield bonds? One way is to compare the "spread" in coupon rates between a junk bond and a less risky asset, such as U.S. Treasury bonds. Generally, if the spread is lower than the historic average, the more attractive high-yield bonds become.

For example, suppose a high-yield bond has a 7.5 percent coupon rate. Bond holders should receive $75 per year per $1,000 face. Suppose a 7-year Treasury note has a 3.0 percent coupon. Holders of these bonds should receive $30.00 annually per $1,000 face.

In this example, the yield spread is 4.50 percentage points—which translates into $45.00 more interest income for the high-yield bond.

Over the past 40 years, the average spread between these two bond classes has been about 4.80 percentage points, according to Mr. Gelfand. The current yield spread is below this historical average. This fact means that, all else equal, high-yield bonds are more appealing than when the spread exceeds the historical average. The lesson: Watch the spread!

Source: Kate Dore, "High-Yield Bonds May Lose Appeal amid Rising Interest Rates," CNBC.com, May 18, 2022.

Of course, actual default rates could turn out to be much different than expected. History suggests that the major determinant of aggregate bond default rates is the state of economic activity. During an expansionary economic period, bond default rates are usually low. But in a recession, default rates can rise dramatically. For this reason, the investment performance of corporate bond portfolios, including junk bond portfolios, largely depends on the health of the economy. In fact, many investors believe that yield spreads and defaults (particularly on junk bonds) are a leading indicator of economic activity, and not just a response to it. As you can see in the nearby *Investment Updates* box, investors pay attention to yield spreads on junk bonds.

Some investors like to keep track of outstanding bonds that were issued by companies that are now in bankruptcy. A Bloomberg screen cap listing some so-called Distressed Debt is displayed in Figure 18.7. For example, look at the 7.5 percent Sears Roebuck Acceptance bond that matures on October 15, 2027. The price of this bond is $0.35 per $100 of face, which makes its Yield to Maturity a whopping 841 percent That is, this yield calculation assumes the company makes the coupon payments and pays the face value. Chances are, however, that these bonds will not make any payments to investors who buy them.

CHECK THIS

18.8c Can junk bond default risk be completely diversified away by large institutional bond investors?

18.8d From an investor's perspective, is there any importance in distinguishing between fallen angels and original-issue junk?

FIGURE 18.7 | Distressed Debt

	Issuer	Coupon	Maturity	Price	Yield	Spread ↓	Amt Out ↑
			Export to Excel				US Distressed Debt
	TRACE data generated from previous day's close						
	110 bonds found for 67 issuers		Amount 76.89BLN		☐ Newly added bonds only		
3)	LUMBERMENS MUTUAL CASLTY	9.150	07/01/26	.001	914994.000	91499200.0	400MM
4)	DEAN FOODS CO	6.500	03/15/23	.299	2457.350	245667.0	700MM
5)	DEAN FOODS CO	6.500	03/15/23	.625	1680.950	168025.0	700MM
6)	INTELSAT LUXEMBOURG SA	8.125	06/01/23	.500	1248.070	124737.0	1MMM
7)	SEARS ROEBUCK ACCEPTANCE	7.500	10/15/27	.350	841.300	84004.3	43MM
8)	SEARS ROEBUCK ACCEPTANCE	6.750	01/15/28	1.612	391.919	39042.0	24MM
9)	SEARS ROEBUCK ACCEPTANCE	7.000	06/01/32	1.220	280.470	27895.8	91MM
10)	BANCO MACRO SA	6.750	11/04/26	84.750	244.894	24419.6	400MM
11)	CFLD CAYMAN INVESTMENT	6.900	01/13/23	27.000	194.362	19366.6	500MM
12)	KEURIG DR PEPPER INC	7.450	05/01/38	152.918	193.466	19154.8	125MM
13)	FANTASIA HOLDINGS GROUP	11.875	06/01/23	22.000	161.196	16048.7	541MM
14)	YUZHOU GROUP	8.500	02/04/23	33.700	148.813	14811.7	500MM
15)	FANTASIA HOLDINGS GROUP	9.250	07/28/23	23.125	143.418	14271.5	344MM
16)	CHINA AOYUAN GROUP LTD	6.350	02/08/24	16.500	129.624	12867.3	460MM
17)	PETROLEOS DE VENEZUELA S	5.375	04/12/27	3.750	126.669	12540.0	3MMM
18)	KAISA GROUP HOLDINGS LTD	10.875	07/23/23	28.000	125.710	12499.5	750MM
19)	TROUSDALE ISSUER LLC	6.500	04/01/25	33.150	121.027	11978.2	11MM
20)	KAISA GROUP HOLDINGS LTD	9.750	09/28/23	27.000	109.673	10896.0	980MM
21)	ALPHA HOLDING SA	9.000	02/10/25	14.000	107.566	10630.3	400MM

Source: Bloomberg Finance L.P.

18.9 Summary and Conclusions

Bonds are a major source of capital used by corporations and governments. This chapter covers many aspects of this market, including the following items—grouped by the chapter's important concepts.

1. **The basic types of corporate bonds.**

A. A corporate bond represents a corporation's promise to pay bondholders a fixed sum of money at maturity, along with periodic payments of interest. The sum paid at maturity is the bond's principal, and the periodic interest payments are coupons. Most bonds pay fixed coupons, but some pay floating coupon rates adjusted regularly according to prevailing market interest rates.

B. The largest category of corporate bond investors is life insurance companies, which own about 20 percent of all outstanding corporate bonds. Remaining ownership shares are roughly equally distributed among individual investors, pension funds, banks, and foreign investors.

2. **How callable and convertible bonds function.**

A. Corporate bonds are usually callable, which means that the issuer has the right to buy back outstanding bonds before maturity. When a bond issue is called, bondholders surrender their bonds in exchange for a prespecified call price.

B. Make-whole call provisions have become common in the corporate bond market. If a callable bond is called and has a make-whole call provision, bondholders receive the approximate value of what the bond is worth. This call provision gets its name because the bondholder does not suffer a loss if the bond is called.

C. Convertible bonds give the holder the right to convert the bond into a specified number of shares of common stock, usually that of the issuing firm.

3. **The different types of government bonds.**

A. The U.S. Treasury sponsors the STRIPS program, where Treasury bonds and notes are broken down into principal strips, which represent face value payments, and coupon strips, which represent individual coupon payments. Because each strip created under the STRIPS program represents a single future payment, strips effectively become zero coupon bonds.

B. Municipal notes and bonds are intermediate- to long-term interest-bearing obligations of state and local governments or agencies of those governments. Municipal debt is commonly called the tax-exempt market because the coupon interest is usually exempt from federal income tax, which makes municipal bonds attractive to investors in the highest income tax brackets. However, yields on municipal debt are less than yields on corporate debt with similar features and credit quality, thus eliminating much of the advantage of the tax exemption.

4. The basics of bond ratings.

A. When an issuer sells a new bond issue to the public, it usually has a credit rating assigned by several independent bond rating agencies. Without a credit rating, a new bond issue would be difficult to sell, which is why almost all bond issues sold to the public have credit ratings assigned.

B. Bonds with a speculative or lower grade rating, commonly called high-yield bonds, or junk bonds, represent corporate debt with higher-than-average credit risk. Credit ratings for junk bonds are frequently revised to reflect changing financial conditions.

GETTING DOWN TO BUSINESS

This chapter explored the world of bonds, an important category of investments for institutions, such as pension funds and life insurance companies, and also for individuals. How should you put this information to work?

Now that you understand the most important features of corporate bonds, you need to buy several different issues to experience the real-world gains and losses that come with managing a bond portfolio. With a simulated brokerage account (such as Stock-Trak), try putting roughly equal dollar amounts into three or four different corporate bond issues. Be sure to include some junk bonds in your selections.

You can find out more information about corporate bonds at the many websites now specializing in bonds, including Investing in Bonds (www.investinginbonds.com). The websites of bond rating agencies such as Moody's (www.moodys.com), Standard & Poor's (www.standardandpoors.com), Kroll (www.kroll.com), and Fitch (www.fitchratings.com) are also quite informative.

As you monitor the prices of your bonds, notice how interest rates influence their prices. You may also notice that for bonds with lower credit ratings, the stock price of the issuing company is an important influence. Why do you think this is so?

Of course, with the convertible issues, the bond price will definitely be influenced by the underlying stock value, but the impact depends on the specific conversion features of the bond, including whether the bond is in the money or not.

For the latest information on the real world of investments, visit us at jmdinvestments.blogspot.com.

Key Terms

adjustable-rate bonds 607
bid-ask spread 613
bond refunding 600
convertible bonds 603
credit rating 619
default risk 615
discount basis 609
exchangeable bonds 605

face value 608
general obligation bonds (GOs) 615
high-yield bonds 621
hybrid bonds 616
imputed interest 609
indenture summary 600
insured municipal bonds 617
in-the-money bond 604

Related Bloomberg Functions

SRCH	Fixed Income Search, 18.1
FIW	Fixed Income Worksheet, 18.1
DDIS	Debt Distribution, 18.1
CAST	Capital Structure, 18.2
NI EQL	Equity-Linked Securities, 18.2
OVCV	Convertible Valuation, 18.2
CSCH	Convertible Search, 18.2
CVM	Convertible Table, 18.2
DEBT	Sovereign Debt Ownership, 18.3
SOVM	Sovereign Debt Monitor, 18.4
USD	U.S. Treasuries Monitor, 18.4
ILBE	World Inflation Breakeven Rates, 18.4
FIT TIPS	Fixed Income Trading: U.S. TIPS, 18.4
ILB	Inflation-Linked Bonds, 18.4
ECO	Economic Calendars, 18.5
AUCR	Auction Results, 18.5
MSRC	Muni Bond Search, 18.7
PICK	Muni Offerings, 18.7
GBY	Municipal Bond Monitor, 18.7
DES	Security Description, 18.8
RATD	Ratings Definitions, 18.8
CSDR	Sovereign Ratings, 18.8
CRPR	Credit Profile, 18.8
YAS	Yield and Spread Analysis, 18.8
SOVR	Sovereign CDS Monitor, 18.8
DIS	Distressed Bonds, 18.8

Chapter Review Problems and Self-Test

1. **Callable Bonds (LO2, CFA3)**   A particular bond matures in 30 years. It is callable in 10 years at 110. The call price is then cut by 1 percent of par each year until the call price reaches par. If the bond is called in 12 years, how much will you receive? Assume a $1,000 face value.

2. **Convertible Bonds (LO2, CFA5)**   A convertible bond has an 8 percent coupon, paid semiannually, and will mature in 15 years. If the bond were not convertible, it would be priced to yield 9 percent. The conversion ratio on the bond is 40, and the stock is currently selling for $24 per share. What is the minimum value of this bond?

3. **Equivalent Yields (LO3, CFA2)**   A particular investor faces a 40 percent tax rate. If an AA-rated municipal bond yields 4 percent, what must a similar taxable issue yield for the investor to be impartial to them?

Answers to Self-Test Problems

1. The call price will be 110% − 2 × 1% = 108% of face value, or $1,080.

2. The minimum value is the larger of the conversion value and the intrinsic bond value. The conversion value is 40 × $24 = $960. To calculate the intrinsic bond value, note that we have a face value of $1,000 (by assumption), a semiannual coupon of $40, an annual yield of 9 percent (4.5 percent per half-year), and 15 years to maturity (30 half-years). Using the standard bond pricing formula from an earlier chapter (or a financial calculator), the bond's price (be sure to verify this) if it were not convertible is $918.56. This convertible bond thus will sell for more than $960.

3. The equivalent taxable yield is the municipal yield "grossed up" by one minus the tax rate:

$$\frac{.04}{1 - .40} = .0667, \text{ or } 6.67\%$$

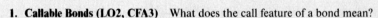

Test Your Investment Quotient

1. **Callable Bonds (LO2, CFA3)**   What does the call feature of a bond mean?
   a. An investor can call for payment on demand.
   b. An investor can only call if the firm defaults on an interest payment.
   c. The issuer can call the bond issue prior to the maturity date.
   d. The issuer can call the issue during the first three years.

2. **Callable Bonds (LO2, CFA3)**   Who primarily benefits from a call provision on a corporate bond?
   a. The issuer
   b. The bondholders
   c. The trustee
   d. The government regulators

3. **Callable Bonds (LO2, CFA3)**   Which of the following describes a bond with a call feature?
   a. It is attractive because the immediate receipt of principal plus premium produces a high return.
   b. It is more likely to be called when interest rates are high because the interest savings will be greater.
   c. It would usually have a higher yield than a similar noncallable bond.
   d. It generally has a higher credit rating than a similar noncallable bond.

4. **Callable Bonds (LO2, CFA3)**   Two bonds are identical, except one is callable and the other is noncallable. Compared to the noncallable bond, the callable bond has:
   a. Negative convexity and a lower price.
   b. Negative convexity and a higher price.
   c. Positive convexity and a lower price.
   d. Positive convexity and a higher price.

5. **Convexity (LO1, CFA3)**   What does positive convexity on a bond imply?
   a. The direction of change in yield is directly related to the change in price.
   b. Prices increase at a faster rate as yields drop than they decrease as yields rise.
   c. Price changes are the same for both increases and decreases in yields.
   d. Prices increase and decrease at a faster rate than the change in yield.

6. **Convexity (LO1, CFA3)**   A bond with negative convexity is best described as having a price-yield relationship displaying:
   a. Positive convexity at high yields and negative convexity at low yields.
   b. Negative convexity at high yields and positive convexity at low yields.
   c. Negative convexity at low and high yields and positive convexity at medium yields.
   d. Positive convexity at low and high yields and negative convexity at medium yields.

7. **Duration (LO1, CFA3)**   Which of the following most accurately measures interest rate sensitivity for bonds with embedded options?
   a. Convexity
   b. Effective duration
   c. Modified duration
   d. Macaulay duration

8. **Refundings (LO1, CFA3)** The refunding provision of an indenture allows bonds to be retired unless:

   a. They are replaced with a new issue having a lower interest cost.
   b. The remaining time to maturity is less than five years.
   c. The stated time period in the indenture has not passed.
   d. The stated time period in the indenture has passed.

9. **Credit Risk (LO4, CFA4)** A fallen angel bond is best described as a bond issued:

   a. Below investment grade.
   b. At an original-issue discount.
   c. As investment grade, but it has declined to speculative grade.
   d. As a secured bond, but the collateral value has declined below par value.

10. **Convertible Bonds (LO2, CFA5)** Which one of the following statements about convertible bonds is false?

    a. The yield on the convertible bond will typically be higher than the yield on the underlying common stock.
    b. The convertible bond will likely participate in a major upward movement in the price of the underlying common stock.
    c. Convertible bonds are typically secured by specific assets of the issuing company.
    d. A convertible bond can be valued as a straight bond with an attached option.

11. **Convertible Bonds (LO2, CFA5)** A convertible bond sells at $1,000 par with a conversion ratio of 40 and an accompanying stock price of $20 per share. The conversion price and conversion value are, respectively:

    a. $20 and $1,000.
    b. $20 and $800.
    c. $25 and $1,000.
    d. $25 and $800.

12. **Convertible Bonds (LO2, CFA5)** A convertible bond has a par value of $1,000 and a conversion ratio of 20. The price of the underlying stock is $40. What is the conversion value?

    a. $20
    b. $800
    c. $1,000
    d. $25

13. **Agency Bonds (LO1, CFA2)** The following are quotes for an agency bond:

Bid	Ask
102:02	102:05

    If the face value of the bond is $1,000, the price an investor should pay for the bond is *closest* to:

    a. $1,020.63.
    b. $1,021.56.
    c. $1,025.00.
    d. $1,026.25.

14. **Treasury STRIPS (LO3, CFA2)** When originally issued, a 10-year-maturity Treasury note can be stripped into how many separate components?

    a. 10
    b. 11
    c. 20
    d. 21

15. **Treasury Bills (LO1, CFA2)** Treasury bills are sold on a discount basis, meaning that the difference between their issue price and their redemption value is:

    a. The same for all T-bill issues.
    b. The imputed interest on the T-bill.
    c. Never less than the issue price.
    d. The bond equivalent yield for the T-bill.

16. **Treasury Auctions (LO1, CFA2)** Which of the following statements about single-price Treasury auctions is true?

   a. Competitive bidders pay their bid prices.
   b. Noncompetitive bidders pay the stop-out bid plus a 10 percent premium.
   c. Noncompetitive bidders pay the stop-out bid.
   d. All of the above are true.

17. **Treasury Dealers (LO1, CFA2)** When trading U.S. Treasury securities, Treasury dealers:

   a. Buy at the bid price and sell at the ask price.
   b. Sell at the bid price and buy at the ask price.
   c. Buy at the stop-out bid price and sell at the market price.
   d. Sell at the stop-out bid price and buy at the market price.

18. **Agency Bonds (LO3, CFA2)** Which statement applies to a bond issued by an agency of the U.S. government?

   a. It is exempt from the federal income tax on interest.
   b. It becomes a direct obligation of the U.S. Treasury in case of default.
   c. It is secured by assets held by the agency.
   d. None of the above.

19. **Agency Bonds (LO3, CFA2)** Which is true for bonds issued by all agencies of the U.S. government?

   a. They become direct obligations of the U.S. Treasury.
   b. They are secured bonds backed by government holdings.
   c. They are exempt from federal income tax.
   d. None of the above.

20. **Municipal Bonds (LO3, CFA2)** Which of the following investors is most likely to invest in locally issued municipal bonds?

   a. High-income individual with a need for liquidity
   b. High-income individual living in a triple income tax municipality
   c. Commercial bank
   d. Life insurance company

21. **Revenue Bonds (LO3, CFA2)** A revenue bond is distinguished from a general obligation bond in that revenue bonds have which of the following characteristics?

   a. They are issued by counties, special districts, cities, towns, and state-controlled authorities, whereas general obligation bonds are issued only by the states themselves.
   b. They are typically secured by limited taxing power, whereas general obligation bonds are secured by unlimited taxing power.
   c. They are issued to finance specific projects and are secured by the revenues of the project being financed.
   d. They have first claim to any revenue increase of the issuing tax authority.

22. **Insured Municipal Bonds (LO3, CFA2)** Which one of the following generally is not true of an insured municipal bond?

   a. The price on an insured bond is higher than that on an otherwise identical uninsured bond.
   b. The insurance can be canceled in the event the issuer fails to maintain predetermined quality standards.
   c. The insurance premium is a one-time payment made at the time of issuance.
   d. The insurance company is obligated to make all defaulted principal and/or interest payments in a prompt and timely fashion.

23. **Taxable Equivalent Yield (LO3, CFA2)** A municipal bond carries a coupon of 6 3/4 percent and is trading at par. To a taxpayer in the 34 percent tax bracket, what would the taxable equivalent yield of this bond be?

   a. 4.5 percent
   b. 10.2 percent
   c. 13.4 percent
   d. 19.9 percent

24. **Taxable Equivalent Yield (LO3, CFA2)** A 20-year municipal bond is currently priced at par to yield 5.53 percent. For a taxpayer in the 33 percent tax bracket, what equivalent taxable yield would this bond offer?

   a. 8.25 percent
   b. 10.75 percent

c. 11.40 percent

d. None of the above

25. **Taxable Equivalent Yield (LO3, CFA2)**   The coupon rate on a tax-exempt bond is 5.6 percent and the coupon rate on a taxable bond is 8 percent. Both bonds sell at par. At what tax bracket (marginal tax rate) would an investor show no preference between the two bonds?

a. 30.0 percent

b. 39.6 percent

c. 41.7 percent

d. 42.9 percent

Concept Questions

1. **Bond Features (LO2, CFA3)**   What is a bond refunding? Is it the same thing as a call?

2. **Callable Bonds (LO2, CFA3)**   With regard to the call feature, what are call protection and the call premium? What typically happens to the call premium through time?

3. **Put Bonds (LO1, CFA5)**   What is a put bond? Is the put feature desirable from the investor's perspective? From the issuer's?

4. **Bond Yields (LO1, CFA4)**   What is the impact on a bond's coupon rate from:

   a. A call feature?

   b. A put feature?

5. **Floaters (LO1, CFA4)**   From the bondholder's perspective, what are the potential advantages and disadvantages of floating coupons?

6. **Embedded Options (LO2, CFA5)**   What are some examples of embedded options in bonds? How do they affect the price of a bond?

7. **Junk Bonds (LO1, CFA3)**   Explain the difference between an original-issue junk bond and a fallen angel bond.

8. **Callable Bonds (LO2, CFA5)**   All else the same, callable bonds have less interest rate sensitivity than noncallable bonds. Why? Is this a good thing?

9. **Callable Bonds (LO2, CFA5)**   Two callable bonds are essentially identical, except that one has a refunding provision while the other has no refunding provision. Which bond is more likely to be called by the issuer? Why?

10. **Bills versus Bonds (LO1, CFA2)**   What are the key differences between T-bills and T-bonds?

11. **Agencies versus Treasuries (LO3, CFA2)**   From an investor's standpoint, what are the key differences between Treasury and agency issues?

12. **Municipals versus Treasuries (LO3, CFA2)**   From an investor's standpoint, what are the main differences between Treasury and municipal issues?

13. **Revenues versus General Obligation Munis (LO3, CFA2)**   What is the difference between a revenue bond and a general obligation bond?

14. **Treasury versus Municipal Bonds (LO3, CFA2)**   Treasury and municipal bond yields are often compared to calculate critical tax rates. What concerns might you have about such a comparison? What do you think is true about the calculated tax rate?

15. **Callable Bonds (LO2, CFA2)**   For a callable bond selling above par, is it necessarily true that the yield to call will be less than the yield to maturity? Why or why not?

Questions and Problems

Core Questions

1. **Conversion Price (LO2, CFA5)**   A convertible bond has a $1,000 face value and a conversion ratio of 45. What is the conversion price?

2. **Conversion Ratio (LO2, CFA5)**   A company just sold a convertible bond at a par value of $1,000. If the conversion price is $58, what is the conversion ratio?

3. **Conversion Value (LO2, CFA5)**   A convertible bond has a $1,000 face value and a conversion ratio of 36. If the stock price is $42, what is the conversion value?

4. **Callable Bonds (LO2, CFA5)** A bond matures in 25 years but is callable in 10 years at 120. The call premium decreases by 2 percent of par per year. If the bond is called in 14 years, how much will you receive?

5. **Call Premium (LO2, CFA5)** You own a bond with a 6 percent coupon rate and a yield to call of 6.90 percent. The bond currently sells for $1,070. If the bond is callable in five years, what is the call premium of the bond?

6. **Convertible Bonds (LO2, CFA5)** A convertible bond has a 5 percent coupon, paid semiannually, and will mature in 10 years. If the bond were not convertible, it would be priced to yield 4 percent. The conversion ratio on the bond is 25 and the stock is currently selling for $49 per share. What is the minimum value of this bond?

7. **Convertible Bonds (LO2, CFA5)** You own a convertible bond with a conversion ratio of 20. The stock is currently selling for $72 per share. The issuer of the bond has announced a call with a call price of 108. What are your options here? What should you do?

8. **STRIPS Price (LO1, CFA2)** What is the price of a STRIPS with a maturity of 12 years, a face value of $10,000, and a yield to maturity of 5.2 percent?

9. **STRIPS YTM (LO1, CFA2)** A STRIPS with nine years until maturity and a face value of $10,000 is trading for $7,693. What is the yield to maturity?

10. **Treasury Auctions (LO1, CFA2)** The Federal Reserve announces an offering of Treasury bills with a face value of $60 billion. Noncompetitive bids are made for $8 billion, along with the following competitive bids:

Bidder	Price Bid	Quantity Bid
A	$9,400	$15 billion
B	9,405	14 billion
C	9,410	11 billion
D	9,415	8 billion
E	9,425	10 billion
F	9,430	9 billion

In a single-price auction, which bids are accepted and what prices are paid by each bidder? How much money is raised by the entire offering?

11. **Municipal Bonds (LO3, CFA2)** A municipal bond with a coupon rate of 2.7 percent has a yield to maturity of 3.9 percent. If the bond has 10 years to maturity, what is the price of the bond? Remember, most municipal bonds have a face value of $5,000.

12. **Yield to Maturity (LO3, CFA1)** A municipal bond with a coupon rate of 6.2 percent sells for $4,920 and has seven years until maturity. What is the yield to maturity of the bond?

13. **Yield to Call (LO2, CFA5)** Assume a municipal bond has 18 years until maturity and sells for $5,640. It has a coupon rate of 5.70 percent and it can be called in 10 years. What is the yield to call if the call price is 110 percent of par?

14. **Tax Equivalent Yields (LO3, CFA2)** A taxable corporate issue yields 6.5 percent. For an investor in a 35 percent tax bracket, what is the equivalent aftertax yield?

15. **Tax Rates (LO3, CFA2)** A taxable issue yields 6.4 percent, and a similar municipal issue yields 4.7 percent. What is the critical marginal tax rate?

Intermediate Questions

16. **Treasury Prices (LO1, CFA2)** A Treasury bill has a bid yield of 2.75 and an ask yield of 2.73. The bill matures in 152 days. What is the least you could pay to acquire a bill? (*Note:* You may need to review material from an earlier chapter for the relevant formula.)

17. **Treasury Prices (LO1, CFA2)** At what price could you sell the Treasury bill referred to in Problem 16? What is the dollar spread for this bill? (*Note:* You may need to review material from an earlier chapter for the relevant formula.)

18. **Treasury Prices (LO1, CFA2)** A Treasury issue is quoted at 102.28125 bid and 102.375 ask. What is the least you could pay to acquire a bond?

19. **Treasury Yields (LO1, CFA2)**   A Treasury bond with the longest maturity (30 years) has an ask price quoted at 99.4375. The coupon rate is 4.6 percent, paid semiannually. What is the yield to maturity of this bond?

20. **Convertible Bonds (LO2, CFA5)**   Ashton Long, a bond analyst, is analyzing a convertible bond. The characteristics of the bond are given below.

Convertible Bond Characteristics	
Par value	$1,000
Annual coupon rate (annual pay)	7.2%
Conversion ratio	25
Market price	105% of par
Straight value	99% of par
Underlying Stock Characteristics	
Current market price	$32 per share

Compute the bond's conversion value and conversion price.

21. **Convertible Bonds (LO2, CFA5)**   Determine whether the value of a callable convertible bond will increase, decrease, or remain unchanged if there is an increase in stock price volatility. What if there is an increase in interest rate volatility? Justify each of your responses.

Use the following information to answer Problems 22 and 23: Stephanie Poden is evaluating her investment alternatives in Sands Incorporated by analyzing a Sands convertible bond and Sands common equity. Characteristics of the two securities are as follows:

Characteristic	Convertible Bond	Common Equity
Par value	$1,000	
Coupon (annual payment)	6%	
Current market price	$960	$42 per share
Straight bond value	$940	
Conversion ratio	25	
Conversion option	At any time	
Dividend		$0
Expected market price in one year	$1,080	$54 per share

22. **Convertible Bonds (LO2, CFA5)**   Calculate the following:
   a. The current market conversion price for the Sands convertible bond.
   b. The expected one-year rate of return for the Sands convertible bond.
   c. The expected one-year rate of return for the Sands common equity.

23. **Convertible Bonds (LO2, CFA5)**   One year has passed and Sands's common equity price has increased to $58 per share. Name the two components of the convertible bond's value. Indicate whether the value of each component should increase, stay the same, or decrease in response to the increase in Sands's common equity.

Spreadsheet Problems

24. **STRIPS Price (LO1, CFA2)**   A STRIPS traded on May 1, 2022, matures in 18 years on May 1, 2040. Assuming a 4.1 percent yield to maturity, what is the STRIPS price?

25. **STRIPS YTM (LO1, CFA2)**   A STRIPS traded on November 1, 2022, matures in 12 years on November 1, 2034. The quoted STRIPS price is 62.75. What is its yield to maturity?

26. **Make-Whole Call Premium (LO2, CFA5)**   Assume that Kendal Corp. has an outstanding bond issue with a par value of $1,000 and a current market price of $1,022.70 per bond. The bond has seven years remaining and a coupon rate of 6 percent.

   a. Find the current yield to maturity for the Kendal Corp. bond.
   b. If the bond trades at a yield spread of 1.5 percent above comparable U.S. Treasury notes, what must the current yield on Treasury notes be?
   c. If the Kendal bond has a make-whole call premium of 130 basis points above the U.S. Treasury rate, what is the make-whole call premium?

CFA Exam Review by Kaplan Schweser

[CFA3, CFA5]

Patrick Wall is a new associate at a large international financial institution. Mr. Wall recently completed his finance degree and is currently a CFA Level I candidate. Mr. Wall has a new position as the assistant to the firm's fixed-income portfolio manager. His boss, Charles Johnson, is responsible for familiarizing Mr. Wall with the basics of fixed-income investing. Mr. Johnson asks Mr. Wall to evaluate the bonds shown below. The bonds are otherwise identical except for the call feature present in one of the bonds. The callable bond is callable at par and exercisable on the coupon dates only.

	Noncallable	Callable
Price	$100.83	$98.79
Time to maturity (years)	5	5
Time to first call date	—	0
Annual coupon	$6.25	$6.25
Interest payment	Semiannual	Semiannual
Yield to maturity	6.0547%	6.5366%
Price value per basis point	428.0360	—

1. Mr. Johnson asks Mr. Wall to compute the value of the call option. Using the given information, what is the value of the embedded call option?

   a. $0.00
   b. $1.21
   c. $2.04

2. Mr. Wall is a little confused over the relationship between the embedded option and the callable bond. How does the value of the embedded call option change when interest rate volatility increases?

   a. It increases.
   b. It may increase or decrease.
   c. It decreases.

3. Mr. Wall believes he understands the relationship between interest rates and straight bonds but is unclear how callable bonds change as interest rates increase. How do prices of callable bonds react to an increase in interest rates? The price:

   a. Increases.
   b. May increase or decrease.
   c. Decreases.

Bloomberg Exercises

1. Find the amount and type of debt that Costco (COST) has outstanding. **(CAST)**
2. Review the current yields on major U.S. Treasury securities. **(SOVM)**
3. Collect a list of inflation-linked bonds that are available to investors. **(ILB)**
4. Examine the credit rating summary for Visa (V). **(CRPR)**

What's on the Web?

1. **Bond Quotes** Go to finra-markets.morningstar.com/BondCenter/Default.jsp and find the corporate bond search. Enter "Ford" for Ford Motor Company in the "Issuer Name" box and search for Ford bonds. How many bonds are listed for sale? What are the different credit ratings for these bonds? What is the yield to maturity for the longest-maturity bond? What is its price?

632 Part 6 ● Topics in Investments

2. **Historical Credit Spreads** The Federal Reserve Bank of St. Louis has files with historical interest rates on its website at www.stlouisfed.org. Go to the site and find the monthly Moody's Seasoned Aaa Corporate Bond Yield and the monthly Moody's Seasoned Baa Corporate Bond Yield. You can calculate a credit spread as the difference between these two returns. When was the largest credit spread? The smallest? What factors do you think led to the large credit spreads and the small credit spreads?

3. **Treasury Auctions** Go to www.treasurydirect.gov and find the next Treasury auctions scheduled. When are the auctions scheduled? What instruments will be offered at these auctions?

4. **Municipal Bond Prices** Go to www.municipalbonds.com and find the municipal bonds traded yesterday for your state. What was the most active bond in terms of the number of trades? Which bond traded the highest dollar amount? How many bonds had a spread of more than one point in trading yesterday?

Projecting Cash Flow and Earnings

"Financial statements are like fine perfume; to be sniffed, but never swallowed."

–Abraham Briloff

Learning Objectives

Help yourself grow as a stock analyst by knowing:

1. How to obtain financial information about companies.

2. How to read basic financial statements.

3. How to use performance and price ratios.

4. How to use the percentage of sales method in financial forecasting.

Cash flow is a company's lifeblood, and, for a healthy company, the primary source of cash flow is earnings. Security analysts strive to make accurate predictions about future cash flow and earnings because an analyst who predicts these well has a head start in forecasting future stock performance.

Like any security analyst, we must examine financial statements to make cash flow and earnings projections. The quality of our financial statement analysis depends on accurate and timely financial statements. Generally, firms issue financial statements that provide a fair and accurate summary of the firm's financial health. You should know, however, that firms do have some discretion in reporting financial information. In rare cases, firms issue inaccurate, or even fraudulent, financial statements. Therefore, Abraham Briloff offers sound advice when he advocates a careful viewing of financial statements.

CFA™ Exam Topics in This Chapter:

1. Introduction to financial statement analysis (L1, S5)
2. Financial reporting standards (L1, S5)
3. Understanding income statements (L1, S6)
4. Understanding balance sheets (L1, S6)
5. Understanding cash flow statements (L1, S6)
6. Financial analysis techniques (L1, S6)
7. Financial reporting quality (L1, S8)
8. Applications of financial statement analysis (L1, S8)
9. Measures of leverage (L1, S10)
10. Evaluating quality of financial reports (L2, S5)
11. Integration of financial statement analysis techniques (L2, S5)

Go to Connect for a guide that aligns your textbook with CFA readings.

In a previous chapter, we examined some important concepts of stock analysis and valuation. Many of these concepts depend on either cash flow or earnings forecasts. In this chapter, we probe more deeply into the topic of stock valuation through an analysis of financial statements. In particular, we focus on cash flow and earnings forecasting. In this chapter, you will become acquainted with the financial accounting concepts necessary to understand basic financial statements and to make forecasts of cash flow and earnings. You may not become an expert analyst—this requires experience. But you will have a solid grasp of the fundamentals, which is a really good start.

Most investors have a difficult time reading the financial statements that are directly issued by firms. These investors rely on secondary sources of financial information. Bear in mind, however, that no one is paid well just for reading secondary sources of financial information.

By studying this chapter, you are taking an important step toward becoming "financial statement literate" (a good course in financial accounting is also very helpful). Ultimately, you learn how to read financial statements by reading financial statements! You know that your golf or tennis game improves with practice. Your financial statement reading skills also improve with practice. If you have an aptitude for it, financial statement analysis is a skill worth mastering. Good analysts are paid well because they provide good analyses. Who knows? Perhaps you, too, will become a financial analyst.

Review Regulation FD at the SEC website: www.sec.gov.

19.1 Sources of Financial Information

Good financial analysis begins with good financial information. An excellent primary source of financial information about any company is its annual report to stockholders. Most companies expend considerable resources preparing and distributing annual reports. In addition to their stockholders, companies also make annual reports available to anyone who requests a copy. In fact, most companies provide electronic copies of their financial statements on their websites, typically under a tab labeled "Investor Information."

A convenient way to access annual reports from several companies at one time is to visit the website of the Securities and Exchange Commission (SEC). The SEC requires corporations with publicly traded securities to prepare and submit financial statements on a regular basis. When received, these documents are made available for immediate public access through the SEC's Electronic Data Gathering, Analysis, and Retrieval (**EDGAR**) archives. Visit sec.gov and click on the "Filings" tab to enter the EDGAR database.

The most important EDGAR document is the annual **10-K** report, often called the "10-K." Companies are required to submit an EDGAR-compatible 10-K file to the SEC at the end of each fiscal year. They are also required to file quarterly updates, called 10-Qs. The **10-Q** is a mini-10-K filed each quarter, except when the 10-K is filed. Every 10-K and 10-Q report contains three important financial statements: a balance sheet, an income statement, and a cash flow statement. You must be familiar with these three financial statements to analyze company earnings and cash flow.

The Securities and Exchange Commission's **Regulation FD (Fair Disclosure)** stipulates that when a company discloses **material nonpublic information** to security analysts and stockholders who may trade on the basis of the information, it must also make a simultaneous disclosure of that information to the general public. Most companies satisfy Regulation FD by distributing important announcements via e-mail alerts. To receive these e-mail alerts automatically, you can register for the service at the company's website. You can usually find the registration page in the investor relations section of the company's website.

Related Bloomberg Functions

FA   Financial Analysis

EDGAR
Electronic archive of company filings with the SEC.

10-K
Annual company report filed with the SEC.

10-Q
Quarterly updates of 10-K reports filed with the SEC.

Regulation FD (Fair Disclosure)
Requires companies making a public disclosure of material nonpublic information to do so fairly, without preferential recipients.

material nonpublic information
Any information that could reasonably be expected to affect the price of a security.

19.2 Financial Statements

Financial statements reveal the hard facts about a company's operating and financial performance. This is why the SEC requires timely dissemination of financial statements to the public. It's also why security analysts spend considerable time poring over a firm's financial

balance sheet
Accounting statement that provides a snapshot view of a company's assets and liabilities on a particular date.

income statement
Summary statement of a firm's revenues and expenses over a specific accounting period, usually a quarter or a year.

cash flow statement
Analysis of a firm's sources and uses of cash over the accounting period, summarizing operating, investing, and financing cash flows.

asset
Anything a company owns that has value.

liability
A firm's financial obligation.

equity
An ownership interest in the company.

statements before making an investment recommendation. A firm's balance sheet, income statement, and cash flow statement are essential reading for security analysts. Each of these interrelated statements offers a distinct perspective. The **balance sheet** provides a snapshot view of a company's assets and liabilities on a particular date. The **income statement** measures operating performance over an accounting period, usually a quarter or a year, and summarizes company revenues and expenses. The **cash flow statement** reports how cash was generated and where it was used over the accounting period. Understanding the format and contents of these three financial statements is a prerequisite for understanding earnings and cash flow analysis.

We begin by considering the basic structure and general format of financial statements through a descriptive analysis of the balance sheet, income statement, and cash flow statement of a hypothetical intergalactic company—Borg Corporation.

THE BALANCE SHEET

Table 19.1 presents year-end 2535 and 2536 balance sheets for Borg Corporation. The format of these balance sheets is typical of those contained in company annual reports distributed to stockholders and company 10-K filings with the SEC. You will quickly see the accounting practice of specifying subtraction with parentheses and calculating subtotals with underlines. For example, Borg's 2536 fixed assets section is reproduced below, with the left numerical column following standard accounting notation and the right numerical column following standard arithmetic notation:

Fixed Assets	Accounting Style	Numeric Style
Plant facilities	$35,000	$35,000
Production equipment	20,000	+20,000
Administrative facilities	15,000	+15,000
Distribution facilities	10,000	+10,000
Accumulated depreciation	(20,000)	−20,000
Total fixed assets	$60,000	= $60,000

In the accounting style column, locate the row labeled "Total fixed assets." The single underline indicates this number will be used in another sum. Referring to Table 19.1, notice that total fixed assets is a subtotal used to calculate total assets, which is indicated by a double underline. With these conventions in mind, let us look over these sample balance sheets and try to become familiar with their format and contents.

The Borg Corporation balance sheet has four major **asset** categories: current assets, fixed assets, goodwill, and other assets. Current assets are cash or items that will be converted to cash or be used within a year. For example, inventory will be sold, accounts receivable will be collected, and materials and supplies will be used within a year. Cash is, of course, the quintessential current asset. Fixed assets have an expected life longer than one year and are used in normal business operations. Fixed assets may be tangible or intangible. Property, plant, and equipment are the most common tangible fixed assets. Borg Corporation has no intangible fixed assets. However, rights, patents, and licenses are examples of intangible assets. Except for land, all fixed assets normally depreciate in value over time. Goodwill measures the premium paid over market value to acquire an asset. Other assets include miscellaneous items that do not readily fit into any of the other asset categories.

The Borg balance sheet has three major **liability** categories: current liabilities, long-term debt, and other liabilities. Current liabilities normally require payment or other action within a one-year period. These include accounts payable and short-term debt. Long-term debt includes notes, bonds, or other loans with a maturity longer than one year. Other liabilities include miscellaneous items that do not belong to any other liability category.

Shareholder **equity** is the difference between total assets and total liabilities. It includes paid-in capital, which is the amount received by the company from issuing common stock, and retained earnings, which represents accumulated income not paid out as dividends but instead used to finance company growth.

TABLE 19.1

Borg Corporation Balance Sheets, 2536 and 2535

	Year 2536	Year 2535
Current assets		
Cash	$ 2,000	$ 1,480
Accounts receivable	6,200	6,200
Prepaid expenses	1,500	1,500
Materials and supplies	1,300	1,300
Inventory	9,000	9,000
Total current assets	$20,000	$19,480
Fixed assets		
Plant facilities	$35,000	$35,000
Production equipment	20,000	20,000
Administrative facilities	15,000	15,000
Distribution facilities	10,000	
Accumulated depreciation	(20,000)	(17,000)
Total fixed assets	$60,000	$53,000
Goodwill	$ 5,000	
Other assets	3,000	3,000
Total assets	$88,000	$75,480
Current liabilities		
Short-term debt	$10,000	$10,000
Accounts payable	5,000	5,000
Total current liabilities	$15,000	$15,000
Long-term debt	$30,000	$20,000
Other liabilities	3,000	3,000
Total liabilities	$48,000	$38,000
Shareholder equity		
Paid-in capital	$10,000	$10,000
Retained earnings	30,000	27,480
Total shareholder equity	$40,000	$37,480
Total liabilities and equity	$88,000	$75,480
Shares outstanding	2,000	2,000
Year-end stock price	$ 40	$ 36

The fundamental accounting equation for balance sheets states that assets are equal to liabilities plus equity:

$$\text{Assets} = \text{Liabilities} + \text{Equity} \qquad (19.1)$$

This equation says that the balance sheet must always "balance" because the left side must always equal the right side. If an imbalance occurs when a balance sheet is created, then an accounting error has been made and needs to be corrected.

Financial analysts often find it useful to condense a balance sheet down to its principal categories. This has the desirable effect of simplifying further analysis while still revealing the basic structure of the company's assets and liabilities. How much a balance sheet can be condensed and still be useful is a subjective judgment of the analyst. When making this decision, recall Albert Einstein's famous dictum: "Simplify as much as possible, but no more."

Table 19.2 is a condensed version of Borg's 2536 balance sheet that still preserves its basic structure. Notice that the current assets rows are reduced to two components: cash and operating assets. We separate cash from operating assets for a good reason.

TABLE 19.2	Borg Corporation	Condensed 2536 Balance Sheet		
Cash	$ 2,000	Current liabilities		$15,000
Operating assets	18,000	Long-term debt		30,000
Fixed assets	60,000	Other liabilities		3,000
Goodwill and other assets	8,000	Shareholder equity		40,000
Total assets	$88,000	Total liabilities and equity		$88,000

Later, we show that the net cash increase from the cash flow statement is used to adjust cash on the balance sheet. This adjustment is more clearly illustrated by first separating current assets into cash and operating assets.

CHECK THIS

19.2a What are some examples of current assets?

19.2b What are some examples of fixed assets?

19.2c What are some examples of current liabilities?

19.2d Which accounts in Table 19.1 show changes between the 2535 and 2536 balance sheets?

THE INCOME STATEMENT

Table 19.3 is a condensed income statement for Borg Corporation. This income statement reports revenues and expenses for the corporation over a one-year accounting period. Examine it carefully and be sure you are familiar with its top-down structure.

The income statement begins with net sales, from which cost of goods sold (COGS) is subtracted to yield gross profit. Cost of goods sold represents direct costs of production and sales, that is, costs that vary directly with the level of production and sales. Next, depreciation and operating expenses are subtracted from gross profit to yield operating **income**. Operating expenses are indirect costs of administration and marketing. That is, these costs do not vary directly with production and sales. Subtracting interest expense on debt from operating income yields pretax income. Finally, subtracting income taxes from pretax income yields net income. Net income is often referred to as the "bottom line" because it is normally the last line of the income statement. In this example, however, we have added dividends and retained earnings information (items that often appear in a separate financial statement). To avoid a

income
The difference between a company's revenues and expenses, used to pay dividends to stockholders or kept as retained earnings within the company to finance future growth.

TABLE 19.3	Borg Corporation	Income Statement, Year 2536
		Year 2536
Net sales		$110,000
Cost of goods sold		(89,000)
Gross profit		$ 21,000
Depreciation		(3,000)
Other operating expenses		(10,000)
Operating income		$ 8,000
Interest expense		(2,000)
Pretax income		$ 6,000
Income taxes		(2,400)
Net income		$ 3,600
Dividends		(1,080)
Retained earnings		$ 2,520

separate statement, we show here that Borg Corporation paid dividends during the year. The sum of dividends and retained earnings is equal to net income:

$$\text{Net income} = \text{Dividends} + \text{Retained earnings} \qquad (19.2)$$

In Table 19.3, note that we assume a 40 percent tax rate.

CHECK THIS

19.2e   What is cost of goods sold (COGS)?

19.2f   What is the difference between gross profit and operating income?

19.2g   What is the difference between net income and pretax income?

19.2h   What is meant by retained earnings?

THE CASH FLOW STATEMENT

The cash flow statement reports where a company generated cash and where cash was used over a specific accounting period. The cash flow statement assigns all cash flows to one of three categories: operating cash flows, investment cash flows, or financing cash flows.

Table 19.4 is a condensed cash flow statement for Borg Corporation. The cash flow statement begins with net income, which is the principal accounting measure of earnings for a corporation. However, net income and **cash flow** are not the same and often deviate greatly from each other. A primary reason why net income differs from cash flow is that net income contains **noncash items**. For example, depreciation is a noncash expense that must be added to net income when calculating cash flow. Adjusting net income for noncash items yields **operating cash flow.**

In your accounting classes, you learned that the difference between earnings and cash flow is generally the result of accrual accounting. Under this system, businesses recognize income and expenses as they are incurred, rather than when the cash flow is actually paid or received. As a result, earnings might not reflect cash flow accurately.

With this thought in mind, analysts generally agree that cash flow is a more reliable measure than earnings and agree that cash flow is better suited for cross-company comparisons. Moreover, analysts often refer to a company as having "high-" (or "low-") quality earnings. This distinction is a judgment of whether earnings accurately reflect the cash flow of the company. If they do, then the company is said to have high-quality earnings.

Operating cash flow is the first of three cash flow categories reported in the cash flow statement. The second and third categories are investment cash flow and financing cash flow. **Investment cash flow** (or "investing" cash flow) includes any purchases or sales of fixed assets and investments. For example, Borg's purchase of Klingon Enterprises's distribution facilities reported in footnote (*) is an investment cash flow. **Financing cash flow** includes any funds raised by issuing securities or expended by a repurchase of outstanding securities. In this example, Borg's $10,000 debt issue and $1,080 dividend payout reported in footnote (†) are examples of financing cash flows.

cash flow
Income realized in cash form.

noncash items
Income and expense items not realized in cash form.

operating cash flow
Cash generated by a firm's normal business operations.

investment cash flow
Cash flow resulting from purchases and sales of fixed assets and investments.

financing cash flow
Cash flow originating from the issuance or repurchase of securities and the payment of dividends.

TABLE 19.4	**Borg Corporation** Condensed 2536 Cash Flow Statement	
		Year 2536
Net income		$ 3,600
Depreciation		3,000
Operating cash flow		$ 6,600
Investment cash flow*		(15,000)
Financing cash flow†		8,920
Net cash increase		$ 520

* December 31, 2536, purchase of distribution facilities from Klingon Enterprises for $15,000 (including $5,000 goodwill).

† Issue of $10,000 par value 5 percent coupon bonds, less a $1,080 dividend payout.

Standard accounting practice specifies that dividend payments to stockholders are financing cash flows, whereas interest payments to bondholders are operating cash flows. One reason is that dividend payments are discretionary, while interest payments are mandatory. Also, dividend payouts are not tax deductible, but interest payments are.

The sum of operating cash flow, investment cash flow, and financing cash flow yields the net change in the firm's cash. This change is the "bottom line" of the cash flow statement and reveals how much cash flowed into or out of the company's cash account during an accounting period. In this case, $520 of cash flowed into Borg Corporation (you can also see this change in cash by comparing the cash columns in Table 19.1).

CHECK THIS

19.2i   What is the difference between net income and operating cash flow?

19.2j   What are some noncash items used to calculate operating cash flow?

19.2k   What is the difference between an investment cash flow and a financing cash flow?

19.2l   What is meant by net increase in cash?

19.2m   Can you explain why a cash item like interest expense does not appear on the cash flow statement?

PERFORMANCE RATIOS AND PRICE RATIOS

Check out the "Investing" section at www.moneyunder30.com.

Annual reports and 10-Ks normally contain various items of supplemental information about the company. For example, certain profitability ratios may be reported to assist interpretation of the company's operating efficiency. For Borg Corporation, some standard profitability ratios for 2536 are calculated immediately below:

Ratio	Formula	Calculation
Gross margin	$\dfrac{\text{Gross profit}}{\text{Net sales}}$	$\dfrac{\$21,000}{\$110,000} = .1909$, or 19.09%
Operating margin	$\dfrac{\text{Operating income}}{\text{Net sales}}$	$\dfrac{\$8,000}{\$110,000} = .0727$, or 7.27%
Return on assets (ROA)	$\dfrac{\text{Net income}}{\text{Total assets}}$	$\dfrac{\$3,600}{\$88,000} = .0409$, or 4.09%
Return on equity (ROE)	$\dfrac{\text{Net income}}{\text{Shareholder equity}}$	$\dfrac{\$3,600}{\$40,000} = .09$, or 9.00%

return on assets (ROA)
Net income stated as a percentage of total assets.

return on equity (ROE)
Net income stated as a percentage of shareholder equity.

Notice that **return on assets (ROA)** and **return on equity (ROE)** are calculated using current year-end values for total assets and shareholder equity. It could be argued that prior-year values should be used for these calculations. However, the use of current year-end values is more common.

Annual reports and 10-Ks may also report per-share calculations of book value, earnings, and operating cash flow, respectively. Per-share calculations require the number of common stock shares outstanding. Borg's balance sheet reports 2,000 shares of common stock outstanding. Thus, for Borg Corporation, these per-share values are calculated as follows:

Ratio	Formula	Calculation
Book value per share (BVPS)	$\dfrac{\text{Shareholder equity}}{\text{Shares outstanding}}$	$\dfrac{\$40,000}{2,000} = \$20.00$
Earnings per share (EPS)	$\dfrac{\text{Net income}}{\text{Shares outstanding}}$	$\dfrac{\$3,600}{2,000} = \$1.80$
Cash flow per share (CFPS)	$\dfrac{\text{Operating cash flow}}{\text{Shares outstanding}}$	$\dfrac{\$6,600}{2,000} = \$3.30$

WORK THE WEB

One of the more frequent uses of financial ratios is in stock screening. Stock screening is the process of selecting stocks based on specific criteria. A popular method used by legendary investor Warren Buffett, among others, is searching for value stocks that have high growth potential. A value stock has a relatively low price-earnings ratio. However, low price-earnings ratios can be an indication of low future growth potential, so we also want to determine if these stocks have future growth possibilities.

We went to www.finviz.com and clicked on the "Screener" tab. You can see that there are three different sets of criteria to choose from: Descriptive, Fundamental, and Technical.

Under Descriptive criteria, we chose to limit our search to U.S. equities with a market cap over $10 billion (i.e., large-cap stocks). Under the Fundamental tab, which we show below, we screened for stocks with a PE less than 15, estimated EPS growth greater than 30 percent, and P/FCF less than 10. The results are shown in the table below. (Try it yourself.)

Using stock screening as an investment tool is not really this simple. What we have done here is narrowed the universe of stocks to a few stocks that meet our criteria. It is now up to us to further examine the companies to determine if they are actually good investments. In other words, stock screening is not the end of the investment process—it narrows the field.

No.	Ticker	Company	Sector	Industry	Country	Market Cap	P/E	Price	Change	Volume
1	COF	Capital One Financial Corporation	Financial	Credit Services	USA	44.30B	7.97	94.26	1.44%	1,683,647
2	CXO	Concho Resources Inc.	Basic Materials	Oil & Gas Drilling & Exploration	USA	22.50B	9.15	109.49	4.42%	2,591,658
3	DFS	Discover Financial Services	Financial	Credit Services	USA	27.31B	10.55	82.27	1.39%	1,561,063
4	DISH	DISH Network Corporation	Services	CATV Systems	USA	15.98B	11.71	35.08	4.40%	4,155,581
5	ETFC	E*TRADE Financial Corporation	Financial	Investment Brokerge - National	USA	12.36B	12.33	50.60	0.28%	1,076,136
6	FCX	Freeport-McMoRan Inc.	Basic Materials	Copper	USA	17.32B	6.32	11.95	3.82%	23,376,976
7	HIG	The Hartford Financial Services Group, Inc.	Financial	Property & Casualty Insurance	USA	18.94B	13.33	52.72	1.11%	1,869,505
8	LNC	Lincoln National Corporation	Financial	Life Insurance	USA	14.20B	9.08	67.15	1.19%	1,359,560
9	MRO	Marathon Oil Corporation	Basic Materials	Independent Oil & Gas	USA	13.26B	12.06	15.68	1.03%	15,512,602
10	MS	Morgan Stanley	Financial	Investment Brokerage - National	USA	80.04B	10.06	48.06	0.52%	5,795,715
11	MU	Micron Technology, Inc.	Technology	Semiconductor- Memory Chips	USA	48.69B	4.07	43.33	1.81%	16,326,559
12	PGR	The Progressive Corporation	Financial	Property & Casualty Insurance	USA	43.39B	14.80	74.43	−1.50%	4,002,476
13	RJF	Raymond James Financial, Inc.	Financial	Investment Brokerage - Regional	USA	12.91B	13.91	91.09	1.29%	530,163
14	STI	SunTrust Banks, Inc.	Financial	Money Center Banks	USA	29.36B	11.65	65.35	0.96%	2,048,256
15	SYF	Synchrony Financial	Financial	Credit Services	USA	24.25B	7.68	34.34	0.56%	2,606,804
16	URI	United Rentals, Inc.	Services	Rental & Leasing Services	USA	11.14B	10.56	140.24	2.36%	1,014,903
17	VLO	Valero Energy Corporation	Basic Materials	Oil & Gas Refining & Marketing	USA	37.24B	12.21	88.44	0.22%	2,993,302

Filters: cap:large fa_epsyoy:o30 fa_pe:u15 fa_pfcf:u10 geo:usa

Source: finviz.com, 2019.

Notice that cash flow per share (CFPS) is calculated using operating cash flow—*not* the bottom line on the cash flow statement (see Table 19.4). Usually, when you hear the term "cash flow," it refers to operating cash flow.

Recall that in a previous chapter, we made extensive use of price ratios to analyze stock values. Using the per-share values calculated immediately above and Borg's year-end stock price of $40 per share, we get the following price ratios:

Ratio	Formula	Calculation
Price-book (P/B)	$\dfrac{\text{Stock price}}{\text{BVPS}}$	$\dfrac{\$40}{\$20} = 2.00$
Price-earnings (PE)	$\dfrac{\text{Stock price}}{\text{EPS}}$	$\dfrac{\$40}{\$1.80} = 22.22$
Price-cash flow (P/CF)	$\dfrac{\text{Stock price}}{\text{CFPS}}$	$\dfrac{\$40}{\$3.30} = 12.12$

We use these price ratios later when assessing the potential impact of a sales campaign on Borg Corporation's future stock price. Our nearby *Work the Web* box shows how we can use price ratios to help screen for potential investments.

19.2n   What is the difference between gross margin and operating margin?

19.2o   What is the difference between return on assets and return on equity?

19.2p   What is the difference between earnings per share and cash flow per share?

19.2q   How is cash flow per share calculated?

Financial Statement Forecasting

Related Bloomberg Functions

BI	Bloomberg Intelligence
EE	Earnings and Estimates
EM	Earnings Trends
EEG	Earnings Estimates Graph

pro forma financial statements
Statements prepared using certain assumptions about future income, cash flow, and other items. "Pro forma" literally means according to prescribed form.

percentage of sales approach
A financial planning method in which some accounts vary with the level of predicted sales.

In December 2536, Borg publicly announces the completion of an acquisition of some distribution outlets from Klingon Enterprises, LLC. The stated purpose of the acquisition is to expand sales. Complementing the acquisition, Borg also announces plans for a marketing campaign to increase next year's net sales to a targeted $137,500.

As a Borg analyst, you must examine the potential impact of these actions. You immediately contact Borg management to inquire about the details of the acquisition and the marketing campaign. Armed with this additional information, you decide to construct **pro forma financial statements** for Borg Corporation for the year 2537.

THE PERCENTAGE OF SALES APPROACH

A simple model to construct pro forma financial statements is one in which every item increases at the same rate as sales. This may be a reasonable assumption for some financial statement items. For others, such as long-term debt, it probably is not because the amount of long-term debt is something set by company management. Therefore, long-term debt levels do not necessarily relate directly to the level of sales.

A more sophisticated model builds on the basic idea of separating the income statement and balance sheet items into two groups: those that do vary directly with sales and those that do not. Given a sales forecast, calculating how much financing the firm will need to support the predicted sales level is easy. This quick and practical model is known as the **percentage of sales approach**. You have decided to use this approach to generate pro forma financial statements for Borg Corporation for the year 2537.

THE PRO FORMA INCOME STATEMENT

The Borg Corporation announced projected sales for the year 2537 of $137,500—an increase of 25 percent over 2536. We use the 2536 Borg Corporation income statement and several assumptions to generate the pro forma income statement. From Table 19.3, we see that in the year 2536, the ratio of total costs to net sales was about 94.55 percent (actually 94.5454 percent). We assume the ratio of total costs to sales will be 94.55 percent in the year 2537 also.

Table 19.5 is our pro forma income statement for Borg Corporation for 2537. To generate Table 19.5, we assume that the ratio of cost of goods sold to net sales will be the same in 2537 as it was in 2536 (80.91 percent).

We see in Table 19.4 that depreciation in the year 2536 was $3,000. Accountants grapple with various methods to produce depreciation schedules. Here, as a practical matter, we apply the percentage of sales approach. Depreciation expense as a percentage of sales in 2536 was $3,000/$110,000 ≈ 2.7272 percent. For the year 2537, we estimate depreciation expense to be ($3,000/$110,000) × $137,500 = $3,750. (Note that we multiplied the actual ratio in 2536 by estimated sales in the year 2537.)

Borg Corporation financed the purchase of the distribution outlets with 5 percent coupon bonds, which represent long-term debt. To estimate the 2537 interest expense, we assume that Borg pays 4 percent simple interest on its short-term debt and 8 percent on its existing long-term debt. Given these assumptions, the 2536 interest expense of $2,000 was split $400 (= $10,000 × .04) for short-term debt and $1,600 (= $20,000 × .08) for long-term debt. Therefore, the additional $10,000 in long-term debt added at the end of 2536 will increase interest expense on long-term debt to $2,100 (= $20,000 × .08 + $10,000 × .05).

TABLE 19.5   **Borg Corporation**   Pro Forma Income Statement, Year 2537

	Year 2536	Year 2537
Net sales	$110,000	$137,500
Cost of goods sold	(89,000)	(111,250)
Gross profit	$ 21,000	$ 26,250
Depreciation	(3,000)	(3,750)
Other operating expenses	(10,000)	(12,500)
Operating income	$ 8,000	$ 10,000
Interest expense	(2,000)	(2,500)
Pretax income	$6,000	$ 7,500
Income taxes	(2,400)	(3,000)
Net income	$ 3,600	$ 4,500
Dividends	(1,080)	(1,350)
Retained earnings	$2,520	$ 3,150
Net profit margin	3.27%	3.27%
Total costs/Net sales	94.55%	94.55%

Adding an assumed $400 for interest on short-term debt, the total interest expense in the year 2537 will be $2,500.

Finally, recall that we assume that the ratio of total costs to net sales will be the same in 2537 as it was in 2536 (about 94.55 percent). To achieve this, we assume that the other operating expenses account is our "plug" and if we set this account to $12,500, we maintain the desired ratio of 94.55 percent.

The effect of assuming that total costs are a constant percentage of sales is to assume that the profit margin (net income/net sales) is constant. To check this, notice that in Table 19.5 Borg Corporation's profit margin was $3,600/$110,000 = 3.27 percent in 2536 and $4,500/$137,500 = 3.27 percent projected for 2537. In this calculation, a tax rate of 40 percent is assumed for both years.

Next, we need to project the dividend payment. The decision of how much of net income will be paid in dividends is a decision that rests with the management of Borg Corporation. However, two dividend payment schemes are reasonable: one where the *dollar* payout is the same from year to year and one where the *percentage* payout is the same from year to year.

We will assume that Borg management has a policy of paying a dividend that is a constant percentage of net income. For 2536, the dividend payout ratio was $1,080/$3,600 = 30 percent. We can also calculate the ratio of the addition to retained earnings to net income, which is $2,520/$3,600 = 70 percent for 2536. This ratio is called the *retention ratio* or *plowback ratio,* and it is equal to one minus the dividend payout ratio. The term "plowback ratio" is logical because if net income is not paid out to the shareholders, it must be retained by the company. Assuming the payout ratio is constant, the projected dividends are $4,500 × .30 = $1,350. Thus, the addition to retained earnings is $3,150.

THE PRO FORMA BALANCE SHEET

To generate a pro forma balance sheet, we start with the balance sheet for 2536 shown in Table 19.1. On this balance sheet, we assume that some of the items vary directly with sales and others do not. For the items that do vary with sales, we express each as a percentage of sales for the year just completed, year 2536. When an item does not vary directly with sales, we write "n/a," for "not applicable." For example, on the asset side, inventory is equal to about 8.2 percent of sales in 2536. We assume that this percentage also applies to 2537, so for each $1 increase in sales, inventory will increase by $.082.

The ratio of total assets to sales for 2536 is $88,000/$110,000 = .80, or 80 percent. The ratio of total assets to sales is sometimes called the **capital intensity ratio**. This ratio tells us

capital intensity ratio
A firm's total assets divided by its sales, or the amount of assets needed to generate $1 in sales.

the amount of assets needed to generate $1 in sales. So the higher this ratio, the more capital-intensive is the firm. For Borg Corporation, $.80 in assets was needed to generate $1 in sales in 2536. If we assume that the capital intensity ratio is constant, total assets of $110,000 will be needed to generate sales of $137,500 in 2537.

On the liability side of the balance sheet, we have assumed that only accounts payable vary with sales. The reason is that we expect Borg to place more orders with its suppliers as sales increase, so payables will change directly with sales. Short-term debt, on the other hand, represents bank borrowing. This account is not likely to vary directly with sales. Therefore, we write n/a in the "Approximate Percent of Sales" column for short-term debt in Table 19.6. Similarly, we write n/a for long-term debt because long-term debt will not vary directly with sales. The same is true for other liabilities and the paid-in capital account.

Retained earnings, however, will change with an increase in sales, but the increase in retained earnings will not be a simple percentage of sales. Instead, we must calculate the change in retained earnings based on our projected net income and dividends, which come from our pro forma income statement.

We can now construct a partial pro forma balance sheet for Borg Corporation, as shown in Table 19.6. We construct the column labeled "2537" by using the percentage of sales wherever possible to calculate projected amounts. For example, inventory in 2537 is projected to be ($9,000/$110,000) × $137,500 = $11,250. More generally, the ratio of total fixed

TABLE 19.6	Borg Corporation	Partial Pro Forma Balance Sheet, Year 2537		
	2536	**Approximate Percent of Sales**	**2537**	**Change**
Current assets				
Cash	$ 2,000	1.8%	$ 2,500	$ 500
Accounts receivable	6,200	5.6	7,750	1,550
Prepaid expenses	1,500	1.4	1,875	375
Materials and supplies	1,300	1.2	1,625	325
Inventory	9,000	8.2	11,250	2,250
Total current assets	$20,000	18.2	$ 25,000	$ 5,000
Total fixed assets	$60,000	54.5	$ 75,000	$15,000
Other assets	$ 8,000	7.3	$ 10,000	$ 2,000
Total assets	$88,000	80.0	$110,000	$22,000
Current liabilities				
Short-term debt	$10,000	n/a	$ 10,000	$ 0
Accounts payable	5,000	4.5	6,250	1,250
Total current liabilities	$15,000		$ 16,250	$ 1,250
Long-term debt	$30,000	n/a	$ 30,000	$ 0
Other liabilities	3,000	n/a	3,000	0
Total liabilities	$48,000		$ 49,250	$ 1,250
Shareholder equity				
Paid-in capital	$10,000	n/a	$ 10,000	$ 0
Retained earnings	30,000	n/a	33,150	3,150
Total shareholder equity	$40,000		$ 43,150	$ 3,150
Total liabilities and equity	$88,000		$ 92,400	$ 4,400
External financing needed:			$ 17,600	$17,600
Through short-term debt:				$ 2,500
Through long-term debt:				$15,100

assets to sales was about 54.5 percent in 2536. For 2537, total fixed assets is projected to be ($60,000/$110,000) × $137,500 = $75,000. This amount represents an increase of $15,000 from the total fixed assets in 2536.

For the items that do not vary directly with sales, note that we initially assume no change and write in the existing amounts. You can see the application of this method in the column labeled "2537" in Table 19.6. Notice that the change in retained earnings is projected to be $3,150, which is the amount shown in Table 19.5.

Inspecting the partial pro forma balance sheet for Borg Corporation, we see that total assets are projected to increase by $22,000 in 2537. However, without additional financing, liabilities and equity will increase by only $4,400, leaving a shortfall, or imbalance, of $22,000 − $4,400 = $17,600. In Table 19.6, to be safe, we have calculated this $17,600 shortfall in two ways: as the difference between total assets ($110,000) and total liabilities and equity ($92,400) and as the difference between the change in total assets ($22,000) and the change in total assets and liabilities ($4,400). We have labeled the shortfall amount as *external financing needed (EFN)*.

SCENARIO ONE

The creation of a pro forma income statement and a pro forma balance sheet points out a potentially serious problem with Borg Corporation's projected sales increase of 25 percent–it isn't going to happen unless Borg can somehow raise $17,600 in new financing. For analysts working for Borg Corporation, this is a good example of how the planning process can point out problems and potential conflicts. For example, if Borg had a goal of not raising new financing, then an increase in sales of 25 percent is not possible.

If we take the need for $17,600 in new financing as given, we know that Borg Corporation has three possible sources: short-term debt, long-term debt, and new equity. The choice of the exact combination of the three sources of financing is a decision that the management of Borg Corporation must make. For illustration, however, we will choose one of the many possible combinations.

Suppose Borg Corporation decides to borrow the needed funds, some via short-term debt and some via long-term debt. In Table 19.6, you can see that current assets increased by $5,000, but current liabilities increased only by $1,250 (the increase in accounts payable). If Borg wants to keep the ratio between current assets and current liabilities constant, it should borrow $2,500 in short-term debt. In 2536, the ratio between total current assets and total current liabilities was 4 to 3, or 1.3333 (= $20,000/$15,000). In 2537, total current assets are $25,000, which means total current liabilities should be $18,750, or $2,500 more than the amount shown in Table 19.6.

If Borg borrows $2,500 in short-term debt, this leaves $15,100 to be raised by issuing additional long-term debt. These financing amounts are shown at the bottom of Table 19.6. Table 19.7 shows a completed pro forma balance sheet given this assumed financing decision.

We have used a combination of short-term debt and long-term debt to solve the financing problem for Borg Corporation. It is extremely important for us to emphasize that this is only one possible strategy–and it might not even be the best strategy for Borg Corporation. As analysts, we could (and should) investigate many other scenarios. For example, we would have to ask how the increased debt load would affect future earnings of the company.

SCENARIO TWO

The assumption that assets are a fixed percentage of sales is convenient, but it may not be suitable in many cases. In particular, we made a hidden assumption when we constructed pro forma financial statements for Borg Corporation: We assumed that Borg was using its fixed assets at 100 percent of capacity because any increase in sales led to an increase in fixed assets. For most businesses, there would be some slack, or excess capacity, and production could be increased by, perhaps, running an extra shift or utilizing spare equipment.

	2536	Approximate Percent of Sales	2537	Change
Current assets				
Cash	$ 2,000	1.8%	$ 2,500	$ 500
Accounts receivable	6,200	5.6	7,750	1,550
Prepaid expenses	1,500	1.4	1,875	375
Materials and supplies	1,300	1.2	1,625	325
Inventory	9,000	8.2	11,250	2,250
Total current assets	$20,000	18.2	$ 25,000	$ 5,000
Total fixed assets	$60,000	54.5	$ 75,000	$15,000
Other assets	$ 8,000	7.3	$ 10,000	$ 2,000
Total assets	$88,000	80.0	$110,000	$22,000
Current liabilities				
Short-term debt	$10,000	n/a	$ 12,500	$ 2,500
Accounts payable	5,000	4.5	6,250	1,250
Total current liabilities	$15,000		$ 18,750	$ 3,750
Long-term debt	$30,000	n/a	$ 45,100	$15,100
Other liabilities	3,000	n/a	3,000	0
Total liabilities	$48,000	n/a	$ 66,850	$18,850
Shareholder equity				
Paid-in capital	$10,000	n/a	$ 10,000	$ 0
Retained earnings	30,000	n/a	33,150	3,150
Total shareholder equity	$40,000		$ 43,150	$ 3,150
Total liabilities and equity	$88,000		$110,000	$22,000
External financing needed (EFN):			$ 0	$ 0

If we assume that Borg Corporation is running at 75 percent of capacity, then the need for external funds will be quite different. When we say "75 percent of capacity," we mean that the current sales level is 75 percent of the full-capacity sales level:

$$\text{Current sales} = \$110,000 = .75 \times \text{Full-capacity sales}$$
$$\text{Full-capacity sales} = \$110,000/.75 = \$146,667$$

This calculation tells us that sales could increase by one-third, from $110,000 to $146,667, before any new fixed assets would be needed.

In Scenario One, we assumed that adding $15,000 in net fixed assets would be necessary. In our current scenario, no spending on fixed assets is needed because sales are projected to rise only to $137,500, which is substantially less than the $146,667 full-capacity sales level. As a result, our Scenario One estimate of $17,600 in external funds needed is too high. In fact, an argument could be made in Scenario Two that the level of external funds needed is $2,600.

To begin, you can see in Table 19.8 that we have now written n/a next to the total fixed assets account, and we have written in a value of $60,000 (the same as for the year 2536). When no change is assumed for the total fixed assets account, total assets increase by $7,000. On the liability side of the balance sheet as shown in Table 19.5, a sales level of $137,500 generates an increase of $3,150 in retained earnings. In addition, this sales level means that the accounts payable account will increase by $1,250. The difference between the increase in total assets and the increase in total liabilities and equity would be $2,600 without any external financing (= $7,000 − $3,150 − $1,250). In Table 19.8, which is a completed year 2537

TABLE 19.8

Borg Corporation Pro Forma Balance Sheet, Year 2537

	2536	Approximate Percent of Sales	2537	Change
Current assets				
Cash	$ 2,000	1.8%	$ 2,500	$ 500
Accounts receivable	6,200	5.6	7,750	1,550
Prepaid expenses	1,500	1.4	1,875	375
Materials and supplies	1,300	1.2	1,625	325
Inventory	9,000	8.2	11,250	2,250
Total current assets	$20,000	18.2	$25,000	$5,000
Total fixed assets	$60,000	n/a	$60,000	$ 0
Other assets	$ 8,000	7.3	$10,000	$2,000
Total assets	$88,000		$95,000	$7,000
Current liabilities				
Short-term debt	$10,000	n/a	$12,600	$2,600
Accounts payable	5,000	4.5	6,250	1,250
Total current liabilities	$15,000		$18,850	$3,850
Long-term debt	$30,000	n/a	$30,000	$ 0
Other liabilities	3,000	n/a	3,000	0
Total liabilities	$48,000	n/a	$51,850	$3,850
Shareholder equity				
Paid-in capital	$10,000	n/a	$10,000	$ 0
Retained earnings	30,000	n/a	33,150	3,150
Total shareholder equity	$40,000		$43,150	$3,150
Total liabilities and equity	$88,000		$95,000	$7,000

pro forma balance sheet, we see that this is the amount that the short-term debt account has increased. That is, we have assumed that Borg Corporation will use only short-term debt as its EFN source. You will note, however, that this assumption means that the ratio between total current assets and total current liabilities will decrease (slightly).

EXAMPLE 19.1

EFN and Capacity Usage

Suppose Borg Corporation was operating at 88 percent of capacity. What would sales be at full capacity? What is the EFN in this case? What is the capital intensity ratio at full capacity?

Full-capacity sales would be $110,000/.88 = $125,000. From Table 19.1, we know that fixed assets are $60,000. At full capacity, the ratio of fixed assets to sales is $60,000/$125,000 = .48. This tells us that Borg Corporation needs $.48 in fixed assets for every $1 in sales once the company reaches full capacity. At the projected sales level of $137,500, Borg needs $137,500 × .48 = $66,000 in fixed assets. This is $9,000 less than the original year 2537 value of $75,000 shown in Table 19.6. Therefore, EFN is $17,600 − $9,000 = $8,600. Current assets and other assets would still be $25,000 and $10,000, respectively, so total assets would be $101,000. The capital intensity ratio would then be $101,000/$137,500 = .7345.

CHECK THIS

19.3a What is the basic idea behind the percentage of sales approach?

19.3b Unless it is modified, what does the percentage of sales approach assume about fixed asset capacity usage?

PROJECTED PROFITABILITY AND PRICE RATIOS

In addition to preparing pro forma financial statements, you also decide to calculate projected profitability ratios and per-share values under the new sales forecast. These values are reported immediately below and compared with their original year-end values.

	Year 2536	Year 2537
Gross margin	19.09%	19.09%
Operating margin	7.27%	7.27%
Return on assets (ROA)	4.09%	4.09%/4.74%
Return on equity (ROE)	9.00%	10.43%
Book value per share (BVPS)	$20.00	$21.58
Earnings per share (EPS)	$ 1.80	$ 2.25
Cash flow per share (CFPS)	$ 3.30	$ 4.13

Note that two ROA numbers are provided for 2537. The first is from Scenario One, where we assume Borg is already running at 100 percent capacity. The second is from Scenario Two, where we assume Borg is running at 75 percent capacity.

One common method of analysis is to calculate projected stock prices under the new sales scenario using prior-period price ratios and projected per-share values from pro forma financial statements. For Borg Corporation, you decide to take your previously calculated year-end 2536 price ratios and multiply each ratio by its corresponding pro forma per-share value. The results of these projected stock price calculations (rounded) are shown immediately below:

$$P/B \times BVPS = 2 \times \$21.58 = \$43.16$$
$$P/E \times EPS = 22.22 \times \$2.25 = \$50.00$$
$$P/CF \times CFPS = 12.12 \times \$4.13 = \$50.06$$

Which projected stock price is correct? Well, it clearly depends on which sales level is realized and which price ratio the financial markets will actually use to value Borg Corporation's stock. This is where experience and breadth of knowledge count immensely. Of course, no one can make perfectly accurate predictions, but the analyst's job is to expertly assess the situation and make an investment recommendation supported by reasonable facts and investigation. But some analysts are better than others. Like professional baseball players, professional stock analysts with better batting averages can do very well financially.

19.4 Starbucks Corporation Case Study

Related Bloomberg Functions

BRC Bloomberg Portal: Single Security

RV Relative Valuation

Visit Starbucks's website at www.starbucks.com.

After carefully reading the analysis of Borg Corporation, you should have a reasonably clear picture of how to do an earnings and cash flow analysis using pro forma financial statements. In this section, we present an analysis based on the 2018 financial statements for Starbucks Corporation. As you will see, using data for a real company is challenging.

This section begins with a review of the 2018 financial statements for Starbucks. We then proceed to analyze the effects on earnings and cash flow that might result from two sales projection scenarios. The analysis is similar to that for Borg Corporation, with a few important differences. Note that amounts shown are in millions of dollars (except earnings per share).

Table 19.9 is the 2018 condensed balance sheet for Starbucks. This balance sheet shows that at fiscal year-end 2018 (September 30, 2018), Starbucks had $24,156 million (or $24.156 billion) of total assets and $1,176 million (or $1.176 billion) of shareholder equity. In Table 19.10, which is the 2018 condensed income statement for Starbucks, the bottom line reveals that Starbucks earned $4.518 billion in net income from $24.720 billion in net revenues.

TABLE 19.9

Starbucks Corporation Balance Sheet for 2018 and 2017
($ in 000,000s)

	2018	2017
Current assets		
Cash and cash equivalents	$ 8,756.3	$ 2,462.3
Short-term investments	181.5	228.6
Accounts receivable	693.1	870.4
Inventory	1,400.5	1,364.0
Other current assets	1,462.8	358.1
Total current assets	$12,494.2	$ 5,283.4
Fixed assets		
Long-term investments	$ 267.7	$ 542.3
Property, plant and equipment, net	6,263.8	5,401.1
Other assets	546.9	1,158.2
Total fixed assets	$ 7,078.4	$ 7,101.6
Goodwill and intangible assets	$ 4,583.8	$ 1,980.6
Total assets	$24,156.4	$14,365.6
Current liabilities		
Accounts payable	$ 1,179.3	$ 782.5
Accrued expenses	2,298.4	1,934.5
Other current liabilities	2,206.5	1,503.7
Total current liabilities	$ 5,684.2	$ 4,220.7
Long-term debt	$ 9,090.2	$ 3,932.6
Other long-term liabilities	8,206.2	755.3
Total liabilities	$22,980.6	$ 8,908.6
Shareholder equity		
Common stock	$ 1.3	$ 1.4
Paid-in capital	41.1	41.1
Retained earnings	1,457.4	5,563.2
Other stockholder equity	(324.0)	(148.7)
Total stockholder equity	$ 1,175.8	$ 5,457.0
Total liabilities and equity	$24,156.4	$14,365.6
Shares outstanding (000,000s)	1,394.6	1,461.5
(Fiscal) Year-end stock price	$ 56.84	$ 53.71

From these values, we calculate Starbucks's return on assets (ROA) as 18.7 percent. Because of a one-time decrease in equity, return on equity (ROE) is calculated as a whopping 384 percent. In 2017, ROE was 52.9 percent, which is roughly in line with recent historical values for Starbucks. As of its 2018 fiscal year-end date, Starbucks Corporation had 1,394.6 million shares outstanding.

Based on the number of shares outstanding, earnings per share in 2018 was $3.24 and book value per share was $.84, which also reflects the one-time decrease in equity. For comparison, book value per share was $3.73 in 2017, which is in line with recent historical values. Remember, book value is defined as a company's net worth (i.e., total assets minus total liabilities), which is measured by total stockholder equity. Based on a fiscal year-end 2018 stock

	2018	2017
Total net revenues	$24,719.5	$22,386.8
Cost of sales	10,174.5	9,034.3
Gross profit	$14,545.0	$13,352.5
Store operating expenses	$ 7,193.2	$ 6,493.3
Other operating expenses	539.3	500.3
Depreciation expense	1,247.0	1,011.4
General and administrative expenses	1,983.4	1,604.2
Total operating expenses	10,962.9	9,609.2
Income from equity investees	301.2	391.4
Operating income	$ 3,883.3	$ 4,134.7
Gains from acquisitions and dispositions	$ 1,875.6	$ 93.5
Interest income and other income	191.4	181.8
Interest expense	(170.3)	(92.5)
Earnings before income taxes (EBT)	$ 5,780.0	$ 4,317.5
Income tax expense	1,261.7	1,432.8
Net income	$ 4,518.3	$ 2,884.7
Earnings per share	$ 3.24	$ 1.97
Shares outstanding (in 000s)	1,394.6	1,461.5
Cash dividend declared per share	$ 1.26	$ 1.00
Cash dividend payout ratio	38.9%	50.7%
Operating margin (OI/Total net revenues)	15.7%	18.5%
Income tax rate (Income tax expense/EBT)	21.8%	33.2%

price of $56.84, the price-book ratio for Starbucks was 67.42, and the price-earnings ratio was 17.54 (= $56.84/$3.24).

PRO FORMA INCOME STATEMENT

To construct a 2019 pro forma income statement for Starbucks, we use forecasted sales and the percentage of sales approach, just as we did for Borg Corporation. As shown in the *Work the Web* box, we visited finance.yahoo.com and entered the ticker symbol for Starbucks, SBUX.

Clicking on the "Analysis" link, we see that the highest estimate for Starbucks's 2019 revenue was $28.1 billion, or an increase of about 13.7 percent from Starbucks' 2018 revenue level of $24.72 billion. The low estimate for 2019 revenue was $26.02 billion. Finding ourselves in a frothy mood, we will take the highest and lowest revenue estimates as two cases as we begin to create our 2019 pro forma income statement.

Table 19.11 is our pro forma income statement for Starbucks for 2019. We included 2018 for comparison. For both the high and low estimates for revenue, we assumed that gross margin, operating margin, and net interest and other income as a percentage of sales will be the same in 2019 as they were in 2018. We assume, however, that the income tax rate will be 33.2 percent. As good analysts do, we judge the actual 2018 income tax rate of 21.8 percent as too low by historical rates. These assumptions have the net effect of assuming that the profit margin will remain the same, about 15.6 percent.

WORK THE WEB

Calculating company growth rates can involve detailed research. A major part of a stock analyst's job is to provide estimates of growth rates. One place to find earnings and sales growth rates is at finance.yahoo.com. We pulled up a quote for Starbucks (SBUX) and followed the "Analysis" link. Below, you will see an abbreviated look at the results.

You can see that analysts expect sales to increase 6.60 percent in the current year and 7.50 percent next year. The estimated earnings growth is 11.60 percent for the current year, 12.60 percent next year, and 12.25 percent for the next five years (per annum).

Earnings Estimate	Current Qtr. (Mar 2019)	Next Qtr. (Jun 2019)	Current Year (2019)	Next Year (2020)
No. of Analysts	25	25	29	30
Avg. Estimate	0.56	0.71	2.7	3.04
Low Estimate	0.52	0.67	2.38	2.82
High Estimate	0.6	0.75	2.75	3.5
Year Ago EPS	0.53	0.62	2.42	2.7

Revenue Estimate	Current Qtr. (Mar 2019)	Next Qtr. (Jun 2019)	Current Year (2019)	Next Year (2020)
No. of Analysts	21	21	27	27
Avg. Estimate	6.31B	6.69B	26.36B	28.34B
Low Estimate	6.21B	6.59B	26.02B	27.99B
High Estimate	6.51B	6.93B	28.1B	29.29B
Year Ago Sales	6.03B	6.31B	24.72B	26.36B
Sales Growth (year/est)	4.70%	6.00%	6.60%	7.50%

Growth Estimates	SBUX	Industry	Sector	S&P 500
Current Qtr.	5.70%	N/A	N/A	−0.02
Next Qtr.	14.50%	N/A	N/A	0.04
Current Year	11.60%	N/A	N/A	0.05
Next Year	12.60%	N/A	N/A	0.11
Next 5 Years (per annum)	12.25%	N/A	N/A	0.10
Past 5 Years (per annum)	15.66%	N/A	N/A	N/A

Source: Yahoo! Finance.

We assume that Starbucks will maintain its dividend payout of about 38.9 percent ($1.08 per share dividend on our restated $2.77 earnings per share) and assume that Starbucks will not issue or repurchase shares. Therefore, 61.1 percent of net income will flow to retained earnings and shares outstanding will remain at 1,394.6 million. Combined, these assumptions and the two sales forecasts result in a rounded earnings per share of $3.15 given the high revenue estimate and $2.91 per share with the low revenue estimate.

PRO FORMA BALANCE SHEET

Table 19.12 contains partial pro forma balance sheets for Starbucks for 2019 using the percentage of sales approach we discussed earlier in the chapter. Again, we included the actual 2018 balance sheet for comparison. Notice that we assumed that all asset accounts, including property, plant, and equipment, will increase with sales. Short-term and long-term investment levels, however, are certainly likely to reflect decisions made by senior management at Starbucks. We will also stick with our assumption that only two liability accounts will vary with sales—accounts payable and accrued expenses. In both cases, this assumption is reasonable.

TABLE 19.11

Starbucks Corporation Pro Forma Income Statement, 2019

	2018 (Restated)	2019 (High Est.)	2019 (Low Est.)
Total net revenues	$ 24,720	$ 28,100	$26,020
Cost of sales	(10,175)	(11,566)	(10,710)
Gross profit	$ 14,545	$ 16,534	$15,310
Operating expenses	(10,963)	(12,462)	(11,540)
Income from equity investees	$ 301	$ 342	$ 317
Operating income	$ 3,883	$ 4,414	$ 4,088
Net interest and other income	$ 1,897	$ 2,156	$ 1,996
Earnings before income taxes (EBT)	$ 5,780	$ 6,570	$ 6,084
Income tax expense (33.2%)	(1,919)	(2,181)	(2,020)
Net income	$ 3,861	$ 4,389	$ 4,064
Dividends (38.9%)	1,502	1,707	1,581
Retained earnings	$ 2,359	$ 2,682	$ 2,483
Gross margin	58.8%	58.8%	58.8%
Operating margin	15.7%	15.7%	15.7%
Interest and other income/Net sales	7.7%	7.7%	7.7%
Income tax rate	33.2%	33.2%	33.2%
Profit margin	15.6%	15.6%	15.6%
Earnings per share	$ 2.77	$ 3.15	$ 2.91
Shares outstanding (000,000s)	1,394.6	1,394.6	1,394.6

Note that we have not rounded intermediate calculations, thus some numbers may not appear to add correctly.

Looking at the partial pro forma balance sheet using the high sales estimate, we see that the external financing needed is $145.8 million. Why does this financing need occur, and what does it mean?

In this scenario, assets will grow by about $3,303.5 million and current liabilities will grow by about $475.6 million. The difference between the growth in assets and the growth in current liabilities is $2,827.9 million. Retained earnings, however, increase by about $2,682.1 million, which is $145.8 million less than the difference between asset growth and the growth in current liabilities and equity. For the low growth scenario, Starbucks generates excess cash to the tune of $1,395.7 million.

This excess cash means that under the low sales growth scenario, Starbucks becomes quite the "cash cow." That is, the existing profit margin Starbucks enjoys is such that considerable future growth can be financed out of sales. At these projected sales growth levels, no external financing is needed to finance this growth, so "excess" cash accumulates.

Senior management at Starbucks could use this additional cash in many ways. In terms of investments, Starbucks could purchase other companies, look for new ways to expand the company, or buy back its own shares in the open market. Management at Starbucks could let this cash accumulate while looking for places to spend it. Or they could choose to declare an increase in the cash dividend and distribute some cash to shareholders.

At this point, we can generate a pro forma balance sheet that actually balances, depending on what sales forecast we use. To conduct ratio analysis, as we will, we need to use a pro forma balance sheet that balances. In both sales growth scenarios, we assume that management uses the long-term debt account to balance the balance sheet. In the high sales growth scenario, we assume management will issue more long-term debt. In the low sales growth

	2018	Percent of Sales	2019 (High Est.)	Change	2019 (Low Est.)	Change
Current assets						
Cash and cash equivalents	$ 8,756.3	35.4%	$ 9,953.8	$1,197.5	$ 9,217.0	$460.7
Short-term investments	$ 181.5	.7%	$ 206.3	$ 24.8	$ 191.0	$9.5
Accounts receivable	$ 693.1	2.8%	$ 787.9	$ 94.8	$ 729.6	$36.5
Inventory	$ 1,400.5	5.7%	$ 1,592.0	$ 191.5	$ 1,474.2	$73.7
Prepaid expenses	$ 1,462.8	5.9%	$ 1,662.8	$ 200.0	$ 1,539.8	$77.0
Total current assets	$12,494.2		$14,202.8	$1,708.6	$13,151.5	$657.3
Fixed assets						
Long-term investments	$ 267.7	1.1%	$ 304.3	$ 36.6	$ 281.8	$14.1
Prop., plant and equip., net	$ 6,263.8	25.3%	$ 7,120.4	$ 856.6	$ 6,593.3	$329.5
Other assets	$ 546.9	2.2%	$ 621.7	$74.8	$ 575.7	$28.8
Total fixed assets	$ 7,078.4		$ 8,046.4	$ 968.0	$ 7,450.8	$372.4
Goodwill and intangibles	$ 4,583.8	18.5%	$ 5,210.7	$ 626.9	$ 4,825.0	$241.2
Total assets	$24,156.4		$27,459.9	$3,303.5	$25,427.3	$ 1,270.9
Current liabilities						
Accounts payable	$ 1,179.3	4.8%	$ 1,340.6	$ 161.3	$ 1,241.3	$62.0
Accrued expenses	$ 2,298.4	9.3%	$ 2,612.7	$ 314.3	$ 2,419.3	$120.9
Other current liabilities	$ 2,206.5	n/a	$ 2,206.5	$ 0.0	$ 2,206.5	$ 0.0
Total current liabilities	$ 5,684.2		$ 6,159.8	$ 475.6	$ 5,867.2	$183.0
Long-term debt	$ 9,090.2	n/a	$ 9,090.2	$ 0.0	$ 9,090.2	$ 0.0
Other long-term liabilities	$ 8,206.2	n/a	$ 8,206.2	$ 0.0	$ 8,206.2	$ 0.0
Total liabilities	$22,980.6		$23,456.2	$ 475.6	$23,163.6	$183.0
Shareholder equity						
Paid-in capital & other equity	($ 281.6)	n/a	($ 281.6)	$ 0.0	($ 281.6)	$ 0.0
Retained earnings	$ 1,457.4	n/a	$ 4,139.5	$2,682.1	$ 3,941.0	$2,483.6
Total stockholder equity	$ 1,175.8		$ 3,857.9	$2,682.1	$ 3,659.4	$2,483.6
Total liabilities and equity	$24,156.4		$27,314.1	$3,157.7	$26,823.0	$ 2,666.6
External financing needed:			$ 145.8	$ 145.8	($ 1,395.7)	($1,395.7)

TABLE 19.12 — **Starbucks Corporation** Partial Pro Forma Balance Sheet, 2018 ($ in 000,000s)

scenario, we assume management will pay down long-term debt. Ask yourself, what other options are available to the management team at Starbucks? Table 19.13 presents these pro forma balance sheets.

CHECK THIS

19.4a Use the high sales estimate and data in Table 19.12 to determine the level of external financing needed if short-term and long-term investments were held at their 2018 levels.

19.4b Using the high sales estimate and data in Table 19.12, do you think it is more likely that Starbucks would use short-term or long-term debt if external financing needed was $3 billion? What financial data support your answer?

TABLE 19.13

Starbucks Corporation Pro Forma Balance Sheet, 2019
($ in 000,000s)

	2018	Percent of Sales	2019 (High)	Change	2019 (Low)	Change
Current assets						
Cash and cash equivalents	$ 8,756.3	35.4%	$ 9,953.8	$1,197.5	$ 9,217.0	$ 460.7
Short-term investments	$ 181.5	.7%	$ 206.3	$ 24.8	$ 191.0	$ 9.5
Accounts receivable	$ 693.1	2.8%	$ 787.9	$ 94.8	$ 729.6	$ 36.5
Inventory	$ 1,400.5	5.7%	$ 1,592.0	$ 191.5	$ 1,474.2	$ 73.7
Prepaid expenses	$ 1,462.8	5.9%	$ 1,662.8	$ 200.0	$ 1,539.8	$ 77.0
Total current assets	$12,494.2		$14,202.8	$1,708.6	$13,151.5	$ 657.3
Fixed assets						
Long-term investments	$ 267.7	1.1%	$ 304.3	$ 36.6	$ 281.8	$ 14.1
Prop., plant and equip., net	$ 6,263.8	25.3%	$ 7,120.4	$ 856.6	$ 6,593.3	$ 329.5
Other assets	$ 546.9	2.2%	$ 621.7	$ 74.8	$ 575.7	$ 28.8
Total fixed assets	$ 7,078.4	28.6%	$ 8,046.4	$ 968.0	$ 7,450.8	$ 372.4
Goodwill	$ 4,583.8	18.5%	$ 5,210.7	$ 626.9	$ 4,825.0	$ 241.2
Total assets	$24,156.4	97.7%	$27,459.9	$3,303.5	$25,427.3	$1,270.9
Current liabilities						
Accounts payable	$ 1,179.3	4.8%	$ 1,340.6	$ 161.3	$ 1,241.3	$ 62.0
Accrued expenses	$ 2,298.4	9.3%	$ 2,612.7	$ 314.3	$ 2,419.3	$ 120.9
Other current liabilities	$ 2,206.5	n/a	$ 2,206.5	$ 0.0	$ 2,206.5	$ 0.0
Total current liabilities	$ 5,684.2		$ 6,159.8	$ 475.6	$ 5,867.2	$ 183.0
Long-term debt	$ 9,090.2	n/a	$ 9,236.0	$ 145.8	$ 7,694.5	($1,395.7)
Other long-term liabilities	$ 8,206.2	n/a	$ 8,206.2	$ 0.0	$ 8,206.2	$ 0.0
Total liabilities	$22,980.6		$23,602.0	$ 621.4	$21,767.9	($1,212.7)
Shareholder equity						
Paid-in capital & other equity	($281.6)	n/a	($281.6)	$ 0.0	($281.6)	$ 0.0
Retained earnings	$ 1,457.4	n/a	$ 4,139.5	$2,682.1	$ 3,941.0	$2,483.6
Total stockholder equity	$ 1,175.8		$ 3,857.9	$2,682.1	$ 3,659.4	$2,483.6
Total liabilities and equity	$24,156.4		$27,459.9	$3,303.5	$25,427.3	$1,270.9
External financing needed:			$ 0	$ 0	$ 0	$ 0

VALUING STARBUCKS USING RATIO ANALYSIS

We now turn our attention to valuing Starbucks using ratio analysis and the pro forma income statement and balance sheets that we generated. Immediately below, we report actual and projected profitability and per-share values for 2018 and 2019.

	2018	2019 (High Sales Forecast)	2019 (Low Sales Forecast)
Gross margin	58.8%	58.8%	58.8%
Operating margin	15.7%	15.7%	15.7%
Return on assets (ROA)	16.0%	16.0%	16.0%
Return on equity (ROE)	328.4%	113.8%	111.1%
Earnings per share (EPS)	$ 2.77	$ 3.15	$ 2.91
Book value per share (BVPS)	$ .84	$ 2.77	$ 2.62

For Starbucks, the low equity value in 2018 gives a book value per share of $.84, much lower than the book value per share we calculated for 2017, which was $3.73. We computed the PE ratio for 2018 and the P/B ratios for 2018 and 2017. Taking these price ratios and multiplying each ratio by its corresponding projected 2019 per-share value results in the following stock price calculations:

Using fiscal year-end stock price of $56.84			2019 (High Sales Forecast)	2019 (Low Sales Forecast)
PE ratio, 2018	20.53	PE × EPS	$ 64.61	$ 59.83
P/B ratio, 2018	67.42	P/B × BVPS	$186.50	$176.90
P/B ratio, 2017	14.38	P/B × BVPS	$ 39.79	$ 37.74

Using ratio analysis, we generate Starbucks's prices, which range from $37.74 to $186.50. We note that both P/B ratios seem to make poorer forecasts than the PE ratio. Looking across sales forecasts, you can see that the prices we generate for Starbucks do not differ greatly. In fact, our projected Starbucks stock prices are more sensitive to the values picked for the price-earnings (PE) ratio and price-book (P/B) ratio than they are to the value of the sales forecast picked.

VALUING STARBUCKS USING A TWO-STAGE DIVIDEND GROWTH MODEL

In a previous chapter, we introduced the two-stage dividend growth model. Fortunately for us, Starbucks pays a dividend, so g_1 for T periods and then grow at rate g_2 forever thereafter. The model is:

$$P_0 = \frac{D_0 \times (1 + g_1)}{k - g_1}\left[1 - \left(\frac{1 + g_1}{1 + k}\right)^T\right] + \left(\frac{1 + g_1}{1 + k}\right)^T\left[\frac{D_0 \times (1 + g_2)}{k - g_2}\right] \qquad (19.3)$$

In Equation 19.3 we need values for dividends per share, D_0, as of Time 0 (2018 in this case). We can pluck this value, $1.08, from the data provided above. We assume that Starbucks pays the same percentage, 38.9 percent, of earnings as a dividend. We need dividend growth rates for the two periods, however, and an appropriate discount rate.

From the preceding *Work the Web* box, we can see that analysts collectively think that Starbucks will be able to grow earnings at 12.25 percent for the next five years. After that, we will assume that Starbucks will be able to grow earnings *forever* by one-fourth of that, 3.0625 percent. Even though this is a significant drop-off from 12.25 percent, it is still higher than the long-term historical real growth rate of the U.S. economy, which is about 3 percent. Therefore, in Equation 19.3, $g_1 = .1225$ and $g_2 = .030625$.

We calculate an initial discount rate using the capital asset pricing model (CAPM). If we use a risk-free rate of 2.5 percent, a market risk premium of 8 percent, and a Starbucks beta of .43, the discount rate, k, is $2.5\% + .43 \times 8.0\% = 5.94\%$.

Plugging these inputs into Equation 19.3, we obtain this value for Starbucks:

$$P_0 = \frac{\$1.08 \times 1.1225}{.0594 - .1225}\left[1 - \left(\frac{1.1225}{1.0594}\right)^5\right] + \left(\frac{1.1225}{1.0594}\right)^5\left[\frac{\$1.08 \times 1.030625}{.0594 - .030625}\right]$$
$$= -\$19.21 \times (-.335) + 1.335 \times \$38.68$$
$$= \$6.44 + \$51.64$$
$$= \$58.08$$

This estimate of $58.08 is only about $1.24 higher than the Starbucks stock price of $56.84, which was observed at the time of Starbucks's fiscal year-end. It looks like we were fortunate in our selection of inputs (or perhaps sly).

We note that the early May share price for Starbucks is about $78. How can we explain that price with the two-stage growth model? Like any good analyst would, we vary our inputs to see how sensitive the estimated price is to changes in these inputs. Even though we *could* change the growth rates, we will not. Instead, we will vary the discount rate and the length of time that Starbucks will exhibit an earnings growth rate of 12.25 percent.

We generate a set of additional discount rates by varying the beta for Starbucks. Recall that we discussed how difficult it is to calculate a true beta and that betas vary by source. Beginning with the beta value we looked up, .43, we selected four other beta values, while keeping the risk-free rate and the market risk premium the same as before. We suspect that the length of time that Starbucks will grow earnings at the rate of 12.25 percent could be too short or too long, but we cannot be sure. Therefore, we vary this length of time from three to six years. We then recalculate a Starbucks price for each of these combinations using the two-stage growth model. The results appear immediately below.

		Number of Years Starbucks Grows Earnings at 12.25%			
Beta	Discount Rate	3	4	5	6
.30	.049	$77.94	$84.55	$91.63	$99.21
.40	.057	$54.20	$58.71	$63.49	$68.57
.50	.065	$41.52	$44.90	$48.46	$52.21
.60	.073	$33.62	$36.30	$39.11	$42.04
.70	.081	$28.23	$30.44	$32.73	$35.11

From this sensitivity analysis, it appears that both the discount rate and the length of time that Starbucks grows its earnings by 12.25 percent are important in estimating a value for Starbucks. For an analyst, performing various "what-if" scenarios concerning input values that are used in valuation formulas is good practice.

VALUING STARBUCKS: WHAT DOES THE MARKET SAY?

As with many publicly traded companies, analysts frequently offer conflicting opinions concerning the future growth prospects of Starbucks and its current value. If you are a believer in the efficient markets hypothesis, the easiest way to value Starbucks is to look at what its shares are selling for in the open market. After all, the market price for Starbucks shares is the result of the collective assessment from thousands of analysts and investors. If, however, you believe that you are an above-average prognosticator for future sales and earnings growth for Starbucks, you can use the methods in this chapter to assist you in your personal investing decisions concerning Starbucks and other companies.

The methods presented in this chapter are intended to help you become a better financial analyst. Calibrating these methods to a publicly traded company is a useful way to get familiar with how inputs and assumptions affect the resulting valuation. These methods could be valuable to you if you are an internal analyst. For example, suppose you are asked to calculate whether the company you work for needs more financing to meet its expected sales growth levels. You can use the percentage of sales approach when you perform this task.

The methods in this chapter are especially useful if you are trying to value a nontraded company after you are given its financial data. Someday, you might find yourself calculating a per-share tender offer in a hostile takeover attempt. In any case, we are confident that this chapter will help you become more "financial statement literate" and help you develop as a financial analyst.

19.5 Summary and Conclusions

In this chapter, we focus on earnings and cash flow analysis using financial statement information. Several important aspects of financial statements and their use were covered. We summarize these points by the important concepts of the chapter.

1. **How to obtain financial information about companies.**

A. Good financial analysis begins with good financial information. A primary source of financial information is a company's annual report. In addition, the annual 10-K report and the quarterly 10-Q updates filed with the SEC are available from the EDGAR archives.

B. The internet is a convenient source of financial information about many companies. For example, the SEC provides a document search portal called "EDGAR."

2. **How to read basic financial statements.**

A. Three financial statements are essential reading for securities analysts: the balance sheet, the income statement, and the cash flow statement. The balance sheet has three sections: assets, liabilities, and equity. A fundamental accounting identity for balance sheets states that assets equal liabilities plus equity.

B. The income statement reports revenues and expenses. Companies use their net income to pay dividends or to finance future growth. Net income is the "bottom line" for a company.

C. The cash flow statement reports how cash was generated and where it was used. The cash flow statement assigns all cash flows to one of three categories: operating cash flow, investment cash flow, or financing cash flow.

3. **How to use performance and price ratios.**

A. Profitability ratios based on financial statement information are often reported to help investors interpret a company's operating efficiency. Standard profitability ratios include gross margin, operating margin, return on assets (ROA), and return on equity (ROE).

B. Annual reports, 10-Ks, and 10-Qs also report per-share calculations of book value, earnings, and operating cash flow, respectively. If we divide the stock price by these per-share values, we get three important ratios: the price to book ratio (P/B), the price-earnings ratio (PE), and the cash flow per share (CFPS).

4. **How to use the percentage of sales method in financial forecasting.**

A. Financial analysts often make projections about sales growth, future costs, and net income. These forecasts can be used to construct a forecasted, or pro forma, set of financial statements.

B. The percentage of sales approach is a method analysts can use to construct pro forma financial statements. This approach is based on the basic idea of separating the income statement and balance sheet items into two groups: those that do vary directly with sales and those that do not. Given a sales forecast, analysts can use the percentage of sales approach to calculate how much financing the firm will need to support the predicted sales level.

GETTING DOWN TO BUSINESS

This chapter delves deeper into earnings and cash flow concepts, which are two of the most important tools of fundamental analysis. It focuses on using financial statement information to develop pro forma numbers to use in stock valuation. How should you, as an investor or investment manager, get started putting this information to work? The answer is that you need to get your fingers dirty! Dig into the financial statements of a few companies and develop your own pro forma financial statements.

An excellent source for financial statement information is the SEC EDGAR database (www.sec.gov). Other useful online sources are The Public Register Online (www.annualreportservice.com) and Corporate Information (www.corporateinformation.com).

A next step is to pick a company you are interested in and examine its financial statements. As you read a company's financial statements, an important exercise is to try to understand what each number really represents. Why is it there? Is it a market value? Or is it just an accounting number (like depreciation)? Once you are familiar with a company's current financial statements, try to develop pro forma statements for various sales scenarios as was done in this chapter. You really can learn a lot by doing this.

Key Terms

Related Bloomberg Functions

FA	Financial Analysis, 19.1
FA BS	Financial Analysis: Standardized Balance Sheet, 19.2
FA IS	Financial Analysis: GAAP Income Statement, 19.2
FA CF	Financial Analysis: Standardized Cash Flow, 19.2
EQRV	Equity Relative Valuation, 19.2
BI	Bloomberg Intelligence, 19.3
EE	Earnings and Estimates, 19.3
EM	Earnings Trends, 19.3
EEG	Earnings Estimates Graph, 19.3
BRC	Bloomberg Portal: Single Security, 19.4
RV	Relative Valuation, 19.4

Chapter Review Problems and Self-Test

1. **Margin Calculations (LO3, CFA7)**   Use the following income statement for Paul Bunyan Lumber Co. to calculate gross and operating margins:

Paul Bunyan Lumber Income Statement	
Net sales	$8,000
Cost of goods sold	(6,400)
Gross profit	$1,600
Operating expenses	(400)
Operating income	$1,200
Other income	80
Net interest expense	(120)
Pretax income	$1,160
Income tax	(464)
Net income	$ 696
Earnings per share	$ 3.48
Recent share price	$76.56

2. **Return Calculations (LO3, CFA7)** Use the following balance sheet for Paul Bunyan Lumber Co. along with the income statement in Question 1 to calculate return on assets and return on equity:

Paul Bunyan Lumber Balance Sheet	
Cash and cash equivalents	$ 400
Operating assets	400
Property, plant, and equipment	3,160
Other assets	216
Total assets	$4,176
Current liabilities	$ 720
Long-term debt	612
Other liabilities	60
Total liabilities	$1,392
Paid-in capital	$ 600
Retained earnings	2,184
Total shareholder equity	$2,784
Total liabilities and equity	$4,176

3. **Pro Forma Income Statements (LO4, CFA2)** Prepare a pro forma income statement for Paul Bunyan Lumber Co. assuming a 5 percent increase in sales. Based only on the pro forma income statement, what is the projected stock price? (*Hint:* What is the price-earnings ratio?)

Answers to Self-Test Problems

1. Gross margin is $1,600/$8,000 = .20, or 20%;
   Operating margin is $1,200/$8,000 = .15, or 15%
2. Return on assets is $696/$4,176 = .1667, or 16.67%;
   Return on equity is $696/$2,784 = .25, or 25%
3. With 5 percent sales growth, sales will rise to $8,400 from $8,000. The pro forma income statement follows. A constant gross margin is assumed, implying that cost of goods sold will also rise by 5 percent. A constant tax rate of 40 percent is used.

Paul Bunyan Lumber Pro Forma 2022 Income Statement	
Net sales	$8,400
Cost of goods sold	(6,720)
Gross profit	$1,680
Operating expenses	(400)
Operating income	$1,280
Other income	80
Net interest expense	(120)
Pretax income	$1,240
Income tax	(496)
Net income	$ 744
Earnings per share	$ 3.72

To get a projected stock price, notice that the 2021 price-earnings ratio was $76.56/$3.48 = 22. Using this ratio as a benchmark, the pro forma earnings of $3.72 imply a stock price of 22 × $3.72 = $81.84.

Test Your Investment Quotient

1. **Balance Sheet Assets (LO2, CFA8)**   White Company assets as of December 31, 2021:

Cash and cash equivalents	$ 150
Operating assets	$1,190
Property, plant, and equipment	$1,460
Total assets	$2,800

White Co. experienced the following events in 2022:

Old equipment that cost $120 and that was fully depreciated was scrapped.

Depreciation expense was $125.

Cash payments for new equipment were $200.

Based on the information above, what was White Co.'s net amount of property, plant, and equipment at the end of 2022?

   a. $1,415
   b. $1,535
   c. $1,655
   d. $1,660

2. **Cash Flow (LO2, CFA5)**   Cash flow per share is typically calculated as:
   a. Net cash flow/Shares outstanding.
   b. Operating cash flow/Shares outstanding.
   c. Investing cash flow/Shares outstanding.
   d. Financing cash flow/Shares outstanding.

3. **Cash Flow (LO2, CFA5)**   Which of the following is not an adjustment to net income used to obtain operating cash flow?
   a. Changes in operating assets
   b. Changes in current liabilities
   c. Depreciation
   d. Dividends paid

4. **Cash Flow (LO2, CFA5)**   The difference between net income and operating cash flow is at least partially accounted for by which of the following items?
   a. Retained earnings
   b. Cash and cash equivalents
   c. Depreciation
   d. Dividends paid

5. **Financial Ratios (LO3, CFA6)**   Which of the following profitability ratios is incorrect?
   a. Gross margin = Gross profit/Cost of goods sold
   b. Operating margin = Operating income/Net sales
   c. Return on assets = Net income/Total assets
   d. Return on equity = Net income/Shareholder equity

6. **Financial Ratios (LO3, CFA6)**   Which of the following per-share ratios is incorrect?
   a. Book value per share = Total assets/Shares outstanding
   b. Earnings per share = Net income/Shares outstanding
   c. Cash flow per share = Operating cash flow/Shares outstanding
   d. Dividends per share = Dividends paid/Shares outstanding

7. **Dividend Payment (LO2, CFA4)**   A dividend payment has which of the following effects on the balance sheet?
   a. An increase in shares outstanding
   b. A decrease in shareholder equity
   c. A decrease in paid-in capital
   d. An increase in retained earnings

8. **Sales Growth (LO4, CFA8)**   A particular firm is operating at less than full capacity. If sales are expected to grow at only a modest rate next year, which of the following is true?

    a. Assets will likely increase faster than sales in the short-term future.

    b. Dividends should be reduced to conserve cash.

    c. No further financial planning should be performed until the sales growth rate increases.

    d. External financing will likely not be needed next year.

9. **Capacity Usage (LO4, CFA9)**   Which of the following is true regarding the full-capacity sales level of a firm?

    a. A firm that is operating at less than full capacity will never need external financing.

    b. For a firm that is operating at less than full capacity, fixed assets will typically increase at the same rate as sales.

    c. A firm with excess capacity has room to expand without increasing its investment in fixed assets.

    d. Only firms operating at full capacity can grow rapidly.

Use the following raw data to answer Questions 10-13:

Net income:	$16
Depreciation/amortization:	$ 4
Repurchase of outstanding common stock:	$10
Issuance of new debt:	$18
Sale of property:	$12
Purchase of equipment:	$14
Dividend payments:	$ 4

10. **Cash Flow Analysis (LO2, CFA5)**   Operating cash flow is:

    a. $20.

    b. $16.

    c. $12.

    d. $30.

11. **Cash Flow Analysis (LO2, CFA5)**   Investing cash flow is:

    a. $2.

    b. ($2).

    c. $12.

    d. ($12).

12. **Cash Flow Analysis (LO2, CFA5)**   Financing cash flow is:

    a. $8.

    b. ($8).

    c. $4.

    d. ($4).

13. **Cash Flow Analysis (LO2, CFA5)**   Net cash increase is:

    a. $18.

    b. $20.

    c. $22.

    d. $24.

Use the following financial data to answer the Questions 14-16:

Cash payments for interest:	($ 12)
Retirement of common stock:	($ 32)
Cash payments to merchandise suppliers:	($ 85)
Purchase of land:	($ 8)
Sale of equipment:	$ 30
Payments of dividends:	($ 37)
Cash payment for salaries:	($ 35)
Cash collection from customers:	$260
Purchase of equipment:	($ 40)

14. **Cash Flow Analysis (LO2, CFA5)**   Cash flows from operating activities are:
    a. $91.
    b. $128.
    c. $140.
    d. $175.

15. **Cash Flow Analysis (LO2, CFA5)**   Cash flows from investing activities are:
    a. ($67).
    b. ($48).
    c. ($18).
    d. ($10).

16. **Cash Flow Analysis (LO2, CFA5)**   Cash flows from financing activities are:
    a. ($81).
    b. ($69).
    c. ($49).
    d. ($37).

17. **Cash Flow Analysis (LO2, CFA5)**   A firm has net sales of $3,000, cash expenses (including taxes) of $1,400, and depreciation of $500. If accounts receivable increase over the period by $400, cash flow from operations equals:
    a. $1,200.
    b. $1,600.
    c. $1,700.
    d. $2,100.

18. **Cash Flow Analysis (LO2, CFA5)**   A firm using straight-line depreciation reports gross investment in fixed assets of $80 million, accumulated depreciation of $45 million, and annual depreciation expense of $5 million. The approximate average age of fixed assets is:
    a. 7 years.
    b. 9 years.
    c. 15 years.
    d. 16 years.

19. **Ratio Analysis (LO3, CFA6)**   An increase in the market price of a company's stock would cause which of the following ratios to increase?
    a. Return on assets (ROA)
    b. Return on equity (ROE)
    c. Price-book (P/B)
    d. Book value per share (BVPS)

20. **Price Ratios (LO3, CFA6)**   All else the same, which of the following ratios is unaffected by an increase in depreciation?
    a. Price-earnings (PE)
    b. Price-book (P/B)
    c. Price-cash flow (P/CF)
    d. Price-sales (P/S)

Concept Questions

1. **10-K and 10-Q (LO1, CFA1)**   What are the 10-K and 10-Q reports? By whom are they filed? What do they contain? With whom are they filed? What is the easiest way to retrieve one?

2. **Sales Forecast (LO4, CFA8)**   Why do you think most long-term financial planning begins with sales forecasts? Put differently, why are future sales the key input?

3. **Current Events (LO2, CFA4)**   What makes current assets and liabilities "current"? Are operating assets "current"?

4. **Income and EPS (LO2, CFA6)**   What is the relationship between net income and earnings per share (EPS)?

5. **Noncash Items (LO2, CFA5)**   Why do we say depreciation is a "noncash item"?

6. **Operating Cash Flow (LO2, CFA5)**   In the context of the standard cash flow statement, what is operating cash flow?

7. **Comparing ROE and ROA (LO3, CFA6)** Both ROA and ROE measure profitability. Which one is more useful for comparing two companies? Why?

8. **Retained Earnings (LO2, CFA1)** What is the difference between the "retained earnings" number on the income statement and that on the balance sheet?

9. **Gross! (LO3, CFA6)** What is the difference between gross margin and operating margin? What do they tell us? Generally speaking, are larger or smaller values better?

10. **More Gross (LO3, CFA6)** Which is larger, gross margin or operating margin? Can either be negative? Can both?

Questions and Problems

Core Questions

1. **Income Statements (LO2, CFA3)** Given the following information for Smashville, Inc., construct an income statement for the year:

Cost of goods sold:	$164,000
Investment income:	$ 1,200
Net sales:	$318,000
Operating expense:	$ 71,000
Interest expense:	$ 7,400
Dividends:	$ 3,200
Tax rate:	21%

What are retained earnings for the year?

2. **Balance Sheets (LO2, CFA4)** Given the following information for Smashville, Inc., construct a balance sheet:

Current liabilities:	$ 42,000
Cash:	$ 21,000
Long-term debt:	$102,000
Other assets:	$ 36,000
Fixed assets:	$150,000
Other liabilities:	$ 11,000
Investments:	$ 32,000
Operating assets:	$ 64,000

3. **Performance Ratios (LO3, CFA6)** Given the information in Problems 1 and 2, calculate the gross margin, the operating margin, return on assets, and return on equity for Smashville, Inc.

4. **Per-Share Ratios (LO3, CFA6)** During the year, Smashville, Inc., had 17,000 shares of stock outstanding and depreciation expense of $15,000. Calculate the book value per share, earnings per share, and cash flow per share.

5. **Price Ratios (LO3, CFA6)** At the end of the year, Smashville stock sold for $48 per share. Calculate the price-book ratio, price-earnings ratio, and price-cash flow ratio.

6. **Calculating EFN (LO4, CFA8)** The most recent financial statements for Bradley, Inc., are shown here (assuming no income taxes):

Income Statement		Balance Sheet			
Sales	$4,800	Assets	$14,200	Debt	$ 9,900
Costs	(3,180)			Equity	4,300
Net income	$1,620	Total	$14,200	Total	$14,200

Assets and costs are proportional to sales. Debt and equity are not. No dividends are paid. Next year's sales are projected to be $6,240. What is the external financing needed?

7. **Operating Cash Flow (LO3, CFA5)** Weston Corporation had earnings per share of $1.64, depreciation expense of $310,000, and 140,000 shares outstanding. What was the operating cash flow per share? If the share price was $43, what was the price-cash flow ratio?

8. **Earnings per Share (LO3, CFA3)** Alphonse, Inc., has a return on equity of 12 percent, 28,000 shares of stock outstanding, and a net income of $98,000. What are earnings per share?

9. **Addition to Retained Earnings (LO2, CFA8)** Lemon Co. has net income of $520,000 and 75,000 shares of stock. If the company pays a dividend of $1.28 per share, what are the additions to retained earnings?

10. **Cash Flow Statement (LO2, CFA5)** Given the following information for Hetrich, Inc., calculate the operating cash flow, investment cash flow, financing cash flow, and net cash flow:

Net income:	$175
Depreciation:	$ 52
Issuance of new stock:	$ 7
Repurchase of debt:	$ 18
Sale of property:	$ 10
Purchase of equipment:	$ 70
Dividend payments:	$ 9
Interest payments:	$ 32

11. **EFN (LO4, CFA8)** The most recent financial statements for Martin, Inc., are shown here:

Income Statement			Balance Sheet			
Sales	$27,500		Assets	$105,000	Debt	$ 43,000
Costs	(19,450)				Equity	62,000
Taxable income	$ 8,050		Total	$105,000	Total	$105,000
Taxes (21%)	(1,691)					
Net income	$ 6,359					

Assets and costs are proportional to sales. Debt and equity are not. A dividend of $850 was paid, and Martin wishes to maintain a constant payout ratio. Next year's sales are projected to be $31,625. What is the external financing needed?

Intermediate Questions

Use the following financial statement information to answer Questions 12–16. Amounts are in thousands of dollars (except number of shares and price per share):

Kiwi Fruit Company Balance Sheet	
Cash and equivalents	$ 570
Operating assets	650
Property, plant, and equipment	2,700
Other assets	110
Total assets	$4,030
Current liabilities	$ 920
Long-term debt	1,280
Other liabilities	120
Total liabilities	$2,320
Paid in capital	$ 340
Retained earnings	1,370
Total equity	$1,710
Total liabilities and equity	$4,030

Kiwi Fruit Company Income Statement	
Net sales	$ 7,800
Cost of goods sold	(5,900)
Gross profit	$ 1,900
Operating expense	(990)
Operating income	$ 910
Other income	70
Net interest expense	(250)
Pretax income	$ 730
Income tax	(200)
Net income	$ 530
Earnings per share	$ 2.00
Shares outstanding	265,000
Recent price	$ 34.50

Kiwi Fruit Company Cash Flow Statement	
Net income	$ 530
Depreciation and amortization	175
Increase in operating assets	(90)
Decrease in current liabilities	(120)
Operating cash flow	$ 495
Net (purchase) sale of property	$ 180
Increase in other assets	(80)
Investing cash flow	$ 100
Net (redemption) issuance of LTD	$(190)
Dividends paid	(220)
Financing cash flow	$(410)
Net cash increase	$ 185

12. **Calculating Margins (LO3, CFA6)** Calculate the gross and operating margins for Kiwi Fruit.

13. **Calculating Profitability Measures (LO3, CFA6)** Calculate ROA and ROE for Kiwi Fruit and interpret these ratios.

14. **Calculating Per-Share Measures (LO3, CFA6)** Calculate the price-book, price-earnings, and price-cash flow ratios for Kiwi Fruit.

15. **Pro Forma Financial Statements (LO4, CFA8)** Following the examples in the chapter, prepare a pro forma income statement, balance sheet, and cash flow statement for Kiwi Fruit assuming a 10 percent increase in sales.

16. **Projected Share Prices (LO4, CFA6)** Based on Problems 14 and 15, what is the projected stock price assuming a 10 percent increase in sales?

17. **Full-Capacity Sales (LO4, CFA9)** Thorpe Mfg., Inc., is currently operating at only 75 percent of fixed asset capacity. Current sales are $480,000. How fast can sales grow before any new fixed assets are needed?

18. **Fixed Assets and Capacity Usage (LO4, CFA9)** For the company in Problem 17, suppose fixed assets are $420,000 and sales are projected to grow to $695,000. How much in new fixed assets is required to support this growth in sales?

19. Calculating EFN (LO4, CFA8) The most recent financial statements for Moose Tours, Inc., follow. Sales for 2023 are projected to grow by 15 percent. Interest expense will remain constant; the tax rate and the dividend payout rate will also remain constant. Costs, other expenses, current assets, and accounts payable increase spontaneously with sales. If the firm is operating at full capacity and no new debt or equity is issued, what is the external financing needed to support the 15 percent growth rate in sales?

MOOSE TOURS, INC. 2022 Income Statement	
Sales	$995,000
Costs	(782,000)
Other expenses	(15,000)
Earnings before interest and taxes	$198,000
Interest paid	(21,670)
Taxable income	$176,330
Taxes (21%)	(37,029)
Net income	$139,301
Dividends	$45,700
Addition to retained earnings	$93,601

MOOSE TOURS, INC. Balance Sheet as of December 31, 2022			
Assets		**Liabilities and Owners' Equity**	
Current assets		Current liabilities	
Cash	$ 27,500	Accounts payable	$ 71,500
Accounts receivable	47,300	Notes payable	9,900
Inventory	83,600	Total	$ 81,400
Total	$158,400	Long-term debt	$171,600
Fixed assets		Owners' equity	
Net plant and		Common stock and paid-in surplus	$ 23,100
equipment	$400,400	Retained earnings	282,700
		Total	$305,800
Total assets	$558,800	Total liabilities and owners' equity	$558,800

20. Capacity Usage and Growth (LO4, CFA8) In Problem 19, suppose the firm was operating at only 90 percent capacity in 2023. What is EFN now?

CFA Exam Review by Kaplan Schweser

[CFA3, CFA5, CFA11]

Laura Bond is a Senior VP of MediaInvests Partners (MIP), a late-stage venture capital firm. MIP is considering an investment in VirtualCon Corp. VirtualCon went public during the dot-com boom, and it currently trades at a small fraction of its IPO value; however, its recent financial statements have shown improvement.

Harry Darling, a former employee of MIP and current VirtualCon board member, thinks that VirtualCon is an excellent candidate to take private. He has presented the idea to MIP's board, pointing out the rising operating cash flows. Ms. Bond has the highest regard for Mr. Darling, but she remains dubious about his assessment of VirtualCon. She has come across several items in the footnotes to the financial statements that have raised concerns.

Ms. Bond noticed that six months ago VirtualCon created a special-purpose entity (SPE) to securitize its receivables. The firm sold off $12 million of its accounts receivable in those two quarters, which represented 80 percent of those outstanding and more than five months of revenue. She notes that a change in the default rate assumption and the discount rate at the time of sale caused the fair value of the receivables to exceed book value by $3.8 million, which VirtualCon booked as revenue.

Mr. Darling also points out, "VirtualCon has become more active in managing its accounts payable. It set up a financial arrangement with its principal bank so the bank makes payments to VirtualCon's suppliers on its behalf, and VirtualCon has 90 days to pay the bank. The suppliers are more willing to do business with VirtualCon because they have the assurance of being paid by the bank."

1. Ignoring interest, what is the effect on VirtualCon's total cash flow (CF) and cash flow from financing (CFF) from its financing arrangement for its accounts payable at the time of payment to the supplier?

	Total CF	CFF
a.	Unaffected	Increase
b.	Decrease	Unaffected
c.	Unaffected	Unaffected

2. Which of the following statements about VirtualCon's securitization of receivables is least accurate?

   a. It accelerates operating cash flow into the current period.
   b. It enables the firm to reclassify financing cash flow as operating cash flow.
   c. It could allow the firm to recognize a reduction in operating expenses.

3. If VirtualCon had decided to slow its payment of accounts payable by 90 days instead of entering into a financing arrangement with the bank, what would be the impact on its operating cash flow (OCF) and financing cash flow (CFF) during the 90 days relative to its cash flow under the financing arrangement, ignoring interest?

	OCF	CFF
a.	Higher	Lower
b.	Higher	Higher
c.	Lower	Higher

Bloomberg Exercises

1. Collect financial statements for Goldman Sachs (GS). **(FA)**
2. Review the price ratios for Delta Air (DAL). **(EQRV)**
3. Evaluate earnings estimates for Harley-Davidson (HOG). **(EE)**

What's on the Web?

1. **Ratio Analysis** Go to finance.yahoo.com and enter the ticker symbol for Pfizer, PFE. Look under the "Statistics" link to find some ratios and other financial information for Pfizer. Discuss Pfizer's performance by interpreting the following ratios (calculating them where necessary): gross margin, operating margin, return on assets, return on equity, book value per share, earnings per share, cash flow per share, price-book, price-earnings, and price-cash flow.

2. **Ratio Calculation** Under the "Investors" link at DuPont's website (www.dupont.com), you will find financial statements for the company. Using the most recent Form 10-K, calculate the following ratios for DuPont over the three years reported: gross margin, operating margin, return on assets, return on equity, book value per share, earnings per share, cash flow per share, price-book, price-earnings, and price-cash flow. How have these ratios changed over this period?

3. **Cash Flow Statement** You can find financial statements for 3M in the company's annual report located in the "Investor Relations" section of the company's website, www.3m.com. Locate the statement of cash flows in the annual report. How have the items changed over the years? Explain 3M's most recent cash flow statement in words.

Global Economic Activity and Industry Analysis

"Blessed are the young, for they will inherit the national debt."

—President Herbert Hoover

If you want the supply of your investment services to be in high demand, you should:

1. Understand the process of top-down analysis.

2. Be able to measure the level of economic activity both globally and domestically.

3. Understand the relation of monetary and fiscal policies to economic activity.

4. Be able to identify industry sensitivity to business cycles.

Do you like roller coasters? If you do, you know some of the thrill is the anticipation of the next dip or loop. Financial markets and economies also have ups and downs (but no loops, we hope). Many of these financial moves, like those of the roller coaster, can be quite extreme. The movement in the fortunes of the overall economy is called the business cycle. Unlike the gyrations of roller coasters, economic cycles can have serious effects on your wealth. As a result, economists and investors spend much time and effort trying to predict these movements.

CFA™ Exam Topics in This Chapter:

1. Topics in demand and supply analysis (L1, S3)
2. Aggregate output, prices, and economic growth (L1, S3)
3. Understanding business cycles (L1, S3)
4. Monetary and fiscal policy (L1, S4)
5. Currency exchange rates (L1, S4)
6. Introduction to industry and company analysis (L1, S12)

Go to Connect for a guide that aligns your textbook with CFA readings.

In this chapter, we answer some general questions about economic activity. For example, what is the business cycle? How is economic activity measured? What are monetary and fiscal policy? How does economic activity impact sectors of the economy and the firms in these sectors? Answering these questions might help us anticipate economic movements. These predictions, in turn, might be valuable for deciding which investments to choose for a particular time period.

As you might imagine, in recent years there has been an increased focus on global economic conditions. This focus is important because the global economy impacts investments abroad and also those "at home." For example, the stock price of domestic firms that operate abroad will be influenced by economic cycles in other countries. Further, political and economic policies of other countries can impact domestic interest rates and relative currency values. Understanding the impact of global economic activity is, therefore, critical to successful investing.

20.1 Top-Down Analysis

Related Bloomberg Functions

EQS	Equity Screening
COUN	Country/Region Guide
ECOW	Economic Data Watch
ECO	Economic Calendars
WECO	Economic Calendars by Country
ECFC	Economic Forecasts
GEW	Global Economy Watch
FX24	FX Session Chart
FXCA	FX Conversion Calculator
PEG	Pegged Currencies
FXTF	FX Ticker Finder
FXC	Currency Rates Matrix
FXFM	FX Rate Forecast Model

What if your professor asked you to identify the single stock that you believe will be the best one to hold for the next six months. Because thousands of stocks are actively traded in the United States alone, this question is difficult, maybe impossible, to answer. Nonetheless, this is the task that active equity portfolio managers face every day—trying to select the stocks that they think will outperform all the others.

In the process of security selection, some managers undertake a "bottom-up" approach. That is, they select securities without regard to perceived economic cycles or industry-specific information. The more common style, however, is called "top-down" analysis. Under this approach, managers essentially take a big-picture perspective of the global economy. With the big picture in view, the manager then filters and sorts potential investments into smaller and smaller groups. As Figure 20.1 illustrates, this process is like a funnel, where all possible investments go in at the top. Then, based on economic, industry, and company analysis, the best potential investments are identified.

To better understand this process, consider this example: An investment manager studies the global economy and predicts an increased U.S. budget deficit will weaken the U.S. dollar. The manager also thinks that economic growth in international markets will be stronger than economic growth in the United States. This manager might then decide to select a group of U.S. companies that receive the bulk of their revenue from outside the United States. Within the major U.S. sectors, this strategy might imply that industrial, consumer staple, or technology companies should receive further attention.

Next, the manager looks at the economic cycle. If the expectation is for strong growth, then industrial companies will be preferred to consumer staple companies, which are more defensive. A "defensive" company, as we discuss later, is one that performs relatively better in a climate of weak growth. As you might expect, everyone still needs toilet paper, and other necessities, even if the economy isn't doing so well.

Once the industry is selected, the manager faces the task of selecting the best company within the industry. As we discussed elsewhere, this decision is largely based on forecasting cash flow, sales growth, earnings growth, and other critical financial information. In this chapter, however, we concentrate on identifying information that helps us see the "big picture" of the economy.

CHECK THIS

20.1a What does it mean to be a top-down analyst?

20.1b How does economic information play into top-down analysis?

FIGURE 20.1   Top-Down Analysis

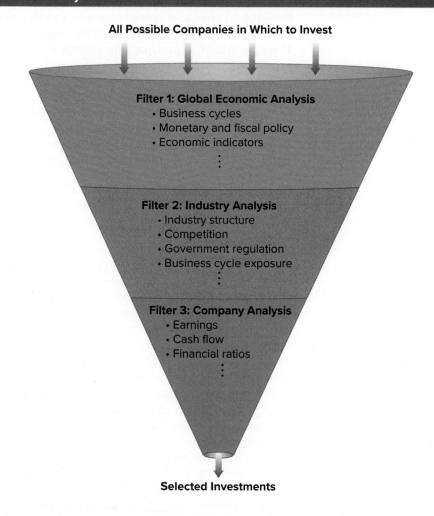

All Possible Companies in Which to Invest

Filter 1: Global Economic Analysis
- Business cycles
- Monetary and fiscal policy
- Economic indicators

Filter 2: Industry Analysis
- Industry structure
- Competition
- Government regulation
- Business cycle exposure

Filter 3: Company Analysis
- Earnings
- Cash flow
- Financial ratios

Selected Investments

20.2 Global Macroeconomic Activity

As we mentioned in the chapter opening, economies all around the world have a significant impact on the investment process. Investors should not only look at domestic activity and invest in only domestic stocks. This notion is particularly true when you consider that the United States makes up under 35 percent of global equity market capitalization. In the following sections, we discuss economic activity measures mainly from a U.S. perspective. The same measures can (and should) be used to evaluate the health of the economy of any country.

gross domestic product (GDP)
The market value of goods and services produced over a period of time.

nominal GDP
The dollar value of economic output in terms of the current year.

real GDP
The value of economic output adjusted for inflation.

REAL GDP

One of the most important measures of the health of an economy is **gross domestic product**, or **GDP**. GDP measures the market value of goods and services produced over a period of time. Thus, GDP effectively reflects a quantity of output. GDP is an indicator, or measure, of the standard of living for people residing in the country.

Typically, GDP is reported on a nominal basis. **Nominal GDP** reflects the dollar value of output in terms of the current year. Many economists, however, prefer to focus on **real GDP**. Real GDP is nominal GDP adjusted for inflation. Because real GDP accounts for the effects of inflation, it is a more consistent comparison of the standard of living across time periods.

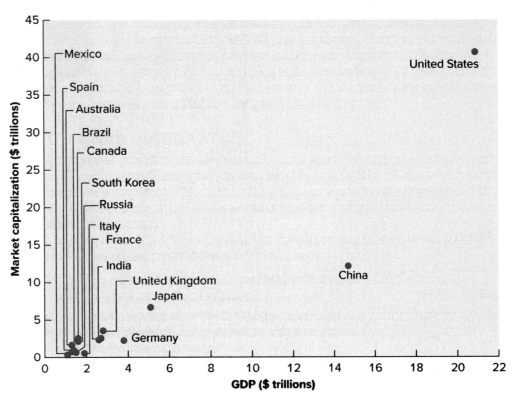

FIGURE 20.2   GDP versus Market Capitalization

Source: World Bank, 2022 (in US$ equivalent).

Why do analysts care about real GDP? As an example, consider a country whose nominal GDP increases in one year from $1.29 trillion to $1.41 trillion. This increase is 9.3 percent. If the country is experiencing high inflation, however, then the real economic growth is much less. For example, if inflation were 7.1 percent during the year, then the real growth rate of the economy is closer to 2.2 percent (i.e., 9.3 percent − 7.1 percent). As investors, if we were using expected growth rates to decide our country investment levels, real GDP is a much better measure of true underlying economic growth than nominal GDP.

Figure 20.2 illustrates this important relationship. This figure plots the GDP and corresponding market capitalization of the 15 leading economies in the world as of 2021. What do you notice about the relationship between GDP and market values? They seem to be significantly correlated–those countries with the highest GDP also have the highest equity market valuations. In fact, the correlation value of .93 is almost perfectly positive. Thus, investors wanting to allocate capital across countries should consider using GDP growth in their decisions.

BUSINESS CYCLES

When analyzing potential GDP growth, investors need to be aware of the business cycle. As we point out in our opening roller coaster analogy, a nation's economy, especially GDP, goes through periods of ups and downs. In the national economy, this up-and-down movement is called the business cycle. Figure 20.3 is a simple illustration of this cycle.

The four stages of the cycle include peak, contraction, trough, and expansion. While Figure 20.3 suggests that the cycle follows a rather smooth pattern, reality is not so simple. For example, look at Figure 20.4A, which illustrates real GDP levels (in 2012 dollars) in the United States since 1959. You might be thinking that you do not see much of a wave pattern in Figure 20.4A. Well, you are right. So, look at Figure 20.4B, which plots yearly growth in real GDP. In this figure, you can see the ups and downs of the business cycle. You can also see that the actual data do not follow the smooth pattern that Figure 20.3 suggests.

FIGURE 20.3

The Business Cycle

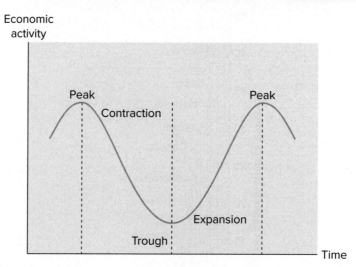

FIGURE 20.4A

U.S. Real GDP, 1959–2021

cyclical sectors
Economic sectors that have a high sensitivity to the business cycle.

defensive sectors
Economic sectors that have a low sensitivity to the business cycle.

If you are conducting a top-down analysis, you must understand the link between the business cycle and GDP growth. An investor who can successfully identify patterns in the cycle might be able to predict which sectors within an economy are better situated for short-term growth. To help you with this process, check out Figure 20.5, which identifies the stages of the business cycle in which some of the major market sectors might perform well.

Sectors are often referred to as **cyclical** or **defensive**. Cyclical sectors, such as industrials and materials, have above-average sensitivity to the business cycle, which means they tend to perform best when the economy is expanding. In contrast, defensive sectors, such as health

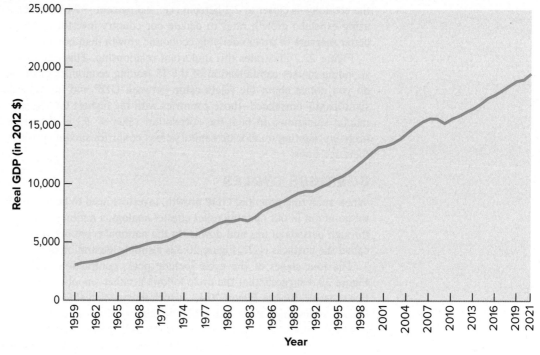

Source: St. Louis Federal Reserve Bank.

FIGURE 20.4B   U.S. Real GDP Growth, 1959–2021

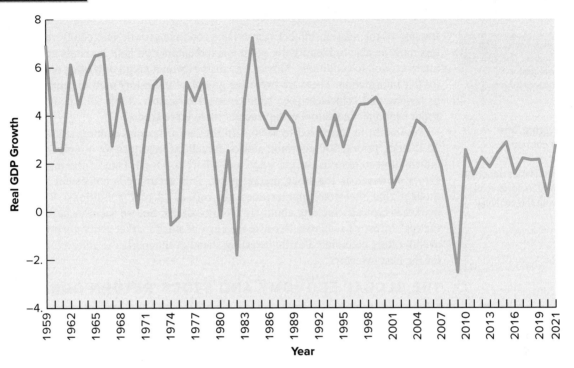

Source: St. Louis Federal Reserve Bank.

FIGURE 20.5   Sector Performance Across the Business Cycle

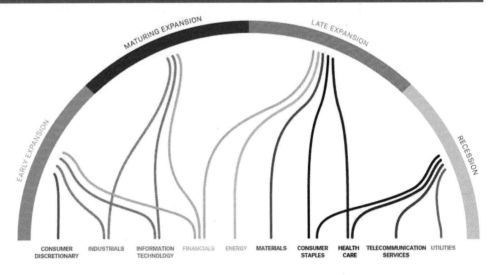

Source: www.schwab.com/resource-center/insights/sites/g/files/eyrktu156/files/2017-08/OnInvesting_Summer16_web.pdf.

care and consumer staples, have relatively little sensitivity to the business cycle, so they perform relatively better during the late stages of the business cycle.

ECONOMIC INDICATORS

leading, lagging, and coincident economic indicators
Economic time series data that tend to change in advance of, behind, or with the economy.

Because of the relationship between GDP, economic growth, and equity value, astute investors must be able to identify the economic indicators that help investors accurately forecast future economic conditions. Most economists rely on a group of **leading economic indicators** for this information. There are two other groups of indicators used to gauge economic activity: **lagging** and **coincident** (i.e., simultaneous) **indicators.** Table 20.1 contains a list of the major economic indicators within each of these three groups.

You might be surprised by Item 7 in the list of leading economic indicators in Table 20.1: stock prices, 500 common stocks. Recall, as investors we attempt to use economic information to help us decide when and where to invest. One of the most accurate indicators, however, is the stock market itself. This accuracy is consistent with the general thought that the stock market does not reflect current conditions. Rather, the stock market is typically looking about six months ahead. So, we seem to have a "chicken and the egg" investing scenario. Because the current stock market generally provides an idea of overall future economic health, investing ahead of the market is quite a difficult task—even for the best investors.

THE GLOBAL ECONOMY AND STOCK RETURN CORRELATIONS

Increased technology and improved supply chain logistics, combined with reduced trade barriers, have significantly increased the integration of economies around the world. Recall that we examined the business cycle in the context of one economy. Today, however, business cycles tend to move together worldwide.

Astute investors know that the principle of diversification predicts that returns from international investments can offset the returns from domestic investments. The amount of the offset depends on the correlation among investments. Over time, correlations across country

TABLE 20.1	Economic Indicators

Leading Indicators

1. Average weekly hours, manufacturing
2. Average weekly initial claims for unemployment insurance
3. Manufacturers' new orders, consumer goods, and materials
4. Index of supplier deliveries
5. Manufacturers' new orders, nondefense capital goods
6. New private housing units authorized by local building permits
7. Stock prices, 500 common stocks
8. Money supply (M2) growth rate
9. Index of consumer expectations
10. Interest rate spread, 10-year Treasury bonds less federal funds rate

Coincident Indicators

1. Employees on nonagricultural payrolls
2. Personal income less transfer payments
3. Industrial production
4. Manufacturing and trade sales

Lagging Indicators

1. Average duration of unemployment
2. Ratio of trade inventories to sales
3. Change in index of labor cost per unit of output
4. Average prime rate charged by banks
5. Commercial and industrial loans outstanding
6. Ratio of consumer installment credit outstanding to personal income
7. Change in Consumer Price Index for services

Source: The Conference Board.

stock market returns have increased. Unfortunately, this increase is especially true during bear markets—which is precisely when investors need protection provided by diversification the most. For example, in the Crash of 2008, correlations across country stock market returns essentially went to +1 because almost all countries were hit with a recession (i.e., a contraction stage).

The major differences in correlations among economic conditions occur in the expansion stage because each country comes out of the trough stage at a different rate. Understanding the differences in economic activity can be helpful in determining investment allocations across countries—especially during expansions.

THE EFFECTS OF EXCHANGE RATES ON GLOBAL INVESTMENTS

Suppose an investor can make accurate predictions of which stock markets around the world will perform relatively better. Even with this enviable skill, another factor affects the rate of return on international investments—the exchange rate. For example, suppose a U.S. investor wants to buy an asset in Germany, whose currency is the euro. The first step for the investor is to convert U.S. dollars into euros. Once the euros are in hand, the investment can be made. When the asset is sold, this U.S. investor converts the euros back into U.S. dollars. The net return will be based on the return of the asset and on whether the euro appreciated or depreciated relative to the U.S. dollar.

Let's consider an example. Suppose we have $10,000 to buy shares of a company listed on the Deutsche Börse, the German stock exchange. At the time of the investment, the exchange rate is $1.29/€. The shares increase in value by 10 percent during the year. At the end of the year, we sell the shares and convert the euros back into dollars at a rate of $1.18/€. What is our net dollar return?

Well, the asset itself had a positive return, so that is good. But what about the impact of the exchange rate? As with any asset, we want to invest in currencies that are appreciating. We were invested in euros, so did the euros appreciate or depreciate relative to the U.S. dollar? At the beginning of the year, one euro could be converted into $1.29. At the end of the year, one euro could be converted into only $1.18. Thus, one euro is worth less in terms of U.S. dollars at the end of the year. This means that the euro has depreciated relative to the U.S. dollar. This depreciation means that the net return to the U.S. investor will not be 10 percent because the asset return is going to be reduced by the depreciation of the euro. Let's calculate the exact return.

Step 1: We convert the U.S. dollars into euros at the beginning of the year. It takes $1.29 to "buy" one euro. Thus, with $10,000 we can purchase $10,000/($1.29/€) = €7,751.94 worth of shares.

Step 2: We calculate the ending value of the shares. If the €7,751.94 investment increases in value by 10 percent, the ending value is €7,751.94 × 1.10 = €8,527.13 when we sell the shares.

Step 3: We convert the euros back into dollars. At the end of the year, one euro can be converted into $1.18. Thus, €8,527.13 × $1.18/€ = $10,062.02.

Check out www.xe.com for a list of exchange rates, as well as a currency converter.

Step 4: We calculate the dollar-denominated return. Because the investment of $10,000 grew to $10,062.02, the return was .62 percent. As we thought, the depreciation of the euro reduced the dollar-denominated return earned on the euro-denominated shares (which was 10 percent).

As international investors, we need to be aware of the impact of exchange rates, as well as think about asset allocation and security selection. Changes in exchange rates will likely increase or decrease our international portfolio returns. Although exchange rate movements complicate the investment process, these movements actually provide some potential diversification benefit over longer periods of time. Nonetheless, some investors prefer to avoid all exchange rate risk. As we discussed in an earlier chapter, international investors can use futures contracts to reduce this currency risk if they so desire.

EXAMPLE 20.1

Exchange Rate Risk and Returns

You have found an attractive stock listed on the Bolsa (the Mexican stock exchange). You decide to invest $25,000. The investment does well, earning 15 percent in one year. During the year, the exchange rate goes from 19.05 pesos per dollar to 18.78 pesos per dollar. What is your dollar-denominated return on this investment? (You should note that whether we multiply or divide depends on the direction of the conversion.)

Step 1: $25,000 × (19.05 pesos/$) = 476,250 pesos

Step 2: 476,250 pesos × 1.15 = 547,687.50 pesos

Step 3: 547,687.50 pesos/(18.78 pesos/$) = 29,163.34

Step 4: ($29,163.34 − 25,000)/$25,000 = .1665, or 16.65%

The investment itself did well. Plus, the peso appreciated. In this case, the net dollar return, 16.65 percent, was higher than the return on the peso-denominated investment (which was 15 percent).

You might be wondering if this discussion is relevant given that most investors can now invest in international companies by simply buying a country-based ETF on the U.S. exchange. While these types of investments have simplified the process of obtaining international exposure, they do not eliminate the impact of exchange rate movements. The underlying fund manager still has to make currency conversions, so the currency movement still impacts overall investor returns. This impact is just "hidden" within the return of the fund itself.

CHECK THIS

20.2a What is the difference between nominal and real GDP?

20.2b In what stages of the business cycle would you prefer to invest in cyclical industries?

20.2c How do exchange rates impact investor returns?

20.3 Monitoring Jobs and the Price Level

LABOR MARKET INDICATORS

Related Bloomberg Functions

ECST World Economic Statistics

IFMO Inflation Monitor

For goods and services to be sold, there must be demand for them. In the United States, about 70 percent of GDP is the result of consumer spending, with the remainder being driven by categories such as investment and government spending. Because so much of GDP is from consumer spending (i.e., consumption), employment levels are critical for the health of the economy.

Most economists believe that unemployment is a lagging indicator because recessions bring about unemployment. Unemployment does not fall until expansion begins. Some economists, however, suggest that unemployment is a leading indicator. Their argument is that high levels of unemployment can signal an even longer contraction—because consumers cannot spend as much if they are unemployed (or underemployed). Whether you believe unemployment is a lagging or a leading indicator, knowing how unemployment is calculated is important.

Economists divide the nonmilitary working-age population into three groups: employed, unemployed but seeking employment, and unemployed and not seeking employment. The **labor force** is defined as all nonmilitary working-age people who are employed or unemployed

labor force
All nonmilitary working-age people who are employed or unemployed but seeking employment.

unemployment rate
The percentage of the labor force that is unemployed but seeking employment.

labor force participation rate
The labor force divided by the nonmilitary working-age population.

but seeking employment. The **unemployment rate** is the percentage of the labor force that is unemployed but seeking employment. The **labor force participation rate** equals the labor force divided by the nonmilitary working-age population. For example, in early 2022 in the United States, the labor force was approximately 162 million people. According to the Federal Reserve, this number represents a participation rate of 61.9 percent. Of the labor force, about 3.9 percent, or 6.3 million people, were unemployed.

As with any statistic, understanding the calculation is important when interpreting the number. For example, at the height of the recession in 2009–2010, unemployment levels surged to over 10 percent. The reduction in the unemployment rate since this time is likely a result, at least in part, of economic growth. There are other underlying issues, however. For example, the participation rate was over 66 percent before the recession. When unemployed people become discouraged, they often drop out of the labor force. All else equal, this exodus reduces the unemployment rate because these people are no longer used to calculate the unemployment rate. The same happened during the COVID-19 pandemic, as workers decided to stay home and not work. Astute investors must disentangle these effects if they want a true picture of the economy's health.

While increasing employment is generally good for the economy, it is only one measure of the health of the economy. Two other important measures are the wage rate and the inflation rate. For example, if unemployed people find work in lower-paying jobs, spending by these consumers will be lower. Or if inflation increases at a higher rate than wages, then purchasing power decreases and workers are actually worse off in real terms. Thus, in addition to employment, the real (or inflation-adjusted) wage rate is an important measure to help gauge economic health.

THE CONSUMER PRICE INDEX

Consumer Price Index (CPI)
Measures the average prices paid by urban consumers for a fixed "basket" of consumer goods and services.

Core CPI
Measures the average prices paid by urban consumers for a fixed "basket" of consumer goods and services, excluding food and energy.

In the previous sections, we saw how important the inflation rate was to calculate real levels of GDP and wages. We now discuss how inflation is measured. The most commonly used measure of inflation is the **Consumer Price Index (CPI)**. The CPI measures the average price of a fixed basket of consumer goods and services. Inflation is the percentage change in the CPI from one period to the next. For example, if the CPI increases from 104.3 to 105.2 during the year, then the inflation rate is .9 percent for that year [= (105.2 − 104.3)/104.3].

Major parts of the CPI basket include housing and food. Smaller parts include medical care, recreation, education, energy, and apparel. There are variations of the CPI. For example, some economists prefer to focus on **Core CPI**, which excludes food and energy prices. The logic used by these economists is that these items are subject to greater volatility because of potential supply disruptions. This issue became particularly relevant in 2011 when energy and food prices rose drastically, but Core CPI remained roughly unchanged. In this case, Core CPI may understate the true impact of inflation on consumers.

Of course, there are others who suggest that the CPI overstates inflation. For example, the CPI does not consider the invention of new goods or quality improvement. Also, so-called substitution effects are ignored. An example of a substitution effect is when consumers switch to chicken and away from beef if beef prices rise relative to chicken prices. A congressional commission studied this issue and concluded that the CPI might be overstated by about 1 percent in any given year as a result of these substitution effects.

Given the debate over the ability of the CPI to measure inflation, it is the responsibility of investors to understand its limitations. Otherwise, return expectations and other analyses might be incomplete.

As Figure 20.6 illustrates, the inverse relationship between inflation and real GDP is quite pronounced. This negative correlation suggests that high inflation is detrimental to real economic growth. This relation might be driven by the fact that high inflation leads to higher interest rates. Providers of funds will demand a higher interest rate to compensate them for their loss in purchasing power brought on by inflation. High interest rates tend to reduce the demand for loanable funds—which, in turn, reduces economic growth.

A common rule of thumb on Wall Street is that the inflation rate plus the market price-to-earnings (PE) ratio equals 20. (Remember we discussed price ratios in an earlier chapter.)

FIGURE 20.6   U.S. Real GDP Growth and CPI, 1959–2021

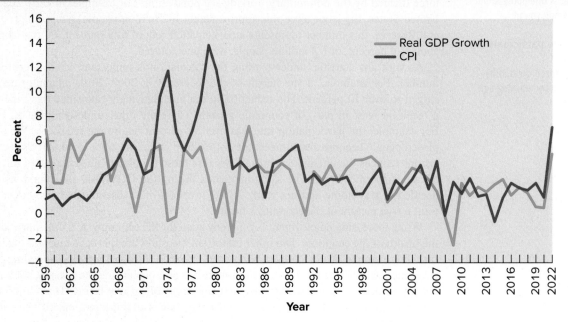

Source: St. Louis Federal Reserve Bank.

While this is not an exact number and obviously varies through time, it does illustrate that inflation can have a negative effect on stock prices.

For example, assume this rule holds true and inflation is 4 percent. Then, the market PE ratio should be about 16. If inflation heats up and increases to 6 percent, then the PE would likely fall, to about 14. For every dollar of earnings a company has, its share price would fall by about two dollars. If earnings increase with inflation, then the full drop in price might not be realized, but the negative effect of inflation will likely still be felt in stock prices.

Given the above relationships, we can identify a "Goldilocks" scenario as a country where economic conditions are not too hot or too cold . . . they are "just right." Such a country will have strong income growth, low unemployment, and low inflation. This combination should result in rapid expansion of the economy and, as a result, benefit the underlying companies that are competing in that economy. Understanding this link will help investors select their allocations across assets, particularly those allocations across geographic regions where different economic conditions exist.

CHECK THIS

20.3a   If all else stayed the same, but the labor force participation rate declined, what would happen to the unemployment rate?

20.3b   What is the "Goldilocks" scenario with regard to economic conditions?

20.4 Monetary and Fiscal Policy

Think about the economy as if it were a car: You want to keep it moving forward but avoid going too slowly or too rapidly. To maintain the desired pace, someone needs to drive the car, monitor the speed, and give the car more (or less) gas as needed. For an economy, the role of maintaining a desired pace generally has been assumed by monetary and fiscal policy makers.

MONETARY POLICY

Money is a generally accepted means of payment. Money functions as a medium of exchange, a unit of account, and a store of value. There are various ways to measure the amount of money, or money supply, that is in the economy. The most basic measure of money supply is called M1, which includes currency and checking deposits. A broader money supply measure, M2, is M1 plus time deposits, savings accounts, and money markets.

The money supply is important for the economy because it represents the "gas" for the economic engine. Giving the economy more gas (i.e., more money) makes it go faster, but giving it too much can result in overheating (i.e., high inflation). In fact, a common saying is that "inflation is always, and everywhere, a monetary phenomenon." So, the goal of policy makers is to keep the money supply growing at just the right pace to keep the economy moving forward at the desired rate. To see the importance of money supply for investors, check out Figure 20.7. You can see the generally positive relationship between money supply growth and stock prices.

THE FEDERAL RESERVE The Federal Reserve (or "Fed" for short) is the central bank of the United States. A central bank is called the "banker's bank" because it provides loans to banks and holds deposits for banks. Besides regulating the nation's banks, the Fed also monitors and changes the money supply. Monitoring the money supply is a difficult task for the Federal Reserve.

The Federal Reserve is an independent federal governmental agency. Technically, the Fed does not answer to any other part of the government. The reason for this independence is to enable the Fed to pursue its goals without political consequences. Whether the Fed is actually independent, however, is a matter of debate because the Fed Board is appointed by the president and approved by the Senate. Nonetheless, the primary goals of the Fed are to keep inflation in check, generate full employment, moderate the business cycle, and help achieve long-term economic growth.

While other countries have similar central banks, the goals of these central banks can differ from those of the Fed. For example, the European Central Bank (ECB) oversees the European Union. The ECB, however, has only one main goal: control inflation. The ECB has little, if any, responsibility to stimulate economic growth. The lack of such a goal might seem unimportant to you, but it can have a big impact on investment allocation. Slow economic growth might be reflected in relatively lower stock prices.

FIGURE 20.7 **U.S. M2 and S&P 500 Index, 1959–2021**

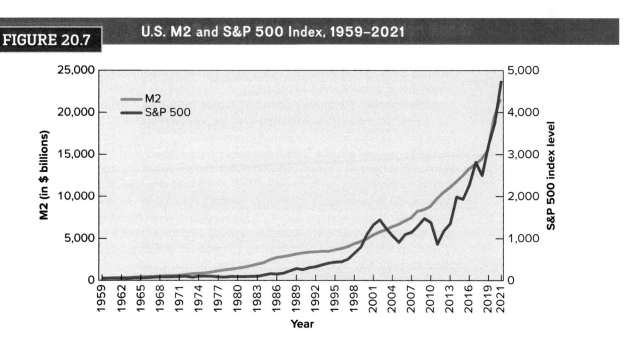

Source: St. Louis Federal Reserve and author calculations.

discount rate
The interest rate the Fed charges its member banks on loans.

federal funds rate
Interest rate that banks charge each other for overnight loans of $1 million or more.

open market operations
The buying and selling of bonds directly on the secondary market for purposes of increasing or decreasing the money supply.

fiscal policy
Government determination of tax rates and spending policies.

For a running tab of the government's debt, check out www.usdebtclock.org.

To achieve its goals, the Fed has primarily relied on its ability to change interest rates. For example, the Fed has control over the **discount rate**, which is the interest rate the Fed charges its member banks on loans. While "discount window" lending is small in comparison to other Fed operations, changing the discount rate has a ripple effect throughout the banking system. The **federal funds rate**, which is the short-term rate at which banks lend to each other, generally changes with the discount rate. In turn, changes in the federal funds rate can even impact longer-term rates for mortgages and other loans. All else equal, reducing the discount rate should stimulate demand for loans, which, in turn, spurs economic growth.

MONEY CREATION The Fed has historically focused on the discount rate, but it also has the ability to "pump" money directly into the financial system. In fact, this activity increased dramatically in the wake of the Crash of 2008. To impact the money supply through the financial markets, the Fed conducts **open market operations**. Through this process, the Fed either buys or sells Treasury bonds in the open market. Buying bonds puts money into the financial system because the Fed pays dollars to the bond sellers. The goal of buying bonds is to spur economic growth. The Fed puts the brakes on the economy by reducing the money supply. When the Fed sells bonds, it takes dollars from the bond buyers.

Adding money to the financial system has a ripple effect because the United States follows a fractional reserve banking system. In this type of banking system, banks must keep only a percentage (or fraction) of their deposits on reserve. This fraction is set by the Fed. Deposits that are not held on reserve can be loaned to borrowers. When borrowers make purchases, the sellers deposit the proceeds into a bank. A fraction of this deposit is set aside, and the remaining funds are lent again. As you can imagine, this process repeats over and over.

How big is this ripple effect? With a 20 percent reserve requirement, total money supply from an initial $100 deposit can become $500 in total money supply. This expansion results from the *money multiplier,* which is calculated as 1 divided by the reserve requirement ($1/.20 = 5$). If banks increase lending standards, or if there is a lack of demand for borrowing, then the money supply will not expand to the level predicted by the money multiplier. In this case, banks would have excess reserves caused by a so-called lower *velocity of money.* The Fed can control the inflow of reserves into the banking system and predict the total money supply using the money multiplier. End-user demand and bank lending standards, however, can prevent the money supply from reaching the amount predicted by the Fed.

FISCAL POLICY

The federal government collects taxes and uses this money to pay for products and services. The determination of tax rates and spending policies is referred to as **fiscal policy**. Potentially, fiscal policy has significant impacts on the overall economy. For example, if the government wanted to spur investment, it could reduce (or even eliminate) taxes on capital gains. Or the federal tax code could allow for a faster depreciation of capital spending by businesses—which would also spur investment. Interestingly, it seems that lower taxes can actually increase government revenue. If economic activity increases enough as a result of lower tax rates, total tax revenue increases. This is referred to as "supply-side economics," a concept that has been hotly debated since Ronald Reagan was president.

Unlike you and me, the federal government is not really forced to abide by, or even set, a restrictive budget. As a result, one of the "hot button" issues in recent years has been the fact that the federal government's expenditures exceed tax revenues. When government expenditures exceed tax revenues, the resulting shortfall is called the *budget deficit.* Over time, these budget deficits grow and increase the national debt because excess spending must be paid for with borrowings. As of early 2022, the national debt was almost $30 trillion.

In theory, the national debt finances government spending, which is part of GDP. Thus, there are some who believe that increased government spending actually aids economic activity. The downside of debt, however, is that it must be financed and repaid. In the long run, continued debt implies higher interest rates and increased taxes, both of which slow growth. To pay off the debt, the federal government could print money. As we learned earlier, however, increasing the money supply would spur inflation and devalue the dollar. The general consensus is that sustained budget deficits are detrimental for the long-run prosperity of an economy.

TABLE 20.2

Country Debt, 2010

	Total Debt as a % of GDP	Bond Yield (10-year)
Greece	140.2	11.3%
Ireland	97.4	8.3
Portugal	82.8	6.8
Spain	64.4	5.5
United States	62.2	3.3

Source: *The Economist.*

For an investor, national debt can be a critical factor in choosing country investment allocations. For example, the impact of high federal debt levels was a driving factor behind the recent European debt crisis. In 2010, the PIGS (Portugal, Ireland, Greece, and Spain) all suffered large budget deficits and increased their level of sovereign debt. As a result, their sovereign debt was downgraded. This downgrade, in turn, increased interest rates on new debt and caused many investors to flee from these four stock markets.

Table 20.2 provides some information on the PIGS's government debt levels as a percent of GDP, as well as their corresponding yields on 10-year government debt. The table also provides comparable statistics for the United States. In 2010, U.S. debt (held by the public) as a percentage of GDP was close to that of Spain, and it was the highest it had been since the 1950s. Recall that the U.S. national debt in the 1950s was a result of spending for World War II.

You can see from Table 20.2 why many people are concerned that the United States may turn into a "European-type" state. This fear has become more pronounced over the last few years as the U.S. debt (held by the public) has increased to over 75 percent of GDP, much of it due to stimulus spending related to the coronavirus. When other debt is considered (such as Treasury bonds held internally by Social Security), the figure rises to over 130 percent of GDP.

CHECK THIS

20.4a Who controls monetary policy? Who controls fiscal policy?

20.4b If the Fed adds $10 billion to the money supply, why would the money supply be expected to grow by more than $10 billion?

20.5 Industry Analysis

Related Bloomberg Functions

ICS	Classification Browser
RRG	Relative Rotation Graph
IMAP	Intraday Market Map
GMM	Global Macro Movers
BI	Bloomberg Intelligence
SPLC	Supply Chain Analysis

Economic information is helpful to investors when they are looking for areas of potential growth (or decline). While much of the discussion in previous sections focused on country-level issues, economic information is also useful for analyzing industries. For example, in an attempt to help the economy recover from the recent economic crisis, the federal government passed a stimulus bill (fiscal policy). Much of this increased spending was supposed to go to capital improvements such as roads. As a result, many investors thought industrial firms would be big beneficiaries of this spending because new equipment would be required.

Earlier in this chapter, we discussed the business cycle and how investments in specific firms can be classified as defensive or cyclical. These classifications are a description of how dependent these firms are on the business cycle. Defensive investments are not as linked to the business cycle as are cyclical investments. To examine these links in more detail, and to learn how to evaluate sectors and industries, we turn our focus to the general process of sector and industry analysis.

TABLE 20.3

Sectors of the S&P, January 2022

Sector	Market Value (%)
Materials	2.60
Energy	3.26
Financials	11.28
Real estate	2.66
Industrials	8.00
Consumer staples	6.13
Utilities	2.53
Health care	13.04
Consumer discretionary	12.18
Technology	28.10
Communication services	10.22
	Total: 100.00

IDENTIFYING SECTORS

S&P SECTORS There are many ways to define a sector. A good starting point is the list of 11 basic sectors used by Standard and Poor's, the creator of the S&P 500 index. Table 20.3 provides a list of the 11 sectors, along with their early 2022 index weights. As you can see, some sectors are quite small (such as materials and real estate), while others (such as health care and technology) are quite large.

While these weights are not extremely volatile, they do change when some sectors do well relative to other sectors. For example, in early 2007, financials comprised over 20 percent of the index weight. Financials were less than 15 percent of the index following the financial crisis and related Crash of 2008. This fluctuation might seem like common sense, but understanding the reasons behind these movements could give you an advantage when you invest.

ROTATIONAL INVESTING As we discussed earlier in the chapter, macroeconomic trends and government actions can favor some industries more than others. Unsophisticated investors might believe that if the S&P 500 return is positive, then the returns for all sectors must be positive. It is possible, however, for some sectors within the S&P 500 to have a negative return over a given period even if the entire index has a positive return. Of course, the reverse is also true. As a result, active investors will decide to enter and exit industries over time. This process of moving investment dollars from one industry to another is often referred to as *rotational investing* because investors "rotate" dollars out of some industries and into others.

Figures 20.8 and 20.9 provide a snapshot of performance differences. Figure 20.8 shows the returns for the sectors over some historical time periods. As of January 11, 2022, you will notice that for the last month (the column labeled "Net (%) 30"), the technology sector had lost about 4.96 percent of its value, while the energy sector was up about 20.07 percent. The other time periods provide different stories. For example, notice that over the last year, for energy all the sectors were positive. So, is this most recent move a sign of sector rotation? We can't say for sure, but it is definitely a possibility.

Figure 20.9 is called a "heat map," and it provides a breakdown of the S&P 500 into its major sectors. Within each sector, the heat map identifies the specific companies in the S&P 500, with the size of each box representing relative market weights. Each box is then color coded to identify whether the stock price for a particular company (and therefore industry) is up or down. The heat map changes throughout the trading day, but at any moment it provides a visual snapshot of the market and its sectors.

To see the current heat map, check out
finviz.com/map.ashx.

FIGURE 20.8

S&P 500 Sector Returns as of January 19, 2022

S&P 500 Sector	Net (%) 5	Net (%) 30	Net (%) 90	Net (%) 180	Net (%) 360
Materials	−2.22	0.05	3.55	10.32	15.42
Energy	1.76	20.07	11.56	38.09	49.02
Financials	−5.23	2.06	−1.64	11.78	26.56
Real estate	−3.13	−4.76	2.19	4.36	31.93
Industrials	−2.37	1.25	−0.10	3.72	16.10
Consumer staples	−0.37	2.25	9.00	9.02	18.57
Utilities	−0.60	−0.94	4.61	5.61	9.73
Health care	−3.84	−4.31	2.29	3.49	11.71
Consumer discretionary	−5.52	−3.64	−1.83	4.89	11.54
Technology	−5.13	−4.96	0.39	7.51	23.29
Communication services	−2.68	−2.65	−7.06	−2.64	17.72

Source: Author calculations.

There are other factors that lead investors to rotate sectors. One particularly relevant factor is the industry life cycle. As Figure 20.10 illustrates, industries often follow a defined life cycle: start-up, consolidation, maturity, and relative decline. Of course, each industry is different and the stages can vary in length. By understanding this framework, however, investors might be able to identify which companies are poised for higher growth and which ones are likely to face a more muted future.

SUBSECTOR (INDUSTRY) DIFFERENCES The 11 S&P sectors provide a good distinction across firms, but they are not without limitation. For example, do you think it would be good to compare Ford Motor Company to Starbucks? Most investors would say that these two businesses are quite distinct. Ford is in automobiles, and Starbucks is in retail. Yet, S&P puts them both into the Consumer Discretionary sector. This example illustrates that sophisticated industry analysis often involves drilling down to uncover more detailed information.

FIGURE 20.9

S&P 500 Heat Map

Source: finviz.com, 2022.

FIGURE 20.10 The Industry Life Cycle

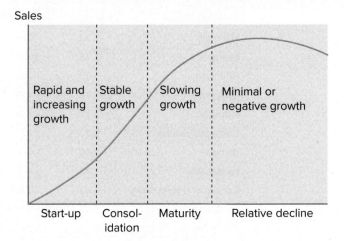

One way to gather information is to make comparisons across subsectors. These subsectors are often referred to as industry groups. One way to separate these groups is to use the Global Industry Classification System (or GICS). This system begins with the 11 S&P sectors, but it then subdivides them into 24 industry groups, 69 industries, and 158 subindustries. The GICS allows for a more defined comparison across firms.

As an example, consider the classifications for Ford and Starbucks as follows:

$$Ford = 25102010$$
$$Starbucks = 25301040$$

The first two digits (25) identify the sector, which is Consumer Discretionary. The next two digits (10 and 30, respectively) identify the industry groups, which are Automobiles and Components (for Ford) and Hotels, Restaurants, and Leisure (for Starbucks). The remaining values further distinguish firms within the industries. Obviously, this more specific breakdown provides a potentially better (but more narrow) list of comparison firms.

PORTER'S FIVE FORCES

Once you have narrowed down the industries in which you are interested, you will want to undertake some additional analysis. One particularly helpful approach is to use *Porter's five forces*, which is named after strategy guru Michael Porter. Figure 20.11 illustrates the basic framework of this industry analysis technique.

The goals of this analysis are to estimate how competitive the industry is and to identify which firms might be best positioned for success. The framework focuses on five core pieces:

1. **Threat of new entrants.** This piece examines the ease with which new firms can enter the market. In turn, the extent of these "barriers to entry" impacts how likely it is that a firm will be able to retain market share. Morningstar, a leading financial analysis firm, refers to these barriers to entry as a company's "economic moat."

2. **Bargaining power of buyers.** This area analyzes how difficult it would be for a buyer to switch to another seller. The easier it is to switch, the more pricing pressure a seller will face. This pressure will affect the ability of a company to maintain its profit margins.

3. **Bargaining power of suppliers.** This piece examines the supplier network for the company and estimates whether suppliers have the power to raise prices. Again, this power will also impact the ability of a firm to control its profit margins.

4. **Threat of substitute products.** This area is similar to new entrants, but it goes a step further. For example, if beef prices increase significantly, a consumer could switch to chicken. Thus, firms need to be concerned about competing products beyond the specific industry.

FIGURE 20.11   Porter's Five Forces Model of Competition

Threat of New Entrants
Barriers to entry
  • Economies of scale
  • Product differentiation
  • Capital requirements
  • Switching cost to buyers
  • Access to distribution channels
  • Other cost advantages
  • Government policies
Defense of market share
Industry growth rate

Bargaining Power of Suppliers
Supplier concentration
Availability of substitute inputs
Importance of suppliers' input to buyer
Suppliers' product differentiation
Importance of industry to suppliers
Buyers' switching cost to other input
Suppliers' threat of forward integration
Buyers' threat of backward integration

Intensity of Rivalry
Number of competitors (concentration)
Relative size of competitors (balance)
Industry growth rate
Fixed costs vs. variable costs
Product differentiation
Capacity augmented in large increments
Buyers' switching costs
Diversity of competitors
Exit barriers
Strategic stakes

Bargaining Power of Buyers
Number of buyers relative to sellers
Product differentiation
Switching costs to use other product
Buyers' profit margins
Buyers' use of multiple sources
Buyers' threat of backward integration
Sellers' threat of forward integration
Importance of product to the buyer
Buyers' volume

Threat of Substitute Products
Relative price of substitute
Relative quality of substitute
Switching costs to buyers

5. **Intensity of rivalry.** Taken together, the above factors help score the intensity of the competition within the industry. Understanding this intensity helps investors identify which industries (and companies) they think are most likely to retain (or gain) market share.

Once an analyst has identified relevant industries, the next step is to select the best companies within these industries. We discussed many of these issues in previous chapters, where we covered relevant financial metrics and valuation approaches. With all of this information, you are now ready to conduct top-down analysis.

CHECK THIS

20.5a   Are all firms in the same sector comparable?

20.5b   How is Porter's five forces model useful in analyzing industries?

20.6 Summary and Conclusions

In this chapter, we present some ways for investors to narrow the set of all possible investments. We discuss many economic conditions that can influence potential investment returns.

1. **Understand the process of top-down analysis.**

A. There are thousands of individual stocks in the United States alone. One method to narrow the list of choices is top-down analysis.

B. The filters used to "funnel" the choices often focus on measures of macroeconomic and industry activity.

2. **Be able to measure the level of economic activity both globally and domestically.**

A. Economic globalization has had a significant impact on the investment process, particularly because the United States represents only about 40 percent of global market values.

B. Gross domestic product (GDP) measures the overall level of economic activity in an economy. Growth in GDP is highly correlated to asset values within the economy.

C. Changes in GDP are often driven by the business cycle, which economists try to predict using leading economic indicators. Other indicators, such as employment and the price level (or inflation), are also important.

D. Aside from asset values, changes in exchange rates also impact the net return to an investor.

3. **Understand the relation of monetary and fiscal policies to economic activity.**

A. Monetary policy is controlled in the United States by the Federal Reserve, or the Fed. The Fed uses changes in interest rates, combined with open market operations, to increase or decrease the amount of money available.

B. Increased money supply is like "gas" for the "economic engine."

C. Government policies on taxes and spending are called fiscal policy.

4. **Be able to identify industry sensitivity to business cycles.**

A. There are 11 basic sectors used to categorize companies. These sectors, though correlated, come in and out of favor at various times. The process of reallocating investment dollars among sectors is known as rotational investing.

B. Companies within a sector are not always similar. Thus, investors often need to drill down to subsectors to provide a better comparison.

C. One method used to evaluate the strength of an industry is Porter's five forces: threat of new entrants, bargaining power of buyers, bargaining power of suppliers, threat of substitute products, and intensity of rivalry.

GETTING DOWN TO BUSINESS

This chapter discusses top-down investment analysis. When investors undertake a top-down analysis, they must know how to measure and interpret economic activity. This knowledge will help them make better decisions about investing across countries and industries.

As investors, there are two primary decisions we must make: asset allocation (percentage allocations across countries and industries) and security selection (picking individual securities within each allocation). Investors tend to believe that security selection is the key determinant of portfolio performance. The general conclusion, however, is that asset allocation is more critical for returns than security selection. In fact, the general consensus among researchers is that asset allocation determines about 90 percent of a portfolio's return, while security selection accounts for only 10 percent. Thus, understanding top-down analysis can be a critical factor for long-term investment success because it plays a key role in choosing allocation strategies.

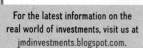

For the latest information on the real world of investments, visit us at jmdinvestments.blogspot.com.

Key Terms

Consumer Price Index (CPI) 677
Core CPI 677
cyclical sectors 672
defensive sectors 672
discount rate 680
federal funds rate 680
fiscal policy 680
gross domestic product (GDP) 670

labor force 676
labor force participation rate 677
leading, lagging, and coincident economic
  indicators 674
nominal GDP 670
open market operations 680
real GDP 670
unemployment rate 677

Related Bloomberg Functions

EQS	Equity Screening, 20.1	
COUN	Country/Region Guide, 20.1	
ECOW	Economic Data Watch, 20.1	
ECO	Economic Calendars, 20.1	
WECO	Economic Calendars by Country, 20.1	
ECFC	Economic Forecasts, 20.1	
GEW	Global Economy Watch, 20.1	
FX24	FX Session Chart, 20.1	
FXCA	FX Conversion Calculator, 20.1	
PEG	Pegged Currencies, 20.1	
FXTF	FX Ticker Finder, 20.1	
FXC	Currency Rates Matrix, 20.1	
FXFM	FX Rate Forecast Model, 20.1	
ECST	World Economic Statistics, 20.3	
IFMO	Inflation Monitor, 20.3	
ECTR	Trade Flow, 20.4	
FOMC	FOMC Activities, 20.4	
IFMO	Inflation Monitor, 20.4	
WCDM	World Countries Debt Monitor, 20.4	
CSDR	Sovereign Ratings, 20.4	
ICS	Classification Browser, 20.5	
RRG	Relative Rotation Graph, 20.5	
IMAP	Intraday Market Map, 20.5	
GMM	Global Macro Movers, 20.5	
BI	Bloomberg Intelligence, 20.5	
SPLC	Supply Chain Analysis, 20.5	

Chapter Review Problems and Self-Test

1. **Exchange Rates (LO2, CFA5)**   You invest $50,000 in Germany when the exchange rate is $1.42/€. Your investment gains 15 percent, and you subsequently exchange the euros back into dollars at a rate of $1.48/€. What is your total return on this investment?

2. **Real vs. Nominal (LO2, CFA2)**   Assume the inflation rate in 2022 is 2.4 percent. If nominal GDP grew 3.5 percent and nominal wages grew 2.8 percent, what are the approximate real growth rates in GDP and wages?

Answers to Self-Test Problems

1. Step 1: $50,000/($1.42/€) = €35,211.27

   Step 2: €35,211.27 × 1.15 = €40,492.96

   Step 3: €40,492.96 × $1.48/€ = $59,929.58

   Step 4: ($59,929.58 − $50,000)/$50,000 = .1986, or 19.86%

2. Real GDP growth ≈ 3.5% − 2.4% = 1.1%

   Real wage growth ≈ 2.8% − 2.4% = .4%

Test Your Investment Quotient

1. **Money Multiplier (LO3, CFA4)**   If the Fed adds $10 billion to the banking system and the reserve requirement is 20 percent, what is the maximum increase in the money supply?

   a. $200 billion
   b. $50 billion
   c. $10 billion
   d. $2 billion

2. **Real GDP (LO2, CFA2)**   If nominal GDP grew by 5 percent and inflation was 3 percent, the closest approximation of real GDP is:

   a. 15 percent.
   b. 8 percent.
   c. 5 percent.
   d. 2 percent.

3. **Inflation (LO2, CFA2)**   If the CPI increased from 123.4 to 125.3, the inflation rate is closest to:

   a. −1.5 percent.
   b. 0 percent.
   c. 1.5 percent.
   d. 3.0 percent.

4. **Industry Analysis (LO4, CFA6)**   Which of the following industries would be considered the most defensive?

   a. Consumer discretionary
   b. Industrials
   c. Technology
   d. Consumer staples

5. **Leading Indicators (LO2, CFA3)**   Which of the following is not considered a leading economic indicator?

   a. Stock prices, 500 common stocks
   b. Money supply (M2) growth rate
   c. Average duration of unemployment
   d. Index of consumer expectations

6. **Business Cycle (LO2, CFA3)**   Which of the following is not one of the four stages of the business cycle?

   a. Peak
   b. Contraction
   c. Trough
   d. Cliff

7. **Exchange Rates (LO2, CFA5)**   Suppose you are a U.S. investor looking to buy assets in Mexico. If you have $10,000 and the current exchange rate is 11.87 pesos/dollar, how many pesos will you have to invest?

   a. 842
   b. 11,245
   c. 78,926
   d. 118,700

8. **Real vs. Nominal (LO2, CFA1)** If the average wage rate increases from $15.23 per hour to $15.65 per hour and the inflation rate over the period is 4.2 percent, what is the approximate real increase in wages?

   a. 2.8 percent
   b. 1.4 percent
   c. −1.4 percent
   d. −2.8 percent

9. **Monetary Policy (LO3, CFA4)** All of the following are ways the Federal Reserve changes the money supply except:

   a. The discount rate.
   b. Open market operations.
   c. The prime rate.
   d. All of the above are used by the Fed.

10. **Industry Analysis (LO4, CFA6)** Which of the following is not one of Porter's five forces?

   a. Bargaining power of buyers
   b. Threat of substitute products
   c. Threat of new entrants
   d. All of the above are part of Porter's five forces.

Concept Questions

1. **Monetary Policy (LO3, CFA4)** If the economy was in recession, what monetary policies might the Fed employ?

2. **Exchange Rates (LO2, CFA5)** If you are a U.S. investor who believes the Australian dollar is going to appreciate, would that make you more or less likely to invest in Australian stocks?

3. **Industry Analysis (LO1, CFA6)** Briefly explain the process of top-down analysis.

4. **Industry Analysis (LO4, CFA6)** Which sector would generally be more sensitive to the business cycle: industrials or health care?

5. **Leading Indicators (LO2, CFA3)** Why do you think that consumer sentiment is considered a leading economic indicator?

6. **Inflation (LO2, CFA2)** If you believed inflation was going to increase over the coming years, would you rather invest in short-term or long-term debt?

7. **Industry Analysis (LO4, CFA6)** Many health care companies depend on patents to sustain profits. In the context of Porter's five forces, how would a patent expiration impact a health care firm?

8. **Fiscal Policy (LO3, CFA4)** Which one of the following propositions would be consistent with a supply-side view of fiscal policy?

   a. Higher marginal tax rates will help reduce the size of the budget deficit.
   b. A tax reduction will increase disposable income and spur economic growth.

9. **Real vs. Nominal (LO2, CFA2)** Why is inflation associated with lower values of real GDP and wages?

10. **Fiscal Policy (LO3, CFA4)** Briefly explain why a high level of national debt may be detrimental for economic growth.

Questions and Problems

Core Questions

1. **Money Multiplier (LO3, CFA4)** Assume that the Federal Reserve injects $2 billion into the financial system. If the reserve requirement is 18 percent, what is the maximum increase in money supply? Why might the maximum increase not be achieved?

2. **Money Multiplier (LO3, CFA4)** Assume that the Federal Reserve injects $60 billion into the financial system. If the money supply increases by a maximum of $300 billion, what must the reserve requirement be?

3. Ms. Van Eaton tells Ms. Smith that she likes the fact that the conclusions in her report are backed up with facts, but she tells her that she is concerned about the section concerning the bargaining power of buyers. She says that while all of the points she listed may be factual, they do not all support her conclusion. Which of Ms. Smith's points support the conclusion that consumers have strong bargaining power over the industry?

   a. Points 2, 3, and 4
   b. Points 2 and 4
   c. Points 1, 2, and 4

4. Regarding Ms. Smith's and Ms. Van Eaton's statements made about the competitive strategy of the South Winery:

   a. Both are incorrect.
   b. Both are correct.
   c. Only one is correct.

Bloomberg Exercises

1. Pick four financial metrics and conduct an equity screen. **(EQS)**
2. Identify which economic statistics are set to be released today. **(ECO)**
3. Determine which countries have the highest/lowest level of inflation. **(IFMO)**
4. Identify which countries have the highest levels of debt to GDP. **(WCDM)**
5. Map out Boeing's (BA) largest suppliers and customers. **(SPLC)**

What's on the Web?

1. **Exchange Rates** Go to www.xe.com and find the current euro/dollar exchange rate. If you had $75,000, how many euros would that be worth at the current exchange rate?

2. **Industry Analysis** Use the heat map at finviz.com/map.ashx to determine which sectors are currently the strongest and weakest in the S&P 500.

3. **Industry Analysis** Visit www.msci.com/gics and click on "GICS Structure & Sub-Industry Definitions." Find the code for the Coal and Consumable Fuels sub-industry.

Mortgage-Backed Securities

"Our houses are such unwieldy property that we are often imprisoned rather than housed in them."

—Henry David Thoreau

Learning Objectives

Before you mortgage your future, you should know:

1. The workings of a fixed-rate mortgage.

2. The government's role in the secondary market for home mortgages.

3. The impact of mortgage prepayments.

4. How collateralized mortgage obligations are created and divided.

Will Rogers wryly advised buying real estate because "they wasn't making any more." Almost all real estate purchases are financed by mortgages. Indeed, most of us become familiar with mortgages by financing the purchase of a home. But did you ever stop to think about what happens to a mortgage after it is originated? Today, mortgages are usually pooled to create mortgage-backed securities. The basic concept is simple. Collect a portfolio of mortgages into a mortgage pool. Then issue securities with pro rata claims on mortgage pool cash flows. These mortgage-backed securities are attractive to investors because they represent a claim on a diversified portfolio of mortgages and, therefore, are considerably less risky than individual mortgage contracts.

Mortgage financing makes home ownership possible for almost everyone. With mortgage financing, a home buyer makes only a down payment and borrows the remaining cost of a home with a mortgage loan. The mortgage loan is obtained from a mortgage originator, usually a local bank or a mortgage broker. Describing this financial transaction, we can say that a home buyer *issues* a mortgage and an originator *writes* a mortgage. A mortgage loan distinguishes itself from other loan contracts by a pledge of real estate as collateral for the loan. In this chapter, we carefully examine the investment characteristics of mortgage pools.

CFA™ Exam Topics in This Chapter:

1. Time value of money (L1, S1)
2. Introduction to asset-backed securities (L1, S14)

Go to Connect for a guide that aligns your textbook with CFA readings.

21.1 A Brief History of Mortgage-Backed Securities

Related Bloomberg Functions

MBSS MBS Pool Search

Visit
www.investinginbonds.com
for more information on mortgage-backed securities.

Traditionally, savings banks and savings and loans (S&Ls) wrote most home mortgages and then held the mortgages in their portfolios of interest-earning assets. This changed radically during the 1970s and 1980s when market interest rates ascended to their highest levels in American history. Entering this financially turbulent period, savings banks and S&Ls held large portfolios of mortgages written at low pre-1970s interest rates. These portfolios were financed from customers' savings deposits. When market interest rates climbed to near 20 percent levels in the early 1980s, customers flocked to withdraw funds from their savings deposits to invest in money market funds that paid higher interest rates. As a result, savings institutions were often forced to sell mortgages at depressed prices to satisfy the onslaught of deposit withdrawals. For this, and other reasons, the ultimate result was the collapse of many savings institutions.

Today, home buyers generally turn to local banks for mortgage financing, but few mortgages are actually held by the banks that originate them. After writing a mortgage, an originator usually sells the mortgage to a mortgage repackager, who accumulates them into mortgage pools. To finance the creation of a mortgage pool, the mortgage repackager issues mortgage-backed bonds, where each bond claims a pro rata share of all cash flows derived from mortgages in the pool. A pro rata share allocation pays cash flows in proportion to a bond's face value. Essentially, each mortgage pool is set up as a trust fund, and a servicing agent for the pool collects all mortgage payments. The servicing agent then passes these cash flows through to bondholders. For this reason, mortgage-backed bonds are often called **mortgage passthroughs,** or *passthroughs.* However, all securities representing claims on mortgage pools are generically called **mortgage-backed securities (MBSs),** The primary collateral for all mortgage-backed securities is the underlying pool of mortgages.

The transformation from mortgages to mortgage-backed securities is called **mortgage securitization,** As of January 2022, there was a total of about $12.2 trillion of outstanding mortgages securitized in mortgage pools. This amount represents tremendous growth in the mortgage securitization business. In the early 1980s, less than $1 billion of home mortgages were securitized in pools. Yet despite the multitrillion-dollar size of the mortgage-backed securities market, the risks involved with these investments are often misunderstood even by experienced investors.

mortgage passthroughs
Bonds representing a claim on the cash flows of an underlying mortgage pool passed through to bondholders.

mortgage-backed securities (MBSs)
Securities whose investment returns are based on a pool of mortgages.

mortgage securitization
The creation of mortgage-backed securities from a pool of mortgages.

21.2 Fixed-Rate Mortgages

fixed-rate mortgage
Loan that specifies constant monthly payments at a fixed interest rate over the life of the mortgage.

Understanding mortgage-backed securities begins with an understanding of the mortgages from which they are created. Most home mortgages are 15-year- or 30-year-maturity **fixed-rate mortgages** requiring constant monthly payments. Even though the monthly payment amount is constant, the principal and interest division of these payments changes each month.

As an example of a fixed-rate mortgage, consider a 30-year mortgage representing a loan of $100,000 financed at an annual interest rate of 8 percent. This annual interest rate translates into a monthly interest rate of 8 percent/12 months = .67% per month. The 30-year mortgage requires 360 monthly payments. The size of the monthly payment is determined by the requirement that the present value of all monthly payments, based on the financing rate specified in the mortgage contract, be equal to the original loan amount of $100,000. The monthly payment for a fixed-rate mortgage is calculated using the following formula:

$$\text{Monthly payment} = \frac{\text{Mortgage amount} \times r/12}{1 - \dfrac{1}{(1 + r/12)^{T \times 12}}} \quad (21.1)$$

where:
r = Annual mortgage financing rate
$r/12$ = Monthly mortgage financing rate
T = Mortgage term in years
$T \times 12$ = Mortgage term in months

In the example of a $100,000, 30-year mortgage financed at 8 percent, the monthly payment is $733.76. That is, using Equation 21.1:

$$\text{Monthly payment} = \frac{\$100{,}000 \times .08/12}{1 - \dfrac{1}{(1 + .08/12)^{360}}}$$
$$= \$733.7646$$

Monthly payments for fixed-rate mortgages are very sensitive to interest rates and number of years in the loan. Table 21.1 provides monthly payments required for 5-year, 10-year, 15-year, 20-year, and 30-year mortgages based on annual interest rates ranging from 5 percent to 15 percent in increments of .5 percent. Notice that monthly payments required for a $100,000, 30-year mortgage financed at 5 percent are only $536.82, while monthly payments for the same mortgage financed at 12 percent are $1,028.61.

EXAMPLE 21.1 **Calculating Monthly Mortgage Payments**

What is the monthly payment for a 15-year, $100,000 mortgage loan financed at 8 percent interest?

A 15-year mortgage specifies 180 monthly payments. Using the monthly payment formula, we get a monthly payment of about $955.65, as follows:

$$\text{Monthly payment} = \frac{\$100{,}000 \times .08/12}{1 - \dfrac{1}{(1 + .08/12)^{180}}}$$
$$= \$955.6521$$

If you wish to calculate mortgage payments for other interest rates, maturities, and loan amounts, we suggest using a built-in spreadsheet function. For example, the *Spreadsheet Analysis* box contains an example mortgage payment calculation using an Excel spreadsheet.

CHECK THIS

21.2a   The most popular fixed-rate mortgages among home buyers are those with 15-year and 30-year maturities. What might be some of the comparative advantages and disadvantages of these two mortgage maturities?

21.2b   Suppose you were to finance a home purchase using a fixed-rate mortgage. Would you prefer a 15-year- or 30-year-maturity mortgage? Why?

FIXED-RATE MORTGAGE AMORTIZATION

mortgage principal
The amount of a mortgage loan outstanding, which is the amount required to pay off the mortgage.

Each monthly mortgage payment has two parts. The first part is the interest payment on the outstanding **mortgage principal**. Outstanding mortgage principal is also called a mortgage's *remaining balance* or *remaining principal*. It is the amount required to pay off a mortgage before it matures. The second part is the pay-down, or *amortization,* of mortgage principal. The relative amounts of each part change throughout the life of a mortgage. For example, a 30-year, $100,000 mortgage financed at 8 percent requires 360 monthly payments of $733.76 (rounded). The first monthly payment consists of a $666.67 payment of interest and a $67.09 pay-down of principal. The first month's interest payment, representing one month's interest on a mortgage balance of $100,000, is calculated as:

$$\$100{,}000 \times .08/12 = \$666.666$$

After rounding this payment of interest, the remainder of the first monthly payment, that is, $733.76 − $666.67 = $67.09, is used to amortize outstanding mortgage principal. Thus, after the first monthly payment, outstanding principal is reduced to $100,000 − $67.09 = $99,932.91.

	A	B	C	D	E	F	G
1							
2			Monthly Payments for a 30-Year Mortgage				
3							
4	A 30-year mortgage specifies an annual interest rate of 8 percent						
5	and a loan amount of $100,000. What are the monthly payments?						
6	*Hint:* Use the Excel function PMT.						
7							
8			−$733.76	= PMT(0.08/12,360,100000,0,0)			
9							
10			Monthly interest is 8%/12 = 0.667%				
11			Number of monthly payments is 12 × 30 = 360.				
12			Initial principal is $100,000.				
13			First zero indicates complete repayment after last monthly payment.				
14			Second zero indicates end-of-month payments.				
15							
16	For a 15-year mortgage, we get a bigger monthly payment.						
17							
18			−$955.65	= PMT(0.08/12,180,100000,0,0)			
19							

Source: Microsoft.

TABLE 21.1 — $100,000 Mortgage Loan Monthly Payments

			Mortgage Maturity		
Interest Rate	30-Year	20-Year	15-Year	10-Year	5-Year
2.0%	$ 369.62	$ 505.88	$ 643.51	$ 920.13	$1,752.78
2.5	395.12	529.90	666.79	942.70	1,774.74
3.0	421.60	554.60	690.58	965.61	1,796.87
3.5	449.04	579.96	714.88	988.86	1,819.17
4.0	477.42	605.98	739.69	1,012.45	1,841.65
4.5	506.69	632.65	764.99	1,036.38	1,864.30
5.0	536.82	659.96	790.79	1,060.66	1,887.12
5.5	567.79	687.89	817.08	1,085.26	1,910.12
6.0	599.55	716.43	843.86	1,110.21	1,933.28
6.5	632.07	745.57	871.11	1,135.48	1,956.61
7.0	665.30	775.30	898.83	1,161.08	1,980.12
7.5	699.21	805.59	927.01	1,187.02	2,003.79
8.0	733.76	836.44	955.65	1,213.28	2,027.64
8.5	768.91	867.82	984.74	1,239.86	2,051.65
9.0	804.62	899.73	1,014.27	1,266.76	2,075.84
9.5	840.85	932.13	1,044.22	1,293.98	2,100.19
10.0	877.57	965.02	1,074.61	1,321.51	2,124.70
10.5	914.74	998.38	1,105.40	1,349.35	2,149.39
11.0	952.32	1,032.19	1,136.60	1,377.50	2,174.24
11.5	990.29	1,066.43	1,168.19	1,405.95	2,199.26
12.0	1,028.61	1,101.09	1,200.17	1,434.71	2,224.44

Source: Author calculations.

The second monthly payment includes a $666.22 payment of interest, calculated as:

$$\$99,932.91 \times .08 / 12 \ = \ \$666.2194$$

The remainder of the second monthly payment, that is, $733.76 − $666.22 = $67.54, is used to reduce mortgage principal to $99,932.91 − $67.54 = $99,865.37.

This process continues throughout the life of the mortgage. The interest payment component gradually declines, and the payment of principal component gradually increases. Finally, the last monthly payment is divided into a $4.86 payment of interest and a final $728.91 paydown of mortgage principal. The process of paying down mortgage principal over the life of a mortgage is called **mortgage amortization.**

mortgage amortization
The process of paying down mortgage principal over the life of the mortgage.

Mortgage amortization is described by an amortization schedule. An amortization schedule states the remaining principal owed on a mortgage at any time and also states the scheduled principal payment and interest payment in any month. Amortization schedules for 15-year and 30-year, $100,000 mortgages financed at a fixed rate of 8 percent are listed in Table 21.2. The payment month is given in the left-hand column. Then, for each maturity, the second column reports remaining mortgage principal immediately after a monthly payment is made. The third and fourth columns for each maturity list the principal payment and the interest payment scheduled for each monthly payment. Notice that immediately after the 180th monthly payment for a 30-year, $100,000 mortgage, $76,781.56 of mortgage principal is still outstanding. Notice also that as late as the 252nd monthly payment, the interest payment component of $378.12 still exceeds the principal payment component of $355.65.

The amortization process for a 30-year, $100,000 mortgage financed at 8 percent interest is illustrated graphically in Figure 21.1. Figure 21.1A graphs the outstanding mortgage principal over the life of the mortgage. Figure 21.1B graphs the rising principal payment component and the falling interest payment component of the mortgage.

EXAMPLE 21.2 **Mortgage Amortization**

After five years of payments on a mortgage loan financed at 8 percent, what are the remaining balance and interest and principal reduction components of the monthly payment?

For the 30-year mortgage, referring to Table 21.1, we see that the monthly payment is $733.76. Referring to the 60th monthly payment in Table 21.2, we find that the remaining balance on the mortgage is $95,069.86. Principal reduction for this payment is $99.30, and the interest payment is $634.46.

For the 15-year mortgage, the monthly payment is $955.65, and after the 60th monthly payment, the remaining balance is $78,766.26, with a principal reduction of $427.69 and interest payment of $527.96. An earlier *Spreadsheet Analysis* box shows how to use Excel to calculate monthly payments for a 30-year and a 15-year mortgage.

If you wish to calculate interest and principal reduction components for other interest rates, maturities, and loan amounts, we suggest using built-in spreadsheet functions. The following *Spreadsheet Analysis* box shows how to obtain the interest and principal reduction components for any given month in a mortgage. The second Excel table that follows also shows how to obtain the remaining balance for a mortgage.

FIXED-RATE MORTGAGE PREPAYMENT AND REFINANCING

A mortgage borrower has the right to pay off an outstanding mortgage at any time. This right is similar to the call feature on corporate bonds, whereby the issuer can buy back outstanding bonds at a prespecified call price. Paying off a mortgage ahead of its amortization schedule is called **mortgage prepayment.**

mortgage prepayment
Paying off all or part of outstanding mortgage principal ahead of its amortization schedule.

Prepayment can be motivated by a variety of factors. A homeowner may pay off a mortgage in order to sell the property when a family moves because of, say, new employment or retirement. After the death of a spouse, a surviving family member may pay off a mortgage with an insurance benefit. These are examples of mortgage prepayment for personal reasons. However, mortgage prepayments often occur for a purely financial reason: An existing mortgage loan may be refinanced at a lower interest rate when a lower rate becomes available.

TABLE 21.2

$100,000 Mortgage Loan Amortization Schedules for 15-Year and 30-Year Mortgages

30-Year Mortgage $733.76 Monthly Payment				15-Year Mortgage $955.65 Monthly Payment			
Payment Month	Remaining Principal	Principal Reduction	Interest Payment	Payment Month	Remaining Principal	Principal Reduction	Interest Payment
1	$99,932.91	$ 67.09	$ 666.67	1	$99,711.01	$288.99	$ 666.67
12	99,164.64	72.19	661.58	12	96,402.15	310.90	644.75
24	98,259.94	78.18	655.59	24	92,505.69	336.70	618.95
36	97,280.15	84.67	649.10	36	88,285.81	364.65	591.00
48	96,219.04	91.69	642.07	48	83,715.70	394.91	560.74
60	95,069.86	99.30	634.46	60	78,766.26	427.69	527.96
72	93,825.29	107.55	626.22	72	73,406.02	463.19	492.46
84	92,477.43	116.47	617.29	84	67,600.89	501.64	454.02
96	91,017.70	126.14	607.63	96	61,313.93	543.27	412.38
108	89,436.81	136.61	597.16	108	54,505.16	588.36	367.29
120	87,724.70	147.95	585.82	120	47,131.26	637.20	318.46
132	85,870.50	160.23	573.54	132	39,145.34	690.08	265.57
144	83,862.39	173.53	560.24	144	30,496.58	747.36	208.29
156	81,687.61	187.93	545.84	156	21,129.99	809.39	146.26
168	79,332.33	203.53	530.24	168	10,985.97	876.57	79.08
180	76,781.56	220.42	513.35	180	.00	949.32	6.33
192	74,019.08	238.71	495.05				
204	71,027.31	258.53	475.24				
216	67,787.23	279.98	453.78				
228	64,278.22	303.22	430.54				
240	60,477.96	328.39	405.38				
252	56,362.29	355.65	378.12				
264	51,905.02	385.16	348.60				
276	47,077.79	417.13	316.63				
288	41,849.91	451.75	282.01				
300	36,188.12	489.25	244.52				
312	30,056.40	529.86	203.91				
324	23,415.75	573.83	159.93				
336	16,223.93	621.46	112.30				
348	8,435.20	673.04	60.72				
360	.00	728.91	4.86				

Source: Author calculations.

Consider a 30-year, $100,000 fixed-rate 8 percent mortgage with a monthly payment of $733.76. Suppose that, 10 years into the mortgage, market interest rates have fallen, and the financing rate on new 20-year mortgages is 6.5 percent. After 10 years (120 months), the remaining balance for the original $100,000 mortgage is $87,724.70. The monthly payment on a new 20-year, $90,000 fixed-rate 6.5 percent mortgage is $671.02, which is $62.74 less than the $733.76 monthly payment on the existing 8 percent mortgage with 20 years of payments remaining. Thus, a homeowner could profit by prepaying the original 8 percent mortgage and refinancing with a new 20-year, 6.5 percent mortgage. Monthly payments would be lower by $62.74, and the $2,275.30 difference between the new $90,000 mortgage balance and the old $87,724.70 mortgage balance would defray any refinancing costs. As this example suggests, during periods of falling interest rates, mortgage refinancings are an important reason for mortgage prepayments.

The possibility of prepayment and refinancing is an advantage to mortgage borrowers but a disadvantage to mortgage investors. For example, consider investors who supply funds to write mortgages at a financing rate of 8 percent. Suppose that mortgage interest rates later

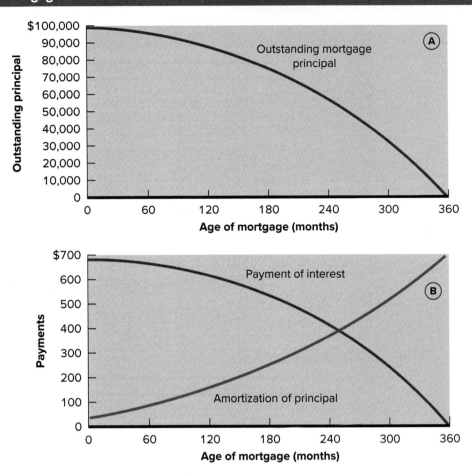

fall to 6.5 percent and, consequently, homeowners rush to prepay their 8 percent mortgages so as to refinance at 6.5 percent. Mortgage investors recover their outstanding investment principal from the prepayments, but the rate of return that they can realize on a new investment is reduced because mortgages can now be written only at the new 6.5 percent financing rate. The possibility that falling interest rates will set off a wave of mortgage refinancings is an ever-present risk that mortgage investors must face.

REVERSE MORTGAGES In a standard mortgage deal, lenders provide a lump sum of money to borrowers. Borrowers then use this money to purchase a home. To repay the loan, borrowers make monthly mortgage payments. In a "reverse" mortgage deal, borrowers (with home equity) receive monthly payments from a lender.

Borrowers generally do not have to repay money received from a reverse mortgage as long as they live in their homes. But the loan becomes due if the borrowers die, sell their home, or move to another principal residence. Borrowers qualify for most reverse mortgages if they are at least 62 years old and live in their home.

The amount of money borrowed in a reverse mortgage depends on factors such as:

- The age of the borrowers.
- The type of reverse mortgage.
- The appraised value and location of the home.

In general, the older the borrower, the more valuable the home, and the less that is owed on the home, the more that can be borrowed. The proceeds from a reverse mortgage are typically tax-free.

Learn more about reverse mortgages by searching aarp.org/money/.

SPREADSHEET ANALYSIS

	A	B	C	D	E	F	G
1							
2			Amortization Schedule for a 30-Year Mortgage				
3							
4	A 30-year mortgage specifies an annual interest rate of 8 percent						
5	and a loan amount of $100,000. What are the monthly interest and principal payments?						
6	*Hint:* Use the Excel functions IPMT and PPMT.						
7							
8	After 10 years, i.e., for the 120th payment, interest and principal payments are:						
9							
10		−$585.82	= IPMT(0.08/12,120,360,100000,0)				
11							
12		−$147.95	= PPMT(0.08/12,120,360,100000,0)				
13							
14							
15	After 20 years, i.e., for the 240th payment, interest and principal payments are:						
16							
17		−$405.38	= IPMT(0.08/12,240,360,100000,0)				
18							
19		−$328.39	= PPMT(0.08/12,240,360,100000,0)				
20							

	A	B	C	D	E	F	G
1							
2			Remaining Balance for a 30-Year Mortgage				
3							
4	A 30-year mortgage specifies an annual interest rate of 8 percent						
5	and a loan amount of $100,000. What is the remaining balance?						
6	*Hint:* Use the Excel function CUMPRINC.						
7							
8	After 8 years and 4 months, the remaining balance is the present value of payment						
9	number 101 through payment number 360.						
10							
11		−$90,504.68	= CUMPRINC(0.08/12,360,100000,101,360,0)				
12							
13	After 16 years and 8 months, the remaining balance is the present value of payment						
14	number 201 through payment number 360.						
15							
16		−$72,051.18	= CUMPRINC(0.08/12,360,100000,201,360,0)				
17							

Source: Microsoft.

Reverse mortgages appeal to "house rich but cash poor" homeowners who want to stay in their homes. However, the terms of reverse mortgages are sometimes highly complicated. Therefore, potential borrowers should fully understand the details of a reverse mortgage deal (including fees). The CFPB has an excellent website devoted to reverse mortgages.

CHECK THIS

21.2c Suppose a 30-year, $100,000 mortgage is financed at an annual interest rate of 4 percent. What are the interest and principal payments for the 120th payment? The 240th payment?

21.2d What is the remaining balance on this mortgage after 100 payments (i.e., after 8 years and 4 months)? After 200 payments?

Government National Mortgage Association

Visit the GNMA and
HUD websites at
www.ginniemae.gov and www.hud.gov.

**Government National
Mortgage Association
(GNMA)**
Government agency charged
with promoting liquidity in the
home mortgage market.

fully modified mortgage pool
Mortgage pool that guarantees
timely payment of interest and
principal.

prepayment risk
Uncertainty faced by mortgage
investors regarding early payment of mortgage principal and
interest.

Check out the FNMA and
FHLMC websites at
fanniemae.com and freddiemac.com.

**Federal Home Loan
Mortgage Corporation
(FHLMC)**
Government-sponsored enterprise charged with promoting
liquidity in the home mortgage
market.

**Federal National Mortgage
Association (FNMA)**
Government-sponsored enterprise charged with promoting
liquidity in the home mortgage
market.

In 1968, Congress established the **Government National Mortgage Association (GNMA),** colloquially called "Ginnie Mae," as a government agency within the Department of Housing and Urban Development (HUD). GNMA was charged with the mission of promoting liquidity in the secondary market for home mortgages. Liquidity is the ability of investors to buy and sell securities quickly at competitive market prices. Essentially, mortgages repackaged into mortgage pools are a more liquid investment product than the original unpooled mortgages. GNMA has successfully sponsored the repackaging of several trillion dollars of mortgages into hundreds of thousands of mortgage-backed securities pools.

GNMA mortgage pools are based on mortgages issued under programs administered by the Federal Housing Administration (FHA), the Veterans Administration (VA), and the Farmers Home Administration (FmHA). Mortgages in GNMA pools are said to be **fully modified** because GNMA guarantees bondholders full and timely payment of both principal and interest even in the event of default of the underlying mortgages. The GNMA guarantee augments guarantees already provided by the FHA, VA, and FmHA. Because GNMA, FHA, VA, and FmHA are all agencies of the federal government, GNMA mortgage passthroughs are thought to be free of default risk. But while investors in GNMA passthroughs face limited default risk, they still face **prepayment risk.**

GNMA operates in cooperation with private underwriters certified by GNMA to create mortgage pools. The underwriters originate or otherwise acquire the mortgages to form a pool. After verifying that the mortgages comply with GNMA requirements, GNMA authorizes the underwriter to issue mortgage-backed securities with a GNMA guarantee.

As a simplified example of how a GNMA pool operates, consider a hypothetical GNMA fully modified mortgage pool containing only a single mortgage. After obtaining approval from GNMA, the pool has a GNMA guarantee and is called a *GNMA bond.* The underwriter then sells the bond, and the buyer is entitled to receive all mortgage payments, less servicing and guarantee fees. If a mortgage payment occurs ahead of schedule, the early payment is passed through to the GNMA bondholder. If a payment is late, GNMA makes a timely payment to the bondholder. If any mortgage principal is prepaid, the early payment is passed through to the bondholder. If a default occurs, GNMA settles with the bondholder by making full payment of remaining mortgage principal. In effect, to a GNMA bondholder, mortgage default is the same thing as a prepayment.

When originally issued, the minimum denomination of a GNMA mortgage-backed bond is $25,000. The minimum size for a GNMA mortgage pool is $1 million, although it could be much larger. Thus, for example, a GNMA mortgage pool might conceivably represent only 40 bonds with an initial bond principal of $25,000 par value per bond. However, initial bond principal only specifies a bond's share of mortgage pool principal. Over time, mortgage-backed bond principal declines because of scheduled mortgage amortization and mortgage prepayments.

GNMA CLONES

Two government-sponsored enterprises (GSEs) are also significant mortgage repackaging sponsors. These are the **Federal Home Loan Mortgage Corporation (FHLMC),** colloquially called "Freddie Mac," and the **Federal National Mortgage Association (FNMA),** called "Fannie Mae." FHLMC was chartered by Congress in 1970 to increase mortgage credit availability for residential housing. It was originally owned by the Federal Home Loan Banks operated under direction of the U.S. Treasury. But in 1989, FHLMC was allowed to become a private corporation with an issue of common stock. Freddie Mac stock traded on the New York Stock Exchange under the ticker symbol FRE until 2010. Freddie Mac now trades OTC under the ticker FMCC.

The Federal National Mortgage Association was originally created in 1938 as a government-owned corporation of the United States. Thirty years later, FNMA was split into two government corporations: GNMA and FNMA. Soon after, in 1970, FNMA was allowed to become a private corporation and has since grown to become one of the major financial corporations in the United States. Fannie Mae stock traded on the New York Stock

Exchange under the ticker symbol FNM until 2010. Fannie Mae now trades OTC under the ticker FNMA.

Like GNMA, both FHLMC and FNMA operate with qualified underwriters who accumulate mortgages into pools financed by an issue of bonds that entitle bondholders to cash flows generated by mortgages in the pools, less the standard servicing and guarantee fees. However, the guarantees on FHLMC and FNMA passthroughs are not exactly the same as for GNMA passthroughs. Essentially, FHLMC and FNMA are only government-sponsored enterprises (GSEs), whereas GNMA is a government agency.

FHLMC and FNMA both performed poorly during the financial crisis of 2008. The combined GSE losses were $14.9 billion. In the past, it was widely thought that Congress would be unwilling to rescue a financially strapped GSE. In September 2008, however, the two GSEs were placed into a conservatorship run by the Federal Housing Finance Agency (FHFA).

The FHFA conservatorship is designed to preserve and conserve the assets and property of the GSEs and restore them to a sound financial condition. The GSEs have a statutory mission to promote liquidity and efficiency in the housing finance markets.

The U.S. Treasury committed to invest as much as $200 billion in preferred stock and extend credit through 2009 to keep the GSEs solvent and operating. This bailout was likely the biggest and costliest government bailout ever of private companies.

As of April 2022, the Federal Housing Finance Agency and the U.S. Treasury are working together to figure out how to get the GSEs out of conservatorship and to operate independently. To do so, however, the GSEs have to meet their new capital requirements.

A 2012 amendment under the 2008 bailout directed that the GSEs sweep capital to the Treasury Department. As a result, the GSEs hold a slim level of capital, about $3 billion each. Most likely, the GSEs would need $150 to $200 billion in capital. The question is, how will the GSEs raise this capital? In addition, will the federal government provide a guarantee for securities issued by Fannie and Freddie? If so, they will no longer be GSEs. But, if they are to operate independently, will they be a government agency, like GNMA, or will they be a private/public hybrid? Time will tell.

CHECK THIS

21.3a Look up prices for Freddie Mac and Fannie Mae common stock under their ticker symbols FMCC and FNMA online at finance.yahoo.com.

21.4 Public Securities Association Mortgage Prepayment Model

Related Bloomberg Functions

CTP CPR to PSA Calculator

PDI Paydown Information

Visit the Securities Industry and Financial Markets Association at www.sifma.org.

prepayment rate
The probability that a mortgage will be prepaid during a given year.

Mortgage prepayments are typically described by stating a **prepayment rate,** which is the probability that a mortgage will be prepaid in a given year. The greater the prepayment rate for a mortgage pool, the faster the mortgage pool principal is paid off, and the more rapid is the decline of bond principal for bonds supported by the underlying mortgage pool. Historical experience shows that prepayment rates can vary substantially from year to year depending on mortgage type and various economic and demographic factors.

Conventional industry practice states prepayment rates using a prepayment model specified by what was the Public Securities Association (PSA). In 2006, the PSA was renamed the Bond Market Association. The Bond Market Association merged with the Securities Industry Association and became the Securities Industry and Financial Markets Association.

According to this model, prepayment rates are stated as a percentage of a PSA benchmark. The PSA benchmark specifies an annual prepayment rate of .2 percent in month 1 of a mortgage, .4 percent in month 2, .6 percent in month 3, and so on. The annual prepayment rate continues to rise by .2 percent per month until reaching an annual prepayment rate of 6 percent in month 30 of a mortgage. Thereafter, the benchmark prepayment rate remains constant at 6 percent per year. This PSA benchmark represents a mortgage prepayment

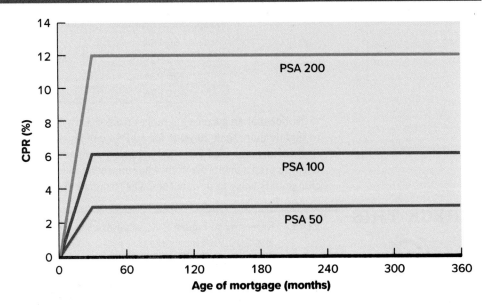

schedule called 100 PSA, which means 100 percent of the PSA benchmark. Deviations from the 100 PSA benchmark are stated as a percentage of the benchmark. For example, 200 PSA means 200 percent of the 100 PSA benchmark, and it doubles all prepayment rates relative to the benchmark. Similarly, 50 PSA means 50 percent of the 100 PSA benchmark, halving all prepayment rates relative to the benchmark. Prepayment rate schedules illustrating 50 PSA, 100 PSA, and 200 PSA are graphically presented in Figure 21.2.

Based on historical experience, the PSA prepayment model makes an important distinction between **seasoned mortgages** and **unseasoned mortgages.** In the PSA model, unseasoned mortgages are those less than 30 months old with rising prepayment rates. Seasoned mortgages are those over 30 months old with constant prepayment rates.

Prepayment rates in the PSA model are stated as **conditional prepayment rates (CPRs)** because they are conditional on the age of mortgages in a pool. For example, the CPR for a seasoned 100 PSA mortgage is 6 percent, which represents a 6 percent probability of mortgage prepayment in a given year. By convention, the probability of prepayment in a given month is stated as a *single monthly mortality (SMM)*. SMM is calculated using a CPR as follows:

$$SMM = 1 - (1 - CPR)^{1/12} \qquad (21.2)$$

seasoned mortgages
Mortgages over 30 months old.

unseasoned mortgages
Mortgages less than 30 months old.

conditional prepayment rate (CPR)
The prepayment rate for a mortgage pool conditional on the age of the mortgages in the pool.

For example, the SMM corresponding to a seasoned 100 PSA mortgage with a 6 percent CPR is .5143 percent, which is calculated as:

$$SMM = 1 - (1 - .06)^{1/12}$$
$$= .005143, \text{ or } .5143\%$$

As another example, the SMM corresponding to an unseasoned 100 PSA mortgage in month 20 of the mortgage with a 4 percent CPR is .3396 percent, which is calculated as:

$$SMM = 1 - (1 - .04)^{1/12} = .003396, \text{ or } .3396\%$$

average life
Average time for a mortgage in a pool to be paid off.

Some mortgages in a pool are prepaid earlier than average, some are prepaid later than average, and some are not prepaid at all. The **average life** of a mortgage in a pool is the average time for a single mortgage in a pool to be paid off, either by prepayment or by making scheduled payments until maturity. Because prepayment shortens the life of a mortgage, the average life of a mortgage is usually much less than a mortgage's stated maturity. We can calculate a mortgage's projected average life by assuming a particular prepayment schedule.

For example, the average life of a mortgage in a pool of 30-year mortgages, assuming several PSA prepayment schedules, is stated immediately below.

Prepayment Schedule	Average Mortgage Life (years)
50 PSA	20.40
100 PSA	14.68
200 PSA	8.87
400 PSA	4.88

Notice that an average life ranges from slightly less than 5 years for 400 PSA prepayments to slightly more than 20 years for 50 PSA prepayments.[1]

Bear in mind that these are expected averages given a particular prepayment schedule. Because prepayments are somewhat unpredictable, the average life of a mortgage in any specific pool is likely to deviate somewhat from an expected average.

CHECK THIS

21.4a   Referring to Figure 21.2, what are the CPRs for seasoned 50 PSA, 100 PSA, and 200 PSA mortgages?

21.4b   Referring to Figure 21.2, what is the CPR for an unseasoned 100 PSA mortgage in month 20 of the mortgage?

21.4c   Referring to Figure 21.2, what is the CPR for an unseasoned 200 PSA mortgage in month 20 of the mortgage?

21.5 Cash Flow Analysis of GNMA Fully Modified Mortgage Pools

Each month, GNMA mortgage-backed bond investors receive pro rata shares of cash flows derived from fully modified mortgage pools. Each monthly cash flow has three distinct components:

1. Payment of interest on outstanding mortgage principal.
2. Scheduled amortization of mortgage principal.
3. Mortgage principal prepayments.

As a sample GNMA mortgage pool, consider a $10 million pool of 30-year, 8 percent mortgages financed by the sale of 100 bonds at a par value price of $100,000 per bond. For simplicity, we ignore servicing and guarantee fees. The decline in bond principal for these GNMA bonds is graphed in Figure 21.3A for the cases of prepayment rates following 50 PSA, 100 PSA, 200 PSA, and 400 PSA schedules. In Figure 21.3A, notice that 50 PSA prepayments yield a nearly straight-line amortization of bond principal. Also notice that for the extreme case of 400 PSA prepayments, over 90 percent of bond principal is amortized within 10 years of mortgage pool origination.

Monthly cash flows for these GNMA bonds are graphed in Figure 21.3B for the cases of 50 PSA, 100 PSA, 200 PSA, and 400 PSA prepayment schedules. In Figure 21.3B, notice the sharp spike in monthly cash flows associated with 400 PSA prepayments at about month 30. Lesser PSA prepayment rates blunt the spike and level the cash flows.

As shown in Figures 21.3A and 21.3B, prepayments significantly affect the cash flow characteristics of GNMA bonds. However, these illustrations assume that prepayment schedules remain unchanged over the life of a mortgage pool. This can be unrealistic because prepayment rates often change from those originally forecast. For example, sharply falling interest rates could easily cause a jump in prepayment rates from 100 PSA to 400 PSA.

---

[1] Formulas used to calculate average mortgage life are complicated and depend on the assumed prepayment model. For this reason, average life formulas are omitted here.

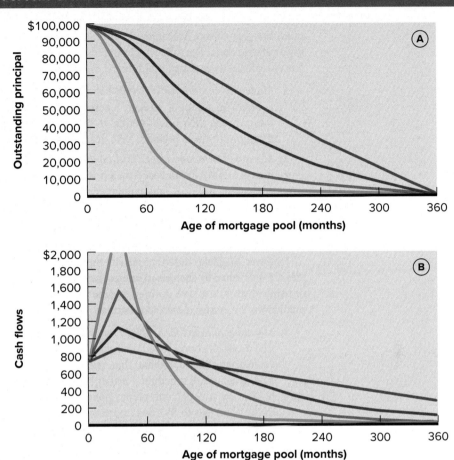

FIGURE 21.3 Principal and Cash Flows for $100,000 Par Value 30-Year, 8 Percent GNMA Bonds

Because large interest rate movements are unpredictable, future prepayment rates can also be unpredictable. Consequently, GNMA mortgage-backed bond investors face substantial cash flow uncertainty. This makes GNMA bonds an unsuitable investment for many investors, especially relatively unsophisticated investors unaware of the risks involved. Nevertheless, GNMA bonds offer higher yields than U.S. Treasury bonds, which makes them attractive to professional fixed-income portfolio managers.

CHECK THIS

21.5a GNMA bond investors face significant cash flow uncertainty. Why might cash flow uncertainty be a problem for many portfolio managers?

21.5b Why might cash flow uncertainty be less of a problem for investors with a very long-term investment horizon?

MACAULAY DURATIONS FOR GNMA MORTGAGE-BACKED BONDS

For mortgage pool investors, prepayment risk is important because it complicates the effects of interest rate risk. With falling interest rates, prepayments speed up and the average life of mortgages in a pool shortens. Similarly, with rising interest rates, prepayments slow down and

Macaulay duration
A measure of interest rate risk for fixed-income securities.

average mortgage life lengthens. Recall from a previous chapter that interest rate risk for a bond is often measured by **Macaulay duration.** Macaulay duration assumes a fixed schedule of cash flow payments. However, the schedule of cash flow payments for mortgage-backed bonds is not fixed because it is affected by mortgage prepayments, which in turn are affected by interest rates. For this reason, Macaulay duration is a deficient measure of interest rate risk for mortgage-backed bonds. The following examples illustrate the deficiency of Macaulay duration when it is unrealistically assumed that interest rates do not affect mortgage prepayment rates:[2]

1. *Macaulay duration for a GNMA bond with zero prepayments.* Suppose a GNMA bond is based on a pool of 30-year, 8 percent fixed-rate mortgages. Assuming an 8 percent interest rate, their price is equal to their initial par value of $100,000. The Macaulay duration for these bonds is 9.56 years.

2. *Macaulay duration for a GNMA bond with a constant 100 PSA prepayment schedule.* Suppose a GNMA bond based on a pool of 30-year, 8 percent fixed-rate mortgages follows a constant 100 PSA prepayment schedule. Accounting for this prepayment schedule when calculating Macaulay duration, we obtain a Macaulay duration of 6.77 years.

Examples 1 and 2 illustrate how Macaulay duration can be affected by mortgage prepayments. Essentially, faster prepayments cause earlier cash flows and shorten Macaulay durations.

However, Macaulay durations are still misleading because they assume that prepayment schedules are unaffected by changes in interest rates. When falling interest rates speed up prepayments, or rising interest rates slow down prepayments, Macaulay durations yield inaccurate price-change predictions for mortgage-backed securities. The following examples illustrate the inaccuracy:

3. *Macaulay duration for a GNMA bond with changing PSA prepayment schedules.* Suppose that a GNMA bond based on a pool of 30-year, 8 percent fixed-rate mortgages has a par value price of $100,000 and that, with no change in interest rates, the pool follows a 100 PSA prepayment schedule. Further suppose that when the market interest rate for these bonds rises to 9 percent, prepayments fall to a 50 PSA schedule. In this case, the price of the bond falls to $92,644, representing a 7.36 percent price drop, which is more than .5 percent larger than the drop predicted by the bond's Macaulay duration of 6.77.

4. *Macaulay duration for a GNMA bond with changing PSA prepayment schedules.* Suppose that a GNMA bond based on a pool of 30-year, 8 percent fixed-rate mortgages has a par value price of $100,000 and that, with no change in interest rates, the pool follows a 100 PSA prepayment schedule. Further suppose that when the market interest rate for these bonds falls to 7 percent, prepayments rise to a 200 PSA schedule. In this case, the bond price rises to $105,486, which is over 1.2 percent less than the price increase predicted by the bond's Macaulay duration of 6.77.

Examples 3 and 4 illustrate that simple Macaulay durations overpredict price increases and underpredict price decreases for changes in mortgage-backed bond prices caused by changing interest rates. These errors are caused by the fact that Macaulay duration does not account for prepayment rates changing in response to interest rate changes. The severity of these errors depends on how strongly interest rates affect prepayment rates. Historical experience indicates that interest rates significantly affect prepayment rates and that Macaulay duration is a very conservative measure of interest rate risk for mortgage-backed securities.

To correct the deficiencies of Macaulay duration, a method often used in practice to assess interest rate risk for mortgage-backed securities is to first develop projections regarding mortgage prepayments. Projecting prepayments for mortgages requires analyzing both economic and demographic variables. In particular, it is necessary to estimate how prepayment rates will respond to changes in interest rates. A duration model that accounts for these factors is called **effective duration.** In practice, effective duration is used to calculate predicted prices for mortgage-backed securities based on hypothetical interest rate and prepayment scenarios. The *Investment Updates* box summarizes the basic structure and some of the risks of asset-backed and mortgage-backed securities.

effective duration for MBS
Duration measure that accounts for how mortgage prepayments are affected by changes in interest rates.

---

[2] The Macaulay duration formula for a mortgage is not presented here because, as our discussion suggests, its use is not recommended.

INVESTMENT UPDATES

DEFINING ASSET-BACKED (ABS) AND MORTGAGE-BACKED SECURITIES (MBS)

Asset-backed securities (ABS) and mortgage-backed securities (MBS) are two of the most important types of asset classes within the fixed-income sector. MBS are created from the pooling of mortgages that are sold to interested investors. ABS are created from the pooling of non-mortgage assets.

The Structures of ABS and MBS

Three parties make up the structure of these types of securities: the seller, the issuer, and the investor. Sellers are the companies that generate loans for sale to issuers and act as the servicer, collecting principal and interest payments from borrowers. ABS and MBS benefit sellers because they can be removed from the balance sheet, allowing sellers to acquire additional funding.

Issuers buy loans from sellers and pool them together to release ABS or MBS to investors, and can be a third-party company or special-purpose vehicle (SPV). Investors of ABS and MBS are typically institutional investors that use ABS and MBS in an attempt to obtain higher yields than government bonds and provide diversification.

Examples of Asset-Backed Securities

There are many types of ABS, each with different characteristics, cash flows and valuations. For example:

Home Equity ABS: Home equity loans are very similar to mortgages, which in turn makes home equity ABS similar to MBS. The major difference between home equity loans and mortgages is that the borrowers of a home equity loan typically do not have good credit ratings.

Auto Loan ABS: Auto loans are types of amortizing assets, and so the cash flows of an auto loan ABS include monthly interest, principal payment, and prepayment. Prepayment risk for an auto loan ABS is much lower when compared to a home equity loan ABS or MBS. Refinancing is rare when the interest rate falls because borrowers won't be able to save significant amounts from refinancing at a lower interest rate.

Credit Card Receivable ABS: Credit card receivables are a type of non-amortizing asset ABS. They don't have scheduled payment amounts, while new loans and changes can be added to the composition of the pool. The cash flows of credit card receivables include interest, principal payments, and annual fees.

Examples of Mortgage-Backed Securities

Most mortgage-backed securities are issued by Ginnie Mae (the Government National Mortgage Association), Fannie Mae (the Federal National Mortgage Association), or Freddie Mac (the Federal Home Loan Mortgage Corporation), which are all U.S. government-sponsored enterprises.

MBS from Ginnie Mae are backed by the full faith and credit of the U.S. government, which guarantees that investors receive full and timely payments of principal and interest. In contrast, Fannie Mae and Freddie Mac MBS are not backed by the full faith and credit of the U.S. government, but both have special authority to borrow from the U.S. Treasury if necessary.

Associated Risks

Both ABS and MBS have prepayment risks, though these are especially pronounced for MBS. Prepayment risk means borrowers are paying more than their required monthly payments, thereby reducing the interest of the loan. To deal with prepayment risk, ABS and MBS have tranching structures to help distribute prepayment risk. Investors can choose a tranche based on their own preferences and risk tolerance. An additional type of risk involved in ABS is credit risk, which is also transferred to investors who want higher returns associated with this risk through tranching.

The Bottom Line

Asset-backed and mortgage-backed securities can be quite complicated in terms of their structures, characteristics, and valuations. Investors have access to these securities through indexes such as the U.S. ABS index. For those who want to invest in ABS or MBS directly, it's imperative to conduct a thorough amount of research and weigh your risk tolerance prior to making any investments.

Source: Mitchell Grant and Alexandra Yan, "Defining Asset-Backed (ABS) and Mortgage-Backed Securities," *Investopedia*, May 9, 2019.

CHECK THIS

21.5c Why is it important for portfolio managers to know by how much a change in interest rates will affect mortgage prepayments?

21.5d Why is it important for portfolio managers to know by how much a change in interest rates will affect mortgage-backed bond prices?

Chapter 21 ● Mortgage-Backed Securities 707

21.6 Collateralized Mortgage Obligations

Related Bloomberg Functions

MSD MBS Settle Dates

collateralized mortgage obligations (CMOs)
Securities created by splitting mortgage pool cash flows according to specific allocation rules.

When a mortgage pool is created, cash flows from the pool are often carved up and distributed according to various allocation rules. Mortgage-backed securities representing specific rules for allocating mortgage cash flows are called **collateralized mortgage obligations (CMOs).** Indeed, a CMO is defined by the rule that created it. Like all mortgage passthroughs, primary collateral for CMOs is the mortgages in the underlying pool. This is true no matter how the rules for cash flow distribution are actually specified.

The three best-known types of CMO structures using specific rules to carve up mortgage pool cash flows are (1) interest-only strips (IOs) and principal-only strips (POs), (2) sequential CMOs, and (3) protected amortization class (PAC) securities. Each of these CMO structures is discussed immediately below. Before beginning, however, we retell an old Wall Street joke that pertains to CMOs: Question: "How many investment bankers does it take to *sell* a lightbulb?" Answer: "401; one to hit it with a hammer, and 400 to sell off the pieces."

The moral of the story is that mortgage-backed securities can be repackaged in many ways, and the resulting products are often quite complex. Even the basic types we consider here are significantly more complicated than the basic fixed-income instruments we considered in earlier chapters. Consequently, we do not go into great detail regarding the underlying calculations for CMOs. Instead, we examine only the basic properties of the most commonly encountered CMOs.

INTEREST-ONLY AND PRINCIPAL-ONLY MORTGAGE STRIPS

interest-only strips (IOs)
Securities that pay only the interest cash flows to investors.

principal-only strips (POs)
Securities that pay only the principal cash flows to investors.

Perhaps the simplest rule for carving up mortgage pool cash flows is to separate payments of principal from payments of interest. Mortgage-backed securities that pay only the interest component of mortgage pool cash flows are called **interest-only strips,** or **IOs.** Mortgage-backed securities that pay only the principal component of mortgage pool cash flows are called **principal-only strips,** or **POs.** Mortgage strips are more complicated than straight mortgage passthroughs. In particular, IO strips and PO strips behave quite differently in response to changes in prepayment rates and interest rates.

Let us begin an examination of mortgage strips by considering a $100,000 par value GNMA bond that has been stripped into a separate IO bond and a PO bond. The whole GNMA bond receives a pro rata share of all cash flows from a pool of 30-year, 8 percent mortgages. From the whole bond cash flow, the IO bond receives the interest component and the PO bond receives the principal component. The sum of IO and PO cash flows reproduces the whole bond cash flow.

Assuming various PSA prepayment schedules, cash flows to IO strips are illustrated in Figure 21.4A, and cash flows to PO strips are illustrated in Figure 21.4B. Holding the interest rate constant at 8 percent, IO and PO strip values for various PSA prepayment schedules are listed immediately below:

Prepayment Schedule	IO Strip Value	PO Strip Value
50 PSA	$63,102.80	$36,897.20
100 PSA	53,726.50	46,273.50
200 PSA	41,366.24	58,633.76
400 PSA	28,764.16	71,235.84

Notice that total bond value is $100,000 for all prepayment schedules because the interest rate is unchanged from its original 8 percent value. Nevertheless, even with no change in interest rates, faster prepayments imply *lower* IO strip values and *higher* PO strip values, and vice versa.

There is a simple reason why PO strip value rises with faster prepayment rates. Essentially, the only cash flow uncertainty facing PO strip holders is the timing of PO cash flows, not the total amount of cash flows. No matter what prepayment schedule applies, total cash

IO Strip

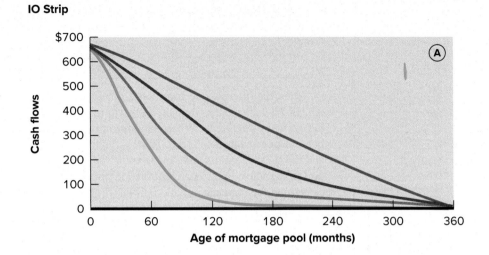

PO Strip

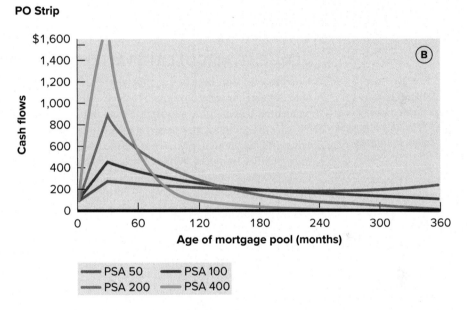

PSA 50   PSA 100
PSA 200   PSA 400

flows paid to PO strip holders over the life of the pool will be equal to the initial principal of $100,000. Therefore, PO strip value increases as principal is paid earlier to PO strip holders because of the time value of money.

In contrast, IO strip holders face considerable uncertainty regarding the total amount of IO cash flows that they will receive. Faster prepayments reduce principal more rapidly, thereby reducing interest payments because interest is paid only on outstanding principal. The best that IO strip holders could hope for is that no mortgages are prepaid, which would maximize total interest payments. Prepayments reduce total interest payments. Indeed, in the extreme case, where all mortgages in a pool are prepaid, IO cash flows stop completely.

The effects of changing interest rates compounded by changing prepayment rates are illustrated by considering IO and PO strips from a $100,000 par value GNMA bond based on a pool of 30-year, 8 percent mortgages. First, suppose that an interest rate of 8 percent yields a 100 PSA prepayment schedule. Also suppose that a lower interest rate of 7 percent yields 200 PSA prepayments and a higher interest rate of 9 percent yields 50 PSA prepayments.

The resulting whole bond values and separate IO and PO strip values for these combinations of interest rates and prepayment rates are listed immediately below:

Interest Rate	Prepayments	IO Strip Value	PO Strip Value	Whole Bond Value
9%	50 PSA	$59,124.79	$35,519.47	$ 94,644.26
8	100 PSA	53,726.50	46,273.50	100,000.00
7	200 PSA	43,319.62	62,166.78	105,486.40

When the interest rate increases from 8 percent to 9 percent, total bond value falls by $5,355.74. This results from the PO strip price *falling* by $10,754.03 and the IO strip price *increasing* by $5,398.29. When the interest rate decreases from 8 percent to 7 percent, total bond value rises by $5,486.40. This results from the PO strip price *increasing* by $15,893.28 and the IO strip price *falling* by $10,406.88. Thus, PO strip values change in the same direction as the whole bond value, but the PO price change is larger. Notice that the IO strip price changes in the opposite direction of the whole bond and PO strip price change.

CHECK THIS

21.6a Suppose a $100,000 mortgage financed at 9 percent (.75 percent monthly) is paid off in the first month after issuance. In this case, what are the cash flows to an IO strip and a PO strip from this mortgage?

SEQUENTIAL COLLATERALIZED MORTGAGE OBLIGATIONS

sequential CMOs
Securities created by splitting a mortgage pool into a number of slices called *tranches*.

One problem with investing in mortgage-backed bonds is the limited range of maturities available. An early method developed to deal with this problem is the creation of **sequential CMOs.** Sequential CMOs carve a mortgage pool into a number of tranches. *Tranche,* the French word for slice, is a commonly used financial term to describe the division of a whole into various parts. Sequential CMOs are defined by rules that distribute mortgage pool cash flows to sequential tranches. While almost any number of tranches are possible, a basic sequential CMO structure might have four tranches: A-tranche, B-tranche, C-tranche, and Z-tranche. Each tranche is entitled to a share of mortgage pool principal and interest on that share of principal. Sequential CMOs are often called collateralized debt obligations, or *CDOs.*

As a hypothetical sequential CMO structure, suppose a 30-year, 8 percent GNMA bond initially represents $100,000 of mortgage principal. Cash flows to this whole bond are then carved up according to a sequential CMO structure with A-, B-, C-, and Z-tranches. The A-, B-, and C-tranches initially represent $30,000 of mortgage principal each. The Z-tranche initially represents $10,000 of principal. The sum of all four tranches reproduces the original whole bond principal of $100,000. The cash flows from the whole bond are passed through to each tranche according to the following rules:

Rule 1: Mortgage principal payments. All payments of mortgage principal, including scheduled amortization and prepayments, are first paid to the A-tranche. When all A-tranche principal is paid off, subsequent payments of mortgage principal are then paid to the B-tranche. After all B-tranche principal is paid off, all principal payments are then paid to the C-tranche. Finally, when all C-tranche principal is paid off, all principal payments go to the Z-tranche.

Rule 2: Interest payments. All tranches receive interest payments in proportion to the amount of outstanding principal in each tranche. Interest on A-, B-, and C-tranche principal is passed through immediately to the A-, B-, and C-tranches. Interest on Z-tranche principal is paid to the A-tranche as cash in exchange for the transfer of an equal amount of principal from the A-tranche to the Z-tranche. After A-tranche principal is fully paid, interest on Z-tranche principal is paid to the B-tranche in exchange for an equal amount of principal from the B-tranche to the Z-tranche. This process continues sequentially through each tranche.

For example, the first month's cash flows from a single whole bond are allocated as follows: Scheduled mortgage payments yield a whole bond cash flow of $733.76, which is divided between $67.09 principal amortization and $666.67 payment of interest. All scheduled principal amortization is paid to the A-tranche, and A-tranche principal is reduced by a like amount. Because outstanding principal was *initially* equal to $30,000 for the A-, B-, and C-tranche bonds, each of these tranches receives an interest payment of $30,000 × .08/12 = $200. In addition, the Z-tranche interest payment of $10,000 × .08/12 = $66.67 is paid to the A-tranche in cash in exchange for transferring $66.67 of principal to the Z-tranche. In summary, A-tranche principal is reduced by $67.09 + $66.67 = $133.76 plus any prepayments, and Z-tranche principal is increased by $66.67.

Remaining principal amounts for the A-, B-, C-, and Z-tranches, assuming 100 PSA prepayments, are graphed in Figure 21.5A. Corresponding cash flows for the A-, B-, C-, and Z-tranches, assuming 100 PSA prepayments, are graphed in Figure 21.5B.

Two questions arise from this structure. First, why would investors, such as the holders of the Z-tranche, be willing to forgo all cash flow early on? As with any investment, the added risk this deferral creates is rewarded with a higher expected return relative to the other tranches.

Second, is there any way for the holders of the Z-tranche to reduce their risk? In a previous chapter, we discussed credit default swaps (CDSs), which are essentially put options that enable the holder to insure a bond. Before the financial crisis of 2008, there was an extremely active CDS market for CMOs. Unfortunately, most CDSs were bought and sold directly between individual investors, meaning that there was significant counterparty risk.

When the real estate market collapsed, default rates on mortgages soared. Because many sellers of CDSs did not have enough capital to make good on their obligations, many of these sellers were financially ruined. For example, one of the most active players in the CDS market was Lehman Brothers. Lehman Brothers, a pillar of Wall Street since the 1850s, filed for bankruptcy in September 2008.

Fortunately, an active public market has developed for CDS trading, so you can now buy and sell contracts as you would a traditional derivative contract. This has reduced the risk in these securities, as standard margin trading rules would apply.

FIGURE 21.5   Sequential CMO Principal and Cash Flows for a $100,000 Par Value GNMA Bond

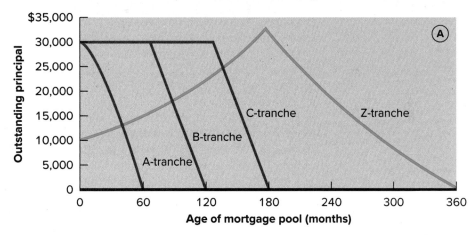

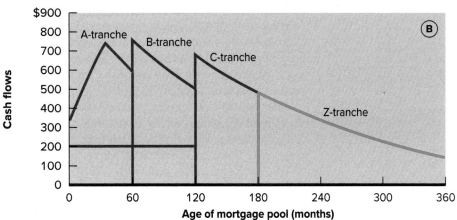

21.6b Figures 21.5A and 21.5B assume a 100 PSA prepayment schedule. How would these figures change for a 200 PSA prepayment schedule or a 50 PSA prepayment schedule?

21.6c While A-, B-, and C-tranche principal is being paid down, Z-tranche interest is used to acquire principal for the Z-tranche. What is the growth rate of Z-tranche principal during this period?

PROTECTED AMORTIZATION CLASS BONDS

protected amortization class (PAC) bond
Mortgage-backed security that takes priority for scheduled payments of principal.

Another popular security used to alleviate the problem of cash flow uncertainty when investing in mortgage-backed bonds is a **protected amortization class (PAC) bond,** or **PAC.** Like all CMOs, PAC bonds are defined by specific rules that carve up cash flows from a mortgage pool. Essentially, a PAC bond carves out a slice of a mortgage pool's cash flows according to a rule that gives PAC bondholders first-priority entitlement to promised PAC cash flows. Consequently, PAC cash flows are predictable so long as mortgage pool prepayments remain within a predetermined band. PAC bonds are attractive to investors who require a high degree of cash flow certainty from their investments.

PAC support bond
Mortgage-backed security that has subordinate priority for scheduled payments of principal. Also called *PAC companion bond.*

After PAC bondholders receive their promised cash flows, residual cash flows from the mortgage pool are paid to non-PAC bonds, often referred to as **PAC support bonds** or *PAC companion bonds.* In effect, almost all cash flow uncertainty is concentrated in the non-PAC bonds. The non-PAC bond supports the PAC bond and serves the same purpose as a Z-tranche bond in a sequential CMO structure. For this reason, a non-PAC bond is sometimes called a PAC Z-tranche.

PAC collar
Range defined by upper and lower prepayment schedules of a PAC bond.

Creation of a PAC bond entails three steps. First, we must specify two PSA prepayment schedules that form the upper and lower prepayment bounds of a PAC bond. These bounds define a **PAC collar.** For example, suppose we create a single PAC bond from a new $100,000 par value GNMA bond based on a pool of 30-year fixed-rate mortgages. The PAC collar specifies a 100 PSA prepayment schedule as a lower bound and a 300 PSA prepayment schedule as an upper bound. Cash flows to the PAC bond are said to enjoy protected amortization so long as mortgage pool prepayments remain within this 100–300 PSA collar.

Our second step in creating a PAC bond is to calculate principal-only (PO) cash flows from our 30-year, $100,000 par value GNMA bond, assuming 100 PSA and 300 PSA prepayment schedules. These PO cash flows, which include both scheduled amortization and prepayments, are plotted in Figure 21.6A. In Figure 21.6A, notice that principal-only cash flows for 100 PSA and 300 PSA prepayment schedules intersect in month 103. Before the 103rd month, 300 PSA PO cash flows are greater. After that month, 100 PSA PO cash flows are greater. PAC bond cash flows are specified by the 100 PSA schedule before month 103 and the 300 PSA schedule after month 103. Because the PAC bond is specified by 100 PSA and 300 PSA prepayment schedules, it is called a PAC 100/300 bond.

Our third step is to specify the cash flows to be paid to PAC bondholders on a priority basis. PAC bondholders receive payments of principal according to the PAC collar's lower PSA prepayment schedule. For the PAC 100/300 bond in this example, principal payments are made according to the 100 PSA prepayment schedule until month 103, when the schedule switches to the 300 PSA prepayment schedule. The sum of all scheduled principal to be paid to PAC 100/300 bondholders represents total initial PAC bond principal. In addition to payment of principal, a PAC bondholder also receives payment of interest on outstanding PAC principal. For example, if the mortgage pool financing rate is 9 percent, the PAC bondholder receives an interest payment of .75 percent per month of outstanding PAC principal.

Total monthly cash flows paid to the PAC bond, including payments of principal and interest, are graphed in Figure 21.6B. As shown, total cash flow reaches a maximum in month 30, thereafter gradually declining. So long as mortgage pool prepayments remain within the 100/300 PSA prepayment collar, PAC bondholders will receive these cash flows exactly as originally specified.

PAC collars are usually sufficiently wide so that actual prepayments move outside the collar only infrequently. In the event that prepayments move outside a collar far enough to interfere with promised PAC cash flows, PAC bonds normally specify the following two contingency rules:

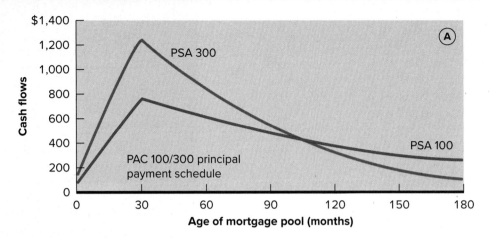

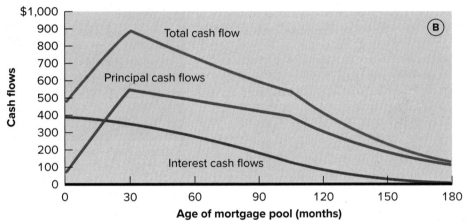

PAC contingency rule 1. When actual prepayments fall below a PAC collar's lower bound, there could be insufficient cash flow to satisfy a PAC bond's promised cash flow schedule. In this case, the PAC bond receives all available cash flow, and any shortfall is carried forward and paid on a first-priority basis from future cash flows. Non-PAC bonds receive no cash flows until all cumulative shortfalls to PAC bonds are paid off.

PAC contingency rule 2. When actual prepayments rise above a PAC collar's upper bound, it is possible that all outstanding principal for the non-PAC support bonds is paid off before the PAC bond. When all non-PAC principal is paid off, the PAC cash flow schedule is abandoned and all mortgage pool cash flows are paid to PAC bondholders.

CHECK THIS

21.6d   A PAC 100/300 bond based on a pool of fully modified 30-year fixed-rate mortgages switches payment schedules after 103 months. Would switching occur earlier or later for a PAC 50/300 bond? For a PAC 100/500 bond?

21.6e   Figures 21.6A and 21.6B assume a PAC 100/300 bond based on a pool of fully modified 30-year fixed-rate mortgages. What would these figures look like for a PAC 50/300 and a PAC 100/500 bond?

21.6f   How might a large change in market interest rates cause mortgage pool prepayments to move outside a PAC collar far enough and long enough to interfere with an originally stated PAC bond cash flow schedule?

FIGURE 21.7   MBS Yields

100% GNSF 6.5 S				7.000(
6/2022	CPR	VPR	CDR SEV	30D
1M ▾	11	11	-- --	3.5

+🔍
0 MED

Settle	06/17/2022
Deal Level Controls	
Index Rates	+0
All Loans	
Prepay	189 PSA
Vary	0
Price	101-29+	34
Yield	1.8583
Avg Life	5.07
Spread Duration	4.66
Prin Win	Date ▾	7/22-11/38

Source: Bloomberg Finance L.P.

Yields for Mortgage-Backed Securities

Related Bloomberg Functions

SYT   Super Yield Table

You can find yields for and indices of mortgage-backed securities (MBSS) for GNMA, FHLMC, and FNMA mortgage pools online at various sources. Figure 21.7 is a **Bloomberg** screen showing information for a Ginnie Mae (GNMA) bond. You can see that the yield on this bond is about 1.86 percent. The bid price is 101 and 29.5 (the "+" is a half).

Summary and Conclusions

This chapter discusses the large and growing market for mortgage-backed securities. The chapter covers many aspects of this market, including the following items—grouped by the chapter's important concepts.

1. **The workings of a fixed-rate mortgage.**

A. Most Americans finance their homes with a down payment and a loan for the remaining amount—known as a mortgage. Mortgages are often repackaged into mortgage-backed securities through a process called mortgage securitization. Currently, about half of all mortgages in the United States have been securitized, yet the risks involved in these investments are often misunderstood.

B. Most home mortgages are 15- or 30-year fixed-rate mortgages with fixed monthly payments. The present value of all monthly payments is equal to the original amount of the mortgage loan. Each monthly payment has two parts: interest on the remaining principal and a scheduled pay-down of the principal. Through time, the interest payment gradually declines, and the pay-down of the principal gradually increases.

C. A mortgage borrower has the right to pay off a mortgage early—known as mortgage prepayment. Borrowers frequently prepay to refinance an existing mortgage at a lower interest rate. Prepayment and refinancing, which are advantages to mortgage borrowers, are disadvantages to mortgage investors. Therefore, mortgage investors face prepayment risk.

D. In a reverse mortgage, borrowers (with home equity) receive monthly payments from a lender. Borrowers generally do not have to repay money received from a reverse mortgage as long as they live in their homes. However, the loan becomes due if the borrowers die, sell their home, or move to another principal residence.

2. The government's role in the secondary market for home mortgages.

A. In 1968, Congress established the Government National Mortgage Association (GNMA) as a government agency charged with promoting liquidity in the secondary market for home mortgages. GNMA is the largest single guarantor of mortgage-backed securities. Two government-sponsored enterprises (GSEs) are also significant mortgage repackaging sponsors: the Federal Home Loan Mortgage Corporation (FHLMC) and the Federal National Mortgage Association (FNMA).

B. Each month, GNMA, FHLMC, and FNMA mortgage-backed bond investors receive cash flows derived from fully modified mortgage pools. Each monthly cash flow has three distinct components: payment of interest on outstanding mortgage principal, scheduled amortization of mortgage principal, and mortgage principal prepayments.

3. The impact of mortgage prepayments.

A. Mortgage prepayments are stated as a prepayment rate. The greater the prepayment rate, the faster mortgage pool principal is paid off. Because they depend on prevailing interest rates, prepayment rates vary substantially from year to year. In practice, the industry states prepayment rates using the Public Securities Association (PSA) prepayment model. This model states prepayment rates as a percentage of a PSA benchmark. This benchmark, called 100 PSA, represents an annual prepayment rate of 6 percent for seasoned mortgages. Deviations from the 100 PSA benchmark are stated as a percentage of the benchmark.

B. Prepayment risk complicates the effects of interest rate risk. Interest rate risk for a bond is related to its effective maturity, as measured by Macaulay duration. Macaulay duration assumes a fixed schedule of cash flow payments. However, the schedule of cash flow payments for mortgage-backed bonds varies because of mortgage prepayments (which, in turn, are affected by interest rates). For this reason, Macaulay duration is a deficient measure of interest rate risk for mortgage-backed bonds.

4. How collateralized mortgage obligations are created and divided.

A. Cash flows from mortgage pools are often carved up and distributed according to various rules. Mortgage-backed securities representing specific rules for allocating mortgage cash flows are called collateralized mortgage obligations (CMOs). The three best-known types of CMO structures are interest-only (IO) and principal-only (PO) strips, sequential CMOs, and protected amortization class securities (PACs).

B. Cash flow yields for mortgage-backed securities (MBSS) and collateralized mortgage obligations (CMOs) for GNMA, FHLMC, and FNMA mortgage pools appear online daily at www.wsj.com. Cash flow yield for a mortgage-backed security corresponds to the yield to maturity for an ordinary bond. Essentially, cash flow yield is the interest rate that discounts all future expected cash flows from a mortgage pool to be equal to the price of the mortgage pool.

GETTING DOWN TO BUSINESS

This chapter covered one of the more complex investments available, mortgage-backed securities (MBSs). These investments are fairly complicated, but unlike most exotic instruments, the basic types of MBSs are very suitable for ordinary individual investors. In fact, GNMAs and similar investments are frequently recommended, and rightly so, for even very conservative investors.

However, directly buying into mortgage pools is not practical for most individual investors. It is also probably unwise because not all pools are equally risky in terms of prepayments, and analysis of individual pools is best left to experts. Instead, most investors in MBSs end up in mutual funds specializing in these instruments, and most of the major mutual fund families have such funds.

If you are interested in learning more about these investments, the internet contains a large amount of information. Some of the first places to visit are the websites for GNMA (www.ginniemae.gov), FNMA (www.fanniemae.com), and FHLMC (www.freddiemac.com). For much information on the home mortgage business, along with current mortgage rates across the country, try Mortgage News Daily (www.mortgagenewsdaily.com). An informative site with good-to-excellent coverage of mortgage-backed securities is Investing in Bonds (www.investinginbonds.com).

For the latest information on the real world of investments, visit us at jmdinvestments.blogspot.com.

Key Terms

average life 703
collateralized mortgage obligations (CMOs) 708
conditional prepayment rate (CPR) 703
effective duration for MBS 706
Federal Home Loan Mortgage Corporation (FHLMC) 701
Federal National Mortgage Association (FNMA) 701
fixed-rate mortgage 694
fully modified mortgage pool 701
Government National Mortgage Association (GNMA) 701
interest-only strips (IOs) 708
Macaulay duration 706
mortgage amortization 697

mortgage passthroughs 694
mortgage prepayment 697
mortgage principal 695
mortgage securitization 694
mortgage-backed securities (MBSS) 694
PAC collar 712
PAC support bond 712
prepayment rate 702
prepayment risk 701
principal-only strips (POs) 708
protected amortization class (PAC) bond 712
seasoned mortgages 703
sequential CMOs 710
unseasoned mortgages 703

Related Bloomberg Functions

MBSS MBS Pool Search, 21.1

GNMA GNMA Pool Information, 21.3

PDI Paydown Information, 21.3 & 21.4

CTP CPR to PSA Calculator, 21.4

MSD MBS Settle Dates, 21.6

SYT Super Yield Table, 21.7

Chapter Review Problems and Self-Test

1. **Mortgage Payments (LO1, CFA1)** What are the monthly payments on a 30-year, $150,000 mortgage if the mortgage rate is 6 percent? What portion of the first payment is interest? Principal?

2. **Mortgage Prepayments (LO3, CFA1)** Consider a 15-year, $210,000 mortgage with a 7 percent interest rate. After 10 years, the borrower (the mortgage issuer) pays it off. How much will the lender receive?

Answers to Self-Test Problems

1. This is a standard time value of money calculation in which we need to find an annuity-type payment. The present value is $150,000. The interest rate is .06/12 = .005, or .5 percent, per month. There are a total of 360 payments. Using the formula from the text, we have:

$$\text{Monthly payment} = \frac{\text{Mortgage amount} \times r/12}{1 - \dfrac{1}{(1 + r/12)^{T \times 12}}}$$

Plugging in $r = .06$ and $T = 30$, we get a payment of $899.33. The interest portion for a month is equal to the mortgage balance at the beginning of the month ($150,000 in this case) multiplied by the interest rate per month (.5 percent), or $150,000 × .005 = $750. The remaining portion of the payment, $899.33 − $750 = $149.33, goes to reduce the principal balance.

2. We first need to know the monthly payment. Here, the original balance is $210,000, the rate is 7 percent, and the original life is 15 years. Plugging in the numbers using the formula above, check that we get a monthly payment of $1,887.54. From here, there are two ways to go. One is relatively easy; the other is relatively tedious. The tedious way would be to construct an amortization table for the mortgage and then locate the balance in the table. However, we need only a single balance, so there is a much faster way. After 10 years, we can treat this mortgage as though it were a five-year mortgage with payments of $1,887.54 and an interest rate of 7 percent. We can then solve for the mortgage balance using the same formula:

$$\text{Monthly payment} = \frac{\text{Mortgage balance} \times .07/12}{1 - \dfrac{1}{(1 + .07/12)^{5 \times 12}}} = \$1,887.54$$

Solving for the mortgage balance gets us $95,324.50.

Test Your Investment Quotient

1. **Fixed-Rate Mortgages (LO1, CFA2)** Which of the following statements about fixed-rate mortgages is false?

   a. Fifteen-year mortgages have higher monthly payments than 30-year mortgages.
   b. Scheduled monthly payments are constant over the life of the mortgage.
   c. Actual monthly payments may vary over the life of the mortgage.
   d. Actual monthly payments are never more than scheduled monthly payments.

2. **Fixed-Rate Mortgages (LO1, CFA2)** The interest component of a monthly payment for a fixed-rate mortgage is:

   a. Highest during the first year of the mortgage.
   b. Highest during the middle year of the mortgage.
   c. Highest during the last year of the mortgage.
   d. Constant throughout the life of the mortgage.

3. **Fixed-Rate Mortgages (LO1, CFA2)** The principal reduction component of a monthly payment for a fixed-rate mortgage is:

   a. Highest during the first year of the mortgage.
   b. Highest during the middle year of the mortgage.
   c. Highest during the last year of the mortgage.
   d. Constant throughout the life of the mortgage.

4. **Fixed-Rate Mortgages (LO1, CFA2)** The remaining balance on a 30-year, $100,000 mortgage loan financed at 8 percent after the 180th payment is (no calculation necessary):

   a. $100,000.
   b. $50,000.
   c. $76,782.
   d. $23,219.

5. **Fixed-Rate Mortgages (LO1, CFA2)** Which of the following mortgages has the lowest monthly payment (no calculation necessary)?

   a. 30-year, 8 percent
   b. 30-year, 10 percent
   c. 15-year, 8 percent
   d. 15-year, 10 percent

6. **Fixed-Rate Mortgages (LO1, CFA2)** Which of the following mortgages will pay the smallest total interest over the life of the mortgage (no calculation necessary)?

   a. 30-year, 8 percent
   b. 30-year, 10 percent
   c. 15-year, 8 percent
   d. 15-year, 10 percent

7. **Fixed-Rate Mortgages (LO1, CFA2)** Which of the following mortgages will have the largest remaining balance after 180 monthly payments (no calculation necessary)?

   a. 30-year, 8 percent
   b. 30-year, 10 percent
   c. 15-year, 8 percent
   d. 15-year, 10 percent

8. **GNMA Bonds (LO2, CFA2)** Mortgages in GNMA pools are said to be fully modified because GNMA guarantees bondholders which of the following?

   a. A minimum rate of return on their investment
   b. A modified schedule of cash flows over the life of the pool.
   c. Full and timely payment of both principal and interest in the event of default
   d. Eventual payment of both principal and interest in the event of default

9. **GNMA Bonds (LO2, CFA2)** Which of the following is not a source of risk for GNMA mortgage pool investors?

   a. Prepayment risk
   b. Default risk
   c. Interest rate risk
   d. Reinvestment risk

10. **GNMA Bonds (LO2, CFA2)** Which of the following should a bond portfolio manager purchase if the manager is looking for mortgage-backed securities that would perform best during a period of rising interest rates?

    a. A 12 percent GNMA with an average life of 5.6 years
    b. An 8 percent GNMA with an average life of 6.0 years
    c. A 10 percent GNMA with an average life of 8.5 years
    d. A 6 percent GNMA with an average life of 9.0 years

11. **Prepayments (LO3, CFA2)** A bond analyst at Omnipotent Bank (OB) notices that the prepayment experience on his holdings of high-coupon GNMA issues has been moving sharply higher. What does this indicate?

    a. Interest rates are falling.
    b. The loans comprising OB's pools have been experiencing lower default rates.
    c. The pools held by OB are older issues.
    d. All of the above.

12. **Collateralized Mortgage Obligations (LO4, CFA2)** For a given mortgage pool, which of the following CMOs based on that pool is most likely to increase in price when market interest rates increase?

    a. 100/300 PAC bond
    b. A-tranche sequential CMO
    c. Interest-only (IO) strip
    d. Principal-only (PO) strip

13. **MBS Duration (LO4, CFA2)** Higher prepayments have what impact on the effective duration of a mortgage passthrough security?

   a. They decrease effective duration for all maturity mortgages.
   b. They increase effective duration for all maturity mortgages.
   c. They increase (decrease) effective duration for short (long) maturity mortgages.
   d. They increase (decrease) effective duration for long (short) maturity mortgages.

14. **MBS Duration (LO4, CFA3)** Which of the following most accurately measures interest rate sensitivity for mortgage passthrough securities with prepayment risk?

   a. Static duration
   b. Effective duration
   c. Modified duration
   d. Macaulay duration

15. **MBS Duration (LO4, CFA2)** The most important difference between effective duration and Macaulay duration for a mortgage passthrough security is that:

   a. Macaulay duration is easier to calculate.
   b. Effective duration is easier to calculate.
   c. Macaulay duration accounts for prepayment sensitivity.
   d. Effective duration accounts for prepayment sensitivity.

Concept Questions

1. **Mortgage Securitization (LO4, CFA2)** How does mortgage securitization benefit borrowers?

2. **Mortgage Securitization (LO4, CFA2)** How does mortgage securitization benefit mortgage originators?

3. **Mortgage Payments (LO1, CFA2)** All else the same, will the payments be higher on a 15-year mortgage or a 30-year mortgage? Why?

4. **Ginnie, Fannie, and Freddie (LO2, CFA2)** From an investor's point of view, what is the difference between mortgage pools backed by GNMA, FNMA, and FHLMC?

5. **Mortgage Pools (LO4, CFA2)** What does it mean for a mortgage pool to be fully modified?

6. **Prepayments (LO3, CFA2)** What are some of the reasons that mortgages are paid off early? Under what circumstances are mortgage prepayments likely to rise sharply? Explain.

7. **Prepayments (LO3, CFA2)** Explain why the right to prepay a mortgage is similar to the call feature contained in most corporate bonds.

8. **Prepayments (LO3, CFA2)** Evaluate the following argument: "Prepayment is not a risk to mortgage investors because prepayment actually means that the investor is paid both in full and ahead of schedule." Is the statement always true or false?

9. **Prepayments (LO3, CFA2)** Mortgage pools also suffer from defaults. Explain how defaults are handled in a fully modified mortgage pool. In the case of a fully modified mortgage pool, explain why defaults appear as prepayments to the mortgage pool investor.

10. **CMOs (LO4, CFA2)** What is a collateralized mortgage obligation? Why do they exist? What are three popular types?

11. **IO and PO Strips (LO4, CFA4)** What are IO and PO strips? Assuming interest rates never change, which is riskier?

12. **IO and PO Strips (LO4, CFA2)** Which has greater interest rate risk, an IO or a PO strip?

13. **Sequential CMOs (LO4, CFA2)** Consider a single whole bond sequential CMO. It has two tranches, an A-tranche and a Z-tranche. Explain how the payments are allocated to the two tranches. Which tranche is riskier?

14. **PACs (LO4, CFA2)** Explain in general terms how a protected amortization class (or PAC) CMO works.

15. **Duration and MBSS (LO4, CFA2)** Why is Macaulay duration an inadequate measure of interest rate risk for an MBS? Why is effective duration a better measure of interest rate risk for an MBS?

Questions and Problems

1. **Mortgage Payments (LO1, CFA1)** What is the monthly payment on a 30-year fixed-rate mortgage if the original balance is $315,000 and the rate is 4.9 percent?

2. **Mortgage Balances (LO1, CFA1)** If a mortgage has monthly payments of $1,240, a life of 30 years, and a rate of 4.5 percent per year, what is the mortgage amount?

3. **Mortgage Payments (LO1, CFA1)** A homeowner takes out a $417,000, 30-year fixed-rate mortgage at a rate of 5.2 percent. What are the monthly mortgage payments?

4. **Mortgage Balances (LO1, CFA1)** You have decided to buy a house. You can get a mortgage rate of 5.25 percent, and you want your payments to be $1,500 or less. How much can you borrow on a 30-year fixed-rate mortgage?

5. **SMM (LO4, CFA2)** What is the single monthly mortality assuming the conditional prepayment rate is 7 percent?

6. **CPR (LO4, CFA2)** What is the conditional prepayment rate if the single monthly mortality is .426 percent?

7. **IO and PO Values (LO4, CFA2)** A $100,000 GNMA passthrough bond issue has a value of $107,680. The value of the interest-only payments is $52,973. What is the value of the principal-only payment?

8. **Mortgage Interest (LO1, CFA1)** A 30-year, $250,000 mortgage has a rate of 5.4 percent. What are the interest and principal portions in the first payment? In the second?

9. **Mortgage Balances (LO1, CFA1)** A homeowner takes a 15-year fixed-rate mortgage for $140,000 at 7.6 percent. After seven years, the homeowner sells the house and pays off the remaining principal. How much is the principal payment?

10. **Mortgage Balances (LO1, CFA1)** Consider a 30-year, $145,000 mortgage with a 6.1 percent interest rate. After eight years, the borrower (the mortgage issuer) pays it off. How much will the lender receive?

11. **Prepayments (LO3, CFA1)** Consider a 30-year, $160,000 mortgage with a rate of 6 percent. Five years into the mortgage, rates have fallen to 5 percent. What would be the monthly saving to a homeowner from refinancing the outstanding mortgage balance at the lower rate?

12. **Prepayments (LO3, CFA1)** Consider a 25-year, $350,000 mortgage with a rate of 7.25 percent. Ten years into the mortgage, rates have fallen to 5.4 percent. What would be the monthly saving to a homeowner from refinancing the outstanding mortgage balance at the lower rate?

13. **Prepayments (LO3, CFA1)** Consider a 30-year, $230,000 mortgage with a rate of 6.90 percent. Five years into the mortgage, rates have fallen to 5.70 percent. Suppose the transaction cost of obtaining a new mortgage is $2,500. Should the homeowner refinance at the lower rate?

14. **Mortgage Prepayments (LO2, CFA2)** A homeowner took out a 30-year fixed-rate mortgage of $220,000. The mortgage was taken out 10 years ago at a rate of 7.20 percent. If the homeowner refinances, the charges will be $3,500. What is the highest interest rate at which it would be beneficial to refinance the mortgage?

15. **Mortgage Prepayments (LO2, CFA2)** A homeowner took out a 30-year fixed-rate mortgage of $120,000. The mortgage was taken out 15 years ago at a rate of 7.95 percent. If the homeowner refinances, the charges will be $2,000. What is the highest interest rate at which it would be beneficial to refinance the mortgage?

16. **CPRs (LO3, CFA2)** What are the conditional prepayment rates for seasoned 50 PSA, 200 PSA, and 400 PSA mortgages if the 100 PSA benchmark is 3 percent per year? How do you interpret these numbers?

17. **SMMs (LO3, CFA2)** In Problem 16, what is the single monthly mortality for seasoned 50 PSA, 200 PSA, and 400 PSA mortgages? How do you interpret these numbers?

18. **Mortgage Payments (LO1, CFA1)** A 30-year mortgage has an annual interest rate of 5.6 percent and a loan amount of $210,000. What are the monthly mortgage payments?

19. **Mortgage Amortization (LO1, CFA1)** A 20-year mortgage has an annual interest rate of 4.9 percent and a loan amount of $250,000. What are the interest and principal for the 120th payment?

20. **Mortgage Balances (LO1, CFA1)** A 30-year mortgage has an annual interest rate of 6.1 percent and a loan amount of $270,000. What is the remaining balance at the 180th payment?

[CFA2]

Mark Houston, a Level I CFA candidate, has just been hired as a junior analyst in the mortgage management department of Fixed Income Strategies. Mr. Houston is asked to perform some analysis on the mortgage pool shown below. All mortgages are conforming 30-year fixed-rate loans.

Pool	Outstanding Mortgage	Weight in Pool	Mortgage Rate	Months Remaining	Service Fee (bp)	Net Interest	Monthly Payment	Conditional Prepayment Rate
1	$100,000	19.61%	8.25%	234	50	7.75%	$ 860.71	6.00%
2	150,000	29.41	7.70	344	55	7.15	1,082.40	3.20
3	175,000	34.31	6.90	344	45	6.45	1,168.88	3.20
4	85,000	16.67	9.20	345	55	8.65	702.02	3.00

Before tackling the job, Mr. Houston does some research on mortgage loans. First, he assembles some facts about the difference between fixed-rate mortgage loans and traditional fixed-income corporate bonds:

- Mortgage loan payments consist of both principal and interest.
- The final payment on a mortgage does not include the par amount of the loan.
- Servicing fees on mortgage pools decline as the loan matures.
- Straight corporate bonds do not include call options.

Marvin Blanda, CFA, CEO of Fixed Income Strategies, tells Mr. Houston to calculate the expected prepayments for the first 12 months for all of the loans in the portfolio. He warns Mr. Houston not to forget about the relationship between conditional prepayment rates (CPRs) and single monthly mortality (SMM) rates.

1. Regarding conditional prepayment rates (CPRs) and single monthly mortality (SMM) rates, which of the following is most accurate?

   a. SMM is computed from the CPR to compute monthly prepayments.
   b. SMM is computed from the CPR to compute changes in loan maturity.
   c. CPR is computed from the SMM to compute monthly prepayments.

2. Mr. Houston made a mistake in his research about the nature of mortgage loans. Which of the following statements regarding mortgage loans as compared to straight bonds is least accurate?

   a. Servicing fees on mortgage pools decline as the loan matures.
   b. The final mortgage payment does not include the par amount of the loan.
   c. Mortgage borrowers do not get call options.

3. Mr. Blanda instructs Mr. Houston to calculate the weighted average coupon rate (WAC) for the mortgage pools. Which of the following is closest to the WAC?

   a. 7.28 percent
   b. 7.78 percent
   c. 8.01 percent

4. Mr. Blanda tells Mr. Houston to recalculate the SMM for Pool 3 based on 200 PSA rather than the current 100 PSA. The revised SMM is closest to:

   a. .36 percent.
   b. .55 percent.
   c. .97 percent.

Bloomberg Exercises

1. Use the search function to identify available mortgage-backed securities. (**MBSS**)
2. Test the CPR to PSA calculator. (**CTP**)

What's on the Web?

1. **Depository Trust and Clearing Corporation (DTCC)** Go to www.dtcc.com. What is the role of the DTCC? What par value of mortgage-backed securities was cleared in each of the last three months?

2. **Fannie Mae** Go to the mortgage-backed security section at www.fanniemae.com. What were the longest-term bonds recently issued by Fannie Mae? What are the coupon rates? What are the coupon rates on the shortest-term bonds issued?

3. **SMBS** Go to the mortgage-backed security section at www.fanniemae.com. Find the SMBS section. What is an SMBS? How do they work? Is an SMBS a suitable investment for most investors?

Answers to Test Your Investment Quotient Questions

Chapter 1

1-1	b
1-2	b
1-3	c
1-4	b
1-5	b
1-6	c
1-7	d
1-8	a
1-9	a
1-10	d
1-11	d
1-12	d
1-13	d
1-14	a
1-15	b

Chapter 2

2-1	a
2-2	c
2-3	c
2-4	c
2-5	b
2-6	b
2-7	b
2-8	a
2-9	c
2-10	b
2-11	a
2-12	a
2-13	c
2-14	c
2-15	d

Chapter 3

3-1	d
3-2	a
3-3	c
3-4	a
3-5	c
3-6	b
3-7	c
3-8	c
3-9	c
3-10	c

Chapter 4

4-1	c
4-2	b
4-3	d
4-4	d
4-5	d
4-6	d
4-7	b
4-8	a
4-9	a
4-10	a
4-11	b
4-12	d
4-13	a
4-14	a
4-15	d

Chapter 5

5-1	b
5-2	a
5-3	b
5-4	c
5-5	a
5-6	b
5-7	c
5-8	a
5-9	a
5-10	b
5-11	c
5-12	b
5-13	a
5-14	c
5-15	c

Chapter 6

6-1	c
6-2	a
6-3	a
6-4	b
6-5	b
6-6	c
6-7	d
6-8	c
6-9	c
6-10	a
6-11	a
6-12	d
6-13	d
6-14	c
6-15	c
6-16	c
6-17	c
6-18	a
6-19	a
6-20	b

Chapter 7

7-1	d
7-2	c
7-3	d
7-4	d
7-5	c
7-6	a
7-7	a
7-8	d
7-9	c
7-10	d
7-11	c
7-12	d
7-13	b
7-14	d
7-15	d

Chapter 8

8-1	d
8-2	c
8-3	d
8-4	b
8-5	a
8-6	b
8-7	c
8-8	b
8-9	a
8-10	d
8-11	c
8-12	b
8-13	c
8-14	b
8-15	d

Chapter 9

9-1	b
9-2	a
9-3	a
9-4	d
9-5	d
9-6	b
9-7	a
9-8	c
9-9	c
9-10	b
9-11	a
9-12	a
9-13	d
9-14	a
9-15	b
9-16	a
9-17	b
9-18	c
9-19	d
9-20	d

Chapter 10

10-1	b
10-2	c
10-3	d
10-4	a
10-5	a
10-6	b
10-7	a
10-8	a
10-9	b
10-10	c
10-11	a

10-12	a
10-13	c
10-14	c
10-15	c
10-16	a
10-17	a
10-18	b
10-19	a
10-20	d
10-21	b
10-22	a
10-23	c
10-24	c
10-25	c

Chapter 11

11-1	d
11-2	c
11-3	c
11-4	b
11-5	c
11-6	a
11-7	a
11-8	b
11-9	b
11-10	a
11-11	d
11-12	b
11-13	d
11-14	c
11-15	a

Chapter 12

12-1	d
12-2	a
12-3	a
12-4	d
12-5	b
12-6	b
12-7	b
12-8	c
12-9	d
12-10	d
12-11	d
12-12	a
12-13	b
12-14	a
12-15	b

Chapter 13

13-1	b
13-2	a
13-3	b
13-4	c
13-5	a
13-6	b
13-7	b
13-8	d
13-9	c
13-10	c
13-11	d
13-12	a
13-13	d
13-14	b
13-15	c

Chapter 14

14-1	a
14-2	d
14-3	a
14-4	d
14-5	d
14-6	c
14-7	d
14-8	a
14-9	d
14-10	b
14-11	b
14-12	d
14-13	c
14-14	a
14-15	d

Chapter 15

15-1	a
15-2	c
15-3	c
15-4	b
15-5	d
15-6	a
15-7	a
15-8	c
15-9	a
15-10	b
15-11	a
15-12	b
15-13	d
15-14	a
15-15	d

Chapter 16

16-1	a
16-2	d
16-3	c
16-4	a
16-5	a
16-6	b
16-7	a
16-8	c
16-9	a
16-10	b
16-11	b
16-12	d
16-13	a
16-14	c
16-15	d

Chapter 17

17-1	a
17-2	c
17-3	b
17-4	b
17-5	d
17-6	a
17-7	a
17-8	a
17-9	c
17-10	c
17-11	d
17-12	a
17-13	d
17-14	c
17-15	c

Chapter 18

18-1	c
18-2	a
18-3	c
18-4	a
18-5	b
18-6	a
18-7	b
18-8	a
18-9	c
18-10	c
18-11	d
18-12	b
18-13	b
18-14	b
18-15	d
18-16	c
18-17	a
18-18	d
18-19	d
18-20	b
18-21	c
18-22	b
18-23	b
18-24	a
18-25	a

Chapter 19

19-1	b
19-2	b
19-3	d
19-4	c
19-5	a
19-6	a
19-7	b
19-8	d
19-9	c
19-10	a
19-11	b
19-12	c
19-13	c
19-14	b
19-15	c
19-16	b
19-17	a
19-18	b
19-19	c
19-20	d

Chapter 20

20-1	b
20-2	d
20-3	c
20-4	d
20-5	c
20-6	d
20-7	d
20-8	c
20-9	c
20-10	d

Chapter 21

21-1	d
21-2	a
21-3	c
21-4	c
21-5	a
21-6	c
21-7	b
21-8	c
21-9	b
21-10	a
21-11	a
21-12	c
21-13	a
21-14	b
21-15	d

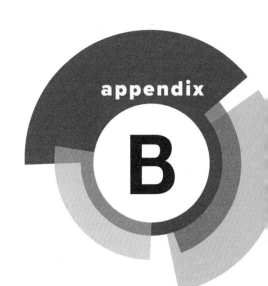

Key Equations

Chapter 1

1. Dividend yield $= D_{t+1}/P_t$ (1.1)

2. Capital gains yield $= (P_{t+1} - P_t)/P_t$ (1.2)

3. Percentage return $= (D_{t+1} + P_{t+1} - P_t)/P_t$ (1.3)

4. $1 + EAR = (1 + \text{Holding period percentage return})^m$ (1.4)

5. $\text{Var}(R) = \dfrac{1}{N-1}\left[(R_1 - \overline{R})^2 + \cdots + (R_N - \overline{R})^2\right]$

6. Geometric average return $= \left[(1 + R_1) \times (1 + R_2) \times \cdots \right.$
$$\left. \times \left(1 + R_N\right)\right]^{1/N} - 1 \quad (1.5)$$

7. Blume's formula:
$$R(T) = \left(\frac{T-1}{N-1} \times \text{Geometric average}\right) + \left(\frac{N-T}{N-1} \times \text{Arithmetic average}\right)$$

Chapter 2

1. $\text{Margin} = \dfrac{\text{Account equity}}{\text{Value of stock}}$

2. Maintenance margin
$$= \frac{(\text{Number of shares} \times P^*) - \text{Amount borrowed}}{\text{Number of shares} \times P^*}$$

3. $P^* = \dfrac{\text{Amount borrowed} / \text{Number of shares}}{1 - \text{Maintenance margin}}$ (2.1)

4. Maintenance margin
$$= \frac{(\text{Initial margin deposit} + \text{Short proceeds}) - \text{Number of shares} \times P^*}{\text{Number of shares} \times P^*}$$

5. $P^* = \dfrac{(\text{Initial margin deposit} + \text{Short proceeds}) / \text{Number of shares}}{1 + \text{Maintenance margin}}$

Chapter 4

1. Net asset value $= \dfrac{\text{Asset value}}{\text{Number of shares outstanding}}$

Chapter 5

1. Price-weighted index level $= \dfrac{\text{Sum of stock prices}}{\text{Divisor}}$

Chapter 6

1. $P_0 = \dfrac{D_1}{1+k} + \dfrac{D_2}{(1+k)^2} + \dfrac{D_3}{(1+k)^3} + \cdots + \dfrac{D_T}{(1+k)^T}$ (6.1)

2. $P_0 = \dfrac{D_0(1+g)}{k-g}\ (g < k)$ (6.2)

3. $P_0 = \dfrac{D_1}{k-g}\ (g < k)$ (6.3)

4. $g = \left[\dfrac{D_N}{D_0}\right]^{1/N} - 1$ (6.7)

5. Payout ratio $= D/EPS$

6. Sustainable growth rate $= \text{ROE} \times \text{Retention ratio}$ (6.8)
$$= \text{ROE} \times (1 - \text{Payout ratio})$$

7. Return on equity (ROE) $= \text{Net income}/\text{Equity}$ (6.9)

8. $\text{ROE} = \dfrac{\text{Net income}}{\text{Sales}} \times \dfrac{\text{Sales}}{\text{Assets}} \times \dfrac{\text{Assets}}{\text{Equity}}$ (6.10)

9. The two-stage dividend growth model: $P_0 = \dfrac{D_0(1+g_1)}{k - g_1}$
$$\left[1 - \left(\frac{1+g_1}{1+k}\right)^T\right] + \left(\frac{1+g_1}{1+k}\right)^T\left[\frac{D_0(1+g_2)}{k - g_2}\right] \quad (6.11)$$

10. Discount rate $= \text{U.S. T-bill rate} + (\text{Stock beta}$
$$\times \text{Stock market risk premium}) \quad (6.12)$$

In this equation:
  U.S. T-bill rate = Return on 90-day U.S. T-bills
  Stock beta = Risk relative to an average stock
  Stock market risk premium = Risk premium for an average stock

11. $P_0 = B_0 + \dfrac{EPS_0(1+g) - B_0 \times k}{k - g}$ (6.14)

12. $P_0 = \dfrac{EPS_1 - B_0 \times g}{k - g}$ (6.15)

13. $\begin{aligned} D_1 &= EPS_1 + B_0 - B_1 = EPS_1 + B_0 - B_0(1+g) \\ &= EPS_1 - B_0 \times g \end{aligned}$ (6.16)

14. $\text{FCF} = \text{EBIT}(1 - \text{Tax rate}) + \text{Depreciation}$
$$- \text{Capital spending} - \text{Change in net working capital} \quad (6.17)$$

15. $V_{Equity} = V_{Firm} - V_{Debt}$ (6.18)

16. $B_{Equity} = B_{Asset} \times \left[1 + (1-t)\dfrac{\text{Debt}}{\text{Equity}}\right]$ (6.19)

17. $V_{Firm} = \dfrac{\text{FCF}_1}{k-g} = \dfrac{\text{FCF}_0(1+g)}{k-g}$ (6.20)

18. Expected price $= \text{Historical PE ratio} \times \text{Projected EPS}$
$$= \text{Historical PE ratio} \times \text{Current EPS}$$
$$\times (1 + \text{Projected EPS growth rate})$$

19. Expected price $= \text{Historical P/CF ratio} \times \text{Projected CFPS}$
$$= \text{Historical P/CF ratio} \times \text{Current CFPS}$$
$$\times (1 + \text{Projected CFPS growth rate})$$

20. Expected price $= \text{Historical P/S ratio} \times \text{Projected SPS}$
$$= \text{Historical P/S ratio} \times \text{Current SPS}$$
$$\times (1 + \text{Projected SPS growth rate})$$

Chapter 7

1. Abnormal return = Observed return − Expected return

Chapter 8

1. Market sentiment index (MSI)

$$= \frac{\text{Number of bearish investors}}{\text{Number of bullish investors} + \text{Number of bearish investors}}$$

2. $\text{Arms} = \dfrac{\text{Declining volume}/\text{Declining stocks}}{\text{Advancing volume}/\text{Advancing stocks}}$ (8.1)

Chapter 9

1. Future value = Present value $\times (1 + r)^N$ (9.1)

2. Present value $= \dfrac{\text{Future value}}{(1 + r)^N}$ (9.2)

3. Present value = Future value $\times (1 + r)^{-N}$ (9.3)

4. Current price

$$= \text{Face value} \times \left(1 - \frac{\text{Days to maturity}}{360} \times \text{Discount yield}\right) \quad (9.4)$$

5. Bond equivalent yield

$$= \frac{365 \times \text{Discount yield}}{360 - \text{Days to maturity} \times \text{Discount yield}} \quad (9.5)$$

6. Bill price

$$= \frac{\text{Face value}}{1 + \text{Bond equivalent yield} \times \text{Days to maturity}/365} \quad (9.6)$$

7. $1 + EAR = \left(1 + \dfrac{APR}{m}\right)^m$ (9.7)

8. $\text{STRIPS price} = \dfrac{\text{Face value}}{(1 + YTM/2)^{2M}}$ (9.8)

9. $YTM = 2 \times \left[\left(\dfrac{\text{Face value}}{\text{STRIPS price}}\right)^{1/2M} - 1\right]$ (9.9)

10. Real interest rate = Nominal interest rate − Inflation rate (9.10)

11. $f_{1,1} = \dfrac{(1 + r_2)^2}{1 + r_1} - 1$

12. NI = RI + IP + RP (9.11)

13. NI = RI + IP + RP + LP + DP (9.12)

    In this equation:

    NI = Nominal interest rate

    RI = Real interest rate

    IP = Inflation premium

    RP = Interest rate risk premium

    LP = Liquidity premium

    DP = Default premium

Chapter 10

1. $\text{Coupon rate} = \dfrac{\text{Annual coupon}}{\text{Par value}}$ (10.1)

2. $\text{Current yield} = \dfrac{\text{Annual coupon}}{\text{Bond price}}$ (10.2)

3. Bond price

$$= \frac{C}{YTM}\left[1 - \frac{1}{(1 + YTM/2)^{2M}}\right] + \frac{FV}{(1 + YTM/2)^{2M}} \quad (10.3)$$

    In this formula:

    C = Annual coupon, the sum of two semiannual coupons

    FV = Face value

    M = Maturity in years

    YTM = Yield to maturity

4. Premium bonds:

    Coupon rate > Current yield > Yield to maturity

5. Discount bonds:

    Coupon rate < Current yield < Yield to maturity

6. Par value bonds:

    Coupon rate = Current yield = Yield to maturity

7. Callable bond price

$$= \frac{C}{YTC}\left[1 - \frac{1}{(1 + YTC/2)^{2T}}\right] + \frac{CP}{(1 + YTC/2)^{2T}} \quad (10.4)$$

    In this formula:

    C = Constant annual coupon

    CP = Call price of the bond

    T = Time in years until earliest possible call date

    YTC = Yield to call assuming semiannual coupons

8. Percentage change in bond price ≈

$$- \text{Duration} \times \frac{\text{Change in YTM}}{(1 + YTM/2)} \quad (10.5)$$

9. $\text{Modified duration} = \dfrac{\text{Macaulay duration}}{(1 + YTM/2)}$ (10.6)

10. Percentage change in bond price ≈

    −Modified duration × Change in YTM (10.7)

11. Par value bond duration

$$= \frac{(1 + YTM/2)}{YTM}\left[1 - \frac{1}{(1 + YTM/2)^{2M}}\right] \quad (10.8)$$

    In this formula:

    M = Bond maturity in years

    YTM = Yield to maturity assuming semiannual coupons

12. Duration

$$= \frac{1 + YTM/2}{YTM} - \frac{(1 + YTM/2) + M(CPR - YTM)}{YTM + CPR[(1 + YTM/2)^{2M} - 1]} \quad (10.9)$$

    In this formula:

    CPR = Constant annual coupon rate

    M = Bond maturity in years

    YTM = Yield to maturity assuming semiannual coupons

13. Dollar value of an 01 ≈ Modified duration

$$\times \text{Bond price} \times 0.001 \quad (10.10)$$

14. $\text{Yield value of a 32nd} \approx \dfrac{1}{32 \times \text{Dollar value of an 01}}$ (10.11)

15. $P = \dfrac{C}{YTM}\left[1 - \dfrac{1}{(1 + YTM/2)^{2M}}\right] + \dfrac{\text{Face value}}{(1 + YTM/2)^{2M}}$

$$P(1 + YTM/2)^{2M} = \frac{C}{YTM}[(1 + YTM/2)^{2M} - 1]$$
$$+ \text{Face value} \quad (10.12)$$

Chapter 11

1. Risk premium = Expected return − Risk-free rate

    Risk premium $= E(R_J) - R_f$ (11.1)

2. Portfolio return for N-asset portfolio:

    $E(R_P) = x_1 \times E(R_1) + x_2 \times E(R_2) + \ldots + x_n \times E(R_n)$ (11.2)

3. Portfolio variance for two-asset portfolio:

    $\sigma_P^2 = x_A^2 \sigma_A^2 + x_B^2 \sigma_B^2 + 2 x_A x_B \sigma_A \sigma_B \text{Corr}(R_A, R_B)$ (11.3)

4. Portfolio variance for three-asset portfolio:

    $\sigma_P^2 = x_A^2 \sigma_A^2 + x_B^2 \sigma_B^2 + x_C^2 \sigma_C^2 + 2 x_A x_B \sigma_A \sigma_B \text{Corr}(R_A, R_B)$
    $+ 2 x_A x_C \sigma_A \sigma_C \text{Corr}(R_A, R_C) + 2 x_B x_C \sigma_B \sigma_C \text{Corr}(R_B, R_C)$ (11.4)

5. The weight in Asset A in the minimum variance portfolio:

    $x_A^* = \dfrac{\sigma_B^2 - \sigma_A \sigma_B \text{Corr}(R_A, R_B)}{\sigma_A^2 + \sigma_B^2 - 2 \sigma_A \sigma_B \text{Corr}(R_A, R_B)}$ (11.5)

6. Portfolio return for three-asset portfolio:

    $R_P = x_F R_F + x_S R_S + x_B R_B$ (11.6)

7. Portfolio variance for three-asset portfolio when all correlations are zero:

    $\sigma_P^2 = x_F^2 \sigma_F^2 + x_S^2 \sigma_S^2 + x_B^2 \sigma_B^2$ (11.7)

Chapter 12

1. Total return − Expected return = Unexpected return

   $$R \quad - \quad E(R) \quad = \quad U \qquad (12.1)$$

2. Announcement = Expected part + Surprise (12.2)

3. $R - E(R) = U$ = Systematic portion + Unsystematic portion (12.3)

4. $R - E(R) = U = m + \varepsilon$ (12.4)

5. Total risk = Systematic risk + Unsystematic risk (12.5)

6. $\dfrac{E(R_A) - R_f}{\beta_A} = \dfrac{E(R_B) - R_f}{\beta_B}$ 12.6)

7. SML slope $= \dfrac{E(R_M) - R_f}{\beta_M} = \dfrac{E(R_M) - R_f}{1} = E(R_M) - R_f$

8. $E(R_i) = R_f + \left[E(R_M) - R_f\right] \times \beta_i$ (12.7)

9. $R - E(R) = m + \varepsilon$ (12.8)

10. $m = \left[R_M - E(R_M)\right] \times \beta$ (12.9)

11. $R - E(R) = m + \varepsilon = \left[R_M - E(R_M)\right] \times \beta + \varepsilon$ (12.10)

12. $\beta_i = \mathrm{Corr}(R_i, R_M) \times \sigma_i / \sigma_M$ (12.11)

Chapter 13

1. Sharpe ratio $= \dfrac{R_p - R_f}{\sigma_p}$ (13.1)

2. Treynor ratio $= \dfrac{R_p - R_f}{\beta_p}$ (13.2)

3. $E(R_p) = R_f + \left[E(R_M) - R_f\right] \times \beta_p$ (13.3)

4. Jensen's alpha $= a_p = R_p - E(R_p)$ (13.4)

   $\qquad = R_p - \left\{R_f + \left[E(R_M) - R_f\right] \times \beta_p\right\}$

5. $E(R_p) - R_f = \left[E(R_m) - R_f\right] \times \beta_p$ (13.5)

6. $E(R_{p,RP}) = E(R_{m,RP}) \times \beta_p$ (13.6)

7. $\dfrac{E(R_p) - R_f}{\sigma_p} = \dfrac{x_S E(R_S) + x_B E(R_B) - R_f}{\sqrt{x_S^2 \sigma_S^2 + x_B^2 \sigma_B^2 + 2 x_S x_B \sigma_S \sigma_B \mathrm{Corr}(R_S, R_B)}}$ (13.7)

8. $E(R_{p,T}) = E(R_p) \times T$ (13.8)

9. $\sigma_{p,T} = \sigma_p \times \sqrt{T}$ (13.9)

10. Value-at-Risk:

    $\mathrm{Prob}[R_{p,T} \le E(R_p) \times T - 2.326 \times \sigma_p \sqrt{T}] = 1\%$

    $\mathrm{Prob}[R_{p,T} \le E(R_p) \times T - 1.96 \times \sigma_p \sqrt{T}] = 2.5\%$ (13.10)

    $\mathrm{Prob}[R_{p,T} \le E(R_p) \times T - 1.645 \times \sigma_p \sqrt{T}] = 5\%$

Chapter 14

1. Carrying-charge market: Basis = Cash price − Futures price < 0

   Inverted market: Basis = Cash price − Futures price > 0

   (14.1)

2. $F = S(1 + r)$ (14.2)

3. Spot-futures parity: $F_T = S(1 + r)^T$ (14.3)

4. $F = S(1 + r) - D$ (14.4)

5. $F = S(1 + r) - D(S/S)$

   $\quad = S(1 + r) - S(D/S)$

   $\quad = S(1 + r) - Sd$

   $\quad = S(1 + r - d)$ (14.5)

6. Spot-futures parity (with dividend yield): (14.6)

   $F_T = S(1 + r - d)^T$

7. Number of index futures contracts, N, needed to hedge fully:

   $N = \dfrac{V_P}{V_F} \times \dfrac{\beta_P}{\beta_F}$ (14.7)

8. Number of U.S. Treasury note futures contracts, N, needed to hedge a bond portfolio:

   $N = \dfrac{D_P \times V_P}{D_F \times V_F}$ (14.8)

9. Duration of an interest rate futures contract (rule of thumb):

   $D_F = D_U + M_F$ (14.9)

Chapter 15

1. Call option intrinsic value = $\mathrm{MAX}(S - K, 0)$ (15.1)

2. Put option intrinsic value = $\mathrm{MAX}(K - S, 0)$ (15.2)

3. American call option price $\ge \mathrm{MAX}(S - K, 0)$ (15.3)

4. American put option price $\ge \mathrm{MAX}(K - S, 0)$ (15.4)

5. European call option price $\ge \mathrm{MAX}[S - K/(1 + r)^T, 0]$ (15.5)

6. European put option price $\ge \mathrm{MAX}[K/(1 + r)^T - S, 0]$ (15.6)

7. $S + P - C = K/(1 + r_f)^T$ (15.7)

8. The put-call parity relationship: $C - P = S - K/(1 + r_f)^T$ (15.8)

   $S = C - P + K/(1 + r_f)^T$ (15.9)

9. The put-call parity relationship (with dividends):

   $C - P = S - \mathrm{Div} - K/(1 + r_f)^T$ (15.10)

Chapter 16

1. Delta, one-period binomial model:

   $\Delta = \dfrac{C_u - C_d}{Su - Sd}$

2. $(\Delta S - C)(1 + r) = \Delta S \times u - C_u$ (16.1)

3. Call value, one-period binomial model:

   $C = \dfrac{\Delta S(1 + r - u) + C_u}{1 + r}$ (16.2)

4. Black-Scholes call option pricing model:

   $C = SN(d_1) - Ke^{-rT}N(d_2)$ (16.3)

5. Black-Scholes put option pricing model:

   $P = Ke^{-rT}N(-d_2) - SN(-d_1)$ (16.4)

   Where, in the Black-Scholes formula, d_1 and d_2 are

6. $d_1 = \dfrac{\ln(S/K) + (r + \sigma^2/2)T}{\sigma\sqrt{T}}$

7. $d_2 = d_1 - \sigma\sqrt{T}$

8. Call option delta = $N(d_1) > 0$

9. Put option delta = $-N(-d_1) < 0$

10. A useful option hedging equation:

    Change in value of stock portfolio + Change in value

    $\qquad\qquad\qquad\qquad$ of options = 0 (16.5)

11. $\Delta S \times$ Shares held + Option delta $\times$

    $\Delta S \times$ Number of options = 0 (16.6)

12. Number of stock options needed to hedge shares held:

    Number of options = $\dfrac{-\text{Shares held}}{\text{Option delta}}$ (16.7)

13. Number of option contracts needed to hedge an equity portfolio:

    $= \dfrac{\text{Portfolio beta} \times \text{Portfolio value}}{\text{Option delta} \times \text{Option contract value}}$ (16.8)

14. Black-Scholes-Merton call option formula:

    $C = Se^{-yT}N(d_1) - Ke^{-rT}N(d_2)$ (16.9)

    Where, in the Black-Scholes-Merton call option formula, d_1 and d_2 are:

15. $d_1 = \dfrac{\ln(S/K) + (r - y + \sigma^2/2)T}{\sigma\sqrt{T}}$

16. $d_2 = d_1 - \sigma\sqrt{T}$

Chapter 17

1. Leverage factor = 1/Margin percentage   (17.1)
2. $F = S \times (1 + r)^T$ (17.2)
3. $F = (S + PVSC) \times (1 + r)^T$ (17.3)
4. Estimate of property value $= \dfrac{NOI}{\text{Market capitalization rate}}$ (17.4)

Chapter 18

Convertible bond-to-stock conversion formulas:

1. Conversion ratio = Number of stock shares acquired by conversion
2. Conversion price $= \dfrac{\text{Bond par value}}{\text{Conversion ratio}}$
3. Conversion value = Price per share of stock × Conversion ratio
4. STRIPS price $= \dfrac{\text{Face value}}{[1 + (YTM/2)]^{2N}}$
5. STRIPS yield $= 2 \times \left[\left(\dfrac{\text{Face value}}{\text{Price}} \right)^{\frac{1}{2N}} - 1 \right]$
6. Bond price $= \dfrac{\text{Annual coupon}}{YTM} \times \left[1 - \dfrac{1}{(1 + YTM/2)^{2M}} \right]$
   $+ \dfrac{\text{Face value}}{(1 + YTM/2)^{2M}}$
7. Equivalent taxable yield = Tax-exempt yield / (1 − Marginal tax rate)
8. Aftertax yield = Taxable yield × (1 − Marginal tax rate)
9. Critical marginal tax rate = 1 − (Tax-exempt yield / Taxable yield)

Chapter 19

1. Assets = Liabilities + Equity   (19.1)
2. Net income = Dividends + Retained earnings   (19.2)

Profitability ratios:

3. Gross margin $= \dfrac{\text{Gross profit}}{\text{Net sales}}$
4. Operating margin $= \dfrac{\text{Operating income}}{\text{Net sales}}$

5. Return on assets (ROA) $= \dfrac{\text{Net income}}{\text{Total assets}}$
6. Return on equity (ROE) $= \dfrac{\text{Net income}}{\text{Shareholder equity}}$

Per-share calculations:

7. Book value per share (BVPS) $= \dfrac{\text{Shareholder equity}}{\text{Shares outstanding}}$
8. Earnings per share (EPS) $= \dfrac{\text{Net income}}{\text{Shares outstanding}}$
9. Cash flow per share (CFPS) $= \dfrac{\text{Operating cash flow}}{\text{Shares outstanding}}$

Price ratios:

10. Price-book (P/B) $= \dfrac{\text{Stock price}}{\text{BVPS}}$
11. Price-earnings (PE) $= \dfrac{\text{Stock price}}{\text{EPS}}$
12. Price-cash flow (P/CF) $= \dfrac{\text{Stock price}}{\text{CFPS}}$
13. Two-stage dividend growth model:

$$P_0 = \frac{D_0 \times (1 + g_1)}{k - g_1} \left[1 - \left(\frac{1 + g_1}{1 + k} \right)^T \right] + \left(\frac{1 + g_1}{1 + k} \right)^T \left[\frac{D_0 \times (1 + g_2)}{k - g_2} \right]$$

     (19.3)

Chapter 20

1. Money multiplier = 1/Reserve requirement

Chapter 21 (online)

1. Monthly payment $= \dfrac{\text{Mortgage amount} \times r/12}{1 - \dfrac{1}{(1 + r/12)^{T \times 12}}}$ (21.1)
2. $SMM = 1 - (1 - CPR)^{1/12}$ (21.2)

NAME INDEX

A

Angel, James, 153
Arms, Richard, 272

B

Bachelier, Louis, 529
Baldwin, William, 311
Bancanovic, Peter, 23
Barber, Brad, 257
Black, Fischer, 539
Blume, Marshall, 26–27
Boehmer, Ekkehart, 61
Bollinger, John, 277
Briloff, Abraham, 634
Buffett, Warren, 173, 224, 255, 490, 589, 641
Burger, Dani, 518

C

Cedarbaum, Miriam, 223
Chang, Kenneth, 214
Corcoran, Barbara, 578
Cramer, Jim, 264

D

de Cervantes, Miguel, 363
Dell, Michael, 573
DeVoe, Raymond, 328
Dimson, Elroy, 16
Dow, Charles, 269

E

Edwards, Lincoln, 518
Einstein, Albert, 637
Elliott, Ralph Nelson, 270

F

Fama, Eugene, 419–420
Feather, William, 137
Ford, Henry, 2
Franklin, Benjamin, 292, 597
French, Kenneth, 419–420

G

Goodman, George J. W., 137
Graham, Benjamin, 74, 251

Grant, Mitchell, 706
Grewal, Kevin, 473
Groome, Todd, 570
Gross, Bill, 125

H

Half, Robert, 459
Haliburton, Thomas Chandler, 292
Harrington, Kevin, 578
Hoover, Herbert, 668

J

James, LeBron, 261
Jensen, Michael C., 435
Jones, Charles, 61

K

Kahneman, Daniel, 260, 262
Kenny, Thomas, 295
Kenyes, John Maynard, 266
Klammer, Franz, 395

L

Leeson, Nicholas, 255–256
Lynch, Peter, 107

M

Macaulay, Frederick, 343, 343n4
Madoff, Bernard, 48
Malkiel, Burton, 341–342
Markowitz, Harry, 364
Marsh, Paul, 16
Massa, Annie, 153
Merton, Robert, 539
Mickelson, Phil, 223
Milligan, Spike, 1
Morgan, J. P., 431, 447

N

Needleman, Sarah E., 578

O

Odean, Terrance, 257
Or, Amy, 570

P

Patton, George S., 98
Petersell, Yakob, 518
Porter, Michael, 684–685

R

Rescate, Rebecca, 578
Rogers, Will, 40, 431, 565, 693
Rooney, Ben, 76, 152

S

Santayana, George, 2, 234n1
Scholes, Myron, 539
Schweser, Kaplan, 38–39, 72–73, 134–135,
171, 212–213, 290–291, 326–327,
361–362, 393–394, 429–430,
457–458, 487–488, 527–528,
563–564, 595–596, 632, 666–667,
691–692, 721
Sharpe, William F., 433, 451
Smith, Adam, 137
Statman, Meir, 371
Staunton, Michael, 16
Stewart, Martha, 223

T

Treynor, Jack L., 434
Tversky, Amos, 260, 262
Twain, Mark, 2, 459

W

Waksal, Sam, 223
Welch, Ivo, 16
Woodard, Jared, 551

Y

Yan, Alexandra, 707

Z

Zhang, Xiaoyan, 61
Zuckerberg, Mark, 79

EQUATION INDEX

A

Abnormal returns, 220
Account balance sheet, margins, 50
Accounting, 637
Aftertax yield, 618
Alpha, calculating, 435
American call option price, 513
American put option price, 513
Announcements, 397
Annualized returns, 6
Annual percentage rate (APR), 302-303
Arbitrage futures contracts, 581-582
Arithmetic average dividend growth rate, 177-179
Average annual returns, 16
Average returns, 23

B

Bank discount basis, 298-299
Bank discount yield, 301-302
Betas
    calculating, 414-415
    expected returns and, 413
    portfolio, 403
    risk premium and, 405
    for securities, 414
    systematic risk measurement, 413
Black-Scholes option pricing model, 539-542, 554-555
Blume's formula, 26-27
Bond equivalent yield
    APRs EARs and, 302-303
    bank discount yield v., 301-302
Bond risk measures
    dollar value of an 01, 347
    yield value of a 32nd, 348
Bonds
    callable bond price, 337
    conversion price for, 603
    conversion ratio for, 603
    conversion value for, 604
    coupon rate, 329-330
    current yield, 329-330
    duration of discount, 345
    duration of par value, 345
    price of callable, 337
    price of discount, 332
    price of premium, 332
    price of straight, 330-331
    price of Treasury, 612
    risk measures based on duration, 343

C

Callable bond price, 337
Call options
    delta (Δ) calculation for, 534
    in-the-money, 500
    intrinsic value of, 498-499
    lower bound for prices of, 513
    out-of-the-money, 500
    put-call parity, 516
    upper bound for prices of, 512
Call price, 337, 513
Capital asset pricing model (CAPM), 410
Capital gains yields, 4-5
Carrying-charge market, 473
Change in value of options held, 547
Clean surplus relationship (CSR), 187
Closing arms ratio, 272
Constant perpetual growth model, 175-176
Conversion price for bonds, 603
Conversion ratio for bonds, 603
Conversion value for bonds, 604
Coupon rate, 329
Critical marginal tax rate, 618
Critical price (P*), 53
Current price, 299
Current yield, 329

D

Diversification
    portfolio variance, standard deviation, 379-380
    variance of return, portfolio, 376
Discount bond price, 333
Dividend-adjusted parity, 476
Dividend discount model (DDM)
    constant perpetual growth model, 175-177
    discount rates for, 185-186
Dividend income, 3
Dividend yield, 4, 5, 23
Dollar value of an 01, 347
Dollar-weighted average returns, 27-29
DuPont formula for ROE, 180
Duration
    bond risk measures based on, 348
    discount bond, 346
    interest rate futures contract, 479
    Macaulay, 343, 344
    modified, 343, 344
    par value bond, 345
    semiannual coupon, 345

E

Earnings per share, 192, 640
Economic value added (EVA), 187
Effective annual rate (EAR), 302
Effective annual return (EAR), 6
Enterprise value (EV) ratios, 196
Equity beta to asset beta conversion, 190-191
Equity value, 190
Equivalent taxable yield, 617-618
Erratic dividend growth, 178-179
European call option price, 513
European put option price, 513
EV to EBITDA ratio, 196-197
Exchange rate risk and returns, 676
Expectations theory, forward rate, 314
Expected price, 195
Expected returns, 364
    calculating, 366
    portfolio, 368
    projected risk premium, 365
    systematic risk and, 402
    unequal probabilities, 367, 369

F

Forward rate, 313
Free flow cash model (FCF), 189
    constant growth DDM v., 190-192
    valuation, 191-192
Full capacity sales, 646

SUBJECT INDEX

A

Aberdeen Global Income Fund, 124
Abnormal earnings, 187
Abnormal return, 215, 433
  cumulative, 221–222
  event study, market reaction to bad news, 219–222
  Jensen's alpha measure of abnormal return, 435–436, 440–441
Absolute return funds, hedge funds, 573
Account balance sheet, 50
  short sales and, 57–58
Account equity, 50, 58
Accounting periods, financial statements and, 636
Accounts, investment
  annualizing returns, margin purchase, 53–54
  cash accounts, 49
  hypothecation/street name registration, 54–55
  margin account, 49–53
  margin purchase, annualizing returns on, 53–54
  retirement, 55–56
  See also entries for specific account types
Accredited investor, 139, 569
Accrued interest, 334n1
Adjustable-rate bonds, corporate, 607–608
Advance/decline line, 271–272
Advanced Medical Optics, Inc., 219–222
Advisor, financial
  choosing, 46–47
  robo, 47
Aftertax return, 42
Agricultural Futures, 463
AIA, 145
Airport bonds, 616
Alibaba Holdings Group, 145
Alphabet, 155
Alpha, calculating, 436–438. *See also* Jensen's alpha measure of abnormal return
Alternative Investment Management Association (AIMA), 570
Alternative investments
  accredited investors, 569
  benefits, 566–567

compensation/costs, 568
hedge funds as, 569–573. *See also* Hedge funds
liquidity, 568
portfolio, traditional/diversified, 567
risks of, 567–569
structure/transparency, 567–568
Altria Group, Inc., 83
Amazon, 81, 193, 194, 273–274
American call option price, 512–513
American Electric Power (AEP), 149, 177, 180
American Express (AXP), 149, 183, 430
American Football Conference, 279
American Funds, 102
American Funds EuroPacific Growth Fund (AEPGX), 105
American options, 491
American put option price, 513
American Stock Exchange, 148
Amex Internet index, 239
Anchoring, 255
Announcements, news and, 396–398
Annual coupon, current yield, 329–330
Annual earnings per share (EPS), 192
Annualizing returns, 5–6, 89
  margin price and, 53–54
Annual percentage rate (APR), 302–303, 308
Annual report, mutual funds and, 103
Answers
  equations, 726–729
  investment quotient questions, 723–725
Anticipated announcement, 397
Apollo and TPG funds, 140
Apple Inc. (APPL), 155, 274, 364
Arbitrage
  cash-futures, 472–474
  futures contracts and, 581–582
  hedge funds, 126, 571
  index, 476–477
  option pricing bounds and, 511–514
  put-call parity and, 517
Arbitrage pricing theory (APT), 410n3
Arbitration, 48
Arithmetic average dividend growth rate, 177–179
Arithmetic average return, 24, 26–27
A-shares, 105

Asian Nikkei index crash of 1990, 237–238
Ask, 82
Ask price, 88
Asset allocation, 44, 686
  diversification and, 378–380
  investor profile and, 64
  Markowitz efficient frontier and, 381–383
  strategic, tactical *v.,* 65
  See also Diversification
Asset allocation funds, 114
Asset-backed securities (ABS), 707
Asset beta, 190
Asset categories, balance sheet, 636
Asset-specific risks, 399, 401
AT&T, 57, 81, 83
At-the money option, 500
Auctions, U.S. Treasury, 613
Availability bias, 263
Average annual value-weighted percentage returns, 420
Average ending wealth by investment holding period, 373
Average geometric returns by investment holding period, 373
Average life, 703
Average returns
  arithmetic, geometric *v.,* 24, 26–27
  calculating, 15, 19
  dollar weighted, 27–29
  geometric, 24–26
  historical record, 15
  risk premiums, 15–16
  risk-return trade-offs, 29–30
  spreadsheet calculations, 23

B

Back-end loads, 105
Backtesting, 268
Backwardation, 473, 474, 581
Balanced funds, 114
Balance sheet
  asset categories, 636
  equations, 637
  financial statements and, 636–638
  pro forma, 643–645, 651–654
  Starbucks example, 649

Bank discount basis, 298
Bank discount yields, bond equivalent
    yields *v.,* 301–302
Banker's acceptance, 297
Bank of America, 148
Barclays Aggregate Bond Index, 404n1
Barclays Bank, 123
Bargaining power of buyers, 691–692
Barings Bank, 255–256
Base-year values, 162
Basis (cash price), 473, 473n1
Basis point, 298
BATS Options Market, 494
Bear call spreads, 510
Bear Market Percentile Rank, 458
Bear raid, 61
Bear Sterns, 240, 506
Beat the market, 215
Behavioral biases, 253
    endowment effect, 256
    loss aversion, 254–256
    myopic loss aversion, 256
    1/n phenomenon, 263–264
    overconfidence, 256–259
    regret aversion, 256
    representativeness heuristic and,
      259–261
    sunk cost fallacy, 256
    See also Behavioral finance; Bias
Behavioral finance
    defining, 252
    herding, 264
    heuristics, 263–264
    investment mistakes, 265
    limits to arbitrage, 265–266
    market sentiment index and, 268–269
    overcoming bias, 264
    prospect theory and, 252–256
    See also Behavioral bias; Bias
Belief perseverance biases, 253
Bell curve, normal distribution, 20–21
Bellwether rate, 295
Bellwether stocks, 151
Beneficial owner, 54
Berkshire Hathaway, 224, 589
Best efforts underwriting, 141–142
Beta, 186
    calculating, 414–415
    decomposing total returns, 413
    graphical representation of
      calculating, 416
    market portfolio and, 410
    portfolio expected returns and,
      406–408
    regression, calculate with, 418
    unexpected returns and, 413
    writing equations for, 412
Beta coefficient
    defined, 402
    measuring systematic risk, 402–403
    portfolio, 403–404

    researching, 405
    risk premium and, 406–407
    total risk *v.,* 405
Bias
    cognitive, 252
    investor, prospect theory and, 253
    loss aversion, 254–256
    overcoming, 264
    survivorship, hedge funds and, 573
    types of investor, 263
    See also Behavioral biases; Behavioral
      finance
Bid, 82
Bid-ask spread, 613
Bid price, 147
Big Board. *See* New York Stock Exchange
    (NYSE)
Binding arbitration, 48
Binomial option pricing model, 537–539
Bitcoin, 586
Black Monday, crash of October 1987,
    235–237
Black-Scholes-Merton call option formula,
    554–555
Black-Scholes option pricing model,
    539–542, 557
    five inputs, volatility and, 551
    hedging, 547
Blackstone Group, 140
Blended funds, 101, 114, 115
Blockchain technology, 145–146, 586–587
Block trades, 271, 272
Bloomberg, 153, 225, 430
Blue Chip Fund, 118
Blue-chip stock, 118n6
Blume's formula, 26–27
Bohr, Neils, 173
Bollinger bands, 276
Bond credit ratings
    alternatives to, 620
    corporate yield spreads through
      time, 621
    importance of, 619–620
    junk bonds, 621–622
    price and, 624
    prudent investment guidelines, 620
    purpose for, 619
    ratings agencies, 619
    symbols, 620
Bond equivalent yield
    annual percentage rate (APR), effective
      annual rate (EAR) and, 302–303
    bank discount yield *v.,* 301–302
    leap year, 301
Bond funds, 101
    characteristics of, 113
    stock funds and, 114–115
    Treasury Inflation-Protected Securities
      (TIPS) and, 311
Bond markets, 362
Bond maturity, corporate bonds, 605–606

Bond par value, 603
Bond principal, 329
Bond refunding, 600
Bond risk measures
    dollar value of an 1, 347
    duration and, 348
    yield value of a 32nd, 348
Bonds
    calculate duration, 345
    corporate trading, 79
    coupon bond, calculate price, 331
    coupon rates and, 77, 329–330
    current yield, 334
    defining, 329
    discount, price, 333
    duration and maturity, 347
    investing in, 624
    Malkiel's bond price theorem,
      341–352
    maturity and, 79
    premium/discount, 332–333
    premium, price, 333
    price quotes, 334
    price, reinvestment rate risk and, 352
    prices and yields, 341, 342
    quotes, 78–80
    straight bonds, 329
    tracking benchmarks of, 305
    Treasury bond prices, 335
    types/yields of, 306
    See also U.S. Treasury Bills; Yields
Bond seniority provisions, corporate bond
    indentures and, 600
Bond-to-stock conversion, 605
Bonus lock-in, 232
Boston Stock Exchange (BSE), 147
Bottom-feeders, 270
Box spreads, 510
Break-even effect, 255
Breaking the buck, 109
British Bankers' Association (BBA), 297
Broker
    choosing/types of, 46–47
    customer relations and, 48–49
    example disclosures, 49
    online, 47
Brokerage, 46
Brokers, 146–147
B-shares, 105
Bubble
    defined, 234
    dot-com, crash and, 238–239
Budget deficit, 680
Bull call spreads, 510
Business cycle, global macroeconomic
    activity, 671–673
    sector performance across, 673
    sectors of, 672
    stages of, 671, 672
Business development, stages of, 573
Business Insider, 265

Company-sponsored retirement plan, 55
Competition
    market efficiency and, 217–218
    Porter's five forces of, 684–685
Conagra Brands, 96
Conditional prepayment rates (CPRs),
    703, 721
Constant growth DDM, free flow cash
    model (FCF) v., 190–191
Constant perpetual growth model, 175–177
    applications of, 177
    formula for, 176–177
Constraints, investor. See Investor
    constraints
Consumer Price Index (CPI), 7
    jobs, monitoring price level and, 677
Contango, 473, 474, 581
Contango effect, 473
Contingent deferred sales charges
    (CDSC), 105
Continuation patterns, 274
Contraction stage, business cycle, 671, 672
Contract terms, common stock
    options, 491
Conversion price, 603
Conversion ratio, 603
Conversion value, 604, 605
Convertible bond, 81
    bond-to-stock conversion, corporate
        bond indentures, 603–604
    graphical analysis, price, 604–605
    in-the money, 604–605
    out of the money, 605
    value, 605
Convertible funds, 114
Convex price-yield relationship, 601
Core CPI, 677
Corporate bond indentures
    adjustable-rate, 607–608
    bond maturity/principle payment
        provisions, 605–606
    bond seniority provisions, 600
    bond-to-stock conversion provisions,
        603–604
    callable bonds, duration and, 602
    call provisions, 600–602
    convertible bond prices, graphical
        analysis, 604–605
    coupon payment provisions, 606–607
    defining, regulation of, 599–600
    issuer's call privilege, restricting, 601
    make-whole premium, 603
    maturity and, 605–606
    private placement, 600
    protective covenants, 607
    put provisions, 602–603
    sinking fund provisions, 606
Corporate bonds
    cash flow matching and, 598
    common stock v., 598

defined/characteristics of, 598–599
    five-year note issue, example, 599
    issue terms, 598
    junk grade, 599
    ownership patterns, 598
    plain vanilla, 598
    unsecured debt, 599
Corporate bond trading, 78
Corporate bond yields, 307
Corporate Information, 657
Corporate risk management
    call options and, 507–508
    protective put strategies and, 507
Corporate trading bonds, 79
Corporate yield spreads through
    time, 621
Corrections, 269
Correlation
    defined, 374
    diversification and, 374–376
    risk determinant, 374–376
    risk-return trade-off, 380–381
    systematic risk principle and, 402
    zero, portfolio, 382
Correlation coefficient, 374
Cost
    ETFs, mutual funds v., 121
    mutual funds and, 100, 105–106
Cost approach valuation, real estate, 584
Coupon payment provisions, corporate
    bond indentures and, 606–607
Coupon rate, 77, 329–330, 609
Coupons, 329
Covariance, 415
Covered call strategy, 509
Covering the position, 56
COVID-19 crash of 2020, 240–241
Crack spread trading, 583
Crash
    of 1929, 235
    defined, 234
    dot-com bubble of 2000–2002,
        238–239
    February 2020 COVID-19 crash,
        240–241
    Flash Crash of 2010, 237
    Nikkei index of 1990, 237–238
    NYSE circuit breakers, 237
    October 1987, 235–237
    October 2008, 239–240
    program trading and, 236
Credit bonds, municipal bonds, 616
Credit default swaps (CDS), 506–507
Credit quality, bond funds and, 113
Credit spread, 620
Critical price, calculate, 53
Crocs, Inc. (CROX), 397
Cross-hedge, 477
Crossing network trades, 155
Crowdfunding, 143

Crush spread trade, 583
Crypto asset, 587
Cryptocurrency
    benefits, 588
    bitcoin, 586
    blockchain technology, 586–587
    as investment, 587–588
    overview, 586
    risks, 588
Cubes (QQQ) fund, 119–120
Cumulative, 80
Cumulative abnormal return (CAR),
    221–222
Curing the short, 56
Current assets, 636
Current liabilities, 636
Current yield, 77, 329–330, 334
Customer relations, brokers and, 48–49
Customer's agreement, 46
CVS Health Corporation, analysis
    dividend discount model (DMM),
        197–199
    free cash flow model (FCF), 200
    price ratio analysis, 201
    residual income model (RIM), 199–200
    summary quote, 197
Cyberbrokers, 47
Cyclical sectors, business cycle, 672

D

Dark pools, 155
Data snooping, market efficiency and, 225
Day-of-the-week effect, market anomalies,
    229–230
Days to Cover, 60
Dealers, 146–147
Deal flow, private equity funds, 575
Deal structure, private equity funds,
    577–578
Death cross, 276
Debentures, 599
Debt
    distressed, 623
    government, 608, 666, 680
    PIGS countries, 681
Decision-making, behavioral finance and,
    263–264
Dedicated portfolios, 349
Deep-discount broker, 46
Default premium (DP), 318, 319
Default risk, municipal bonds and, 615
Defensive sectors, business cycle, 672
Deferred call provision, callable bonds, 601
Defined benefit plan 401(k), 99
Defined contribution plans, 99
Delayed reaction, stock price and, 219
Delivery-options, futures contract,
    479–480
Dell Technologies, 364, 573

Electronic Data Gathering, Analysis, and Retrieval (EDGAR), 635
Elliot wave theory, 270
Emerging markets funds, 111
E-mini Dow Futures contract, 462
E-Minis, 152
Employee stock options (ESOs)
   Black-Scholes-Merton call option formula, 554–555
   Coca-Cola employee stock options, 555
   defined, 553
   features of, 553–554
   Gap, Inc., 554
   repricing, 554
   valuing, 554–555
Endowment effect, 255, 256
Enel S.p.A., 145
Enterprise value (EV) ratio, 196–197
Environmental, social, and governance (ESG)
   funds, 112
   scores, 113
Equities, 75
   common stock, 79–80
   defined, 79
   preferred stock, 80–81
   price quotes, common stock, 81–83
Equity beta, 190
Equity crowdfunding, 143
Equity income, funds and, 111
Equity investors, hedging and, 551
Equity LEAPS, 97
Equity, shareholder, 636
Equivalent taxable yield, municipal bonds, 617–618
Errors
   investment mistakes, 265
   prospect theory and, 253
ESG funds, 112
ESG scores, 113
ETF permutations, 551
E*TRADE, 46
EURIBOR interest rate, 297
Eurodollars, 297, 460
Euro LIBOR, 297
European call option price, 513
European Central Bank (ECB), 679
European options, 491, 497
European put option price, 513
European-style options, 87
European Union, 148
European Union interbank, 297
Evaluating investors/money managers, market efficiency and, 224–225
Events, systematic, unsystematic v., 400
Event study, market reaction to bad news, 219–222
Excel™, 300–302, 331, 336, 338, 345
Excess return, 15, 433
   Sharpe ratio of, 433–434
   Treynor ratio of, 434–435

Exchangeable bonds, corporate, 605
Exchange members (NYSE), 147–149
Exchange rate, effects on global investments, 675–676
Exchange-traded funds (ETFs), 103, 473
   advantages, 120
   from Bloomberg, 120
   commodities, 582–583
   defining/types, 119–120
   exchange-traded notes (ETNs), 123
   leveraged, 122–123
   mutual funds v., 121–122
   taxes and, 122
Exchange-traded futures contracts, 84
Exchange-traded notes (ETNs), 123, 473, 582–583
Exercise price, 87
Exercising option, 87
Expansion stage, business cycle, 671–673
Expectations theory, 313–314
   expectations/forward rates, 313–314
   Fisher Hypothesis and, 314
Expected returns, 364–366
   announcements/news and, 396–398
   beta and, 406–408, 412
   calculating, 365, 366
   capital asset pricing model (CAPM) and, 410
   decomposing total returns, 413
   portfolio, 368
   states of the economy and, 365
   systematic risk and, 402, 412
   unequal probabilities, 365, 367, 369
   unexpected returns and, 396
   variance of, calculate, 366–367
Expected risk premium, 365
Expected volatility, 126
Expiration day, 87, 538
Expiry, 540
Exponential moving average, 275
Extendible bonds, 602
External financing needed (EFN), 645, 647
ExxonMobil, 72, 83, 502

F

Facebook (FB), 79, 143, 145
Face value, 329, 330, 598, 608–609
Factor analysis, 420–421
Factor beta, 420–421
Factor loading, 420–421
Factor portfolios, 420–421
Fallen angels (unforeseen economic events), 621
False consensus, 263
False piercings, 275
Fama-French three-factor model, 419–420
Fannie Mae, 298, 306, 614
FCOJ futures contracts, 488
Federal Deposit Insurance Corporation (FDIC), 47, 110

Federal Financing Bank, 614
Federal funds rate, 295, 680
Federal government agency securities, 614
Federal Home Loan Mortgage Corporation (FHLMC), 298, 306, 701, 702
Federal Housing Finance Agency (FHFA), 614
Federal National Mortgage Association (FNMA), 298, 306, 701, 702
Federal Reserve Bank (Fed), 296
   hedge funds and, 569
   minimum percentage and, 50
   monetary policy and, 679–680
   Treasury security auctions, 613
Federal Reserve Board, 294
Federal Reserve Board Regulation T, 51
FedEx (FDX), 494
Fees
   hedge fund, 126, 570–571
   impact of mutual fund, 108
   listing, 149
   management, private equity funds, 574
   mutual funds and, 104–105
   why pay load and, 107
Fibonacci numbers, technical analysis, 279
Fidelity Investments, 102–103, 107, 121
Fidelity Low-Priced Stock Fund (FLPSX), 442
Fidelity Magellan Fund, 107, 218
Fiduciary, 48
Financial advisor, choosing, 46–47
Financial assets, classifying, 75
Financial buyer, private equity fund exit, 578
Financial calculator, using, 339–340
Financial futures, 84, 461, 462
Financial Industry Regulatory Authority (FINRA), 77, 78, 143
Financial information, sources of, 635
Financial leverage, 52
Financial statement forecasting
   percentage of sales approach, 642
   pro forma balance sheet, 643–645
   pro forma income statement, 642–643
   projected profitability/price ratios and, 648
   scenario one, 645
   scenario two, 645–647
Financial statements
   balance sheet, 636–638
   cash flow, 639–640
   documents of, 635–636
   income, 638–639
   performance ratios/price ratios, 640–641
Financing cash flow, 639
Financing, venture capital, 139
Firm commitment underwriting, 141
Firm-specific risk, 265
First-stage, venture capital, 139

Interest rate risk
  defined, 340
  maturity and, 341
  promised yield/realized yield, 340–341
  See also Bond risk measures
Interest rate risk premium (RP), 316
Intermediate-term bond funds, 113
Internal rate of return (IRR), 28
Internal Revenue Service (IRS), 55, 103
International emerging markets
    index, 567
International funds, 111–112
International Monetary Market
    (IMM), 460
International Securities Exchange
    (ISE), 494
In-the-money bond, convertible bonds and,
    604–605
In-the-money options, 500–501
Intraday price quotes, 82
Intrinsic bond value, convertible
    bonds, 605
Intrinsic value, options
  call options, 498–500
  defined, 498
  facts regarding, 501
  in-the-money, 500–501
  put options, 499, 500
Inverse floaters, adjustable rate
    bonds, 608
Inverted market, 473
Inverted yield curve, 304, 306
Invesco brokage, 102
Investment banking firm, 141
Investment cash flow, 639
Investment company
  mutual fund types and, 100–102
  organization creation, 102–103
  taxation of, 103
  See also Mutual fund
Investment horizon, 41–42, 63
Investment management, 43–44
Investment objectives, mutual fund, 115
Investment opportunity set, 379
Investment performance data, 441
Investment policy statement
  constraints, investor, 41–43. *See also*
      Investor constraints
  risk, return and, 41
  strategies/policies, 43–45
Investment professionals
  broker, choosing, 46–47
  broker-customer relations, 48–49
  defining, 46
Investment returns, compounding
    and, 25
Investment risk management
  defined, 447
  value-at-risk (VaR), 447
Investment value, convertible bones, 605
Investor bias, prospect theory and, 253

Investor constraints
  horizon, 41–42
  liquidity, 42
  portfolio, forming investment, 63
  resources, 41
  short sale ban, 61–62
  special circumstances, 43
  taxes and, 42–43
Investor profile, asset allocations and, 65
Investor protections. *See* Protection,
    investor
Invoice price, 334
iPath S&P GSCI Crude Oil Total Return
    Index ETN (NYSE:OIL), 473
Iron Mountain Inc., 83
Issuer's call privilege, restricting, 601
Italy Index (EWI), 120

J

January effect, market anomaly, 230–232
Jensen's alpha measure of abnormal return,
    435–436, 440–441
Jobs, labor market indicators, 676–677
Johnson & Johnson (JNJ), 213, 430
JPMorgan, 151, 297
Jumpstart Our Business Startups
    (JOBS), 143
Junk bonds, credit ratings, 621–622
Junk grade corporate bonds, 599
Junk municipal funds, 114

K

Kansas City Board of Trade (KBT), 460,
    461, 464
Kickstarter, 143
Kinder Morgan, Inc., 83
Kiplinger's Personal Finance, 265
Kroll, LLC, 619

L

Labor force, 676
Labor force participation rate, 677
Labor market indicators, 676–677
Lagging economic indicators, 674
Lake Wobegon effect, 116, 116n4
Large-cap stocks, 7
Large-company funds, 111
Large-company stocks, 31
Last trading day, 87
Late expansion, business cycle, 673
Late stage, business development, 573
Law of small numbers, 263
Leading economic indicators, 674
LEAPS, 528
Legal insider trading, 223
Lehman Brothers, 240, 506
Letter of intent (LOI), private equity
    funds, 576
Leveraged buyouts (LBOs), 140

Leveraged equity, real estate, 584
Leveraged ETFs, 122–123
Leverage factor, futures contract, 580–581
Leveraging instrument, margin and, 52
Liability categories, 636
Lifecycle fund, 55
Limited tax bonds, municipal bonds, 616
Limit order, 150–151
Limits to arbitrage
  firm-specific risk, 265
  implementation costs, 266
  noise trader risk, 266
  Royal Dutch/Shell price ratio, 267–268
  3Com/Palm mispricing, 266–267
Lipper Inc., 115
Liquidity, 63
  alternative investments, 568
  investor constraint, 42
Liquidity preference theory, 315n1
Liquidity premium (LP), 315n1, 318
Listing fees, 149
Listing requirements, alternative trading
    forums and, 157
Load, 104, 107
Load funds, 104
Lockup periods, hedge funds and, 568
London Interbank Offered-Rate
    (LIBOR), 297
London Metals Exchange (LME), 481
Long call, 510
Long hedge, 468
Long position, 56, 465
Long put, 510
Long-short funds, 127, 571
Long straddle spread, long call/long
    put, 510
Long-Term Capital Management, 569
Long-term debt liability, 636
Long-term funds, 101
  defined, 110
  stock funds, 110–112
Long-term U.S. government bonds, 31
Loss-averse investors, 254–256
Loss aversion, behavioral bias, 254–256
Lower bounds, call/put option prices, 513
  American calls/puts, 512–513
  European call/put, 513
  stronger bounds, 513–514
Low-load funds, 104
Lumen Technologies, Inc., 83

M

Macaulay duration, 343, 602, 706
  calculating, 344–346
  modified duration, calculating, 346
MACD (moving average convergence
    divergence), 277
MACD line, 277
MACD trading rule, 277
Macro hedge funds, 127, 572

Mad Money, 264
Maintenance margin, 53, 471
Make-whole call premium, 602
Make-whole call price, 336
Make-whole call provision, corporate bond
    indentures, 602
Make-whole premium, 602
Malkiel's bond price theorem, 341–352
Managed futures, commodities and, 583
Management fees
    mutual funds, 105
    private equity funds, 574
Managing investments, 43–44
Margin, 50
Margin accounts
    account balance sheet and, 50
    annualizing returns on purchase, 53–54
    defining, 49–50
    financial leverage, 52–53
    hypothecation, 54
    initial margin, 51
    maintenance margin, 51–52
    street name registration, 54–55
Margin call, 51, 53, 59, 471
Margin deposit, 58
Margin purchase, 49
Marketable securities, 608
Market anomalies
    day-of-the-week effect, 229–230
    earnings announcement, 233
    January effect, 230–232
    price-earnings (PE) ratio, 233–234
    turn-of-the-month effect, 233
    turn-of-the-year effect, 232–233
Market cap, 7
Market capitalization (Market Cap), 82, 671
Market Diary: Closing Snapshot, 271
Market efficiency, 215
    causes of, 215–216
    competition, profit motive and, 217–218
    economic conditions leading to, 252
    event study, market reaction to bad news,
        219–222
    information sets for, 217
    market timing and, 225–226
    new information, price and, 219
    positive news reaction, 219
    random walk, price and, 218–219
    semistrong form, 217
    stock price, past information and, 218
    strong form, 217
    testing for, 224–225
    weak form, 217
    See also Market anomalies
Market excess returns, index funds excess
    returns v., 436
Market liquidity, 61
Market neutral, hedge funds, 126, 571
Market order, 150, 151
Market portfolios, security market line
    (SML) and, 410

Market returns, security returns v., 437
Market risk premium, 410
Market risks, 399, 401
Market segmentation theory, 315
Market sentiment index (MSI), 268–269
Market timers, 27
Market timing, 44, 64
    day-of-the-week effect and, 229–230
    hedge fund, 127, 572
    January effect, 230–232
    market efficiency and, 225–226
Market volume, 291
MarketWatch, 402, 403, 417
Marking to market, 470
Markowitz efficient frontier, 381–383
Markowitz efficient portfolio, 383
Markowitz portfolio analysis, 383
Martha Stewart Living Omnimedia, 223
Material nonpublic information,
    222–223, 635
Maturing expansion, business cycle, 673
Maturity
    bond duration and, 347
    bond fund and, 113
    bonds and, 79
    interest rate risk and, 341
    serial bonds, 606
    term bonds and, 605–606
    treasury bills, 608–609
Maturity preference theory, 315
Maturity premium, 315, 315n1
McDonald's, Inc., 98
Measures of performance, 432–440.
    See also Performance evaluation;
    Performance measures, comparing
Mental accounting, house money and, 254
Merrill Lynch, 46, 72, 102, 148
Metal & Petroleum Futures, 462
Mezzanine funds, private equity funds, 577
Mezzanine-level financing, venture
    capital, 139
Microcaps, 157
Microsoft Corporation, 74, 98, 155, 157,
    260, 276, 278, 397, 402
MidAmerica Commodity Exchange, 460
Mid-cap funds, 111
Middle market, private equity funds,
    139–140
Minimum investments, mutual funds and,
    99–100
Minimum portfolio variance, 389
Minneapolis Grain Exchange (MPLS), 460
Minnesota Mining and Manufacturing
    Company (MMM), 78
Mispricing, limits to arbitrage and
    Royal Dutch/Shell price ratio and,
        267–268
    3Com/Palm, 266–267
Modern portfolio theory (MPT), 364
Modern term structure theory, 316–317
Modified duration, 343–344, 346, 602

Momentum effect, 264
Monday, daily average returns and, 229
Monetary policy
    defining, 678
    Federal Reserve Bank, 679–680
    fiscal policy, 680–681
    money creation, 680
    money supply, stock prices and, 679–680
Money creation, monetary policy, 680
Money flow, charting, 277–278
Money market deposit accounts
    (MMDAs), 110
Money market funds, 101
Money market instruments, 75–76
Money market mutual fund (MMMf)
    accounting and, 109
    defined, 108
    deposit accounts, 110
    long-term funds, 110
    taxes and, 109
Money market prices, 298
Money market rates
    defining/types of, 293–298
    "Money Rates" report (WSJ), 293–298
Money multiplier, 680
Money options, 500
"Money Rates" report (WSJ), 290–293
Monthly returns, January effect and,
    230–232
Moody's Investors Service (Moody's),
    619, 620
Moral obligation bonds, 616
Morningstar, 116, 117, 117n5, 197, 422,
    438, 458
Morningstar fund screener, 116
Morningstar Fund Selector, 136
Mortgage amortization, 697
Mortgage-backed securities (MBSs), 584
    cash flow analysis of GNMA, 704–706
    fixed-rate mortgages, 694–700
    Ginnie Mae, 707
    GNMA mortgage pools, 701–702
    history of, 694
    interest-only strips (IOs), 708
    mortgage amortization, 697
    mortgage prepayment, 697
    mortgage principal, 695
    prepayment risks, 707
    principal-only strips (POs), 708
    PSA benchmark, 702–704
    reverse mortgages, 699–700
    securitization, 694
    SMBS, 722
    structures of, 707
    yields for, 714
Mortgage passthroughs, 694
Mortgage prepayment, 697
Mortgage principal, 695
Mortgage repackager, 306
Mortgage securitization, 694
Moving averages, chart patterns, 275–276

Multifamily housing bonds, 616
Municipal bond funds, 113, 306
Municipal bonds
  default risk, 615
  defining characteristics of, 615–616
  equivalent taxable yield, 617–618
  features of, 615–616
  general obligation bonds (GOs), 615
  insured, 617
  put/tender bonds, 616
  taxable, 618
  taxes and, 614
  types of, 616–617
Municipal-debt funds, investment
    objectives, 115
Municipal funds, 109
Mutual fund
  closing quotes, 119
  cost and, 100
  defined, 99
  diversification and, 99
  ETFs v., 121–122
  example prospectus, 107
  expense reporting, 106–107
  expenses/fees, 104
  impact of fees, 108
  investment companies, open-end/closed-
    end funds, 100–102
  investment objectives, 115
  long-term, 110–117. See also Long-term
    funds
  management fees, 105
  management, professional, 99
  minimum investments, 99–100
  net asset value, 101–102
  organization/creation, 102–103
  performance benchmark, 118
  performance information, 117–118
  portfolio values, impact of fees on, 108
  prospectus/annual report, 103
  risk and, 100
  sales charge, 104–105
  screeners, 116
  short-term funds. See Short-term funds
  style box, 117
  taxes and, 100, 103, 122
  trading costs, 105–106
  transactions, 103–104
  turnover, 105–106
  12B-1 fees, 105
  types, 101
  using performance ratings, 18
  why pay loads/fees?, 107
  yardsticks, 117
Mutual fund companies, 102
Myopic loss aversion, 256

N

Nabisco, Inc., 397
Nanocaps, 157

NASDAQ, 60, 98, 137, 147
  competitors, third/fourth market,
    155–156
  dealer market, participants, 155
  electronic communications network
    (ECN) and, 155
  major indexes, 159
  operations, 153–154
  order types, importance of, 154
  OTC market, 155
  quote-driven market, 153
  ticker symbols, 81
  trading, ticker tape, 82
NASDAQ Capital Market, 155
NASDAQ Global Market, 155
NASDAQ Global Select Market, 155
NASDAQ Options Market, 494
NASDAQ 100 Volatility Index (VXN),
  552–553
National Association of Securities Dealers
  Automated Quotations System
  (NASDAQ). See NASDAQ
National Distillers Products Corp., 80
National Football Conference (NFC), 279
National Football League (NFL), 280
National Futures Association (NFA), 481
National Stock Exchange (NSX), 147
Neckline support, chart pattern, 275
Negative average returns, 229
Negative convexity, 601
Negative covenant, corporate bonds, 607
Negative pledge cause, 600
Negative roll yield, 473
Negotiable certificates of deposit, 297
Neste market efficiency, 216
Net asset value, mutual funds and,
  101–102
Net operating income (NOI), real estate
  valuation, 585
News, announcements and, 396–398
News components, 424
News effects, 424
New York Board of Trade (NYBOT), 461
New York Coffee Exchange, 460
New York Cotton Exchange (NYCE),
  460, 461
New York Futures Exchange (NYFE),
  460, 461
New York Mercantile Exchange (NYMEX),
  460, 461, 467
New York Stock Exchange (NYSE), 7, 51,
  61, 98, 137, 147
  competitors, third/fourth market,
    155–156
  crash of October 1987 and, 237
  ending stop orders, 153
  flash crash of 2010, 151–152
  floor activity, 149–150
  goal of, liquidity, 148
  listed stocks, 149
  major indexes, 159

  members, 147–149
  order types, 151
  special order types, 150–152
Nike, Inc., 88, 89, 382, 404
Nobel Prize, economics, 364
Noise trader risk, 266
Noise trading, 259
No-load funds, 104
Nominal GDP, 670
Nominal interest rate (NI), 317–318
Nominal interest rates
  defined, 309
  modern term structure theory, 316–317
  traditional theories, critiques of, 316
Noncallable bonds, 600, 601
Noncash items, 639
Nonconstant growth, first stage, 183–185
Nonconvertible bonds, 604, 605
Nondiversifiable risk, 401
Nonmarketable securities, 608
Nordstrom, Inc., 81, 82, 154, 505–506,
  508–509
Normal distribution, 20–21
NTT DoCoMo, 145
NYSE Arca, 148, 494
NYSE circuit breakers, 237
NYSE Euronext, 137, 148
NYSE most active stocks, 81

O

October 1987 market crash, 235–237
Odd-lot indicators, 279
Offering price, 104
1/n phenomenon, 263–264
Oneok, Inc., 83
One-period binomial option pricing model
  (BOPM)
  assumptions/setup/inputs, 531
  delta, 532, 534
  formula, 532–534
  fractional share (delta) portfolio
    tree, 532
  stock price tree/option priced tree, 532
One-way vol bets, 518
Online brokers, 47
Open-end mutual funds, 100–102, 108
Open-high-low-close charts (OHLC), 273–274
Open market operations, 680
Open Marketplace, 157
Option chain, 494
Option contracts, derivative
  defined, 86
  futures v., 87
  gains/losses, 88
  price quotes, 87
  put options, 88, 89
  put returns, 89
  stock investing v., 89
  terminology, 87
  trading, 87–88

Put dates, 602
Put option, 87-89, 491
    hedging stock, stock options, 548-549
    intrinsic value, 499
    lower bounds prices, 512-513
    payoffs, 503
    profits, 505
    protective, corporate risk management
        and, 507-508
    upper bound prices, 512
Put option deltas, computing, 546
Put price, 602
Put provisions, corporate bond indentures
    and, 602-603
Put returns, 89
Put writer, 502

Q

Quaker State Corporation, 336
Quarterly updates, 10-Qs, 635
Quote-driven market, NASDAQ, 153

R

Randomness. *See also* Representativeness
    heuristic
Random walk, price market efficiency and,
    218-219
Rating agencies, bond credit, 619
Ratio analysis, valuing with, 654-655
Raw return, 432
Real estate
    cost approach valuation, 584
    defining investment in, 584
    leveraged equity, 584
    mortgage-backed security, 584
    net operating income (NOI) approach,
        valuation, 585
    REITs/CREFs, 585
    sales comparison, 585
    valuation, 584-585
Real estate investment trusts (REITs),
    585, 596
Real gross domestic product,
    670-673, 678
Real interest rate (RI), 309-310, 316
Realized return, 364
Realized yield, 340-341
Reasoning, errors in, 252
Recency bias, 263
Recession, 620, 659, 675
Redemption fee, 106
Redemption value, 608-609
Red herring, 143
Refunding provision, corporate bond
    indentures, 601
Registration requirements, SEC, 567-568
Regression, calculating beta with, 418
Regret aversion, 256
Regulated investment company, 103

Regulation
    corporate bond indentures and, 599-600
    hedge funds and, 125, 569, 570
    OTC Markets Group marketplaces, 157
Regulation FD (Fair Disclosure, SEC), 635
Reindexing, 162
Reinvestment rate risk
    bond price and, 352
    example, 350
    price risk *v.,* 351
Reinvestment risk, 349-351
Relative strength charts, technical analysis,
    272-273, 291
Relevant information, market efficiency
    and, 224
Representativeness heuristic (randomness/
    chance events)
    biases, investor, 263
    clustering illusion, 262
    coin flip patterns, 260-261
    defined, 259-260
    gambler's fallacy, 262
    hot-hand fallacy, 261-262
Repriced employee stock options, 554
Required earnings per share, 187
Reserve Primary Fund, 109
Residual income model (RIM), 187-188,
    199-200
Resistance level, technical analysis, 270-271
Resources, investments and, 41, 63
Retained earnings, 179
Retention ratio, 179, 643
Retirement accounts
    company-sponsored, 55
    individual retirement accounts (IRAs),
        55-56
Return on assets (ROA), 640
Return on equity (RO)
    analyzing, 180-181
    retention ratio and, 179
Return on equity (ROE), 640
Return on investment (ROI)
    annualizing, 5-6
    average. *See* Average returns
    dollar returns, 2-4
    historical portfolio returns, 7-14
    percentage returns, 4
    total dollar return, 3
    See also Historical rates of return; Risk
        and return
Returns
    sector, 682
    systematic/unsystematic components
        of, 400
Return variability
    frequency distributions/variability, 17-18
    historical record, 19-20
    historical variance/standard deviation,
        18-19
    normal distribution, 20-21
    risk/reward, 21-22

Revenue bonds, 306, 616-617
Reversal patterns, 274-275
Reverse mortgages, 699-700
Reverse trade, 471
Reward-to-risk ratio, security market line
    (SML) and, 406, 408, 411
Rights offer, 140
Risk
    alternative investments and, 567-569
    beta measures, 190
    commodity-based investment funds
        and, 473
    corporate management. *See* Corporate
        risk management
    cryptocurrency, 588
    efficient portfolio and, 379
    equity beta and, 190
    firm-specific, 265
    fixed-income securities and, 79
    gender overtrading and, 257
    hedging contracts and, 468-469,
        477-478
    historical rates of return and, 8
    interest rate, Malkiel's theorems and,
        340-343
    interest rate risk premium, 316-317
    January effect and, 230
    money market mutual funds and, 109
    mutual funds and, 100
    noise trader/sentiment-based, 266
    options and. *See also* Options, manage
        risk with
    portfolio, diversification and. *See also*
        Diversification
    price, reinvestment rate risk *v.,* 351
    reward, return variability and, 21-22
    systematic, diversification and, 401
    systematic/unsystematic, 399
    unsystematic, diversification and, 400
    variance and, 369-370
    venture capital and, 573
    See also Bond risk measures;
        Reinvestment rate risk
Risk adjustment, market efficiency and, 224
Risk and return
    capital asset pricing model (CAPM)
        and, 410
    exchange rate, 676
    investment policy statement and, 41
    portfolios and, 63
    stocks and bonds, 378, 379
    summary, 411
    two assets, 381
    See also Return on investment (ROI)
Risk-averse behavior, 41, 252-254
Risk-free rate, 15-16
Risk management, 447-448
Risk premiums, 185, 186, 395
    average returns, 15-16
    betas and, 406-407
    expected return and, 365

Risk-return trade-off, 29–30, 380–381
Risk-taking behavior, 252–253
Risk tolerance quiz, 43, 62–63
Risk tolerance score, 42, 62–63
Risky asset allocation. *See* Diversification
Robo-advisors, 47
ROI. *See* Return on investment (ROI)
Rotational investing, sector identification, 682–683
Roth individual retirement account, 55–56
Royal Dutch, 267–268
R-squared, 439, 442

S

Sales comparison valuation, real estate, 585
Saudi Aramco, 145
Scatter plot, 416
Scheduled sinking fund redemption, 606
Seaport bonds, 616
Seasoned equity offering (SEO), 140
Seasoned mortgages, 703
Secondary market, 140, 146
Secondary reactions, 269
Second-stage financing, venture capital, 139
Sector funds, 112
Sector identification
    heat map, 683, 692
    rotational investing, 682–683
    sector returns, 683
    S&P, 682, 683
    subsector (industry) differences, 683–684
Sector performance, business cycle, 673
Securities
    federal government agency, 614
    marketable/nonmarketable, 608
    overvalued, expected return and, 409
    selling to public, private equity funds and, 140
    U.S. Treasury, 608
Securities and Exchange Act of 1934, 51, 222–223
Securities and Exchange Commission (SEC), 152
    defined, 142
    financial information, 635
    hedge fund regulation and, 569, 570
    OCC and, 494
    regulation, corporate bond indentures, 599–600
    security law enforcement, 567–568
    short selling ban, 61
    12B-1 fees and, 105
Securities broker, 46, 147
Securities dealers, 147
Securities, financial asset classification, 75
Securities Investor Protection Corporation (SIPC), 48
Security analysis, 45, 174

Security market line (SML), 395
    beta, risk premium and, 405
    capital asset pricing model and, 410, 411
    defining, 409
    expected returns, beta and, 406–408
    market portfolios and, 410
    reward-to-risk ratio, 406, 408, 411
    slope of, 411
Security returns, market returns *v.*, 437
Security selection, 44–45, 64, 686
Seed stage, business development, 573
Self-attribution bias, 263
Semiannual coupons, duration, 345
Semistrong form market efficiency, 217
Senior debentures, 600
Sentiment-based risk, 266
Separate Trading of Registered Interest and Principal of Securities (STRIPS), 307–309, 609
Sequential Brands Group, 223
Sequential collateralized mortgage obligations, 710–711
Serial bonds, 606
Settle price, 460
Shanghai Stock Exchange, 145
Shark Tank (ABC), 578
Sharpe-optimal portfolios, 443–446
Sharpe ratio of portfolio excess return, 433–434, 440–441
Shell Oil, 267–268
Short hedge, 467, 470
Shorting stock, 56
Short interest, 60
Short position, 56, 58, 59, 465
Short ratio, 72
Short sale
    basics of, 56–57
    constraints, SEC ban, 61
    defined, 56
Short selling, hedge funds, 127, 572
Short-term bond funds, 113
Short-term funds
    money market deposit account, 110
    money market mutual fund (MMMf), 108–109
Sigma, option prices and, 544
Signal line, 277
Single monthly mortality (SMM) rates, 721
Simon Property Group, Inc., 83
Simple moving average, 275
Simultaneous economic indicators, 674
Single-state municipal funds, 114
Sinking fund, 606
Sinking fund call price, 606
Sinking fund provisions, corporate bonds, 605, 606
"Sleeping Beauty" bonds, 606
Slope coefficient, 419
Small company funds, 111
Small-company stocks, 31
Smartstops, 473

Snakebite effect, overconfidence and, 259
Social conscience funds, 112
Socially responsible investing (SRI), 113
Social responsibility funds, 112
Social Security Administration trust fund, 608
Society of Risk Management Consultants, 451
SoftBank, 145
Soft commodities, 461
Soft dollars, 106
Solver tool, 444, 445
Sortino ratio of portfolio excess return, 433
South African Krugerrand, 580
Southwest Airlines Co., 402
Special call price, 336
Special circumstances, 63
Special order types, NYSE, 150–152
Special purpose acquisition company (SPAC), 146
Speculating, futures contracts, 465–466
Speculator, 465
Spot-futures parity, 474–475
Spot market, 472
Spot market transactions, commodities, 580
Spot price, 472
Spreads
    bid/ask prices and, 147
    defined, 508
    money accounts and, 49
    options trading strategies, 509–510
    tutorial website, 510
    types of, 509–510
SPX options, 549
Standard deviation, 18–20, 23
    annual, risk-return trade-off, 29
    beta coefficient *v.*, 403
    calculate, spreadsheet, 23
    implied, 551–553. *See also* Implied standard deviations
    measuring, 411
    portfolio, 371
    portfolio variance, 377
    return, total risk, 433
Standardized exchange-traded futures contracts, 84
Standard normal distribution, 454
Standard & Poor's Corporation (S&P), 1, 7, 159, 497, 619, 620, 624
    S&P 100 (OEX), 497
    S&P 500, 119, 239, 404n1, 497, 549–550
    S&P Depositary Receipt (SPDR), 119
    S&P 500® Index Options, 97
    S&P sectors, 682
    S&P 100 Volatility Index (VXO), 552–553
    S&P 500 Volatility Index (VIX), 552–553
Standard & Poor's Depositary Receipt, 119
Starbucks Corporation, 155, 404, 553

Super Bowl indicator, 279
support/resistance levels, 270–271
technical indicators, 271–272
Triple Crown indicator, 280
Technical indicators, 271–272
Tender offer bonds, 616
10-K report, EDGAR, 635
Tennessee Valley Authority, 614
10-Qs, quarterly updates, 635
Term bonds, 605–606
Term structure, expectations theory and, 313–315
Tesla, 60, 402
Tesla, Inc., 492
Testing, capital asset pricing model (CAPM), 419
Texas Instruments BAII Plus financial calculator, 339–340
Third market competitors, 155
Third-party managers, spot-market commodity transactions and, 582–583
3M Co., 78, 495
3M Com/Palm mispricing, 266–267
Ticker symbols, 81
Ticker tape, 82
Time diversification fallacy, 372–374
Time remaining option expiration, 543
Time to maturity, 514n1
Time value of money, 30, 186, 308
Time value, option, 499
Timing trades, ETFs, mutual funds v, 121
Tippee, insider trading, 222–223
Tipper, insider trading, 222–223
T-notes, 608
Token sales, 145
Tokens, initial coin offerings (ICO), 143, 145
Top-down analysis, 669–670
Top-yielding stocks, S&P500, 83
Total amount, management fee, 574
Total dollar return, 3
Total market capitalization, 7
Total percent return, 4
Total return indexes, 9
Total returns, decomposing, 412
Total risk. See Standard deviation
Tracking surprises, 398
Trade Reporting and Compliance Engine (TRACE), 77
Trade time, NYSE, 148
Trading accounts, 46
Trading costs, mutual funds, 105–106
Trading frequency, overconfidence and, 257
Trading strategies, options
    combination, 510–511
    covered call strategy, 509
    spreads, 509–510
Traditional fixed-price call provisions, 600–601
Treasure bond prices, 611–613

Treasury Inflation-Protected Securities (TIPS), 310–313
Treasury note prices, 611–613
Treasury notes, 609
Treasury STRIPS. See U.S. Treasury STRIPS
Treynor index, 406n2
Treynor ratio of portfolio excess return, 434–435, 440–441
Triangles, 291
TRIN "Closing Arms" ratio, 272
Triple A credit rating, municipal bonds, 617–618
Triple Crown indicator, 280
Trough stage, business cycle, 671, 672
Turn-of-the-year effect, market anomaly, 232–233
Turnover, mutual funds and, 105–106
TVGoods, Inc., 578
12B-1fees, 105
Two-period binomial option pricing model, 534–537
Two-stage dividend growth model
    capital asset pricing model (CAPM), 185–186
    defined equations for, 181–183
    H-model, 185
    nonconstant growth, first stage, 183–185
    valuing Starbucks using, 655–656
Two states of the economy, 364
TXU (energy firm), 140

U

Uncorrelated assets, 374
Under Armour, 57
Underlying asset, 467
Underwriter spread, 141
Underwrite stocks, 141
Underwriting, 141–142
Unemployment rate, 677
Unequal probabilities, 365, 367, 369
Unexpected returns
    beta and, 413
    expected returns and, 396
Uniform price auction, 142
Unique risks, 401
United Technologies, 430
Unlimited tax bonds, municipal bonds, 616
Unseasoned equity offering, 140
Unseasoned mortgages, 703
Unsecured debt. corporate bonds, 599
Unsystematic components of return, 400
Unsystematic events, systematic v., 400
Unsystematic risk, 399
    diversification and, 400
    summary, 411
Upper bound
    call option prices, 511
    put option prices, 512

Uptick rule, 61
U.S. equity risk premium, historical/international perspectives, 15–16
U.S. Food and Drug Administration, 223
U.S. Forum for Sustainable and Responsible Investing, 113
U.S. Gold Eagle, 580
U.S. Natural Gas Fund, 473
US Oil Fund, 473
U.S. Savings Bonds, 608
U.S. Sentencing Commission, 48
U.S. Treasury auctions, 613
U.S. Treasury Bills, 7, 12, 31, 461, 608
    bid/ask price, 299
    defining, 297
    futures trading, 85
    inflation rates, interest rates and, 311
    price and yield calculations, 300
    prices, calculate, 300
    quotes, 298–299
    real interest rates, 1950-2021, 311
    research prices, 335
    Treasury yield curve, 304, 305
    See also Treasury Inflation-Protected Securities (TIPS)
U.S. Treasury Bonds (T-bonds), 85
U.S. Treasury quotes, 612
U.S. Treasury, securities, 608
U.S. Treasury STRIPS, 307–309
    calculating prices, 610, 611
    yields for, 308–309
U.S. zero-coupon strips, 307–309

V

Valero Energy Corp., 83
Valuation
    deal structure, private equity funds, 577–578
    private equity funds, 576
    real estate, 584–585
    venture capital method, 577
Value-at-risk
    computing, 448–450
    risk management, 447
Value creation, private equity funds and, 578–579
Value indexes, 160
Value Line, 117n5
Value stocks, 192
Value-weighted index, 159, 161
Valuing
    market analysis, 656
    ratio analysis and, 654–655
    two-stage growth model and, 655–656
Vanguard, 102
Vanguard Group, 121
Vanguard 500 Index Fund (VFINX), 105, 226–228
Vanguard REIT ETF, 120
Vanguard Small-Cap ETF, 120